Collected Works of Northrop Frye

VOLUME 8

The Diaries of Northrop Frye
1942–1955

Collected Works of Northrop Frye

Alvin A. Lee, General Editor

Jean O'Grady, Associate Editor

Nicholas Halmi, Assistant Editor

The Collected Edition of the Works of Northrop Frye has been planned and is being directed by an editorial committee under the aegis of Victoria University, through its Northrop Frye Centre. The purpose of the edition is to make available authoritative texts of both published and unpublished works, based on an analysis and comparison of all available materials, and supported by scholarly apparatus, including annotation and introductions. The Northrop Frye Centre gratefully acknowledges financial support, through McMaster University, from the Michael G. DeGroote family.

The Diaries of Northrop Frye

1942–1955

VOLUME 8

Edited by Robert D. Denham

For Jane, this collection of early Norrie stories, with affection & thanks for all your help over the years —

Bob

UNIVERSITY OF TORONTO PRESS
Toronto Buffalo London

© Victoria University, University of Toronto (diaries) and Robert D. Denham
(preface, introduction, annotation, appendixes) 2001

Toronto Buffalo London
Printed in Canada

ISBN 0-8020-3538

Printed on acid-free paper

National Library of Canada Cataloguing in Publication Data

Frye, Northrop, 1912–1991
The diaries of Northrop Frye, 1942–1955

(Collected works of Northrop Frye ; v. 8)
Includes bibliographical references and index.
ISBN 0-8020-3538-8

1. Frye, Northrop, 1912–1991 – Diaries.   2. Critics – Canada –
Correspondence.   I. Denham, Robert D.   II. Title.   III. Series.

PN75.F7A3 2001   801′.95′092   C2001-901451-1

This volume has been published with the assistance of a grant from
Victoria University.

University of Toronto Press acknowledges the financial assistance to its
publishing program of the Canada Council and the Ontario Arts Council.

University of Toronto Press acknowledges the financial support for its
publishing activities of the Government of Canada through the
Book Publishing Industry Development Program (BPIDP).

For Evelyn, Beatrice, Ivy, Ella, and Jack
ab imo pectore

Contents

Preface

This volume contains a transcription of the diaries that Northrop Frye kept intermittently from 1942 until 1955. Altogether there are seven diaries, or at least seven different books in which Frye recorded his daily activities. The 1950 and 1951 Diaries form a chronological unit, though they are in two different bound books. Two of the diaries are quite brief: the 1951 Diary (13 days) and the 1953 Diary (4 days). Two cover somewhat longer periods: the 1942 Diary (89 days) and the 1955 Diary (81 days). These two diaries are similar in chronological scope, though in terms of the actual amount of writing, the former is twice as extensive as the latter. Three diaries are devoted to longer periods of time: the 1949 Diary (five months), the 1950 Diary (eight months and three days), and the 1952 Diary (almost four months). All of the diaries are in Frye's hand, and all but the 1949 and 1953 Diaries were written in relatively small bound books of varying sizes. The 1949 Diary was written on 130 ruled sheets that had been inserted in a ring binder; the 1953 Diary, on seven ruled sheets, also with punched holes for a ring binder. The headnotes in the present volume give the provenance, present location, and further physical description for each of the diaries.

My aim in transcribing the diaries has been to reproduce the content of the text exactly as Frye wrote it, with the following exceptions. On ten occasions Frye characterizes people in ways that I think would be overly hurtful or embarrassing. I have deleted the phrases containing these epithets, which amount to thirty-six words altogether. I have regularized Frye's use of the comma and period within quotation marks, following the standard North American practice, and I have italicized words and phrases he underlined. I have not noted any of the minor changes that Frye himself made to his own handwriting, such as spellings he corrected or, except in one case, words he marked through. And I have not followed Frye's practice of elevating and underlining the affixes following ordinal numbers (e.g., 3ʳᵈ) and centuries (e.g., 19ᵗʰ). All editorial additions have been placed in square brackets. Other material in square brackets includes paragraph numbers, expansions of abbreviations, and an occasional omission or mistake. When I have been uncertain about my deciphering of a word, usually a person's name, Frye wrote, I have also put the word, followed by a question mark, in square brackets. When Frye himself refers to entries or pages within a diary, I have placed the number of the entry or the page within square brackets in the text. In the 1949 and 1950 Diaries Frye uses a symbolic code, explained in the introduction, to refer to various parts of his lifelong writing project. He refers to this project, formulated when he was quite young, as his ogdoad, and he gave a name to each of the eight parts: Liberal, Tragicomedy, Anticlimax, Rencontre, Mirage, Paradox, Ignoramus, and Twilight. When Frye uses one of his shorthand symbols, I have given its name in square brackets following the symbol, though I have not repeated the name if the symbol reappears within a single paragraph. In the three places where Frye himself uses square brackets, I have replaced them with braces: { }.

As one might expect in diaries such as Frye's, many characters come onto the stage of his daily life. Some exit and are never heard from again, while others make repeated appearances. Rather than identifying people in a note each time they are referred to, I have listed the names of people Frye mentions in Appendix 1, along with a brief biography or at least some identifying information. Sometimes this information is scanty, such as a year of graduation only. The biographical notes do not generally project what might be said about the lives of Frye's contemporaries beyond the years covered by the diaries. I have not been able to identify several dozen people in the cast of more than 1,200.

The annotations will doubtless be too copious for some, too slight for others. Their intent is simply to provide additional information for those who might want it. One of the virtues of notes is that they can be ignored.

In citing the diaries I have used a shortened form that incorporates the last two digits of the year followed by a period and the paragraph or note number. Thus, "49.27" refers to the 1949 Diary, paragraph 27, and "42.n. 57" refers to note 57 of the 1942 Diary. In the notes of a given diary, references both to paragraphs and to notes within that diary omit the year. They are of the form "See par. 18, above" and "See n. 84, below." In both the notes and the directory I have followed the University of Toronto convention of referring to a year of graduation by inserting "T" between the last two digits of the year, as in "3T3" for the graduating class of 1933, or for Emmanuel College, "5E6."

Acknowledgments

In annotating Frye's diaries I have drawn on the special knowledge and good will of many people. Frye's students from the 1940s and 1950s have been especially generous in their replies to my enquiries. I owe special debts of gratitude to Victoria University in the University of Toronto and to the Victoria University Library for permitting me to edit Frye's manuscripts; to Margaret Bennett, who took on a number of my queries as a special project and whose sleuthing skills identified several dozen of the diaries' cast of characters; to Michael Happy, who provided information for more than forty of the notes; to Alvin Lee and the Frye Centre, for funding Michael Happy's assistance. Alvin Lee, General Editor of Frye's Collected Works, and Associate Editor Jean O'Grady (who prepared the index) have supported me in ways too numerous to catalogue. The largest debt I owe is to Margaret Burgess, on whose exemplary skills as a copy-editor I have come to depend and who has continued to assist me in ways that go far beyond copy-editing. Special thanks are also due to William Blissett, George Johnston, Gordon Wood, and Ian Singer for their generous help; to Ken Wilson of the Emmanuel College/United Church Archives; to Lisa Sherlock of the Victoria University Library; to the reference staffs of the Metropolitan Library of Toronto and National Library of Canada; to Ron Schoeffel, Editor-in-Chief at the University of Toronto Press, and Anne Laughlin, Managing Editor of the Press; and to the following people, who helped me in one way or another in annotating the diaries: M.H. Abrams, Jessie Day Adams, Johan Aitken, Ruth Manning Alexander, Hugh Anson-Cartwright, Harriett Coltham Armson, Margaret Avison, Ruth Bagworth, Arnold Tate Bailey, Paul Banfield, Peter Barker, Bruce Bashford, Barbara Tubman Beardsley, Munro Beattie, Karl Beckson, Patricia Beharriell, Allen Bentley, Carol Bishop, Ann Black, Michael Bliss, Josephine Benyon Boos, Judy Livingston Bowler, Robert Brandeis, Willard Brehaut, Patricia Smith Broadhurst, Patricia Butts, Reed Carson, Don Carter, Erin Carter, Morley G. Clarke, Muriel A. Code, Donald Coles, R.G. Colgrove, Isobel (Toni) Routly Collins, John Robert Colombo, Helen Conger, C. Abbott Conway, Ramsay Cook, Ellen E.

Cullen, Mary Lane Culley, Jean Dancey, Kerry Dean, Elsie Del Bianco, W. Thomas Delworth, Robert DeMaria, Jr., Philippe Desan, Kay Brown Dills, Barbara Sagar Doran, Leone Earls, David Eastwood, Joan Eddis, Shirley Endicott, Sharon English, Peter J.A. Evans, William Fennell, G.W. Field, John B. Findlay, Richard J. Finneran, Amy E. Fisher, Douglas Fisher, Joyce Fleming, Edith Fowke, Evelyn Fullerton, Colin Furness, Onalee Walter Gage, Marie Bond Gardner, Margaret Gayfer, Mary Gibson, Tom Gibson, Ray Godfrey, Homer Goldberg, Susan Gould, Warwick Gould, Harry Greene, Oscar A. Haac, Don Haddow, A.C. Hamilton, Don Harron, Jonathan Hart, Patty Hawkins, Catharine Card Hay, Ronald Haycock, Veronica Healy, Helen Holt Heath, Ruth Dingman Hebb, Standish Henning, Janet Fulton Hibberd, F. David Hoeniger, Diana J. Ironside, Scott James, Donna Jeynes, Anne Kavelman, Dorothy Kealey, Hugh S. Keeping, David Kent, Ralph E. King, Roger Kingsley, James D. (Dan) Kinney, Shirley Kirkland, David Knight, Mary Louise Knight, Martine Lachance, Norman Langford, John R. Latimer, J. Philip Lautenslager, Madeline Bomberg Lavender, Julie LeBlanc, Hope Arnott Lee, Gene Lees, Debbie Lindsay, Jean Little, Frank Lynch, Lucille Hoffman McBeth, Sally McCrae, Kenneth MacLean, Roland McMaster, Barbara McNabb, David McNeil, Amy Marshall, A.E. Wallace Maurer, Martin Maw, John Meisel, Glenn E. Menard, Alan Mendelson, Brian Merrilees, Audrey Milne, Benton Misener, Arthur Mitzman, Melissa Monteiro, Hugh Moorhouse, Phyllis Foreman Moorhouse, Ken Morgan, Jan Narveson, Kim G. Ness, Sophie Nina, Mary-Anne Nichols, June Noble, Barbara Norman, Margaret Dillon Norquay, Ernst M. Oppenheimer, Richard Outram, Debra Ozema, Reta Horner Parna, David S.J. Parsons, Jill Patrick, David Pitt, Komala Prabhakar, Colleen Thibaudeau Reaney, James Reaney, Margaret J. Ritchie, Diane Rogers, Barbara Rooke, A. Doreen Ross, Malcolm Ross, Barbara Ruchkall, Florinda Ruiz, John Rutherford, Doris Mosdell Sangster, Nancy Schenk, Ron Schoeffel, Jane Reddick Schofield, Judi Schwartz, Helen Searing, Elizabeth Seymour, Grace Dempster Shabaeff, Martin Shubik, John Slater, Jean Brown Sonnenfeld, Francis Sparshott, Thomas Steman, Dave Stephens, Mary-jo Stevenson, Douglas Stewart, Isobel M. Stewart, Richard M. Stingle, Dabney Stuart, Brian Sullivan, Lois G. Taylor, Caroline Temple, Phyllis Thompson, Nik Thomson, Hugh G. Thorburn, James L. Thorson, Bogusia Trojan, Lagring Ulanday, Steven Vincent, Margaret Kell Virany, Gloria Fisher Vizinczey, Dawn Wanless, Richard S. Warren, Donald Weinert,

Marilyn Wells, Hayden White, Jane Widdi-combe, Mary McCosh Williams, Nora Wilson, Rosemarie Schawlow Wolfe, Shawn Wong, and Ross Woodman.

I express my thanks also to Clara Thomas and William Blissett, who served as external readers of the manuscript and whose special knowledge helped to make the book better than it would have otherwise been. Part of the work on this volume was completed under a fellowship from the National Endowment for the Humanities and a summer grant from Roanoke College. I remain indebted to both, not merely for their generous support.

My greatest debt, of another kind altogether, is to Northrop Frye, teacher *in saecula saeculorum*.

Abbreviations and Shortened Forms

Frye's own abbreviations have been expanded in square brackets, with the following exceptions: R.K (Religious Knowledge), O.T. (Old Testament), N.T. (New Testament), CBC (Canadian Broadcasting Corporation), and F.S. (*Fearful Symmetry*).

AC	*Anatomy of Criticism: Four Essays*. Princeton, N.J.: Princeton University Press, 1957.
AGT	Art Gallery of Toronto
Ayre	John Ayre. *Northrop Frye: A Biography*. Toronto: Random House, 1989.
BG	*The Bush Garden: Essays on the Canadian Imagination*. Toronto: Anansi, 1971.
CCF	Co-operative Commonwealth Federation
Correspondence	*The Correspondence of Northrop Frye and Helen Kemp, 1932–1939*. Ed. Robert D. Denham. Collected Works of Northrop Frye, vols. 1 and 2. Toronto: University of Toronto Press, 1996.
EC	Emmanuel College
Erdman	*The Complete Poetry and Prose of William Blake*. Ed. David Erdman. Rev. ed. Berkeley: University of California Press, 1982.
FI	*Fables of Identity: Studies in Poetic Mythology*. New York: Harcourt, Brace and World, 1963.
FS	*Fearful Symmetry: A Study of William Blake*. Princeton, N.J.: Princeton University Press, 1947.
HKF	Helen Kemp Frye

Hughes	John Milton. *Complete Poems and Major Prose*. Ed. Merritt Y. Hughes. New York: Odyssey Press, 1957.
LN	*Northrop Frye's Late Notebooks, 1982–1990: Architecture of the Spiritual World*. Ed. Robert D. Denham. Collected Works of Northrop Frye, vols. 5–6. Toronto: University of Toronto Press, 2000.
MD	*The Myth of Deliverance: Reflections on Shakespeare's Problem Comedies*. Toronto: University of Toronto Press, 1983.
MM	*Myth and Metaphor: Selected Essays, 1974–1988*. Ed. Robert D. Denham. Charlottesville: University Press of Virginia, 1990.
NB	Notebook
NF	Northrop Frye
NFC	*Northrop Frye in Conversation*. Ed. David Cayley. Concord, Ont.: Anansi, 1992.
NFCL	*Northrop Frye on Culture and Literature: A Collection of Review Essays*. Ed. Robert D. Denham. Chicago: University of Chicago Press, 1978.
NFF	Northrop Frye Fonds, Victoria University Library
NFL	Works in Northrop Frye's own library, now in the Victoria University Library
NFR	*Northrop Frye on Religion*. Ed. Alvin A. Lee and Jean O'Grady. Collected Works of Northrop Frye, vol. 4. Toronto: University of Toronto Press, 2000.
NGC	National Gallery of Canada
OCA	Ontario College of Art
OCE	Ontario College of Education
RCMT	Royal Conservatory of Music of Toronto
RE	*The Return of Eden: A Study of Milton's Epics*. Toronto: University of Toronto Press, 1965.
ROM	Royal Ontario Museum
RW	*Reading the World: Selected Writings, 1935–1976*. Ed. Robert D. Denham. New York: Peter Lang, 1990.
SMC	St. Michael's College, University of Toronto
TC	Trinity College, University of Toronto
TCM	Toronto Conservatory of Music
TSO	Toronto Symphony Orchestra
TTC	Toronto Transportation (later Transit) Commission

UBC	University of British Columbia
UC	University College, University of Toronto
UCC	United Church of Canada
UNB	University of New Brunswick
U of T	University of Toronto
USk	University of Saskatchewan
UWO	University of Western Ontario
VC	Victoria College, University of Toronto
VU	Victoria University, University of Toronto
WE	*Northrop Frye's Writings on Education.* Ed. Goldwin French and Jean O'Grady. Collected Works of Northrop Frye, vol. 7. Toronto: University of Toronto Press, 2000.

Introduction

"The literary instinct," according to Samuel Butler, is demonstrated by those who find themselves "writing at all odd times," just "as people show the artistic instinct by sketching in season and out of season."[1] Northrop Frye, paraphrasing Butler, notes that "incessant recording is the literary habit" (49.9), and for Frye the habit developed into an addiction. When he wasn't at his typewriter pounding out the manuscripts for the books, essays, letters, reviews, addresses, and lectures that now fill a large shelf, he was scribbling away in the margins of the books he was reading, recording the Odyssean adventures of his imaginative and critical quest in his notebooks, the expansiveness of which approaches that of Pepys's diaries.[2] Moreover, Frye was a faithful and constant correspondent: thousands of his letters have been preserved.[3] The present volume now adds Frye's diaries to this large body of work.

Although Frye was an irrepressible writer of notebooks, we cannot say that about him as a diarist, even during those seven years that he was chronicling his daily activities. Still, the diaries that have survived do run to more than a quarter of a million words. The earliest extant diary is from 1942. In the next one that has survived, written in 1949, Frye remarks that during the course of his life he has made "several efforts to keep a diary" (49.1), indicating that he kept more diaries before 1949 than the one we have. He does refer to a 1943 diary,[4] which is not extant, and, as we know that he disposed of some of his early notebooks,[5] he may have discarded some of his diaries as well. Or they may have simply been misplaced or lost. About all we can say is that before 1949 Frye may have kept a few diaries in addition to the one that was preserved (1942) and the one that wasn't (1943).[6] Following 1955, the date of the last diary we have, the possibility that Frye kept additional diaries seems remote. Why did he abandon diary writing during the last thirty-five years of his life? For one thing, after *Anatomy of Criticism* (1957) thrust Frye into prominence, he simply became too absorbed in other projects for the diary to continue as a literary habit. As he says in a notebook from the early 1960s, "I have occasionally wondered why I couldn't keep diaries. The answer is that I'm too busy with other writing—the only times I succeeded in keeping a diary more than a week or two were in doldrum periods of writing. Now I'm so full of commissions & deadlines I can't even keep notebooks" (NB 18, par. 105). "A week or two" is plainly an understatement, but in the 1960s Frye had embarked upon the expansive project of what he called his third book. This was an undertaking that consumed him for most of the rest of his life, and outside of the various "commissions & deadlines," he poured an enormous amount of energy into the notebooks for that unrealized book,[7] as well as into the books and articles and addresses that he did write. The diary, in short, was replaced by other writing commitments. Frye also gave up keeping a diary because he conceived of such writing to begin with only as "an experimental form of discipline" and not "as a Pepys ten-year project" (49.5).

II

Frye typically wrote in his diaries at the end of the day. The actual amount of writing he did each day was determined, to a large extent, for four of the diaries (1950, 1951, 1952, and 1955) by the format of the book he was using. These four diaries were written in day-books or daily journals, having a single, lined page for each day with the date printed in the top margin. For these four diaries Frye almost always confined what he had to say at the end of the day to the space allotted for that day, and he almost always filled an entire page with his small script. The 1955 Diary, which was kept in a small book measuring only 3 × 4½ inches, is more like an appointment book, each page containing space for two days. For this diary Frye's entries are much briefer, and sometimes he carries the entry over from one day to the next. The 1942 Diary was written on lined sheets in a bound notebook; the 1949 and 1953 Diaries, on loose, lined sheets that Frye kept in a ring binder. For these three diaries he was not, of course, constrained by the format of the day-book, and he did typically write more than a single page for each day's entry. Once Frye had developed the rhythm of diary writing in the day-books (1950 and following), the entries regularly follow a two- or three-paragraph form for a single day.

As a genre, the diary has as many subspecies as drama or lyric poetry—those conventional forms that Frye catalogues in such detail in his own theory of genres in *Anatomy of Criticism*. In his engaging study of diaries, *A Book of One's Own*, Thomas Mallon discovers seven types of diarists: chroniclers, travellers, pilgrims, creators, apologists, confessors, and prisoners.[8] Frye's diaries contain elements that could be a part of all of these species, except perhaps the last. As a genre, the diary is often an introverted and intellectual form, and so shares features with the autobiography or confession. The word "diary" also has the suggestion of a personal and private document, and the feeling does linger that to read another's diary is to invade his or her privacy. Most diaries, however, will eventually find an audience, even if unpublished, and those who do not want their diaries read will surely do the only sensible thing they can do to have their wish fulfilled—destroy the manuscripts. During one of the several times Frye feels particularly anxious about the future of Victoria College, thinking that he has reached the end of his career in Canada, he writes, "after all, nobody is going to read this diary except me and I don't mind boring myself" (50.386). But whatever Frye might have felt about the audience for his diary when he was thirty-seven, he obviously came to a different opinion in the 1980s, when he turned over his 1949 diary to his biographer John Ayre.[9] It is worth noting in this regard that Frye writes in his 1952 Diary that "a man has to die and leave a diary behind before what he has to say can be published at all, if he thinks in an unconventional form" (52.202).

Frye used the conventional phrase *keeping a diary* to refer to his own project.[10] To *keep* a diary does imply a certain degree of protection, which is why diaries sometimes come with lock and key. Of course, "keep" may mean simply to maintain by writing. We don't attach the verb "keep" to forms of writing other than the diary and its cousins (the journal, the daybook, the notebook, the chronicle, the log).[11] But the word suggests things in addition to simple maintenance: preservation (we keep meat by freezing it), to hold under guard (we keep prisoners in jail), to withhold from the knowledge of others (we keep secrets), to hold things confidential (we are instructed to keep things to ourselves). Mallon believes that "diaries are so much about the preservation and protection of the self that they demand the word right from the moment they're being composed. Diaries are *for* keeps: in fact they *are* keeps (Noun: FORTRESS, CASTLE: specif: the strongest and securest part)."[12] But what does it mean to say that Frye *kept* a diary in this sense? What is being kept and from whom? What was he trying to preserve within the fortress of these little bound books? Fortunately, we have Frye's own explicit reflections on the purposes of his daily writing, found in the prologue to his 1949 Diary, to help us answer these questions.

From the beginning Frye's diaries had been a means for recording the current state of his imaginative life. He would return to his diaries, at least occasionally, to read them. But a much better source for the record of Frye's creative life is contained, not in his diaries, but in his notebooks, and he seems to have realized this at the beginning of 1949, when he takes up diary writing with renewed vigour and with a different, or at least an additional, purpose. The diary now becomes a way for him to systematize his life and impose a sense of discipline on his daily activities. It even has a moral function:

> I'm not working hard enough, and I feel that a diary would be useful, as my job is mainly thinking & writing, & I need some machinery for recording everything of importance I think of. As a moral discipline, too, it's important for a natural introvert to keep his letters answered, his social engagements up to date, and his knowledge of people and events set out in greater detail. . . . I also hope it will be of some moral benefit, in passing a kind of value judgment, implicit or explicit, on whether I've wasted the day or not, whether my schedule is in shape, whether my unanswered letters are piling up, etc. The feeling of meeting my own conscience at the end of the day may cut down my dithering time. I should be careful, however, not to ascribe exaggerated values to secondary duties merely because they are duties & I don't like them, but always to put writing, thinking & reading first. (49.2–3)

Diary writing, then, is something Frye wants to develop into a habit. For Frye, there are two kinds of habit: the positive kind that, as he learned from Samuel Butler's *Life and Habit*, comes from continual practice and can lead to genuine freedom, and the negative kind, born of inertia and leading to entropy. The flurry of activity recorded in these diaries gives the impression of anything but indolence, yet Frye does see inertia as his "great enemy" (52 .3) and "the chief enemy of the soul" (49.6). When it manifests itself, as it frequently does, Frye will typically declare that he has "buggered" the day. The practice of diary writing, then, as Frye conceives it at the beginning of 1949, will be an exercise in Butler's practice-habit, standing as a kind of moral imperative for him to cut down on wasted time and keep up with his primary duties and secondary obligations.

But Frye announces that the diary will be, in addition, a tool for recording "everything of importance" he thinks of, noting that he should not be upset by the miscellaneous character of his life; a place for interpreting his dreams ("field work for anagogic interpretation," as he calls it); a source for two novels that he plans to write, one of which, he proclaims with casual assurance, "could be finished this year"; and a means for passing judgment on whether or not he is maintaining his relations with his students, keeping up with scholarship, and completing more mundane tasks, such as ordering books for the library. He even speaks of recording things from his student papers as material for writing a book on English. Frye does not rule out anything as worthy of being recorded: "one should avoid all taboos." The one thing he does not want the diaries to be used for is the "actual writing" of his books and essays.[13]

Frye is by no means able to exclude his writing projects from his diaries, but he does come close to achieving the ends he sets forth in the prologue to the 1949 Diary. The diaries record thousands of the most miscellaneous and mundane of daily activities, they reproduce almost two dozen dream interpretations, they contain scene after scene that might be incorporated into a novel, and they do provide the occasion for Frye to determine whether or not he is systematizing his life. But this description tells us very little about the scope and richness of the diaries, which are an intimate record of twenty-six months in the life of a man who usually deflected attention away from his own life. Whatever else they are, they are the raw material for biography.

III

Frye placed a high priority on privacy, and after he became a name, his secretary, Jane Widdicombe, did succeed in protecting him from most of the countless potential invasions of that privacy. He was fond of telling interviewers that he had unconsciously arranged his life to be without incident, the result being, he claimed, that no biographer would have the slightest interest in him as a subject. John Ayre's biography is, of course, evidence to the contrary. And however much we might like to agree in theory with Eliot's principle that there is a difference between the man who suffers and the mind which creates, in practice the principle is very difficult to maintain. When one becomes a public figure, there is a natural curiosity on the part of the public to learn about his or her life. Frye was also fond of insisting that his life *was* his published work, just as he was fond of quoting Montaigne's remark that his life was consubstantial with his book. One can understand what he meant by that, and yet this opposition between life and work, at the deepest level, cannot finally be sustained, as Michael Dolzani has shown.[14]

Frye is aware, of course, that whatever aims the diarist might have, what will emerge from all diaries is necessarily self-revelation. The self-revelation may be minimal, but it is there. The absence of sufficient self-revelation is what worried Frye about Samuel Pepys's *Diary*:

> I've been reading in Pepys, to avoid work. I can't understand him at all. I mean, the notion that he tells us more about himself & gives us a more intimate glimpse of the age than anyone else doesn't strike me. I find him more elusive and baffling than anyone. He has a curious combination of apparent frankness and real reticence that masks him more than anything else could do. One could call it a "typically English" trait, but there were no typical Englishmen then and Montaigne performs a miracle of disguise in a far subtler & bigger way. Pepys is not exactly conventional: he is socially disciplined. He tells us nothing about himself except what is generic. His gaze is directed out: he tells us where he has been & what he has done, but there is no reflection, far less self-analysis. The most important problem of the Diary & of related works is whether this absence of reflection is an accident, an individual design, or simply impossible to anyone before the beginning of Rousseauist modes of interior thought. (42.67)

A few entries later Frye writes that Pepys's "*genre*, the diary, is not a branch of autobiography, as Evelyn's is. . . . When I try to visualize Pepys I visualize clothes & a cultured life-force. I have a much clearer vision of the man who annoyed Hotspur or Juliet's Nurse's husband. . . . He does not observe character either: I can't visualize his wife or my Lord. Even music he talks about as though it were simply a part of his retiring for physic" (42.69). Frye, on the other hand, engages in a great deal of character observation—the character of his colleagues, his students, his family, his wife, and, most of all, himself. His diaries provide a rich and extensive psychological portrait. He does not set out to write a confession, but by the time we have come to the end of the diaries, he has confessed more than he perhaps realized.

But the diaries are also a chronicle. We peer over Frye's shoulder as he trudges to his office, teaches his classes, attends *Canadian Forum* meetings, reflects on movies, socializes with neighbours and other friends, discusses Blake with his student Peter Fisher, works on his various commissions, eyes attractive women, records his dreams, plans his career, judges his colleagues and his university, registers his frank reactions to the hundreds of people who cross his path, travels to Chicago, Wisconsin, and Cambridge, plans his fiction projects, reflects on music, religion, and politics, shovels his sidewalk, suffers through committee meetings, describes his various physical and psychological ailments, practises the piano, visits bookstores, frequents Toronto restaurants, reflects on his reading, and records scores of additional activities, mundane and otherwise. As a chronicle, Frye's diaries are like Virginia Woolf's, putting the most inconsequential event, such as cutting the grass, alongside the most sober reflection, such as the nature of the contemporary church or the unspeakable uselessness of war. His speculations on a wide range of critical and social and religious issues are not unlike those in a typical notebook entry. His notebooks occasionally become quite personal and thus move in the direction of the diary. His diaries very often become quite impersonal and thus move in the direction of the notebook. The context of the speculative passages is sometimes a contemporary event, as when the Korean War triggers his prescient views on the path that Communism will take during the last half of the century. Most often, however, the contexts for Frye's speculations are the courses he is teaching or his writing projects.

IV

What, then, do we learn about Frye as a person in the diaries? The question can be answered in part by what he does, by noting those things to which he devotes his time and energy—his sessions with students, his commitments as an academic citizen, his rather full social calendar, his involvement in his community (especially the countless hours he gives to public lecturing and to the *Canadian Forum*). Many of his activities outside the classroom Frye finds to be joyless and dull, but he does dutifully take on a wide range of commitments. The sheer number of things that occupy Frye's life is so extensive that little time would seem to be left over for periods of sustained writing. We have to remind ourselves that during six of the seven years covered by the diaries Frye was at work on *Anatomy of Criticism*. It was during these years as well that he wrote more than fifty major articles and reviews.

Still, finding time to write is one of Frye's great struggles. A case in point is the production of his seminal essay "The Archetypes of Literature," which turned out to be the most frequently anthologized of all his articles. The paper arose from a request on 23 June 1950 by the editor of the *Kenyon Review*, who asked Frye to write an article on poetry, the request having been motivated by the *Review*'s response to the essay he had previously submitted, "Levels of Meaning in Literature." Frye replies that he would prefer to write an essay on archetypes. For the next fortnight, he busies himself with three talks for CBC Radio's "Writer as Prophet" series and with preparing to leave Toronto for his Guggenheim year at Harvard. There is no time for additional writing, though on 25 June he does report that he has begun "drafting out a tentative plan" for his archetypes essay. The Fryes fly to Cambridge on 10 July, and four days later, on his birthday, Frye gets down to work, drafting the opening part of his essay, which he calls "a bit speculative," and producing "a lot of rubbish on the theory that [he] could always cut later." His writing is interrupted by a two-day trip to the beach, but on 18 July he begins to see the general shape of his paper, and he devotes the better part of the next two days to writing, though the first day results in very little but false starts. Meanwhile the Fryes' classmate Jean Elder, along with her father and Helen's parents, arrive for a week-long visit. Finally, on 24 July Frye begins "to organize [his] instruments of production," buying paper and pen and renting a typewriter. By 25 July the first part of the article "is in pretty fair shape." He then spends the better part of 28 July typing it, and the next day posts it from Ipswich, Massachusetts, of all places, where the Fryes had set out for another beach trip with Ruth Jenking, a Victoria College colleague who was enrolled in the Harvard summer school. The time from conception to the birth, then, has been just over a month, but it has been a fitful month, and the actual writing of "The Archetypes of Literature" appears to have taken no longer than a couple of days. But the process is typical: Frye is always scrambling to find time amid a hectic schedule to write. The archetypes essay appears to have almost written itself once Frye had determined its general three-part shape. He certainly worried less about it, and spent less time in preparing to write it, than he did, say, for his fifteen-minute CBC talk on Shaw. In any case, the diaries as chronicle contain scores of vignettes that reveal how a man who desperately wants a settled routine for his writing projects has great difficulty finding such a routine because of the demands made on his time by external factors of every variety.

V

The most obvious of the external demands was, of course, teaching. The diaries provide little evidence that Frye spent much time in the daily preparation for his classes, and in March of 1950 he notes that he hasn't done any reading for his lectures in years (50.226). Frye's teaching schedule was relatively full, at least by today's standards. The most extensive accounts of his teaching are in the diaries for 1949, 1950, and 1952, years during which he taught three two-hour English courses, two one-hour Religious Knowledge courses, and one graduate seminar. All were year-long courses. For 1949 and 1950 Frye's teaching schedule was this:

Monday
English 2i: English Poetry and Prose, 1500–1660
Graduate seminar in Spenser (1950 only)

Tuesday
Religious Knowledge, fourth year
English 4k: Nineteenth-Century Thought

Wednesday
English 2i: English Poetry and Prose, 1500–1660
English 4k: Nineteenth-Century Thought

Thursday
English 3j: Spenser and Milton
Religious Knowledge, first year
Graduate seminar in Blake (1949 only)

Friday
English 3j: Spenser and Milton

Frye taught the same courses in 1952, though his schedule was ar-ranged a bit differently: Monday, 2i and 4k; Tuesday, 4k and Religious Knowledge (fourth year); Wednesday, 2i; Thursday, 3j and Religious

Knowledge (first year); and Friday, 3j and the graduate seminar (on allegory). Religious Knowledge (or a Religious Knowledge option) was a subject that all arts students, except those in commerce and finance, were required to take during each of their years at the University of Toronto. Frye taught one of the several offerings for both first- and fourth-year students in the Honour Course. The first-year course, on the English Bible, was intended primarily for students in language and literature. The fourth-year course, also on the English Bible, was "a course in the appreciation of Biblical literature." Both of the Religious Knowledge courses met for one hour each week.[15] In addition to his regular teaching responsibilities, Frye gave lectures in a course on drama taught principally by E.J. Pratt, a course that met two hours a week. Toward the end of the course Frye would give the Thursday lectures on Jonson and Webster, among other playwrights. Informally, Frye also met with the Writers' Group, which had been organized by students about ten years earlier as a way of generating interest in creative writing and in the Victoria literary magazine, *Acta Victoriana*. In 1949 the group met in the evenings, but by the next year it had become a Tuesday afternoon session, and in 1952 it met at 10:00 A.M. on Monday. In these more or less informal but regular meetings Frye became the sounding board for undergraduates— all women—who would meet in his office to read their stories and poems. This was not a credit-bearing course, but in 1950 and 1952 it did occupy an hour in Frye's weekly calendar. Altogether, then, Frye met with students for ten or eleven hours each week. This was at a time when Frye was already a full professor and a recognized, published scholar: Victoria College appears not to have rewarded senior faculty members who were active professionally with light teaching schedules. Outside of his university teaching responsibilities, we also find Frye conducting funerals, giving sermons, lecturing to secondary school English teachers, community reading groups, and librarians, and giving talks to audiences at the School of Social Work, the Royal Ontario Museum, Emmanuel College, the English Institute, the Modern Language Association, the Royal Society of Canada, and the Universities of Chicago and Michigan.

Teaching for Frye was, at least in part, an occasion for testing his ideas. He took no lecture notes into the classroom, and what lecture notes he did write came only after he had gone back to his office.[16] The diaries themselves are a source of some of these notes, as Frye frequently records the ideas that emerged from his lectures. These entries are some of the richest in the diaries.

VI

As already said, Frye's diaries are much more than a chronicle. A strong current of the confession runs throughout, part of the confession being the self-revelation that Frye wished Pepys's *Diary* had contained. Frye reveals a great deal through self-analysis, writing about his abnormal fears, his physical insecurity, his self-consciousness, his introversion, his sanguine humour and his dark moods, his claustrophobia and paranoia, his grieving over the death of a colleague, his phobia about animals. He writes about his various bodily deficiencies and physical ailments (for example, his deviated septum, hay fever attacks, constipation, insomnia, and various states of stupor induced by too much alcohol). He probes his own ego, often from a Jungian perspective, and there is no small measure of self-congratulation, even before he reaches his thirtieth birthday.

"I have always believed," Frye writes in an entry for the second day of his 1942 Diary, "that to have several competing firms scrambling for my business on all lines was Utopia. A delight in this and a horror of any monopoly that could get along without me is my one real economic feeling" (42.8). Frye's awareness of his genius leads not so much toward vanity as toward self-possession: "I glory in my intelligence, & should, yet in me a universal intelligence reaches a certain focus" (49.162). Or at least egoism can provide a perspective on life and need not be seen as one of the seven deadly sins:

> I think one's view of the world ought to be periodically corrected by an insane & megalomaniac egoism. Suppose I pretend for a moment that the whole world I live in was created especially for me, & every event that happened to me was done for my benefit. It follows that the events of one's life would show a unified providential design. Looking at one's life from this point of view, everything about one's life with which one is dissatisfied is the result of a missed opportunity of grasping the real significance of past events, the real significance being, on this theory, its meaning to me. This would be the only way of making sense of the notion of the sinlessness of Jesus' life—a notion I'm not very interested in anyway. (49.363)[17]

Still, there is no question that Frye is very much aware of his special gifts. When he is irritated about having been asked by the Guggenheim committee for more information than he has provided about his knowledge of Spenser scholarship, he quips, "It's very lonely being a genius:

you're just an arrogant crank who happens to be bright" (50.116). The following day, in connection with his article on Spenser, he laments his not yet having reached the point "where people would know in advance how important I am, & be ready to study my next collection of axioms as that, instead of just looking over it as though it were one more article" (50.120). About the list of Guggenheim candidates, he remarks, "Except for me, it's a pretty undistinguished list" (50.260). And when he is at Harvard, Frye, having scrutinized the English department there and finding it not particularly distinguished, notes that Toronto is not such a bad place to be after all, and then writes, "at times, in my delusions of grandeur, I wonder if the world of English scholars isn't waiting for someone, maybe me, to give them a lead" (50.501).

Sometimes Frye is less confident. He has only "a hope that posterity will recognize the greatness of such books as *Fearful Symmetry*" (49.199). At other times he recognizes the dangers of his growing reputation as a guru of sorts. Reacting to a remark by a female student that he "was the best Christian she knew," Frye muses that "there are dangers in the fact that I have developed, without being able to help it, the kind of facile pseudo-sanctity which comes from having pleasant security & no major problems" (49.175). Or again, wondering about the joke circulating at Victoria College that he was God, he complains to his diary, "I don't like it at all, especially the emotional stampede it makes on me. It tempts me to take myself far too seriously, not as a hero (that's easy) but as a fender-off of hero-worship. Like Julius Caesar, I have to keep making ostentatious gestures of refusing the crown" (49.304). Or still again, "I am almost the only critic I know who can really see criticism, and, like the man in H.G. Wells's very profound story about the seeing man in the blind community, I find myself isolated with my superior power instead of being able to benefit others directly with it" (50.515). The ego, Frye says after recording some praise that has come his way, can be "a spur to imagination" (49.230); but if being the only one who can see has its powers, it has its limitations as well. Frye's loneliness, in the middle of a half-dozen communities of which he is a part, is not simply the result of his introversion.

VII

As indicated above, Frye sets out to record his dreams in his diary, using them as his "field work for anagogic interpretation." We sleep, Frye speculates, not to provide periodic respite for the weary brain, but "to sink it into the domain of creative archetypal imagery & free association, whence it emerges to give direction & basis to the wakened mind" (50.110). He understands dreams as existing halfway between waking consciousness (the world of becoming) and archetypes (the world of being or the creative world of art and thought). Dreams can work positively or negatively. If they work positively, they assimilate what happens in the chaotic world of ordinary experience, including the experience of childhood, to the grand epic of the archetypal world. This is the world of what Frye calls, following Jung, "the universal comedy of the human collective unconscious" (49.30). If the small dramas of our dream life become episodes in the universal epic, then our psyches will progress into a more or less healthy state, which Frye describes as a state of relaxation and concentration—Jung's individuation. The collective form of such progress is the unity Frye finds in Spengler's idea of culture (49.77). If our dreams work negatively or regressively, then we are jerked back and forth between waking reality and either Freudian wish-fulfilment or Adlerian will-to-power fantasies. Here we are simply caught up in an anxious escape from reality and in forming substitute reactions that will never overcome the antithesis between reality and desire.

Frye's psychic universe, then, is three-storied: between the world of consciousness on top and the world of archetypes below is the dream world of erotic desires and will-to-power fantasies. Progress in shaping a self comes from connecting dreams to the archetypes below. Regression results from our inability to get beyond (or, in Frye's model, below) the shuttling back and forth between the two top levels. But Frye's psychic model has another, still lower level, for below the archetypal world of concentration and art "is the world of meditation, which seizes the moment Satan can't find," as Blake says in *Milton*,

> & in which the soul emerges through the mind as well as the body. Blavatsky says that if you could remember your deep dreams you could remember your previous incarnations. I don't think it's necessary to accept this, but it's possible that if you could take a golden bough with you all the way in the original plunge to sleep, Alice's fall down the well, you would never need to sleep again. The Tibetan Bardo has something of this idea of an initial plunge & then a gradual rise back to the same old grind. (49.77)

Most dreams are a "wandering in the limbo of the past, just outside that gate we have as yet no golden bough to enter" (49.117). Frye records nineteen dreams altogether.[18] Most are either wish-fulfilments or nightmares. One is a purely Oedipal dream, combining anxiety and desire.

Others, which are difficult to label, involve lost keys and returns to childhood, the latent content of which mystifies Frye. On only three occasions does he see his dreams as assimilating archetypal content and so directly connected to the third level. One is a complicated dream in which he is able to recognize most of the sources of the manifest content, and he believes the dream reveals certain "erotic or even wish-fulfilment" latent content. But the real archetype of the dream, he speculates, has to do with "the Catholic-Protestant antinomy which is always in my mind" (49.91).

A second dream with archetypal import begins with characteristic erotic and anxiety features, but the end of the dream is what Frye finds most significant: "As I staggered around I saw two huge & rather frightening stone heads on the side of the square I'd been on, one that I was looking directly at, of a woman, & another on the left, that I didn't look at, of a man. I record this dream because the statues seem archetypal—I feel sure that the last two were my father & mother" (49.189). On 21 March 1949 Frye records the third archetypal dream:

> To bed early, & had a long series of strange dreams. One had me on the roof of a house with the house apparently moving about under me; some nervousness but above all a great puzzle as to what was moving it. . . . Another one had me a student again kidnapped by S.P.S. [School of Practical Science] for hazing purposes. They knew me well & a friend of mine deserted me at their approach, whispering that it would be good for me. However, I was busy trying to talk myself out of the situation when I woke. The purpose of the hazing was the slighting remarks I was alleged to have made about engineering, which I was busily denying. May be some reference to a phenomenon Jung doesn't mention: an introvert trying to project before him his own extroverted self, or vice versa. This is the theme of Sitwell's Man Who Lost Himself, which I read in my Freshman days & is an extrovert > introvert pattern. Henry James' *Jolly Corner* seems to be reversing the pattern: I was reading it just before I fell asleep. I was also looking at *FW* [*Finnegans Wake*], as I've rashly tied myself up to a "What To Do until Finnegan Wakes" talk at Michigan. Kenner is all wet about the "keys" on the last page being the keys of the church. The phrase is "the keys *to*," & it means the keys to the Church, & to all churches. Shem looks at churches from behind, & holds the keys *of*, no *to*, dreamland—that phrase turns up a few pages earlier. (49.284)

Frye is especially interested in the hazing episode of this dream, and the next day he speculates about the man who wanted to haze him, saying that in this episode of the dream, "I came face to face with a real archetype, one, as I say, that Jung doesn't know about, a kind of compensatory extroverted censor figure, not unfriendly, not completely unsympathetic, but utterly contemptuous of all the introvert vices (self-abuse, cowardice, insolence, physical weakness) & profoundly suspicious of many of the virtues" (49.288). Frye glances at his "introvert vices" from time to time, noting that he is an abnormal conductor of fear (42.31), that he has "a persistent sense of physical insecurity engendered by [his] weak & awkward body" (49.20), that he hates to be dominating (49.98), that while he is gregarious enough, he nevertheless prefers the solitude of social introversion (49.112), and that he wants to rid himself of self-consciousness, which leads to *Angst* and claustrophobia (50.5, 106).

In *Anatomy of Criticism* Frye would argue that the concern of the literary critic should be the "dream patterns which are actually in what he is studying, however they got there" (109), and that Jung's idea of the collective unconscious is "an unnecessary hypothesis in literary criticism" (112). But Jung is very close to Frye's side in his diaries. He had taken notes on Jung's *Psychology of the Unconscious* in the early 1940s,[19] and by the end of the 1950 Diary he had read Jung's *Psychological Types* and his commentary on *The Secret of the Golden Flower*; and he had waded through two commentaries on Jung as well, Wickes's *The Inner World of Man* and Jacobi's *The Psychology of C.G. Jung*. The result is that in his diaries Frye draws frequently on Jung's work ("I think I've pretty well got the hang of Jung now," he writes on 13 April 1949), and he calls on Jung's anima/animus distinction in his brief commentaries on Hamlet, Blackmore's *Lorna Doone*, James's *The Sense of the Past*, and Nathan's *Portrait of Jennie*.[20] He speaks of writing a paper on Blake and Jung;[21] he sees Jung's individuated self in Huck Finn, in the *Inferno* as a body of regressive symbols,[22] and, as seen above, in James's *Jolly Corner* as a reversal of the extrovert/introvert pattern. He writes, moreover, of having arrived, with the publication of *Fearful Symmetry*, at the stage of Jungian individuation: "It occurs to me that what I did in writing FS was perform the act described in much the same way by Freud & Jung. This is the act of swallowing the father, integrating oneself with the old wise man. Presumably I shall never find another father, not even in Shakespeare, & should realize that I am essentially *on my own*. I've really reached an individuated stage of thinking, if not of personal life" (49.110).

Even though Jung has his limitations (he conventionalizes dream symbolism, he has no conception of the form of society, and his account of the archetypes of the self is restricted),[23] his insights into the psyche are clearly useful for Frye's locating and understanding conventional psychic patterns in the works he glances at; thus, Jung makes repeated appearances in the 1949 and 1950 Diaries. And Frye even turns to Jung in trying to understand his own psyche, seeing himself, for example, as one of Jung's intuitive thinking types, one for whom "sensational thinking is undifferentiated" (49.47).[24] In a particularly telling series of entries in the 1949 Diary, he turns to Jung's anima/animus distinction to try to understand his relationship with women. His problem, in short, is that his anima, the feminine nature within his masculine soul, or what he calls at one point "the aggregate of all the female characters in me" (49.361), is not recognized by women. After having had lunch with Margaret Avison, Frye writes,

> I made the mistake with her of allowing her to make me into an animus figure. That in itself isn't a mistake, but it's a transference that a real friend should mature & dissolve. I never did that, but tried to act like an animus. I talked to her as a woman dances, trying to sense her lead and articulate it. It worked well for a while, but it stereotyped me, & she gradually realized the physical male object before her & declared her love for it. As that is only deadlock, and I had no further animus resources, the dance is over, & we're standing around, both facing the orchestra & not each other, patting our hands nervously to signify our approval of what has been done. I made the same mistake with Elizabeth Frazer [Fraser].[25] Part of the error comes in my very animus nature: I respond by idealizing the woman into an anima. I have thought of both Elizabeth & Margaret as wonderfully subtle and accurate creatures, & of their instincts as invested with a superior insight, which I could educate myself by following. I have learned little from these women, & have not helped them much to learn from me. (49.48)

They have not learned much from him because he has been unable completely to shake off his animus role: "Intelligent & sensitive women have often quite literally laid down the law to me" (49.238); that is, he yearns to develop the anima nature within himself but cowers in the face of the female animus. At the same time Frye has difficulty with women who project their own masculine soul onto him: "Women who make me their animus & then desert when I can't fill *that* role get me down. I spend a fair amount of emotional time in a state of baffled tenderness, & it's a positive relief to have so self-absorbed a youngster [as Norma Arnett] come in, get what she wants out of me, shake her curls & flounce out again" (49.197). This is why Frye says that he has so much difficulty with his female students. His animus is too strong for their anima and his anima too weak for their animus: "I can't really teach a woman, because, being a woman, the things organic to her learning process are female, & shut me out. All I could do would be to identify myself with her animus, which puts me, as I've discovered & elsewhere remarked, in a hell of a spot" (49.101).

VIII

Frye often takes a liberated view of women—it distresses him, for example, that his colleague Kathleen Coburn is excluded from gatherings in that male institution at Victoria University, the Senior Common Room (50.86). Nevertheless, his male gaze is often directed at women as attractive physical objects. Frye remarks at one point that

> People are human beings first and men and women afterwards. Their bodily functions are different; their environments are different, though the difference in this century has been greatly decreased. So there may be generalizations of the "men are like *this* whereas women are like *that*" kind which may have some hazy and approximate truth. I don't know. Men's conversation is more abstract & less personal than women's, but whether that's an accident of training or an essential sexual trait I don't know. I do know that the kind of mind that thinks along these lines of facile antitheses is a dull & tiresome mind. It betrays a fixation on sex-differences which is mere adolescence, & in an adult unhealthy. (42.77)

But throughout the diaries Frye violates his own injunction against stereotyping. The economic dependence of women on men, he says, produces shrewishness and silliness (49.97). "What the average woman wants," he writes, "is something maudlin to attach her complex of self-pity and I-get-left-at-home and my-work-is-never-done and nobody-appreciates-it-anyway to" (42.90). He explains the inability of his female students to follow what he says in one of his lectures about archetypes as "the difference between the male & the female mind" (50.152).

Frye takes a good measure of delight in providing Freudian interpretations of the stories of what he calls "my writing girls," the informal creative writing group he met with regularly. "Really, those kids," he says, "they're very attractive youngsters, they've only got one thing on their little minds, & it ain't writing. Today it was a red stain on a clean dress, from wine. Last week it was a blood-red moon. Before that it was Jean Inglis' triangular-piece-out-of-the-lamp story" (50.133). The writing group, in fact, provides the occasion for Frye to engage in his own form of male exhibitionism: "I find having all that beauty & charm & health & youth in my office a bit overpowering: I find, not unnaturally, that I want to show off. I never worked that out of my system because, not being athletic, I couldn't show off in the approved ways during the mating season" (50.153). When Frye finds himself surrounded by a large number of women ("so much female flesh") in a Toronto restaurant in 1942, he begins to feel "a little like a stud," and he muses that if the war goes on for too long, civilians may have to be drafted for "stud duty" (42.105). What attracts Frye at the beach in Ipswich, Massachusetts, are "the lovely American bodies" (50.508). At Wells Beach he finds that the "lovely & nearly naked figure [of an eighteen-year-old girl] hovering on my line of vision" causes him, in a witty understatement, "some difficulty in concentrating on the formal causes of literature" (50.580). Sometimes Frye can almost wilt in the presence of feminine charm. When the novelist Frances Wees calls him, her "cuddly viscerotomic sentimental female self" projecting itself over the phone, he muses that "something in her approach is so intimate that I feel rude unless I start becoming earnest & avuncular. Even over a phone a hand steals out to pat her backside, & by the time I hang up I'm lowing at her like a cow" (49.247). A certain light-hearted innocence emerges from such remarks: one can see Frye grinning wryly at himself. It is nevertheless true that in the diary entries that focus on women, including women students, he is typically unable to get beyond physical appearance. "Cute" is his favourite epithet, followed by "attractive, "pretty," and "beautiful."[26] There is nothing perverse in all this, and whatever libidinous urges Frye has, they are most often disguised or displaced. But a catalogue of his references to women leaves the impression that Frye's male gaze reveals more about himself than he perhaps realized.

IX

What then of Frye's wife Helen? When the Fryes were married in 1937, Helen had been working at the Art Gallery of Toronto, arranging gallery talks, organizing children's educational programs, and writing an occasional radio script about the gallery for CBC Radio. By the early 1940s, however, she had given up her job at the Art Gallery, and, except for some freelance newspaper writing, she busied herself with other activities at Victoria College and in the community. She writes occasional reviews and articles on art and artists—eighteen altogether from 1942 to 1955 (see Appendix 2). She devotes some energy to the *Canadian Forum*: Frye himself was appointed editor in 1948, a position he held until he took his Guggenheim year at Harvard in 1950, and Helen became a member of the editorial board. They were both still active on the board when the diaries come to a close in 1955. The diaries reveal nothing about Helen's work as art editor of the *Forum*, which mainly involved her selecting the graphic art for each issue, but she did attend at least some of the weekly staff meetings.

Helen also takes an active role in the Faculty Women's Council during these years, though, as the diaries reveal, she attends the various functions of this group more from a sense of duty than for pleasure or other benefit. She occasionally participates in the *Citizens' Forum*, a popular weekly radio program, broadcast over CBC, which made use of listening groups that met in people's homes. Otherwise, Helen seems mostly to have stayed at home, where she had the burden of the domestic chores. She could occasionally cajole Frye into helping with the shopping, furniture moving, or yard work. He sometimes feels guilty about his failure to lend a hand. When it comes time to paint their house before leaving for Harvard in 1950, Frye writes,

> One member of the caucus inside my brain says I'm a lazy & selfish bastard to let her do all the painting without raising a finger to help. Another member, speaking for the government, says I have my own work to do, and the fact I keep on doing it is the guarantee of the contribution I make to the family fortunes. Also that the self-accusation is one of the ready-made formulas of an infantile conscience, which, in an introvert, insists that practical and manipulative activities alone can be called work. Helen herself doesn't feel that way, as she can't help me with my writing. (50.325)

Frye's urge is to steal away from the house on Saturday mornings, going to his office to catch up on his letter writing and other obligations. It is clear that Helen would prefer to have him at home, and he occasionally does stay home on Saturday, if only to read.[27] He takes pleasure in putting himself in Helen's care. Once, in reflecting on how her article in the *Star Weekly*, with its circulation of almost a million, will receive wider circulation than anything he will ever write, he muses, "Curious how little that means. It occurs to me that the marriage vow, where the man says cherish & protect & the woman honour & obey (or used to) ought to be reversed for a matriarchal society like ours, where the woman affords the man protection in her home in return for unquestioning obedience within it" (49.184). Frye does relish the protection, but whether he is unquestioningly obedient, and in what sense, is less clear.

Helen makes well over three hundred appearances in the diaries, but we never get a rounded picture of her interior life. We do see from time to time her sense of humour, her judgments about Frye's various lectures, radio talks, and sermons (he seeks her critiques and values them), and her devotion to her family. We learn about her presiding over meals and other social events at their home, her various missions of mercy in the community, and her sundry physical ailments. But what Helen really thinks and feels remains something of a mystery. Her restlessness is the chief thing we discover about her psychological state. This manifests itself sometimes as the normal anxieties associated with domestic life. At other times it borders on depression. Her dark moods seem to result partly from her general melancholic humour, as Frye calls it (50.276), but more often than not the reason for these moods is something external: she is weary from housework; sulky because Frye gets home late; uneasy about the values of the propertied middle class; anxious about her father and mother, Frye's own father (who spends the Christmas season with them during these years), Frye's sister Vera, and her own brother Roy and his wife; bored by pouring tea at the faculty women's functions; and apprehensive about becoming middle-aged. When Helen is "feeling that way again" (50.125), the typical cure is to go to the Park Plaza Hotel for drinks and then out to lunch or dinner at one of the dozen or so restaurants they frequent.

Frye records his disagreement with Montaigne about marriage:

> Montaigne says that one should not love a wife too much, for that is attachment: she might die and then where would you be? The doctrine of non-attachment is mine; the application is not: I feel that in such a passage as that wisdom has outfoxed itself. One should withdraw attachment from possessions & machines, but you remain attached to your right arm, & life without it is a mutilated life. With wives as with arms, one is attached, & simply has to take the chance. The metaphor of "one flesh" is not an idle one. (49.139)

From what we know about Frye's feelings for Helen at the beginning of their relationship, as this is recorded in their correspondence, and from the almost debilitating grief he suffered when she died in 1986, as this is recorded in his late notebooks, it is clear that their attachment was one of genuinely deep devotion. Few expressions of love are as poignant and powerful as Frye's for his wife in the notebooks. But the years covered in the diaries do not seem particularly gratifying or fulfilling years for her. The present diaries are of course Frye's, not Helen's. For one who comes on stage so frequently in the diaries, however, we would expect to learn more about Helen than we do. She comes across, finally, as one who is given little space to develop her potential.

X

Frye used his notebooks for developing the ideas for his books and essays, and, as indicated above, he warns himself against letting the diaries turn into notebooks. It is impossible, however, for Frye completely to eliminate his intellectual life from the diaries. His speculations—motivated by a lecture, a conversation, a book he has been reading, a current event, or simply by an idea flashing across his inward eye—spill over onto almost every page. Not infrequently the thoughts he records do make their way into one of his writing projects. He is not too far into his 1942 Diary, for example, before he devotes several entries to Gérard de Nerval, whose visions of creation and apocalypse in *Le Rêve et la Vie* he finds especially fascinating, and he does use Nerval in *Fearful Symmetry*, which appeared five years later, to make a point about the importance of the analogue, rather than the source, in studying Blake.

Frye's speculations cover a range of philosophical, literary, musical, political, and religious topics. Sometimes they are triggered by a thesis advanced in a lecture, and he occasionally provides fairly full abstracts of what he said in class, as in his 1949 account of one of his lectures on Newman in Nineteenth-Century Thought. "I had nothing to say," Frye begins, "so fell back on rehashing the old Verstand-Vernunft distinction" (49.30). Frye then rehearses his lecture, or at least that part of it having to do with the emotions, and we follow the free association of his own running commentary on what he had said. He takes us through Cassirer and *Gestalt* theory, through Carlyle and Tennyson and Blake, carrying us, six hundred words later, into the world of Jungian archetypes.

In entries such as this one we have Frye the creator, to use one of Mallon's categories. Many notebook-like passages reveal Frye's fertile mind speculating on the nature of the city (49.120), on *Lorna Doone* (49.161) and Charles Williams's novels (49.200–1), on the idea of receptivity in *The Tibetan Book of the Dead* (49.223), on the social values of democracy (49.312–15), on C.D. Broad's conception of metaphysics

(50.145), on the revolutionary, "existentialist" thinkers of the nineteenth century (50.172), on the distinction between form and formula (50.541), on Swift (50.423, 426, 427) and Blake (50.531–2, 534–5, 538), on homosexuality (52.8), and on scores of other topics.

The diaries from 1949 on were written during the period Frye was at work on what was to become *Anatomy of Criticism*—"the vast . . . thing in my brain that's trying to get born" (50.202). As we might expect, Frye does not restrict his thoughts about the *Anatomy* to his notebooks. By the time of his 1950 Guggenheim year Frye had already written "Music in Poetry," "The Anatomy in Prose Fiction," "The Nature of Satire," "The Function of Criticism at the Present Time," "The Argument of Comedy," "The Four Forms of Prose Fiction," and "Levels of Meaning in Literature"—all of which would be incorporated into *Anatomy of Criticism*. By May of 1950 Frye is beginning to realize that his original Guggenheim project on Spenser is transforming itself into a more theoretical book:

> My head is full of ideas of various kinds. What I really should do is plunge straight into the second chapter of L and just hope to God I can work out a conspectus of archetypes. I've been confusing myself by doodling with a lot of cabbalistic diagrams, & should get my nose closer to the whole problem. Obviously L is basically going to be FS over again, deduced from general principles & then verified by application, instead of induced from the practice of one poet. That means the book's sunk if I can't work out a general theory of archetypes. That doesn't worry me, because I can. But the Spenser particularly can't be just a six-book commentary: I have to read Spenser until he comes apart deductively, the great archetypes that sprawl across the books emerging from a single central principle. All that's clear: what isn't clear is the extent to which L is likely to become a general theory of poetry, or could do so without losing its girlish figure. I mustn't let general symmetries spoil particular ones. (50.349)

"L" is Frye's shorthand for Liberal, the name he gave to the first volume of his lifelong eight-book project—what he referred to as the "ogdoad." Liberal was initially conceived as representing *Fearful Symmetry*, but when Frye completed that book, he renumbered it zero, and Liberal then became a study of the epic. The scheme of eight masterworks was never rigid, and it went through various permutations over the years, but it did correspond, as Frye explains it, "to some major divisions in my actual thinking."[28] If his "general theory of poetry" is not clear to Frye in May of 1950, by January 1951 the essential components of the book, which Frye is calling *Essay on Criticism* at this point,[29] have cleared up, except for his treatment of the epic:

> I seem to be at the point of looking down on literature from a height, no longer working inside it. I have three major ideas, each a part of a logically coherent structure. First is the area covered by my Kenyon Review articles, on meaning & the verbal universe, on archetypes & genres, & on the structure of symbolism. Second is the area covered in my three-volume Guggenheim prospectus, the analysis of the essential modes of verbal expression, scripture, epic, drama, lyric & prose. Third is the area covered by my "Church & Society" article & my interest in 19th c. subjects, especially Morris, Butler & Yeats. This is actually an apology for criticism: a statement of the social function of the arts & of the place of criticism as a social science. Several things are not clear to me yet, & one of these is, curiously enough, the precise way to tackle the epic. Another is the relation of the elements of the trivium, grammar, rhetoric & logic, & of the function of dialectic as a verbal element. I have a hunch about "verbal determinism" that may not work out. So my draft of the last four chapters, or Part Three, is loose: something like this perhaps: 9, The Limits of Verbal Expression (i.e., Literature & the Other Arts); 10, Art & Spiritual Authority (raising the point that comes out of Arnold, even Newman, & goes back to Roger Bacon, of the non-compulsive authority of *all* scripture); 11, Criticism as a Social Science, and art as a continuously expanding force cracking up all dogmatic *a priori* systems & closed societies like the "monologue" of the Church; 12, The Dialectics of Criticism, following out my concentric scheme. (51.10)

The organization of *Anatomy of Criticism* would, of course, go through many changes over the next half-dozen years, but here the general contours of the book are easily recognizable.

XI

Michael Dolzani has provided what he calls a "skeleton key" to Frye's ogdoadic code, and the introduction to Frye's late notebooks includes a briefer account of the eight-book schema, with particular reference to the way it served Frye during the last decade of his life.[30] Frye's diaries contain further variations on this large conceptual structure, and in the interest of having a more complete understanding of his thinking about the major books of his life, we can summarize the several ways they appear in the diaries in the following table:[31]

	The Ogdoad	
	The Trivium	The Seven Pillars
Liberal L	Grammar of verbal structures or narratives. Linear sense of all forms of verbal expression. Containing form: interconnection of Christian Bible and Christian year. Associated with the theory of poetry, the study of anagogics, and the Renaissance epic.	*Liberal, Tragicomedy,* and *Anticlimax* are to be an outline of the three main divisions of the hypothetical verbal universe: Poetry
Tragicomedy ⌐	Rhetorical encyclopedia or ordered presentation of definitive myth. Containing form: total vision. Associated with the theory of drama and Shakespearean comedy.	Drama
Anticlimax ∧	Logical and verbal universes are identified. Containing form: something conceptual. Associated with a commentary on the Bible, with a theory of prose, with Jonathan Swift. A transitional book that expands into *Rencontre*.	Prose
	The Quadrivium	
Rencontre ∧	Primary anagogy. Music provides the transition to the quadrivium. "Blake's Treatment of the Archetype" provides a sketch of *Rencontre*. Associated with "the form of the fourth" (prophecy), with Romanticism, Blake, and modern thought, with the systole and diastole rhythm of induction and deduction	*Rencontre, Mirage, Paradox,* and *Ignoramus* are an outline for four containing myths or hypotheses of the four divisions of the factual verbal universe, which are the four divisions of Scripture: *Law:* contrast between visionary law (gospel) and causal law

The Quadrivium (*concluded*)

Mirage ∨	Quadrivial logic or geometry. Diagrammatic basis of thinking. Linked with "Levels of Meaning in Literature" and the total form of human creative power.	*Prophecy* or active idea: general survey of informing of fact by myth and of relation of different arts (e.g., sculpture as the hypothesis of biology)
Paradox ⊢	Quadrivial rhetoric or astronomy. Comparative religion. Groundwork for archetypes and a conspectus of the verbal universe.	*History*: the event done, as opposed to law (the event doing). Philosophy of history. Vico–Spengler. The Marxist element.
Ignoramus ⊥	Quadrivial grammar or arithmetic. Linear progression on a deeper level. Associated with the dialectic of Marxism and Thomism, with free thought, Mill, the university, the symposium.	*Wisdom*: philosophy (the idea done), as opposed to prophecy
Twilight ⊤ or Γ	Quadrivial music. Secondary anagogy. Second coming or the return to the source.	

Frye used the ogdoad as a roadmap for his writing career, and it is possible in retrospect to see that *A Study of English Romanticism* is associated with Rencontre, his late notebooks with Twilight, *A Natural Perspective* with Tragicomedy, *The Great Code* and *Words with Power* with both Liberal and Anticlimax. We can even see in the last four of "the seven pillars" an embryonic form of the phases of revelation in *The Great Code*. But Frye also used the ogdoad, which was never rigidly fixed in his mind, as a way of generating both ideas and deductive frameworks of various kinds. So it is also possible to see in each of the eight parts of Frye's "medieval curriculum" (he cheats a bit by making his quadrivium into a quintivium) structures and concepts that make their way into *Anatomy of Criticism*. By 1952, thanks to his Guggenheim year at Harvard, Frye had worked out the key features of the theory of poetry that had displaced the Spenser book, and in the 1950 Diary especially Frye is continually working through parts of the argument that will find their place in the *Anatomy*. The following passage—Frye's speculations about his conspectus of the verbal universe—is typical of the rapid-fire movement of his schematic thinking:

Barth talks about the Word spoken, the Word written & the Word revealed. The first two may account for the poetry & prose distinction. If poetry & prose fiction *both* are imagistic, synthesizing the event & the idea, I've got a total of *six* categories: law & history are two types of event: the doing & the done—that's a point I've never worked out. Prophecy & philosophy, the latter being a new category, are then the idea doing & done. Oh, hell, I don't know: but I am clear that the four kernels, commandment, parable, aphorism & oracle[,] are not the kernels of prose fiction. The kernels of prose fiction, reading from left to right, are probably plot, situation, theme and Joyce's "epiphany," the moment of insight. I worry about false symmetries, but actually I may be working my way toward a table of literary elements. The four kernels above are the kernels of scripture, & their objective counterparts are, of course, law, history, wisdom & prophecy, respectively: in the N.T., Gospel, apostolic act, epistle & apocalypse. Note carefully how in scripture the hypothetical contains the actual. It's possible that there are four forms of fiction or hypothetical history (i.e. of a philosophy of history). Spenglerian cycle & Marxist exodus (Augustinian Christian too) would correspond to tragedy & comedy, & the various dialectics (Whig & so on, also Hegel) would be the third section. Hypothetical, remember, means mythical or containing form. I suppose too the two conceptions myth & ritual broaden out the distinction I dredged out of Mill between a university of *free* thought and a society of act controlled by the dialectic of free thought. Only free thought means free imagery too, of course: the poet, as Norman [J.] Endicott once remarked to me, is a playing man. (50.296)

XII

There are many, well-furnished rooms in the mansion that Frye built. Some of the rooms are medieval, some are Baroque, some are topped with Gothic spires; others are enclosed with glass to let the light in, and still others are dark dungeons. Most are elaborately designed. The mansion has large open spaces and secret rooms, clear hallways and labyrinthine passages. It has playrooms and studies and chapels. It has ample space to accommodate each of Frye's primary concerns: food, sex, property, and freedom of movement. And it rests upon a foundation of extraordinary knowledge. Because Frye's architecture is so expansive and ingenious, it is reductive to label his work as belonging to this or that school. He has been called a structuralist, a Romantic, a myth critic, a New Critic, a totalizing liberal humanist, a Platonic synthesizer, an Aristotelian analyser. One recent anthologist of criticism even put Frye into the camp of the psychological theorists. All of the labels are reductive, even though one could find proof-texts in Frye to support any one of them.

It is nonetheless true that some things in Frye are more fundamental than others, and in our efforts to try to understand Frye's universe it is natural for us to search for his ultimate concerns. In this search we still have a long way to go. But as more and more of Frye's previously unpublished writing becomes available, and as we are able to step back from his large body of work and get a perspective on it from at least a middle distance, the spiritual dimension of his thought has emerged as a more important dimension than previously thought. A number of Frye's readers, in any event, are less reluctant to speak of Frye's work in religious terms than they were several decades ago, when Frye himself was arguing that all determinisms, including the religious, should be purged from criticism. One indication of this is the recent conference on "Frye and the Word," which was devoted to examining the religious contexts of Frye's criticism.[32]

What, then, do we learn from the diaries that might advance our understanding of Frye's religious position? For all his interest in Mahayana Buddhism, the *Yoga-Sutras*, the world of fairies and elementals, the occult, the *I Ching*, the bardo state in *The Tibetan Book of the Dead*, theosophy, and numerous varieties of esoteric spirituality, Frye remained within the orbit of liberal Protestantism, even though he had rather given up on most of its institutional forms. The diaries, like the rest of Frye's work, contain a great deal of anti-Catholic sentiment. He wonders at one point why he gets so depressed when he learns that someone has converted to Roman Catholicism. Part of his depression comes from the institution of Catholicism itself: "I hate & fear this totalitarian, sleepless, relentless, anti-liberal, anti-Protestant, anti-democratic [Catholic] machine" (49.27), a Church that is Machiavellian in its militancy (49.103). But he is just as depressed about institutional Protestantism, including his own United Church of Canada:

> It isn't the fact that Catholic converts have to assent that they believe absurd doctrines that bothers me. It's really, at bottom, resentment against Protestantism, especially this fatuous United Church, for being so miserably lacking in intellectual integrity. Protestantism is done for here, unless it listens to a few prophets. I don't want a Church of any kind, but if, say, a student of mine were quavering over conversion to Catholicism, I'd like to be able to point to something better than a committee of temperance cranks, which is about all the United Church is now. (49.27)

Upon taking his father to the Eaton Memorial Church in Toronto and discovering that the service consists of a movie, Frye immediately leaves. Later, in reflecting on the experience, he writes,

> Any sensitive person with any accuracy of instinct would, it seems to me, find what the Eaton Memorial substitutes for Christianity a pretty phony & pinchbeck thing. Even I, who am not attached to the ceremonial side of religion, would have been a little chagrined at being caught in the Assembly Hall by one of my friends, at any rate without a pained expression on my face. I can also see that if I went to the United Church more regularly I should understand better why people turn Anglican & Catholic. My objection to conversion is not that the church you join is no better than the one you leave, but rather that I feel, for myself, that any coincidence of any church's service with what I'm looking for would be accidental. (49.90)

Frye can say jokingly that he rather likes the United Church because it contains within it the church-destroying principle, having already swallowed up three churches within itself (49.133). He preaches occasionally but seldom takes much comfort from preaching any of the half dozen sermons he records. He says on one occasion that he still fears the church (49.232) and on another that all of the talks he is asked to give on religious topics bore him: "I wish people would stop forcing me to be a religious special pleader. Nine-tenths of my appearances this year have been religious—both as writer & speaker, & I'm tired of it" (52.159). Part of Frye's anxieties spring from the guilt he has about how he uses his Sundays. After delivering a sermon on wisdom at the Howard Park United Church (an invitation he accepts as a way of doing penance), he is confronted by Elizabeth Lautenslager, the minister's wife, who "asked me abruptly why if I believed 'all that,' I didn't go to church. . . . I could see her point clearly. She works like a galley slave to help her husband, who works like a galley slave to keep a church going, & here's a high-powered intellectual from the college who draws a crowd & works out a beautiful theological pattern & doesn't even attend church. It was too complicated however to explain the grounds I base my dispensation on" (49.266). At the beginning of 1952 Frye has "some vague notion of making a regular practice of going to church this year," but he never acts on his indeterminate urge because, he says, inertia wins out (52.15). Later in the year, however, he does manage to justify his dispensation, arguing that Sundays provide him the occasion for "listening to the Word" in his own way:

> I haven't yet figured out what to do with Sunday, and my anxiety to have it all to myself gives me Kierkegaard's "dread" or *angst*, & [*sic*] about which he talks very well, except that he doesn't see that *angst* is the state of Blake's Spectre of Urthona: the egocentric or proud desire to *possess time*, the revolt against the consciousness of death. My possessive attitude, not only to Sundays, but to time generally, is bothering me a good deal, but hanging on to time is the last infirmity of noble mind. The Jewish Sabbath was a day of rest at the end of the week: the Christian Sunday is a day of leisure at the beginning of the week. Leisure is the opposite of laziness, & hasn't really any more to do with rest than with work. It's the essential condition of creative life, the relaxation from ritual, the removal of the censorious urgency of routine, in which that free association of ideas which begins the creative process is allowed to function. In short, it's listening to the Word. Surely that's what a member of the leisure class should do with Sunday. (50.25)

Here and there Frye does record some of what results from his listening to the Word: the difference between religious wisdom and religious knowledge (49.98), the distinction between the fear generated

by an orthodox notion of hell and the fear that comes from utter exclusion, which is what Jesus suffered when abandoned by all the
disciples (49.164, 262), the contrast between thought (talking to oneself) and prayer (talking to God) (49.242), the sense of liberation that
comes from those, like his student Peter Fisher, who have an "open
top" view of religion (49.246), the relationship among the Holy Spirit,
Sophia or the feminine personification of wisdom, and the Virgin
Mary (49.263), the relation between Creation and Apocalypse, on the
one hand, and the Incarnation, on the other (49.285), the idea of God,
not as a subjective presence, but as a community (49.350), and the
dangerous absolutizing of religious dialectic versus the freedom of
liberal Protestantism (49.364). This catalogue, drawn only from the
1949 Diary, is but a brief sampler of the religious ideas that are forever swirling through Frye's head.

Again, the diaries are not notebooks. Their occasional speculations are
discontinuous and frequently cryptic. But they do contain the seeds of
what Frye developed in his later essays and books. It is possible, for
example, to reconstruct one of the central elements of Frye's Christology
from what he records from time to time about Jesus as suffering humanity.[33] One of Frye's most substantial essays on religion, "The Church: Its
Relation to Society,"[34] was written in 1949, and in two of the entries for
that year (351 and 364) we get a partial abstract of the argument he
develops in that essay. That argument derives from what Frye calls the
"mandala vision," a vision in which "the privacy of prayer & spiritual
communion is not introspection, but the discovery of a community, and
charity is action in the light of such a discovery" (50.259). These visionary
words, which Frye could have written in 1990, will have to be set beside
his many cranky and irreverent outbursts.

Because Frye's diaries are a potpourri, an introduction can point the
reader to but a few of those features of thought, action, and passion that
his opening this little window onto his life permits us to see. It is a life,
like all lives, filled with ironies, contradictions, and multiple masks.
Montaigne remarks that "every sort of contradiction can be found in me,
depending upon some twist or attribute: timid, insolent; chaste, lecher-
ous; talkative, taciturn; tough, sickly; clever, dull; brooding, affable; lying, truthful; learned, ignorant; generous, miserly and then prodigal—I
can see something of all that in myself, depending on how I gyrate; and
anyone who studies himself attentively finds in himself and in his very
judgment this whirring about and this discordancy."[35] So, as these diaries reveal, Frye might have said about himself.

1. From the 1942 Diary (in Notebook 4), p. 9, NFF, 1991, box 22
(courtesy of Victoria University Library).

2. From the 1949 Diary, p. 23, NFF, 1991, box 50, file 9 (courtesy of Victoria University Library).

3. From the 1950 Diary, NFF, 1991, box 50 (courtesy of
Victoria University Library).

Still reading: I can't seem to settle either on letters or writing. Next week, after I send the Blake & the drama articles out, I want to get down to serious work on a series of epic articles. I ought to publish something on Spenser, for God's sake. Then there's that Paradise Regained article: something by me in the Milton bibliographies wouldn't hurt either, and I doubt if the Rinehart introduction will get there very soon. I feel as though I'd like to see some result from the four pieces of proof I read half all before writing anything more. But that's nonsense: I've got to plunge into the epic and clear up that part of the next book. I'm reverting to the idea of a series on the different books of the F.Q. With all I know about symbolism, it's silly not to be pouring out articles on the subject: even the job I did for Elmer on Rilke could probably be published, & that should keep me busy for months.

It's growing on me that my next published book will be the "Essay on Criticism" after all. But I think it's now as richer & more complex than my original idea, also more unified. I seem to be at the point of looking down on literature from a height, no longer working inside it. I have three major ideas, each a part of a topically coherent structure. First is the area covered by my Kenyon Review articles, on meaning & the verbal universe, or archetypes & genres, or on the structure of symbolism. Second is the area covered in my three-volume Guggenheim prospectus, the analysis of the essential modes of verbal expression, scripture, epic, drama, lyric & prose. Third is the area covered by my "Church & Society" articles & my interest in 19th c. subjects, especially Morris, Butler & Yeats. This is actually an apology for criticism: a statement of the social function of the arts & the place of criticism as a social science. Several things are not clear to me yet, & one of these is, curiously enough, the precise way to tackle the epic. Another is the relation of the elements of the Trinity, grammar, rhetoric & logic; & of the function of dialectic as a verbal element. I have a hunch about "verbal determinism" that may not work out. So my draft of the last four chapters, or Book Three, is loose: something like this, perhaps: 9, The Limits of Verbal Expression (i.e., Literature & the Other Arts); 10, Art & Opinion & Authority (revising the point that comes out of Arnold, even Newman goes back to Roger Bacon, & the non-compulsive authority of all "scripture"); 11, Criticism as a social science, or art as a continuously expanding force cracking up all dogmatic & a priori systems & closed societies like the mythology of the Church; 12, The Dialectic of Criticism following out my concentric scheme.

4. From the 1951 Diary, NFF, 1993, box 5 (courtesy of
Victoria University Library).

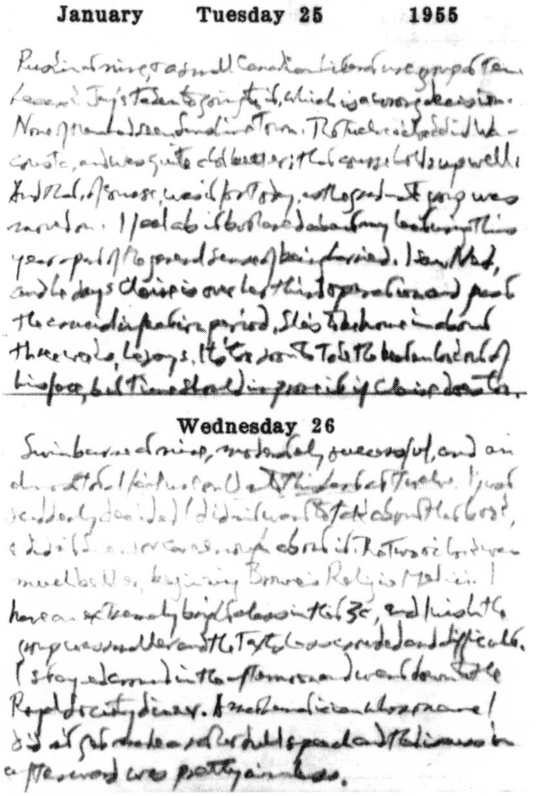
January Tuesday 25 1955

Wednesday 26

5. From the 1955 Diary, NFF, 1993, box 2, file 2 (courtesy of Victoria University Library).

Collected Works of Northrop Frye

VOLUME 8

The Diaries of Northrop Frye
1942–1955

1942 Diary

[12 July – 12 November 1942]

The manuscript for this diary is contained, along with some early notes on a work of fiction, in Frye's Notebook 4, which is in the NFF, 1991, box 22. The notebook, measuring 21.1 × 13.1 cm., is bound in black leatherette with a maroon spine. Toward the beginning of Notebook 4 (par. 24) Frye refers to the first section of the notebook he is writing in as a "diary." But this section of the book mostly contains ideas for a work of fiction. Because its form is closer to that of a notebook than a diary, it has not been included in the present volume. This early section dates from Frye's second year at Merton College, Oxford—three years before he began the diary proper. In the first paragraph of his 1949 Diary Frye remarks that his 1942 diary was a "better than average" effort.

July 12. [Sunday]

[1] A pleasant Sunday discovering how the other half lives: out with Beth & Ruth Jenking to Beth's boss's (say that five times quickly) palace in Port Credit.[1] Theatrical Hollywood black bathrooms, Second Empire bedroom, seven acres of dried-out vegetation (can't get men to manage it), a swimming pool, bar (uninhabited), etc. etc. First time in about four years for Helen & me to go swimming. Two very well-built women— Beth particularly most asymmetrical in a bathing suit. The boss, a mining engineer whose wife got sleeping sickness in Korea, belongs to the Bohemian Club in California (founded about 1880 & originally an artists' club: still has a summer camp where professionals give their all).[2] A tamarisk is a very delicate & lovely tree covered with tiny purple blossoms. Helen & I with our small white bodies looked inhibited & modest, as though born in a caul.

[2] Beginning to work my first piano programme, to consist of a Byrd group, some Debussy Préludes, some Bach (probably the 3–part Inventions, though I'd love to open W.T.C. [*Well-Tempered Clavier*] 2 again, perhaps a Mozart sonata, and some romantic, doubtless the Brahms Ballades op. 10. Debussy is really not so hard to play, at any rate not in the Preludes—he's for the most part a thoroughly practical pianist, and though when played he sounds like an ectoplasmic evocation, when worked at he feels like impromptu. I'm doing a group from the 2nd bk. now, *Bruyères* and *Les Terrasses*, going on to *Ondine* later. Langford says (I *must* remember to get him a wedding present) that even *Feux d'Artifice* isn't bad, but as long as I'm in an apartment I shall postpone it.[3] The discovery of the impromptu effect is rather disenchanting, except in *Des Pas sur la Neige*, a powerfully disturbing and sinister piece of music.[4] That's one of the few the programme of which I think I understand: steps on snow is a pattern of white on white, recalling Melville's great chapter on the symbolism of white as a "colorless all-color of atheism," symbol of the materia prima or substratum which is all colors & yet no color. Also the white fog into which Pym disappears in Poe's story—an underlying symbol in Henry James' *Golden Bowl*, incidentally—is connected with a curious black-and-white pattern there. I dare say Ben Nicholson's white-on-white abstract belongs too.[5] As steps on snow make no noise, Debussy's irony rather bites its arse, but I don't mind that. It's the Rameau tradition, if it's true that Rameau predicted the eventual exhaustion of melodic combinations—one of the phrases of John Stuart Mill's accidie, by the way—in his treatise on harmony.[6]

[3] The French have consistently ignored the great forms, the sonata and the fugue, and have stuck to dainty descriptive pieces not to be taken too seriously. It seems to be an outlet for their crotch-bound paralytically caesured poetry. The pictorial tendency, often with a dance basis, is so persistent it should be worked out in some detail. The nihilist one too, referred to above & also in Ravel's Bolero. Of course the Bolero isn't limited to that: its blow-up-and-bust orgasm rhythm is in *The Turn of the Screw*, but it's of perhaps wider application, to the crescendo-repeat-and-pounce technique of modern propaganda of all kinds, including advertising, and of the boom-and-crash periods of cyclic capitalism. The French are not a rhythmically-moving race—a Celtic-Latin alloy. Michelet says they hesitated between Rabelais & Ronsard & then chose Ronsard, but hesitation is impossible on such a point.[7] Vulgar French is of course mere constipation disguised as Classical reticence & understatement: that's

the exportable kind. The highlights of a musical history would probably be Couperin-Rameau fanciful titles, with some of Landowska's notes (lunatic but interesting).[8] The attack on opera centring on the Gluck & the Tannhauser [*Tannhäuser*] fights: the impossibility of producing music while pretending to be a Roman (Revolution: Cherubini & Napoleon were both Italians): the 19th c. partition into a Provençal, a Belgian and a Pole (Franck is purely Teutonic and Chopin's music is entirely pictorial. His non-committal titles are a pose: one doesn't expect any other music to follow his Preludes. There's a closer link between Chopin & Debussy than one would at first think): the *opéra bouffe* parodies of the *Faust* type: revival of the Rameau tradition with Debussy & Ravel: Saint-Saen's [Saint-Saëns's] last-war journal. Do the French hate music? Why is it there's no lust of the flesh & pride of the eyes in it? no Renoir or Boucher or Hugo even? I'm getting cultural dysentery again. Hangnail is an incorrect form of angnail, a clear case of false etymology.

July 13. [Monday]

[4] Stiff from exertion yesterday. Helen is worse. We went back to Jenking's last night and everybody was very sleepy & tired & wished to hell we'd go. Some went: I did some playing but my left hand would hardly function. The old boy[9] asked for Chopin & I played the A♭ Prelude. It's always been a theory of mine that the clock really strikes twelve in that piece but one beat is missed because the sound waves go in the wrong direction.

[5] Somebody named Stanley Fewster, advertising manager of the T.T.C., has written an ad for them saying: "The more a product is advertised, the greater are its sales which reduces manufacturing costs and creates low prices to the consumer." I'm thinking of putting that beside a line from Dumbo: "I suppose you and no elephant ain't up in no tree," and asking my kids which is worse English. The answer is that one has to be translated into English before it makes sense and the other doesn't. If he had a French name one could understand it: "which" here means "the which," the French *lequel*, and "create to" could be the ambiguity of "créer à."

[6] A man in a pub evidently just returned from England said "I can't see religion at all." The word "religion" in that sentence is tautological, except that he was talking about Catholics.

[7] All minds are passive to impressions 90% of the time, and probably people are more affected by oracles than they admit. When I'm sleeping peacefully & Helen flashes a light suddenly in my eyes, my sense of confidence gives way in a curiously disturbing fashion and I lie awake for the next half-hour. The same thing happens when I give a confident tug on my shoelace and it breaks with a sickening jerk. On a larger scale, it must be the breakdown of the tentative pragmatic synthesis of experience which is the basis of confidence that accounts for the stunned paralysis following a catastrophe.

[8] I have always believed that to have several competing firms scrambling for my business on all lines was Utopia. A delight in this and a horror of any monopoly that could get along without me is my one real economic feeling. It has a censor in the fact that all my intellectually respectable friends are socialists & therefore it must be all wrong (no doubt because delightful: the feeling of jealousy of the gods leaks through every open pore of my imagination), but it persists. It's intensified now that business is all ganging up into a kind of super-monopoly, using the war for its entering wedge and adopting the motto of "help win the war by combining the maximum of inconvenience for you with the minimum for us."

July 14. [Tuesday]

[9] Thirty today. Many good resolutions, most broken already. I've come across a most remarkable katabasis, Gérard de Nerval's *Le Rêve et la Vie*, very useful for Blake. According to Symons he, when asked why he was leading around a lobster on a blue ribbon, said "because it does not bark, & knows the secrets of the sea." He carried around an apron string which he said first was the girdle Mme. de Maintenon wore to the first performance of *Esther* at St. Cyr, then the garter of the Queen of Sheba, then hanged himself with it.[10]

[10] He begins by analyzing the relation of dreams to waking life, citing Swedenborg, Apuleius & Dante as forerunners. He loved somebody named Aurélia who gave him the gate, & his whole life is built on a Beatrice pattern. She becomes for him a Mother-God, at once Isis, Venus & the Madonna. He tries to pray to the Virgin but says she's dead: Aurélia has died in fact. There are several early hallucinations resulting

from "l'épanchement du songe dans la vie réelle" & in one of these he is in the spiritual world in a garden guided by an old woman. She becomes identified with Nature & tends to disappear into it, & Gérard cries: "Oh! ne fuis pas; [...] car la nature meurt avec toi!" But she vanishes, "le jardin [avait] pris l'aspect d'un cimetière," voices say "L'Univers est dans la nuit," and Aurélia at that moment is dead. After a long struggle between relapsing into various conventional things, including pietistic Catholicism & wondering if "plutôt elle s'absorbait dans la somme des êtres: c'était le dieu (meaning la déese [déesse], Venus) de Lucrétius, impuissant et perdu dans son immensité"—a female God according to Blake—he is finally saved by his Beatrice. She says "Je suis la même que Marie, la même que ta mère, la même aussi que sous toutes les formes tu as toujours aimée. A chacune de tes épreuves, j'ai quitté l'un des masques dont je voile mes traits, et bientôt tu me verras telle que je suis."[11]

[11] Some of his adventures in the spiritual world & his transfiguration of the commonplace—as when his friend wants him to go past a corner & it becomes a conflict on a lonely plain among vast hills between two spirits—are not remarkable. Much of the second part is an account of his madness, which, while it is very pathetic, is also a bit dull. The high points for me are his visions of the creation & of the apocalypse.

[12] He begins by saying "emporté sans souffrance par un courant de métal fondu, et mille fleuves pareils, dont les teintes indiquaient les différences chimiques, sillonnaient le sein de la terre comme les vaisseaux et les veines qui serpentent parmi les lobes du cerveau"—an amazing Dali-ish double image, with Blakean overtones. Then he sees the people of the Golden Age beneath all the "couches successives" of "différents âges"; "comme au souvenir d'un paradis perdu" is what he weeps for. Then he goes to a diagrammatic cosmology of the Boehme type: a curious remark about "j'avais essayé de réunir les pierres de la *Table sacrée*" shows one of the weaknesses of his thought. He absolutizes good & evil: his trip into foreign countries didn't succeed in showing him the relativity of good & evil. There may be of course some Osiris overtones. Creation goes on with some amazing geology, considering the date: "les figures arides des rochers s'élançaient comme des squelettes de cette ébauche de création, et de hideux reptiles serpentaient ... au milieu de l'inextricable réseau d'une végétation sauvage." The seven Elohims (seven is a sacred number to him) divide the world. Four kingdoms of birds,

beasts, fish & reptiles are created, then a quintessence from above produces a race of "Afrites." This begins a civil war among the Eternals: three Elohims (he adds the s) were shut up within the earth, where they founded vast kingdoms, & begot a race of necromancers. He regards these imprisoned giants as evil, unfortunately. This took place in the centre of Africa, which gradually becomes desert & assumes a monotonous hieratic civilization.[12] One curious remark links Blake with Frazer: "chacun de leurs souverains s'était assuré de pouvoir renaître sous la forme d'un de ses enfants." Ramifications of this thought haunt him: the race lives on as an individual. Then comes a plague & the flood (caused by the opening of Orion), from which 3 Elohims took refuge in Africa, where they lurk to tempt the progeny of Noah. Meanwhile, "partout mourait, pleurait ou languissait l'image souffrante de la Mère éternelle"— Enion—and there's general war & sacrifice. Some day these eternal enemies must "rejoignent dans un hideux baiser cimenté par le sang des hommes," for they are halves of the world-engirdling serpent.[13]

[13] In his "descente aux enfers"—notice the plural—he thinks in terms of a harmony of things his vision has disturbed. This gradually, as all harmony-thinking does, becomes a mathematical nightmare in his madhouse. But he says "je crois que l'imagination humaine n'a rien inventé qui ne soit vrai," and, after his apocalypse, he begins to realize why he is mad: "Pourquoi, me dis-je, ne point enfin forcer ces portes mystiques, armé de toute ma volonté, et dominer mes sensations au lieu de les subir?" He says that disorder of the spirits distorts the link between spiritual & natural worlds, "semblables à ces reflets [regrets] grimaçants d'objets réels qui s'agitent sur l'eau troublée."[14]

[14] He is saved in the madhouse by his kindness to a boy he significantly calls Saturnin, & his Beatrice announces the end of his katabasis. He leaves the boy, identified with his Selfhood, in the madhouse, calling himself dead & expiating his sins in purgatory. But he himself throws off his mother-image (up to a point) and understands the importance of the freeing of the body, though he still thinks of it as Bower of Bliss rather than Gardens of Adonis. "Le cor enchanté d'Adonis résonnait à travers les bois": he sees a New Jerusalem; he hears two notes, "l'une grave, l'autre aiguë," in an octave, "qui commenças l'hymne divin"—Milton's diapason, and then "le choeur des astres se déroule dans l'infini; il

s'écarte et revient sur lui-même, se resserre et s'épanouit, et sème au loin les germes des créations nouvelles." He says Thor broke with his hammer the holy table of the seven metals, but couldn't break the "Perle rose" in the centre which opens into eternity. "Le *macrocosme,* ou grande monde, a été construit par art cabalistique; le *microcosme,* ou petite monde, est son image réfléchie dans tous les coeurs. La Perle rose a été teinte du sang royal des Walkyries." He ends up blessing Thor, Héla his mother, ton frère Loki, ton chien Garnur, & even the world serpent, "car il relâche ses anneaux, et sa gueule béante aspire la fleur d'anxoka (whatever that is), la fleur soufrée,—la fleur éclatante du soleil"—thus he reaches the Marriage. There follows a delightful little augury of innocence: a little girl opens a green door & is knocked down by a cat: "Tiens! ce n'est qu'un chat!" she says: "Un chat, c'est quelque chose!" says a voice. Then he sees the abyss open in the North: "je vis se creuser devant moi un abîme profond où s'engouffraient tumultueusement les flots de la Baltique glacée." Then a vision of France as arbitrating a quarrel between Russia and the East, or perhaps with Russia.[15]

July 15. [*Wednesday*]

[15] Chapter 5 [of *FS*] is going fairly well. Got Yeats' Vision out of the library. Now Yeats is neither fool nor liar, & if I have received any help from spirits myself in the course of writing on Blake I am very grateful for it. But I'm sure he's all wrong. Submission to automatic writing is relaxation or passivity of the mind. If it's imaginative, it creates the spirits itself—Yeats himself has difficulty in not believing this. His spirits seem to be a rather dim-witted bunch of boobs and if he'd told them to go to hell, where they perhaps belonged, & worked his system out himself, it would have been clearer, surely. It may have been one such dope who persuaded me to get the book out of the library: such a dose of "mathematic form" is confusing at this point, and whenever he refers to or quotes from Blake, as he constantly does, Blake goes immediately out of focus like a pair of wrong glasses. He doesn't understand Blake at all: calls his prophecies unfinished. But he says he's figured out the M.T. [*The Mental Traveller*].[16]

[16] I wonder why he doesn't? Thinking in racial terms is always a sign of confusion in me, but there is something Teutonic in Blake's almost

sentimental receptivity to the infinite which Yeats' Irish mind can't grasp. Blake's links are German & American, apart from a few things like this wonderful de Nerval book.[17]

[17] Helen at work on a Standard article today—cut stems of flowers with a good sharp knife, she says.[18] I made her cut the adjectives, which are a feature of bad writing: if they mean nothing they're filler: if they mean something it's an insult: "You're such a dumb cluck you'd probably go to work on it with a file."

July 16. [Thursday]

[18] Helen away to Hamilton: nothing more eventful than a haircut. Went down to the station for dinner & felt vaguely nostalgic. I wonder what sort of people find languages easy. Any I ever tackled let me in for fearsome complications of paradigms, idioms, irregular verbs, & syntax, followed, if at all, by looking fifty thousand words up in a dictionary. But then I'm bad at languages anyway: too careful & panicky—a curious combination, but it exists. Mother's deafness was made a lot worse by her habit of staring hard at people while they choked nervously through a sentence under the pressure of her lurid green eyes, and then saying in her terrific voice "Now I got it all but one word."

[19] Obscenity in language is an ornament except when it becomes routine, & in the latter event it approaches mere idiocy. The most horrid example of passivity & inertia of mind I know is Woodside's story of the soldier who gazed into a shell hole at the bottom of which a dead mule was lying, and said: "Well, that fuckin' fucker's fucked." (What sort of person is it, incidentally, whose feelings would be spared by printing the above as "that ____in' ____er's ____ed," or "that obscene obscenity's obscenitied"?) Probably much the same as the temperance crank reported in the *Star* (which is run by one & gives publicity to such vaporings) who said in effect "if they must have a beer pub (beverage rooms, they're called here) they should see that there's a good solid partition between the men's & the women's side," as though it were a urinal—as a matter of fact that's how Ontario thinks of it, as a slightly salacious necessity for the vulgar people who don't stay home. I remember being in Richmond Hill,[19] which is as dry as a paper cinder, with [Bert] Arnold & asking where we could get a beer. The natives' expressions, confidentially com-

ing out to meet the outside world or else shrinking correctly from it, were exactly what they would have been had we asked for whores.

July 17. [Friday]

[20] Beer with Bobby Morrison in the Babloor.[20] He says Nick, the bald-headed waiter, was once a terrific ballet dancer. His friends, teamsters & what not, ribbed him about this until he put on a show for them after hours that knocked them speechless & stopped all ribbing. He says he knew Boris Volkoff when he was begging pennies at the stage door, & that he never got any nearer the stage. George, the brunet on the men's side, is a sergeant in the Indian service, on pension (pension & salary add up to about $100 a week) & has a sort of country estate. All his friends are sahibs, nabobs, cheroots, pahits[21] and the like. Kelly the manager was a prize-fighter & owned a string of race horses (with the picture of a famous one on the walls); Van the head waiter was in the army of occupation last war. Bobby doesn't like the Coldwell-McMann investigation into Gladstone Murray because they don't know anything about radio. Coldwell says it's true that some speaker (Earl of Bristowe I think) was withdrawn for Fred Allen ? & McMann says that shows how our liberties are being curtailed.[22] He says Cary Grant & Barbara Hutton's marriage drew a tabloid headline of "Cash and Cary." He says R.E. Knowles' son was jailed for 9 months for printing a story about necrophiles in *Flash*, then went into the Air Force & was killed. Interesting man, Bobby. He says at Newmarket they imported about 800 adolescent girls for a dance & at the entrance two sergeants were selling safes saying: "Here you are, boys, step right up & get 'em; you'll be needin' 'em tonight; here's your chance to get 'em cheap; get 'em while they're goin'." Next morning they rounded them all up again in a rubber salvage campaign. The girls ranged from 13 to 18, fighting to get in. When you think what the law says about under the age of consent! Jail, lashes, terrific curses from a judge gone all queasy in the belly: all the trimmings.

[21] I apologize to the spirits: it was a good idea to get Yeats out.[23] Indirectly.

July 18. [Saturday]

[22] Hell of a holiday; sat around and panted, like Dol Common's fa-

ther.[24] Ned [Pratt], Earle [Birney], Esther [Birney] & Peter Fisher in in the evening. Ned dead tired, Earle with a broken ankle, Esther gone without sleep for a night or two. Lively party. More talk about Marcus Adeney & his magazine,[25] supported by I.B.M. which also supports *Think*.[26] Earle wrote a twelve-page letter to the editors during his convalescence, mostly about dangling participles. Earle doesn't like Margaret Avison's poetry, which is a crime. Margaret told me once that she was picked up by some boys in a car who started to get fresh, whereupon she started reciting poetry at the top of her voice. "Say, are you nuts?" one of the boys asked. "No, I'm a genius," she said & continued to recite. "By God, I believe she is," they said, & she at once became an oracle: they asked her about God & the soul. That would do for a prelude or something some time. Well, anyway, Marcus & his magazine are in bad with Earle, Ned, Sirluck & to some extent [A.J.M.] Smith. Marcus is a pathetic example of an adolescent fixation. In his teens he must have gone through the usual stages, building dream-castles, striking attitudes, receiving homage and developing through a brilliant career. But instead of settling down to a gruelling routine of reading & practice in writing, his image got in his own way, and here he is in middle thirties challenging men who have done the reading & the practice, posturing, scheming & sounding off exactly like a sixteen-year-old. Of course literature is strewn with such wrecks of the Selfhood—Gertrude Stein is an example—but these hole-in-corner cases, these unrecognized Emma Bovarys, are more pathetic than those who have accidentally broadened into charlatans. Eugene Cassidy is another, but cruder. I'd like to do a novel on a small-town genius *in vacuo*, by the way, ending up with a de Nerval finish: subjective apocalypse, objective collapse. That's really the kind of thing I've been trying to dope out all along.

[23] I bought my first hard liquor today: the process is typically Canadian.

[24] Every normal man has an alternative career he sometimes dreams about: [Walter T.] Brown told [Wilmot] Lane, with a touch of bravado, that he'd like to chuck his chancellorship & go back to building boats. I have music. Corresponding to this is the holding of an opposite mental state up as a reflector to the one one has. I'm a Blakean, a visionary disciple: hence the complement is scientific materialism & skepticism of the crudest kind. It used to tempt, or rather tease, but it's losing its

appeal, which is perhaps unfortunate. But I'm always torn between feeling that the cock crows because he has a vision of the dawn, or because he feels stimulated by standing on top of a pile of horseshit.

July 19. [Sunday]

[25] Sunday. Didn't feel like working: too hot to move. Sat on ass reading Rimbaud & discovering what the French language can really do when it gets going.

July 20. [Monday]

[26] Writing spurt on the Blake. Chapter Four finished & in type. Went over to [John F.] MacDonald consulting on 2nd yr. Pass paper & dumped Lane's *Closed Book* on him (a viciously apt title, by the way).[27] Then to collect Helen at Esther's [Esther Birney's], buggering around with the baby & going out for dinner. Set me back several hours, but finished in a burst of speed at eleven o'clock. I must cut down on beer in hot weather when I'm working: it makes me stupid & lazy. William is a charming baby, & I think Esther will be sensible about him. Most of my intellectual friends have brats. She said she took lectures from Karl Bernhardt in child-fluttering & asked when to "correct" a child. He said, "I am sure you did not intend to use that word, Mrs. Birney: the child is always right." Matter of terminology: the child is never "wrong": it is merely ignorant & unformed—still, Karl's a dope. Glanced over a book on nudism. I don't see the point myself: I don't wear clothes out of modesty. I wear them because they have pockets. Earle apparently has gone in for the straight what's-the-use-in-times-like-these line, which hardly seems intelligent enough for him. He has a very simple & honest mind, & tends to be attracted by the simplified clarity of extreme positions. Helps him as a poet, maybe.

July 21. [Tuesday] .

[27] Chapter Five. The Blake takes all my time & energy: I shall never write a book under such conditions again. I've stopped playing the piano & stopped reading. And every once in a while I suspect I'm writing shit. If the public doesn't like it I shall write a novel which shall earn me a million tax-free dollars, exclusive of movie rights, & lose me my job. The

Verlaine-Rimbaud story would make a swell novel, as I dare say two or
three thousand people have thought before. It could be combined with
the de Nerval one.

July 22. [Wednesday]

[28] Eleanor in for dinner.[28] We discussed how it felt to write books and
I said I had two audiences in mind: my friends that I could talk to, who
inspired me to eloquence & short cuts, & the sort of barbaric academic
who would probably read it, who made me repeat myself endlessly &
pound the pulpit. A certain amount of gossip, of the kind Eleanor rather
goes in for. Ray [Godfrey] & her social work: I said I thought social
services were very healthy in their attitude, tolerant but not spineless,
clean but not caustic or even antiseptic. A great many pretty, shiny,
marcelled girls, waitresses & what not, do piecework on the side & come
from homes where you'd prefer to breathe in a handkerchief.

July 23. [Thursday]

[29] Oh, God, when I finish this book I shall learn to compose music.
I shall get my teeth fixed. I shall go to a horse race and bet on the horse
that looks most like Aunt Dolly [Garratt]. I shall go to the Riverdale Zoo
and sneer at the Great Crested Macaw (*Accius Pacuvius*).[29]

July 24. [Friday]

[30] Eleanor [Godfrey] once more, calling at the office to take Helen &
me out to the pub. George Beattie, who comes from a clerical family,
talks about his god-damned priestly brother with gravy on his surplice,
and has a little [of] the *mauvais prêtre* look of Baudelaire, and a pleasant
Catholic female exhibitionist who claimed to have an infantile uterus.

[31] I don't know why I have such a horror of animals. A recurrent
nightmare is badly hurting an animal and then stomping it furiously into
a battered wreck in a paroxysm of cowardly mercy. And that is to some
extent what I'm like. Any intimate contact with any animal I dislike, &
their convulsive movements give me panic. If I go to hell, Satan will
probably give me a wet bird to hold. For one thing, they're afraid, & fear
is something I'm an abnormal conductor of. There's a pigeon sitting
outside my window now giving me pigeon-flesh.

July 25. [Saturday]

[32] Helen slept all afternoon and I got some books out of the library, determined to relapse into a couple of detective stories. I don't think that I have either a highbrow or a lowbrow pose about detective stories, but I don't really quite understand why I like reading them. I read them partly for the sake of the overtones. I'm not a connoisseur of them: I can never guess what the hell's up when the detective suddenly pulls out a watch and shouts: "My God, we may yet be in time!", shoves the narrator and half the country's police force into a taxi, dashes madly across town and finds the girl I'd placidly thought was the heroine all equipped with a blunt instrument & an animal snarl. I'm always led by the nose up the garden path in search of a false clue, and I never notice inconsistencies. And I always get let down when I find out who dun it. As I say, I like the overtones. A good style, some traces of wit & characterization, a sense of atmosphere, and a lot of the professional intricacies of the game can go to hell. Yet I want a novel in that particular convention & no other. The answer is, I think, that I'm naturally a slow & reflective reader, & make copious marginalia. In the detective story I live for a moment in the pure present: I'm passively pulled along from stimulus to stimulus, and, ignorant & idle as that doubtless is, I'm fascinated by it. Yet I seldom finish without disappointment. The detective story is the opposite of the ghost story; the former is all intellectual resolution and poetic justice, the latter all emotional response & brooding evil. I'm also quite fond of good ghost stories, & a good ghost story is usually far better written than a good detective story—has to be, because of the importance of atmosphere. But I want to eat my cake & have it: I want a sustained emotional thrill, & when the wavering index stops & points the thrill goes out like a light. This is apart altogether from the highly implausible complications of alibis & time-tables and so on which usually disfigure the denouement. It's something to be carried off by sheer writing: I'm very fond of The Moonstone[30] although I think the denouement is a lot of eyewash. Organically new developments of the form are very rare. And why are all detective story writers, at least all English ones, stinking snobs? An offensive Jew almost always turns up; all radicals are long-haired heels; the hero or another detective is always a well-fed member of the British upper-middlers. Dorothy Sayers is the worst; Margery Allingham comes next. In the two I have, one, by Anthony Berkeley, contains a lot of pro-Conservative propaganda; the other, by John Dickson Carr, says the hero (another well-fed Tory: Carr seems to

be a sort of Chestertonian Fascist Catholic) expected the manager of the hotel to be a Jew but found him belonging to the "island" instead. I suppose the ability to write a good detective story comes from a competence in complications and an intensive training in social conventions.[31] In a train wreck the most useful person present would probably be a woman, and an I.O.D.E. Past Mistress, or whatever they call them.[32] Or, if a man, a reactionary executive or a senior army officer. These are stereotypes, but so are detective stories. I should think a story in symposium form, with a Marlow [Marlowe]-narrator supplying the clues and his auditors all guessing shrewdly & wrong,[33] would have its points.

[33] Two difficulties in relating a detective story to a novel: (1) 99.9% of all the people who get murdered thoroughly deserve it. The rest are victims of homicidal maniacs who aren't allowed in detective stories. A motive strong enough to lead to murder is a justifiable one, nearly always. That's one reason for letdown, the feeling that the law isn't worth maintaining. (2) Most detective stories turn on a concealed clue: the character of the murderer. Hence character-analysis is out of place. For that reason I think the orang-utang of Poe was a good scheme,[34] though my students don't like it. There is no mystery in *Crime & Punishment*, as the whole point of the book is that Raskolnikoff has the only character in it capable of murder.

[34] The stimulus of the pure present I mentioned [par. 32]: it's the basis of movies and comic-strips & in fact nearly all stimulus-amusements. And a spoiled society playing with toys, like that of the 20–yr. truce, is a society which resents being reminded of anything that happened six months ago, and will elect a stupid politician on the strength of his wrong guesses: I mean, if he supplies a new stimulus. Hepburn knows that. He was so badly beaten in the Noseworthy & the other two by-elections he should have been finished. But was he? No: he instantly yells: "Where's the American navy? Their fleet's in hiding!" and everyone is so outraged at this they forget all about the elections.[35]

July 26. [Sunday]

[35] Marjorie King in to supper. Says she's always been frank with her young Tony about sexual matters and he finally asked her why she

didn't have another baby. She put him off, not thinking he could understand the economic implications of birth control, when he at once began to tell her how to go about having one. A good example of the breakdown of an educational theory.

July 27. [Monday]

[36] Terrific thunderstorm in the afternoon: over to Walter's at night: MacDougalls there. Arnold Walter is a heavy Teutonic bastard for whom small talk is difficult & very generalized discussions in very pedantic terminology about art & life in order. He feels that Spenglerian history-worship has been the ruin of Germany and is trying to fight it with a sentimental Catholic devolutionary version of the same thesis: everything clicked in the Middle Ages, Renaissance a staggering disaster but things held up until 1750–1800 with that awful revolutionary spirit & that dreadful democracy & that horrible Rousseauism. Romanticism was the complete buggeration of culture & things went from worse to worser until we came to Dadaism and that Pretty Pass we're in now. Meanwhile he composes music that sounds like bad Schumann. I tried some Blake on them: no fizz.

July 28. [Tuesday]

[37] Hot weather. Went to show, an English mystery, "Ghost Train."[36] Swell. One of the things that interested me about it was the way the English can put the most typically English frozen-faced sourpussed jerks into a picture and preserve intact all their stupid social stereotypes, & then when you're just about to curse them for being such god-damned English jerks you suddenly realize the English have put them there. It's known, well-known in fact, as the "English Ability to Laugh at Themselves." I only hope it doesn't breed a self-conscious paralysis the way the discovery of their ability to muddle through did.

July 29. [Wednesday]

[38] Dullish evening at the Romans: the Miseners are going to Ottawa. Graham Millar says moonlight scenes in the movies are invariably sunlight ones taken with a red filter. He knows this because they're always daytime clouds.

[39] I think I'll ask my kids in the fall how many movie titles they can get: *This Above All* (Hamlet); *Come Live with Me; We Who Are Young* (with Lana Turner); *Blossoms in the Dust* (with Greer Garson); *The Grapes of Wrath; The Little Foxes.* Or books: *Brave New World, In Dubious Battle* (P.L. I), *Antic Hay, Look Homeward Angel.*[37] Probably been on an Information Please programme.[38]

July 30. [Thursday]

[40] About this Rimbaud–Verlaine idea: I'd have to make something a bit more exciting out of Verlaine than he actually was. I get fed up with those people who act like bad little boys & finally collapse on the bosom of Mother Church, with a big floppy teat in each ear, and spend the rest of the time bragging about what bad little boys they used to be and how pneumatic the bliss is. Rimbaud stayed tough.

July 31. [Friday]

[41] I'd like to write a book on *How to Write Literary Cant*: I've had the idea for some time, but can't do more than just outline it now. I have my Shakespeare-Milton-Shelley thing somewhere. That would do as a preliminary exercise. Also a chapter on "The Art of Belittling"—source-hunting (plagiarism in a contemporary, & by inference in a classic), committee theories (Homer & Langland). Also one on "Manicheanism" or the art of reducing men & masterpieces to abstract nouns. Was Euripides a romantic? Was Lucretius, having no religion, a "truly great" poet (useful phrase in conversation if not publishing). Under belittling goes the bright young Strachey-Guedalla imitator with a target: New Statesman type.[39] Good e.g. in Fausset's book on Tennyson.[40] "Dialectics": the evolutionary, clearing throat for century to utter a masterpiece; devolutionary, Catholic Spenglerian or Pretty Pass school (see above), etc. etc. Could do the sort of paragraph-shit + quote type of Shakespearean criticism. Introductory chapter on "Useful Words": note, essential, element, aspect; the Cautious Cough type of thing I cut out of my kid's essays.

Aug. 1. [Saturday]

[42] In the meantime I have to do that satire paper, but it should be simple.[41] 1. Satire in Roman lit. (Bennett) a form: with us, outside the

Renaissance, a tone or attitude. Often involves parody of form. Comic rhymes: Butler, Gilbert, Ogden Nash. Prose: Tristram Shandy.

2. Tone is humorous. Humor in Jonson shows it depends on convention. Humor of Popeye to eat spinach, Wimpy to eat hamburgers. Husband-beating in comics. Wife-beating isn't but once was: Punch & Judy. Dubious! I think the female will makes the former inherently funny. Mother-in-law (Freud).

3. Are these conventions arbitrary? Moral selection: cripples & lunatics aren't funny. Missing link here: conventions not arbitrary but go back to state of society. Cf. brutality of Roman satire: Cinna wants to be seen a pauper & is one (Martial) [*Epigrams* 7.19 (Loeb 2.17)].

4. Sting in satire involves upsetting emotional tone: a peculiarly English trick. G. & S. [Gilbert & Sullivan] & Katisha. Cuckolds: Brute. Dickens laughter-&-tears formula. Shylock & Falstaff. Outside English rare but cf. Quixote.

5. Note effectiveness of debtor's jail in Pickwick vs. Little Nell. Former socialist challenge. Hence revy. [revolutionary] tone of satire. Cockney impudence of Eng. satire. Ridicule of institutional dignity. Clergy: Chaucer's Pardoner, Milton's bishop, Trollope's Proudie. Royalty, Lear & French horror at it. Bourgeois massacre of aristocratic Eng. drama. Amory. Self-deprecatory tone of English toward courage. Surtees, Gilbert, Baims father. H5 [*Henry V*] & Kipling show same picture of stuffed-shirt & grouser. Obscenity a bodily democracy, also danse macabre. Body ridicules soul: Quixote & Sancho Panza. Ned's [Ned Pratt's] grapnel hook poem.[42] Chaplin & the absurdity of pompous dictators. Scientist: Butler's EM [*The Elephant in the Moon*].

6. Everything that consolidates is silly. Contempt for dignity is Christian. Bunyan's Xn [Christian] & Apollyon vs. Hotspur or Macbeth (note his breakdown in Act 5). Rises to prophetic denunciation of society as demonic. Swift, Shelley, Blake, & Huck Finn. Satirist himself remains invulnerable, hence pose of common sense: Falstaff on honour. Thurber.

7. Two tones: (1.) The Prophetic—Alazon swashbuckling tone, long wind, long words, catalogues, invective & abuse. Theological origin: Isaiah 4, Luther & Calvin (find good e.g.'s) (one of Calvin's in Pareto,[43] Nashe on Harvey,[44] Burton (the Love-Melancholy sentence I always read),[45] Milton & Colasterion,[46] Carlyle. (2.) The Socratic. Socrates & Thrasymachus:[47] the eiron. Chaucer, Dryden & Pope, most moderns. Ours not an alazon age: S. Johnson's "laughing & exulting" not our cup of tea.[48] Why are invective & abuse so extraordinarily readable? Panegyric so dull? Latter

has his reward: former the divine dissatisfaction. Danger of crude satire in making us smug.

8. Satire as a powerful English weapon in the war. Germans may conquer but can never convince the English. Greater effectiveness of Chaplin & law vs. literature: Mein Kampf's ridicule of Germans inoculates against satire. Wagner has no upsetting humour; Shakespeare has. Americans have: imgve. [imaginative] hyperbole of Mark Twain's yawn. Auden's "negativism" passage in Dog Beneath the Skin.[49]

Aug. 2. [Sunday]

[43] Sunday. Harold [Kemp] came with his girl friend. Late adolescence. She was "afraid" of us, and at first started to carry on a flirtation with him & ignoring us. Harold being a good friend of ours & an extremely sensible lad, she collapsed & sulked for the rest of the evening, apart from one or two remarks, addressed to him, but indicative of ownership to us.

Aug. 3. [Monday]

[44] Reading the *Four Zoas* all day. Blake *did* write a certain amount of shit, I'm afraid, and a certain amount of automatically produced drivel. Maybe not: maybe the F.Z. is just a draft & every letter of J [*Jerusalem*] goes into its fit place. But he *did* write shit, all the same.

Aug. 4. [Tuesday]

[45] There's a series of *New Directions* studies on "Makers of Modern Literature," by Harry Levin on Joyce, very well reviewed, & now one by David Daiches on Woolf, said to be not so good.[50] Wilson Knight is producing another book, this time on Milton.[51] A new Simenon translated, two stories again.[52] He's so good that his stories don't even depend for their interest on the puzzle.

Aug. 5. [Wednesday]

[46] Absolutely nothing has been happening lately. Conditions are ideal for work but I don't seem to be doing any. Nevertheless, I want them to stay ideal. All evil is unnecessary; superfluous & evitable, as Thoreau called it.[53]

Aug. 6. [Thursday]

[47] Lunch with Aunt Lily [Lilly Maidment] in the park. Aunt Lil[l]y's programme for winning the war is worry, hoard, and boycott Italian stores. Dinner with Ruth Home in the evening. She showed me a swell book on Japanese prints, privately printed by some American amateur. Many of them are parodies of Chinese moral tales: it's a witty, sophisticated, middle-class development. Dropped in to Godfrey's after for a drink.

Aug 7. [Friday]

[48] When I start learning to compose I shall investigate modal harmony: I find myself quite baffled by the stupidity of musicians in ever dropping it. Arranged in order of sharpness, they are Lydian, Ionian or major, Mixolydian, Dorian, Aeolian or minor, Phrygian, Locrian. Lydian is a shade brighter than major, Dorian a shade more majestic than minor, Phrygian & Mixolydian, Phrygian especially, gloomy and plaintive. I dare say a lot of Bach's minor music is really Dorian, a lot of Chopin's Phrygian, a lot of Beethoven's major Lydian, a lot of Mendelssohn's Mixolydian. You see, it's an interlocking scheme. A piece of B Lydian would have a key signature of 6♯; in B major, of 5♯; B Mixolydian, 4; B Dorian, 3; B minor, 2; B Phrygian, 1; B Locrian, none. I ran across a piece in G♯ by Sibelius (a set of tree-pieces op. I think about 85)[54] with 4♯—G♯ Phrygian, in other words. Debussy's Hommage à Rameau ends in G♯ Dorian. Wonder if a spectrum association would ever be made by some future Scriabine: Lydian red, etc. I've got more notes on this in Elizabethan music somewhere.

Aug 8. [Saturday]

[49] Mary Winspear in for dinner: still no certainty of a job in Alberta, but as usual she has hopes. The Eng. Dept. told her quite frankly they didn't want her: they're a small department and she'd "break up the gang." Mary has adopted a curiously bitter & sterile cynicism about the war to cover some much deeper feelings. She says if the war stopped tomorrow they'd have to throw thousands of planes into a junkpile & leave them for salvage in the next war, & isn't that amusing? The answer, as she knows damn well, is no. E.K. [Brown] has bounced back to Cornell, maybe to get his hat: A.S.P.W. [Woodhouse] has lost 30 lbs. &

probably has a skinfold on his abdomen. I think a war job (she says Wees may put her in "ordinance" [ordnance], whatever that is) would be almost as good for her as for the army. I saw once where E.K. got his namesake Audrey Alexandra[55] into a P.M. speech: they'd left in a lot of prefatory harrumphing about her & her sublime thought, but cut the actual quotation of the s. t. [sublime thought]. She says George & Kitty won't hitch: one likes talking & the other parties; one's academic & the other Anglo-Saxon snobbery & upper-muddle class.

Aug 9. [Sunday]

[50] Sunday again: the usual soul-crushing bore with Fulton Ave.[56] & the usual muddle of not taking a book out. Never do that again. I get isolated with the Star Weekly every time, and the amount of unreadable drivel that pulpy mass purveys is incredible. The Montreal Standard is infinitely better, even when Helen isn't in it.

Aug. 10. [Monday]

[51] Mary [Winspear] said the last person to have real intellectual guts was Bernard Shaw. I said writers were becoming a stereotype, a Brahmin caste, and I trotted out my anatomy theory. If I ever get around to writing a novel called *Liberal*, the motto for which will be Isaiah 32:8,[57] I want a sentimental weather-cocky Craggish hero with an anatomic "Jack" counterpoint and a fantastic "Regillus" one.[58] When my ideas are major, why is my execution so miserably stupid: is it just lack of practice? My opening scene with Kennedy is all right if he reinforces the liberalism. But it's so bloody Quixotic to think in terms of Dostoievsky and produce something on the level of *Cosmopolitan* or *Maclean's*. I'm getting fed up with it and all my wool-gathering dreary accidia.

[52] Bitched the day, celebrating because Ned [Pratt] liked the Blake. Show at night. Thurber's "Male Animal."[59] Not bad: but Henry James was a bad dramatist and a master of Thurber's. The main theme,—a hot-headed undergraduate editor turning a piece of ordinary teaching routine into a crusade, is sound. The episodic clowning with his wife was a bit weak. But the Chairman of Trustees was too crude: one never gets them like that. They always turn up quoting Holy Scripture and John

Stuart Mill on Liberty. A novel about a similar situation with the weakling's endlessly rationalizing would be all right. The other show was a
bad English thriller based on fake "psychology": Flora Robson writing
poison-pen letters because she was a spinster & her maternal impulse
was frustrated.[60]

Aug. 11. [Tuesday]

[53] Bitched the day again. Lunch with Norm Langford, who is gradually trying to piece his musical & theological interests together & make a
pattern out of them, which, if he succeeds, will bring him very close to
Blake. We discussed the failure of the R.C.'s [Roman Catholics] to make
anything of the present situation, and I said I thought they'd overesti-
mated the consistent importance of Latin civilization.

Aug. 12. [Wednesday]

[54] Bitched the day. Lunch with Peter Fisher & beer all afternoon.
Discussed Blake: I've recorded the results in my notes. I seem to be
suffering from schizophrenia. Helen had the fidgets too and I took her
over to the island[61] for dinner.

Aug. 13. [Thursday]

[55] Bitched the day: finished ch. 6., what there was of it. My first sneeze
of the hayfever season began at Yonge & McGill: I'd gone down with
Helen to meet Harold [King] & Thornhill on Gould St. My mental life is a
riot.

Aug. 14. [Friday]

[56] Bitching the day: the change of tense is not significant. I wish I knew
what the hell was going wrong with me. Robins told me of a dream he
had. He was in a committee meeting in which a proposal demanding
large property qualifications for municipal offices was being discussed.
Robins spoke long and eloquently against the measure. At the end a man
rose holding a paper bag. "I agree with you absolutely, sir," he said. "My
name is Ramsay MacDonald. Have a doughnut." This was 15 years ago.

Aug. 15. [Saturday]

[57] The paper refers to Mr. Churchill & Mr. Stalin. If the London *Times* does that, the second front is under way. The *Times* got along fine with M. Daladier and Signor Mussolini & Herr Hitler, balked at Tovarisch Stalin and, exotic to the last, substituted "M. Stalin." Stag at Earle Birney's for Sirluck.[62] Ned [Pratt] read us a new poem: general theme of the conflict of Orc & Urizen. Swell poem too. Infinitely better than a silly fantasia on Hitler's nightmare he'd been discussing with me. The only contribution I made to that was to suggest that in Wagner's general scheme Hitler would not be Siegfried but Alberich. Went to see Woodhouse.

Aug. 16. [Sunday]

[58] Sirluck's wedding reception. I hate all such affairs. I cannot make a remark worth throwing at a dead ape when I'm standing up. Took Helen down to Diet Kitchen afterwards for dinner.[63]

[59] Events started early today. Helen was wakened at six or five or some equally esoteric hour by a bat that had flown in. Helen is deathly afraid of bats, because some fool woman once told her that bats got in women's hair and hung on. So when this creature appeared she dived under the bed clothes. My moral code is based on the central principle "Never do anything about anything until absolutely necessary." Particularly when, in the middle of sleeping off a hangover early Sunday morning, one is required to get up and chase bats. The subsection of my code dealing with bats is to the effect that if they can find their way in they can find their way out if one just leaves them alone. So I shut the creature up in the bathroom hoping it would find its way to the vent pipe: I couldn't see how else it could have got in. In the morning it had presumably done so. This evening a bat flew in the front window—whether a new one or an old one that had hung around all day we shall never know. I wanted to coax it back out the window, but it had got involved in the bedroom by that time and there was nothing to do but kill it. I hate killing things: its plaintive dying squeak will haunt me. The sparrows and squirrels in the park who flock around when we're eating know this, and they take no notice whatever of the most menacing gestures.

Aug. 17. [Monday]

[60] Hay fever much worse: yesterday I walked home through the ravine without a single sneeze. It's cool, though. Langford says Andy Lytle once called the penalty box the "sin bin."[64] Says a book on evangelical revivals pronounced one socially beneficial because it had decreased the number admitted to lunatic asylums for chronic alcoholism more than it had increased the number admitted for religious mania. His comment was that humanitarians are cold-blooded.

Aug. 18. [Tuesday]

[61] Hell of a day, close & muggy. "Devils, Drugs & Doctors" by Howard Haggard,[65] is crude & its view of history naive, & I know most of what I need of it, but it has some stuff I could use on my kids. Spittle as a cure is all over Pliny & in the N.T. [11]. Acosta, 16th c., says of the Panama Canal: "I am of opinion that human power should not be allowed to cut through the strong & impenetrable bounds which God has put between two oceans, of mountains & iron rocks, which can stand the fury of the raging seas. And, if it were possible it would appear to me very just that we should fear the justice of Heaven for attempting to improve that which the Creator in His Almighty will & providence has ordained from the creation of the world."[66] Burton mentions a Panama Canal.[67] I know all about the mandrake. Bone of Luz (resurrection bone) & extra rib of woman disproved by Vesalius [130]. Galen dissected only animals. Hip bones flared like oxen: when disproved, excuse of man changing shape through wearing tight trousers [130]. John XII (Pope) burned unsuccessful surgeon of Florence: surgeon who failed to keep him alive flayed by survivors. Regimen Sanitatis Salernitanum, ca. 1100, tr. Harrington: this is the "Quiet, Merryman & Diet" source [137–40]. Dissection of executed criminals: reading of Papal indulgence permitting it, then removal of head (brain seat of soul & shouldn't be exposed). Introductory oration, choral song, body opened by servant while physician read aloud from Galen, pointing with wand at organs [144]. Celebration, concert, banquet or show, ceremonious burial of corpse. Took two days [144]. Vesalius stole a hanged skeleton (very daring): till then anatomy of skeleton very inaccurate. Much pro-Galen opposition: link with painting. That blood goes from one side of heart to other *through lungs,* upheld by Seuetus,

hinted at by Vesalius, violently opposed by clergy: he doesn't say why [147]. Thought (V.[Vesalius]) like Galen mucus from brain: purging of brains frequent. Paré tied ligatures instead of cauterizing wounds: lessened pain but increased risk of infection. St. Anthony's fire (burning & blackening of limbs) caused by ergotism or rye poisoning. Control began in 17th c. Syphilis business I think I know, and Fracastoro's poem [240]. Wolsey accused of giving it to H 8 [Henry VIII] by whispering in his ear [238]. Bacon assigned the cause to cannibalism, frequent in West Indies. He says Neopolitan merchants pickled human flesh instead of tunny & gave it to the French [246]. Cf. Diodorus Siculus. Mandeville wrote *A Modest Defense of Publick Stews*, advocating inspection & segregation of prostitutes [260–1]. Belief that continence would lead to corruption of flesh, medieval & perhaps Arabic in origin, useful to monks (wonder if it is connected with the celibacy-chastity distinction?) & found in Franklin [272–3]. Licensed prostitution common in M.A. [Middle Ages] (Stowe) [chap. 11, *passim*]. Liver seat of passion (sexual): Pistol's "liver burning hot" in Shakespeare [291]. "Blood" thinking still very common: the PM negro blood scandals. King's evil touch I know: crampings as well [294]. Also potable gold, unicorn's horn, mummy (Browne), Digby sympathy cures, usnea (moss from criminal's skull), bezoar, etc. Spice trade which caused much 15th–16th c. discovery was largely medical, according to this [322–34]. C 2's [King Charles II's] treatment: pint of blood from arm, 8 oz. cupped from shoulder. Emetic, 2 purges. Enema containing antimony, sacred bitters, rock salt, mallow leaves, violets, beet root, camomile flowers, fennel seed, linseed, cinnamon, cardamon seed, saphron, cochineal & aloes [334]. Head shaved & blister raised on scalp. Sneezing powder of hellebore & cowslip powder to strengthen brain. Purges frequent, interspersed with soothing drink of barley water, licorice & sweet almond. White wine, absinthe, anise, thistle leaves, mint, rue & angelica are also given. Plaster of Burgandy pitch & pigeon dung applied to feet. As bleeding & purging went on, he got melon seeds, manna, slippery elm, black cherry water, extract of flowers of lime, lily-of-the-valley, peony, lavender & dissolved pearls. The gentian root, nutmeg, quinine & cloves. He got worse & 40 drops of extract of human skull. Then "Raleigh's antidote" which had everything in it, then bezoar stone. Then Raleigh's a[ntidote], pearl julep & ammonia finished him off. This is known in medical parlance as the works. Get that Cloister & the Hearth thing, also Gil Blas [343] & Sisam.[68] Kings of course could afford the works [334–5]. Rather ironical that the founder of the R.S. [Royal

Society][69] & the most intelligent king we ever had should be torn to pieces in such a Bacchanalian orgy. In Egypt a faithful wife's urine was good for sore eyes [336]. Mithridates was looking for a universal antidote, particularly against snake bites. Viper's flesh, which Digby fed his wife to improve her complexion [331], good because viper's immune from own poison. This was the basis of theriac [337]. Dioscordes (time of Nero) drew up a drug list, basis of later herbals [338]. Galen's balance of humour theory I know [338–40]. Paracelsians discovered that mercury was good for syphilis; Galenists wouldn't treat it because it wasn't in Galen [345–9]. "Venereal" originally an astrological term. Purging common as without vegetables people were full of shit. *Triumphal* [*Triumphant*] *Chariot of Antimony*, 1604, author who calls himself Basil[e] Valentine, a monk, says he fed a. [antimony] to pigs & they got fat, fed it to fasting monks & they all died. Hence antimony, anti-monks, for stibium [349]. Examples of "signatures": orchid for testicles, euphrasia or eyebright for eye, nutmeg for brain. In 1624, pope threatened to excommunicate snufflers, death for smoking in Turkey, in Russia noses slit, flogged, sent to Siberia [354–5]. Tom o' Bedlams were graduates of Bedlam: used to blow horn to have drink put in it, hence "horn is dry" in Lear [372].

[62] Check S. Wolff, *The Greek Romances in Elizabethan Prose Fiction*, and a paper by Howard in PMLA 24 (Mar 00) on εκφρασεις [ecphrasis, "description"] and Ut pictura poesis. Miss Mainwaring [Manwaring], *Italian Landscape in 18th c. England*. Price, *The Distinct Characters of the Picturesque & Beautiful*, 1801. Richard Graves, *Columella, or the Distres't Anchoret*, 1779, caricature of chinoiserie in 18th c. parks.[70]

Aug. 19. [Wednesday]

[63] Today the news was all about the Dieppe raid, & the Russian front also got a front-page splash. The fact that the Chinese stormed & captured Wenchow, a city of 100,000 on the coast, was recorded in a tiny box in the second section. I simply cannot understand this assumption that the Chinese front is of no importance or interest. It's all the sillier when one realizes that the current of world history is now going through Asia & that Europe has ceased to be of any organic historical significance. China will probably have the next century pretty well to itself as far as culture, & perhaps even civilization, are concerned.

[64] Western historical dialectic gives me a pain anyway. God thought of us. He started us back in Nile slime & Euphrates mud, then the Greeks added reason, the Hebrews God, the Romans law and the British fair play, until here we are. Asia is irrelevant: it has no real history because it didn't contribute anything to our great Western omelette. Phooey. In Sept. 1939 the New Yorker wrote a stentorous leader about a world of peace being plunged into war.[71] Two hundred million people, if that, go to war in Western Europe and that's a world at war. Half a billion people have been fighting for years in Asia and that's peace. I expected something better from the New Yorker.

[65] I read for the first time a story by Edgar Wallace, The Shadow Man[72] or something, which I found unexpectedly well written. There's a creative energy in story-telling of a kind little short of major in him. It isn't a good detective story because he's got so much narrative skill he moves along from incident to incident & pulls the detective along: the detective doesn't really manipulate the circumstances. But I suspect he's worth looking into.

[66] Was told by someone that Woman of the Year with Katherine Hepburn was good, & went down to see it.[73] It was with a quite good propaganda film, Confirm or Deny.[74] Our propaganda films are surprisingly adult. The other show was about a quasi-Dorothy Thompson, who gave up a brilliant public career for the man she really luhved. She could speak every language in Europe but she couldn't cook, & all the housewives in the audience gurgled. There was one good line, the moral of the picture, that women should be illiterate and clean, like canaries. All foreigners are funny. For small-town Midwestern isolationist consumption.

Aug. 20. [Thursday]

[67] I've been reading in Pepys, to avoid work. I can't understand him at all. I mean, the notion that he tells us more about himself & gives us a more intimate glimpse of the age than anyone else doesn't strike me. I find him more elusive and baffling than anyone. He has a curious combination of apparent frankness and real reticence that masks him more than anything else could do. One could call it a "typically English" trait, but there were no typical Englishmen then and Montaigne performs a miracle of disguise in a far subtler & bigger way. Pepys is not

exactly conventional: he is socially disciplined. He tells us nothing about himself except what is generic. His gaze is directed out: he tells us where he has been & what he has done, but there is no reflection, far less self-analysis. The most important problem of the Diary & of related works is whether this absence of reflection is an accident, an individual design, or simply impossible to anyone before the beginning of Rousseauist modes of interior thought. Cf. Logan Pearsall Smith on the language.[75] There simply weren't the words for it, maybe.

[68] A man can tell me all about his tastes in food, clothes & women & tell me nothing. One remark about, say, Beethoven and I've got him: but if I sifted the stools of his subconscious for years I should learn only that, in common with all human beings, he possesses a sex instinct. And I can imagine a period like the Restoration so highly civilized that a socially disciplined member of it could actually send out a barrage of this generic information as a smokescreen. Why?

[69] Pepys knew perfectly well what he was doing: he wrote a book which he well knew to be an art-form. His motive in doing so is not obvious, because his *genre*, the diary, is not a branch of autobiography, as Evelyn's is.[76] He was a supreme observer, making himself a visionary, *se faire voyant*, as much as Blake or Rimbaud. And he knew perfectly how effective & oracular the random is: his camera keeps on clicking after he gets in bed with his wife because he knows better than to shut it off. A real & artistic passion for observation in itself with no attempt at a creative follow-through is rare, but it exists. And there's a riddling, gnomic quality in the photograph absent from the painting. When I try to visualize Pepys I visualize clothes & a cultured life-force. I have a much clearer vision of the man who annoyed Hotspur or Juliet's Nurse's husband. I feel that Pepys makes the dead eerie and transplanetary, not our kind of species at all. He does not observe character either: I can't visualize his wife or my Lord. Even music he talks about as though it were simply a part of his retiring for physic.

[70] Harold [Kemp] had lunch with us at Feinsod's on his way to Camp Borden.[77] Poor boy, he was bored, hot & feverish—hay feverish, that is. His course has got its dullest stretch just now. For a while I was afraid his lack of experience would make him a sucker for the military, but as the novelty wears off that appears less likely.

[71] It's a bugger to know how much I have to explain to my kids. I've just realized today, for instance, that they probably couldn't answer such questions as: what are the five orders of English peerage, with their feminines? What is a lord? Is a bishop a lord? Who sits in the House of Lords? What are the gentry? What is a baronet? What is an esquire, & why did Pepys throw handsprings when he was first called one? What would a contemporary of Shakespeare or Milton mean by a gentleman? Who is the head of the Church of England? (My kids will say the Archbishop of Canterbury). What is a deacon? Why are rector, vicar & curate rare terms among Catholics, or are they? (I don't know that one myself). What does the word "county" mean? When was the Catholic hierarchy restored in England? Are there any Catholic cathedrals in England? What is the difference between a deacon and an elder? As for such points as that a Lord of the Bedchamber is discreetly called a Lord in waiting when a Queen is reigning, I needn't go into that.

Aug. 21. [Friday]

[72] Connected with this is a sketch somebody should do sometime on the personal background of English literature: what families lived where, who was related to whom, who patronized whom. William Herbert Earl of Pembroke; connected with the Herberts, George & Lord H. of Cherbury; connected with the Countess of Pembroke who was Sidney's sister—that sort of thing.

[73] [Peter] Fisher claims that the reason Westerners can't get any charge out of Buddhist monks is that the average Western scholar to them is not a seeker of wisdom but a scribe: it's a question of class. Ella Martin & Gordon Webber were in last night.

Aug. 22. [Saturday]

[74] Cool weather, thank God, but I made the fatal mistake of going to the Kings' [Harold and Marjorie] at night. I paid for it with an asthmatic night. I wish I could develop the art of automatically avoiding the echoes which are a major source of revision in my writing: why couldn't I have said "Kings in the evening"? Harold showed us his summer paintings which are unusually competent and assured. He's one of our few educated painters.

Aug. 23. [Sunday]

[75] Stayed in bed all day: even so not a good night. Read Jane Austen's *Love and Friendship*, a skit which proves to me, as none of her novels prove, that she is an important & not merely an intelligent & amusing writer. Jane is a blind spot to me: I enjoy reading her for relaxation and I admire her skill and ingenuity, but I never feel much sense of cultural infusion, of the kind I require from a great writer. This boils down to the fact that I have nothing to say or discover about her, & so take her merits on faith. In the same volume there is a "History of England" on the *1066 and all that* plan which contains a takeoff of the Jacobitism of sentimental romantics, of the kind also ridiculed in George Borrow.[78] I can't forgive Jane for the vulgarity and Philistinism of *Mansfield Park*: if she hadn't written that absurd book I could enjoy her without reservations. But her explicit preference for her dim-witted Fanny to her intelligent and sensible Mary Crawford means that in the long run she accepted her county families, and had no positive basis for her satire of Lady Catherine or Collins or Sir whatsisname [Walter Elliot] in *Persuasion*. In the long run she stands for the "dismal & illiberal," for the exclusion of the free air of culture & intelligence. *Mansfield Park* gives her away—well, it gives the whole 19th c. away.

Aug. 24. [Monday]

[76] Our fifth wedding anniversary but even so an irritating day. Discovered at Britnells [Britnell's][79] that Freud has been banned in Canada. Helen was restless & we went to the show: two irritating pictures. In one a D.A. accused the wrong man of a murder: his wife, the accused's aunt, nagged & bullied her husband, plundered his office and lied extensively about it, seized her suspect and tortured him to exact a confession, which he gave finally in the usual slapdash way of a sloppy movie. I suppose this woman, who, instead of being well strapped and locked in her room, was finally justified on the ground that "feminine intuition" is infallible, is more escape for housewives. There'd be more point to it if women were not so spoiled already. "Intuition" as generally understood is a mental short cut employed by the unintelligent, who are no doubt pleased to be told that it's superior to intelligence.[80]

[77] People are human beings first and men and women afterwards.

Their bodily functions are different; their environments are different, though the difference in this century has been greatly decreased. So there may be generalizations of the "men are like *this* whereas women are like *that*" kind which may have some hazy and approximate truth. I don't know. Men's conversation is more abstract & less personal than women's, but whether that's an accident of training or an essential sexual trait I don't know. I do know that the kind of mind that thinks along these lines of facile antitheses is a dull & tiresome mind. It betrays a fixation on sex-differences which is mere adolescence, & in an adult unhealthy.

[78] In literature I find the war of the sexes a most unheroic theme. I'm enough of a disciple of Blake to believe that the domination of the female will is evil, and therefore I just don't find the wife-beats-husband theme funny. James Thurber does, or pretends to; Bernard Shaw does, & pretends not to, the comic strips do & the movies do. I'm sorry, but I don't. I don't find Mrs. Pinchwife's final line funny;[81] I don't find the Venus of *The Merchant's Tale* funny; I just don't find any irresistible female funny. And it's not funny now because it's not the inverse of a convention. True, women's labor is exploited more than that of men, & the various prostitute rackets that are allowed to run, notably the alimony, the "breach of promise" and the "rape" rackets, are superficial compared to that fact. But there is no real subjection of women today of the kind that makes *Bringing up Father* a criticism of life. I don't want male authority reestablished: I just want the whole silly business of inferior sexes and self-conscious "equality" of sexes dropped & forgotten about. It's no longer amusing, if it ever was.

[79] The other show, about a man who scrimped on his tiny salary (half as much again as I get) to buy a yacht while he was young enough to enjoy it, was a good illustration of a muddle inferior writers often get into, of being able to work out a plot. That is, push the characters around within certain complications only by making the characters so stupid that they cease to become interesting as characters. It's a dreary but frequently encountered dilemma.[82]

Aug. 25. [Tuesday]

[80] The Vicar of Bray never got to be a bishop.[83]

Aug. 26. [Wednesday]

[81] I don't know why I keep reading this idiotic Braybrooke Pepys, for which Everyman's Library obtains money under false pretenses.[84] It's not only heavily expurgated but some of the most important musical references are left out. For the expurgation there is only the faint excuse of 19th c. publication and the facts (a) that milord B. [Braybrooke] was in the Pepys family (b) that he was presenting a historical rather than a literary document. That Everyman should ask $1.50 for his croquette is nonsense. I'd like to write an article on Everyman prudery sometime. Geoffrey of Monmouth; the translator's smug sneer on p. 248.[85] Malory, according to Blunden. The Gulliver's Travels "For Young People" has been modified. The Pepys is the worst, of course, for B. [Braybrooke] has even been allowed to tamper with the family text to the extent of printing "prostitute" for "whore," on the three-point landing principle: I remember the New Yorker's account of a play, I think Sean O'Casey's, where Lilian [Lillian] Russell was billed as a "Young Whore." Several papers printed it as a "Young Harlot" (more cushion for sensitive moral fundaments in two syllables). One "blushed prettily and whispered 'A Young Girl Who Has Gone Astray.'" One said "with Miss Russell and the following cast."

[82] This combined with the banning of Freud makes me wonder if we are in for a wave of prudery as a defence against the licentiousness of war. That is, it puts me in a gloomy state of mind in which I wonder. I hope we'll continue the tendency to greater frankness and less bother about it which the popularity of, say, *The Grapes of Wrath*, would seem to indicate. But as people instinctively do the sillier things, there's a danger of a huge wave of sullen prurience pouring over us again, welling up from the deep & bitter hatred of culture in our middle class: especially, I think, the women and the women-dominated males. The sexual obsessions of our civilization are not settled yet, by a long way.

[83] Magda [Arnold] was in and told us about her rats. Seems she picks them up and shoves a hypodermic needle full of adrenalin into their peritoneums, and they droop. Proves the James-Lange emotional theory wrong, the theory of reducing all emotions to "fight or flight" (anger & fear) wrong, and the theory that the physiological states of all emotions are the same wrong. The last always did sound pretty silly: Cannon, in

1915, thought it up.[86] Bitter opposition from the head of the pharmacology department, who saw himself on the skids, evidently, but she got her Senate Chamber.

Aug. 27. [Thursday]

[84] I resolved today to (1.) keep up my diary (2.) read all the books I own, before reading much else (3.) write Blake (4.) practise Byrd. Saw Beverley Burwell, who looks taller & older & tells me Jerry Riddell has gone to Ottawa for {censored}.[87] He's pessimistic about the war. Bickersteth's letters home are mimeographed & circulated & contain many vicious comments about the War Office: full of antiquated crocks hanging on to their salaries & avoiding being pensioned off on various pleas of emergency. He seems to feel that the German account of Dieppe as a foozled invasion attempt was correct: I'm not sure: it's too symmetrical. Of course if it proved only that Canadians are not cowards it didn't prove much.[88]

[85] Lunch accidentally with the Langfords & [John] Line, discussing the negative nature of evil. Line not in too good form: scared of me, maybe. Then Norman [Langford] came in in the evening with his long-legged wife. He tells me that Gieseking was one of the few people who successfully snubbed Bickersteth. He had lunch at Hart House & then the Warden casually mentioned that their Steinway was a very good piano, if, uh—. The great man went to it, played a scale & an arpeggio, tapped one note for the repeating action, and then said: "Ja, good piano!"

[86] I remember Woodhouse once telling me that Will once gave a series of Room 8 lectures. One was on Pascal & Lafontaine, a weird combination he did nothing to ameliorate. At the end he proudly boasted to [Herbert] Davis that he had performed a masterpiece. Then he gave an account of writing it the day before, sitting before some papers & having nothing emerge until 11:00 p.m. or thereabouts, when he suddenly began to write furiously. "Why is it, Davis," he spluttered, "why is it that I can only work under the most terrific pressure? Is it because I'm so *damned* phlegmatic?"

Aug. 28. [Friday]

[87] Discovered something called Allergitabs, which make me feel funny

but seem to work. Picked up that souse George Beattie at the pub & then went to a kosher place on College & Spadina, George making love furiously to Helen all the way. Then to Ruth Jenking's where we pounded hell out of a couple of Mozart fantasias—amazing things he wrote in 1791 for music boxes, his last year when he was picking up anything he could get in the way of a commission.

Aug. 29. [Saturday]

[88] Hot day. Read Oscar Levant's *Smattering of Ignorance.* Gossipy & malicious: quite good on Hollywood's bag-of-tricks approach to sound tracks. If a producer gets less than tutti he feels gypped. Conventional "sweep" for opening: i.e., harp glissando, ascending-scale violin passages & woodwinds, ff [fortissimo], then cymbals crash on first beat, then grandiose tuttis.[89]

Aug. 30. [Sunday]

[89] Out to Fulton Ave., finding Roy [Kemp] very gloomy about the draft. The draft is getting rather horrible, with this hypocritical pretence that they're only calling "single" men, including all men married since summer 1940 who now have businesses & small children coming along. Our three noisy female neighbors are getting it: one husband in army, one in air force, one category E with a game knee expecting to be re-examined and shoved in.

Aug. 31. [Monday]

[90] Speaking of war, I sometimes feel that women are bad for morale: they go in for catastrophe, funerals & oracles. They're the sex of Cassandra, and they're extremely short on humor. They hate obscenity, an essential part of humor, and the female magazines never go in for it. Cartoons, jokes, breezy comic stories, have little place in the *Ladies Home Journal.* It isn't just mediocrity: the male magazines for mediocrities always have humor: but what the average woman wants is something maudlin to attach her complex of self-pity and I-get-left-at-home and my-work-is-never-done and nobody-appreciates-it-anyway to. There's something morbid about the domestic mind which weeps at weddings & gets ecstatic over calamities. During the war they keep making woo-woo

noises prophesying large drafts & taxes with no we'll-get-along-some-how reserve. Partly of course because they're not in it. If people only believed in immortality & a world of spiritual values! But it might only make the war more ferocious.

Sept. 1. [Tuesday]

[91] Spent the morning buggering around with little odd jobs. Saw Archie Hare, who looks haggard. My druggist tells me that a new drug act has been passed preventing several drugs, including codeine and phenobarbol [phenobarbitol], to be sold over the counter without a doctor's prescription, thus greatly reducing the effectiveness of such potent medicines as the one that's helping me. Sounds like a medical stranglehold on their apothecary enemies of 3000 yrs. There may be a lot to be said on both sides, but doctors today are such ignorant barbarians, & their sense of heresy is priestly rather than scientific. They are in fact the modern priests, supported by women, with the advantage over the priests of being able to tickle their bellies as well as ask them about their sex lives. They shouldn't win too complete a victory over anyone.

Sept. 2. [Wednesday]

[92] The radio is going: why is so much dance music thin, wailing, dismally melancholy and wistful, like a train going through a forest at night? Is it intended to reproduce the complaining of the libido? Certainly it's aimed at below the waist, & suited to a dimly lit dance hall with adolescents shuffling up & down the floor rhythmically rubbing their genitals together.

[93] I'm acquiring too many vulgar expressions, like bum's rush for W.C. & cowflop for female wallflower.

Sept. 3. [Thursday]

[94] Day buggered by being stood up for an hour at lunch by George Beattie. He outlined an interesting family situation: father an upright if narrow Plymouth Brother, who according to his lights has tried to be a good father, is detested & ignored by his family, especially a daughter who yanked her mother away from him. Another son is an Anglican

priest. When he comes to town he finds that only his unrighteous souse George really respects the old boy, sees what he's driving at, and will go to church with him.

[95] Anniversary of the war, so we're told: see Aug. 19. It occurred to me a short while ago that I never really considered the possibility of our losing the war. I mean by that that I had never sat down and figured out how I could conscientiously go on living if we did. I'm beginning to understand how paralyzed, hopeless, hag-ridden and stupefied the average intellectual anti-Nazi on the European continent must be—or rather have been.

Sept. 4. [Friday]

[96] Mary Louise & Peter [Cameron] got married today, by Betty [MacCree's?] father, who did an awful job but let me out. I hate wedding receptions, & the only thing the service reminds me of is that "for fairer, for loather" was the original form of "for better, for worse." Helen probing to see how much Jerry's house would cost us to live in: too much. Helen's been restless lately: the war gives her claustrophobia & she has the feeling that everyone else is doing something more interesting. Jerry [Riddell] going to Ottawa to take a government job, Eleanor being mysterious about a career in advertising or publicity or something & taking a trip,[90] Mary [Winspear] going out to Edmonton to be Dean of women, Beattie collecting a salary of $6100 a year: with my hopelessly non-essential background she feels that everyone's playing a game she's left out of.

Sept. 5. [Saturday]

[97] Listened to Information Please programme last night. I wonder what the popular appeal of that programme is based on: I think partly on the enormous prestige enjoyed by a man who is well-informed on non-controversial subjects. The amount of actual erudition Kieran gets a chance to display is not impressive, as such things go, but such things go a long way, like the polysyllables of Goldsmith's schoolmaster [The Deserted Village, l. 213]. By means of it I succeed in scaring the shit out of [Bobby] Morrison & Beattie, who make three times the money I do. One doesn't realize the immense social prestige of the university until one

gets a little outside it. Speaking of them, I wonder if the dry rot at the basis of their lives is significant of an economic change in which the bustling, successful, money-making, super-selling young man is no longer a pure clear-eyed Alger hero but an embittered souse.

Sept. 6. [Sunday]

[98] A cousin of Helen's living in Forest dropped in. Interested in music, & apparently planning to teach it. Asked her what she was working on & she said "Grade Ten." Probed farther & she said "Beethoven." "One of the sonatas?" I suggested. "Guess so," she said. She has a voice like a kitchen stove falling downstairs. I can't understand the superstitious & barbaric notion in this country that it's sissified to cultivate an accent. The idea that correct & well-modulated speech is a fundamental corner-stone of culture doesn't occur to my students, many of whom make noises like the cry of the great bronze grackle in the mating season. As it isn't part of one's education, I can't teach it: I'm just the best friend who won't tell them. The Yankee method of talking through the nowse and hawnking like a fahghowrrn is very widespread; some whine like flying shells, some mutter like priests, some chew & gurgle like cement mixers. Ten minutes of frank talking to this girl and I could raise her several notches in the scale of culture: she's a bright kid and can take things on.

[99] The problem has two complications. One is the Victorian native Canadian, i.e. American, prejudice that an educated & cultivated accent is an English one. I've been told I have an English accent because I speak standard American. I remember trying to get Harold [Kemp] at the age of twelve to say "I've got ants in my pants, I can't dance": he protested violently because he thought I wanted an English a, or what he thought was an English a. I said I wanted a flat Canadian a, but I did not want *his* a, which defies all phonetic analysis and sounds like an unsuccessful attempt to imitate a cockatoo. To Victoria, anyone who cultivates an Oxford accent is a hypocrite, a sissy, a snob & probably a Fascist. The fact that it is far better to cultivate an Oxford accent than not to cultivate an accent at all is something that just never penetrates. The other is a hazy pseudo-democratic impression that correct speech is stuck-up. A great deal of what Mencken calls the vulgate is produced by a deliberate & conscious attempt—this, I perceive, is drifting into an article, & I'd better make it one. Written for the Forum as "Reflections at a Movie."[91]

Sept. 7. [Monday]

[100] Labor Day. Read Peter Quennell's "Caroline of England,"[92] mostly out of the Harvey Memoirs, but intelligent & well written. It would be an amusing idea to write a skit on an English professor waking up in, say, Pepys' time and trying to get hold of the language & customs. You'd have to know your stuff, but it would make good if somewhat obvious slapstick.

Sept. 8. [Tuesday]

[101] Howard Smith has a book out: "Last Train from Berlin."[93] Howard was a very likeable boy, frank & open-hearted in the best American way, somewhat naive, & a little sentimental, as Americans are. He is one of those who are so unwilling to be cynical that they tend to lack humor. I remember his showing me some Russian kopecks with "Workers of the World Unite" on them and saying: "*Now* have the Russians forgotten the world revolution?" I said something about the profound Christianity indicated by the "In God We Trust" on American coins and he laughed, though somewhat unwillingly.[94]

Sept. 9. [Wednesday]

[102] Stayed in bed all day: the process doesn't seem successful, as I'm worse off than ever. Went out last night to Fulton Ave.: poor old Harold [Kemp] still finds the Air Force tough going & Roy [Kemp] is still worried.

Sept. 10. [Thursday]

[103] The hay fever seems to have passed its meridian: maybe I'm just getting asthma & I shall regret ever having given up hay fever. Got check today, the incredible sum of $165.11: I thought with the new tax it would be far less. So we went to the Eglinton, meeting Saunders on the way, who said he thinks Jenny's job is some form of counter-espionage (he said "National Research Council" to me), to see a new Dashiell Hammett, "The Glass Key."[95] Beautifully paced, very well acted, directed & photographed: a swell tough and utterly amoral movie about a successful, ruthless & quite likeable Tammany gangster. A curious color-cartoon, on the invasion of Holland, done in puppets.

Sept. 11. [Friday]

[104] Restless & at a loose end, besides being full of shit owing to my giving Helen breakfast in bed & lying down to eat it with her. At a loose end, bitching the day apart from a memorandum for the Retreat discussion on the 27th, which [Walter] Brown has asked me to take. I had Jessie [Macpherson] to lunch yesterday to see if she had any ideas about it: she hadn't. I don't know why I've written down "at a loose end" twice, unless it's a Freudian wish that I had one.

Sept. 12. [Saturday]

[105] Down to collect Helen & we went to downtown Diana's: absolutely jammed with females.[96] I never knew there were so many women in the world, or so few men. I felt a little like a stud: if I'd been in uniform I'd have felt completely so. There's a curious sensation about being surrounded with so much female flesh that's hard to analyze. Also on the street, but not quite so bad there. If the war lasts long enough they may start drafting civilian males for stud duty: they're very near it in Germany now and we generally do what Germany does a year or so later. I'd be category E for the Army, but I'm afraid 1–A for studding. The sedentary are the most sex-ridden of all men, despite a popular superstition to the contrary largely invented by them. The Kings had lunch with Brough Macpherson today, who is leaving for U.N.B. A cheap & lousy second-hand bookstore has opened on Yonge & Charles. I went all through it to the back, where they had a shelf of semi-erotic books on what they refer to as "sex harmony" and emerged with a Hanford Milton Handbook for 15¢.[97] It's about time to read it.

[106] Possible novel situation: man's mother dies when he's about 17 & entering college. Father marries again, has a daughter & dies himself when the son's about 20. Widow wants to remarry & get rid of the kid, so the man marries earlier than he would otherwise have done, around 22 or 23, & brings up his half-sister as a daughter. On second thought, the situation would be quite normal.

[107] I wonder how far-reaching the stopping of travel & touring will be: an enormous amount of our economy was tied up with it: in the Maritimes, for instance, the roads were a solid line of piss-and-postcard places

between villages, where they thickened. Unsound economy, certainly, but wiping it out is a revolution of no small proportions. The effect will be healthiest in Quebec, I think, which was freezing into a Maria Chapdelaine pose of ye olde picturesque rutting & rooting queynte paysan, with of course the Fascist Catholic twist—the Vichious circle of church, pub, field & kitchen.[98]

[108] I've been brooding about that movie: I have to do more under the Sept. 6 title.[99] Friends of democracy are seldom frank about its failings & I don't know if anyone has researched the persistence in it of the Aristides complex.[100] The great heart of the people can put up with conscientious, honest, efficient government just so long and then they arise in their wrath and demand some form of picturesque graft or colorful tyranny. Recently the Socialist mayor of Milwaukee, who had served his city faithfully for years, was defeated by an obviously incompetent crooner. Now that "Glass Key" picture showed that it's gangsters, not saints, who attract fanatical loyalty and are impossible finally to crush. Cf. the frank support of child labour in "The Great McGinty":[101] another film along much the same lines. As compared with the intellectualized & comparatively superficial analysis of a Fascist type in Citizen Kane, I think that's an important thing for the films to do.

[109] Met [George] Beattie & Morrison again. George says Judith Robinson is subsidized by a reactionary firm of publicity agents called Judson or something. Said she was fired from the Globe & Mail for technical errors only: mainly handing in her copy 20 minutes before the deadline. Says Drew hired a flesh peddler at $300 a month so he can sell his stuff in the States: hence the Hong Kong bust. Evidently he didn't hire a good one. Says that "Raymond Arthur Davies" is a Bronx kike named Rabinovich who steals his stuff from PM, so true to type he's even anti-Semitic.[102]

Sept. 13. [Sunday]

[110] Lunch out at the [Graham] Millars & came back discussing the usual question why we dearly love & don't much like the [Gordon] Romans. Last night I dreamed I was living in Stalingrad with a Russian family: the wife a beautiful slim girl copied from some picture of a ballerina. They asked me how I got there & I said quite simple,

B.C.-Pacific-Siberia, the Russian transportation system is wonderful east of Stalingrad—you'd never know there was a war on. An old woman came & knocked on the door: she was an evil malicious gossip, inquisitive & interfering, & well known to be a German spy. The girl said "No, you can't come in; go away, you old tart." Yet we all had the feeling that sooner or later she *would* come in, & would order us around as she liked. Then I suddenly heard cannonading, which I'd been only vaguely conscious of before, & I knew the Russians had retreated another ten miles. Gradually the old hag forced her way into the vestibule, soldiers (German) started pouring in, & I woke up.

[111] I often wonder about intuitive racial-stereotype thinking: a lot of it's balls. For instance, there's a big good-natured German in Moncton called Lichtenberg who had been a peaceful, thrifty, industrious contractor there for thirty years. For two wars the local Gestapo have cut their teeth on him: when the news is bad or they get tired of reading spy stories they'd go up and practise on him. Recently the Gestapo combed his whole house over, in response to some silly anonymous "tip," & one of them found two large knobs in a dark closet. "Aha!" he said, stepped into the closet & gave one a twist, thinking of course it was a private transmitter set. It was an extra shower he'd installed. Incidentally, he's a naturalized Canadian citizen, but married before that, so his wife, who belongs to one of the oldest Maritime families, is an enemy alien. Well, Dad's friendship for Lichtenberg has come in for much unfavorable comment in that stinking little kraal Moncton, & the stinkers point out gleefully that "Frye" is really a German name, & that I look just like a German. It's a beautiful theory, only it just happens to be wrong.

[112] Kermes, the house that produced scarlet dye in the Middle Ages, is the source of carmine, crimson, & vermillion (little worm).

Sept. 14. [Monday]

[113] I'd like to do a New Yorker type of story with echoes from a club like our S.C.R. [Senior Common Room]. Krating: ". . . you see it isn't the Espinani Jews,[103] the real Jews, that are the trouble; it's the Polish kind that cause . . ." ". . . So when the inspectors arrived they found the coal all stacked up in the bathtub. You see, you can't just . . ."

[114] Alice Eedy was in tonight: she's been doing social service work & seems depressed by various anomalies about the situation of our forgotten men.

Sept. 15. [Tuesday]

[115] Called for Helen & took her to see "The Magnificent Ambersons,"[104] highly recommended by some people including Eleanor [Godfrey], but I found it a blowsy and turgid piece of Byrony. I've been writing out a paper on William Byrd,[105] which is taking too much time but seems to be inspired. If I'm going to do movie articles I should get Leo Rosten's book on Hollywood: he's the Leonard Q. Ross of Hyman Kaplan.[106] Peter Fisher was in in the morning with a hint he might be going overseas. Discussed German-Russian war as based on a Rajas-Tamas[107] clash of Albion & millennial ideals: both proximate apocalyptics.

Sept. 16. [Wednesday]

[116] Dull morning on committee for admissions: one of Jessica Lambert's: her father being referred to as a refugee. Gabriel Wells, the New York bookseller, has two Coleridge notebooks, offered to Yale at a terrific price they won't pay. Kay [Coburn] says they're probably stolen, as the Coleridges had a book thief for butler once. Down on streetcar with Hugh MacTaggart [Mactaggart], now at Honeywood, who talks as though he had a brass plate stretched across his windpipe.

[117] Ideas for article on movie music:[108] Orson Wells' incessant woo-woo noises, a dull series of drum rolls & trombones slithering from solemn burp to gloomy blop. Most incidental music is just "flourish," "sennet," "exeunt with a dead march" stuff, a bag of tricks: "sound effects," in short. Oscar Levant describes the "sweep" (Aug. 29)[109] & feels that the producer always wants tutti, like the parvenu who wouldn't have any second violins in his orchestra. He quotes a Russian film (Shostakovich) opening with a lone piccolo, followed by a flute. This indicates lack of enterprise in experimenting with timbre.[110] Hollywood can't use woodwinds: they can't shiver their timbers: only brass. The piano's very effective percussion tone they leave out: they overdo harps & leave out tom-toms & gongs even for horror films. Conventional

orchestra background for everything: no regrouping. Motto from Ecclesiasticus. Nobody listens, so no leitmotif, an obvious point, one would think. Quotation, of course, & plagiarism. Uniformly heavy scoring: all harmonic tricks & a general air of having found the lost chord, mostly the dominant discords. Why not long stretches of scenery & music for real drama, towards an operatic movie? Because nobody listens. This all the more essential as real music has dropped behind. There's no amusing popular song: just bawling & nasal honks. Swing is stuck on a treadmill of rhythm, even Duke Ellington. Might recall "motion picture moods" of Rapee as showing plagiarism basis. Often more effective. Farmyard Symphony vs. Fantasia, use of Beethoven Pastoral. Even good tricks, high pedal-point on Snow White, 19th c. What I mean by vocal music is that musical comedies can't last. Songs are painful to photograph, singers even more so, & the camera is too relentless in its pursuit: musical comedy plots are pretty fragile. Moncton & O Katherina. Need more Gershwins? Might explain about "syncopation" of jazz. If chromatic harmony is played out the movie is the place for new experiments, not the concert hall. Of course there is a good deal going on, the train-boat sequence in *The Reluctant Dragon*. Oh, we're getting there: that should be enough for a necessarily rather vague & ill-informed article. After all, I don't know anything about montages or pan shots or fadeins or the rest of the patter.

[118] The Garretts dropped in suddenly: Helen's a week late with the curse & was asking my Helen for advice. Apparently you have to know what to ask for at the drug store: if you just ask for help they can't do a thing. The hands of the law are as clean and pure as the devil's arse hole: at any rate in its attitude to abortion & its support of the various prostitute rackets, alimony, breach of promise & rape.

Sept. 17. [*Thursday*]

[119] Another point about "what the public wants" is that there isn't anywhere else for a young couple to go. Hence out of sheer self-respect they can't allow themselves to be bored. The dollar they paid to get in is a hole in their expense money: they're not going to walk out of it & leave the dollar behind. Besides, what else are they to do with their evening, read Shakespeare? There's no use telling them to practise the art of boredom & improve their taste. The situation is there & nobody can do anything about it—I guess that's got it.

Sept. 18. [Friday]

[120] College creeping back: for the first time I don't want to see it open. I didn't get enough of the Blake done. Faculty reunion dinner tonight, very dull. There's going to be occupational therapy for the girl patriots, there's a lot of pro-Vichy propaganda in Quebec, arts colleges are now being closed up right away—ho hum. Havelock back—his Socrates will run to two volumes.[111]

Sept. 19. [Saturday]

[121] Helen down with a cold. Bust my glasses for the first time in eight years, which vexed me, as Pepys would say.

Sept. 20. [Sunday]

[122] Staggered around with my glasses trying to read Morris' Early Romances, which I got yesterday morning from Britnell's along with several other second-hand Everymans for my new course. Harold & parents[112] dropped in with the Lambert kids. Jessica goes into Trinity—a very sweet kid as far as I could see, which of course wasn't very far.

Sept. 21. [Monday]

[123] Still without glasses, so spoiled myself loafing. Nobody can tell me impressionist painting of the Pissaro type is myopic. I find that when outlines are fuzzy I become very sensitive to splashes of color.

Sept. 22. [Tuesday]

[124] Had to go down to Dundas St. to collect my glasses, then Conservatory, then Music Library, picking up Byrd, then Convocation: an unqualified disaster which it bores me to write about. Helen down with a cold, as I said before.

Sept. 23. [Wednesday]

[125] Lectures began this morning: all lectures begin half an hour early: T.T.C. request for staggered hours. I told my kids they'd been staggering into 9 o'clocks at 9:30 for years. Opening lecture to 2e[113] thorough but

dull. I don't do the Trinity this year: Child does it, or part of it. To Marion Darte's for a party including Eleanor [Godfrey], Ray [Godfrey], the Callaghans & a chap with one leg from Winnipeg.[114] Very dull evening: tiresome discussion with wild generalizations about the sexes which I engaged in only because I didn't want to sulk. Eleanor was stewed and sullen and Morley has a thick streak of ham in him anyway. But he does tell a story well—when he does.

Sept. 24. [Thursday]

[126] Morley [Callaghan] & Eleanor [Godfrey] dislike the English but don't fully understand why: it's because they're Catholics, of course. The confusions of interests today are curious. Heywood Broun turned R.C. after he'd become convinced, wrongly of course, that it wasn't inherently Fascist. He judged the church by a political standard assumed superior to it. Yet if he had realized this he'd have sold out to the reactionaries. Funny deadlock.

[127] The theory of democracy about the will of the people being the source of government is, in that form, just will-worship like Calvin's.

Sept. 25. [Friday]

[128] Full of shit again. Every once in a while I get shocked by the callousness and brutality of members of my class: I was thinking of that Sunday afternoon at Millars. Mildred [Oldfield Millar] was speaking of her young David's tendencies to run across the road, & I said, "You can imagine the state of mind of mothers on Charles St., or places where kids have to play on the streets." One woman said "Oh, I don't think those people care much." *Cats* would care, and *hens* would care, but the mothers of Charles St. don't give a damn.

Sept. 26. [Saturday]

[129] Chancellor Wallace in a sermon quoted George H. Palmer on the death of his wife: "Who can contemplate the fact of her death & not call the world irrational if out of deference to a few particles of disordered matter it excludes so fair a spirit?" Remarks like that don't usually impress me, but this one does.

Sept. 27. [Sunday]

[130] Well, today was the Retreat. I got through it somehow, dividing it into "The Search for Wisdom" (morning) and "The Search for the Word" (afternoon). I said everything is learned by the scientific method and absorbed in the personality as an art, a knack or flair. The former is knowledge, the latter wisdom & the goal of an "arts" course. Knowledge of itself is lumber or a machine: a liberal education implies the elimination of pedantry & vulgarity & the achievement of a fully integrated personality. Students come to college because they want to grow. Mental growth is a fact like physical growth. But the possessor of a liberal education is not his own end, nor do his class affiliations or social responsibilities exhaust his duties, for there are no *douanes* in culture. Hence wisdom is the entry into a universal order and a world of spiritual values. The discussion was good but the staff talked too much. I stressed "scientia," knowledge, as against "love of wisdom," philosophy, which defines the human attitude towards the knowledge. Love today is interest, the difference between the good & mediocre student of equal intelligence. In the afternoon I went on with "The Search for the Word": wisdom reveals spiritual values but does not save more than a few Stoics of exceptional strength who have the very rare quality of *heroic* wisdom from an evil physical world. Besides, the personal is superior to the impersonal. Hence wisdom becomes less an abstract noun & more a concrete entity of mind, or person: a saviour, furthermore, a God also man. Hence wisdom which arrives at the Logos has expanded into revelation or vision. The kids couldn't get that, of course, and fought over whether you could know if God exists or not. However, I really think the Retreat was less hideously futile than usual.

Sept. 28. [Monday]

[131] Three lectures and busting with shit: went home early this afternoon. Then to Havelock's for a debating society executive meeting. Eric has taken quite a shine to me evidently & he certainly does work hard at debates. They varied between political and local-scandal subjects, suggesting "should formal parties be suspended?" I said it would be more interesting to say "should formal dresses be suspended?" They came to no conclusions but are planning a group of inter-year debates.

Sept. 29. [Tuesday]

[132] Add to S.C.R. [Senior Common Room] catchwords (Sept. 14): "I don't see why unconventional people aren't willing to take the consequences of being unconventional."

[133] At that party of Marion Darte's Eleanor [Godfrey], stewed, said she didn't like divorced people: Ray [Godfrey] said: "Say you don't like the system of divorce, not that you don't like divorced people." I was very impressed with that for several days, but not anymore. To dislike divorce is a vague approximation: to dislike divorced people is concrete as far as it goes. I don't trust approximate remarks. Thus you say: "throw out all the old men & put in young ones," meaning "throw out incompetents and put in good men," but as the former looks vaguely like a more practical suggestion you hope it will approximate the latter. Similarly with the peacetime "don't let young people drive cars." Man named Bishop in to sign up for the Spenser course.

Sept. 30. [Wednesday]

[134] Met Kay Mabee at Feinsod's: Children's Aid on Isabella. Just through with taking five kids to court, packed in rumble seat, to charge parents with neglect & get custody. She noticed they seemed to be playing some sort of game, & she discovered it was seeing who could amass the biggest collection of fleas. Tonight Helen stayed down & I strolled over to Yonge for dinner, found Murray's[115] jammed, drifted down to Bloor, picked up Roy [Kemp] & had dinner at Babloor. Full of his draft, of course. So I'm depressed, irritated, nostalgic & half-sick, & I suspect that tooth, which bothered me last year at exactly this time, is acting up again. The Forum sent up a ragtag staff too & that adds to the depression. Oh, God, I'm bored with the war: I can't even rise to a nobler expression.

Oct. 1. [Thursday]

[135] Another S.C.R. [Senior Common Room] one: "they always assassinate the wrong man."

[136] Jingle has been underestimated: a great deal could be done by a

novelist in making the actual cuts of ordinary speech. Coming home with young Victor Butts after the retreat, I said it was too bad Brown had preached his entire sermon at three boys. He said, "Yeah, did rather. Wave length."

[137] Rosemarie [Schawlow] in for lunch: thrown up C.I.L. & is considering a job leading to personnel work in Scarboro where she'll be on a shift, 7–3 one week, 3–11 next. Wants to take a course with me on top of that. Frances Bower, a girl who lives all the time in a Beulah of enthusiasm, being happily without a sense of criticism, breezed in from O.C.E., where everything is wonderful, including Diltz, who easily replaces the English people here in her affections. She wants essentially to study anthropology (Indian) in Chicago & do field work in South America. A girl without beauty or exceptional brains, she's made the most of what she has. She says her grandfather, having retired at 70, promptly went to Northern Vocational to do machine-shop work. He wanted to build the road to Alaska but his womenfolk intervened.

Oct. 2. [Friday]

[138] Reading the *Golden Bough* again and Blake & Spenser chase each other's tails all through it. My graduate Spenser course is waving gently in the breeze: Bishop dropped out, a Ph.D. man named Grant is pending, Rosemarie [Schawlow] is pending, Ruth Jenking is pending.

Oct. 3. [Saturday]

[139] Quiet day, mostly at home reading.

Oct. 23. [Friday]

[140] There are times when I don't feel in the least like keeping a diary. In the last twenty days I've been ploughing through the Golden Bough, collecting a Spenser bibliography, and dodging my lectures. We visited the Langfords at Laurel, a dull prairie, over Thanksgiving.

[141] Reading Wooley's book on Ur last night.[116] The Sumerians mystify

me. There's nothing archaic about them. Their art is blocky, unrhythmical, realistic, over-sophisticated. Their government is typical monarchy and their royal sacrifices seem to be less barbaric than the Charge of the Light Brigade. They must have had millennia of development behind them wherever they came from.

[142] Anthology of war stories: Hemingway. He says in his preface: "Cowardice, as distinguished from panic, is almost always simply a lack of ability to suspend the functioning of the imagination."[117] So *that's* why I'm afraid of the dentist. Anthology of light verse by F.P.A. looks better than Auden's in some ways.[118] Hell, Christopher Isherwood in this New Yorker has swiped an idea I had years ago: married couple arguing with each other by diary.[119]

[143] I've had three fan letters on my Forum article, described on Sept. 6.[120] One was a mash note from an Alberta girl who said she was a schoolteacher, had a high I.Q., wrote poetry, was quite pretty and was twenty years old. If I was interested, would I write?

[144] Today I learned the Hebrew alphabet from Ps. 119.

....

Nov. 1. [Sunday]

[145] Well, let's try again. Today I preached a sermon on Job 24:1,[121] a good text and not a bad sermon, but Helen said not loud enough. Yesterday I walked down behind a woman, not fat, but mature and solidly built. She had rayon stockings on, and her thighs rubbed together with a little cricket chirp at every step. At the [Norman J.] Endicotts the other night Bee Wallace said she went over on a boat with some undertakers going to a conference in England. One said "Know what's the latest thing in caskets? Sagless springs, the bed of eternity." We've come a long way from ancient Egypt. It was last Thursday we were at the Endicotts. Norman said he thought my anatomy article[122] was erudite, which is spoiling me. Last Friday we had tea (apple juice) at the [Walter] Browns to consummate the Lawson wedding by proxy.[123] Mrs. Barber & some other women were laying into the apple juice as though it were what it obviously wasn't. "I never touch intoxicants," said Mrs. B. "If I did, I'd just roll around."

1949 Diary

[31 December 1948 – 31 May 1949]

The original holograph of this diary is in the NFF, 1991, box 50, file 9. It is written in ink on lined, 14.4 × 22.1 cm. notebook paper. The holes punched in the margin suggest the leaves were originally in a ring binder. Frye wrote from margin to margin on the front and back of 130 unnumbered pages.

Prologue to the Diary of 1949.

[1] In the course of my life I have made several efforts to keep a diary, & in fact have produced some better than average ones, notably one that ran from July 12, 1942 until the opening of term. They have always proved to be sizeable writing jobs, but have been useful in recording the contemporary stage of my imaginative development.

[2] This year I want to tackle the diary scheme again on a bigger scale, as a means of systematizing my life. I'm not working hard enough, and I feel that a diary would be useful, as my job is mainly thinking & writing, & I need some machinery for recording everything of importance I think of. As a moral discipline, too, it's important for a natural introvert to keep his letters answered, his social engagements up to date, and his knowledge of people and events set out in greater detail.

[3] There is hardly any phase of my life that a diary would not be useful for. Reading the morning paper & mail leading to recording the social side of my life, marking essays affords material for a possible book on how to write English. Conversation, even at Victoria, occasionally produces ideas; lectures are very productive of ideas I often just let go to

waste. The thing is not to be alarmed at the miscellaneous character of one's life & stylize the diary accordingly, as I've tended to do. It should be a continuous imaginative draft, not itself a work of literature. I also hope it will be of some moral benefit, in passing a kind of value judgment, implicit or explicit, on whether I've wasted the day or not, whether my schedule is in shape, whether my unanswered letters are piling up, etc. The feeling of meeting my own conscience at the end of the day may cut down my dithering time. I should be careful, however, not to ascribe exaggerated values to secondary duties merely because they are duties & I don't like them, but always to put writing, thinking & reading first.

[4] I have discovered that the stability of my whole day depends on getting up early. I seem to feel that I need eight hour's sleep—I hope this is untrue, as that's a terrible waste of time. I have recently taken to examining my dreams, as a kind of field work in anagogic interpretation, & that could be, if not overdone, a legitimate diary source. I'd like to put some of the early morning on piano practice, as it's often difficult to get at the piano later, and it's the one thing I can't do at the office. Practice pedal of course if too early. I'd like to build up a memorized repertoire of 18th c. music for this year, starting with the English school, going on to the Italians, then the Germans & finally the French. It's an advantage not to plan too extensively for piano work. Another piece of daily routine is this unending nightmare of languages. I had thought of German, Italian & Latin for this year.

[5] Because of the reasons noted, I think it best to retain the conventional basis of the diary form, a chronological narrative dated. There was a time when I disliked the idea of reading back over my past life, & several of my diary efforts made a point of ignoring the linear dated narrative.[1] Of course I don't think of the present diary as a Pepys ten-year project, but merely as an experimental form of discipline at my present imaginative stage.

[6] I don't think I should put all my effort into morning hours—the worst time for dither for me is afternoons, especially the period before dinner, which is often so late in our house as to leave little for the evening. The primary aim of my life at present must be to avoid entropy. Inertia is the chief enemy of the soul, and is far more persistent & pervasive than temptation, at least for me.

[7] On beginning a project like this, one should avoid all taboos—
I shouldn't be too careful to avoid a miscellaneous, even sloppy, appearance. The only thing that bothers me is the size of this paper, but I think
it'll do. I shouldn't read it over too much either. The only thing the diary
won't cover is the actual writing I do. I thought of simply going on with
my dozen-paper project this year, beginning with one on Blake & Jung,
& going on to a general-principles paper to be done for the Humanities
Colloquium.[2] Then perhaps the Spenser & Milton papers. I could leave
the romance project for the summer.

[8] Years ending in 9's have been Wanderjahre for me: 1919 supplied the
pleasantest & the most unpleasant periods of my childhood—summer at
Ayer's Cliff, winter at Burges.[3] I think I didn't go to the Maritimes until
1920, which spoils the pattern. 1929 I came to College. 1939 I returned
from Europe and began my permanent job. 1949 I'm beginning to feel a
bit restless—impatient with Victoria's corniness, & wondering if it is
really the best place in the world to work.

[9] As Samuel Butler says, incessant recording is the literary habit.[4]
I want to write a couple of novels, of which at least one could be finished
this year, on college education. I cannot do this properly without recording every absurd freak of education I hear of or get in the mail.

[10] The things I must be particularly careful to pass judgement on are:
keeping posted on bibliography, and ordering library books, & getting
into closer personal touch with my students. I have taken too little care of
these things.

New Year's Eve.

[11] Went to see the Laurence Olivier *Hamlet* this afternoon—its elev-
enth filming, according to the program. As Olivier directed the film &
played Hamlet too, it was still the subjective fallacy, the conception of
the play which derives from the accident that Hamlet is a fat actor's role,
not in the least scant of breath. In any production the actor who takes
Hamlet's part has a lot to say about the production, and in fact he is
usually in charge of the production, & his first care is usually to ensure
that if any part is cut it won't be his. Olivier wasn't crude about it: he
slashed the soliloquies to ribbons & turned it into a play of action. The

subjective fallacy showed up chiefly in his treatment of Ophelia—he manipulated her part to make her just the "anima" of Hamlet, & deliberately cut out her mature intensity of feeling & her sharp sly humor. Consistently with this he made her death pure accident, thus making all the references to her "doubtful" death in the fifth act entirely pointless. The foils to Hamlet were also weakened—Laertes of course has a very badly written part, but the stability of Horatio was hardly in evidence & Fortinbras was abolished altogether, along with those dismal robot clowns Rosencrantz & Guildenstern. On the other hand, the king & queen were fully & excellently treated.

[12] *Hamlet* is not about Hamlet at all, but about a situation into which Hamlet fits, and all attempts to treat the play as though it were primarily a character study of Hamlet destroy the symmetry of the play. For one thing, one needs all the rich counterpoint of the Polonius family, which plays the same role in *Hamlet* that the Gloucester family does in *Lear*. We have to see this subplot from its own perspective as well as from Hamlet's. Ophelia corresponds to Gertrude, & her attraction toward Hamlet is, from Polonius' point of view, a desertion to vice, just as Gertrude's attraction toward Claudius is from Hamlet's. The father-daughter hold here is as palpable as the bigger mother-son one. But more important, *Hamlet* is not a play about Hamlet's indecision, but about the ritual element in revenge. In Hamlet the stimulus to revenge takes the creative form of the play: in Claudius it takes the form of a ritual sword-dance, a Druidical drama punctuated with choruses of toasts & cannon shots. But the question "why did Hamlet delay?" is no more important to the play than the question "why did Claudius delay?" for Claudius also has shallow excuses and self-analyzing soliloquies. There is something comic in the elephantine fumbling on both sides, especially in the fourth act.

[13] There were excellent things in Olivier's version, though: the winding stair & the general Piranesi setting, Hamlet as the Orc-hero brandishing the torch in Claudius' face, a grotesque little wooden statue of Christ to which Claudius prays, the use of the cross on the sword-hilt in the Hamlet-Ghost scene, the whole Saturnalia or Balshazzar's feast aspect of Claudius' revels. The camera, by pushing closer to the characters, brings out the horror of tragedy that stage plays often gloss over, & reminds us that tragedy is after all about people getting hurt.

[14] A very quiet New Year's Eve—we went over to the Hebbs for a while. Vera's [Vera Frye's] thesis was on parental attitudes to higher education. She says lower middle-class immigrants want their children to work hard & avoid higher education—they get their ideas of universities from the movies, & think of them as playgrounds for spoiled rich children. The comic professor of the movies is proof that people are in grave danger of spraining their brains if they study too hard. That belief in overworking the brain is very common, not as a belief but as a rationalization of inertia. It's part of the guilt complex about not meeting the physical standards of frontier ancestors which runs all through our society and is kept alive by such agencies as the Saturday Evening Post, as well as a growing realization that the social expression of the virtues of initiative & enterprise belong[s] in the past. A good deal of my own unhandiness is an inner protest against the social prestige of hawbuck virtues. I suffered a good deal from being called a "sissy" in my childhood, but an unconscious determination to live up to that role was only strengthened thereby.

New Year's Day. [Saturday]

[15] Cold & snowy: my first duty, after the furnace, was digging the real estate out from under the snow—my legal thirty feet. Difficult to get much done—I'm determined to learn to read German fluently before the year is out, & I'm facing a copy of *Wilhelm Meister* with some apprehension, as I don't really want to plough through all that damned stuff about puppets again. Voted, for a two-year term, May Birchard, & Kay Morris. Tried to memorize the last movement of a pretty little Arne sonata in A major that came in a book Helen gave me for Christmas. In connection with censorship the phrase "meddle class" came into my head. Tea with the Haddows: he says that termites are getting into the city's wood. He had a beautiful European pine Christmas Tree, from a nursery near here that sells them to Buffalo & Detroit, where there's a large Polish population nostalgic for what would be their national tree. He says red pines are better than white pines for reforestation, & that a jack pine is a small & scrubby looking tree, native to Ontario.

[16] Mem [Memorandum]: get Chauvin or someone to review *Refus Global* for the Forum.[5] Also ask Allan [Sangster] again about Dr. Faustus.[6]

[17] Ninety-two Christmas cards came in. The Constants, Ralph Hicklin (ask about Evelyn Waugh article), Jodine Beynon (a difficult avuncular letter), perhaps the Lipsets, the Johnstons (return story),[7] Mac Ross, the Stobies, Kay Coburn, the Maynards, the Oughtons (suggest the Lysenko piece), Clara [Utes?], the Sirlucks & Baby Nancy need personal notes.[8] I have to be responsible for thanking verbally Wilfred Watson, Charles Comfort, John Robins, Mrs. Hubener, Ronald Bates, Doug Valleau, Don Harron (tickets),[9] Ross Beharriell, Jo Fisher, John Morgan, Martin Shubik, Gordon Wood & Victor Whatton.

[18] New Year's is a dull holiday: Christmas provides a definite ritual of things to do, but New Year's is just a day to dither & dawdle through, overeating & underthinking. A huge chicken pie for dinner, which gave me a terrific heartburn—wonder how a smothered burp ever acquired so romantic a name. Vera [Frye] went back tonight. If there is one thing in Jung that rings true to experience, it's his doctrine of the argumentative animus in women. He writes about it with great feeling, & it's clear that some of his women patients must really have put him on the spot. I've served as animus-projection for several women, & I know how bitchy even normal ones can be, to say nothing of neurotics. Vera's animus is a council symbolizing Chicago, or the American way of life. There's always a let down when someone leaves, but this holiday has been an unusually concentrated dose of family, & the emotions generated by a family, even when most tender and solicitous, are sterile emotions. Dad is still left.[10] I wonder about the anecdotal mechanism of age—do old people really forget that they've told their stories many times before?

[19] I'm veering round to the idea of a short & simple book on Spenser for this year's work, if such a thing is possible. Of course there's the opening Colloquium paper,[11] designed to boil down my L [Liberal] ideas[12] and that may take some time to work out. Actually that paper is ye next thynge. While listening to the Messiah, it occurred to me that sometime I might take a try at writing the popular novel that gets written every ten years on the life of Christ or the early Church, & has been called, during the last century, the Last Days of Pompeii, Quo Vadis, Ben Hur, Unto Caesar, The Robe, & God knows what else. Mine wouldn't be popular: it would be more along the Merejkowski or Sholem Asch line, but it would attempt to reconstruct what really happened according to my ideas of it. Robert Graves appears to have messed it up by not

digesting the anthropological pattern. It's true that I think the Gospels are designed to conceal the historical Jesus, but even so something happened, & to present that something in a way that would satisfy me & still convey something to the public might be a job worth thinking about.

[20] On the street car home Helen was irritated by the woman sitting next to her, who kept digging her elbows in her ribs. Helen loses her temper with a conscious effort—throws it away, so to speak. People do things on various levels of consciousness, & sensitive & imaginative people are often unusually irritable because they recognize the deliberate element in unconscious actions. I feel irritated by people who block up doors on street cars, because I recognize in it a deliberate assertion of an aggressive egocentric to-hell-with-you attitude. I call it deliberate, though the person himself may be a) partly conscious of it b) unaware of it though capable of recognizing it in some form or other if brought to his attention c) wholly unaware of it. Naturally it's much more explicit in drunks and people of low intelligence. Selfhood contemplates Selfhood with irritation & the imagination with resentment; imagination contemplates Selfhood with wrath and imagination with love.[13] I find it difficult to stay on the imaginative level because of a persistent sense of physical insecurity engendered by my weak & awkward body. The same is true of Helen, except that she has the additional courage of a woman who knows that nobody will take a sock at her. The usual female notion that if they were men they would be a fortiori more audacious than they are as women in bawling out truck drivers & attacking brutes with umbrellas who flog horses, kick dogs & pinch maidenly bottoms is, of course, nonsense, except as a trump card in the female game. If they were men the question of how they would get along in a fight would be present; they would be involved in the constant weight-guessing competition that goes on among men, & if they couldn't count on much help from Brother Ass[14] they'd fold their tents and silently steal away, just like other men.

Jan. 2. [Sunday]

[21] Sunday, for God's sake—it's time I was back to work. Reading Wilhelm Meister with a few glints of dawning insight into the damn language. I had a dream last night pointing very laboriously to an imaginary street called Weston Ave. in Moncton[15] south of Park Street, at the

blindest end of which I found Wilson & an old man & a baker shop where I was to hand in some old biscuits and get them renewed or something. Some circumference-centre antithesis in contrasting the limits of Toronto (Weston and Wilson Ave.) with the interior of Moncton. The baker's shop turned into a theatre where I saw a lot of my students.

[22] Not wholly a wasted day—I read some German & wrote a bit of my paper[16]—but it felt like one. I did practically no piano work. Staying in has affected my nose, & I must have an operation on my septum soon; as girls say when their lovers leave them chewing their nails, we can't go on like this. Helen has turned on the radio and a "pops" orchestra is chasing a tonic chord. Gives every sign of eventually catching it, too.

Jan. 3. [Monday]

[23] I should stop trying to cuddle my Sundays: complete inactivity, I notice, makes it hard to sleep nights. That happened to both of us, & the result next day is more exhausting than two church services and a Sunday school would have been the previous day.

[24] [Peter] Fisher came in wanting to know if MHH [*The Marriage of Heaven and Hell*] presents the Apollo-Dionysius [Dionysus] antithesis. I said yes, except for the marriage part: the Olympian setup always eventually turns out female (Enitharmon) & has to be fucked. Nietzsche, I said, following a hint of Jung's, was an Adlerian & spectral will to power, the S of U [Spectre of Urthona] caught by Luvah, a nihilistic activity of linear will without telos. Wagner, on the other hand, is all murmuring & rippling female will, spider web Freudian Vala symbolism, Isolde dying like Cleopatra, the Grail standing up in Parsifal like a huge cunt. How anybody can miss that opera as the apotheosis of the Whore's gold cup I don't see. He [Fisher] said he thought Hitler had produced an expurgated version of Zarathustra, as Nietzsche ridicules the identification of state & folk. He also said Magda Arnold had turned *Roman* Catholic—a disgusting piece of news if true, but, as he said, what can you do if you have Jung and nothing else? I said I supposed the principle of divination was based on the notion of enough psychic life hovering around the carcass to provide some sort of golden bough to the underworld. He was remarking on how Plato in *Phaedrus* derives augury from prophecy

[244b–d]: I said the temptation to make prophecy easier by using a crystal would be the starting point on the downward path to bird's guts.

[25] David Knight for lunch: he has the same inconsequential burble Eleanor Coutts has, but he makes Yale sound pleasanter than most places in the States. He works mainly with Wimsatt & Cleanth Brooks, & seems to be doing us credit.

[26] It's not impossible that my remark about psychic life in entrails [par. 24] may have emanated from a curious dream, the only one I can remember of a long series. I was playing the Schumann Papillons, which I seemed to remember fairly well, except that I substituted one of the Novelettes for the last long one. At first I seemed to be playing opposite Marie Bond on another piano (the name may be significant as well as a recent meeting with her)[17] on my right, then Connie Blewett got mixed up with it, & finally was lying on her back on top of the piano with a mysterious dark girl standing behind me. All these things are I think dramatizations of Jungian ideas I've recently been reading about. It's curious how dreams seem to point silently to certain things, like the ghost of Christmas Future. So does Shakespeare point silently to certain key points like the death of Ophelia. I think Shakespeare dreamed his plays: I find no evidence that he did anything but hold the nozzle of the hose, so to speak. I picture him as vaguely bewildered & irritated by his own genius, perhaps frightened by it into comporting his conscious life in a deliberately trivial manner. He just didn't give a damn: all speculation about his personality breaks down on that central point, and his inscrutability is a major source of his eternal fascination. But he leaves the critic absolutely free to do as he likes, & the editor too.

[27] I wonder why the information that so-&-so has turned Roman Catholic depresses me so. I think it's not so much that Church, though, as a liberal Protestant democrat, I hate & fear this totalitarian, sleepless, relentless, anti-liberal, anti-Protestant, anti-democratic machine. It isn't the fact that Catholic converts have to assent that they believe absurd doctrines that bothers me. It's really, at bottom, resentment against Protestantism, especially this fatuous United Church, for being so miserably lacking in intellectual integrity. Protestantism is done for here, unless it listens to a few prophets. I don't want a Church of any kind, but if, say, a

student of mine were quavering over conversion to Catholicism, I'd like to be able to point to something better than a committee of temperance cranks, which is about all the United Church is now.

[28] Eleanor Coutts dropped in to say goodbye. She tells me of a good movie (British) about Palestine: "My Father's House."[18] The New Yorker speaks of a French one on the Auschwitz camp, "La Derniere Etape."[19]

[29] I'm not satisfied with the day. Very little German, no music, little reading, no writing & a good deal of buggering around. A new New Yorker was part of the trouble: the rest was mainly lack of energy. No essays marked either, & no letters written.

Jan. 4. [Tuesday]

[30] Got up all right for work, but with many groans & protests from the asinine brother.[20] My first lecture was on Newman:[21] I had nothing to say, so fell back on rehashing the old Verstand-Vernunft distinction. I said Vernunft could be interpreted a) as whole as opposed to partial reason b) as an intuitive comprehension articulated by Verstand c) vulgarly, as an emotion. That a & b were reconcilable—I showed how, via Cassirer and the *Gestalt* theory—but emotion remained the accompanying criticism of activity and not the goal or characteristic of activity. I suppose this is the real point of Jung's counterpoising principle—the unconscious being the realm of the pleasure principle in its upper regions as well as the realm of intuitive apprehension in its deeper ones. Intuition, what I call literal apprehension, begins all creative activity. Intelligible articulation of this is progressive; emotional reaction to it is regressive, at least in itself. If thinking or creating strikes a snag, the emotions register anxiety or bewilderment: if everything goes well, they register buoyant pleasure. Naturally we try to get to a point which will register pleasure on the emotions, but we cannot pursue the pleasure unless we avoid the possibility of anxiety, bewilderment, even suffering, that comes with progressive articulation. That's why the pursuit of happiness is, in itself, regressive. In thought it leads to the state of mind many theosophists are in, of confusing profound thoughts with pleasure at the idea of having profound thoughts. Anyway, I said that the emotional vulgarization of the romantic conception of Vernunft, which Carlyle did so much to foster, was popular in the 19th c.: it's behind Methodism

& pietism, & behind the whole notion that science is progressive & busy proving something, leaving a regressive last stand at the least—for religion. This is written all over In Memoriam. It's still operant in our notion that science is primarily progressive, & that the best the humanities can do is imitate the sciences in research, literary criticism, unrecognized as science, sinking thereby into emotional or subjective regression. I wonder if a certain cyclic process goes on in the mind whereby intuitions are born in the unconscious, hammered by Los into a generative form, & then fall back (never mind the metaphors) into the unconscious again through the upper unconscious dream-world. Everyone admits that the dream comments on the previous day, & everyone knows that the problems of that day are sometimes solved by sleep alone. Does not this imply that the dreaming consciousness rearranges material from waking consciousness in a wish-fulfilment form, & that this material, now dramatized, is assimilated to the archetypes below it, from whence it reemerges to consciousness? This would explain how dreams hook themselves onto the key experiences of childhood, as I'm convinced that impressions taken in the first few years of life recreate for the individual all the primary archetypes. Thus the dream assimilates the haphazard and involuntary experiences of waking life, the becoming world, into the archetypal world of being where everything is a wish-fulfilment comedy. Each dream is a personal episode of a universal comedy of the human collective unconscious, a drama broken off from the one great epic. If the individual is not progressing, then his dreams will be Freudian sex-dreams or Adlerian power-dreams, concerned solely with an antithesis between reality & desire. These fall into the childhood archetypes & reemerge autonomously in life: the whole process is involuntary, sterile, & regressive—or rather, it follows the organic curve of life, & becomes regressive from 35 on, ending in the dismal poverty of ideas one sees in age.[22] If he is progressing, his individuality, Jung's self, takes form at the centre of the wheel, instead of being one of the foci of an ellipse, the other being a point in the dark.

[31] R.K. lecture[23] which I had to cut to 75 minutes. I said some more along the same line, that doctrines of "faith" were germs of thought, art & action, that religion implied progress in the sense of fulfilment of one's own being, & that such progress was the articulation in thought & action of faith. That unrealized faith was intellectual lumber, & emotional religion regressive—that sort of thing. That man is born attached to nature

& religious progress is detachment. That the ego is the parody of the real self. That consciousness of existence is consciousness of existence in a parabola, a cycle running from birth to death, therefore such consciousness is *Angst*. That the universal form of this was the Creation-Apocalypse cycle of the Word. In the 4k lecture I said in answer to a question on Toynbee, that the advantage of studying a dead language or an *accomplished* history is that it's relatively in the realm of essence—a living language is a glacier with you as part of a terminal moraine being pushed backwards.

[32] Lunch with Osbert Sitwell at the University Club—Lionel Massey gave the party, & Doug LePan & Paul Arthur & a man I didn't know were there. Sitwell was a high-coloured solid-looking aristocrat with iron-grey hair, who until he opened his mouth could have been either a cultivated man or a barbarian. Wonderful lunch—oysters & a fine dry red Portuguese wine. The conversation was commonplaces, though highly cultivated commonplaces. He is deeply impressed by my book—says he's recommended it to a lot of people including the painter John Piper. Edith [Sitwell] is at the St. Regis on East 50th St, New York. He's Jung's sensation type, not a thinker primarily.

[33] Back to Victoria, found Helen, & took her out for a cocktail. Then to Knox's office for a committee to draft the new 3b,[24] with Roper plugging Americans & McLuhan contemporaries generally. We finally picked Tennyson, Browning & Whitman, Sartor Resartus, Culture & Anarchy & Mill's Liberty, Vanity Fair & Joyce's Portrait for special study. Then somebody—I think Bissell—decided we bloody well didn't have to recommend Sartor if we bloody well didn't want to, so we tossed it off and put Middlemarch on instead. Then home. Knox says the new 18th c. man, [Douglas] Grant, has arrived.

[34] Margaret [Newton] has her new job, God help her, with the government. Means starting work at 8:30. Trethewey & his wife went to New York for the M.L.A. Peterborough wants me for the 21st.[25]

Jan. 5. [Wednesday]

[35] My mental life at the moment is slack & lazy & disorganized. Yesterday I did no music, marked no essays, wrote no letters. Today I'm

marking essays as the easiest thing to do. Lunch, S.C.R. [Senior Common Room]. Ned [Pratt] and Ken [MacLean] back from New York[26]—Ned had a wonderful time being feted by the [Mark] van Dorens & met Fadiman: Ken said the weather was sloppy & hard to get around in. Evidently [Osbert] Sitwell said very little about the novel last night, apart from a few carefully phrased wisecracks. I complained about my second year, & Joe Evans, who is Registrar now, says it goes back to a pernicious experiment in pseudo-progressivism undertaken by people he named as Thornton Mustard & [Stanley] Watson about ten years ago, featuring among other things the abolition of grammar.[27]

[36] Second year lecture dull: only a remark about the Renaissance taking to Plato because he reflected their own city-state set up as opposed to the Christendom founded intellectually by the imperialist & federalist Aristotle, had any overtones. The Newman was better. I pointed out how "liberal" means free (gentlemen's education beginning in leisure) & freedom must lead either to Christian liberty or to Liberalism, his horror of which helped drive him into the R.C.Ch. [Roman Catholic Church], & which was represented by Julian. I said Newman, like Toynbee, was a great historian whose metaphysical outfit was curiously ramshackle, put together with hunches & intuitions. His interest in ideas is genetic: his best books are Church histories like the one on the Arians. His mind is purely dialectic, proceeding from dilemma to dilemma & committing himself at each step. That the Apologia tried to present his conversion as conscious, instead of the autonomous subconscious explosion dealt with by William James. Finally I tackled a more difficult question I haven't worked out yet. I think if Newman had remained Anglican or perhaps even been born R.C., he'd have been in the Neoplatonic tradition. Clement & Origen affected him powerfully; he loved the Dionysiac doctrine of angels, & his theory of sacramentalism is right down that line. Dialectic, controversy & the need to assert the substantiality of the Church pushed him into a somewhat uncongenial Aristotelianism (it's partly too just a straight Victorian itch for getting something definite done, or down) which comes out in things like the Grammar of Assent, which I characterized as shoddy. I also spoke of the spiritual pragmatism in his view of certitude & probability, & connected it with his dialectic.

[37] Marked a few essays & took Helen, who had just finished writing an article for the Star Weekly, out for a cocktail. I had a sidecar, which,

I've been told, works on the backfire principle: you swallow down one lemonade after another trying to get a faint alcoholic taste in your mouth, when suddenly there's a dull boom in your stomach, a sudden ringing in the ears, crimson clouds before the eyes, & there you are as drunk as a coot. I had only one, so I don't know. A businessmen's dinner was in the dining room, and as I came out I heard the hostess say to the waiter, "How are they getting along with eleven bottles among twelve men?"

[38] Margaret [Newton] says Cam Hillmer has finally succeeded in getting stomach ulcers: he had, as I said, been asking for them with both hands out. The Wednesday night program was Twelfth Night, done, as Lister Sinclair had remarked to me with great pride some days ago, on Twelfth Night, or rather on Twelfth Eve. The title means something, I think, with the extraordinary convivial atmosphere. I think more money is handed out for tips than in any other Shakespeare comedy. It was cut very little. Then a woman named van Berenson [Barentzen] played the Appassionata, technically brilliant, but not at all subtle or profound. Dad, who had whimpered over the length of the play, got his revenge by talking all through the first movement. Debussy—a brittle and hurried version of *Undine*, which should flow in a liquid caress.[28] Very little German, no music, no letters.

Jan. 6. [Thursday]

[39] Lectures all morning. In Milton I dealt with the paradox of evil as a metaphysical negation & a moral fact, comparing it with the conception of cold in physics. Somebody asked me why chaos existed. I said all conceptions of the universe, not just the Einsteinian, are limited, & chaos marks the limit of that which is created by God yet is not God. There can be nothing beyond chaos, because there can be nothing beyond God; but God's power radiates to the limit of matter, or creation, hence there has to be chaos, or as near to pure matter as is conceivable, at that limit. I said that God's power is a vision to angels, a mystery to men, an automatic instinct in animals, plants &, according to the 17th c., minerals, and operates as luck or chance in chaos, hence Satan's footslip.[29] That the 19th c, influenced by the prestige of biological & other sciences, had looked downward from the human mystery & seen the world as a mechanism, and that the 20th c., peering through that, had struck probability & the "principle of indeterminacy" at the bottom of it. A touch of glibness there, as there is in a lot of what I say.

[40] The Blake was dull: Woodman read a paper on Blake & Milton.[30] In dealing with the female will, I said the polarizing of regressive & progressive female was in Homer (Calypso-Penelope) & in a sense in Virgil too—Dido vs. the real bride, the city he built. The complete pattern in the Bible says that the bride (Jerusalem) *is* the forgiven harlot, & a dim perception of that made Samuel Butler write that curious essay about the whitewashing of Penelope.[31] Not much naturally in the First Year lecture except a realization that the use of the messenger in Job may have a touch of Greek influence.

[41] At lunch I completely forgot about Hart House—a rather rare piece of absentmindedness. I wanted to speak to Barker[32] too, about Charles Bell. I must never do that sort of thing again. I've been sleepy & tired all day: I can't understand why I slept so badly last night, unless the sidecar did explode after all. I dreamed about waiting a long time for Roy Daniells & some unknown stranger to visit me. They arrived very late, were connected somehow with two light switches with covers removed and works showing, & when they arrived the unknown stranger seeped *into* me in a way that made the dream the nearest thing to a nightmare I've had in a long time. The references are to the visit some years ago of Maynard & the composer, to the appearance of Daniells' & Finch's new poems, to Margaret's [Margaret Avison's] review of them[33]—she'd phoned me about it that night, to the wedding present for Roy Helen & I had been discussing that night, & to the Jungian symbolism in his title, Deeper into the Forest. The stranger seems to be the neglected music, Finch, who doesn't like me, & some other principle corresponding to my brother Howard, with whom Roy seemed linked—possibly the brother with my name who died in infancy.[34] Sinister little bugger, though: I woke up feeling I was experiencing the first of the autonomous breakthroughs Jung talks about.

[42] David Hoeniger, who wants to go to Wisconsin, says Council yesterday was terribly fatuous—low standards caused by too many women; should Alumni Hall stay open till 9, 9:30 or 10? New York is organizing a State University. Bill Fennell was worrying away on the moral problem of tragedy: isn't it that Hamlet is involved in guilt no matter what he does, & isn't *that* the essence of tragedy? I think not, for if Hamlet had killed Claudius on schedule there would have been no tragedy. He mentioned Antigone, but even so you can't treat *Hamlet*, an experimental tragedy without catharsis, as a typical tragedy. Hoeniger says there are

18,000 institutions in U.S.A. that grant the degree of B.A. If so, I don't see why I can't sell more copies of *Fearful Symmetry*, as all of them must teach some English. But perhaps they haven't heard of Blake.

[43] Mill illustrates in a curious way the regular social rule that doctrines become most articulate in opposition. His utilitarianism is like my Protestantism. He's deeply ashamed of the intellectual tawdriness of Bentham & can't understand why more aren't converted to Coleridge than are; yet he's convinced that the real dynamic is in Bentham & not in Coleridge. He defends Bentham, not encouraged by the social ascendancy of the utilitarian school, of which he is also somewhat ashamed, but out of a clear knowledge of the intellectual domain in which Benthamism looks cheap, shoddy & almost outcast.

[44] Marjorie King has just phoned to say that Harold [King] is dead. Heart attack striking without warning last night. Harold was as lovable a person as I knew, & I shall miss him intensely: it's one of the few deaths I have experienced that hurt. She wants me to do the funeral: I always refuse marriages, but I don't see how I can refuse this—actually my attitude to marriages may be ungracious. I suppose when people ask me they want either a personal touch or less religion than they get from professionals. Personal touches are out of place at funerals—there one wants only to see the great wheels of the Church rolling by. It is much more of an imposition than Marjorie realizes, as the death is a considerable shock to me, even if it cannot be compared with the shock to her. As for the religion, all one can do at a funeral is proclaim the fact of resurrection: any funeral that doesn't do that is just variations on "Behold, he stinketh" [John 11:39].

[45] Cameron Caesar came in tonight, a great relief, as I thought the name on the phone was Ken Peacock, whom I have very little to say to. Two or three acres & a rebuilt house (by himself & wife) on the shore of Lake Huron have made him happy. They both hate cities. He's assistant director of research in Standard Oil. I found his description of the structure of Standard Oil very interesting, though vague—that is, I had assumed that all institutions whatever followed or at least approximated the structure developed by the Catholic Church out of the Roman Empire: the pyramid, with one man at the top and a broadening base of delegated authority. Cam held out the vision of endless interlocking

directorates in which no one has complete control or even understanding of the whole structure. Here there is, according to him, a certain latent managerial flexibility in which you can take authority rather than have it delegated to you, where salary isn't important because you can make a fortune out of your "contacts," and where you can, without recourse to any mysterious board or committee, gain an immense & expanding influence. The conception of an organization which interlocks but does not pyramid—a Presbyterian economy—will bear thinking about. He says the big men are curiously terrified of being "legislated out of existence"—perhaps industrial anarchism, or laissez faire, does supply the germ of the ultimate anarchism, or maximum freedom, that we all want. He reports that a man named Fegley, whom I met with him in London after he'd had a bicycle tour of Russia, was then a Communist who published an exposé of interlocking directorates in British Transport, showing how one firm could break a strike by shifting its resources to another & proclaiming that the strike had ruined it. The pamphlet itself prompted a huge transport strike, also a libel suit, which Fegley wiggled out of because, though there were errors, the directors couldn't find them & declared other things erroneous that were right. Then he returned to America & joined the Methodist ministry (his father was in it) with a vague idea of making Protestantism a Communist front. Methodism won: he's completely absorbed in it now, is Secretary of the World Federation of Churches, is immersed in Church politics & has developed a passionate interest in home cooking. Also a German Jew who has invented some interesting things, including a process for extracting salt from milk for invalids who feel about salt the way diabetics feel about sugar. Something else about dialysis I can't remember.

Jan. 7. [Friday]

[46] My head is full of this bother about the funeral—I went over to the funeral parlor this afternoon to talk to Marjorie about it. Margaret Fairley was there, & remarked that there shouldn't be any compulsion for the audience to join into anything, as there'd be everyone there from devout Baptists to party members. I dismissed the idea of a hymn, which produces a terrible caterwauling at funerals, but I think there should be a prayer, in spite of the brethren's scruples, for the sake of the relatives at least. I shall read the paragraph in the Book of Wisdom about the souls of the righteous being in the hands of God, & the paragraph following

about people who die in the prime of life [Wisdom of Solomon 3:1–9]. Marjorie asked for "These Things Shall Be"[35] & Blake's Jerusalem, & something about social justice from the Bible, which I'm afraid isn't very interested in social justice, as such. Margaret [Fairley] suggested Amos, but he's rather thundery weather for funerals. I thought of James, but I dunno. Jeremiah is too dismal & Isaiah just hits & runs. I'd like to read the paragraph in Religio Medici which is the teacher's statement of faith,[36] & I'd dearly love to find something decent about painters, perhaps from Van Gogh. The only Biblical thing I can find, & that's not very good, is from Zechariah.

[47] I think it may be valuable to me to do this job: it's closer to me than just a service to Marjorie. It's a way of letting the light shine, so to speak: psychologically, it's a help in trampling on the heaving monster underneath. Jung would classify me as an intuitive thinker, which means that my sensational feeling is undifferentiated. Certain emotional stimuli have a way of making me emotionally seasick: I start weeping to myself when I think of that passage in Religio Medici as a teacher's confession of faith. This is sentimentality, not bad, but undeveloped & undifferentiated emotional power that has to be integrated & harnessed. By myself, the service I'm planning would start me snivelling—well, not that, but emotional explosions, or beating waves. The wave image is very close, & the analogy of seasickness apt—it isn't precise or differentiated feeling directed *at* something, is what I mean. In front of a crowd with Marjorie depending on me at a critical point in her life, I shan't break down, but will ride the damn beast for all his bucking & plunging.

[48] Milton lecture—the old line about the impossibility of approaching the Father directly, the quibble in Book 3 as connected with the withdrawal from causation, etc. Nothing new except the Limbo of Vanities being the god of pride in salvation by works, reaching the same god as Satan by the opposite route. Talked to Irving, a man so extroverted he baffles me, much as I like him. He says hang on to graduate work because next year, thank God, is [Walter T.] Brown's last, & after that [Harold] Bennett, whether the next president or not, should carry more weight. He mentions Oswald McCoskey, professor of agronomy in Guelph, as the man to do the Lysenko job I have in mind.[37] Lunch with Margaret Avison. I feel that there is very little real intimacy between us now. I made the mistake with her of allowing her to make me into an

animus figure. That in itself isn't a mistake, but it's a transference that a real friend should mature & dissolve. I never did that, but tried to act like an animus. I talked to her as a woman dances, trying to sense her lead and articulate it. It worked well for a while, but it stereotyped me, & she gradually realized the physical male object before her & declared her love for it. As that is only deadlock, and I had no further animus resources, the dance is over, & we're standing around, both facing the orchestra & not each other, patting our hands nervously to signify our approval of what has been done. I made the same mistake with Elizabeth Frazer [Fraser].[38] Part of the error comes in my very animus nature: I respond by idealizing the woman into an anima. I have thought of both Elizabeth & Margaret as wonderfully subtle and accurate creatures, & of their instincts as invested with a superior insight, which I could educate myself by following. I have learned little from these women, & have not helped them much to learn from me.

[49] But Margaret is relaxing her hold, not only on me, but on life itself. She is dying, and she is moving toward death with a fascinated sleep-walker's gaze, brushing aside everything that gets in her way, Guggenheim fellowships & offers of help in everything from jobs to mere food & shelter. The experience of death is about all that seems deeply to interest her. I described her to Margaret Newton as a conscientious objector to life, & while that goes too far, it indicates something of her current attitude. The attitude I suppose is partly a pose, but so are all attitudes, & the trouble with any attitude is that it tends to sharpen itself into the entering wedge of activity. A psychoanalyst could tell Margaret that she is willing to draw attention to herself by appearing to fix her gaze on death, & she would know that. It wouldn't stop her from dying. Because of the "animated" nature of our relationship, there is a boring & irritating element in our friendship, which Margaret herself noticed, and, with the ruthlessness that women have in such matters, eliminated from my behavior & at least cleared up my thoughts. I am also bored with having my friends die, however, & wish that Margaret would come to live with us & eat steaks, & let herself grow fat and stupid and contented.

[50] She isn't half in love with easeful death by any means:[39] she is in no position to commit suicide with dignity & courage like George Beattie, & she doesn't want to. But some years ago she practically asked me if she

should commit herself to Communism. I said no. Then, without consulting me, she considered Roman Catholicism, & laid it aside. I found both of these manoeuvres crude & obvious, & was rather impatient with them. I think I see now what she is after. Death is the intellectual synthesis that makes sense, the dialectic shearing off unreality that she is ready to commit herself to. Only in this case she doesn't have to *do* anything: she can merely wait for death to accept her. How can one protest against an attitude like that? Half the world is on one side of the pillars of Hercules, the other half on the other side, and in front is the great open ocean. What can one do? It's as though Lady Macbeth were awake.

[51] Eleanor[40] has phoned, wanting to know if the Sitwell lecture was as bad in my estimation as in hers. I hadn't heard it, thank God. If I didn't know him to be brilliant I'd say he was a dope: in any case he's a kind of caricature of the Englishman fleecing the semi-cultured colonials.

Jan. 8. [Saturday]

[52] This morning I went down to the office and went to work on the funeral service, which I held at two o'clock. It went all right. It is a quite genuine nervous strain; it took a lot out of me & I'm glad it's over, yet there is a strong part of me that is excited at having a new toy to play with, at the chance to appear before people in a new light, and, above all, at the chance to dither & bugger around & upset my routine. I need hardly comment on the fact that there has been no German, no music, no letters & no essays. I can only hope that the dithering, which I do as a form of inner cackling over every egg I've extroverted, represents some kind of inner reintegration.

[53] There was a big crowd at the funeral. All the left-wing intelligentsia turned up: the Jim Endicotts, the Fairleys, Margaret Gould, Dora Wechsler, Dorothy Marks & her husband Oscar Rogers, who read the service at Bill Fairley's funeral; a lot of Artists' Federation people like Tillie Cowan & Eleanor Baker; some Social Work people like Dorothy Morgan; Northern Vocational people & assorted painters like the Halls, & relatives. I had hard-shell Baptists who wouldn't want liturgy, Jews who would wince at any reference to Jesus, & Communists who would object to the whole practice of spiritual processing. I read first "the souls of the righteous" passage from Wisdom,[41] then a passage further down about those who

die before their time; then I read a passage from one of the Van Gogh–
Theo letters—one of the early ones with a strongly evangelical tone, then
the Religio Medici passage,[42] then, after a remark or two about charity,
Zechariah 7–8 instead of Rev. 21. Then the two poems Marjorie asked for,
These Things Shall Be (which I find corny) and Blake's Jerusalem (which
I don't). I was going to compose a prayer, but thought better of it & read
the 90th Psalm as a prayer instead. The crematorium business was pretty
awful, but funerals are grim, I think intentionally grim, & any clergyman
who tries to pretend that they're not grim is in danger of making an
obscene jackass of himself. The committal was my own composition,
though based on the traditional form. I had no idea what the hell to do,
but the undertaker pushed me around. I had to lead the way in in front
of the casket, & it was quite a strain not to scamper or dawdle or keep
glancing behind me. I'm not much of a priest.

[54] Tea, or rather sherry, at Marjorie's afterward. Oscar Rogers, Panton,
the Vice-Principal of Northern, a man named [William J.] Brown, and a
boy from the school of Social Work named Bob Short, who married
Margaret Gayfer's sister.[43] Marjorie's own sister had come from Chicago,
a charming woman. Her husband is in music & they want to go to
Oberlin, which sounds to me like a thoroughly decent, if somewhat
demure, place. I'm collecting names of American universities I think I
might be able to live in, just for the record. Harold has a brother, a doctor
in London, but he was over in September & is not coming again, though
he tried to. The conversation, led mainly by Panton, who was Harold's
[Harold King's] colleague for twenty years, was reminiscent of early
trips to Europe, & such questions were discussed as what the French did
when they wanted a long cold drink of something.

[55] Helen, who took the funeral pretty hard (Harold had worked on the
magnolia trays with her & the fact that his name was Harold didn't help
either),[44] said that after the service Margaret Gould said to Dora Wechsler
"that shows you what a great man he was, & how much he'll be missed."
Death is a great begetter of clichés, but that indicates that I did what I set
out to do. One needs to counter blast the grisly & repulsive Egyptian
mummery of the undertaking business—the last look & the whole "Loved
One" nonsense.[45]

[56] Physically I felt like bed: psychologically I felt like going out, so we

went out to Ruth Home's place. A healthy English spring [mattress?] was there named Pamela Gifford, who teaches Latin (& English) at some girls' place I didn't know about called Hatfield.[46] Earl Wilson, a sensitive & slightly immature lad from the College of Art, was there, & Harold Whitley. I drank a lot of beer, not enough to stupefy me, though, & played the piano a little. Ruth's father is a gentle old soul: he discussed their country place at Cheltenham near Orangeville: the farms around Guelph, he says, are completely exhausted in regard to soil. They were originally forest land which should never have been cleared, as it never had more than a few inches of topsoil on it, but which was cleared, & ruthlessly: the grants of land to pioneers stipulated that ten or twelve acres a year should be cleared. Piles of oak logs, two feet through, simply set on fire because of no demand for lumber. Farmers now quite uninterested in reforestation, as they won't live to see anything more than saplings, & they haven't the children they used to have, so that the best friend of the land is the city slicker.

[57] Dad says that terrapin are boiled alive like lobsters, but are dumped on a board & allowed to make their own way to the boiling water, as they're attracted by its smell & never fail to head for it. The New Yorker has an interesting article on embezzlement which points out that it's not, after all, a crime against the people, but against an employer or employing corporation, so that it's really a civil rather than a criminal matter.[47] Not entirely, but that's its reference. A curious dream last night about living in a huge crystal palace full of doors & windows I was trying to keep shut & locked against intruders.

[58] This week has not come up to expectations, due only in part to the funeral. I suppose "due" there is ungrammatical, but I notice that professors get so inhibited on that point that they tend to use "owing" where they should use "due." But I have not got the work done that I wanted to do, I'm in a worse state of dither than ever, and my music in particular is disorganized. I still suffer from a fundamental lack of energy & drive.

Jan. 9. [Sunday]

[59] Sunday, thank God: I'm trying to add myself together. Margaret [Newton] down for breakfast, & we were speaking of the way Gordon Domm in Bathurst United had cleaned up the Beanery gang. There was an article in Maclean's about them designed to give them "constructive

publicity."[48] Lawbreakers of all ages have a craving, & consequently some need, for publicity, & merely to cut it off doesn't work. She also mentioned a new paper started in New York featuring good news, i.e. the positive & constructive things done in society rather than sheer calamity. It occurs to me that the newspaper convention of reporting disasters is completely irresponsible. Not that they should ignore the odd ten-year-old girl who gets raped by a pervert and concentrate on the beautiful lives of all the ten-year-olds who don't, that's silly. But a chronicle of the diseases of society ought to be coherently related to the analysis of society which would show those evils in perspective, give some idea of what their causes are, & what steps are or should be taken to prevent them. As it is, the newspaper tradition that interesting things are calamities, & that they are interesting because they are calamities, is pure nihilism, & breeds the feeling that peace provides no "moral equivalent of war." I imagine that in every gang of tough kids there are a few genuinely bitter ones who hold it together, & the rest have as much strain in living up to their tough persona as everyone has with any unnatural stylization of character.

[60] Nothing happened except a party at Mrs. Haddow's, & nothing happened there. A girl with pear-shaped buttons—huge things—on the front of her dress which were greatly admired by the women. I wanted to say "Great is Diana of the Ephesians" [Acts 19:23–40], but thought better of it.

Jan. 10. [Monday]

[61] Nothing much said at the 2i[49] lecture: I can't seem to get into that course, yet the conception of a planned state excites me. A bad day: I slept badly for some reason. I seem to depend now on Benedryl for my sleep & nightmares are beginning to come through. Peter Fisher came in & I was very glad to see him, as I'm still wound up about Harold [King] & Margaret [Avison]. He talked, and very well, about T.E. Lawrence, & about how it infuriates people to see relaxation, floating down the river like Ophelia, moving with the power of something else yet different from the river, neither deliberately swimming nor deliberately drowning, & so dying a "doubtful" death. He was convinced in the war that those about to die had the mark on them. I had felt that way about Harold Kemp, though it could be rationalizing.[50] Lunch at S.C.R. [Senior Common Room]: a Judge Mott there who said married people had no

rights as such. I said I was under the impression that when I married I had entered into a civil contract to support my wife, & that she could sue me if I didn't. He admitted that, but said that when that sort of question came up the marriage had already broken down, which is doubtless true but it didn't strike me as very sharply pointed. René Wellek sends me his review of the Blake in Modern Language Notes.[51] A stupid and ignorant review by a stuffed shirt. It was certainly tough luck to appear in America along with another book written reassuringly in conventional academese.[52] Then two women came in from that intelligent group of dear good ladies who paid me thirty bucks per lecture last term, possibly by mistake. I signed up for two, one on chivalric romances & the other on the Court of Love. 2i kids were in all afternoon, followed by that dithering idiot Stephen Gibson, who is rapidly becoming associated in my mind with whatzasname—David McKee. Having committed himself to working for three whole months on a PhD. at the age of 34, he feels tired, & wants to go away for a year. I'm all for any scheme that will keep him away from my office. The kids came in so fast I didn't really get the look at them the interviews were designed for. Graydon Bell is one of the better boys, & I liked a cheerful girl called Judy Livingston, though she'll never be much as student.[53] They're such nice kids, & so illiterate, & have been so infernally cheated. After marking an essay you expect a thing to come shambling in drooling and saying "boo-boo-boo-boo," but what you get is an attractive self-respecting youngster who looks you straight in the eye & says he or she always did have trouble with comp.

[62] Robins phoned in the evening to say that Arthur Barker had had a heart attack & would be in bed for three weeks & would have to take it easy the rest of the term. The occupational hazards of the teaching profession are getting alarming. Barker has been working like a horse for several years, & he's not a horse. I get his Milton people. Trinity hired an R.K. man last term who said he had an Oxford M.A. & turned out to have nothing from nowhere, so they let him go at Christmas. Margaret[54] says she's heard a rumor he's been confined to a mental institution. The students say they didn't notice any difference. They wouldn't, of course: but the guy might have been good. After the funeral Saturday I decided that the only person present I was trying to please was the corpse, & that reflection has cheered me greatly with respect to lecturing.

[63] I should do a lot of things: see Lacey, take Eleanor[55] out for a drink, phone up about [Arthur] Barker, get those fucking letters written, in-

cluding some for the Forum, see Marjorie [King], & so on. There's no rest for the wicked, & even less for the very, very good.

Jan. 11. [Tuesday]

[64] Today I finally grappled with the question of Newman's conversion. My point was mainly the analogy he felt between his position and the Monophysite controversy. The Church, like Christ, had to have a human as well as a divine nature. It had to be a physical, substantial thing, a social organization as well as a communion of saints. In the Church of England he tried to find the two marks of the true Church, Catholicity and Apostolicity. He soon ceased to deny that the Roman Church was Catholic, & that meant that the differences in its doctrines thereby ceased to be heresies & became corruptions. Then they became exaggerations, changes in emphasis rather than in doctrine, like the cult of the Virgin. Then the dialectic went into action, & the organism analogy of the Development said they had to be organic additions rather than corruptions. On the other hand the Via Media was a Monophysite Church: it had the divine ideas, but in substance it was full of heresy. The Church of England was irremediably in the grip of heresy, & the Roman corruptions were nothing to its corruption. Superstition can be corrected, but not heresy. I'm getting a much clearer notion of dialectic as an argument that proceeds along a direct is-or-is-not dilemma line, & commits the dialectician personally & emotionally to the real & substantial side. That may actually be the "way of the philosophers": in any case, it helps articulate my hunch that dialectic is the consolidation-of-Beulah stage just short of anagogy.

[65] The R.K. lecture was all right, but I just unloaded the English Institute paper on them.[56] Then lunch, where Bill Fennell & Joe [Fisher] & I discussed the priesthood of the lecturer. It was a figure Joe raised. I said that the priest was under no temptation to pretend that he was God—that's true in this context—if I lecture on Newman I'm under no *direct* temptation to present myself as someone better & more attractive than Newman. But the audience is under a constant temptation to see the priest instead of God, to discuss Norrie Frye's lectures instead of the subject, & substitute a passive entertainment for active participation in eating the body and drinking the blood of Newman. That's due to the accident of their ignorance—the university being ideally a community participating in learning, not a community of learned teaching unlearned.

There isn't a damned thing you can do about it: as long as the job *is* teaching there'll always be a paradox. Students consist of a majority of just kids & a few seekers, & the university exists because the seeker's need is real enough to be worth collecting money from the others. Lecturers train themselves to greater & greater efficiency, & the more efficient they become the more they stamp the students' minds, so that the seekers after truth become followers of them.

[66] In Adam all die because Adam was all humanity: every man in his situation would have seized the apple. In Christ's death all are condemned because every man would have done what Pilate & Caiaphas did. *All* the disciples forsook him & fled; the winepress was trodden *alone*; Peter, the cornerstone of the Church, denied him. It is this *separation* of all human nature from the humanity of Christ that gives the written record autonomy & destroys the "monologue with itself" claim of the Church. I'm not clear just how, but the humanity of Christ is set over against human social structures, and attachments & commitments to the latter must be tentative. The regenerative leap of individuation is what is required. Why is extroverted sanctity (miracles of healing & the like) found only in the Roman Church?

[67] Reading some lyrics of Campion, it occurs to me that the function of convention, in lyric poetry at least, is to detach personal from literary sincerity.

[68] Ran into Ned [Pratt] & told him my woes. He says Markowitz tells him that evening drinking is the best way to ward off heart disease. He went to the liquor store with me & bought me a bottle of rye. Promised him faithfully I would not have a heart attack in ten years. Told him to stop Deacon from calling him the author of Collected Poems. Forum meeting in the evening[57] Andrew [Hebb] not there, & Helen went to hear Joe McCulley on crime. Dull meeting, but the February issue is in the bag anyway. Penguin books print 75,000 copies, & when they sell out never reprint. I must keep Stykolt in mind for reviews. World news is in the doldrums just now.

Jan. 12. [Wednesday]

[69] Forum first, then the College. The Hudson Review wrote finally to

say they'd take my article.[58] Nice of them. That's the four forms of fiction one, & it's damn good. Dick Preston sent me application forms for the Headship of the R.M.C. [Royal Military College] Department. $6600, evidently: not bad, & that's initial salary. A poor lad named D.L. Weinert came in to see me: very nice boy. Wanted to know if I'd ever seen him in classes. I had, but my heart sank, as I had no idea of his name. He'd been in that god-awful 1st yr. pass group I had three years ago once a week, & have been trying to forget ever since. He wants to go to the Columbia School of Journalism, & has to have a recommendation from a senior professor. He is in Pol-Sci entirely in classes of two hundred odd. None of them remembered him: the one he thought would, who had him in a group, said she remembered his face vaguely but not him, & couldn't fill out any form. It's a grim parable of what universities are doing these days.[59]

[70] Brilliant lecture on Arnold—the opening one, dealing with his just-beautiful-true diagram, & its integration into culture, the form of the fourth, his Jungian conception of orthodoxy as a threefold synthesis, three-fourths of life, needing to close with the demonic form of the fourth, the pagan & dangerous beauty. I said pretty well all I have to say about Arnold, but I feel that if you do grab a man by his balls right away he's not so likely to get away afterwards, whereas if you start harrumphing & preluding and building up you never get to him at all. As I said last night, though in a very different context, I'm one of these people who go sneaking through life saying they have everything to declare. Anyway, I drew a diagram on the board, thus:

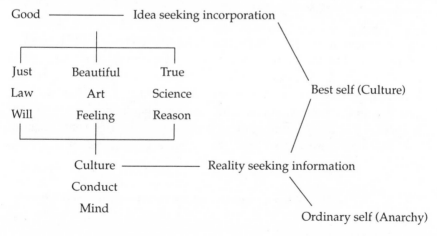

[71] Thus there's a four-power alliance, of which the orthodox synthesis, by leaving out the middle term of beauty, achieves three-fourths of the good. Same 3–4 symbolism as in Blake & Jung. As in Jung too, & perhaps in Blake, the form of the fourth is demonic. I feel that my idea of the seven liberal arts really has something, & I think someday I shall be able to write a book (v [Mirage], according to the scheme) on the geometry of vision, which will analyze the diagrammatic patterns present in thought which emerge unconsciously in the metaphors of speech, particularly prepositions (up, down, beside & the like). This threefold division of the good is in Poe & Emerson too. At the moment I see no distinction between the geometric & the arithmetic.

[72] Over to Andrew [Hebb] tonight after copyreading the Forum articles & taking them over. He told us of a J.W.A. Nicholson (I think) a Maritimer who has written for the Forum[60] & is a United Church minister & C.C.F. supporter. The latter fact has prevented any advancement in the former. It's extraordinary how many saints & martyrs there are whom no official God recognizes.

[73] Irving said when I was talking to him that [Walter T.] Brown is typical of Canadian university administrators in making the error of pretending to businessmen that he's a businessman, an error easily discovered. He says idealism & a determination to stick to the university as an idea may impress businessmen, but if you speak, as Larry Mackenzie did, on "Universities are Big Business," & then quote a budget that any businessman worth talking to would consider peanuts, you don't get far.

[74] Bert Hamilton came in this morning & asked me what a woman meant when she talked about security. I said patiently that it depended on the woman & the context. He said "this" woman seemed to mean by it complete self-sacrifice of a man to her. I said that any woman who attached such a meaning to security was neurotic, & should be avoided. It appears that he has escaped (for "this" woman married someone else) an emotional commitment that would have been disastrous, & feels greatly relieved.

[75] Marjorie King sends a note asking for the transcript of the funeral service.

Jan. 13. [Thursday]

[76] The usual four-lecture grind, exceedingly unrewarding. Nancy Rowland came in. She says she tried convent life for three weeks, didn't like it, & now wants to marry Bill Orwen,[61] doing a Ph.D. on Marvell in the graduate school, with Rochester connections. She thought marriage would be psychologically very suitable in providing a home, etc. I had a hard job not to laugh while I was being gravely offered logical excuses for wanting to get married, but said I was very pleased, which I am, particularly if he's a Catholic. I suppose it's the convent in her that makes her such a funny little dry stick. After the grind I came home & wrote six notes, to [Ernest] Sirluck, Danuta Constant, Fredelle Maynard, Jodine Beynon, Ralph Hicklin & Nancy. I don't understand why I attach so overwhelming an importance to letter writing.[62] I found it easier to understand why I wasted the evening—Dad wanted to talk. A.D. Branscombe is dead: it's a nice point whether I should drop a note to John, now in the Baptist ministry in Springhill, Nova Scotia, or not. I think not, on the whole. Dick Preston has written to suggest that I should apply for the Headship of the English Department at R.M.C. [Royal Military College]. The fact seems to amuse people, but the amount of money they offer—$6600 initially—is startling. It's a Civil Service job, and if I had any military experience whatever I'd be strongly tempted.

[77] I told my Milton kids this morning—by the way, Trinity did not turn up[63]—re Eve's dream & her decision to work alone next day, that dreams do slightly condition one's waking life the next day. I'm beginning to feel that dreams rise in level through a normal night's sleep, from an unknown depth in beauty sleep, which is never, or practically never, remembered, through symbolic archetypal dreams very seldom remembered, at least in detail, through erotic fantasies occasionally remembered, though too carefully disguised to make much impression, through will-to-power fantasies or Adlerian dreams relatively easy to remember, into dreams which are substitutes for waking actions, which are often dozes following the alarm ring. If we study conscious behavior we see the same thing. The subsidence of consciousness into doing things without noticing corresponds to substitute dreams. Listening to street-car conversations of the so-I-says-to-him variety shows how near the surface of consciousness the will-to-power fantasy is—even "normal" people are continually mistaking it for reality, or at least allowing it to condition

reality. It's the real "guardian of the threshold." The erotic wish-fulfilment fantasy demands what for "normal" people is a deliberate withdrawal from reality, a voluntary escape. Below this is the creative world
of art & thought, which demands not only relaxation from the world but
concentration as well. Below this is the world of meditation, which seizes
the moment Satan can't find,[64] & in which the soul emerges through the
mind as well as the body. Blavatsky says that if you could remember
your deep dreams you could remember your previous incarnations.[65]
I don't think it's necessary to accept this, but it's possible that if you
could take a golden bough with you all the way in the original plunge to
sleep, Alice's fall down the well, you would never need to sleep again.
The Tibetan Bardo has something of this idea of an initial plunge & then
a gradual rise back to the same old grind.[66] The trouble is you have to
hypnotize yourself somehow to fall asleep: without some initial giddiness you just get insomnia. This progression, if it exists, corresponds
roughly to the Spenglerian progression of a cultural cycle, & if so is
doubtless involved in the argument of Finnegans Wake.

Jan. 14. [Friday]

[78] A curious dream about going into a bookshop of law books run by
Doug LePan, trying to get out of it again, taking the wrong turn &
becoming involved with a narrow dusty door I could hardly squeeze
through & which let me out into a blind alley anyway. Some dreams
doubtless are monitory, but they're not much use if you can't remember
them. In any case, I found my way back & got the right turning.

[79] Helen says Arnold Walter has made rather a bungle of administer-
ing the Conservatory in one respect: he brought in Kolessa, Parlow &
Vinci & compels all scholarship students to use their scholarships on
them. As Kolessa can't teach & isn't the musician he thinks she is that
policy doesn't work out for piano. Being a gesturing ham in the grand
style tradition, complete with a corny resonance intended to be sublime
which she applies to the most precise Mozart, & of course with showers
of wrong notes, she teaches her pupils to plunge their hands on the keys
with all their weight to get "tone." During lessons on the grand her ten-
year-old brat walks up & down the keys of an upright in the same room.
Kolessa decided, reasonably enough, that Walter's admiration for her
could be explained only as love, & when he began to neglect her, as she

thought, she put private detectives on him who even put dictaphone wires in his office. She ran up a bill of $1800, & was detected in her turn when the hapless flatfeet came in to try to garnishee her salary check. I think she's been fired.

[80] Irving says the point I made in the Lawren Harris article[67] about mathematics as a set of possible systems was first realized by Leibnitz, whose "best of all possible worlds" was "possible" in a mathematical sense: one possible mathematical system is the one that exists. It took 19th c. mathematics & logical positivism to clinch the idea. He says the major problem of philosophy now, or rather for the "realist" school, is to reconcile the structure with the content of experience, which means bringing together mathematics & psychology. That Dewey, lacking mathematics, speaks only to the social sciences, & Whitehead, lacking psychology, only to the natural sciences. That Wittgenstein came out purely for structure in the Tractatus, leaving the content as a separate problem which he approaches as solipsism, epistemological solitude. The American realists gave the question up entirely & turned to other matters, Montague to the mysticism implicit in nuclear science, Northrop to fame & fortune in the cultural-synthesis field, Pitkin to best-sellers, Spalding to "eating chocolate bars & sharing an office with me." Perry to history. That's the way Irving talks—an extroverted conception of philosophy which sees it as flowing out of and around people. It mystifies an introvert like me, but fascinates me. He and Robins both liked the Lawren Harris article: he tells me I'm a better essayist than Aldous Huxley, which I daresay is true, & urged me, or Helen through me, to make a bibliography of everything I've written. I think I shall do so, & preface it to this diary. There's a fair amount of it, but I have a genius for writing things that do nothing to advance my career.

[81] It occurs to me that the reason for the Cartesian view that consciousness is existence, & that everything below consciousness, e.g. animals, are [is] mechanistic, is a revolutionary doctrine:[68] it recognizes Blake's upper limit of Beulah, the apocalyptic vortex from the animal to the conscious perception, nature to imagination, and insists on a clear break in the chain of being at that point. It gets everything else wrong, however.

[82] I'm beginning to feel more clearly that the quadrivium as well as the trivium is involved in the complete job given in embryo by *Fearful*

Symmetry. I've already visualized the first four with some clarity, and this idea of isolating the diagrammatic basis of thought as the essential V [Mirage] job[69] sounds promising. ⊢ [Paradox] in that case would be concerned with such matters as the psychology of conversion, accepting say the Roman Catholic pattern because of the consolidation of its symbols in a sort of projected mandala. ⊥ [Ignoramus] then would perhaps really have to tackle the job Irving suggests, on some level anyway. I wonder if the seven pillars aren't a job of book writing separate and distinct from the bulk of my books? That is, they're not, or not all, mammoth tomes, but rather essential clarifications of the seven steps of a sort of jnana-yoga ascent.[70] If I could only get this thoroughly through my head I could shake off a lot of phobias. At the moment I'm fussing over a variant of the Arnold diagram:

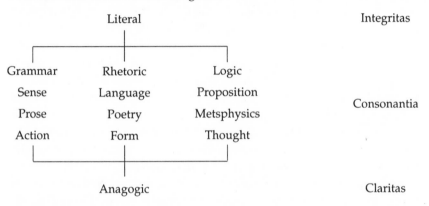

and wondering if there's any point in trying to link this with the Dante four levels thus:

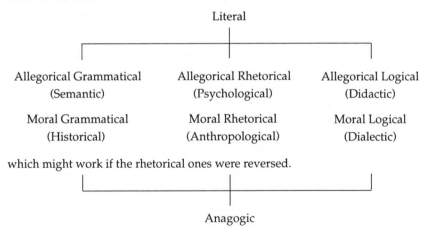

which might work if the rhetorical ones were reversed.

[83] Doris Mosdell phoned to say she'd been working on a Forum editorial on censorship (movie) & went to see a man called Silverthorne who turned out to be a quite intelligent & cultivated person. He's under pressure from the local Bawling Boys, who can stampede vote-grabbing politicians, from the Mayor down.[71] She phoned the chairman of the Moral Uplift Committee, who referred her with considerable regret to the chairman of the Cinema Committee, cautioning her not to believe that the latter did everything because they got all the publicity, but the Uplift Committee really did a lot of work too in suppressing things & ought to get some credit in every news writeup. Doris is favorably impressed by the real censors, & very depressed by the boys. She says there's an article in it, but not an editorial.

Jan. 15. [Saturday]

[84] Margaret [Newton] left this morning for Washington. [Walter T.] Brown has had what sounds like a stroke, though they say it's not one. Anyway his motor reflexes failed to function. He couldn't lecture & walked bumping into things. Strain & overwork. Then downtown to send a couple of silver spoons to Roy Daniells & the Bretts.[72] Fifteen bucks just for checking a couple of social obligations off our list.

[85] There seems little chance of much reduction in income tax: we will still have to pay interest on the bonds we sold. Curious warped mentality of the capitalist system—we can skimp on relief & essential social services & all the charitable aspects of life & still do nothing *wrong*: but the moment we think of defaulting on debts owed to more-or-less well-to-do people who wouldn't suffer if the interest were withheld, a tremendous moral outcry goes up. That's honour, & honesty, the natural virtues of the upper & middle classes respectively, the former in our social system being conceived in terms of the latter. Essential virtues they are too, but there's a point at which they block the view of charity.

[86] I've been thinking about the St. John's College scheme.[73] Parts of it appeal to me very much, but it seems more like a professor's program of self-culture than something to teach to students—also, the requirement on the teacher to be able to teach everything including mathematics & science seems to me to confuse an amateur ideal of culture with a professional technique of instruction. I could do it—at least there was a time when I could have done it, & I imagine I still could—but it would

be, not real teaching, but a deliberate *tour de force*. No one can be a great lecturer—I think I have the adjective coming to me—without sublimating a considerable amount of exhibitionism, but a teaching job that was a deliberate exhibition of versatility would focus on that, & turn me into a hopeless show-off. Of course every improvement in teaching methods, or in education generally, is primarily extra work for the teacher.

[87] A pleasant, though late, evening at the Hallman's [Hallmans'], home at two a.m. Cumberlands there, Jack as exuberant as ever. Re television: "I'm an old-fashioned man: I don't believe the telephone will ever replace the horse; and when you can hear radio, & in most cases smell it, I see no reason why it should also be seen." Actually the expense of television is a formidable economic barrier to surmount: who's going to pay for costumes & scenery, advertising sponsors? If so, there won't be much reduction in the cost of living for a while. Also, what will happen to good music, as the movies have proved that photographing concerts is a mistake?

[88] Dorothy [Cumberland] says Mustard's educational ideas weren't so bad; but that they were misunderstood & only partially applied.[74] I said that the trouble with my kids is not that they don't know any grammar, but that they haven't any ideas in their poor little noggins, & they haven't any ideas because in education we can no longer distinguish interest, which leads to the passive receptivity of being entertained, from concentration, which is active & self-coordinating.

[89] The trip out & back was evidence of how lousy the transportation services are in this city. St. Clair car to Yonge, Yonge to Bloor, Bloor from Yonge to the end of the carline at Jane, then after some wait, the Kingsway bus, getting off that after quite a while & walking along a dark puddly road with no sidewalk for four sizeable blocks. Total, an hour & twenty minutes. A taxi would have ruined us, & the driver couldn't have found the place anyway.

Jan. 16. [Sunday]

[90] Dull day, me with what the 18th century would call a loosening. The incredibly mild weather continues. Tretheweys & Hebbs in for tea, & in the evening we made the gross error of taking Dad to the Eaton

Memorial Church. Apparently they never hold services there in the evening: last time they put on an incredibly stupid nativity play, & this time it was a movie. I lit out, & Helen & Dad soon followed. I suppose the ritual is a psychological reality, & therefore a need for many, & the instinct to find a church service that wouldn't insult one's self-respect is important for many people, though not apparently for me. Any sensitive person with any accuracy of instinct would, it seems to me, find what the Eaton Memorial substitutes for Christianity a pretty phony & pinchbeck thing. Even I, who am not attached to the ceremonial side of religion, would have been a little chagrined at being caught in the Assembly Hall by one of my friends, at any rate without a pained expression on my face. I can also see that if I went to the United Church more regularly I should understand better why people turn Anglican & Catholic. My objection to conversion is not that the church you join is no better than the one you leave, but rather that I feel, for myself, that any coincidence of any church's service with what I'm looking for would be accidental.

[91] Helen's reports of the meeting—I mean the movie, of which she saw a couple of reels, were worse than my forebodings. I was tired & went to bed early, & dreamed very mixed up dreams. One concerned a tiger cub whose eyes had been removed—I saw the sockets. Some discussions about the value of glass eyes. Some monk was involved, & so was the attic of a large house, perhaps a boarding house, with a landlady making beds. The theme shifted to Blake's tiger & my attempts to explain the integration of creatures within the body of Albion to a class. I had the feeling that I understood but did not really grasp the principle involved. The scene dissolved and took on vaguely Muskoka-ish attributes—something about climbing up a steep path to the top of a hill with Helen's mother & meeting Helen part way up (ref. to a walk I took with Jean Cameron, who had been referred to that day). A figure blended of Allan [Hamer?] and Andrew Hebb appeared dimly in the background. Then finally my finding in a big encyclopaedic book like Toynbee's, but not Toynbee's, a footnote on Moncton which asserted that its original name was Ronamonde, Portuguese in origin, before it had been named after a "British general." The references here are to the footnote on the United Church in Toynbee,[75] which of course had been occupying my mind, & to a remark Trethewey made last Friday about a possible Portuguese origin for many Maritime names, e.g., Tantramar.[76] The general shape of this dream is the Catholic-Protestant antinomy which is always in my

mind. The great difficulty in evaluating dreams is, I think, the difficulty of remembering the *narrative* sequence: one can remember episodes, but their interconnection, which must be an important part of their meaning, gets blurred. Thus dreams are easier to understand as comment than as content, just as literary criticism, which is very like the interpretation of dreams, finds it easier to explain works of art in terms of their sources than in terms of their integrated meaning. I recognize most of the *sources* of last night's dream, & remember more content than usual, but what is, to use Freud's terms, latent in its manifest content? It doesn't seem to me to be "Freudian," i.e. of primarily erotic or even wish-fulfilment significance. Someday the meaning of such a dream will be as clear as the meaning of a dream of a tower in a virgin, but it isn't yet, & even Jung conventionalizes dream symbolism.

Jan. 17. [Monday]

[92] In any case I think it was partly the "monk" element in my dream (cf. the *real* etymology of *Moncton*) that made me think, when talking this morning of the monastic overtones in Utopia, of Joachim of Floris & the monastery militant, so to speak: the conquest of the world by the monastic ideal. Of course one of my favorite ideas is that the real form of society is not the Church but the university, which can never become autonomous because it always has to listen to something, & that the clearest visualization of this is Rabelais' Abbey of Thélème.[77]

[93] [Peter] Fisher in. I raised the point I've recorded elsewhere about Blake's failure to distinguish the spectral Ulro memory he hates from the cumulative practice-memory that Samuel Butler equates with heredity. We agreed that recognition, recollection, Plato's real anamnesis, was something far more fundamental. I said that the fundamental act of the conscious revolution, the vortex through which humanity breaks away from the animal, is the capacity for variable symbolism, that is, or that works out to, the ability to symbolize objects. Habitual or recognized symbolization is language. It's learned anew & traditionally by each individual, & that's why symbols are always esoteric. This conception of language as habitual, traditional or residual symbolism, assigning to poetry the function of recreating language by expanding the symbolization process, will bear thinking about.

[94] Fisher asked why 18th c. historians were so concerned with the topography of history, the superficial progress of great names & events, & never sought the small significant symbol, the trivial revealing anecdote, the essential phrase. They practise a sort of historical phrenology, trying to divine the mind from the conformations of its external continent. I said the avoidance of what we should call the "interesting" was part of the 18th c.'s rage for keeping consciousness on top.

[95] [Walter T.] Brown evidently had a real stroke, on Saturday. Robins says he thinks he'll never be back, though he'll doubtless try. If he has the sense to get scared his terrific constitution may pull him out of it. Jack Garrett is going to New Zealand to head the Department at Canterbury. I find that quite a blow, personally & for the Forum. Archie [Hare] says it's tough talking to Lacey, because he knows, & you know, & you know that he knows, & he knows that you know, & you know that he knows that you know, & he knows that you know that he knows, & so on. Woodhouse wants me to read a paper on Spenser he's doing for a Johns Hopkins special lecture. Ph.D. committee meeting: a woman of 50 named Mrs. [Mabel] Mackenzie, who is planning on going back to B.C. where she came from, came into this new man [Douglas] Grant about a Ph.D. thesis, about his first interview. She's evidently a most determined female whose husband lives in Florida. She came in & said (according to Grant): "Have you a Ph.D. subject for me on the 18th c.? If not, I know a professor in another university who has his drawer full of Ph.D. subjects." The official letter of recommendation, from Sedgewick, said: "You may not like her, but by God you'd better respect her."

[96] It's beginning to dawn on me that the seven pillars are consolidations of the books I'll be writing, not my total output. This ⅂ [Tragicomedy] isn't necessarily a book on Shakespeare, or even on the drama, at all, any more than L [Liberal] was necessarily a book on Blake, or will be necessarily a book on Spenser or Dante or the Bible. The seven pillars are all definitive statements about the facts of life, drawn from a prodigious erudition & the writing of a great number of books & articles & essays. So at that point I can maybe get down to work on a tiny handbook to Spenser. A casual remark of Harold Wilson's about the problem of form in a book that contained the FQ [*The Faerie Queene*] did the trick.

Jan. 18. [Tuesday]

[97] Two brilliant lectures, but otherwise a wasted day. David McKee was in here drivelling again: this time I managed to give him a slight hint of my opinion of him, but he's such a masochist he'd probably welcome it. A poet named Roskolenko to lunch,[78] via Paul Arthur, who didn't realize he was to come too. Another extrovert, a former Trotskyite, now an S.D. [Social Democrat], born in Picton, Ont., lives in New York, has been a good deal in the Orient (his wife is an Irish-Chinese Eurasian; interested in Blake & has read my book); wants a Guggenheim to go back & write poetry about it; is sponsored by Herbert Read, Lewis Mumford & William Carlos Williams but doesn't think he'll get it with Malcolm Cowley on the committee; wants to get a novel published in Canada & was on his way to Collins. Busy little man. Paul Corbett in, in the line of duty. Some aimless buggering around & then I went home, to find Helen's parents & Jean Elder there. Beer completed the knockout. Dad is beginning to talk of leaving, & will probably do so next week. Poor Jean has family trouble a lot worse than we have. I suppose just as the economic dependence of woman on man produces the bulk of female shrewishness & silliness, & of children on parents a great deal of perverse rebelliousness & superfluity of naughtiness, so the dependence, as much emotional as economic, of the old on their children produces a great deal of the egomania of senility. Jean says it hits 104 in Kansas in the summer, re an approaching automobile trip. I said the answer was to stay out of Kansas, but she said her father's brother lives there.

[98] The R.K. lecture, theoretically on Job, was devoted to the proposition that in wisdom, as opposed to knowledge, no questions are ever answered & no problems solved, because religions answer questions only by trying to raise the level of the questioner's mind to the point at which he sees the question as unreal. I cited the trial by ordeal & the Catholic "is this beer-bottle real?" dilemma, to which my answer is that I don't feel any psychological impulsion either to assert or deny its reality. I think I shocked them all right, even if I did have to use a beer bottle to do it. Afterwards Clarence Lemke said: "Did you know that Cathy Nicholls was in your class?" I said: "no; who's Cathy Nicholls?" ["]Evidently she's the rabble-rouser that the current preaching mission has assigned to Victoria women." Jean says she's one of God's Lesbians, who tries to get girls emotionally dependent on her. "You know," said Lemke,

"people get a phrase or two from you and start a big hubbub about it, & when they don't know your whole philosophy it isn't fair." Discipleship embarrasses me, I think on the whole more than it pleases me. I hate dominating.

[99] The Arnold lecture said that the three classes, as classes, were partial & therefore sectarian; as parts of society, they had positive things to contribute. The aristocracy contributes the idea of the Gentle Man; the middle class, the Free Man; the lower class, the Equal Man: Fraternity (initiate brotherhood whose morality is morale), Liberty & Equality respectively. That Arnold regarded the Church as a function of the State; Newman regarded the State as ultimately a function of the Church: that's one of the things the "securus iudicat orbis terrarum" tag means.[79] Newman, like Toynbee, is a historian whose telos is "Christian civilization," & it's the visibility, the social & political importance of the Church of Rome that helped push him into it.

Jan. 19. [Wednesday]

[100] A lot of work on Hart House lately: the Committee met Monday, & today Abba [Aba] Bayefsky reviewed his own show. Talked into [in] a very low voice about the social challenge of painting. Said Europe, which he pronounced as a monosyllable, Yurp, is stuck in the 1910 groove, especially France, that the cartoon is a more highly developed form of pictorial expression today than what is now orthodox painting. I suppose painting, like literature, has a trivial reference: rhetorical to composition & balance, grammatical to narrative values & social comment. I'm just beginning to realize that the point of my statement about prose fiction as grammatically organized means the predominance of narrative, that is, the sequential representation of "life." Its logical or propositional basis I'm not clear on. Comfort congratulated me on my Lawren Harris article but said Harris himself resented the "contemplative yogi" remark about the portraits.[80] Some New Statesman critic once remarked that when a writer reads a review of his own book, he dismisses the praise as mere justice, the least the fool could have said, & pounces on the dispraise as a screaming outrage. Charles [Comfort] of course would never have made a statement like that: I think, though, that he's getting to be recognized as a bit of a smoothie. I wish he'd read, & absorb, Montague's *Hind Let Loose*, the first part of it. Barker Fairley says

he leaves for Columbia next week & that I'm to go ahead on my Colloquium paper.[81] He suggested a Harold King memorial show for Hart
House next term—I was a dithering fool not to have thought of that
myself. One of Bayefsky's pictures had all the pictorial values—color
contrast & harmony, composition & structure—of a Homer Watson.
Curious. Martin Shubik wanted to know about the Forum, so I'm on the
point of having to reap the fruits of my impulsiveness.[82] Ideally, one
should be as ruthless as possible in dealing with a situation like that, but
I can be ruthless only on my own possibly sentimental morality. I mean
by that that I'm going to lie like a son of a bitch in order to spare his
feelings.

[101] University lecturing is not teaching but a form of intellectualized
preaching. You can go into all the world & preach the gospel, but if you
try to teach any more than about twelve disciples you've had it. Teaching
relates two individuals through Socratic love, which has to be homosexual. I can't really teach a woman, because, being a woman, the things
organic to her learning process are female, & shut me out. All I could do
would be to identify myself with her animus, which puts me, as I've
discovered & elsewhere remarked, in a hell of a spot. To teach a boy is to
form his character, which means partly to unite him to the males of the
tribe. It also involves the sort of love which sees with complete clarity what
the boy's character is: you can't, that is, teach a frivolous person in the way
you would teach a preternaturally solemn one. I'm not a teacher according
to this line of thought; and I wonder if it's possible without some physical
interest in men, or sublimation of it. Even Jesus had a beloved disciple, as
Marlowe pointed out.[83] I can trace no such interest in myself.

[102] A long erudite discussion about Federation at tea, led by Sissons
and followed by Surerus & [Joe] Fisher. They're Senate members, of
course, & I didn't really belong. [George Munro] Grant of Queen's had
some critical role to play: I couldn't figure out what. Nelles was old &
timid & Burwash had to carry it through: the Senate opposed it & held it
up for a year, & so did John Sandfield Macdonald, then Premier, who,
though a Catholic, had no use for separate schools.[84] The trouble now is
ground rents which Victoria owes to the University under the Clergy
Reserves agreement, & which might amount to $6000 a year. The ac-
countant feels we ought to pay taxes on a business-value basis. Brown
never cleared the matter up & I have an idea that that was the grave

negotiations that were on foot when he got the stroke. Surerus hinted that a group of businessmen on the Board were trying to take it out of Brown's hands & do some poker-playing. Why did Trinity, who didn't join until 1903, get so much land & the best campus playing field? Why did Brown insist on letting Trinity have the same Senate representation as Victoria (5) when U.C. [University College] has 12? On a proportional basis that's nonsense. And so on: Sissons then went into details of Federation, & he's fine on his regular *laudator temporis acti* line—it's when he moves from 1849 to 1949 that he becomes a bore.

[103] The 2i lecture was on Machiavelli: I'm clarifying my view of a militant organization as pyramidal. In Machiavelli all peacetime activities are geared to a war economy, of course: it's a state militant as the R.C.Ch. is a Church militant. (I suppose that's why, if, say, a daughter of mine turned Catholic, I'd feel more bitter than if she turned anything else: I have to be the enemy of a militant church I'm not in, & it's the only really militant church.) The more militant an organization becomes, the more important a single leader is, & the more everything is subordinated to a shearing dialectic, committing the entire life to one side of a dilemma. Plato's Republic integrates dialectic & the Pope, the philosopher-ruler chosen to rule because he was born golden. I see now a bit more clearly what the shape of the Beulah-consolidation is, but ∧ [Anticlimax] and ʎ [Rencontre] are beginning to stick together in a curious way.

[104] The Arnold lecture dealt with the Hellenic-Hebraic business—regular stuff, but I committed myself at the end to saying it was baloney & next Tuesday I shall have to say why—the Hegelian fallacy of transforming truths into half-truths. I shouldn't make statements like that: they sound adolescent, & I think rather bother the kids. Every once in a while my undifferentiated sensuous feeling quality, the opposite of the intuitive thinking I specialize in, gets loose, & gallops around the room on a hobby-horse squawking & cackling & generally carrying on. I did it at the Van Doren lecture & at the final lecture at the Institute. I must realize that that side of me is not under complete control, & I can't trust it.

Jan. 20. [Thursday]

[105] Lectures 9–1; lunch; student appointment; pageproofing the Forum; purchasing subcommittee at Hart House; dinner down & the Writ-

ers' Group in the evening. The sort of day it's easy to brag about. Actually it's profoundly soothing to be busy all the time: it's like a holiday to have no time to do what you ought to do. Creation without toil, Yeats calls it.[85] The Milton lecture moved another inch on this pyramidal business: I took the cube and pyramid from somewhere in the anti-Episcopal tracts[86] & showed how Satanic organization, springing from an identification of freedom with having nothing over one's head, becomes pyramidal, the structure of the "first prelate angel" reproduced in the R.C.Ch., the episcopal system ("a sawed-off pyramid"), monarchy, & hence the Nimrod & Tower of Babel passage in Book 12. Chapel, where I saw who Cathy Nicholls was, and where Ken [MacLean] told me that Theodore Spencer had died—heart attack, believe it or not. The Blake was a bit easier—Pitt's paper re. 18th c. poetry was not only good but long.[87] It seems like a dull group. He had things to say about Cowper's conception of liberty that made me realize how much I'd neglected him in FS. Then my poor frosh, very sleepy & window-gazing. [Harold] Bennett is now acting president, poor little bugger.

[106] A girl who I think is named Rita Horner came in to ask me about taking an M.A.[88] I've made mistakes with this before, & tried to be a bit more careful. She's low second at best, so no scholarships—just wants to complete a rhythm, & has only wakened up to the possibilities of education. Comes to me because my lectures woke her up. So I warned her carefully that there'd be a big let-down & she'd feel like a ghost, with no organic relationship to the College any more. Also that the graduate school was a professional training centre, & really made no provision for amateurs who just wanted to do some more directed reading. It developed then that she wanted to go to England, & finally it came out that it was time she had a holiday from mamma. I encouraged her to work a year & then go on her own steam—it'll work out, as she's very fond of her family & isn't unhappy—just needs transplanting.

[107] The Forum looks passable: Jack [Garrett], evidently, is leaving in the middle of March, with all his exams unread. If [Arthur] Barker's out too that'll be quite a mess. At Hart House Bloore & Sandy Best & I picked out four Bayefskys to show the Art Committee, to pick I suppose two of. Considering his manifesto about social realism, his stuff is pretty rigidly composed, mannered, & as much stuck in the sort of Derain-Modigliani groove as anything he'd have seen in France—wonder if he knows about

people like Kathe Kollwitz. Came back to the Library to get the Figgis Blake[89] out of the "Treasure Room," but that bitchy dame whose name I don't know said she was late as it was. Then to dinner, with the Fugger Group fuggering about.[90] [Walter T.] Brown went to the hospital today for X-ray treatment.

[108] Even the Writers' Group was dull & stupid—it *must* be the weather. Some good-for-not-much poems & two quite brilliant stories by a lad named Jim Dickinson in second year pass. He says he hasn't written before, but his competence is professional. A long story called *Narcissus* about a schizophrenic: if I'd met it in a good anthology I'd say it was derivative, but only then. Also a fine dry story about a primitive tribe who were nomads on the march for the winter & decided to kill a "fool" who was pottering around with some strangely marked rocks which the "Wise Ones" insisted were the effects of rain & decay. The rock marking his grave was dated 1957. What was good about it was the absence of all nudges in the ribs. He's a very good lad, & will bear watching. I wish to hell I could organize my social life better: such people ought to be picked out & invited up to the house. Isabel [Isobel] Routly Stewart, now a most handsome matron, was there: she claimed the credit for having organized the Writers' Group in 1938 or 9. Her husband Dick is on D.V.A.[91] in the Teachers' College Columbia writing a thesis in psychology of Education on problems of marital adjustment. Clearly he hasn't any of his own. Two children, seven & two: Isabel [Isobel] is up for her mother, who was injured by a car on New Year's. Evidently she did graduate work in Fine Arts & knows Barbara Brieger, with whom she's been attending my R.K. lectures. Said she regretted not doing an M.A. when her husband was at war, but didn't like to beat him in the degree when he was busy defending democracy—interesting point of delicacy. She takes courses in Columbia from Tyndall [Tindall] and Trilling, one in short story writing and one on "Christianity & the Human Tragedy" at Union Seminary which she said was like my R.K. course—I'll bet it isn't.[92] Molly Brown turned in a fair but unfinished sketch. The freshie who sits by herself is Ann Carnwath. Came home to find Helen a bit sulky because I was out so late—Dad decided today, of all days, to make chili con carne, & she had the whole social & conversational burden of the evening. I gather the discussion about religion on the Varsity radio program was the flop young Hornyansky said it would be at lunch yesterday. Helen had the Faculty Women affair, with a cocktail with Vo Love afterward.

Jan. 21. [Friday]

[109] Decided to take the Mt. Pleasant bus to save time getting to the train—a mistake. The usual overheated, stuffy, poorly lighted coach left over from a Harvester's Excursion. There are times when I wonder if the healthy-competition people haven't got something.

[110] It occurs to me that what I did in writing FS was perform the act described in much the same way by Freud & Jung. This is the act of swallowing the father, integrating oneself with the old wise man. Presumably I shall never find another father, not even in Shakespeare, & should realize that I am essentially *on my own*. I've really reached an individuated stage of thinking, if not of personal life. There's more to it than that—Blake is right in a way no one else is—but that's the psychological aspect of the book. What I should do now, or one of the things I should do now, is explore mandalas. This is linked with the ideas I've had about the geometry of thinking—I could, perhaps, work them out from the 19th c. people. Perhaps, too, if every poem is necessarily a perfect unity, every thinker is necessarily perfectly right. That is doubtless just another way of saying that one seeks understanding rather than a judgment of value. Yes, it was certainly a father-swallowing—look at the people I sent my free copies to—Dad, Pelham [Edgar], the dedicatee, [Herbert J.] Davis, Keynes, [Wilmot B.] Lane, Currelly: every one a father-figure, with the possible exception of Keynes. That may have been partly the reason it was so personal a book.

[111] Norma Arnett came up to me last night & wanted to know why a poem she (and I to some extent) thought was good had not been considered even for honourable mention in the Varsity contest—such neglect of response to her talents "drove her more into herself"—a child's threat, of course, but I knew what she was going through. I said the judge was just plain wrong (I think it was McLuhan, so it's a reasonable enough assumption). I said I used to feel that perfect clarity of expression would automatically produce an adequate response from intelligent & cultivated people, but that after reading the reviews of FS I had realized that people were just stupid. Apart from the fact that hardly any of them knew Blake from buggery. I didn't make this last remark to Norma.[93]

[112] The trip to Peterborough was damn dull, & I regretted it. Mrs.

Seaton, my hostess, didn't ask me to lunch, so I went to a hotel & tried to eat up something like the value of the dollar & a half they charged, naturally without success. The women I talked to were on a pretty primitive level, but there was a certain pallid interest in trying to get their range. I'm still, of course, intensely introverted, but in some ways my dramatic imagination is consolidating. It's curious how introverted I am at my age. Solitude is still a delicious luxury to me, especially solitude in a crowd, drifting around cities. In such a case I prefer tried & worn paths: I dislike exploring & using any effort meeting new situations. Naturally I don't want to talk to people (at least people with nothing in common with me, such as one would meet) & in that state regard all official surliness, like the librarian yesterday, as a kind of violation. Like my father, I'm gregarious enough: it's quite possible to be a social introvert.

Jan. 22. [Saturday]

[113] Decided to stay home this morning, with the usual result of having to go shopping & lug home great piles of food. In the afternoon I went down to the office, where of course nothing was doing. I finally blasted out of Dad the information that he was leaving a week from Monday. I had more or less figured that out anyway: he wants to change his rooming house to that of a woman who returns to Moncton the beginning of February. His curious, childish unwillingness to tell anyone what his plans are is part of an intense introversion: he's not so much selfish as egocentric, not inconsiderate so much as unwilling to admit the reality of other people's existence. This habit of his was mainly what drove Mother into turning her dominating aggressiveness into a squalid & miserable shrewishness. Yet it had no effect whatever on him, as her shrewishness was external & therefore unreal, whereas his introversion was the circumference of reality. A curious paradox: his sweetness of disposition was the product of an invulnerable & inviolate childishness; the bitterness of hers the product of an affronted & neglected maturity.

[114] Went to Morley Callaghan's play, "To Tell the Truth," a Saroyanesque fantasy with one scene, a brewery counter, & all sorts of people wandering into it to demonstrate that life can be beautiful. It was fortunate that Morley asked me how I liked it in the intermission, when it was still only placidly bad; it was only in the last two acts that

its badness became acutely embarrassing. A most inept & fatuous play, but maybe he can sell it to the movies. Its central doctrine, that if you dream of something beautiful that dream really is you, would be very grateful to the movies. I don't know quite what to say to Don Harron, except that he struggled valiantly with a role that was half male ingénue (or is it ingénus?) & half leprechaun. The audience was mainly sisters & cousins & aunts.[94]

[115] The Ariosto & Tasso arrived today from Italy. The Tasso seems all right, but the Ariosto has been gutted all to hell by some slobbering fool who cuts out even half-lines. His introduction is full of exclamation points: he seems to like cuddling the poet's testicles while he cuts them off. On Milton's principles, expurgating a book is the same as castrating a man,[95] and those who enjoy doing the former are only sublimating their desire to do the latter. It's a moral principle with me not to keep an expurgated book on my shelves, & I shall have to ask Goggio to recommend a better one.

Jan. 23. [Sunday]

[116] Overtired after a strenuous week: will I *never* learn not to accept invitations outside Toronto? A very dull day: out to hear Sclater at Old St. Andrews talk about the gap (curtain he called it) between youth & age. He's a frivolous person & seemed to assume that after 1913 the world lost a point of stability it had up to that time. Life goes in a parabola, thus: $_1\cap_{70}^{35}$, & on the descending curve you're apt to be fascinated by the point opposite you on the up curve. I think there may be even a physiological basis to this, indicated by the way young childhood crowds into the minds of the very aged. I didn't actually hear much of the sermon. The Wilsons came in for supper & Margaret [Newton] returned from Washington. Says the Truman inaugural wasn't, like most American parades, exuberant & good-humored, but a grim military march-past for the benefit of the Soviet Ambassador. If I were a leading Russian Communist I'd say: we now have Russia, one-sixth of the world. We have East Europe & the West is in our pocket—we could occupy it in two weeks anyway. The revolt of Asia is the great political fact in the contemporary world, & we're in a position to exploit that: the Americans can only prop up beaten & discredited governments. The revolt of Africa hasn't yet come, but is certainly coming. The only power able to oppose

our conquest of the world is the U.S.A. There's no use fighting her: she's too strong: she has the atom bomb & an economic system that works best under wartime conditions. With the three continents in our grip, we can sit tight & let her blow up & burst with her economy which demands continuous centrifugal expansion & which we are continuously curtailing. That's what it looks like from where they sit, I think. Why should they start a war? Margaret's on the Reserve Army list & has been told to report to H.Q. It doesn't look like war yet, to me, but that may be just a "wistful vista."[96] The Americans could start a war to forestall their blowup; but the Russians could start one too to forestall the blowing up of the contradictions in the argument I've just outlined.

Jan. 24. [Monday]

[117] An almost deliberately wasted day: my gut seems to prefer the evening to the morning now, & the changeover bothers me. [Peter] Fisher came in & I filled up on too much beer: I don't know why, except a certain urge to write the day off & wait for another one that I occasionally get. I staggered home & was dopey the rest of the day, trying to read Johnson's England[97] for my Museum lecture. I suppose heaven could be defined as the gaining of the ability to explore the underground caverns of time at will. I wish H.G. Wells' Time Machine had been turned toward the past, & made a radio set capable of picking up the impressions made on whatever it is—the theosophists call it Akasa—by actual events. The future is potential only, & is actualized only in experience. The past is actualized in memory, & I suppose such memory (dependent on the sense experience of books) could be transformed into vision, as it was for a moment by those two women in Versailles.[98] The vast organization of memory known as scholarship seems to me to be what the dreams we can remember are: wandering in the limbo of the past, just outside that gate we have as yet no golden bough to enter. I have already referred to Blavatsky's remark that if you could remember your deep dreams you could remember your past incarnations [par. 77]. I don't think one needs to concede the question begged here, though it does come into James' Sense of the Past: I mean the question of participating in rebirth. But the something new that came into the world with the Industrial Revolution was partly an intensification of memory, the apocalyptic sense of the deliverance from an accomplished time.

[118] The Castiglione lecture said very little except to point out the Prince-Courtier link, & link Machiavelli's doctrine that appearance (e.g. of virtue) is essential in government with Castiglione's similar doctrine of the continuous epiphany of culture. Fisher pointed out how military a commander Moses was, constantly in conference with an invisible High Command, constantly issuing communiques & orders designed to minimize idleness & boredom, concerned for the welfare & morale of his men yet a ferocious punisher of rebellion—and all the time he's lost his way & has no idea where the hell he is. To look at a map of the wanderings of the children of Israel through a territory that any dimwit could have got through in a month is to get some idea of the sardonic quality of the Hebrew imagination. He also said he didn't trust the people who went through intense emotional, almost visionary, experiences on the battlefront & then when they returned denied the normality of those experiences, & insisted that only safety & security provide a normality you can trust. He also spoke of a yoga called Agni-yoga. Just as a fish lives in water, so man lives in air, & shows his embryonic state by doing so. Just as Christ's disciples were fishermen, so we have to escape from the Leviathan who is, not for us a sea-monster, but the prince of the power of the air. Fire is the apocalyptic or vortical element, for it destroys the others. From there we went on to Plato's pyramid which is the element & seed of fire (πυρ), the "pyre" on which the burning hero becomes a god, the burnt-offering the food of the gods—this clears up a point I've been worried about in relation to the symbolism of sacrifice—I could understand the communion but not the holocaust. The pyramid is of course the Tower of Babel, the essential militant form, & the number of Plato's state is probably pyramidal. The man on the top of the pyramid, Ikhnaton or Julian, is necessarily the son of the sun. If I can work out the Orc-Urizen element in this I'll have something.

[119] The Seven Books are mine: they are a creative effort built up from a series of critical studies, & by no means identical with them. The first of these are, respectively, L [Liberal], a grammar of verbal structures or narratives giving the linear sense of all forms of verbal expression; ר [[Tragicomedy], a rhetorical encyclopedia or ordered presentation of the definitive myth; and ∧ [Anticlimax], a logic identifying the logical & verbal universes. A music follows ∧ [Rencontre], music being the transition to the quadrivium, & the book a primary anagogy. The next three

are, V [Mirage], a quadrivial logic or geometry, concerned more deeply with the diagrammatic basis of thinking, ⊢ [Paradox], a quadrivial rhetoric or astronomy doing a real "comparative religion" job & ⊥ [Ignoramus], a quadrivial grammar or arithmetic doing the linear progression idea on a deeper level. Then, perhaps, ⱨ [Twilight], a quadrivial music or secondary anagogy, a second coming or return to the source.[99] But my studies of the Bible, Dante, Shakespeare, Spenser, Milton, Blake, the romantics & the Victorians are something else, the material from which the seven are drawn. I suppose I should attempt none of these books for about fifteen years, while I practice my six languages & collect ideas through my studies, & then write out the first three very quickly. I suppose there's no real reason why I shouldn't start the drama book right away, except for prior projects.

[120] I think there is a real meaning in the conception of a "capital" city, not in the technical sense (i.e. New York is the real capital of the U.S.A., of North America, perhaps of the world). The city is the community become conscious: it is to the country what man is to animals. Animals live; man knows that he lives; people live in the country & often live very well, but in the city some additional consciousness comes to life. I've said before that only the bourgeois is creative man: in some respects I think culture is impossible except in a capital city. There are more people in Cincinnati than in Shakespeare's London; but Cincinnati *cannot* produce genius. It isn't the capital of anything: no organization of state or nation or anything else with a body comes to a head in it. The only exception to the monopoly of cities in culture is the medieval church & monastery, & those were linked by iron bonds to the invisible empire of Rome. For culture there must be something centripetal: the Holy Roman Empire & Church were the old Empire turned inside out, focussed on Rome instead of spreading out from it. The empire is centrifugal, & weakens culture. New York, however fascinating, is not producing the culture it should partly because the social unit of which it is the capital is ill-defined, as we are moving from nations to world-empires. Here's a difficulty when I come to Morris & the Shelley theory of decentralization: small towns don't work unless they're the heads of social organisms, and there's no known way of breaking up, say, England, into such organisms. I don't know why an organism can be as small as Attica at one time and as big as half the world at another.

Jan. 25. [Tuesday]

[121] The Tuesday lectures are generally good, but I still feel tired & nervous, & I'm still struggling with my gut. A lot of the deficiencies in my schedule are deliberate sins of omission & commission: I stupefy myself with beer, for instance, & allow an overmastering inertia to dominate me most of the day, but apart from all that I really am conscious of a continuous, pervasive fatigue. Part of it is simply lack of exercise: I should make a point of walking to the College at least twice a week, & oftener when possible. Possibly I eat too much for lunch, but I don't know. Even if these were all cleared up, though, two points remain about sleeping. One is, that I apparently (it may be only a bad habit) need eight hours' sleep, & if I go out in the evening I don't get it. The other is, that my deteriorated septum prevents me from sleeping well, & after Helen has had her operation I'm going to plan to have mine as soon as I can. I can never get used to sleeping on my back. Without complete relaxation in sleep, I'm under a nervous strain that works itself out in attacks of constipation & the like. It's a shame to bugger up a constitution so well adapted to scholarship, though, & one thing I *must* do is run away from hay fever this summer.

[122] There isn't much to say about either lecture: the Arnold said that anarchy is a competitive scramble of sects, schools & writers: culture is a normal standard possessing spiritual authority which it is advantageous to have embodied in temporal establishments: an established church, an established educational system, an academy of letters. Ties together a certain amount of Arnold. The R.K. lecture finished Job, & dealt with the Leviathan symbol. Neither up to my top mark. Came home early & buggered around.

Jan. 26. [Wednesday]

[123] Lectures routine: one on Ascham which said what there is to say about Ascham, & another Arnold one: I thought I had a point but it got away from me, & must stop talking about Arnold. Discussion with Joe [Fisher] & Charlie [Leslie] about students: Joe said they weren't intellectually curious, & wanted the problems of the universe handed them all wrapped up. I said students of today were existentialists, knowing that

the "ideas are weapons" catchword of our day was bullshit, & trying to find centrality in the balance of living: they weren't cynical or argumentative or even depressed, but just resigned to a mad world. Joe said they responded to mysticism: I said that was partly because of the practical element in mysticism, & its technique of attaching & detaching oneself simultaneously to & from life. Barker Fairley's lecture was a brilliant job trying, to put it unsympathetically, to show that Goethe's influence & power is radical & progressive even if he wasn't. His interest in science & his refusal to attach mystical priorities to poetry links [link] him in modern thought most closely with the Marxists, who unite art & science on a basis of philosophy. During it I consolidated a little my conception of art as explorable on two levels, the deeper or quadrivial level being the one that includes science, the astronomy of Dante, the biology ("arithmetic") of Goethe, the geometry of Plato.

[124] I came across a passage in *Culture & Anarchy* today which said that the presentation of the perfect man is the theme of poetry[100]—an interesting link between Arnold & Renaissance criticism I could well follow up. I tried today to link him with the Cambridge Platonists, not very successfully.

Jan. 27. [Thursday]

[125] The usual grim morning: Nancy Rowland read the Blake paper: it's amazing how commonplace her mind really is. Some buggering around in the afternoon: I tried to get to Blanshard's lecture, but what with Rosemarie handing me a Wordsworth bibliography[101] sent her once by Abbie Potts of Rockford College, Rockford, Ill, I didn't get started until five, & by then the crowd outside the door was so big I just came home. Amazing how they swarm to lectures around here. Then dinner with the great man [Brand Blanshard], me sitting beside [Derwyn] Owen & Savan. I spotted Owen as another [George] Edison, a bright & agreeable young man on the make, & talked mainly to Savan, about the superiority of Canadian radio drama. (The bad writing is due to a curious nervous twitch in my arm.) Discussion afterwards dullish—he's a simple-minded old bugger, & claims to be the only surviving practising "rationalist." Irving brought up the question of seven professors dismissed for Communism from Washington & others who had to sign

statements that they wouldn't engage in Communist activities & "believed the doctrines of Marx to be erroneous," the president saying that no Marxist could teach "the Truth." I said, perhaps a trifle too loudly, that one should distinguish Communist activity, which, or the control over which, was a matter of policy, from the theoretical statements, which were the silliest kind of hysterical witch-baiting. The others fuffled & foofled around the question, including Blanshard. He was at Merton when Eliot was, & was impressed by Eliot's technical attainments in philosophy. Said he was a cold fish who didn't know or want to know anyone, read the Principia Mathematica, said he'd read all Plato in Greek, studied with Joachim, & said, aged 24, of Emerson: "What a lazy fellow he was!" He didn't know Eliot was at Merton to find Bradley until I told him; said Bradley lunched off two duck's eggs & something else I forget—goat's milk, probably. Said the English had more tolerance for colorful personalities in universities—some sighing generally over the great days of eccentrics & how dull everyone is now. I found this insincere: I think we regard the old eccentrics with affection because they're gone, & don't really want them back. He's full of lecturer's jokes, like: "Bishop Manning was a point with position & no magnitude." "You can lead a girl to Vassar but you can't make her think." One eccentric had trouble with his eyes, was told by his doctor not to look into a bright light, found his classroom had a window at the opposite end, so announced that in future he would lecture with his back to the class, which he did. Another, with a powerful visual memory, used to keep drawing diagrams in the air, & at the end of the lecture was practically crawling under the table so the students could "see" the imaginary blackboard . . . Modern philosophy seems to me to be a lot of highly rarefied gossip, a discussion of what professor is defending what position in which university. I suppose it always was.

[126] Don Harron, poor lad, was trying to get some suggestions out of me about what Morley [Callaghan] was getting at in the part of George. Whatever it was is not clear to Morley, as he keeps changing his lines on him. I said the idea Morley had was the magnetic power of innocence, which, like chastity in Comus, is something that baffles, fascinates & in a measure exasperates other people, & that in the play it was a fixed point, acting as a magnet & a redeeming force on the heroine. That was the best I could do.

Jan. 28. [Friday]

[127] Irving gets over-enthusiastic at times—I had to go over to sit through two hours of an alleged "seminar" by this Blanshard person, who *is* so amiable & charming, & has *so* much wit & eloquence, & yet just doesn't interest me—he lacks the power of flight. He kicked around Herbert Spencer a bit: Spencer, starting from a Leibnitzian problem of finding among many possible universes the real one, brought in evolution to show that we call the universe "actual" that we are united with by our bodily contract. He messed up the argument in his desire to prove an anti-empirical position on logical necessity, which he based on the Meno slave-boy episode. I couldn't always follow him—he seemed to be saying that such a proposition as "all crows are black" had something to do with logical necessity. Little June Clark tackled him from an existentialist Heidegger approach, which he seemed to think was a kind of half-assed romantic Kantianism. He said—he's a fairly consistent rationalist—that there were no particulars, picked up an ash-tray and said there was nothing there but a set of duplicatable accidents & relations. I said to June afterwards: "He made that ash-tray disappear very neatly, didn't he?" & she said "Yeah, but I can always get it back whenever I like." I like June.[102]

[128] Lunch with Earle Sanborn & wife—he told me about Woodhouse & Alexander of Queen's at the M.L.A. running into a bumptious & impudent elevator boy who spotted Alexander as a professor of English & insisted that Woodhouse was a professor of Geography—Woodhouse wasn't amused. This led to talk about progressive education—Mustard went down on the Athenia.[103] I said "How did he sink?", a brutal remark in that context, but one I may be able to use in another.

[129] Committee meeting for the essay contest—I'm still Chairman, but Joe [Fisher] has taken it over. He wanted one on the teen-age hoodlum gang—said the students would be able to tell him something about that because they were all existentialists. He may or may not have forgotten where he got the idea. There's been a lot of sombre brooding about the hoodlum problem lately. I think myself that an angry & aroused public opinion demanding punishment would be the healthiest reaction—developing recreational facilities as a long-term project is all right, but

shouldn't be offered as blackmail. A remark of McAree's about the hoodlum gangs of his day struck me forcibly: he said there were lots of places for them to play, but that they were too lazy to play as well as too lazy to work. Many well-meaning and gentle people suffer from a vicious streak of masochism—they feel helpless in the midst of a brutal society, & in some warped way they want to feel so: they like saying they can't do anything about, say, the American hold on Canada, or say it with a significant grin. In the last decade they helped the rise of fascism, & now they show a sneaking fondness for communism because of the nihilistic element in it. I suppose guilt feelings are involved, but another thing is the cult of individual detachment, the desire to become a disembodied watcher, which acts as a powerful imaginative narcotic. Incidentally, the young hoodlum who is admired because he does nothing & is supported by the women in his gang is a curious confirmation of the soundness of Veblen's theory of the leisure class.[104]

[130] It occurs to me that the difference between being selfish & being egocentric is that the selfish person is aware of his ego; he's aggressive & defiant about it, & feels the need of protecting it. The egocentric person is like the child who refers to himself in the third person; he's a kind of parody of a mystic, & feels toward other people a kind of perverted love: they are his creatures, things he has allowed to find their shadowy being in his dream. He appears selfish only when disturbed, when some incongruity between dream & reality forces its way in. But conscious selfishness is an imaginative advance. This links up with what I was saying about the Herbert Spencer argument. We could have created any kind of world, but actually did create this one.

[131] At three a second-year child came in for help with an essay on the 17th century—she was trying to find the Biblical source for the Leveller doctrine, & had been consulting a concordance to find out where it said in the Bible that all men were created free & equal. Then, she said, she'd "even asked her minister"—Philip Ross of Eaton Memorial—but all he said was "Go see Professor Frye."

[132] In the evening we went over to see Marjorie [King]. Tony is admirable—very adolescent & a bit bumptious, but extremely good-humored & shows signs of a developing wit. Second form high, & shows strong university tendencies. It's wonderful that he's such a decent kid, as poor

Marjorie is certainly having a thin time of it. Her sister has gone back to Chicago, & the sort of exhilaration which catastrophe always seems to bring has all ebbed away. Great bags under her eyes, & she was going to work this morning but was overcome by sleep & slept till two.

Jan. 29. [Saturday]

[133] Ran into Norman Langford this morning. It's awkward asking him about his family: what you have to say is, "What news of Grace & Felicity?" He's quit the Wesley Buildings & wants to get into the American Presbyterian Church. Says he's given the United Church up: it doesn't stand for anything but a principle of union, & has no evangelical cutting edge—this last phrase was mine. Personally, I rather like the United Church because it contains a sort of church-destroying principle within itself, having already destroyed three. I'd be sorry to see him go, & I find the restlessness of a nomadic civilization contagious, even though I don't share it. Ran into Murdo Mackinnon too—nothing particular—he had laryngitis. Margaret Avison, or rather that vicious thing in her, saw that her poem wasn't in the current Forum & demanded it back. However, I've worried enough about her. Norman said the U.S.A. was affecting him like a line of Vaughan's about a happy land not far away "couldst thou but get thither."[105] I said it reminded me of another one: "How brave a prospect is a bright backside!" I told him he should muscle Lloyd Douglas out of the Jesus-book business & live on his royalties.[106] If he's too intellectual for that, there's still a hell of a big demand for nearer-my-God-to-thee books of the what-can-a-man-believe variety. There's a lot of dough in religion, & if you didn't have any religion you could get the dough.

[134] Preface to a book on *The Faerie Queene*: "The aims of this book are simple & strictly limited. There are several excellent studies of Spenser on the market, and this book makes no attempt to rival or supplement any of them. There are many scholarly studies of the background, tradition & origin of *The Faerie Queene*, and this book adds nothing that is new in the way of research. What seems to me to be missing from Spenserian criticism is a commentary on *The Faerie Queene*, not a running commentary elucidating the obscurities,[107] but an organized commentary articulating the complete argument of the poem. That is what this book attempts to supply.["][108]

[135] "The fact that so obvious a requirement has not yet been met indicates a considerable barrier between Spenser's conception of poetry and ours. The introduction, comprising the first two chapters, tries to remove this barrier, or at least make a breach in it, by explaining the theory of continuous allegory which underlies *The Faerie Queene* in modern terminology.["]

[136] "I have not made any judgement of value on either the poem or the poet. My reason for this is that contemporary criticism is not highly enough organized to know what the factors of value in critical judgement are. It is hoped that this study (like its predecessor) will call attention to one of the most greatly neglected of such factors: the quality of a poet's thinking as demonstrated by the integrity of his argument."

[137] In the evening we made another journey into the hinterland—the Cumberlands in Mimico, & returned again at two in the morning. I don't know how people with small children manage. The Hallmans, Muriel Code & people called the Summers—he a B.C. man now with National Carbon.[109] Muriel is now a teacher in Mimico, living with her family & coining money, beautifully dressed, & a most typical teacher, except that she's an unusually awe-inspiring one. Her brother married Wyn Horwood, and so is Howe Martyn's brother-in-law—Howe has moved to England to take a top job with Lever.[110] Jack [Cumberland] turned on an endless Paganini concerto. Few forms of art seem to me quite such aimless doodling as the cadenza of a violin concerto. Gene Hallman says the weather business is in a silly mess—the older men who had learned the art of forecasting are pushed aside to make room for over-qualified university graduates who are sitting around waiting for meteorology to complicate itself to the point at which their training might be useful. Present forecasters are pretty bad. Muriel is going to Sweden this summer. It's curious that while you hear little of Swedish literature, music or painting, you hear a great deal about its furniture, glass, interior decorating, apartment & housing schemes & handcrafts—it's a sort of William Morris heaven. This may have something to do with the fact that it's the most socially stable country in the world. I must remember this when I get to Morris & his moral distrust of the great arts. The turning point between fine & useful arts is architecture, which is fine when conspicuous (cathedral & castle) & useful when essentially a matter of housing. It occurred to me too, in discussing swing music, that the restlessness of a

nomadic civilization I referred to above [par. 133] is mirrored in its art: its music is designed to set your feet moving, & the movies (significant name) to lead you toward a mirage-world in the distance.

Jan. 30. [Sunday]

[138] Quiet Sunday unspoiled by Church, though in the afternoon I took Helen to the hospital for some minor repair job in the uterus. As they gave her a private ward & the Blue Cross calls for a semi-private, it looks as though I'll be stuck for some storage charges. Went down to see her in the evening: she was still a bit inclined to worry herself over trifles, largely out of nervousness. It's vividness of imagination that produces cowardice—not imagination in Blake's sense, but in the Renaissance sense. The operation is pure routine, the merest trifle, yet a little imp inside one keeps nagging constantly "yes, but just supposing." Such cowardice is a perversion of imagination, from its true function of establishing patterns of possibilities into a false one of probabilities or future developments. The realm of eternal possibility belongs to art; the realm of future probability to science. One of the major functions of science is prophetic, predicting the future. Science & therefore future probability are in this case on the side of the doctor.

[139] Montaigne says that one should not love a wife too much, for that is attachment: she might die and then where would you be? The doctrine of non-attachment is mine; the application is not: I feel that in such a passage as that wisdom has outfoxed itself. One should withdraw attachment from possessions & machines, but you remain attached to your right arm, & life without it is a mutilated life. With wives as with arms, one is attached, & simply has to take the chance. The metaphor of "one flesh" is not an idle one.

[140] I wonder about extra-sensory perception of books—I don't mean simply the capacity of people hag-ridden by erotic fantasies to open any book at whatever erotic passage it contains. I have had some experiences of having the books I wanted fall out of the shelves at the time I wanted them. Four years ago I bought, on a pure impulse, a Viking Library collection of novels of the supernatural.[111] I regretted the impulse instantly, kicked myself for wasting the money, &, trying to salvage the purchase, dawdled through de la Mare's *Return* & Machen's *Terror*, also

an opening story by Mrs. Oliphant which actually gave me a calendar idea, though it was more an instance of an idea than the idea itself. Yesterday, for no reason at all, I suddenly pull the book out of the shelves & read Nathan's *Portrait of Jennie*, which I'd completely ignored before, & it turns out to be an anima story that may be an opening lead into my romance study.[112]

Jan. 31. [Monday]

[141] Dad left today—his presence has been a constraint on both of us, but I certainly can't blame any of my failures of the month on him, except perhaps the music, & that one is more or less chronically bitched anyway. Now that I'm ready to take some musical advantage of his absence, the damper falls off the soprano E, just as in my violin-playing in childhood the E string was always breaking—we used gut. I went to see Helen in the evening,[113] who slept the whole time, and ended a month very badly indeed by forgetting a Hart House engagement. I hate doing that. I consoled myself by drinking beer with Margaret [Newton] till midnight.

[142] Discussing with [Peter] Fisher today the relation of bard to chief, of prophet to king. It's a very pervasive distinction. In medieval culture there's the theory that the Pope informs the Emperor. Dante holds the political aspect of this view: there should, in the first place, *be* an Emperor, and the Pope is his spiritual preceptor. The evils of Europe spring from an autonomous or temporal Pope & a weak or non-existent Emperor. In Dante the historical apocalypse is the released energy of man, the returning Emperor. In the Renaissance the relation becomes that of courtier & prince, the courtier who acquires all culture to put it at the service of the Prince, the prince who is the principle of autonomous action—well, not autonomous altogether, because he is informed by the courtier principle. In Chinese culture the relation of adviser to Emperor is one of the chief preoccupations of both Taoism & Confucianism. In Hebrew culture the relation of prophet to king, of Isaiah to Ahaz & Nathan to the real David, is historical & actual; the poet-king David & the wisdom-king Solomon are dreams. Saul is the prototype of the king who assumes prophecy, the manic will-to-power conqueror whose instincts are a parody of inspiration; who is enthusiastic but not informed. Hitler is a very Saul-like figure. The relation, I said, works only in a

Prospero-Ferdinand form, when the informer is Jung's old wise man or second (& therefore never the first) father & the actor a youthful Eros whose education has been an act of Socratic love. I said the only such relationship that seemed to fit the typical form was that of Aristotle to Alexander. Note that the adviser, whether Merlin or Prospero, has a faint magician touch about him. Fisher referred to the "who shall revenge oneself on the witness?"[114] question of Nietzsche's ugliest man, who requires, not pity, but shame from Zarathustra. The reference is to the Promethean horror of being watched, a point I forgot to make in my Job lectures.

[143] Margaret [Newton] was concerned largely with the psychosomatic woes of her Hillmer friends, and with the sort of intense personality study she does—she really has love in her, & I respect her a great deal, apart from being very fond of her—I don't respect all the people I'm fond of. All day a feeling of irritation with Margaret Avison for demanding that poem back has been nagging me. I knew that she would if I didn't print it at once, & I was damned if I would—why should I coddle her? I don't mind getting kicked in the face if there's any point to it, but I feel she's not serious about her poetry—she's just diddling with it, & using it for some form of personal satisfaction that has nothing to do with poetry. I hope I don't have to quarrel with her.

[144] Fisher says the Brockville camp used to sing:

> Oh, I don't want to go & be a soldier
> I don't want to have my ballocks shot away,
> I just want to stay in dear old Brockville
> And fart & fuck my life away.

[145] I asked Fisher why Don Quixote stood alone: why there was only one great army satire when there were so many church ones. He didn't really know, but mentioned the tie-up of officers (retired) of the major-colonel-brigadier sort of rank with mysticism.

Feb. 1. [Tuesday]

[146] I start the month with something gained: a clear sense that the Seven Books are to be built up from my critical studies, including the

Blake, as the Bible was from Hebrew literature. Thus they are to be autonomous syntheses, not hiding behind anyone's skirts. That's why the Blake is not one of them, & I feel relieved at having identified it as the swallowing of the father. It doesn't matter how many, if any, critical studies accompany them. If I realize this I should be less afraid of using Blake.

[147] The 4k lecture started Ruskin: I spoke of the work of art as timeless & in time, & of historical criticism as a branch of history treating works of art as historical allegories. Of the parabolas of classical & romantic philosophies of history, & of the way that Spenglerian conception of cultural age solved the problem of the so-called "decadence" of Western culture from the Middle Ages. Of the universal rationalization of history to make the preceding age, the age of the father, an aberration from the great tradition (the second father or old wise man) which is now being carried on by the new people. Thus music does fine as far as Mozart, is just awful until modern times, & starts again with Debussy. How this affects Ruskin's championing of Turner & his denigration of the rococo & baroque. The R.K. lecture was on the Leviathan symbol & how he's the inside as well as the outside, human nature & nature, & about the separating of human nature from humanity, illustrated in the complete isolation of Christ in the Passion. I said there was no soul, only a spiritual body.

[148] Young Sawyer came in to instruct me about Charles Williams. Like me he has difficulty, though an Anglican, in following the Anglican line of mediation between Protestant & Catholic dialectic. Evidently Williams is keen on the transcending of dialectic, which means I should try to get interested in him, though the powerful Anglo-Catholic smell of his books is a bit repulsive. I said the one form or mandala is not seen but swallowed, hence there's no final beatific vision. He said that Williams suggests that Luther, Calvin & Loyola were each *right*, not only that they made sense, but that they each responded to a spirit that bloweth as it listeth. He said on that basis you have to say Buddhism was right too: I said Williams would have to say, as a Christian, that the spirit that bloweth is the third person of a Trinity of which the second person is Christ. I find Sawyer extremely likeable. He suggested we toss for the check, & lost—or won—anyway he paid.

[149] At lunch today they were discussing *The Naked and the Dead*[115] & the effort to impart realism in dialogue. Joe [Fisher] said that dialogue was not so immediate a matter as the conventions of the novel made it. He cited the case of an army cook who had just got everything unpacked in new quarters & a fire lit when the order came to pack up & move. He stood stunned & motionless for a few seconds, then suddenly leaped & grabbed a large pile of soup plates & flung them in the air & watched them fall & shatter on the floor. Then he jumped on them. "And then," said Joe, "he spoke."

[150] Reading Williams on Arthurian romance—he seems to be trying to cultivate the literary thrills in diabolism in his novels & plays.[116] Diabolism seems to me to combine all the disadvantages of superstition with none of the advantages of religion.

Feb. 2. [Wednesday]

[151] Shuttling day—breakfast for Margaret [Newton], lecture, bank, lecture, Hart House for lunch, chairing Sidney Key's talk, over to the hospital, back home in a taxi with Helen, down to the College to hear Ken's [Ken MacLean's] lecture,[117] back home for supper & out to Evelyn Macdonald's [McDonald's] for an A.T.E. [Association of Teachers of English] executive meeting.[118] I embarrassed Key slightly by saying: "If a painter calls his painting 'Composition' we know where we are, but if he calls it 'struggle between good & evil' or 'pertaining to a Fool's Paradise' (the name of two pictures in the undergraduate show he was reviewing) is the title part of the picture or the painter's way of telling us to go to hell?" I had to answer the question myself, & in the course of doing so distinguished a tradition of fantasy from surrealism, primitivism & abstraction.

[152] Ken's lecture I thought was beautiful, a very sensitive & subtle piece of writing that I'm going to try to get him to print.[119] A flank attack on Locke, most unexpected, & yet completely inevitable once done. He used this American dodge of rhetoric, looking at the quality of imagery to show how it conditioned his ideas. It was full of haunting phrases like "Locke makes us aware of the image-population of the mind," and "Locke loved white things," followed by a long list & a link with the

tabula rasa. Sat beside Ned [Pratt], who was still crowing over his New-foundland reception[120]—ate & drank so much he couldn't do it any more, but said he'd go back to die there, as he couldn't think of a better end than their homicidal hospitality. Dale, when he head this story, said it was a remark to link with "Die of a rose in aromatic pain."[121] Hilliard [Trethewey] drove me home with Irving in the car & we were discussing [Fulton] Anderson. I said the strain of living up to his persona must be terrific; a fool would think it was something you could take off & put on at any time, but Andy knew it had to be on for good, & if you woke him up at two in the morning there he'd be with the mask still on. Irving thought that was pretty funny—I'm not so sure.

[153] The meeting at Evelyn Macdonald's [McDonald's] was mainly about a publicity campaign to get well-to-do people to issue statements saying English is a good thing. I said that was fine, & a publicity cam-paign to get ourselves right in there with Vocational Guidance was fine too, as English can't blast money out of the Department for anything & V.G. & other things that are fashionable can. But, suppose I were Goldring & English people came to me with all these statements: what's to stop me from saying: O.K., English is important. So we'll take all this goddam shit we're under political pressure to teach, like character building & personality development & religion & God knows what else, & put it into one course & *call it English*?[122] The question was not too well re-ceived, as, though I modified my language, I did talk about political pressure & the teaching of religion, & the Macdonald bag anyway, & Diltz & Woodhouse to a lesser extent, only criticize the nonsense that the P.C. [Progressive Conservative] government doesn't endorse. The one man there, apart from Milne, who seemed to be in His Majesty's loyal opposition, was a man from Northern named, confusingly, Macdonald.[123] I mean North Toronto. He called me Norrie, but I'm not clear where I met him. He said that what I had described had already taken place, because of the ignorance of "English" "teachers." Of 300–odd people in O.C.E., 280 take English from Diltz, & of those 16, from four universities, are Honour English specialists. Add to that 280 P.H.E. [Physical and Health Education] people & others whose certificates are marked "French, Mathematics, Natural History" who are nevertheless assigned to Eng-lish, & you've got quite an association of English teachers. We never think of our Pass Course as the main source of High School teachers of English, but it is. The first time I opened my mouth in that organization I said I hoped it would be professional rather than cultural, as such things

can turn into Boy-Scout do-gooder efforts to improve the mind very quickly. Woodhouse sat all over me by talking about "the best subject-matter in the world," so they organized groups—complete evenings donated by professors. The only group was about fifteen people who thought it would be just lovely to have Norrie Frye talk to them about Blake. Four evenings, to be exact. After I've done it, I'm going to insist that any other professor who does it should collect the Extension fee for doing it. Otherwise, here we are on the same damned old merry-go-round, trying to save ourselves by good works, & forgetting the fact that we formed the organization to raise a professional morale which is low because we do so much for nothing, not out of charity like the doctors, but through the infection of a public impression that that's what our work's worth.

Feb. 3. [Thursday]

[154] Tired & nervous for some reason—apparently I *must* have eight hours' sleep. I came home to find Helen's father, & later her mother, whose birthday it was, along with Aunt Lily's [Lilly Maidment's].[124] I drank nearly three bottles of beer & staggered into bed at nine & slept right through, so I write this the next day. The lectures were surprisingly good considering how tired I was. Even the Blake gave me an idea for my Blake-Jung paper: in the hierarchy of Zoas we have to go through the Tharmas world on our own way from Generation to Eden. Now Tharmas & Enion are, respectively, the old wise man & the Magna Mater, Prospero & Isis. The first-year lecture I think really woke those kids up—I was playing with the notion that art : social science :: mathematics : natural science, a body of symbolic relationships & possibilities. We say, because literature is so helpless, that it is being influenced by psychology. Isn't the real influence the other way around? Surely it's not that psychology teaches us the Oedipus motivation in Hamlet so much as Hamlet beginning to form a conceptual framework for psychology? This reminds me that after lunch I went over to Priestley's office & signed up for the Colloquium paper on Feb. 28: "First steps in literary criticism."[125]

Feb. 4. [Friday]

[155] Paradise Regained is going according to plan, with no surprises—this morning I dealt a bit with the storm & pinnacle temptations. The former is the moral anxiety engendered by the sense of chaos under

nature—our own atomic bomb fears. The latter is of course the giddiness of tragedy—the man on the pinnacle.

[156] Several people in this morning, & in the afternoon. I went over to Woodhouse's office for exam-setting. 4k[126] at two with Mrs. Kirkwood, who was setting, & Shook's replacer, a Father Madden. I suggested "How far is it true to say of Mill that in his thought culture produces anarchy?" but there were no takers, & I shall have to use it myself later. Woodhouse went to another office at 3 & I asked if I could stay in his, as I had nowhere to go. He said of course, & he'd get me something to read, & placed in my hands the page proofs of a formidable article written by himself on Milton's view of creation. Terrific job of weaving in & out of ex nihilo & de Deo & the eternity of matter & so on. As it was in page proofs, I couldn't suggest my real criticism, which was that he was too anxious to refute Saurat[127] to deal adequately with the very real doctrine of retraction that I think is in Milton, linked to the chain of being. That cute nun Sister Marion [Madeleine Norman] was there, very happy with the prospect of doing some work on Sprat. I suggested a Lycidas question on it as a complete Christian epic in miniature. No takers, though Woodhouse was much struck with the idea.

[157] I think my stomach must be shrinking—Tuesday night I went out to dinner at a hearty place at Spadina & College that gave me a large plate of food I couldn't touch & the waitress thought I was a sissy— should have had a soft-boiled egg & a slice of toast, she said. The dime tip I left her was pure cringe. I no longer find full-course lunches a matter of course.

[158] Among [Peter] Fisher's remarks I forgot to include one about Nietzsche & Wagner: "the trouble with the Germans is not that they haven't any sense of humor, but that they are always trying to laugh like gods."

[159] A very nice first-year lad whose name I haven't got came in to see me: he didn't come to ask me anything, but to tell me something. The something was, that all his courses fitted together into a single pattern he could almost grasp an intuition of at times, & that this modulated into a general feeling that life was wonderful & being at university was wonderful. He began by saying: "I've been thinking a lot about symbolism

lately, though I perhaps haven't gone into it as deeply as you have."
I said I thought that was unlikely. Then he fished a Christopher medal
out of his pocket & tried to say something about the feeling & texture of
silver. I don't understand why people regard the professional training
school of graduate studies a promotion from that sort of contact.

Feb. 5. [Saturday]

[160] Spent the morning writing letters of recommendation including
one for Ernst Oppenheimer for Illinois.[128] Some vocational guidance
genius had dreamed up a form in which I was supposed to check things.
Categories like "leader" were graded from "unnoticed" through "leads
in minor affairs" & "leads in major affairs" to Messiahship (top 1% or
A+) & the personality of course went from objectionable through generally liked to Queen of the May. There followed a series of things I was
supposed to check: "assertive," "over-assertive," "confident," "given to
ups & downs," "erratic," "retiring" & God knows what else. I wanted to
check them all & write underneath "I assume the applicant is all of these
things in turn, like any other normal human being"—but you have to do
your best for the student, and save your wisecracks for your friends.
There wasn't room to write it anyway. Not one word about scholarship
except a category that ranged from "needs prodding" to "does things on
his own." The work of somebody who thought that a Tammany ward
boss was the finest flowering of the human spirit. One significant category was that of grammar—"adequate-inadequate."

[161] Helen has been reading *Lorna Doone* during her convalescence—
I must soon reread it if I am to do anything on the romance, as I imagine
it lies deep in my mind, just above the very lowest, or Sherbrooke, layer
of archetypes. To write in the first person is excellent for a romance, &
the identification of author & narrator by means of a persona would
approximate a single or definitive effort. Blackmore is, I think, one of the
many romancers who wrote only one great book. The romance is the
clearest example obtainable of the predominance of grammatical or narrative rhythm: its only pauses are suspensions, hence its serial technique,
& the romancer gravitates toward prose, as the poetry of the romance
tends to a breathless prosaic doggerel. The archetypes are very clear: the
gigantic libido-hero, the fragile anima who is kidnapped by the armed
men & discovered to be of different blood from them, the villainous

shadow who sinks into the bog at the moment that the anima dies & recovers—which is really what happens—the oppression of the waste land (hence the great snow) by the robbers and the slaughter-of-suitors rise of yeomen against the insolent parasitic aristocrats, the opening of the centre symbol when he crushes the gold nugget in the mine, the Mary-Martha opposition of Lorna & Ruth Huckaback (note that symbolically John should have married Ruth, the wife principle who has to be distinguished from the anima. The romancer always pretends that we can eat the anima & have her too), the "sundering flood" symbolism involved in the meeting of hero & heroine, the evil forces imprisoned within the mysterious mountains, the roaming knight errant Faggus with his wonder horse. Everything is there—even the hero dies & revives in the "Kide's lambs" scene.

Feb. 6. [Sunday]

[162] Samuel Butler seems to me to take one further than almost anyone else in the mystery of predestination. Our notions of free will & moral responsibility seem to me to be rationalizings of something given, data, données. The possession of beauty or strength is obviously to some extent a datum, & so is intelligence. I glory in my intelligence, & should, yet in me a universal intelligence reaches a certain focus. We back into such questions through our reversed perspective which sees only the Tower of Babel, the ranking pyramid of egos. We like to compare, & ascribe guilt or culpability to those who are compared against.

[163] Failures are wicked people: there is no other kind of failure. We see this in reverse when we blame people for "failing" in any other sense.

[164] The teaching of hell fire is undoubtedly bad, yet it has some psychological point: it brings one face to face with one of the limits of the human mind, & instils a fear which often acts as a spur to an imagination that without it might get nowhere. Also it enables one to see other horrors such as Nazism in proportion, & with less bewildered astonishment. Perhaps if it isn't stirred up it will remain, acting on us if we don't act on it, conditioning our fears of security, of war, of the atom bomb, of death itself—the fear of death is less deep than the fear of hell. Yet there must be better ways of getting at it than by telling indignant lies about God. Orthodox hell though is a populous & even gregarious community:

there is a still deeper fear, the fear of being unwanted, absolutely unacceptable to anybody. Jesus went through that when *all* the disciples forsook him & fled.

[165] I don't much care to be busy: one side of me pulls away from activity on the plea of wanting to write, & urges me to a real psychosomatic blowout, catching flu & going to bed & be coddled for a week. I can resist that, but don't want to be pulled over to the other side of getting fascinated with activity, the way Woodhouse has been. Neither loving nor hating good works is a difficult position to maintain.

[166] Helen asked off her own bat today if there were any connection between *Lorna Doone* & Morris. She didn't know that I'm reading *The Roots of the Mountains* now. She thought Lorna's giving up of her estate & marrying a yeoman, even a knighted one, might have a social meaning other than just a Victorian hero not wanting to live on his wife's money. It was just the coincidence that seemed unusual.

[167] Fearful Symmetry has nearly sold out the first edition: the type has gone, but they'll do an offset reprint. I'd like to revise the footnotes someday. Not the text: if I started revising that I'd soon get involved in L [Liberal] or ⅂ [Tragicomedy].

[168] Reading Williams' *Arthurian Torso*: in Geoffrey Arthur can conquer Rome but can't fight the real Emperor, who lives in Byzantium. That's his father, the English-Roman New Troy struggle being a war of the brothers. Sailing to Byzantium, the Eastern goal of the Prester John Emperor-Messiah, the land the Grand Can will return from—that must run all through.

Feb. 7. [Monday]

[169] Busy day: nine o'clock lecture, Acta kids[129] in 10–11, Fisher 11–1, 2i exam committee 2–4;[130] wrote statement for Acta 4–5:30; dinner; wrote Margaret; lecture to women on romances of chivalry, 8–9:30. A thirteen-hour day is one that makes me hysterically tired, the way I saw Woodhouse get on Friday. A stranger would have said he was in excellent spirits: to me he was like a little child on the point of tears. However, Fisher was full of fascinating ideas about Plato, some of them from

Collingwood's Principles of Art. Plato was rejecting the representational element in art, & was trying to purify art by restoring its magical basis—hence the emphasis on music & the mode-mood connection, which is pure magic. He attacked the Iliad not as epic but as tragedy—tragedy to him, as to the Iudians, was *bad taste*, spiritual defeatism. If you see the world turning on the spindle of Necessity you see it in the comic context which the symposium is—the Plato-Aristophanes tie-up is very deep, as I've guessed. Theseus in Shakespeare's MND [*A Midsummer Night's Dream*] is a pure philosopher-ruler, & has many Platonic characteristics, including his view of art. Then we went on to discuss the life-Bardo cycle. Normally we are dragged backwards through life & pushed forwards through Bardo, & attempt to find some anastasis at the crucial points, or else go through a vortex or Paravritti which leads us, not to escape, but to implement charity by going forwards through life, as Jesus did, & withdraw in retreat from Bardo.[131] There was something about the shades in Homer I haven't got quite straight.

Feb. 8. [Tuesday]

[170] Another hysterical day: nine lecture repeated to the Barker girl,[132] Sawyer in at 11, R.K. lecture at 12, lunch, hair cut & shoeshine, tea & general buggering around owing to a headache, dinner with Lemke & three of his friends, a Bob Lederman, working for the Evangelical Brethern in Listowel[133] & trained in philosophy & apparently psychiatry. Talks a great deal & has a mind as sharp as a razor. Two quieter lads, one named Boissoneau [Boissonneau], in forestry, & knows Haddow. I'd like to see them again. Lederman spoke of the establishing of a community as necessary in the cure of, say, alcoholics, & that to him was one of the main functions of the Church. Had been trained in the little theological school of the Brethren in Illinois, whose President had the strength of character to remark in a lecture: "We have nothing distinctive to contribute to theology." Went over to Hart House to hear Lister Sinclair on poetry as dramatic spectacle in Shakespeare. He looked unhealthy, with a front tooth missing, but was in excellent form & he has extraordinary wit & charm. We went home in a taxi & discussed Morley's play,[134] which he didn't like either.

[171] Talked to Douglas Fisher & Molly Brown about last night's meeting. Evidently my statement was quite helpful,[135] & Fisher himself seems

to have made an excellent speech. The main attack came from the V.C.U. [Victoria College Union] President Keith Davey, who I think means well. Both he and the Associate, Anne Templeton, are complete chucks, & make one wonder about student government. Fisher seemed very browned off about it. The whole fallacy about university life is that it isn't regarded as a community of learners, but as a dichotomy of scholar-teachers & students, & the false analogies from democracy that build up student government separate them & drive the teachers into the graduate school, where they feel they can find their community. Davey, not being able to work, is a great plugger for "activities," which have multiplied around the place so fast the kids have no time to do anything. He has diligently spread around the College the notion that if you're applying for a job down town your employers will be mainly interested in what your extra-curricular activities were. If you give promise of joining the firm's bowling team & its light opera society, & can be counted on to take up collections for everything around the office & to be out to dances every Saturday night, they'll take you on: they won't say "What was your job before & what sort of job did you make of that?" Fisher said one of the things he saw in the war was a German tank blown up by a lucky shot. Hours later he got a look at it: it was still red hot, & inside were three rows of teeth, the heads around them blackened to a crisp.[136]

[172] I was looking through the Britannica & struck an article on pre-existence, Blake's doctrine that the human nature of Christ was eternal.[137] The writer said it had met with little support, but was held by Isaac Watts—a possible link.

[173] Continuing the art : history :: mathematics : science analogy [par. 154], doesn't it follow that, while art never improves, the pattern of its possibilities does consolidate, as does that of mathematics? Thus ⅂ [Tragicomedy], for instance, might demonstrate the possibility, or rather the fact, of such consolidation—I hint at the idea in FS [chap. 12].

[174] Sawyer was arguing with me about Charles Williams, & I was maintaining that there could be civilized Christianity but no Christian civilization. He brought in an article on Abraham in a Jewish magazine which proved my essentially Protestant point about the break and separation from the civitas terrena which Abraham represents.

[175] I got a sort of manic-depressive reaction to my reputation today: Mrs. Hubener told me how anxious she was to hear my R.K. lectures because in one of her classes a row had broken out between Vic kids & some Trinity people in which one of the former girls had said the latter should come over & hear Professor Frye, who was the best Christian she knew. Mrs. H. pointed out a certain looseness in that expression, which the child qualified into the best representative of Christianity she knew. I suppose that's all right really: she didn't mean me; but still there are dangers in the fact that I have developed, without being able to help it, the kind of facile pseudo-sanctity which comes from having pleasant security & no major problems. I think my life at present is as close to an age of innocence as it well could be. So far, however, the sort of hero-worship that would turn me opaque instead of translucent isn't a very deadly point—I don't actually give the impression of being different from other people, surely. Well, anyway: at lunch Irving & Ken [MacLean] were discussing how Canada, as usual, had taken up Wissenschaft after U.S.A. had got a bit tired of it. Ken said there was a lot of it here & Irving said not: "Look at Norrie," he said, "a living example." "He's living, all right," said Ken, "but they'd kill him if they could"—meaning Woodhouse & Priestley. Irving made further objections & Ken told him he didn't know what he was talking about, to shut up & eat his soup. Ken over-subtilizes situations at times, but I think I see what he means.

Feb. 9. [Wednesday]

[176] I'll be glad when this week is over: I'm trying to fight off the flu by going to bed. I took some Benedryl & slept all afternoon, then got up & went to a Forum meeting. Talked into doing a front cover for next issue on a new national library & theatre,[138] as per speech from throne. Also a Mindszenty editorial.[139] Very few ideas about either. Struggled through a Nashe lecture & used some stuff I stole from Lister Sinclair. Stage direction in Titus Andronicus: Lavinia's hands cut off & tongue cut out, ravished—however they did that. Titus chops his hand off on the stage to prevent Aaron killing his two sons, but is too late & Aaron sends back the two heads along with the hand. Titus announces that he thinks this is a dirty trick, & plans revenge. Puzzle: how to get all the cold cuts off the stage? He takes the two heads in one hand: that being full of heads, he can't carry the other hand—*his* hand, which Aaron has returned. So he gives it to Lavinia, who hasn't any hands at all, has to take it with her

mouth, and goes out like a retriever with the hand dangling from her puss. It amused my kids, & the brightest of them mentioned the Grand Guignol.[140]

[177] At the Ruskin lecture the Wallace boy gave me quite a fight. I was saying that no critic can ever say to an artist: "What you did was well done, but not worth doing." He objected, & perhaps I shouted him down. Next time I shall try to approach it from the next point I'm making, the art-as-symbol-of-society point. That is, a certain kind of society produces a certain kind of art, & some kinds of art are always anachronistic, as the epic poem would be for us or the novel for the age of Charlemagne. Perhaps it's difficult for my students, as it apparently was for readers of *Fearful Symmetry*, to know where exposition stops & commentary begins. Went over to Hart House and listened to J.W.G. Macdonald on the Calgary group show, which looks fresh & youthful, & has no trace of the Group of Seven influence in it. Evidently someone named Maxwell Bates, a prisoner in Germany during the war, & who shows strong Picasso & Henry Moore influences, is the ring leader. I didn't hear much of the talk, as I was too full of the miseries. Also I missed Wally Field's lecture & an Art Committee meeting which would have clashed with it anyway.

Feb. 10. [Thursday]

[178] My students wouldn't let me go on with Samson Agonistes, but asked unanswerable questions about P.L. [*Paradise Lost*] & P.R. [*Paradise Regained*]. Why did Satan fall? Could Christ really have fallen? I had to take refuge in paradox: if Christ had fallen, it would have been inevitable that he should have fallen. On the way down Mr. Haddow talked to me about forestry & how commercial & what he called "aesthetic" interests clashed over reforestation—the latter wanted some hardwood in with the pulp & paper supply. I'd asked him about speaking to the outfit called "Men of the Trees," who he said were mainly women. I suggested "Men of the Trees & Nymphs" as an alternative title, but he said he didn't think that would be accurate.

[179] The sitting squad has departed in a chuff from the Blake group, because we've come to papers now. There were so few today that I took them into my office, where I can think better. The paper was lousy. What

came out (of me, I mean) was the very simple statement, which might just as well have gone into chapter 4 of FS, that Blake regarded "generalization" in portrait-painting as a rationalization of a profitable pseudo-artistic racket. You didn't paint Sir Cloudesby Shovel in particular, but the hero in general, which looked enough like Sir C.S. to make him cough up. Also, more important, that a work of art is a focus of a community. Its unit is the symbol, & even degraded symbols, of religion & the state, are of vast power in making such a focus. The word is the audible symbol, & this in analogy produces the nation, the nation being essentially the language-group. Art is the *growing point* of language, a direct recreation of myth, language itself being the fossilized, vestigial, second-hand mythology which forms the body of tradition. The metaphors imprisoned in abstract nouns are an elementary example of this. Jargon or ready-made writing shows the connection between commonplace thought & second-hand ideas.

[180] My R.K. lectures have been working out the principle that there is an apocalyptic epistemology, in which the aggregate of individuals & the one form become the same thing. Thus the chain of being becomes the vortex:

Leviathan	natural man	←human world→	society→	One Man	Jesus
	serpent, dragon	←animal world→	flock of sheep→	One Lamb	
	wilderness	←vegetable world→	garden→	One Tree (vine, rose)	
	rock, desert	←mineral world→	city→	One Home (stone)	

It seems to go across too, for first year as well as fourth. I suppose it's the basis of ⅂ [Tragicomedy], though the epistemological part of it seems related to ∧ [Anticlimax]. Better on left side:

Antichrist or Der Führer	←tyranny	←human world
The Dragon or Old Serpent	←beasts of prey	←animal world
The Barren Tree	←wilderness	←vegetable world
The Rock of Sepulture	←desert	←mineral world

Feb. 11. [Friday]

[181] The hump is over—I don't think things will be quite so bad from now on. Started Samson, & unloaded my stock of ideas on tragedy,

including one about Samson as the exarchon of a chorus which is Israel. The people in that class who come in at 9:10, notably McLellan, do it so consistently that I feel they must be making some sort of point of it, & I am seriously thinking of announcing that in future lectures will begin at 9:10. Two of that depressed band of 48 people[141] came in—Stingle & Parsons. The latter has been in a terrible nervous jitter all year, & this morning he was nearly in tears. Wouldn't tell me what it was, just said it was personal. As for Stingle & Co., they've all been very browned off, what with so many people in the graduate school to feel superior to, ranging from fellow-students to Priestley. I sympathize, of course, but still they *are* a bunch of spoiled babies, who came back because they didn't want to grow up, & are busy looking for splendid & inspiring leadership in a community fit for culture-heroes to live in. Patchell dropped out entirely, & is now loafing.[142] My throat is still sore, & I came home after lunch & stayed in, going to bed early.

[182] Last night I gave my final museum lecture—I was dead tired & it wasn't my best work at all, but I suppose it wasn't too bad. The next one will be better. The only original ideas concerned the decline of the court as a cultural centre, Swift, Pope, & Johnson all being Tories, courtiers deprived of a king, wanting an ideal king ruling by divine right, but in opposition to the actual one, who, being a Whig nominee, wasn't even clear of party politics. This withdrawal of the intellectuals both from court & the bourgeois city can be seen even geographically, as the London of 18th c. culture is based on the neutral territory between Westminster & the City: or the Strand & the Fleet, where Johnson lived, up through Covent Garden & Drury Lane, where Will's coffee-house was, over in Soho & pushing north into Bloomsbury from its axis on Charing Cross Road, where Johnson said the full tide of human existence was. This withdrawal marks the consolidation (so far as it can ever be consolidated) of the Fourth Estate, that drifting mass of newspapermen, authors, publishers, publicists (whatever they are), professors, scientists & scientific amateurs, & cultivated professional men. At the same time the economy of the nation seemed to strike a balance between the excitement of the city & the repose of the country, London & the squirearchy being its focal points. This balance, which accounts for the themes of Cockney satire & the Petition for Absolute Retreat,[143] is the key to the "Augustan" business. Virgil & Horace, more than any other poets, express that balance between the centrifugal imperium &

the keeping of bees, between animated urbanity & the farm in the Sabine hills.

Feb. 12. [*Saturday*]

[183] Stayed home & decided to hell with it—I mean correspondence & Forum editorials & such. I'm a Methodist; I hate taking time from the Lord's work. The Lord's work for me is sitting still in a comfortable chair thinking beautiful thoughts, & occasionally writing them down. This also happens to be what I like to do, which just shows you how wise the Lord is. I had a curious collection of very interesting dreams—as usual, I can't remember details, but there was travelling & mountain-climbing & agreeable company, including women, & tulip-beds and in general a sort of change of pace in my dream life, as though spring were coming in the unconscious. I told my Milton kids that dreams commented on the preceding day, & if they watched their own dreams carefully they'd find that they conditioned the mood, & so often the events, of the next day. This in connection with Eve's dream. It's part of the Beulah withdrawal & return.

[184] Helen's article in the Star Weekly came out today & we went over to the corner to have tea & take a look at it. Nearly a million copies— much wider circulation than anything I write will ever have.[144] Curious how little that means. It occurs to me that the marriage vow, where the man says cherish & protect & the woman honour & obey (or used to) ought to be reversed for a matriarchal society like ours, where the woman affords the man protection in her home in return for unquestioning obedience within it.

[185] This week my mind has been working on a train of thought started by [Peter] Fisher on Monday—it's a wonderful arrangement having him come in Monday. That's the difference between the Aristotelian theory that art grows naturally out of nature & the Platonic theory that art is manic & mantic, a flooding of the mind by a larger mind with magical potency. It came up in Ruskin, in the Museum lecture (where it's the basis of the distinction between the Augustans & the age of Blake) and it's a ⋏ [Rencontre] point, with Plato lining up on the analogy side. I suppose they're objective & subjective fallacies respectively, but that's a bit too easy. What's the middle ground? In my own mind I've made

Blake both Aristotelian & Platonic on this point. The antithesis probably doesn't exist, but if not how does one restate the problem? The modern Platonic anamnesis theory is the Jungian unconscious; the modern Aristotelian one is the evolution doctrine in Goethe & Samuel Butler. There it seems less an antithesis.

Feb. 13. [Sunday]

[186] A cuddled Sunday: I did nothing but sit. Also I wrote out a good bit of my colloquium paper.[145] Sitting solid all day produces a headache with me, & by evening I felt quite miserable. Margaret [Newton] stayed in & drank beer all day, which added to the confusion. She had a very decent Esthonian D.P. [displaced person] named Elmo [Leunk?], who was her driver in Europe, in to see her: she was to take him out to dinner, but as it came seven o'clock & she wasn't even dressed he naturally decided to go home. Margaret is a bit overpowering when she's full of beer & claustrophobia.

Feb. 14. [Monday]

[187] St. Valentine's day, not that I paid any attention to it. Lecture, & then this Kay Fowler infant, who I thought I'd got rid of last year, came in to tell me all about a love affair with Harry Boyd in fourth year which was going badly. She took up exactly the time [Peter] Fisher would have taken if he hadn't begged off the night before—I don't know how she knew. I dimly divined that the boy figures she's got something with a dotted line on it up her sleeve, & is developing very, very cold feet. He picked a remark about marriage as a rat-trap out of Berdyaev & a sentence which seems to countenance free love out of Blake—I mean FS. The world is dissolving in flux for him & he's trying to hold a pattern together—meanwhile, there's this girl with her head shoved through the pattern, very obtrusively a real something to come to terms with. She'll hook him: he hasn't a chance.

[188] Lunch with Francis Chapman—a delightful lad with a beautifully speculative mind. His father, who has had a stroke, still can't talk. His doctor says it's nouns that are the block. We discussed the $\alpha\pi\epsilon\iota\rho\text{o}\nu$ [infinite]—the shadow of negation that rises from philosophy, Wittgenstein's thing that is not significant, or rather signifiable. I told

him that coincidence was mentally unusable design—he liked that. Then to the Forum to type out an editoral on Mindszenty.[146] Kay Morris, who was trying to write an editorial on juvenile delinquency, was so tired she could hardly focus her eyes. Then home, & out again to talk to the women on courtly love. I guess they were more interested than they looked. I wound up with my astrology & humours spiel, which they loved. I guess I'm a favorite of theirs now, but Moff Woodside's idea of getting long-term good will for the College out of them is baloney. One who was a Victoria graduate asked me, knowing perfectly well who I was, if I thought Victoria would be a fit place to send her daughter. Both she & another woman in the car were greatly impressed by the prestige of Trinity, & not at all impressed by Victoria's hospitality—at least not in that direction.

Feb. 15. [Tuesday]

[189] Curious disturbed dream last night—evidently I can't sleep properly without Benedryl, even when I seem to be feeling all right. I was crossing the ocean in a ship which nevertheless stopped at small French towns. A feeling that the voyage was four days & two had passed—some reference to the four-day panic of last week & to some extent this. I seemed to be inside a small square in the centre of a small French town where the boat had stopped—I knew the town, as a stop anyway, or at least recognized a huge statue on my left looking out of the square as Bourdelle's Vierge d'Alsace—the name Bourdelle didn't come to me.[147] Young Chapman had asked that day about de la Motte Fouque[148] & I'd said it was Alsatian. (The name has a highly improper reference to intercourse before going to sleep & Helen's nervous exhausted state, with some anxiety about my own technique.) Anyway, I seemed to be carrying Helen in my arms, & the stopping of the ship (it all fitted together quite logically, really) made me stagger around the square unsteadily carrying her. I felt appallingly weary at the prospect of carrying her & not sleeping properly (a direct reference, as I wasn't) for four days. As I staggered around I saw two huge & rather frightening stone heads on the side of the square I'd been on, one that I was looking directly at, of a woman, & another on the left, that I didn't look at, of a man. I record this dream because the statues seem archetypal—I feel sure that the last two were my father & mother. After that there were long & tedious dreams about being in the army & in an American university: one of the former had a sort of pit-&-pendulum scene.

[190] A fairly good, & certainly entertaining, lecture on Ruskin & a good R.K. one that went over much the same ground again, except that it provoked a great many questions—even Barbara Brieger asked one. I'm beginning to realize that the Biblical doctrine of all individuals of a class constituting a single individual (society or the Church is the body of one man, etc.) so that the individual & the universal are the same thing, is the Thomist doctrine of real universals, & accounts for the "approved" nature of Thomism as a definitive conception of the Church. Then to lunch: Brown still has aphasia but his father-in-law died, which is a minor blessing—or maybe it was his father. Then the Forum again, after writing the front-page editorial,[149] which I hope is all right, & home from there.

Feb. 16. [Wednesday]

[191] Two lectures & the afternoon spent doing various joe-jobs. The number of letters of recommendation I'm writing these days is terrific— Oppenheimer alone has twenty. Also various stenographic irritations like Acta copyreading & essay contest theses, etc., etc. Laurette's [Laure Rièse's] lecture at 5: pleasant but thin, not up to the standard of the other two. Moff Woodside confirmed the impression I made on the good ladies—one of them said to me: "Your knowledge is so abysmal!" Bless their hearts. Just before the lecture I was assaulted by this Morris lunatic and asked how I reconciled my C.C.F. interests with Christianity. He has some notion in his addled head that socialism & "liberal" theology go together. I was very patient, because I really think he is touched in the head, & has no idea how absurdly rude he is. Hilliard [Trethewey] drove me home & says Lacey hasn't much longer to last, as he's stopped taking food. A dullish day, with very little thought in it. The Ruskin lecture tried to split the real production-consumption cycle from the false exchange-for-profit cycle which has evolved out of it, but I don't know enough economics to do the job properly.

Feb. 17. [Thursday]

[192] Four lectures of course in the morning, pageproofing of the Forum in the afternoon & a two-hour lecture at the Museum in the evening. Talking about Samson Agonistes along lines I think I know pretty well. The R.K. lecture completed a point in my chart:

human—community	= One Man
animal—flock of sheep	= One Lamb = blood (through the "blood as life" in the law).
vegetable—garden	= One Tree = water (assoc. w. trees in Gen., Ezek. & Rev.)
mineral—city	= One Stone = body

Hence eucharist & baptism. The tree has a more direct reference to the vegetable blood, or olive oil & the anointing symbol. I should shift that city business up to the human level: it's silly to keep it at the stone level. Note the sacrificial Lamb, the seven-branched candlestick, with the two olive trees (Zech. [4:2–14] & Rev. xi [11:3–6]) & the breastplate of Judaism. I suppose the refusal of wine in the R.C. [Roman Catholic] communion is derived from the sense of the Lamb as holocaust, the Jewish prohibition of drinking blood. The bread & wine business comes out of the vegetable level somehow—maybe water comes out of the rock. It comes out of the temple, which is on that level, in Ezekiel.

[193] Beharriell read a fair paper on romanticism in the Blake course, which is now meeting in my office. Never again will I allow a sitting squad in a graduate course. To have a whole body of people with no sense of responsibility to the course trooping in & out as they feel like it, coming in a body if they think they're going to be entertained, & leaving in a body if they think they're going to be bored, demoralizes the others, & I'm not having any more of it. One thing which emerged was the two conceptions of Adam: if we think of Adam as born, or natural (nature meaning that which is born), we can't help (nor should we) thinking of the Fall as evolution, the arrival of human consciousness. Only when we think of him as unborn does it become a fall.

[194] I got home from the Forum to find Muriel [Code] here—George has just been asked to do an outdoor column: I though that, like Jack Cumberland, he was a lover of the great indoors. But he seems very pleased. Then I tried to read Birkhead['s] *Tale of Terror*,[150] which I like very much—evidently Godwin started the Rosicrucian novel that Bulwer-Lytton developed. The lecture wasn't my best work at all: I was terribly tired & nervous, couldn't keep from tensing up & couldn't get the range of the audience.[151] They spread from quite naive people to a girl who had read Virginia Woolf's essay on the Sentimental Journey.[152] I said I thought that book had the pervading irony in it of a takeoff on a travel book—the traveller doesn't do anything he's supposed to do, just ambles along picking up oddities, like Bemelman's in our day.[153] In view of the fact

that the SJ ends, probably, in the word "cunt" I don't think there's much to that essay.

Feb. 18. [Friday]

[195] Started Spenser with third year—I've been an unconscionable time on Milton, considering that I haven't said a word about the Christian Doctrine, Milton's view of creation & matter, & all the other things Woodhouse puts in the foreground. I couldn't seem to bring myself to keep on doing joe-jobs, & insisted on the luxury of reading instead. Cut the goddam Commission on Culture,[154] which is a hell of a waste of time, & came home.

[196] For years I've been pondering the possibility of a genuinely new formula in prose fiction. I've been interested in turn in all of my four forms, but I don't see anything new in any of them (for me, that is: I'm not making a general judgement). There remains the fifth form, the Finnegans Wake cyclic myth. I've thought of a novel on the life of Christ, & will collect things to put in it: but I wonder what would come of a Bardo novel.[155] Huxley appears to be one of the few who have tried the story of the persistence of consciousness after death, & I gather it's a bad novel (Time Must Have a Stop). Yet here might be a formula to handle my interest in fantasy & the tale of terror in that novel way I've been looking for. Let's say a man dies. His personality splits into a ghost that hangs around the body & another focus of consciousness. He realizes that he's "saved," whatever that means, because he's committed his consciousness to the latter. Those who commit themselves to the former are demonic. He becomes the centre of a world, or rather its circumference: the world is apparently in dream space. He's a *Lare*, a fixed point, no longer a living body rolling from place to place, but a watcher, & things come to him—a psychoanalytic analysis of his past first, a pure vision of his "damned" self (on my principle that the mouth of hell is the previous moment), other perspectives of the world, & so on. There isn't anything that couldn't fit a scheme like that. (Re extrasensory perception of books: Sawyer shoved Williams' *All Hallows' Eve* through my door today & I didn't open it until I'd written the above as far as "looking for." The rest was thought out independently.)

[197] Norma Arnett came in today with a defense of her poem she wants to print in Acta.[156] I don't know if she has much on the ball, but she's a

good kid, & I like the tense egocentric childlike offhand way she just uses me & takes my help for granted. Women who make me their animus & then desert when I can't fill *that* role get me down. I spend a fair amount of emotional time in a state of baffled tenderness, & it's a positive relief to have so self-absorbed a youngster come in, get what she wants out of me, shake her curls & flounce out again.

[198] Citizens' Forum in the evening—very nice people putting up patiently with a lot of bullshit about World Government.[157] Silcox & a P.C. M.P. [Progressive Conservative Member of Parliament] from Kamloops named [Davie] Fulton saying "Well, there's Russia" & somebody called Priest and Phelps of McGill saying "Yes, but still." A Mrs. Renshaw visited the group to hand out propaganda for a World Government organization—same vague Mildred Fahrni type who can't answer the most elementary objections to what she's supposed to be supporting & who a hundred years ago would be handing out missionary tracts.

Feb. 19. [Saturday]

[199] Still reading *All Hallows' Eve*: extraordinary to find the Cagliostro Rosicrucian thriller still going strong, & with an introduction by T.S. Eliot. It's a measure of our civilization that a type done in clinical disbelief by Godwin & with detachment by Bulwer Lytton should now be taken so seriously. Somehow the book, & the way I've picked it up, & its theme, remind me that reading books is a form of necromancy, as no book attains its full meaning until its author is dead & reading becomes a form of communicating with the dead. Milton's conception of the book as the consolidation of a man's soul is true enough, but in time it's his preserved & mummified body. Speaking of a book as a man's soul, I've often wondered if there isn't a real world of creative value withdrawn from our judgement of it. Posterity brings a great deal to light & levels out much injustice, but it's not infallible, & even when it's right its rightness isn't relevant. There must be a world in which every artist *has* the greatness he dreamed of & tried to achieve. The Beerbohm Enoch Soames story is an ironic frameup: it shows how inadequate the future is as a substitute for eternity. There must be a world in which Benjamin Robert Haydon is exactly the genius he thought he was—the future, like the past, is the mouth of hell, & confirms his own doubts. I wouldn't give

the devil two cents for a peep at the B.M. [British Museum] catalogue in 2049 without a written guarantee that it would be interesting. I'm quite sure that a hope that posterity will recognize the greatness of such books as *Fearful Symmetry* doesn't really support me. I'm so detached from that that it surprises me: it's either the mercy of God or the fact that I have a job & a steady salary cheque coming in. Or a combination of the two: Williams calls it luxury.

[200] *All Hallows' Eve* is a Bardo novel, & a type of fantasy that is not popular now because it will be later. I notice he's a bit cute: his Antichrist's servant, whom he's cured of a brain tumor, says: "We all carry his mark in our bodies." But then the ingenuity of familiar reference is one of the main points of such a book. The (by now to me) rather readymade distinction between remorse & repentance is made: the hero is "not yet mature enough to repent." If repentance is metanoia, is it something you *do*? Isn't it rather a profound desire for guidance? Isn't it at most a withdrawal from good works? I've talked myself about remorse as a luxury, but I think it's just an intellectual's catchword.

[201] I must collect my impressions of Bardo novels: this *Portrait of Jennie* that I picked up[158] is one, & Henry James' *Sense of the Past* is another. These last two are Dunneish stories,[159] where the collision of two time tables is a main point, & the heroines are animas. Williams' story seems to be purer Bardo, & to grasp, imaginatively, the point that Purgatory was invented by the R.C.Ch. [Roman Catholic Church] to bring Bardo into Xy [Christianity]. In Huxley it would be the pure Eastern thing. Yeats combines them too. Also the fact that in Williams the heroine goes into the future & reports its knowledge to Simon puts a Dunne stamp on it too.

[202] I have deliberately fucked going to see Lacey. I tell myself now that it's too late, that I should do him no good & relieve myself only of a neurotic compulsion. How much of that is true I can't say. James i, 27,[160] is very silly: the rhetorical effort of a fashionable preacher who wants to make an effect & doesn't know how. Not that I get light on my problem by cursing James. I come back to my Chik-hai Bardo point:[161] time affords the opportunity for the inspired act: to neglect it is original if not actual sin, and all such sins are a waste of time, loss of time, a surrender of a bit more of oneself to the devouring mouth of hell. That's what Blake

meant about the moment in each day.[162] I wish I could find a way of living by faith that was not an abdication of decision—a break with the rhythm of original sin is what one is after, I suppose.

[203] *All Hallows' Eve* was exactly the book I was looking for: I have temporarily lost my ambition to write a Bardo novel myself, & consolidated my impulse to write an article, perhaps for that *Trollopian* magazine, on the occult novels of Bulwer Lytton. After fifty pages of Williams' book, one has to pass a special critical Order-in-Council[163] to keep oneself from dismissing it as a lot of blithering nonsense. That kept me reading it, but it's still as crude & tasteless a performance as the genre supplies. His public is too sophisticated to worry about the factual basis of magic, so there's none of Lytton's naive & detached curiosity, & Lytton's normal Victorian prejudices are replaced by a fetid, miasmic, oppressive & appallingly obtrusive priestly morality. The ingenuity & intelligence with which he gears his fantasy to Christian doctrine makes the book positively bad instead of negatively inept, but reveals how completely ritual, the physical transmission & recreation of the divine community in time, is white magic, & exists & has influence only insofar as the forces of evil are conceived as black magic. I can't help feeling that the Christian drama of heaven & hell is one thing & Bardo another; that Bardo is essentially bound up with Karma & reincarnation, & though purgatory is the point of contact, it still wouldn't come together even if one didn't feel that the purgatory idea was alien to Christianity. I'm not clear on this point yet. In terms of my four forms, *All Hallows' Eve* is a romance-anatomy, a Gothic horror tale in which the villain is (as he is occasionally in the cruder examples) the devil, & in which the anima moves in Bardo, as Lilian does in *A Strange Story*, which also ends with a magician destroyed within his own magic circle.[164] This Gothic horror romance is linked to an auctorius theory of Bardo: someone like Yeats who didn't feel a compulsion to make Bardo rationalize priestcraft might have brought it off.

[204] In the evening I went out to the New Play Society to see Oedipus Rex, followed by Sheridan's *Critic*.[165] The cool air of eighteenth-century sanity was what I wanted right then. Note carefully that Oedipus is *not* killed, but is a pharmakos. I must be careful about my communion theory of tragedy, with the hero falling on the stage. Greek tragedy, linked to a religion of sacrifice, has to report the fall by a messenger:

drama is to that extent τα επη, told to us only, as the Bible is the messenger of the death of Christ. A religion of sacrament can use a visibly dying hero: if it doesn't, as in *Samson Agonistes*, it's not only Classical tradition but is, like *Samson*, best done in an Old Testament theme, where the hero is prototypical. For a modern audience that doesn't believe in pharmakoi, pity at least is not purged. We feel pity for Oedipus & terror for fate, & so get primarily the moral effect of irony. However, the hero falling on the stage is half-way to the blasphemous ritual of the gladiator show. What does Seneca do?

Feb. 20. [Sunday]

[205] Very pleasant Sunday, spent partly in writing my paper.[166] Helen seemed to have been waiting for the attack of flu that knocked her out yesterday afternoon, & is now very cheerful. As usual, her cheerfulness includes the suggestion that I should learn to dance—I'd quite like to, of course—and reveries of exotic places to spend the spring.

Feb. 21. [Monday]

[206] Nine o'clock lecture with Mary Louise Kilgour & Doug Fisher hot on my heels. Mary Louise wanted to know about printing Norma Arnett's letter,[167] which I thought would be all right sans blither, & Fisher tells me that a lad in Pol. Sci. named Harry Green is refusing a V.C.U. [Victoria College Union] job he could have (Pres) for Acta.[168] If so, things look good. Then a lad named [Kenneth] Knox came in, sent by Charlie Leslie. He was born with half his guts missing, & after he hit puberty he spent about ten years in hell. Then he thought the hell with this (not being able to digest his food, etc.) & got up & joined the Air Force, & has been running quite normally ever since. He picked up Christian Science but of course had its number before he started, then he picked up Swedenborg & that's where he is now. After an anti-intellectual period he finally came to university, & has discovered that science is all right if it's translucent rather than opaque. "The experience was determined by the coming to life of the Word." I liked him & he seemed to need a talk, but I had very little to say to anyone so full of certainties—the right kind, no smugness. He's got a lot out of Kant, & seemed pleased that his first name, like Swedenborg's, was Emmanuel. Then Peter Fisher, then Doris Mosdell with another Forum complaint. She sounded very unreason-

able, & probably had the curse, but the gravamen of her charge was, as usual, Lew's domination.[169] Also the Shubik-Sangster business.[170] Then a most infernal Department meeting. One bright spot: Rinehart wants me to do a Milton in their series.[171]

[207] [Peter] Fisher & I talked of a lot of things: how people like myself, for whom things generally resolve, feel guilty about those who seem born for bad luck, a Cain responsible for a bleeding Abel. It's partly the tough luck Christ ran into, not that that can be called luck. I complained loudly about Williams' book & he said the Christian fear of the Jew (Antichrist in the book was a Jew)[172] was like Tibetan Buddhism's fear of Bön.[173] He denies the purgatorial element in Bardo, in fact in all Karma. He seems to feel though that if you want moral purgation you'll get it, as you can only go into the house you build yourself. We discussed the geometry of thought, how Jung's unconscious is obsessed by a diagram that places it underneath (in contrast to Freud, who puts it underneath because he's talking about deliberate repressions. All he says is that if you sit on a stool dropping things out of your bottom the hole underneath gets to be fairly shitty after a while). But while it might be good exercise to work out the whole thing on another diagram that puts it above & calls it superconscious, one couldn't attach oneself to the diagram either, because it would just lead (as so many translations of Oriental scriptures do) to renaming the sky-god. If you must have a diagram, putting the conscious & the other mind *beside* each other is perhaps best, & that's what Fisher thinks the "para" in such words as Parabrahman actually means.[174]

[208] He referred to a book called *Science & Reality* by a Pole named Korzybsky [Korzybski] who is hipped on semantics,[175] & maintains, something that I thought was foolish at first, that it is almost if not quite impossible to learn your native language. You learn & understand only other languages. I think there's a lot in that. I told my kids re Sidney that the Renaissance social system was reflected in literary categories, epic & tragedy being aristocratic & comedy & satire concerned with low life. Thus putting comic scenes into a tragedy was socially subversive; furthermore, it's a revolt against tragedy. Falstaff by stealing the show makes a monkey out of H4 [King Henry IV] & becomes the carnival king. Fisher asked me what I was going to do with things like ludian drama & Japanese No plays. I said they belonged in the pattern of *The Tempest*,

which is, like the No plays, a Bardo play. That was the kind of comedy that absorbed tragedy into itself, & was no longer revolting against tragedy.

[209] Helen tonight described the walk of the intellectual Englishman, with the arse stuck up like a ship's poop, as the Oxford lurch.

Feb. 22. [*Tuesday*]

[210] Got tired of Ruskin & went on to Morris. I said that Morris' thought turned on the etymology of manufacture, & that he thought of the useful arts as the growing point of a revolutionary movement. He thought of the creative vitality of the Middle Ages as revolutionary, & as expressing itself in John Ball.[176] If you start passing aesthetic judgements on the things around you it won't be long before you realize you're getting gypped. The point is would useful arts (as in Sweden) achieve so much social stability they'd wipe out the fine arts?—Morris after all is fairly Tolstoyan about things like tragedy. Maybe; but Morris raises the question: isn't the romantic theory of genius just the artistic equivalent of this cancerous exchange-for-profit excrescence on the real production-consumption cycle? Just as in economics you start with the profit-seeking man, so in the arts you start with genius-millionaires who have far more than their fair share, & then masses who haven't enough. The greatest artists after all are craftsmen—Chaucer, Morris' favorite, Shakespeare, & the artists who grew out of the useful arts of the 18th c., Mozart, Watteau, Blake.

[211] The women came in at 11 to draft out a Renaissance course.[177] I fixed it up for them & was of course signed up for several—I think four. One on Castiglione, one perhaps on the Italian epic, two on the Elizabethans. Then the R.K. lecture, in which I added little to the chart except that a girl (Eleanor Thompson) asked me about the shearing of sheep—I said that if it was anything it was a death-&-revival thing corresponding to the opposite number, the snake, who sheds its skin. Also the tree of life, Zechariah's candlestick, flanked by the olive trees, as Jesus with Moses & Elijah, or the past law & the future prophecy contained in the present. This goes opposite the three crosses. The regenerate-redeemed-reprobate pattern of the crosses applies to cities, & explained the "third part" business in Rev. 8.[178] The same three patterns on the stone level

too: Samson between the pillars, the dying sun god, is on the other side[,] the Stonehenge figure in the doorway, the man against the rising sun between the stones, the high priest between Joachim & Boaz, Jesus emerging at the spring equinox out of the cave of rock.

[212] I typed my paper all afternoon & came home with 17 pages.[179]

Feb. 23. [Wednesday]

[213] More Morris. A witty lecture but not much in it—my usual line about the state of innocence in *News from Nowhere*. However, Morris is going very well. I like Room 30 to lecture in. I made several points I already have—the Robot Utopia (Bellamy, Wells, Campanella) as the actualization of the aim of the primitive society to achieve a pure ritual out of life, the progressive-education context of American society being competitive capitalism, & so having a bumptiousness & aggressiveness about it that Morris' society wouldn't have, etc. The Bacon lecture at ten was good & highly concentrated, but stock: only I noticed the *Advancement of Learning* has the history-poetry-philosophy triad again, history including "natural history" or biology, as it should. Curious that not until the theory of evolution was it proved that natural history was really history.

[214] At four a new committee sparked by Mary Jackman, with Jessie [Macpherson] as Chairman & Douglas Duncan on it, opened a show of Douglas' pictures in Alumni Hall. Douglas made a not very good speech, & I drifted around aimlessly trying to introduce artists to professors & vice versa, & finding them in separate clumps. All the artists were there, & the cornier members of staff disappeared very quickly. Coincidence, of course, but I think it marks the beginning of a new rhythm in Victoria life. I took Helen out for cocktails & dinner, our first party in three months.

[215] David Parsons is in a far better temper—he'd discovered a good book of Shaw that is giving him leads.[180] I said I thought *Heartbreak House*, a study of accidie in which pure destruction appears as a release, was remarkable prophecy for 1916 & contained the whole existentialist thesis. *Back to Methuselah* was more what Shaw thought & argued about, the other what he saw. *Man & Superman* as the dead end of Courtly Love

& a return to the scholastic view—passion cheapens & binds; it cannot ennoble or emancipate. Considering Shaw's contempt of Thackeray, there's a lot of *Vanity Fair* in it. The cutting out of motivation, of reflection, of the knowledge of good & evil, is common to Nietzsche's mastery, Bergson's intuition, Butler's practice-skill, Shaw's housewiferly cleaning-up hero. St. Joan's belief in her voices is just that: that's why she's innocent—no sense of good & evil, though all her doubters try to persuade her of it.

Feb. 24. [Thursday]

[216] The Spenser was stock, though I got a little clearer the contrast between medieval Arthurian romance, where the knights steal the show, & the Tudor propaganda for the king, which wanted the "historical" figure of Arthur & wanted to get rid of the legendary & adulterous knights. Last night at 4 [Mel] Breen, who was supposed to read a paper at the Blake today, came to say he was dropping out of the course—been offered a job on Mayfair.[181] What with our evening date, I had nothing ready for the seminar. So I talked. Don Harron was there & helped a good deal.[182] Ken Maclean [MacLean] told me yesterday he'd met Fyles of McGill who'd read my book & was very impressed with it. "This man Frye," he said, "does he—does he *teach*?" He evidently thought of me as some high-powered sustaining fund. Irving commented at that point that I was the Nietzschean Superman—I feel much more like the rope-dancer, on the point of busting his conk. Well, anyway, I taught, & thanks to Harron I had a good time—I don't know about the others. Nothing new in the first-year lecture. Very pleasant note this morning from Richard Ellmann of Harvard, who said he's spoken to a colleague of mine about my book at the M.L.A.—I thought Ken, who knows him, but Ken said no. Anyway, he said he admired the book's courage, & was using it as a compulsory text in a Blake & Yeats course he gives at Harvard.

[217] Robins kidding me at lunch about the tide at Moncton laying waste the whole countryside. I said it was primitive, mesozoic & out of time, which he corrected to full of slime. I said the bore had given me my idea of Leviathan, the sporting sea-monster who *is* the sea, & as for Muskoka Lakes, nothing ever *happened* there—that sort of thing. Then Ned [Pratt] wondering how to get crows out of his back yard, getting

permits to discharge firearms, etc. Someone suggested cats, but Ned said he'd rather have crows than cats, & in fact had bought himself an air-rifle to shoot amorous felines with. The spectacle of Ned lying on his bed drawing a bead on a tom-cat's prick with an air-rifle & chuckling over the silence of his deadly weapon is something I like dwelling on.[183] Rinehart's parcel of books came today:[184] some of their editors don't do much for their $250.

[218] Several good things consolidated out of the Blake seminar. My mind is still on Morris, & I repeated the "manufacture" point. Machines, Butler said, ought to be bodily organs: once they become autonomous it's the sign of tyrannical conditions in society. Morris could never have strung along permanently with Marx's idea of seizing the machines, because to him the only instrument of production is the human hand. Society doesn't plan for the artist; the artist plans for society, because the artist creates & society is created. Now the printing-press is a machine, & something that Milton may dimly have realized in Areopagitica is that wherever you have a book-machine you have the possibility of censorship. Hence Blake's manufactured book, the free form of the book as a manuscript in the strictest sense. Blake is a purer medievalist than the pre-Raphaelites, whose "pre" is Florentine 15th-c. realism, & his book is an illuminated manuscript, whereas the Kelmscott press sort of coloured-capital thing goes back to the incunabula block-printing stage. I *must* do an essay on Morris.[185] Anyway, there's a real Blake point that didn't get into *Fearful Symmetry*. The only prophecy Blake tried to get printed was probably suppressed in proof.

[219] I traced the sentiment-sensibility-melodrama progression in 18th c. prose. First a revolt against the Augustan supremacy of the reasoning consciousness in the name of emotion as a mature instead of a childish or primitive element; then the Byronic pose of misunderstood nobility, where you find yourself in a revolutionary attitude to society because you're refined & the world is coarse; then the gloomy misanthrope-hero & the exploring of the dark side of the moon—the night half of the mind. Gothic horror novels written for an insular Protestant middle-class public present wild caricatures of foreign, Catholic, aristocratic life as a kind of psychological katabasis. This goes with the *poète maudit* period & the business of "abandoning" (Johnson's very penetrating remark on Ossian) the conscious mind, Platonic fashion, to a titanic or daimonic involun-

tary upsurge of power. Enthusiasm becomes creative & the Muse & god mean something again. This is a revolutionary period, the period of Chatterton, Collins, Smart, Cowper & Ossian in poetry, all of whom abandoned their minds to some extent, & Monk Lewis & his cohorts in prose. The English culture, like English society, recovered its balance & got over its revolutionary scare. Romantic poetry puts the consciousness back on top with more democratic representation—the subconscious is the mythopoeic source of power & the consciousness damn well better remember it or else, but then the subconscious ceases to be titanic & becomes tender, erotic, even gay; the subconscious of Lewis Carroll & Kingsley & George Macdonald & Morris. Victorian society is an introverted society. Tennyson is seriously praised for never writing a line a mother couldn't read her daughter & yet allowed to get away with terrific aphrodisiac drenches as "Now sleeps the crimson petal, now the white." Re the introversion, you think of London in 1660 or 1760 as a public place, Johnson & his circle & coffee-houses & plays. London in 1860 you think of as empty, all the culture confined to homes. France on the other hand was extroverted: it had impressionist painting & Paris was still a public city.

[220] The use of frustration in art, the separated lovers of romance & the suspended episodes of serials, are closely connected with the presence in art of linear time. This element is in the serialized & episodic romance but *not* in the epic, which begins *in medias res*; it is in the chronicle play, where the rejection of Falstaff symbolizes the continuous frustration of life (the separation of the green world from the court), but not in tragedy or comedy. It is in tragedy only to the extent that tragedy is incomplete comedy. Soap operas & comic strips are as close to endless art as we can get: their unreality has something to do with the intolerable realism of their form.

Feb. 25. [Friday]

[221] Young Sawyer in after the nine o'clock lecture. A dismal day, with most of the people I met in a foul temper, including Hilliard [Trethewey] in the morning. Margaret [Newton] has gone on one of her heavy extroverted binges, & sat up playing cribbage with Jack Goldschmidt until about three in the morning. Both Helen & I are perverse about having other people up there,[186] & can't sleep until they leave. I don't know

why, but we reinforce one another. Stumbled at length into an uneasy dozing dream that I was in the Merton Library pointing out the Mob Quad[187] to Woodhouse, very proud of my knowledge, of being able to display it, & of having been connected with it. Curious. Sawyer, as I say, was in: he's a very eager learner & is hard to talk to because he interrupts so much. I was trying to articulate my dislike of *All Hallows' Eve*, but was too sleepy to get far. He gave me another one called *The Place of the Lion*, which looks much more promising. At lunch another long gossip about de Beaumont's compulsion neuroses: his hatred of the common room chair, his fighting with his office door (Ned [Pratt] claims he's finally torn the knob off, & Archie [Hare] says there's nothing in his office now anyway), his lecture-room mannerisms (diabolical laughter with rolling of shoulder at every witticism), and his refusal to buy stout for his wife's insomnia because of the expense. Came home & went to bed.

[222] David Parsons in in the evening, shillyshallying in the original sense. Wants to write & thinks South Africa is his writing home, knows he isn't fitted for graduate work, & is full of adolescent arse-bites. I couldn't help him much except to tell him that he didn't have to prove anything to anybody, even himself, that he was young enough & unmarried enough to play his hunch about writing, but that if it didn't work out he was to regard it as a negative experiment & not as a defeat. He's full of "testing" nonsense, & resolves to change his life-style by efforts of will. I said he could imitate only his best self, which isn't profound, but for someone in his situation might be useful. Talked to Margaret [Newton] afterwards—she was lonesome & Helen went to Newmarket for the Citizens' Forum meeting.[188] One of her child welfare concentration camps is trying to cure a little girl's fear of the dark by making her sleep alone in a huge gloomy attic: the child is going crazy & has big black circles under her eyes. It's a most progressive place; they don't do any strapping. The official reason for torturing the child is: "Dr. Blatz recommends isolation."

[223] The moment of illumination, the flash of Chik-hai Bardo,[189] the instant that Satan can't find:[190] that's the anastasis that arrests the time-rhythm of original sin, the Karma of being dragged involuntarily backwards. That is apocalypse: that's what each life leads to as its own fulfilment. Nobody can move toward it: inspiration, providence, instinct, intuition, all the metaphors of involuntary accuracy, including grace

itself, are groundswells carrying us along in a counter-movement, forward to the moment. We go by relaxing ourselves, & trying to put ourselves in the organized receptivity, the "negative capability," of being ready to listen to or look at whatever comes along. If it never comes, that's not our business. If death brings it, as the Tibetans say, that's the point about death. But to have something shown you & then refuse to admit that you saw anything of the kind: that's the sin against the Holy Spirit of inspiration which is not forgiven (i.e. makes it impossible for you to arrive at release or anastasis) either in this world or the next (Bardo). You can't expect something, or you'll find an oracle in every spiritual breeze that passes over you; you can't expect nothing, or you'll have in yourself no principle of escape.

[224] David Hoeniger asked me if T.S. Eliot were one of the books I wanted to write. I said no: I could write only about people who were open at the top, & he was sealed off at the top. I had no idea what I meant, but he understood. People who enter into religious systems as he has done deny the integrity of the verbal universe: the open top has something to do with the *als ob* basis of poetic truth. That's their affair: it merely leaves *me* with nothing to say. One thinks of the Pantheon with its hole in the roof, though I don't think I'm quite talking about religious eclecticism.

Feb. 26. [Saturday]

[225] Arsed around reading Williams' *Place of the Lion*, a much better book than All Hallows' Eve, but still bad: he's no artist. For about fifty pages he tries to let his story tell itself, but then gets morally itchy & starts fussing & mussing & grimacing & making points & preaching sermons & scolding his characters & twisting his allegory into cute little patterns. An unbelievably pedantic writer. This book makes Eliot's point about the Chesterton influence[191] much clearer. Like Chesterton, he can't think of the arts except as a source of homiletic points. C.S. Lewis must be an influence too, & a bad one. Well, anyway, I finished the damn book & went to the President's reception for the F's at four. Margaret Fairley, Robert Finch, the Fords, Miss Fernold [Fernald], Wally Field, the Fishers—some of my best friends are F's. Some W's & a few B's, or sons of B's. Lacey died today at around noon. Satan the accuser is very busy with me these days: it isn't so bad when he quotes Scripture: the trouble

is that he also knows the law. However, there was a brief flurry with [Harold] Bennett, who loses his head easily, over a supposed clash between the funeral & the colloquium. Eventually he phoned the family & learned that the funeral will be Tuesday. The Fishers had planned to eat sandwiches in Joe's office before going out for the evening, but Joe forgot his keys, so they came home & ate sandwiches in our parlor, as they didn't want to go home & confuse their dog. After that we went over to the Brieger's to see Kathleen Fenwick, down from Ottawa to continue the series I started. Energetic but not reflective conversation. The Telegram interviewed me this morning on a statement of Dana Porter's against using novels as models of English in schools. I said it brought together the spoken & written word. The Telegram is an excellent paper under McCullagh, I'm afraid.[192] Jim Scott does a good book page.

Feb. 27. [Sunday]

[226] Spent Sunday reading & writing the end of my paper.[193] The trick was to bite off a single point & make it clearly, so I made the verbal universe point. It seems to be led up to with some logic. Various irrelevant speculations occurred to me. One was that Dante is in the final canto of Paradiso really looking into the secrets of God, as per I Cor. ii, 10. Three circles with Christ in the middle, but Christ elongates into a cruciform shape in which Dante recognizes the source & seed of his own life. That's the three-formed genital organ of creation, of which the mystic rose of the creature is the feminine counterpart. I daresay that would shock a lot of people, including Dante himself, but only because we're afraid of the other sterile prick of the mountain of purgatory, aimed at paradise but not quite getting there. Dante was misled by the false doctrine of purgatory, I think, & couldn't see that the mountain was the Tower of Babel, ejaculating a seed that never fertilizes but, like Onan's [Genesis 38:8–9], falls back to the earth. He has this pattern in, but for human souls he buggers it with purgatory. I still haven't the relation of Bardo to purgatory clear, but I feel that purgatory must be an illegitimate adaptation of Bardo. Not that Yeats & Charles Williams have done any better. Once more I skipped the offer of a Hart House concert.

Feb. 28. [Monday]

[227] February closes effectively with my paper;[194] but I deliberately let myself get into a dither over the paper in order to let my work go—

essays, letters, reading even, God knows what, just to gloat over twenty pages of stuff that could just as well, from the time I've put on it, be fifty pages. (For the time was *not* spent in the usual revision.) Nothing much happened in the morning—the lecture was dull (Bacon's essays, which I've never figured out how to lecture on), [Peter] Fisher was dull, though we discussed tragedy & comedy, & lunch was dull. The paper was all right. Finch didn't show up, & must have been puzzled by my remarks to him at Smith's reception, which implied that he knew about it. I seem fated to say the wrong thing to Finch. Priestley chaired the meeting. I borrowed his watch & timed it beautifully, except that that damned tickle on the right side of my throat woke up half way through. Someone brought me a glass of water & as I kept on [Fulton] Anderson solemnly marched out & returned with a jug. However, I got through. The attendance was mainly English—Anderson was the only non-English person who talked; he gave a short summary of my paper, said he liked it, & walked out. Marshall McLuhan went after me with talk about essences & so on—Helen Garrett reported from Jack that he'd said he was out to get me. He didn't, quite, though a stranger would have been startled by his tone. Actually, I imagine he agreed with a fair amount of the paper, though he didn't say so when I went home with him. Jack Garrett said it was magnificent. Woodhouse (who seemed tired and may possibly have thought himself glanced at, though nothing was further from my intentions: Woodhouse tries to sound like a pedant, but he's really a great man, & doesn't fool me for a minute) said I should print it as it is in spite of my disclaimer, & Priestley & [Harold] Wilson seemed to approve—Wilson especially; Priestley is pure *Wissenschaft* after all. He said I was as agile as a lightweight boxing champion, & possibly part of his mind thinks of agile people as lightweights. I was disappointed only in the quality of attendance: too much my own crowd of M.A. English people (even one undergraduate, Gloria Fisher) & too few from other departments.

[228] McLuhan again on his anti-English line—I think Jack Garrett is right in regarding it as a phobia. Met Helen for cocktails at the Park Plaza, & then dinner at Maison Doré—a sudden impulse of hers broke our boycott of that place & we had a wonderful dinner very well & promptly served.[195] It was a fine celebration altogether. The bar waiter overcharged me a dime on my second Martini, which he said was imported vermouth & the best gin because he didn't want to serve anything cheap to a person of taste. I couldn't have distinguished the two Martinis to save my life, so it was worth a dime.

[229] [Peter] Fisher's only idea was that the fool at the end of Yeats' phases is regarded by the world as a comic hero in a tragic context, whereas the point that stops the wheel turning is the point at which he becomes the tragic hero in the comic context: the ambiguity of Samson, Jesus & Lear. Macbeth is the opposite of Lear, the Saul usurper. Lear is royal Lear, always. The comic hero in the comic context is, if anything, the Quixote-Malvolio carnival butt. The tragic hero in the tragic context is much the same—the pharmakos. The rejection of Falstaff *must* come in the chronicle play—the endless serial which has no dramatic resolution inherent in its form—for that makes Falstaff the fool, the comic hero in the tragic context; the green world never uniting with the red & white world, the cycle going through & starting over.

Mar. 1. [Tuesday]

[230] Tried to get a jump on work today by marking ten essays & starting one of the Kaplan books I have to do for C.B.C. More views on the paper. Irving was silent about it, curiously for him; it may be an accident. Maclean [Ken MacLean] said it was wonderful, especially the first part: said somebody there said that nobody like me had been around for five hundred years. That brings us smack into Lydgate & Occleve, very clumping & pedantic people. I record praise partly because I think the ego is perhaps the spur of the imagination, & the gratifying of its vanity acts as a spark plug to creation. Also, it confirms the feeling of being on the right track. Shrove Tuesday, so, as I said, I didn't really need to start my essays till tomorrow.

[231] Lacey's funeral at Eaton Memorial. [Harold] Bennett read the service & [John] Line did the eulogy. The college came out of [it] with great dignity & the choir's *Nunc Dimittis* was fine, but Maclennan's voice is unpleasantly synthetic—chants & moans. I said impatiently that they should read the account of the Struldbrugs[196] at funerals—not too tasteful a remark.

[232] Morris is still going strong—anarchism this morning. Nothing new except that a state grows into an empire because the first principle of a state is to fight its neighbors until it eats or is eaten. The empire grows into a world-state & becomes a dinosaur of bulging flesh & a peanut brain in a capital city, breaks down, small states arise, & the same

process goes around again. Morris' interest in useful arts & his anarchism come together on a decentralization of the state of which the Dark Ages is the analogy. His Utopia has no World State, but in it nothing exists but the *community* of England, which has been rediscovered once the state has been destroyed. R.K. lecture an attempt to begin a deductive review—I started off on the Word of God as book, but didn't dredge up anything fresh. Too many questions perhaps. I said *maybe* the Reformation, by making the Bible autonomous, introduced a principle of infinite emancipation of which liberalism, democracy, toleration, equalization of opportunity, were all by-products—at least the belief in them was. I don't know if that's true historically, but it is in other respects. Lautenslager, blast him, wants me to preach at Howard Park on Mar. 13. I will, too, partly for a penance I suspect I need & partly for a test to see whether I can behave normally in a Church without getting solemn & oracular & emotionally stampeded & influenced by my audience. All those things mean I'm still afraid of the Church.

[233] McLuhan did say something after all yesterday, about Germans. Said when a German met another human being it was like a root meeting a stone: he had to warp & twist himself into the most extraordinary convolutions to get around the unpleasant fact of someone else's existence. I also brought up a point Ken [MacLean] mentioned which has been worrying me: Edmund Wilson is as informed and precise a critic I know on everything since about Rousseau. Behind that (Swift or Ben Jonson) he's an ignoramus, & the more earnest & explicit he gets the more fatuous he sounds. I have experienced myself some feeling of culture as reaching a great divide around 1776, when the American phase of history began, & of a great difficulty in fitting the traditional & modern sets of values together. The contrast between say ⌐ [Tragicomedy] & ʎ [Rencontre] is linked with this.[197]

Mar. 2. [*Wednesday*]

[234] Nothing happened today except that I skipped Council again, in order to come home & do papers. The Morris lecture was very good, what with remarks about community centres, with good fellowship & endless folk dances & picnics & other forms of extroverted cheer. I didn't say so much that's new, except that I'm beginning to get clearer in my mind the real significance of Morris' "manufacture": the sort of thing

Zen Buddhism brings out in its doctrine of work. Also my culture-begins-in-the-Sabbath doctrine of leisure as the growing point of creativity: a good point for the first day of Lent, not that I think much of Lent. Spent a long time in the Forum office, mostly assigning books. The 2i lecture was on Browne—nothing there, except that I'm beginning to speculate on a link between my cutting-out-of-motivation point and the Spinozistic tradition of the rejection of final causes—whether *that* has anything to do with the present "existentialist" incubus, as perhaps a rejection of evolutionary teleology. Speaking of evolution, that's coming up again soon, & I should do some thinking about what Shaw means by metabiology.

Mar. 3. [Thursday]

[235] I think there's a jinx on my Blake & Jung paper, also on the damn course. Benton Misener is a man I should never have let into the course—an emotional lame brain who got converted to God knows what by my Milton lectures & took the Blake course for inspiration. He has, according to Beharriell, been talking about his paper for weeks, but didn't turn up to do it. Coming right after Breen it makes me look pretty silly, & unlike Breen, who will be quite happy on Mayfair, I probably haven't heard the end of it. I'm getting fed up with being the cynosure of mental spastics. Of course the paper was too much for him, but why didn't he duck out of it in time? The last time I assigned a Blake & Jung paper was to Thorburn, who not only didn't turn up, but had a complete nervous breakdown & became a violent homosexual. However, I'm ungrateful to destiny: I wanted to expound Jung in order to get a detached view of a possible paper on the subject. I expounded Jung beautifully, but I didn't get him related to Blake much. In the first place, Jung's later thought loses its grip on the original libido book,[198] where he's closest to Blake, & in the second place all that stuff about types, introversion & extroversion, persona & soul-image, isn't particularly Blakean. It throws a suggestive light on the romance & perhaps even on the drama, but Jung is a ⅂ [Tragicomedy] man, not an L [Liberal] one.[199]

[236] The R.K. lecture tried to make some sort of pattern out of the three meanings of Word of God, as Christ, as the Bible, as the original or ground of created objects, Son, Spirit & Father. I'll try to bounce the Trinity off my fourth-year kids next Tuesday. It's clearing a little, but not much.

Mar. 4. [Friday]

[237] Helen got flu today and spent most of the morning upside down. I expected her to have Tillie Cowan for lunch, but she called that off, & I left her alone until about half-past two. She was all right fundamentally: it's the hit & run kind. However, I finished the 2i essays.[200] Fifty of them on More's Utopia. At least thirty-five of them said you can't have a perfect society without perfect individuals, & all social improvement must begin in the human heart. It's so nice to be living under a democracy, where people can think for themselves & aren't ideologically indoctrinated. The Spenser lecture said that imitative harmony made the poetry a third allegory of the subject, a rhetorical allegory as the historical allegory is grammatical & the philosophical a logical or propositional one.

Mar. 5. [Saturday]

[238] This morning I went down to finish up odds & ends—letters to Jack Nicol & Richard Ellmann, a letter to the New Statesman bawling the beejesus out of them for a review on Blake that hadn't mentioned me, etc.[201] After listening to the voice of the accuser for a long time, I'm gradually getting a slight feeling of deliverance from the law. That is, I'm really completely detached from my book, as I think I've said, & I don't mind in the least squawking like hell about it on occasion. I feel almost that I am outgrowing, not only the desire for dignity, but the desire for integrity. It has something to do with shaking off my animus role, which I hope I'm gradually doing. Intelligent & sensitive women have often quite literally laid down the law to me.

[239] I ran into Jerry Riddell this morning & explained the status of the college to him—about the way my kids are consolidating into a middle-class united front—their indifference to social problems, their apathy about the revolutionary situation, their intense religiosity, & the gradual wiping out of the earnest evangelical basis of the college, & so on. Jerry has an uneasy manner & he has the knack of making me feel profoundly embarrassed for no particular reason.

[240] This afternoon I did various odd jobs like reading overdue essays, & Helen on an impulse asked Jean Elder in tonight. She seemed to be

recovering from flu & seemed gloomy about the approach of middle age (her feet get bigger, a contingency that wasn't in the books about the problems of middle-aged spinsters) & seemed to be very conscious of all the women she knew who were younger & had more energy & better clothes.

[241] I've been reading Kafka today for my broadcast—a silly biography by Max Brod & his own published stories. Some of them very fine—the audacity of his imagination is very bracing, & his sardonic humor is usually in charge, except when he feels he isn't being honest unless he includes the irony of the situation. I think I'll do a good broadcast on him: my main points are the Chaplinesque figure at the centre & the Book of Job as the sun he revolves around.

[242] Another point I must start to think about is this. All thought is talking to oneself. All prayer is talking to God. The difference between thought & prayer thus depends on one's conception of where God is. If you accept the Thou Art That doctrine,[202] prayer is controlled & directed thinking. Similarly the difference between grace & inspiration depends on the location of God.

Mar. 6. [Sunday]

[243] Rather an aimless Sunday in which I tried to begin the Kafka paper, without much success. Not the usual play of mind I usually cherish Sunday for—I'm working too hard, or at any rate have too many things on my mind. Yesterday I sent six reasons for teaching English off to Bob Macdonald [McDonald], who is in charge of the A.T.E. [Association of Teachers of English] publicity campaign, with a note at the bottom saying I owed my success as an English teacher to never thinking why I was doing it. That was just another little something dropped on me—it came Thursday night when the Acta kids were in. Incidentally, that Harry Green lad who is to be next year's editor seems a very bright boy. Listened to Beethoven's Serenade op. 8 this morning: it has the same episodic structure as the late quartets, & I wonder what the connection is. The Stage 49[203] tonight did Moby Dick, quite well as I thought.

Mar. 7. [Monday]

[244] I gave my second year kids back their essays,[204] & bawled them

out for being prudish & over-moralizing. The slightest shock at this time is enough to push them out of that giggily self-conscious adolescent state of being stimulated by the slightest reference to copulation or excretion. But if the shock doesn't come they'll make it a fixation & become really prudish—at least some of them will.

[245] [Peter] Fisher left this Korzybski book[205] with me—a "non-Aristotelian" synthesis of what he's after. He's discovered that nature is the mirror of the human mind or body, & is trying to relate verbal patterns to physiological neural reflexes. Sounds interesting but, as far as I've gone, which isn't far, quixotic. In any case it's quadrivial. Fisher obviously didn't think much, either of my paper, which he called high & dry, or of the colloquium as an idea. It didn't work out properly, either, from my point of view. I spoke of the wistful way the Nazis had developed Plato's infernal doctrine of the "golden men" (in the Nazis gold is taken literally, so that you can see the gold in the Nordic hair) as a socially necessary lie. Also of the conception of rhetoric, which ought to be only the study of figures, as oratory, the debased interested form of magical verbal vibrations. He doesn't altogether approve of my editing the Forum—at least, he remarked that it must take a lot of time from the sort of thing I really want to do. I said the voice of the accuser encouraged me to believe that when I died he would be judge and say: "What have you done that you didn't want to do? Nothing else counts here."

[246] Fisher is one of the few people I relax with, because I don't give out to him. He's also one of the few who defines his attitude in a way that doesn't tie me down. I am never satisfied with professing Christians, even though I may be one myself, & of course I am still less satisfied with the people who don't get the point of religion. His Orientalism is an open top, so to speak, & I get claustrophobia if I can't find someone with an open top. Like the ape in Kafka's story,[206] I don't want freedom; I just want a way out. Lately I've become more conscious of the limitations of his mind. Partly morbidity, I suppose: the same compulsion Eleanor has of fastening on a weak spot somewhere in all her friends, & looking at every wart as a potential cancer. (That's a frenzy of honesty that Oliver Cromwell, talking to his portrait painter, didn't arrive at. If he had he'd have been a more typical Puritan, a Puritan with the everlasting-no sense of the indwelling accuser, & so would never have become Carlyle's hero, a Shaun to Carlyle's Shem.) However, the tendency to idealize friends & project archetypes on them has to be checked too.

[247] Frances Wees phoned me tonight—she's so pure an example of herself she bewilders me. She's got to be a widely recognized female novelist just by being her cuddly viscerotomic sentimental female self. Something in her approach is so intimate that I feel rude unless I start becoming earnest & avuncular. Even over a phone a hand steals out to pat her backside, & by the time I hang up I'm lowing at her like a cow.

Mar. 8. [Tuesday]

[248] Huxley began today in a shower of protests about my ignorance of evolution. I noted the Hegelian dialectic in him but did not take it far. The R.K. was the one where I hoped a doctrine of the Trinity would emerge, & it did, up to a point, like this:

	as creative power of God	— Father
Word of God	as person of Christ	— Son
	as mental or spiritual form of Bible	— Spirit

I said the Spirit is the indwelling Everlasting Gospel which articulates itself, the Father the power on the other side of Nature who can never be approached directly or we get Fate and a Final Cause, at best an old goat with whiskers. I got into some deep water over three persons as *masks*, united in One Word, not one substance, their real form concealed, revealed only as operations of the Word. The opening of Genesis makes it obvious that all objects are in their real or uncreated (unborn) form words of God.

[249] I was tired & staggered home early—a luncheon date with Marjorie King fell through, & I went home to find Tillie Cowan having lunch with Helen. I revised my Kafka paper and read Korzybsky [Korzybski], who seems to me to have something on the ball, though perhaps not all he thinks he has. My Kafka paper says his main figure has three allegorical strands: the Jew in a Gentile community, the artist in society, & Kafka as the son of his father. Put them together & you have, besides Kafka, Joyce's Shem.

Mar. 9. [Wednesday]

[250] Two lectures, a lunch for de Tolnay, a god-damned Library com-

mittee meeting, a hell of a waste of time because of a general administrative bitch-up—they were going to build a new Library, Robins & Peggy Ray drew up plans, & then the Board funked the building plans which we were nevertheless supposed to consider. Then de Tolnay's lecture—fascinating stuff about the Protestantism of Valdes & Ochino coming through Vittoria Colonna into Michelangelo. The Last Judgement shows the uselessness of intercession of saints. The Virgin is supported by the Dove, souls rise without wings borne up by faith alone, & so on. Some of the influences seemed to me to be gazelle-like leaps but I suppose his erudition covers them, & it's amusing to think of the Sistine harboring Lutheranism—maybe that was why they befouled it with candle grease & breeches. He didn't sufficiently consider the fact that Protestant & Catholic differences aren't visible once the Last Judgement begins, as the activity of the Church militant then stops. The lunch was mainly [Norman J.] Endicott protesting about me as a theological critic. I attempted to assure him that I wasn't, without success.

[251] Huxley seems to interest the kids, but he doesn't go so well from my point of view. The ideas he starts are germinal & I've barely formulated them. There's a lot of potential Freud in Huxley: he describes conscience very much as a superego, & he seems to suggest that a class society is a Saturnalia of the pleasure-principle (the struggle for profits) over against a reality principle which begins as struggle for existence in nature & ends as struggle for the fulfilment of natural powers in art. He's not crude, & doesn't try to identify evolution with progress. The distinction between artifice & artificiality, between the art that grows naturally out of nature & the art that falls from nature through pride, is there too. Something Pelagian too: redemption of nature by free will.

[252] I didn't realize the Renaissance painters sketched their figures in the nude before completing the finished painting. Hence some very powerful drawings of Michelangelo that actually show a nude virgin.[207]

[253] A very bad habit is developing in the College of asking retired people back after the customary two years. The pernicious practice extends the actual retiring age to 70. Sissons' sense of proportion completely collapsed this year & he's now essentially a neurotic. Now Trethewey tells me they're going to do the same thing with that poor old lunatic de Beaumont. His reasons are purely economic: de Beaumont's had an excellent salary (ten times what he's worth) for many years but

has been paying heavy income tax on it, so now he'll need the money. Of course rules aren't perfect: de Beaumont should have been pensioned off years ago, Sissons should have gone on the dot, & Pratt & Robins shouldn't go for a long time yet. I know Trethewey feels about de Beaumont as I do about Robins, but the hell with this mealy-mouthed fair-mindedness.

Mar. 10. [Thursday]

[254] Terrific snowfall all day: I was out twice, but didn't make much impression on it. I got into conversation with a four-year-old girl who was busy with a broom. "You can't sweep, can you?" she said. "No," I said, "I haven't a broom." She said very sympathetically: "Didn't your mummy let you have a broom?" My feeling of vague tiredness still persists. I didn't work so hard this morning either, because that cute Mallinson girl took the full two hours to read her paper. Don Harron asked about a possible Eros-hero link (etymological or at least paronomasia), and she suggested that the Golden Net was partly Jung's enmeshing hair symbol. I want to say something next week about Yeats' symbols being those of the law in the wilderness: the mountain with the moon-god sitting on it. The first year R.K. lecture was a repetitive flop, but the third year nine o'clock began to chop a little bit out of Book II [of *The Faerie Queene*]. Via media, in the historical allegory Anglicanism, in the moral one Aristotelian temperance, is between extremes superficially contrasted but essentially one. Hence the integration of the soul against the bondage of externality, the defense of Alma against Maleger, falls between two tests for Guyon alone:[208] Mammon or over-activity (grabbing money as an end instead of a means is the external fallacy too) and the Bower of Bliss or passivity. The free man is active, the man bound by the tyranny-anarchy of desire (vs. the order of reason) bound to externalize the source of his compulsion, hence idolatry. "Beauty & money" are explicitly referred to. Mammon is Charybdis, the gulf of greediness, the BB [Bower of Bliss] Scylla, the siren magnetic rock. One sucks down (cave), & the other is the illusory island that turns out to be a rock or a Leviathan. Historically, the cave is Puritan capitalism & the BB Catholic eroticism.

[255] Last night was the damndest meeting of the A.T.E. [Association of Teachers of English]—Dana Porter turned up, made some aimless & stupid remarks, & got well grilled. He's not a bad sort really, & seemed

impressed. As Woodhouse said, if he didn't bring much illumination, he may have taken some away with him. I was very pleased at the way the women spoke up, which is unusual in public meetings. Some very genuine idealism came through. It's clear that our good English teachers are good because of a very genuine idealism. I don't know why I write the same phrase twice, unless it's to shout myself down.

Mar. 11. [Friday]

[256] Today a very decent & unaffected Englishman named [Ronald] Peacock turned up. He's at Manchester in German, succeeding Barker Fairley, & did our second colloquium for us on T.S. Eliot & poetic drama. I was disappointed, as I'd rather have had his other talk to the German people on German romanticism. I told Priestly beforehand I thought the colloquium would succeed only if it refrained from discussing sex, politics, religion & T.S. Eliot. He wasn't a very good discussion leader, & the topic was so specialized it was a purely English show anyway. Not much of importance said. I'm afraid Toronto will get a bad reputation for murdering its guests. However, Peacock gave me a warm invitation to visit him at Manchester. I might do it too. At lunch Woodhouse on my left and Flenley on my right were discussing Nuffield scholarships, which, though very badly publicized, offer a married man free passage over & back with wife plus £600, which would be not bad even if the College didn't make it up.[209] Woodhouse is a terrific power, being on the Selection Committee, & he's given a scholarship next year to his other favorite Priestley: I hope he doesn't feel he'll have to cool off with me. I suppose there'll be no harm in applying for both that and a Guggenheim. A lot of discussion afterward about British universities which I found very dull. In the evening we went to see Eleanor [Godfrey] & Bill [Graham]. Rosie cuddled up to me all evening: as I said, she's the only living creature who's discovered that I'm just a person at heart.[210] The Drainies came in later: he's on the radio, was Ishmael in a very good Moby Dick they did last Sunday. Don Harron brought him to my lectures & he's one of my worshippers. His very pretty wife was in on the adulation too, & it was very good to see them in the company of Eleanor & Bill, who don't think of me as someone likely to take off for the sky at a moment's notice. Peter Fisher says of dogs, re Rosie, that they seem intelligent to man only because, like sheep, they're stupid as animals. He says T.E. Lawrence hated zoos & was embarrassed by animals, because

they reminded him of his imperfect development from them. They get along better with children, who are more like them. Cats in particular ignore all the silly efforts that dogs make to comprehend man.

[257] Look into & away from a bright light & you see a red spot. Close your eyes & it turns green. Thus Jung is right: the world of closed eyes is complementary & compensatory. The green world in Shakespearean comedy is not strictly a dream-world, but it has dream links.

[258] I said of Marjorie Hope Nicolson that she was a very masculine woman who, unlike a real man, was afraid to reveal the feminine side of her nature.

[259] When automobiles began, their shape was that of the old buggy, & it's taken them some time to evolve away from it. They aren't yet at their proper shape, but are getting there. I understand that human Robots are getting fantastically elaborate, & I suppose their shape too is influenced by the conventional form of the human body. It'll be interesting to see what shape it develops into—might be a theme for a story. What, psychologically, is the connection in eeriness between the robot & the ghost?

[260] Helen showed me with great glee a Tampax ad that said "the principle of internal absorption was known for many years, but it was only after Tampax was invented that you could actually wear it right in your own home."

[261] Bowman said cemeteries in Okinawa, which is as much Chinese as Japanese, were womb-shaped, & full of beautiful jars containing the bones of the dead which had been carefully scraped by virgins (symbols I suppose of the return to the mother). I said it was a most ingenious way of discouraging virginity. Robins said the same custom is B.C. Indian.

[262] The reason Jesus is so tough about calling people fools is that "thou fool" is psychologically quite different from "you're a fool." He is talking about the central situation of pathos, as I call it, the utter exclusion of an individual from a group, the determination to shut him off from everything that makes up his individuality except his own ego or Selfhood. As this imprisonment is the definition of hell according to

Blake, Jesus also means that no one can send another to hell, & if he tries he lands there himself. It's a pretty grim thing to say "go to hell" and mean it: that's the bottomless pit that opens during Claudius' prayer in *Hamlet*. To say "thou fool" in the sense of denying a person's right to belong to any human group whatever is worse than murder, because it aims at a deeper extinction of the spirit, at despair rather than death. But if a man tells me he has stolen money & I say "you're a fool," that's the opposite: it means he is acting in the way I'd want him to act if I desired his damnation, & so, as I don't want him to be a fool, the remark is charitable. This is all very simple, but it's part of a growing pattern. Jesus' fundamental act is to cast out devils, to locate the pharmakos in man & by driving it out achieve his catharsis. To identify the devil-state with an individual, to make him a scapegoat or a pure devil is the ultimate act of evil, & can come only from one who has made himself into a pure accuser, & so by a ghastly paradox becomes the Satan he attempts to project on another.

Mar. 12. [*Saturday*]

[263] Went down in an aimless sort of way to try to work on my sermon, but didn't. The pattern that's emerging is the same old goddamn pattern, & it's too complicated for a sermon. I was reading the stuff about wisdom in Proverbs and realized to what an extent the conception of Holy Spirit, the Sophia or feminine figure personifying wisdom, & the mother of Jesus fit together. The Holy Spirit is surely that of which the Virgin is an analogy. Somebody asked me about the Virgin Birth on Tuesday & I was afraid to say I thought it was nonsense, not because of the repercussions, but because of the nature of my influence. I may return to the point & say something like this: the Virgin Birth is in the Gospels because of Isaiah's prophecy where the word translated in the Septuagint as παρθενος [*parthenos*] means simply young woman. Hence, though the Virgin Birth is scriptural, there is another sense in which it is apocryphal, & so, while Protestantism accepts it, it tends, in striking contrast to the Catholic doctrine, to become unfunctional. This business of the larger basis of dogma is a difficult point of dialectic. It's easy for the idiot questioner to grin at a failure to fit his so-called logical patterns, such as, for instance, the question of canon. The basis of admitting only Hebrew texts to the O.T. is absurdly arbitrary, & while there's no logical way of

rebuilding the canon, it is none the less true that it does you far more good to read the Book of Wisdom than Chronicles. It is of course possible that a complete symbolic pattern would define the true canon.

[264] Well, anyway, the general direction of my idea is that all knowledge strikes root in the whole organism, & develops into wisdom. To know, e.g. a science, is not to think as an ego, but to follow the pattern of thought in the science, as though one's knowledge were a thought in a vast universal human mind. Similarly love is not "John loves Mary," but the following of the pattern of love. Hence value: we find by experience that science is better than superstition, art than vulgarity, love than hatred, because the former enter into a larger order, so that you lose yourself & find themselves [yourself] again in the former, & try to save yourself & get lost in the latter. Eventually you begin to wonder if this view of the world as a lot of egos trying to find love & science & art in the middle of hatred & superstition & vulgarity isn't a pretty relative one. Suppose the world is really just one man who is all art & science & love, with the hatred & so on infinitely removed from it? What I originally had in mind was the full trinitarian pattern, the community of men emerging from the coordination of art & science in the form of love, the objective coordination of nature emerging as mysterious power, & both making sense only as the same thing—separate they are, respectively, atomic humanitarianism & the ghost of the father, or Leviathan. I write this of course in my own shorthand.

[265] Party for the Garretts tonight: I hated to have to say goodbye to them, & I don't think Jack will be particularly happy in New Zealand. He will certainly turn violently anti-Labor; he & Helen are both social democrats only to the extent that that's opposition. Apparently they've been in touch with relatives in N.Z. & have been angling for the job a long time. The party was crowded & noisy, but I suppose people had the sort of good time they're supposed to have at such jams.

Mar. 13. [Sunday]

[266] Got through the church service all right: I think that it was technically quite a brilliant performance. My flock were there: Margaret Gayfer, Patchell, Stingle, Jamie Reaney. Ted Thompson [Thomson] & his brother [sister] Eleanor were obviously responsible for getting me there: Don

[Dawn] Wanless and Barbara Ewing were also there.[211] Outline of sermon pretty well as above: actually, though I didn't quite realize it at the time, it was the doctrine of Citta-matra. Elizabeth Lautenslager asked me abruptly why if I believed "all that," I didn't go to church. If I was right, weren't they fools? She's a very blunt, honest girl, & I could see her point clearly. She works like a galley slave to help her husband, who works like a galley slave to keep a church going, & here's a high-powered intellectual from the college who draws a crowd & works out a beautiful theological pattern & doesn't even attend church. It was too complicated however to explain the grounds I base my dispensation on. Then came a "fireside" discussion on Sunday observance, ironically enough. Earl finally released us at nine & drove us home, when we went up to drink beer with Margaret [Newton]. Ten bucks. Earl was full of College politics; the committee those dismal shitsacks on the Board, stampeded by the McKelcan sow, organized to check upon the morals of Acta after Peter Grant's poem,[212] & a long string of possibilities for the Presidency—Lockhart, [Art] Cragg, Vaughan, & so on. I thought it would be fulsome to say I preferred him to any of his candidates, though I do. Also the mistake the United Church made in putting up Willard Brewing, who is as deaf as a post & stupid, as Moderator. The trouble with having a layman as President is that then he has authority over theological appointments, an authority which of course [Walter T.] Brown not only used but abused.

Mar. 14. [Monday]

[267] The usual Monday of far too much beer with Peter Fisher, who was in slightly better form. We banged our heads against the wall of Plato's Republic, but nothing new emerged. A bloody meeting of the Art Committee: joint. Day, Boggs, Thurston, Watson, Christenson, Creighton, Grube & a man named Noxon who was absent are the new members. Purchasing sub-committee is a hangover responsibility for me. I drove the meeting hard & held it to an hour & a half. Undemocratic, maybe, but the Chairman's duty is to interpret the will of the meeting, & the will of that meeting was to get the hell out of there. Douglas Stewart, in Fine Art, is the new secretary.[213]

[268] Over to Woodhouse's to meet the exchange man, one [Walter P.] Bowman of Western Reserve. Very decent sort; rather commonplace, &

with a somewhat limited range of ideas. After trying to draw him out for a while, Woodhouse said the hell with it & proceeded to reopen the first colloquium. Apparently I'm the exchange from here to Michigan.[214]

Mar. 15. [Tuesday]

[269] Opened Samuel Butler this morning. I said that satire is an intellectual conception of society, & deals with pedants & bigots & cranks, & so requires a norm to bounce them off of, so to speak. It usually implies a low norm, or commonplace conventional person, & a high norm, or genuinely detached conventional person. Gulliver & Higgs are low norms: it isn't Swift's moral to say we should all be like Gulliver. The commonplace conventional is strong by virtue of his common-sense attitude, but is involved in the absurdity of the conventions themselves. But he & the absurd world reflect one another, like the normal & green worlds in Shakespeare, & the satiric resolution comes out of their interpenetration. Similarly with the Alice books, though that's the pure comedy pattern rather than the satiric one. I must work on the relationship of comic & satiric resolutions from this point of view: my old "parabasis" problem. In Swift the high norm comes out in things like the humanity of the king of Brobdingnag: the Houyhnhnms, however, are intended to represent the fact that the high norm is unattainable. In Erewhon the low norm is Higgs & the high one the high Ydgrunites, people with an attitude like Montaigne's. Butler of course developed this into his gospel of worldly wisdom, which I just began to expound. The R.K. lecture said some more on the Trinity. Exploring nature leads to a search for concealed power in or behind nature; liberal humanism explores history. So we get a humanized power in nature & a deified love or sense of community in history. There is no natural religion & no historical religion: Christianity teaches that these two gods will remain forever apart unless seen to be the same thing. Both are essential & valid, & both are essentially antithetical. That leaves me with the nature of Christ to expound next Tuesday.

[270] Lunch with Bowman, who continued amiable & a bit naive. Then I went back home for a bath & a rest, & had two cocktails before dinner, which made me feel sophisticated for the moment & sleepy for the rest of the evening & set me back two bucks. It biteth like a serpent & stingeth like an adder,[215] & costeth me two ruddy bucks. The dinner was wonderful: a superb steak. Bowman's paper wasn't much, but he was so disarm-

ing that an excellent discussion finally got going. The important principle that emerged for me was: in my music & poetry article[216] I discovered that the ordinary term "musical," meaning pleasant-sounding, was not, & in fact tended to be the opposite of, the kind of poetry that showed the influence of the art of music. I am now convinced that exactly the same thing is true of the word "pictorial." Tennyson tries to produce elaborate harmonies of sound, & does, but that doesn't convince me that he knows or cares about music. He also builds up very elaborate pictures, like the nude Venus in *Oenone*, but that doesn't convince me that he knows or cares about painting, & it's a matter of record that he didn't. But when Browning says "to get on faster" in The Flight of the Duchess [l. 829] I know he knows music, & when his tulip blows out its bell like a bubble of blood[217] I know he knows painting. It isn't pictorialism that's the mark of an unpainterly poet: it's the transfer to poetry of the sense of vivid quick sketching (Herrick's *Upon Julia's Clothes*) (also of course Finch's poem),[218] of pictorial masses & composition & recession of planes & color-tones. *Not* shades of color: Bowman seemed to assume that an interest in differentiating colors marked an interest in painting. I said Blake's color-words in poetry were completely heraldic, & one would never dream that Blake thought of his poems as being simultaneously paintings if we had only the former. He said you don't buy a picture by color any more than you would a horse. Grant said many excellent things, among them the fashion of heavy varnishing (1700–00) in order to monotonize color & bring out masses: when we clean National Gallery pictures today we bring out the color, & so see them as we want to see them, which we naturally assume to be the true way. I'll think about this and try to organize a pictorial sequel or appendix to the *Music & Poetry*.

Mar. 16. [Wednesday]

[271] I seem to be becoming more and more of a priest. Also the little buggers signal to each other about my lectures. Joan Arnold, who of course has turned Anglo-Catholic, came to 2i today because somebody had told her that it was Hooker. So she listened to all that damn stuff about law & came up with Hope Arnott afterward to ask me if marital love bred idolatry. I said no. Then Barbara Ewing, who made an appointment Sunday night after the service, came in to tell me that the Last Judgement had passed on her & she wanted to turn Roman Catholic. It

was my first actual encounter with the process. It's the thing Jung is talking about, all right, & I'm convinced that one should wait till the dust settles. She'll do that anyway: there's far more involved. The ego in its last desperate stand wants to apotheosize itself in the one real human institution, & that's why so many Catholic converts, Thomas Merton for instance, are sanctified demons, arrogant snobs who find, not the rule of charity, but the charitable rule. I told her to wait until the problem of what *she* was to do looked less important, because I'm sure that if you just wait & hold yourself together, the real thing comes through, & it never quite does if you turn Catholic. I worried a bit over "whether I'd done the right thing," but with my convictions I had to say that or nothing. She's a very good girl, so good that she said, not "should I turn Catholic?" but "why are you not a Catholic?" which was the question I could answer. I was agreeably surprised to find how detached I was, not stampeded in either direction.

[272] I went to Hart House for lunch & George Pepper did a really brilliant job of reviewing some unpretentious but rather dull mountain pictures by Mr. & Mrs. Peter Whyte of Banff, obviously very cultivated people who have fun painting. All top-of-the-spectrum color range, afraid of the reds & yellows that are like brass in a choir. Then I went to hear Irving's lecture, which I'm afraid I didn't attend to very carefully. I'm worried about my own, & I don't know quite where to take off from. Urwick evidently felt that mere social work is all very well, but, after all, the spiritual values of life are what count. I think that's horseshit. I came home with Margaret [Newton]—Helen had been cleaning house all day & was a little petulant, as Mrs. Horton didn't show up. Went to the Morgans for dinner. [J.S.] Morgan talked very well & is an enthusiastic Oxonian—I'm a lukewarm one, but I kept going. A friend of his named Isaacs, like Morgan a Jesus [College] man, was the war's first casualty— up in a training plane when the first sirens sounded, & for some reason burst into flames and crashed, killed within two minutes of Chamberlain's speech. Morgan said he learned that at a Jesus Gaudy,[219] which sounded profane. Margaret Fairley was there, & David Hoag & his wife. I didn't get much impression of him. He has a low voice & Morgan's deaf. He showed me a remark from the Vice-Chancellor's speech: "fortunately the College system prevents plans of expanding the university population from getting very far." I also complained mildly about a letter I got this morning from somebody in Minnesota named David

Erdman who's finished 600 pages of a book on Blake & has roughed out 300 more, & will I read it?[220] Morgan gave me several pointers to use for Forum material.

[273] Samuel Butler is opening up: the importance of heredity & privilege in society means the importance of the state of nature in society, for society speaks with the deep conservatism of nature. That unites the natural & counter-natural or artificial aspects of society more closely— well, no, it doesn't really, but defines the forms of natural society more clearly than Huxley. The individualized dislike of cooperation (prosecuting people for bad luck) is natural too.

Mar. 17. [Thursday]

[274] Grim morning: Ann Carnwath was in in what may be the first stage of dementia praecox. I mean that: a terrible magic circle she can't break out of: a mixture of self-love and self-hatred in which she knows everything about herself. Great-grandfather a drunk, grandfather a Methodist in reaction who wouldn't let his children have any fun; father, & apparently mother too, work out their parental revolt by forcing *their* children, a boy & a girl, into dancing schools & parties; both are studious & religious; both have breakdowns. The parents get stubborn & Ann is terrified they'll return any moment from Virginia & say what's all this nonsense; we went through it all with your brother and we're damned if you—and so on & so on. I failed completely, did no good & may have done some harm. If I could only pick her up by accident & take her out for coffee or something. Jessie [Macpherson], I'm glad to learn, sees her every day & if she goes over will get her to the Psychiatric. I feel so helpless confronted by this sort of thing: and I'm so damned good on semicolons and dangling participles.

[275] Lunch at the Heliconian Club for Frances Wees.[221] At the head table with Lotta Dempsey, a fine beautiful creature who asked me what the six most beautiful words in the language were. I'm not very proud of my choice—the first six that came into my head, of course: chrysanthemum, parchment, explosion, multitudinous, oriole & flageolet. Marjorie Campbell, who evidently does some writing, was on my other side. I thought Frances' speech was excellent—completely professional, quite detached about the relation of her stuff to real literature, & yet not

belittling or patronizing herself beyond a certain point, & recognizing too that if she practises writing on any level long enough she goes through the same process of improvement & concentration that the greatest writers do on the highest level. I was much more impressed than I expected to be.

[276] Forum meeting this evening: I met Doris' [Doris Mosdell's] objections I think quite adroitly: Helen said so anyway. I guess the Board will hold together, but I deeply regret my bungle over Shubik. There is a certain decadent luxury in remorse, of course, but not much, & it's silly to laugh hollowly about it. I continue to be convinced that repentance, as distinct from remorse, is something you have done for you.[222]

[277] Not much in the lectures: contrast of spiritual & physical effort in Books I & II of F.Q. [The Faerie Queene]. House of Holiness is the place of vision; House of Alma the physical body. Ross Beharriell & his wife were at church. I sometimes wonder about the workings of Providence— I seem to have touched a good many people as the result of an almost involuntary impulse. It may be an important event in Barbara Ewing's life (though I must be careful not to take her decision, whatever it is, as oracular), & possibly one of the people touched was myself. But I still think I should stick to semicolons & participles. After I got home from the Forum meeting Nancy Rowland phoned, so the day ended with me giving an impromptu lecture on Sartor Resartus over the telephone to a bewildered graduate student at a quarter to twelve . . .

[278] Occasionally people like Benton Misener do something silly & avoid me, thereby making the situation worse all around. I think it must be the rule of charity not to let them stew as I have done, but close the little buggers up.

Mar. 18. [Friday]

[279] For instance, Mary McFarlane had an appointment with me which she made Sunday evening & didn't turn up, & probably the same thing is involved. One thing in the Blake yesterday (1st yr. R.K., incidentally, on the Trinity, was a total flop): Byzantium is Magian culture, conceived by Yeats as classical tomb & Western womb, hence not only on the historical cycle but on the Bardo one, as the axis of both. I spoke of a

certain prudery in making moral judgements, e.g. about Fascism: "it's all very terrible of course, but after all it *is* what's coming, isn't it?" Contrast that with the poetry that he really feels deeply: "the ceremony of innocence is drowned" [Yeats, *The Second Coming*, l. 6].

[280] Lunch at S.C.R. [Senior Common Room] with Ned [Pratt] trying to find out who once told him the "one fucking medal" story. I owned up, & had to tell it twice, with great success both times. Curious about laughter: here it's simply (the joke, I mean) an elaborate pretext for letting one of the Bad Words emerge. I felt like the devil & after doing some copyreading at the Forum office went home, skipping yet another Culture Commission. I went to bed intending to go to sleep, but Helen climbed in beside me stark naked, so I didn't. In the evening Clarence Lemke, Duke Boissoneau[223] & June Clark came in. Mostly questions from Lemke about what he refers to as "The Book." June is worried over my rejection of the historical Jesus: she wants a reality in the past to balance her present experience. I think she dimly surmises that I'm keeping it for the sake of an out that might let me out of Christianity altogether. My foreground reason is that the historical Jesus belongs logically only to an autonomous church with an unshakable tradition, which is the Roman Catholic Church in my opinion, though I think I understand Greek & Anglican claims. Once you see that historical tradition is the apocryphal shadow of the body of Christ, you realize that when you are changed by the Word of God into the Word of God you are absorbed into an eternal body: it isn't a Second Coming polarized by a First. I guess I do believe in pre-existence (eternal humanity of Jesus) as far as it goes. But if NNR [*There Is No Natural Religion*] really does include ARO [*All Religions Are One*] you need to come to terms with certain wise men of the east who were led to the same spot but departed another way. I said catharsis is achieved in tragedy, but the figures on the stage who produce it are purely figures on the stage: there's no actor in the dressing rooms & no saintly Jewish rabbi in Galilee. The person, or mask, is visible; the substance to a Protestant is forever invisible.

Mar. 19. [Saturday]

[281] In a state of complete nervous exhaustion—partly too much priestcraft & cure of souls. I seem however to have to go on with theological speculations. One involves the translation of the Bible. I keep

telling my kids that you can't just translate the Bible, but have to make up your mind on the basis of your own theology about ecclesia, metanoia, arton epiousion, presbyteros & episcope.[224] I say that there are consistent Catholic & Protestant translations of the Bible, but no consistent impartial ones. Now I know what the Catholic consistency is: it's a belief in the priority of the Church to the Bible, so from that point of view you can translate the Bible only into the language of Church doctrine. That for me is a circular but very efficient paradox. But what is Protestant consistency? Doesn't it stake its case on the possibility of an absolutely impartial translation, so as to keep the Word over the Church's head? If not, isn't a Protestant translation just as sacerdotal, & if so what's the shape of its Church? To me the Catholic case is overthrown by the mere possibility of an alternative translation, but what Protestantism implies I don't know, except that it certainly is not private judgement or reason or conscience or archaeological evidence that takes priority. In every case the Catholic church-consistency must be polarized by something with an open top.

[282] The other question is a reversion to Blake: what is immortal is a spiritual body, & that includes both the ego & its own, not that I've read Stirner's book.[225] The natural abstraction of the ego or body has nothing to do with the soul or spirit, the first act of which is to reach beyond the body into other relations. A man's social life, for instance, is clearly a part of himself, & it's impossible to think of life after death as a mere survival of the ego-abstraction. Everything I have loved—my emanation, Blake would call it—is as much a part of me as anything else in my character, & must survive if anything else in my character does. Helen is eternally part of my life as I am of hers, & so we are all members of one body & yet not married, for the Helen in my life is mine, & not the ego-abstraction people refer to when they name her. I attach my love to that abstraction, but love it only approximately. Your spiritual body is the invisible house you build of which the ego-abstraction is the doorkeeper or covering cherub. The person is the incarnation or visible mask of the real Self or Atman.[226]

Mar. 20. [Sunday]

[283] Headache & nervous exhaustion continued until I went out to Fulton Ave.[227] & ate one of my mother-in-law's dinners. Gave the Kafka broadcast at 5:45 & I think it was good: it was right on the nose as regards

timing, though as the movie review was ten seconds over I had to speed up. I think I read it quite well & it was good stuff: as good a review of Kafka in 750 words as anyone could reasonably expect. Read Henry James' *The Other House* all day, not yet finished, but it's very, very good—a curious folktale legend with all the Jungian patterns I'm looking for in romance.

Mar. 21. [Monday]

[284] First day of spring, which has started in in earnest. 2i lecture on Burton, then I learned that Hamilton has got a Beaver Club Overseas Scholarship & Peter Fisher, & perhaps H.N. Maclean, likely to go to R.M.C. [Royal Military College]. Things seem to be looking up. Uneventful lunch. Irving tells me the rumor that the U.B.C. budget is cut 70% is a canard, based on a cut of $70,000 from the Arts Budget which means only that the Legislature has finally caught up with Larry Mackenzie & his splurges. I then went & read the Forum editorials, writing one that isn't the masterpiece I thought it might be,[228] & went home & devoted the rest of the day to coddling myself. More specifically, to finishing *The Other House*, which proved disappointing, a beautifully finished mediocrity, I think. To bed early, & had a long series of strange dreams. One had me on the roof of a house with the house apparently moving about under me; some nervousness but above all a great puzzle as to what was moving it. Some reference evidently to the "doorkeeper" imagery above [par. 282]. Another one had me a student again kidnapped by S.P.S. [School of Practical Science] for hazing purposes. They knew me well & a friend of mine deserted me at their approach, whispering that it would be good for me. However, I was busy trying to talk myself out of the situation when I woke. The purpose of the hazing was the slighting remarks I was alleged to have made about engineering, which I was busily denying. May be some reference to a phenomenon Jung doesn't mention: an introvert trying to project before him his own extroverted self, or vice versa. This is the theme of Sitwell's Man Who Lost Himself,[229] which I read in my Freshman days & is an extrovert > introvert pattern. Henry James' *Jolly Corner* seems to be reversing the pattern: I was reading it just before I fell asleep. I was also looking at FW [*Finnegans Wake*], as I've rashly tied myself up to a "What To Do until Finnegan Wakes" talk at Michigan. Kenner is all wet about the "keys" on the last page being the keys of the church. The phrase is "the keys *to*," & it means

the keys to the Church, & to all churches. Shem looks at churches from behind, & holds the keys *of*, no *to*, dreamland—that phrase turns up a few pages earlier.[230]

Mar. 22. [Tuesday]

[285] I think I can work out FW by way of the Menippean satire: I've given a brilliant lecture on Butler I must write out here. The R.K. one was the last, thank God. June Clark seized the occasion to read me an open letter in the last fifteen minutes. The kids didn't like it, it was a corny & egotistic gesture, & it upset me a good deal, but I carried it off well except for a silly throaty peroration ending with the words "through the mercy of God.[231] I was sick afterwards at her stampeding me that way—I *must* keep my head absolutely clear & cool. It wasn't her fault, it was mine. Of course, for some silly reason I was nervous about that lecture, & in fact was quite dizzy & faint: I'd taken a chapel service—on Judas—& in general was being tempted not to keep it clean. Anyway I'm damn glad *that's* over. My point, such as it was, was that Creation & Apocalypse are not events in time but are psychological polarizations between the world which has been manifest & the world which is to be manifest. I explained Creation as Maya, magic, not illusion but a deliberately created illusion. Once Creation & Apocalypse disappear from time the Incarnation ceases to be an objective centre, & we realize that just as God redeems Job from nature by blocking him off at the first cause, so he redeems us from history by blocking us off at the First Coming. The hell with it. Moff Woodside gave me a tolerable limerick:

> There was a young curate of Ban,
> Who had loved a stained-glass St. Anne:
> With the aid of a ladder
> He eventually had her
> But came down no longer a man.

[286] Well, anyway, the Butler lecture said Butler was, like all satirists, something that it is now fashionable to call existential. Satire for him, as often for Browning, consists of putting the logical case for & the human case against, the latter arising as a kind of total human revolt against the rat-traps the former leads to. In considering the dumping of bananas at Halifax & the digging of gold out of Ontario ground & putting it under-

ground again in Kentucky, one can see simultaneously the logical case for it & the utter absurdity of it. This expands to a general high Ydgrunite attitude of preserving the human values while remaining detached from the logical case. Butler despises the zeal that makes religion logical, as in the Oxford Movement,[232] & above all he despises the religion of science. I also said that he puts the logical case for with such thoroughness that he often misses his satiric target through over-subtlety, fooling not only the general public, as in *The Fair Haven*, but himself, as in his Odyssey & Resurrection nonsense.[233] That's old: what's new is the sense of the satiric norm which upholds organism against machine, detached conventionality against living according to the law & the machinery of logic. Whenever ritual, or logical act, seems bound or confined, the total human reaction appears as an emancipating force. I don't know where the hell I'm going from here—I thought, until June Clark buggered it up, that I had an idea leading to the Social Work lecture, which could deal with rational man discovering that reason leads to law, machinery, ritual & Utopias, versus the existentialist conception of a total human being. I think the Social Work lecture should deal with the conception of charity, good works without attachment springing from vision, though of course in terms they can get. Not "another" world, but this world properly seen; also the folly of chopping up emotion, intellect, mind, body, etc. etc. Note that the word "essentially" is always so helpful at this point. Well, anyway, Butler was fanning out in another direction toward Joyce, who is in that tradition & often mentions Erewhon. Not that Joyce is a high Ydgrunite, but I think he gets his keys to dreamland through some deep plunge into the habit-energy that Butler deals with. Damn June Clark. Came home to find Helen sick again. *Morley* Clarke, who's in Princeton normally doing some thesis, phoned me "just to check on my views of the fallen world." Damn the fallen world.

[287] I think I'll begin the Social Work talk by saying that I think that the "*mere* social work is all very well, but of course a sense of spiritual values is what we *really* need" sort of line is bullshit. I may say something about the liberal dynamic in the humanities & religion, the need of keeping society open at the top & about the social work conception of charity contrasted with the handing out of the necessities of life to the underprivileged by the privileged to keep the former from revolting & the latter from thinking too meanly of themselves. Also the Mill point: democracy combines majority rule & minority right; but what gives a

minority a right? I may also develop my statement that the age of specialization is working itself out as an apology for being such a fish out of water. Also the old line that the psychiatrist adjusts us to our environment & the object of all culture & education is to get us dissatisfied with it again. That's a good opening lead in defining the difference between the social sciences & the humanities.

[288] I think in my dream about the S.P.S. [School of Practical Science] man [par. 284] who wanted to haze me I came face to face with a real archetype, one, as I say, that Jung doesn't know about, a kind of compensatory extroverted censor figure, not unfriendly, not completely unsympathetic, but utterly contemptuous of all the introvert vices (self-abuse, cowardice, insolence, physical weakness) & profoundly suspicious of many of the virtues. Something of him in Peter Fisher, perhaps.

[289] Helen Stephenson tells me she's pulling out of her dither. And just as I was beginning to pull out of mine, along comes Mossie Kirkwood & will I inspire the St. Hilda girls April 2?[234] That with the Baccalaureate on the 3rd cuts my time for the Social Work talk down.

Mar. 23. [Wednesday]

[290] A fairly decent lecture on Walton suggests that I could & should make more of these bits & pieces at the end of 2i. No ideas however. And then what should happen but that Sawyer should come in with another damned Charles Williams thriller.[235] This one, of course, is about the Tarot pack. I suppose the order he gives is authentic: 1) Juggler 2) Empress 3) High Priestess or Woman Pope 4) Pope or Hierophant 5) Emperor or Ruler 6) Chariot 7) Lovers 8) Hermit 9) Temperance 10) Fortitude 11) Justice 12) Wheel of Fortune 13) Hanged Man. The Greater Trumps are: 14) Death 15) Devil 16) Falling Tower 17) Star 18) Moon 19) Sun 20) Last Judgement 21) Universe 0) Fool. No, they're all greater trumps. Actually this book looks more like the real thing, a cosy, snuggly, cuddly intellectual's thriller, which I trust will not turn moral on me. It does: just the same blathering nonsense, gurgling girls & endless moral needling. McLuhan's Forum article suggests that he suffered abominably from the kind of self-consciousness he denies.[236]

[291] The Samuel Butler lecture unconsciously began to pick up the

rhythm of peroration. I can't spin him out for two more, not that I want to. I said that Butler has a real doctrine of active vs. passive mind which produces such analogical antitheses as the following: organism evolving within a will vs. Darwinian adaptation to environment; organisms making tools or machines (= extra organs) vs. man strangled in the machinery he dances attendance on; organism reasoning vs. crank yielding to the rules of logic; organism making gods vs. superstition of self-abandonment & sacrifice; & finally, subtlest of all, organism creating a larger organism in society vs. surrendering oneself to society. This last is the antithesis between the high norm or true Ydgrunite & the low norm of the commonplace conventional. The latter is what the Colleges of Unreason represent, which is why they preach Butler's own views & yet are ridiculous. Also the organism producing art vs. clinging to tradition (no way of making an aged art young again). I also repeated the point that the Erewhon-19th c. England relationship is more or less that of Huxley's nature & civilization antithesis. The Erewhonians are almost a natural society; their behavior is Darwinian & as what they do is to some extent buried under moral ideas in England, its overt emergence from suppression in Erewhon looks funny. Particularly their natural respect for money. I think I should write a series of reviews of my favorite novels. Erewhon could be one, Huckleberry Finn another; perhaps Morris (Sundering Flood looks logical); perhaps Hawthorne (Blithedale Romance?); perhaps a Virginia Woolf; perhaps my stuff on Handley Cross;[237] perhaps Pierre; not impossibly Sense & Sensibility; quite possibly Bleak House or The Chimes. It would involve a good deal of reading because I'd want to see each book as the epitome of the author's work. Antic Hay (a very short note on the symbolism). Then a series on dramas that could include my Chaplin review.[238]

[292] Helen was still very much under the weather & I spent the rest of the day fucking the dog.

Mar. 24. [Thursday]

[293] Quite a day, what with Spenser at 9: Book 3 is clearing up beautifully, & before long I think the little book I have in mind will take shape. Then the Blake, with Ruth Siddall: a very bright girl but a somewhat aimless paper. Then a frigid 1st yr. R.K. in which I said you approached the Bible as you would the study of comparative religion: first as a

historical product, then as a pattern of symbols, then as a dialectic pattern. It's the old grouping again, of course. The drama lectures[239] were as usual: in Jonson's EMIH [*Every Man in His Humour*] I put the social centre of gravity in Westminster, the London gentry vs. both the cits [*sic*] & the country squires (Stephen). Then over to page proof the *Forum* & home with an agreeable sense of being much put upon.

[294] Henry James' *Jolly Corner* is about an American expatriate who comes to the house of his birth in New York to haunt it & find there the apparition of what he would have become if he had grown up there. An introverted aesthete (more or less) trying to create his own extroverted self. A Hawthorne sense of ghostly life sprouting from a rooted spot, but the larger implications of the return to the place of birth are there too. He hates what he evokes, but his girl friend, who has dreamed of the extroverted self, says she would love him in any form, though naturally she prefers the one he's in. Thus the situation is a Jungian version of the triangle of lover, woman & rival: the rival is the shadow & the hero comes to terms with it through the interposition of the anima. The story closely resembles The Sense of the Past, with the hero again in a house which is haunted because *he* is doing the haunting. Curious how in Henry James the Ishmael & Isaac roles are reversed: the American returning home is Jacob in Edom.

Mar. 25. [*Friday*]

[295] Another Book 3 lecture, assorted interviews, lunch, where I told my story about Sid & Ernie Gould with great success, & off to the Forum, where I had a most delightful surprise: Lew [Lou Morris] had bought a lot of dusty old music on spec, & in it were two volumes constituting a complete Bischoff Bach. I need hardly say how I felt the rest of the day, with the Brother Capriccio, the Goldberg Variations, the Sonatas, the French Overture & the A minor Fugue all falling into my lap at once. I must find out what a fair price on it would be.

Mar. 26. [*Saturday*]

[296] Quiet day, an aimless journey to the office where I picked up Gordon Wood and took him out for coffee. To Britnell's,[240] where I considered buying the Edel collection of James' Ghost Stories for six

dollars, but didn't as there was evidently no essential story in it I didn't have except the Altar of the Dead. Kay Coburn is currently advertised in two catalogues at once: Coleridge Phil. Lectures in Phil. Library, & a novel called *The Grandmothers* in Oxford.[241] I thought she was going to do that pseudonymously, but perhaps it's difficult to get novels published that way, advertising being so personal these days: I wouldn't put it past them to show a picture of Kay with her hair down to her shoulders and her breasts falling out of her dress. Home in the afternoon, where I wrote the Preface to my new Spenser book (a different one from the one I have above [pars. 134–6]), & to the New Play Society's revue, Spring Thaw,[242] at night. Funny in spots, some of the humor very labored. I'd like to work on something like that: I could have brightened up some of the gags. The paper says (Irving told me in the intermission) that the American Gestapo raided a New York fellow travellers' dinner, nabbed the Fairleys & grilled them for two hours, & ordered Margaret home on the next train. Irving thinks that may lead to a Toronto heresy hunt. When U.S.A. is so enormously strong it's disturbing to see it act in the stampeding-bourgeois way the Communists want it to: it makes the Communists look so right. David Knight's father phoned, leaving a message at the College "re David Knight." However, it turned out to be re John Knight, his piano debut & how wonderful he was. His recital here is on the 9th.[243]

Mar. 27. [Sunday]

[297] Charles Williams has started me thinking about the infantilism of the modern "intellectual." The introverted intellectual wants his mamma, he chooses a sedentary occupation so he can cuddle himself, & he's intelligent enough to know how pervasive the desire to be cuddled is. He's full of fantasies of being neglected or snubbed, & so is liable to a chronic childish irritation. Hence, by contrast, a thirst for a genuine cuddle, a happy serenity of love that is an approximation to the virtues of a mother. In *The Greater Trumps* this mother-figure is a virgin mother named appropriately Sibyl. The old man, the father to be put off, is her brother, & there's a daughter who's supposed to be a Beatrice & talks like little Nell going under ether. I see this mixture of childish irritability & a childish desire for the sort of virtue that would please a mother in myself, but I also see it in Huxley, in C.S. Lewis, & it's not unknown even to Bernard Shaw, though he has a clearer idea of what it is. I'm glad to

have got this clear, as it indicates that for myself, while I have to avoid the selfishness & irritability, still the please-mamma type of goodness is a dead end.

[298] Went out for a walk in the afternoon on the ground that I have to walk (think on my feet) when preparing a speech. It's the right formula but I didn't get far, though I walked past Oakwood along St. Clair. I wish I hadn't made such a damn good Senior Dinner speech in 1944: it blocks me everywhere I turn. The point is I can use some of it but not the best parts: not the stuff about the semicolon, for instance.

Mar. 28. [Monday]

[299] Second year lecture, but didn't finish. Peter Fisher, then lunch with Margaret Avison & Colleen Thibaudeau; the latter is really a very cute little girl & I think Margaret & she took to each other. Then an R.K. teachers' meeting, where nothing much happened, tea, with Surerus talking about the [Margaret and Barker] Fairley case,[244] & home. I thought Alvin [Surerus] was trying to be fair-minded, & succeeding quite well; Ken [MacLean] much better; Joe Fisher talking like the fool he can sometimes be, or sound like. Like Irving, Surerus fears a heresy-hunt here: I'm not sure.

[300] Fisher's (Peter) main theme was the philosopher-ruler, who he identifies with the Pratyekabuddha.[245] I pointed out his manifestations: the Pope in the R.C.Ch., the king, Eisenhower in the U.S.A., etc. They're all frauds, more or less (the king, for instance, as "Head of the Church" as well as the army & state). They differ from the sun-king, Alexander, Julian, Ikhnaton, the Mikado, in that the latter is attached to society by every muscle of his body, a crucified sun, whereas the philosopher-ruler is, as in Plato, attached not to society at all—he's withdrawn from that— but to dialectic. The Pope can only articulate the evolving dogma of the Church. Fisher pointed out that the Pope, an ex-Cardinal, speaks to Mindszenty of "your college." The Lankavatara suggests that the Pratyekabuddha is attached to his detachment: that's why he can also be a hermit. Nazism left out the philosopher-ruler: Hitler insisted on being the operative hero, & thus became personally responsible for the collapse of Nazism.

Mar. 30. [Wednesday]²⁴⁶

[301] Wound up my second year lectures: the bits & pieces of prose are beginning to take more shape. Maybe if I'd read the stuff I could lecture about it. I said of Jeremy Taylor that gorgeous brocaded prose belongs to funerals, partly because you want the impersonality of ritual, & gorgeousness in the proper context is impersonal (purple is both penitential & royal), & partly because it presents death as a high adventure of the soul in which the dignity of man is preserved. I should go further with this. I said too, what is fairly obvious, that the erudition of Donne's sermons shows the age's pride in the traditions of their church.

[302] The fourth year wind up was a general survey of the main themes of the course, which I expect to take as the basis for my Social Work lecture. The attempt to find the "governor" principle in society, the thing that has spiritual but not temporal authority, turns out to be the principle of life, the thing that makes a society an organism & not a mechanism. From there I can go into religion, because the spiritual authority can be nothing but a vision of a spiritual world. That's where Milton takes over. I think that'll be all right: now for something that will penetrate the St. Hilda's girls who want intercourse with me.²⁴⁷

[303] Everybody liked my speech, apparently: Archie Hare said he was glad Dana Porter left before I got up.²⁴⁸ So did Surerus. I spent the afternoon at a Ph.D. committee meeting, which began at two & went on until six fifteen. Mostly assignment of teaching fellowships. Evidently Stoll has decided to attempt to tear Sedgewick limb from limb in the J.Q. Adams essays. Sedgewick had said in the Alexander lectures that (apropos of Stoll on Othello) marriage in Minnesota was a compound of something-or-other, private enterprise, no doubt, & the grace of God. As Stoll is a very ill-tempered shrew anyway, he must have foamed blood if Sedgewick left this remark in the printed version.²⁴⁹ I came home very tired & went to bed early.

Mar. 31. [Thursday]

[304] Last day of lectures, & a rather queer day altogether. People still full of compliments about the Senior Dinner: Bill Little called me into his

office to say he liked it, & Ned Pratt called on me with a bottle of Bacardi. Ned's gestures are so damn concrete. Thanks for everything, he said: it seemed to be some kind of valedictory. I think that some kind of Epistle Dedicatory in the drama book is the appropriate thing. A third year girl, Kathlyn Smith, sent me a six-page letter about what a wonderful lecturer I was. She recognized the possibility & the dangers of hero-worship, but still they were all there: I wonder when the hell all this business of confusing me with God began. I feel like signing myself up to write next year's Spring Thaw. I don't like it at all, especially the emotional stampede it makes on me. It tempts me to take myself far too seriously, not as a hero (that's easy) but as a fender-off of hero-worship. Like Julius Caesar, I have to keep making ostentatious gestures of refusing the crown. But my mother's emotional blocks keep coming in: June Clark pushed me into one at the last R.K. lecture, & I notice that "I am the Duchess of Malfi still"[250] seems even yet to get under my defenses. I don't know what the hell it symbolizes for me.

[305] Well, anyway, after the drama lectures[251] Isabel [Isobel] Stewart came in and stayed for an hour trying to convert me to Christianity. She's at the Toronto Bible College this year, is in love with MacNichol [McNicol], the head of it, and wants to sic him on me. The point is my R.K. course is an evangelical possibility she wants to manipulate, & I daresay she's the first of a long string of people who will be waiting on me to tell me that my course is a wonderful one, & would be so much better if I'd just reconstruct it more along the lines that they have in mind. I should be tough, & treat them as a Cabinet Minister of Health would an anti-vivisectionist secretary, but I'm not tough, & I stampede easily. The perfect female missionary, buck teeth, determined smiles, nervous titters, vague clothes, slip showing, & completely earnest, sincere of course, inaccessible to all ideas not already her own ("knowledge grows out of the knower"), completely sure of her right to pin me down in my office for an hour & make me answer questions. This last is something I can't figure out: why my assertion of a certain vitality in religious matters gives her the right to grill me about my beliefs, gives Barbara Ewing the right to ask me why I'm not a Catholic, gives June Clark the right to assault me wherever she sees me, gives the Morris idiot the right to quiz me like an R.C.M.P. [Royal Canadian Mounted Police] snoop on my politics, gives the [Douglas] Latimer oaf the right to (practically) call me a corrupter of youth, gives Lemke the right to tell me I'm too highbrow

for most people, & so on & so on & so fucking on & on & on. Meanwhile Helen had her hat on for an hour. Three Martinis & a Chinese dinner & an early bed helped some, but it was a bewildering anti-climax to what I had thought would be an innocent celebration. At first I thought that this sort of attack would lead to my giving up the course as something undesirable. Right now I'm beginning to get a bit stubborn about it: I am not ashamed of the gospel of Northrop Frye, whatever it is. Also I have to follow the Master's example & give evasive answers. I say nothing of the rights of Margaret Avison & Doris Mosdell—they're possessive & proprietary rather than inquisitional. They're all women too: I seem to be a collective animus.

Apr. 1. [Friday]

[306] My first holiday from lectures, but, like most first days, not a very profitable one. The luxury of not having to get down at nine was real, but the ritual gestures of letdown that one makes on such occasions. However, Isabel [Isobel] Stewart's visit yesterday was letdown enough, & the celebration with Helen afterwards perfunctory. I didn't finish the last sentence, which is a good indication of my dithering state of mind. weren't. The Picasso show opened tonight and the Whitleys drove us down & back. It's a good show, small, but many famous pictures. Ran first into George Edison, who was in a bad temper & pronounced Picasso a fraud. I can remember George asking me if I thought it would matter that his wife wasn't a university graduate. I said the important thing was for her to know what a professor's life was like & be willing to share it. Now George pontificates like a self-made president of Elks, and his wife covers up for him. There was a sculpture show too, but it wasn't any good. Bill Graham came in at the end from Spring Thaw, which he hated.

April 2. [Saturday]

[307] St. Hilda's for dinner & then my speech, which came off as a considerable triumph, somewhat to my surprise, as I'd got into a dither over it. Dinner with Mossie [May Kirkwood] on one side of me and a cute little (or big rather) fourth year girl with a snub nose & breasts bursting out of her dress. Also a lovely Scotch girl whose husband discouraged her from smoking with the remark that you wouldn't want to see a nun smoke—evidently he thinks of women as more or less

accessible nuns. I said I bet a lot did. I like the small & intimate atmosphere of St. Hilda's very much, but understand what [W.A.] Kirkwood means when he says he's given up trying to follow his wife's aberrations. I took off from a general "Blake & Vision" topic, saying that art frequently looked obscure because you had to grow up with it, just as wisdom looks riddling & ambiguous because it's trying to expand your mind. But it was popular art that really was obscure. My focus was Reynolds' praise of obscurity & Blake's deprecation of it, the former being linked with the grand style of portrait-painting, which of course was a popular & commercial vehicle, assimilating the subject to a flattering heroic archetype. I said this obscurity was reflected in the photographer's clouds of a later day. Also that interested art is obscure because it conceals its motive. I brought out my allegory & irony point & said that advertising & propaganda were ironic arts, addressed directly to a theoretical audience of dopes & indirectly to its real public who weren't expected to believe it & would arouse dismay or contempt if they did. It's a good line to keep in mind for a future occasion. I brought in the verbal universe too & they worried over that like puppies over a bone—very keen kids, & nice kids. I really put on a good show—even Helen liked it. I said, re the importance of a good prose style & of using it properly: "The Churchill who stood hurling defiance at real enemies in the summer of 1940 was a figure of unforgettable dignity & power: the same Churchill, hurling the same kind of defiance at such prosaically honest people as Attlee & Bevin, begins to sound like a performing elephant."

April 3. [Sunday]

[308] Baccalaureate sermon bitched up the morning—they dragged that old fuddy-duddy Willard Brewing out of the moth balls, & he said all the wrong things. Even to the silly crack about sociology. Man shall not live by bread alone, he says. It's true Jesus said it first, but he said it when he was damn near starving to death, & was in a position to say it. He didn't say it out of an overflowing breadbasket in a comfortable middle-class income bracket. I think the kids were depressed, & the staff was certainly discouraged. [Harold] Bennett almost rescued it with his charge—whatever he does he does with dignity & a sense of his audience. If [Walter T.] Brown had been there instead it really would have been a rout. I played a curious collection of hymns, & some Bach, W.T.C. [*The Well-Tempered Clavier*] II, including the old E major chestnut for the postlude. After all,

different people hear it every time. I came home but didn't feel like concentrating on my next job, & tried to read some Henry James instead.

April 4. [Monday]

[309] Fisher came in but was a bit preoccupied, though he suggested a few things I may be able to use on Wednesday.[252] Lunch with Helen, who was on her way to the doctor's for a cold, & out to hear David Hoeniger's *Winter's Tale* paper. It didn't give me many ideas, partly because I'm not yet in the Winter's Tale mood, & partly because David is one of those people who are interested in symbols & say all the right things & yet somehow don't quite bring them to life. However, his concurrent patterns, winter & spring, death & resurrection, nature & art, discord & concord, are all quite right. The paper was dreadfully long: part of the blunted & insulated feeling of his paper was due to the fact that he hasn't learned to cut. Rosemarie [Schawlow] was there, & drove us home in her new car, an Austin. She wants to take her brother in it to Washington: he's got to the preaching-for-a-call stage.[253]

April 5. [Tuesday]

[310] Somewhat aimless day—I seem to have got in quite a yank over my Social Work talk— psychologically it was bad to have it come after my other lectures, as it looms up too much. Of course I know damn well I'm kidding myself into a dither in order to have something to do besides mark essays. Doug Fisher was in—another big V.C.U. [Victoria College Union] Assembly row—motion of censure on Acta defeated by one vote.[254] He's going to Library School, of all places. His tastes are more consistently bookish than I thought they would be. He evidently felt the June Clark episode as an acute personal embarrassment, & so I gather did most of the class. Mary Louise Kilgour in too, to thank me for the things I'd taught her. Lunch by myself at Eaton's College Street, where I picked up two tickets for John Knight's recital. Also some correspondence with Rinehart over the Milton—I've finally decided to work out a text of my own.[255]

April 6. [Wednesday]

[311] Tizzy, of course, all day: prowled around, & found myself out at Dundas & Keele by three o'clock. However, I got through it all right.[256]

I began by having tea with the staff: [John S.] Morgan was my host, & I met Cassidy, a most pleasant roly-poly little man named Al Rose, who is writing an article on the Regent's Park project for the Forum,[257] Mel Gamble, Norm Knight, Sophie Boyd, who turned out to be a very gentle & soft-spoken girl like Marjorie King—I'd pictured her metallic & efficient for some reason—and others. Margaret [Newton] was there of course, & Jessie [Macpherson], who had come to hear what she thought might be an anti-sociology line but remained to approve, & David Savan & his wife. He'd phoned me last night he was coming, & that helped the dither. Margaret put me straight by telling me to talk to the students in the school, as no one else had any right to be there. Marjorie King, by the way, is just back from Chicago—that beautiful sister of hers I met in January lost her husband in exactly the same way.[258]

[312] The lecture wasn't my very top form, but I knew it couldn't be. The room was a brutal place to lecture in,[259] for one thing, & as I was tired & nervous my lower jaw tightened badly. Also I got no water & it was just luck my throat didn't tighten up too. However, I think it went over all right. They're quite formal, what with Morgan introducing & concluding me & Norm Knight thanking me. I said I didn't know what the hell I was doing there, but I thought the age of specialization was breaking down anyway. Then I started to try to outline a common framework of assumptions within which both critics & social workers act ("democracy"). For this I used Burke, Mill & Arnold. Burke says participation in society is involuntary, society precedes individual, all social problems are therefore inductive & empiric, social tensions are resolved in law (an axiom both for the social worker who has to start with legislation & the social democratic, as opposed to the communist, view of the class struggle) & unconditioned will makes for tyranny whether it's the will of the people or not. Mill takes over from there. He says democracy isn't just majority rule (will), but a combination of that with minority right, & that what gives a minority a right is the possession of value. He's inductive like Burke, & induction is not a pure logic but allows for the hunch, & so leads to an open society (as opposed to, e.g., Marxism, which is systematic, deductive, a priori, & works from canonical texts of revealed religion). The central form of this open society is the discussion group, for permitting freedom of thought automatically restricts freedom of action (not by compulsion, but by making so much of it seem ill-considered). Hence the discussion group possesses the value or end of society, & this

value is wisdom, which cannot be a purely subjective thing. Arnold makes this explicit, basing wisdom on culture, the liberal education of the free man which is also the form of society. This form is a classless society which preserves the values of the classes: leisure & privilege, liberty & enterprise, work & security. (This essential point that wisdom is not subjective I don't think I made clear.) Hence "democracy," an open inductive social ideal, not the name of our society, which is an oligarchy, but a process within it. Its movement toward freedom is not the subjective existentialists' freedom, nor the other form of the same fallacy, the laissez faire idea of the destruction of institutions. Individual & social freedom are the same thing, & just as the free man shows himself free by his rigid inner discipline, so the free society shows its freedom in its dependence on law & the complication of its institutions.

[313] Wisdom, the goal of society from the humanities' point of view, is represented by the Symposium of Plato. Plato's Republic is inside the Symposium, which stands at the head of the Laws too, & the university (Newman's conversation) doesn't add anything essential. The séance, where individuality is lost in the contemplation of a medium of a hidden & mysterious will, is the corresponding pattern of the slave state. (I'm not quite clear about this: the Hitler-Saul analogy may have carried me away; & what about the Quaker meeting?).

[314] Charity, the goal of social work, is often misconceived as reactionary (privilege-class handouts) or neurotic (good works proceeding from the ego, regarding others as helpless), but is really the activity of what wisdom contemplates, setting people free. Compared with wisdom, both engage the whole man, no chopping up into emotion & intellect; both are unmotivated (you can't set people free unless you're free yourself, & you're not free if you're dependent on a satisfactory or justifiable compulsion); both work with values rather than morals {this is Blake: value judgements are on states and moral judgements on individuals}; both are without purpose or ulterior motive (i.e., in the future. Art never develops, & the cult of posterity is a dismal superstition). Both may hope for general future improvements, but are concerned with making appear what is really here, Blake's Jerusalem.

[315] The party at Cassidy's afterward was a very good party, but both of us were a bit crocked. I was very tired & Helen's cold is still riding her.

The Jaffarys, the Irvings, Sophie Boyd, F.C. Auld in law, Miss Hatch from the school, a Mrs. Rachel Dennison I'd met at Haddow's, & poor old Brady were there. I say poor old Brady because he spent the whole evening upstairs in a coma. Diet, I think. Cassidy tried to turn the meeting into a symposium because of what I'd said, but he started the topic of what was wrong with the Toronto conversation, & it didn't take, or rather proved his point too quickly. Irving continues to say kind things to me—he went over with me to the school.

[316] This morning, for instance—well, not for instance—he was asking me what I thought of religious training for young Allan [Irving] & said he didn't want to send him to Sunday School at four. The question suddenly reminded me how important being sprawled out on my belly reading Hurlburt's Story of the Bible was for me, & how miserably my time was wasted at Sunday School. Irving even suggested a connection between the rise of the Sunday School and the decline of the Church. I'd like to do a long story someday on my return to Sherbrooke trying to find archetypes.

April 7. [Thursday]

[317] Blake group resumed operations today—I've started reading *Jerusalem* to them & letting them ask the questions.[260] They seem to go for it, but of course no general ideas emerge. The vale of Entuthon Benython is a female phallic symbol,[261] I discovered, but the rest was familiar ground. That beautiful boy Donald Harron was there & I took him to lunch—he's started work on this Duchess of Malfi "collaboration" with me.[262] I'll have to talk him out of his fifty-fifty proposal. He's a brilliant lad, bursting with dramatic ideas. Long dull afternoon at a Graduate English meeting, mainly to report on the work we'd done in committee the week before. Exacerbating to the bum.

April 8. [Friday]

[318] I still can't seem to get down to work: Mary McFarlane was in. She's had a long complicated winter with Bert Hamilton & David McKee—well, she's pulled away from the latter, who she thinks is working himself up to suicide, but apparently Hamilton got himself in a hell of a snarl over her & some other woman.[263] The one he mentioned to me who

wanted "security" was the other woman,[264] & I gathered that he'd called on her & found her in bed with someone else. Purely circumstantial evidence, of course. To get to a more cheerful subject, her thesis on Smart is likely to be very good—she *is* a most intelligent & sensitive girl. I met her again with Marg Dillon in the Promenade record shop, where I bought a lot of madrigal records—that's Peter Fisher's work again. I skipped a Scholarship & Bursary Committee meeting. Took Feilding to lunch & succeeded in getting him on the Forum board.

April 9. [*Saturday*]

[319] Stayed home in the morning & did the essay competition[265]—one job more or less off. In the afternoon A.J.M. Smith, who had phoned me last night, was to be in the pub,[266] so I met him there, with a curious death's head also from Michigan State named John Clark, & James Reaney & Stingle. This R.M.C. [Royal Military College] job is getting complicated. After failing to get me & Priestley, they applied to Woodhouse, who recommended Fisher & Maclean—Peter & H.N., of course, not ours.[267] Evidently they want to make only the chief appointment this year, & as Maclean dropped out that left Fisher. I wanted a job there for Love, which, up till now, was working out perfectly, as Love will be here another year & then Fisher can appoint him. But now Smith tells me that Earle Birney & Roy Daniells have both applied for the job. Earle I can understand: he's under a vague boss no older than himself & wants to be mamma's soldier boy anyway, but Roy's interest I find hard to account for. I wonder if my own unconscious is hankering for the job—I've had a lot of dreams about being in the army lately. Last night a flight of tank-carrying aeroplanes, ready to land on the Balkan mountains, flew in my dream over a slate-blue sky, darkening the air like an eclipse, & all looking like black bats. Well, to get back to Smith, who is here on a white-slaver raiding party involving McGee, Pitt[268] & perhaps Hoeniger, he proposed that I take in Michigan State on my Ann Arbor trip & perhaps repeat my Finnegans Wake lecture there. Stingle asked me if I were leaving—said it's spring and the usual crop of rumors to that effect are about. He was at the Social Work lecture & said it was interesting to see my technique on people who didn't grant any of my postulates. Then to [Reid] MacCallum's, where I picked up Helen & paid a mortgage instalment. Alice wasn't there, but signs of her recent interest—book-binding— were. I missed a seminar on Tuesday with a

Polish logical positivist named Mehlberg, & Reid said he was good. I gathered that the Eddington conception of the irreversibility of time inferred from the second law of thermodynamics is on its way to the ash can. Home for dinner & then out to hear John Knight's recital, which was quite an event—a big crowd there, & the boy is really good. I didn't care for all the music—of the four 18th c. items three were fakes—but he has a great deal of poetic feeling, & approached a lot of different things in different ways, many of them very fresh & individual ways. Even the Liszt Rakoczy march he ended with emerged with great clarity, & so did that broken-winded old plug, the Beethoven 32 C minor variations. A "Bridal Suite" of Ken Peacock's[269] seemed to me to have more individuality than most contemporary piano music. Four movements: Something Old (a sort of gavotte a l'antique style I liked very much), Something New (moderne writing), Something Borrowed (Ravel's Pavane, Debussy's Cathedral & Tea for Two)[270] & Something Blue (which wasn't the blues it should have been).

April 10. [Sunday]

[320] The hundredth day of the year, for God's sake. Just finished a wonderful story of Henry James's called the Altar of the Dead, an elaborate spectre, emanation, animus-anima pattern that combines ordinary religious symbolism with the lighted pathway of the Halloween feast of all souls. Grace Dempster, now Madame Shabaeff, came in for tea.[271] She's deliriously happy, now that she's married a 50–year old Russian ceramic artist whom she regards as one of the world's great masters. She brought us samples of his work—it's an unfamiliar convention to me, madonnas & such in gold & platinum ("only the best is good enough for Mr Shabaeff") surrounded with stones polished to look like semi-precious stones. She's learning the trade gradually, & they work together, like the Deichmanns, in a country place shut in for the winter. He's had quite a career: conscripted by the Red army, he got his brother, who was a White conscript, out of the country with his Red passport, then made his own way to Vladivostock where ("being completely impartial and of course an artist first and always") he supported himself doing cartoons for both Red & White newspapers. They caught up with him (he's still blacklisted in Russia) & he made his way, sleeping on park benches, to Harbin, Shanghai, San Francisco & New York. He couldn't stand Americans & came to Canada—his best friend in Montreal is Fritz Brandtner.

He's color-blind, which may account for the curious magenta lips on the Madonna & Child that make them look a bit like perfume ads in the New Yorker. Actually, he sounds like Bill Howard with a genius complex & a Russian accent—a sort of cultural handyman. She's here to get his stuff into Toronto stores. She's had a hell of a tough time with her own family, & deserves a break. Her questions about the College had the curious unreality of a woman who doesn't give a damn about the world outside her own home. As the bracketed remarks indicate, her conversation is indistinguishable from a sales talk. She's so proud of her husband's artistic characteristics such as his simplicity, his inefficiency in business & his bad temper (she says Lismer said "Shabaeff is the greatest artist in Canada, but he's a devil," which I put among the New Yorker's Remarks We Doubt ever Got Made Department, but perhaps she hypnotizes people into murmuring the right responses) & the way he'll round off a sculpture of a girl and say "There! Ass all finished!" Grace was a bit exhausting, but I was very glad to see what had happened to her.

[321] In the evening we went to David Savan's to meet Morris Ginsberg, a kindly & gentle old man who listened very patiently & attentively to a lot of Canadian gossip. The McCurdys & David Spring & his wife in history were there. Mrs. Savan is an English girl, a Quaker, & very appealing in a little-girl sort of way—walks like a penguin & makes deprecatory flutters with her hands.

April 11. [Monday]

[322] Had a very good talk with [Peter] Fisher though little that was new emerged. Evidently it's true about Roy's application to R.M.C. [Royal Military College] as well as Earle's [Earle Birney's], but Fisher is still very hopeful of getting it—the Vice-Commandant wants him. He's very keen to get the job & is a little resentful that it's being gossiped about so much. We drank a lot of beers & had lunch & then, although I was very sleepy, I came home & worked all afternoon & evening on my R.K. tests—about 130, all of which I got marked. The first year people seemed to get more out of the course than I expected, but I'm still doubtful about that course, & I think I'd better write it off. The fourth year one, on the other hand, seems to me to fit the pattern of what Victoria tries to do for people. I gather this partly from the little notes they write at the end of their exams. Edythe O'Brien German [Germain] tells me the course has given

her an insight into Catholicism, which is important to her because she's married a Catholic, a former Jesuit novice, & feels the difference has been keeping them apart. Madeline Bomberger wants something to go on with to replace a now very unsatisfactory evangelical spasm in her adolescence,[272] & has got it from the course; Diana Ironside, who never got above a 66 in her poor bedeviled life, was inspired by the wisdom lecture to go on with her studies & if possible do graduate work.[273] There are a lot of confused people in Household Ec & the like who take it because they're the sort of people who do take R.K. & it's the only course available to Honour students in 4th year. I think I shall talk over with King Joblin the possibility of organizing four courses on the English Bible designed to lead up to my course. I also got a letter today from a Social Work student named Michael Roth who objected to my Psalm-of-Life counsel to act in the present & not toward the future. Said he'd learned to believe in results in the future from Marcus Aurelius, of all people.

April 12. [Tuesday]

[323] Went down & had an interview with [Fred] MacRae, who is doing a thesis on Canadian literature, wants to know how to understand Picasso, & had questions to ask about Samuel Butler—three points. Came home and worked very hard at 3j essays,[274] getting them all done but seven. I wish to hell I'd stop getting in a panic about all the work I have to do: here I yowl about being smothered under a pile of term work I actually do, once I get down to it, very comfortably in two afternoons & evenings. The reason is, of course, that I keep protesting inwardly that I have very little time to read & almost no time to write during the term. But even so I shouldn't kid myself into a tizzy & let my work get so damned disorganized.

April 13. [Wednesday]

[324] Finished my seven essays and went down town on a sudden impulse & bought Frances Wickes' *The Inner World of Man* for $6.25—a fearful price, but the book isn't in the library yet.[275] Spent the afternoon in the Reference Room reading Jung's Secret of the Golden Flower.[276] I think I've pretty well got the hang of Jung now, & should start serious work on Freud. I'm very dissatisfied with the way Jung jumped over the libido Orc-hero to his archetypes without incorporating him—neither

Jacobi[277] nor Wickes seem interested in the old libido-symbolism. In quest of what I'm in quest of I have to unite Jung as well as add Freud to him. The only idea I got from the Golden Flower book was the conception of individuality as a temenos, a cut-off sacred place of universal holiness (in the innocent sense). He also says that Chinese science is based not on causality but on synchronization & that the truth of astrology is in divination, the real "constellations" being the pattern formed at each instant of time. I haven't got it quite clear yet, but it will bear thinking about. I picked Helen up from a Women's Council meeting with Laurette [Laure Rièse], then Laurette took us to her room where we drank a synthetic cocktail mixture that wasn't at all good for us, & then the four of us—Jessie Mac [Macpherson] joined us—went out to dinner. Then we came home & listened to what was left of the St. Matthew Passion on the radio—a somewhat listless performance, with Bill Morton's voice (the narrator) quavering like a banshee over whatever notes Bach had written, following their melodic curves approximately. Why is the St. Matthew such terrific music, & the St. John, though written in the same idiom, without grip, to me at least?

April 14. [Thursday]

[325] Blake group met for an hour. I met the temenos idea again in Jerusalem, where it's linked with the Jewish temple. The holy of holies is the fallen Selfhood ego, the dark-shrouded nothingness; the inner court is the ego-home, family & friends; the outer court is the world of money-changing & competition. Cleansing the temple & casting out devils are the same thing, obviously. Somebody asked me if Golgonooza & Golgotha were connected, & I said yes—I hadn't realized before what was meant by the fact that Jesus was crucified in the place of the skull. Then we met on term marks, but got only the third year done. Forum meeting tonight—a very pleasant & good-humored meeting with a full turnout, for once. Feilding was there & kept his vow of silence, more or less. I guess I can't tell high church Anglicans that I think Charles Williams is a ham: they're determined to make a cult of him, & why should I spoil their fun?

April 15. [Friday]

[326] Good Friday (I ate fish for both meals) but nevertheless I went down to the office & we finished up term marks. Then I had lunch with Robins, which I was glad of, as I haven't talked with him much lately &

felt I'd been growing away from him—well, he chills me a bit by his appearance of giving things up. De Beaumont has taken everything out of his office, but at least he still rattles his door. I still think he is rather giving up, but his mind & mine run parallel such a long distance that we seem to have a lot in common even though we never meet. In some respects the conversation was quite like one with Fisher. I mentioned Roth's letter & Isabel [Isobel] Stewart's assault on me & we speculated on the source of the Christian disease for "results," counting the saved souls & hearing a clock tick all the time you're not doing the Lord's work. We agreed that Jesus' strategy indicated that he was clear of the idea even if Paul wasn't. I feel a very profound peace in the idea of an energy set free to work & quite unconcerned about results.

[327] These two lovely children Don Harron & Gloria Fisher were in for dinner. I don't know how this "collaboration" with Donald on the radio version of *The Duchess of Malfi* he wants to do will work out, but I certainly can't accept his original fifty-fifty proposal—too many of the ideas are his.[278]

April 16. [Saturday]

[328] Quiet day, very cold—snow in the morning. Helen was restless with spring fever & dragged me down town to look at furniture. There wasn't any. Actually the idea was to buy Easter presents for her family: I note with some concern that the store keepers are actually succeeding in getting people stampeded to buy Easter presents. Still, there'd be something to be said for three folklore festivals: a red & green one in the winter, a yellow & purple one in the spring & an orange & blue one in the fall, if the Halloween color-scheme would change its black to blue. In the evening we went over to see Marjorie King & found Mary Campbell there. Looked at a lot of Harold's paintings & took some of them home on approval.[279]

April 17. [Sunday]

[329] Easter Sunday, & a beautiful day. Went out to Fulton Ave.[280] & to the Kemp's church—St. Andrew & St. Luke. A charming little church, packed to the doors, & their new rector seemed to me a most likeable young man. Obviously the women think so after so many years of the old goat. Then to the family dinner. The letters from Roy [Kemp] &

Marion [Kemp][281] were fairly dismal: Mary [Kemp] has an ear affection that could become a mastoid, & Marion's three letters each contained the phrase "I guess I am just getting to be an old grouse pot." We went for a walk, somewhat to Helen's disgust, as she had her twenty-five dollar shoes on, & went to our own home for supper.

April 18. [Monday]

[330] Rained like hell all day. Peter Fisher is fairly certain of the R.M.C. [Royal Military College] job—he was closeted with the Vice-Commandant over the weekend. He has the whole curriculum to organize but doesn't get the full salary—a mere $4550 is all he gets to struggle along on. I came home in the afternoon & in the evening went out to a meeting of the Canadian Literature Club—that very naive organization that practically strangled me to death last year. Helen refused to go with me, but it wasn't really so bad. Dale & I were involved in judging a contest of reviews—I had poetry & he prose. Mine were all fairly footling, but I tried to make a good story out of it, & I think I succeeded. They seemed pathetically grateful to have a couple of live professors, & treated us well—taxi there & back, which got me home by 10:30.

[331] Fisher told me a good tough-colonel story. "You young men don't know what war is all about these days. Why I remember once in '79 there I was, the only man defending a fort against nine Fuzzy-wuzzies. Killed eight of 'em; last man pinned me to the wall with his spear. Hung there for three days." "God, sir, that must have been painful!" "Oh no, not really, except when I laughed."

[332] Voice out of the past: Mrs. Hickman of my mission field in 1934 wrote to say she'd heard my voice over the radio.[282] Her Carol, that tubby little girl of twelve, is twenty-seven now, & a wife & mother. I was delighted to get her letter, as that field has been haunting me for a long time: it was one of the worst of my correspondence blocks.

April 19. [Tuesday]

[333] Supervised an R.K. exam all morning—mine. Helen reported from Jan Meisel tonight that some didn't like it, but I don't see how it could have been fairer. Anyway, nobody fainted. World's dullest job. Over to the Forum again (I went yesterday) to read editorials. Ivon's [Ivon Owen's]

front page one is very good.[283] Filled up on beer: I have a mental block about my Michigan lectures. Hell with them—if I turn up with nothing prepared, they may conceivably be able to understand me. I've just finished the Wickes book—not very profound, but a good practical introduction to Jung.[284] I think I've more or less got the point of Jung now, & I'd like to take the next step, which I think would be through anthropology into some consideration of the social or ritual aspect of symbolism. Jung, like Freud, has no form of society: he just says the individual has to adjust himself to it.

April 20. [Wednesday]

[334] My intellectual life continues to be something of an interregnum. However, I cleared up letters & various odds & ends, & came home to listen to a complete Don Giovanni & a German lieder singer—Uta Graf. I wrote to Mrs. Hickman,[285] & my sense of the historical nature of that achievement sent me out for a Martini. Helen phoned Mary [Kemp] last night, but didn't get much beyond a general sense of emotional infantilism. My spring hay fever has struck in full force.

April 21. [Thursday]

[335] Blake group, quite dull. Poor Nancy Rowland, with her precise unimaginative mind & her total lack of humor, finds Blake very difficult to follow, & is in a bit of a stew over it. In the afternoon I pageproofed the Forum & then went over to Hart House to look at a Cosgrove painting I wasn't much impressed with. Dead trees in a forest, huge, monochromatic, left side only properly organized, & a squeezed-down top. Five hundred bucks. He's tied up by contract to Stern, who I gather (from Grace Shabaeff) is not only a crook, but is recognized as one by all Montreal artists. Then I went to the Fudger group and read my anti-Deist paper.[286] It didn't go over well: too dull a group, & someone who I think must have been Gordon Sisco was furious, & attacked it violently. His objections were of course all solidly Deist ones: said I'd overlooked the "homespun" virtues & so on. He evidently regarded me as not only an intellectual but a Barthian intellectual—Barthian as a smear term in the United Church is considerably worse than Communist. Bert Arnold was the only Victoria man there & [Norman J.] Endicott, as usual, was my only real defender. Irving left early & [Harold] Bennett forgot it. Munro Beattie turned up at lunch today—he's got very heavy, but seems to like

being at Carleton, and wants naturally to do a Ph.D.—here, evidently,
though he's now doing graduate work at Columbia in the summer.

April 22. [Friday]

[336] Mostly running around, getting tickets & money. Last night I
dreamed I said to a Dr. Gopal of India (there was such a person, but I
never met him) that I wanted a piano, & he took me too literally and sent
one up to 205 Fulton Ave., where I found my mother-in-law, metamor-
phosed to Kay Morris, warding off its delivery. There was quite a fuss:
Ken MacLean was most prominent among my sympathizers, but I was
aware simultaneously that our piano was there & I couldn't have another one in, & that our piano wasn't there but had been moved to our
own place. The prototype, & part of the name Gopal, was Goggio who so
kindly *lent* me an Ariosto instead of telling me where I could get one for
myself. I'd have to buy this piano, though, evidently, & thought I was
lucky to get off with cartage charges of $16.64, plus a $3 tip given to one
of the movers. The prototype for the bill was a hydro bill. I record this
dream because it puzzles me, & because I remember so *very* few dreams
these days. Well, I went to the Reference Library, & in spite of it read
Jung's Secret of the Golden Flower & the Tibetan Book of the Dead.[287]
Then came home & went to bed early—I don't know why I feel tired &
listless these days, beyond a fairly mild dose of hay fever. I'm not
thinking much either, though I'm thinking of beginning to think about
the social & anthropological side of Jungian symbolism. Also I've begun
Kierkegaard's Concept of Dread again, though what I've read so far is
mainly horseshit.

April 23. [Saturday]

[337] Nothing at all happened today: I went out for one shopping expedition & that was that. These lectures[288] are so childishly easy and at the
same time I'm so childishly delighted at getting the break that I take out
my restlessness in a feeble pretence at working at them.

April 24. [Sunday]

[338] Got to the train all right, though I would have missed it again if
this time the ticket seller hadn't shown a ray of intelligence & warned
me. Times changed to daylight saving, & when that happens trains for

some reason leave *half* an hour earlier. I noticed that the train didn't actually leave until 8:30, though, this being the first day. I had a chair car & thought I might jot down the points of my lectures, but Sharon Kirsch had other ideas about how I was to spend my time. Sharon was six, & was travelling alone, back to her parents in London. She said her mother had warned her against speaking to strangers because "now I'm not saying *you* would, or anything"— she might get kidnapped. However, she decided fairly soon that I wasn't in the kidnapping business. She was a very sweet little girl, & very ingenious about getting me to amuse her— she had nothing to do but sit in that chair, & if they'd experimented for years they couldn't have designed anything less comfortable for a child to sit on. I feel rather helpless about amusing kids, not having any of my own, & was grateful for her resourcefulness.

[339] I wasn't expecting a three-hour wait in Detroit, but there was one, & Detroit on Sunday afternoon for three hours ought to stop Morley Callaghan & other such dimwits from writing about Toronto. The station is in the slums too. However, I got to Ann Arbor without incident & was met by Hereward Price. He put me in a hotel room in the men's residence or Michigan Union. Then we went to dinner at a hotel downtown: Americans seem to entertain a good deal in this way. Price & his wife, a charming old German lady, [Warner] Rice & his wife, who looked like Miss Honey, a younger man named John Arthos, who has just written a book on eighteenth-century diction,[289] & an older man named Thorpe, a Romantic man, whose wife is an invalid & who told me of his current interest in Leigh Hunt. The conversation was about the Communist victory in China. Americans are probably very jittery these days, & small blame to them. Then we went out to Price's house & some younger people turned up: young Willkinson, whom I met at the English Institute & who is perplexed about his thesis, which is supposed to do with myth, & a Jewish-looking lad named Donald Pearce, who is very bright, Canadian in origin, & who is a friend of Claude Bissell's, doing a thesis on Yeats.[290] The conversation was miscellaneous & gossipy: nobody here has Woodhouse's intensity.

Ann Arbor, Mich., April 25. [Monday]

[340] Woke up with a raging headache—a blocked nose again. Breakfast here and then met John Arthos for coffee at 10:15—everybody is on

standard time in Michigan. Arthos is the man I should recommend to come to Toronto. He's apparently very interested in the very kind of thing that interests me, and is also going to work on Spenser. Apparently he had an important Army job in the war—his father is Greek & his mother a Philadelphia Quaker. These bits of information were picked up later at lunch. He's read Cassirer, for instance, & yet has done this 18th c. job on poetic diction.[291] Price turned up, somewhat depressed because his application for exchange work in Germany had been turned down: they want younger people, to come back & do good-neighbouring after-wards. There's an elaborate scheme of using American credits in foreign countries for academic exchanges. Arthos mentioned a book to me on allegory & ancient art by Roger Hinks—a Warburg Institute thing.[292] Then he took me over to the Library, into a rare book collection, & an enthusiastic woman made me pretend to be very interested in 17th c. Latin medical treatises & the like, which with a headache was difficult. Then lunch, with Thorpe, Bredvold & two other people whose names I didn't get. Aimless discussion of a bill to prevent any past or present Communist from holding a teaching job. I said the insertion of "past" was pure hysteria. Bredvold, who is something of a blockhead, was supporting the bill—one of the others was a Jew who looked like Nims & said he'd been made to sign a statement saying he wasn't Communist before he got on the staff, & added to it the words "or Fascist." American liberals can't get far beyond such futile gestures, I imagine. He said, quite correctly, that the bill was designed to show the legislature's contempt of the teaching profession. I couldn't support him too warmly, being a guest. Then Thorpe took me through the administration building & the Horace Rackham building for graduates. Incredibly lush surroundings that made me feel like one of the Dead End kids. Thorpe hadn't been in the former building before himself, & it's clear that there is some resent-ment over the preference given to administration: Rice has plans for a new Library drawn up, but that clearly is last on the building pro-gramme list. Meanwhile books are being stacked double. The extraordi-narily imaginative use of color in decorating was what got me. The Rackham building has huge reading rooms filled with oak panelling, carpets costing thousands of dollars, expensive stuffed upholstered chairs (one for each of the fifty-odd who came out to hear me), two or three theatres (if I'd been a really famous lecturer I'd have got one that looked like the New York Planetarium) & padded cells for professors writing books. We came out & Thorpe, a perfect absent-minded professor, said:

"Now I wonder if that is my car? No, it can't be: the license number isn't the same." He drove me around a bit & took me home—his wife is an invalid & he has to feed her. He's written a book on "The Mind of John Keats."293

[341] Well, the Spenser lecture wasn't so hot. I'd counted on a black-board, & with their luxury they didn't have that. Then again, what with a long introduction from Thorpe, I didn't get started until about 4:30, & Rice had warned me to cut it off at 5 to let people catch the bus to Willow Run. So I had to leave out about a third of what I was going to say, & of course no diagrams. Oh, well. Rice had dinner with me alone in the Women's residence. He's much more sensitive & intelligent alone than in company, & I was pleased with the intimacy. We discussed Woodhouse, Bush, Price & other personalities. Then the Finnegans Wake lecture, which was very much better, & better attended. I had time to get through most of my stuff, & then a discussion followed that was very lively & lasted over an hour—until, in fact, janitors came to kick us out at 10:30. It was different from Toronto, where professors embarrass the hell out of the poor bugger by talking nervously in order not to embarrass him. The kids seemed very keen & of course I'm at my best in that sort of seminar work. I went back with Arthos & we had a chaste milk with somebody named Morley Greenhut & I went to bed.

Ann Arbor, April 26. [Tuesday]

[342] Got up & wandered around the town, noting that nude wax mod-els in stores are draped, & that half-mast means a hell of a long way down the pole in this country. Then met Arthos again, & [he] brought along a character named Nelson, who claims to be the only man at Ann Arbor interested in Finnegans Wake. He's a most amusing blighter, calls himself an Aristotelian rationalist, & kidded Arthos a good deal—I won-dered if all of it was as good-natured as it sounded. Then Art Smith (whom I'd phoned) turned up from Lansing in his car—he has the term off—with Jean, & I said goodbye to the Ann Arbor people—well, to Arthos and Donald Pearce. Then we went into record & book shops: he's got very interested in the Columbia long-playing records, & bought a Beethoven trio (op. 70 no. 1), a lovely thing, with Serkin playing the F$\sharp$ on the other side, along with a Fantasy in G minor op. 77 I didn't know, which ended in C major. We had lunch & drove to Lansing, & then had

dinner after Art drove me all around the campus of Michigan State College—a huge "plant" which seemed even bigger as a whole than Ann Arbor, though it has only a mere 15000 students as against Ann Arbor's 21000. The women's residence has two reception parlors, one for girls with dates and one without, if my syntax is clear. The English department however lives in a squalor that reminded me of Victoria College.

[343] Art had most of this department in for the evening. The head, Russell Nye, whom I'd met at the Detroit M.L.A., an old goat named Newlin, a spectacled young man named Adrian Jaffey (?) [Jaffe], an older man named Elwood Laurence [Lawrence], a businessman named Bill MacCann, a young chap named Shirley interested in Spenser & Elizabethan science, & John Clarke [Clark], who was with Art in Toronto & who has written an article for the South Atlantic Quarterly (Duke) proving that a hell of a lot of the phrasing & imagery of Prufrock, Gerontion & Waste Land was swiped out of E.F. Benson's Life of Fitzgerald. The conversation alternated between the highbrow & the scabrous: I tried to report some of my Finnegans Wake talk, & some I think were interested. Nye spoke of a mink farm (the quadruped, I discovered, usually has a bone in his prick—all the time, I mean) & the sad fate of the "punk," a third-rate male mink who is thrown into a group of females, takes all the chewing & biting & gouging that go with the sex war among the minks, & is then yanked just at the crisis-point & a real breed mink, whose fur is too valuable to get chewed up, sent in to reap the fruits of his suffering. Someday, says Nye, he's going to buy a mink farm just to give the punk his chance. There was also discussion of an attempt to get a new school board elected & the progressive educators, who are in charge now, thrown out. Art showed me a very short letter from the principal with five gross errors in it, all on the "if their is anything I can do" level. The stenographer might be to blame for some of the spelling, though he should have read it over if he signed it, but after all she was a product of the same system. MacCann said his little daughter had got a new kind of report: her determination to get all her arithmetic problems right was isolating her from her community.

East Lansing, April 27. [Wednesday]

[344] Slept badly on the Smith couch—I'm a very fussy sleeper these days, with my snoot. I looked at the latest manifestation of that endless

table of contents for the book of Canadian prose,[294] which seems to be greatly improved. He said a committee of about four of us should get together & write the great Canadian novel & I suggested for a title "The Wind Shall Break." He showed me a book called Miss Lonelyhearts I must read.[295] Then he drove me to the bus station & I got a bus to Detroit, which still seems a most unattractive city. There I got to the station & out, & the trip to Toronto was without incident, as I like trips to be. I wish I knew where I get this terrific agoraphobia that besets me when I travel alone: the worst case of it was, of course, going to England in 1936. It has something to do with an introverted attitude combined with a withdrawal of the persona, to use Jungian terms. My thinking apparatus seems to go all to pieces in unfamiliar territory: there's a profound disturbance in what I should guess was the sympathetic nervous system. This time I was better off: my bowels have the same rhythm as my brains, & at Ann Arbor I had a private room & bath. But exploring, finding new experiences & surroundings, constipates my brains, & all my observations are superficial and out of perspective. I'd be a hell of a reporter. A profound resentment of change, linked to an intense desire to root my thinking organically in a home, wells up in me & makes me deliberately create fears. Of course no one can think at will—thought's only use of will-power is to release something below the will, & a profound organic disturbance leaves the will flapping & clacking around by itself in a fruitlessness of resolution.

[345] Margaret [Newton] was in when I got home but Helen was out with the Hebbs at a show—a French movie on the life of St. Vincent de Paul.[296] She'd been at a tea for the Faculty Women while I was away: Margaret reported her comment as "We opened with prayer, & Jesus am I tired of the smell of middle-aged women!" Part of my insecurity during the trip was due to my having sent all my American money in a postal note to Roy [Kemp] at Lansing, & I gather that, as Mary refuses to go back to Toronto, there may be a separation. I feel very sorry for Roy, tied up to a girl who is emotionally about seven years old.

April 28. [Thursday]

[346] Staggered down & held my Blake group—nothing new, only I wonder if Woodman is dropping out. Not much in the mail—the Davidson memorial volume[297] is up again, & Hal Vaughan is in charge

of it. Came home early & went to bed early—Don Harron was in with a nicely completed Duchess of Malfi script.

April 29. [Friday]

[347] Down in the morning & started on my fourth year R.K. papers. Ned [Pratt] was in, & I told him of a proposal at Ann Arbor to get him down for a lecture on Canadian literature this summer. There's a creative writing job available at Manitoba—$3000, & he evidently wants a fourth year student to have it. I suggested Donald Coles, Doug Fisher & Doug Valleau in that order, but I think all of them are blind leads.[298] Sybil Hutchinson was in, & plunked down a 500-page novel by Len Peterson, the CBC writer, for a hurry-up report for Wednesday.[299] Norm Langford came in & I had lunch with him—he's of course preoccupied with trying to get across the border, or rather past the Covering Cherub, a dithering & bungling American Consulate. Nothing otherwise new. The Commission on Culture met at 4, & I went for the first time since they made [John F.] Macdonald chairman. Hell of a waste of time. Altogether I got 70 R.K. papers done.

April 30. [Saturday]

[348] Finished the R.K. papers, also the novel, which I didn't think much of. It's in the idiom of a proletarian novel of the 30s, a scared rabbit of the working class caught between his bourgeois desire to cuddle into his family & the imperious dialectic leading him to the communion of saints, alias the trade union. But he can't make up his mind about his own approach (the author, that is) & what he's produced is just a meddle-some soap opera. The story, or rather formula, just takes a poor droopy-drawers & kicks him around. I find novels like that not only depressing but subtly corrupting. My own life might so easily have been like that if I'd been born without brains, & where does that reflection get me?

[349] Joyce seems to be a little like Ned Pratt, who is also Irish, as well as like nearly all Irish writers except Yeats: his feelings are undifferentiated, that is, corny & sentimental, & hence solemnity is his worst enemy, & his only possible *persona* is the comic mask. *Stephen Hero* is a miserable performance; the lyrics are very minor, & his claims to their merit are ridiculous; *Exiles* seems to be tired Ibsen, & the opening episodes of

Ulysses are strangled by stage fright. With the newspaper office scene Joyce seems to go into his "Witches Brew" conversion, & here the whole idea of the great masterpiece with its dense erudition & original techniques begins to become comic as well as the subject matter. From there on he's all right: but I'm glad he didn't try, or at any rate didn't live to finish, a *Paradiso*. He has enough for epic comedy, but not enough for *commedia*. If he'd been born Protestant, like all the other important Irish writers, he'd have been all right.

May 1. [Sunday]

[350] I've been thinking a good deal along the lines started by my Social Science lecture.[300] One thing about Mill I hadn't really got clear was his commitment to the Liberal party. To be disinterested is one thing; to be neutral is quite another thing—that's where the Communists drive their wedge. They got the idea from Christianity that life is a battlefield in which neutrality is impossible, but they make that an absolute principle. Before committing yourself for or against, say, Communism, you should make a disinterested judgement of value, & I rather resent lining up with reactionaries against Communists because I have to make this judgement & realize that they talk horseshit about religion & wouldn't allow me to operate freely in their society. Actually they don't make moral claims any more: they just say their side is winning. Well, anyway, society precedes the individual, as Burke says, & we go through an adolescent rebellious phase in which society seems the "wholly other," an objective thing apart from ourselves that threatens the full life we think of as subjective. Education is a form of initiation into a predetermined social organism. Thinking along these lines, I find closer rapprochement between my religious & political feelings, & find myself disapproving of all forms of Rousseauism, or doctrine of the anterior individual, whether in Deweyism in education, existentialism in philosophy, Kierkegaardism (& possibly Barthianism) in religion, or Americanism in politics & social life. All those things seem to me preoccupied with the adolescent's conviction of subjective reality. God is one person, or one substance or whatever it is—actually God is not one person, & we confuse ourselves by using "Thou" & "He" into thinking of God as a lonely individual. God is a community, a kingdom of Heaven, & fellowship & the communion of saints precede all our experience. Hence the Church—but physical embodiments or incarnations of fellowship all

define themselves dialectically—Plato's state, the Church militant, & the trade union & revolutionary movements, the political party (which exists only in a revolutionary society).

[351] The direction I'm working in is an article on "The Idea of a Protestant University," which I've offered to Hal Vaughan for his book.[301] The university impinges on the adolescent at the climax of his adolescence, just when he is beginning to get the idea that all knowledge proceeds from the knower, & provides him with the community of learning which paradoxically completes & organizes his sense of individual freedom. The university, like the Protestant Church & the democratic state, does not define itself dialectically. It forms the keystone of life, between a childhood where the subjective has reality & an adult life in which the objective dialectically determined social unit has reality. It concerns itself, not with the dialectic choice which properly follows it, Plato's state & Newman's Church, but with the disinterested community of vision, which includes the dialectic, Plato's symposium & Newman's liberal conversation. To the Protestant it's *that* that embodies Christian liberty, the pure act of listening to the Word which enfranchises both Church & State & breaks down all the dialectic barriers. In the University science is presented as a community; the work of art is the focus of a community, & we see how a community of people & a community of ideas, the symposium which is the form both of society & of education, come into alignment. We are too apt to think of freedom as individuality—the child's sense of a self-sufficient individual uncommitted to dialectic choices, which is an "escapist" narcotic for the adult. The university teacher is disinterested but not neutral. Mill is a liberal and a Liberal. If he were a liberal and therefore a Liberal, he would be, like Communists, absolutizing the dialectic choice, & would see nothing but error in Conservatism. If he were a liberal & not necessarily a Liberal, he would be in the phase of suspended induction so dear to so many academics, refusing to reason downward deductively from a priori induction (revolutionaries who absolutize dialectic are wholly deductive) & assuming that the commitment is not worth making: that's escapism, & the phase I've been in up to now, perhaps.

[352] Milton insists that freedom is a release of energy, also that the individual as such has no energy, though he may be able to tap the source of it. Idolatry to him was closely linked with the absolutizing of

social communities, the incarnations of which were the bishop in the church, the king in the state & the censor in the symposium. It appears that communities are on four levels: an Ulro or subjective community of involuntary participation through birth, mainly of the family & symbolized by father & mother; a Generation objective community of voluntary participation through choice, mainly of the party & symbolized by the comrade; a Beulah symposium community of affinity, mainly of the university & symbolized by the fellow, & an Eden community of supervoluntary incorporation of one divine & human body & symbolized by the (communion of) saints. I think I've got something here, in spite of all the blather—nice to have it on the first of May. I thus need to add to Newman Arnold's conception of culture, without confounding culture, as Arnold tends to do, with a dialectically determined Church.

[353] My present idea is to make the ∧ [Anticlimax] a commentary on the Bible, for God's sake.

May 2. [Monday]

[354] Reid MacCallum died very suddenly & without any kind of warning yesterday. At a retreat with the Cowley Fathers in Bracebridge; lay down on his bed after Church, & evidently his heart just stopped beating. It's a baffling business—I never realized before how strong the impulse is to find a satisfactory cause of death. Up to now I had always believed in a sort of "will to live" that made all organic deaths predictable. Now I seem to feel detached from life much more. The company of the dead increases in attractiveness as one goes on—migravit ad plures [he joined the majority]. I can't think of any death closer to me personally: I keep thinking of all the ways I shall miss him, & it doesn't take long to get quite a list.

[355] Peter Fisher in & we talked of little else—he's in a strong Bardo phase at the moment, & feels that it's all the same world anyway. Committee meeting of the colloquium at one with Priestley & Flenley, then a Ph.D. Cee [Committee] meeting that went on until five. A terrific heat wave has struck, & something of that may have affected Reid—I notice my heart stepping up a good deal. Meanwhile I don't see how Woodhouse survives.

May 3. [Tuesday]

[356] Went over to MacCallum's in the afternoon—Alice had gone for a walk with Finch,[302] but returned before we left. Betty Endicott was in charge. Then we went for some drinks at Park Plaza & dinner at the La Chaumière, on the wake principle. Ned Pratt has heard from Michigan about the lecture they talked of to me.[303]

May 4. [Wednesday]

[357] MacCallum's funeral in the morning—St. Mary Magdalene, of course, gave him the works. If it had lasted another hour they'd have had at least one more corpse on their hands. Helen went instead to help prepare a lunch at the MacCallum home. She looked me up afterwards & we went home where I continued to try to mark papers. To bed early: the heat continues insufferable, like my temper.

May 5. [Thursday]

[358] Blake group, getting more listless all the time. Came home crazy with the heat but revived in time to get out to hear the Albeneri Trio, a superb outfit. I've never heard Trio playing like it. Beethoven Kakadu variations,[304] wonderful jolly music; the Ravel, & everybody sent home happy with a Schubert. Jessie [Macpherson] there, & the [Harold] Bennetts: they introduced an English female named Morris who seems to be looking over the English (departmental) ground. From St. Anne's, Oxford, whatever that is. Jessie thinks Alice [MacCallum] is likely to get a bit fanatical with Reid gone: evidently she was talking to her, as she was to Helen, about Reid's becoming a kind of tutelary angel for, among others, me. I don't know how far one could go with such speculations; one has to consider the intensity of Alice's desire to keep Reid alive in some form. By alive I mean in touch with the temporal world. Blissett was there, & I wanted to ask him if music could say anything outside the range of L'Allegro & Il Penseroso, but he'd gone. Tillie Cowan was there too, though I doubt if she cares much for music: when I said isn't it good she thought I meant the metalcraft show outside. Rosemarie [Schawlow] was in in the afternoon to announce her engagement to someone in graduate Geography named Roy Wolfe—Jewish, though unreligious, so

there's a pall with the family, who want her to become Jewish. Ethnically she is, of course, but her strong United Church principles pull the other way. He has a deafness that may be traumatic, & is very shy—she says it'll be some time before I meet him. She's back from Washington, where her brother gave a paper.

May 6. [Friday]

[359] Went down to Hart House for a special meeting of the Art Committee & got most of the fall lined up: we plan a Canadian Group & an O.S.A. [Ontario Society of Artists] show (the Art Gallery has its 50th anniversary next year & plans only one big pooled show, so we can get things like that), Bertram Brooker, John Hall, Casson & Panton, a Western Ontario group, & so on. Comfort tells me he's been asked to exhibit at Victoria. If [Walter T.] Brown would only retire I think the [Harold] Bennetts would do a fine job making the place less corny.[305] Incidentally, I've planned the Public Lectures for next year: Trethewey on Phèdre or Andromaque, a new man named Davison, of Manchester, who will be visiting Professor of Classics, to do a Greek play, Ned [Pratt] on King Lear, and somebody, probably McLean (C.V.) on Job. It is still hot, & after lunch at Eaton's I came home & finished the 2i papers.

May 7. [Saturday]

[360] I am still avoiding the Forum, though I did try: I was there at 9:45, but the Morrises weren't up and Alan [Creighton] evidently does a five-day week. So I went to the College & wrote six letters, to my own tremendous relief: letters still panic me. The temperature dropped 40 degrees, & I had lunch at this new place on Yonge Street, the Brass Rail. Cocktail bars appear to have absorbed most of the modern tendencies in decorating & design, & it's probably the right place for them. Came home & finished the 1st yr. R.K. papers. Little by little I nibble & nibble.

[361] The individual man comprises a multitude of other characters—Jung's archetypes are surely only a few threshold dwellers. There is at least a good-sized village inside me. Many are children, some are women, & a few may be animals or even monsters. Some are replicas of other people I know, either in personal acquaintance or in reading. They die, but new ones move in & grow up. All this is not pure whimsy—I'm

trying to get at a real fact of existence. Ever since Plato people have talked of the state in terms of the individual: what would happen if one were to look at the individual in terms of a society? Suppose Jung's "anima" were not *a* feminine figure in me, but the aggregate of all the female characters in me? He says himself that the animus is regularly a group or council. So with me: in the course of a day, even a day spent in pure solitude, I should go through a bigger dramatic repertoire than any commedia dell'arte. Pedants, buffoons, comedians, debaters, politicians, hermits, saints, sages, middling-sensual men, suburban bourgeoisie, all dispute within me, & everything I do & say is the calculus of probabilities resulting from their competition within me. A good deal of behavior shows this. The "censor" could be a whole Sanhedrin, & the kind of experience of conversion described by William James in his chapter on healthy-mindedness corresponds point for point to a political revolution.[306] In Victorian times it was fashionable to be patriarchal or matriarchal: only the older & graver heads spoke, & within the individual, as within society, children were seen but not heard. Nowadays democracy is fashionable: we disapprove of censors, allow our women & even children a voice in our assemblies, & if we do not allow our perverts or Calibans to speak, at least we try to locate them & keep a police record of them. Democracy turns easily into a police state, & it is easy for people with liberal & open societies inside them to become converted to a rigorous totalitarian dialectic. I suppose two-party opposition-patterns are more common—nearly everyone is aware of some dividing contrast in his attitudes & moods. I think of all these characters as dramatis personae, speaking masks. Perhaps most of them inhabit a sort of Gentiles' outer court, the real decisions (every thought is a decision, a bill that's had two readings & committee in a well-regulated mind) being made by a small cabinet within of high priests. Whether there is one high priest or supreme pontiff I don't know. This veers toward an idea I've had for a long time, that Jesus' cleansing of the temple & his casting of devils out of individuals were exactly the same act. The thing that's difficult to grasp is that it's only the holiest of holies that are socially visible: all the outer courts are hidden. Thus each man looks consistently like one man: only in anarchy do the money-changers & dove-sellers suddenly appear in his face or conversation. Ordinarily he presents the appearance of one man interpreting the will of a small & fairly homogeneous group. Thus for an elect Christian, Christ cleanses the temple, *or* casts out devils, *or* harrows hell, redeeming & releasing the bound spirits, *or* separates sheep from goats, all of these activities being the same.

[362] "Some [of us] call it autumn & others call it God"[307]—one is much wiser to stick with autumn in such a case.

[363] Another thing: I think one's view of the world ought to be periodically corrected by an insane & megalomaniac egoism. Suppose I pretend for a moment that the whole world I live in was created especially for me, & every event that happened to me was done for my benefit. It follows that the events of one's life would show a unified providential design. Looking at one's life from this point of view, everything about one's life with which one is dissatisfied is the result of a missed opportunity of grasping the real significance of past events, the real significance being, on this theory, its meaning to me. This would be the only way of making sense of the notion of the sinlessness of Jesus' life—a notion I'm not very interested in anyway. But sin is one aspect of a general life-situation of which ignorance, impotence, vulgarity, stupidity, false judgement, etc. are other aspects, quite inseparable from it. The sins of the "indifferent honest" [*Hamlet*, 3.1.125] man are the results as a rule of simply being in moral dilemmas. If Jesus were sinless he must have kept out of moral dilemmas with extraordinary agility, & if this agility were not purely the result of omniscience and/or omnipotence, which would take away the credit of his incarnation, it must have come from a continuous ability to make the most of every situation he was in from childhood up. Hence he would never have fallen into that state which paradoxically is both fate and chance, & which affects all of us. Things happen unpredictably & involuntarily to us which involves us in moral dilemmas, & more or less sin enters into, not getting out of them, but simply through them. Perhaps the origin of such unpredictable events is always some deficiency in our previous handling of a previous situation. Believers in reincarnation say "man is born into the world he has made"— we believe that only of Christ. Of course for anyone to dodge sin in early childhood not only the family training but the heredity must have been carefully taken care of, which is why so much hullabaloo is made about the Virgin & her immaculate conception, in spite of Jesus' irony on the subject. All this is most irreverent, & I mean to make something of irreverence, to carry the attitude of, say, Shaw into the citadel of faith itself. If I keep my nerve I may encourage & put heart in all those queasy

intellectuals who can't resist cutting the throats of their critical reason on the altar of an introverted acceptance of tradition.

May 8. [Sunday]

[364] The trouble with this latter attitude is that of the convert. Kierkegaard, whom I've been reading, was a convert, though not *to* anything. It is characteristic of the convert, I think, to think of himself first as an antecedent individual, then lose that individuality by joining a communion, whether Catholic or Communist or anything in between. That means accepting all the social & moral things this communion stands for in a lump, as secondary. Kierkegaard talks very well about the necessity, not only of going all the way to faith, but of coming back all the way to the recreated (or "repeated") personality. But there remain things like the pernicious political influence of the Catholic Church, the Protestant fatuities about liquor, Communist tactical hooliganism, & with all groups the miserable & cantankerous moral hypocrisies, which Kierkegaard is quite indifferent to. This is the result of absolutizing the dialectically determined group. Conversion as such is always toward the absolutized dialectic, & so differs from the tactical freedom of the true liberal Protestant. There are no "converts" to Protestantism, no single dialectic sucking one in: there are a dozen churches one may join. For Vaughan's article[308] I must work out the open society ("democracy") as the social tendency of the open Church (a *position* reached from the negation that God is no respecter of persons), as the inductive or empiric listening to the Word that precedes the free choice of the dialectically determined. Catholics take this free approach to society, of course, but don't get it in religion.

[365] Went down to Hart House for a tea that's next Sunday. Met Yvonne Hackenbroch, as earnest as ever about her kittenish ability to light on her feet. She's going to curate Judge Untermeyer's private collection of 17th c. textiles & such, on 5th Ave. opposite the Metropolitan, which the latter hopes to acquire at the Judge's death along with her. He's dead already as far as her ambitions are concerned.

May 9. [Monday]

[366] Fisher in, quoting somebody on Aristotle as a biologist, & remark-

ing (with some help from me) that biological understanding is characteristic of the "civilization" phase of culture, suggesting a link Spengler
missed between Aristotle & Goethe. The somebody I think was de Wulf.
Fisher's Blake thesis is going to be very good. Also something that
clicked with my recent speculations: where did the West get its idea, not
of the logos, but of the "ology"? The conception of the democratic discourse seems bound up with the self-sufficient church in some way. It's
opposed to Hinduism, Judaism & what Protestantism perhaps should
consistently be: a centripetal commentary on a central Word (actually
identified as Om in Hinduism & the Tetragrammaton in Judaism). The
characteristic of the demarcated discourse seems to be the exclusion of
poetry. Prose expresses narrative (causality) & proposition (abstraction):
hence it's hard for us to develop the sciences of synchronization or the
philosophies of concretion. The theologians & scientists would never
take Dante & Goethe seriously as theologians or scientists unless they
wrote prose. The epic tradition stands out against that, of course. Over to
the Forum office, & then home.

May 10. [Tuesday]

[367] Holiday today, or I considered it one, so I bummed around &
finally dragged out my old novel, & typed out what I'd written.[309] I have
to admit it's pretty witty writing: if I can keep it up I may have something. I don't want to put too much time on it, but I'd like to carry it
around in my mind again. The pedantry, stiffness & tendency to tactless
allusiveness are largely gone. Helen had to pour for an examination tea,
& I went over to Wymilwood[310] to pick her up, & talked to some of the
kids there. Helen proved to be feeling restless, so we went to the Park
Plaza & had cocktails—I had far too many—then dinner at the Brass Rail,
obviously an American speculation, & a movie—the main feature, a very
poor hash of Margery Sharp's *Nutmeg Tree*, was a washout,[311] but an
incidental account of South Pole exploration was admirable. Last night I
dreamed a small group of professors was meeting in an upstairs Hart
House room, just talking. Reid [MacCallum] was one of them—he was
dead, & everyone knew he was, but he was one of the party anyway. I
think his influence had something to do with the magnetism of innocence. Most of us get very knowing & sophisticated in spite of ourselves,
but he remained primitive.

May 11. [*Wednesday*]

[368] Dull day, with the Library Committee meeting for two hours & a Forum meeting in the evening. I've become rather fascinated by the sketch of my novel: I like its wit. That happens to me every year: then I begin to get a bad conscience about wasting my time trying to add just one more damn novel to the world's stock of them when I could add something unique in the way of criticism.

May 12. [*Thursday*]

[369] Forum in the morning: I think Lew's [Lou Morris is] getting rambunctious again. Marshall McLuhan in to lunch & we set the graduate moderns paper. It's tough, & shows his influence. In the evening we went to Pete Colgrove's to hear him read his paper on the fourth dimension.[312] I'm glad he's got interested in something that will give his rather childish religious intuitions a concrete subject to get into. I tried to help his party go, & I think I did, but I must say I'm not much impressed by the arguments about how four-dimensional people would be to us as we would be to two-dimensional people—an analogy to something that doesn't exist seems to me a shaky argument. I suggested that having two eyes in one plane was more reason for the three-dimensional nature of our perception, but I don't think much of that. Don Harron & Gloria [Fisher] were there, & two other couples, the Bochners, the girl a lovely Jewess who's going to Palestine this summer to work on a farm, & the [Howie] Harrises (son of Lawren), also a very pretty girl, Barbara Pentland & Fred Hagan. Pleasant enough evening, though Pete looked so much like Monsieur Verdoux discoursing on murder that it was a bit eerie. I wonder though about my eyes remark: to perceive four-dimensionally, e.g. a sphere, we'd need a third eye on the other side of the object. Four dimensional perception is circumferential. I wonder if the creation of this third eye facing us is the point about crystal-gazing & mirror-divination: combining them might be interesting.

May 13. [*Friday*]

[370] Aimless buggering day—some papers marked, in one of which I found the sentence, "It shows his depthness into the behind scenes of

nature." Every once in a while one gets a glimpse of what the language will be like when the Dark Ages really hit us. I can't seem to get going on any sort of work, & for some reason I don't think I'm very well. I wish I could shake off the valetudinarian attitude Reid's [Reid McCallum's] death has inspired in me. Norah McCullough in from Saskatchewan. Adult education there is taking a beating from ignorant CCF politicians. She left me a brief David Smith had submitted to the government, & went into a complex rigmarole of conflicting personalities I can't go into now. I always associate Norah with worthy causes, misunderstandings, & packets of unreadable prose. The best things in her conversation are the quick pencil sketches: a little girl pulling off her parka & hair falling over her face like a poodle.

May 14. [Saturday]

[371] Somewhat better today, but the marking is much slower than I expected. I really do seem to be under the weather, & I went to bed in the afternoon. I seem to need sleep, though why God only knows—I get enough of it.

May 15. [Sunday]

[372] Isabel's baby was christened today, & her father, the bishop, did a much smoother job than Woodcock did on Nancy.[313] No howls from Hilary, only a pleasant succession of burps. The bishop has revised the service, cutting out the "conceived in sin" passage. Then a tea party, at which I met archdeacon Marsh & wife, a pleasant example of muscular Christianity, also a girl named [Jessie] Day, who was Vic 37 & teaching English at Danforth Tech, engaged to a man—a friend of Harold's [Harold Whitley's], who was godfather. The Bretts were there, & asked us to dinner. Hilary is a lovely baby.[314] In the evening we asked Marjorie [King] in—she looks dreadfully tired. Margaret [Newton] also came in with Mary & Wilf Hamilton—they're very pleasant people. The day wasn't quite as inane as it sounds.

May 16. [Monday]

[373] Fisher in: some rather aimless discussion of the Isa Upanishad.[315] We were wondering whether there wasn't some intellectual snobbery

about a cult of orthodoxy—Kierkegaard, for instance, seems to imply by his speculativeness a discouragement of other forms of speculation. I know that I have many qualities in my thinking that he would call spiritless. Also whether (we touched on this *very* delicately) sanctity couldn't be a kind of refuge—whether Reid [McCallum], for instance, didn't find a certain escape in doing his duty. A nice point, & no doubt an ungracious one. In the evening we went down to the Forum & I reviewed four books while others read proof. Ivan [Ivon Owen] & Pat were there, tee-heeing in a rather self-conscious way about their unborn child. At least Helen said it was unborn. Ivan [Ivon] was doing the front page feature, on the election.[316] Very pro-CCF, though less of a party plug after I got through with it. Andrew [Hebb] won't approve,[317] but on the other hand a lot of our readers are still pro-CCF, & if the papers will all yell that we get back on the bandwagon for an election, still they'd yell something slanderous anyway. I think the female will aspect of our manoeuvres, holding off & then being coy, will keep the CCF people in the right state of dither.

[374] I started recording my dreams again today: I had one last night about a key I had lost that interested me, but I couldn't get a clue to the meaning of the key.

May 17. [Tuesday]

[375] Finished 2b exams[318] & in the afternoon I slobbered another bibful of deathless prose for the benefit of Here & Now on criticism & book-reviewing.[319] Then on an impulse I bought two Everymans, the Koran & George Macdonald's Phantastes, & a rather dubious Jungian book. The Koran still baffles me: I can't figure out why the hell anybody went for that book. It probably makes a lot more sense in Arabic as a prose-poetry synthesis of the Word in which rhetorical & dialectic aspects are indistinguishable.

May 18. [Wednesday]

[376] Set a Blake exam I take a certain pride in: annotating five passages—very tough ones—in the Prophecies.[320] My kids had quite a struggle with it: they started at two, & though none of them wrote much, Nancy Rowland broke into summary at a time she listed as 7:15. Depart-

ment meeting in the afternoon, very dull, & picked up Helen, who was struggling with her annual report for her women. We went out for a beer & met Henry Kreisel, on his way to England for the summer, & Jim Scott, who had dinner with us. I was going to take him until he revealed incautiously that he was getting half as much again as I am. He tells me Fisher got the R.M.C. [Royal Military College] job, which pleased me greatly.

May 19. [Thursday]

[377] Ph.D. exams all day. Hamilton will I think get through. [Robert L.] MacDougall far more fluent. If I am to get anywhere this summer I must minimize drinking, & not use this diary perfunctorily as a duplicate of my engagement pad. This by the way. MacDougall was followed by Dougherty, who was very bright & quick, & knew nothing whatever. We'll pass him: I can't understand why we go through this gloomy ritual, & waste our time & exacerbate our rumps, when we pay no attention whatever to the results. Came home to find Helen in an embarrassed dither over her reports: the sort of pure embarrassment with no definite basis for it that I often get into after a public appearance I wasn't very interested in making. Margaret [Newton] says David Hoag is now manic-depressive & he's had to go to Whitby.[321]

May 20. [Friday]

[378] I wonder if the theme of the blinding of Gulliver in Lilliput has Samson overtones. I saw the Blake Studies book of Keynes today—a magnificent printing job, & the reference to me in the second sentence is very pleasant to behold.[322] I gather Margoliouth has reviewed me in RES [Review of English Studies], & made a joke of an incautious remark about using the Scone stone to "crown the Kings of England."[323] Curses. The [Allan] Bevan exam was a solemn farce, & we let all four through, including Dougherty. The whole business makes my arse sag. Oh, well. [Joseph] Fisher, as usual, being pathological about "fairness." A man puts on a really monumental display of ignorance, & we all rush in at once to see who can be most fair to him. If he puts it on at the end of his exam, he's tired, if at the beginning, he's nervous, if in the middle, he's really the type of mind that does better on some other subject. I saw Dougherty's 18th c. paper, marked by [Douglas] Grant & [Joseph] Fisher.

It got 60: I don't know why, & neither do they. The correct mark for it was zero, & we should have kept stumbling over that zero until we realized that Dougherty wasn't good enough.

May 21. [Saturday]

[379] Went out to the Bretts [Gerard and Betty] for dinner with the Briegers & Whitleys, & the Chinese-collection person at the Museum, Helen Fernauld. Today I started editing Milton, dammit: I'd like to edit Blake, & did the Minor poems & two books of P.L. [Paradise Lost]. A cheap job, of course, but a blind-staggering one none the less.

May 22. [Sunday]

[380] There's a horrid fascination about this stupid job[324] that keeps me busy at it: I finished to the end of Book 8, & nearly killed myself. Margaret [Newton] came in from a weekend of driving around the country. Oh, well, $250. Less withholding.

May 23. [Monday]

[381] Did Book 9 before [Peter] Fisher (and Gordon Wood) came in,[325] & finished P.L. [Paradise Lost] in the evening. I let Fisher pay for my lunch in view of his job.

May 24. [Tuesday]

[382] Holiday. Went out for lunch with [Marshall] McLuhan and Ned [Pratt]. They wanted me to do a graduate course on modern poetry but I didn't bite. Woodhouse wants it given every year, & of course wants to push a U.C. [University College] man into every graduate course he can. I want to stick to allegory & cultivate that field. McLuhan brought up the subject of his magazine again.[326]

May 25. [Wednesday]

[383] Finished editing the prose today, & went out in the evening to a party given by Norah McCullough. Rik Kettle was telling me about the wheat market: he says wheat acreage in U.S.A. has increased 30% since

1939 & that there's terrific pressure on the State Department to force recipients of the Marshall Plan to turn back the money into American goods for export, which is exactly what the Russians said would happen. Every farmer is swarming into wheat now, & other crops are suffering. Massey-Harris[327] of course is breaking all records.

May 26. [Thursday]

[384] Went over to discuss 3e papers[328] with [Harold] Wilson and Woodhouse, which I read in a fit of absence of mind yesterday. I was rather taken aback by the way Woodhouse fought over every work, as it seemed to me linked with his original practice of giving too many marks to his own notes. Wilson is getting off next year to go to Huntington Library, so Woodhouse will have both Wilson & Priestley to replace next year. I wonder if Wilson is preaching for a call. Temperamentally, he'd be far happier in a big library than in teaching, I imagine, & most of his American friends are librarians and bibliographers. I'd be sorry to see him go for good. Woodhouse told me I should apply for a Nuffield next year, that no one else would stand a chance, & that he will probably still be on the committee. A benevolent despot, is Woodhouse, and at times an enlightened one.

[385] Then I went to Hart House, where the Warden was holding a meeting of the curators of local galleries. Besides Comfort and Key, there was Edna Breithaupt of Wakunda, a Miss McLaughlin (Isabel's sister, Helen says, though she doesn't look like her), Clare Bice of London, a McDonnell [Thomas Reid Macdonald] (or some such name) from Hamilton, a man named Graff from Peterborough, who said he was in my 41 classes, & Saltmarsh [Saltmarche] of Windsor. Then Philip Clarke [Clark] and A.J. Casson came in for lunch. I was a little startled at the importance of the meeting when my own summons to it, & I gather Comfort's too, was so casual. I think the Warden may have an important idea in his mind, but I think he may not be too clear himself just what it is. Anyway, I was the watchdog of the Committee, & saw nothing that affected the Committee's interests adversely. He put me in the chair, & at the head of the lunch, which struck me as curious, as it made them almost ancillary to the Art Committee.

[386] Then a Library Committee meeting, at which we looked dully at plans for extending the Library eastward. Nothing to that, except Peggy

Ray's brilliant reorganization of the dungeons in the cellar. Then to the Royal York, picking up McLuhan and Fr. Bondy on the way. After a lot of running around from the foyer to the cocktail lounge, & from there over to the Station & staring at a deserted bulletin board, McLuhan finally phoned the York Club. The object of this manoeuvre was to intercept Harrison, & Ned's [Ned Pratt's] idea—I don't know why. Harrison did exactly what he said he was going to do, as Ned realized when he took out his letter in the taxi & read it on the way up to the York Club. Anyway, we had a very pleasant evening & a wonderful dinner: a Martini before, a red Medoc during, & a Benedictine after. The conversation was of course anecdotal: Harrison doesn't care to talk, & meets every conversational effort with a clasping of hands, as though to say "well, that's been handled; now for the next challenge to geniality." McLuhan says his rudeness, of which he has a great deal, is a middle-class Englishman's conception of aristocratic English behavior. Then we adjourned to the Institute:[329] Harrison had specified "an evening with the Basilians," being of course a recent convert. Rome put on a somewhat perfunctory exhibition of urbanity, which broke down halfway through on a discussion of T.T. Shields, in which tolerant amusement was attempted, with a certain amount of success. Ned stole the evening & talked the whole time about himself, which probably pleased Harrison & was certainly entertaining enough for the rest of us. Frs. Muckle, Denomy, O'Donnell, & Flahiff all in robes, which certainly convey an overwhelmingly substantial impression of dignity & power. Larry Lynch not in robes, which made him look like an errand boy. He was one, too.

May 27. [Friday]

[387] Friday morning I was up bright & early to attend MacLure's Senate Chamber,[330] which was not held there but in the garret of 44 Hoskin. Cold too. MacLure put on a most impressive show: MacDougall & Underhill were there from history, & they certainly seemed impressed. The Paul's Cross sermon was a subject that no one knew anything about except MacLure & Harrison,[331] so Woodhouse, for instance, had to relapse into the catechism about grace & nature & the three Mosaic laws, ceremonial, moral, & judicial, which Luther held to be abrogated. Lunch afterwards in the Hart House round room—very pleasant, but unsubstantial. I mean the conversation, not the lunch. Came back to discover Hopwood on my doorstep: I'd forgotten about his appointment but fortunately wasn't very late. The poor boy was utterly orphaned by

Reid's [Reid MacCallum's] death: Reid had part of his thesis at Bracebridge without his name on it,[332] & he had quite a time getting it back. I then went home, ignoring a Commission-on-Culture meeting. MacLure is to be head of United College, the Peterson wench leaving.

May 28. [Saturday]

[388] Buggered around a good deal pretending to work on the Milton job, and actually read a good bit of Erdman's book,[333] which has arrived. Six hundred odd pages and he's only at the end of the 4 Zoas! I typed out the manuscript of the sonnets, sweated out a chronological table, & thought the hell with a bibliography—that involves a trip to the Library, which is a long way to go for $250. MLN wants me to review Blackstone's book.[334]

May 29. [Sunday]

[389] Sunday, & worked feverishly (at last) on the Introduction which I got, in a way, so to speak, done. It's a very short introduction, but I thought from the last few letters that my space was pretty circum-scribed.[335] Irving dropped in with a review of an evangelical blast by Sorokin he wants me to check.[336]

May 30. [Monday]

[390] Fisher in, of course: many beers. Parsons dropped by: I didn't want to see him, & I'm afraid we baited him a bit on some very unformed ideas about the uniformity of life in Canada. Sleepy & stupid in the afternoon, of course too; I don't really know why I do it. Helen came down for a Women's Faculty Dinner & we had a cocktail. Then I oddly discovered I wasn't hungry, ate a sandwich & went home. The introduc-tion (of course) has to be extensively revised. At 4 I went over for a colloquium committee meeting with Barker Fairley, Tom Goudge & Priestley.

May 31. [Tuesday]

[391] Last day of this dithering month. Got the Milton stuff all ready & sent it off, with a wire saying it was coming. Had lunch with Graham

Cotter,[337] who mentioned a book called The Shape of the Liturgy, by Dom Gregory Dix, Anglo-Catholic Benedictine, which sounds interesting.[338] Roy Daniells is in town, on his way to Halifax, & Helen threw a beautiful dinner for him, asking the [Norman J.] Endicotts. They stayed till midnight, so I think enjoyed themselves. A good deal of gossip, with the very concrete, almost sensational, approach to ideas that both Roy & Norman have. Roy raised the questions of a B.C. summer school, for me.

1950 Diary

[1 January – 7 September 1950]

The diary is in the NFF, 1991, box 50. It is in a bound notebook (13.6 × 19.6 cm.), entitled The Canadian Line Daily Journal 1950, *published in Toronto by Brown Brothers, Ltd.*

Memorandum from 1949

[1] 1949 was not a very eventful year for me, but it was an exceedingly happy year, except for the deaths of Harold King and Reid MacCallum. 1948–9 was easily my best teaching year to date: this year isn't coming up to it, except that my graduate course is infinitely better this time. The year (the first part of it) was full of little local personal triumphs: the colloquium, the Social Work talk, the Senior Dinner, the St. Hilda's evening, the Howard Park sermon.[1] Not much writing. I dictated a draft of L [Liberal][2] in the summer, but that was only a joke, really. The only important writing I did was the colloquium paper, & I still think it's one of the best things I've done. The meaning paper[3] really didn't come up to it, & I'll have to do some more work on it. I also wrote an essay for the Davidson book,[4] which was a most important thing to write at that point, as it consolidated my thinking along lines that had preoccupied me for months. It disposed of those preoccupations almost too neatly, as I feel I've reached the end of a phase of discovery in 4k lectures, for one thing. One unexpected result was that ⊢ [Paradox],[5] of all things, came clear, or relatively clear, just at the end of the year. I have that general sense of completing a phase of discovery in all my lectures, and it's one of the things that make me feel it's time for me to take a year off.

[2] So I've applied for a Guggenheim, and hope that 1950 may see a bit of a change of scene. Two important things that I wrote in 1948—the prose fiction article and the comedy one—are appearing now along with the Quarterly article,[6] and the impact of all three should keep me in the market for a bit. I also received a note from Bonamy Dobrée asking me if I'd like to visit England as a lecturer, & that may lead to something. Roy Daniells & Des Pacey have suggested summer schools at their respective ends of Canada.[7] I don't particularly want to travel, though Helen does, but I feel I should, as the glimpse of Harvard I got this summer made me realize how much I missed by not being on the circuit.[8] I don't ordinarily write at my best without my roots growing around me: the Blake emerged out of pure routine. But the Blake after all was an intensely personal book, a kind of subjective academic lyric, a hymn to the Father, and I think I'm entering on a more public phase of my life.

Sunday, January 1

[3] A typical holiday, with late breakfast and aimless lunch: I finally got a headache from too much sedentary idling, and went out for a walk. It was a desperately dull and gloomy day, and the streets were largely deserted. I show little enterprise in my walks: I've always preferred obvious paths. I want to think when I walk, and I can't both think and wonder where the hell I'm going next. So I just slugged my way along St. Clair Ave. west to the end of the car line (nearly) and came back on the car. I was thinking mainly about the prose book, and the sort of discussions I'll be involved in after I've worked out the four forms, the theory of satire, and the annexation by literature of metaphysics. It's the last chance I'll have for some time to do any strategic planning.

[4] After dinner we took Vera [Frye] down to the station. She seems in wonderful health, except for some sciatica in her hip that seems to bother her. I've never seen her in better spirits. Both she and Dad seemed far more relaxed and less querulous and on the defensive than usual.[9] She no longer assumed that I was just on the point of adverse criticism of the American way of life: maybe in ten years she won't take it as a direct personal remark if I do make such a criticism. It's very interesting to me that the pure American and the pure Communist are identical. Vera's whole life is service to the state: she has completely identified herself

with her community, and most of her sentences start with the word "we." She has no religion, and needs none: her country is infallible, not statically infallible like a god, but dynamically infallible, always in the process of working out the right solution—or rather a workable solution, "right" being still a static word.

[5] New Year's is a dull holiday, an anticlimax after Christmas, but as my New Year's Eve potations were confined to one glass of sherry there's little point in soul-searching. I feel Micawberish, full of a vague hope that something may turn up if I don't work too hard trying to make it do so. I expect great things of 1950, but I don't feel like undertaking any ritual disciplines as yet, not even languages. I'm too anxious to get started on the tactics of the trilogy,[10] the general shape of which is becoming almost overpoweringly clear. Teaching bores me at the moment because it's a product of self-consciousness, and I'm getting anxious to start work & forget self-consciousness.

Monday, January 2

[6] This being the New Year's Day of practice, as distinct from theory, I paid tribute to it by buggering around aimlessly all morning, and then went down to the office in the afternoon. It was a foggy day—one of the heaviest fogs I've ever seen here, and I should think that those who obediently get gloomy in gloomy weather would go into reverse & feel exhilarated with the mystery & glamour that a fog spreads over things. My Hudson Review was in the mail,[11] and I spent some time gloating over it: I'm getting to be a terrible intellectual narcist. Saw Ned [Pratt], who has been converted to John Sutherland by a friendly letter, & who tells me Mrs. Ford is dead.[12] Came home and voted. I plumped for May Birchard for alderman again, but she still didn't make it, though she was close.[13] The Sunday sport issue went pro, greatly to my surprise.[14] Both Protestants & the Cardinal had gone against it, two of the three papers who had been for it had ratted midway (the third, the Star, was against it anyway) and not a candidate except Lamport had dared to open his mouth in favor if it.[15] It indicates that "public opinion" that everyone is afraid of is largely a matter of lobbying and organized minorities.

[7] Mrs. Haddow was having a "tea" that lasted from 4 to 10, and I went over with Helen, who had been asked to do some pouring. The Erichsen Browns [Erichsen-Browns] were there, along with Mrs. Le Bourdais

(their daughter). They've met us a dozen times and never remember us, so it's difficult to work up much interest in them. The Kemenis again, with a juicy cutie from Hungary who is looking for a job and, like most refugees, knows exactly what she wants and how to get it. Mrs. Cotts was there and said admiring things about the book—suggested I write fiction.

[8] Des Pacey in in the evening: I got a better idea of his sense of responsibility, even of his sensitivity to other people, than ever before. Last summer he took a $12000 house, sat down to write a novel to help pay for it, & batted out a first draft in 28 consecutive evenings. The story lacks its proper climax: he hasn't placed the novel yet. He says [Malcolm] Ross is going to Queen's, Tracy (perhaps) to Saskatchewan. I recommended Love for his vacant associateship.[16]

Tuesday, January 3

[9] Got up and went down for my nine o'clock, on Newman—the last discourse. All that stuff about Julian.[17] It was a smoothly presented lecture, though with nothing particularly new in it, and, for a nine o'clock and the first lecture of the term, the kids seemed unusually interested. I'm trying to be less bothered by late comers. Then I dithered around, went to the bank, and the station to get my Huntsville ticket,[18] and finally turned up again for my opening lecture on Job. I talked too much, but seemed to hold them: again a smooth enough performance. Lunch at the S.C.R. [Senior Common Room]: not much there. Some aimless Sunday sport discussion. Charlie Leslie said frankly the people were tired of being dictated to by churchified fools, but Hugh Moorhouse yammered, the way a fundamentally honest man does when he feels obliged to be dishonest about something for high motives. Then the writing girls, most of them asleep. Rita MacLean read a story about a boy who drank too much beer in a pub and thought he went to heaven—a pleasant but rather too facile fantasy, of the sort that schoolgirls go for. Afterwards a procession of people: Eleanor Coutts, to show me a book on Jewish mysticism by a Jerusalem scholar whose name I think is Gershom Scholem,[19] & Norma Arnett, to tell me she wants to do an M.A. thesis on Traherne. She's put her hair up recently, and it seems to have affected her mind: she's very nervous & giggly, whereas last year, though tense enough, she seemed much more secure of herself. I wonder if she's in danger of some crackup. Then Jack Vickery, who looks much better—

he seems to like Wisconsin.[20] Stingle didn't come over for the holiday: he's busy finishing up his Morris thesis. Vickery seems to feel that Wisconsin isn't doing much for him, but that it's intellectually respectable enough. He's doing Wordsworth with Jerry[21] and, he says, some Spenser with a man I didn't get the name of. They must have a terrific Renaissance department. Maybe this man got the bid intended for me. [22]

[10] Helen came in and we went off to the Plaza roof[23] to have our first party since the holiday started. It didn't make much for my evening, but I love the sense of quiet detachment that that place and the contemplative materials they supply give me. We came home in a taxi and went to bed early—Helen with an incipient hangover.

Wednesday, January 4

[11] I caught the train to Huntsville (a euphemism: I'm a great coward about trains and am generally to be found crouching and ready to spring in front of the gate an hour before it opens) and the trip up was without incident. No snow, except a few patches in deep woods north of Washago, and the ground was a mass of subtle colors: maroons and russets, tan and straw, and something—I think a moss—covering the ground with a lovely burnt orange. In Muskoka there were the outcropping rocks, gray and green, with pinkish streaks from the granite. It sounds a bit sugary, but it wasn't really.

[12] Huntsville (pop. 3600) is a pretty little town set in rolling hills beside the lake. The hotel was as luxurious as the Royal York, and I had two baths. A Mr. Kenneth Prueter phoned: he turned out to be the inspector of schools for the district. Huntsville is a bit down on its luck: temporarily (no skiing) and in the long run. Its lumbering has suffered a good deal from cut-and-run profiteers and evidently there's no legislation to stop that sort of destruction. Prueter said that the Muskoka Wood Co., the largest lumber firm there, was more enlightened: it's run by the Hutchinson family (two members, cousins, at my lecture) who have a more permanent sense of values. Fishing has also been largely destroyed by rich locusts in airplanes.

[13] I think the talk was all right—a hash of my Culture Commission stuff,[24] with some of the Library Association one unloaded during the

question period. I made them laugh towards the end, and of course the questions brightened it up a lot. A Dr. Milligan, uncle of Don, says Don died three years ago of brain tumor. An Indian whose name sounded like DeSyce had been speaking to the Rotary Club & he spoke in the middle of my talk: they usually ask for a recess, & had him instead of music. Curious custom. Nice guy, very pro-Gandhi. Like so many Indians, solemn & obviously ambitious. I went to the home of a pleasant couple named Conway, & was interested that everyone drank liquor although they were clearly all church workers—some I think United Church. Maybe those boobs at 299 Queen[25] don't know their own strength: they certainly don't know their own weakness.

Thursday, January 5

[14] I decided that on the whole I'd waste less time if I got some sleep, so I came in at 12:30 and slept till 7:30 in the morning. The alternative was to get a train at 4:18 a.m. I got up and prowled around the town: it was much colder and began to snow. The streets were deserted except for a vast concourse of dogs: evidently everybody in Huntsville has a dog, and as it was garbage collection day, they were all out investigating the garbage and each other. The next train out was at half past one, so I got it and tried to atone for my quixotic wasting of two days by slugging at my Milton paper.[26] That paper is without exception the most unrewarding piece of writing I've ever tried: I mean the greatest effort for the least result. However, such as it is, I think I've got to within a paragraph or two of the very end.

[15] Got home in time for dinner, and then Helen dismayed me by dragging me out to Yvonne Williams['] place to listen to Norah McCullough talk. She was ever a talker, so, one talk more. She's a really pathological talker: she held all five of us (the Halls were there) with her eye, and when one or two would squirm or look away or make a tentative remark to someone else, she'd hold the remainder; she was occasionally reduced to one (me) but she never stopped. I mean that almost literally. Mostly about Saskatchewan, and the personalities in the Adult Education Department. I was startled to learn that the C.C.F. don't expect to win the next Saskatchewan provincial. Norah still keeps assuming that I'm a prominent and influential member of the C.C.F. and could do something about their bad Adult Education policy in Saskatch-

ewan if I wanted to. Unfortunately her own unending blither about personalities would confirm any C.C.F.er in thinking the Department was a bunch of longhairs, & any non-C.C.F.er in thinking that the whole government was a bunch of incompetent amateurs.

[16] She released us at last, and the Halls told us on the way home that Elizabeth Scott's liver has quit functioning, & she's going to die. Grim piece of news. Yvonne's studio is a beautiful and spacious job, with wide lovely windows in the studio and very compact and well designed living quarters.[27] After the squalor of Lismer's, she must feel stimulated by such a symbol of success.

Friday, January 6

[17] A somewhat wasted day: I guess I'm not one of the wise men. The nine-o'clock was the first of a series of running comments on *Paradise Lost*, dealing with the first two books. I thought my material on that was in better shape, but I sprawled around a good deal. Judy Livingston yawned in my face the whole time, which didn't help any. Then I had a chapel service to do, and as the prescribed Scripture reading was from Peter's Pentecost sermon in Acts, I tried to say something about the Holy Spirit, without much success. I seemed to be dull and tired. Hilliard [Trethewey] drove me down—I haven't got him that Joan Evans book[28] I was thinking of getting him for Christmas, and I don't quite know what to do about it. Robins tells me that on the Comprehensive someone had given, as an example of a picaresque novel, "Turvey," by Frances Birney.[29] Speaking of the Birneys, we got an exceedingly corny New Year's card from them—sometimes I wonder about that family. Also in the mail was a pleasant fan letter from someone named Keith Rinehart, who's doing a Ph.D. in Wisconsin: my connections with that place are certainly stronger than anywhere else.

[18] Came home for lunch—Lucy Massey is in town, and she'd been invited. She's a really wonderful woman in her way, and my father behaves like a twelve-year-old child when she's around. Being human, she likes the homage. I think she's putting a mild pressure on him to stay up here, as it's hardly fair for her to assume the responsibility for looking after him if he collapses in Moncton suddenly.[30] On the other hand, I know perfectly well that he's putting off as long as possible the day

when he'll have to come here permanently. When he does, something in his organic unconscious will raise the question, "Why shouldn't I die now?" So I'm in no hurry to force the issue.

[19] In the afternoon the three of them went off to an English movie called "The Chiltern Hundreds,"[31] evidently a very easy-going and good-tempered picture, and a big success for all concerned. I might just as well have gone, for all the work I did. Helen has just bought a rug and armchair for my study, and for some reason I can't relax in a room without a rug.

Saturday, January 7

[20] Yesterday I met Murdoch MacKinnon, who is planning to write a book on Sir John Harington—an admirable subject, though I doubt that MacKinnon is an admirable person to do the job. I think he wants a Nuffield,[32] and is sounding me out. He says John Graham is fitting in very well at Western—that's a relief. Prueter,[33] incidentally, told me that Western men were compelled by the Extension department, which has a lot of power, to do three & four evenings a week lecturing in nearby small towns in addition to their regular work. Part of Western's policy of digging itself into the community, at the expense of course of their staff.

[21] I got out very late: a heavy snowfall kept me busy with my legal thirty feet.[34] I didn't mark any essays, but spent my time getting letters written. I have a phobia about letters anyway, and I got rid of a number of accumulating neuroses. Letters to Edith Sitwell and Dallas Kenmare in England,[35] Beaver Scholarship recommendations for Doug Fisher & John Nicol, various bills paid: it doesn't sound like much, but it means a lot to get them done.

[22] Peter [Kemp] was brought over this afternoon, and Helen's parents stayed for dinner. Dad was out with Lucy [Massey], & didn't return until eight o'clock. Helen was worried, but I pointed out that we let him stay in Moncton from one year's end to another without worrying, & he seemed to survive. Actually he (and she) got confused by the street cars, & went all over hell's half acre (I don't know what process transmuted that phrase into the meaning of a large area). Helen's father seems dead tired, querulous and in need of a rest from grandchildren.

[23] Murray Thomson and Don Franco were over tonight: I'd heard enough about Saskatchewan, but actually Murray was very decent. We talked about religion mostly, & his feeling that a church sermon built up a habit of uncritical acceptance of external authority. I see what he means, though I find that sort of liberal-secularist dialectic pretty frivolous. Franco is teaching school in Welland, which he says is a fascinating town for watching cultural minorities and class stratifications.

Sunday, January 8

[24] I don't quite know what to say about today: I have seldom wasted a day so completely. Of course all the work I had lined up for myself to do was irksome—letters, essays, the final paragraph of the Milton—so naturally none of that was done. But I didn't even do any reading of importance, nor even try to get a decent radio programme. Yet in spite of this I felt profoundly at peace with the world, playing with the baby,[36] listening to Dad talk (he's far less repetitive this year than usual), and just buggering around. The day was gone before I realized what had happened to it.

[25] Nevertheless, this sort of thing can't really be condoned: I haven't yet figured out what to do with Sunday, and my anxiety to have it all to myself gives me Kierkegaard's "dread" or *angst*, & [sic] about which he talks very well, except that he doesn't see that *angst* is the state of Blake's Spectre of Urthona: the egocentric or proud desire to *possess time*, the revolt against the consciousness of death. My possessive attitude, not only to Sundays, but to time generally, is bothering me a good deal, but hanging on to time is the last infirmity of noble mind. The Jewish Sabbath was a day of rest at the end of the week: the Christian Sunday is a day of leisure at the beginning of the week. Leisure is the opposite of laziness, & hasn't really any more to do with rest than with work. It's the essential condition of creative life, the relaxation from ritual, the removal of the censorious urgency of routine, in which that free association of ideas which begins the creative process is allowed to function. In short, it's listening to the Word. Surely that's what a member of the leisure class should do with Sunday. A day spent in a synthetic waste of time—sports & the like—seems to me an inevitable but hysterical reaction from drudgery.

[26] All theology is designed to persuade people to go to church, but I'm rather obstinate about not going to church, even when I do nothing better—and it's very easy for me to do better. As I don't believe in a substantial real presence, I don't believe anything *happens* at a church service. I don't understand the "this do in remembrance of me" aspect of Christianity: it seems silly, & I must think about it. Religion is still where medicine was in, say, 1750: its practitioners are sincere, but it can't really cure.

Monday, January 9

[27] I think constipation is to nervous sedentary academics what boils were to Job: a certain humiliation & a possible test of faith. The strain of getting back to work hasn't been recorded further down than the neck, and my gut still bucks up and says "who, me?" when I request it to function on schedule. However, I got out and started talking. The Hooker lecture was dreadfully dull, to me as well as to them—full of theological issues I've only very imperfectly grasped myself. I picked up a little in the graduate group, where I started to try to work out the progressive & regressive characters of romance: virgin or heroine-anima against the harlot, wise old man against the malignant old man, and so on. I must realize that, as the monster usually contains the old man, so the hero is supported by the bearing animal (horse), in which, as Jung showed, there's some suggestion of a progressive mother.[37] It also occurred to me that the hero-monster antithesis is always a victim-tyrant one. The hero is always in a revolutionary role: he releases the victim from the tyrant, which is why the giant is usually an enemy. Feudal or chivalric aristocracy owed its power to its militant struggle for order against rapacity: its decline began with the regularizing of the crusading impulse on which it was founded into an external war, & so a defence of the *senex* order in Christendom. Also, if the bearing animal can become a machine, the old-man monster could too—the labyrinth is a machine, & so is the mill with its revolving wheels. I rather shot the works this morning.

[28] To Emmanuel to get my picture taken by Leroy [LeRoy] Toll with the 5T1 executive[38] & asked them to supper the 22nd. They said they wanted Sunday as the residence people get gypped out of a meal then. I expected six, but there are nine: three "members at large" have been added. They are large, too. However, the executive lasts all year instead

of just one term. I tried to assume my usual kindly & benignant smile for the camera, which will doubtless reproduce the usual fatuous leer. Came home to find Helen worn out with Peter [Kemp], who by that time of course had recovered his temper. He howled dismally for half an hour after he went to bed, so I finally broke all the rules & went up to him. He'd lost his bottle (the present focus of his sexual life, Freud says) in the bed clothes, so I dug it out & plugged it into his puss & heard no more from him. Marked fifteen essays.

Tuesday, January 10

[29] Got out fairly early and my Newman lecture wasn't bad: the straight stuff about the evolution of dogma, but in the middle of it I got a strong vision of the identity of the Roman law and the Roman Church, and of both, especially the law, as intimately connected with the Aristotelian entelechy or law of the organized being, a biological conception that seems to permeate all our thinking. Obvious, but as a vision it's worth having: it may be involved in ⊥ [Ignoramus] as well as ⊢ [Paradox]. I think I almost shot a sitting target when I wrote that Church & Society paper:[39] it seems almost to have paralyzed further intuitive movements in that direction. Certainly there was a great contrast between it and the dry precise accuracy of my three other papers,[40] where I'm completely on top of the subject. Irving told me today he'd written four or five pages to the Guggenheim about me, stating in reply to their question about the importance of my work that it made everything else English professors were trying to do look trivial. Also that the editor of the Kenyon Review (Price?)[41] wanted the name of a "real writer" in Canada—they pay $10 a page, & I gather he doesn't want to be bothered with run-of-the-mine academics. All very pleasant. My R.K. lecture was on Job, and not bad: more Leviathan symbolism, but nothing new.

[30] I don't quite know how it happened that seven or eight attractive young ladies turn up on my doorstep every Tuesday afternoon to read me stories, but they do and I don't mind.[42] This time it was that luscious child Mary Lane—Liz they call her—with a story about mountain-climbing. Good story too—full of opulent & lush description and a mystical experience of being out of time—evidently the girl herself has done some climbing. Then a melodious little poem by Sylvia Moss. Kay Brown wants to join the group. I managed to get my quota of essays done, and

so stayed down to the lecture—Thomson on Thompson (Francis).⁴³ Quite a decent lecture, if you care about Thompson—I don't for some reason. Post-romantic religiosity seems to me a lot like diabolism—it combines all the disadvantages of superstition with none of the advantages of religion. Hilliard [Trethewey] drove me home: he seems keen to get at his Racine lecture & I'm very glad I asked him to do it. My copies of the English Institute book⁴⁴ came today & I gave one to Ned [Pratt]. Went home and did a few more essays, but felt very tired.

Wednesday, January 11

[31] Dawdled around in the morning, enjoying the absence of a nine o'clock—I *am* a lazy bastard. The second year lecture, again on Hooker, was much better: I gave them the idea of law spread out over the chain of being. Man halfway between the angelic & the animal, hence a threefold law; the law of the church, which is "intuitive," a symbol or Butlerian "analogy" of Eternal law;⁴⁵ the law of society, which is rational & distinctively human, & the law of instinct, which produces the army of Caesar (I added this for completeness). How law begins as external & arbitrary command, then becomes the inner discipline of reason, then the reconstructed accuracy of instinct, via ceremonial & ritual, on the higher level. Not bad: I'm gradually getting this point a little clearer. Then the twelve o'clock on Newman, where I linked his genetic & pragmatic ("skeptical," he calls it) view of probability with his choice of the genetic confession form and his primarily historical cast of mind. Then tried to develop the idea of sacramental analogy via his view of Butler, without much success.

[32] Went over to the Forum office: they say they can't let me off Christmas editorials for a while yet: they give the Forum too much publicity. Some Indianapolis paper that scrounges quotable things covered the back of its Xmas issue with it: somebody in the States mimeographed it & sent it out as a Xmas card; McAree (this I didn't know) referred to it & quoted a slab of it.⁴⁶ I generally read McAree, too. Sneaked off from the second Armstrong lecture⁴⁷ & went & had a couple of drinks. Back to dinner in Burwash & assembled for a discussion afterwards. Thomson seemed a decent enough sort, but unfortunately that lugubrious whippoorwill Malcolm Wallace was there, so we all leaned on the wailing wall & boo-hooed for two hours about how nobody loved us. The trou-

ble is that an old twirp like that is not only tiresome, but malignant as well—that came out in the Dana Porter meeting last year.[48] We hear a lot about the wonderful respect for the humanities everybody had around 1900. Well, what did they do with it? Was Canada, in 1900, turning out poets & novelists worth a shit in a cow barn? Was it turning out real scholars who could write important & lasting books? Nonsense. All the educational process in Canada was doing then was putting silk hats on middle-class farmers like him.

Thursday, January 12

[33] The Milton lecture was addressed to some pretty unresponsive & yawny kids, but still I got a few things clear that I'd never realized before. The allegory of Sin & Death, for instance, incorporates the theme of the female monster Scylla & the devouring Charybdis. The Limbo of Vanities, the goal of human good works, is the upper limit of Beulah, the moment of vision where the cycle still whirls you around. The outside of Eden, where we first see Satan, is the forest or jungle, the other side of the garden. The sheep in the pasture are thus contrasted with (as in Dante) the wolf in the forest. Also that the "myopic" visualization is in Book IV shifted to perfumes, smell being the most languorous & least critical of the senses. Then we suddenly get the stinking fish of Tobit: Milton doesn't give you the ridiculous farting devils of the Middle Ages, but still the devil stinks. The first year lecture, on Job, had nothing new in it. King Joblin said his kids, when he got to Buddhism, had dug up the Buddhist priest at Huron St. & brought him along.

[34] In the afternoon I ordered posters for the public lectures, then went to a tea for Jean Ross Skoggard's chinoiserie—not bad either. I said it was good to her, & she said wistfully "I guess you'd have to say that anyway." Then to tea with Clarke Irwin, for Farrar of Farrar & Strauss, a shy man full of bursts of confidence. George W. Doran, the last half of Doubleday Doran, now a very old man with a goatee, was there. Knoxes, Inneses,[49] Kay Coburn & of course the Clarkes. Irene [Clarke] is very unhappy about the Library. So am I. Says she thinks the place needs a blood transfusion. So do I. We got along. Helen had sent me word she couldn't get to it, & I came home to find her painfully ill & Aunt Lily [Lilly Maidment] in charge. A flu germ apparently hit her suddenly at noon and gave her a stiff neck: her whole left arm was put out of

commission. I helped her with her bath & got her into bed, but I had to go out to a Forum meeting & she wanted to sit up till I came home. She was worse then, but I plugged her full of aspirin & hot milk & she got to sleep, after a fashion. Her main trouble was claustrophobia. I'd hoped Peter Morgan would drive me home, but he could only take me to Yonge Street, & in trying to get out he locked bumpers with Edith's [Edith Fowke's] car & we were held up a good half hour. When you accept a ride you never feel like walking out on your host. The meeting itself was relatively uneventful: the February issue is more or less in hand.

Friday, January 13

[35] The Kemps are wonderful in emergencies: Helen's mother arrived at 7:15 a.m. I left the whole house in her charge and went off to my nine o'clock. Milton again: I tried to work out something on the "He for God only" line [*Paradise Lost*, bk. 4, l. 299] about how humanity is descended from *Eve* in its natural form & needs a mediator with God who can only be a new Adam. More on the dream as the revolt of the egocentric libido, the principle of pride, against a law which it regards as an external censor—this clicks with an old hunch I've had that Freud describes the man under the law—it's not an accident that he wrote a book on Moses and regards the conquest of the Promised Land as the "future of an illusion." Then how Satan in the temptation communicates directly with the proud libido in Eve, a parody of the way the Holy Spirit in man answers to the Word. The problem of the ultimate externality of both libido & Spirit remains unsolved. Also of the fact that unfallen Eve is the "passion" part of Adam's own body, whereas the fallen Eve is the entering wedge of an external "nature."

[36] Lunch with Earle Grey at the Arts & Letters about a proposed series of Elizabethan lectures in June. Not much there: he's clearly a man of impulses & enthusiasms: got the idea of doing "A Day in the Life of an Elizabethan" parallel to Lister Sinclair's Johnson one. My work & his credit line, apparently. Nuts. Went back to the College and picked up the third issue of Acta, with a staff picture in it that I said made me look like a homosexual judge.[50] Went home (because I'd phoned without getting an answer: everybody was asleep) but found things in good order & Helen much better, so went back to listen to Irving at the Culture Commission.[51] Stated a "disequilibrium" theory of modern culture arising

from the over-intellectualized ideas of Renaissance. He pointed to Galileo as the basis of what Descartes popularized, & quoted him as saying that while he didn't know what man was, man was clearly a spectator. As he rather slighted the role of Bacon in science, I said that to call man a spectator makes nature theatrical, and that Bacon denounced the speculative abstract system as an "idol of the theatre."[52] For him, I said, man & nature interpenetrated: they were, so to speak, in it together: sometimes man & sometimes nature appeared to be the creative half of the partnership, but that their relation was always active & manipulative. Hence Bacon is a kind of springboard for the social sciences, taking the final step by making natural science socially respectable.[53]

Saturday, January 14

[37] Helen was much better this morning, but didn't want me to go to the office, so I stayed home all day, somewhat to my chagrin: I really need a spell at the office on Saturday to pick up odds & ends of correspondence & such. So I felt I rather wasted the day—I'm not implying that anybody wasted it except me, of course—and consoled myself by starting to read the Inferno for the fourth time, with the general idea of really getting a grip on Dante. I think I may, too: I noticed how the encounter with the three beasts indicates Dante's break with the conventional epic structure. (They represent, by the way, Milton's chaos, sin & death.) He's in the position of a knight-errant ready to encounter the monster, but he has to dodge the monster & go a roundabout way. What he does, of course, is enter the belly of Leviathan. The fact that the agent of his redemption is Virgil with his *belle stile* makes the identification of the "hero" & the poet complete. He & Milton are thus progressive in relation to the dialectic of the epic: Spenser & the Renaissance Italians, in going back to the Christian worthy, were regressive.

[38] I've been looking at my meaning paper[54] & I'm not satisfied with it. It's not bad, but the fact that there is a cognitive element in centripetal meaning is asserted only, not demonstrated. I need to do some more work on the evolution of the verbal structure out of free association, ambiguity & paronomasia—also on what the completed structure *means*, if it does. I don't know: I can't seem to get back to firm ground. The general pattern emerging is too long & complicated. I don't know that I can really break off a nice clean chunk like my "Function" article.[55]

[39] Nothing "happened" today except that I went over to the corner for some shopping & dropped into the Deer Park Library:⁵⁶ something I very seldom do. I approached it in the spirit of a querulous invalid: I wanted to read *something*, didn't know just what, & nothing the stacks offered me would quite do. I finally went off with a copy of Hudson's *Purple Land*, which I have no intention of reading.⁵⁷ I met David Parsons there: he seems to be back to normal, & neither of us mentioned his silly letter of last summer. He even spoke of coming to terms with the thesis again. Meisterschaft naturally bores him,⁵⁸ but I told him that to have some definite target to hit was an advantage: university students had no idea what their minimum demands were.

Sunday, January 15

[40] Another aimless Sunday: we went out for supper to the Grubes. The Morgans⁵⁹ were there, & Kay Coburn. Very pleasant party. We listened to Mary Winspear review Kay's "Grandmothers" on the radio.⁶⁰ Just general chatter: John [Grube], who is in Orientals,⁶¹ had to go out to a group of Moslem friends celebrating the birthday of Mohammed. George [Grube] has never mentioned my letter to him, but it's clear to me that he's read it. We got home about ten & listened to a very masterly performance of the second Brandenburg & A minor violin concerto on the air from the CBC orchestra. As Roy [Kemp] used to say when he played trio with Helen & Harold [Kemp]: "Every man for himself, & I'll see you at the coda."

[41] Some more Dante: I hate the Inferno, because Dante so obviously believed, not only in a substantial & objective region of torture that never ends, but in all the legal quibbles that entrap divine "love" into sending people there, such as failure to have been baptized. It's too easy to work out the imaginative aspect of it, the symbolic reasons why Virgil can't be saved & a perfunctory Christian can be. One still remains stupefied by the perversity of the human mind. Dante saw everything in hell except the fact that to create an imaginative hell and then suggest that it's real is an act of intellectual treachery to the God in man lower than that of Judas, who may conceivably have acted from better motives. I can't help feeling that there *is* some development in literature, for all I say to the contrary. George Orwell's 1984 presents a real hell, not just one we happen to be more scared of, & his book is morally an infinitely better

book than the Inferno. Surely this moral superiority has some relevance to critical standards.

[42] Re Burke: prejudice is always a major premise, & sets up a deductive *a priori* pattern of reasoning in the mind. If I read Burke with a prejudice against him, the proposition: "everything Burke says is wrong" is submerged in my mind like an iceberg. I don't consciously admit it, or wouldn't without heavy qualifications, but still a large part of my reaction to Burke will be a syllogistic rationalization of a premise that he must somehow be wrong. The prejudice is not in itself emotional: it may be caused by an emotion, but in itself it's simply an inadequate & premature major premise. Mill's in and out movement, of principles fed by observation & observation illumined by principles, seems to me a pretty definitive statement of something or other.

Monday, January 16

[43] The nine o'clock was the first on Religio Medici: the usual stuff—I find it hard to say anything either new or significant to 2i. The graduate group was, as usual, better: I worked out the analysis of Milton's three-fold act for them & showed them how the creative act, which is prophetic, is the Christian form of the epic quest: the monster in this case is Nimrod, the Leviathan of tyranny, and the impotent old king who is redeemed is ultimately Adam, which explains why the dragon & the old man aren't identical, but are related as tyrant & victim. It's an important link. I let them go ten minutes early in order to think of something to say to the librarians.

[44] The librarians were a very keen & appreciative bunch, & fed me extremely well. Sanderson was on my right, [Dorie?] opposite, & the chairman, a woman named Dean, on my left. We started with sherry, which was unusual, & then after lunch I gave them a bit of a rehash of my Guelph talk, of which I still have the notes. Not altogether, though: I said that the changeover from passive to active education, whenever it occurred, put the student in the hands of the librarian. Also that the first step in attaining freedom of choice & individuality of character in education was marked by the choice of books. The rest of the talk was inspirational, I think. They presented me, or rather Helen, with a huge white cyclamen—fortunately a girl named McCann drove me back to the College.

[45] Over to the colloquium, with Bob McCrea [McRae] giving what seemed to me a rather indecisive paper on the antithesis between rationalists who thought history was predictable & "historicists" who thought there was nothing to do but play your hunches. Bob isn't as adroit in dodging questions as I am, & got into some trouble with people like Pucetti [Puccetti] needling him from one side & Fackenheim from another. A paper like that shouldn't ignore the social sciences, or, say, economics, where the predictable element is unquestionable. The delivery was very good & clear, but I still think philosophers are a bit oblivious, somehow.

[46] Well, well. On the way back Woodhouse told me Don Cameron Allen of Johns Hopkins had written him asking him if he thought anyone in Canada was capable of filling a full professorship there: 19th c. preferred, but failing that, history of criticism & general problems. At the end of his letter he said "What about Frye?" I said "please don't slam that door." Salary $7000, leading (they don't say how soon) to $8000. Clark of U.B.C., who wrote that very useful book on Boileau, was there:[62] he's reading my book now & likes it very much.

Tuesday, January 17

[47] The nine o'clock began on Arnold: I thought the most promising thing to bite off was the relation of classes to society. How upper, middle & lower classes could, if they dissolved themselves as classes, contribute culture, liberty & equality respectively to society; how *qua* classes they were only barbarians (i.e. an occupying army), philistines (i.e. merely anti-cultural) and popular (i.e. merely anti-democratic). In each case the natural self of the class resists the better self of the class directly above it (it goes round in a circle: the barbarians are merely anti-egalitarians)[.] I think this is extremely important because it illustrates a point that seemed inconsistent when I stated it in my discussion of romance in the prose fiction paper: that the feudal aristocracy was a militant revolutionary group, whose strength was in subduing the internal proletariat (chivalry) & whose weakness was in trying to take on the external one (crusades).[63] Hence not only are Carlyle, Bentham & Marx wrong in attempting to solve class conflict through a dictatorship of one class, but a pseudo-aristocratic revolution (Nazism) cannot produce anything but a race myth, & a pseudo-proletarian one nothing but an anti-democratic one. (The pseudo-bourgeois revolution is that of the "intellectuals," or

"natural aristocracy," that attempts to make like the goose that laid golden eggs, but only produces turds.)

[48] The R.K. lecture tried to finish up Job, but got involved with a mass of questions—I want questions, of course, but it continually surprises me how novel an idea the existence of the physical world in a spiritual form—surely the most elementary idea that one could find among any of the higher religions—is to them. As soon as it hits them, they fire all the questions at me that theologians have been racking their brains over for centuries, as though I had snap answers for them all. Bless their poor little innocent hearts. I went to the Forum office in the afternoon and read over the editorials, then wrote my own on Sunday sport[64] & tottered home. I seemed to feel a cold coming on, & went to bed early. I got beside Bill Little at lunch & we discussed the Browns. He said that Maud was sore that [Walter T.] Brown's portrait didn't show him smiling. As he says, few of us have ever seen Brown with his mouth shut.

Wednesday, January 18

[49] The Browne lecture was technically quite good: I recovered my Gertrude Stein technique, which on the whole I've lost this year, of repeating a point in fifty different ways until they begin to see some of the facets. It made an impression, but of course I don't like Browne & his perverse anti-intellectualism: he seems to me fundamentally frivolous, at least in that first book. Then I dodged over to the bank and back for my twelve o'clock. More Arnold: nothing very new & a rather disappointing lecture, as I'd expected great things of it. However, I did say that civilization was the idea of culture actualizing itself & informing history, & identical with his fourth "power" of culture, social life & manners.

[50] I missed lunch, rather a risky thing to do as it gave me heart flutters half the night, & got over to Hart House at 1:30 just in time to introduce George Johnston on the New Brunswick art show. He was very good, after a slow start. Then I collected the purchasing sub-committee and we decided to recommend a small & unpretentious Lucy Jarvis for $40 & a moderately competent Jack Humprheys [Humphrey] for $60. Some argument about a rather slick Alex Colville—windmill against a blue sky—and a Miller Brittain "Morning Stars Sang Together"—I felt it was interesting but unsuccessful.[65] I'd like to see an all-Colville & Brittain

show next year, with more to pick from. Then I went to Tuck Shop & talked to young Boggs—a very intelligent & sensitive lad, who knows Barbara Pentland (now at UBC)—while I ate two very indifferent doughnuts. Then I buggered half an hour at Simcoe Hall listening to Laidlaw say that Biology 17 had been changed by statute to Biology 19. General Course Committee, they called this nonsense. Picked up Blissett, who took me to tea at U.C., & then, realizing I was missing Greta Kraus & some Bach, went to a Ph.D Committee meeting. Met [F.H.] Anderson at tea, & he said he'd like to see my meaning paper.[66] He's broken his left arm, & looks very tired. At the Ph.D. meeting I urged the drawing up of a basic reading list, which will no doubt involve me in extra work. Norman [J. Endicott] said he liked my Quixote paper very much though he still worried about my "unconscious intention" theories.[67] Jean Elder came over for dinner, by herself—her father had been asked, but he fell downstairs & hurt himself.

Thursday, January 19

[51] The Milton lecture wasn't as fresh as last week's lectures, but it wasn't bad: I tried to work out Book X as a kind of archetypal flood, a destruction (largely) of the order of nature set up in VII. Then I marked the first year class essays, very approximately. Gordon Wood was in: he's got that Tracy offer from Pacey[68] & I'd advised him to see Robins. But Robins just dithered & yammered & wouldn't say anything definite. Robins' refusal to play any sort of cooperative or social role has been past the boundary of neurosis for some years, & the sooner he quits the better, I think, as far as responsibility is concerned. I have been very disappointed in him for some time. In fact I am worried about my future as a first-class scholar in a second-class institution, but that's another story. I don't know what to do for Gordon, except try to prod Robins again. George Johnston was in too, & some of my second-year kids (Catherine Wilson & Patricia Smith). George hasn't begun his thesis yet: that's an iniquitous system we go in for: Woodhouse keeps saying he wants people to have their third year free & then they take till Christmas buggering over their generals.[69] I don't know why I'm so irritable. I think I woke up the first year people over Job, but nothing new emerged.

[52] At lunch Irving told me about a Scotch theologian named Bowman, who has written a book on *The Sacramental Universe*.[70] This was notes

from extempore lectures at Princeton—largely Irving's notes, & he showed me an article he'd written about Bowman for the Princeton Alumni magazine.[71] He (Bowman) appears to be a kind of neo-Gnostic, regarding the world as an emanation of spirit on four levels: *physical* (unconscious-objective), *natural* (including I gather the rationally intelligible, as "natural" differs from "physical" in being an object with a subject looking at it), *valuable* (moral & aesthetic apprehensions), and purely *spiritual*. Seems to have some link with my four levels. He says the lower level is in every case a function of the higher, & derives the Incarnation accordingly.

[53] Went over to the Forum & page-proofed it, or most of it. Bertie Wilkinson says we're "doctrinaire." Good old Bertie. I wish we were. They decided to put my Sunday editorial on the front page,[72] which makes me wince a little. Found Margaret Newton at home, but she couldn't stay to dinner.

Friday, January 20

[54] Today I started to clean up the last two books of *Paradise Lost*, and a lot of things suddenly cleared up, not wholly to my surprise. I found myself writing on the blackboard the whole time, which pleased them. I said the divine, human & demonic levels produced order or reason (creation), disorder or chaos (disobedience) & inverted order or passion (rebellion). Man like the will must be attracted to one or the other. In society these produced liberty, anarchy & tyranny respectively. Law could be a movement of the disobedient or unattached will to either. From there I went on to three levels of redemption: lowest, prefigured coming or law, the separation of good from evil & of one society from other tyrannies—Israel here means a human society. Next, individual coming or gospel; the release of positive good & of the individual from the law—Israel here means the body of prophets which forms the Christian Church. Lastly, second coming or apocalypse, the release of the whole people of God in the form of a single body—Israel here means both an individual body and a society. The movement appears to be Hegelian—I wonder if I'm veering toward Joachimism, though I suppose all Protestants take off from Joachim.

[55] Marked my graduate papers all day—some very good stuff. Whatton

said the first book establishes a Christian context for all those that follow it—that could be Woodhouse. I'm wondering about the antithetical nature of Books I & II. The Mallinson girl wrote the best essay: a fine study of Book VI bringing out the connection between courtesy & rhetoric, & the stress put on words.

[56] Otherwise I kept to myself: had lunch at Feinsod's[73] & seemed to want solitude. I went home early & found Helen in low spirits: Dad had got into one of his poor-mouth moods. However, she pulled out of it— she finds that mood contagious, & so hard to handle—and we all went to bed early. January is the month of heavy slogging. I dug a little deeper into Dante's hell, but am almost as anxious as Dante was himself to get out of it & on to purgatory. I am very pleased to find that I can, in a manner of speaking, read Italian—I don't mean the Inferno, which I've largely memorized anyway. After I've pulled my Latin up I'll really be ready for work. The New Yorker quotes Saroyan as saying that children are the only real aristocracy, which, believe it or not, really means something.[74]

Saturday, January 21

[57] I finally escaped to the office today & wrote a few letters & paid a few bills. I think it's a good thing to reserve Saturday for assorted nonsense I don't feel like doing on working days. Especially in the slugging season. Helen came down & we had lunch at the Chez Paris [Paree],[75] but I still hadn't got much work done & let her go on to the Museum by herself. I'm trying to put that damn Milton Preface in shape, & am not having much luck with it. It's very difficult for me to believe that anything I take no pleasure in writing is any good at all. I felt restless & kept talking to Helen about the chances of getting a better job in the States. I don't actually want a better job in the States, but my account is sixty dollars overdrawn & I could certainly use more money. One obvious move is to finish the Milton & collect that miserable $250. I have a savings account, but this is the big year for the second mortgage; also the year we'd like to get the house painted. Logically, this ought to be the last year for feeling any sort of financial squeeze.

[58] Reading the Inferno is depressing: I'm not sophisticated enough not to resent the leer behind it. This is why I can't accept the "conscious

intention" argument of Norman Endicott:[76] one of Dante's conscious intentions was certainly to scare the shit out of me, & it's hard not to protest against that intention. I know all about the difference between the imaginative & the spectral Dante, & that only the latter is trying to suggest the substantial existence of hell. I know too that it's a great tribute to Dante to feel he's demonic when reading the Inferno, heroic in reading the Purgatorio, & simply illuminated when reading the Paradiso. It's the same as feeling that Shakespeare is a militarist in Henry V, an anti-Semite in the MV [*The Merchant of Venice*], an atheist in Lear, & a benevolent sentimentalist in The Tempest. But the pseudo-literal aspect of hell is so psychologically regressive that it's bound to pull some of one down. Israel as law is Jacob, the seizer of the hero's vulnerable heel, & the traitor-accuser among the twelve, Dan the serpent. Meanwhile I'm trying to see if I can add anything to what Jung says by trying to figure out the Inferno as an analytical disgorging of regressive symbols. As the terrible mother (Fortune) & father (the Veglio [old man]) get disgorged fairly soon, maybe the actual sequence peters out in the long series of guttersnipes in the ten pockets of fraud.

Sunday, January 22

[59] The one event of the day was having the 5T1 executive kids in to supper. I didn't realize they'd abolished the office of Vice-President, and as the biggest of their members at large couldn't come, there were only seven. Three of the seven were girls, so it turned out to be a charming party. Helen made a ham & scalloped potatoes for them, & it was wonderful to see them eat. Lively kids, all in different courses, & very keen kids. John Finley [Finlay], who's in biology, upholding the power of the mind—besides, he'd learned how to find water with a hazelwand. Ian Outerbridge, who comes from that Chinese missionary family & talked about hurricanes in Bermuda (when houses collapse they explode from the *inside* because the storm lowers atmospheric pressure), Glenn Ross, a quiet boy I had lunch with earlier with Tom Dyke, & a hockey (Senior Intercollegiate) player named something like Hausman,[77] were the other boys. Peggy Quiggin (who seems to be a natural leader: she got them to wash dishes & told them when it was time to go home), Lucille Hoffman,[78] & a Barbara Sagar who's the daughter of an S.P.S. [School of Practical Science] professor, were the girls.

[60] I'm beginning to wonder if the foreground problem of ⊥ [Ignoramus] isn't a philosophical statement of the Marriage of heaven & hell. Or perhaps that's the theme of ⋏ [Rencontre] after all. Anyway, heaven in modern thought is involved in the dialectic of Thomism: the demonic dialectic has a lot to do with Marx, & I suppose a synthesis of Thomism & Marxism would be a very crude & approximate way of stating what I have in mind. The Thomist idea of the real universal, stripped of all the nonsense about substance, is certainly part of the "perennial philosophy": Marx' doctrines of a classless society, the humanization of deity, & of the causal role of instruments of production, are part of it too, when stripped of all the Hegelian clap trap about antithesis of classes & that metaphysical materialism that seems to keep buggering the dialectic one. I wonder if a reformed Thomism, a "dialectic realism," wouldn't be something like the answer. I don't know why the solution of this problem doesn't seem to me as far away as ⊥, but I guess it'll have to be: I *must* remember that time is fleeting even if art is long. In any case I have to get the main principles through my skull before too long: maybe Tillich, who is coming here, will have suggestions.

Monday, January 23

[61] Hilliard [Trethewey] drove me down & turning left at the Yonge-Rowanwood corner he hit the rear fender of a crazy antique cruising through the red light. The man, whose name was Peacock, showed no disposition to resist, & gave his name meekly. The nine o'clock was on Browne & not very good: my dislike (it's almost that) of Browne is aggravated by my students' refusal to read him. The graduate group waded into the Bible: I feel nervous about having the Harrons and John Drainie there who have heard it all before, which is a silly piece of vanity on my part. Even they seemed a bit apathetic. Underhill was in to lunch & I put the case of the Forum to him. He doesn't want to do it himself, but I was astonished that he would consider doing it. He took it for granted that I would get a Guggenheim. I suggested that the most promising places to look were, first, among younger academics of assistant-professor rank; second, among liberal & socially-minded clergymen of Anglican or United Church persuasion; third, among married women with not too many family responsibilities, as well as no job. Eleanor [Godfrey] was in an ideal position. But we can't ask back anyone we've

had, as the town is strewn with the wrecks of people who have quar-
relled with the Morrises [Lou and Kay]. He said he'd think about it, &
went off to the dentist.

[62] I finally decided (a very foolish decision) to go to the Department
meeting, as Blissett had come in for his thesis Friday & I'd forgotten to
bring it down. We started to beat the bejeezus out of the calendar again &
finally stalled on the new 3b course I'd been on a committee to draft last
year. Woodhouse, who always sabotages every meeting he's not chairman of, quoted Knox & Bissell, who weren't there, as saying there wasn't
enough to teach. When I left there was a string of six or seven proposals,
all of which had still to be voted on. I was so bored when I got home that
I let Helen take me out to a movie, called "Saints and Sinners."[79] It was
the same old plot that's been worn out on ten thousand other movies
already, but it was in a new setting (Irish village) with some good acting
(Abbey players) & fair characterization. The plot turned on a fear of the
end of the world: I suppose there would be a strong apocalyptic sense in
a country that felt oppressed, as well as a strong will toward private
revelation (in this case an old woman's prophecy) in a country that is
Catholic. Yeats & Joyce both show how strong this is, in different ways.

Tuesday, January 24

[63] A miserable sleety day, & my fourth-year kids' upper jaws reached
an all-time high. Arnold again, getting rid of the Hellenic-Hebraic nonsense with a blast at the Hegelian technique of oversimplifying com-
plexities, including the Marxist deliberate creation of an antithetical
"class struggle" pattern in society. I suppose Christianity—no, hell, that's
not Hegelian. I got anarchy into the blackboard pattern. Then I buggered
around feeling aimless, & started on my famous demonstration of the
anatomy of the spiritual world from Revelation. So far, it seems to take
all right. The writing kids were in & Jean Inglis read another story, very
good too: she really has ability if she'd do a little work. A Christmas
story, unfortunately, & at this time of year it's difficult to accept it for the
Forum: otherwise I'd have done so. A young couple in the dead calm of
marriage between courtship & children, very lonely in a new & hideous
"house beautiful" immaculately decorated according to the magazines.
Finally the girl pushed a lamp off & broke a "triangular piece" out of it.
Poor Jean had no idea what her story meant, & I explained as delicately

as I could that brides who were neurotically fussy housekeepers just after marriage thought of their houses as symbols of continuing virginity, that the "house beautiful" people knew that & exploited it unmercifully, & that the girl's final act was her mind righting itself. They looked thoughtful because they were trying not to look self-conscious. Catharine Card also read a pleasant fairy tale about toads—in form a little like the Oscar Wilde things.

[64] In the evening the Haddows took us to the symphony: very decent of them, as it was a special concert & they bought the tickets for us. Not many there. A long & varied programme. An overture by a Czech named Morawetz, who has clearly chosen freedom, a suite of Britten's based on Rossini themes & a rather undistinguished piece of movie music by a New Brunswicker named Eldon Rathburn, who's in the National Film Board. Also a Haydn concerto played by a fourteen-year-old girl got up to look like an infant prodigy: pig tails & short socks & a very little-girl sort of dress. The only really childish thing about her was her nervous little jerky curtsey, which consisted of sticking her backside into the concertmaster's face. The second half was the Silbelius second, somewhat ploddingly played.[80] Then we went home & had cocoa with them—very pleasant evening.

Wednesday, January 25

[65] The ten o'clock finished Browne & began on Burton—I have to step on it. The Arnold one turned out better than I expected: a discussion of his conception of culture as a kind of secularized Protestantism. I cited Hegel as an extremely immanent thinker, putting the idea entirely inside history; Newman as a transcendent one, putting the idea inside a self-enclosed Church which the world has to join, & Arnold as trying to work out a sort of "informing" middle role. Culture as creation is a transcendent Word of God, a canon of classics; culture as criticism is a growing & improving immanent force. If some outfit like the Hazen conference[81] had the sense to ask me to do a series of lectures on the idea of a Protestant university they'd be surprised at the results.

[66] Woodhouse had been phoning me frantically about a Ph.D. committee meeting, so I went over at three and we got Sawyer's thesis out of the way. He turned in an excellent statement on Conrad, & he'll be all

right. I'm not chairman, but I'm on. The graduate meeting itself thrashed over a petition of Percy Janes to substitute a novel for a thesis (M.A.). After about an hour of wrangling, Arthur Barker remarked that there was nothing in the calendar, or next year's calendar for that matter, which could possibly permit us to grant the request. So we turned it down, but appointed a committee to look into the question of bringing "creative writing" (what a revealing phrase that is!) in at the graduate level. Child and [Norman J.] Endicott are to go to Michigan to see what cooks there. The sort of impression Joe Fisher makes on me at such meetings has me bothered. I'm sure he's utterly the wrong choice as the next departmental head.

[67] Got home late & gobbled supper (macaroni & cheese, made by Dad) & then dashed back again to hear George Johnston's paper on The Phoenix & the Turtle.[82] I'm glad I never went further with my idea of writing a critical Golden Bough on that poem, but it still interests me.[83] George said afterwards that Shakespeare tends to push the catastrophe further & further forwards as he goes on, until in The Tempest it's in the first scene. Interesting as showing the development of late comedy out of tragedy, & approximation to the Book of Job form of analyzing tragedy. I also noted the link between the vanished phoenix of the threnos & the empty tomb of Fidele in Cymbeline.

Thursday, January 26

[68] Began on Paradise Regained today: my stuff on that is really too well in hand, & I think they felt overstuffed. The trouble is that it's what no poem should be: a great theme superbly handled by a profound & powerful mind, & yet a damned dull poem. Mary MacFarlane brought along the poems of Smart (still not complete) & a request to write a letter for her to the University Women's outfit. Nice ethical problem involved: should one mention the fact that she's engaged to be married? In the mail there was the last issue of Contemporary Verse with a long (& most friendly) analysis of my old Forum article by John Sutherland.[84] He must have fallen in love or something. I wrote him at once & told him to develop his ideas himself, as I would never have time to write much more on Canadian literature. The first year lecture wasn't very good, though I'm gradually getting my dialectic a little clearer. I went home early & read some more Inferno.

[69] In the evening the Citizens' Forum came to our house, so I had to sit around for that.[85] A very small group turned up—Ruth, Mrs. Saunders, Mrs. Cartier & the Baileys from Newmarket. The subject, debated by Blair Fraser, Lister Sinclair, Roger Ouimet & Agnes Macphail, was, who are the six great Canadians of the past half-century?[86] For God's sake. We thrashed that over a long time & finally decided to pick the six most inclusive categories & nominated one for each. In Politics, Government, Defence & Law, we picked [Mackenzie] King—all four had him. In Economics, Agriculture, Mining & Business, we picked Saunders, the Marquis wheat man. In Art, Literature, Music & the Drama we picked Arthur Lismer, because of his educational influence. Archie Bailey, by the way, talked very well about the importance of art. In Science & Medicine we picked Banting; in Education & the Press Coady [Cody]; in Social Welfare & Religion J.S. Woodsworth, also on all four radio lists. This question of great men is filler for a lot of magazines these days, & what impresses me is the amount one would have to know to make an interesting choice. I added a note to our report that we were entirely dependent on the publicity machine for our list. In literature, for instance, what Canadian has done the biggest job? Well, that's foolish, as are all questions about the greatness of men. What painter has done the most to reeducate our visual associations? Picasso gets the publicity, but maybe Braque did the essential job.[87]

Friday, January 27

[70] My tiresome nervous system is still bothering me: for some years now I've been needing my spark plugs cleaned without knowing how to do it. If I work or loaf, I'm still usually dead tired by 6 o'clock. If I do anything at all in the evening, I seem to wind up to a certain point of tension. If I have a nine o'clock lecture, & have to get up early, I haven't unwound sufficiently, & then my gut refuses to relax. This has happened four times—every day I've had a nine o'clock—this week. So today I felt utterly demoralized, unable to go back home because I knew Helen's mother & Mrs. Smith & the baby would be there. I gave my nine o'clock, on Paradise Regained, & it worked out all right, then went off to the Reference library. If I hadn't been so lazy & tired & sleepy & stupid & demoralized it would have been a wonderful day. But it wasn't: it was just a wasted day. I couldn't work at my paper; I couldn't do anything. This sort of thing has been going on for years. I don't know whether a

year off to knock a couple of books out of the way would improve matters or not, but I don't see how it could hurt. The point is that the situation is so completely *silly*. I don't really work so damn hard, but I have to pretend to myself & others that I do in order to account for my continuous exhaustion. I doubt if any doctor could put a diagnosis on it: I imagine that the terrible strain of producing the Blake & the feeling of anticlimax that's followed it has taken its toll: but there I am dramatizing myself again. At the moment, of course, I feel dreadfully bored because two things dangling in front of me all month like the apples of Tantalus haven't moved any closer. One is the Johns Hopkins offer,[88] the other the English invitation.[89] I've more or less written off the former, & the latter is fading. Then again, by not applying for the Nuffield I've stuck my neck out on the Guggenheim, & if I miss it I've really had it. Oh, well, I suppose I should set all this down, as I have at least another month of it to go through. More important is my recurring restlessness about Victoria, wondering if they'll really adopt [Walter T.] Brown's policy of running it at a third-rate level. If so, I must make up my mind to leave, & that won't be easy. As I've said, I don't think much of Joe as the next head, but he couldn't be much worse than Robins has been lately. Well, that's enough ego-squalling for the present. Light—I mean Lead, kindly Light, amid the encircling gloom. I don't care about choosing my path, but I'd like to get a glimpse of it occasionally.[90]

Saturday, January 28

[71] Saturday seems the day for writing letters of recommendation: two for the University Women's Scholarship & one (Ronald Bates) for a job in Sweden—Liljegren of Upsalla [Uppsala], the man who wrote that book on Milton that ought to be burned by the public hangman.[91] I said to Ronald: "I'll recommend you to him with great pleasure, but I can't recommend him to you." The women were Mary MacFarlane & Winifred Nelson at Bryn Mawr, who wrote me a most perfunctory letter without giving me the slightest hint about her graduate work or what she wanted me to do. I said she was a student of mine & a good girl. Clarence Lemke was in again: he's much better, his father's sick & he's taken over his business, which seems to be good for him. He's very pleased at having left the university, & it seems to have set him up.

[72] The more I think about my meaning paper[92] the more involved I get. I've been thinking of Smart's Jubilate Agno as a very good example

of how the creative process starts, in paronomasia & free association. Wherever we have "madness" we have glimpses of the creative process in action: Lear is a good example. Finnegans Wake may be something else again. (As I write this Dad decided he wanted to listen to a "Share the Wealth" radio program. A woman has just been offered $2450 to spell four words. The third was "psychology," & the poor creature, who was utterly unnerved anyway by the size of what was dangled in front of her nose, began on some "scy" combination & missed it. She'll remember it all her life, probably with feelings of humiliation if not actual guilt. I don't like the radio.) Jubilate Agno also has a passage on rhyme words & the orchestral sounds of words that shows how the original paronomasia process articulates itself into a metrical structure. The counterpart to this is the elaboration of diagrams in thought.

[73] Another thing that's just occurred to me: I've thought of the distinction between hypothetical (art) & natural (science) universes as actually taking the form of a one-to-one correspondence. Thus sculpture, I say, is the hypothesis of biology. Now, wouldn't I be in a fine mess if literature turned out to be the hypothesis of theology? Because that, if I stick to my "dialectic realism" line, would imply the descriptive or existential scientific validity of metaphysical realism. Or is the ontological argument necessarily an assertion only, & so hypothetical?

Sunday, January 29

[74] Dad left today & we took him down to the station in the afternoon. He seems quite cheerful. A.Y. Jackson had the seat in front of him & said the Art Gallery had an option on two Miller Brittains (I don't know how he spells it). Jackson is a nervous man: made enough gestures telling me this to represent the confusion of tongues at Babel. It was a dreary day, & what with Dad leaving Helen felt restless, so we went over to see the Hebbs. Andrew was messing about with that Overstreet book, "The Mature Mind," another example of a psychological person who has hit the jackpot of the Women's Clubs.[93] Even Ethel Fulton has read it. Overstreet quotes incessantly from Brock Chisholm: one of the things he says is, so help me God, that to end war we must persuade people to mitigate their combative instincts.

[75] I hope Dad didn't feel that he was under any obligation to leave: I think he feels, as we do, the constant pressure of his presence on the

ego—a selfish, even a despicable, part of one's nature, but still a part that's inseparable & will always be there, like an incurable neuralgia. I find I don't have much luck trying to apply Christian Science methods to the ego. But I'm sure I communicate nothing of this to him: I mean rather that *his* ego, or diabolic accuser, calls him a parasite just as mine calls him a nuisance.

[76] I should like to systematize my reading more along the lines suggested by the chapters of my Blake book. First, psychology & epistemology; second, metaphysics & theology; third, political science, economics & law; fourth, aesthetics & the criticism of the arts; fifth, comparative religion & anthropology; sixth, history; seventh, biology. The other sciences go on from there. I want to try to get the essential principles of Aristotle through my head in the second group, & then go on to St. Thomas. I think what I'm looking for in one is primarily the archetype. I've been reading Dante's Convivio, & I notice that he says, very calmly & flatly, that the Platonic idea, the Aristotelian telos & the Thomist universal are all the same thing. Also that the pagan gods are vulgarizations of this conception, just as "angels" are vulgarizations of the stellar intelligences. If I could link this up with a psychological archetype I'd be all set. I don't mean just Jung's archetypes either: I probably mean several categories of them.

Monday, January 30

[77] The nine o'clock was the usual nine o'clock, & the graduate group was only fair. I'm on the outlines of the verbal universe in the Bible now & I think I lost them. That is, they couldn't make the jump from the exposition of meaning leading up to the hypothetical verbal universe to the details of the symbolic parts of that universe. Nor did I get much out of it all that was new. In the afternoon I drifted over to U.C. again & Blissett again took me in to tea. He said something that struck me—that E.M. Forster is an essentially Meredithian novelist, his dislike of Meredith being protective. I said I couldn't take Meredith because of the latent sadism in him—in Evan Harrington, for example, about every third page has some image of flogging.[94] Blissett referred me to a remark in Aspects of the Novel about using "sharper instruments" than Meredith. He could be right at that—certainly those German females in Howard's End do seem to be in a constant state of Meredither. The meeting was for Pass

Course examiners—I'm on 1b with Woodhouse. I felt a bit depressed as a result of having collided with Wood & Laidlaw at lunch over what they called the cult of unintelligibility in modern poetry. They disgorged all the usual clichés & assumed that the strong liking I expressed for Valery's Cimetière Marin was either hypocritical or imaginary. (As a matter of fact it was largely both, but that wasn't their business.) I don't know why people of first-class critical ability just don't seem to be attracted to French when it's such a magnificent literature.

[78] I've been reading the Convivio, & it's much duller than I expected. It gives me a hint, though, on how to handle Milton's Christian Doctrine: it's the same rather tentative (and often contradicted later) working out of rather pedantic & fanciful ratiocinations that are set aside when the great poems come & clear them up. Some parts, like the association of the seven planets with the seven liberal arts, are just doodling. Yes, I think the archetype is what I look for first. After I've learned a little bit about Aristotle, I'd like to explore the way he got absorbed into conceptions derived from law: in Dante, for instance, the word "ragione" means both reason & Roman law: "reason teaches," he says, & then quotes Justinian.

Tuesday, January 31

[79] A hurried exit again this morning: several inches of snow fell, so I left the unpleasant duty until I got home. The nine o'clock finished Arnold, & nearly finished a blonde youngster who nearly dislocated her jaw. The R.K. lecture was fair, though I ran out of material early. The writing group provided a story by Sylvia Moss. Stephen tells the hero that, as fate is inevitable, suicide is the only free act. The hero, who is rather drunk, walks across the viaduct & contemplates a light shining below. He almost jumps over, but makes his decision to live. Then he sees a mysterious figure scrambling up the other side, dashes across to help him & is knocked sky-high by a car. His last thought is that Stephen was right. I said Stephen was wrong still, because if you will to live your death is accidental: only when you're preoccupied with your fate does it become inevitable, & this holds no matter what corny & contrived jokes "fate" plays to prove it's something more than accident. They said I was criticizing on moral grounds: I said I was holding out for the detachment of the author (and the reader of course) from the contrivance in the story.

[80] Gordon Wood came in: he's about decided to accept Pacey's offer. Damn Robins. I don't see what else he (I mean Wood) can do. We went out for a beer and discussed various things—my teaching (he says the graduate group was baffled yesterday), Peter Fisher (who is apparently not so detached politically as he seems when I'm around) and Fredericton as a place to live. Robins seems to feel that we can always whistle him back from N.B., but I dunno.[95] Then I went to an Art Committee meeting. They voted 6 to 5 for the Lucy Jarvis & against the others. They may have been right, but I didn't like Charles Comfort being so damn stuffy about it just because he wasn't there at the Subcommittee. It was a long meeting, but I didn't see how to speed it up. Charles says Louise's [Louise Comfort's] thyroid is acting up. Speaking of sick women, Helen spent all yesterday with Joan Grant, who is in some danger of losing her baby. She was back home all day. I find these ten-to-twelve hour days very trying, & went to bed early. I went over to Britnell's & checked over their stock yesterday, but bought only a Nicomachean Ethics, in Greek.

Wednesday, February 1

[81] Busy day: a ten o'clock scavaging the bits of prose in 2i: a job I hate, & am always glad to get over, & a twelve o'clock starting Ruskin. I drew my two parabolas on the board & gave my usual cultural history line. And then, so help me, I had a one o'clock. About 60 people turned up to hear me talk to the C.C.F. club about "Liberalism & laissez faire." I said the Tories had the advantage of realizing that "democracy" didn't mean anything unless you attached it to some economic context. I then tried to draw a contrast between the oligarchic tendencies of laissez faire & the revolutionary democratic action against it that finds its champion in representative government & works toward, not complete control of industry, but toward establishing a central authority to which all industry must defer. Thus it saps the autonomous secret power of oligarchy which is withdrawn from popular control, from publicity, & from in short the community as a whole. Somewhat to my surprise, an obviously non-Socialist audience turned up. They grilled me pretty hard, & of course I know very little about economics, but I got through by some artful dodging.

[82] Meanwhile I wrote a letter to Miss Elizabeth Nitchie of Goucher

College, who wrote asking me to write a paper on Blake at the English Institute this summer. So that gives me something definite to do, at last. Sept. 8–12, it runs. Interesting that they've decided to do a group on Blake. I suggested four topics, with a preference for one on Jungian archetypes.[96] I skipped Cecil Bald's Donne seminar, but turned up to Council. No Essay Competition this year, thank god. Then Hilliard's [Hilliard Trethewey's] lecture on Athalie—as Robins said, he should have been wholly serious, like Matthew Arnold, but after some dismal facetiousness he turned in a sincere & quite powerful exposition of the play. The crowd wasn't bad, & that was the one I was worried about. Helen & I took them to a French dinner at the Chaumière afterwards, which I think they enjoyed—they even took a glass of sherry. Then Helen went off to a Healey Willan recital & I to Woodhouse's stag for Cecil Bald. Bald is a rather dry stick of a man, but pleasant enough. We talked about the Renaissance origins of Donne's imagery—funny how we always seem to talk over the heads of most of our visitors. Then Woodhouse & I settled Gordon Wood's future: good old Woodhouse came through with a readership.

Thursday, February 2

[83] I got down to the nine o'clock & talked about the storm & the pinnacle in Paradise Regained. About the storm as an epiphany of Satan to Christ, the prince of the power of the air showing the extension of chaos or the Leviathan-principle over the world. There's also some connection between the vision of eternity, which is a single detached symbol, & the "sign of the times" which is the oracular stimulus from nature to premature action—the atomic bomb, in short. I'm getting the end of L [Liberal] a bit clearer, but I need a lot more on the nature of archetypal meaning & on the importance of intensional as opposed to the old-fashioned extensional methods of source-hunting. The first-year lecture was routine: that R.K. course, at any rate the first-year one, is the chief thing I'm trying to run away from next year.

[84] In the afternoon I went over for a few minutes to a picture committee meeting. Mary Jackman said she'd seen a copy of the Forum for the first time in years & here was my name as editor. She wanted to know why we didn't reproduce pictures, & there was a latent hostility in her tone that made me bridle a bit. I cleared out & went to Tillich's lecture—

a huge crowd in Wycliffe. He talked on the "theology of despair": the attempt to start with despair as a "limit-situation." It disappointed me a little, as I'd read enough Kierkegaard to figure it out myself. Even the feeling it gave me of being on top of Tillich was hollow: I didn't want to feel on top of Tillich: I wanted to feel a contact with something fresh. Anyway, I went off to the Park Plaza & picked up Helen & we had a string of cocktails. Then we had dinner at Diana's, where we acquired Madelaine Page, & drifted over to hear Cecil Bald talk about Australian literature. We heard about three poets, Drury(?),[97] FitzGerald & Manifold—the last sounded interesting. Then he read from one of Furphy's novels—pleasant & a bit dated—& from a short story by someone called Barbara Bainton [Baynton], who evidently wrote around the turn of the century & sounded amazingly good—far better than anything we were producing at that date. I mentioned Seven Poor Men of Sydney,[98] the only Australian novel I've ever read, but Bald hadn't read it.

Friday, February 3

[85] At the nine o'clock I tried to work out my conception of the climax of Paradise Regained: it's the epiphany of Christ to Satan, the divorce of heaven & hell, which is actually the climax of Blake's Jerusalem too. I said something about the central symbol of Christ's life being the casting out of devils, which involved me in speculations I naturally couldn't work out on the spot. For instance, I said that the story of the sheep & goats takes place within the soul, & that consequently the sheep & goats are not people. At that point I was violently assaulted by a lad named Peter Grant. He started all the row last year by talking about "woodworker Joe" in a poem assimilating a virgin's fantasies to the Virgin Mary,[99] and now, it appears, he's backfired & got a V.C.F. [Varsity Christian Fellowship] type of religion. So naturally he didn't like the suggestion that there wasn't any red-hot hell to hasten a similar backfiring to others. I refused to argue the point, as I felt I was wrong in raising it.

[86] After the usual buggering I went into lunch with the males in the English department, Cecil Bald, & Bennett. I had mildly suggested moving the party to Chez Paris [Paree], in view of the fact that Bald has a special interest in Coleridge & it was silly to leave Kay Coburn out. Robins said he couldn't make the switch because Bennett didn't want to

take the party "off the campus."[100] That's the kind of thing that makes me restless about staying at Victoria. I then went over to his seminar on Donne's Anniversaries. I nearly went crazy sitting on a hard chair in a hot stuffy room listening to all that god-damned crap once more about the decay of the world & Aristotle & Averroes versus Cyprian (he forgot II Esdras), & Goodman & Hakewell,[101] & R.F. Jones' important study & that book of Coffin.[102] So I left at three & didn't stay for the discussion: it looked a bit rude, but I didn't feel I could do anything else. So I went home, reflecting on the folly of wasting my time & energies going to other people's lectures out of politeness & idle curiosity. Four this week. So I cut the one I really wanted to go to—Tillich's on principle & substance tonight—& spent the evening in bed reading Jung's Psychological Types, with a general sense of recharging my batteries & beginning a systematic hunt for the formulas of archetypal meaning.

Saturday, February 4

[87] Went down to my usual letter-answering stint, & actually did answer some, in spite of a nuisance of a Varsity editor asking me yesterday for an editorial on democracy for some damn foolishness or other. It's Charlie Leslie's job, & he unloaded it on me. So I took most of the morning on that,[103] with the boy waiting in the office for it, & didn't get a letter off to Peggy Roseborough. I'm still preoccupied by the idea of democracy as the attempt to transcend the concept of "rule" & hence of a ruler & ruling class, & as exposed to two threats of a *coup d'etat* coming from the economic structure, either from the executive (Fascist) or the soviet end. Both end in managerial despotism. Oh, the hell with it. Helen came down & we had lunch at Chez Paris [Paree], then walked down to the Art Gallery. Very pleasant walk, as it was a beautiful day, going past streets & buildings that looked so familiar & yet were so strange. The fact that this city is just on the point of emerging into a metropolis (subway, new by-pass, widened streets, projected building in the slum-center, proposed amalgamation of York, liberalizing of mores in regard e.g. to Sunday, etc.) forms part of my present restless feeling.

[88] The Lismer show at the Gallery was good: nothing unexpected: very little in fact unfamiliar, but still it's pleasant to see it all at once. He's certainly a painter of tangle: the enthusiasm with which he tackles an insanely complicated mass of planes & twisting rhythms is infectious, &,

as in his lecturing, one is ready to believe he's solved the problems involved because he talks so gracefully about solving them. I think his recent Maritime studies of fishing wharves, stones, fish, hawsers, killicks, & anchors are among the best things he's ever done.

[89] We had a cup of tea there in the Grange[104] & then went home for dinner & out in the evening to hear the Music Club do Ruddigore. I'd never seen it before. It's not absolutely first-class G & S [Gilbert and Sullivan]: S, though tuneful as usual, misses fire occasionally, especially at the beginning, & he doesn't warm up at all to the mock-gruesome atmosphere. Still, there's a lovely madrigal—well, part-song—in the finale of the first act. G has a tendency to beat his jokes into insensibility: the theme with variations is a dangerous form for jest. But I was very grateful to them for giving me a new show—I'm so out of patience with Patience, which I understand is the choice for next year. Lovely girls in the show—I didn't see much of the men, who were concealed by complex & very badly fitting uniforms.

Sunday, February 5

[90] Stayed home all day: as usual, I don't know whether I'm really tired or just bone lazy. I slept in the afternoon & sleep affects me like alcohol: it relaxes some sort of threshold & makes my mind more freely associative than usual. As this involves the dredging up of unfamiliar memories, it also makes me sentimental & nostalgic. On a Sunday, particularly when I'm reading a commentary on Genesis, this makes me pious as well. In Jungian terms, I'm a thinking type, with feeling undifferentiated & likely to break over me in waves. As a thinker, I'm committed to detachment: my feeling works as tempter trying to make me attach myself. If I could turn Roman Catholic, for instance (which would appeal to me more than my inherited evangelism because of its legal completeness of ideal phrasing), that would be the tempter's supreme triumph, the achievement of giddiness designed to make me throw myself off the pinnacle & trust to angels to get buoyed up. Jung would call it sacrificium intellectus.

[91] Abandoning these reflections, & going on with Jung, I'm somewhat teased by a vague intuition floating in the back of my mind derived partly from the final Paradise Lost lecture. The Joachim dialectic of *three* ages seems to me now inescapable, & I feel, as Joachimites always do,

that it's starting about next Tuesday. The age of the law was not only Hebraic but Classical, the age of society which afforded primarily the social differentiation of the slave state. The age of the gospel was primarily an age of subjective individuality: it set up a differentiation within the individual, & so produced the Papacy at one end & the dictator at the other. Democracy & its effort to transcend rule marks the beginning of a movement toward an apocalyptic or second coming way of looking at things, a Bergsonian recreation of a non-differentiated organism above individuality. In this age Christ is no longer a peculiar society nor a historical individual, but the body of man. The law is a polarity between a past contract & a future Messiah; the gospel is a polarity between a past Messiah & a future contract (in Newman, the total actualizing of dogma). The emergence of the Protestant-democratic-inductive science complex & the sharpening of the three-fold analogy I speak of in my essay[105] is the vanguard of it. This actually transcends Blake, who saw only the Druid side of induction, & would have made a similar bungle of democracy if he'd had the chance. Now I have to keep this out of the hair of my meaning & archetype articles.

Monday, February 6

[92] The nine o'clock started the poetry part of 2i, & as it's easy for me it came off all right. I had a bad headache, caused, as my headaches always are, by the backing up of mucus in my deviated septum. That in its turn was the result of spending a second night without Benadryl: experiment rationalizing laziness. Guess I'm a dope addict, for the present anyway. But then Helen Garrett couldn't sleep either without that stuff she took. The graduate group wasn't bad: Miss Page is useful to me, because I feel that when I've made a point clear to Miss Page I've made it clear to everybody, including myself. I wish she weren't quite so obtuse—I can't even say an epic is a long poem without her asking me if I'm not confusing greatness with size—but still I'd rather have it, because I suspect the others get equally crude misunderstandings & don't say anything about them. I tried to make the transition clearer between the four levels & the listing of archetypes, & think I may have succeeded, in part at least.

[93] It was important for me to do this because I was thrown into a tizzy & a twitter by a letter that arrived this morning from Rice, the Kenyon

Review editor. He's read my articles, pronounced them "very brilliant & very original" & wants to get one for the Kenyon Review by Feb. 15. So I dug out my meaning paper & after brooding over it for a while I saw what to do with it. I'd originally begun it as a restatement of the theory of the four levels of meaning, & then altered it for the Philosophical Club, taking on the logical positivists & getting involved in questions I couldn't really handle. For this all I have to do is recast the paper in its original form, which means sticking entirely to my own stuff. So I got the first level done & the second roughed out, & I think I'll have it done in time, & quite a good article too.[106]

[94] At noon I went over to Hart House to supervise the hanging of the Western show, which isn't as bad as reported. The Warden called me in to tick me off for railroading too many motions through & to say that Simmons, the Keeper of the Prints, had got the wind up & left college: I suggested Earle Sanborn as a possible substitute.[107]

Tuesday, February 7

[95] Yesterday I got my Benadryl supply & was all right again this morning. The nine o'clock on Ruskin was pretty fair: the pre-Raphaelite stuff is straightforward enough. The Varsity held over my editorial & printed it under my name. Poor Doug Dryer got the job of writing up communism,[108] & his anxiety to dissociate himself from what he was talking about gave him a mild form of schizophrenia. My own job turned out to be a fairly concise bit of writing, though after all it isn't much of a trick to defend democracy. I was very disappointed in my R.K. lecture: I'm really falling down on that course this year. This one was just a parsonical harangue. I must pull up my socks & see what I was doing last year at this time.

[96] I kept on with the paper & got, I think, the second level done, which wasn't so bad, as the second level has all that stuff about the three areas of literature. I still wonder if that isn't a digression; it probably would be one if criticism weren't so disorganized that I have to explain everything from the ground up. A more serious matter is the condensation: I'm just beginning to realize that a certain type of compression in my writing isn't a virtue.

[97] The writing group produced a bad poem by Kathlyn Smith, which I had to be polite about, & a story by Rita Maclean that we didn't really have much time to discuss. None of these kids, except possibly Jean Inglis, will make writers, but they certainly provide a pleasant interval in the week, or would if I weren't so damn busy. I hear Joe Fisher may be sick again. This morning an ape named de Vries came in to sell me a suit of clothes at a bargain—a Dutchman, probably a Jew, who talks big about the English importing business he's in. The thing that got him into my office was his sixteen-year friendship with Howard Layhew, who's still in a remarkably vague business of investment counselling—"if you have any money to invest, he's the man to see." He talks about him as though he were prosperous again—he's been promoted to being a reader in the Christian Science Church. I think it's the man that gets to read Mary Baker Eddy, & a woman reads the other Bible—it's a fairly hermaphroditic set up. Joe [Fisher] seems to be all right, but was off his feed for some days.

Wednesday, February 8

[98] Wednesday is like a half-holiday because I have no lecture until ten, & when I did get down I sailed easily through the Court of Love & typed out what I've done of my paper. I think the first two levels will pretty well do. The twelve o'clock on Ruskin I made very amusing, but I didn't say much of consequence. As usual, I forgot on practically every occasion to announce the public lecture. I don't know, though, that the lectures are principally for students even if students would attend them. The hall was full anyway, & as the next two are on big examinations we'll be flooded out, which is fine. Davison didn't hurt himself lecturing on Oedipus Rex; he gave an outline of the history & conditions of the Greek stage & then a long summary of the plot. Finally he suggested that Oedipus was Pericles. That counts as originality, I suppose. I decided I needed a drink, & took Helen out & had three Martinis, then dinner, which effectively wasted the evening. I damn well wanted to waste the evening. Helen had spent the day admiring the little baby boy the Hamiltons have just adopted, & I think she's about ready to call off her domestic superego complex.

[99] The article is hanging fire, & as I have to waste some time this week

fussing over examinations I'll just have to hope & pray that I can get Saturday as well as Sunday clear. I don't really think it'll be so bad once I really get at it. And it really is important to me, anyway.

[100] George Johnston says Robins told him there was nothing for him at Victoria. I suppose Robins' excuse for all this inertia is that he can't be sure I'm getting the Guggenheim. In this case it doesn't matter, because George still feels the same way about Mt. Allison.[109] He wants to write, & a routine teaching job that will let him write, & scholarship is a full-time job here that sucks all one's capacity for framing ideas & impressions into itself. I feel too that George's rhythms are slow & easy-going—if he can ever add up all the charm he has he'll be a most readable writer, but he's been a fair length of time in the world & hasn't shown very striking talents yet. I told him his last stories were all in pastel shades. But he's made the right decision if it's right with Jean. He'll never do his thesis.

Thursday, February 9

[101] A very tiring day, for one reason & another. The nine o'clock cleared up Samson Agonistes & gave them something to talk about. Then some god-damned gump named Murphy barged in & proceeded to recite a long summary of a book he'd written called "The Root of the Matter."[110] After twenty minutes of this he saw that I looked annoyed, so I finally got rid of him, though not without getting winged in three places a) a request to review the book for the Varsity b) a long brochure about the book c) an interview next Tuesday. I turned down the first, sent back the second & enclosed a note calling off the third. I was so infuriated that I put a sign up on my door telling pests to keep away, but of course I took it down. It was my Varsity editorial that attracted him, so let that be a lesson to me.

[102] After the twelve o'clock, which made me feel just a little bit better, I went over to have lunch with Woodhouse. Watson Kirkconnell, a most undistinguished little man, came along. I'd read Woodhouse's article & wanted to discuss it with him, but got little chance. My point was that The Faerie Queene grows out of romance as late Shakespeare comedy does out of tragedy, & as the catastrophe comes first, so in Spenser the essential quest comes first, & sets the Christian tone: the other five books may not be explicitly Christian, but the Christian perspective enables

one to distinguish the redeemable from the irredeemable. I pointed out that the Maleger water-business is linked with the bloody-handed babe & that a baptismal reference ("living well") [*The Faerie Queene*, bk. 1, canto 2, st. 3] is explicit: this he hadn't noticed. We stayed all afternoon doing 4k, 1b, & 1b supplemental.[111] He'd set the whole of 1b, & said that if I'd thought up any questions we could put them into the supplemental. Mrs. Kirkwood came in & I told her that the reason her students came to me for 4k was that I gave them what they wanted—smart bright lectures—& didn't try to educate them. They don't want to read or study or think, but they find it socially exciting to feel that they're living in an intellectually stimulating atmosphere, & so I'm "stimulating," but under no illusions as to the essential educational value of the job I'm doing. I know that I'm just standing on my smart bright head. I think it made her feel a lot more encouraged. That was my one good deed for the day: I came home feeling very tired & rather depressed, & in no condition to go out again to a Forum meeting. However, of course I did.

Friday, February 10

[103] The Forum meeting last night was again uneventful: I was very tired, & I'm afraid I rather imposed that feeling on the board. Alan Sangster said he wouldn't do anything but his column, which was reasonable enough, but made me feel suddenly very bored with getting people to do something for nothing & very anxious to get out of the Forum. I'm turning pro as a writer as fast as I can & I've really outgrown worthy causes. I had a hell of a job getting editorials & suggestions out of them: maybe the news *is* in a bit of doldrums. The issue itself is in fair shape. I agreed tentatively to do a front-page feature on the death of Orwell, God help me.[112]

[104] The nine o'clock was on Milton: questions from them—a good class would have made something of it, but 5T1 is damn well not a good class. I made a few suggestions about books, & a fresh kid—I think Judy Livingston—asked me if it was really necessary to read these books. That sort of level. Then I had to cook up a supplemental 1B & it really took a fair amount of time typing it & the others out. Looking up references for a spotter takes a lot of time—I'm just interested in Woodhouse's manoeuvres. I went in to lunch early—Irving, who has sold my article already, says he wants a drink as commission. He'll get the whole bottle

if I do sell it, but I'm not counting any chickens before I've laid the egg, especially remembering that Virginia fiasco.[113]

[105] In the afternoon I typed out my report for Hopwood's thesis & took it over.[114] I hadn't seen a copy of the thesis since it was bound, & the girl looked at me very suspiciously & said: "didn't you need a copy for this appraisal?" I mumbled something about having read it before & beat a retreat. Hopwood, considering his almost pathological shyness, really did very well. I started him off asking about myth & archetype & so on in relation to his thesis. The philosophers grilled him pretty hard, but he seemed to come through. McRae's report wasn't nearly as favorable as mine, & he disliked the chapter I thought was the best. [F.H.] Anderson wasn't there. Woodhouse was the chairman, & he seemed quite favorably impressed. So was everybody except Thorburn—I was glad he hadn't read more than one chapter. Came home & went to bed while Helen went out to a show.

Saturday, February 11

[106] Well, this was the day I'd been waiting for, so I started in to work in the morning & worked pretty consistently all day until nearly six. I got the third level done, all but a sentence or two at the end, which has really broken the back of the present job. It's a square egg, though, & doesn't come easily. One trouble was Helen, who can't help feeling just a little jealous of anything that takes my full attention, & who seemed anyway to feel very depressed & miserable. I don't know why: she always blames it on a flu bug. Another trouble was being in my study with the door shut: I want quiet, but when I get it it seems to bother me. I get self-conscious with myself, which is a most involved state of mind. It's a form of *angst* or claustrophobia. It was lunch time before I got the opening section straightened out: as usual, I'd backed into it the wrong way. It's beginning to shape up now & take the dry precise bite I want. In the afternoon we went out for a walk and I staggered home under a huge cineraria we bought at a florist. Had tea in Murray's, which is in very subdued lighting, almost like a cocktail bar. I got the third level to cover most of what I'd thought of for the fourth, so tomorrow shouldn't be so bad. I knocked off for the evening, but was too tired to do anything but play solitaire.

[107] This paper is beginning to give me a glimmer of what will probably be an essential argument of V [Mirage]. I say that the study of physics does not imply that the physical universe exists, but that it is totally intelligible. Similarly with the verbal universe. Theology goes on to make an existential affirmation about each (the unmoved mover *is* God, the one word *is* Christ) which makes them descriptive & the subject of affirmation an object. That's the essential fallacy about Thomism, that, as I say, it's metaphysical rather than dialectic realism. I can't indefinitely go on saying that literature refuses to affirm or deny the identification of the verbal universe with Christ. Sooner or later (this is the V [Mirage] job) I have to come to grips with the total form of human creative power. Now that, as I see it (and as Blake saw it) contains divinity within its intelligibility: it doesn't add divinity to it existentially. I know Thomism comes within a hair's breadth of saying what I say, but it can't quite say it or it couldn't remain within the Church. What I say is the straight Lankavatara line: the doctrine of Mind-only arising out of Paratantra.[115]

Sunday, February 12

[108] Got to work at a fair time & was finished by half-past one—the fourth level didn't take more than two or three paragraphs. As usual, I couldn't understand what all the fuss was about once it was over. I played around with it most of the afternoon & recast several sentences. But, except for the conclusion of the third level where I stalled yesterday, it's done. Curious how closely the pattern of this year follows last year, even to busting a gut getting a paper done in the middle of February. I feel now like sailing straight into my Blake archetype paper, which I think should be the last of my prefatory studies. I haven't heard from Miss Nitchie yet, but the hell with that.[116]

[109] I heard some good music: the Philharmonic did a Haydn, very stodgily, & the Mahler first. I find Mahler very pleasant & easy to listen to—the theme of the Funeral march haunted me all day—but I certainly don't find the profundities in him that I gather I'm supposed to find. Or, if they're there, they're romantic & introspective profundities only: no objective plumbing into the world. Two lovely Bach things—Fourth Brandenburg & one of the Ricercare. Now those really are profound. We went out for a walk along residential streets, seeing the lighted windows

against the graying sky. It's the kind of thing that always fascinates me & always depresses Helen. I guess she thinks of the propertied middle class in terms of its facade, & I tend more to look under the skin—I don't know. I love the propertied middle class, though not for being that, & never walk along residential streets in Toronto without thinking that it really is a very great civilization. I see it now somewhat as our envious great-grandchildren will.

[110] With regard to this "leisure" question: I say that the gospel Sabbath is not a day of rest at the end of the week, but a day of leisure at the beginning of the week. I wonder if sleeping should be conceived, not as rest at the end of the day, but as leisure at the beginning of it? Hence our "small hours" conception of the day as beginning at midnight. I've often wondered *why* we sleep: it surely isn't to "rest" the brain, which doesn't rest & doesn't need it (except perhaps for the initial "beauty sleep") but to sink it into the domain of creative archetypal imagery & free association, whence it emerges to give direction & basis to the wakened mind.

Monday, February 13

[111] Down to my nine o'clock, which was damned dull, and then to the graduate group. Miss Page was right in there bitching. What that poor girl needs is success—lots of coarse, vulgar, materialistic success. So do we all, but one sees it more clearly in some than in others. I excreted my article all over them, & it seemed to go all right. The modern initiates get their contact with the divine power in a bath of bullshit. Lunch with Margaret Avison, who had sent me a long poem to make sense of. She has no narrative or constructive ability at all, & I suggested that she should stick to her one essential gift of seeing things very sharply & one at a time, & let the inner unity emerge from the common intensity of the different visions. It's almost grotesque to see her fine technique trying to assimilate narrative, like a python swallowing a sheep. Eliot's *Waste Land* bothered her a great deal, & an unsympathetic critic would have said it was bad Eliot. I never say things like that. I did say that life was as private a matter as death, & ought to be treated with equal respect. This was in an incidental connection, but I had Woodhouse, Joe Fisher & Margaret herself in my mind.

[112] I got caught in the 2i meeting after all, & had to go over to U.C. Shook set it, & it's all right. It's about the toughest paper in the curriculum to set, & he seemed to feel self-conscious about it—as he said to me afterwards, one sets papers for the other professors as well as the students. I had to skip Robert Finch's colloquium, as I'd wasted enough of the afternoon, & went back to the office to work. A storm blew up around four o'clock & appears all set to go on the whole night. I was too absent-minded to look out the window, & persuaded Helen to meet me for dinner. At the cocktail lounge we met Jim Scott, who seemed cheerful, Helen James & Bob Weaver. Later a Saskatchewan man named Leddy came along: I'd been writing him about Blissett, & it certainly looks as though Blissett will get the job. Poor Helen had been spending the afternoon trying to buy a girdle, which from her account is a most humiliating process, & would be if she didn't have a sense of humour. She went on to the Forum office to proofread, & I went back to my typewriter. At eleven o'clock I dropped it* in the post office on Yonge Street. It's a damned good article too, whatever the Kenyon Review thinks. If they don't want it I shan't change it. *Now* all I have to do is get an archetype paper done—maybe two papers—and then I'll be all set for L [Liberal]. *The article, not the typewriter.[117]

Tuesday, February 14

[113] Storm still, as the Lear stage directions say. It stayed at almost exactly 32° all day & deposited several inches of the wettest snow I've ever seen on the ground, with a few intervals of sleet & hail. It wasn't so bad in the morning, but in the afternoon it was impossible to walk without going up to one's ankles crossing streets. I began my nine o'clock by saying "everybody who isn't here is a sissy," and then turned in a surprisingly good lecture on Ruskin. Drudgery can only produce hysterical quests for entertainment or laziness; men shall not live by bread alone, but by circuses; Work that is not drudgery is creative & a life of creative work is the same thing as a life of leisure. Set the ideal & test drudgery by it; most luxurious art is built on sweated labour, but the Philistine solution that doesn't distinguish the necessary from the important won't do either. The R.K. lecture was still parsonical, but not too bad: history of religion breaks down at two points: the attempt to find God outside man (power past nature, giving us the old man in the sky) &

the attempt to find God inside man (love in natural society, giving us mandarinism). They grilled me pretty hard: there's a great variety of needs in that class.

[114] I felt tired after two exhausting efforts, & was rather disconcerted to get tabbed by Robins for an alumni version of the faculty debate. Especially if I have to amuse the kids too. I don't want to do both, & actually I'd rather amuse the kids. The writing group produced a story by Liz Lane—very good too: really those youngsters keep up an amazing standard. I think that in a small way I am keeping in direct touch with a creative process, & I'm amazed how my own theory holds up about writers not actually knowing the meaning of their own symbolism. This story had two pieces, beautifully connected together by a single symbol, but with all her very intelligent & in fact discursive mind she wasn't really aware of the connection.

[115] Went out to the Forum office & sat there with dripping feet typing out an editorial on George Orwell.[118] I hadn't had time to think about it, & it was a poor job: as unsatisfactory a piece of writing as I've ever done. I suppose it wasn't actually bad: just something I shall reread with no pleasure & less profit. Came home, changed my shoes & socks & shovelled something else for a change.

Wednesday, February 15

[116] I got quite a let-down today from two letters, one from Vera [Frye] saying that the "arthritis" condition she complained of last year (Christmas) was more serious than she thought, & she'll have to wear a brace. Eventually it'll mean an operation. Also that her apartment is sold up & the Aldridges [Aldriches] will have to move. The other was from the Guggenheim committee saying that their "advisers" wanted to know about my knowledge of existing scholarship on Spenser & my view of the difference between my own & other studies of him.[119] I thought the first question was insulting and the second fuddy-duddy, & I suddenly realized how disappointed I'd be if I *didn't* get the fellowship & if an incompetent committee decided against me. It's very lonely being a genius: you're just an arrogant crank who happens to be bright.

[117] Neither lecture was bad nor new. I did the pastoral convention &

some more Ruskin. I think I made a fair job of expounding *Unto This Last*, which I've always found difficult. Jim Service asked me if the difference between the necessary & the important corresponds to the difference between self-interest & self-respect, which of course it does: there's a lead there. I said that for Ruskin profit comes out of labor, & should never come out of exchange.

[118] I'm getting a split personality the way my engagements are piling up: March 13, the day I have to look after Abrams,[120] had the students' faculty debate & the St. Hilda's Literary Society dinner in the evening. I had to turn both down, as I got asked to both. Tomorrow both Vic & Hart House are reviewing art shows at 1:30.

[119] Ned's [Ned Pratt's] lecture was very, very good. I was pretty sure it would be, but he *does* write so well, & reads (prose, not poetry) with such great charm of manner. He's quite a showman in his way, & has integrated his style beautifully with his showmanship. Watching him, I couldn't help wishing that I were less of a personal Puritan—I'm so determined to let my stuff go over on its sheer merits that I ask a lot more of my audience. Perhaps it's just the inimitable mellowing that comes with age. He didn't open up Lear so much for me, but he reminded one eloquently of the play, which is what is wanted for a public lecture. I felt like going out for a drink again, & we did go & had two, but came home for dinner. I don't know why this silly Guggenheim letter has got under my skin—I suppose I just assumed I'd go sailing through with no questions asked.

Thursday, February 16

[120] The nine o'clock began Spenser, & I tried approaching it *via* my article. I guess some of it went over, but the implications are too packed, and I wonder if even the article itself isn't really pretty dense stuff. I wish I could get to a point where people would know in advance how important I am, & be ready to study my next collection of axioms as that, instead of just looking over it as though it were one more article. Well, anyway, I spent the next two hours (in quite a nervous state) typing out a crowded two-page single-space letter to the Guggenheim people. I replied to their literacy test with what I hope was just the right amount of injured merit, & then shot them a terrific line about Spenser. Two tact-

lessly worded letters in one week (another from Miss Nitchie) have sent me desperately scratching my ego. I'm in a miserable February mood, & wish I could snap out of it. It's partly hangover from finishing the article.

[121] At the twelve o'clock I asked my kids to let me know when it was a quarter to one, as I had to go then. They gurgled: they love getting out early from twelve o'clocks. I began to get the feeling that I'm actually beginning to make the transition from fourth year to first year.[121] It's a welcome feeling, but I wish it weren't associated with a feeling of botching the fourth year. Well, anyway, I had Marshall McLuhan & Douglas Duncan in to lunch. The relation with Marshall had one awkward point: the refusal of a Forum article. Douglas says the show was written up by Rose Macdonald & reviewed over the radio, which is all good for the college's publicity. Marshall talked quite well about Wyndham Lewis: first he read a statement, in rather stilted language, about Lewis' conception of the mask, & then read some amusing bits from the autobiography. He says the Time & Western Man attack was part of a deliberate Shaun-&-Shem game he played with Joyce. Considering that Lewis at Rugby got a cup the boys give for six floggings in one day (after getting five & finding the day nearly at an end, he went & bounced a tennis ball against the headmaster's door) & was kicked out of the Slade in two weeks, I don't know that Toronto's attitude was as provincial as he seems to think. I went over to the Forum office & read the page proofs of a somewhat undistinguished issue & came home. Helen says the news from Roy & Mary [Kemp] is quite cheerful & they'll be looking for the baby soon.[122]

Friday, February 17

[122] Driving down with Hilliard [Trethewey] I learned that [John] Wood is staying on in French. Maybe Laidlaw will get a bid somewhere else: anyway I got a call from Tommy Goudge asking for recommendations for him. Hilliard himself is getting next year off & will likely go to Boston, as, I suppose, will Joe. The fly in the ointment is his mother, who lives a few miles out & is very ill. I didn't get this from him: Helen got it from her. If the Guggenheim comes through I don't know about joining the Vic colony in Boston.

[123] The nine o'clock was straight routine about Spenser: I don't know

but what the form of this year's diary may be inhibiting my lectures a bit: sounds silly, but it could be. Anyway, it was all on the total scheme, soft-pedalling the chastity business because Woodhouse is setting the paper. I've learned a lot from pacing myself against Woodhouse, but I wonder whether I haven't come to the point where I should strike out for myself. That doesn't involve any change of feeling towards him, of course. Maybe when his Milton book is done he'll be less obtrusive. Maybe when mine is done he'll be more so, as it'll likely be done first. God, I hate myself these days. I think I'm so restless because I'm anxious to get my *Wanderjahre* over & done with, & then settle down to a recreation of routine.

[124] Typed out the three exam papers & sent them off, then went over to Trinity for lunch. I was early & Roper was there: he really is a very decent sort, & seems not only friendly but anxious to know me better. We discussed Huck Finn: I said the raft was a pure *Bateau Ivre* symbol, & that the reason for all the Katzenjammer stuff at the end was that when Huck, who is the pure individuated self, in Jung's terminology, gets kidnapped in the cellar of a white slave-owning family & has to act under the domination of Tom Sawyer, who is pure ego, both he and the ego-principle become poltergeists. Not that I said all this. Arthur Barker & Milton Wilson then came along & we went in to lunch. Barker's criticism of my Milton thing[123] was exactly what I wanted: it was very careful & very appreciative: his suggestions rounded out my argument at every point and I think I shall adopt them all. I wish to God I'd had him on the Kenyon article, though that would perhaps need an ideal Barker. Anyhow, I went & got a haircut & came home with a load off my mind, physically and mentally speaking.

Saturday, February 18

[125] So I felt encouraged to set this weekend as a deadline for the Milton job, & did the alterations Barker had recommended in the morning. Some of them, including the final paragraph on *Samson Agonistes*, were a bit tricky, but they came all right. Helen was feeling that way again, so I took her out to Simpson's for lunch & she cheered up. We plodded through part of the store—or at least I did—I find overheated stores in winter pretty trying in a heavy coat. My body temperature in any case seems to lack a thermostat. We came home on the bus & I

tackled the last part, on the "poetry as poetry," to quote Bledsoe's phrase. It was the stuff I ground out on the Huntsville train, & isn't so bloody awful as I thought if it's shifted around a bit. It will be an anticlimax though: I can't help that. Anyway, I got my watch back today.

[126] Some of Barker's remarks made me realize that I should do a bit of thinking about the conception of angels. After all, it's damn important in the Thomist set up. Lycidas joins the "solemn troops & sweet societies" of the city of God & gives it his full attention while being at the same time "Genius of the shore," a guardian or watcher of human fortunes. I suppose angels are personal archetypes, & belong on the third level with gods & myths as parts of the whole, the whole being the divine-human society. As substantial existences, therefore, they're covering cherubs, part of the chain of being, Atlases who hold up the sky-god on top of man. That's what the prohibition about worshipping them really amounts to (in the N.T.). Thus far I'm just repeating the ideas I have now: what's new is the ambiguity of the collective "intelligence" that watches human society from outside & simultaneously acts within a divine society. In Dante that's linked with the dreadful pervasive vulgarity which identifies God, not with suffering humanity, but with ruling humanity, & so continually cuts God down to human size, using him just to rubber stamp the standards arrived at by Popes & Emperors down here. Milton has a lot less of that, mainly because his political ideas are in better shape: his heaven is a place of *spiritual* authority, not a series of astral barracks labelled "for officers only." I only wish Milton had done his poem on the Passion.

Sunday, February 19

[127] Today I didn't seem to work properly, in contrast to yesterday, when everything seemed to come very quickly & easily. Mysterious. Anyway, I'm within two paragraphs of the end, & those are blocked out. As usual, it's the peroration on Milton's imagery that stops me. I can't imagine where the afternoon went to—well, yes I can—some of it went to bed, as for some reason I was dreadfully sleepy. In the evening we went to Ruth Home's for dinner to talk to a couple of girls from the Boston Museum. One was named Alice McInnis (spelling by ear) who's in Orientals, & a very charming girl named Morna or Lorna Crawford, a medievalist. Both, I think, Irish Catholics. A man named Sidney [Syd-

ney] Watson from the College of Art—stocky & pleasant, who disagreed very strongly with my statement that the centre of Canadian painting has moved from Toronto to Montreal. Helen Fernauld [Fernald] was there too, & talked about Winter Park, Florida, which is a colony of retired specialists in everything under the sun, & give lectures to each other. We both had a very good time.

[128] I think I've got the approach to my archetype paper now. Myth is an attempt to explain a ritual & the verbal containing form of ritual. Hence both myth & ritual grow toward encyclopaedic completion: the myth in Scripture, the ritual in the annual calendar, & each mirrors the other, more or less. That begins to straighten out my original fussing over the two forms of Scripture & what I called the Druid analogy. It hasn't really cleared it up, as the total mythical vision is still a lot bigger than the Bible, but it's starting. It seems to me that this point, & the interconnection of the Christian Bible & the Christian year, is the containing form of L [Liberal], whereas the total vision might conceivably be the container of ⌐ [Tragicomedy], as it seems to suit better what I say in FS 12 about drama [404–5, 427–8]. What contains ∧ [Anticlimax] in that case? Something conceptual—possibly a lead from FW [*Finnegans Wake*]. Minor points: the climax of PR [*Paradise Regained*] follows the *real* argument of Job—the one I've figured out—very carefully, & so the argument of L will hang together a lot more clearly, especially in connection with FQ [*The Faerie Queene*] 1, as Job is the real dragon-slaying myth of the tenth canto. The fall of Satan at the end of PR is possibly—just possibly— the only one mentioned in the Bible, & perhaps Milton knew it. There's no reason to suppose that Jesus' reference to the fall of Satan [Luke 10:18] is to be cast far back in time—on the other hand, if it is, it's his only reference to his pre-existence.

Monday, February 20

[129] The nine o'clock was the Geoffrey of Monmouth lecture, which I usually enjoy giving, but this year I feel pressed for time. It's their essay day, so I'm snowed under again. The graduate group went well: even Miss Page co-operated. I gave them some stuff about tragedy as a vision of law, the first step in seeing reality: [Thomas] Hardy was right there. I spoke of the romantic fallacy of an undigestible ineffable sitting in the middle of art & buggering up the verbal universe—that led to what

I called the "existential fallacy" of Kafka & others: the attempt to render tragedy as pure bewilderment & lost direction. I mean that the conception of an unknown unconscious like Hardy's immanent will limits & bedevils art. Re centripetal symbols as images & centrifugal ones as signs, I said that if there were no meaning but centrifugal meaning a dog could learn to read. I'm getting places with L [Liberal], or wherever the hell this goes.

[130] I went over to Hart House to have lunch with Marcus Long & a man called Preston, an Assistant Professor of Physics. The radio kids roped me in on one of their programmes—I have to discuss the H-bomb with these blokes, for God's sake. As nobody but people with FM radios can hear it anyway, I think we'll be pretty well left to ourselves. I threw some money down the drain by accepting, as Frank Peers of the CBC phoned this morning & asked me to come on the Citizens' Forum to discuss film censorship.[124] Oh, well. I only wish this weren't on quite such a footling subject. Then I dropped in on a table with Woodhouse & Blissett & [Douglas] Grant. Blissett has the Saskatchewan job; Grant thanked me for the loan of my wife, & then I sat down & we discussed, well, the H-bomb. I said I felt distressed at the thought of a city going up in smoke, but the thought of a chain-reaction blowing the whole world to pieces filled me with profound peace. Woodhouse got Abrams' undergraduate lecture fixed for the West Hall on Tuesday.[125]

[131] I came back & typed all afternoon, except for Duncan Robertson & another lad whose name I forget at the moment. Both want to do Ph.D. theses with me, one on modern criticism and one (we decided) on the theme of apocalypse in Blake, Shelley & Carlyle.[126] I think that's a most promising subject, & he's a very intelligent person who will, I think, do it well. I met Robert Finch on the street car coming home & said I was sorry to miss his colloquium—an asinine type of remark, but I don't know how not to make it.

Tuesday, February 21

[132] The nine o'clock finished Ruskin, I trust—I'm skating on pretty thin ice talking about his attack on the free market, & if it weren't for their readiness to co-operate with me in keeping up the pretence of my omniscience (which in turn is caused by their own lack of reading)

I could be made pretty uncomfortable. The parenthesis is unfair: there really is a pretty deep sense of courtesy in students, I think. At eleven a student in architecture whose name sounded like Crang came in—he'd phoned Sunday to say he was tackling a fifth-year thesis on religion in architecture. He wanted to know if there were a common factor in religions he could base his study on. I said no. The poor lad has never had time all through his course to think of anything: now he's thinking & ideas are pouring into his head in a swirling mass from all sides. He'll be all right—he's a bright boy. I told him religious architecture was an exception to his form-follows-function rule, as that rule assumed an inhabited building, & nobody lives in the sacred building except the god.

[133] The twelve o'clock just made my Word-of-God in three forms point, & then I held up under questions. I suppose I should remember the large religious population in that class. I worry still about being too parsonical, but with the type of question I get it's hard to avoid it. King Joblin tells me I'm slated to follow Charlie Leslie on the university sermon. That's of course. Then my writing girls. Really, those kids: they're very attractive youngsters, they've only got one thing on their little minds, & it ain't writing. Today it was a red stain on a clean dress, from wine. Last week it was a blood-red moon. Before that it was Jean Inglis' triangular-piece-out-of-the-lamp story. Kay Brown however turned in a very expert piece on a Bella Coola[127] initiation ceremony.

[134] Well, Mary MacFarlane came in at three & then I went to an Art Committee meeting. Day & Boggs were carried over—a good choice. Creighton & Grube, in other words, weren't.[128] I guess my handling of it was democratic enough. Charles Comfort wasn't there. Came home in a terrific storm to find Margaret Newton in for dinner. She's getting a little restless about her job, I think, as well as disillusioned about her friends— the Oakville Hillmer is more neurotic than ever & she thinks they may be headed for a marital smash-up.

Wednesday, February 22

[135] I forgot the ashes, too.[129] There was a good foot of snow on the ground to clear off this morning, and another eight inches tonight. My lectures are brightening up a bit, I think. I made something fairly lively out of the Elizabethan sonnet, one of English literature's duller subjects,

at least as portrayed by Representative Poetry.[130] I said in connection with a Shakespearean sonnet that one feels that that order of words had existed since the beginning of time & were just waiting for the right person to set them free. Hyperboles like that increase the snob value of one's lectures, as the brighter kid's feel they've got something the others have missed. They have, too. Also, they aren't pure hyperboles—I believe of course in an order of words.

[136] Kenyon Review accepted the article,[131] so that's that. Thinking it over, it doesn't seem as good technically as my other things. Rice is certainly under the impression that I've written an article on the forms of poetry corresponding to the one on prose—he's asked for it twice now. It's a long way off—at least the lyric part of it is. The twelve o'clock was on the beginning of Morris, & very good too: Morris I can do. The only new thing, apart from the Sweden point and the revolutionary significance of the small arts as involving an anarchist decentralizing plan,[132] is the revolutionary nature of the chivalric ideal: theoretically, the knight was supposed to defend the oppressed against the extortioner, exploiter & robber. So the aristocracy was in theory what the Peasants' Revolt was in practice. There's a point or two still to get clear about Morris' medievalism: notably the exact interpretation he gives to spiritual authority: it's mostly the projection of the social order, but it's linked with the romance too & its combination of revolutionary & aristocratic elements.

[137] I worked on the last two pages of the Milton: the part about the imagery that had been sticking me. I got it done, & I think it's not so bad. In fact, I feel very relieved in my mind about that whole infernal business that's been haunting me for a year. Twenty-four pages of exceedingly compact information about Milton. So I went & had a drink with Helen to celebrate & dropped it in the box. If they object now they'll have a fight on their hands.

Thursday, February 23

[138] Maclean's [C.V. McLean's] lecture yesterday was well attended, but otherwise pretty poor: he hasn't the literary sense of a roadscraper. Also has no style. I'd have done a lot better with [John] Macpherson, only I picked Maclean [McLean] because I thought he had more presence & a more resonant voice. Helen hated it. We went out for a drink &

dinner at Murray's, where we saw Ruth Jenking, & then went down to hear the Mendelssohn choir do the Beethoven Mass. As I said, we went from a solemn ass to a solemn mass. It was quite a good performance, except that the principals, though very attractive, were also a bit young & inexperienced. I couldn't always follow the sudden changes in the balance of tone, but it was a wonderful improvement on the shambles of a few years ago, when they tried to sing it at sight. It's a profoundly sobering work, not exhilarating like Bach & Handel.

[139] More digging this morning.[133] The nine o'clock was about Ariosto & Tasso. I took my conscience in my hands, tore it in two, & withdrew the second essay. I just don't feel I can go through two big sets. The twelve o'clock did Jesus as the spiritual Israel. I forget what all I've done in that second year. I mean first year. Ned tells me I've been made an F.R.S.C. [Fellow of the Royal Society of Canada], which is fine—I could use another degree. Priestley & Collin (who's been waiting fifteen years) went through too. Ned says he'll try to get Kay Coburn one: in my opinion she's far better entitled to it than Priestley, to say nothing of that Collin idiot. What's good about it for me is getting it before I'm forty (Ned thinks I'm probably the youngest F.R.S.C. in the country) & without any solicitation on my part. There are advantages in staying with Canada. Nobody else in Victoria has one except Ned himself & DeWitt.

[140] I went down to the library this afternoon intending to do some work on an archetype paper, but didn't concentrate. Then I buggered off for a drink, had dinner, drifted in to the library & got out Broad on the mind—God knows why.[134] Then I walked down to the Ryerson Institute & did my radio program with Preston & Long. It sounded pretty god-dreadful to me, but the boys seemed to like it. I still feel that the H-bomb is entirely beyond the scope of rational discussion—there just isn't anything to say. However, we said it for our half-hour.

Friday, February 24

[141] I went down & struggled through my nine o'clock, which was like lead to lift: 5T1 again. They're like babies in their fierce aggressive resistance, expressed in yawns & bored looks, and, from the unusually bright ones, a question of the "why do we hafta?" variety. The lecture wore me out, & I just diddled around until it was time to get through lunch, which I had to stay down for, otherwise I'd have gone home. The

lunch was Robins collecting King Joblin & me & a man named White (not a black man, though), who has a daughter in second year.[135] Karl Bernhardt, the fourth, had dropped out, & we expressed such strong resistance that the whole thing fell apart. We finally agreed to get Bennett to put the bite on Wood, who is Labour, Davison, who is probably Tory, & a third visiting Englishman, Guthrie of Emmanuel, who is a home-rule Scotchman & therefore (apparently it is a therefore) a Liberal,[136] to discuss the English election.

[142] After that I went home, skipping the culture commission,[137] & intending to mark some essays. I discovered that I was really suffering from considerable nervous exhaustion. I wondered if I just wanted to coddle myself, & decided it didn't particularly matter. The feeling of depression was real enough. I keep involuntarily making up fantasies in which I play a dignified insulted-and-injured role when I'm in that mood. God, how I need a year off: if I miss the Guggenheim I shall have to talk to myself quietly all summer. I haven't felt this way since the summer of 1947: that, by the way, was the time I really should have applied for a year off.

[143] I went to bed very early, & tried reading the Bible before I went to sleep. I find the Gospels most unpleasant reading for the most part. The mysterious parables with their lurking & menacing threats, the emphasis placed by Christ on himself & his uniqueness & on a "me or else" attitude, the displaying of miracles as irrefutable stunts, & the pervading sense of delusion about the end of the world—those are things for intellectual ingenuity to explain away, & the fact that they're there recurrently comes to me up out of the delicate tissue of rationalization. The Christian Church with all its manias had started to form when the Gospels were written, & one can see it at work smoothing things away & making it possible for Christianity to be kidnapped by a deformed & neurotic society. I wonder how long & how far one can dodge or resist the suggestion that the editorial shaping of Scripture is a fundamentally dishonest process.

Saturday, February 25

[144] I seemed to feel the need of sitting still for a certain length of time. So I sat, the whole day. I did nothing but read a book "The God that Failed" which Weaver wants me to do for CBC.[138] Confessions of Koestler,

Silone, Wright, Gide, Fischer & Spender on why they're no longer Communists or fellow travellers. Doesn't tell me anything I didn't know, but it's a readable enough book. I wonder if I can get away with saying, "The mental processes of scientists are much simpler & more innocent than those of writers."

[145] Also I've been trying to read Broad on the mind.[139] He was Irving's tutor, & I see a little more clearly the source of Irving's gossipy & discursive approach to philosophy. What Broad says strikes me as profoundly unreal, but one remark he makes in passing makes me wonder just how far the conception of metaphysics as a grammatical fantasy can be pushed. The noun & verb represent respectively the sources of being & becoming, of the ideas of the substantially existent & of the motor-genetic. The universal (this was Broad's suggestion) comes out of the adjective, & the universe of value springs from the adverb. Note that the universal modifies substance (as in Thomism) & that value modifies manifestation or coming into being. Conjunctions & prepositions are then the source of the essential associative machinery, such as causality, & the pronoun involves the whole question of persona, the person in the substance & standing in place of it.

[146] Also I'm trying to gather up the threads of an archetype paper. I think I can distinguish three kinds of myths, narrative, imagistic & conceptual. Narrative myths approximate the death & resurrection theme by way of the quest, the hero killing the dragon in which life conquerors death. Imagistic myths consolidate the city-garden form of heaven over against the stone & pole form of hell. Conceptual myths are based on the struggle (though that's a narrative word) between the word & nature for the control of reason. That, of course, means the incorporation of law into gospel. The general parallelism of hero = kingdom of heaven = intelligible word and dragon = kingdom of hell = reasonable nature needs working out in detail. The idea of manifestation & disappearance seems to belong to hell; the idea of concealment and realization seems to belong to heaven: one is creation, the other apocalypse.

Sunday, February 26

[147] More sitting, this time with my nose-blocked headache. I don't know whether I brought on the headache by concentrated sitting or not. Anyway, I continued to sit, & Helen to wait on me, even to looking after

the furnace. I put in some time by writing out my radio talk,[140] which seems easy. As I've said before, it's no trick to defend democracy. I only wish I would get a reputation for doing so that would get to American ears, in case I have any difficulty getting a visa, in case I have any occasion to apply for one.

[148] I went out for a walk—it's quite cold weather—& struggled out with the ashes, which was more of an effort than it should have been. I hated missing the student composers' concert, but that was precisely the sort of thing I organized this collapse to avoid. I went to bed early & in the morning I had a very, very Oedipus dream. I don't remember having dreamed of sexual intercourse before—the censor usually requires that package gift-wrapped—but here I was screwing the hell out of one of my students—not one who would attract me if I were in the market—who has mother's name, & who, I discovered, had previously been pawed by my father, now too old, etc. Long before I read Freud or Jung, I had been interested in my relatively uncensored dreams, notably nightmares (this dream was half a nightmare), & I have always felt that they represented a kind of emotional excretion. Psychoanalysis is just the old purging & bleeding routine anyway, and a certain amount of purging can be done by the healthy organism itself. So I feel that I may very well have fished up the emotional core of what's been bothering me, especially when I've been feeling so infantile & masochistic.

[149] The thing I was trying to say to that fool Guggenheim committee was this: Spenser scholarship is still stuck at the second level, where the narrative runs parallel to a historical and a moral allegory. There are acres & acres of Spenser where there just isn't any second-level pattern at all. Book III is entirely on the third level of myth & archetype, & so is IV. The fact that V isn't buggered V, & the whole epic with it. What's more, once one understands Spenser on the third level, second-level interpretations even where they're possible cease to be interesting. In fact, I'm really committed to avoiding second-level interpretation altogether, as was Milton.

Monday, February 27

[150] I feel I've turned the crisis this morning, & feel now that I can sit down & write L [Liberal] no matter what happens. What's more, I feel like doing it. It annoys me to think that I'm subject to "black moods," for

all the world like a spoiled Victorian papa with liver complaint, but I think it's over now. My nine o'clock had a faint trace of a new idea, for once: I divided the Platonic ladder into three stages (I was talking about the Fowre Hymnes [by Spenser]): lowest stage, possessive desire of body for desirable object (clutching baby stage); highest stage, the reestablishment of this; incorporation of the idea or form of beauty within the (universal) soul. In between, the soul-body-as-substantial-unit stage, which is the reproductive or permanent desire of the persisting body for the persisting beauty in the object. In the graduate group I took up the same idea again in relation to the FQ [*The Faerie Queene*] & the alchemic tradition. On the bottom was the hermaphroditic Venus, the serpent with its tail in its mouth; at the top the golden world, & in between is the sexual tension of opposites, the red king & the white queen. As before, the high stage reestablishes the unity of the low stage (this is a Bergson progression), & hence there must be a green world between the gold one & the red & white one (the green lion world is really black). I still haven't figured out this pattern in any consistent way. I suggested that there were three levels of the green world, Blake's Beulah, the upper limit or vision of Paradise which passes (end of Book VI); the dead centre or Gardens of Adonis, & the lower limit of the Bower of Bliss. Points here are by no means clear to me yet. The Page got off on a discussion of whether Socrates was real or not: she still can't get over this "or not" *pons asinorum*, & as soon as I think it's clear off she goes again.

[151] I had lunch with Dona Edgar & we discussed Pelham's [Pelham Edgar's] opus:[141] I couldn't decide whether she thinks I really let her down over the book or whether her manner is just naturally brusque. I'm inclined to think that she's a bit unreasonable about it, though in her circumstances I suppose that's natural enough. I came home & marked fifteen essays: if I can repeat that tomorrow & Wednesday, I'll be through. In the evening I went down & talked to the extension-course women about Spenser. They fall in love with all their professors: I think George Edison is slightly in the lead. They're quite fun to talk to, & don't yawn in my face like the undergraduates.

Tuesday, February 28

[152] I still felt better today, & kept on with Morris: I must do an essay on him sometime.[142] The remark I quoted from Saroyan about children

being the only real aristocracy [par. 56] has a lot to do with NN [*News from Nowhere*] & his whole romance feeling. The R.K. developed the point I made last Saturday about the three kinds of archetype [par. 146]. Curious the difference between the male & the female mind: some of the men stayed right with me, but I could feel the women giving up *en masse*. I said the essential narrative myth, death & resurrection, contained the opposition between the Messiah who dies as an individual man but lives eternally as the large human body of his people & the dragon-hero who lives as an individual & in whom all his followers die to themselves. The essential conceptual myth, the opposition of intelligible word or gospel & reasonable nature or law, I associated with my neither is nor is not point. I haven't got all this clear: I said "is" as predicate was really "is there" & had to expand into an "is here": that may actually be Kant's argument.

[153] The writing kids produced a very pleasant story by Catharine Card, who is a really sweet girl. Darcy Green tells me that her shyness actually is neurotic & she's been under psychiatric treatment. It's a women's magazine formula, but very nicely done. Gloria Thompson did a parody of *My Last Duchess*. I find having all that beauty & charm & health & youth in my office a bit overpowering: I find, not unnaturally, that I want to show off. I never worked that out of my system because, not being athletic, I couldn't show off in the approved ways during the mating season.[143]

[154] I came home & marked a few essays, but got drinking beer with Helen, who promptly went to sleep. I think it may have been about time for a holiday anyway after my sick spell. The Guggenheim people wrote asking how much more money I think I'll need in case they decide to give me some. I wish to hell they'd shut up & shell out. How do I know what it'll cost to live in the States next year? Also they want to know where I'm going. I want to go anywhere I can settle down. The invention of microfilm makes all the talk about having to go here for this & there for that a lot of hypocritical nonsense. I gather from Ned [Pratt] that the F.R.S.C. [Fellow of the Royal Society of Canada] business is a false alarm: Christ, I wish he wouldn't speed good news without checking his facts.[144]

Wednesday, March 1

[155] I skipped over the Epithalamion & went on to Ben Jonson: I've

worked out a pretty fair lecture on him, & now I can start Donne next week. The twelve o'clock did a bit more Morris, only I got bogged down in the Tolstoyan criticism of art & the glorification of the Sidney ideal over the Shakespeare one. They didn't help out, either: they don't recognize their Philistine prejudices when they meet them. I think the boredom & impatience I find so hard to shake off this year is highly contagious. Then lunch, where Robins & Pratt & Little & I discussed cats & dogs, & then I got rid of some of my correspondence: recommendations & the like. I decided to go to Council, noticing that Ned [Pratt], though he was in for tea, skipped it. I must start skipping things. It was the goddamndest dull meeting, except for a complaint by [John] Wood about the untouched filth of his office. They appointed a committee to see if that vague woman who sits in the basement all day can be prodded into doing something about the dusting.

[156] I phoned Woodhouse this evening about the Guggenheim letter: he says his own award was $2500, [Malcolm] Ross's last year, $3000, & they may be considering raising the ante to $3500. So I think I'll hit them up for that. I think too that I may go to Harvard after all: a real research man would prefer Washington or even Pasadena, but that's too lonely for me: I want to be near a real university where I know, or could get to know, some people. Also I'd want to be on the Atlantic seaboard, as Chicago or California would pretty well leave me stuck in Chicago or California. I also asked him about the F.R.S.C. business & he says my name is on a waiting list, & it'll be a year or two before I go on. The list this year is Roy Daniells, Sidney Smith, Collin, Pegis, Wilson of Dalhousie & Britnell of Saskatchewan. Proportional representation is obviously pretty important, & it seems to be a perquisite of departmental & other administrative heads. Roy's Traherne job is a pretty footling thing to get an F.R.S.C. on.[145] Marked no essays, & went to bed early again.

[157] I'm beginning to feel that L [Liberal] is essentially a statement of the theory of poetry, as ⅂ [Tragicomedy] is of drama & ∧ [Anticlimax] of prose. Drama is not a form of poetry, but a separate form, & as I've now come to think of lyric in terms of epic fragmentation epic, diffuse, brief & microcosmic,[146] is beginning to take shape as a kind of "normative" form of poetry in general. I don't know how far one can go with classifying formulae.

Thursday, March 2

[158] The nine o'clock opened Spenser up in terms of a poetic narrative flanked by a moral & a historical allegory, & opposite it a Biblical one. This is more important than it sounds, as the Biblical allegory is the core of the transition to the third level, and in it the second-level allegories find their archetypal meaning. The twelve-o'clock tried out my Trinity as Word of God point on the first year, but it's too tough for them. In the afternoon I went to the Library Committee meeting, damned dull, where we discussed a new way of saving money by taking all the unreadable stuff off to Bell House. The morale of Victoria is so low that I wonder if even a blood transfusion would save it. Then I went off to the periodical room of the Library & saw some 13th-c. reproductions of the Apocalypse that Peter Brieger had got up from the Morgan Library. He wants to know the origin of apocalyptic interest in England: I suggested of course Joachim, & he agreed that Joachim was probably important, but can't pick up his trail in England. One of the books he had showed the two witnesses of ch. xi as medieval friars [Revelation 11:3–14].

[159] It was a very cold day, & I nearly froze my balls off waiting for a bus. The bus took me over to Yonge St., & after six cars had gone by without even stopping, I thought the hell with it & dropped in to the Famous Door to get warm.[147] Evidently nobody ever treats these minor pubs as anything but beer parlors, but I, like a fool, ordered a dry Martini & got one smothered in vermouth. So I had a beer chaser. Then Dorothy Clarke Hay came in with a man whose name I didn't get: he's from Chicago, knows Martin Loeb & Lou Morris, & is currently reviewing a book for the Forum. Dorothy was less raucous than usual, & is a most charming girl when she's quiet. She says Mary Louise & Peter [Cameron] are living in Scarborough & are a bit lonely, as they hesitate to ask people to come all that way to see them. I finally got home &, believe it or not, went to bed early, as Helen went out to her radio program. Doesn't hurt me. Broad on the mind turned out to be a fairly good choice of book after all.[148] I'm beginning to feel that that paper the Kenyon Review wants on the forms of poetry is the next job, & how to work it out I *don't* know.[149] My principle that archetypes inform literature, & so create forms, is so far just a pious hope.

Friday, March 3

[160] I got pretty well through F.Q. I [*The Faerie Queene*, Book I] this morning, though it was rather a bad lecture. Robins tells me my replacer's salary will take $2500 to $3000 off mine. As that's Canadian money, I may have a thin time of it next year, and am beginning to wish I'd either applied for the Nuffield or just waited my turn. However, I may be getting just cheesed off. I went over to the Forum office & read stories all afternoon: I can't understand why we get so many stories & so few poems. Helen sent a message to get a furnace poker on the way home. I asked for one with a hook on the end, but the man said he didn't have any bent pokers. So I took his straight poker home, inserted it in the furnace, gave one tug at a clinker, & had a bent poker in two seconds— bent double, that is.

[161] I think I may have a bit of a lead on the poetry article, which I now think of as "The Problem of Genres in Poetry." The only suggestion we have is the Greek lyric-epic-drama one; but with us drama is not a form of poetry, but a separate form of literature in general. Its essential genres, however, appear still to be tragedy & comedy. Also the relation of music to poetry with us is accidental, & hence τα μελη [*ta mele*, song or melody] hardly exists as a definable separate form. That leaves epic, which can be examined as the normative form of poetic synthesis deriving from scripture, & verging off to narrative poetry (romance & ballad) on one side & treatise poetry (descriptive landscape poem, essay, satire & the rest) on the other. Perhaps there isn't any central form, or the central form is scripture itself, & the parietal principles are epic & encyclopaedia. That's a point that's been bothering me a great deal. But this is cold hash. So is my point that the distinction between "diffuse" and "brief" epic in Milton pares down to a "microcosmic" epic which is simply the lyric at its most concentrated. But the lyric seems to me closely related to drama, & its axial forms seem to be also comedy & tragedy, L'Allegro & Il Penseroso. Out of the comic axis I can see a general distinction of paean & dithyramb, Apollonian and Dionysiac enthusiasm, emerging. Out of the tragic axis I think I see an agon-poem or poem of conflict (intellectual or emotional-erotic) and a pathos-poem or poem of death or self-abnegation. The overtones of "ode" are mainly comic, & of "elegy" mainly tragic.

Saturday, March 4

[162] I went down to slough off a lot of irritating bills & letters that have been on my conscience for some time. We're cutting it fairly fine without Margaret's money,[150] & will have to sit pretty quiet to get through next year. I've about decided that if those blasted Guggenheim people don't give me enough money I'll let their award go for a year. MacGregor Dawson, who was away over age anyway, did just that—also he talked them into letting him take it to England. Of course I haven't got the award, but I'm over the feeling I might not get it. But after all this is the year we pay off the second mortgage, and it will mean a bit of a squeeze getting through, in spite of certain resources we have like renting the house. I still think they shouldn't have put me in the situation of saying how much I'd need.

[163] In the evening I went out to Ned's [Ned Pratt's] birthday party, taking a bottle of Napoleon brandy along as hostage. Everybody there asked except Corbett, who had a cold. I don't find him *sympathique* anyway. Goudge, McRae, Hare, Johnston, Knox, Jim Scott, & John Wood & Blissett. The last two are more or less guests of honour—Wood is getting married next month. The conversation was a bit too anecdotal for my taste, particularly when I'd heard all the anecdotes before. McNaughton's profanity, Hook's [Hooke's] exhibitionism, Bell's arrogance, the Potter-Michael limerick feud. Then we got onto mathematicians, Sid Gould (I told my story), Infeld & how Einstein is a mediocre mathematician in respect to finesse, as Beethoven might be called a mediocre composer, or Shakespeare, from the point of view of someone else like Wolcott Gibbs, a mediocre dramatist. Actually, we all had a wonderful time: I just wonder sometimes if Ned gets what he wants, or knows what he wants.

[164] More about the poetry article: drama, whether poetry or prose, is *threefold* in structure, & its three forms, once more, are respectively narrative, visionary & conceptual. The three essential forms of drama are thus tragedy, comedy, *and symposium*, which ought to disentangle some of ∧ [Anticlimax] from ⊐ [Tragicomedy], & clear up my old ideas on this. All drama is fundamentally *eventual*, assimilated to ritual: it's τα δρομεϝα [*ta dromena*], the things done. What happens in tragedy is catastrophe; what happens in comedy is triumph; what happens in symposium is

illumination. The process of symposium, or dialectic, moves toward this: it implies commitment.

Sunday, March 5

[165] This morning Helen seemed nervous again, & we went out for a walk through the fashionable suburb section around Lawrence Park east of Yonge. A very pleasant walk, except for picking up a large assortment of dogs, including a Great Dane who seemed to be guarding the whole damned street. Helen is terrified of big dogs, & I dislike & distrust them: I feel they have a very bad effect on the humans who own them. So we beat a retreat: I felt foolish, because I felt I had failed, not so much in courage as in savoir faire. The two things are much the same: a soldier's courage is the expression of knowing what to do, as his whole training consists in being told what to do. We met Barbara McNabb on the way home: she asked if I'd like to meet John Wedgwood, Veronica's brother, who is coming to Toronto. If he's as nice as Veronica I certainly would.[151]

[166] Marjorie King in in the evening: Tony was invited but had to stay home with a bellyache. She's full of plans for her trip to Europe this summer: they go on the Isle de France & will be going to her brother-in-law's place in Dorset. She still looks utterly exhausted, but the trip is having its automatic effect on her even in anticipation.

[167] I'm quite pleased with my drama point, as I think it pretty well settles the form of ⅂ [Tragicomedy]. Also it gives me a handle on Shakespeare's dialectic, though I hope figuring out ⅂ won't involve ∧ [Anticlimax] as completely as ∟ [Liberal] does ⅂. I don't know if I can use anything like the same formula on the lyric, but I think Schiller may give me a lead. My distinction between the "singing" lyric and the "autonomous" lyric is close enough to his "naive & sentimental," though I don't like his words. His division of sentimental into elegiac, idyllic & satiric is suggestive too, as it corresponds roughly to my dramatic three, after, again, reforming his words. Certainly those seem to be real genres, as distinct from pseudo-genres. A pseudo-genre may be an arbitrary form like the sonnet which may have any content, or an arbitrary content like the pastoral which may have any form. On the other hand, we do have pastoral elegies, pastoral idyls, & pastoral satires. Milton's sonnets are elegiac (Piedmont, Blindness, Second Wife), idyllic (Margaret Ley, Cyriack

Skinner) & satiric (i.e. intellectualized or occasional) (Tetrachordon, Cromwell, Vane).[152]

Monday, March 6

[168] Late getting out, & nearly missed Hilliard's [Hilliard Trethewey's] bus: my watch loses time & has to be watched, so to speak. The nine o'clock started Donne, & took a more conventional line than usual with me: this is no time to fuddle their poor brains. Besides, I'm bothered myself over classifications of lyrics. The graduate group was mostly theorizing: I tried out my drama idea on them, & I think it's all right. Whatton asked me about satire. I said there were three levels of apprehension, divine comedy, human tragedy, & human comedy. That laughter ranges from the laugh of pure freedom (child at play) on the first level, to laughter at the agony of suffering on the third (heaven to hell). The tragic vision is of course the moral vision of law. Satire looks at the human comedy from a moral standard above it implying a vision of freedom above that. The vision of freedom is a precarious thing that we hold on trust: that door might slam shut & leave us on the moral level of pure repulsion & horror, as in *1984*. This is a point I never got clear before, & it's an essential part of the ⅂ [Tragicomedy] pattern. I wish more people would ask me questions: I'm not like Socrates, & don't know where the dialectic is going.

[169] I used lunch to hand Robins my subcommittee report on Library policy, & King Joblin my hymns & Scripture lesson. Then I went to Hart House to arrange the Playfair show & Abrams' accommodation & lunch, & then back to Vic to get a notice about his lecture sent around. Then I went home, finished my radio talk, & settled down with Helen for a pleasant evening. Then came a tap on the door, & there stood Carol. Carol is a cute blonde high-school girl who accompanied her mother when the latter drove me home from the talk to the extension-course women last Monday. They'd promised to pick me up on the way down, & I guess my subconscious took that as an invitation to forget about the whole business. So Carol sat down in the litter of beer bottles, with Helen babbling hysterically while I was upstairs jumping into a pair of pants. We hadn't finished dinner either, & were having it in the front room because Helen was waxing the dining-room table. However, I was ready

in three minutes, & gave a lecture on drama without stopping for breath. It's their final meeting. Not my best work, needless to say.

Tuesday, March 7

[170] Woke up with a bad headache that stayed with me most of the day—nose again. The nine o'clock finished Morris, slightly to my regret, as I think I do him fairly well. Then I typed out my radio talk & sent it down to Helen James, & tried to think of something to say to the R.K. people. I attached my threefold scheme to ritual, myth & doctrine, & thence to Church, Bible & University, defining the latter as the "idea" of the university. I don't like the way I get tangled up in threefold schemes: I *must* remember that three is a Beulah number. But I haven't located the demonic fourth: in Blake the fourth is time, whereas with me time is one of the three. After a relatively uneventful lunch I staggered home & went to bed, but that didn't seem to work, so I got up again, ate dinner & then buggered off down to the college again for the Alumni meeting. Davison is in the hospital with a chest condition, but [John] Wood's body, as I said, was still warm, & they got Brian Barton to sub for Davison. Wood gave a longish speech, based, he told me, on old copies of the Spectator & the Statesman, which was most dispassionate & objective. Guthrie spoke for the liberals, but didn't profess to know anything about politics: Brian Barton did very well. It was a very successful discussion, though both Wood & Guthrie were intensely nervous—curious how inhibited the academic mind is, & what easy game it would be, in itself, for totalitarians: I mean by that their failure to understand that their lack of specialized knowledge of the subject was not a disqualification, as democracy ought to be government by amateurs for amateurs. I told King Joblin I'd take the whole service. Dearly as I love King, I don't go for his corncrake voice ("granulated," as Pete Colgrove used to call it) & could do better in that way myself.

[171] I don't think I can make a lyric classification convincing unless I can demonstrate that at a certain pitch of concentration archetypal symbols begin to appear. Thus the elegiac lyric seems to have an introverted aspect, ranging from pensiveness to despair, which one might call the melancholy poem, & in this the figure of the veiled woman seems to be prominent: in Il Penseroso, in Keats' Ode to Melancholy, in Baudelaire.

Father & mother symbols appear in the poem, which is, I think Tharmatic rather than Urizenic. Keats' Autumn is really a mother-symbol.

Wednesday, March 8

[172] The ten o'clock charged through Donne, &, as usual, said nothing very new or true. I'm getting more accustomed to thinking in terms of a "satiric" genre of lyric, & I think it works. The twelve o'clock was much better: I started Huxley, but got off on the general anti-Cartesian or existential movement which, I said, produced in Darwinism a reversal of the Cartesian derivation of existence from consciousness. I went on to show the connection of this with Schopenhauer's will & idea, Nietzsche's will to power & the "all too human," Marx's ruling-class & dispossessed, Freud's ego & libido & the whole psychological conception of that which is mental & yet not conscious (I linked the anti-Freudian French existentialist doctrine of conscious freedom with the Cartesian tradition) & Kierkegaard's "spiritless" natural reason & dread (which, as I saw for the first time, links both with the Nietzsche-Marx revolutionary pattern & with Bergson's identification of the subconscious will with duration: the existential is always the Spectre of Urthona).

[173] Munro Beattie dropped in for lunch. He's nigger-trading, & the best man on his list was George Johnston, so George will at least get the offer.[153] Both Love & Hoeniger came up & made a good deal of him, & I'll try to push one of them in his direction if I can. Beattie takes very well to being a big shot—I don't mean that in any catty sort of way. He told me that now I'd made the Kenyon Review he knew exactly where I was academically. He did an M.A. at Columbia on Canadian poetry. I wish I knew where I was academically.

[174] I buggered around & took a couple of drinks, rather rashly, & then came back for the tea for Peter Haworth's exhibition. Jessie [Macpherson] asked me to make a speech thanking him & I made a very good one—I quite surprised myself. Helen poured for a while, & then Barbara Brieger, who makes a great fuss about being bored on such occasions. Barker Fairley was there, sulky as the devil about having to go to England. We (us, Comforts, Haworths, Briegers, Jessie & others) piled into cars & went up to the Jackman's [Jackmans'] for drinks. In spite of taking the precaution of eating a good deal, I was fairly high. We had a quick

dinner in Murray's & talked to Douglas Duncan, who had coffee with us, & then got a street car & arrived home half expecting to see Acta kids on our doorstep, but we got there just ahead of them.

Thursday, March 9

[175] The kids were excited about their exams, & got a terrific slug of powerful coffee from Helen, & left at ten minutes after one. I don't think I've ever seen students so wound up. They talked & talked & talked, & couldn't seem to stop talking. About their courses mostly, the deficiencies of high school teaching, vocational guidance & the like. I was interested, though not surprised, by their contempt for progressivist tendencies. I talked mainly to the men, who kept the conversation on a fairly personal plane.

[176] So naturally, I was pretty rocky for my nine o'clock, but it turned out to be a very good lecture, opening up the second book [of *The Faerie Queene*]. They got interested in censorship for some reason, & I tried to draw a distinction between censorship & education. In the latter things are presented in a certain order: you present Andersen to a child rather than Rabelais for the same reason that you present arithmetic to him rather than calculus. Rabelais is for adults. Milton's Areopagitica implies that people have gone through an educational program & are now proceeding in self-education. They choose, for reason is but choosing.[154] Society cannot survive except on the assumption of this. Most biological adults are uneducated & are still children, but nothing can now be done for them. If the mind doesn't keep pace with the body no extension of the educational process is feasible. Here comes a Catholic-Protestant antithesis: for the Catholic the Church educates until death & can therefore withdraw things permanently: the Protestant Church is itself educable, & those within it must therefore be autonomously educated. This got a bit off the track, but not so far as it sounds. I said Mammon & Acrasia were bourgeois-Puritan (religion & the rise of capitalism) & aristocratic-Catholic (Great Whore & Court of Love) clusters. I don't see why one isn't free to make the second point when so many books dwell gleefully on the first. I must read Tawney & Darcy respectively.[155] The first year was straight on translation.

[177] The Ph.D. committee lasted for two ~~years~~ hours (Freudian slip)

.

figuring out the permutations & combinations of orals. As usual, I contribute too much too soon. Jitter set in & I was a bit demoralized by four o'clock. Woodhouse is full of the "London Lectures" he's been asked to do.[156]

Friday, March 10

[178] The writing group kids came in for supper last night & produced some pretty fair stuff: poems by Sylvia Moss, a sketch by Kathlyn Smith, & another very good story by Jean Inglis, so good I asked her to send it to the Forum.[157] I found their conversation a bit dull and school-girlish; men certainly are necessary in keeping up an impersonal level. I got to bed by midnight, but in the morning I felt very tired, and my nine o'clock was bloody awful. I tried to say something about how the cult of youth in the Bower of Bliss was really a denial of life because it opposed the process of maturing, but it didn't come quite off: in fact it didn't come off at all. I staggered in to lunch & talked to Robins & Woodside about the growing cleavage between staff & students & about how the Senior Dinner came at the worst possible time, at least for students, & should come with the other graduation exercises, which really do impress them. Then I went home & found the Kemp family in possession, with old Mr. [Patrick] Cronin & Mary Boulton due to arrive for tea. I stayed upstairs for the whole performance, as my nerves were jumping out of my skin in all directions, & waited until everyone was gone. Then I went to bed early & got some real sleep, which I badly needed, or felt I needed.

[179] I've been worrying about the clash of threes & fours in my classifications. Finally, I've been slowly forced into a general extension of my prose forms to other departments. I now think of the four forms of drama as tragedy (corresponding to romance), novel (corresponding to comedy: I mean the other way around: I'm listening to the Franck symphony at the moment & I like the Franck symphony), symposium (corresponding to anatomy), *and mime*, corresponding to confession. The mime involves the whole question of persona, Yeats' mask, & of course of soliloquy. Hamlet is a tragedy-mime mixture, & the function of the chorus in Greek drama is mimic. The mime brings up the question of "hypocrisy" along with persona & manifestation, & has overtones extending as far as the God of the Trinity who is three persons (personae) in one substance. If I've really located the form of the fourth in drama &

prose, it should work out in poetry too: in epic, as a confession of the type represented by Wordsworth's Prelude; in lyric, as a sort of reflective meditation different from both the satiric & the elegiac.

Saturday, March 11

[180] Got up late & went down to send a wire off to Abrams telling him where to go tomorrow night, which is when he's coming. Then I phoned Hart House & got that arranged, & walked up in the slush to the liquor store. There I met Major Howarth, who was looking a bit seedy, & who has spent the last three years in the hospital in more or less constant pain. No circulation in hands or feet. Something about scar tissue. They've been burning him alive with electric treatments, & it seems to do him good. He said he'd met Ned [Pratt] downtown & Ned has asked him up to lunch. Then I waited in various queues for various food items & came home in a bad temper & badly fussed. Shopping is not for the weaker sex. I spent the rest of the day buggering over my sermon tomorrow: as always, I work too hard on sermons. Blissett came in to dump the Milton part of his thesis on me, but changed his mind, as I said I couldn't possibly read it this week anyway.[158]

[181] This general fourfold scheme I've hit on should, I think, clear up ʎ [Rencontre]. I have, for my complete theory of the verbal universe, one book to do on the theory of poetry (epic-lyric), which is ∟ [Liberal], one on drama, which is ⅂ [Tragicomedy], & one on prose forms, or ⋀ [Anticlimax]. That takes in my trivium. ʎ, then, deals with the fourth form of literature, the prophecy, which is peculiarly associated with mime, prelude & confession. As the other three relate to rhetoric, grammar & logic (as I think now) so the form of the fourth relates to music, the ambiguous link between trivium & quadrivium, the verbal & the numerical universes. I've always felt that ʎ had something to do with romanticism on its narrative side, with the interaction of the Hegelian triad & the Kantian dichotomy on the logical, with fragmentation & the lyric rhetorically— and with music. Also, the strong feeling of persona about it was there from the beginning. The link with Blake in the form of prophecy is right too. Well, that's on the shelf, but I must go over my ⅂ notes & see what I've said about "persona" & translate it as mime. The theme of disguise in comedy has a link with this, & so has the leviathan theme in Job. Most of my ideas about mime are pure hunches as yet, but they're coming.

Note how in prose forms the mime appears not only in the confession itself but in the growing persona preoccupation of the novel & its sense of the contrast between action & motive.

Sunday, March 12

[182] Brooded over my wind-egg[159] all day. In the afternoon we went out for a walk and met Mrs. Manning with two boys which were hers & two girls that weren't. I haven't seen her for years—since a party at Pincoe's in fact, and she turned out to be a very pleasant & friendly girl, with bright laughing eyes—she sounded actually as though she were a bit lonely, & as Ed Manning strikes me as a dull & rather humorless person she may be. She said calmly that her eldest son was too phlegmatic: take him to a circus, she said, and no starry eyes: he acts as though he'd lived through it all before in another world. The younger one is much more what she'd like.

[183] Went out to chapel & turned in a technically beautiful performance. Text: "then all the disciples forsook him, & fled" [Matthew 26:56]. Theme: the constant sense of alienation of Jesus from human society: not the withdrawal of John the Baptist, which sets up a magnetic pole in the desert, but a permanent sense of being excluded from the human community, in the world & not of it. How the trial of Jesus marks a total consolidation of society against the prophet: there is no human being that does not consent to God's death. Here is a demonstration of original sin far deeper than any fall of Adam, which is only a legal fiction. Democracy is the least superstitious form of government because of its conviction that people are not fit to be trusted with power. And so on. The "long prayer" was a paraphrase of the Lord's Prayer & the short one was simply the reading of the 90th Psalm. I understand very well the remark attributed to McNaughton: he didn't mind preaching sermons: it was the goddam prayers that got him down. Margaret Carmichael, the mad girl in Ruddigore,[160] who has a remarkable contralto voice, sang a solo, & I think it all passed off very smoothly. Even Helen was impressed, & she isn't usually by my theological efforts.

[184] I naturally didn't have time to do any thinking. I worked out the whole service, prayers & all, around the theme of an initial total withdrawal from physical society which rediscovers a different principle of

community. In *that* world even prayer has a point as a wireless message through a medium that will carry it. I say this because I've never got the point of prayer. I didn't have time to develop this, but the inner world as a source of all *value* in particular is becoming a more suggestive idea to me. On the whole, though, preaching is something I want very little of.

Monday, March 13

[185] Staggered out very tired & went through a pointless nine o'clock on Herbert & Crashaw, then tried out my new fourfold scheme on the graduate group. If they don't mind the fact that I'm a long way off Spenser I sure don't. Anyway, I was surprised at the way ʎ [Rencontre] is clearing up around the ideas of fragmentation & epiphany. I now feel that scripture is not so much a form as a tendency, the anagogic tendency to unification as opposed to the oracular tendency to epiphany. I wish somebody would have sense enough to ask me to do a series of lectures somewhere.

[186] Well, anyway, I went in to lunch & Abrams turned up all right: a friendly-looking & rather undistinguished person in appearance, which is good: he's obviously the type to get down to business. All the English staff came except Robins, which was no surprise to me: Ned [Pratt] did the honours. I can't remember much of the conversation: a certain amount of Cornell gossip. The paper was very good: it traced the development of the idea that the poet is to his poem as God is to the universe from its theological origins down to the remark of Dean Inge that for understanding the relation of God to the world the relation of poet to poem might offer a helpful analogy: a beautifully turned conclusion.[161] What I particularly liked was the way it made Woodhouse so happy:[162] it was about the history of ideas & the origin & development of romanticism & contained a flattering allusion to Woodhouse's Collins essay.[163] So the discussion was mainly Woodhouse, with a bit of [Barker] Fairley & Frye. Graham Cotter also spoke up in favor of criticism as a science. I talked a bit about Blake, but he doesn't fit these orders of grace & nature discussions: with him it's an epistemological basis of active & passive minds. I note a tendency to the overuse of the colon in my writing: I must try more—uh—dashes.

[187] Helen got in quite a stew over the dinner, but it was a good dinner

& went off all right. Kay Coburn was a bit shaky on her pins from her cold, but turned out, & so did the Dunns. Charlie had got an offer from Cincinnati, but I don't know how it turned out. My writing is turning out to many turning outs. Gordon Roper & his wife came in later. Kay is our exchange to Cornell this year,[164] which is certainly the right choice, but strikes me as funny—I wonder how the stag line will function next year with her as chairman. I like Abrams very much; & he grows on one, & is not at all the bright boy on the make that one sees so often.

Tuesday, March 14

[188] Roper was a good person to have along, as he knows all about Chicago & Abrams seems very interested in Chicago. A bit too much party line about it, but this Crane lead should probably be followed up. Housing is difficult too: I'd better stick to the Atlantic seaboard.[165]

[189] I got through Huxley after a fashion, but a Hegelian pattern corresponding to the Darwinian one wouldn't come. Then I went over to Abrams' Coleridge lecture, which I introduced badly and couldn't hear. I think the fourth year honour people liked it, but the second year pass course didn't know what the hell the score was. Abrams makes a very good impression: honest, intelligent, & respects his job & his audience. He even had mimeographed copies of the Dejection Ode ready. Then I went through an R.K. lecture on Ecclesiastes: fair, but I seem to have got derailed on that course. Then back to Hart House for lunch: everybody I asked turned up. It was all right, though some very corny jokes were told. I let Abrams wander for the afternoon: he went to the Library, however, & I went home to read that other book I was supposed to do for the radio, & that got delayed in the mail. Carlo Levi's *Of Fear and Freedom*: a passable piece of musing on life. After dinner I went out to Woodhouse's party & ran into Norman Endicott on the way.

[190] The party was all right except that I was tired. So was everybody, apparently, except McLuhan, Abrams, Joe Fisher, who talked very well, & of course Woodhouse. Woodhouse has been asked to do a Milton paper at M.L.A. & his opposite number is Cleanth Brooks,[166] who apparently belongs to a group called the "New Critics" who are supposed to ignore historical criticism & concentrate on texture, whatever texture is. Abrams is a historical critic, & is on Woodhouse's side. The general

consensus was that, as I said to MacGillivray afterward, the critic ought to say everything relevant, but not necessarily all at once. I don't go for the sort of discussion which seems to be academic & is really just gossip. I prefer to listen to Abrams talking about 18th c. German Leibnitzians—Bodmer & Breitlinger, they sounded like—who equated the "possible" fantasies of artists—chimeras & the like—with Leibnitz's possible but non-existent worlds.[167] I asked Abrams if being in the Kenyon Review would make me a new critic: I certainly can't claim to be *au courant* in such matters.

Wednesday, March 15

[191] Felt very sleepy after Woodhouse's whisky & didn't make much out of Vaughan or Traherne. The kids didn't cooperate either: the final Huxley lecture was brilliant—Freudian slip again—I meant to write wasn't brilliant. I said the Hegelian pattern was a bad one when stretched out in history: in Marxism, for instance, it was just a donkey-&-carrot arrangement. In the intervening hour I wrote out my review of Levi's book. Another half-pound of Erdman arrived in the mail:[168] he's found not only a publisher but a $500 advance. So he gave me one of his dollars to use on return postage.

[192] At lunch today they said I'd impressed the V.C.F. [Varsity Christian Fellowship], & Irving prophesied gloomily that I'd probably be hooked for more sermons. Bill Little thought the closing of the frontier, which began to hit Canadian life around the thirties, had developed not only a demand for social but for intellectual security. I suppose it's a common American thesis, but there may be something in it even if I don't like it. But surely people turned Mormon & Christian Scientist & Catholic (Paulists) and stood around waiting for the end of the world when the frontier was open. I like Bill Little very much when he gets on his real interests.

[193] Bledsoe came in this afternoon & for the first time I heard about a possible cheque.[169] He says Rinehart is going ahead to produce texts in a series—say the romantic poets—to replace the old dinosaur anthologies. He asked about Erdman for the Blake & I told him about the English Institute.[170] They don't want to duplicate editors. He spoke with marked coldness of Mark Schorer, who did their Wuthering Heights—I don't

know what's up in that quarter.[171] He says he's turned the introduction over to Douglas Bush,[172] who will probably snoot the bibliography—he can hardly fail to like the introduction itself.

[194] Then I went to the C.B.C. and read my review, beautifully, in rehearsal. Then I read it again, loudly, inflexibly & far too slow, for performance. I was convinced that I was reading it even faster the second time. I don't know what gets into me on these occasions. Helen James thought my reviews were excellent, but I think she was naturally disappointed too. She wants me to join a discussion on religion—the B.B.C. bans religious discussion & all expression of atheistical views, and she naturally wants the C.B.C. to improve on this a bit.

Thursday, March 16

[195] Got up very tired: I think there is a flu bug biting me, & all day I felt as though I had gone without sleep for about three days. I had rumbles in the guts & a general feeling that my skeleton had been replaced by something rubber. The nine o'clock opened up Book Three [of *The Faerie Queene*], & wasn't too bad: I tried to work out the idea that occurred to me Monday in connection with the relation of the orders of grace & nature as complicated by a contrast between the active & passive mind, which is what explains the contrast between the Bower of Bliss & the Gardens of Adonis. It's not a new idea, of course, but a flank attack on an old one. The twelve o'clock went on with the is-it-true-or-not problem of the Gospels. Then I went over to Hart House, and, still feeling like hell, introduced Playfair, who was reviewing his own show. He gave an impression of great sincerity, talked entirely about himself & with complete modesty, & finished all he had to say in fifteen minutes. He said he'd begun with a strong Picasso influence, & went back from him to earlier masters, which, as I said, was what Picasso had done himself. Chirico went back to the point of going back on himself—I thought of that because of a strong Chirico influence in some of his work along with the Picasso. His main point was simply that the fine brush-work of an El Greco was explicable only as the product of a great mind. Doesn't sound like much, but I liked him. George Johnston got the Ottawa job.[173]

[196] Then I went down to the station & met Helen there & we got on the train for London. An uneventful trip, except that Helen claimed not to

know it was a dinner, & we blew up a last minute scare about formal clothes. However, the Mackinnons [Murdo MacKinnons], who met us at the train, soon reassured us. They drove us a bit around the town & we saw the famous public library, which is also an art gallery, a film & record library, & a community centre generally. It is a most pleasant little building, & I'd have liked to see more of it. However, we had to drive off to the Western campus to make my speech. John Graham was there, & Frank Stiling & Klinck, who was late, also two other people, Ready (?) & MacCrae [John McRae], whom I remember from the graduate school. Collin wasn't there: he was ill. The Dolores Garrod I'd been corresponding with turned out to be a most self-possessed little damsel, & very attractive. But on the whole the women were dull, taking no part in the discussions during or afterward.

Friday, March 17

[197] The talk was my usual line, & I think it wasn't too bad, but I was feeling so lousy and had to force myself so much that it was certainly nowhere near my top form. However, the questions were frequent enough to show some interest, & they came up & crowded around me afterwards, & I guess all told I gave them a fair enough evening. We went over to the Klincks for a drink afterward—also food, as Mrs. K is the comfortable sort of woman that makes rich chocolate cakes. By the irony of fate I couldn't eat anything except a couple of ripe olives. I couldn't even eat my dessert at dinner, which was strawberry shortcake. Oh, well. A boy named Glen (I think) Hyatt, who is interested in T.S. Eliot, attracted me.

[198] The visit to Western almost exactly duplicated my visit last year to Michigan University & Michigan State, on a reduced scale. The Western people are a compact, friendly, rather folksy group, holding the humanities line in the middle of a place given over to business administration, journalism, extension courses & rugby teams. They are slightly in awe of us & our high-powered graduate school, but they obviously have qualities that make them essential in a place where Woodhouse & I would be hopeless. I was particularly impressed by Murdo & Elizabeth [MacKinnon]: no apologies, just frankness & cordiality.

[199] I was nearly hysterical when I finally got to bed after midnight, but in the morning I felt almost recovered. The Mackinnons [MacKinnons]

had told us not to get up until the youngsters were fed, but as we awakened to the sound of a small child getting shushed into a whisper by its mother Helen said we had to put the kids out of their misery, & we got up. There are two little girls, Ann & "Tinker Bell," four & three, & as cute as they come. After breakfast & after hearing Ned [Pratt] on a school radio programme, we said goodbye to Elizabeth[,] & Murdo took us around Western—the Arts building, the library, the tiny little museum, & a concert hall with a badminton net stretched across the middle of it & four girls playing badminton. We didn't have time to see the downtown Aeolian Hall with its baroque organ. I talked to John Graham, but there's nothing new there, and—last night—to Klinck about someone to replace Murdo, who's getting next year off. At least he has leave of absence. I spoke highly of Victor Whatton, and may land him something. Their staff is a young group, & Murdo seems very well adjusted both to Western & to the little village outside London he lives in.

Saturday, March 18

[200] Slight kick-back after that tough Thursday, but better. It's always a bit cheerless coming back home after leaving it in the winter. It was only a coincidence that the furnace was all choked up with dust & not working properly, & only a coincidence too that Friday was the bloodiest god-damned snowstorm of the whole year; but they were both depressing coincidences. It snowed all the way from London & took us an hour to come home on the street car, which we were foolish enough to take. So we dug ourselves in for the rest of the day.

[201] Today was completely wasted. I don't know why. I shovelled the damn place out this morning, taking it very easily, & still had to sit down afterwards with all sorts of orange & sky blue solar systems spinning in front of me. So I got out to the office & told myself & Helen I had to write some letters. I did, too, but when I got there I just looked at the letters & got out again. There was a letter from Norman Langford asking me about a line from Donne's Litany: "From light affecting, in religion, news,"[174] & a note from Graham Cotter asking me if my four categories of literature were efficient causes. I think they are: they're certainly controlling rhythms, & so operating powers. Oh, God, I wish I could just sit down & start writing, with no essays to read or lectures to give or magazine to edit or speeches to make. I feel that I've been dissipating my

energies for so long that it would be a tremendous relief just to concentrate them for a while. Two more weeks of it. This is the month the Guggenheim is supposed to do its stuff. The part of me that I'm interested in living with doesn't give a damn whether I get next year off or not, but dreads not getting it because of the hullabaloo that would be set up by the part of me that I'm not much interested in living with. Hell of a mixed-up state of mind, when they're both me.

[202] I feel dull & spoiled, like a constipated lapdog. Next week I'm going to do some concentrated essay reading & get *that* out of the way, & then I may be able to see where the hell I am. Otherwise I just have to sit tight & wait for April 1, when most of my lectures will be finished. Two weeks today. I skipped the Forum meeting by going to London, & shall have to catch up on that too. I'm really not working or being worked hard: it's just the vast size of this thing in my brain that's trying to get born.

Sunday, March 19

[203] Stayed around indoors all day, listening to the radio, hearing some good music—a program from Halifax of recorded music featuring Purcell, Boyce & Arne. At six I heard a most curious noise over the radio purporting to come from some Professor named Frye who was talking about books. It's the first time I've heard my voice, except for a few remarks in that Infeld programme. I would never have recognized it as my own voice: that nasal honking grating buzz-saw of a Middle-Western corncrake. I need a few years in England. The reading wasn't as bad as I thought it might be, but Clyde Gilmour on movies was a hell of a lot better.

[204] My idea of a fourth prophetic category has expanded into a threefold active counterpart to my original threefold scheme. Thus to drama, the thing done, there corresponds ritual, the doer, & the four forms of drama evolve out of the four corresponding forms of ritual: tragedy from sacrifice, carnival from comedy (I mean the other way round), symposium from communion, mime from dance. That's clear to me: it's not so clear that the four forms of epic, narrative, commedia, treatise & prelude evolve from four forms of lyric, elegiac, idyllic, satiric & dithyrambic. Here $\tau\alpha$ $\epsilon\pi\eta$ [ta epe], the thing said, is contrasted with the sayer, & poetry is the projection of song. And it's not clear at all that the four forms of

prose evolve from four forms of prophecy. Here the thing thought is projected from the thinker. Romance then evolves from the commandment, the prophecy of judgment on the wilderness-wandering, the compulsion of the quest. Novel evolves from parable, midrash, sutra, upanishad—that sort of thing. Anatomy evolves from aphorism, & confession from oracle. A considerable amount of this must be bullshit.

[205] Douglas Grant was in for dinner, very tired & jittery. Joan's just had her baby, whom he proposes to call Abigail. He says he's been promised a villa in Sicily, & if he could make $500 a year out of writing he'd live there. I have an idea he won't remain in the teaching game, at least not over here. I suggested "Energy Enslaved" (Blake, of course) as a title for his war book, which is coming out now.[175] He seems to be reliving the war with great intensity, & it makes him restless & inclined to keep passing the sort of activist value-judgements that war begets. A good deal too about such things as premonitions of death in war time, which he's experienced.

Monday, March 20

[206] Dug myself out very unwillingly and staggered through some nonsense about Marvell & Herrick. The graduate group went very smoothly, with a lot of absentees, but for once I got somewhere near Spenser. It was just the straight stuff about the rhetorical allegory, or decorum, being largely a matter of imitative harmony, the sound being an echo of the sense. Also all of the funny noises in Spenser. I've got enough new ideas out of that course to last me for a while, & it was a relief to relapse for once into routine.

[207] The afternoon was broken up, partly by my own desire for a drink, partly by Barker's [Barker Fairley's] calling a meeting of the colloquium executive. I'm the new chairman, for a time at least. We put Rossi, the coming visitor in philosophy, down for November, & put Creighton & Finch on the committee. Poor old Barker still feels pretty blue: he was just beginning to start exploring U.S.A. & get some real recognition when they slammed the door on him & he has to pick up a trip to England as consolation prize, & of course he knows all about England.[176] I then drifted in to the department meeting, where matters of monumental unimportance were being discussed. I went home with Knox, who

tells me the A.T.E. [Association of Teachers of English] is getting B.K. Sandwell to harangue them. I said that really tore it, & he agreed.

[208] At lunch there was some discussion of the recent invasion of Victoria by some louts from the Westminster Seminary in Philadelphia, the arsehole of Biblical literalism, who spoke in the chapel last night to get converts, but I gather were quite a flop. The best things they did were to quote Barth & Brunner out of context—though, as Hugh Moorhouse pointed out, literalists don't recognize the existence of context. Peter Grant, Douglas Latimer & Clinton Lawson were the Rahabs who let them in. Everyone agrees that it's a good thing that they've finally manifested themselves on their real intellectual level. Barth, said one lout, got all his ideas from Kant. "I can explain Kant. Here's this pulpit. I turn away & it disappears. Mind's everything. That's Kant." I said I bet a lot of students wished it were. Anti-intellectualism among students is increasing, as it naturally goes with the growing separation of staff & students. It isn't part of a closed-frontier demand for security, but a childish desire to pretend that the frontier is still open & Philistine values still primary.

Tuesday, March 21

[209] The first Butler lecture said about what I expected to say, except for one link that may be important: the low norm of satire has performed the minimum feat of Darwinian adaptation to environment, & the high norm has exhibited the Lamarckian "cunning" of becoming a free individual within society. I said that the final cause of the evolutionary process for Butler was some kind of entelechy or fulfilment of being like that of Aristotle, who was also a biologist. My Butler lectures are rushed this year, but last year I can't count more than four either, so I may just be in a greater hurry to get through.

[210] The R.K. lecture was confined to receiving questions, some very stupid ones, like what is the Bahai movement? Also one or two people who have been sleeping soundly all year wake up & give evidence of that fact. But on the whole I think they're interested, & my conception of the word as the resolver of the antithesis between reason & nature by setting up a free structure of active vision including both is beginning to take shape. I imagine that the current genetics controversy in Russia

marks the beginning of some difficulty in defining the Father in Marxism.[177] The body of revelation is clear, & the "historical process" or Holy Spirit is all right, but Marx's failure to do anything about the power of nature, Huxley's reality-principle or struggle for existence, is bothering them.

[211] The writing group produced Mary Lane's third story, her best yet: pretty lively account of a minister in a small Western village with a dead wife, a defeated & embittered housekeeper, unruly kids, a bum of a farmer, & a very convincing study of community life. In short, a fine story full of all sorts of insights & sympathies. Rita Maclean did a story about a pink house in Rosedale—her best yet too. They write well, these kids, & they've really worked hard. I stayed around and went in to tea, where nothing happened, came home and started reading essays. Calendino's thesis on Spenser & Ariosto turned out to be the goddamnedest blithering bloody nonsense—80 pages, & he gets down to his subject around p. 68. However, I'm gradually getting through all the stuff I'm supposed to get through. Blissett too: the Milton caboose of his, & perfunctory enough.[178] The conception of tragedy as a vision of time, as that which slowly passes over the wheel of fortune into that which has irrevocably been, will bear thinking about.

Wednesday, March 22

[212] Two more lectures nearer the end. The 2i was stuff about satire: the Butler lecture was the book of the Machines business,[179] in which I was morbidly conscious of my ignorance of the biological situation involved. I wish I could feel that Butler's grasp of it were clearer, or that the issue between him & Darwin was something more than just a verbal one. Unfortunately my key lecture on Butler was last year on the day of the Senior Dinner, the day I didn't record.[180] I made a brilliant summary of the kinds of idolatry Butler's iconoclasm was directed against that I must try to recapture.

[213] I struggled all afternoon—well, nearly two hours—with a Telegram reporter named Dorothy Howarth, who apparently does a series of "human-interest" studies of professors. As she wanted to know only incidentals about me, & didn't give a damn about my work or my writing, I tremble to see the result.[181] My life apart from my work has

been very colorless, and I'm afraid I'm not a good subject for interviewing. Then I went in & had tea. James was in,[182] & as I appreciated his interest in the College I tried to talk to him, but it was uphill work with Alta Lind [Cook] there—she's in one of her grousing moods, having just had a summons for not shovelling off her sidewalk.

[214] The Art Committee met at five—joint meeting. Grube & Watson were re-elected, so there's more continuity than usual. Boggs was made the new secretary. Stewart turned in a curious annual report, asserting that a decline of undergraduate interest had been evident, & caused by too many abstract pictures. Evidently the Warden,[183] in a meeting Monday night I couldn't get to (=didn't feel like attending) had spoken of a growing cleavage between staff & students, the moral of which for him is fewer deadheads & more young people on his committees. Came home very tired & headachy, went to bed very early & slept like a baby.

[215] It occurs to me that my four forms have something to do with the four movements of the sonata: let's take the lyric ones, as they're closest to "song." The first movement is in sonata form, & the sonata form is comic, as I've worked it out elsewhere.[184] Hence it belongs to the paean or idyll. The slow movement then is elegiac, the scherzo satiric, & the finale mimic or dithyrambic.

Thursday, March 23

[216] Today was given over chiefly to lectures: the nine o'clock brought the third book [of The Faerie Queene] a little more into focus for me. There actually is a highly schematic form of it, & I must get its graphic formula clearer. The thing I haven't got clear is the relation of Cupid & Psyche to Venus & Adonis. I traced the VA pattern in the Britomart-Artegall relationship (redeemable love); in the Belphoebe-Timias one (virginity, hence C of L [Court of Love] frustration); in the Mariell-Florimell one (the VA level, hence pure nature-myth) & in the Argante-Squire of Dames (parody). Also I linked the bondage of Amoret to Busirane with jealousy or possessive love, & hence as cpt. [counterpoint] to Malbecco & Hellenore, which in turn links with the allegory of Troy. So the masque may be love in bondage, & Psyche, the soul, may represent the release of love from a virgin-mother complex. As I say, it's getting a bit clearer. The twelve o'clock finished off the Frosh, who wanted to know what I thought of

this nonsense in the Readers' Digest about explaining Old Testament miracles by planetary collisions.[185] I said I didn't think much of it. Then they wanted to know what I thought of "all this pyramid stuff." Same answer.

[217] In the afternoon I had the drama lectures on Jonson,[186] & forgot my book, so talked more or less at random. I said all the usual things—that lecture is getting pretty threadbare—but in the course of wondering what the hell to say about *The Alchemist* I got a new sense of the place of that comedy in the general ⌐ [Tragicomedy] pattern. Its Saturnalia form represents the *containing* of a potentially tragic pattern. The apocalyptic mind aware of a world under judgement but perverted into a Satanic ambitiousness is held impotent in a comic situation. This is old: I thought I had something new. It arose out of a discussion of the Kitely episode in EMH [*Every Man in His Humour*], & how the "serious scene" in comedy is a tragic germ.[187] I need to think more about the ironic suspended conclusion of a play like *Troilus and Cressida*, which seems to cut across my four categories. It may be a Bardo or mime resolution.

[218] In any case I'm beginning to think more & more of making at least a big initial assault on ⌐ [Tragicomedy]. It's in many ways an easier book to write than L [Liberal], & it would certainly be nice to have it out reasonably soon & present it to Ned [Pratt]. If I keep up a certain amount of work on L, finishing Spenser annotation & so forth, it really shouldn't get in the way too much.

Friday, March 24

[219] Another dithering day, this time largely because I was bothered about the speech tonight, & wanted to dodge doing both it & anything else, the way I do. I finished 3j this morning by dint of some fast talking about the Mutability Cantoes, some perfunctory aligning of them with the Gardens of Adonis, some bothered & hesitant remarks about the Irish question, & not doing anything more about the Cupid & Psyche business. They gave me a clap: I wish I could feel more charitable about that class, & I wish my ego didn't ride me so hard. At lunch David Hoeniger brought along a couple of lads from Saskatchewan, Mandel & Steadman [Stedmond]. Mandel has applied for a Beaver Club Scholarship, & seems to think he'll get it. He did an M.A. on Christopher Smart

& wants to go on for a Ph.D.,[188] & was on his way to meet Mary MacFarlane [McFarlane] in order to work out a *modus vivendi* with her in case he does have to stay here. He's a good lad: I liked him very much, & as I wouldn't put a plugged nickel on Mary's chances of finishing her thesis I'd hate to see him forced out of Smart.[189] He told me some charming stories about Saskatchewan: about Bentley, who, cherubic & fiftyish, is engaged to be married & has founded a Gabriel Fauré society in Saskatoon, & about a Pole who was being tutored in English & said he'd read a Shakespeare play called "How You Like It." "As You Like It," said Mandel. "Oh, fine," said the Pole.

[220] Irving was in, a little worried about Francis Chapman, who wants to go to Paris & study philosophy with the Thomist people there: of course he's got caught in the [Reid] MacCallum spider web and, as Irving says, is cultivating the MacCallum manner. Alice [MacCallum] wants him to edit Reid's unfinished book: an absurd notion.[190] Rinehart sent back my introduction, with Bush's comments. His general reaction was highly favorable, but some of his minor suggestions irritated me, or my ego. There's a curious literalness about Bush's mind that makes him an admirable reader for this type of thing. For my phrase "The Sixth Elegy is in Classical language," meaning that it uses Classical imagery, he suggested reading simply "in Latin."[191] I made the corrections & sent them back, but still have a bibliography to do. April will see me yearning to do my books, & actually getting mired in that Pelham Edgar nonsense,[192] graduate theses like Calendino's, proofs of Milton, the Institute paper[193] & other clogs to my soul.

Saturday, March 25

[221] Helen turned up at five-thirty yesterday & we went over to the Godfreys[194] on Charles St: he's a medical student, & both are friends of the Morrises & very interested in the Forum. Then we were driven over to Hart House. I sat beside Fillmore & Joan Eddis, the latter a most charming girl, not only very pretty but as sharp & bright as a cricket.[195] Helen was beside Alec Macdonald. No faculty, unless you count him & Miss Parkes. Two toasts, one to the Varsity proposed by a girl named Wilkinson, very pretty but insipid, & replied to by next year's editor, whose name is Moritsugu. All the speeches were bad except mine, & mine turned out surprisingly well, mainly because I threw half of it out

& began with a lot of wisecracks about the Varsity I thought up after I got there. My general line was that censorship was the negative aspect of propaganda, alias advertising, that it should be distinguished from the gradualism of an educational process, & that the freedom of a free press referred to its educational value & nothing else. I said the importance of a free press could be measured against the hell of 1984, with its jargon, its obliteration of the sense of continuity, & its control over records, & against on the other side the ideal of a free society in Areopagitica. We went back to the Godfreys afterwards. Conversation was students rowing & worrying over the things I'd suggested. I love listening to students, say twice a year. I like students, but not only can't afford much time for them but feel I'd lose my impersonal standing with them if I played around with them too much.

[222] This morning I went down & did a few incidentals, including sending off a pound or two more of Erdman's book back to him. Ned [Pratt] was in, very tired from Montreal. I must get going on a party for him of some kind,[196] as I can't believe that Robins will get much further than a worried expression. U.C. is giving one for Clawson. I went to lunch & Hugh Moorhouse told me that he'd been in miserable health all year, most of it due to the fact that he was biting only on one tooth & wasn't digesting his food properly. After a dentist filed the tooth down the indigestion stopped. [John] Wood was in, a little embarrassed over the fact that they need a sessional appointment in French next year & the only person whose qualifications fit perfectly he knows of is the girl he's going to marry next month.

Sunday, March 26

[223] Yesterday afternoon I went down to the Art Gallery to look at the Canadian show, & it was unusually good—all sorts of lively & varied stuff, & a bewildering variety of new names & styles. I seldom get a chance to look at pictures these days, & found the experience really exhilarating. The Art Committee was down too, & we picked up a small Brandtner, a J.W.G. Macdonald, & I think were considering a Murray Bonnycastle when I left. I saw only the paintings & sculpture, & will have to go back for furniture & stuff. The idea was to get a selection of current working art, not stuff from other galleries, & most things had prices attached in the catalogue. The great big oils were disappointing &

rather meaningless, but there were quantities of lovely pastels & water colours & etchings, many at very low prices. I picked up Helen there & we started to go home, as she wasn't feeling well.

[224] However, she changed her mind on the streetcar after smelling several drunks & a woman on the first day of the curse, very unprotected. So we got out to get some air & headed for the Park Plaza, where we looked over the Telegram article.[197] Not at all good, but I was thankful it wasn't worse. The picture of me was god-awful, but I suppose I look like that some of the time to some of the people. One drink led to another, & I had five, Helen three. Then we went down to 22A Elizabeth for dinner, and met Aba Bayefsky, & his wife. He's a charming lad, & wants another Hart House show, but he talked so badly at his last one he won't get another for a time. They left soon, & we went home & to bed after a record-breaking bust. I don't know exactly what we were celebrating.

[225] Nothing happened today except that I went down to parade for the Baccalaureate sermon & found I had the wrong day. Must be next week. That sort of thing happens to me at least once every year. Came home & dawdled around. Helen James phoned about her projected discussion of religion.[198] I advised against having a Catholic on, but it won't do any good. I could be wrong about that anyway. Funny how the radio has dramatized the symposium. That actually is one of the most significant things about the radio: the way it's focussed on the "quiz program," the roundtable discussion, the dramatic monologue (news) & other symposium elements. Television will bring back the mime, & go on with the regular debasing process of a late Spenglerian era.

Monday, March 27

[226] The nine o'clock got through Elizabethan song, after a fashion. I think one reason why I find my lectures such a drag this year is my feeling that they're so thin: I haven't done any real reading on them for years. The graduate group turned up some relatively interesting points. I started on the decorum of the Spenserian stanza & pointed to a deliberate technique of breaking up the quest narrative which increases from the first two books, where there's a will & a way, to the collapse of all narrative values in 4 & 6. The reason is the spatial elaboration of the

central idea, & it gets narrative tension in reverse: instead of looking to see what happens next, we're in a world where anything may happen & we take things as they come. This is consistent with an allegory of states: Dante's is an allegory of individuals, & we finish the Inferno feeling that that's a state individuals are in all right, but not a place individuals can be isolated as such against. What Spenser gives us is the *dialectic* of the quest, in which the real form of the virtue is clarified & the illusion rejected: that's the Castiglione symposium form.

[227] I got through lunch & an interview with a charming freshie named Barbara Coleman, an unusually precocious child, & stage struck. She has asthma, & has missed a lot of lectures. Then I went home & marked fifteen essays: if I mark any more than that in the course of a day I get gloomy. Helen spent the day with Elinor MacGillivray cleaning the Grants' house: it was pretty dirty, & I gather it was probably the best real cleanup it had had since away back in the Priestley regime. Helen was naturally very tired: too tired even to sleep properly.[199]

[228] I think if I settle down to it I could take quite a bite out of ⅂ [Tragicomedy], taking L [Liberal] by essay stages, with a view to making it a more or less definitive study of anagogics. I could start right away on an outline of the exposition of ⅂, beginning with the stuff I have on the structure of New Comedy, then something on Old Comedy & the ritual calendar, then an analysis of the relation of comedy to tragedy, symposium & mime. It's for the development that I need more knowledge of symbolism, especially of the WT [*The Winter's Tale*] pattern. For the recapitulation I need to think a lot about the meaning of persona & the Bardo play.

Tuesday, March 28

[229] My nine o'clock finished up the Butler irony business, but I'm not in the groove on Butler the way I was last year: my lectures are a series of echoes from what were once brilliant & inspired lectures. It's very disappointing. Part of the trouble is that I lose what I call my Gertrude Stein technique of repeating a point a dozen different ways, so that they not only get the idea, but get it in all its contexts. I do that when I'm discovering things. Then next year I just make them as single points, & what I gain in concentration I lose in every other way. Curious process, & apparently inevitable, up to a point.

[230] The twelve o'clock, the last R.K. lecture, was again given over to questions. No June Clarke [Clark] this year, thank God.[200] They want to know about the after-life. It's true what Jessie [Macpherson] said: they do think I'm in possession of secrets. I think, by & large, the course has gone over, though the concentrating process I mentioned above has affected it too, & far too much of the course was simply not on the Bible at all. I got a fair ovation after it, & I think the presence of people like Audrey Renwicke & Norman [A.] Endicott perhaps doesn't matter.[201] But I've felt very self-conscious now that the course has become an institution.

[231] The writing group also met for the last time today & produced three ash-trays (I'd been hinting I needed some), a brown bunny of Easter chocolate, & an accompanying limerick. Bless their little hearts. No other writing, except a few of the M'Lellan girl's "fragments," some not bad, though her apologetic manner is overdone.[202] Her insensibility to the outer world is the product of an intense withdrawn ego. I think they've had a good time, & I certainly enjoyed having them amuse me.

[232] I skipped a picture committee meeting & went home to something I regarded as more important: finishing my 2i essays. George Johnston was in to thank me for having got him the Ottawa job, but seems very bemused. I still think he may never do his thesis. Robins was in to lunch & I needled him some more about a dinner for Ned. Robins is feeling the same way I am, but his whole life is involved, & he hasn't the concrete project that I have to change his rhythm to. No man should be so vulnerable at his age.

Wednesday, March 29

[233] For some reason I was as nervous & jumpy as a cat all morning, trying to get rid of my lectures. The 2i was a dithering series of useless notes about this and that, and the 4k, the last on Samuel Butler, was a bit foolish too. I got a lot of applause, especially from fourth year, but my tenseness was part of a general tendency in my character, which I notice I've inherited from Dad, to write off anything that's not going so well & make a fresh start—in this case, next year. However, I felt in a very holidayish mood, naturally, & went over to Britnell's to see if I could buy some books. But I'm in that state of mind again—I don't want to collect books or even read them. I want to write one. However, Stanley Russell's

copy of Frazer's *Folklore in the Old Testament* was being offered at two dollars a volume, so I bought it & lugged it home: it's a book I obviously ought to own, & there's a lot of stuff in it I've never really gone through. If I could find a copy of A.B. Cook's *Zeus* somewhere I'd be all set.

[234] Helen got spring fever too today & went out to see Connie Howard, so she was late. My spring fever generates ideas about writing; hers, about decorating—her advantage is that she can talk about her ideas & I can't. I'm swinging over to ⅂ [Tragicomedy] again now, & I'll have a shot at working out, say the exposition, this summer. I think that instead of beginning with a vast cosmological harrumphing burp about meaning & reality & events & concepts, I shall just expand the stuff I have about the structure of New Comedy & make that Chapter One, which will make an arresting and inductive beginning. Then my stuff, or rather Cornford's stuff, on Old Comedy, in which I take the Aristophanic pattern as a clearer & more explicit statement of the symbolic patterns in New Comedy. That's Chapter Two. Then a third chapter on the Christian comedy myth & the final dialectic of comedy as separating the eiron world from the alazonic myth—or rather bound ritual. Actually, that's more logically Chapter Five, three & four dealing with comedy's relation to tragedy & symposium respectively. Yes, that's easier, & I think more logical. I'm beginning to weaken considerably on this mime business, which no longer looks to me like a separate form of drama.

Thursday, March 30

[235] Today was the final break in my lecture routine, so I celebrated it by not going to the Forum office & by drifting around until I finally wound up at Eaton's Round Room for lunch. I'm trying to catch the rhythm of free thought again, & am coddling myself accordingly. I fished out the unabridged version of my comedy paper & I think I can draft out a chapter or two fairly soon. However, sooner or later I had to find my way back to the college & give my final drama lectures.[203] The one on *The Duchess of Malfi*, the second & last one, was by far the better of the two: it was the same old lecture, but a brilliant job of presenting it. They received it in silence: the Huggett girl looked at me and smiled to show her appreciation, but the others were just 5T1ers. No particularly new ideas, except that I noted the insular Sicily-England parallel in *Philaster* & the suggestive female name "Arethusa."[204] It's hard work

trying to interest a poor class in plays that it's not occurred to them to read, & of course having my time cut down makes them seem just stuck on the course. Not that I really want more time. I got a clearer sense of the illusory nature of the melancholy society in Webster: the echo & mist images, & Delio's final speech, indicate very strongly that the sick society isn't really there—that is, isn't eternally there. That's what's involved in the assault on the Duchess to break her sense of her own identity: I compared her refusal of Bosola's chloroform conception of death to Christ's refusal of the vinegar sponge.

[236] I went & had two drinks, then out to Fulton Ave., where Helen was sitting with Peter [Kemp]. She'd taken him out on a walk, & he insisted, for the first time, in toddling along by himself. Milestone. We stayed there the whole evening, as Helen's parents went out again to their club. I sat & read Plautus' *Poenulus*, a dull & foolish play even by Plautine standards—it's one where he does some kidding of the conventions to show he's bored with it too. The Kemps seem well, but fagged out with little Peter. It's a heavy strain on them, cute as he is, & I can't help wondering if Peter's parents will ever assume their responsibilities. In the meantime everyone's cheerful enough.

Friday, March 31

[237] Slept in a bit this morning, & when I got out I skipped the Forum office again. I don't know why I should choose that to play hookey from—well yes I do. But I've got to stop this nonsense. I went & had a shoeshine & a haircut instead, & read the New Yorker. Then I went in to lunch, where the usual conversation was being carried on—Archie [Hare] doing a puzzle & somebody joking about the Hare brain. In the afternoon I went over to assist in the Graham Cotter obsequies. Saw Charlie Dunn, who told me he'd decided to stay here "in spite of Toronto's offer." I think he's inclined to be a bit of a yowler, but evidently Cincinnati couldn't come through with much. Cotter was awful. Woodhouse & I took him through Victorian thought & as I left I recommended failing him. Afterwards I had the usual trouble with my conscience, but it's time we made these exams less of a farce. Woodhouse is a poor examiner, as his questions are essentially lectures addressed to his colleagues, but in spite of that it was clear that he hadn't read much, or absorbed what he read. There's some block in his mind that

makes him bemuse himself with speculation. [Norman J.] Endicott said his Marvell paper was full of improper puns in the Coy Mistress that aren't there. Shook wanted me to see his romantics paper because instead of answering any of his questions he blattered away about Kenneth Burke, and so on & so on. Listening to his answers, or gargles, about *Sartor Resartus*, I reflected on the tyranny of fashion: he probably would have been quite interested in talking about Kierkegaard's conception of *angst* & its relation to Kafka & Auden, but exactly the same thing, the everlasting no in *Sartor Resartus*, derived from exactly the same background & contemporary with Kierkegaard, he's completely incurious about because it's attached to an unfashionable name. Woodhouse told me it was a "good sign" I hadn't heard from the Guggenheim people because some girl in McGill *had* heard that she hadn't got one. I follow the logic all right, but I resent having to wait for "signs" this way. The next book is like the kingdom of God—it won't come by observing signs. Woodhouse is alarmingly tired: he's driving himself nuts trying to clear his desk by the 12th.

Saturday, April 1

[238] The Senior Dinner last night was, on the whole, a good party. All the men & a good number of the women were informal, so this year I had nothing to do with the dinner except eat it—the first time in about five years. At my table were Bob Edmonds & two girls in moderns I didn't know, Helen Holt & Mary McCosh. Helen had a couple of boys in modern history; the girl didn't show up. [Robert Charles] Wallace of Queen's was the main speaker, & for my money he did an expert job of turning out all the commencement-day platitudes, but it was technically a very good performance, & I think very acceptable to the students. Jessie Mac [Macpherson] did the toast, very well. She ended by singing a ditty she'd composed for the Annesley dinner: I wasn't quite sure what I thought of that, & was inclined to agree with Jessie that she was mixing her roles. I mean Helen, of course: dittography. However, I think the students liked it, & she certainly was a good sport to try it. The Tretheweys drove us & the Irvings down & back, which simplified the party still further. As I say, it went off well—the students, Dick Bowles & Joan Webster, were relaxed (Irving, who is chairman of the committee this year took some credit for that, so he must have given them better advice than he did the poor Walters [Walter] girl last year),[205] and Grant

Robertson made an excellent chairman by the simple device of cutting out all the chairman's remarks. Helen teased me afterwards about having wanted to make a speech again myself. I suppose she's right in a way: I hate hearing other people speak, & when I'm forced to I always sit & think up the speech I'd have made in his or her place.

[239] Today I skipped Honeyford[206] in the morning but went over in a pouring rain to take part in the examination of one [Allistair] Macdonald. Another bloody inarticulate boob, but for some reason we passed him. Joe Fisher is still being sentimental about nerves & so on: I spoke up & said a Ph.D. candidate was proposing to undertake a career involving a lot of talking, even of answering unforeseen oral questions, & shouldn't be encouraged to embark on such a career until he showed signs of some ability to talk. Everywhere else we assume some connection between nervousness & insufficient preparation: why not in graduate orals?

Sunday, April 2

[240] At the end of the meeting yesterday Woodhouse said wearily, "any more business?" The last man in the department one would expect to respond to such a challenge got up & said he had something to say. The dissolving department had to be peremptorily summoned back to hear Ned's [Ned Pratt's] "further business." Ned, beaming, produced a bottle of rye from his bag & we all adjourned for a drink. Then I went home to dinner & we got out to the end of the St. Clair car line for Hope Arnott's Acta party. It was fun, though exhausting fun, & Helen was a bit fractious both before & after. We played the same charade game we played years ago at Alta Lind's [Alta Lind Cook's]: I suggested most of the titles for the other side, so our side won handily. Those kids have terrific energy; they must make up for it by sleeping in lectures. Alison Jeffries summarized Senior Day for us: evidently Ann Carnwath's work. I like catching up on student gossip occasionally. The Arnott parents & twin sister were there: Barbara has the same cast in her eye that Hope has.

[241] This morning I got to the Baccalaureate service: I knew it was the right morning this time,[207] as I had to play the piano. It wasn't so bad, even if I was badly out of practice. Harold Young did it, not as well as last time, but acceptably enough: he has some idea what a student is. I thought it went on about seven minutes too long: I have a very exact

limit of recipience to sermons, & beyond that limit I curse every sentence that isn't the last one. It usually sounds as though it were going to be, too, in parsonical oratory—nothing is so hard on the nerves as a prolonged peroration. Bennett was fair, not as good as last year. But on the whole it was easy enough to take.

[242] In the evening we went to the [Douglas] Grants to toast the new baby in champagne. The MacGillivrays were there, & as they're abnormally temperate people & Joan was afraid to drink (she's nursing the baby) I had a fair amount of champagne, not that it's a favourite drink of mine. Abigail squalled dismally & refused to go to sleep, so the Grants brought her down—they wanted to show her off anyway. I think it will do Douglas a hell of a lot of good to have a healthy infant to look after—I don't mean that smugly. On the way home the MacGillivrays told us that F.O. Matthiessen of Harvard had committed suicide. He said it was the state of the world, which is hardly possible: there are too many better reasons.[208]

Monday, April 3

[243] This morning a letter arrived from the Guggenheim people saying they'd awarded me a fellowship of $3000. So that's that. It makes me sick to think what a fuss I've made over it. I got out to my graduate group & harangued them on my three joining points, & it went over very well. I spoke of the island-as-individual symbol in F.Q. 2 [*The Faerie Queene*, bk. 2]: note that such a "people island" has rivers (humors then, blood later) but no sea. The "humor" in comedy is a liquid progress toward an external goal: the temperate man is not dramatic: he's the norm that contains the drama (i.e. the comedy) in himself.

[244] At lunch I told Ned [Pratt], John [Robins], Bennett & Irving the news. Ned was very pleased; Bennett's reaction was chiefly one of worry, but I don't blame him. In the afternoon I had students in wanting to know about the power of prayer. Alison Jeffries was the ringleader, as she had been able to keep her father from being a hopeless drunk by prayer, & she'd been arguing about it.[209] Then I started to clean off my desk: letters of recommendation and such. After five letters—my absolute limit for any one day—I went over to the Forum office. Not really so much to do there—I told *them* the news[210] & *they* looked glum, though

less so when they realized it was only for a year. They want me to make a *pro tem* arrangement with them, but of course I won't. I'll write Feilding & see if he'll take it over. Came home to find Isabel [Whitley], Helen's mother & little Peter there, but they all left almost immediately. Then I took Helen out for a drink & a dinner at Angelo's. She's still fractious, as well as dazed, and worried more over the backed up basement drain than about next year. However, I suppose that's natural enough. Owing to a foolish exuberant letter of Mary's [Mary Kemp's], we (or rather she) was expecting her & Roy [Kemp] tonight, but of course they didn't come. Roy phoned from New York & said he'd be up the week after Easter. A letter from Dad, who seems to be feeling better, & one from the long-forgotten Luella Thomson, who'd seen the Star (Telegram rather) writeup.²¹¹ A very kittenish letter. She could hardly believe she was forty. According to my tally, the evidence of that fact has been accumulating for seven or eight years, which ought to break down any normal skepticism. The Guggenheim story won't be released to the press until April 17.

Tuesday, April 4

[245] Spent a lot of the morning fussing over my R.K. term test, which was harder than usual. I don't think it's as bright a class as usual either. Kenneth Fulford was quite aggressive about the test, but the good ones were good. Norman [A.] Endicott said: "The only professor who's ever united theory & practice," which of course is high praise for a Marxist. I'm not giving them quite so much chance to bullshit me this year. Several people in again to discuss the course: they're chiefly interested this year in my point that the privacy of the spiritual life isn't simply introspection, but an attempt to get in touch with a real community.

[246] Now that I know about next year, these are my aims. First, to draft out and write as much as possible of two major studies, one of the Renaissance epic (L) [Liberal] based mainly on Spenser's FQ [*The Faerie Queene*], and one on Shakespearean comedy in relation to the whole theory of drama (ꟾ) [Tragicomedy]. At the moment it looks as though ꟾ will take the lead, & I hope that five chapters of it will be ready before fall. Then I start real research, & perhaps the writing of L as well. Both books will probably have 12 chapters & be in sonata form, 5 chapters expository, 4 development, & 3 recapitulation. The maximum goal is

both books done: a reasonable goal would be one and a complete draft of the other.

[247] Second, to do some intensive reading around my three courses[212] to freshen them up, give me a securer sense of background, & a more vivid grasp of primary sources. Third, to acquire a fluent reading knowledge of at least two languages other than French and Italian, both of which are more or less in the word-looking-up stage. These two would presumably be Latin & German, in that order. I might also pick up some Spanish, as I'd hardly want to publish ٦ [Tragicomedy] without some knowledge of Calderon, even granted that my desire to know about him is largely curiosity. I think I'll take some Greek books along, but can hardly hope to get far with that language.

[248] My first stop will be Harvard, & from there we can start to plan for other trips. If the Guggenheim conditions are only six months in the States, there's no reason we couldn't go off to Europe—say the south of France—in the spring. I'll inquire about that later. Meanwhile, I'm hoping for a reasonably complete ٦ [Tragicomedy] at the end of 1950.

Wednesday, April 5

[249] This was my first day entirely without lecture commitments, & I've started fussing over the opening chapters of ٦ [Tragicomedy]. The main event of the day was the Council meeting. They put me on several committees: I'll have to fix up the Public Lectures again before I leave. But they'll miss me on the Library Committee about as much as I'll miss them, Ken [MacLean] can take my place on the picture committee, & I guess Kay Coburn can take over Acta. It was a sad blow for poor old Tom Delworth, who was in this morning, & who has to be next year's editor along with Hope Arnot [Arnott]. He called a meeting for tonight, but that was pretty sudden notice for me. Kay will be all right.[213]

[250] After the Council Bennett reported from the Board of Regent's meeting. Said Victoria would try to get their floor salaries level with U.C. ones. U.C. has lecturers 2000–3500, with automatic promotions each year of $200: when they hit the maximum they're either made associates or fired. No wonder Woodhouse uses his lectureships as jumping off places for his bright boys. Assistants are 3500–4500, associates 4500–5500, and

full 5500–7000. Damn few are getting 7000—Barker Fairley is one of them. So getting our floor level will take a certain amount of dough, but Bennett has really done wonders in the year he's had. I asked about promotions on the professorial level, & Bennett said Sid Smith had gone a bit vague at that point & had talked about merit and market value. I said that answered my question, which was actually whether promotions were primarily due to offers from other universities. Smith had said that the average professorial (full) salary was around $5800, & Surerus said practically everybody at U.C. is stuck at the lowest possible level of his salary. It looks as though I'd better scratch around for some more offers. Not a word about the Presidency yet.[214] I hope they persuade Bennett to stay on; Joe Fisher tells me the job was offered to Woodside, who, very sensibly, turned it down. Sensibly because of his stomach ulcers. Also I don't think he has much courage, & I think he'd fold up in a crisis. Otherwise I haven't heard even a ripple of a rumor. I'll know before I leave, and it's important to me that I should know, as their choice will probably determine mine for some years to come.[215]

Thursday, April 6

[251] Maundy Thursday, but I didn't see anyone licking someone else's boots, which is the modern substitute for the rite. Hilliard [Trethewey] drove me home last night and I broke the news to him: he was surprised and, as he always is when surprised, a bit gruff, but recovered. I want to talk to him about such problems as renting the house. On the way home Irving was energetically canvassing votes for his motion (announced yesterday) in the fall that the Senior Dinner should be abolished. The point is that its cost—well over $2000—is considerably larger, for one thing, than our year's appropriation for books for the library ($1300). As for me, I was feeling perfectly happy, as Bennett had told me near the end of the meeting that he was going to try to get me put on half salary for next year. So when I came home and found Helen weary from housework, I took her out for a drink & then we went to La Chaumière for dinner. As it turned out, we didn't manage things too well: we had dinner too late and ate it too fast, and after we came home we slept very badly. So this morning I was feeling very hangoverish, and so was she.

[252] This morning Robins called a meeting of the English department, not about term marks, but about the question of dropping our refusal

scheme for late essays, which won't work anyway, and substituting an automatic docking scheme. Chris Love & of course Kay [Coburn] thought that this was treating them too much like children: I said they were children, Robins said we're penalized in the adult world for lateness anyway: cf. the income tax. After the meeting he asked me if I were still opposed to Love's appointment, and I said no. But I still am: it's a second-rate appointment, made out of pure inertia, and is the first move in bringing the English department down to the level of the other departments. I pressed hard for giving Gord Wood something definite: say two-thirds the cost of the Senior Dinner—but obviously Victoria is going to do some terrific belt-tightening next year. They're sending my 3j and not impossibly the 4k course over to Trinity: I don't know who inherits 2i, but that's something Wood could do. If they muff Wood I don't see what there is in Victoria for me, except a small puddle & delusions of grandeur.

Friday, April 7

[253] I left early yesterday & walked home, dropping in to Creasser's bookstore[216] on the way home—the first time I've had a chance to see it since they moved. That was years ago, and the new place is exactly the same as the old one—some of the same books, in fact. The same yappy pups, even, who don't seem to have grown a day older, though they must be the next generation. I picked up a Riverside Swinburne and a little volume of Jane Austen's scraps, including *Love and Friendship*. That's a favorite book of mine: I borrowed it from Marjorie King years ago, who said it was a favorite of hers too. I was startled and a little shocked, in that irrational way one is, to discover when I got home that I had Marjorie's copy. I don't wonder that she's selling her books, but I hadn't expected her to sell that one.[217]

[254] Today I sat. More explicitly, I sat through some Plautus, as I'm trying to collect notes for my opening chapter on the structure of New Comedy. I think it'll come all right. In the evening we went out to a show: there was quite a line up, being a holiday & still a Nonconformist town, and in the line up were the Connors, who had the apartment next to us on Bathurst St. many years ago—we'd forgotten about them, & about the party there we took Harold [Kemp] & his girl to (I think at that stage Dottie). The show itself was pleasant: "Tight Little Island,"[218] about

a small Hebridean community & how it dealt with a wreck bearing fifty thousand cases of whisky. An immemorial theme, but pleasantly handled. As I was looking for comic archetypes, I noted that the Saturnalia is an upsetting of an existing social order which recalls a Golden Age before that order was established, & which is therefore the Saturnalia's grandfather, so to speak. Hence the existing social order is a kind of deputy rule, a vicegerent custom, like the rule of Angelo in MM [*Measure for Measure*]. In this movie the only antagonist, a Malvolio churl, was captain of the home guard, & tried, like Malvolio, to act like a steward locking up the drinks. One of the most unsympathetic people was his own colonel. This, of course, was as corny as Plautus himself really: the drunks weren't slaves, but they were poor people, & there was a restive agin-the-government tone to the whole picture.

Saturday, April 8

[255] More sitting—Helen obviously didn't want me to go to the office, though there was a lot of work to do there. More Plautus, and the general drift of the exposition is beginning to shape up. After all, I can always leave my letters another day, and it's certainly luxurious to work on a book. Not many kids are dropping in. Eleanor Coutts phoned tonight, & she'll be in, of course: she catches me with deadly accuracy. I appreciate her coming, of course, but she tells me all her news in her letters, & she isn't what one might call the reflective type. She wants to go to Europe for the summer on one of those Quaker work camp things. She says Ruth Wallerstein is in Italy, & of course Helen White is jazzing off somewhere—I think New York. Work on Alabaster is progressing,[219] & she's learning Hebrew. David Knight was in the other day too, from Yale. He's been very busy, & has his thesis to do next year. He wants a Canadian subject, & furthermore wants to come back here: I hope I don't have to make a decision on him, as for some reason I don't think he quite fits the mood of Victoria. His news was mainly about his brother Jack, who's been on tour with great success. He really is quite good: I heard him last year, and David is bursting with fraternal pride. He quoted a listener as saying "Well, I'm through with Horowitz: in fifteen years this lad will have wiped him off the map." I'm not prepared to go all that way, but a programme that includes the Bach G minor organ fugue, the Beethoven Apassionata, the Chopin A flat Polonaise & a flock of other stuff is quite a mitt full for anyone so young. Speaking of overheard remarks, I heard a

youngster (female) say on the Victoria staircase: "—and then I have to hurry through my lunch, & come over here with indigestion and have to burp French all afternoon."

[256] Another thing I said to the graduate group is that words come to us atomically, little hard pellets of significance. In our minds they become digested just as food does, and eventually build up one's real language, which is not dictionary language but one's total power of expressing oneself. This total power is waste & void, a milky chaos of rumbles & rumors & chance associations. Then the verbal spirit broods on it & brings it to its real life, the structure of the creative word. Naturally, I think more is involved here than a figure of speech.

Sunday, April 9 [Easter Sunday]

[257] I didn't get out to church, but we did go for a walk on a beautiful morning. The Kemps and Peter arrived for noon, which was when we had dinner. Peter has got to the stage of wanting everything he sees that's out of reach, & insisting on getting it in an endless monotonous whine. Nothing like a small child to bugger the conversation. Helen's father was trying to tell me that his vision of Harold [Kemp] after Harold died[220] was neither delusion nor anything occult, but simply an experience in the spiritual world—the risen world that Easter is all about.

[258] In the evening we went out to see the Fairleys, who leave for England tomorrow[,] tonight. The gathering was partly academic & partly Communist. Kay Coburn, Barbara Rooke, the Boeschensteins & the Milnes; the Hopwoods, the sinister young man who runs the bookstore, & a couple named Park, recently back from Moscow. The woman used to be a wife (two children) of a Ford executive, divorced him, went into social work, & is now one of the brethren, or sistern. We used to see her at Douglas Duncan's. They were attending Communist conferences (the only way you can get into Russia now). Her answers were straight out of the primer, but his showed a more first-hand impression. He spoke of seeing plays—Wilde's Ideal Husband, Shaw's Pygmalion: I wonder how they did *that* in Russian. Barker [Fairley] is taking the C.P.R. [Canadian Pacific Railway] train to St. John that goes across Maine, so he says he'll have a chance to piss on the United States. Just the same Barker has been deeply hurt by his exclusion.[221] I wish the

Americans didn't do all the silly things the Communists expect them to do and know in advance how to take advantage of.

[259] To get back to the subject of resurrection [in par. 257], I'd like to think more about the nature of mandala vision. I've got it clear now that the privacy of prayer & spiritual communion is not introspection, but the discovery of a community, and charity is action in the light of such a discovery. Things like Jesus' apocalypses, Paul's conversion [Acts 22:1–21] & his third heaven passage [2 Corinthians 12:1–8], Stephen's vision [Acts 7:55–6], Pentecost [Acts 2:1–13], Revelation, all show that vision of this community is a physical possibility, & that the veil of nature was getting pretty thin around the first century. This seems to me the real form of the "eschatological" nonsense, which is a perversion of it.

Monday, April 10

[260] I read essays all morning—mostly those General-course pests. I wrote on Audrey Renwicke's that the style was that of a modestly bright eleven-year-old child—stronger sentiments than I usually permit myself. It took me the whole morning, & then I went in to lunch. The Globe & Mail broke the Guggenheim story this morning. They phoned up last night for a photograph, which they didn't use. They listed six. Jean Hubener, now I believe in Boston, got one, of all things.[222] Gregory Vlastos got one, though I don't see how he could have applied in Canada, as he's moved to Cornell—maybe it was just a list of those interesting to Canadians.[223] A Manitoba man in history & two scientists.[224] No poets, novelists or painters, though I know Gustafson & Livesay applied. Except for me, it's a pretty undistinguished list.

[261] At lunch I came in for a certain amount of ribbing about sharing fellowships with the merry widow. Also some gossip about Stapleford ("The Lord is my goatherd," I said, in connection with his nickname).[225] I notice a much cosier & more relaxed feeling about the S.C.R. [Senior Common Room]—maybe it's because Robins isn't bolting his lunch & rushing off to an appointment. Robins says Ned [Pratt] refuses point blank to have anything to do with a dinner that requires him to make a speech.

[262] Two o'clock found me waiting to get into Woodhouse's office.

I certainly will be glad when Woodhouse gets away: he's so exhausted now that I'd say it was about nip & tuck. His mother's sick, for one thing, which doesn't help the getting away process any. Ph.D. Committee—not much business. Somebody named Cole from B.C. we have to get rid of, also Duncan Robertson. However, it took an hour. Then Blissett's thesis oral. Blissett turned up with a patch on his face he'd got walking into a lamp-post while trying to send home a dog. A very good exam. Woodhouse tackled him on the Mutability Cantoes: the interesting thing there is his identification of Mutability with the sinister side of Gloriana—Cynthia in her Hecate aspect, as I would say. I took him through the pinnacle scene in P.R. [*Paradise Regained*], which I said showed Christ on the wheel of fortune, arresting the whole course of time by his refusal to fall, & so telling clock time to go to hell. That impressed even [Norman J.] Endicott.

Tuesday, April 11

[263] McLuhan said the medieval critics distinguished epic from romance on an ethos-pathos basis—the association of romance & pathos (passivity, stress on event) made me prick my ears, & I must look into it. Blissett stood up very well, & had none of the cockiness that made him a bit unpleasant in his generals.

[264] Claude Bissell had a few drinks ready for us afterwards before Clawson's dinner. Very typical of Clawson that his dinner should come on a day when congratulations were being showered on Blissett & me. I drank Scotch very hard & fast & was quite high until I had my dinner. I sat beside Douglas Grant but have no idea what I said to him. Woodhouse did the speech, but of course was nowhere near his normal standard. At the Ph.D. meeting I was feeling good & said if he wanted to make a joke about Clawson's retiring into a life of final ease he could have it for free. He made the joke, but it sure as hell didn't save the speech. [Malcolm] Wallace spoke at the end, but shouldn't have. Clawson's own speech was almost eerily self-effacing, yet full of unself-conscious quiet dignity. He made one feel, quite without realizing it, that the life of a fine scholar & teacher is a really monumental achievement. I discovered that he was a Maritimer, which was illuminating—he's quite a typical one in many ways.

[265] Jean & Ruth Elder were here when I got home—Jean had been to a conference in Atlantic City—stayed in a hotel where she paid four bucks a day & slept (or tried to sleep) on a straw tick bed. The O.E.A. [Ontario Education Association] is on now, & Jean's been busy discussing sex.

[266] To get down to today, I spent it marking my eighty R.K. tests. They're dull, & only one student wrote me a note to say my course was good—about a half-dozen did last year at least. I think actually the course was a bit more austere and intellectualized this year. Only three failed it—it's exceptional though even to have three. One student said that Job thought his situation was "unjusted." I bet myself a drink it was an Honour Psychology student, & it was, but I haven't paid myself yet. I told that to Woodside, & he said that a student from some shoddy place in the States where he'd taken a lot of assorted trash had on his record "Maladjustment: Third Class."

Wednesday, April 12

[267] Kay Coburn came in yesterday to congratulate me: she says the year will spoil me, but I'm willing to take the chance. She doesn't think much of Mrs. Hubener. Eleanor Coutts also came in, & held my marking schedule up an hour. However, as I say, I appreciate her coming. She showed me a letter from Ruth Wallerstein in Italy, or rather on the boat headed for there. The Wisconsin people sound nice, but I'm glad I didn't go there.

[268] Today I went over to Roper's office to Ross Behariell's M.A. oral, who is also up from Wisconsin. He's obviously written an excellent thesis on Hawthorne, though I didn't read it. Incidentally, Eleanor [Coutts] said something yesterday that struck me about St. Joan: the kingfisher, which used to be hung up as a weathercock, as a symbol of the bird (the messenger from the blue heaven, the dove whispering the word) symbolism which begins with the hens laying eggs & ends with Joan's revolt against being imprisoned in a cage. This is all me. Today she brought along a copy of a novel called "The Horse's Mouth," which everyone thinks I ought to read because the hero keeps quoting Blake. I opened it & on page one was a garbled gabble from *Europe* of which the final line was more or less Blake[226] & the other two were, as the White Knight says in Alice, his own invention:[227] I shut the book.

[269] A Library Committee meeting followed the M.A. oral, & it was the damnedest meeting. The Emmanuel people don't turn up, the lazy bastards, & Irene Clarke wasn't there, so the board that was to tell Robins what to do consisted of [Raymond Arthur] Davies as chairman, Bennett, Joe [Fisher], Hilliard [Trethewey], Charlie [Leslie] & myself. Bennett was in one of his panicky blustering moods, telling us how the planning committee didn't see why we had to expand at all if we'd just throw out our junk. Robins told me afterwards that he'd give anything to get out of his job, that for the first time in his life he finds difficulty in sleeping, that he thinks Peggy Ray ought to succeed him & that of course there's no chance of it,[228] that whereas he could tell the planning committee to go plump to hell if they interfered in the English department, as librarian he's completely vulnerable. Well, he shouldn't have taken the job. Obviously heavy retrenchment is the order of the day, or disorder.

Thursday, April 13

[270] The Forum meeting was last night. A fair meeting, but nobody takes any initiative in editorial subjects, including me, & it's a struggle to get them lined up. Sandwell had a very silly editorial[229] on our thirtieth anniversary—silly and malicious. He's been dressing for dinner in the colonies so long the starch has stuck to him. I don't know who'll succeed me: I'm sure Feilding won't, & it's getting to be an intolerable burden to me. Today I went over to read some stuff. The Reader's Guide has taken us off their index—they have some idiotic system of collecting votes from librarians, & we didn't get enough votes. There's a Canadian index, but it costs fifty dollars, & nobody will buy it—it's full of trash anyway. Some harebrained Carnegie scheme. The voting system is interesting, as it's a good way of eliminating the little mag. and consolidating the monopoly of the big commercial ones. The modern world makes me tired.

[271] Margaret Newton was in to dinner: she's definitely planning to quit her job soon and she wants to go back to Europe: Brock Chisholm has told her there's a job waiting for her in child welfare. She spent the evening dreaming up a trip for us to Rio de Janeiro: that's her idea of where we should go. (Betty Endicott, on the other hand, favors the south of France.) I'm not on a junket, but I didn't tell her that. After all, if I can really shake off the mortal coil of Toronto & get some work done I might

get my project "finished" in time for a longer vacation than they say they'll allow me (one month). In the meantime, my time continues to be wasted: I spent the whole morning marking two late essays from those General-course nuisances. The interest in Plautus I started last weekend has been shelved again & left me more frustrated than ever, & I still haven't got the bibliography of Milton done or that Pelham Edgar blight & murrain started.[230] Even when I begin to think of my project I can feel suggestive patterns begin to form & curl around each other. I must just stop thinking until all this excrement is cleared away and I can work without getting fouled by it. One thing, I must get started earlier in the mornings: I keep snoring like a hog until after eight. I don't know why: lack of exercise, maybe.

Friday, April 14

[272] Today I went down to the office congratulating myself on having got my desk cleared to the point at which I could see it. That mood lasted approximately ten minutes. When I got there a bound copy of Anne Bolgan's M.A. thesis, 250 pages long, was waiting for me. I started to leaf through it, and Victor Whatton came in with a little term paper on Spenser he'd just dashed off. In terms of 8 x 11 double-spaced typing, I'd estimate its length at 120 pages. Five minutes later a very excited boy named Gene Lees arrived with a bound copy of a novel he's just written, & of course nothing would do but Norrie Frye had to read it.[231] He's a close friend of Bill Mathers [Mather] in second year, who's an ardent disciple of mine. He's very young & naive, & I don't hope for much from the novel, though he's probably a writer all right. He phoned up again tonight, ostensibly to say he'd noticed some grammatical errors, but really to see if I'd had time to look at it yet. Youth & creative instinct are both things that seem ferociously ruthless & egocentric, but they aren't, because they're so vulnerable. It isn't only authors who feel I ought to read things either: apart from Eleanor & her "Horse's Mouth," Margaret Avison sent me a play of E.E. Cummings called "Him." I want to read plays & get ideas from them, but I didn't get much out of this one—very suggestive, but I'm sure it really doesn't work out, & it ought to. Too much Pirandello, maybe, & certainly too much 1927 smarty-pants. That's its date. Everything concerned with the soul of the artist is evidently dead serious, & everything else is brilliantly written but fantastic. The main characters, labelled Him & Me, seem to be indwelling genius & ego

respectively, & there's a lot of by-play about masks & personae: the room they sit in has four walls, the audience one invisible, & of course there's a mirror on that wall which is sometimes the other self & sometimes the audience itself—but I'm certain he's just playing around. It's so damned easy once you get going on these masque & mime paradoxes. It ends in a circus & a barker announcing a series of freaks ending with one called Ananke who turns out to be the woman called Me. There's also a You, naturally, but he doesn't get anywhere. I'll have to look at it again, however, as I haven't yet got the central principle of the mime.

Saturday, April 15

[273] I stayed around yesterday for the Culture Commission meeting because I got a nice letter from Chalmers & found they'd put "Congratulations to Professor Frye" on the minutes. Bill Fennell, Mrs. Innes [Innis], Brailey, Callum Thompson, the Chairman & I were there to hear Chalmers read the same paper on the contemporary significance of religion that's already been written & read a dozen times.[232] I think Irving's criticism, which I got this morning, is sound. All their stuff is just patter from Berdyaev & Tillich about the dilemma of modern man, & instead of reading that & rehashing it they ought to be reading Lower & Underhill and Innes [Innis] & [Donald] Creighton & MacGregor Dawson & [Samuel D.] Clark on church & sect & trying to get somehow or other in direct touch with their own community & saying things applicable to it.[233]

[274] I went over to Anne Bolgan's oral at 11: Knox & Barker in the Trinity Board Room. The thesis was pretty naive: she's not Ph.D. material but she's bound she's going to come here & get one.[234] She says she doesn't like Cornell: too much spoon feeding. Barker & Knox are worried about Love's thesis: they think, though they don't say, that he had bad guidance from Woodhouse, who didn't let him deal either with Samson or the dramatic part of P.L. [Paradise Lost]. So his thesis on Renaissance Latin plays & Milton is restricted to the Trinity MS notes, & I gather his handling of the plays is pretty superficial: summaries of plots & the like. So he had to shove it all into an appendix, which has left damn little thesis.[235] Barker felicitated me on being out of all this next year, but I'll probably get my wings limed with Love's thesis before I spread them. So I came back & finished a report on Calendino's effort & then went out for a drink. I've also been doing a fair amount of correspondence: I got a

lot of congratulatory notes. One from Olive Howard, bless her heart: the family news is that Uncle John [Howard] is dead. Clawson was very pleased with the note I sent him, but I no longer think he was unconscious of what he was doing.[236] In common with the rest of the human race, I've been underestimating that man. Helen is getting into quite a stew over renting the house: counting taxes, mortgages, & painting, it'll take us $1150 just to keep the house here next year. So at $100 a month we'd barely break even, & will have to ask $125. No sense going in the red over it.

Sunday, April 16

[275] Blodwen Davies came in yesterday to spend a few days with us: the simple life got her down for a bit. I like Blodwen & enjoy having her around: she has unusual interests, & is comfortably gossipy without being malicious. She was talking last night about old people who went senile & made life miserable for younger people, who insisted on being spoiled & so on. She's had trouble with her own mother, & her friend Yvonne McKague is having it now. She's interested in geriatrics anyway. She quotes a theosophical source as saying the "soul" hangs on until a point—they say about 56—when it's clear whether there's anything there for it or not. Senility is the result of the soul's giving up. Too simple, but it may give me a lead on the "lost soul" business my kids are so keen about. The theosophists of course make the event decisive for another reincarnation. Helen and I walked down to the Museum in the afternoon.

[276] We were also discussing astrological types—I know nothing about them, but I've been convinced for a long time of the essential correctness of the humor theory. Not that I think there are humors, but I am sure there are four types of temperament, sanguine, phlegmatic, choleric & melancholy. I, for instance, am sanguine, & Helen, like all the Kemps, is melancholy. Her mother is sanguine, Blodwen is phlegmatic, & so on. It's possible that, as in Jung's four types, there's a differentiating & an auxiliary humor: thus Bill Little is choleric & phlegmatic & Norman [J.] Endicott choleric & melancholy. This is fun. It's a big advantage having it simply as types, without pinning it down to actual bodily substances, though there may be such substances. The astrological types would complicate it a good deal more, of course.

[277] Sunday reflection: for a long time I have realized that the moral perfection of Jesus' life was an imaginatively sterile idea: if you try to imagine Jesus doing the morally right thing in all situations you vulgarize him into whatever happens at the moment to be your moral ideal. The fewer situations one can imagine him in, the more powerful a figure he becomes. Hence the *essential* life of Jesus must be discontinuous, a series of epiphanic appearances called up, like the presence in the mass, in response to a significant situation.

Monday, April 17

[278] Got out to the graduate group: I thought it would be a terrific struggle to get back to lecturing, but it wasn't, particularly. I went on with my humor stuff. The passionate man has his humor running into a sea of non-being ("all to run one way," as Jonson says):[237] the temperate man keeps his humors coursing around like the four rivers of Paradise, instead of spilling like the Ecce Homo Luvah Christ or the Veglio of Dante. Thus in Book II original sin is symbolized as irrevocably spilt blood, & we have the "living well," the natural spring which is part of the cycle of waters in nature (rebirth from seas as rain) & insufficient, & the standing pool into which Maleger is thrown & in which Tantalus is stuck.[238] This water theme, on the natural level, is tied up at the end of the fourth book. I then went on to my criticism of Woodhouse, that his antithesis between a genial Anglican & a sourpuss Puritan view of the order of nature won't work. As in Blake, there's an epistemological apocalypse or Paravritti to take place in nature, which is nothing but the field of it: hence the crucial place of the allegory of Temperance. Ultimately the Bower of Bliss is Narcissus' illusory reflection in the standing pool, so it's under water too—hence the bathing beauties. After the lecture Don Harron told me he & Gloria were going to England to look out for jobs—only for a while, though, he thinks.

[279] Helen was still in a stew over renting the house, so in the evening we went over to see the Tretheweys. They think $125 a month isn't bad, & that we'll get it all right. Anything we spend on the house can be deducted from the income tax we have to pay on the rent, including interest on mortgage. The Tretheweys themselves are undertaking a really heroic project, taking two kids to France & England, destinations unknown, on the $5000 or whatever it is he gets. Perhaps he's saved

some money—he's made a fair amount—matriculation papers & such. He told us of another family on *both* a Guggenheim & a Fullbright [Fulbright] who can't make ends meet in Paris, partly because they have to move so often—being more sophisticated than the Tretheweys, they've spoiled their children. Apparently *American* Guggenheims go abroad, & non-American ones have to come to the States.

Tuesday, April 18

[280] I dropped in to see the immigration people today & they seem hopeful of getting us into the States without a consular visa. I hope that doesn't mean no documents at all, or we'll never get through on the train. They seemed pleasant enough. Then I finished young Lee's novel,[239] went in to lunch, over to the Forum office to read editorials, & then to Wymilwood for a tea the Hares were throwing for the [John] Woods. It was a very pleasant party, & the staff seemed to feel like one. Mrs. Woods is a pleasant looking girl. Talked to [Bert] Arnold, who's developed a tendency to abuse the bourgeoisie and idealize aristocracy—says he'd rather be under the lions than the foxes. Hangover of his earlier Nazi sympathies, I suppose. We'd been discussing Anglo-Catholic converts, which he's bitter about because of Magda [Arnold] and Joan [Arnold]. I said I taught people that symbols were things to use, not worship, & we agreed it was the intellectual's self-conscious sense of insecurity that made him take to masochistic paradox. Even if I weren't a Protestant I'd be grateful for well organized heresy. If a patient is under the care of two doctors, & one tells him to lie flat on his back & the other tells him to move around, he has to use his own judgement, & his chances of good health are better when doctors disagree. We went out for a drink afterward: I had to sit down because I could hardly bend my knees. Then dinner at Chinatown & home to bed.

[281] Two possibly inter-related hunches. Myth comes from the people as a whole, & a class structure results from their attempt to realize myth instead of hypothesizing it. Class structure produces a dispossessed proletariat, as Toynbee says, out of whom comes a new Church. If people could stop trying to realize myth the class struggle & the cyclic movement of history would end. I visualize this argument as a restatement of Marx, not of Toynbee, & as ⊥ [Ignoramus] material. Two: the impulse to dance to music is Lockian, including the impulse to beat the feet & nod

the head at a concert—that's all relegated to the appendix of applause. Motionless response means that the real music is within the universal Mind. Now, applied to the conception of mime in drama as developing from dance, one gets the conception of pure mime as a masque of contemplation like The Tempest. I thought I had a big fish here, but it's got away for the moment.

Wednesday, April 19

[282] The Bach festival began today with an organ recital by Power-Biggs [Power Biggs] at the Eaton Auditorium in the afternoon. Did one of the things after Vivaldi, the six Schubler [Schübler] preludes, a trio-sonata in E♭, three preludes from the Little Organ book, & of course the G-minor fugue & the D minor Toccata. Saw Jessie Mac [Macpherson], who said she'd invite us to tea after if some visitors from Cleveland didn't come. They didn't & she did, & I sat at a table with Barbara Rooke. I didn't realize she was a singer, but she's a first alto in the Mendelssohn choir—a man named Wrestaway [Westaway], a woman named Mrs. Harrison, who used to sing in the Eaton Memorial Church, & another woman named Capling, a soprano. All musical gossip. Pleasant interlude. It was raining & we eventually found our way to the Park Plaza for another drink, had dinner at Murray's & then went down in a taxi (picking up Hugh Moorhouse & Phyllis Foreman)[240] to Massey Hall to hear the B Minor Mass. I was in a good mood, not only because of Bach but because my Kenyon Review article[241] arrived today & it looks better than I expected.

[283] The B minor Mass was a glorious performance[242]—I hadn't heard it since the old Fricker days, when they had to pause every eight bars to give the old ladies a chance to get their wind back. For the first time I realized what a brilliant & buoyant set piece it is. Our tickets were smack in the middle of the front row of the second balcony, as though we were two-thirds of the Trinity. Though a very Protestant mass, with the weight thrown on the Kyrie & the Credo, it's pure revelation, & that's why it's so brilliant & buoyant. It's such a contrast to the Beethoven mass, where the predominant feeling is mystery, & the big climax is the Messianic Benedictus, which is dependent on a violin solo. Bach takes mystery in his stride: the key word of the mass, for him, is "gloria," & he gives you pure mandala vision. He's also given the real meaning of sacrament,

which is commedia, recognition, anagnorisis, epiphany. It's the exact opposite of sacrifice: in sacrifice, which is tragedy, something is killed: in sacrament something is brought to life. That something is the real presence of a single mind which contains both the Mass & the participating audience. No external God can be adored with music He did not compose.

Thursday, April 20

[284] Got out to the Forum office to pageproof it, & down to Eaton's to have lunch with Helen. The afternoon concert was superb: a small chamber orchestra conducted by Mazzoleni with Greta Kraus. They did an Overture in C major, a triple concerto in A minor, where G.K. turned in some of the best harpsichord playing I've ever heard in my life, a Concerto in D minor, a wonderfully dramatic & striking thing, & the Fourth Brandenburg.[243] For my money, it was pretty close to an ideal concert. Then, at Helen's insistence, we went home & ate fish & drank beer, & hared down in another taxi to hear the St. Matthew Passion. In the interval we met Brough Macpherson & Marjorie King, who proposed that we should go down to the first balcony & sneak some seats there. We accepted, as our bottoms were getting calloused & we were sitting next to some schizophrenic old bag who obviously wished she hadn't come. Afterwards the four of us went home to Brough's for some coffee & he drove us home. I like Brough very much & wish he weren't so left-wing—in this age of suspicion & fear I've got to the "some of my best friends are Communists" stage.

[285] In the twenty years that I've been listening to the Passion I've changed my mind about it. I used to feel that the narration was something to sit through, & one waited for the arias & choruses. Now I feel that the work is primarily narration, as the arias & choruses, with greater familiarity, fall into the background as commentaries. This, of course, brings out its real tragic structure, as it's like Greek tragedy, not only in its use of a chorus, but in its *reporting* of the events. Even Christ, though he does his own singing, is contained within the narration.

[286] Audiences bother me, & always have. It's partly because I've always had a naive desire to participate in a group as intensely as possible, & this makes one priggish. Then, I can see, not only in every whisper, but

in every cough & twitch, the sign of a nervous refusal to participate, to set up one's own song & dance instead. As this is in me as well as them, it's a corresponding perversity in me that allows me to be distracted. I know this, & when I try to resist it self-consciousness intensifies & helps the perversity.

Friday, April 21

[287] I went down early to preside over my own R.K. exam. Di Rogers said: "I may not know what Job thought, but I know what he felt like," and showed me a large boil on her neck. I phoned Helen directly it was over—it must have been a fairly easy exam, as relatively few were still writing at twelve. Helen met me at Eaton's for lunch—I ran into Roloff (as he now calls himself) Beny, which reminded me that I *must* have a look at his show.[244] Helen was in company with Wesley Hicks, who does a column for the Telegram and is also a Canadian *Time* correspondent. *Time* had given him an assignment on the thirtieth anniversary of the Canadian Forum, & he was trying to pin it on me and my Guggenheim. I hope to God *Time* does run a piece on the Forum—it would be a terrific break for them, and they certainly have a break coming.[245] Anyway they certainly gave out the assignment—he showed me the flimsy. He's a very decent sort—as Helen said, he shows it possible to be even a *Time* reporter and a gentleman too. Then we went in to the concert. Power Biggs again. He did the St. Anne Prelude & Fugue, the Schmucke Dich Chorale & the Passacaglia; then, after the intermission, the Pastoral organ sonata in F, some things from the Art of Fugue, & the last chorale. He requested no applause, but in such a low mumble that he got it. The program was based on the famous Mendelssohn program of 1840. He's a very restrained player, & lets the structure emerge very clearly—he uses only three manuals, & lays a photographed copy of the music, much reduced in size, on top of the fourth.

[288] After the concert we walked over to the Forum office & the *Time* photographer eventually turned up. They stuck me in Alan Creighton's swivel chair, which no one can sit in except Alan, told me to lean back & relax, so I leaned back & relaxed onto the floor. I was limping for the rest of the day—told Helen I'd fallen in love with Lois Marshall & wanted to do everything she did.[246] The photographer had a wonderful chance to take a shot of me & call it reversed decision or the like, but damned if *he* wasn't a gentleman too.

[289] Another thing that's happened in this eventful week is that the British Council has finally been heard from—they & the Registrar of Leeds. So I've got *that* to think about too. Apparently it's all fixed, only they talk about "next session," whatever that means. I'd love to go, but I won't take any time off the Guggenheim.

Saturday, April 22

[290] The evening's concert, perhaps almost the best yet, was a sort of "Pops" concert after the other two. It began with the D Major Overture, then Herta Glaz singing Schlage Doch—she's a very mature musician— the sopranos are charming kids, & one bursts with local pride listening to them, but still one *does* hope they'll get through all right—and then the Peasants' Cantata. I don't find that as thrilling as the other comparable Bach, but I certainly enjoyed it thoroughly—and then the Magnificat. That has completely destroyed the distinction between sacred & secular music—even more than the B minor, I think, it tears the veil of the temple clear away. We staggered out in a daze and had a cup of coffee at Child's, then on to a party at the Arts & Letters Club Jessie'd asked us to.[247] Free drinks, by God—I don't know who paid for them, & I wondered a little at the sort of social hierarchy that cuts straight across an institution like the Mendelssohn choir & puts those who have money & social connections & get on the Woman's Committee or the Board of Directors in a special category. However, George Edison dragged me over to the bar— I was tired and didn't want to drink heavily, but I had to match him. He said, very truly, that musicians can't talk but can only gossip. The Dalton Wells joined us, & as the crowd thinned out very quickly we had a wonderful time. Mary Morrison looked more hard-faced close up than I expected, but I didn't meet her: I did tell Greta Kraus how good I thought she was. Voaden & Brooker also spoke to me. The Edisons drove us home, & so ended the Bach festival. Three of the happiest days I have ever spent in my life. Not only because of all that glorious music: not only because of getting some social life I was about ready for outside the college: not only because a lot of flattering things happened to me all at once at the same time. A New Statesman critic quotes Sean O'Faolain as speaking of "that bridge, which every artist longs for, between the loneliness of his private dreams and the gaiety of the public square." That's the sort of thing I mean. Perhaps the moral is that I've made myself lonelier during the long winter pull than I needed to—but even so the festival was so completely festive—no routine work except the presiding[248] was

even attempted—that my childish dreams of being a remarked individual in a brilliant company suddenly, for once, came true.

Sunday, April 23

[291] Yesterday we did little except shop in the morning. I bought a bottle of sherry, & the woman ahead of me handed $32 in to the cashier. We also picked up the little kitchen table that is now a bedroom table, Boles having put a walnut top on it. So it finally is "the little walnut table" that Helen used to speak of. In the evening Rose Macdonald, Winifred Needler & this Thompson (no, [D.F.S.] Thomson: he's Scotch) man from Classics—alas from Merton College. It was a very quiet but very pleasant party—it turned out that Thomson as well as Friedl had been in Egypt, that Thomson as well as Rose were strongly Presbyterian, & so on. Thomson is quiet & a bit diffident, but he certainly makes his efforts, he's been around, & he's no fool. Deacon burst loose this morning with a piece on me in the Fly Leaf where he said I was the ablest editor the Forum had ever had.[249] The constellation of fame I've had this week is enough to make anyone believe in astrology, not that I was ever unwilling to believe in it, or at least in synchronization. Meanwhile the statement, though nonsense as fact, won't do the Forum any harm by its appearance at this time. People like to feel that things are going well.

[292] Today we spent recuperating. Helen was keeping a lookout for Roy & Mary [Kemp], who have made one of their periodical threats to descend on Peter, but they didn't turn up. In the afternoon a man who is a friend of Mrs. MacBride's, and is getting married, came over to look at the house. It's a silly thing for newlyweds to take on. Hugh Keeping also has a bid in for it: that's more possible, particularly if they rent the attic or share it with another couple, but I still can't be sure that it would be a wise move for them. Incidentally, this Jewish book on Old Testament miracles, explaining them all by colliding planets & so forth, was reviewed in the Globe & Mail by Frank Hogg of the Observatory.[250] His review, which was pretty contemptuous, will help me a lot, as my first year kids took to asking me about it in tones that suggested it refuted me (it made the Readers' Digest). I suppose it's really impossible to make a hypothesis connecting a number of natural sciences together that isn't fundamentally a mathematical hypothesis.

Monday, April 24

[293] Got out to my last graduate lecture & gave them my duplicate Rineharts.[251] I didn't think they'd want many of them, but they all disappeared instantly. I had a bad headache (nose-block) that increased in virulence until late in the afternoon—too little food yesterday, I think. Then I dealt with the three levels of law, gospel & second coming that dawned on me during one of my *Paradise Lost* lectures (Jan. 20) & linked it with a threefold level of hell, nature & heaven that I applied to Spenser. The hell level of time is pure duration: the heaven level is the pure present of eternity: in between is the cycle, the world of the Gardens of Adonis. The purpose of the Mutability Cantoes is to show that the cycle is redeemable, for Jove is confined in his see by Nature even though Mutability really wins the argument. Nature is an order only to the extent that grace occupies it like an arbitrary invading army. When grace is withdrawn from it, it becomes pure illusion or hell ("meer nature or hell," as Blake says).[252] That brings us back to Beulah, or the Gardens of Adonis, with its two gates, the upper one leading to Eden & the lower one to ἡδονή [pleasure], the Bower of Bliss. The jingle is from Henry Reynolds.[253]

[294] On an impulse I asked a lad named Alec Manson in to lunch. He's working on an M.Th. on the philosophy of history, or thinks he is, and thought he'd try Niebuhr. He'd asked me about my own stuff on the subject at an intermission last week. I told him that Schweitzer, Berdyaev, Löwith, Butterfield, Dawson, Toynbee & Eliot's Notes on Culture were all better than Niebuhr. He seemed dull, but said I'd opened up the subject for him. Incidentally, I saw Lemke Friday, who's got woman-trouble now instead of God-trouble—much better for him. The Lees boy phoned Helen & was evidently very pleased at what I'd done with his novel with my offer to recommend it to Sybil Hutchinson. He said, in fact, "How grateful can you get?" So *he's* all right, but I'm a bit worried about Lemke—I don't know what to do with visionary diabetics—people who crave illumination but don't know how to absorb it. It seems cruel to push them away, but it may be more so to encourage them. Helen phoned a house painter tonight who said his estimate was $375—about a hundred more than she'd bargained for. She's a depression child, & regards this news as a calamity.

Tuesday, April 25

[295] Yesterday afternoon we cleaned up term marks: routine seems to be a bit easier this year. Today I went over to a series of dull meetings at U.C. The first was on the 1b exam, which Woodhouse had set, leaving me to explain his questions. The next was a department meeting, an emergency one called to decide that we really couldn't do anything about the Representative Prose idea for at least another six months.[254] Then a 2b exam meeting, from which I gloomily lugged away 73 exams. I skipped a tea at Victoria designed to celebrate the gift of an astrolabe,[255] & went off home.

[296] I don't know how I feel right now about my conspectus. Barth talks about the Word spoken, the Word written & the Word revealed.[256] The first two may account for the poetry & prose distinction. If poetry & prose fiction *both* are imagistic, synthesizing the event & the idea, I've got a total of *six* categories: law & history are two types of event: the doing & the done—that's a point I've never worked out. Prophecy & philosophy, the latter being a new category, are then the idea doing & done. Oh, hell, I don't know: but I am clear that the four kernels, commandment, parable, aphorism & oracle[,] are not the kernels of prose fiction. The kernels of prose fiction, reading from left to right, are probably plot, situation, theme and Joyce's "epiphany," the moment of insight. I worry about false symmetries, but actually I may be working my way toward a table of literary elements. The four kernels above are the kernels of scripture, & their objective counterparts are, of course, law, history, wisdom & prophecy, respectively: in the N.T., Gospel, apostolic act, epistle & apocalypse. Note carefully how in scripture the hypothetical contains the actual. It's possible that there are four forms of fiction or hypothetical history (i.e. of a philosophy of history). Spenglerian cycle & Marxist exodus (Augustinian Christian too) would correspond to tragedy & comedy, & the various dialectics (Whig & so on, also Hegel) would be the third section. Hypothetical, remember, means mythical or containing form. I suppose too the two conceptions myth & ritual broaden out the distinction I dredged out of Mill between a university of *free* thought and a society of act controlled by the dialectic of free thought. Only free thought means free imagery too, of course: the poet, as Norman [J.] Endicott once remarked to me, is a playing man.

Wednesday, April 26

[297] Today I started exams: finished the first year R.K. lot, which didn't amount to much, and started to make a dint in the fourth year ones. I got down to about Catherine Card's paper—what a farce these pseudonyms are!—and then went out for a drink & went home. In the meantime I'd written six letters—three recommendations, a note to Hugh Layhew, a letter propositioning Feilding about the Forum (it was rather a delicate trick to write it)[257] & a note to Sybil Hutchinson about Lee's novel.[258] So I felt virtuous, as though for once I'd done an honest day's work—that favorite phrase of sedentary people. The exams were dispiriting. I don't expect ever to give a first year R.K. course again—it's too tough for them. They try to reinforce their confusion by smugness, as undergraduates will.

[298] Came home to find Helen a bit restless: the family is really getting a bit worried over Roy & Mary [Kemp], who said they were leaving New York Sunday morning. However, they're not famous for thoughtfulness, & one can't just disappear on a New York highway. She'd taken her mother to a Victoria tea, which she found pretty perfunctory. So we decided to go out for the evening. We went & had an outrageously bad dinner at a Coles dump on Eglinton Avenue. I can't understand why all the restaurants here are so bad once you get off the beaten track—it's nearly as bad as England. Well, anyway, the movie was very good: Graham Greene & Orson Welles collaborating in a thriller: "The Third Man."[259] The musical accompaniment—a zither playing the same series of chords over & over—was very effective, & the whole atmosphere of post-war Vienna, its spirit broken by occupation & its poverty grinding everyone down to a squalid sort of mutual prostitution, was horribly convincing. The villain, done by Orson Welles himself, was the type Hollywood movies generally idealize—a cheerful, handsome, appealing boy who was a complete psychopath, & the curiously empty & helpless horror that such a character inspires came through in a magnificent scene—the only one where he said anything—on a Ferris wheel with the American hero, whose inept honesty made just the right foil. The ferocity of the heroine's devotion to the man whom she knew had betrayed her tied up what was really a pretty grim story, for all the melodramatic chase-through-sewers touches that made it more reassuring for the young women behind us.

Thursday, April 27

[299] Today's mail brought a cheque from the Kenyon Review of $144 American dollars—more than I expected—and a statement from the radio that I'd earned nearly $200 on it last year. Ah me: I haven't faced my income tax yet. My letters to Harvard have produced extremely kindly responses from both Bush & Ellmann. Today *Mrs.* Bush wrote to tell us about a house, bless her heart. Indiana Press wrote to say they'd like to look at any book I happened to have been writing lately. I think I'm going to like being at Harvard. Time was supposed to run its piece today, but didn't. Betty Endicott says there's a rumor that Luce has bought the Partisan Review. Wish he'd buy the Forum.

[300] More slugging with papers—all the 4th year R.K. It took longer than I thought it would—I worked hard on it all day & I'm only down to Walter Murton, who is the alphabetic half-way mark. Madelaine Page was in this morning to tell me that for her Spenser exam she wants to do a comparison of Spenser & Debussy, & would in *fact* like to do a doctoral thesis on it. I said I thought it would be a difficult thesis to put into words, & one needed so many words for a doctoral thesis. However, she's chosen the Renaissance versus the medieval treatment of angels, & wants to focus on Massinger, who apparently does something interesting with angels.

[301] The women whose extension course roared to a beery finish on March 6 want to do the 17th c. next year, & Mrs. Kilbourn & Mrs. Whatsername—Carol's mother—were in. I drafted a course of seventeen lectures for them & sent them away happy. They were gloomy about the prospect of my staying in the states. I dunno. Anyway, I planned a good course for them, with lectures on painting and music. Wilbur, I think is her name. They're very pleasant creatures. Nothing reminds me of my advancing age so much as the growing antiquity of the women I find attractive.

[302] God, exams are dull. The students have all the fun & excitement of cramming & plugging & staying up late & feeling that they're running big risks & holding post mortems & forcing their lazy little brains into a spasm of hectic activity. What we do is the dishwashing afterwards.

[303] Roy & Mary [Kemp] arrived at eleven tonight. They've been up in the mountains. Breezy.

Friday, April 28

[304] Finished the R.K. lot this afternoon & am ready for some real exam-marking next week. Just a lot of regurgitated lecture notes— I know I didn't give them much chance to do anything else, but they haven't been thinking or trying to think, and I find it very depressing. I hope the feeling I have of a gradual decline in intellectual curiosity is just an occupational disease. Anyway, the R.K. course, like all the others, needs a year's incubation.

[305] Mary, the Kemps & Peter[260] were over for dinner. Everybody seemed exhausted, including the poor little boy, who'd had no afternoon sleep. So they left early to take him home. It's going to be tough having Mary around: she's a pure "Bohemian," a disease I should diagnose as a fixation of the child's unawareness of time. The amount of disorganization *that* can cause in a household has to be experienced to be believed. I sent off my income tax today—$18.55, which isn't as much as I thought it might be.

[306] I wonder if the development of ⊥ [Ignoramus] won't be something like this: first the expansion of the distinction between myth & ritual into the free thought, discussion & imagery of Mill's university and the controlled act of custom or ritual which follows its dialectic. This I have. Myth thus becomes the "word," the verbal containing form (not the stimulus) of action. The insistence on the absolute liberty of the creative process, which goes farther than Mill dreamed, keeps me from falling into the different fallacies that beset this idea. The university or social symposium thus transcends all churches, vs. Newman, which buggers any attempt to make the symposium a form of commentary on something else. This something else may be a religion, or a mysterious creative process (as, apparently, in Arnold's critical conception of culture), or the universe of "nature" described by reason. It seems to me at the moment that I shall have to give up the conception of a definitive Word like the Bible. The Catholic argument that the Word is contained by the Church seems to me at present right—i.e., the Bible seems to me a clerical

forgery, though a very wonderful one, & I want to avoid both the pitfall of the "subjectivity" rat-trap, which I can get around by redefining myth, and the other pitfall of making a critical *tour de force* of interpreting the Bible that's there just because of the cheap logical dilemma of the fact that it is there.

Saturday, April 29

[307] Spent most of the morning & a fair amount of the afternoon getting photographed by Roy [Kemp]. Evidently he feels he made a mistake in not getting me when he had the chance, & brought over all his equipment to mug me. Mary [Kemp] told the immigration man, who was curious, that I was an atom expert. She seems rather hysterical, & says she is suffering constantly from arthritis. Self-consciousness, weak eyes, light hair & glasses must combine to make me the world's least photogenic author. The situation in the younger Kemp family is that Mary has finally dithered her way towards getting Peter baptized a Catholic, so we're going to have a christening party sprung on us tomorrow.

[308] In the afternoon Roy took us all for a ride in his station wagon— first to the Goudges to return the crib they lent us, then out east. We finally dropped in on Bill & Connie Howard in Scarboro [Scarborough] & saw their new house. Bill had spent the day pouring concrete & was getting ready for the Arts & Letters Club monthly dinner. Helen decided I'd had enough family & that I should go to it, so I did, but Ned [Pratt] had previously called to offer me a drink beforehand, & as at that time I hadn't thought of going I had to pass it up. The dinner was all right except that I didn't know many people: R.A. Daly, Gordon Davies, George Pepper, A.Y. Jackson were the people I talked to, besides John Coulter, who wanted to beef about a bad review Doris [Mosdell] had given his play in the Forum."[261] I sat with strangers, as I muffed it going in—Gordon Alderson was opposite me. There was a musical program. Samuel Hersenhoren, played three movements of a "Hasidic Suite" by a New York Jew named Saminsky, & a Bloch encore. Nicholas Goldschmidt sang the last verse of *The Triumph of Charis*, a lovely Hugo Wolf, & a group of Czechoslovakian folksongs. The last one said: "I have to die, but in the grave I'll hop around and sing." Then a pianist from the Conservatory, a Bela followed by an enormous Hungarian surname.[262] He played the Bach Toccata in E minor, the lovely slow movement from

the Schubert B♭ sonata, a Bartok, and, for encore, a Chopin Mazurka. I thought he was very good. So I got pretty decent value for my dollar and a half, although I still feel that apart from some Conservatory people, most of the Arts & Letters membership is just a lot of overweight Babbitts. Very few university people belong, not that that's a bad thing.

Sunday, April 30

[309] Got off to a late start (Daylight Saving Time robbed us of an hour's sleep) and rushed in to the christening party. It turned out to be a most remarkable feat of organization on the part of those two very remarkable women, Helen & her mother. Mary [Kemp], with poor old Alec waiting to take her to dinner, was on the phone until ten last night, but the trick was turned by the Cronin family, six of whom came. With three Kemps, three Hyrchenuks,[263] two Fryes & three of Mary's friends that made quite a convincing party. Helen Cronin & Alec were godparents. Peter screamed bloody murder during the entire service, greatly to the delight of his grandparents and of me. I thought Helen was a little brick to give the party, considering how everyone disapproved of the whole performance. I felt almost a personal dislike for Mary, not that I'm fool enough to be prejudiced against Catholics (though I confess to a strong prejudice against converts) but I really have a horror of Catholicism & of the way it exploits a bird-brain like her. And I don't think the horror is a purely irrational one. Tolerance means carelessness, & carelessness is not possible outside the Orient—well, it's vanished there too. I have to care about Peter in opposition to the care that Stephen Hyrchenuk S.J. feels for him, a care which I regard as demonic, however silly that word may sound in any sort of personal connection with him. We missed lunch, but got some dinner and some beer after everyone left.

[310] Going on with ⊥ [Ignoramus]: I think of it as the final wind-up, of course, of a total series. The solution of the myth-ritual situation is in habit or practice, which is ritual controlled by myth—this is, I think, Thomistic. The question is of the nature of the total myth of which all art, as well as all Scripture, forms part. For this I need a clear articulation of archetypes & a conspectus of the verbal universe. I'm expecting ⊢ [Paradox] to do the groundwork of that.

[311] Sunday reflection: the Gospels contain few if any obvious or unan-

swerable prescriptions about ordinary kindliness. Cruelty to animals, for instance, would be a most common phenomenon in Palestine: Jesus must often have witnessed it, and, as no statement from him has been recorded, he must have passed by on the other side, like his own priests & Levites.

Monday, May 1

[312] I rather muffed the day in some ways: Roy & Mary [Kemp] slept over at Fulton Ave., thank God, and *we* slept late. In the morning we finally decided about the Shakespeare Festival lectures—pro, which means we don't leave here until July 15. *Then* we wrote to both Bushes (or Bush's), Ellmann, & a couple of leads. Roy & Mary came over about noon to pick up the rest of their stuff & then I drove down with them to Bloor St. & said goodbye to them at the corner. Mary's final remark to Helen about her kindness in getting Peter "launched" set me to wondering just what is going on in that pinball machine she uses for a mind. Like the average spoiled child, she blames Roy for everything she doesn't like, & he'll never amount to anything until he gets away from her. I sound irritated, but she's a real menace, as she has all the malignancy that goes with selfishness, arising from a kind of censorship in reverse: she stops herself from knowing her reasons for trying to get her own way. I must see if Freud says anything about a censorship in the interests of narcism.

[313] Well, anyway, I had lunch down there & came home to do papers. For some reason I felt that I couldn't do more than a very few hours' work on them, which is what I mean by muffing the day. I'd thought there'd be some mail for me, but there wasn't: I guess I've had it. We were tired & went to bed early, & I read flood stories in Frazer's Folklore in the O.T. till I nearly wet the bed. Perhaps that's what they're about anyway.

[314] The papers are awful: nothing but lecture notes, not all mine either. I hope it's sun spots or something, but I feel very depressed about the current generation of college students. However, it brought the 19th c. prose course back to my mind: I'm impressed by the forcefulness of the contrast between the Burke-Butler sense of organic continuity, which logically *must* find its solution in a church, and the revolutionary sense of immediate break, which *must* deny, not only immortality, but the fact of

continuity itself. The current genetics controversy in Russia[264] is an attempt to break with the whole biological-legal basis of bourgeois conservatism, which in this course can be seen so clearly going from Burke to Butler. I must remember that in its original medieval setting reason means law & nature means biology. They coincide in the conception of history, of course: the historical basis of Christianity is what involved them in the crisis of the West.

Tuesday, May 2

[315] More papers: I got more done this time, but it's a slow and dull job, bringing in its train the feeling that we're not doing a teaching job & that we encourage them to substitute a hazy remembrance of lecture notes for a clear recollection of the texts, which ought to be our minimum requirement.

[316] My present view of the seven pillars—I know I get a new one every month or so—is that the first three, L [Liberal], ⌐ [Tragicomedy], and ∧ [Anticlimax], outline the three major divisions of the hypothetical verbal universe, or poetry, drama and prose. The next four, the quadrivium, outline the four containing myths or hypotheses of the four divisions of the factual verbal universe. These four are the four divisions of Scripture, law, history, wisdom, and prophecy. As the theme in each is the relation of myth to substance and act, each focusses in the vision-analogy pattern. Thus ⋏ [Rencontre] deals with the law, and hence with the contrast between the visionary law, which is the gospel or the inner spiritual life of the God-Man, and the causal, stimulating, eventual law which is the contract propelled by a divine Caesar. This seems to take ⋏ further away from a 19th c. setting, and from music, but that's just for now. Then ∨ [Mirage], at present the least clearly visualized of the seven, deals with prophecy or the active idea, which I see now as a general "aesthetic" survey of the informing of fact by myth, and of the relation of the different arts: sculpture as the hypothesis of biology, for instance. The last two deal with the substantial or passive side: ⊢ [Paradox] with history, the event done as opposed to law, the event doing, and ⊥ [Ignoramus] with philosophy, the idea done as opposed to prophecy. Note that history and philosophy belong to the written word, law & prophecy to its informing power: hence law may have a definite relation to music & prophecy to the plastic arts, or some of them. Perhaps music

contains the real secret of my "mime" business, the mysterious form of the fourth. Anyway ⊢ is the philosophy of history, the book that takes up all my Spengler-Vico interests and works out the development of the Logos as the evolving principle of history, the attempt to realize the Logos, the recurrent Fall, being the source of the movement of the historical cycle. The real Logos is hypothetical. There's a strong Marxist element in ⊢ I must work out too.

Wednesday, May 3

[317] Today Douglas Grant phoned us up & we went out to their new flat for the evening. Douglas himself picked us up. I'd rather wasted the afternoon, as a bunch of students—Ruth Elizabeth McLellan was the ringleader—took me out for coffee. I paid the bill, which may have been bad manners. Then I ran into Hope Arnot [Arnott] & went out for a drink. So 4k suffered, but the hell with it. Douglas drove away the hell and gone out to the Lansing cut-off, where there's a big new development. The [Joe] Fishers, & the McLuhans later, were there. It's a nice little flat, but, as Helen remarked, it may be lonely for Joan. Two reflections occur to me in connection with the 4k course, which now looks to me like one of the major patterns in the whole quadrivium. One is, is it hopelessly fanciful to see the Aristotelian middle way, the middle class & the middle ages as interconnected phenomena in bourgeois ideology? Like its modern modulation into left & right extremists, it seems to emerge everywhere as a pattern. Second: re the Marxist elements in ⊢ [Paradox], I notice in my threefold diagram a constant association between the Fascist hero and history ("the historical moment") and between the Communist hero as the incarnation of a dialectic. In Arnold's diagrams I repeatedly find that equality, populace & the power of truth coincide. Marx himself associates the revolutionary victory over history, the dialectic triumph over the whole conservative alignment of history, biology & law, with the victory of a *deracinated* class. The climax of Milton's P.R. [*Paradise Regained*] is actually this, as Christ refuses to do what Proudhon said he should have done (along with Dostoievsky's Inquisitor), push the tragic wheel around once more.[265] The *stasis* in P.R. is the union of the symposium achieved outside time. Marxism turns the wheel, of course, & so does Jung's compromise with the demonic which integrates the personality and turns Germany to Hitler. This conception of the triumph of deracination is part of the whole revolution of consciousness

against the organic, Descartes' basis, which turns up in Burke as "this metaphysical revolution," the doctrine of the a priori rights of man.[266] Rights belong to myth, duties to ritual, & the former have to be visualized freely in order to clarify the latter: this leads to a liberal or Millish moral rather than the Marxist seizure of the sun or a conservative acquiescence in ritual *data*, the uncreated visions. Both are Luvah fallacies.

Thursday, May 4

[318] Went down to the office & had lunch with Feilding. Tried to talk him into taking over the Forum editorship, but, not greatly to my surprise, he said no. I don't know what to do next. I've finished the 4k papers, I think, but there won't be many for Shook to read. I've made a start on 2b, the last pile of shit. The mail contained a note from Trimble, who's still Chairman of the Moncton School Board, congratulating me. Also the house tax bill—$269. Ouch. They promised the reassessment wouldn't raise taxes, but included a statement saying it hurts them worse than it does us. In the evening we went over to see Ruth Hebb to try to persuade her to keep the front door turquoise instead of apple green. Irving says Chalmers wants 1000 words from me about modern literature.[267]

[319] The forms of drama seem to me to be polarized between the act without scene, which is music, and the scene without act, which is the symposium. Similarly words themselves range between the point in lyric where they disappear into music (cf. the more elaborate madrigals) and the point in hieroglyphic where they disappear into pictures (cf. the Book of Kells and Blake's Job). I think that as I find the four elements of scripture (= the factual verbal universe) are law (social sciences), history, prophecy & wisdom (the active & passive event, the active & passive idea), so the four verbal (audible) hypotheses are music, drama, poetry & prose. Putting the mime over on the *left* side makes things come a lot clearer, I think. Also a *fifth* form of tragicomedy, absorbing such *scherzo* ideas as sparagmos, the satiric lyric, the wandering in the wilderness, and the Saturday between Good Friday & Easter, the "interlunar" night, is slowly beginning to emerge between tragedy & comedy. This should form a reservoir for my ideas on fragmentation. In musical drama too there's mime (ballet), tragedy (oratorio), tragicomedy (perhaps the song-cycle), comedy (opera) and symposium (chorale). A lot of this is still just

bullshit, but in L [Liberal] I want to try to demonstrate the kernels of
poetry (which I now think of as dithyramb, elegy, satire, paean and idyll)
by showing how they find fulfilment in the essential parts of epic. The
katabasis, for instance, may form part of the tragicomedy wandering
archetype & so link up with a danse macabre satire, as in Lucian.

Friday, May 5

[320] Marked 2b papers all day, learning among other things that Gray
was famous for his "ellergy." The Blake answers (there were a few) were
weird: the instructors had been telling them something about FS in the
lecture or two they had to put on Blake, & getting these remarks strained
through a second year pass noodle makes me wonder why I ever did it.
We went down to Town & Country to have dinner with Harrons—
supper rather, as it's one of those help-yourself-at-the-buffet places. I
asked the girl if we could reserve a table & have a drink beforehand &
she said: "certainly, that's the idea." It was too: one man was even asked
if he wanted a liqueur after his meal. Then we went off to the Museum to
hear Spring Thaw 50.[268] It was very good fun—a hundred times funnier
than last year, & that depressing idiot Eric Christmas wasn't around, so
we had a revue that, for me, was something quite different & our own. It
was like an extraordinarily good Vic Bob.[269] A lot of it was Donald's
[Donald Harron's]: his humour has improved a good deal and seems
very original: he asks quite a lot of his audience, what with making puns
in four languages, & he packs his jokes in so one listens too hard to be
always laughing—like an early Marx Brothers, & quite different from the
gabble-gabble-*punch* formula of radio gagsters. But he is a very good
boy, & I wish the pair of them the best luck in England, where they're off
to next week.[270]

[321] I gathered afterwards that the good music was Mavor Moore's:
Pete Colgrove & Ada played the pianos, & I noted with a touch of envy
that Pete has kept up his piano playing better than I have.[271] The closing
tune was a very lively and catchy one, based on a skit called "The Last
Resort," where a travelling salesman—I mean a man at a travel bureau—
finally broke down in front of a difficult family and a song called "Go to
Hell" started. The theme was the Royal Commission on Culture trying to
find some, & deciding to boil down their results in a "revue." They
finally decided that Canada's culture was primarily physical—hockey,

pea soup & the mounties, & they presented the "Mrs. Mackenzie King medal" to a "Nature Woman," a sort of Girl Guide mistress. The leading actress was Jane Mallett, and a very competent actress she is too. Donald [Harron] did a wonderful skit on a naive Canadian author bringing a drama about a mounted policeman and a bear to Hollywood.

Saturday, May 6

[322] There was a take-off on Italian opera called "La Traviesti," in which a bandit called Taranna was forcing amalgamation on a group of villagers. That was Donald's [Donald Harron's] too. We got the usual view of Pegi Brown's legs, but the corny features of last year weren't there. We went out to Diana's afterwards with the Harrons & a big good-natured Jew named Lou Jacobi, who does monologues at banquets. Hell of a way to make a living, but he had a series of good stories, & told them very well.[272] I wonder if the technique of the revue, a series of short skits connected by a theme, couldn't be incorporated into drama as a new type of comedy.

[323] Today I finished 2b and a dull week—dull of course because of the papers. On a question "What qualities of character do you think Jane Austen admired?" I derived the answer "I think Jane Austen liked the kind of girl who could be interested in something besides balls" from a paper that said almost that—anyway, the story is a success. Ned [Pratt] has big plans for a party for me June 3: F.R. Scott & Phelps are to come from McGill & he'd like to get A.J.M. Smith & Sirluck. Sounds like a wonderful party: he was asking me whom I'd like, which of course, to anyone who knows him, means whom *he'd* like—however, I like them too. Gene Lees was in again, & in the mail was a note from Sybil Hutchinson. She's quit McClelland & Stewart because *Jack* McClelland, the son, wanted to be editor & muscled her out. She said he wrote supps[273] all through a pass arts course. So that means that M & S are reverting to normal—they probably wanted her out because she raised their standards too much. They used to be dishonest, according to Ned. However she speaks of joining some other firm. What Lees wanted to know was, should he go to college, & would I be around the year after next. The two questions are interdependent for him.

[324] Spring hay fever struck in force today with a warm day. The

bedroom painting proceeds apace, and Helen's mother & father came over to help. They worked very hard, & he got very tired—he's aged rapidly in the last few years. They brought over a lousy-looking pulp called "Glance," where Roy [Kemp] has several pages of pictures—the only good things in the magazine.

Sunday, May 7

[325] I wanted Helen to take a rest from painting today, but she's anxious to finish, and worked until four. After that I made her dress up and come out for dinner with me at Angelo's, which I think helped her morale. One member of the caucus inside my brain says I'm a lazy & selfish bastard to let her do all the painting without raising a finger to help. Another member, speaking for the government, says I have my own work to do, and the fact I keep on doing it is the guarantee of the contribution I make to the family fortunes. Also that the self-accusation is one of the ready-made formulas of an infantile conscience, which, in an introvert, insists that practical and manipulative activities alone can be called work. Helen herself doesn't feel that way, as she can't help me with my writing.

[326] So I let her paint, and wrote up notes. I think L [Liberal] is potentially a very great book, but I have to make sure it takes the proper form. I think my present meaning paper forms an admirable introduction to it, with a few points expanded here & there, notably the fact that criticism today is better & more mature & assured than poetry or fiction because it's systematically organized on a basis of stealing from previous authorities—something poetry & fiction did too in better days. But I have to work out the division of epic forms, the rationale of features in the epic (catalogue, council, katabasis, flashback, battle, games, etc.) and the place of symbolism in the verbal universe, in such a way as to provide an intelligible theory of poetry in general by linking it all up with the "kernels" of lyric.

[327] The point is that chapters 1–3 are fairly clear, & 7 to the end are fairly clear, being a commentary on Spenser & Milton. It's 4 to 6 that are boggy. Now 4 logically ought to deal with the forms of poetry, the article Rice wants for the Kenyon Review; 5 ought to deal with the rationale of the features of the epic form, & 6 with the Renaissance setting. In any

case I can start by expanding & clarifying my meaning paper for the opening chapter, & my function-of-criticism one for the second one— the thing that's been sticking me is the ass-end-to conception of those chapters I've had. The third chapter is the one on archetypes of Scripture that I've always thought of for 3, & my Blake paper will outline part of it.

Monday, May 8

[328] Went down and read Stingle's thesis on William Morris—a pretty perfunctory job, especially towards the end. But his interpretation of "the idle singer of an empty day" struck me: idleness in an artist is either creative or useless, depending on whether his time is creative or "empty." In the latter case the power of myth & archetype remains unreleased. Hence—I'm moving away from Stingle now—all the images of paralysis and imprisonment in the early poems. I still think I could write a damn good article on Morris. Actually two essays, on Morris & Butler, could sum up everything I have to say just now about 4k in a fine contrast.[274] Morris inherits the radical tradition that runs from Paine & the utilitarians through Mill's essays on socialism, combining it with the really radical elements in Carlyle & Ruskin, & leads to a fine statement of English Marxism, the conscious revolutionary triumph of myth. Butler picks up the conservative case of Burke & Arnold, even of Newman, & combines it with Darwin to produce the status quo acquiescence in ritual data.

[329] Then I read graduate essays, with the authors dropping in at intervals to tell me their mothers had gone crazy. To be accurate, two did that: Gordon Brooks and Summersgill. Also a couple in because I wouldn't be around next year to hold their left hands while they wrote their theses. I took Ronald Bates in to lunch & encouraged him to work at that high-brow thriller subject that Sawyer was considering.[275] The thriller is quite a suggestive form actually: it's the opposite of the detective story, where we get the smug primitive identification with the group & see the individual marked down by a process of hocus-pocus. In the thriller we're identified rather with the fugitive from society. The archetype of all thrillers is The Pilgrim's Progress, where the refugee from the city of destruction is hounded on by a nameless fear, & has to do battle with various members of its police force like Apollyon.

[330] I came home to find all the Kemps painting, & Helen rather discouraged because the color she'd chosen, a soft brown beige, has turned out to be as pink as a monkey's arse. Not that it will matter when we get the furniture moved back and bugger off to Boston.

Tuesday, May 9

[331] Got an unusually early start today and wrote a lot of letters & sent off a lot of checks. Felt a little more virtuous, but not much. I began, like the fool I am, to start thinking once more about an essay on Morris. I spent most of the morning sitting around the American Immigration Office: that very nice girl I talked to last time wasn't there, and I got a considerably more dismal specimen—well, he was a very good type, really, only he didn't understand why these Guggenheim people should be paying me three thousand bucks to write a book that wouldn't belong to them afterwards. In other words, he wanted to send me off to the consul, but I fought that, & he finally said: "O.K. You're a visitor. The hell with it." So I'm a visitor, I trust.

[332] Forum meeting in the evening. I feel gloomy about the Forum: the Morrises have worked so hard for so little reward, & the two most obvious successors, Feilding & Andrew Hebb, won't do the job. God, I wish *Time* had written us up: it really is grotesque the way a magazine like that can play God in this dithering mindless society. However, the present issues seem to draw favorable comment.[276] George Morrison is dead.

[333] The simplest way to break down L [Liberal] is into four parts of three chapters each: the second part, 4–6, being the one at present largely unclarified. One thing: according to the evidence I myself presented in my Music & Poetry article,[277] music intellectualizes poetry & brings it nearer my "satiric" division. It seems to have nothing to do with the dithyrambic, & dithyrambic poets—Swinburne, for instance—aren't musical. If I'm going to get a complete theory of poetry into L, I'm going to have to do a lot of hard reading of "lyric" poetry. Maybe I should bypass the whole question & just go from Scripture to the three kinds of epic, if there are three kinds. As I've said before, my notion that archetypes are the creators of forms in literature is just a pious hope.

[334] Peter Fisher was in town today & we went over & had a beer in the late afternoon. Ronald Bates tagged along, so we didn't have much to say, though I'm not sure we would have had much anyhow. He gets $4800 now, and drives a brand new Pontiac. He's been lucky, but he's got the ability to hold on to his luck, and I certainly think he's well placed, even if he doesn't write.

Wednesday, May 10

[335] Yesterday two Yeats books arrived from the CBC, Ellmann's & a symposium of cultured gabble called "The Permanence of Yeats," meaning the intensity of the authors' desire to get their names in print by talking about him.[278] One point I must get clear: second-level criticism is research; third-level is reconstruction; fourth-level, where the critic gives place to the critical reader, is proclamation. Today, there's no organized third-level criticism, and to the extent that it is unorganized proclamation will just be gabble.

[336] Spent the day mostly reading Ellmann's book. It gets off to a very slow start, its attempt to dodge around the course of Hone being unconvincing.[279] But when he gets to the Golden Dawn period he begins to use a lot of new material, diaries & the like, & it becomes much better & more thoughtful.[280] I must develop my ideas about Yeats. It's just possible that Yeats can be explained as an extrovert who thought he must be an introvert because he was a poet, a shy man, and a diffident lover. His whole life is ridden by a passion for community: the group of courtiers in Castiglione would be heaven for him if he belonged to it. But it had to be a secure community: conspiratorial revolutionary work that was below instead of above the middle class he couldn't stand. Hence he explores his mind with the clueless & desperate fascination that the introvert has for society. Organizing drama for him is "creation without toil":[281] he gets his secret society going first, and it's only when he turns from people to a dogma & a set of ideas that he goes haywire. He didn't want a religion; he wanted an aristocracy.

[337] Blake's distinction between Los & the Spectre of Urthona means that there are at least two forms of the time-world. One is the world made from time, Los's halls. The other is the work done, the world that

simply *has happened*. As I've said so often, the mouth of hell is the previous moment, the devouring jaws of time where the irrevocably done thing is forever imprisoned.[282] This gains more & more over man as his life becomes more predictable. This world is the spiritualists' world: a huge slag-dump of echoes, rumors, murmurs & sighing recurrences to a "fatal" moment, where the unconscious family continuity of the "creative will," only by itself it isn't creative, persists.

Thursday, May 11

[338] I finished Ellmann, a minor but very respectable job, which improves as it goes on, & brings out the outlines of his life in a very sensitive way, I think. As for that other goddamn book, I have no idea what to say about it. Half of it is from the Southern Review & the Kenyon Review, & a lot of it is just incredible shit.

[339] I wish I knew why Yeats fascinates me so: I'm quite seriously thinking of rewriting my essay on him,[283] for God's sake. A lot of that essay was tentative, though it sure was a hell of a lot better than anything in this "Permanence" book, with one or two exceptions. This time he comes to me in connection with Morris instead of as a pendant to Blake, and that way certain values come clearer. One thing is his search for community that would govern, but not cause, a "creative minority" or secret order that holds the essential archetypes of the world, the makers of the myths the world dreams as history. The "true mask" of this is the council of wise men, the sages standing in God's holy fire who seem impotent (this impotence is the theme of Morris's Earthly Paradise and of much early Maeterlinck) from the causative point of view, but are all the time building up the artifice of eternity.[284] The "false mask" is the conspiratorial order, the Rosicrucians, the Irish revolutionaries, the Blue Shirts & other Druidisms.[285] These are select. The redeemable symbols are the Cheshire Cheese group, the Irish House of Lords that haunts his later dreams (including the Bishop Berkeley and the near-bishop Swift) and the audience of his real plays (Cathleen ni Houlihan being part of the false mask).[286] As for Eliot & that "minor mythology" stuff,[287] I've learned from Blake that there's no such thing as a private mythology, or rather, that all mythologies are private to the poet and it's the critic's business to see that they aren't private to anyone else. The mythology of the Christian Church was doing a bit better when Isaiah saw God in the temple, &

when Elijah heard the still small voice, than it ever did when it was able to force millions of people to say they believed it or get burnt alive. The critic proper is to the biographer what law is to history—a spatial cross-section. Besides, it's the dispossessed mythologies—Jewish & Celtic—the despised & rejected ones, that really get there: I don't understand Eliot & Arnold on the nose-counting.

Friday, May 12

[340] Shook came in with the Nineteenth Century Prose rereads, but didn't suggest any changes, so I think I can say that the marking is over. Then we went to Joe Fisher's office for Victor Whatton's oral. M.A., but a most unusual thesis: an incredibly thorough edition, with introduction & variant readings, of Swift's fragment of autobiography. I think Whatton is an extraordinary worker—he's going to Regina College, and seems to be quite happy about it—says he needs time to teach, read & think. I think we could do a lot worse than get him on Victoria: at his age he'll not find it so easy to get the job he deserves. He's absorbed my "verbal universe" teachings very completely.

[341] Ken Maclean [MacLean] was in to lunch, bless his heart—he looks wonderfully well, rested and tanned. We'll be getting in touch with him this summer, I hope, as he's going to be in West Cornwall a good deal. The program of the English Institute arrived today. I give the opening paper of the first afternoon section, so I'm not as well placed as before.[288] That's on Friday, Sept. 8. Monday afternoon we have our meetings in the Morgan Library, & there'll be a Blake show. They're continuing the editing series & Duthie of McGill is giving a paper.[289] Another group is on medieval literature, where there likely won't be too much discussion, & another on "The Assumptions of Criticism," where there will be too much. It's being conducted by Hubler of Princeton, whom I'm pretty sure I don't like.

[342] The Public Lectures Committee met in solemn conclave in my office after lunch. Kay [Coburn] & Irving—Alta Lind [Cook], as usual, didn't show up. She may be sulking. I drafted a scheme of "Four Epics," Grant Robertson on the Odyssey, Surerus on the Niebelungenlied, Robins on something English, & something French.[290] We may have to get an outsider for the French one, unless [John S.] Wood can do something,

anywhere between the Chanson de Roland and Victor Hugo. I think that's about my last College fatigue.

[343] Went home and shifted furniture, & we slept in our own bed at night, for the first time in nearly two weeks. I prefer a mattress that doesn't imprint Yeats's gyres all over my backside. I went to sleep wondering what the hell an intermittent male voice over a loudspeaker was doing: he was calling numbers for a street dance held to celebrate the opening of the Mt. Pleasant Rd. extension.

Saturday, May 13

[344] I think my Public Lectures will work out fairly well: I nailed down Grant Robertson & Robins & O.K'd it with Bennett. Grant was actually quite pleased to be asked: he fluttered around me half the morning asking if I had any suggestions. Robins said he'd had a warning from his doctor to go easy, but, as I pointed out, the doctor meant easy on all that library nonsense, not on his own work. I don't know where Surerus is: he must be up north. For the fourth one I think I'll get Denomy on the Chanson de Roland, & if not I'll try to get Leo on Ariosto. Hell, what have I got to lose? Or Goggio.

[345] Hugh & Margaret Keeping were in about the renting of the place. They're currently our best prospects. They want the house, though Helen feels doubtful about them, & have a complicated deal in mind about subletting their apartment, furnished ("personally selected furniture," as Margaret says), for $125 (if they get that I'll start thinking up a few deals myself) and bringing their sister in with them. The deal is contingent on a) permission to sublet b) their getting the rent they expect c) her sister's wanting to throw up her present comfortable flat. But Hugh is a most buoyant lad, Margaret is an unreasonably pretty girl, & I always feel that young people like that generally get what they want—and at the moment they want this house.[291]

[346] The opening of L [Liberal] is gradually getting clearer: my ideas about higher criticism in the Bible are beginning to mesh with my meaning paper. Second-level criticism is allegorical "lower" criticism, research into background and genesis; third-level is archetypal, & incorporates the traditional criticism both in the Bible & in secular literature. This is

the real "higher criticism": everything now called that is still lower. This idea is already in my writing: I don't know why it's taken me so long to see it. This means that the trouble with medieval criticism was that it was too purely archetypal: paradoxically enough, it lacked a real sense of allegory (maybe because on the second level it related everything to Christ as a real presence, & so slighted the centrifugal movement of Scripture into autonomous event and idea). Colet's lectures on St. Paul are real second-level stuff,[292] & the Protestant "plain sense" doctrine reversed the medieval error by cutting off the third level: it was therefore a simple antithesis (based perhaps on principle alone instead of on substance alone).

Sunday, May 14

[347] Today we had Laure Rièse in to lunch: she leaves Wednesday for Europe. She's been working hard, & looks tired, also older. But she should get more mature, & I notice that her judgements on people are far more in focus than they used to be—that reckless childish cattiness of hers bothered me, not only for itself but as evidence for what university people prejudiced against women say university women do. Now, however, she seems to be slowly discovering reality. She made a remark about Hilliard [Trethewey] that struck me: this is his last big chance, & it's a shame to take a wife & two kids to Paris & become the head of a Canadian family in France when his spoken French is so bad. It was a beautiful day, & we went out later for a brisk bustle about the boneyard.[293] I said that for the alliteration: it was actually a very slow & meditative walk.

[348] If the first chapter of L [Liberal] contains my function-of-criticism stuff as well as the levels of meaning, two will have the Scripture and archetypes stuff. This morning the sixth chapter (as I think now) on the Renaissance situation began to clear up. So that puts the boggy ground in 3–5. Part of my point is that for a variety of reasons the essential dialectic of the Renaissance epic runs through Spenser & Milton because (in part) of their Protestantism. Catholic epics (Camoens & Tasso) are thus inorganic & repetitive set pieces, *tours de force* in short. If I can establish this, or anything like this, the sequence, after the first chapter, should logically go: Two, Scripture; Three, the relation of Scripture to epic; the primitive epic & the archetypes & essential episodes of epic.

Four, the Classical epic, the types of epic that then formed (romance, commedia, treatise & prelude) and five, the Catholic sacramental epic (Dante). What that leaves out, at present, is: a) the informing of poetry in general, & of lyric in particular, by epic archetypes b) the development of dialectic *from* Milton. The horrid suspicion is dawning on me that I may be working toward a sort of Forsyte-Saga construction, with a series of essays (Blake, Keats, Mill, Newman, Ruskin, Morris, Butler, Yeats, Shaw) forming a transition from L to ⅂ [Tragicomedy], besides picking up some of the sparagmos of ⅄ [Rencontre]. The list of names breaks down into a poetry (L–⅂) & a prose (⅂–⅄ [Mirage]) group.

Monday, May 15

[349] I don't quite know what I did today except get my graduate exam ready. Whatton came in to write it in the afternoon & I went home. My head is full of ideas of various kinds. What I really should do is plunge straight into the second chapter of L [Liberal] and just hope to God I can work out a conspectus of archetypes. I've been confusing myself by doodling with a lot of cabbalistic diagrams, & should get my nose closer to the whole problem. Obviously L is basically going to be FS over again, deduced from general principles & then verified by application, instead of induced from the practice of one poet. That means the book's sunk if I can't work out a general theory of archetypes. That doesn't worry me, because I can. But the Spenser particularly can't be just a six-book commentary: I have to read Spenser until he comes apart deductively, the great archetypes that sprawl across the books emerging from a single central principle. All that's clear: what isn't clear is the extent to which L is likely to become a general theory of poetry, or could do so without losing its girlish figure. I mustn't let general symmetries spoil particular ones.

[350] I can't really say much more just now until the archetype section clears up, taking the Blake paper with it. It looks as if L [Liberal] ought to reverse the general scheme of FS: first the complete conspectus of archetypes is ch. xi of FS, following a theory of meaning roughly corresponding to ch. xii. Then a discussion of the epic tradition (FS x), which takes at least four chapters. Then a discussion of Spenser which starts with Albion (FS ix, L vii), goes on to Adonis & Beulah & the Los & Mutability principles (viii in both) & then the Orc quest (FS vii, L ix). The Los

principle has to be replaced in L by, I think, my general doctrine of the hypothetical containing myth, & by the conception of culture as the resolution of the doctrine of the Word. I could try this out on the dog by casting my Blake paper in a general *a priori* form. The doctrine of analogy precedes the discussion of the redeemable middle ground. What has to come next is a statement of my theory of myth as a hypothetical expanding containing form, transcending all assertions, which is the basis for the doctrine of the transferability of images within archetypes.

Tuesday, May 16

[351] Got out in time to set my exam, & sat around in my office reading all morning—I seemed to feel the need of some vicarious invigilating. I think the exam was a good one: one specific question on points in Spenser, one specific one on historical background. Both compulsory, but with lots of options, & the Page can do her stuff on Debussy if she likes.[294] Some of them wrote until 1:30. I hope the shower of disasters in that class is slackening off. Gordon Brooks' mother died: Ralph King's wife & children are all sick: Burgener's in the hospital & can't write the exam.

[352] Took Helen out to the Park Plaza for a drink: she was getting house bound. We had several drinks, & dinner at Diana's, then home in a taxi to find the Cronins on our doorstep. They (Helen, Margaret, Catherine) took us down to a family called the Greenes, who live in Sir Wyly Grier's old house on Crescent Road. He's a publisher, evidently: Canadian Who's Who, & she's the former Margaret Lawrence, a writer of sorts for a Toronto paper.[295] His education is by no means out of the top drawer, but he has good hobbies. He collects paintings, & he has the portrait of Michelangelo that Peter Brieger was being so damned discreet about last year. He thinks it's a Titian. He has a godawful picture of a souse clutching a jug by some follower of Caravaggio: he gives his name as Valentin. Then there's a Ribera—a very late one, & the best on the Continent, he says. St. Bartholomew, Ribera's favorite saint. A Madonna by (I think he said) Francesco Bigio, a pretty wooden imitator of Raphael. A small & quite pleasant van Ostade, a "workshop" Reubens (his word) which I remember as a Madonna too—anyway, it was a woman with clothes on, which in Reubens means either a Madonna or a duchess. A kneeling acolyte by Bassano and a profile portrait by some follower of

what he called "gentle" Bellini. That was the only picture I liked: a fine group of circular receding planes. It was quite a strain admiring them, as I'm totally out of sympathy with all that Baroque nonsense. He also has a record collection, & a terrific gadget that does everything but show pictures of the players on his gramophone. It's the only one in Canada & it certainly does give a very high-fidelity recording—at least the few minutes I heard of it did, as it didn't work. The son of a Rabbi, the Cronins said, though they're evidently Catholics now, hence the Cronin connection.[296]

Wednesday, May 17

[353] Went down very late, after mowing the front lawn, and started marking my papers. A few of them were very good—so good I think I'll keep them around. Whatton, the Mallinson girl, Sawyer, and, curiously enough, Baxter, wrote good papers. The Page's [Madelaine Page's] comparison of Spenser & Debussy, however, showed such an exhaustive knowledge of both that I think I'll give her a first too. The comparison was interesting, but not particularly clinching, for my taste.

[354] A rather silly thing happened: the fourth year English kids decided to give a tea in Annesley today at the same time that a Library Committee meeting was called. I'd been to a lot of Library Committee meetings, and I wanted to see my kids, so I sent a note to Robins telling him I had a conflicting engagement. Well, I shall never understand the rules about time: I was asked for three, & showed up at three, but nobody else came—well, a lot of people didn't come—until four, when in came Robins & Joe Fisher from the Library Committee meeting. So I sneaked off to collect Helen from some women's meeting at Wymilwood, and we went down to the Oxford Press to a cocktail, or rather a whisky, party, given for Geoffrey Cumberlege. I couldn't get much charge out of Cumberlege, but enjoyed the party. Helen didn't: I think she was a bit disillusioned by a closer view of C.C. Johnson, who had attracted her considerably at first meeting. He tends rather to exploit big brown spaniel eyes and the sort of manner that goes with that. Anyway, I talked to Colleen Thibaudeau, who's talking of starting a publisher's co-operative enterprise with Sybil Hutchinson; to Underhill, who seems completely recovered; to Sclater, who wrote Haida;[297] to Arnold Walter, who wanted a book on Elizabethan England; to Donald Creighton, who was concerned over the general dither of Americans; to

George Brown, who wanted to tell me that the Toronto Press would consider anything I wrote, and to Ivan [Ivon] Owen, who wanted to tell me that the *Oxford* Press would consider anything I wrote. Ho hum. I'm convinced that Ivan [Ivon] is the next man to ask for the Forum editorship. Afterwards we went down to Chinatown (22A) for dinner. I drank too much, of course: I always do when it's within reach. It's a bad thing to drink heavily *before* dinner.

Thursday, May 18

[355] Another dithering day: a late start, & did nothing in the morning except go down to the theatre & get tickets for tomorrow night, then lunch by myself at Simpson's. Then I went over to 44 Hoskin[298] & dug out one of three Ph.D. theses I'm supposed to read by next week. John Reymes-King on Morley's madrigals. Enormous apparatus criticus: half a dozen bibliographies, photostats of a rare book of canzonets, several appendices, including Morley's textbook reprinted in full, and introduction on psychology and aesthetics, a section on the historical background of what he calls "madrigalism," & a note-for-note analysis of all the madrigals. I think he's just showing off.[299]

[356] Pageproofed the Forum in the afternoon: a fine issue, I think. I'm a little embarrassed at how little credit I can take for the Forum's improvement. The only really weak thing in the issue was my nonsense on the Peace Congress which I wrote Tuesday afternoon.[300] The mail had an airmail special delivery letter from Stingle in Wisconsin telling me he wanted his M.A. oral this weekend or next week, but without condescending to say when he'd actually produce the body. A negative answer, though a very courteous one, from the landlord at Harvard I'd written to, and a phone call from Hugh Keeping calling off *his* deal. Her sister doesn't want to come in with them. Yvonne Williams was in for dinner: a lovely quiet girl when she's by herself. I generally see her in the company of blatherskites. She's currently doing a war memorial window for Deer Park Church: as I said, the wasteland is a hard thing to put into stained glass.

[357] I notice that the news about the Winnipeg flood relief has completely crowded poor old Rimouski & that other town that got burnt up. As Hugh Moorhouse remarked at lunch, organizing a relief fund for

Rimouski would have been wonderful for Canadian relations, but there isn't a line about it in the papers now: Winnipeg has all the sop sisters.[301] The simple precepts of the gospels about charity & almsgiving just don't fit, it seems to me, a world where need is publicized, & emotions of pity & terror are churned up by the press to the exact point that the press thinks desirable. Impulse, good or bad, became an anachronism with the Industrial Revolution.

Friday, May 19

[358] Got down & started writing my dope on literature for the bloody Culture Commission.[302] Like all my writing efforts, it took longer than I expected. I got it about half done when I went over to Hart House to drop in on a meeting of the minor art-gallery directors. The one last year was fun, but this was nothing but freight rates & insurance. I got out & on to lunch at Chez Paris [Paree] with Tom Delworth & Hope Arnot [Arnott]. They didn't talk much about Acta, as they were still suffering from exam nerves. Incidentally I saw the Art Class show at Hart House, which had only still life & figure drawing, & remarked to McLachlan that they were a lot better on still life. He said "yes, but of course apples & oranges are things they have seen before." I suppose the psychological impact of the nude on youth is a point. Well, I got back to the College & finished the damn thing as Helen came in from the Faculty Women. So we went out for cocktails, & then dinner at a pub called The Pilot I'd never been to before.[303] Then to the Royal Alec to see "The Madwoman of Chaillot,"[304] which I thought was quite a charming play. It reminded me oddly of something I'd been reading in Frazer the same day. It appears that in Senegambia they don't believe in death by natural causes: if somebody dies he's been killed by sorcerers. As people are always dying in Senegambia, they're always looking for sorcerers, & every so often the priests summon everybody to an ordeal by poison—if you puke it up you're innocent, & your chances of not surviving this drench are about one in four. After they've killed off about a quarter of the population this way, the survivors go home happy as hell because they've killed all the sorcerers and nobody is going to die any more.[305] The theme of Giraudoux's play was precisely similar, only the sorcerers were called pimps, in the straight Plautine tradition. Helen had had lunch yesterday with Rose Macdonald, who'd taken her to the Women's Press

Club & introduced her to Estelle Winwood, one of the madwomen. The lead role was taken by a woman named Eleanora Mendelssohn, great granddaughter of the composer, who was understudy for the part, but did a fine job. The Pratts were behind us & the Bennetts in front of us, & the Bennetts drove us home. Helen's first ride over the new by-pass—I was on it yesterday. The papers griped about a traffic jam, but that's just copy. No sidewalk on it, even: nothing but pure destruction of a once beautiful park.

Saturday, May 20

[359] Wrote a few letters & marked some essays: I get very irritated at the way graduate essays keep placidly dribbling through my door at this time of year. I didn't do anything about Stingle, but I *did* buy a couple of dusters, & hope to start cleaning up the office on Monday. When I got home I beheaded the dandelions on the back lawn: more of a job than it sounds, in view of the shape our lawn mower's in.

[360] I seem to have stopped thinking for the moment. My mind is hovering around a definitive statement of my ritual & myth ideas, destined to lead in the Lankavatara direction. But I can't seem to keep all this clear of ideas swarming around Mill, Morris & Yeats. Also I've just finished the three volumes of *Folklore in the Old Testament*. I get very annoyed with books that are like vacuum cleaner bags: trying to find things in them is like trying to wash gold dust out of yellow sand. [Diagram on p. 356 follows here.]

Sunday, May 21

[361] Today was a day of rest, all right. The Irvings came over for tea with their two kids. Allan is a very nice little boy, but just beginning to get into a bratty stage. The adage about children being seen & not heard was all that made large families & civilized gatherings (sexual & social intercourse, in short) simultaneously possible for the Victorians. Allan is still interested in furnaces, so we went down & I showed him how the blower works, & then he got to the workbench & began asking the names of everything. Not all desire to learn: it was mostly teasing, with some souvenir-hunting. The Irvings seemed a bit tired.

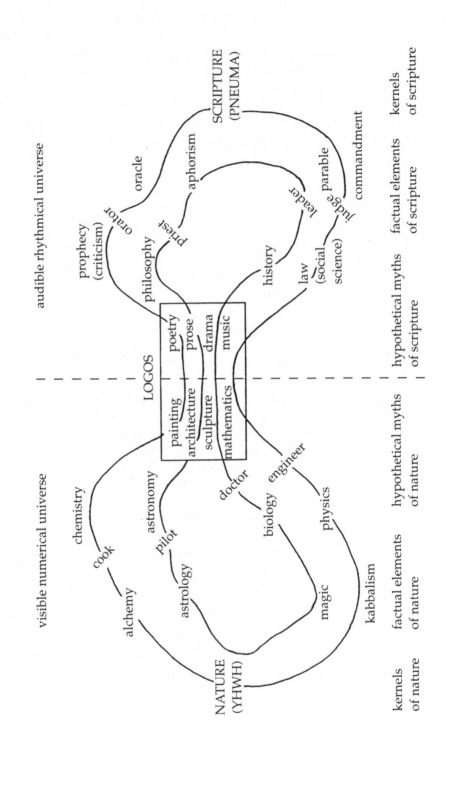

[362] He told me a curious story about Reymes-King, whose thesis he saw in my study. Reymes-King used to be at Alberta, which means he was under not only Newton, who is a bastard, but Mrs. Newton, who is one of the great bitches of all time. I've heard a lot of stories about her before, from people like Mary Winspear who know the place, & was prepared to hear that the way she abuses her position is, in that most inaccurate phrase, out of this world. She's clearly a lunatic, but unfortunately a malignant lunatic, & one of her little tricks is to sit in on professor's classes & take over the discussion. Usually the poor jerk who is the victim of this royal favor has to stand there with a glassy smile & pretend to like it, because it's his job, but Reymes-King didn't: he told her to get the hell out. So she went raging back to Newton & told him to fire Reymes-King, and, as she's never a woman to do things by halves, added that he'd tried to seduce her. That, I gather, would take a man who was blind, deaf, a sexual pervert & a total stranger to her. Newton brought the case to the Board of Governors, most of whom are, like himself, machine-tooled Social Credit politicians. But one of the old guard brought in a motion that Reymes-King should not be fired & that Newton should be, & it almost carried. That's why Hunter lasted two years longer: Newton was trying to fire him when he was interrupted by the screams of his wife clutching her pants. So Reymes-King went to Western Reserve, where he has to get a Ph.D to hold the chairmanship of the Department.[306]

Monday, May 22

[363] I made out a list of all the things I ought to do today, but I didn't get any of them done. However, I did get a start on that damn Milton bibliography, & spent most of the morning in the library. I broke the back of it, but it's amazing how much fussing there is to do over even the simplest bibliography. But of course even the simplest kinds of scholarly apparatus baffle me: as I said once, I don't understand the people who say: "I bet what I want is in the Public Records Office," and go & find it there, when I couldn't even find the Public Records Office.[307] Came home eventually to find Haddow tearing up the pavement: he's building an extension on his garage for his trailer.

[364] Things are shaping up. Bush's friend Sindall has written that he'll let us have his house (or two floors of it) for the summer, till Sept. 1,

which will give us plenty of time to look round. It'll be wonderful to have a house even for six weeks. As for our end, it looks as though the David Lewises will want it. He came in today with Margaret Lazarus. In his manner of speech he's startlingly like George Grube. He said that the place would be a "godsend" for him & his four children, & that he'd pay our full price if he had to, but didn't want to. I think it was just a nervous man's gesture in the direction of driving a hard bargain. Two boys, 12 & 5, & two girls, twins, Peter's [Peter Kemp's] age.[308] Social planning, he said. I outlined the expenses he'd have in addition to his rent: he'd forgotten he'd have to buy coal. Social planning, I thought. He's just starting again in law practice—Jolliffe's firm—and as he should have a near monopoly of labor cases now that Cohen's dead he should have enough money.[309]

[365] I took Helen out to dinner at the Northgate, the new pub on Yonge Street, and we got very good food, though otherwise the place was just the typical synthetic fodder den of a cocktail bar. We liked the Pilot better, but it's curious how different Toronto public eating is now from what it was when I came twenty years ago, with every third house a tea room, and every third shop a Chinese joint. We dropped in on the [Norman J.] Endicotts on the way home. Betty has acquired a crabby poodle from Enid that bites at every sudden movement. She says it's better than a ladies' finishing school for her lunging daughters. I said I thought animals should be seen & not felt, & Finch, who was there, agreed.

Tuesday, May 23

[366] Today I went down to Hoskin Ave. to be chairman for a PhD in Modern History. Ken McNaught, Carlton McNaught's son, & now a professor at Manitoba, I think in United College. The thesis was on J.S. Woodsworth's career to 1921. I was rather pleased to be asked to be chairman, as it's evidence of seniority, & I think I did the job with great aplomb. I think it would be quite easy for me to become a bustling executive & committee-sitter—I probably give the impression of being one now.

[367] Anyway, [Chester] Martin took him up on his unconditional defense of Woodsworth: said there were too many occasions when he was a

minority of one to believe that he was always right & his opponents totally wrong—for instance, his unqualified opposition to war in 1939, where he broke with his whole party. I asked McNaught if he thought there was some analogy between the Woodsworth-Methodist situation in 1920 and the Endicott-United Church one in 1950.[310] He didn't answer the question, which obviously made him uncomfortable: I'd like to know myself what the chances are of Endicott's reaching secular canonization by 1980. Martyrs are essentially witnesses of a real, invisible & ideal community: they have to be judged by the relation this community bears to the one they identify or associate it with. Underhill raised the question of a public's right to protect itself in a general strike. He got through all right: Modern History rehearses the thesis examination.

[368] Back to Victoria & saw Norma Arnett in the Library. She's going to marry Don Coles in the fall. She's had a nervous crackup & gave me the usual line about how graduate work limed the struggling soul. But I don't have to worry about her going to Madras, & when she gets legally screwed she'll be all right. I don't envy the Coles boy, though: she'll probably bite like a black widow spider. I finished the bibliography & sent it off, & then went out to a Forum meeting in the evening. John Nicol had typed out a fine list of topics, & we got a fair-sized agenda planned. The summer is confusing with everybody going off, but we're all right so far. Kay [Morris] thinks Helen should hold [David] Lewis to her price.

Wednesday, May 24

[369] This was a holiday[311] I'd been waiting for, & we got off to the train for Brantford by 9:30. We hadn't seen Jim & Elizabeth Brown for years, & were very keen on going to see them. The visit was exactly what, I think, both of us hoped it would be. They have a charming little house in the middle of town, about at 1865–70 date, & three of the cutest kids I've seen in a long time. Jamie, so he informed me, was four. Cathy was a little older, six or seven, & the baby, Sarah Ellen, is about Peter's [Peter Kemp's] age. I never was much attracted to Elizabeth as an undergradu- ate, but as a plump matron of forty she's really something. And Jim is a small-town lawyer, which is an excellent thing to be; they've got well settled into the community, & go to Hal Vaughan's church. I was a little surprised that they pronounced Hal "very immature." They have a car, & went to Mexico in it last January, taking two of the kids, & brought

back a picture by a Canadian girl they met in Taxco, who has married & settled down there & turned amateur painter.[312]

[370] They took us to the hotel for lunch, which was very sensible, & then Jim drove us all over Brantford & environs. We saw a pleasant square in the middle of town with a statue of Brant in it—better than most municipal statuary: I thought the head was fine. Then we drove out to A.G. [Alexander Graham] Bell's old home, which has been turned into a little museum by the telephone company. We saw two churches, one built for the Mohawks in the 18th c., but no longer used by them, & a charming little church belonging to a Wesleyan splinter called the "Inghamites," I think: the only one here: its headquarters I believe is in Cornwall.[313] The Cockshutts, who own the town, support it. Farringdon Independent Church, it's called: the elders can marry people. Jim also showed us into Hal's [Hal Vaughan's] Zion Church, a fine old Victorian Gothic pile spoiled by a flat ceiling & some curious stained glass. These were modern improvements. We came back & the whole family drove out to a hillside for a picnic. We came back on an evening train & were home before midnight, seeing bits of fireworks at various spots in the city. The Haddows' building project has run into bad drains.[314]

Thursday, May 25

[371] I got out very late but in time to get to Ellen Stevenson's oral. I don't know why the hell Ellen Stevenson wants to take graduate English, but anyway, there she was, with a thesis all hand done on the influence of Scott on Buchan. Her committee was Child, who's supposed to read modern novels, Clawson, the only man in the department who'd read any Scott, Kay Coburn & me. In the middle of Child's quiz I saw something on page two that interested me, so I said: "What's the subtitle of *Waverley*?" She had it down in her thesis as "Tis Sixty Years Hence," & stuck to it it was hence.[315] Hysteria, of course. Poor old Clawson had been saving that one up for his own point—that sort of thing is always happening to Clawson. Anyway, we passed her & I went back to the College with Kay, who's trying to go up north & skip graduation.[316] I had lunch by myself & read a couple of late essays, Chapman's and Robertson's. Duncan Robertson is a most unpredictable bird: I told [Norman J.] Endicott he was the genius type but without any genius. I don't know, though: after a first essay that was no good and an exam that he

blacked out in he goes & turns in one of the best second essays I got: full of the most original & stimulating ideas.

[372] This evening two more people came in to look at the place. Becker, is the name. A long-legged guy in some sort of mining business, I think, & a cute American wife. He knows Art Brandt, being connected with the geophysics people. They also have four children. I was very much taken by them, & felt I'd rather do business with them than with the Lewises, but after all the Lewises *were* here first.

[373] I had a bad headache from all the pollen yesterday & went to lunch at the Pilot hoping to get a lot of food & try to anchor it. I got the food, all right: a vast plate of spaghetti, but the headache didn't ease off until evening. I overheard two remarks from the man next to me, who was from Winnipeg. First, that any fool could have recognized the Red River for a flooding river, because it has a delta like the Nile. Second, that as the Red flows north, it moves through colder & colder country, & so more & more snow & ice gets collected into its progress as it goes on, so it's more likely to flood badly than a southbound river.

Friday, May 26

[374] Well, this was it. I got down in time to get some money out of the bank for Helen, & then went over, slightly late, to Love's oral. It wasn't bad, & I'd read the thesis quite carefully last night. The Scriptural Latin plays of the Renaissance are a minor subject, but quite a genuine one, & I think Chris can do quite a good textbook on them by doing just the sort of easy-going job—summarizing plots & the like—that made it a somewhat indifferent thesis. I mean, he could write a profitable text for junior instructors who haven't the energy or the Latin to work through the stuff themselves. I said that to [Norman J.] Endicott, who said, "And senior instructors too." Yeah. I didn't like the connection of the thesis with Milton: that was clearly a mistake from the beginning.[317] He made two errors of taste: he kept talking about the contrast between an Old Testament Jehovah & a New Testament Christ, which was an anachronism, and he kept saying that a last act that dealt with redemption ruined a play as a tragedy—this in a Scriptural play! I felt very proud of myself for being able to criticize a statement that Barthelemy's *Christus Xilonicus* had no Plautine influence when I recognized two phrases in the bits he

quoted as coming from *Amphitryon*. As I said, the *Amphityron* has a weird relationship to the Christian conception of an incarnate god.

[375] Reymes-King turned out to be as muddle-headed as his thesis. Jeanneret read a vague appraisal by Sir Ernest [MacMillan], who was there, & a very dubious one by Jessie [Macpherson], who wasn't. I said that if he planned publication he should do a modern edition of Morley's dialogue with introduction & notes, which would involve cutting the whole of his psychological & aesthetic introduction, which, I said, was a lot of baloney anyway. Jeanneret asked Ketchum & Dryer if they concurred in that judgement, & they did. I thought Reymes-King was also bumptious, arrogant & insensitive, besides being totally unable to understand the process of reasoning. I showed how poets hated the madrigal, & how the principle of "imitare le parole" represented an annexation of poetry by music. He said he agreed, which, as he'd written the thesis to prove the opposite, confused me. Ketchum said he almost felt some sympathy with Mrs. Newton,[318] & finally said: "Well, the Americans can have him." So we put him through.

Saturday, May 27

[376] On my way back from the Reymes-King orgy I met Kay Coburn, & took her out for a drink. She could have done with it, too: her older brother, Wes, was at that moment sleeping off a hangover in her apartment. Carroll usually takes care of him, but he's away, and Frank, the psychiatrist, is in Iowa. Wes was invalided out of the first world war, got into jewelry, is an unemployable expert on diamonds & works in a retail store, & is divorced from a bitchy wife, with custody of a ten-year-old boy. A whoring wife, too, hence the divorce. So he lives at home & occasionally goes on bats. His father knows it, too—really, the jokes played by fate are sometimes in damn poor taste. Not that it isn't pretty frequent—Mark McClung, for instance.

[377] Got out this morning to a revising committee meeting in the Board Room at Simcoe Hall. Those meetings are of course dull, but I'm glad to see we've returned to a more human form of meeting. On the way back I ran into Finch, who spoke of Reymes-King in terms that suggest that my remarks about him on the previous page are unfair. Anyway, he got the degree. I went back to my office & started to sweat out my Yeats pa-

per.[319] I was a damned fool about that paper—I should have written it
out when I read the books, & not let it go stale & then do it at the last
possible moment. It took me all afternoon until well after five—for one
thing, I'd thrown away all my carbon paper & of course had to make two
copies. I produced what to me was a dull summary of Yeats's life instead
of a review of Ellmann's book, but Helen said she liked it, and it should
be all right for the general public.

[378] In the evening we went out to a party at the Briegers. The Dunns,
Bissells, Taits, Coxeters, Vickers, Ruth Home & a bunch of dum furriners.
Good enough party, only I wasn't terribly enterprising—talked mainly
to Charles [Dunn] & Claude [Bissell], & was talked at by the Vickers.
They've managed to get possession of a house on Walmer Rd., next the
LePans, by evicting a guy with a whore & seven horrible kids who'd
muscled in on his poor old mother. The story of how they got in was a
real saga, but I couldn't follow it all. Their predecessors used a broom
closet for a toilet. Barbara Brieger said she never knew what to talk to me
about, & Thorburn had said so too, the ungrateful old goat.

Sunday, May 28

[379] Slept in & dawdled in the morning: I have a sort of feeling of
gathering my forces together, but that's a feeling I can't trust. Got down
to the CBC for my Yeats talk,[320] & found that my producer was a short
pleasant Jewish boy named Arthur Hiller. This time I was determined to
read through it in time & covered it in 8 minutes. So I had three-quarters
of an hour to sit around, & the CBC has no canteen open on Sunday & no
reading room. Gordon Sinclair, who was to give the radio talk, turned up
in a bright yellow jacket, green breeches, & white shoes. (Harold Whitley
told me later he'd tried the yellow jacket, with a red shirt, out on the
primary teachers in 1946, to their consternation.) He was a friendly
person who talked easily, & we liked him. He said he'd met Yeats in
New York at the Dutch Treat Club, along with Yeats-Brown, & was
embarrassed at having to sound off about his India book[321] & talk like a
literary big-shot in front of the world's greatest poet. He told us stories
about Hemingway, who was one of a brilliant group around 1923—
Morley Callaghan, Griffen [Griffin], Mary Lowery (Ross), Sinclair himself, & others—on the Star, who quit in disgust when they made him
publicize Baby Stella, the Zoo's elephant. His letter of resignation was

posted on several yards of copy paper, but was unfortunately destroyed. It began: "I wish to resign from this paper. I wish to resign because I do not like this paper. I do not like this paper because it degrades me. And the way it chooses to degrade me"—and so on to Baby Stella.[322] Also about his chasing a woman who'd been in the Japanese earthquake & wouldn't talk, came out of her bath & leaned over the staircase & her breasts fell out of her dressing gown & told him to get the hell out, so Hemingway printed just that story—a good Hemingway miniature in itself—in the Star, breasts & all.[323] My talk was all right except for getting an infernal frog in my throat that ruined the final paragraph. Or so I thought—they were very good about it. We went back to the Pilot for dinner, as it was open, & gorged ourselves. I hate to say it, but they give too much food, and in Toronto too. Then we came back home & over to see the Whitleys, who have a new Dodge.

Monday, May 29

[380] Got out to a late start & was heavy & sleepy all morning. I think Helen is right when she says you can get a hangover on excess food as well as excess drink. Neither of us slept well, & I went over at noon and filled up on beer, for God's sake, thereby throwing the rest of the day down the drain. In the morning I started dusting out my bookcases, accompanying myself by composing indignant speeches about the way things are run around this place. I cleaned out the whole of the bookcase opposite me, & feel far less cluttered & panicky. Curious experience, throwing out all the various excreta I'd been saving since before my Oxford days. Notebooks full of dead wood. I don't know why I have such a passion for collecting notebooks when I don't think I've ever filled one completely up. Even the original Blake one has a couple of blank pages at the end.

[381] Stingle phoned in the morning & I had his oral with Barker at 2:30. He didn't seem to know much. Then I took him over to the corner & we had still more beer.[324] He's a pleasant boy, but very bored with Wisconsin, and he certainly makes it sound as though the kind of teaching he did were second-form high school stuff here. Like trying to get them to suggest meanings for words without any, like "un-American." The first suggestion was "not believing in private enterprise." He and Jack Vickery & a girl named Olga Westland (originally Wassylchuk [Wasylchuk],

which she thought sounded un-American) form a Toronto trio:[325] the professors have taken to making jokes about "small fry." He says my great admirer there is Quintana.[326] Graduates & undergraduates take the same courses, so at all levels of teaching you have to get used to all levels of students.[327] No, I'm sure I didn't make any mistake.[328]

[382] Read Gummow's thesis, which will do, & came home. Bill Haddow, bless his heart, got us started on—well, he did most of the former himself—two very small jobs that had been bothering us. One was getting a hole dug and cemented for the clothes line, the other was repairing a hole in the fence that had got to be a runway for dogs. Went to bed with a general feeling of wanting to write the day off and start another.

Tuesday, May 30

[383] Late again, & dropped into Coles' bookstore. Bought the second volume of the Riverside Swinburne ("tragedies") for 59¢. I went into the bank, but the manager said it was too soon to apply for foreign exchange. Irving nipped me & I guess I'll have to grind out another 1000 words before they let me go. However, Chalmers said very admiring things about the last 1000—didn't see how anybody could say so much in so few words, & the like.[329] Irving certainly has a capacity to take activities like this thing seriously (though he's quite detached about it too) that neither Helen nor I possess.

[384] Robert Weaver at lunch: he wants me to do a series of four talks on the radio on poetry generally. I suggested Donne, Milton, Blake & Yeats just to get the range, & he seemed to think it a good idea.[330] It's not cleared with the mighty yet, but should be soon. I'd like it, as it would be a good way to pick up some extra dough without too much work. Also it would tend to establish me as a radio personality, & I think I'd make as good a one as Roy Daniells or Art Phelps. Came home to find Roy's [Roy Kemp's] pictures of me, & a pleasant letter from Roy suggesting that *Time* might run the Forum story after all. Doris Mosdell is going to take Clyde Gilmour's place on *Critically Speaking* for the summer.[331] She'll do a good job, though speaking is new to her & I gather is scaring the pants off her. A nice letter from Eric Havelock yesterday & one today from Harold Wilson, enclosing an article he'd just done on *All's Well*. A good article too, though he should let himself go more.[332]

[385] More dusting, this time of the other bookcase. I turned up my 1943 diary and decided I was expressing myself with more vigour than I am now. It was very pleasant then, even with the war on, drifting around pubs & restaurants when Helen was working, meeting Eleanor[333] & talking to my students as an equal, & we seemed to go to more parties then. It's more lonely being a mature & successful figure, with a reputation growing in three countries. (Four—somebody sent FS off to a professor in Japan interested in Blake the other day.) Stephen Gibson was in, discussing his perennial graduate work, & this evening Ellmann, bless his sweet heart, phoned from Cambridge to tell me about a house.

Wednesday, May 31

[386] It would be terribly easy to dawdle & dither one's whole life away, and still be under the impression that one was constantly busy. I don't know what the hell I did today. By the way, the new President is a man called A.B.B. Moore, now Principal of St. Andrews College in Saskatoon. Go west young man, but only long enough to attract some attention back east. He better be good. On paper it sounds like a dull appointment— churchman employed to smooth down Emmanuel's ruffled feathers. The trouble is—after all, nobody is going to read this diary except me and I don't mind boring myself—that my restlessness is due to a loss of faith in Victoria's future, but I sure as hell don't want to leave Canada or stop being a Canadian, yet technically I've reached the end of the line in Canada for my kind of job. Theoretically, there ought to be many advantages in being in the University of Toronto and not under its jurisdiction. But Victoria's position in federation is indefensible now, and can't be rectified without financial loss which we can't very well stand. If I were President, I'd first appoint a Property Commissioner who would take over some of Bill Little's over-enlarged functions[334] & start operating our buildings in a less wasteful way. Then I think I'd appoint a full-time publicity man. Then I think I'd hire a lot of cheap teaching labor out of the graduate school & try to bring our teaching & tutoring, in our subjects, into line with the other three colleges.[335] Then, if this paid off, I'd start expanding departments, very slowly. All philosophy first, then Spanish & Italian, then medieval & eventually modern history. Kay Coburn once suggested the possibility of Victoria's operating an Institute of Social Studies on the analogy of St. Michael's Medieval Institute,

and I think I'd look into that possibility, in connection with making the social outlook of the Church & its recruits a bit more realistic. This may be all screwy, but we can't just coast, because we're coasting behind the whole time, trying to compete with a first-class university without a first-class staff or second-class resources.

Thursday, June 1

[387] Well, the month has arrived in which I promised to do something about the Edgar MS[336] in [sic], so with heavy sighs I dug it out & stared at it. I'm beginning to see what to do. There are five chunks of the memoir that are salvageable. First, there's the account of his family, Ridouts & Edgars, with the long excerpt about great grandfather Ridout getting chased by the Indians. Secondly, there's a reasonably straightforward account of his own life from birth to graduation from Toronto—I think the Johns Hopkins part is a bit too fragmentary. Third, there's a chapter on the English visit, with the [Arnold] Bennett appendix. Fourth, the Egypt chapter. Fifth, the long account of the trip with D.C. Scott. That, with my introduction, will be Part One, called perhaps "Fragments from a Memoir." The second part will consist of short essays on Canadians, some published, some in MS. Leacock, [Sir Andrew] Macphail, Roberts, & Pratt were published.[337] The criticism chapter on me is in the MS, & Peggy Ray brought over a scrapbook with a few reviews & things in it. A not too flattering sketch of John Macnaughton will do for here.[338] The third part will have to be the miscellaneous stuff wherever I can dig it up. The article on R.O.M. [Royal Ontario Museum] goes into Part Two.

[388] After standing us up yesterday, David Lewis phoned to say they'd decided to look for a house to buy. This after asking us to hold it open for them. However, we're through doing business with friends, & will have to be fairly impersonal from now on. Robert Weaver says the radio series is on, & all right.[339] I had lunch with Ned [Pratt], who tells me that Duthie of McGill, after inviting him to Montreal to speak, & spending a fair amount of money getting him there, opposed the idea of paying him an honorarium on the ground that he'd come at Duthie's invitation. I don't follow the reasoning, nor does Ned. Ned heard it from Phelps, who was furious. Phelps, by the way, isn't coming to my dinner because he didn't open Ned's letter until two weeks after he got it—a curious pose.

Friday, June 2

[389] Today I arrived at a tentative table of contents, wrote a draft of my introduction, which will have to be considerably expanded, and got the editing of the first two sections of Part One done. Part Three is shaping up: Peggy Ray has dug up all sorts of stuff—essays on Meredith, Hardy & James, longhand MSS on Galsworthy & Morris I probably won't type out, a curious essay called "The United States in Fact & Fiction," & a rather silly one on modern (1937) poetry. This with the two Arnold things should set up that part of it. When you add it all up Pelham did a hell of a lot more writing than most of the people who called him lazy ever did. A pathetic amount of it is later than his first wife's death: pathetic because it illustrates what he might have done otherwise. I don't say he had a tremendous amount on the ball, but, hell, he kept the party going. With these reflections in my mind I went into Irving's office & saw the sixteen volumes written by John Watson when he was professor of philosophy at Queen's. As he said, people who complain they can't write because of being intellectually isolated ought to see that output by someone who was practically in Greenland as far as isolation was concerned. He (Watson) was a Kantian, & one of his books was reviewed at great length by T.H. Greene.[340]

[390] I finally decided to treat the Culture Commission to my attendance, but found they'd moved away past me into recommendations to General Council. I couldn't—or didn't—follow the discussion, and met Helen at the Park Plaza. She's house bound again, & the strain of letting the house is bothering her a good deal. Damn the Lewises. So we went for our regular academic cure, & then had dinner—at Diana's because it was raining. We picked up that very nice lad Thomson[341] & he took us back to the bar—only the basement or rather rez-de-chaussée one this time, for yet another drink. He's hoping to go to the Maritimes this summer after marking matriculation papers. Meanwhile, he's working at the cello, which he appears to be good at.

Saturday, June 3

[391] Tonight was the night of Ned's great party, and it was quite a good party, though I still can't help wondering if Ned really gets what he wants. Underhill, Jim Scott, Archie [Hare], Claude Bissell, George Edison,

Tommy Goudge, who drove me home, John Robins, at long last, very quiet & subdued, & Frank Scott from Montreal, who came down for it, though he was going to Kingston anyway. Apart from what he had to say about Montreal, the conversation was much as ever. George Edison told us all over again about his friend who thinks he's God, only he seems more impressed with him than before; the same Pelham [Edgar] stories, much the same gossip. Scott is defending the case of a Jehovah's witness restauranteur who has had his license arbitrarily revoked by Duplessis, the defendant, solely because of his religion.[342] He paints a pretty gloomy picture of Quebec clerical fascism, though he admits that even Catholic labor unions have had to smarten up a bit under pressure from below. But they've just brought in an absurdly arbitrary censorship law, & it looks as though the black plague will keep its stranglehold on Quebec for some time. Tommy tells me that [John] Thorburn is getting ready (I think) to publish something on astrology.

[392] Before long I may give birth to some sort of "Essays on Myth & Ritual," which could be the germ of ⋏ [Rencontre], though it seems closer to the second part. Everything I've been thinking about lately seems to be going in that direction. The world of myth is the world of final causes, the visions of the ends of all acts. All teleological acts (rituals) are informed by this world of myth. Deductive & a priori thinking takes the world of myth as data, and, in itself, refuses to regard it as subject to reformation. That's the attitude of Catholicism and its Shadow, Communism. Inductive thinking concentrates on law, the act as data, & that refuses to examine the myth: the attitude of Judaism & its Shadow of Nazism. Protestantism ought to be the proper form of J.S. Mill: an inductive attitude which eventually takes a "leap" & creates a new vision. The world of myth is the idea of the university.

Sunday, June 4

[393] Sat around furtively trying to write my introduction,[343] & I think when I get it to a typewriter it'll be done. Also diddled with the Culture Commission nonsense. Rosemarie & Roy Wolfe came over in the afternoon with the baby. Nine weeks old, pudgy face, looks like any other child his age, which is fairly nondescript, but Rosemarie doesn't think so. They've just started running a boarding house. Poor kids. Helen got Gene Hallman of the CBC interested in Roy & that may land him some-

thing. He certainly is struggling hard enough to get a job. Griffiths [Griffith] Taylor is using Roy's deafness as an excuse not to recommend him for a job, but it's mainly just indolence & scatterbrain, I think—that is if it's not just straight anti-Jewish prejudice, which I daresay he's capable of too.[344] If all heads of graduate departments were as conscientious as Woodhouse a university would be a better place. On the other hand, as Joe Gargary would say, candor compels for to admit that the first impression of Roy is a buster.[345] We also listened to Doris Mosdell over the radio: she's taking over on movies from Clyde Gilmour, who's on his honeymoon. She was all right: I heard she was nervous, & she's such a little girl that voice production would be a problem. But she had lots of stuff, & I'm glad to know that writing gratis for the Forum does still get you some recognition eventually, if only from somewhere else.

[394] I'm convinced that the way to make social studies an integral part of the idea of the university is to group them around law. As it is law is an inorganic study, for it breeds nothing but lawyers, & makes judges come out of an esoteric professional group, which is bad, particularly when they're so close to the police. You can dither around with silly little courses in sociology, but the minute you start to take it seriously you're involved in evaluating the quality of legislation. Anthropology is the history of law, as law is the articulated form of custom. Economics is the dynamic of law: without law there is no answer to the unconditioned will of dialectic materialism. Law is the final cause of social science, and the efficient cause of freedom.

Monday, June 5

[395] Went down & did some more editing.[346] Helen protested that I was leaving her too much with the house letting, so I buggered back in time to meet a Mr. Whipps, of Athol, Mass. Whipps practically said he'd take it, or try to, but he won't. Like many men, he blusters a bit to impress one with his personality & then begins to count his money. He has to a) phone his wife in Massachusetts & get her O.K. b) see if there's a reasonable chance of letting his house down there, where rents, I understand, are relatively cheaper, as they're ahead in housing; c) see if his boss approves d) hit the boss up for a raise. So I don't think *he's* a very bright prospect, but for a while I had higher hopes of one Addison B.

Poland, of the Prudential Life. Jean Elder had told us about them: she was offered a job chaperoning hundreds of Canadian high school youngsters they're importing to Newark, their head office, to train in the sort of work they're going to start doing in Toronto. They've taken over the campuses of Drew & Upsala for the summer. A lot of people are going to be moved to Toronto, some permanently, & for a while we thought we had seventy or eighty prospects with a powerful firm to back them. But, alas & alack, he phoned down to Newark & it was no go: no one is being moved for a year with his family. Helen thinks he got ticked off: I don't understand American business, giving a man a job to do & no data to do it with. They're probably only interested in half a dozen big shots. Anyway, we had Lou & Kay Morris in in the evening. They brought their own beer—today was one of those half-hearted holidays & we couldn't get any—and they took back the baby stuff they'd lent us for Peter [Kemp]. So our hospitality was a bit more qualified than I like it to be, but I guess they won't mind. Helen was asking about the University Settlement[347]—Kay, who's just been fired by the present manageress, one Gorrie, who I gather is exceptionally inadequate even for that place, thinks it may be in some danger of becoming a Communist nest. Of course Kay is apt to see a crypto-Communist under every tree—still, her training has given her some sense of where they are.

Tuesday, June 6

[396] Nothing happened today except Mrs. Mallinson's M.A. oral, which was painless. Her thesis was a "new criticism" analysis of some religious poems of Donne, & [Norman J.] Endicott & Clawson read it. Norman sure doesn't care for the new criticism, though, as he doesn't go for the history of ideas either, I don't quite know what he does want. Neither, I think, does he, & that's kept him unproductive, perhaps. In the evening two very pleasant & gentle people named Keenleyside came in to look at the house. They decided it was out of their range financially, but they were more our sort of people. They're living in the house of Alan Barr, Pelham's [Pelham Edgar's] portrait painter, & are just down the street. No furniture at all; one baby. He's in Photographic Survey, which does air photography for mining & lumbering firms. They're doing a complete mile-to-inch survey of Alberta, & evidently air photography is like X-ray photography for mining: it shows up patches under the soil, & in

lumbering they can estimate the height of trees to within three feet out of fifty. In other words, he's very enthusiastic about his job. I wish we could let them have it, but I don't think we can.

[397] Irving goes to Kingston tomorrow to read his paper.[348] Kickback from the Culture Commission—two foolscap pages of recommendations, as I said, all shit except two specific proposals to encourage Arts & Theology students to take more social sciences. They were Irving's: I wasn't too keen on them, but still they were proposals, & after I left one was thrown out & the other modified till it was shit too. Bill Fennell told me this, also that Irving has been bawling the bejeesus out of him for wasting his time by throwing out his recommendations. I'm sorry Irving feels let down, but I can't imagine why he ever took the Culture Commission seriously in the first place, & said as much to Bill. Bill said he thought Irving had a mania for getting into print. So do I, but God! what print! Incidentally, I don't know that I've recorded the fact that Love has been made Senior Tutor, as Bill doesn't want the job after he comes back. Now *that* is a sensible appointment, I think.

Wednesday, June 7

[398] Today we were all plunged into an unseasonable heat wave: it's been coming on for a few days, but is really bad now. We went up to the Leslies['] for supper and then went down to the Pass Course reception. As I haven't one Pass Course student, not one, & as Janet Angel Fulton & her parents didn't turn up,[349] it was a pretty dull party. I should have sat it out upstairs in the Chapel, where there were lots of empty seats (the prize-winners consisted of three A's), but we stayed downstairs instead. [D.O.] Robson suggested that I might disc my last radio talk, which would enable us to get away on July 1 if a hell of a lot of other things worked out. Possible. I saw Jerry Riddell there—his father, who has gone pretty glassy-eyed, is being featured in the current orgies as the sixty-year graduate, or something. Jerry is now the Canadian permanent delegate to the United Nations, so I suppose they'll be moving to New York. He suggested we should let them know when we'll be in New York, so they can get play tickets for us.

[399] We had a good time with the Leslies, with their funny gangling kids—two girls, Gwyneth & Marion, early high school age. Gwyneth

asked me to play for her, & I didn't do so badly considering. Helen was bored to death by the reception & the heat & listening to all the faculty women chatter. She feels the College is in a bad case of doldrums & interregnum, & of course so do I. *Nobody* seems to know bugger-all about Moore. I hear he's a good preacher. Yeah. I hear he's liked by all his staff at St. Andrew's. His staff at St. Andrew's consists of three people. I hear nothing to suggest that he's an able administrator or has any ideas about education or any notion of what he's walking into. One more house-gawker—name of Jones, from London. In at four—early, Helen still getting dressed—had to get a train at four back to his wife, who's having a baby tomorrow. Hobbs glass.350 He looked over the house in five minutes, wouldn't even go down to the basement, muttered something about letting us know & scrammed.

Thursday, June 8

[400] Today the proofs of that infernal Rinehart book began to arrive—the first six books of *Paradise Lost*. The donkey job was complicated by the fact that L [Liberal] ideas keep busting out of me in all directions. Oh, God, the entanglements that permanent residence involve one in. However, I got the proofs all read, without benefit of my original MS, so there may be even more inconsistencies than usual—the only ones that bother me, though, are capitalization, & surely that's just guesswork anyway. I went home in the sweltering heat to find Blodwen Davies sitting in what looked like her slip, but wasn't. She left very soon, and Helen soon collapsed in tears. She's got terribly involved with the house-letting & has sat crouched over the phone all day & nobody's phoned. So I phoned Whipps, and, as expected, his boss wouldn't let him sign a long lease. The last thing the poor girl wanted to do was go to an Honour Course reception, but she got dressed and looked very pretty and we slugged through the damned reception—however it was a hell of a lot better party. Kay Brown, Kathlyn Smith, Mary Lane, Gloria Thompson, Ruth Manning—mostly women, I see—however, that McFayden lad was there & another boy who took my R.K. course. Alison Jeffries, who got a first; Di Rogers & Bridget Drugan & Francis Chapman, ditto. We had a long list of first-class honour people, but none in straight English—the highest there was Harriett Coltham, first in seconds. I nailed Surerus for the Public Lectures, so I have only Denomy to worry about. These affairs are pretty hopeless—however,

Helen enjoyed the Chapel affair, & apparently Moff Woodside did us all proud. I couldn't stand the heat & carbon dioxide. The Fishers drove us home & we found the Haddows also in a temper because they wanted to get to bed & couldn't because some relatives were standing them up. It must be the weather. Went to bed obsessed by the idiotic jingle of the College (U. of T.) song, which has been drunkenly staggering around the carillon for days on end.

Friday, June 9

[401] Skipped Convocation, which I really should have gone to, but it was another bloody hot day. Peggy Ray, bless her heart, has dug up more duplicates and is getting the two Arnold papers typed for me.[351] So that'll pretty well clear up the MS. Haven't heard from Pierce yet: probably don't need to. Dona [Edgar] says she'll send Currelly's corrections on the Egypt chapter.[352] More proofs from Rinehart. The proofs are rather bad in spots, but these were better than the first set. American business again: air mail *and* special delivery, price 93¢ for 80 sheets of page-proofs—thank God I've only one set to read. I sent them back parcel post, like the cautious Canadian I am. I doubt if they got here two hours sooner with all that nonsense.

[402] Helen has put another ad in the Star & phoned six agents, & just about decided to cut the price from $150 to $125. She's panicking a bit, of course, but the registration with agencies is wise. One funny old girl named Gertrude Tait turned up with a sick Pekinese mutt—broke his lower jaw & she wondered if he'd grown new bone. Nine years old. I said no. I didn't know, but she thinks $150 is a profiteering price, & if she wasn't going to be optimistic about the house I wasn't going to be optimistic about her damn dog's bones. The agents tell Helen what she ought to do about making her house look more attractive, & it gets her down. Helen's mother & father were over for dinner, bringing a letter from Roy [Kemp]. Mary [Kemp] is bitching again, this time about her "career," and so they still haven't got a working partnership going. It's beginning to look like separation, Peter [Kemp] or no Peter.

[403] This is a very wild speculation indeed: I wonder if some of the psychological fools could conceivably be right that early contact with the magical element in religion—I'm thinking of the miraculous powers of

Jesus—*does* dislocate one's sense of reality to the extent of magnifying one's will power through an unrecognized link of self-identification? It happened that way with me, that's why I raise the point: it would account for much in Jesuitism.

Saturday, June 10

[404] This morning Mary Simon turned up: she was more cheerful about the house & thought we'd make our $150. Then a dreadful little man from Chalmers & Meredith, who explained carefully that his firm was only listing it for rental for "good will": that they really preferred selling houses, & thought it was a bother to pick up a measly hundred bucks for renting it. As I said to Helen afterwards, if I were in business I'd do anything for a dollar, & I don't trust people who claim to have only a wholesale interest in money. So he pushed our rickety porch to see if it would fall over, said our house needed decorating very badly & instanced the plaster crack in the hall, asked suspiciously why our hot water tap was still leaking, & wound up by reminding us of the deep debt of gratitude we'd owe Chambers & Meredith if they *did* rent the place for us. Meanwhile the Star had put our ad under the "Houses Wanted" column. I trust this is just what Blodwen [Davies] would call a lunar phase of temporary difficulty. But it *is* rather tough on Helen, even if it was only revenge for, in Mary Simon's words, "not givin' it to me exclusive."

[405] Regarding what I said last Saturday [par. 392]: it's a sort of rehash of my Church & Society article, except that it looks more closely into the relation of Protestantism & its analogy laissez faire. Mill falls exactly into the "redeemable" middle of that dialectic. His doctrine of liberty really amounts to a doctrine of freedom of thought, that being the essential principle to be safeguarded. It's much the same in Milton—for instance in *Areopagitica*. Keep the censor out of the creative process & then let temporal authority do its damnedest. And although the world of myth is essentially art (because it's free act or creation, not just free thought), its incarnation is the university. The university deals with myth *in process*, continually subject to reformation. In all branches of knowledge inductive pioneering has to do with novelty, & the inductive leap with the reforming metamorphosis, the presence of which in science buggers Newman's whole thesis. Saw the MacGillivrays tonight.

Sunday, June 11

[406] Helen pushed me out into the garden to help prune, but in temper she was more like Eve after the fall than before. I didn't blame her, but it was a bit tough getting through the morning. I'd gone over yesterday to get her a detective story to read to take some of her mind off her troubles, but she still couldn't read, so I read it myself. It was "Stop Press," by Michael Innes, and I found it tepidly amusing. It's a very gabby story, full of high-flown literary allusions, which he deprecates but keeps right on making, and is obviously constructed on the "all this and a murder story too" principle. One bright spot was that we phoned the Sindalls & confirmed the house at Harvard.[353] He comes in two days a week & when we leave we're to let them know & they'll meet us & show us around. Another bright spot (yesterday) was a letter from Di Rogers telling me how good my R.K. course was.

[407] Sunday reflection: I recently saw a spaniel sniffing with great concentration at a little girl's wet diapers, & reflected on the fact that although, as Smollett says, we snuff up our own with great complacency,[354] still we regard that type of experience with nausea, & the nausea must be (as I think nausea always is, from Sartrean existentialism to sea sickness) the result of panic. Being just a bit "above" that, we feel dizzy in contemplating a plunge back into those depths. Now, why is smell below us? Does the great mystic take a similar nauseated view of sight & sound? (Actually he'd presumably lose the nausea, with regard to smell too, because he wouldn't panic.) We tolerate smell only in sublimated forms. A woman can put perfume, usually derived from animal excreta, on to excite sexual appetite, but such perfumes are significantly described as "essences." Taste seems to be just teetering on our present level: we can only just tolerate the gourmet if we concentrate on the objective aspect of eating: but if we applied aesthetic theories of empathy & einfühlung to taste we'd promptly get nauseated again. Note that the senses of nausea are those of contact, & lie along the Luvah-Tharmas axis.

Monday, June 12

[408] Nothing much happened today: I couldn't seem to settle down to any of my work. Two of my kids came in this afternoon—Ruth-Elizabeth

McLellan and a girl whose name I think is Frances Hopper. They wanted a list of books to read. Farewells to students falling over their feet & saying "thanks for everything" leave me a bit distraught—when they're so affectionate & mean so well I get sentimental—because it *is* sentimental to prolong what must necessarily be a brief & impersonal relationship. Nothing happened about the house today except that one person who dug the ad out of the wrong column phoned yesterday to see it today at five & then stood us up. Gave his name as Doctor Johnson, though in speech he sounded more like Daniel Boone. Giving the phone number in the ad makes it impossible to get any protection from that kind of thing.

[409] I keep chattering like this because there's no point in trying to do any serious work. I did a lot of pasting today on the Edgar thing. But whenever I get anywhere near my real job things start to bust loose. I noticed for instance how Paradise Lost ends: the last book is really focussed on vision & analogy, on Jesus and Nimrod. That's the only new point likely to emerge from my radio talk.[355] Then again, my technique of distance criticism keeps banging things out as I move further back. For instance, close up the Mutability Cantoes are a mass of impressionistic brushwork derived from Ovid & Irish geography, but as you go back from it, all you see is a great dark mass in the lower centre foreground rising up in defiance of a surrounding background of light—in other words the archetype of the Book of Job.[356] Also I noticed what a struggle Milton has in trying to express one of my own points: that wrath is the opposite of irritation, and that if God is capable of wrath he's incapable of irritation. Milton shows this by making God into a hideous hypocrite, pretending to love & care for his creatures, & then just grinning when he hears that one third of his angels have revolted. But the presence of a community of angels will enable me to keep my original-city point: Adam & Eve are really suburban.

Tuesday, June 13

[410] Today I went down & fixed up the Edgar MS so that it will be ready to take down to Lorne Pierce. It took me all morning, but I hope I won't have to do anything more now except page proofs. At the last minute I decided to cut out the unpublished D.C. Scott essay (there's better stuff on Scott in the memoir) and the Meredith poetry essay,

which is pretty dated now.[357] Also I rewrote my introduction, which is now, I think, quite a graceful & well turned piece of writing. After that I settled down to my damned Culture Commission fatigue, the last one I have to do.[358] I was just getting down to that when Eleanor Coutts came in. I don't know why I get so impatient with her: it's just that she writes me a letter & tells me all the news, then comes to town & phones me (Sunday) and tells me all the news, then comes to see me & tells me all the news, & hell, it's always the same news. She's got a job in Washington for the summer with the Quakers. However, I got the Culture Commission nonsense finished and sent off. So that's *that* disentangled. Then I went over to the Forum office and found another huge pile of stories, a few poems, & no bloody articles. I don't know what the hell's the matter with Canadians. Lou wants Edith [Fowke] as next editor. I want Ivan [Ivon Owen], so we'll compromise on Edith.

[411] The Star ran us a free ad today, so we spent the evening phoning, or rather being phoned. Some people named the Macdonalds came up to look at it. Working class people, two families of three kids each, interested only in gadgets and in nothing that we have. Thank god it's still possible in our society to overawe them. I don't mean that seriously, but caste differences are real even when class differences distort them. Then two earnest young couples named Yearsley & Orcutt came up—they're the cooperating type, & think of sharing the house. I'm leery of the scheme, but I liked them very much. One of the girls is a linotypist & the other one's pregnant & a dietitian. The men are interested in painting and in Oriental philosophy: Orcutt says he's half Quaker & half Zen Buddhist. His job is in "two-dimensional puppets"—in other words movie cartoons.

Wednesday, June 14

[412] Well, the great day has arrived: the damn house is, apparently, all rented. And not to the Yearsleys either. A tremulous little old lady named Mrs. Bright turned the trick. She sounded exactly like the unproductive kind of prospect, & Helen nearly turned her off the phone last night, but she came this morning with her son. And her son is a lawyer and a 3To graduate of Victoria—Charlie Leslie married him, & Johnny Arnup, who's our lawyer, knows him very well. You can't beat the old school tie. The house is for another son, a medical officer in the Air Force

now in Edmonton. $135 a month, and the 14–month period is all right.[359] They phoned him, and, as they said, it would have been a little longer if he'd been in Nome, Alaska. The lawyer gave Helen five bucks & a letter to close the deal. Two kids, seven & eight. The reason for the old lady's timidity, Helen said, was that she was somewhat in awe of her daughter-in-law, who's used to more gadgets than we have, and then she began to whimper a little about the price, but fortunately her son overruled her, as he saw it was pretty well what was needed.

[413] I got this news by phoning in the afternoon, & then Helen spent some time in high glee phoning the agents it was all off. (We save a hundred bucks.) I had to go over to Norman's [Norman Endicott's] office for a Ph.D committee meeting, where we sat on Anne Bolgan & Desmond Cole, in the manner of suppressing applause described by Lewis Carroll.[360] After that I met Helen at the Park Plaza and we adjourned for a drink. She had Luella Creighton with her, appropriately enough.[361] We were in a condition to get tight on a glass of chlorinated water, and as we had three Martinis I think we were fairly high. Luella, who only had two Old-fashioneds, drove us up to Maggie Newton's, where we were to go for dinner. Donald Creighton got his Guggenheim in 1939, I think, the first year they gave them to Canadians.[362] They lived in a beautiful little Virginia village named Fairfax, near Alexandria, where Dorothy Ladd lives, & from which Donald commuted to the Library of Congress.

Thursday, June 15

[414] Margaret's [Margaret Newton's] friend Ruth was in for dinner: Connie Harrison, whom I've never liked for some reason, came in later. Margaret's used to us, but I don't know what on earth Ruth must have made of us. Margaret gave us two heavy eyes, and I at least must have talked like an old maid coming out of ether. However, I've very seldom had a party where I felt more like just letting go.

[415] Only a very slight hangover this morning, but enough to prevent me from going ahead with my Milton paper. Another shipment of Milton proofs arrived, however (postage $1.77), so I started reading them. Then in came Frederick W. Sternfeld from Dartmouth, editor of *Renaissance News*: he'd warned me he might be dropping in. He's a close friend of Schanzer's father, so we went over with him to Schanzer's digs on Sutton

St. There we picked up Mrs. Sternfeld and a man named Russell Hitchcock, of Smith, who teaches art & has a beard to match. I liked him. We all had lunch at the Diet Kitchen. Like so many American scholars, especially those whose universities are in small towns, they run to gossip, & of course *Renaissance News* is basically gossip anyway. Sternfeld himself is doing what sounds like a very interesting and important work on the songs in Shakespeare & Goethe: I think he said he could reconstruct the tunes they had in their heads. I must look at his book, which is being published by the New York Public Library.[363]

[416] Forum meeting in the evening: it could be my last. I offered to meet Lou's [Lou Morris's] preference for Edith [Fowke], but by that time Lou had sold himself the idea of a rotating chairmanship. So I asked Edith to take it for next month, and then asked her privately about taking it over permanently. But she won't get rid of *Food for Thought* until the end of 1950, & meanwhile has her radio program to do, which apparently is going very well.[364] Lou's argument is that it'll give all the Board some editing experience, & so will make it that much easier to pick a permanent editor from that board—his real idea is of course to make it a stop-gap for me.

Friday, June 16

[417] Today was a rather harrowing day: I hate leaving things to the last minute, but here I was ready for work at ten in the morning with a two thousand word essay on Milton to read over the radio at a quarter to eight still undone. After about an hour's effort Bill Little came paddling all the way up to my office to tell me that Roy Daniells was in town. That impressed me, because I never thought Bill was very interested in Roy. So I hared over to Ryerson House & we went out for coffee. Roy looks wonderful, I think: that perpetually harried expression on his face was completely gone. He repeated the summer school invitation he made last year, so I guess now I can write him when I want it. He's back from Kingston, of course. He tells me that Irving's paper[365] was a great success & that F.R. Scott did a very good job too on the legal revolutions among the British dominions. Andison is staying in B.C. Earle Birney looks very relaxed after *Turvey*:[366] practically everything in it was a personal gripe he wanted to get rid of. The reproductive & excretory processes are closely connected, as I've said, but there's no doubt about what the

nature of catharsis is for the author himself. Also Roy claims to have democratized the English department, which under Sedgwick simply radiated from a great man, & to have got rid of most of the dead wood. Roy was obviously quite touched by the fact that I looked him up when I had a paper to write, and so I didn't tell him it was Bill Little's idea. He's very pleased about my Guggenheim, but unlike others of my well-wishers, didn't suggest that I should leave what he called my closely-woven life in southern Ontario.

[418] I worked very hard all afternoon on the paper, but my writing remains obstinately slow. I must never do this again. Of course, I find working over Milton again in a broad public way a good deal of a bore, but writing is invariably slow & painful for me no matter what it is. I wish I could rearrange the exits in my brain, which now is like the C.P.R. [Canadian Pacific Railway] Hamilton station, where the trains have to leave the main line and back in.

Saturday, June 17

[419] Anyway, I finished typing the paper out at five minutes to seven, but owing to good street car service I was only five minutes late, which by CBC standards is not late at all. The only interruption was Sissons, whom I met on the way back from Murray's. He wanted to know how much the Guggenheim was, & how much the College allows me. I think his interest in me is genuinely kindly, and I rather resent, in a way, having to make such a to-do about Pelham [Edgar], which I know makes Sissons jealous. He tells me that Ruth Jenking is going to be in Harvard this summer: we're hardly going to notice we're not home. (Incidentally, Roy [Daniells] says that Leddy, who is a Catholic & not unduly preju-diced in favor of Methodist parsons, has nothing but praise for Moore.)

[420] I realized some hours before the broadcast that my throat was going to act up: I seem to have acquired a more or less permanent tickle, which is rather serious for me. Helen James, who turned up from New York looking very beautiful, said it was probably nervous exhaustion from a hard year. They put me in a hell of a big studio and couldn't see me when I signalled to them to cut me off (my throat stayed put until the very last page). However, a thunderstorm had suddenly started up, so it probably passed off as just one more atmospheric disturbance, & be-

sides, no one but my nearest & dearest would be listening anyway. A Norwegian named Howe came to listen to the rehearsal, which as usual was fine. I better see what a doctor can do about my *gueule de bois*.

[421] Helen had been spending the day—or the afternoon—at a garden party for Ethel Bennett—I mean at her place for the University Settlement. They made two hundred dollars. She was pretty cool about the broadcast: thought I read the second half too fast. I was tired, having had very little food, and in no condition to entertain the Morgans,[367] who came in at half-past nine and stayed till after one—Margaret Newton joined them on her way back from the nearer Hillmers.

Sunday, June 18

[422] It's taking me an unconscionable time to get through Friday. The Morgans had been approached by Helen (*and* by Chambers and Meredith) to rent our house. They decided to buy, very sensibly—place on Farnham. I forgot to record Helen's reaction to renting our house—she took a bath & left a ring around the tub. Margaret [Newton] talks more & more of leaving her job—they say Ontario has the worst Welfare Department in Canada, except Quebec which has none at all.

[423] Well, yesterday I took it easy, slept in, didn't go to the office, & read Swift. I ought to enjoy reading Swift, for the change if nothing else, but what I'm to say about him doesn't quite come. I keep noticing ∧ [Anticlimax] forms in him, naturally. The Modest Proposal is the satiric analogy of cannibalism which is also in Montaigne (*and* in Dante & the Thyestes theme in Greek tragedy, tragedy being the other side of satire. If tragedy is a vision of law, satire ought to be a criticism of myth, which in Swift is particularly in the *Tub* and in all the parodies of "projects," the project being the new vision of a new ritual. I guess this is the place for the other bracket). *Polite Conversation* is the Lucianic take-off on the Platonic dialogue (the satire on dialectic runs through the Letter to the clergymen). *Directions to Servants* is more difficult to get: I think it's partly a saturnalia form. The Hospital for Incurables is straight vision of hell, in the encyclopaedic *Praise of Folly* tradition. The poem on his death is the Villon testament form. In the letter to the clergymen he says it's his duty to preach & practise the contempt of human things,[368] which not only establishes the link between preaching & satire, but associates both

with the whole *Paradise Regained* withdrawn vision of wrath, the rejection of all act, within which the universe of myth is reborn.

[424] Sunday reflection: if Jesus were to re-enter the world today, he
would not be crucified for calling himself God: he would be made to
stand on tip toe facing a wall with his hands against it until he finally
admitted that he had tried to poison Stalin and blow up the Kremlin.
There would be no Church.

Monday, June 19

[425] Today was a somewhat unsatisfactory day from a general psychological point of view: nothing got rounded off. I read some Milton
proofs, but I have to read more Milton proofs. I phoned a doctor for an
appointment, but I have to *go* to the damn doctor. I did some Swift, but I
have to do some more Swift. One of those days.

[426] Swift is another one of that Irish group overshadowing Yeats, of
course, but I've only just realized why. Swift is an extrovert, so you have
to figure out what he believes in by implication, more or less, but I think
he has a vision of simplicity at the centre of society. Simple writing,
simple living (hence cleanliness)[,] simple thinking. Human beings can't
make this kind of society, the natural man favoring affectation, private
enterprise (Whiggish laissez-faire) and esoteric professional techniques,
especially in religion, law and science. Hence the Yahoo-Houyhnhnm
deadlock, the inability of achieving Houyhnhnm ideals with Yahoo material. Hence Swift is thrown back on the church, which has got its
standards of simplicity (which includes also all the liberty, equality &
fraternity possible to man) from God. Sure it can get corrupt, but still it's
responsible to God for those standards, & so isn't quite the world. So
Swift also has that governor-principle I found all through the 4k course,
and with him it's the Church, as, in different contexts, it is too for Milton
& Coleridge. Perhaps it is the Church.

[427] Anyway, ∧ [Anticlimax] is going to do a lot of sniffling around
Swift, & I'm beginning to see that ∧ may expand into ⋏ [Rencontre] in
somewhat the same way that L [Liberal] does into ⅂ [Tragicomedy].
Because ⋏ is going to be the "Essay on Myth & Ritual" I've been talking
about. It's going to be concerned with the search for the "governor" & for

the recreation mutually of myth & ritual on a systole-diastole rhythm of deduction & induction. That puts its centre in the 19th c. & in "Blake & Modern Thought," as planned. The central area is, as I've said, the "redemption" of democratic liberalism by the Protestant tradition: flanking it are the historical & dialectic double analogy-patterns, the first of which includes all my original Orc-cycle stuff & the second the stage that was supposed to follow on from that.

Tuesday, June 20

[428] Well, I went to the doctor & he tells me I have a flu infection in my gozzle, and is going to fill me up with sulfanilamide. He tends to minimize the deviated septum: says I'd do better to wait until they find the answer to the ragweed allergy. No immediate prospect of my ever sleeping on my right side again. I went over to the Forum office and typed out an utterly meaningless piece of nonsense on the Schuman plan[369]—they were stuck with an editorial because Don Gardner had let them down. I think he may be a bit too erratic for the Board: he's too busy to do anything for the Forum, but missed the meeting last Thursday because he fell alseep. Lou is very pleased with the rotation scheme,[370] as it will enable him to run things his own way. The Forum would be perfectly set up if Allan Creighton had brains: the fact that he hasn't has always been its sticker.

[429] The painters finally arrived today so the other side of Helen's face should relax. Two men named Hocking, father & son, & incredibly efficient. The woodwork is going to be a soft gray, with the doors slightly darker, & they're to mall the vine down. The result is astonishing: from one of the most mousy-looking houses on the street we're suddenly becoming impressive & imposing & noticeable. Doubtless it's a portent, as so many things are.

[430] Tonight Jessie Mac [Macpherson] had a party with us, the Grahams [Bill Graham and Eleanor Godfrey] (including Ray [Godfrey]) & the McLuhans (including a third party there too: Corinne's pregnant again. They never miss, those two). Very pleasant party, except that I was asked to serve the drinks & wasn't very efficient at it. Ray is giving seminars at the School [of Social Work] that are being recorded & relayed to Ottawa. The discussion is supposed to be spontaneous. I told Marshall that

anything I said about any writing I was going to do was just official communiqué & meant go 'way & don't bother me, & he said he'd heard that was the line I took with the Guggenheim Committee. I don't know who told him. Some discussion about a magazine called Neurotica, which Luce has bought.[371] Marshall has a tremendous fund of literary gossip.

Wednesday, June 21

[431] Got out & had lunch with Margaret Avison. Not much there: Margaret seems tired & drained of energy. Part of the trouble is her new room on Washington Ave., north on northside, overlooking a room in OCE where the Leslie Bell singers practise from seven to past ten two nights a week. Drives her nuts.

[432] Dinner with Jean Elder. Dorothy Drever & Isabel Thomas there, along with Ruth [Elder], who left early, & the old man, who got me to carve the chicken. I'm getting to be not too bad at that as far as whittling off wings & legs & slicing the breast is concerned: it's finding those two pieces of dark meat in the small of the back that gets me. Isabel had enough drinks to get her started, & she pontificated the whole evening. A long story about Lou [Morris] & the Forum which had led to the cancelling of her subscription, which I resented her telling. She has all of Eleanor's [Eleanor Godfrey's] most irritating mannerisms, but the platitudes of a school teacher on top of it: Eleanor has a sharp, if limited intelligence.

[433] Poor old Haddow next door must be going nuts—he's at the hardest part of his garage-building now & his plaster won't work—not enough hair in it, he says. On top of that the painter asked him to clear the rubbish out of between the garages. It's mostly his, but I hope he won't resent being asked. Her [Jean Haddow's] sister is there now, doing a two-week refresher course with Boszormeny-Nagy, if that's all the letters.[372] She teaches in that girls' school at Compton, & evidently thinks it proper to overawe her girls by learning to play the Liszt E major Polonaise. When one thinks of all the Bach fugues, Mozart & Beethoven sonatas, Chopin & Debussy preludes & Brahms intermezzi she could learn in the time it would take to play that damned thing (not that it isn't an attractive enough piece of music in its way), one feels melancholy

about the future of music. I gather she has a bad genius complex, & so must be a bad influence on Jean [Haddow]. Helen's parents have had to cancel a trip out to the Ayres in Cooksville, because Harold has had a heart attack. Harold seems to be a somewhat unlucky name among my friends.[373]

Thursday, June 22

[434] Today I finished proofreading the last section of the Milton text. The only part left to do is my own introduction. The text won't be too bad: I think, though, that I made a mistake in leaving out the motto to Areopagitica. I don't care about the footnote: that's only a fart anyway. Otherwise, I think the text should be all right for its limited purposes. 542 pages. It was raining like hell and I'd picked up a slight cold on top of my irritable throat, & with one eye on the talk tomorrow I begged off pageproofing the Forum & went home to bed & stayed there. Didn't do me any harm: slight nervous exhaustion too. I'd done a draft of the Swift talk, so I wrote the talk between the lines of the draft: it's the Balzac method, only he did it with proofsheets, which was much more expensive.

[435] Dropped in to see Irving & told him I heard his paper was a big success.[374] He was engaged in writing it out for publication & had just got to the footnotes. The footnotes concerned the non-academic philosophers, a man named LeSueur & Bucke, the author of *Cosmic Consciousness*.[375] I'd often seen that book at Britnell's, but had no idea Bucke was a Canadian, or that he was one of Whitman's closest friends—almost got Whitman to settle permanently in Ontario. He did some exploring in the West around the 1850's, then went through medicine at McGill & became a pioneering psychiatrist—head of the Hamilton insane asylum. He abolished corporal restraints and liquor—gives one an idea of what it was like before. I was of course able to tell Irving that Bucke's book was a theosophical Scripture, and hence important in the development of Canadian painting, the Group of Seven being excited about theosophy—hence abstraction in Lawren Harris.[376] He was very pleased to hear this—I told him to phone Robins. Canadian philosophy, in Toronto, Queen's & McGill, which is all he's doing, was Scotch rationalism—Reid & Dugald Stewart—at first, & then, with Watson, Kantian idealism. He says Watson was keener on making philosophy rationalize religion than the genuine reverends were: one thinks of Brown again.[377]

Friday, June 23

[436] Today I went down & typed out the script, taking care to make it shorter than the Milton talk. Weaver had phoned to tell me to make it less concentrated (everybody tells me my stuff is too concentrated, but nobody can tell me how to pad it out: what the hell am I supposed to do, write deliberate bullshit?) and to stress the "prophet" angle—this after first telling me to ignore the series title. So the Swift thing was more anecdotal and gossipy, & I guess went off all right. My throat brooded about whether to act up or not, but finally, thank God, decided against it. I've never had mike fright, but to have a tickly throat on page three of a seven-page talk & wonder if you're going to get through the rest of it or not is a quite unpleasant situation to be in. I did it standing up, which helped.

[437] The Kenyon Review editor wrote me about my form of poetry article—this is the third time. So I've written him to say that I'll do him an archetype paper for his next deadline, & if he doesn't like it I'll try to work out the poetry one after that.[378] Also I went over to the bank & found my export permission had gone through all right—the $2100 for the next twelve months. Now after I see a G.P. [general practitioner] I don't think there'll be anything else.

[438] Helen James tells me (from Jim Scott's Telegram column) that Roy Daniells has decided to christen his daughter S, so that when she grows up she can choose her own name with that one limitation. Jim said he'd asked his little three-year-old what she thought of that, but she didn't think much of it because she's got a lisp.[379] Bessie MacAgy was in for dinner. She's a most pleasant & attractive woman—whatever her husband was, he didn't know a good thing when he saw it. She referred to him as a boozer last night—her only comment I've heard. Douglas [MacAgy] has left the Art School to take a promotion job with the movies—the only sort of job one could get with the movies in their depressed state, I imagine. Douglas has acquired the insignia of a successful young American executive—a stomach ulcer.[380]

Saturday, June 24

[439] I let that idiot Gummow talk me into giving him an M.A. oral today, so I went down & gave it to him. Vickers was second reader. The

thesis wasn't really any damn good, and here he wants me to write him a letter of recommendation about a Ph.D thesis on Blake & Wordsworth— he's rather forced my hand there. He needs the letter because he hasn't a course with a first in his special field. Our trouble is that we've developed an enormous Cabbala of oral tradition of equal authority with the written word in the calendar, & the students only find it out by rumor. I don't think he's at all Ph.D material. I overslept & had to hurry down, so I went straight back home & on the Yonge-St. Clair corner Peter Fisher picked me up in his gorgeous new Pontiac. We really must get a car sometime soon. Peter stayed for lunch & I drew out for him the kabbalistic diagram on May 20,[381] which I think may have something. He's been out to Victoria to mark papers—it's the way the Army—or the Civil Service—does things. Out to the family for dinner[382] and Mrs. Cameron came along. She's retiring this year. I found her prattle a bit stupefying, or rather I found an intensely hot night so, what with a very noisy radio next door. Helen's father & mother were in quite good form, however, and her father showed me some old photographs of Grip Ltd: very interesting seeing early pictures of J.E.H. Macdonald, A.H. Robson, Ivor Lewis, & some of his Wyclif [Wycliffe] classmates,[383] including Bishop Hallam, Isabel's [Isabel Whitley's] father. Also, of course, the Kemp family in earlier stages.

[440] The form of the fourth, otherwise λ [Rencontre], is getting pretty clear now, as is the whole shape of the great four-movement verbal symphony that I have in mind. That means that λ won't be an anticlimax or a transitional book, but will rumble to a tremendous close right smack in the middle of modern thought. The thing that isn't clear is the role of music in λ, but that's all right. The thing that pleases me, as I say, is the way it opens out from Λ [Anticlimax] and the way that all the themes are anticipated (and in some measure contained) in L [Liberal]. Now all I have to do is start work on the assumption that the job is as great as I think it is.

Sunday, June 25

[441] Took a rest cure today, except for going out to see Aunt Lily [Lilly Maidment]. I made a mistake on the street car & we got out there at noon—however, she'd already fixed lunch. We saw her rose garden & the alterations in the house, both extensive. Came back and lazed around.

We've about decided to fly to Boston: the difference in fare is very slight, & I've never been up in the air.

[442] I've started drafting out a tentative plan for my next Kenyon Review paper, assuming they'd be interested in one on archetypes. The opening stages are a fairly beaten track: ritual is pre-conscious & animal, myth conscious & human. Ritual is the vestigial human form of synchronization, & myth begins as an effort to explain it. Ritual eventually finds its rationale in the yearly cycle, & so myth becomes cyclic too. Working along these lines I think I can get to the narrative archetypes, & from there to the cycles, the approximation of the day-night cycle to the sleep-waking one being the entering wedge. That's fairly standard, but it's fairly well known too. What isn't so well known is my famous demonstration of the anatomy of the spiritual world that I astonish my kids with every January. Well, when I've got that done, & gone from there to the narrative archetypes of epic, I have another job, & possibly a second article, in hand, namely the working out of my essential thesis that archetypes are the informing powers of poetry. If I can make a passable article out of that the book will be all over but the footnotes. I think I'd be wiser to cook up a hell of a convincing sounding article on archetypes & shoot it at him by his August 1 deadline, & never mind whether it clashes with the English Institute paper or not. Then I can take my time working out its sequel—which, incidentally, involves drama too. The four forms of ritual produce the four forms of drama, & the four forms of myth the four types of prose fiction, or at least so I devoutly hope. In between them is song, and the four forms of song ($\tau\alpha$ $\mu\epsilon\lambda\eta$)[384] produce the four kinds of epic, epic being, so to speak, normative or projected poetry. Some bullshit in this, in fact a lot.

Monday, June 26

[443] Worked perfunctorily at my Blake paper today:[385] that's a subject I feel I've had. Helen called me home at noon to interview the man who's taking the house. Name of Hugh Bright, very decent chap. First month's rent cheque and evidently his name on the lease. Whoopee, if I may allow myself a somewhat dated expression. Quite business-like: took down the names of the neighbors even. Busy day for Helen, as this morning Edna & Nancy[386] turned up. Evidently my little godchild has turned from a redhead into a blonde, & wants to know if there aren't any

men blonds. So she's to have a look at me tomorrow. I received another reminder of the egotism of the creative, or would-be creative, today: a cub-like youth I took to lunch last summer sent me 118 pages of blank verse drama. It's a delicate point in casuistry to know when charity becomes fulsome sentimentality, but I think it's somewhere short of this, so I'm sending it back unread.

[444] A war scene in the papers over Korea: the first real one in five years.[387] It makes me irritable & depressed, & it would be easy to mistake that for genuine concern. I haven't any feeling about war except that I wish it would go away and leave me alone to do my work. I don't care if people have wars if they wouldn't bother me. The last war didn't bother me except when it killed my friends. And I utterly refuse to sanction the notion that the war is something bigger & more important than my concerns. The war is not important unless it makes too much damage to leave a surviving public interested in the work I'm doing, in which case it's important because it's Antichrist. What other attitude any sane man with real work to do can take towards a war I can't even conceive. I'm not a pacifist because that would still mean that war was taking up too much of my thoughts and actions. I want to run away from war as long as possible, & do as little as possible for it if I can't. I'm always optimistic because I assume I'll do better if my community wins, & I wish it would win in a hurry. I take the same attitude toward it that I do to team sports: one of an amiable pretence of an interest I don't in the least feel. The only objective factor is my realization that war is unspeakably useless.

Tuesday, June 27

[445] Well, Nancy came, a leggy tow-headed urchin who sat beside me casting side-long glances at me but hadn't a word to say for herself. Cat got her tongue, I think is the phrase. The fact that she's lost all her baby fat at five means she'll be tall like her mother, who, incidentally, is looking wonderful, & is apparently about to marry a man named Fulford, whom she brought to Toronto with her. That took most of the morning: then I went down to the office and on to a doctor's appointment. He hasn't done me any harm, and gave me a certificate for the Guggenheim people. He seemed brusque, but was bothered about Korea. Back to the office & typed out a few pages of the Blake talk,[388] which is going to be dull, I'm afraid. Helen picked me up from a prolonged hairdo and we

went out for drinks and dinner. She likes the Blake talk better than I do, but this life of idleness—it's really that—and clearing up loose ends is a bore. The painters are through today, & so is the upholstering.

[446] I think the Blake is well in hand, and I'm starting on Shaw. My adolescent interest in Shaw pretty well faded out when I came to college—well, no, it didn't, as I re-read all of his stuff later, but for some reason I'd never read any play of his later than *The Apple Cart*.[389] Doesn't look as though I've really missed much. *Too True to be Good* is an interesting comedy of humors: his trouble is he can't just let humors be enlightened by each other: he wants a central character. In that particular play the nearest norm is Private Meek, an ingenious tricky-slave modulation. On the strength of *The Apple Cart* and the name of *Good King Charles* I'd been saying that Shaw had finally revealed himself as a frustrated Royalist, & I don't think I was so far out. Meek is actually a Caesar in disguise, Charles II is certainly the one idealized figure in his play, the Judge in *Geneva* is a practically royal centre of gravity, & the fact that the king is missing from *On the Rocks* is what makes that such a silly play: it's Shaw's version of England in 1659, waiting for its monarch to appear. Of course Shaw points out the vulnerable point of hereditary kingship, the non-transmissibility of genius, which he gets around in Major Barbara— significant he has to speak of it. But there's more to it than that.

Wednesday, June 28

[447] The first thing today was the dentist, who found two cavities—not bad for six years. He filled one, freezing it. On the way out I talked to the next patient, a little girl who was going to take my R.K. course, & was disconsolate to find she'd be missing "the talk of the campus." Back to the office & picked up Irving & Robins for lunch. Not much there. The jejune nature of my life these days makes me wonder about scholars having nothing to do but $\sigma\chi o\lambda\eta$ [*schole*], leisure. Intense thinking is a by-product of an active life: surely it dries up when it becomes an end in itself, like happiness. Anyway, I have a feeling (it's all I have left) that I'm not thinking because I'm not working. The general bother of getting away upsets me, of course. The hell with me: only I do wish I could concentrate on archetypes.

[448] Going on with Shaw, he's preoccupied by the search for the "ruler":

he simply can't understand that the world is trying to outgrow all that nonsense about rulers. He has very little sense of the governor-principle as that which has authority without power: it's there in the middle of *Geneva*, I know, but he's not satisfied with it. The dialogue of Christ & Pilate ends in a deadlock. He can see through Pilate, & doesn't really want a dictator, though he's enough of a senile *enfant terrible* to play with the notion. The closest he comes to it is in the preface to *Geneva*, where he speaks of Mill & of the right to criticize. He naturally sees that Stalin is a Pope, the incarnation of a dialectic, & rejects the Papacy, which he's consistent in regarding as the only possible form of Christianity. But in a rare flash of real insight he makes King Charles say that the Pope is always a Whig. And he doesn't *really* go for the Platonic philosopher-ruler. No, it's the royal epiphany, the king and queen (it's very funny how he plops the "coupled vote" business into the preface to *Good King Charles*)[390] who are also normative in *The Apple Cart*, the rejuvenated father & mother (cf. "Mopsy & Popsy" in TTG [*To True to Be Good*]: the process doesn't carry through there). Not national royalty ultimately, of course: a Caesar or Charlemagne: Dante's Feltro or super-Constantine: but still nostalgia for the days "when loyalty no harm meant"[391] & when a representative of Louis XIV could be the comic Last Judgement on *Tartuffe*.

Thursday, June 29

[449] Lunch with Mac Ross, from California on his way to Queens. Looks well. Conversation mainly gossip. Evidently I'm now classed as a "new critic" across the line, so some old goat who thinks all new critics are psychopaths is letting off a blast at English Institute Essays 1948. He says the Stobies are in a hell of a spot, & that Bill is a much poorer teacher & colleague than I thought. Mother fixation, evidently, & Peggy mothers him, which is bad for them both. He's been really trying to do something for them, & hasn't succeeded. He says Gillson has all the characteristics of paresis. Speers is to come to Toronto next year: another reason for being grateful to the Guggenheim committee. Ross seems to have had a rather lonely year—anyway he's firm about wanting to stay in Canada.

[450] Down to dump the Edgar MS[392] on Lorne Pierce, who retires tomorrow after 30 years. He raised the question again about my succeeding him:[393] he thinks it ought to be done by an unfrocked parson like me.

The very idea makes my toes curl up, as Douglas Grant said about being at Western. I said whatever royalties there were ought to go to Dona [Edgar], but he'll try to arrange an honorarium for me. It now occurs to me that the honorarium should go to Peggy Ray.[394]

[451] Out to see the Grahams [Bill Graham and Eleanor Godfrey] tonight, Marvin Gelber coming in later. Everybody else was out of town. General discussion: a bit too literary for Gelber's taste—or Helen's. Eleanor certainly keeps up with magazines, & is clearly impressed with the fact that I've made the Kenyon Review—more than she ever was with the book. She and Bill have "settled down," as the saying is, & are talking of buying a place in the country, seeing their friends about once a year apiece, which they suggest is enough. Maybe, but if I were Bill, I'd hesitate to forgo the advantage of having two wives: Ray [Godfrey] got the dinner & knit socks for him all evening. I'm very fond of that menage. I like Gelber too: evidently he's made more than one attempt to buy the Forum, & says Graham Spry promised it to him,[395] then changed his mind at the last minute. Last year he tried again; according to Lou [Morris] he wants to make it a Zionist organ.

Friday, June 30

[452] I'd had all the Blake talk except a page & a bit done since Tuesday, but getting that page finished took a lot of the day. But when I got it finished it was apparently a lot better than I thought. I read it I think quite well, standing up of course: I don't ever want to sit down again. Much faster reading than I've ever done, & for the first time I got a slow-down signal. Only one more:[396] they're a real fag, & I'm actually very well pleased not to have to do the Shakespeare lectures. And, believe it or not, I think I almost got an idea about approaching my archetype paper—that is, the Blake paper.[397] The innocent world is a vision of childhood, not remembered but kept as a real presence—real because people can be united in charity only within that world. I may as well make the Blake paper a sketch of ʎ [Rencontre] as I now conceive it. The innocent world becomes the city-garden, the world in imagery of the integration of myth & in concept the world of final causes.

[453] The Irvings had Helen in to dinner and I joined them after the broadcast, feeling particularly jubilant because my throat hadn't acted

up. Irving was feeling happy too, about being the first man in the history of the human race to write about the history of Canadian philosophy. His paper for the C.H.R.,[398] an expansion of what he had read at Kingston, extends to fifty pages. I have to go over it, of course—or, as St. Thomas Aquinas says in discussing the basis of law, natch.[399] Also over an offprint he gave me a year & a half ago that I put aside hoping he'd forget about it. He didn't. His Alberta study ought to be finished pretty soon.[400]

[454] More Shaw: he has all the comic patterns, and I wish he'd stop teasing them. *The Simpleton of the Unexpected Isles* is a Lucianic *danse macabre*: it has allegory (the four fallen powers of history; a Beulah & of course insular setting, the *Ingenu* type of hero, an agon-death at the beginning & a general sense of sea-change {they dive into the water} for the others). In short, it's Shaw's *Tempest* play. Not bad either. The Last Judgement itself has a slightly Marxist twist: the idlers are "liquidated" (sea-change word again) by disappearing, hell being of course nonentity.

Saturday, July 1

[455] Didn't do anything today: my usual response to crucial days. I've been reading Shaw on Ibsen & Wagner: he was really at his best when these studies were siphoning off his critical abilities & when he was feeling that he was part of a great world movement. When Picasso & Stravinsky succeeded Manet & Wagner he became more isolated & cranky. However, the real thing that he couldn't fit into was the revival of mythopoeia. He thought, being a good Victorian, of a coming third age, the first religious but superstitious, the second rational but impersonal, & the third an apotheosis of human will, the Nietzschean superman, the Marxist destruction of class, the Wagnerian gods, the Ibsenite dismantling of ideals & masks, all fitting the same pattern. But, for all the world like a crazy "social gospel" Methodist parson of the A.E. Smith variety, he thought of the communion of saints not as a real presence but as an allegory of something to be realized in the future.

[456] I got a glimmering vision today of the golden city that, like the old-fashioned myth of the ether, permeates & interpenetrates the here & now, the medium of charitable communication. I think the Blake paper

will begin with my point that childhood is the beginning of life, sleep the beginning of day, Sunday the beginning of the week, leisure (*not* rest) the beginning of activity, & so myth the beginner (and begetter) of ritual. Of the folly of not recognizing the real presence of a charitable community, the binding of the infant Orc until he becomes a terrible babe demanding to be born. Of the *ganz anderes* nature of the babe,[401] & so taken as hellish or daimonic. Of the lurking sense of the unreality of the babe that binds him to the historical cycle, the unrecognized informing power of the alleged "progress" of the world of experience. Of the helplessness or impotence of the innocent world when regarded as unreal: Thel, & compare Morris, Earthly Paradise. Of its true form (shown in dreams) as the eald enta geweorc ["the old work of giants" (*Beowulf*, 1. 2774)], the informing Promethean giants who are the kernel of reality in the Shaw-Nietzsche-Wagner myth of the surpassing of man.

Sunday, July 2

[457] Nothing happened today except that Isabel [Whitley] came over with little Hilary, who is a very pretty & piquant baby. Roy [Kemp] is thinking of buying a place in Londonderry, Vermont, & Mary is pregnant again.[402] Tried to write the Shaw paper, & did write about half of it, but I'm getting browned off & don't know what else to say about him that the public would want to hear. The opening of *The Quintessence of Ibsenism* contains a remark about the "mere literary critic" that I ought to quote in the first chapter of L [Liberal]. Read Irving's philosophy paper,[403] which isn't bad. Irving has taught me a good deal about the importance of extroverted values: keeping up with the journalism, the gossip, the personalities of the academic world. I have taken too little care of these things.

[458] The QI [*Quintessence of Ibsenism*] is about as frank a statement as one could get anywhere of the "play of ideas" thesis. As it's a genuine archetype, the symposium, Shaw's conception of a discussion-play certainly has force. You can't answer it by talking about characterization, either, because Shaw doesn't say that a playwright should or that Ibsen does skimp his character-study. What the argument overlooks, in its implied attack on the Elizabethan school, is the importance of the dream-pattern. For Shaw, at least there, there's nothing but waking rational consciousness in the audience. He says Claudius is more affected by the

mouse-trap play than he would have been by Oedipus, because it's about him. What he doesn't know (no modern critic could very well until Freud) is just how & to what extent Oedipus is about the audience individually. This point at once restores the archetype, & traditional values with it, to prominence. I don't know if I've said that the royal figure who looms up at the end of Shaw is the archon of the feast. As for Ibsen himself, the chief thing there is that the humor has become the persona-absorbed idealist—a very simple modulation. Also I note a tendency to examine the spoiled bourgeois in terms of his isolation from the comic community: the dead end of this is the *Huit* [*Huis*] *Clos* of Sartre—in Ibsen himself the prison-attic of John Gabriel Borkman. It's perhaps the essential form of bourgeois tragedy, which takes the comedy as normative.

Monday, July 3

[459] Today's mail brought an official letter about my going on half salary ($2620, as I go up a notch) and, at the office, a request from *Chicago* Press to let them see my next MS. Ho hum. I must find out why there's so much competition. Spent most of the morning on Irving's *other* paper: the Social Credit one I should have read two years ago.[404] Took both opera in to him & hurried down town to meet Helen for lunch. Ate at Simpson's, a big noisy impersonal barn. Then went over to Johnny Arnup's to get the lease signed & delivered, and to make arrangements for a will. To each other, of course, & if we both conk the lettuce is to be split equally between Fryes & Kemps; my father & Vera, Helen's father, mother & Roy, in that order. Then over to the air lines. The American Air Lines is better than the TCA [Trans-Canada Airlines]: I can take Helen for half fare, for one thing, & the immigration nonsense is over at this end. At the A.A.L. office I ran into D.M. LeBourdais, who introduced himself. He's an old man (63, he told me, with a young wife & two young children who call him grandpa), writing two books on the Arctic, one a school text-book.[405] I think—this wasn't very clear—he finances his plane trips to the north through mining companies for whom he does public-ity. He's a free-lance writer, with a lot of Blodwen Davies' interests as well as her profession. Not "mysticism," though—says he doesn't care about Blake. Enthusiastic about Brooker's *The Robber*, which he says is one of the best books ever to come out of Canada. Went to the King Edward (now one of the Cardy chains of hotels) for a cocktail, then home

on an interminable street car. Mowed both lawns in the evening & diddled at my paper: one more paragraph.[406] Eleanor [Godfrey] phoned to say Bill [Graham] & Ray [Godfrey] have bought a $15000 house on Walmer Rd. & that *she's* pregnant. Three months. Talked to Bill Haddow, who says poor old Donny has failed his year again. I don't know what ails that boy—probably house rot, which is a name I've invented for staying too long with one's parents. We are going to have an income of about $8000 next year, so we shouldn't starve. The Korea business apparently isn't going to catch fire: it's a miserable government to make the first example of resisted aggression without world war, though.[407]

Tuesday, July 4

[460] I wrote seventeen letters today: when I write a dozen more I think I can tentatively say that my desk will be clear. People still keep tripping me up: Clarence Lemke this morning, who wanted me to read a sermon based on my teaching which everyone said was incomprehensible. I gave him no encouragement: I console myself with the reflection that even Jesus got pretty damn impatient at requests for assistance. Also Mrs. Davidson,[408] to tell me she thought Moff Woodside should have been at least offered the Presidency: says I'm wrong in thinking he was. However, she seems reconciled to Moore. Irving again, who's full of enthusiasm about the American edition of his history-of-Canadian philosophy paper, which is to be brought up to date: I'm to go into it as one of the Brett school.[409] Then the dentist, who's an expert on remarks that require only a gargle in reply: spoke of the sullenness of CCF leaders & the hollowness of their efforts to be good fellows. Downtown to pick up the air tickets from the cute girl I talked to yesterday; back to the women's shoeshop for Helen's shoes (there was a shoe sale on and the store was jammed with women standing around and stamping); then a very late lunch, wire to Sindalls, back to the office for more letters, & home with several shopping errands. Not the sort of life that's too highly favorable to the inner life. In the evening another of the tribe of Dan phoned: Stephen Gibson. Another letter. I tried to finish the Shaw paper, but I've got stuck in a bad idiom and will have to start all over again.

[461] Yes, I think the principle of taking comedy as the norm & seeing tragedy as the isolation of individuals from its community is the right formula for the modern "problem" tragedy. That's Ibsen: note in connec-

tion with the archetype the central importance of reclaiming land: Faust, & an example of the same general type in the redemptive charity at the end of Little Eyolf. The incest theme is tragic partly because endogamy is also withdrawal from community. Shaw's treatment of Wagner is interesting, but I don't think Wagner's really very important except as a case history in weak-minded anarchism. However, the Wotan-law & Alberich-laissez faire links may be important.[410]

Wednesday, July 5

[462] Went down to the office and worked like hell at my paper: I finished it, but came home with a sore throat & a sick headache. Some kind of flu bug, I suppose. I went to bed after supper but in spite of that I had a miserable night: like the old lady Dad tells about who said she couldn't lay nor set. Terrific nose-blocked headache, couldn't stand being stretched out in the only position I could sleep in & couldn't stand any of the alternatives. Manic-depressive temperature, first boiling hot & then shivering. The first real sick spell I've had this year, the off-color days I've recorded being no more than that. No visitors except Burgener, who seems to be all right again & was very pleased at what I did for him. James Reaney phoned at supper-time: says he isn't a hero & skipped the Winnipeg flood. A horrible lunch at Diana's[411] may have helped set me off.

[463] The Shaw paper didn't really come up to my expectations, whatever they were. His chief archetype, which he reads into Ibsen, perhaps correctly, is the idealist-as-humor, as I've said.[412] His superman is just there as the comic society as man—what I now call the Ghibelline epiphany—and to represent a transcendence of all humorous (or all-too-human) syntheses. I must work out the connection between the superman and the angel. Meanwhile, the Shavian hero is a superman deputy or regent: the busy, simple, unpretentious, efficient housewife, Caesar & St. Joan. He's a complete pragmatist, of course, all dogmatics proceeding from the learned-doctor or humor. I think *Good King Charles*, which shows a variety of types being liberalized by one another with a royal archon in charge, is about as concentrated a comedy form as he gives us. The only thing I haven't found is a real communion symbol: I could be wrong about that, of course. The relation to dialectic comes out in a lot of places—Major Barbara, for instance—it's linked with the fact that crea-

tive evolution in a conscious being is partly an act of conscious will, & hence dialectic decisions have transcendental consequences, or may have. Also, of course, the link between this symposium-comedy & Fabian tactics.

Thursday, July 6

[464] Got up early, & felt a little better when I was up, as it relieved the pressure on my nose. Felt weak & dizzy all morning, otherwise O.K. Last session with the dentist, who was worried about losing his case-record book & his cash book. A serious loss to him: I hope he finds them. Clarence Lemke was in again, wanting the scripts of my radio talks, for God's sake. Met Helen for lunch—well, on our way to lunch we dropped in to the American Immigration Bureau. My permit had expired & Helen hadn't got one, so we had to wait nearly an hour. However, *that's* cleared up, as I don't think customs will be any trouble. Then lunch, where Helen wouldn't let me have cream in my coffee, butter on my roll, or ice-cream for dessert. Theory she's working on. Then we went down to Johnny Arnup's & got our wills signed, & then back to the locksmith, to collect a suitcase & pay an outrageous bill—$8.75—which left us absolutely broke. It was just three o'clock, but we just managed to get under the wire at the bank & got a cheque cashed—we didn't try to get our Form H's at that time, & will have to go back tomorrow. Then a couple of beers at the Babloor, which we haven't been to for months, perhaps years, & home. Helen had to spend part of the morning listening to Mrs. Haddow's version of a long quarrel between her & her husband. She thinks her husband is dotty, but of course the same observation has been made about her. Too bad. She says Donny [Haddow] failed his exams on purpose, & is very anxious to leave home.

[465] Curious that memories of my childhood and adolescence are beginning to swarm into my mind at this time. I find myself doing the same daydreaming & rebuilding of my earlier life that I did last summer. I suppose it's partly reaction to going away, but I'd better snap out of it once I get to work. It's a good thing to know what you have done wrong, but a bad thing to take refuge in dreaming about an ideal life that didn't happen. The Bible is certainly right when it says that the essential traitor in the soul is the accuser of sin.

Friday, July 7

[466] Thrown off schedule today by the furnace man, who didn't leave until lunch time. We grabbed lunch at Eaton's—that Chippel place where we had tea with the Mendelssohn choir—and then on to the CBC. Helen James had asked me to do my talk early & can it, as she wanted to get away for the weekend. Helen—my Helen, that is—stayed out in the control room—what I called the paternity ward—and I read it standing up again with just one very natural-sounding harrumph. Both Helens said it was a fine script & a very smooth performance. I heard it myself later on in the day and was rather shocked, as I always am when I hear my own voice, at the nasal honk that emerged. That's the result of speaking too far back in the throat and working my mouth muscles too much. Apart altogether from the fact that my sore throat continues to afflict me, of course. We dodged into the downtown area: it was bloody hot, and I went home by myself. One of those days: I had to go back for a forgotten hat, & in the morning I started out by myself & of course forgot everything, including my script.

[467] The Forum party at Markowitz's was quite a success, I think. I drank too much & too fast: I don't know why the hell I do that. One reason is that I'm just nervous, & keep drinking as a nervous habit. The other is that it's one of the few ways in which the undying accusing child in me can claim to make a real man of me. So I talked fast & mixed up my words and got myself all set for a terrific hangover in the morning. Underhill made a little speech & presented me with a copy of the complete piano works of Brahms (except the Paganini Variations). For some reason it hadn't occurred to me that they would make such a presentation. I hope my speech made sense. A number of people, notably Alan [Allan] Sangster, made pleasant comments on my broadcast. It was an amazing turnout: everybody was there, I think. I hate saying good-bye to people I like.

Saturday, July 8

[468] Well, I got the hangover all right, though not nearly as badly as I deserved. I was dizzy and constipated all day and my voice has gone down to a Spectre of the Haunted Grange level: if it goes any lower it'll just be a lot of vibrations. I hope it isn't mental in origin: I don't want to

feel I'm the sort of person who can always be counted on to take to his bed in a crisis. We dashed down to the bank & got our Form H business done—at the last minute, but we'd had bad luck the last two days. I'm probably solvent and overdrawn. Then I went along to get my hair cut in order not to frighten the proper Bostonians. Then I took my last look at that filthy hole I work in—last for fourteen months, anyway—and came home in a taxi with the typewriter. The rest of the day was spent at home: I tried to go to bed but it didn't work. It's very hot, & a bad time for spring cleaning. George Haddow is next door: I met him on the street today & didn't recognize him. My pathologically bad memory for faces makes me sometimes dread even going out on the street alone without Helen to see people for me.

[469] The rush of adolescent memories continues: I'm just at the "change of life" period in Jung's psychology, I suppose.[413] They now take the form of wishing I'd spent my youth practising writing fiction: it's silly, of course, but it's part of a general recognition of the damage I did my future life in my earlier years. A certain amount of daydreaming is normal, I suppose, but I daydreamed to excess, and hesitated to start any real work on fulfilling my ambitions because I was so afraid my first efforts wouldn't show true genius. I worried a lot about genius. I think too that my present excess of embarrassment over various failures to achieve perfect life rhythm in social behavior is largely due to an exaggerated picture of myself built up in reverie during adolescence. I suppose that repentance or metanoia consists first of all in determining the conditions under which your life must henceforth operate. The irrelevant emotion of regret thereby built up is remorse.

Sunday, July 9

[470] Today was pushing & shoving & carrying & throwing out day. I helped a little, but in my usual fashion, which a French woman once described as Continental, I left Helen to do the bulk of it & went upstairs to write a lot of letters. Yvonne Williams phoned: there's a prostitute of the same name who's been in practice for at least fifteen years, & a man had just phoned *her* to tell her she had lovely breasts. Or breath— I couldn't hear which. Aunt Lily [Lilly Maidment] too, bless her heart. When away we'll have to keep in touch with a lot of people: I'm just thinking of Marjorie King, for instance, who's evidently given us that

picture behind me. And I certainly must keep in touch with Ned [Pratt] & John [Robins]: I hope I'll get a better sense of proportion about my work when I'm away. I wrote fourteen letters.

[471] The [Kemp] family came over in the evening and we all had a chicken dinner got ready by Helen's mother. Harold Whitley came over by himself to say goodbye (Isabelle [Isabel Whitley] was over earlier & offered to drive us to the airport), and the Haddows came in. Helen & her mother worked terrifically hard all day: I helped some, but they were in charge and knew what to do. A lot of my letters were pretty perfunctory and silly, I'm afraid, especially those to Mike [Joseph], Charlie Bell and Davis (Peg Stobie too) which I feel apologetic about.

[472] More about the distinction between repentance & remorse,[414] which are always confused even by those who insist that they're distinguishing them. Remorse is the comparison of one's actual self with an idealized self, of what one actually is with what one naturally might have been. Hence it is a reaction of wounded pride. Repentance is, first, the same dissatisfaction with the actual natural self, but from then on it seeks reality instead of regrets. Writing off the debt of the past (the forgiveness of sins), what powers remain in the present? To write off the debt of the past doesn't annihilate the consequences of the past: it merely adjusts one to the position from which to meet the present. And so to work.

Monday, July 10

[473] We got up early, of course, and headed for more pushing & packing. But Helen had really got things wonderfully well organized, and her family were, as usual, right in there. Isabelle [Isabel Whitley] was over at 10:15 & we bundled into the car (after saying goodbye to Jean Haddow) with six pieces of luggage—our four suitcases (so-called: two overnight bags & a briefcase), a blanket & a hat box. We got out to the airport in good time without the slightest trouble from either immigration or (Canadian) customs. Then we piled into the plane & took off. The plane riding was exactly what I expected it to be except for the slowness with which the patchwork below one moves by. Cruising at 250 m.p.h. one still seems to be motionless compared to a train. There was a tedious wait at Buffalo, partly a matter of lining up for American customs, but we got to Boston without incident & caught a taxi, which took nearly an hour to

get through the heavy traffic from East Boston to Cambridge. The Sindalls were here & waiting. Not a single hitch in the whole trip.

[474] The Sindalls are obviously very kindly & considerate people: he had made out a long & careful list of the difficult points: the fact that the curtains are too short in the upstairs bathtub for showering, for instance. We saw one child, a pudgy girl in her early teens named Susie: there's another girl, seven years old. So the "three bedrooms" dwindled to one bedroom & two children's rooms. However, we can put people up all right. The house is a modern one, but built in a quasi-antique style, with a maid's attic & an enormous fireplace. Clapboard & picket fences, tiny lawn & garden, and a quite interesting looking neighborhood. There's a piano, to my great joy, and the radio is busted—sure sign of a peaceful home. Oil furnace, not that that interests us, a huge & noisy frigidaire. Three damn bathrooms. Sindall gives the meticulous explanations that go with a certain lack of practicality—Reid MacCallum had the same habit.[415] He made some of the furniture, & it does tricks he carefully warned us against.

Tuesday, July 11

[475] The Sindalls pulled out to Gloucester, & we went down to that Viennese place on Brattle Street, where we had an excellent dinner served by a cute little German girl of about seventeen with red hair & freckled nose. Then we walked down to Harvard Square, walked back home, & went to bed. I had a hell of a night: I was evidently far more exhausted than I realized, and my throat gave me by far the worst time I've yet had with it. By six o'clock I felt I'd had enough & tried to get up, but couldn't. Helen got up, though, & made me some coffee, & I slept till about nine. After that I decided I'd better spend my first day at Cambridge in a complete rest. Helen had done all the unpacking before I woke up (I don't know why the hell *she* wasn't the one to be worn out: as I told her, the terrible mental strain of sitting around & watching her work had finally taken its toll) and we went down to open a bank account (there I made my first slip: I went first to a Savings Bank where you can't use cheques, a natural enough mistake for a Canadian, I suppose) and shopped for bedding & groceries, & then came home & stayed there. It rained in the afternoon anyway. While Helen was in Woolworth's I met Helen Willard, the girl at the Fogg we'd taken to lunch last

year. If I keep up this average we'll soon meet everyone we know—
though if I'm alone I probably won't recognize them. I spent the rest of
the day in a Sunday mood—after all we missed Sunday this week, & I
always feel it if I do that—reading a Gilbert & Sullivan collection they
have & telling myself it may be useful for comedy patterns—after all, I
have a most effective spot planned for *The Mikado* in ⅂ [Tragicomedy]
and Aristophanic mimic deaths are fairly frequent—not so damn mimic
either in *The Yeomen of the Guard*. Also Gilbert's use of the law, especially
in *Iolanthe*, where it's the symbol of the world set over against the green
world, will bear looking at. Also the use of doubled leads, as in *Patience*
(where there's some connection with trying to prevent stars from starring & so demanding too much money) reminds one of Terence.

Wednesday, July 12

[476] A dreadfully hot day—I hope the whole summer won't be like
this. Helen decided the first thing to do was to retrieve my hat, which I'd
left on the aeroplane. So we did, taking a considerably longer time over it
than it had taken us on Monday to come from Buffalo. The tube fares are
fifteen cents now. Sindall was in again in the morning & gave us tips on
laundry, milk & other services. We took the tram out here at Mt. Auburn
& our fifteen cents lasted (or should have lasted) until the Maverick tube
station in East Boston, where we got a bus to the airport. On the way
back we stopped in the city to do some shopping. My throat kicked up a
terrific protest and the stores (White's & Jordan Marsh) were very far
from being air-conditioned. We had lunch at the Schraft's on Boylston St.
that we'd eaten our first meal in [in] Boston last summer. That time it
was a wonderful day, we were in great spirits & the place seemed fine,
but today we felt very depressed & irritable with the heat & it seemed
just a noisy & crowded dump.

[477] But we really lit on our feet—the house is cool and inviting and
charming. One feeble attempt to preserve the social decencies: the little
strip of back yard is cut in two by a partition, with the place to garden &
sit out on one side & the drying yard on the other. The little doorway
between is absurdly narrow: I can't get the lawn mower through it. But
the lawn mower is big enough to keep the Harvard University grounds
in trim, let alone this tiny yard, which I've christened witch-Grass Ter-
race.[416] I kept on relaxing, & looked through a song book got out by

Simon & Schuster called something like the Fireside Book—Elizabeth Brown had a copy.[417] Illustrations (colored) & settings both very witty & competent. I wonder how long it would take me to learn to write witty & competent harmonic settings for tunes. Because I still think periodically of my idea of A Musical Companion to English Literature, for which I wouldn't want to be too dependent on an arranger.[418] I wonder too how Helen would do on the illustrating. Just pipe-dreaming, of course, but the tunes in this song book will always be the theme songs of my Guggenheim year—or the ones new to me will.

Thursday, July 13

[478] Today I finally got down to the Library, meeting Hilliard [Trethewey] on the way there and Ruth [Jenking] in the Library itself. Both look very well. I asked Ruth over for the evening, but she couldn't come: she was to spend the evening, very typically of Ruth, in tutoring (free) one of the youngsters in the Chaucer course who was lost on the subject of Chaucer's pronunciation. She's taking four summer courses— Robins told her to observe teaching methods, & she's observing that the teaching methods of Ridley & Magoun are no better than the ones she's worked out for herself. The Library put me through all right: the stalls are filled, but they let me have my stack card & a place to put my books out in the reading room. I wandered around the stacks for some time: it's a hell of a big library, of course, but not a superhuman one, and I think I'll soon get the feel of it. Then I went over to the Lamont Library, which is certainly the beautifully laid out reading room it's advertised as being. I think they've slightly overdone the easy-chair side of the publicity— one young man lay down on the floor for a nap. Two young girls saw him & went all over the library looking for a place to giggle. I was a bit worried, as it was a hell of a hot day and I thought he might just possibly have a heart condition, but when I saw him look at his watch I concluded he was all right. It was, as I say, a very hot day, and as I'd worn a shirt in which Helen had removed the tail to make a new collar, I couldn't take my heavy jacket off. I lost my way coming home: I haven't quite got used to the idea of the wheel-shaped arrangement in Cambridge and took the wrong turning when I finally got to Sparks St. We had dinner at home and Hilliard came in for the evening. This Ancren Riwle job he's laid out for himself is a very nice year's work: it'll take him the whole year, but he can do it quite comfortably in a

year, & he has to go to Paris, Cambridge & Oxford besides Harvard. It's a job he obviously knows exactly how to do: something to do with Anglo-Norman recensions of it.[419]

Friday, July 14

[479] Today was my thirty-eighth birthday. Helen & I went down to the Harvard Co-operative Store (they call & pronounce it the "Harvard Coop") & got me a summer suit & a lot of miscellaneous things, socks, a tie & so on. I tried to join the Coop, but they said no—it's reasonable enough, as I'm not a member of Harvard University, but it would have been ten percent discount. It's a good enough store anyway. I have to get a portable typewriter: I think that's my only major purchase now. Helen doesn't think we saved anything by buying my clothes in the States. We had lunch at Howard Johnson's & came home with our purchases, & then I started out again for the Library. This time I found I'd been assigned a stall, No. 227 on the English Literature stack floor. I'm supposed to share it with somebody called Barnett, but he didn't appear. I stayed in my stall until five, trying to write the opening of my Kenyon Review article, which is a bit speculative. I wrote a lot of rubbish on the theory that I could always cut later. I think the opening will be easy enough: it's the real centre of the article that bothers me.[420] On the way back I stopped at a liquor store & asked if there were any formalities about purchasing liquor. He said the formality consisted only in the possession of cash. Even so I didn't know what to buy, and Canadian rye is $5.75 a bottle—though I think a larger bottle than what we're allowed to buy. I got a cheaper rye for $3.75, a Corby's. I must investigate California wines. We came home & had dinner in, after speculating about going out & deciding to renounce the gesture.

[480] It's important for me to get going on a concentrated job as soon as possible, because travel, which is said to broaden the mind, only flattens mine. The exposure of my naturally introverted mind to a whole lot of new impressions confuses me, because I'm more at home with ideas, I'm not naturally observant, and what impressions I do get are random & badly selected. Also they're compared with the more familiar environment back home and, as I don't know the new environment, the comparison is all out of focus.

Saturday, July 15

[481] Ruth [Jenking] and Hilliard [Trethewey] turned up at nine today, & half an hour later we got started for the beach in Ruth's car. We drove out past a lot of rather dingy looking suburbs: Somerville, Everett, Malden—and then onto a road known as Newberryport Turnpike. We finally got out to a pretty little village called Ipswich, and down a lovely tree-bordered road to the beach. We learned later that the beach, which is called Crane's Beach, is run by a committee in the town with the object of making it a family beach. No dance hall or other means of perverting youth. The beach was kept remarkably clean (the only thing that shocked us was a damn dog, a setter, that came up and shat all over where four very lovely young women had just been lying. And that of course was nobody's fault.) by a little jeep that runs up & down it all day. It was pure white sand, & behind the beach were sand dunes. I don't know how full-sized trees came to be growing within half a mile of the shore on such pure sand, but there they were, & the green & blue & white made a wonderful background for the colored bathing costumes. They looked like fairly well-heeled people who patronized the beach (it cost a dollar per car & I don't see how you could get to it without a car) and the bathing suits were really rich lovely colors—not garish or harsh at all. It got fairly crowded in the afternoon, but not too much so. It was a lovely day—I went in twice, Ruth, who has enough energy for the whole party, about four times. We rented a beach umbrella—two in fact—and I tried to keep covered, as with my blond skin I don't take too well to water, but I got my arms & shins pretty badly burned anyway. I mean sun, not water—I take to that all right, & if I'd been just a little more used to it I'd have gone in oftener. Helen & I bought bathing suits, sun glasses & sunhats—we're spending quite a bit of money, but it's so difficult to know what to take when you don't know what you're going to be in for. Ruth went for a walk along the beach & came back loaded with clam shells & seaweed, like a mermaid. She loves beaches—a student at the summer school had told her about this one.

Sunday, July 16

[482] So we got organized to leave at about five & came home without incident. We stopped at a Howard Johnson's for dinner. Evidently

Howard Johnson is a businessman who runs a restaurant organization as
a sideline. They're all financially on their own: he just supplies the name
& a uniform menu & enforces certain standards. I suppose he collects a
royalty on the name, which isn't impressive. We sat on stools and ate
fried clams, which Ruth & Hilliard pronounced delicious & which Helen
& I didn't go for. I found them greasy & a bit nauseating—too hot a day.
No trouble getting back, but the outskirts of Boston—Malden, Everett,
Somerville, East Cambridge—are grim to behold—*and* to smell. The
dividing line between commercial and fashionable Cambridge is dra-
matically sharp—a single street seemed to do that.

[483] I tried to keep out of the sun to some extent, as I'm not very
friendly to the sun, being a blond. Now *that's* a slip-up in symbolism—
surely the fair-haired & blue-eyed ought to take to the sun instead of
scowling & shuddering away from it. But I stayed under the shade of the
umbrella & kept my clothes on and played in the sand like a baby. So I
got away with badly sunburned forearms and shins. I spent most of the
day nursing a tight skin and reading an enormous collection of short
stories made by Somerset Maugham.[421] I think Sindall must be a Book-
of-the-Month man. But a day in the sun beside the sea was for some
reason exactly what my constitution seemed to be waiting for, as that
infernal tickle in my throat, which was rapidly developing into a kind of
asthma, seems to have cleared up, at least temporarily. The climate is
after all more what I've been used to in the Maritimes, and it seems to be
making its own kind of sense: a hot day, a breeze from the sea, and a rain,
& then the cycle begins again. My feeling of nervous tension is slowly
relaxing—it's very boring to have to concentrate on it, or rather be preoccupied with it. I phoned Ellmann today, & got him, but we didn't
make any arrangements for meeting.

Monday, July 17

[484] Today, feeling full of conscious virtue, I went along to my stall at
the Widener at nine-thirty and found it apparently occupied by the ghost
of Barnett. So I went out into the big reading room, sat down opposite an
attractive young girl reading a book on business cycles, & looking as
though she understood it, and began my first serious effort to write. The
writing went surprisingly well, and by the time Helen came to pick me
up at four-thirty I'd actually completed a draft of the first section (it's

beginning to look as though it will have three parts). On the way out we ran into Jean Hubener, who is leaving for New York. She had a long complex story to tell about how she got the Guggenheim: her publisher got it for her, her application was several months late & she was put on the Canadian list by special arrangement. If she's good it's all right, I suppose, & if Kay [Coburn] and Jessie [Macpherson] are correct in thinking her an utter charlatan, then the Guggenheim people have given way to an enthusiasm that amounts to a kind of insult to Canada. So I hope she'll be all right—besides, she seems to be taking her project seriously enough.[422] I was a bit leery of her at Victoria—she took a great shine to me but I always felt she was trying to get me on her side against others, mainly Alvin Surerus, and she *was* a button-holder.[423] It's better seeing her out of the Victorian context. We went out to a place on Brattle Square to have a couple of beers & a dinner.

[485] I think I may as well come out flat-footed for calling literary criticism a science & go on from there.[424] The damn fools wouldn't listen to me when I expounded the general shape of criticism in the Blake book, so maybe the prospect of their being able to acquire something of the scientist's self respect may make them pick up their unpredestinating ears a bit. So I've got it clear to start with that the transitive learning & teaching process is one of criticism & not one of literature itself. I think I'll play down the verbal universe this time and concentrate on immediate tactical considerations—chiefly a marshalling job, assembling the current critical techniques & seeing how many are still missing.

Tuesday, July 18

[486] On these hot days I think the air-conditioned Lamont is a better place to work, at least until my papers are over. A big library is no good to me now, as I can't read & write at the same time, & this paper in particular I have to make up as I go along. I ran into Hilliard [Trethewey] having a cigarette outside: he seems quite contented sitting on the top floor of the Widener with a microfilm reader and transcribing. He's in a comfortable holiday mood, reacting against domesticity, and obviously loves being alone & grabbing his meals in Mass. Avenue coffeeshops. The Lamont Library is quite a place. Six floors, the top one for "Conference Rooms"—in a democracy they evidently don't admit that anyone gives a lecture. Special reading rooms, one for poetry & one for miscella-

neous male interests, smoking rooms, typing rooms, & other rooms marked printing and (I think) photography. I feel much more reassured by a big working open-shelf library than by the Widener stacks.

[487] The paper is falling into three sections, as I've said. First a general introduction & general harrumph about the general situation. I'm taking a few cracks at logical positivism in order to be able later to clear up the role of logic in the trivium without having to meet this sort of confusion. Also I'm trying to point out the utter unreality of the conflict between the new critics & the old-fashioned inquiries, which is directly on my path, because the reconciling principle is genre, and from genre we get to archetypes. The next two sections outline inductive & deductive methods of reaching these conceptions. The inductive section will show the implications in the current practice of criticism: it will probably refer to Auden's *Enchafed Flood* & to my general point about functional analysis expanding from structural analysis. The deductive section, which I'm trying to start on now, will deal with my own particular points of approach. First the verbal universe (in criticism the postulate of a single totally intelligible form), then a conspectus of archetypes or myths, then a conspectus of genres. The last I shan't get to: that's for another article, while the Blake one may clear up the caboose of this one.[425]

Wednesday, July 19

[488] While having lunch today I ran into Tom Easterbrooks [Easterbrook], who's down here with his wife & family doing what sounds like a sort of project with a group of economic historians here, living in Wellesley for the sake of, I think he said, swimming for the kids. He was taking a nine-year-old named Michael to a ball game. He sounds a bit fed up with the economists he meets here: says they don't know anything but an Americanized version of the Whig interpretation of history, and that their identification of economic laissez faire & political democracy is as naive as one occasionally, out of the field or in Canada, suspects it to be. It looks as though a general level of competent mediocrity, very skilful in techniques & somewhat blinkered in philosophical attitude, were the picture of Harvard right across the board.

[489] I'm trying to work out the ritual & myth section of Part Three now, & have a feeling of wading through glue. One thing I hadn't expected

was the sudden recrudesence of the *Greek* classifications of drama, epic &
lyric instead of my "modern" reclassification of drama, poetry with epic
as the synthetic principle, & prose fiction. The last certainly exists now,
but its origin & derivation from the older one has still to be worked out.
The reason for this was that, in working at ritual & myth, I discovered
that my old simple theory of myth descending from ritual won't work.
Myth is the archetypal combination of ritual and epiphany, which are
the original forms of narrative & significance, the temporal & spatial
recurrences of literature respectively. Behind both ritual & epiphany is
the unfallen world which here is split between the "real" world of
experience & the desirable world of the dream. I can't say all that yet, I
suppose. So there are *two* tables to be put in, one of narrative, which is
the quest of the hero, and one of images—which, by the way, are the
corresponding worlds of innocence and experience. The former is the
final cause of art, leading, in so far as finality implies futurity, to a
Marxist conception of art as the vision of the goal of social work, such as
Hopwood had in mind.[426]

Thursday, July 20

[490] I seem to have taken to working rather neurotically at my paper. I
plod out in the morning, go out for lunch, and by four (I seem unable to
write much after four) I discover the whole day has gone and I've
accomplished very little. Today was a day of utter & absolute frustration:
I tried to rewrite the second part & got involved with a long and boring
conceit about a student finding that his learning processes were forming
archetypes out of impressions, and it's all horseshit. At best a single
paragraph. I don't know whether an occasional day like this is inevitable
or whether I could (& if I could I sure as hell should) develop a technique
of recognizing & cutting a pure loss. Of course I was really being a sort of
Childe Roland about the paper: I had no notion of where the hell I was
going when I started it.

[491] My recurrent suspicion, in fact a generally accepted realization up
to the end of 1949, that the prelude setting forth the new critical techniques in studying Spenser is actually going to form a book of its own is
slowly taking hold of me again. It looks as though I were getting the
sense of an expanding body of criticism. In the article it's going to be
concentric: rhetoric first, the structural analysis of the text, flanked by

grammar (i.e. philology) on one side and logic, the semantic pattern of imagery, on the other. Then a functional analysis in which grammar expands into history, leading to Spenglerian containing forms, and logic into philosophy, leading in particular to the Thomist real universal. Then an analysis in terms of the verbal universe, in which grammar & logic meet behind & form the general structure of symbolic forms. These are flanked by two new critical disciplines: critical anthropology, which deals with ritual, & critical psychology, which deals with dream & other patterns of archetypal significance. I introduce these new disciplines, but perhaps not very coherently. Too many ideas: for instance, just as the humanistic dialectic of criticism isn't purely Marxism, so there may be a theology which isn't just anti-Marxist & is a science without being essentially a rationalization of a certain kind of human institution.

Friday, July 21

[492] The gang arrived last night at about a quarter to two. It sure as hell doesn't agree with me to miss my beauty sleep: I wasn't only sleepy, but dizzy & rather sick. However, we got them all stowed away, somehow or other. The Kemps on the sofa in the living room which opens out into a bed (and I gather an uncomfortable one, with a ridge in the middle), Jean [Elder] in little Joan's room, & her father in Susie's. The Elder's brought their own bedding & the Kemps an old auto rug. Apparently they had quite a good trip from Kingston: they went across the border at Gananoque, had dinner on Wolfe Island & spent the night at Watertown. They didn't get far because they didn't start till five and there was a detour. Next day Jean took them over a mountain (Whiteside, I think) which scared them all out of their growth but thrilled them too, & drove through Vermont & New Hampshire, coming into Boston through Lawrence. They got to Harvard Square & picked up a police car, who gave them an escort to Fenway Street.[427] Damn decent of them, but New Englanders have a reputation for being hospitable to strangers. The Kemps, as I expected, didn't go for the Cambridge practice of using nothing but elm trees for privacy, but they turned out the lights.

[493] Today the general bustle & confusion of a large party set in, but everybody was very tired after the long ride, & sat around & snoozed most of the day. Helen's father read Weininger's *Sex & Character*, which Sindall has in his library, & decided, no doubt correctly, that it was a silly

book. Jean took us for a ride into downtown Boston: she drives very well, but says there are hardly any traffic rules in Boston, & nobody observes them anyway. There are a lot of one-way streets, though: however, I got her piloted, with the aid of a map, into downtown Boston, and we went to see Louisburg Square and the Beacon Hill area. Most of the company was too tired to take anything in, and it's curious how even the grace & dignity of metropolitan Boston seems to dwindle in size when one speeds past it in a car. New York is the only city really built for an automobile's perspective—not that it's worth having.

Saturday, July 22

[494] Today we got in touch with Ruth [Jenking] & with the two cars we made an expedition to Lexington. It was a beautiful day, if somewhat hot. We went to three museums in turn, all much the same. (Actually all this "historical interest" stuff is pure nostalgia: people go to see the Longfellow House down here because Longfellow, like Caesar, was an inferior writer who wrote for the Lower School, & they feel sentimental over childhood associations.) The first, run by two old ladies, was Buckman's Tavern, something of a Colonial headquarters, I gathered. The original door was there, with the inevitable bullet-hole; the fireplace had been restored, & there were flintlocks, which fascinated Helen's father, old pistols, lanterns, bottles, farm & household implements, & generally all the litter of an antiquarian museum. The next place was John Hancock's house, where Paul Revere stopped in his highly publicized ride. Here we were taken in tow by an old girl whom Jean described as the best guide she'd ever seen, though she was a bit too obtrusive for my taste. She showed us the very drum that made the first Revolutionary noise, the bed two women were sleeping in on that great night, the table where John Hancock & Samuel Adams rested their consecrated elbows & talked rebellion, & so on & so on. I was not in the least surprised to find that she was an ex-Canadian. Her sidekick had started us off, but this dame pushed her out of the way—the tension between the two women was amusing. She had a very school-teachery manner and the way she put us through the Hancock pedigree was really something. Also, of course, the apparatus of turnspits, churns, spinning wheels, leather fire buckets, samplers, poke bonnets, & other relics of expired housewifery & husbandry. The third place was Monroe Tavern, the British headquarters. Here a man was in charge, a very

pleasant man too, who used exactly the opposite technique. As the
Monroe family still runs it, I thought he might be a late & not great
Monroe who needed a job &, like Henry Adams, was prevented from
getting complete freedom by an illustrious name. However, that's only a
guess: I just wondered because he was so civilized a type. Also, I'd be
curious to know how far the grotesque ancestor-worship in this country
really extends, & what sort of social patterns it traces.

Sunday, July 23

[495] Anyway, the original Monroe was a Scottish baron taken prisoner
at Worcester & sold into slavery in Virginia: I hadn't heard of white
slavery before except in the West Indies. Apparently you were inden-
tured & got money & could buy your freedom (it took Monroe seven
years), but lost all your civil rights in the meantime. We saw a list of rules
of the tavern—no more than five in a bed, tinkers & peddlers in the
outhouses, no boots to be worn in bed, & the like. He showed us old
doors with hinges made in the shape Ͱ, for, he said "Holy Lord"
(perhaps Aaron's "Holiness to the Lord") to keep off evil spirits, & the
cross in the panelling for the same purpose. I knew about the fear of
ghosts & witches in New England, but hadn't expected to find an
apotropaic cross among Puritans.

[496] Then we went on to Walden Pond for a picnic lunch. We had an
enormous supply of food (Helen's mother had bought and cooked a
fifteen-pound turkey) and drink (Ruth brought along a great supply of
soft concoctions). Walden Pond is a quite busy resort now, & very pretty
it is too, although the atmosphere is not exactly Thoreauish. (Nobody
knows exactly where his hut stood.) There was a big crowd of picnickers
and swimmers, and an abundant supply of life guards. (a sudden drop
in the level near the shore makes it a bit dangerous for wading children).

[497] Today Helen & I went over to the Harvard Yard with her father &
mother & we showed them all the buildings we knew, which weren't
many. It was very hot, and we came home in a taxi, to their great relief.
Elder & Jean[428] in the mean time had gone to the Swedenborgian church
over at Quincy Street. After lunch we let the afternoon go: a party of six
in which three are women and two of the men old & deaf is extraordinarily cumbersome to manoeuvre. We had an idea that the Harvard

museum closed at five, but it closes at four-thirty, which was exactly the time we arrived. I got a bit irritable, though I trust I didn't show it, with all the frustrating & clashing rhythms of such a group, beginning with an inconclusive argument about what we're to go [to] & ending with the five of us sitting in the car & waiting for poor old Elder to finish a shit.

Monday, July 24

[498] Anyway—that's the second day I've started with that word—it was a beautiful evening, & I proposed driving out to the sea coast. I had Salem in mind, but for some reason I changed my mind & steered Jean to Marblehead instead. We went through Revere & got an appalling glimpse of a really crowded beach: enormously mis-shapen figures in far too revealing clothes, dirt, horrible food, noise & stench, and a nakedness which it troubled me to be shocked at, because I thought if it weren't prudery it must be snobbery. It was primarily a vision of the Yahoo in human nature. Well, we got from Revere into a respectable middle-class district, where I had no more sense of the Yahoo. Marblehead looked very quaint & pretty in the soft evening light—I gather it's an old fishing town now turned into a tourist & more or less wealthy resort, where they still remember that they once fished. We had dinner at a middling restaurant, where I ordered a waffle and got three hunks of wall board. The others filled up on seafood.

[499] Today I went again to the Lamont Library & worked until shortly after lunch, & then began to organize my instruments of production. First of all I went and rented a typewriter—a very heavy old Royal, $8.25 for three months. Then I got paper & bought a new fountain pen that actually writes. These sound like small matters, as filling a cavity in a fast-rotting tooth might be a small matter, but they were important to me. The Sindalls came in, looking very contented with being at Glouces- ter & having us here. Helen took her father through Harvard, including the three libraries. The woman in charge of the Keats collection at the Houghton seems to have given him the works: he mentioned me & she's going to put him on the mailing list for bulletins. Also he saw the glass flowers[429] & the Longfellow House. He had a wonderful time: I think the fact that Helen's mother hasn't any cultural interests encourages him in a certain inertia, but being alone with Helen he was able to remember that

he's an educated man & enjoy it. Jean & Helen's mother went to the
department stores & Elder poked off by himself & showed what to me
was surprising resourcefulness. A very successful day.

Tuesday, July 25

[500] Today I luxuriated in my typewriter: the first part of the article is
in pretty fair shape, as I see it—and for the first time I can see it. I stayed
home while the others went out. Helen took her father & mother to the
Museum & then to the Gardner Museum—they liked the latter better, as
I'd more or less expected. This time the treatment didn't work so well—
as I suspected, Helen's mother was a slightly subduing influence—she's
a very game sport, but her feet get tired. At four-thirty I joined them in
the cocktail bar at the Kenmore, after a late (4 p.m.) lunch. They were
very ready to sit down, and of course the Kemps can always get drunk
on pure excitement. The hostess, who had an extraordinary Jewish Yankee accent, came around & jollied Helen's father a good deal, which
tickled everybody. We got out of there and drove to the T wharf for
dinner. Sometimes I don't know what to make of Jean—she seems to get
perverse or naughty-girl streaks, & when she does she wrecks the nerves
of everybody in her car by the way she drives—I know she doesn't
wreck the car too, but why she doesn't I don't know. She drove through
a red light on Harvard Square Sunday in one of those moods, & tonight
there were two near-accidents as she took her hands off the wheel and
turned around to speak to people in the back seat. However, the dinner
and its location were a success: the wharf was smelly, but hearty. We
drove through South Boston & saw a big new housing development,
then home through downtown Boston, where the Kemps, with nervousness & the winding streets & darkness & claustrophobia, suddenly got
tired and fractious, like children. We came home just as Elder was
turning in the gate. He'd been out to see young Knox & his wife—he
didn't know I knew Knox, but of course I remember very well his
coming to see me last year.[430] The cocktails & dinner cost me seventeen
dollars, but it's something Helen has had in her mind for a long—
perhaps years—and it's fun for us if they're enjoying themselves, as I
think they are. Jean is much fonder of her father than I realized, and he's
getting about very cheerfully & pursuing his own interests. It'll be a
great deal harder when my own immobile family descends on us, as I
expect them to do sometime next month.

Wednesday, July 26

[501] Today was a day of relaxation for everybody: Jean took her father through M.I.T., and was prodigiously impressed by the "plant." I must go and see it too: I suppose it's far more impressive physically than Harvard, which would probably seem pretty run down to anybody but an impoverished Canadian. Even Lamont Library might not be so wonderful to somebody from Ann Arbor or Wisconsin, to say nothing of California. These reflections were stimulated by the fact that Dick Ellmann dropped in tonight. He'd left a note in my stall, but of course I hadn't been there. Now Ellmann is quite one of the best younger people at Harvard, & he could surely use a good offer to get permanent tenure here & a substantial promotion. Well, he got the offer—a full professorship at Northwestern, by no means the best of the Middle Western universities. So off he goes next year to Northwestern: it evidently didn't occur to him to try to stay here. I'm gradually coming to realize that Harvard is a place where there is a great library and a great tradition. But in English it's just one more English department, & I gather it's much the same elsewhere. Now education is clearly a major New England industry, & if one of its chief centres is willing to rest on its laurels I don't know how long the whole structure can last—except, of course, for expensive playgrounds like Wellesley & Dartmouth, where the professor's social position can hardly be much more than a head waiter's. I think it's a good thing that there's no "best" English department & no centre of English studies, but I also feel that the Department of English at the University of Toronto is not so damn bad a place to be. I must find out more about this: at times, in my delusions of grandeur, I wonder if the world of English scholars isn't waiting for someone, maybe me, to give them a lead. Here at Harvard the best man is Bush, an excellent man in his own somewhat limited way, then there's Sherburn, obviously a stuffed shirt, Ridley, an Oxford cast-off, and that poor lunatic Magoun to sustain the magnificent linguistic tradition of fifty years ago. Spencer & Matthiessen are dead, Ellmann leaving, & Levin's in Comparative Literature. It doesn't add up to anything very impressive.

Thursday, July 27

[502] Well, the party ended this afternoon & Jean's car drove off. They're headed for Roy's [Roy Kemp's] place in Vermont—there was some

complication about it suggesting that Roy had encountered another of those irresponsible infants he seems to attract, but this was cleared up in another letter. They didn't actually have to leave until tomorrow, but they were all set for leaving, & Helen's father spent the morning packing & strapping a bag & then unstrapping it as more things had to go in. He has some sort of neurosis about straps & packing, even with no train to catch. On the whole it's been a most successful week from the entertaining point of view.

[503] I was particularly glad to have a talk or two with old Elder. He's not an impressive man, being old (82), deaf, a button-holer & a face-breather-into, and with an Andy Gump face (the phrase "weak chin" seems to be one of the bits of popular phrenology that are still kicking around) and a fussy & indecisive manner. I set down all these trivia to account for a certain impatience in my own attitude to him. But he certainly is no fool. He's a self-converted Swedenborgian, but is very chagrined to find that the Swedenborgians are stuck in exactly the same middle-class mudhole as all the other sects. So, at 82, he's busy trying to get the Swedenborgians concerned with social reform. They seem unusually stuffy even for a sect: as Swedenborg's own attitude was apocalyptic, the organization of their church was half-hearted from the start, & now it's a dwindling body that has very little to appeal to younger men like Knox. So Elder keeps attending Swedenborgian conferences & forcing them, with many sighs & groans & expressions of reluctance, to admit that the world still exists in an unsatisfactory state. He gets them to pass resolutions, then forces them to dig out the resolutions & form a Social Action Committee, then forces the damn Committee to bring in some sort of report. Very uphill work. His other passion is Henry George, whom he connects very ingeniously with the doctrine of correspondence. The church in the spiritual world is a community, and so the material church body, which he equates with the land, should be a communal possession too.

Friday, July 28

[504] My Canadian mail is beginning to trickle through now, & I've had two letters reacting to my radio talks. One was from an English teacher in Buffalo, who said he'd made tape recordings of them, and had listened to them several times to use for teaching purposes. He's a Catholic,

& disagrees with me on Swift's view of original sin as orthodox. The other was from a poor mad creature in Sydney who'd been fired from a high-school teaching job in 1916 & had woven it into a complex occult fantasy. Some sort of numerology connected with chess and some Chinese thing she calls wun-tzu—I wonder if someone's playing a joke on her, as it sounds like the "Wun hung" type of joke.[431] I always try to reply to such people, as they're dreadfully lonely, and usually I can catch a glimmer of reason, or at least something I can put into a sane formula, but this time I can't get even a glimmer. Poor old soul. I wonder why they seek me out.

[505] Everything very quiet today with the company gone: I stayed home all day and typed. I've moved into Susie's room, where there's a desk. I finally got the damn thing done at eleven at night—twenty-three pages. The third part is still a bit spotty, but on the whole it's worked out, I think. We strolled down to the Vienna place (the Window Shop) for dinner. I find the food there excellent, though Dick Ellmann doesn't think so much of it. We were outside and it almost rained, but held off. Staying around Kenway Street does impress one rather with domesticity—there are *so* many squalling kids about & so little else doing.

[506] I keep avoiding the news & dodging my civic responsibilities as an essential part of having a year "off." But the Korean business was a fiendishly clever move: the Russians sitting in a huge land mass able to strike anywhere, the democracies having to run around everywhere from Germany to Korea to patch things up (I must read McKinder),[432] the prestige situation so bad that probably all the intelligent South Koreans regard the Americans as the real invaders, and a hopeless military situation that makes it as bad for the Americans as, say, the Boer War was for the British Empire.

Saturday, July 29

[507] Today Ruth [Jenking] came in her car to take us out to Ipswich again. We got started at about nine-thirty, me with a completed MS I wanted very badly to mail. The stationer's shops on Harvard Square were all closed for the weekend, so we got on our way and we picked up envelopes in a place in Everett. Then we discovered that the post offices were all closed for the weekend too, but fortunately found one open in

Ipswich, so away it went. We went through the old 1642 house we'd seen earlier from the road, and it turned out to be utterly charming: far more appealing for some reason than the Lexington places. Well, there's less school book documentary about it.

[508] When I was about seven years old our family acquired a book of duets, of which the most difficult & attractive was called the Agawam Quickstep. This did nothing but register on my infantile consciousness, and when I came to teach American literature I found that the two seventeenth-century people who struck me as having most on the ball were Nathaniel Ward, who wrote *The Simple Cobbler of Agawam*, and Anne Bradstreet. Now I discover that this pretty little town of Ipswich was originally called Agawam, & that Ward & she were among the original settlers. It's difficult to say what simple pleasure it gave me to discover this. They had reprints of *The Simple Cobbler* for sale at a dollar & I bought one. The woman who showed us over was an admirable cicerone & besides had braided the biggest damn braided rug I ever saw in my life. Well, the stuff in the museum was the regular stuff, but, as she said, it was over fifty years ago that they decided to add it up, & so it's better integrated than most of these vague shrines. We went out & had lunch at a very good restaurant—clam chowder with Ipswich clams & homemade pies. I like Ipswich: it has traditions, but it obviously has morale besides. So it was pretty late before Ruth could get her swim. Hot as hell, & as we got there late we had to wait for an umbrella. I went for one swim, but my constitution is still haywire: my hands froze & wouldn't warm up. I wish I could get several days of swimming in succession. But even wiggling one's toes in the sand is relaxing enough, besides all those lovely American bodies to look at.

Sunday, July 30

[509] We drove home and had a quick and somewhat inadequate dinner on a stool: I hate eating on stools. Then Ruth drove us out to Wellesley to see the Easterbrooks. Tom had given me most careful directions & if I'd stuck to them, and to the turnpike road, I'd have been all right. But we turned off at the Wellesley sign, and wandered all over the infernal town for nearly an hour & asked at least two dozen people where to go. A cop & a nine-year-old boy finally got us there: Tom's house, 44 Brookfield Rd., was a separate one detached from the street itself of that name & stuck away down off another street.

[510] So Ruth went off home, bless her heart, & we walked into the Easterbrook's front parlor, where a huge television set was in operation. Michael, who'd been promised he could stay up till nine listening to some damn programme or other, was quite sullen to us because he wanted to hear his programme. So we went out with Mrs. E., whose name I think is Dorothy, to find Tom, who in the meantime had missed *his* way & gone off to Worcester, or rather toward Worcester. Then he took us around the Wellesley campus, which looked a little like a more expensive Mount Allison,[433] & when we got back there was only about fifteen minutes left of the programme. They are in a great big house, tastelessly furnished in a flamboyant Jewish way—the man's name is Buxbaum—but extremely convenient for them. The Easterbrooks impressed me as being in a bit of a rut—he said all over again what he'd said at lunch a few days ago, and she seems absorbed in shopping and bargains—but I suppose that's inevitable in a situation involving small children. We got the bus home all right—the last one.

[511] Today was dreadfully hot: I sat around panting all morning and Ruth [Jenking] came around again in the afternoon to take us to the Museum. I don't know why altogether: none of us wanted to go, but Ruth is so bored with her courses that she seems to need a conscious effort to break her routine on weekends. We only lasted about an hour, and spent most of that time close to the exit.

Monday, July 31

[512] There was an exhibition of Daumier drawings, which I liked very much. A man beside me who said "misanthrope" irritated me—people *do* think in such sentimental stereotypes. What's misanthropic about sharp observation and humorous comment? I also saw contemporary American painting, which continues to bore me—more sentimental stereotypes. It's all so photographic—not in technique but in conception. The same deliberately picturesque or obviously epigrammatic subjects, usually with a corny title attached, that one gets at photographic exhibitions. Like a series of New Yorker covers without detachment or humor. Maybe I was just hot: I didn't get much out of a room of Rembrandt etchings either. The next time I go I shall make for the archaeology.

[513] We staggered back—Ruth wouldn't come in—and drank iced tea until it was time to go to the Ellmann's for dinner. They live in an

apartment near Mass. Avenue. George Williamson of Chicago, who's here doing a summer course, was there: I don't know where I got the impression he was English. I got American hospitality with a vengeance—four drinks (different kinds of drinks, I mean) and a wonderful shrimps-and-rice dinner. Mary Ellmann is an English Ph.D. & teaches at Wellesley. Williamson is a bit on the dull side, which meant a great deal of gossip—Chicago must be a hotbed of it, whatever a hotbed is. Crane, McKeon, the Inquisition, & above all E.K. Brown, who evidently has a national reputation as a man on the make. Some talk about Magoun and a curious story of a Jew who seemed to be something of a masochist & wrote a book on Céline.[434] We stayed until one—I don't quite know why except that of course I liked my surroundings. I told Mary all about Canada & wound up by getting into an argument over teaching methods. I said the teacher wasn't concerned with saying what he liked & disliked, but with isolating the permanent reality of what he was talking about, even it he hated it as much as I hate [Carlyle's] *Past & Present*.

Tuesday, August 1

[514] Yesterday it was as hot as hell and today it rained, so I stayed here both days. Not wise: I get involved in taking care of Helen & don't keep my mind driving ahead. I've been reading a long & tiresome book by somebody in New York University—Holzknecht—on what he calls the "backgrounds" of Shakespeare's plays.[435] It's a useful compilation of Shakespearean scholarship, but he has no critical ability whatever—for some reason there seems to be a quite sharp cleavage between scholarship & criticism in the study of Shakespeare. The mark of the earnest & unimaginative teacher is over it: he rides the "healthy & normal" stuff to death, &, as his introduction makes clear, is writing for a lumbering hawbuck of an undergraduate who'd much rather play football. So his chapter on Shakespeare's English, which is otherwise quite good, hasn't a syllable about the important & extensive subject of Shakespeare's bawdy. Whenever he touches on intangibles, like internal evidence in dating the plays, he's lost, & even when he tries to contrast Elizabethan & Jacobean he does it in terms of the characters of the two sovereigns, which he oversimplifies to an absurd degree: he calls James "squalid" twice, whatever that means—I think he just doesn't know the words. I have to review it for whatever journal is published in Washington.

[515] I've also got Ruth Wallerstein's book,[436] but have only read bits of

it. I ought to be very excited about it, because so far as I know it's the first real attempt to incorporate the anagogic tradition of biblical scholarship into English literary criticism, and of course I want to read it very carefully. But she seems bemused by the apparatus of scholarship, & as I read the text it seems to keep going out of focus in a curious way. One of the great mysteries to me is the way people can move nimbly & sensitively over an area of ideas like a blind man, aware of every nuance of texture and fibre & yet unable to see what is there. I am almost the only critic I know who can really see criticism, and, like the man in H.G. Wells's very profound story about the seeing man in the blind community,[437] I find myself isolated with my superior power instead of being able to benefit others directly with it.

Wednesday, August 2

[516] Went to the library and came back to find Helen somewhat depressed as a result of going to see the landlady the Goudges had stayed with & finding the place pretty awful. As she said, the Goudges had said she was like somebody out of Dickens but they didn't say which chapter. Meanwhile I'd got interested in a sequel to the archetype paper—one on genres this time—and got a little way into it, but it's foolish to postpone the Blake with the sneezon coming up in two weeks.[438] We had Hilliard [Trethewey] in for dinner. He enjoys his life here, I think: it's outwardly dull, but he's an introvert & likes it that way. I like talking about French literature to Hilliard: he's a very ordinary mind, of course, but he knows it & on the other hand is genuinely interested in his subject. I think I had at least as good a conversation with him as I had with Williamson, who has a big reputation. Hilliard's mother is probably dying, which adds to his worries.

[517] I don't know why I seem to have developed a nervous habit of going out to piddle every hour or so. Every time I enter the men's can there are at least two doors shut & people sitting & presumably straining inside. But so far I haven't heard a single plop or even smelled a smell, and I deduce that academic constipation is as common in the land of the free as everywhere else.

[518] The news from the family is disturbing. Dad, of course, is very anxious to come down & stay with Lilian [Noyes] in Lowell. That I could manage, but Vera is apparently in really bad shape. She got a bad

diagnosis at the hospital & has to go in again for an operation. They don't seem to know anything about backs—they talk about a lot of discs missing and "damage" to the back—I don't know when she did it any damage. Things don't sound quite as serious as they were last year, but you never can tell. She still speaks of coming here, but I've given that up. And I don't really much want to have Dad come down just at this time, as it's just possible that one of us will have to go to Chicago. And I know damn well he hasn't written Lilian a line, & she won't have the faintest inkling that he'd be coming.

[519] In Cambridge garbage is fed to pigs, & has to be distinguished from "trash." To distinguish them you have to decide whether you'd eat it or not if you were a pig.

Thursday, August 3

[520] Today was devoted to house-hunting. We started off with the Commander Hotel, where the Ellmann's had told us we might get a self-contained suite for $105 per month, but the lowest they had was $175. Damn dull, too. I suggested looking in on the Brattle Inn to see what they had, and they showed us a room at 6, Story St., on the ground floor, now occupied by Jessica Tandy and her husband, whose name is Cronin [Cronyn], now at the Brattle Thea-tre (the hyphen corresponds to the housekeeper's pronunciation). We have the ground floor except for her room—her name's Baillio, and she's clearly a good sort. The bathroom is private: the cooking arrangements exceedingly primitive. Good furniture, & rather too much of it.

[521] In the afternoon we went to look at a room on Garfield St., where a young couple named Leipholz are trying to sublet. There the cooking arrangements were slightly better (gas stove) and it was only $100, but Helen had pretty clearly settled for the Brattle Inn. The Garfield place was built in a bad pretentious period, & the place, though very clean, smelled of suburbia and seemed more a place for young graduates. We liked the Leipholz couple. The girl works at Filene's[439] to help with the rent: he's a graduate student in Fine Art & is interested in religious architecture—going to do a text-book on it. I gave him an invitation to look me up at Toronto. I was sorry to disappoint them, though I don't suppose the disappointment really amounted to much. Anyway, we

went back to the Brattle Inn and signed up with the owner, a Mrs. Groves. She seems all right—Helen liked her better than I did—and has a son-in-law doing anthropology at Dartmouth who—I think she said—has dug up (alive) 800 Beothuks[440] in the wilds of Newfoundland. He'd also done important digging in Alaska—seems to have a nose for it. Well, we settled, as I say, & have about fifty bucks to live on for about three weeks. So our housing problem is settled until March & we're paid up till October. It was another emotional debauch for Helen, and I'm glad it's over.

Friday, August 4

[522] The mail brought a letter from a man at Pennsylvania saying he was bringing a friend to the Institute who's doing a Blake handbook. I was going to put a summary of Blake's symbolism on the blackboard, but if I do all this goon has to do is copy it down & there's the hardest part of his book done, the sales of which would then proceed to undercut mine. Damn these textbook vampires; I have to watch my step.

[523] Ruth [Jenking] came around at noon after lunch and we piled into her car and started south. We got to Plymouth in good time and went to see the damn rock. A man who looked about as Puritan as Mickey Rooney was there, dressed up in a pink & black outfit that was evidently supposed to be 17th c. & gave a lecture on it. The lecture wasn't bad, but the general approach struck me as somewhat phoney. Plymouth was an attractive enough town, but there didn't really seem to be so much to see there. There was a replica of a 1620 hut which struck me as somewhat dubious in details—I suppose it wasn't though. It was a beautiful day, and we breezed on to Cape Cod in wonderful spirits. We crossed a huge bridge over a canal to get to it and made for Wood's Hole.

[524] Wood's Hole was a very pretty little village, the place where the boats come & leave for Martha's Vineyard & Nantucket. It's also a fisheries centre & is full of marine scientists. But there was one disappointment, chiefly for Ruth, who's crazy about fish. When she was here last there was a big aquarium full of very rare deep-sea fish, which she said opened up a whole new world of beauty—it would, too. But we gathered that that had been mostly destroyed in a couple of hurricanes, & all that was left was a tiny series of local fish & crabs. That was

interesting & amusing enough, of course, but nothing like what we were all set for. However, we had dinner there & went to look for rooms. We got a room with a Mrs Stuart, who we decided was a typical Cape Cod Yankee. She's a Canadian, from Montreal. Ruth got a place around the corner. There was a pretty little arm of the sea outside the house, a bright half-moon, and a pleasant view of an extraordinary number of well-kept lawns, recently painted houses & carefully clipped hedges.

Saturday, August 5

[525] Another beautiful day. We had a lousy breakfast & then a cup of coffee with Ruth at a far better place. Ruth slept in, for which we were rather glad, as her terrific energy is somewhat abashing. We left Wood's Hole & drove along the south shore of Cape Cod through a countryside that remained almost excessively prosperous looking. We stopped at Hyannis & had lunch there, & Helen & Ruth went around to look at the shops. Everything was geared for tourists, but in a nice way, and the town was clearly one of America's playgrounds. Girls in shorts—I re-marked to Ruth that girls in shorts never got to the point of losing their self-consciousness, and she said they had no intention of doing so. She's a bit fed up with the way the kids she has to live with in her summer school residence behave—they have no supervision as Harvard doesn't want to spend money on a summer school that's only intended to make it. However: we went through an unusually fine antique shop—well, it sold interior decorations generally—every third house on Cape Cod has a sign saying antiques, some that Helen spotted having the paint still fresh on them. This shop follows the tourist trade around to Florida for the winter and reposes on Newbury Street in Boston in between seasons.

[526] On our way up the coast we stopped to look at an old grist mill, built in 1700, with huge wooden greased wheels and a windmill. I couldn't make much out of the machinery without seeing it operate, but it looked impressive enough. Up the coast the country became sandier & the vegetation scrubbier; the sea appeared more frequently and sand dunes appeared. Then Provincetown. We enjoyed driving slowly along the very narrow street: there's nothing like a narrow street to heighten a sense of festivity—but then we dismounted & walked through it, & the illusion of gaiety and brilliance vanished. It was nothing but a horrid little midway, the stores full of junk & the people looking rather gross.

A large number of quiet middle-aged Negroes, obviously at some convention, made things look a little better, but it was as discouraging to us as the sand and scrub must have been for the Pilgrims, who first landed there.

Sunday, August 6

[527] We stopped and looked at the sea, but decided to get the hell out of Provincetown. Seeing somebody eating a purple ice-cream cone was the last straw for me. We drove back along the north shore to East Sandwich, where Ruth had spent two weeks ten years ago, & finally found a place to stay at a rambling old house off the road. The people had turned what was obviously a big clothes closet into an extra room, which Ruth got: we took the main room with its double bed. The walls were an electric blue & the furniture was all crowned with huge mirrors six feet from the floor. Then we went & had dinner: the first we went to was called the Yankee Clipper & Ruth walked out of it—thought it was too well named. We had to go back to the Cambridge before we found one that looked all right.

[528] Sandwich is supposed to be famous for glass, but all we saw was junk. It was raining so we had to cancel our plans for a morning on the beach & I proposed going home through New Bedford. We stopped to look at a fish hatchery on the way, a very small one, for rainbow & brown trout. We went through the canal again, or rather across it, & on to New Bedford, which reminded me—I don't know why—of the Maritimes, especially Saint John & Halifax. It also looked as though its prosperous days were over, as I gather they are. We had lunch at a quite good Chinese place: the waitress was a laconic woman whom Ruth tried to ask about local sights, but all she knew about the museum was that it was open. Ruth said: "We're going to see the Museum this afternoon," & the waitress said "You can dear." After a tremendous feed of chow mein & fried rice we went to see the Seaman's Bethel that comes into *Moby Dick*, & were shown around by an old sailor from the hostel next door that was built in the eighteenth century. It was just what Melville said it was, a plain little wooden church, Methodist, I think, with plaques along the wall to the memory of sailors drowned at sea. Negroes were all called Kanaka. Some of the verses had real feeling, & the whole effect was one of great simplicity & charm. The main auditorium is up a storey: they meet in the basement when it's too cold in the winter.

Monday, August 7

[529] The whaling museum was dusty, dirty, junky & badly labelled: it was run by a local antiquarian society with very little money and had to accept every footling thing that a local resident wanted to get rid of—but for all that it had very good stuff in it and a good director would really do something with it. It was popular enough anyway. A model of a whaling bark, three-masted & half size—it was a little disconcerting to go prowling through the galley & bunks multiplying everything by two, but I got a very clear impression of it, I think. Around the walls were whaling apparatus & pieces of whale's skeletons, & in gallery rooms there were replicas of cooperage & shops & rigging lofts that would have been more interesting to me with a bit more information about them. A large collection of "scrimshaw," which apparently is carved whalebone, & odds & ends of seafaring litter.

[530] We went on to Providence & looked at Brown University, which seemed charming & rather small stuff. The surroundings reminded me vaguely of McGill for some reason. I liked the look of Providence, & want to go back there: it had the appearance of a community as solid & well integrated as Boston, with the advantage of being relatively small. We had a look too at the Rhode Island School of Design, where Alford & his second wife are—she's "acting director," we saw from a notice. We went into the museum, but it was ten to five then, & we had time for only the briefest glance. It looked like a tiny but exquisitely exhibited collection—a teaching collection with a bit of everything in it—what they had got lots of space & good backgrounds—black velvet, I think, for the Greek vases. Some famous impressionist pictures I saw in passing—two Renoirs & a Degas particularly. In contrast to the whaling museum, it was deserted. I wonder if it's the only Providence Museum—probably, as after all it's a small town. The surroundings of Providence aren't impressive: Fall River, which we passed through on the way there, is more depressed & down at the heels than Lowell, & Pawtucket & East Providence aren't much better. I must find out what happened to that part of the country. Such a contrast to the superb park land along the road to Boston.

Tuesday, August 8

[531] I wish I'd never undertaken to write a paper on Blake: it's like wading through glue and I can't seem to get on with it. The previous

paper had the excitement of discovery about it nearly all the way—it kept surprising me by what it turned up and it pretty well tore the balls out of my next book. But the next job is a paper on the morphology of poetry, & this damn thing is on an uneasy boundary line between them, continually overlapping with both. As I work along it, I naturally discover very little, as the whole surrounding territory has been surveyed thoroughly long ago. I'm working out a fair enough popular exposition of the central myth, but that isn't directly on the treatment of the archetype. I need ten pages at least to outline my theory of the archetype, which would only rehash the article I've just done & give a scrambled & confused notion of it at that; then ten pages to give my exposition of Blake, then ten pages to work out the different archetypes, or rather fifteen pages with a five-page summary & conclusion. Forty pages to write a bad article with all its real points made better elsewhere. I can't possibly go beyond twenty pages & would much rather do it in, say, twelve.

[532] Well, as I see it, Blake gives us four archetypal moods or states in which poetry can be written. These are the moods of Eden, Beulah, Generation & Ulro: the dithyrambic, or song of rapture; the idyllic, or song of innocence; the elegiac, or song of experience, & the satiric, or song of discontent. Such moods are tonalities: you don't keep to them all through a poem any more than you stay in C minor all through a piece in C minor—but you resolve on them. The satire, incidentally, is too specifically identified as a song of discontent: it's really a song of isolation or detachment. The four moods are actually four degrees of detachment, the lowest or zero point being the total identification of the poet with his environment. This really does begin to make sense of some of my "lyric" yammerings.

Wednesday, August 9

[533] I met the Ellmanns on the street today & as I was talking to them a beautiful looking boy passed & they called to him & asked him to meet a namesake. He turned out to be Richard Nelson Frye, who's been in the navy & I think has been in the diplomatic service—anyway he knows something about the Near East & is here for a Near East Conference. He's been on a Rockefeller grant, & I remember him because I've been confused with him, & sent mail intended for him. Maybe as my fame grows he'll be confused with me.

[534] Going on with Blake, the archetypal moods or states are the most prominent things I've struck so far. It clears up Schiller's distinctions too, if we identify his "naive" poetry with a fourth type of the sentimental.[441] There is still something about the interpenetration of tragedy & comedy in each of these moods I haven't got clear, & which may not be there. Now there's the archetypal imagery or significance which derives from the relation of every image in nature to its unfallen form. All unfallen forms are the same form, & yet because they are universal they are real, & because they are real they are immortal minute particulars, though they are so only as forms, & are not atomic or substantial. According to Blake metamorphosis, or the dissolving of form, is at best a vision of the fall. I suppose if "whatever can be created can be annihilated" [*Milton*, pl. 32, l. 36], art is not strictly a creation at all, but only has to appear as such in this world, as Christ appeared as an individual man in time and space. The real or eternal Christ is the form of man, and the real body of art is that which art reveals.

[535] Blake plays down his archetypal narratives: partly because he's a painter, he leans heavily toward the significant rhythm, & it's the absence of clear narrative structure, especially in *Jerusalem*, that makes his prophecies so difficult to read. Communication, as I say, begins by constructing narrative, and it's Blake's lack of interest in narrative that makes him seem incommunicable to the general reader, or at least uncommunicative.

Thursday, August 10

[536] Tonight we had George Williamson in for dinner: we'd also asked Ruth [Jenking], but she couldn't come. He got our note, mailed Tuesday morning, this morning, in the same mail as a letter from his wife, mailed Tuesday morning from Monterey, California. I *must* remember how lousy the mail service is in this country—they recently cut it down as an economy measure.

[537] Well, Williamson remains, as I'd found him before, a gentle & honest soul, & a genuine scholar—he reminded me a little of Harold Wilson. He has two books he's trying to publish—one on Attic, which he calls Senecan, prose in the 17th c—Norman Endicott's field—and one a general introduction to T.S. Eliot. He's had trouble placing them, &

seemed surprised at the way presses were chasing me, so that I regretted telling him they were. Faber & Faber took the Senecan book, but of course not the Eliot, which he hasn't placed yet, & which is badly timed, coming on the heels of Drew & Mrs. Gardiner. The Donne tradition book was his thesis, & since then he's written articles—one called "Strong lines" is referred to regularly in Ruth Wallerstein's book.[442]

[538] The tactic of the Blake article is shaping up a little. After I outline his archetypal imagery, which derives from the unfallen world, I go on to archetype of narrative. The archetypal narrative is the heroic quest, which is the Orc cycle. This is in Blake, but he's not primarily interested in it, as he sees the cyclic shape of it too clearly. That's the reason for the difficulty in trying to wedge Jungian archetypes, which are all narrative ones, into Blake. The shift over from the Orc cycle to the Los pattern of progressive & redemptive work is really the centre of the problem in L [Liberal] that converges on what I call the dialectic development of the conception of the hero. In Blake the cycle of narrative emanating from & returning to the unfallen world is seen so constantly as a simultaneous pattern of significance that the reader has to get this perspective before he can read: it isn't unfolded to him passively in a narrative sequence.

Friday, August 11

[539] All that happened today was a luncheon date with the Ellmanns. We met at a place called the Wursthaus I hadn't been to before, and as it was much better than Howard Johnson's I think I'll go back to it. They're motoring out to Detroit & Chicago at the end of the month—his family is in Detroit & they want to buy a house in Evanston. Mary says she has a graduate student in Wellesley who has signed up for a course in Blake's Prophecies, & some day she's going to ask me up without telling me why.

[540] I've been wondering vaguely about beginning my paper with a distinction between "archetypal" poets like Dante & Milton & Blake who work deductively from the verbal universe, & "ectypal" poets like Shakespeare who work inductively from experience—or rather from the tactical requirements of the job in hand, "experience" being the illusion of an outside life again. Once Shakespeare gets into a play, he tells the whole truth about that particular dramatic situation. But Blake's honesty, though

equally intense, is of a different kind: he seems interested in clarifying his total view of the verbal universe, not in choosing a genre & working out the problems involved there.

[541] What is implied by the fact that revision is possible in writing a poem? It seems to me clear that a poet enters into and discovers a form in the act of writing. There are no pre-existing forms, and if a bad poet writes a sonnet the fourteen lines & rhyme scheme won't give him form: it'll only give him a formula. As such, it won't give form to mediocre thinking or sloppy technique, but can only act as an external or drill-sergeant discipline. But forms, as distinct from formulas, are part of the real presence revealed by art. Once a critic has discovered a form, and nobody but a critic can discover one, it's apt to become a formula for future poets. But in itself it's the formal cause of poetry, which expands from the work of art to the genre, from the genre to the archetype, and from the archetype to the verbal universe. External & objective formal qualities, such as the twelve books of the epic, belong to accident instead of substance.

Saturday, August 12

[542] Today Ruth [Jenking] collected us in her car, as usual, & we went out to Ipswich for a "Seventeenth Century Day" they were having. Seventeen houses on view—well, fourteen, with two churches, a bridge & a boneyard. Thirteen. Seventeen points of interest. It was fundamentally, of course, a series of Mrs. van Pluysh Lynes opening their homes— it's clear that the centrifugal movement from New England to the West, after reaching the coast, is now rippling back & making a wealthy tourist resort out of New England, which takes the form of exploiting its traditions. Thus the "Crane's beach" we've been at derives its name from the Crane who runs the huge bathroom fixture business, & which has its headquarters in Chicago. It's now a fashionable hobby to buy a seventeenth or eighteenth century house & proceed to "restore" it along lines suggested in such magazines as *The American Home*, which I saw in several of the houses I went into. And as Ipswich has a lot of old houses, it's become the centre of a well-heeled restoring group. I sound as though I were trying to be cynical about it, but I'm just trying to see what the facts are. Actually, they put on a very good show.

[543] We went first to an inn dating from 1640—the best room had been taken to the Metropolitan Museum & there was an irritable notice about that. In each house we found several women dressed up in antique costumes—generally Victorian. Here there was a man—the manager— in a Puritan outfit. Slight touch of the commercial harpy's claws about it—the only place where we met that. We saw nine or ten houses, mostly late seventeenth century & early eighteenth century. They might be summarized as low ceilings with huge cross beams, big open fireplaces with places for warming ovens, wide floorboards, old chests instead of cupboards, woodwork with two centuries of paint & varnish scrubbed off, & bits of antique litter like flintlocks, Hitchkock [Hitchcock] chairs, spinning wheels & the like. One house, moved down from Newburyport, belonged to the head of the Boston Museum.

Sunday, August 13

[544] We also saw an old Congregational church & a parish hall where they said there was a collection of Ipswich photographs, but there wasn't, only a wide open women's toilet I practically walked into. One of the houses, which belonged to the Ipswich Historical Society and was the headquarters, was full of gorgeous Chinese stuff—soapstone carvings & the like, though some of it was junky. The original owner had been in the China trade: there was a dulcimer there & Ruth found some other musical instruments in the attic.

[545] By sheer accident, I suppose, an association of New England firemen who go around shooting at targets with hoses & exhibiting old-fashioned fire equipment was there too, & it looked as though the native population of Ipswich was there, & had left the old houses to the tourists & the nobs. On a park called the South Green there were a whole lot of handcraft exhibitions: weaving & spinning, shingle-making, square dancing (kids enjoying themselves & adolescents looking self-conscious & as though they wished they could see the firemen) and bell ringers. The bell ringers were very funny: an older woman like a Girl Guide mistress who ran the group, a young girl concentrating furiously on her part, an old lady who had no notion when to come in & got everyone so concerned with getting her in that they forgot their own parts, and a man whose reflexes were always a bit slow. A goofy art-form, but I got very fond of the bell-ringers.

[546] Ruth drove us to Gloucester, & we saw a bit of the town—much poorer than Ipswich. A beautiful harbour & lots of sailing ships, a telescope you put a dime into & then had to lift a series of persistent kids up to, and an art colony that looked a bit less phony than the one in Provincetown. So we had dinner at a new & very clean roadside restaurant & came home. Today we spent recuperating. Hilliard [Trethewey] came in in the evening. He says B.K. Sandwell has got hold of my Church & Society paper & has mentioned it in *Saturday Night*.[443] He himself has bought a Morris car, in Ontario, & expects to go back & start for Europe around the end of the month.

Monday, August 14

[547] The news from Vera [Frye] makes us feel pretty edgy. Esta Aldrich wants to go on a vacation with her daughter and son-in-law on the 18th. She doesn't want to leave Vera, and wants us to go out there. Otherwise she'll feel like cancelling a vacation she's been looking forward to for years. She doesn't know who else could look after Vera in the interval between Vera's return from the hospital and her return to her apartment. She evidently feels that Vera is pretty isolated in Chicago, & at this time of year she may be. Well, we got two very depressing letters from her, & Helen phoned her yesterday to say we didn't want to go if we could avoid it. (We're flat broke at the moment after paying in advance for the Brattle Inn place). She made a very bad job of the phoning—she's catching too many of my own weaknesses—and I can only hope things will work out. Vera evidently had a terrible time for a while, but is clearly better now. We got a letter from her which was far more cheerful, & she asked us to phone her doctor, a Toronto man named Harvey whom I've met at Ken Maclean's [MacLean's]. So I phoned him, & he took a relatively serene view. It's really a matter now of dealing with Esta. But at the moment it looks as though Helen will have to go out to Chicago & sit around in the Aldrich apartment for a couple of weeks—"huggin' that goddamn cat"—as she says—seeing Vera an hour a day & then looking after her when she comes out, which will mean missing the New York trip, for one thing. If Vera really were isolated & friendless I'd feel differently about it, but as it is, it illustrates the insanity of living in a big city—Helen has to go halfway across the continent to assume the sort of responsibility that in a small town or village any decent neighbour would do as a matter of course. The trouble with Vera is evidently one

disc pressing on the nerves of her spine, & the operation, though of course serious, is apparently not thought of as dangerous. I also phoned Lilian [Noyes] & got the front more or less established.[444]

Tuesday, August 15

[548] The Kenyon Review said my article[445] was a better exposition of the "myth criticism school" (the Americans have to have me in a school) than the myth critics had been able to make for themselves, but would I cut 2000 words out of it so they could put it into a whole series of critical "credos" they're doing so they could later fit it into a book? I'm glad to have the chance to recast it: some sentences in it were bad.

[549] Last night I went to a Poetry Conference organized by the summer school. Ransom, to whom I'd just written a letter, Spender & Viereck spoke. I thought Ransom dull, Spender rather impressive & Viereck brash, noisy, and adolescent & obvious. At about ten o'clock he finally shut up & they began a half-hearted discussion of why poetry wasn't "heroic" any more. I could have told them, but nobody asked me. And who should be there but Klein, Frank Scott & Art Smith. So I made a date for lunch. I'd never met Klein before: he's an orthodox Jew & whenever I've been in Montreal it's always Rosh Hashanah or Yom Kippur or some other devotional reason for disconnecting his telephone.[446]

[550] Today I went to Art's [Art Smith's] room at the top of Wadsworth House. Eric Havelock dropped in briefly, but couldn't come to lunch. We went to the Faculty Union, & I signed in as "Guest of Poetry Group." A man named Coleman from Johns Hopkins was along, & a Frenchman named Pierre Emmanuel, who runs a magazine called *Esprit*. Scott told Emmanuel all about French Canada, & Emmanuel, who seems quite a liberal person, says the Catholic Church is about to come out against all liberal political movements within the Church. He told a story about Bernanos, evidently a cultured bum who rationalizes that fact by regarding all writers who aren't bums, notably Mauriac, as hypocrites & compromisers. He finally was induced to see Mauriac, & as he plodded up the shabby stairs he noted the *petit bourgeois* surroundings with approval & thought that maybe he'd underestimated Mauriac. He'd gone up the back stairs & went into the kitchen, where the servants laughed at him when he said he wanted to see Mauriac & finally was pushed into an

elegant drawing room full of guests from the kitchen: Mauriac had sent for him but hadn't gone to bring him in. It seems to me a curious example of obeying an inner self-caricaturing force.

Wednesday, August 16

[551] In the afternoon there was a "Forum" in Lamont Library. Spender spoke again: the discussion last night had made it rather painfully obvious that he was the only articulate one of the three. Harry Levin was chairman again, & very good. But the discussion got off again on the poetry-vs.-prose line, & was a complete waste of time.[447] I don't know why it's assumed that because a man's a poet he must be an intellectual with a discursive mind & critical ability. Finally, unable to solve a critical problem by themselves, they appealed to Kenneth Burke & asked him what the difference between poetry and prose was, but even he didn't know. *I* knew, but nobody asked me. Mary McCarthy was there, & a very attractive girl. I spoke to Ransom Monday night, & had a closer look at Spender. He's certainly handsome, but with a self-conscious look, as though he'd been spoiled by too many adoring women—and men, of course. There was another meeting last night, which I skipped.

[552] This morning who should I run into on my way to the library but Smith, Klein, and Scott? So I went along & a lad named Robert Lowell, whom I'd seen before as a poet and whom I took to at once. We discussed Joyce: Klein had taken over Kain's class on Tuesday morning & a student had said: "Sir, do you mean that every word in *Ulysses* has a meaning?" Klein said: "I do, & I have discovered them all but three." I gathered that Emmanuel spoke eloquently, Marianne Moore (a sweet-faced old girl that just misses looking hard & sharp as well) very badly (I'd heard her trying to beg off from Eliot [Elliott], the big shambling man who runs the summer school) and (I think) Randall Jarrell, at great length.[448] So long they couldn't have Burke.[449] They seemed bored.

[553] I went to lunch again at the Faculty Union, but this time with Eric Havelock. I called to see him at Leverett House & met a lad named Rosenmeyer, in Classics at Iowa, who's been in Toronto. At the Faculty Club I met his boss, a man named Elles (?)[450] who asked to be introduced to Klein at the afternoon do but didn't turn up. A man named Stirling [Sterling] Dow I didn't cotton to, a fat man named Wolfe I thought I'd

probably like, & a charming old girl named Lily Ross Taylor, who's head
of Bryn Mawr & has written on the deification of the Caesars.[451]

Thursday, August 17

[554] After lunch Havelock took me over to the Widener & gave me the
key to his office, 790. Damn decent of him, though I shall continue to
work in Lamont till the last possible gasp. I mean gasp quite literally, as
the sneezon began punctually at 6 p.m. on Monday, Aug. 14, when a
trifling draft started off about fifty sneezes. Then I shuffled along to the
Forum room again for another session. This time we heard a series of
recordings from the Harvard collection. Dylan Thomas is a wonderful
reader: he did Peacock's Dinas Vawr song in a slow barbaric chant & &
made a superb job out of *Captain Carpenter*,[452] which has always been a
favorite poem of mine. Pound doing his *Sea Farer* with an improvised
kettle-drum accompaniment, Dyer-Bennet singing the *Golden Vanity*,[453] a
badly scratched record of Joyce doing the Moses speech in *Ulysses*, a very
dull & to me very embarrassing extract from *Brébeuf*—the letter—[454]
some Auden, F.N. Robinson's record of *The Pardoner's Tale*, Yeats doing
Innisfree in that phony chant of his, & bits of Eliot. Then the poets
present read their own stuff. The general effect was solemn, youthful, &
a bit owlish. The two Canadians had all the wit, & Klein was very
contemptuous of the Americans afterward, but he perhaps forgets how
mature he is in comparison with them.[455] I liked young Lowell, a very
poor showman, which I thought was all to his credit, and I liked Richard
Eberhardt [Eberhart] better than I expected to. Spender & Marianne Moore
& Ransom wouldn't read. Viereck I thought dull & bad, Coleman, who sat
beside me, just dull, John Ciardi was, I think, bad. A man named Wilbur &
Theodore Roethke I thought had a bit more on the ball, but in general I
thought there was too much romantic whinny & too much straining after
profound thought & too little after disciplined speech. They're confused
by the notion that poetry ought to be socially effective or morally elevating, I think. But above all, the reason for the curiously strangled & muffled
sound that came from them was the absence of any sense of decisive
tonality. The terrific impact of *Captain Carpenter* & of the *Golden Vanity* is
due to the presence of the hard, concrete, impersonal form of tragedy in
them. And here Spender yesterday was raising the question whether there
really was objective form in poetry or not—he rather thought not. Eliot
[Elliott] also mucked in like a good sport & read two of his poems.

Friday, August 18

[555] Last night Ruth [Jenking] took us out to hear Howard [Harlow] Shapley, the astronomer, give a popular lecture on astronomy. It was excellent: exactly what popular lecturing ought to be. Fast, well organized & very clear, & the questions answered with great courtesy. Afterwards we wandered around to see the various things they have there to amuse the public. We saw several telescopes, the big fifteen-inch one being trained on what looked like a patch of torn grey cloth which we were told what [*sic*] was a nebula in (I think) Hercules. I got a much bigger kick out of seeing Jupiter & some of its moons in a much smaller telescope. But then I like astronomy to be spectacular & obvious. I'll take the galaxies millions of light years away on faith, or rather trust, and as for seeing, if I can see mountains on the moon I'm perfectly happy. I don't think there was a moon last night, & there was some cloudiness. The place was full of graduate students & good will. I asked Shapley afterwards about the term "metagalaxy" he'd used: he meant more or less all the galaxies of the stellar universe conceived as a single system. Apparently Toronto is doing some important pioneer work in a new phase of astronomy, but I haven't enough background to understand what it was. I had a good time.

[556] Today we went over to the station & got tickets for New Haven: $10.90 return, which was a bit of a shock. We lined up for the coach, & noted that for all the bus & plane competition there are still a hell of a lot of people travelling by train. Also the people here seemed to push & crash queue lines more than I'm used to in our more phlegmatic country. The trip was a dull one, though with some fine views of the sea & marshlands and of Narragansett Bay.[456] I noticed the extraordinary number of slums near the railway equipped with television aerials. Ken [MacLean] met us and drove us a bit around the town, which is not a particularly attractive town: rather like Cambridge without the Harvard Pale. The medical school & an outfit called the Institute of Human Relations, which is I think where Hutchins got his start when Dean of Law, are near the station.[457] The I.H.R., if that's its name, is concerned mostly with psychology.

Saturday, August 19

[557] Ken took us to Sara's mother's house on Prospect Street, which is a

huge and rambling old house full of old furniture & objects d'art: it would have been a prize catch in Ipswich. Three stories & an enormous number of rooms, many old portraits, including Copleys & Smiberts, several generations of little girls' samplers, including one done by Sara at the age of ten, four-poster beds, old highboys & chests, & so on. Sara's father & grandfather were professors at Yale & her great grand-grandfather—the name is Wolsey [Woolsey]—was a famous president of Yale. There's still quite a bit of money in the Wolsey [Woolsey] family, apparently. Ken is, as I hadn't quite realized, an almost neurotically conservative person, and what he'd have done if he'd married a Miss Biddy O'Flanagan I shudder to think. We ate sandwiches in the parlor & gossiped. Ken enjoyed his summer school at Duke very much, apparently, and met the Chapel Hill staff as well. No offer from Duke as yet, but it may come later. It may be refused, too, as Ken speaks with great affection of Toronto & of things Canadian.[458]

[558] This came out during our tour around Yale. Evidently nearly all the big Yale building was done, & the college system there organized, after 1930, when Ken graduated. He thinks Toronto, especially Victoria, for all its down-at-the-heels shabbiness, is still "unspoiled," and more like what Yale was in his impressionable time. We saw the buildings, but I'll have to get a map if I'm to get any notion of it in my mind. The most attractive of the colleges was his, Pearson, a lovely Georgian quadrangle. Yale is a mixture of Georgian & Gothic. The library is a rather affected Gothic: a long nave leading up to the main desk as a sort of high altar, & dimly lit transepts leading to the reading room apses. We didn't go into the stacks, but did see where the rare book collection was, & peeped into Tinker's office. He has everything critical on Blake except me. We then went up to Pottle's study, where three graduate students were working on Yale's great laboratory: the edition of the Malahide & Fettercairn papers. The first volume will be out this fall.[459]

Sunday, August 20

[559] I took the address of a pleasant lad called Weingrove, & met Pottle, who's going to do a course on Blake next year & is preparing himself to read my book. Then we went on to the Art Museum & saw something of the Dura-Palmyra digs there, & a wonderful collection of Siennese stuff: I hadn't realized how much Siennese painting was there. Also some modern paintings gathered by a Yale society—Abstracts Anonymous or

some such name: we saw a show of theirs in Boston last summer. Some good, some bad.

[560] We eventually left Yale, at shortly after five, & started for Cornwall: I hadn't realized it was nearly across the state. A breath-takingly beautiful drive, especially the latter part of it. Cornwall—there are about six places of that name—is an expensive looking village, a rotten borough Ken says, that gets far more than its share of state money. So its schools are pretty well equipped, and young Kenny isn't too keen about going back to Canada, though Sally is. All three kids looked wonderful, & so did Sara. We saw a copy of Ken's book, *The Agrarian Age*, a nice little book, not impossibly, as Ken says, a bit simple-minded, only about a hundred pages long, & illustrated with Bewick woodcuts.[460] The house is a big rambling farm house dated 1815, with two self-contained "tourist cabins" (Mary Jackman suggested they should run them as such, & they're certainly equipped for it), in one of which we stayed. Van Wyck Brooks was their most recent tenant: it's amusing to think of him scribbling in that luxurious padded cell and lowing like a wounded cow buffalo about the decline of New England. I also gathered that Ken has taken to writing short stories.

[561] We went to bed early & next day—that's Saturday—we went for a walk through the neighboring fields. It's dairy country, so the beauty of the landscape is more or less intact. A long trail for hikers, running from New Hampshire to Virginia & blazed with white marks on trees, runs through the woods there. There's a very old—I think nearly virginal—stand of trees there. My nose behaved beautifully although the roads were lined with ragweed. Then we had lunch & everybody had a sleep for the afternoon. At least Helen did, & I read *The Cocktail Party*—a competent but by no means impressive play.

Monday, August 21

[562] At five-thirty—I'm still on Saturday—we went to a cocktail party given by some people named Foote. I met Mark van Doren there & gave him Ned's regards. I also met a mural painter named Bradford. I tried out Blake's portable frescoes on him & he didn't like them: said a real fresco had to sink several inches into plaster. But then Blake was a fourth-rate painter—nobody went for him but li'erary people. I men-

tioned Michelangelo, but he was li'erary too—second or third-rate. I said who's first-rate & he said Rubens. I said the bulk of Rubens' inspiration was li'erary too, but he said no, that was only the demands of his time. I didn't like Bradford. Well, I drank several Manhattans & we moved on to the Thurbers. There I had a lot more drinks & dinner—well, supper—wasn't served until very late, so I got horribly sick and had two long agonizing sessions in the can puking my guts up. I forgot I had hay fever. Apart from that I enjoyed talking to James Thurber, who told me all about Harold Ross, who seems to be a strange and attractive mixture of toughness and innocence—possibly a much stronger character than Thurber himself, who seems to me to have the insecurity of someone from central Ohio who's still trying to adjust himself to the big bad city. Now how in God's name—I'm not drunk now—did I manage to compose a sentence like that, plopping one clause after another like horse turds and who-whoing like an owl?

[563] The Macleans [MacLeans] seemed to be a little frightened by the smart set in Cornwall, with their multiple divorces and their frenetic lives. Thurber's wife Helen, a tall & competent looking woman, is his second: he has a 17–year old daughter by his first. Lewis Gannett of the Herald Tribune was there—I liked him very much, incidentally, with *his* second wife. Thurber's parties go on all night—this one broke up at five—and after midnight, when we left, the conversation turns bawdy & often abusive. Both Ken & Sara have been insulted by Thurber in the most pointless way—it's not supposed to mean anything, of course, and it certainly doesn't alter their very considerable affection for him. It's just the pattern of life it forms part of that bewilders them. But as far as I saw Thurber, he was completely charming and appealing—almost entirely blind, as I realized with a slight shock.

Tuesday, August 22

[564] Sunday we nursed our hangovers and some people came in for yet another drink before lunch. Their neighbors the Lansings came: Mrs. Lansing, who's called City, is a writer of children's books, & breezed in surrounded with her own kids, like the Sistine Madonna.[461] She was at the party last night, and I liked her. Also her red-headed brother Tom (don't know the last name), a Harvard graduate & a reporter on a Providence paper.

[565] It poured rain from Saturday noon on, so we didn't see much of the countryside, & Ken was rather disappointed. After lunch—something of an understatement for a superb turkey dinner—we drove back to New Haven. Ken is still pretty broody, worrying about everything from South Korea to Joe Fisher (whom he's a bit browned off on), feeling that America can survive only by hanging on to its traditions, and so on. I said the Russians were in a far stronger position than we because they didn't have a museum complex (what I think of as a "Saito" attitude), & regarded their entire civilization as expendable. But he does seem to be well adjusted to Canada—he's half a Loyalist already—and I'm glad of that.

[566] I forgot to say that on Friday Ken took us into one of the most beautiful modern churches I've ever seen. A little Catholic parish church dedicated to St. Thomas More, with clear glass windows & designs etched on them. All the furnishings (I especially noted the chandeliers) showed an extraordinarily imaginative use of copper & aluminum & chromium, but there was nothing freakish or self-conscious about it— the whole effect was completely serene. I suppose the great appeal of Catholicism in the States today has a lot to do with the sense that the degenerate pseudo-Protestants who ought to be leading the country's culture are shaking their nerves to pieces with indiscriminate drinking and fucking and chattering. Well, we got on the train & went home to Boston. We went into the buffet car for a snack. Mem: don't ever go again into a buffet car for a snack. Swindling the public on food has really got to be a fine art: all eating places are getting assimilated to the supper-dance clip joints.

Wednesday, August 23

[567] Monday morning I went down for a haircut & got a rather bad one, I think. I came out onto Mass. Ave. and who should loom up in front of me but Rodney Montgomery Baine, bless his old heart.[462] So we went & had a cup of coffee together—Rodney, true to form, also had a jellied doughnut. I had no notion he'd be anywhere near Harvard. He doesn't particularly care for Richmond, a small Baptist college run by a dictatorial president he doesn't like & doesn't trust, and salaries in the South are pretty small. So he wants to move, & has to acquire a Ph.D. to get enough motive power. (He was forced out of his M.I.T. job by being called up, &

he had, I think, two years in the navy). So he's just now finishing a thesis on Thomas Holcroft, working mainly with Sherburn. He's living in Holden Green with Alice & his three kids, two boys, Wade & Jimmy (Wade Baine: somebody in that family hasn't too sensitive an ear) and a two-year old girl, Alice. He looks less roly-poly, but is probably even heavier and more viscerotonic than he was. Evidently he was closely involved in the Charlie-Mildred bust up: in fact he had a hand in drawing up the articles of separation, & is still friendly & still corresponds with both. He says that when we saw them they probably weren't even living together, as Mildred had kicked him out of the house soon after he got back from Italy. Charlie has the oldest girl, Nona, & Mildred, who's remarried to, I think, a science professor from Indiana, has the other two. Charlie's present wife is a Quaker, & he reports that he has had the happiest year of his life.[463]

[568] He didn't say much about Holcroft, except that he's written & torn up the thesis several times, & is now fairly well satisfied with it & is going to publish it if he has to put all his own money into it.[464] He said he liked my book, though, again very typically of Rodney, he prefaced this by saying he'd found some errors in it, & almost wrote me about them. That leaves me a bit up in the air, as he's forgotten what they were: however, Rodney's criticized my stuff before now, & what he calls errors I don't invariably recognize as such. He seems also to have done a lot of work on Godwin.

Thursday, August 24

[569] On Tuesday, a very hot day, I went over to Boston with Helen to buy a bed jacket for Vera [Frye]. We went to Bonwit Teller's, a very flossy shop Helen would have been afraid to go into if I hadn't been with her—besides, the rather tight financial squeeze we've had lately makes her fretful & panicky. (I should remind myself, perhaps, that such comments are not complaints.) We found a very pleasant woman (I suppose the word "woman" always means somebody middle-aged & not obviously attractive physically: all other females are called girls) who sold us a bed jacket for the five bucks we were willing to pay, and then, under her solicitations, we opened a charge account. Helen was delighted. Then we went over to the Boston Public Library, where I tried to get a reader's card for Helen, but the creature at the registration desk nearly set the

dogs on us. "Cambridge isn't Boston, you know," she snapped. So we came home and yesterday Helen called for me & for some occult reason dragged me over to the *Cambridge* Public Library, which is not an impressive place. She's got the curse, and is full of woes and worries. Hot weather, my disease, no drinks, & crossing Broadway, Cambridge, Kirkland, Massachusetts, Garden, Concord & Brattle Streets in rush hour on our way home didn't improve matters much, for either of us.

[570] Today, however, was our wedding anniversary—the thirteenth. We went to the Bella Vista for dinner, which Dick Ellmann had recommended as the best place in town, but it wasn't any hell—not nearly as good as the Viennese place. However, it was all right, though we were outdoors on a roof under an umbrella, and I'd have done better in an airconditioned interior. Beside us was a young man who'd just got his Ph.D. and was celebrating. His conversation got louder with his drinks & was a mixture of cultural & personal remarks that, considered as a pattern, gave me quite an insight into the Harvard level of student sophistication, though it's difficult to say just what it was. Hilliard [Trethewey] came over in the evening to say goodbye—he leaves tomorrow for Toronto & Muskoka, & we'll hardly see him when he comes back to New York.

Friday, August 25

[571] The news from Vera is, apparently, very encouraging, except that none of it comes from Vera. I phoned Dr. Harvey again tonight & he seemed to think she was coming along beautifully after her operation. They're thinking of sending her home sometime next week, but he said he'd tell her I'd phoned and find out if she still thought she'd need us. In the meantime he said it would be all right to go away for the weekend. Not a syllable out of Dad either, of course.

[572] Alice Baine came in to take Helen out for a shopping expedition. As I rather expected, she's cute, cheerful, cuddly and obviously a homemaker. She brought along young Alice, who didn't take to Helen & proceeded to try to push her face in. Helen reported later that Alice is a terrific expert on bargains & shopping places & that the two boys are stamp collectors who insist that Helen should reopen her correspondence with Marion so as to get some Rhodesia stamps.[465]

[573] I keep giving up trying to push my Blake paper along & dither & dawdle instead. My disease encourages me to sleep in even later in the morning. Today I gave up entirely & read a book on psychosomatic medicine by Helen Flanders Dunbar. I don't see how she can be the same person as the author of that book on Dante's symbolism, but the coincidence of names is curious.[466] She doesn't say much about hay fever, but she says the emotional pattern behind asthma is often one of repression due to a sense of neglect: if people can manage to break down and weep their asthma gets better. I've been told that mother was very sick at my birth & that I was consigned to a nurse who kept me doped with soothing syrup. The strong & irradicable resentment I feel against mother, and especially my feeling that most of her illnesses were due to a morbid mental condition in which self-indulgence predominated, is doubtless fed from some such infantile springs. I can even remember resenting her sleeping half the afternoon. But I doubt very much that any knowledge of my infantile feelings will stop my blood from curdling when the ragweed busts loose, nor does the Dunbar woman suggest that it will. There's also a strong introverted resistance to duty behind all my illnesses, of course.

Saturday, August 26

[574] Rodney [Baine] celebrated finishing his thesis tonight by taking us over to Tufts College to see the Oxford Players put on *The Alchemist*. A group of very young people—the ages were all carefully given in the programme and the oldest was twenty-eight—very attractive (Dol Common made even Elizabethan prostitution seem attractive) and full of life & bounce.

Sunday, August 27

[575] A bright sunny day as Ruth [Jenking] came around again. Two of her three room-mates had come along with us to the observatory: Anne Freedman, who's a cuddly and sentimental Jewess who lives in Long Island, phoned just before Ruth came to tell us she'd be glad if we looked her up in New York. I don't quite see how we can, but it was nice of her, & she seems good-hearted. The other woman, a Miss Wasser from Rochester, came along with us for the trip. She's one of the thinnest women I've ever seen, & she has a hell of a lot of things wrong with her.

Probably the curse was one. She sat in the back seat with a headache & looked like a starving Chinaman, but got a little better as the ride proceeded. It was a very hot day.

[576] I find the Newburyport turnpike a bit dull, as a road, but Ruth talked easily, she was so relieved to get through with Harvard. The one thing she has got from her summer is some understanding of Pope's study of *The Rhythm of Beowulf*, which, incidentally, appeared in 1942, the year of my *Music & Poetry* article,[467] and if I reprint my essays I may say that this article is a footnote to Pope's book. Or, in the words of the oracular cliché, I may not. Anyway, the proper way to read Old English is crystal clear to her now, and as it's a revelation in itself she feels it almost makes up for a very dull summer.

[577] We had lunch at Salisbury Beach, where Helen had steamed clams, for the improvement of her education & the broadening of her mind. Ruth did too, but Ruth's attitude towards everything in the sea is a bit irrational & she either didn't mind or didn't have the sand that Helen choked on. We went on up through that strip of sea coast that New Hampshire has. Ruth was intending to stop at Rye Beach, where she had been two—I mean *ten*—years ago. But in those ten years it had got impossibly crowded and public, and so it didn't take us very long to decide that we ought to push on to Maine. We stopped at Portsmouth, but it was as hot as hell, my hay fever was giving me the devil, and we (Helen & I) were very glad to discover that the Aldrich home & some relic of Paul Jones were both closed for the day & we didn't have to stop & look at them.

Monday, August 28

[578] I picked up slightly in Maine: there seemed to be at that moment a slight ragweed pocket between Kittery & Ogunquit. We went through York Beach, & I found everything very attractive, though the sheer number of tourist places is a bit overpowering and the sense of everybody in the U.S.A. trying like hell to get somewhere else is confusing. But it's interesting to realize that it isn't just a small country and a soft dollar that makes Canada so dependent on tourist trade. Naturally, Maine begins to look more like home too.

[579] We dropped the Wasser woman at Ogunquit & went on to Wells Beach, skipping the painting show advertised at the former place. We inquired first at a hotel, but it looked noisy, & we finally found an excellent place at what was obviously an old ladies home complete with rocking chairs, which is just what we wanted. The man who runs it is I think a widower & acquired it after his mother died, from her. Taxes would be damn high. He doesn't live there just now, & it's in charge of a cute & cheerful woman named Rose Daigle, whom we took to at once. She's French but not from Canada but native—she calls herself Acadian. I hadn't realized that the French in Maine are that—it's of course a territory that should have been part of Canada.

[580] Well, today the sea breezes blew ragweed at me all day long, & I had, quite simply, one hell of a time. I didn't feel able to go swimming—I knew that if I tried I'd start sneezing my fool head off. So I stayed on the verandah or on the beach & scribbled at my paper. A young girl here about eighteen (her name's Vivian Dowling & I noticed that in a copy of some music she'd carefully altered the i's to y's) kept playing around me with a dog. She wasn't especially pretty or intelligent looking, but her body—she was in a bathing suit—had that extraordinarily beautiful feeling of youth & health about it, & with this lovely & nearly naked figure hovering on my line of vision I had some difficulty in concentrating on the formal causes of literature. It was also another reason for cursing my disease.

Tuesday, August 29

[581] Today I was still very groggy & still didn't feel I could go in swimming. One good thing is that my Kenyon Review paper[468] has suddenly started to clear up. It's clearing up so damn fast I can hardly keep up with it. Part One has boiled down perfectly out of what I had & Part Two came along beautifully this afternoon: it meant cutting out a lot of stuff, but the net result is one of the most concentrated & best integrated articles I've ever produced. No splutter, no gargle, no leers, no attempt to fasten pedantic teeth in the arse of somebody else. Nothing but dry fact and obvious truth, expressed with overwhelming concentration but great simplicity. In short, an article to rank with the Argument of Comedy and the Forms of Prose Fiction, only on an even bigger subject.[469]

[582] The afternoon was devoted to more riding: we went up the highway to Kennebunkport. Very pretty place and fine building, but with a
lurking feeling of high price & a general air of genteel stick-em-up. Helen
laughed at me for buying jelly beans, but it turned out that Ruth [Jenking]
is very fond of them. So we ate jelly beans and looked at the ocean: the
rocky coasts make a wonderful blue and brown picture with the surf
giving just a touch of white. A lovely drive along the shore, & then back
to the town, where we had tea in an old barn made into an antique shop,
or shoppe. Helen loves places like that & actually I liked having a really
good tea, for once in this coffee-ridden country. The woman showed us
through the house, which was eighteenth century, long & narrow, one
room after the other, with a flanking parlor added in Victorian times
(they say Victorian here too, it seems) to make the regular five-window
pattern. She said she knew we were Canadians. Meanwhile, we'd got a
postcard in the town—a birthday card—& shipped it off to Dad: I hope
he's not sulking about having his trip cancelled, but I don't see what the
hell else we could have done. Came back and went to bed early. Vyvyan
turns out to be musical in a rather more ambitious way than I expected,
& as I dropped off to a drugged sleep I heard her assaulting the last
movement of the Moonlight. It came right back at her too, like a punch-
ing bag.

Wednesday, August 30

[583] We checked out in the morning & got into the car again & headed
north. We stopped in Kennebunk, on the main highway, to look at a
small museum that the tea woman yesterday had mentioned. Some local
painting & handcrafts, some children's art, & some antiques & relics in
the attic. Rather impressive as evidence of a community solidarity, I
thought; apparently the county it's in, York, has that feeling generally.
Helen didn't like it, though mainly for personal reasons: they were
changing the exhibition upstairs & a woman slammed the door in her
face. We went on to Biddeford & then Ruth wanted to drive out to the sea
again. Eight miles to a spot called Biddeford Pool, & eight miles back.
Helen got hungry, in that way she does, so we ate lunch in Biddeford,
which is a little industrial milltown, mostly French, & very like a little
Quebec town like Drummondville or St. Hyacinthe. We sat next to the
squallbox, & asked the girl to turn it down, which she did with both
reluctance & mystification. I went out to the men's room, opened the

door & there in full view of me & a woman waiting her turn in the other place was somebody who'd gotten squatter's rights, so what I had I held.

[584] We drove on to Portland & got bus tickets for home. We drove around Portland, which is a largish town about Lowell's size & evidently attempts to dedicate itself to Longfellow, but looks tough. We made a half-hearted attempt to find the local museum—Ruth is very conscientious about such things but we had no desire whatever to be instructed by Portland. So we said goodbye to Ruth in a very hole-in-the-corner sort of way, as she was wriggling out of the wrong end of a one-way street. We have had some wonderful times with Ruth this summer, & hated to see them end. Helen has a theory that groups of three don't work out properly, but Ruth destroyed that theory. So we got on the bus, which said it was air-conditioned, and I rather think was. No stops, except one enforced by a deaf woman at Portsmouth who went out to piss after informing the driver that the "other" bus driver always stopped at Portsmouth. So we went on without further mishap down the turnpike & got into Boston just after supper time.

Thursday, August 31

[585] The mail we found when we returned wasn't as important as we'd expected. We had a card from Lilian [Noyes]—very nice of her—and a letter from Vera, very cheerful & courageous all things considered, but she's had a very serious illness and an extremely dull time. There was also a letter from Irving attached to his new essay for the Americans.[470] A story in it about a freshman coming to Victoria to take an R.K. course from Professor Frye. When he begins it he believes in God: when he gets to Christmas he believes in Frye's God: when he comes to the end of the year he believes Frye is God. As a matter of fact I've known for some time that undergraduates used to refer to me casually as "God" in their conversations. It's a strain to live up to that, & doubtless of some theological interest to know that God gets a hell of a dose of hay fever every year at this time: maybe that's why so many wars start in August & September.

Friday, September 1

[586] Today we completed our move to Story St. The moving men

arrived at nine and collected $4.58, which I thought was plenty for a steamer truck[471] & bits & pieces to go a couple of blocks. Helen feels just a little bit guilty at having got so expensive & obvious a place & having funked the job of looking around more extensively. I'm rather glad she does feel that way, because her usual tendency to brood and mope about being confined to such a small space is being counteracted by a desire to rationalize her choice. So she expresses enthusiasm for the conciseness of the arranging & doesn't complain too much about washing dishes in the bath room & eating breakfast in the bedroom. As a matter of fact the place is much better set up for working than the house was: it has an excellent desk and a place to put books. It was hot & we got tired quickly: I did actually most of the unpacking in the evening. (It rained & we'd left our luggage keys at the house, which was why it took so long.) Mrs. Baillio (she's Louisana [Louisiana] French by the way) continues to be a dear; they've put a new double bed in the place of the twin beds they had before; they've moved in new furniture (two enormous easy chairs, one a rocker) & in general I think we'll live comfortably, if not luxuriously.

Tuesday, September 5[472]

[587] It was a relief to get back to work: the Lamont of course is closed for the time being, so I go to Havelock's office. A hot & dusty place to work it is, too: I'd rather be in the stacks. At noon I ran into Jean Hubener again along with Beth Thomson, whom I of course didn't recognize. Beth had come down with Ruth Jenking from Barbara Tubman's wedding: she's been doing social work in South Boston for the past year & wants to quit. She says it's too confining & that she thinks graduate work in English would suit her better. Which, I suppose, may be translated as: I wish I could get married & that some decent man would ask me. Nice kid.[473] Mrs. Hubener continues to flourish: she's seen the Guggenheim people, but nothing new there. Her information about Fairley had been derived from me in the first place.

Thursday, September 7[474]

[588] Alice [Baine] was as good as her word & took us to the station.[475] She's a remarkable driver, considering what she has to contend with. Three kids in the back, & Alice, who's rather a sulky little girl, climbing either into the front seat or, by way of diversion, out the window. So

Alice closes the door with one hand, grabs Alice's thigh with the other, & continues to talk amiably in that sing-song Southern voice. We got to the bus station in very good time & said goodbye—the boys were almost friendly because I'd given them a couple of Canadian air-mail stamps. After a long time of pressing & squeezing we finally got on the bus, along with a philosophical old lady who wished her husband would let her fly.

[589] It was foolhardly to take the bus with my disease. The first part of it was fine. We stopped at a dreadful clip joint for a piss & a sandwich (bus food concessions are the worst thing about a bus) and then drove for miles through the woods until we came to Hartford. By the time we got to New Haven I was still doing all right, but Helen was getting a headache. I'd assumed for some reason that the back of the trip would be broken by that time, but there seemed to be no end to the number of Connecticut villages to go through before we hit even New York State. My nose lasted about as far as Larchmont, & then broke down, & by the time we hit 50th St (the trip had taken over eight hours instead of the six & a half we were expecting) both of us were complete crocks.

[590] We swallowed a glass of milk each at the station & came up to the hotel, where we got a bath all to ourselves—we had to share it last time. The King's Crown looks as though it had tried to lift its face a bit. We went out to Butler Hall for dinner, & as that's an excellent place to eat we felt a bit more cheerful. Also it's much cooler weather than in 1948, which augurs well. But when I got home I was still a mess and it took three Benadryl pills to knock me out. A tickly throat is a new misery to contend with, and one that gives me a bad case of stage fright I wouldn't otherwise have. I wish I didn't associate New York so persistently with hay fever.[476]

1951 Diary

[1 – 13 January 1951]

The entries in this brief diary extend for only thirteen days. Portions of the pages for 4, 6, 7, 8, and 10–13 January are devoted to outlines and notes for Anatomy of Criticism, *and the entries from 14 January to 16 February contain further notes, outlines, and drafts for that book, along with a ten-section outline for "A Musical Companion to English Literature." In the remainder of the diary are forty-six pages of cancelled material, including the drafts of several of Frye's articles and lectures and his poetry reviews for the* University of Toronto Quarterly. *None of the material that is not clearly a diary entry has been reproduced. Frye had broken his right arm in an automobile wreck in September 1950, and although he had begun typing some by November, the fact that his right arm was still stiff at the beginning of the year might help to explain the sketchy nature of the 1951 Diary. The diary, in a bound daily journal (14.7 × 21 cm.), is in the NFF, 1993, box 5.*

Monday, January 1

[1] The second half of the century opened with me drinking some rather oversweet Cointreau with Helen after seeing Vera [Frye] off on the plane. We went to bed soon after midnight. New Years is a dull holiday if one makes one's festive effort at Christmas, and the news from Korea was bad enough to spoil whatever of that spirit remained. But, if the first half of the century saw the passing of Fascism, the second half may see the passing of Communism. I don't look for catastrophic war, but for restricted bleeding wars, threats, interdicts, and an attempt on the part of each side to wait for the enemy to blow up through internal contradictions.

[2] Fortunately, the Bush's dinner lightened the day considerably. Besides George Sherburn and a most personable lad here named Shannon, there were two couples: Rogers of Urbana, evidently finishing a Ph.D. with Sherburn, and Sutherland. James Sutherland is the Defoe and early 18th c. man: his wife Helen works for Penguin Books. Sutherland, Shannon and I are all Merton men, and we held a dutiful reunion. I never got much interested in Oxford, for personal reasons that had little to do with Oxford, and I find it difficult to respond with enthusiasm to gossip about Eights Week, Henley, the different ways of climbing in, and the eccentricities of Garrod, who always bored me stiff as both man and writer.[1] Geoffrey Mure is Warden now, and new buildings are up on the northeast side. Sutherland said he was on an examining board that failed Douglas Grant, evidently in prelims for a D.Phil on Churchill. Or B.Litt: I didn't know he'd ever tried any such exam. Sutherland had also met both Woodhouse & Endicott, & spoke of the latter with spontaneous affection. (Incidentally, the Nov. 18 New Statesman, in a somewhat belated fall list, mentions the James Thomson book as out, along with the war book, the title of which is "The Fuel of the Fire," an abominably insipid title.[2] He'd have done a lot better to stay with the "Energy Enslaved" I suggested.)[3] Bush told me that he and Rice & Woodhouse went to a show last Wednesday, & that Woodhouse got heart flutters & they had to take a taxi.

Tuesday, January 2

[3] Bush was also gloomy about the war news, and the prospects of men's colleges next year. He says there's a rumor that Kenyon College may have to close up. After some desultory conversation with the Sutherlands (he used to be in Saskatchewan) we left & walked back home. We took Dad to dinner at Howard Johnson's, where an already very tired girl told me she'd be working till five in the morning. We got back to find a message from the Sternfelds saying they wanted to see us before they went back to Hanover.[4] Fred was a bit depressed about the musicologists' convention: a couple of sprained brains who wield a lot of power & influence used it against his plan to include composers & performers in the society. He gave me another article he'd done on a Kubik movie score, much smaller in scope than the other one.[5]

[4] Today I spent cleaning out some of my arrears of correspondence in Havelock's office. Three letters of recommendation: a general one to

Margaret Moffit, much overdue, and two more specific ones. James Reaney for a Guggenheim: perhaps too judiciously worded. I restrained my impulse to say that at least he was a Canadian. It will neither get nor lose him a fellowship. David Hoeniger for a junior fellowship here: much more committal, if there is such a word. I think he'd be all right for that. Two acceptances: one to Smith College, one to the Hudson Review. Also I got rid of a story sent me by Jodine Beynon, who's lonely & going through some female crisis that produces verbal menstruations. I told her, with a calculated brusqueness that I hope will help her, that she was too involved emotionally in her story, & that such involvement produced clichés. (Because it's personal sincerity combined with a sophistication about words.) Dad spent the evening gossiping about Moncton, which he loves doing. Babbitt Parlee is mayor now, & evidently doing very well, for which I'm glad. Dad's changed his view of him to a more favorable one. It's clear that Dad is more comfortably situated at Dobson's than he's ever been before, is accepted as one of the family, & has a good arrangement about his meals. He's still self-supporting, though he has only thirty American dollars, and did no Christmas shopping. He claims to be out of debt in Moncton, and doubtless is. He looks frailer, and his presages of death seem, at least to him, less of an old man's clichés than before; but his spirits are good.

Wednesday, January 3

[5] Dad left tonight, sitting up in a coach. Helen took him out in the morning & made him buy scarves for his two fair charmers, & then taxied him out to the glass flowers,[6] to which he had, like myself, little positive reaction. We got his bag checked & saw him to the gate, & he looked so pathetic plodding down the track by himself that I was glad when a good-natured guard let me through because "I looked worried." I waited talking to him in the carriage until other people started to flow in. He seems more cheerful than ever. The physical disadvantages of having him in such restricted quarters would have been pretty hard on both of us if they had lasted longer, & I'm very glad to have those disadvantages removed, a quite different thing from being glad to see him go.

[6] I started working in the Widener, but found that Honig had started

off with a New Year's resolution and had completely filled the bookshelf with Jonson books. So I drifted off to the Lamont, where I spoke to that nice boy Beckjord, who was Cob in the Eliot House play. I didn't stay long & came back to the room for dinner. At present I find reading easier than writing, though next week I hope to finish my drama article.[7] I want first of all to read what I call the "secondary" Aristotle: *Ethics, Politics, Rhetoric & Poetics,* and at the same time begin organizing materials for my Washington job.[8] The first ford to take there is clearly Coleridge, & in any case any speculative work on criticism, such as the one I'm contemplating, has to involve a pretty thorough knowledge of Coleridge. Also one should be able to partake knowingly in the gossip, though the Chicago game of toy soldiers is no doubt dying down. (Incidentally, the notion of a Plato-Aristotle antithesis is itself a Coleridgian idea.) So I'm reading Chambers for the biography:[9] pretty unrewarding book, but gets the sisters-in-law unscrambled. He makes it clear that Coleridge lacked the habits of persevering application that got him his knighthood. Also, to get a grip on the bibliography of the period I'm shockingly ignorant of, I dug out Bernbaum's *Guide through the Romantic Movement.* A primer, with all the critical statements that aren't utterly commonplace either demonstrably false or meaningless. And even I can see that the bibliographies are very bad. What dreadful charlatans there are in American scholarship, some with formidable reputations! It started me wondering again about the possibility of making some money out of a *Blake Handbook* after *Fearful Symmetry* stops selling. Waste of time, though.

Thursday, January 4

[7] Kept on reading at the Widener and spent the day, as I occasionally do, dodging letter-writing. I hate letters, & when I devote a day to them I'm apt to feel I've "accomplished something," & so begins the insidious process of transferring value to secondary activities. It's a tendency in myself I have to watch, along with another that's recently raised its head. Owing to our fathers' chronic inability to make money, Helen & I belonged originally to the semi-depressed class, the shabby-genteel; and this has left us with feelings of apologetic guilt about having a salary & property that we can live on. Such feelings, with us, lead to emotions of sham piety (jealous gods) or sham radicalism: with Helen they tend to recoil back & become worries about her family, especially Roy.

[8] Helen was restless after being so confined to the barracks, so we went out and filled up on Martinis, then had dinner at the Vienna Shop. While there I was amused by the feeding habits of a big and quite handsome blonde girl who was by herself: she'd hold a loaded fork poised six inches from her mouth, open her mouth very wide, and plunge it in. Her check arrived, & she carefully dug out the exact change, down to the pennies for the old age tax, then dumped all the coins on the floor. She was clearly a bit tight, & while the Fryes scrambled around the floor recovering her fortune she was asking with some urgency for the "ladies room." We went to bed early: I can't seem to shake off a flu bug or something that gives me a raspy throat, and Helen seems depressed & low in vitality.

Friday, January 5

[9] Still reading: I can't seem to settle either on letters or writing. Next week, after I send the Blake & the drama articles out,[10] I want to get down to serious work on a series of epic articles. I ought to publish *something* on Spenser, for God's sake.[11] Then there's the *Paradise Regained* article:[12] something by me in the Milton bibliographies wouldn't hurt either, and I doubt if the Rinehart introduction will get there very soon. I feel as though I'd like to see *some* result from the four pieces of proof I read last fall before writing anything more. But that's nonsense: I've got to plunge into the epic and clear up that part of the next book. I'm reverting to the idea of a series on the different books of the F.Q. [*The Faerie Queene*]. With all I know about symbolism, it's silly not to be pouring out articles on the subject: even the job I did for Ernst on Rilke could probably be published,[13] & Dante should keep me busy for months.

[10] It's growing on me that my next published book will be the "Essay on Criticism" after all. But I think of it now as richer & more complex than my original idea, also more unified. I seem to be at the point of looking down on literature from a height, no longer working inside it. I have three major ideas, each a part of a logically coherent structure. First is the area covered by my Kenyon Review articles, on meaning & the verbal universe, on archetypes & genres, & on the structure of symbolism. Second is the area covered in my three-volume Guggenheim prospectus, the analysis of the essential modes of verbal expression, scripture,

epic, drama, lyric & prose.[14] Third is the area covered by my "Church & Society" article[15] & my interest in 19th c. subjects, especially Morris, Butler & Yeats. This is actually an apology for criticism: a statement of the social function of the arts & of the place of criticism as a social science. Several things are not clear to me yet, & one of these is, curiously enough, the precise way to tackle the epic. Another is the relation of the elements of the trivium, grammar, rhetoric & logic, & of the function of dialectic as a verbal element. I have a hunch about "verbal determinism" that may not work out. So my draft of the last four chapters, or Part Three, is loose: something like this perhaps: 9, The Limits of Verbal Expression (i.e., Literature & the Other Arts); 10, Art & Spiritual Authority (raising the point that comes out of Arnold, even Newman, & goes back to Roger Bacon, of the non-compulsive authority of *all* scripture); 11, Criticism as a Social Science, and art as a continuously expanding force cracking up all dogmatic *a priori* systems & closed societies like the "monologue" of the Church; 12, The Dialectics of Criticism, following out my concentric scheme.

Saturday, January 6

[11] I went over to the library in the morning & made a feeble tentative effort to start classifying my notes for the Essay, but didn't get far. In the afternoon I dictated some letters to Helen. I made a beginning on my English Institute series, & wrote to Josephine Bennett, Alfred Harbage and Mike Abrams for papers on Spenser, Shakespeare & Coleridge respectively. After I get their refusals I'll start on Rosemond Tuve and maybe a couple of Harvard people.[16] The Forum came in the mail—some good things, including an excellent review of Huxley's new book by Ivon Owen, under his usual pseudonym.[17] We also got some of the regular muck off to the Blue Cross & Physicians' Services: if we get nothing out of them we'll stop our payments to them. I also dropped a note to Philip [Wheelwright], who proposed meeting us in Newark.

[12] In the evening the Honigs came in. They're very gentle people, & this gentleness, like Ken Macleans [MacLean's], redeems his rather unhappy introspectiveness. He writes with difficulty, & has little faith in his criticism, so he doesn't get along so well in university circles. Hasn't a Ph.D & writes poetry—tsk, tsk.

Sunday, January 7

[13] We seem to sleep very late in the mornings: I wake up regularly with a heavy head and inflamed eyes. Partly the damned oil heating. Boswell's Journal, to do for the Hudson Review, arrived yesterday and I had a preliminary look at it. I think reviewing it will be a pretty straight-forward job.[18] Today was the first big snow of the year: a soft snow that was part rain, & went on & on & on all day. In the afternoon we ploughed through slush & a filthy subway to hear *Don Giovanni*. Very fine, well sung & staged & costumed, but of course had nothing like the immediacy of the Lemonade Opera performance we saw two years ago. Some physical discomforts: the theatre was dreadfully overheated & we had to stare at a black curtain while they pushed the scenery around, & that took the edge off. On the whole, there was a sense of effort & strain about the performance I didn't like, & wasn't there in *Figaro* & *The Finta Giardiniera*.

[14] I don't know what to make of *Don Giovanni* anyway. I like listening to the music, naturally, but it doesn't add up as a drama in the way *Figaro* does.

Monday, January 8

[15] Curious that this diary, covering the year of a gradually warming up cold war, should think it necessary to mark the anniversary of a totally pointless massacre that took place two weeks after peace was signed.[19] Well, the Hudson Review has arrived with my article in it.[20] Not my best work, apart from the fact, which in itself doesn't worry me, that I'm not nearly as knowing as their other critics. Helen went into Boston today to buy a dress: I returned to the house at four and found her in quite a stew. Impulse, which isn't the Kemp forte, had pushed her into buying a kelly green dress, size 12 (she's a 14, of course), for $39 plus $5 for alterations—more than she'd ever paid for a dress before. So I proposed going back to the store (Stearns), and found it had already gone to the fitting room. She put it on & looked rather pathetic in it: I mistakenly decided that, as she'd already paid for it, my role was to encourage her in taking it. But she felt very miserable, and two drinks at the nearest bar only made things worse. That was the Touraine, where they get very shapely and statuesque waitresses and make them strip

their breasts down to the nipples. It bothers Helen, who has so little frontage. Dinner at Child's, which was dull.

Tuesday, January 9

[16] Today Helen phoned Hazel Bush to ask her what to do about her dress, & Hazel told her to phone the store & cancel the order, which she did. But they also said they'd return her money. She was so happy she forgot to be broody about my news, which was a phone call from Tom Bledsoe in New York, explaining what he wanted to see me about at the M.L.A. Notes. Notes to the whole bloody text.[21] They can only do it by adding another form to the binding, so they want sixty-four pages of notes. Apologies for being "so late" with the idea, like God making the world. I had presence of mind enough to ask for some more money that wouldn't be an "advance on royalties," and got promised $100. That means that my text will represent about fifteen times as much work as anything in their series—pressure of competition, of course. The thing is that I'm *not* an editor, & if I were I'd still be demoralized by their habit of making up the book as they go along. The only thing good in it is the renewed study of a text which after all *is* relevant to my project. And they're quite right. The book won't sell without notes.

[17] Margarets Avison & Newton tell us that Eleanor [Godfrey] has had a miscarriage at the same time that Rosie died.[22] I'm very sorry about Eleanor, but I can't work up much feeling about a stiff mutt. I have no love for parasitic fauna of any kind, & I think pets have a bad influence on people, the bigger the creature the worse the influence: look how bad Moby Dick was for Ahab. But while I am not fond of dogs, dogs are very fond of me, & I'm always fending off the embraces of some maudlin yap who's out to show me that he's man's best friend. Now Eleanor & Ray are very sensible & intelligent girls, but I'm certain that the fact that Rosie always cuddled up to me (because I ignored her and she's female) impressed them favorably with me, just as they always felt there was some occult evil in the people she bit. Animals' minds are still an unexplored mystery of nature, & hence become a hideout of superstition of all kinds, from anti-vivisection to the popular (because anti-intellectual) beliefs in the mysterious accuracy and insight of animal instinct. The Reader's Digest, which seldom makes a mistake about the sort of vulgar error that people want encouraged, runs columns going to prove that

every animal is directly inspired by God. The story of the cat who's abandoned two thousand miles from home & eventually turns up with a loyal but reproachful expression on its face is dug out of the newspaper morgue every three weeks or so. I suppose this is all covered in the *Natural History of Nonsense*, but it's a phobia of mine, as animals symbolize something to me: I dream of injuring them.

Wednesday, January 10

[18] Today I went over to the Lamont and looked over their Milton texts. I'm handicapped by not having my own books within reach, of course: I would I were at home. I met Ross Macdonald and he explained the reason for the jam in the library: they have a set of final exams at the end of January, and most of January is reading period. In any case the two annotated Milton texts I wanted, Fletcher's revised Cambridge and, more important, Merritt Hughes' Odyssey Press one, were both missing.[23] I dug out a Hanford text[24] & savagely attacked the notes, completing the first two books before I stopped to take breath. Then I found that the stupid ass Hanford had annotated only Books four & nine besides, so I skipped three & cribbed his notes to four—a foolish practice, but I didn't know what else to do at that point. However, three books done in a day isn't bad. I worked till nearly six on it.

Thursday, January 11

[19] This time I tackled the Widener, & found that everything was out except a bunch of old Veritas.[25] He's useful, but he's a hell of a gabby old bugger, and I only managed to get Book three done, & the other three revised. I've slugged through *Paradise Lost* so damned many times for Rinehart it's affecting me like the stone of Sisyphus, & I tend to forget Camus' remark that we have to think of Sisyphus as a happy man.[26] I find that Honig's New Year resolution is persisting, & we were chasing each other in & out of stall 227 all day: the first time we've clashed. In the morning we went out and scratched a few flea-bites: a notary public to swear at for Larner's briefs and my muzzle for not biting the State of Washington while they feed me;[27] a wire to Smith College, and an interview with a man at the Harvard Trust who represents the owners of Isabel Pope's apartment.[28]

Friday, January 12

[20] Well, after starting a new year and beginning a new diary, what should I do but collapse into the dumpiest, slumpiest, glumpiest week I've had since I came to this country. Three reasons: I want to break the back of this note-taking job quickly, and before I start to think about what an imposition it is;[29] Helen has completed her arrangements for moving to Isabel Pope's and is impatient to get going; and there's the usual post-Christmas January slump, aggravated at Harvard by this exam period.

Saturday, January 13

[21] Today I went back to the Child room and finished books seven and eight, apart from a note on Milton's view of the Creation, for which I'll have to read Woodhouse's article.[30] The mail brought a refusal from Harbage: he has to live in New York anyway and the English Institute spoils his vacation, so he never goes to it. Rosamund Tuve next, I think: though Blackmur's only a postage stamp. Harold Wilson for Shakespeare is a possibility; Alba Warren, whose book on English Poetic Theory 1825–65 is just out,[31] though he's on call from the Navy and it probably makes him restless. The rest of the mail, mostly letters from home, was more cheering.

1952 Diary

[1 January – 27 April 1952]

The diary is in the NFF, 1991, box 50, file 9. It is in a bound notebook (13.6 × 19.6 cm.), entitled The Canadian Line Daily Journal 1952, *published in Toronto by Brown Brothers, Ltd.*

Memorandum from 1951

[1] 1951 was my year for wandering, relaxing, getting new perspectives, listening to gossip, picking up friends, and generally indulging myself in mildly extroverted pursuits. This year, my fortieth one, will, I hope, be a year of writing. My main ambition is to write a small, incisive book (eight chapters), to be called, for the public, *Essay on Poetics*. Its private name is *A First Essay on Poetics*. For a second essay, first attached to and then dropped from the one I'm immediately going to write, is also in my mind. I have also a number of articles to finish, including one on comedy that I have some hopes of. A subordinate activity is collecting a bit more information about English 2i.[1]

[2] I suppose from one point of view it's the silliest kind of superstition to imagine discontinuity in the continuousness of time, to think that one has a fresh start in a New Year or that one should write tired poetry during a *fin de siècle*. But it seems the basis of ritual, and it's one of the techniques of detachment. Every year I think with some awe that my lines have fallen to me in pleasant places,[2] and that if one's luck depended on one's merit, the burden of responsibility would be too great to bear.

[3] For the first two months nothing will be possible except summary on the book. Duty articles include the poetry one, the Edgar book, and the Royal Society paper.[3] This last I could make an epic study for the book.[4] I have some hopes of finishing all this truck by the end of March, along with my lectures. Then I hope devoutly for a spell of relatively uninterrupted writing, and, if I get it, there's a distinct possibility of getting the book done, if I'm not sidetracked. A great many sidetracks have opened invitingly during the relaxation of the holiday season, and I must remember to preserve the shape of my cogitations. I manage to keep my pride, wrath, envy, avarice, gluttony and lechery within moral bounds to some extent: the great enemy is inertia.

Tuesday, January 1

[4] Today was sacrificed to the Ghost of Christmas Present, alias Santa Claus, alias Blake's Urizen worked over by a public relations man. Last night we had the Elders in, with Olive Brownlee, and Mrs. Allan dropped in from down the street. She had interesting things to say about crèches in Provence, where she was brought up. There you can represent your own farmhouse as the manger, and do carved portraits of the people in the village. Something about a *santon* I don't remember. I got a bottle of Bristol Cream sherry for the great moment, but it wasn't any better than the stuff that costs $2.50 less. The Whitleys were in *seriatim*, but neither stayed for midnight. Quiet, pleasant party: Dad made his effort and stayed up. Mr. Elder, aged 84, was wondering why he was stiff: at a Christmas party he was assigned the stunt of turning a somersault, and did.

[5] We didn't stay up much after midnight, but for all that we slept late. Dinner was in the middle of the day: a vast and succulent chicken pie made by Vera [Frye]. The Kemps were over for it. The Cronins were in in the afternoon, bless their hearts: Margaret, Helen, Catherine, and Mary Boulton. Pat is confined to bed now, and Martha, the nun, is doing most of the nursing. Catherine has a new job, working with that man Green [Greene] who lives in Sir Wyly Grier's house on Who's Who, & it's quite set her up.[5] They stayed till after seven and then we had a rudimentary supper, & the Kemps left at ten or so. Helen was exhausted by her social efforts, and when she crawled into bed her morale was very low. Too

much family. I explained to her that she was the centre of a social activity that made the holiday pleasant, and in fact possible, for two families and six people, most of them old, apart from friends, and that her sense of responsibility was about all that made life worth living for people she was closest to in life. I suppose if God thinks of everybody as children, lovable in their own right & full of potentialities, Satan the accuser thinks of everybody as already set in the mold of age, their conversation a response of cliché or stock anecdote to a conditioned reflex, their thinking a mechanical imitation of having thoughts, their future a narrowing repetition of vapid and silly mannerisms. God has hope and a few successes; Satan most of the facts and the balance of probabilities.

Wednesday, January 2

[6] Today I continued the holiday routine by sleeping in and not getting to work until lunch time. By then, of course, there wasn't much to do except scratch a few fleabites of correspondence. But I did get two bits of writing finished: my radio talk for next Sunday, and my Forum review of the book of nursery rhymes.[6] I emptied my usual line about nursery rhymes into that so that I'd be discouraged from making that speech again, and would have to think up another one. I didn't meet anybody at the College except Irving. I didn't ask him how he got along at Philadelphia, but he seemed to approve my remark that I thought I could waste time with less energy by staying home, so I can draw my own conclusions. However, the Hardin Craig paper on four-dimensional time in Shakespeare looks interesting.[7] Woodhouse was elected to the M.L.A. council.[8]

[7] The mail brought a letter from Datus Smith asking if I'd reread Roe's book on the Dante illustrations, which he's cut from 750 to 350 pages. I took the opportunity to recommend David Erdman's book,[9] and said I would. In the evening we all listened to the *Messiah* over the radio. The event, which has been annual with us for about five years, has lost its novelty for Dad, who couldn't have gone out for it, but he stayed for it. The choruses were very muffled and strangled by the radio, but the arias were clear enough.

[8] I was looking at the Second Eclogue of Virgil today: the notorious Corydon-Alexis one that was enough to keep Coleridge slanging away

at Virgil all his life. I have never myself felt any physical basis to my affectionate feelings for other men, but there must be one, and it seems to me as pointless to speak of all male love as buggery as it would be to speak of all marriage as legalized whoring. When Marlowe said that the beloved disciple was Christ's Alexis, he wasn't just being a bad boy:[10] the sense of his remark is that Christ's love, being human, must have had a substantial quality in it. I think—I'm just guessing—that our sentiment against the open physical expressions of love among men—embraces, for instance, and remarks about a boy's shape—may have made "normal" male relationships needlessly abstract, and forced all the "abnormal" people to become a separate caste of fairies. However, I'm so strongly "normal" in emotion myself that I don't really feel this.

Thursday, January 3

[9] I got out very late again and went down to the Royal York to get a haircut: I'd got a good cut there before, and did again: at any rate I won't have to cut it again or even comb it for some time, which is a relief. Then I went back to my office and went out for lunch about 2:30 to Murray's. That was a mistake, because I ran into that menace Irving again. Dearly as I love Irving, his fondness for getting into print and ether does take up one's time. He's anxious to get into—and have me get into—a *new* series of radio talks. He doesn't want to do lectures on natural theology, which is the one they're doing, partly because I backed out of that and advised him to do the same. But he wants to persuade the CBC people to do a second series on values in the humanities & social sciences, where he and I would shine. An hour or so later I picked up my symbolism paper and started working on it again.[11] Some of its proportions are straightening out, but it's only mildly interesting to me. It would be a lot more interesting if I knew what the hell I was talking about. I'm only guessing at what Mallarmé means, and the paper is closely bound up with a lyric chapter I haven't worked out yet.

[10] In the evening we went over to the Whitleys. Harold is now a sort of psychologist to twelve schools in his own right, so he and Vera [Frye] have a lot in common, mostly machines with long names that they use to test kids with: I suppose all this cumbersome apparatus may be essential for coping with the problem of universal education, but I dunno. The motivation behind it seems charitable enough. It was another hard day

for Helen: she'd got everyone—Vera, Dad, her mother and Aunt Lily [Lilly Maidment]—to go to see *The River*, a big Jean Renoir job in technicolor about India.[12] Aunt Lily [Lilly] gets up every morning at 5:30 and works hard until after ten at night, so when she relaxes on her day off she just goes to sleep. They came home for dinner & she fell asleep once or twice at the table. I gather that the movie was pretty sophisticated for most of the audience, and Helen was worried about her party going off properly. She may give the impression outwardly of being a sort of Mrs. Ramsey,[13] but actually she is like me, an introvert for whom social occasions are a conscious effort and not a means of relaxation.

Friday, January 4

[11] Last night the T.T.C. strike, which had been brewing for some weeks, suddenly wild-catted without warning, and left the city without any street cars. So I walked down to the office, and when I got there my shins were sore. So I decided I was badly out of condition and would keep on walking no matter what the street cars did. I met Archie Hare in the hall, who was laughing about the way Pelham's [Pelham Edgar's] mantle has descended on Ned [Pratt]. Ned had complained about the expense of coming down in a taxi—$1.75—and Archie asked him why the hell he came down when there were no classes. "Well," says Ned, "I had to take some friends to lunch at the York Club." I worked some more at my paper[14] and got it all done except for another paragraph that has to be written about archetypes. I don't like the paper, but it's probably all right. In the evening I walked over to Bessie McAgy's [MacAgy's] for supper & met the girls there: they'd got a taxi all right, and we got another to go home without difficulty. The evening was very pleasant, though we were running out of conversation when we left, which was early because I thought taxis would be hard to get later. Snapshots of Douglas & Jerry [MacAgy]. She said she was up playing bridge near us and there was a lot of excitement over a woman attempting suicide in her garage. Police up & so on. The only place I can think of where religion still influences the common law are the obstacles placed on divorce and the law against attempting suicide. Obstacles to birth control perhaps too. Whatever they are, they're invariably nonsense. Not that I approve of the natural man's approach to divorce, suicide or rutting in rubber: it's just that Jesus never said anything that even remotely sounded like "there oughta be a law."

[12] Helen seems to think Vera [Frye] will marry Teddy Downs, but I dunno. It would certainly double the patter of little shop talk around this house at Christmas if she did. She's also talking—probably more to make conversations than anything else—of going back to the Star to read fiction. I told her she wouldn't last long reading "he clasped her to his bosom until her garters popped" eight hours a day. It's tough enough even reading a higher grade of fiction: rereading Virginia Woolf's *Between the Acts* was a disappointing experience. Something in that woman's mind that slithers.

Saturday, January 5

[13] I stayed at home all day, as it seemed pointless to do all that walking, and the day had all the suspended animation of the last of a holiday. I think Vera's [Vera Frye's] much more rested this year, having had two weeks instead of one; and she speaks of having got more away from her school, which may be true even if we don't notice it. She and Dad talked about their trip last summer, and she plans to come in the spring with her car, and suggested bringing Peggy Craig, which rather surprised me. The Haddows, bless their hearts, drove us down: Donny and his mother came along.[15] The Fenian they brought in for Christmas stayed with them until yesterday, & has the chance of a job here. Not bad for a man who came up with a Yale friend going to Collingwood & just stopped here. We got Vera out & off without incident.

[14] I don't like what I'm doing, or not doing, on the Forum. This time we splashed at an article by Lyndon Smith on church & state, Anglican view, all over the front page.[16] The schoolmen drew up a table of fallacies in logic, but it seems to me high time that somebody drew up a corresponding list of fallacies in rhetoric: I doubt that it's really been done. One is the whitewash fallacy: Early Christians, says Smith, believed that forced belief was no belief. What he probably means is that in a few writers a few theoretical concessions in that direction may be detected. That is enough, apparently, to make a facade for the ferocious bigotry, superstition and sadism that was the bulk of Early Christianity. More serious is the half-truth fallacy. His main point is that the separation of church & state is not an unqualified success because of the tendency of the state to seize spiritual authority. But you can't just say that and then snigger, because it's only half the truth: the half modern times have

discovered. The other half, the evil of the temporal power of the Church, was discovered as early as the *Defensor Pacis*,[17] and can't just be ignored. Whatever value Catholicism has today is due to the fact that it's confined, greatly against its will, to spiritual authority. I'm beginning to wonder if the doctrine of the inseparability of theory and practice, which Christianity shares with Communism, isn't a pretty pernicious doctrine.

Sunday, January 6

[15] The usual slovenly Sunday morning: I had some vague notion of making a regular practice of going to church this year, but of course inertia triumphed. In the afternoon we walked down the Clifton Road cut off. There turned out to be a sidewalk of sorts all the way. It was a beautiful day, and a lovely walk. It took us only an hour, so we were forty minutes early at the studio. So many people were there I asked Helen James if Denton Massey's Bible class was broadcasting, but she said they were all musicians. I think I read my talk fairly well: I'm beginning to learn to read slightly faster, after long practice in reading slowly. I don't think I'll ever make three syllables of "every," and I may as well give up trying. My announcer was Rawhide—Max Ferguson. I was preceded by Clyde Gilmour and Gordon Sinclair, both in their top form. Helen James said Roy Daniells was very dull last week on— I think—the Literature of Power. I had good stuff, but must have sounded a bit flat after the other two. *Barabbas* is good, but after all it's nothing but crucifixion, stoning, flogging and torture all through, and *I Promessi Sposi* is, I think, really nothing but a muzzy and maudlin bore. Nothing takes hold. All I can remember is a remark that when tyrants force people to suppress their resentment, they actually feel less of it, which struck me partly because it was uncharacteristically incisive.[18]

[16] The thing I was afraid would happen has happened. Dad has been counting on a trip in Vera's [Vera Frye's] car next summer: says she talked about it all last summer. Vera, who doesn't think he could take such a trip (he does) & thought he'd lost interest (because of course he wouldn't mention it when *she* was here) thought that, after so many years of faithfully plodding back there every year, she was entitled for once to take a trip on her own to California—but that isn't definite. And I, of course, would consider it maudlin nonsense to buy a car, learn to drive it, take a very dull trip & force Helen to, all so he can see Main

Street again. I'll offer to pay his expenses for a plane trip, but I won't throw away a chance to write if I can help it. The reason I worry is that, having spent such a hell of a childhood building upon his vague promises that he had no intention of keeping, I hate to return him in kind. Incidentally, I wonder if psychologists have done any work on the son or daughter figure as a superego symbol for older people?

Monday, January 7

[17] Considering how long a holiday I had, I didn't do so badly this morning. That is, I only slept an hour after the alarm went off. I woke up dreaming I'd just wowed an audience by two wonderful jokes about Katy, my old Flanders mare.[19] It grew out of my regular recurrent dream about a troublesome animal: this time a horse. My two jokes were evidently the same joke. I said, don't sit on a horse's neck, because a horse who will let you sit on his neck will let you sit anywhere, and you might as well be out of reach of his teeth. I thought this lugubrious epigram was about the wittiest remark I'd ever made—maybe it is at that—and why it should have struck my subconscious as funny I don't know.

[18] Hilliard [Trethewey] drove me down, but was preoccupied by traffic, & didn't say much about Detroit. Del [Trethewey] & the kids heard me over the radio, but nobody around Victoria mentioned it—usually several do. The papers are writing up the strike the way they used to write up the war, and it makes for rather silly reading. Everything is so much better with the streetcars out of the way, is the line. One result is certainly that every heap that will roll downhill on four wheels is rolling. No mail at the office, somewhat to my surprise. John Graham said he'd be in today to collect his thesis, so I read it, but he wasn't. The nine o'clock was on Utopia: nothing special. My kids made a real effort to get there. Lunch at the S.C.R. [Senior Common Room]: the committee has bought a new clock, eight packs of cards, a cribbage board and a chess set. [Harold] Bennett wants to know where the money's coming from. The papers say Eisenhower's going to take the Republican nomination, in very "correct" terms which practically force the Americans to elect him. I'd glad I'm not an American. This year anyway. I finished my damn paper, all but the typing, and I was even going to start on that, but the letter e stuck. I can make do with a stuck a and a lot of profanity, but when it comes to a stuck e I can't do the subject justice. However, that

beat-up old pile of arthritic levers has typed out some of the world's best criticism. Hilliard drove me home again, and the traffic was fiendish, but he seems to like driving when it gets to be a sort of chess game. When I got home Helen told me that Jack Grant of U.B.C. died very suddenly, on Christmas Day. No details. So no wonder Roy's talk was dull.[20] I'm glad we got to see him in August.

Tuesday, January 8

[19] Got out late again: I'm not sleeping in: I set the alarm at 7:30 during the holidays and forgot to move it back to 6:30. Anyway, I could only choke down a cup of coffee and start out on the trek. I assumed my most heroic expression and walked one block. Then McCullough, in Orientals at U.C., offered me a lift. A man across the street named Weavers [Wevers], also in Orientals, & so recently from Princeton that his car still has a New Jersey license plate—horresco referens—drove down, with McCullough's two kids, Sheila, second year geography, and a boy in UTS.[21] So I was in time for my fourth year lecture,[22] but of course my kids weren't. I did say something about Utopia yesterday: I said that freedom for most people consisted in doing what they were accustomed to do, & unaccustomed habit was similarly the popular conception of bondage. I didn't say anything new about Newman, and my R.K. lecture gave them the regular table of imagery. More and more strangers appear in that room, most of them introduced by Lemke. I was told by Robins I'd have to move 4k from Wednesday at 12 for Crane,[23] so I moved it to Monday at 12 in Room 36. I spent most of the morning typing out my paper. The end of it is bloody awful, but I can't fix it now. I got two letters from Kingston about my broadcast. Marsh Laverty and Alexander, who said that book he did with Princeton has a Lagerkvist play in it.[24] In the evening Don Urquhart phoned to ask me if I'd discuss the meaning of the word "symbolism" with other students, or rather in front of them, and with Carpenter of anthropology.[25] Apparently Carpenter tells his students that he attaches *this* meaning to symbolism, & that certain other meanings are bullshit; at which point he reads a long passage from *Fearful Symmetry*: I wouldn't ordinarily go for the idea, but I think this business about symbolism constitutes a real difficulty for students. Several of Carpenter's students are, after all, in my R.K. course. I think I know what his objection would be, & I think I know how to meet it. Graham Cotter came to lunch, along with his thesis. I get a bit impatient with these

maudlin Anglo-Catholic converts with their party line on literature, though I try to restrict my disapproval to literary grounds. I can't altogether: there's too much real fixation present.

Wednesday, January 9

[20] Slept badly, for some reason, but got up early and found some more god-damned snow. So I got out and shovelled it off. The man who said that dirt was matter in the wrong place didn't make a very thorough analysis: the snow that falls on my sidewalk is very clean snow, but it certainly is matter in the wrong place. Anyway, I started to walk, and this time walked all the way down. Tough walking too, being very sloppy. I got down in plenty of time to write some letters, and went in to chapel. Kay took it. I went back to my office and got interested in the letter again—to Douglas Bush thanking him for his recommendations—and forgot all about the lecture I went down to give. Well, not all about it, but they were getting ready to leave when I walked in. However, I cleaned up my desk, except of course for the Christmas letters. And I mailed the blasted article to Peyre.[26] If he doesn't like it he can take his rectal temperature with it. A second year student of mine named Hornett died of pneumonia and Ruth Jenking's father had a stroke yesterday and is probably done for. I glanced at Hornett's essay, and it was pretty awful. Too bad: If it had been good I'd have sent it to his mother.

[21] The Council of Four met again in Kay's [Kay Coburn's] office. I think Joe [Fisher] is over-dramatic & Ken [MacLean] a bit fuzzy-headed, but they're all congenial, and the number four is wonderful. I suppose the fascination of bridge is in the number four: there's a hint of Charles Lamb to that effect.[27] Anyway, Bennett & Moore are very keen on Chairman as opposed to Head. de Beaumont made a silly Head, & because they were too yellow to deal with de Beaumont they make their own failure a precedent for weakening another department. Also Sid Smith is turning Head into Chairman, as part, Kay thinks, of a general (and largely unconscious) tendency of administrations to absorb power over departments. Irving is also Chairman, & came on that basis. Joe doesn't think the issue is worth fighting about. David Knight seems the leading candidate at present.[28] (Incidentally, I've seen no writeup of Jack's [Jack Knight's] concert, not that I've looked very hard). The Fishers drove me home, along with Ned [Pratt], & I got thirteen essays marked. Helen had

spent the day tidying drawers & the like & felt very depressed. But I got a note from Nancy saying she'd made "two skirts and a blouse" with the stuff we sent her.

Thursday, January 10

[22] Walked down again: I've approached the end of one of my winter rubber cycles. I buy a pair that's too tight, stretch & split them by stepping into them, & then, when I cross a street, the sticky slush sucks them off my feet. I started a review of Paradise Lost, & covered the first two books. Usual line: nothing new. In the R.K. lecture, on Job, I was trying to distinguish two kinds of endurance: a kind that accepts death, & a kind that accepts the necessity of death but rejects it. In Job's squawk & in Jesus' agony in the garden you reach the depth of misery but the spring of full life still breaks out. Something there, though it's old. I got twelve essays marked and in the morning Danuta Landau (Constant) came in. Things are looking up in the Film Board—a big grant of money. Douglas Valleau is in Meaford, working like hell on Meaford's music and drama: the former includes Pergolesi's Stabat Mater. Alan Brown has married a nice Victoria girl & has a job in Ottawa. Bev Burwell has not only got religion but wants to chuck all his art training & go into the Anglican ministry.[29]

[23] Helen came down and we had a quick dinner in Murrays: she told me to let her into the building if she was late, & I told her that for once in my life I'd respond to female whistles. We then walked down to the CBC & got there in good time. On the programme with me were an American named Geary, from Atlas Steel in Welland & a very decent & intelligent sort, and Pierre Berton of Maclean's. Berton was paired off with Hugh Kemp in New York, whom he knew, & they put on by far the best show: they knew each other & they know their stuff. Geary was paired with a man named Cummings, in Cadbury-Fry, & that was a good pair too, though Geary was better. But I was paired off, as a teacher, with some dame in Chappaqua, New York, who was a "reading consultant" in a private elementary school—a solemn owl who talked all the teachers' college platitudes about democracy. As Yvonne Williams said, phoning up afterwards, even if we had known what each other knew we wouldn't have had much in common. As it was, my part in the broadcast was confined to a crack about loyalty oaths and to observing that Canadians

in the States, with their "exciting" and "stimulating," talked as though they were hopped up with benzedrine. She thought I was referring to the dope problem among juveniles. [30]

Friday, January 11

[24] Went down with Hilliard [Trethewey]: the nine o'clock on Milton covered the third book, and tried to straighten out the business of God withdrawing from causation. Nothing new, but it went all right. My two-hour graduate group was completely bad: I'd prepared nothing for it, & just filled in repeating myself.[31] It would have been all right if they'd wakened up & asked a few questions, but they were as sleepy as a bunch of frosh after a seven o'clock football game, and did nothing. Either they understood nothing of what I've said to them or they understood it as well as I do. However, it did occur to me that Aristotelian or mimetic criticism is my second level. Platonic or enthusiastic-archetypal-erotic-comic-romantic criticism is my third level, and Christian or apocalyptic criticism is my fourth (and I suppose first) level. Anyway, I got rid of them and went over to a lunch for Crane at Hart House.[32] He & I were early and I talked to him: he was (to me) surprisingly friendly. Nothing much emerged at the lunch: I sat between Barker Fairley and Woodhouse. Barker is going to publish the lectures he was to do for Bryn Mawr[33] on his own, he says: Bryn Mawr offered to "try," but he thinks the situation's so fantastic he'd do better to go back to England.[34]

[25] I decided to walk back home in the afternoon. There was an Acta meeting at 4:30, but I had to skip it. On the way I met Norman Endicott and told him I was brooding about a speech for the first-class honour dinner, an institution I didn't approve of in the first place. He said: "They're good speeches too: that's what makes the rest of us so annoyed." Well, I went home and stewed, but of course did nothing. The Bennetts took us down & to my great surprise the event really turned into a party for me. Bennetts, Moores & Jessie [Macpherson] the only other staff present, but what with putting us in the receiving line (the Moores & Jessie ducked out of it), Bennett's introduction of me, & Moore's speech thanking me, there was quite a lot about me. I guess I amused them: I told them my story about the convocation at Andover Newton, gave a few random remarks about the States, said there was only one university however many buildings there were, told them

thinking was not a process like eating & sleeping but a habit founded on practice, & sat down. Not a major effort, but what the hell. The thing that depressed me about it was the difficulty of trying the [to] sense the unity of the audience and the occasion.[35] One of Brown's ideas, that dinner.

Saturday, January 12

[26] Slept in late this morning and walked down. Frittered the rest of the morning: I'd made a fair output of energy yesterday & the day before. Wrote to David Erdman telling him Princeton was willing to look at his book. A lad named Rowe, an Anglican clergyman who runs a magazine for the SCM called *Bias*[,] came in to ask for an article on Christianity & democracy. Several people had let him down and he was in quite a spot. I liked him & let him talk me into doing it—silly of me, & a definitely weak moment.[36] I must toughen up. Edith Fowke nicked me for a Woodsworth job in March.[37] I think the real reason I gave in was that I rather wanted to write out a hunch of mine about the separating of ritual & myth: a curious juxtaposing of Karl Barth on the Word & the Church & John Stuart Mill on liberty of thought & action. Also Irving came in to suggest putting A.F.B. Clark on the Forum board with possibility of editorship in mind.[38] The book of culture essays arrived yesterday,[39] and the binding is a lot simpler & less pretentious than the Davidson job.

[27] Helen came down for lunch and then went into the museum while I marked ten essays. That leaves only three more to do. We had some cocktails, came home for dinner, and then went down to see the Victoria play: [J.B.] Priestley's *An Inspector Calls*.[40] Poorish house: I must ask Archie if they went in the hole. Down to a rather cheap theatrical trick at the end, the play was a study in the contrast between the religious & the moral conceptions of guilt. A girl commits suicide & a family of five is proved to have been guilty, the father by firing her from her first job, the daughter by getting her fired from her second one, the mother by refusing her charity, the son & son-in-law by seducing her. As long as the inspector can attach their class-conscious selfishness to a specific crime, the younger people are convicted of sin; as long as a public scandal to the family is threatened, the older ones are. The inspector leaves & the whole thing is proved a hoax, whereupon the parents pick up where they left off. The younger people—son and daughter at least—are more deeply touched, but even they don't appear to have the strength of mind to face

the fact that all that guilt is potential in them whatever the accidents of consequence may be. At that point the phone rings and the real action starts, the inspector having been of course God. I saw Bert Arnold on the way out and said, "that's the way we do Kafka in English Literature."

Sunday, January 13

[28] The Leslies came in after the play last night. Charlie told us a bit about the English Exhibition, but of course he went to see England, so hadn't bothered much with it. He did go through some pottery works, and was fascinated by it. They left around one, and this morning I found I'd hit the bottom of one of my nose cycles. My nose keeps draining inside until it wakes up a couple of sore spots in my throat. Then I cough. Then I puke. This happened after breakfast, and the sensation of warm coffee going the wrong way made me puke some more. That in turn made me weak and shaky, so I went back to bed and stayed there till 4:30 in the afternoon. I scribbled a few notes for the paper I promised Rowe, and the fact that I'd promised it made me sick at the stomach again. At intervals I fell into an uneasy doze. Yuk. Aghk. Ye-oop.

[29] I ran into Ira Dilworth yesterday, and he told me how impressed he was by the sentence or two I got out on *Citizens' Forum.*[41] He's a smoothie. At least I rather think he is: Irving says not: just a professional culture-monger. He used to be principal of a high school in Victoria: Molly was a student there & she had the job of putting the flowers on the desk, every day. Something reminded me, too, of a very funny story about Sissons, or Mrs. Sissons, who of course has sensed that C.B.S is fundamentally a baby. She is reading minutes at the Walchia and the phone rings. For her. Conversation: "Yes, Charles. Yes. Very soon now. Very soon, Charles." Goes back, continues reading. Phone rings. For her. Conversation: "Charles. Thee knows very well. If thee interrupts again, thee will get no supper at all."

[30] I'm trying to say in this article that democracy, or rather what it tries to bring into the world, is the real natural society.[42] Rousseau was right in thinking that natural society was buried under history, wrong in the (eventually Nazi) notion that the natural society of the future would reconstruct one in the past, instead of realizing that the analogy afforded by the past was inner structure. Hence the notion that we're evolving

towards democracy is a vulgarism. This seems to me the basis of an important unifying formula.

Monday, January 14

[31] I seemed all right again today & got out for my nine o'clock: finished the Utopia. It's getting a little clearer now that what writers look for theoretically in Utopias, & we are trying to realize now in democracy, is a secular analogy of Christianity, the legal basis appropriate to its gospel. Any less adequate basis will cause a mutation of Christianity. It seems clear to me that More means that a Christianity that tries to interfere with a basis of natural religion broader & more tolerant than itself is asking for trouble with its own integrity.

[32] My writing students didn't show up so I typed out what I wrote yesterday and went into my new twelve o'clock. Talked about Newman and the evolution of dogma. Nothing new, but the intensity of the Protestant opposition my students build up amuses me. In the afternoon I did odds and ends & got John Graham's chapter off to him, finished the 2i essays, and tried to do some work on my Richardson-Fielding lecture. Ruth [Jenking] was very blue at tea: we were alone together, and she was oppressed by her father & the dreadful monotony of being with a man who can't live and can't die. She said she felt she'd thrown her youth away for nothing, & that her parents had dragged out of her all the promise she ever had as a scholar. Well, she didn't say quite that, but the trouble was I couldn't do anything except agree.

[33] It's very tiring to stay down for the evening, and it was rather foolish of me to do so: Hilliard [Trethewey] would have driven me up & Mrs. Wilbur down again.[43] Still, it's pleasant reading about a new subject, drifting over to the Park Plaza for a couple of martinis (also unwise, but very luxurious), having dinner alone (dreary, but part of the luxury of solitude) and coming back to the college in the dead hours. But my lecture wasn't at all my best work. Perhaps it was better than I think—no, it just wasn't up to my standard. It's hard to talk to those women—hard, that is, for *me* to talk to them, because they don't respond to anything discursive.[44] I don't know how George Edison gets along with them, but he sure as hell does. Apparently Gordon Roper made a terrific

hit with them on Addison & Steele the day before. I must tell him that. A letter from Roy [Daniells] confirmed the news about Jack Grant.[45]

Tuesday, January 15

[34] Very tired all day, but I walked down and started in on Arnold. Arnold is relatively easy to work on. My Hudson Review copies arrived: I reread my review of Kenner's Pound book[46] and was relieved to find that it didn't really sound as though I were sympathetic to fascism: I was afraid it would be evidence, for such people as this man who's attacked Eliot (Robins, I think), of the extent of the conspiracy against democracy.[47] My R.K. lecture was rather a flop: I sense a strong hostility in that class coming from somewhere, and it makes me self-conscious. Also I don't seem able to get going: I've lost the sense of discovery in archetypes. That goes for my graduate lectures too. What I now know seems obvious & dull: what I don't know I just plain don't know. I haven't the impetus of inspired guessing & getting hunches. Either I'm tired or I'm nervous—unless I'm just anxious to get at my book.

[35] I gave back essays through the afternoon, but as a means of getting to know the kids' names it's a long way from being foolproof. They come in too fast and they all look alike. Nice kids. This time I went home— Hilliard [Trethewey] drove me—and Peter Morgan picked us up for the Forum meeting. The new man, Roby Kidd, if that's it, was there. He's successor to Corbett on the ation of ation.[48] Nice guy with a lot of new ideas. I think he'll be fine, & might even take over the Chairmanship. Ivon Owen sent me a letter resigning from the Board. I never wonder why other people get out of the Forum: I just wonder why the hell I don't. Otherwise the meeting was fine: I seemed to be unusually fertile in suggestions myself. We loaded up Alan [Creighton] with a hell of a lot of stuff to do, anyway, and something should emerge. Allan Sangster drove us home, strong & silent. One bit of good news is that John Nicol's landed a job I recommended him for. Not the CBC, but another one Sword wrote me about. Helen was over at Isabelle's [Isabel Whitley's] all afternoon. She has a small lump in her breast and has killed and buried herself with cancer several times. Then she found Isabelle had a pain in her hip and was stewing about cancer too. Dull weather, and a slumpy time of year, made so much worse by this damn strike.

Wednesday, January 16

[36] A terrific package of guck arrived from Carol Ely Harper today: a great floundering letter with annotations, an earlier letter not sent, & several enclosures. Her poem *The City* has gone into its sixth book, & she wonders if it'll ever stop. Also she wonders if she's going nuts, & proceeds to document the case for the prosecution by talking to me as though I were everything from God to Satan. It made me feel very depressed, just as it would to stand in a maternity hospital listening to all the moans. Only this is worse, because it includes delirium, transference, & a considerable amount of talking up the situation.

[37] This term I have nothing on Wednesday except my ten o'clock, which, being on Ascham, hadn't much new. I did say that the Elizabethan conception of grammar was one that arranged reading, writing & speaking according to the rules of decorum: you didn't take one as a norm: didn't try to write as you speak or speak as you write. Something there. Somebody in one of my classes asked me about the Gospel teaching on childlikeness, & I said the core of innocence, the ability to treat the world as still alive, was itself the child in man and the spark of life in him. Without it a man just became a machine of conditioned reflex and response, to all practical purposes dead, & just waiting for the mechanism to run down. I note that the Robot aspect of man is easiest to see across a gap of generations: the young see it in the old, the old in the young.

[38] Norah McCullough has been in town, and Helen brought her in this afternoon. I was edgy because my 2i kids were coming in, or trying to. However, it passed off as shyness. Norah looks older, but there's so far no hint of her leaving Saskatchewan. Evidently the Davises are getting out of Montreal—I say the Davises because she seems to make a fanfare of bitching when she leaves a place—did at Portland, according to the Chitticks, & here she called Gordie Webber to her home to tell him he'd misbehaved at her party the day before. I stayed down late and went home with the Fishers. We had a quiet evening listening to the Marriage of Figaro on CBC: but that opera is pretty pointless without a stage. That is, you remember what good fun it is on the stage, but if one heard it first on the air it would just be a lot of complicated cackle interspersed with a few lyrics of meaningless beauty.

Thursday, January 17

[39] Overslept: I don't know whether I didn't set the alarm or just ignored it. I figured I'd better take a taxi. The poor guy got jammed in a heavy lineup & cut out of line by a ham driver, so he said: "Did you see what that son of a bitch did to me? Jeez, so help me God, I'll get that bugger if it's last fuckin' thing I do . . . Sorry, professor. Parn my French. You know, I was in the army, an' you know what that does to a guy's language. But when I think of what them god-damned bastards get away with . . ." I got him soothed down & went in to my nine o'clock, covering the war in heaven. I said that just as Christ in heaven, Jesus in history & Christ in the Church were identical in form, so the City of God, the human body and the Church were identical in form. I don't know why I said that. Something for the R.K. lecture.

[40] There was a letter in the paper this morning from a certain Edward J. Pratt, who often writes. Ned says he's a nuisance to him, & that he got Deacon to put a note in his column explaining that his name was Edwin.[49] Once this guy wrote a letter advocating birth control & Ned was phoned up by all the stumblebums on the Knights of Columbus executive telling him he shouldn't interfere with natural processes. I note, however, that Ned got into the argument a bit before he admitted he wasn't the man, bless his heart.

[41] Helen went to a concert: Boszormenyi-Nagy playing. He plays too damn much. Women's Musical Club at Eatons: first performance of Arnold Walter's piano sonata. She took Mrs. Matheson, whom she picked up at Eaton's, & who drove her to the college ten minutes after I started to walk home. It was a dismal day, and I tried to cheer myself up in my usual fashion, by buying some music (at Gordon Thompson's).[50] I got Arnold Walter's sonata, which so far I don't much like: it belongs to what in my Philistine moods I call the eek and blop school. I also got some more Soler—three sonatas from that bunch he published in London, a Dussek sonata, some Villa-Lobos trifles, and the Schirmer Schubert collection of fantasies & stuff—badly overdue in my library. Also some bits of early Brahms—sarabands & gigues. Not too bad a haul: cost me eight bucks. However, I resisted the urge to buy some liquor, so I saved *some* money, for a few days.

Friday, January 18

[42] In the Milton this morning I said that the creation *de Deo*, as opposed to one by God out of something else, which, as the prepositions show, would be a *female* power, is the prototype of the Virgin Birth, in which there is incarnation but not copulation. Creation excludes Satan, hence no "Manichean" alliance of the material and the evil is possible. Chaos is neither a thing nor nothing, but the negative aspect of God's will. The rest was old stuff: Raphael on the planets and so on.

[43] The graduate group had Mary Waugh's paper on *Descent into Hell*. Not bad: she's a bright child. The conception of Gomorrah as the place of auto-erotic love is interesting. I dislike Williams so much—he pushes in, hectors & preaches, and in general writes archetypal fiction the way Samuel Smiles writes representational fiction—that it's hard for me to settle down to him. When I do, he's better than one would think. I still haven't isolated the archetypal strain in prose fiction—Bunyan, Swift's *Tale of a Tub*, George Macdonald, Chesterton, Lewis, Williams. It isn't the anatomy, and I doubt if it's the romance-anatomy combination I used to think it was.

[44] I tried to do some work on that fool paper,[51] & then Helen came down & we went into the tea for Paraskeva Clark's exhibition—good exhibition it is too. Paraskeva was charming. Murray Adaskin has a job in music at Saskatchewan, which will give him time to compose. He's a very serious composer, evidently: his recommendations for the job included letters from Milhaud and Stravinsky.[52] I told him about Bentley & his Gabriel Fauré society. John Hall has had pneumonia, & looks it. I talked to the Ignatieffs, to Art Moore, to A.Y. Jackson (who I think hears very little of what one says) to Douglas Duncan, Mrs. Alford (I hear that the *second* Mrs. Alford is now leaving John A.) and others. It was hard work: I hate those affairs. We came back to find a letter from Moore giving us all a $300 hike, so we went out to the Park Plaza. There we picked up Ira Dilworth, who turned out to be a very good companion: I didn't realize he'd been a graduate student at Harvard, closely associated with Babbitt. Then we had dinner at that French place on Church & Charles, filet mignon, & caught a taxi home. Dilworth says he's working on Emily Carr's journals, & says they're fascinating.[53] Uh huh.

Saturday, January 19

[45] The morning paper carried Deacon's highly eulogistic review of the *Heritage* book.[54] I wrote a far better essay for the Davidson book,[55] but the publishing and publicizing of that book were both badly buggered. Deacon said I was brilliant, that I'd ignored the arts, & quoted my peroration. Letter from Helen James saying people liked my Citizen's Forum effort: the Ottawa Citizen editorialized on it, calling me an "educationist" & so may *Time*.[56] I started to walk down, but R.A. Daly picked me up. His son Tom produced the *Royal Journey* film.[57] He's very impressed by *Ti-Coq*—I think he said he'd seen it four times, twice in French & twice in English.[58] I got in and finished my damn article:[59] it's not very good as an article, but it begins to say something of what I want to say. In any case it's too good for *Bias*. What ails me anyway? Don't I know I'm good?

[46] Helen came down for lunch & met Peggy Ray, whose exasperated frustration has finally got to that vicious circle where it isn't really trustworthy any more, so that the people who have always ignored her now feel justified in doing so. The slattern complex in her has of course destroyed her *authority* long ago. Well, anyway, a lot of people weren't "consulted" about the students' union, so they're mad. Something about no driveway for trucks. Her bitterness about the Library Board was more understandable: she says Irene Clark [Clarke] resigned because they got somebody else (I don't know who) on the Board just to fight her, who's never come since she's quit. I dropped into Murray's for a cup of coffee & found Archie [Hare], Moff [Woodside], Bill Fennell & Art Moore there. Some gossip that sounded interesting, but I was too bemused by having finished an article too quickly & having it snatched out from under my nose to listen to it.

[47] We went over to Ely's & I bought some clothes: flannels, a new suit (blue & double-breasted, no vest—another racket), and what women call accessories. Also a pair of black clothes—I mean shoes—Dad's yapping at me about the cost of living. We got a taxi home, sharing it with a lame girl who lives at Millwood & Bayview & works at Dundas & Keele. Maybe I just feel like a mean old Fascist because I'm reading the Globe & Mail, but I think that, if fairness to workmen is guaranteed, legal arbitra-

tion as a final settlement of public utility strikes ought to be compulsory & anything else should be treated as an act of civil rebellion.

Sunday, January 20

[48] Tried to read some of the music I bought: the Soler is most interesting. The Dussek is full of some real feeling, but can't get far away from its tonic chord. The Schubert, like so much of his instrumental music, is café music. A pretty tune starts, & people look up and notice it; then it goes into commonplace figuration of a Czerny exercise type, and people go back to their drinks and conversation. It's fine for cafés, but it makes dull reading.

[49] I've been meditating an article for something like *The American Scholar* on "The Return of Inflections." That is, I've been wondering if I could find any evidence for tendencies in the "vulgate" to build up inflectional endings out of the present mass of slurred particles. The reason it interests me is that at the other end of speech poets are trying to cut out the mass of analytic prepositions & stuff in order to put their images (nouns & verbs) more directly together—hence so much obscurity. For one thing, the vulgate tendency to break down sentences with subordinate clauses into a series of coordinate ones gives conjunctions a quite new syntactic ambiguity. I think of the man in the hospital who said to me "I'm the guy that the tractor fell on his foot." To translate that into conventional grammar we'd need two sentences, one personal ("I'm the guy on whose foot the tractor fell") and one impersonal ("I'm the guy of whom it is said: 'the tractor fell on his foot'"). Or I think of the "no trunks only" sign I saw at a swimming pool—the concentration of that is like many grammatical devices in modern poetry.

[50] I got out some books of Canadian poetry and started looking at *that* job. What a job. Here's Philip Child gone and written a long poem that's complete bullshit from beginning to end, and who am I to say so?—a friend of Philip Child's. However, the growth of hypocrisy in public criticism doesn't alarm me as much as it did. What some people regard as a loss of honesty is often just an outgrowing of their own emotional attachment to symbols of their emancipation from mediocrity. Anyway, if I get through this job without outraging either the people who write Canadian poetry or the people who read it, if any, I'm going to apply for

the honorary degree of D.C.L. (Doctor of Canadian Letters). It seems to
be a Maritimer's year: Charles Bruce is the best of the conservatives, Kay
Smith of the more cosmopolitan people, & Elizabeth Brewster of the
amateurs.[60]

Monday, January 21

[51] The mail brought a wistful note and poem from Charlie Bell which
exacerbated my conscience, Erdman's thank-you note, John Graham's
response to my annotations on his thesis, and—the climax—a letter from
Merritt Hughes asking me to take a key spot in the English One sequence
at the M.L.A. this year.[61] A really very flattering proposal. I think I'll do
my eiron-alazon stuff for it, though it leaves the publication of that paper
pretty late.

[52] The nine o'clock was on Hakluyt, pleasant but not new. At ten my
three geniuses arrived. Ann Carnwath is the only one who has anything
at all on the ball. This time she turned up with a very business-like
summary of a novel with its scene in Ceylon. Two sisters, the older one
menstruating late & so falling behind her younger sister, only to forge
ahead more strongly in later years. What one might call a late riser.
I think Ann may get somewhere as a writer. Anyway, she's certainly
reading up on Ceylon. The twelve o'clock did some of the Arnold culture
diagram.

[53] I got a letter off to Carol Ely Harper, doing my damnedest to say
what I thought the occasion called for. I tried to interpret her situation as
the taking over of the will by the imagination, so that what's been used to
controlling things in a linear direction panics when it's swung around
the cyclic rhythms of creation. Not all Muses, I said, are soft & cuddly
nudes: some are just obscene harpies that swoop and snatch and fly off.
The business of the transference was tougher, but I told her that her
column of light was the pillar of fire, that it had never left Seattle, and
that it would eventually separate from me. I sure as hell hope it does.
Also I hope I discouraged her from coming to Toronto, and for all the
self-indulgent adolescence in her letter she might do that.[62]

[54] There was a department meeting, but I skipped it and went home
with Hilliard [Trethewey]. He was inducted as an elder in Deer Park

Church yesterday, and in a rather shy way he's very proud of it. He says it's because the kids go there. Christianity went officially on the rampage yesterday on the campus: this year it's in charge of Canon Milford, who looks like a harmless & rather dim-witted person. I hope they'll all remember the ancient text: "The Kingdom of God cometh not with yackity-yackity-yack."

Tuesday, January 22

[55] I really didn't get much done today: I typed out what I had on the poetry, but I gather there's more stuff to come.[63] The nine o'clock was the worst I've ever struggled through. When I finished I told them they could go back to bed. But sooner or later I'm going to break down and tell them that a lecture, like other public performances, can't be indefinitely better than its audience, and that when they complain about dull lectures, they should realize that a professor doesn't produce dullness nearly so often as he reflects it. I know the light's bad & so on, but the real reason is just self-indulgence.

[56] The twelve o'clock was on Leviathan symbols. That's a relatively dead class too, I think, though I suspect myself a bit there. They're not moving with me in the rhythm of discovery, which may mean that I'm not in it myself. I went in to lunch & found Chalmers there. He's very pleased with my chapter, somewhat to my surprise.[64] He said "You're prophetic, boy." The very word I was groping for. One thing I do have in common with most of the prophets is a profound unwillingness to be a prophet. A chilly review in the Varsity, probably by Ann Carnwath. I wonder where the royalties on that book go. The Varsity is full of the preaching mission, on this week, but on its book review page had a beautiful cartoon by Hugh Niblock representing a sheep saying "Lost, hell—I'm hiding." Mrs. Niebuhr, who I understand is an Anglo-Catholic, came up to talk on "The Christian view of Sex."[65] According to reports, the view is dim but clearing.

[57] I started to walk down, but some people on Inglewood Drive picked me up. Hilliard [Trethewey] drove me home, and Del [Trethewey], from a faculty tea at the Loves. It was a filthy day, with a freezing rain, and there was a terrific tie-up later. The end of the TTC strike was announced some time before six—the wage dispute submitted to arbitration, for

God's sake. The worst feature of it was the aggravation of a normal January claustrophobia. Helen didn't go to the faculty tea because she went to Mrs. Arnold Walter's. She (W.) says she likes to collect dreamers. Not my impression of Helen, but a certain Lady Robinson was there who gets ideas in her bath. One was buying Eaton's College Street cheap "because it's losing money anyway" and turning it into a civic centre. I think old Arnold's sonata is really pretty good stuff, though I'm only what you might call familiar with the slow movement, for obvious reasons.

Wednesday, January 23

[58] Walked down, ignoring the street cars, which seemed empty. I finished Hakluyt & started on Deloney. Damn it, I've still got Hooker & Bacon & Browne to do, & I'd better step on it. Last night Alistair Mackinnon [Alastair McKinnon] phoned & said he had something on his mind that Irving and Leslie had told him he would have to come to me with. Very mysterious. He came in on the dot of his appointment, plumped down on a chair, & said: "What sex is God?" I didn't exactly bring him to the point of nosing the divine balls, like Moses, but I told him what occurred to me. The mail brought a letter from the Royal Society saying B.K. Sandwell was trying to get Mazo de la Roche nominated for the Nobel Prize. Fellows of Section II were asked to assent or dissent, and failure to reply (to Alexander) would be taken as assent.[66] They were also asked to state reasons. I said, dissenting, "it's not all that important to have a Canadian win the Nobel Prize." Last year I was rather proud of being an F.R.S.C.—but that was only because my official name is short of degrees. Lobbying for a writer to get a prize which, if she won it, would become worthless because she won it doesn't strike me as a very dignified occupation.

[59] Laurie Cragg was over to give a talk on Science & Religion at 1:30. I stayed up in my room until 1:33, & then thought why be so damn ill-natured. So I went down to hear him—very good, in a rather conventional way. The questions were good too, some of them—one asked him what the religious analogy was to the scientist's suspension of judgement—he'd walked into that by calling it doubt. Walter Stewart came in & we discussed the financial failure of the play. I get more & more worried about the type of goon who gets on the V.C.U. [Victoria College

Union] executive—next year it may be Ed File, which would be Keith Davey all over again. Well, then I went over to U.C. with Irving, who's all steamed up about Christianity, what with the flurry of publicity for the book. Evidently, as I feared, Canon Milford was a flop. Well, what I went over for was Gilson's paper on medieval scholarship. Terrific crowd, so that we had to move into Room 8. I know a Frenchman's idea of a formal lecture is different from a colloquium, but he wasn't as disconcerted as he pretended to be. The paper had a great deal of wit & charm, & only when one thought it over afterwards did one realize that after all the old bugger really hadn't *said* anything. Or at least, what he did say, that historical abstractions like "Renaissance" are not things, I didn't need to be told.

Thursday, January 24

[60] In the discussion afterwards he had quite a field day, and at times was a bit unscrupulous. He'd said that the Romans had contributed nothing to philosophy & science, & about six people tried to explain that Roman law actually was a contribution to philosophy. One very inarticulate lad was, I think, trying to say that the social realization of a thing is as important as its individual discovery: in other words if you fill Europe with aqueducts & paved roads you're surely making *some* contribution to science. But Gilson would have none of it.

[61] Afterwards, I walked up to the Park Plaza & had some drinks with Helen. It looks as though I'm going to have to cut out cocktails in the middle of the week. Ira Dilworth was there again, and seemed a little more relaxed. He's got an apartment, on Blythwood, in a house 110 years old, but, I gather, beautifully furnished. Then we got into a taxi & went down to the Service Line to proofread the Forum. I was sleepy from the drinks & they were late, so I'm not sure if this arrangement really will work. But next time I try it I'll have no drinks & will take a book with me. It was a poor issue, which depressed me additionally.

[62] Today was rather a wasted day: being keyed up the night before & not getting enough sleep does that to me. I took a streetcar this time, & I think everything will soon be back to normal. I came down with John Finlay & what appears to be his girl friend. The nine o'clock was on Book IX [of *Paradise Lost*], & got some relatively interested inquiries. Kierkegaard's distinction of dread & leap corresponds roughly to the distinc-

tion between Eve's fall and Adam's, not that the distinction works. The twelve o'clock, curiously enough, opened out beautifully into Leviathan symbolism from Job: the thing was that they had their Bibles with them. The afternoon was dull. I got my picture taken with the Acta staff & made the dull jokes I always make, went back to the office & typed out a dull review of Child's dull poem,[67] went into a dull tea with everybody yapping shop, walked home on a dull cold day to find Dad in a dull mood. Helen had been out shopping for remnants & had also been to tea in Ruth Hebb's new house, which I gather is pretty wonderful. Separate rooms for all four children and huge closets. It made Helen a bit restless about 27 Clifton. Letter from Vera [Frye] threatening to bring Marvel Hiller for her week at Easter.

Friday, January 25

[63] The nine o'clock finished P.L. [*Paradise Lost*] to all practical extent: the kids were sleepy & didn't say much. They depress me when they just sit & yawn & scribble & look over each other's shoulders to see what their neighbors are writing. It's so eloquent a testimony to the failure of the university to stimulate high school children into a new & participating maturity. The mail brought a note from Henri Peyre thanking me for my symbolism article—evidently my feeling about it was wrong & it is somewhere very near my standard.[68] It won't be out until April, though.

[64] The graduate group had Smallbridge's paper on Rappaccini's Daughter: quite a good analysis, & one much better related to my approach than Mary Waugh's. It worked out, of course, to another one of Hawthorne's anti-Puritan fantasies, the folly of counteracting original sin (the poison) by moral good (the antidote). The poison flower Beatrice wears is the scarlet letter over again. The archetype, however, is the Sleeping Beauty, the young virgin discovered in a perilous place, & of course the logical 19th c. development of Archimago is the mad scientist. I pointed out the sexual things: the germ of love or the child-virgin is in the perilous place of the mother (ring of fire, thorns, labyrinth, & so on); also the identification of flowers, jewels & water. The fact that it explicitly *wasn't* a romantic-agony vampire story, but just skirted being one. Smallbridge mentioned Spenser and the story of Vertumnus & Pomona as sources. It was quite a good session, though they're a fairly mute lot except for Gordon Smith.

[65] I thought I was going to have a clear afternoon, but Norman Endicott turned up at lunch with that desperate look in his eye that means things aren't going so well with his figuring. He wouldn't stay to lunch: had a date, he said. M.A. Committee meeting. So *that* bitched my afternoon. I went to tea at U.C. & found MacGillivray there, & then Knox & Fisher. Knox said the Page [Madelaine] had written a fine paper on music in Marston's plays. She should do her thesis on that & not angels. The M.A. thesis subjects were a very strange lot: nothing earlier than 1660. I have Mary Waugh & Hugh MacCallum, & took the second reader place for a symbolism-in-early-Browning one.

[66] I keep wondering if I'd clarify my mind by getting a few "Second Essay" topics out of the way. I remember what an experience it was to do my religion and society paper[69] and if I could work out my "Fallacy of the Selected Tradition" thesis in a good lively polemic article it would help. The point is, where would it end? I suppose in an Arnoldian classless society.

Saturday, January 26

[67] Very lazy day. The only work I did was to read Graham Cotter's thesis—I certainly hope he's right that I *am* doing an appraisal of it. It's a disappointing thesis—a strong beginning with a Lowes-type of job on *Childe Roland* from the letters & earlier poems: very good. But all the rest of it is a rather commonplace job. Some good aperçus here & there. I note that he rejected Jung because, quite properly, he couldn't swallow the race-consciousness bullshit, but that the rejection involves, for him, a rejection of archetypes as such. I trace here the principle that the attraction of the sacramental analogy is that it relieves poet and critic from the larger responsibilities. I've always known that, but to see something at work increases knowledge of it.

[68] I've been reading Kierkegaard's *Repetition* for the second time, as one wouldn't expect a book with a name like that to yield much on the first reading. It's basically an anatomy, I think, but of course an existential genetic 19th c. anatomy would have to be a confession too, so it's the *Sartor Resartus* hybrid. The trouble is that he disguises the confession & approaches the anatomy quizzically, so it's hard to figure out just what the hell he does mean. Like his Victorian contemporaries in England, he

has a stentorian censor at his elbow ready to roar down any irony it doesn't feel it can control. By that I mean that one has to distinguish irony within a convention from irony that threatens the convention. Or humor, perhaps, even more than irony. One can recognize humor in Wagner's Ring, for instance, in such things as Mime & Alberich, & yet simultaneously realize that the Ring is fundamentally humorless. One thinks of Sir Dinadan in Malory: as long as it's established that he's a brave knight & has us quarrel with the *idea* of trying to break up the hardware of everyone he meets, he can joke about his courage: "then the king & queen laughed that they might not sit." The censor himself has a noisy, guffawing relish for jokes held in leash & prides himself on his sense of humor, but when the joke shows a power of biting him in the ankle it's a different story. So with Kierkegaard: he's a great humorist, like Carlyle, yet his final sympathies are anti-humorous. I think the fear of subversive humor is clear even in Dante. However, this *Repetition* book deals with my epic circle idea, that the essential quest is cyclic, but returns, not to the same point, but to the same point renewed and transformed. As opposed to recollection, it's the Protestant justification by faith as opposed to the Catholic sacramental repetition of substantial presence. At least I think it is: whether he knows it or not is another matter.

Sunday, January 27

[69] Anne Bolgan phoned up in a bit of a tizzy because she'd missed her comprehensive by two marks. So she came to see me, a mass of confusions and resentments I tried to calm down. I suppose every attempt at a charitable act has a bit of the "peace be still" taming of chaos in it. She started off with a very bad relation—no details—with her father, taught in an ignorant & superstitious convent, guilt feelings & a fixation on a neurotic mother superior led her towards becoming a nun. Then a rebelliousness asserted itself & she bought eighteen volumes of Freud & read through them, ending with a pronounced list to port. Now she's educating herself, slowly & through deep realization. I asked her what she did summers, & she said she handed out bath house keys. Twenty hours a week, sixty dollars a week & a free cottage. Obviously a plum like that has to be pulled by someone else—in her case a Supreme Court Justice who's just died, so she's not sure of this summer. What a country. She says, very truly, that it's at least honest corruption, if that makes sense.

[70] The Staples came in in the evening: Helen thought they would be suitable for Dad apart from being our own guests, & they tried to be, but Dad doesn't do much with what's handed him socially. They know a lot of gossip—too much, Helen thought. I like to hear gossip, not for its own sake, but for the sake of knowing what other people know. We missed the Massey money because Mrs. M. took offence when her offer to build a women's residence, subject to putting Lillian Smith in as dean of women, was refused. Mrs. McLaughlin (I think) wanted to come on the Board of Regents & Brown refused because her sister or daughter or something had run off with Clara MacEachren's husband. So we missed McLaughlin money, apart altogether from the Havelock business. Hook brought money in—he was not only an expert figure skater but a golfer good enough to be offered a professional job, & his golfing friends included Dunlop. Ned doesn't seem to do the trick. Jim Endicott was engaged to a plain older girl named Nina Yeomans, had the wedding all set, & a week before went to Chicago for a conference, fell in with Mary Austin who'd just inherited a lot of money, got engaged to her, told Nina abruptly he was calling it off, had his wedding the same day & his honeymoon in the same spot as the one planned, but with a different girl. Tried to square himself by telling people Nina had "chased" him, & was "told off" by Marion Hilliard.[70] Douglas Bush had weak eyes, a bad heart, thyroid trouble & arthritis (he gave lectures at Ann Arbor in a wheelchair), was envious of athletes, tried very hard to enlist in the First World War, even to the extent of calling himself Dubois & coming up before a very anti-French judge.

Monday, January 28

[71] They're best, of course, on Palestine, & told stories of how they deal with locusts there: trenches and flame-throwers, mostly. Storks eat locusts until they're so full they can't take off, and men beat pans all night to scare away the jackals who would otherwise eat *them*.

[72] They stayed till eleven, and I was rather tired for my nine o'clock on Deloney. Nothing there. The twelve o'clock was on Arnold, also nothing much. The President's Report is out now, and there's quite a lively education controversy afoot in the Varsity.[71] Also a religious one, with a St. Mike's lad proving the existence of God by the argument from design.[72] So I told my kids what I thought of complaints about dull lectures.

They took it very well: they're very decent kids. I also edged a little closer to my identification of Arnold's culture and Plato's Symposium.

[73] Graduate English meeting this afternoon in Woodhouse's office. I had to go because I'd promised Anne Bolgan I'd speak for her. What that little nuisance hadn't told me was that she'd tried her comprehensive *twice*, and was technically out. I spoke for her all right, & we granted her the special concession of a third try. I was reminded of what Bill Graham told me about his father, a judge, who after years of trying to take human factors into account finally realized that all he could really do was just administer the law. Now I've got Anne Bolgan on my hands, who will get married long before she finishes her thesis,[73] and so neutralize whatever it was I spoke for. It's a type of action that is neither wrong nor regrettable, but superfluous. I also asked about auditors, & a remark Claude Bissell made implied that he thought I was showing off a bit. I was, too. Joe Fisher sat beside me: it's clear that that's going to be his position for some time to come.

[74] I stayed down for cocktails and dinner, and then went to the Graduate English Club. Earle Sanborn on Yeats' view of history. I sure as hell didn't want to go, but I'm his supervisor and I didn't see how I could help it. It was a very good paper, delivered with that mature authority that has always impressed me about Sanborn. The handling of the discussion afterwards was even more impressive. He's a born teacher. I don't know why he didn't mention my article, as his thesis was the web spun from its bowels: probably thought it would be fulsome. Woodhouse was there: his conscientiousness never ceases to amaze me, and he brought Crane. Patchell & [David] Knight came & talked to me in the interval; and Parr got me into a corner afterward, so it was midnight before I got to bed.

Tuesday, January 29

[75] I must remember that it's dangerous to stay down, foolish to drink heavily (three Martinis is a fair amount of straight gin) the evening before a nine o'clock day, and murderous to swallow two cups of strong coffee late in the evening before a nine o'clock. I slept badly, & the tight grip of my nerves didn't relax in any part of me. Burwash used to say that a raw recruit, who shoots and can't hit, is the opposite of a consti-

pated owl, who hoots and can't shit. Getting up to lecture after a night
like that gives me a fellow-feeling with such owls. The nine o'clock
began Ruskin, but just gave the stuff on the Whistler trial and so on. The
twelve o'clock was, I think, a wasted lecture, on the nature of the charitable act. That is, I felt it was irrelevant, and I can't seem to shake off a
feeling of marking time in that course. I asked them to bring their Bibles
next time in the hope of doing as well as I quite unexpectedly did in the
first year.

[76] The Varsity had an editorial today on page 4 of the President's
Report, where he quotes one Galbraith, Regius History in Oxford (they
reproduced his name as "Gilbreth" in the Varsity) as saying that the
lecture, as it shouldn't be a substitute for student reading, should be as
far as possible a discussion, the lecturer being *en rapport* with his audience & then speaking as impromptu as possible.[74] That actually works
out to a terrific plug for me, as I lecture that way & always have.

[77] I went home in the afternoon, and out to the ballet—the new Canadian ballet, that is—in the evening. I know I've assigned a place to the
ballet in my drama article,[75] but every time I see a ballet I feel it's a damn
silly form of art. They did the second act of "Giselle," a long romantic story
with music by Adam first done in 1842 in London—I wonder what they
did about female legs in ballets then. Tragic tale of dead lovers & cemetery
spirits called Wilis—very typical German romanticism. I found the music
stodgy, the drama posed and labored, and in general it gave me the Wilis.
The second was a formal design, men in red & women in blue, & I
generally like those best. But the music was Brahms variations on a theme
of Haydn, which I think is pretty wonderful music, and the music was so
self-sufficient & the dancing to it so damned unnecessary and irrelevant
that I couldn't seem to get feeling right at all. The second act of the
Nutcracker Suite I did enjoy, because, for one thing, it kidded itself a bit
and wasn't too damn portentous, and for another the use of puppets and
doll figures seems to me to be right. I'd like to see Petrouchka sometime.

Wednesday, January 30

[78] Today I composed a letter to the Varsity which I may as well
reproduce here, as it will never have any other existence: "Dear Sir, or
Miss I guess it is: I read a piece in your editorial Tuesday where you said

that President Smith said that Professor Galbraith said that a good lecturer shouldn't write out his lecture and then just read it off, he should get en rapport with his audience and then say just whatever comes into his head. Well, I generally say whatever comes into my head all right, but this en rapport stuff was a new one on me, and I didn't know how to do it, but of course I knew anything that would be in both the President's Rapport—I mean Report—and a Varsity editorial would be pretty good stuff, so I thought maybe if I shut my eyes tight and concentrated hard I'd get it, and I looked it up in the dictionary and it said "having the same ideas and attitudes as," so I tried it for a morning's lectures. Well, in my nine o'clock I fell asleep; in my ten o'clock I made fun of the things I do when I lecture; in my eleven o'clock I started yawning and then found I was singing the choruses from Pinafore, and in my twelve o'clock I walked straight off the platform and went in to lunch. I think this way of lecturing is lots more fun than the old slow way, and I think Professor Galbraith must be an awfully clever man to have thought up this en rapport idea all by himself." My immediate purpose in this effusion was to take advantage of my position as an impromptu lecturer to come to the defense of others who can't do that. But I showed it to Robins & he advised against it, & his judgement on a point like that isn't likely to be wrong.

[79] No lectures today except the ten o'clock, which I think amused the kids, as it got on to bestiaries and fabulous animals (re euphuism). In the afternoon there was a council meeting. The main business was the defining of the functions of chairmen as opposed to the former heads. They haven't got the idea clear, but I couldn't say anything because one of their main ideas (Bennett & Moore, I mean) was recognizing the importance of people like me, who didn't want to be heads. I think Kay [Coburn] was right in speaking of a (largely unconscious) tendency to weaken departmental autonomy & engross power themselves, and it's unfortunate because U.C. is apparently (I didn't know this) proceeding in the opposite direction. All the present Chairmen, including even chairmen like Hilliard and myself,[76] were very displeased, or at least disconcerted. They haven't yet distinguished the Head from a sort of secretarial job.

Thursday, January 31

[80] Today I buggered myself up properly. I woke up with that pro-

found distaste for going to work that seems to hit me on Thursday mornings, repeated Tuesday morning's experience, or lack of experience, and got out to my nine o'clock on Paradise Regained. Nothing really new, except that the *tempestas* complex is clearer in relation to the storm: it's not just the indifference of nature, but the dangling of omens & signs in front of Christ to make him dizzy. Like the omen of Adam's fall in Book X, & related to my point about Raphael's obscurantism in Book VIII. P.R. is a very good example of how important the archetypal unification of literature through tradition and convention actually is: it's a great poem but, for me, a pretty perfunctory piece of writing, so that its greatness is more transmitted than created.

[81] Well, then I ate two big chocolate bars, for no particular reason, and then went into the twelve o'clock, where I slugged through some more leviathan symbols. Afterwards two boys who'd been reading Kafka's *Trial* came up to see me about it, and a very Kafka-like situation developed, as I've never read the *Trial* & had recommended it because I thought I knew what was in it. Well, I didn't. Very nice boys: I shall read the god-damned book pronto and take them out to lunch. They kept me till 1:30, so I decided to miss lunch and, still full of chocolate bars, got a belated answer off to Abbie Potts, ate wheatcakes in Murrays, & went home. We had a somewhat melancholy stew for dinner, & then went out to O.C.E. to listen to two clucks responsible for mucking up the public school system explain why they were doing it. One was named Cavell & the other one [Thomas H.W.] Martin. They faced a stony & hostile audience with some courage, perhaps: I couldn't decide what I thought of them. That is, they're unquestionably wrong to the verge of being criminally insane, & everyone there believed it. Whether they were really malignant bastards or just stupid & well-meaning opinionated fools was what I couldn't decide. Cavell talked well over an hour & Martin promised 20 minutes & talked 45, so the discussion was pretty short. Priestley used the word "filibuster" to me: he was half-serious, & may have been wholly right. (He's president of the A.T.E. [Association of Teachers of English] this year). Anyway, what they said, Cavell especially, was more full of slop and shit than I was, which was saying plenty. If you can believe them their Grade 8 has better training than we get from university students. What do they take in high school, a concentrated course in general amnesia?

Friday, February 1

[82] I got back last night very late & with my nerves keyed up again—the only thing I did was refuse their coffee. This morning, of course, I ate my breakfast and promptly lost it again, & in fact practically pitched my guts after it. So much for the busy life. The reason I'd gone to the blasted meeting was that Joe Fisher thinks somebody from Victoria should turn up to A.T.E. meetings, & he couldn't because he's got a flu bug. Maybe I have too, but I think it was just two hours of swallowing the Cavell-Martin educational philosophy.

[83] The nine o'clock finished Paradise Regained, partly because I'm in a hurry and that always freezes me up, & partly because I'm not really discovering much in that poem anymore. The graduate group had Hugh MacCallum's paper on Yeats' *Tower*. Good paper, and quite a promising start for a thesis. I told them a little (what very little I know) about the tower as a symbol of the individual vision, the top being, as in Dante, the place you either look down or up. At that point I tried to bring in Kierkegaard, equating looking down the spirals of the tower with his "recollection" and looking up with his repetition or anagogical vision of all things new. Also the lighthouse in Browning & Virginia Woolf. I was too weary to make much of it even if I'd known more. I was about to go into lunch—I don't know why the hell I didn't make the pinnacle link in P.R. that was staring me straight in the face—and met Helen, whom I'd sent downtown after that Roe MS Princeton wants me to reread.[77] They said he'd reduced it from 750 to 350 pages, but it still weighs thirteen pounds, and Helen was pretty tired of carrying it. So I lugged it upstairs and went to lunch with her at the Chez Paris [Paree], the first settled meal I'd had since Wednesday night. Then Helen fussed around with a birthday party she's planning Sunday & bought gloves for Aunt Lily [Lilly Maidment], & I picked up a copy of Graves' *White Goddess* I'd ordered from Britnell and went home and I crawled into bed. Wonder if I've got an ulcer.

[84] The *White Goddess* is not unimpressive, but if you're going to try that sort of job you should be reasonably clear of dubious motivations. I think Graves has, obvious as it sounds, a real mother fixation—it probably comes out in the *Wife to Mr. Milton*,[78] too. It's "true" poetry when it

makes your (Graves') hair stand on end, & when your hair stands on end it's about momma. A secret tradition of Druids and stuff interrupted by a lot of Classical and Jewish and Christian crap about nasty old daddy that spoiled everything.

Saturday, February 2

[85] Today I took it easy. Providentially I occasionally get a day when I can, and today was it. I didn't stir out of the house all day and spent my time reading, mostly *The White Goddess*. I find that type of book intensely interesting to read, and for all my remarks about a mother complex, it's a very considerable intellectual feat to work out all those damned tree alphabets and stuff. Only I must keep clear the fact that an exhaustive comparative study of symbolism is not an immediate part of my job—in my master plan I've postponed it as late as ⊢ [Paradox], a possible retirement, or just the edge of retirement job. So I must be careful not to get flustered by my fascination.

[86] One thing, the nature and argument of the third chapter is clearer. It's on structural archetypes, and it deals with the myth of the quest of the hero. (Chapter Four is on modal archetypes, starting from the same point, the Messianic God-Man, but working out the imagery patterns). Chapter Three then lays out the ground: structures, or phases, are classified according to the degree of action accorded the hero—degree of freedom or power in his action. There are five phases: mythical, where the hero is a god; romantic, where he's human but in some degree supernatural, and superhuman to the extent of being an individual in a class by himself; high mimetic, where he's within humanity & nature but socially exceptional, a king or captain or leader of some kind; low mimetic, where he's "realistically" conceived as a counterpart to the reader norm; and ironic, where he has less freedom of action than is conceivable by the reader norm. An approximate historical progression here, from sagas to modern novels.[79] After that I outline the mythical narrative (Orc cycle); then the romance narrative, using Spenser for the different levels; then I jump to the argument of comedy, dealing with the whole thing from the pastoral down through Shakespeare to Plautus: the mother-wife-daughter triplet & so on. Then the elegiac with its three forms of pleasant pain; then tragedy and domestic tragedy (note that the elegiac descends, mainly via the C of L [Court of Love] mistress, from the *auto*,

or non-human god, side of the mythical). Three and Four will be wonderful chapters: if Five comes up to them, maybe the exposition could be a complete book in itself. The only difficulty would be the way I visualize the present chapter nine as rounding the whole argument off and up by shifting the whole reference of it from Orc to Los via "repetition" and the cycle of the epic. But that might be suggested even in 5.

Sunday, February 3

[87] This being Helen's mother's birthday and Aunt Lily's [Lilly Maidment's] as well, we had a party with them and Helen's father. Dinner was served close to three o'clock, with presents and a roast chicken. It was quite a concession for Aunt Lily to come. They left by suppertime and then we went out to the Barkers. The party was for Crane: Helen talked to his wife and liked her very much. The Woodhouses, Ropers, Owens, Kay Coburn, Keith Hicks & Mary White were there. I ought to do something with the Victoria people. Mrs. Woodhouse, who's 84, seemed cheerful but had recently been knocked down by a couple of stupid biddies horsing around in an elevator—stupid because they didn't pay any attention to her. So she's stiff. There wasn't actually much conversation worth recording, at least on my side. Woodhouse is still being badgered by reporters, and says the next time the President issues a report *he'll* go to India.

[88] Incidentally, Irving tells me that the Council decision to abolish the Senior Dinner wasn't too effective. Students headed by Charles Catto, Will Haddow's nephew, tramped into Bennett's office and, as Catto boasted to Irving, "turned the heat on," saying, like Canada with the St. Lawrence seaway, that they'd go it alone if the College didn't help. The result was that Bennett agreed to fork out eight hundred bucks to match the four hundred the students had. I imagine Bennett figured it would only last one year, and that it would be an easy way out. A weak and arbitrary decision, but Bennett is a weak, and therefore somewhat arbitrary, man.

[89] Creation can never be a conception digestible by science, for it is not an event or a datum, or still less a verifiable fact, and it has outlived whatever use it had as a hypothesis. It is a different way of looking at the order of nature, which the scientist sees only as an order. To think of

light as created is to think of it as potentially lovable, its real source the Word that produces it. Thus the Christian idea of Creation turns out to be the same thing as the Eastern doctrine of Maya: the created world is not reality but manifestation, a fact that doesn't make it "unreal," of course. The same ambiguity is in Job's Leviathan, which means both creation and chaos. It looks as though I can hardly avoid a climax in the triumph of hypothesis over thesis, when the conceivable becomes our closest approach to the existent. That is getting increasingly clear as the goal of my speculations about Christianity, as it has always been my understanding of such things as the Lankavatara Sutra.

Monday, February 4

[90] Well, today was the great day,[80] apart from its being the birthday of Art Moore, Connie Blewett, and, I think, it's the authentic natal day of Ned Pratt, if there is one—his mother got the year of his birth wrong, so he may have been celebrating the wrong day too. Lots of birthdays— June is the month for weddings, & it's nine months back. Anyway, I got down with Hilliard [Trethewey], who said: "First Pinafore (which of course I didn't bother with) and now this—maybe *tomorrow* we can get to work."[81] My nine o'clock, on Nashe, was pleasant but uneventful; then a spell with Ann Carnwath & Joyce Upshall:[82] that useless wench Evelyn Linton didn't come—they said apologetically that she had her "ups and downs." Ann is a very bright girl: she spoke of Yeats as a man who seemed to have transcended his own possibilities. The mail brought a big letter from Abbie Potts about her group: I have to write to Fred Sternfeld, among other things. The twelve o'clock was on Ruskin, which of course I had to cut short. I reported for my ushering job promptly on time, which, as usual, was ten minutes early. As I've said before, punctu- ality is the thief of time. Well, I took poor old Tyrrell over,[83] but all the other guests went to the cloakroom like little lambs, so what Moff Woodside had called a "difficult and complicated operation" turned out to be a cinch. Burwash was full-staff, Board & Alumni—I sat next to the Alumni President, Donald Cook. The head table had Frost & the Mayor besides the obvious dignitaries. Our main speaker, Breithaupt, the Lieu- tenant-Governor, came down with stomach flu and the shits, and sent his fizzling regrets. The Chairman was a dope named Heywood who runs the Evangeline shops—female underpinning. He said Victoria could use more endowment, & then "digressed" portentously to attack the

"creeping paralysis" of social security. Being of course P.C. [Progressive Conservative], there were labored jests at Pearson's liberalism. Pearson said we needed deliverance from the clutching capitalist hand as much as from the "dead hand" (Heywood's phrase) of the State.[84] I remarked afterwards that it would be too bad for Victoria to suffer from the creeping paralysis of the social security brought about by a bigger endowment. Those goons never stop to think of what they're saying. Moore spoke very well.[85]

[91] I didn't do much work in the afternoon, and met Helen & her father & took them out to dinner. A very good dinner too, at Chez Paris [Paree]: what with that and the lunch I was pretty full. A miserable sloppy day spoiled my shoes, but otherwise I was presentable enough. The installation was pretty fair—Moore & Pearson have brought us a long way from Brown with his buck teeth and his yeas and Spencer with his academatic.[86]

Tuesday, February 5

[92] Pearson, of course, simply said what had to be said—the university helps to defend freedom against Communism—but he said it gracefully enough. Mackintosh of Queens spoke well,[87] and so did Moore again. Everything was done decently and in order. Horsing around: Gate House boys (Pearson was Gate) dropped balloons, set off firecrackers (very hard for Helen's father's hearing aid) and showered feathers.[88] I walked back to the College & so did a lot of others: the procession of dark figures going up to a brightly lit college was the pleasantest experience I had. The reception was awful: a jam that nearly crushed the floor in; the lights went off & a near panic occurred in the receiving line. I think the food ran out, but that always happens. We saw the Craggs, & got a warm invitation from Florence to see them in Waterloo; the McGibbons, back from the Barbadoes, & Mrs. LePan. We had to come home by ourselves. I've seldom seen the staff so demoralized.

[93] Well, I pried myself out this morning and went down to talk about Ruskin. On his moral view of art: a question brought out the fact that morality, like beauty, is not the object but a by-product of art, & as the same is true of truth, I wonder if I really have the answer to Maritain's statement that poetry has no object.[89] The nearest I can get to it is that literature, as a total form, is the object of the individual poem. Another

letter, a very disturbing one, from Carol Harper—she's still writing, is very ill, and feels the compulsion will never stop. I need a night's sleep to answer it. Merritt Hughes, in a curiously abrupt letter, accepted my paper. My twelve o'clock was, I thought, unexpectedly good. I gave them four aspects of the Bible with a creator, a creature and a residue in each. Thus: mythical: Creator, cosmos & the deep (Leviathan); historical: covenanting god, Israel and Babylon-Egypt; messianic: Christ, Church, & Pilate-Caiaphas; apocalyptic: real presence, City of God, hell. That's one of the diagrams I've been working for, and I can go places from there: the male-female symbolism in the first two, for instance.

[94] Went to an Acta meeting at 4:30. Walt Stewart, the obvious candidate for next year's editorship, is talking of not coming back.[90] So the plan is to put John Rutherford in, with Ricky Arnold as an adviser.[91] Josephine Boyd is favored for the Associate job, but the Liberal Arts wants her instead, so that's undecided, as the present ones agree with me that Olga Bruchovsky would be quite hopeless. I suggested getting a V.C.U. [Victoria College Union] man on their staff, in case they turn out to be a bunch of thugs.

Wednesday, February 6

[95] Today King George VI died and was succeeded by Elizabeth II. The kids are all terrified for fear the Vic At-Home will be called off: if it is, we'll have two sets of mourning here. I'm hoping for a funeral Tuesday or Thursday, and not Wednesday, which is my easy day anyway.

[96] I didn't get much done today: I sent another blasted letter off to Carol Harper: she *would* crack up in February. However, that's silly. Also I read (for the second time) Albert Roe's book on the Blake illustrations to Dante. Good job this time, and I sent to Princeton a brief note saying so, with a few points of detail that occurred to me. Now if Erdman's book comes out Blake criticism will be in pretty fair shape.

[97] The ten o'clock was dull, on Nashe and Sidney's Apology. I was dull, but at the same time the kids obviously haven't got anywhere near reading a line of Nashe, & it's not too easy to put on a complete show all by oneself, particularly when one is in the same position they are, more or less. I don't do enough reading in the 16th c. to make it alive for me—

I just slug through the same old stuff every year. I went over to lunch at Hart House with Bill Morris & Ted Nichols, of the Hart House Chaplain's Committee. After lunch at high table I went to the Debates Room to speak in a series called "Grounds for Hope: A Personal Statement." I hate personal statements & I don't like that kind of job. I thought I had the audience with me, but I dunno: it wasn't my best work. I tried to talk about hope as a virtue, & said it began in the perception of the absurd: digging gold out of Ontario to put it back underground is logical (the logic of bondage) and simultaneously absurd (the basis of the logic of freedom). Hopelessness, or life in hell, is the inescapable logic of events, as in 1984. And so on: I hadn't really thought it out very clearly, and I'm not too happy in the recollection of it. I think it was difficult for them.

[98] Back to the college and went in to hear Joe Fisher's paper on Lawrence. Not bad, very deliberately read. I regretted the long quotation of the "white slug" passage from *Point Counterpoint*.[92] There's enough crap in Lawrence that he's responsible for without shoving Huxley's crap on top of it. An impressive quotation from a letter to Garnett, defending the essential nobility of his vision in spite of all the nonsense he knew he talked, rounded off the lecture. The letter wasn't egocentric because he'd taken care of that by writing the letter. It was almost enough to send me back to see what Lawrence had to say after all. He's dreary, but not as dreary as Ezra Pound.

Thursday, February 7

[99] The radio and press have started a stentorian boo-hooing, and will probably keep it up all week. Helen said there was nothing on the radio yesterday but dirges and news. Half the fascination of public events for me during the last fifteen years has been watching poor old Masefield grind out his quatrains. This one was better than usual—he probably wrote it a while back—but in any case I thought I'd anticipate him:

> Let's give the Queen the honour due her,
> King George the Sixth is now manure,
> And when she is by death decoyed,
> We all will hail King Charles de Toid.

[100] My nine o'clock did Samson Agonistes and seemed to arouse a

flicker of interest. I also took chapel, on Luke 5:1–11, a hopeless passage to do anything with.[93] For me, anyway. The twelve o'clock was fair—I gave them the same line I gave the fourth year. Live for the moment, I always say—I may be dead when *they* get to fourth year. Kay [Coburn] tells me that Douglas Bush's story about the draft was a blind—that Geoffrey [Bush] had definitely turned down our offer. The main reason seems to be that he's a neurotically patriotic American & won't have anything to do with British or Canadian ways of life. Some father-trouble, maybe.[94] This comes from his Oxford Tutor Miss Seaton, who says we were well rid of him, because, though a charming boy, he'll never make a scholar or teacher, though he may become something of an artist. I suppose the word "neurotically" is wrong—I'm not thinking of him, but of America's present Atlas mood. In connection with son-father tensions—again I'm not thinking of him—it occurs to me that that remark I picked up in Manzoni, that to suppress resentment is often to decrease it,[95] is at least as true as its opposite. We have something in us that admires & comes to terms with tyranny. Sympathy & understanding are often the most favorable atmosphere in which resentments may develop. I think, for instance, of John Riddell, who, in a family where he gets nothing but intelligence, sympathy and understanding, goes through all the behavior patterns of resentment against a thunderous Victorian papa. To say instinctively, "Well, but perhaps the parents—" is just an intellectual's masochism. He's a little bastard, and has been made so by sympathy, tolerance and understanding. I'm not saying that this is generally true: I'm saying it's as true as its sentimental opposite, and that truth lies in a middle that recognizes both the natural and the redeemable elements in the human being.

Friday, February 8

[101] I went over to hear Barker Fairley lecture on Heine last night: his treatment of the fable form, or rather animal imagery in Heine. A most entertaining one, Heine's work being full of sardonic jokes that he put across very well. Thus Fichte's notion that the subject is involved with his own thought-processes Heine compares to a monkey cooking broth & dipping his tail in the pot to keep himself personally involved with the process. However, the thing I mainly noticed about it was its superb success as a piece of technique. Barker is technically the best lecturer

I have ever heard. His voice is beautifully modulated, his delivery perfectly timed, and his asides are just right. There were, I think, a few things alluding allegorically to the States and his exclusion therefrom, enough to make the lecture a piece of quiet resistance literature, but nothing out of place.[96] He seemed to enjoy giving the lecture, and according to Joan [Fairley] it was a new one, not English-tour. We had a couple of drinks and dinner with Kay afterward, & went home to bed.

[102] The nine o'clock finished Samson, with little enthusiasm, and Milton with him. I don't know why I seem to have relatively little enthusiasm for Milton this year—rush, probably. I finished a few old jobs: got Roe's thirteen pounds back to Princeton, for one thing. Also I wrote Charlie Bell a somewhat perfunctory letter. I don't know why *he* should be the selected victim of my sins of omission. I'm afraid Charlie hasn't got a hell of a lot on the ball, for one thing, & I dread to see the misery catch up with him of having the egoism of real genius & the productivity of rather commonplace talent. Well, I went in to tea, and had a long, intimate & to me very pleasant conversation with Charlie [Leslie], Kay [Coburn], Joe [Fisher], Moff [Woodside] and Archie [Hare]. It was more the pleasant feeling of friends around than of anything said—Joe was the ringleader, & dearly as I love him he's a very obvious thinker. I feel however that I spend too much time in sociality—Archie, who with all his charm shows potentially the boredom of senility—he comes up automatically with stories he told twenty years ago—is the dead end of that. I must modify my views about the central importance of the symposium.

[103] The evening was a disaster—my graduate group with that infernal woman Ann [Anne] Bolgan reading the paper and throwing all her emotional attachments into it. Gordon Smith then got obtuse about my anagogical level and my mind went completely blank. I was hysterically tired and this kind of evening was exactly what I didn't want. I sat smothered in the excreta of exasperated irritation until nearly midnight.

Saturday, February 9

[104] Today I spent relaxing: my nerves were in very bad shape this morning. I slept badly, and in general was a breeding ground for ulcers, flu bugs, nervous breakdowns and heart attacks. I took a hot bath and a

spell in bed after lunch. In February you slug it out, and this kind of thing is what gets me by. Year after year I've gone along without cutting a single lecture and, publicly, in a fairly good temper, which for a nervous irascible weakling is the result of pretty sustained attention to oneself. In the evening we went out and had dinner with the LePans, a most pleasant and relaxing evening I thoroughly enjoyed: it was exactly the kind of thing I wanted after that terrific session last night. Douglas is in Washington now,[97] and two years ago took a trip round the world with Mike Pearson, meeting Blunden in Tokyo & somebody else in Rangoon.

[105] My book is shifting its form again, and this time the order of chapters exactly follows the course of my writing since 1949. First, an introductory polemic—my colloquium and UTQ paper.[98] Then an investigation of meaning—my philosophy club-Kenyon paper—chapter two.[99] Then my second Kenyon paper on archetypes, the organizing principle of chapters three and four.[100] Then my third Kenyon article on drama, now chapter five.[101] Then the note-scribbling I did at Seattle, now connected with Chapter six. Then the Pound review and the symbolism article, connected most closely with seven, in spite of the rehash of two. Then the Royal Society paper[102] I'll have to do, linked with eight. The only thing that I decided was a bit out of line was the paper on techniques of criticism. I'm now veering toward the possibility of making that a two-chapter summary of the book, but I'll cut it if I can.

[106] I justify my indolence by telling myself that one can build up a community negatively. As you approach middle age, the number of things you can't do well & shouldn't do at all begins to clarify, and the fierce egotism & ambition of youth that wants to do everything itself and has all time to do it in dies down. Now to cut something off from one's personality is to transfer it to someone else. The fact that this someone else is frequently one's wife is the weak spot. Anyway, I shan't be indolent for long. The ATE [Association of Teachers of English] has dumped the job on me of talking on "What is Poetry?" at their next meeting on the 26th, as though I didn't know. Well, it's excitement (nursery rhymes, Skelton, Longinus), incantation (the romantics), authority (the prophets) and clarification (the Classicists). Excitement includes puns of course: I'd do some Finnegans Wake if it weren't that [Norman] Endicott takes the modern field.

Sunday, February 10

[107] Another day spent resting up and idling—well, not idling exactly, as I finished reading Graves' book. An amazing technical triumph, in its reading of riddles, but philosophically it's junk. The book is dedicated to Vala,[103] and he regards the Orc cycle (which for him doesn't involve the conception of Urizen as an aged Orc: it's pure antithesis & violent death of Orc) as the only theme for poetry. In other words, he can't distinguish Urizen from Los. Hence his book has the fundamental irrationality that all cyclic people have—Jung, Spengler, Yeats & the rest.

[108] I've been thinking about various applications of William James' "moral equivalent of war" thesis.[104] I don't like "equivalent," with its Sanka-coffee and substitution overtones—it suggests the soda pop and chewing gum with which the infantile relieve the tedium of not being allowed liquor and tobacco. It's rather that war is a perversion of something genuine. It's evil, but if you do nothing but simply abolish it you get a social problem of equal size in what Falstaff calls the cankers of a calm world and a long peace [*Henry IV, Part I*, 4.2.32]. The thing is to make it possible for heroism, sacrifice and the sense of holiday excitement to take their rightful place in a peaceful society. The role of a doctor in an epidemic is one example, or an explorer. Similarly religion badly needs the moral equivalent of Communism, a revolutionary consuming zeal. And in connection with what I've been thinking of a good deal lately, I think education needs the moral equivalent of flogging. Flogging itself is not a simple or unnecessary evil: it is, like war, a perversion (largely a sexual perversion, like war too) of a genuine thing in education. For that reason it didn't do the things educators assume it did, like killing the desire to learn, though it was no less an evil for that. It dramatized the awful authority of the subject; it dramatized the sin of laziness; it brought fearful questionings of one's adequacy & sickening apprehensions of ordeals into education. It brought responsibility & reverence, and the thing it perverted would be a good thing. It brought excitement too, and violent emotions into play. No, we've abolished it without releasing what it accompanied, and if the student is no longer apt to hate school, he is in some danger of growing to despise it. The modern high school class, the brilliant students bored to death, cretins capable of grade five work sitting in the back and believing they're in high school, and the teacher driven crazy by the lack of unity and morale

in the class, is not an image of democracy: it's a clear satire on it, and a picture of what democracy is trying not to be.

Monday, February 11

[109] Today I did a queer thing. I went down to my nine o'clock telling myself I had nothing whatever to do after it was over, and promising myself a long quiet spell at the Reference Library, where I like going because it's clear of my environment. I forgot, until the evening, absolutely & totally about the twelve o'clock I've shifted to Monday. I seem to black out about once a year this way, a sort of sacrifice to the ego. It was mysterious the way it was so deliberately planned by the subconscious. I wonder what relation it has to my boasting over the weekend that I've never missed a lecture. Strange the variety of dramatis personae we contain: we have mockers, accusers, even saboteurs and traitors, and doubtless at the centre a judge with a black cap, waiting to put it on. We objectify and project all these things first as gods, then we dramatize them in human society. The extent to which we dramatize is only just beginning to dawn on me. With the death of the king, press and radio are full of people asserting solemnly that they feel emotions they can't possibly feel. They must be either congenital liars or actors in a play: it's more charitable to assume the latter. The people who acquire feelings after they've been suggested to them, or have emotional vacancies in their lives that need filling, are another matter.

[110] The nine o'clock, the lecture I did give, was illuminating to me if not to them. It was on Sidney, the Apology, and that Aristotelian conception of art as a second nature, linked to the Renaissance conception of poetry as social rhetoric combining precept and example in a single informing ideal image, began to glow as one of my second-chapter ideas. Chris Love told me at chapel today that Ned [Pratt] has fallen on the sidewalk and cracked his shoulder.[105] So Saturday's party will be out: I trust it's not more serious. Well, I had lunch at Eaton's College Street all through my lecture,[106] and then went to the Library, which I did enjoy, though perhaps not as much as I'd anticipated. I've bought sermon books for chapters two to five, the last preparatory stage before actual writing, and the thing that chilled me a bit was that while the spurt of energy lasted I had to write out all that stuff about literal and descriptive meaning I've already thrashed over so often.[107] Then when

I came to the new part I was fogged—funny what trifles life depends on. In the evening I went out to a Forum meeting. It's amazing how that magazine wags on. I phoned A.F.B. Clark and he was very pleased, evidently, to come on the board.[108] Feilding threatens resignation, but newcomers seem to keep coming. Joyce Grimshaw is a very capable and useful girl, and if Kidd comes on the board for good I think we'll be all set.

Tuesday, February 12

[111] I got down in good time to my nine o'clock and apologized for standing them up the day before. I said professors were absent-minded & that it wasn't the fun for them it was for professional jokers. Then I started on Ruskin and pretty well finished *Stones of Venice*. There's still a fair amount in that course to do. The twelve o'clock kept on thrashing my new diagram, and one kid protested that a "professor of history" had told them about how solidly established a historical fact the life of Jesus was. Sounds like George Brown in a pious mood. Whoever it was is clearly not very well informed about criticism of Mark during the last twenty years or so. I also talked about marriage symbolism and the Word of God. The whole course bores me stiff this year. I suppose if I could talk to them it wouldn't sound so bad from their point of view.

[112] Irving tells me that B.K. Sandwell is very impressed by the *Heritage* book,[109] will probably give it a spread in Saturday Night; also that he plans to send a copy to T.S. Eliot with instructions to read my chapter. I didn't know what his entry to Eliot is supposed to be, if anything. It was too much even for Irving, who urged Sandwell to tell Eliot to read *his* chapter instead. Fortunately I don't think Eliot will hurt his eyes on it—it's not the way I want to be introduced to him. I went into lunch & Crane was there—Chris Love had brought him over. We talked American politics with Ken [MacLean]. Nothing especially new—he says if Taft gets the Republican nomination the election will be practically civil war, as Taft could win only with the kind of all-out support he'd get from McCarthy. We told him there was no television here; he said he'd seen a lot of aerials around where he lives—Bathurst way—and Ken said that part of the city was called Tel-Aviv, for many reasons. More aimless gossip: the New Yorker going phut[110] after Ross's death, & the like. However, I like Crane very much, and hope to have him up before long.

[113] In the evening I phoned Underhill: nobody seems to be doing a bloody thing about the Royal Society, so I have to. I proposed either two papers on Milton, or three on humor, with Barker Fairley being the third one. He jumped at the second alternative, leaving me to approach Barker, natch. He may—or rather might—do something on Keller, it seems to me. What the hell *I* do now I can't imagine—go back to my unfinished comedy paper, I suppose. And that runs into my MLA paper, and both run into my book.[111] I hope I can spend part of the summer hiding a few talents.

Wednesday, February 13

[114] I used today as Helen's birthday party—sorry, I mean Valentine party—the birthday is in October. I got down to my ten o'clock and finished Sidney, digressing—I don't like digressions, but if they don't read the stuff digressing is sometimes the only way to get them interested—on drama and the role of the unities—action, time, place, social class and mood. (Time & place being subordinate characteristics of action, that leaves action, class & mood as the three fundamental unities. These are respectively mythos, ethos and dianoia.) I used some of my new stuff on high & low mimetic & the difference between a tragic and a pathetic climax.

[115] Well, I picked Helen up at Eaton's College Street and we had lunch there, going around after to look at chairs she wants to buy. Black chairs with stick-out legs I didn't go for; Italian rush chairs I liked better. Then a session at the Wedgwood showroom on Bay. A woman showed us around—secretary with, at the moment, nothing to do. You can't buy anything there—four stores carry a quarter of their stock each. Funny business people the English. It interested me, because I think the whole 1760–1830 period in English culture is really the Age of Wedgwood. What with all that rococo classicism, nostalgic ruin-romanticism and so on. I gave the woman all my contacts: Blake worked for Wedgwood, Coleridge was a pensioner, Keats' Grecian Urn may have been the Flaxman frieze, I know Sir Ralph [Wedgwood] & Veronica [Wedgwood], & finally Barbara McNabb.[112] She clung a bit, but we got out and went to the College for tea & to Wood's lecture. Fair. A lot of academic harrumphing: I will now demonstrate three things, and the like. Huge crowd. Window open and I nearly froze my pinballs off (analogy: you

can have pin buttocks). Very cold day. The lecture was on Proust & told me nothing. I talked to Barker Fairley, who isn't keen to do Keller, but I think will do something. We then had drinks and dinner at Murray's, taxied down to Massey Hall & heard the Mendelssohn Choir, with [Arthur R.] Bartlett & Robertson. Good show but very poor house. It was very nearly a Pops concert in fact, though they did a wonderful Palestrina—*Surge Illuminare*—and a thing of Healey Willan's called Apostrophe to the Heavenly Host—Greek liturgy and very colorful and lively. We talked to Lois Gordon & Elspeth Latimer in the intermission and saw, but didn't talk to, Corinne McLuhan. Another taxi home. Total cost about fifteen dollars, but Helen enjoyed herself and everything seemed to go right. I knew it cost that because I started with that and was broke when I got home.

Thursday, February 14

[116] Got out (damn this pen)[113] to my nine o'clock and started Spenser. I made a silly remark to them about not wanting to go to the memorial service for the king that I regretted: I must remember that I'm likely to start saying silly things at this time of year, and must watch myself. Particularly with so many student talks coming up. It's at this time of year too that students begin to get on my nerves. I begin to resent the fact that they don't read anything and that most of their questions are largely motivated by a desire not to think. It's an infinitely small vision of what I've noted in the Gospels: that the questions asked Jesus were unanswerable because they were so badly motivated that they were really temptations. Anyway, I got Spenser started. Then I read and fooled around—my 2i essays are staring at me but I'm not staring back—and went in to my twelve o'clock. That fundamentalist was on my trail again, but he's not an unintelligent person. I wish though that he weren't there, because that's by far the brightest class I have, and they'd come along a lot faster without him.

[117] After lunch Ken [MacLean] & Joe [Fisher] & I got together. There are three appointments coming up: Knight, being first on the list, will presumably get a nod right away; Kee, who is high because we need a philologist, is next. Both Ken and I are very doubtful about Kee, and even more doubtful about Joe when he starts talking himself into a sentimental view of Kee. However, sometimes I feel that Victoria is

pretty deeply committed to an absurd cult of mediocrity, though probably I feel that only because Joe suggested, swearing us all to secrecy, that Archie Hare is being considered for the next Librarian, because Bennett's prejudice against Peggy Ray is so strong. But surely this notion is too infernally silly even for Bennett to commit himself to, and perhaps the real plan is to have Woodside in there & make Archie registrar, which would be possible if not inspired. Anyway, if David Knight comes on I'll get rid of the writing course, and possibly Acta, and as I'm dropping at least one R.K. course, & may very soon drop both, I should soon be ready to streamline my work a bit more. If I can pass on that Forum goldfish bowl I'll be all set. Again, I may drop 2i and take over 3k: Joe says it doesn't matter about having two courses in the same year. That would arrange things even more neatly. Things are looking up: the four of us have gone all the way up to full Professor in the last ten years without any junior assistance whatever, and as a result my work is all bits and pieces.

Friday, February 15

[118] I gave a two-hour lecture to the drama people yesterday afternoon, filling in for Ned [Pratt]. He usually allows me one lecture per play, but I forgot to bring the text so filled in and, though I covered *Every Man In* fairly well, I didn't get near *The Alchemist*.[114] But it's beginning to look as though Ned will be knocked out for longer than at first appeared, so I don't need to worry *too* much. It's not impossible that I may do some of the Shakespeare. Anyway, I don't know that anything really new emerged, but they were outstandingly brilliant lectures: my stock stuff very well organized. The insight I got Wednesday into the mythos-ethos-dianoia business helped a good deal.

[119] Today the king got buried, so I stayed home all day: the queen had not requested a holiday, but we got one anyway. I spent it, perhaps mistakenly, in trying to think about my book. In fact I don't know where the hell the time went: I certainly didn't do any reading. I did stroll over to the corner and have tea at Murray's by myself,[115] but otherwise it was a day devoted to pure thought, and I got so damned little thinking done, all of it highly impure, that the day seemed wasted. I don't know whether I should just start to scribble or not, but to get involved with the vast complications that would result would be a real heartbreak, and I seem

to feel it would be better pushing & poking ideas around until the general scheme of the book is clear enough to do fairly straight writing. Or what I hope will be fairly straight writing.

[120] The archetype section will start with chapter four, and will have either two or three chapters. After the introduction and the meaning chapter (I've been wondering if I should reverse the chapters on meaning and narrative, now Two & Three, because of my general preference for moving from left to right along my diagrams, but I don't yet see my way clear to doing so) there will be a chapter on levels of narrative. This has the five levels of Feb 2 [par. 86], but how much more it has I'm not clear. Well, the archetypes of the quest, chapter IV, give the story of the quest in myth, the argument of romance, the argument of comedy, and the argument of irony, or at any rate satire. Hell, I don't know. Myth, romance and comedy seem relatively clear, anyway. That's the hero and the dragon. Chapter Five, the chapter on the dialectic of the quest, will then deal with the heroine, and follow her up the various levels until she disappears in the pure vision of union with the Father, which is all male. Shadow > anima > counsellor: is that what Virginia Woolf's *Orlando* was getting at?

Saturday, February 16

[121] Today I went down to the office to see John Graham. That was a bit of a bungle on my part: I wrote him as amiably as I could, telling him I'd be glad to see him, and he took that to mean that I'd summoned him down. I didn't waste his time and I don't think it hurt him any to come, but I cursed myself for a damned fool anyway. I like John, though he's a somewhat progressively educated person, and he's highly intelligent without being particularly intellectual. That CBC job he had was an excellent one for him, and he should be all right at Western. He'll also do a very good job on Virginia Woolf, I think, without ever really wanting to. Mysterious. We had a few beers & a lunch at Chez Paris [Paree]. I was trying to work out something about what I called a secular eucharist theme in VW. Jacob's room is the body of Jacob, just as Mrs. Ramsay's house becomes the theme after the death of Mrs. Ramsay.[116] The suicide of Septimus is an external, futile & ironic "attempt to communicate"— not altogether futile, as the last page of *Mrs Dalloway* shows. *The Waves* & *The Years* are simply attempts to communicate strangled by time, time

being presented as the spectre of Urthona, the enemy of communication. (He is in Shakespeare, too. I mean time, which is him, not it, as the Mad Hatter said.)[117]

[122] The third chapter, after establishing the five levels of narrative (I guess it's narrative, though in fact it's really a chapter on themes), then establishes a mythical and an ethical pole for each. This is best approached by outlining the distinction between the tragic and the comic, via my unfinished paper. From there I can go on to the low mimetic counterparts: I can identify one as pathetic all right, but I haven't yet a better word than "individualistic" for the sort of thing that happens when Pamela's virtue gets rewarded (note how it's so often a *female* triumph, thereby descending from the high mimetic heroines of Shakespeare). On the other side of high mimetic, the poles of romance are individualized, lonely, dreamy, wish-fulfilment specializations of the tragic & comic I call elegiac & idyllic respectively. In comedy the plot is still the soul of the play, but it's a mother bringing the hero to life, not a father killing him: this encircling mother is what revives as the heroine. Cf. All's Well. The ironic pattern has as one pole the pharmakos, I think. Its positive pole (or ethical one) is, I suppose, satire. Anyway, it's an ethical interest in frustration, the sort of thing, to return to the original subject, that Virginia Woolf gives in a novel like The Years, or that we get in the ironic parable of the Kafka type.

Sunday, February 17

[123] I didn't do anything today except get out to see Ned [Pratt] in the afternoon. I found him pretty blue, and his morale low. He wouldn't be a patient patient at best, & he's had enough pain with that shoulder to weaken his morale anyway. He's fretting about being pulled away from his routine, but in fact it may do him some good to have an enforced rest. Vi wasn't too chipper herself, and Claire was out seeing a young friend in hospital who's dying of cancer. What Ned broke was what is called the surgical neck in the shoulder: sounds like a nasty business. He was asking me hopefully about my accident and I tried to give him a minimum estimate on the period of pain.[118] That last phrase reminds me of a discussion we got into about Fortune—via this Carpenter thing that's coming up. Vi spoke of the time she arranged for him to give a lecture to the University Women's Club. She didn't tell us what he said, but I

know. Fortune had two interests. One was the anthropological significance of the menstrual cycle, and the other was the social significance of the position taken by the male in sexual intercourse. And he wasn't the man to modify his interests for anything like the University Women's Club. I wish I'd heard that lecture, and in fact I wish Fortune had stayed here: he'd be useful around this damn place.

[124] Miscellany: if I can persuade Barker Fairley to do something that I could classify as humor, I wonder if I could consider doing my own paper, not on comedy, which I should be able to siphon quite easily into the book, but on "A Recommendation of Finnegans Wake"—i.e., as a hell of a funny book. I'd like to look up the criticism on it anyway, and the thought of doing a Royal Society paper on it amuses me. Two ideas: the sun and moon are *eyes*: that's a very obvious link that I've still missed. We see with the eye by means of the sun; the end of vision is identification with the solar hero and seeing *as it*. Halfway to it is seeing in the dark as the moon: i.e. the halfway mark between actual sleeping and final awakening. That would order and *rationalize* the solar and lunar complexes of symbols as I've never yet had them. The other thing is the importance of heterophonic parody in the five themes, and the way it works. Thus Chaucer, with great low mimetic talents in an age of romance, treats his low mimetic tales as essentially parodies of the romance themes he's more contemporary with—actually the parody is of the low mimetic by the romance. Jonson's *Alchemist* is of the mythical by the low mimetic: Don Quixote is simpler but involves perhaps three levels.

Monday, February 18

[125] Got down to my nine o'clock, on Hooker, & tried to say that law was Hooker's way of finding the middle ground between grace, revelation & faith on the Puritan side and will, reason & works on the Catholic one. The present generation of students seems to react pretty automatically: they just gawped. That is, I find a lack of intellectual curiosity in them. Of course sometimes one student will make all the difference. My fourth year is hopeless except when that nice red-headed girl comes, and I discovered this morning the secret of her liveliness: she was out working for a while after high school. No doubt about it, the progress from secondary to tertiary education is a mistake: if there's no break in be-

tween, there's just no power of articulation. But that one girl sparks the whole class. The class *is* dumb though: to have got all the way to fourth year and still ask if concern with food and money isn't just being lowdown "materialistic" seems to me pretty naive. I tried to make Ruskin's "cause of death" thesis into my Utopia informing ideal point, with some success.

[126] Ann Carnwath was in in the morning: I wonder why the only really interesting people in fourth year aren't in English. Neither is Donald Urquhart. I enjoy very much talking to that girl: she told me about the movie "Detective Story" which sounds like a sardonic master-piece, and we discussed Marxism. At lunch Irving was quite excited about the prospect of chairing the Frye-Carpenter duel, in that way he gets. Evidently Carpenter tries the shock principle in education, and the difficulty with that method is that if you underestimate your audience you really bore them. John Coulter suggested that something of the sort had come into the Burwash talk he did. Irving was also talking about university president types: Larry Mackenzie was quoted as saying "Any-one that can read or write has excellent chance of being appointed (to U.B.C. staff)." I suggested that universities were becoming assimilated to the trades union pattern, where not a great musician but Petrella is the head man. I went in to tea and found Ruth Jenking quite wound up about things in general. We discussed Shakespeare and about how tough it is, if it's possible at all, to get to the bottom of such words as time, nature, fortune, honest, fool and the like in his work. When you try, you find yourself solving cryptograms instead. She said she also thought that Shakespeare's pentameters actually fall mainly into four-beat lines, which is one of my points if it's true. Her father is, naturally, still alive, & is even trying to talk, but there's no hope for anything but a long wait. Mean-while they have a nurse, and the strain of an extra person.

Tuesday, February 19

[127] The nine o'clock was a test I set my fourth year—an easy way out of marking essays. God knows I had enough to do. I had one job to do that really annoyed me to have to do—a description of the lunch of Feb. 4 for Bill James' infernal Victoria Reports.[119] It was a straight piece of advertising copy that anyone else could have done as well, and it took me a disproportionate amount of time and cursing. Then I got two overdue recommendations off to Eleanor Coutts & David Hoeniger—

I know they have to have them, & they have a right to demand them, but the ego in me wants a pretty please. David's all right: I'm thinking of Eleanor, whose letters get pretty brusque at times. Also I got a Forum editorial done on education[120] which looks as though it will be very badly timed, as it's a defence of grammar & an attack on those pirates of the ATE [Association of Teachers of English] which will come out when the issue will be a hysterical public stampede on the senior school and a stupid blast about "frills" from Dunlop. Damn this journal. I mean the Forum. My twelve o'clock wasn't any worse than usual. Actually I got a fair number of interested inquiries, only that dumb girl who sits straight in front of me yawned every time I tried to answer one, which paralyzed me.

[128] I got over to the Forum office with my editorial and found everything turned upside down there. The Woodsworth House annual meeting is coming up, the last day for receiving memberships is tomorrow, the unions are sending in all the memberships they can, and it looks like an organized effort to seize control of Woodsworth House and destroy the attempt at disinterested social study.[121] Not that it will matter a damn to the Morrises [Kay and Lou] personally, but Kay is still capable of getting into a stew about principle. I don't really see why or how a centre of social research is to be attached to a $75,000 property.[122] Anyway, I stayed upstairs in my office and let Helen go to the tea for Doris McCarthy & Virginia Luz. I'm coddling myself, as I have a hard week. Irving is slowly wrecking my nerves and morale about this bloody Carpenter affair: what I had thought of as a pleasant & easy thing to do is now becoming a major ordeal. I had a couple of drinks with Helen, who enjoyed the tea but was in a bad temper, and went home. Letter from Carol Harper saying she'd stopped writing. My affair with that woman has given me a single laboratory specimen of the charismatic leader, and I don't like it. Apart from that, however, it stylizes one so. I couldn't step out of the role she puts me in even to break her trance, and if it were a general relation to the community about me the hypnotism would soon start flowing back on me.

Wednesday, February 20

[129] Took it easy until my ten o'clock, which was still on Hooker. I found a sentence in him to the effect that the best proof that man has a spiritual destiny lies in the fact that his desires cannot be fulfilled by

nature. So I lectured on that, more or less. At eleven o'clock Shirley Endicott came in, ostensibly to ask me whether I was going to require her to say she believed a lot of things she didn't believe in order to pass as an R.K. student. Considering that her two brothers have got through the same course without any Test Acts, I was a little surprised by this, but it turned out that all she wanted to do was sell me a subscription to *New Frontiers*, their new Communist magazine. Theory and practice are inseparable in Marxism. I note that the brethren are still plugging the old social realism line: they've dug up old Robert Harris's schoolteacher picture and reproduced it in color as an example of the sort of art you can look at without taking your mind off the class struggle.[123] I don't see how communism can fight bourgeois philistinism with the latter's discarded weapons, but that's their affair. In fact democracy and Communism seem to have exchanged weapons, like Hamlet and Laertes: democracy fights with promises of liberation & fair play & appeals to crusading idealism and Communism with paternalistic loyalty, prudery, the sanctity of the family, and obvious art.

[130] A girl named Pearl Parnes, an earnest Jewish lass, came in to write me up for the Varsity: they're doing a profile on me.[124] Then I went in to hear Bert Arnold's lecture on Thomas Mann, which I thought was a very fine job. Just what may be called the physical aspect of it alone—condensing all those thousands of pages of pother—was impressive, and the treatment was detached and unstereotyped. I suppose I should look into the Joseph cycle, but oh God. Then I stayed down and had dinner by myself, avoiding drinks, and went over to talk to the Dramatic Society, a rather futile episode in my distinguished career. The meeting was postponed a couple of times and there were only a few there—the president, Jane Reddick, a pretty but somewhat ineffectual looking girl, said a lot of them were coming out to hear me tomorrow night & didn't want to waste both evenings on me, or that was the general sense of it.[125] I said I wished I could take the same attitude. I tried to say something about the difference between the popular tragicomic spectacle and the educated verbal drama split between tragedy and comedy, but I was weary with well doing and I didn't put anything across really. Funny how when a meeting is wrong it's all wrong.

Thursday, February 21

[131] The nine o'clock did the Arthurian business on Spenser—straight

enough stuff—and then I dashed over to the Forum office and read the proofs, which were bad, though the issue itself is quite good. Except that Stella Harrison went all female and slobbery over the king's death, which I should think would rather disgust our readers.[126] I'm damned if I see what the point of the Forum is. Kay [Morris] still in a sweat over trades union skullduggery. I hate the thought of wasting one evening on it, but I seem to be stuck. The twelve o'clock was on the Holy Spirit: I seem to be putting it across all right, but I'll never convert that damn fundamentalist to Christianity, and in the meantime he's a nuisance, because he's so typical of his kind. He's so much better informed about the text of the Bible and the general trade slang of evangelical religion than they are, and yet his cultural level is infantile. He quotes the Reader's Digest to prove that an ass can talk, for instance. Well, I talked for an hour on *The Alchemist* and cut the second lecture—I thought I sure as hell had I right to do *that*.[127] As usual, I'm deeply impressed by the contrast in that play between what a number of very commonplace crooks and gulls do and what they would do if they had the power—the apocalyptic overtones of this last are what make the whole show so wonderful and a major triumph of creative genius and not just a clever and well-contrived comedy.

[132] I went home, relaxed in a hot bath and changed my clothes, & then came down in a taxi to Wymilwood. I met Carpenter in the basement and took to him at once, as I had rather expected to do. We talked in the reading room while the crowd gathered—I should estimate between two and three hundred. We spoke from a table at the far end of the sun room. The sun room was jammed, the piano room above it jammed, with people standing in droves at the back, and even the cafeteria was full of standees. At that point occupancy by more persons became dangerous and unlawful, so the front door was locked, and I have no idea how many were turned away. Staff present included Bill Fennell, Kay [Coburn] & Jessie [Macpherson], Dave Savan, McLuhan & Bert Arnold; nearly all my students, graduate & undergraduate, seemed to be there. Carpenter, I gather, had told his students to come along and see him butchered, so *they* were all there. Margaret Avison, Mary & Stephen Gibson—well, as I say, there was the biggest crowd in history.

Friday, February 22

[133] I was disconcerted and annoyed, partly because, as I've said before, what I had originally thought of as a harmless and pleasant discus-

sion had snowballed into an academic wrestling match. In other words, I thought the attendance had been very badly motivated. Carpenter told me that the night before, at an extension lecture, an old lady had tottered up to him, asked him if he were going to "debate" with me, and then said, "Well, remember—Professor Frye is a genius." I *must* get my hair cut. So what was an ordeal for me was an act of real courage for him, as he's an Assistant Professor with his way still to make, our guest, and still half a stranger to Toronto.[128]

[134] Oh well, the hell with that. Nobody got hurt, and I think we put on a fair show. Carpenter brought a short paper and read it, then I spoke, & then the questions began. I was very glad of the discussion itself, if not of the atmosphere it was held in, because it forced me to clarify an issue I've not yet honestly faced—what in hell is an archetype? The question was, "Are there Universal Symbols?" and I was supposed to be defending the affirmative. Well, I obviously couldn't claim that there was a code book of fixed symbols, with invariable meanings attached, held by every human society in history without exception. What I did say was that, in addition to the symbol, which I admitted was both neutral and learned, there was the archetype carrying the symbol from one culture to another. That as art was a technique of communication, criticism studied the potential communicability of symbols. That in view of the unity of man, of nature, and of the impulse to symbolize, the tactical difficulties in communication—differences of language, the interested rivalry of cultures and the like—were not final: there is no Spenglerian *plurality* of minds, as overemphasis on the variety of cultures would suggest. That because of this pattern of ultimate unity, the tremendous expanding force of symbolic structures (Athens & Judea covering the whole world) had no discernible limits, and in that sense could be called universal. That at the centre of this would be found the symbols of food, drink, shelter & sex; the city & the garden, the father & the mother, the word & the breath, the marriage and the sacramental meal, & the like. That value-judgements could be founded on the ability of a group of culture-symbols to survive incorporation in the larger community: Sparta's were "bad" because Sparta blew to bits when it hit the outside world. That as regards the "learning" of symbols you couldn't argue from the analogy of a scheming scientist and a drooling dog to a spontaneous creative effort and a similarly creative effort of response, which I called presentation and recognition.

Saturday, February 23

[135] Yesterday I picked up the pieces: gave another lecture on the Arthurian tradition in Spenser, quite easy and relaxed, and in my graduate group listened to Don Coles read a paper on a story by Sansom called "The Invited," an ironic parable a little like Rex Warner's *Aerodrome*,[129] and like it very close to the anxiety-dream techniques of German expressionism and Kafka. I'd just managed to get it read on Wednesday afternoon. Then I began on my five levels of theme line. I took a taxi to work, but I didn't need to: I wasn't that exhausted. At lunch, of course, everybody wanted to know who won the fight. The Varsity account was so confused that anyone who hadn't been there would have thought that I was attacking universal symbols & Carpenter defending them.[130] My publicity seems to be snowballing fast: B.K. Sandwell's writeup of the *Heritage* book arrived[131] and sure enough I'm the only one he quotes. An appreciative but not very illuminating review. Irving says he remarked at Britnells [Britnell's] on the stack of "Barabbas" they had, and they said it had started selling since "some guy" had reviewed it on the radio.[132] There's getting to be too damn much God in my life. After lunch I went over to hear Crane's paper on the history of ideas, but instead of staying for the discussion after tea I went off and had three Martinis—Carpenter doesn't drink and I decided against giving him the handicap of a slug of Scotch, so it was the first drink I'd had in three days. Then I went home and stayed put for the evening. Crane's paper was intelligible enough, but its main thesis, that in literature we study the history of ideas in order to see what writers do with their ideas in works of literature, didn't strike me as any blockbuster bomb. But of course I never did pay so much attention to the Lovejoy people anyway.[133] Also his treatment of Fielding, his example, struck me as curious: he compared his moral views with the illustration of them in the novels. Well, hell, I don't think Fielding's a very interesting moralist: the interesting ideas in him are social ones. When he says great men are nuisances and good men "low," he's reflecting the bourgeois revolution of his time, and his Parson Supple shows the relations of church to squirearchy in the 18th century. I wish people weren't so frightened of Marxism that they unconsciously eliminate material factors from their thinking. I kept going to sleep & waking up again throughout the paper: my mind was still on universal symbols. I find it difficult to switch my attention from a big public occasion anyway, and the diffi-

culty is greater when the occasion involves the thing I'm thinking about all the time in any case.

Sunday, February 24

[136] I went down to the office and made out a list of all the things I had to do. Then I stared at the list until it was time to go into lunch. Some people like being busy: I've long suspected that there was a Judas inside Woodhouse that makes him surround himself with odd jobs so that he won't get his Milton book done. But I don't seem to have the same Judas: I desperately want to get my book done, and when my fiddly jobs get to a sufficient point of concentration that I can't keep taking time out to think about more important things, I get panic and claustrophobia. When that happens, the only thing to do is make out an orderly list and then fuck the dog for the rest of the day.

[137] I got a haircut—a bad one this time—and went home. In the evening—I'm talking about Saturday, incidentally—we went out to hear The Magic Flute—the first time I'd seen it done on the stage. It was of course a wonderful show, though a very long one, made longer by an infuriating number of long curtain drops in the second act. Lois Marshall was Queen of the Night, & Mary Morrison, who has an excellent stage presence, & looks from a distance like a very pretty girl, was Pamina. The males were less happy. Tamino was a fat homosexual-looking import from the States;[134] Sarastro, a man named Skitch, lacked weight; but the Papageno was pretty fair.[135] Ernest Adams, formerly a Moncton man,[136] was the Moor. The Masonic symbolism is shallow and platitudinous, but The Magic Flute is more or less what it ought to be, regardless of what the accident-prone school of criticism would say about it. The only modern master of ideal comedy to rank with Aristophanes & Shakespeare is Mozart; Mozart was, it is true, dependent on others for the *lexis* or verbal structure of his drama, and Schikaneder was not a great poet. But a librettist has no business being a great poet, and Schikaneder, who was trained in the Austrian *Zauberspiel* school of Nestroy and Reinhard [Reinhardt], knew what archetypes ought to go into the successor to the *Birds* and the *Tempest*. I still haven't got the *exact* meaning of the bird archetype. In Shakespeare it's Puck & Ariel, & they, especially the "tricksy sprite" Ariel, are descended from the New Comedy tricky slave, who carries out the comic action and, after being threatened with the cross, is

set free. In Christianity it's the Holy Spirit, bird and spirit of air, who brings about the birthe [birth] of the divine comedy & then escapes. His analogy is Barabbas, who descends from the leprosy bird rite of Leviticus [14:4–7]. In Shakespeare the bird fairies act under orders from a father-figure of sorts. The ordeals of fire & water, which make Tamino divine, are above & below the air where the bird man Papageno is.

Monday, February 25

[138] Last night we went out to see the Fairleys: Helen Goudge drove us there & back, but Tommy couldn't come because Stephen still has to be sat with. So it was an extremely quiet party, but a most pleasant one: the Fairleys are such utterly charming and gentle people, and I can't believe, even yet, that Margaret has any real notion of what sort of thing she's conniving at by being a Communist. Barker I think will do a paper on "Comic Myth in Heine," which would be exactly right for us, I should think: I don't know why I'm arranging it.[137]

[139] Today's nine o'clock was on Bacon's Advancement of Learning, which went all right, but wasn't exciting. This time I'm stressing the fact that while his sense of the practical reference of knowledge makes him a prophet of, more particularly, the social sciences where man is involved with nature, in contrast to the Galileo school who talk of man as spectator & so make nature theatrical, still he's very far from the utilitarian people who don't read him say he is: he's a strong believe[r] in disinterested contemplation of the works of God as central to knowledge. Well, the twelve o'clock was still on Ruskin, and not bad: the kids woke up and rode me pretty hard on his economics, which as I don't know bugger-all about economics wasn't easy to deal with.

[140] In the afternoon I went over to Woodhouse's office to do exams. Every once in a while I get something done that rather cheers me up about my own efficiency. For some reason (I'm tired and bored with fiddling while my book is burning inside me) I'd been stewing all weekend over the 4k exam I had to set, and of course did nothing about it. Well, in my two free hours this morning I concocted a 4k exam, took it over and showed it to Woodhouse, Shook & Mrs. Kirkwood, and five minutes later a job that was supposed to take an hour was done and we'd started to gossip. In other words, it was practically a foolproof paper—

I boast of this trifle because I need to cheer myself up. The 3j paper—Barker's—followed at 3 o'clock. Not nearly so good a paper. Hmmm. I went home and phoned Ned [Pratt] up. He's developed bursitis—the same thing that Knox has—in his shoulder as a complication of the break, so it's unlikely that he'll be back this term. The next time I go to see him I think I'll take a copy of Pogo, although I doubt if he really goes for that kind of fantasy. He likes the quantitative hyperbolic kind, not the fantasy of juxtaposition and irrelevance and Finnegans Wake assonance that you get in that superb strip, which seems to me almost the definitive example of its type.

Tuesday, February 26

[141] Finished Ruskin and got a start on Morris, which is more attractive territory. It's dismaying though to discover how much detail I've forgotten since 1949 about his life and work. The twelve o'clock was just bloody awful, except that I gave them a few books to read, and got the odd question or two. Then I went in to lunch & found Harold Wilson ready waiting. I fed him Shrove Tuesday pancakes, which he liked, and then we went upstairs to set the 3b paper, with supplemental. Sounds like a long job, but we got it done in good time. I went home fairly early and got a hot bath and relaxed with a drink before I went out to my next assignment.

[142] This, of course, was to talk to the A.T.E. [Association of Teachers of English] on "What is Poetry?" A terrible assignment, but it turned out to be quite an interesting one from my point of view. There was a fairish crowd, & staff included Woodhouse, Clawson, Shook & Macdonald besides Priestley & [Norman J.] Endicott. Norman did a fine job on modern poets, of a quieter kind than mine: we complemented one another very well, I think. Woodhouse was perturbed by the fact that my answer to the question was simply "verse," & that I ignored the Aristotelian meanings of the word as literature. I'd been given the whole field from *Beowulf* to *The Waste Land,* & I roamed up & down seeking what I might devour. I said that in prose there were at least two rhythms, the rhythm of style, or the way one writes (c'est l'homme) and the rhythm of decorum. Note that there's a positive place for the latter—I mean rather the former, vs. Kenner's nonsense that temporarily took me in. Then in poetry, I said, the metrical pattern was often more complicated than it

looked. The metrical basis of English iambic pentameter has *at least* (nobody heard that) two metrical patterns. One is the iambic pentameter; the other is the old four-thump line that's come down from Anglo-Saxon through Layamon, Lydgate, Skelton (where it has rests, as in Pope's reading of Beowulf), nursery rhymes, ballads (where every other line has a rest) and finally *Christabel*. I then recited the opening lines of the *Canterbury Tales* & of Paradise Lost, as well as a few lines from Shakespeare, to show that one would naturally read them as four-stress lines. (The value of this is, I think, in establishing the idea of a metrical complex as distinct from *a* metre: a notion that would delight the heart of the new critics if they could think of it. If I were a career man I'd do that for them and a bibliography of Blake, to parallel the MLA book on the other romantics, for PMLA. Maybe I can do that anyway if I do get to Cambridge this summer: it wouldn't take much work).

Wednesday, February 27

[143] The ten o'clock went on, in defiance of Lent, with Bacon, but just went through the motions. They haven't read a line of Bacon yet, and their expressions when I say "Are there any questions?" respond, as clearly as silence can, "Start talkin', yuh rat." I fooled & diddled, the way I do when I have things to do I don't want to do. The Library Committee met at 3, and it appears that the rumor about Archie [Hare] is something of a canard. Anyway, the President called for a sub-committee to advise him in the choice of a new librarian, so I promptly put Joe Fisher on it. Joe retorted by sticking me on the next sub-committee, which is supposed to consider shelving space in the new students' union. As I've remarked before, playing goal for the girls' hockey team is about the only job I *haven't* been assigned around this place yet. Well, this was probably the last meeting for both Robins and Trevor Davies. I'm glad Robins is getting clear of it. Davies, according to Surerus, is one of those retired job-clutchers, and practically broke down and cried when they tried to get rid of him some years ago. However, he's through now, and went around solemnly shaking hands with everybody. Money was voted (indirectly, of course) to clean up that filthy library. We went in to tea afterwards. The President remarked that he was pretty sure that the day of big private money for universities was over, and that the era of state aid had begun. He says he decided to have Victoria ask for state aid independently of Toronto, to Sidney Smith's considerable annoyance,

and that Trinity, who had at first decided to go in with Toronto, "reconsidered" after Moore's move.

[144] Claude Bissell's lecture on Grove was very good: the whole series has been excellent. As I told him, it was a hell of a lot better than the subject. He treated Grove with the one quality Grove conspicuously lacked—urbanity. I thought that perhaps the treatment was a bit over-general, as there are some extraordinary scenes in Grove that he could have made a lot of, and he spent—for me—rather too much time on Grove's very second-rate critical views. The central point—again for me—of the autobiography, that so much of the dreadful poverty & misery and groping *clumsiness* of Grove's life originated in a terrific protest against having to earn his own living was glossed over, but implied by the fact that Claude obviously didn't see heroism or grandeur in Grove's personality.

Thursday, February 28

[145] Well, I took Helen out to dinner and then plodded glumly along to my most unwelcome assignment. This was attending the annual meeting of Woodsworth House. Kay [Morris] had warned me to get there at 7:30, but that I couldn't do, and I got there at about 8:15. The meeting room was jam packed with trades union people, and I had to sit in the hall. After a while I couldn't take that, so I wandered in to the other room and talked to various people, including Lew [Lou] Morris, Mrs. George Tatham, Loeb, & others. The McCurdys, Leila, Helen James & in fact a large number of my friends were there. I got the impression that a lot of people were showing their teeth at each other without anything to bite into. The Woodsworth House executive has been feeling its autonomy like green oats, resenting CCF interference, & finally climaxing its defiance by bringing up for discussion an alleged "offer" of sale, which of course would evict the CCF offices. So the CCF packed the membership of Woodsworth House with trade unionists & came with an "amendment" (David Lewis) to the President's report (H.N. Wilkinson) giving the CCF pretty strong interests, if not control, over the House, & forbidding sale without consulting the CCF. That amendment passed, & I sneaked out at nearly midnight exasperated and exhausted. What it all proved except that the Woodsworth House executive are a bunch of irresponsible do-gooders and that the CCF isn't fit to keep a dozen dog-

catchers in public office, I don't know. It remains to be seen just how it will affect the educational policy of the House, which isn't terribly exciting anyway even from a non-socialist point of view. If it lets me out of wasting a Sunday night on them it'll be something gained. My own sympathies were divided, though I'd been lobbied by only one side. I think the *Provincial* CCF organization are a bunch of goons as far as any idea of education is concerned, and I think that Woodsworth House might well be salvaged from them if possible. There's the charitable tax exemption argument too. But it was silly to provoke the CCF so unnecessarily into a display of ruthlessness that was quite unwarranted and irrelevant. And I don't know that I see why *total* separation of House & party should be involved. I heard Margot Thompson putting up a pretty vigorous argument to George Tatham, and I thought she had a case. Oh, well, the hell with it. It was very bad luck for me to have to go: I didn't do anything anyway. Lew [Lou Morris] says Kay's father died suddenly, without illness, at the age of 102, and that Feilding did a beautiful & simple funeral service for him.

Friday, February 29

[146] Somewhere or other I managed to stagger through yesterday's lectures, and today's. The Spenser nine o'clock was routine, and afterwards I spent a couple of hours trying to focus my eyes. I'm ready to believe that there is such a thing as spring fever: an exhaustion that makes me feel as though I'd gone entirely without sleep for about three days can hardly be accounted for in terms of actual sleep lost, though it's true that this week I've not been getting the eight hours I seem to need, psychologically at least. Well, the twelve o'clock[138] was very good, as I suddenly realized that I hadn't yet given them my table of imagery. So I gave them that, and they loved it. God, they're bright kids. After lunch I went in to a meeting of a matriculation scholarship committee they put me on, but can't remember much of what happened, as I had to fight so hard to stay awake. The main question was whether we should extend & increase our scholarships. Offering them is in a sense competing with U.C., so we shouldn't violate a certain gentleman's agreement about "parity." But parity right now means 20 Victoria scholarships against 37 U.C. ones. Well, then I went in to my drama lectures, finished *The Alchemist*, did *Philaster*, & did nearly all of *The Duchess of Malfi*, a play I still do supremely well. I must write out my lecture on that some time.

Well, Ned's left five Shakespeare plays undone, so I'd better get busy.
Then I staggered home, ate dinner, and was in bed by 7:30.[139] Helen
unfortunately had to go out to an infernal Citizen's Forum group[140] at
Ruth Hebb's, so I dozed fitfully & unpleasantly until she came in at
midnight, and then I lay awake for hours, my head spinning in utter
exhaustion, my body temperature boiling, & my nose so full I couldn't
even turn over.

[147] So I was still tired this morning, but I slugged through another
Spenser. The graduate group had a paper by that very cute Margaret
Allen girl on William Morris's *East of the Sun & West of the Moon*, which I
hadn't had time to reread.[141] I went ahead with my table of themes & got
all the mythical & ethical ones done, only I shifted the top one, so now I
have Dionysiac-elegiac-tragic-pathetic-pharmakos (whatever the adjective is) on the *mythos* side, and Apollonian (because it's an ethical divine
society)-idyllic-comic-aggressive-satiric (perhaps this word will do after
all) on the *ethos* one. That switch makes things a bit neater. Maybe I
shouldn't confine the satiric to the more specific theme of the ironic
parable, the integrity of which is showing up in Hawthorne & Melville
now & leading to a lot of clarification.

Saturday, March 1

[148] Meanwhile I was working at every odd moment to get my radio
talk done, and finished it just on the nose. I wrote a bit more than usual
and tried to read it a shade faster, with more variety of pacing and pitch.
I think I may have partly succeeded. The writing jelled at the last minute,
and I think I turned in a fair job on the Laurence Hyde book, considering
that it's engravings and the radio's a blind man's medium. The nursery
rhyme review wasn't bad either: better in some respects than the Forum
article.[142] Helen James, who'd stayed to the end Wednesday night, said
the Trade union assault wasn't too lethal: most of the nominating slate is
back except that David Lewis is in as Vice-President. She said there were
at least twenty resignations from the Party as a result. She was on the
other side. I think they'll lose a lot of middle-class stooges, including me:
my inglorious career as a Fabian Dean of Canterbury is evidently through.

[149] I got home & we went out to see *The Bartered Bride*,[143] a much better
show than *The Magic Flute* simply because there were fewer halts &

curtain-drops. The Czech colony was out in full force—a great many clergymen. This time Mary Morrison was the bride, & showed a talent for straight comedy that was even more impressive than her Pamina. The hero was a balding pot-belly, but the import—the match-maker—was very successful. Towards the end an extremely shapely little girl named Ruth Gillis turned up in a pleasantly rudimentary circus costume—she was Esmerelda, & was, I think, Papagena, though the costume there hadn't shown her in her true colors, so to speak. Nora Conklin was the stepmother, & as massive as ever. There were dancers and in general a lively colorful good-humored show. I think the Opera Festival has done extraordinarily well.[144] The plot was rivalry between step-brothers, the hero the rightful eldest son who has disappeared & gets the matchmaker (*leno* type)[145] to draw up a contract marrying the bride to a son of his father. The rival is the stepmother's boy, an idiot who appears finally as a circus bear & is driven off the stage. Libretti of operas are useful for my comedy thesis because they're less inhibited by the plausibility-principle than *lexis* plays. One can see a summer-winter contest in this quite easily, the bear being regularly a minor behemoth image of a cyclic kind—he's the animal form of the romance giant. The attaching of the foolish rival to the community of the circus is an interesting idea, as the circus has connections with a spectacle *below* comedy.

Sunday, March 2

[150] Yesterday I lay as flat as an unwilling bride—well, no, I didn't quite. I went down to the office in the morning, stared gloomily at my book, went into the can, found the endemic Irving there, and listened to him tell me how he'd stalled off the SCM [Student Christian Movement] attempt at a return match between Carpenter and me for at least the fourth time. I was developing a headache, so I staggered out to lunch & went home again. My morale is so low that I've bought a book of crossword puzzles—the Elizabeth Kingsley double-crostic kind. It's a form of nervous doodling that preoccupies me and is probably less lethal than smoking—though I sometimes think I make a mistake by not smoking. For the most part the puzzles are very easy to do—in fact, if they don't break open in three or four minutes I go on to another puzzle.

[151] Today I was still miserable—sat around fiddling with my goddamned sermon and listened to myself on the radio. People tell me I

have an excellent radio voice, but I don't see it. I sounded nasal and echoic, as though I were talking from the bottom of a rain barrel, and I say "ta" instead of "to." I don't know where I developed this terrific nasal honk. We had a wonderful roast chicken for dinner and I went out glumly to meet my fate. I was "assisted" by two students on the VCU [Victoria College Union] executive, Bill Andrews [Andrew] & Lois White—lovely children, though only in a Nonconformist setting would one call them the acolyte type.[146] They'd come to me in the middle of my frantically busy week for a title, so I cracked open a Bible at random, it fell open at the first chapter of Proverbs, and I stuck myself for a sermon on "The Hatred of Knowledge." I added the Jesus-and-doctors passage from Luke to the lesson, and tried to say that knowledge was in three degrees. One was practical: all men, to paraphrase Aristotle on this level, by nature desire to know what they have to know to adjust to their community. The second is liberal, the pleasure of satisfied curiosity & of seeing one's horizon enlarge. Both are founded on habit & practice, on regularity of expectation and a calculus of probabilities. The third degree of knowledge begins with the bewildered effort to adjust to originality & radical revaluation, & reaches its climax in the apocalyptic paralysis of habit in vision. It sounds complicated, and it doubtless was. I said that justification by faith was based on a conception of faith as the axioms of conduct that were effective in conduct & that the skeptical reserve distinguished the free spirit from the bigot who doesn't doubt his own mind.

Monday, March 3

[152] The chapel was about two-thirds full, & we adjourned afterwards to some non-Eucharist "refreshments"—a paper cup of green ginger ale, not that I wanted more. I think the sermon was largely a failure. Addressed to the wrong people, for one thing. I can't imagine who the right people would have been. So I said fuck the whole business and went over to hear Greta Kraus at Wymilwood. Met Anne Carnwath, who remarked sardonically that I seemed to have solved the problem of what to do on a Toronto Sunday. Lovely concert, including the Fifth Partita, a Teleman fantasia and a wonderful Scarlatti sonata I'd never heard before.[147] I still can't understand why, when they invented the piano, they left off the double keyboard & the couplers: if they'd had those, people like Liszt would have had to stop playing around and settle down to some serious composing. I wonder how much a harpsichord actually

would cost, & whether it really is such a headache to keep it in tune. You can certainly get more out of it with its eight pedals than you can out of a piano. Because of the loveliness of the music and the resourcefulness of the instrument, she scored a great personal triumph—on a piano she'd have sounded pretty sloppy. I mean this to be in praise of harpsichords, not damaging to her—she gave me a wonderful evening. I was too weary to go in for coffee afterward, & we drove home with the Tretheweys. Gordon Davies sat beside me—Doris had a cold—but our conversation was inconclusive.

[153] There seems to be no doubt that part of my fatigue this last week was a gradually gathering protest against this bloody sermon. And yet I don't know: without it I wouldn't have had an excuse to postpone my essay-reading and the like and talk myself into a real nervous strain. The strain was there all right, & yet I have a feeling that I avoided something worse—flu or the like—homeopathically, by deliberately increasing my own disturbance. That's the only way I can account for the tremendous relaxed relief I feel today. My nine o'clock was on Bacon—an uphill fight, as I'm worried by the clock, bored with the course, and have to struggle with students who haven't yet cracked the book. Then Anne Carnwath came in—the two other girls have dropped out of the course,[148] and she just wants to talk about the ideas that come to her. It's too bad she has so mediocre an undergraduate record, but on the other hand I doubt that she'd really have much interest in an academic career.

Tuesday, March 4

[154] The twelve o'clock was on Morris—my lecturing continues a consolidating rhythm I'd hoped to break by going away for a year.[149] I don't get many new ideas this year because I'm preoccupied by my book. And the old ones, as I get accustomed to them, tend to crystallize into aphorisms. That, of course, greatly decreases their effectiveness, as students aren't mature enough for aphorisms. What I call the Gertrude Stein style, of hypnotic repetitiveness, is the style of discovery and of teaching. It's the style of the First Epistle of John & of most mystical literature—Boehme, for instance—and of my lecturing at its best. Fortunately that class is waking up a little. I went over to Trinity to have lunch with Child & listen to his 2i paper. Norman [J.] Endicott & Larry Shook were along. The paper was a good 2i paper—plenty of options and very long. I put in

my usual complaint about 2i, but it's clear that Woodhouse is an immovable object on that point.

[155] The rest of the day I spent in relative idleness: got Abbie Potts's paper off to Fred Sternfeld, but answered no other letters. What with Bert Hamilton sending over his thesis and that drivelling idiot Lorne Pierce sending that god-damned manuscript of Edgar's back to me *again*, my desk is cluttering up a good deal.[150] Today I did some more Morris and actually got a reaction out of them at nine o'clock. Oh, God, the whole *rhythm* of university life is all wrong as it gets inflated in size. When I first came on the staff, students used to flock into my office to talk over their work. Now they never come, and the ones who would hesitate because they know I'm busy. Well, why should I be busy? I'm supposed to be a scholar, not an executive. I'm busy haranguing masses of people as the university picks up the rhythm of mass movement. Well, anyway, I think my twelve o'clock was a fair success—a review of apocalyptic symbols. Instead of my old "chaos" level I added the ordeals of fire & water, the elements of the fourfold man as distinct from his natural inheritance of spirit (air) & body (earth). I also added "vehicular movement" to the animal category, drawing a distinction between the aristocratic horse (hippes, equites, cavaliers) and the proletarian ass & mule with which Jesus is associated. The symbol of the ass is a very complex one, and how it all fits together I'm not sure yet. But it's socially proletarian (cf. Sancho's Dapple vs. Quixote's "once a good horse") and cosmologically the brother who is the body.[151]

Wednesday, March 5

[156] Another thing I did yesterday was attend that subcommittee on the Students' Union in Robins' office. I didn't realize that a library extension was included in that building, or that it's where our archives are to go. Well, I went home and early to bed—Helen went out to a fashion show at Eaton's. I'm still relaxing, and of course avoiding essays & correspondence.

[157] Today I lectured on Bacon's *Essays*. After forty minutes of it I asked them where Aldous Huxley had got the title "Jesting Pilate" for his book. They didn't know. However, I myself began to feel that I was expanding a little on the matter of the rhythmic *genres* or elements of literature—the

aphorism can be, & according to Bacon normally is, the unit of consolidated or crystallized knowledge. The law of nature—e.g. gravitation—is, when verbal, an aphorism. I'm vague on this point because I still don't know whether there's to be a separate chapter on the theory of genres or not, nor where it will go if there is.

[158] I'd been asked by Sidney Smith to go to lunch to meet Hutchins of Chicago, who's in town giving the Marfleet lectures. Eighteen people there: apparently a sort of ginger group, mainly of younger people, to start a discussion and give Hutchins the atmosphere. I sat between Blatz, who told me he was a Catholic & a Vic graduate, & Wetmore in Chemistry, another Maritimer (Saint John). There were also Bill Line & Tupper for the devil's party, & Derwent [Derwyn] Owen, McLuhan, Woodhouse, Innes,[152] Brough Macpherson, Claude Bissell, Crane, & the Deans of Medicine [MacFarlane] & Law (Wright). McLuhan knows Hutchins, evidently. Anderson was there, but scrammed after lunch. I don't know what impression we gave Hutchins—my impression of him was that of a man without quite as much charm as he'd need to get his ideas through to people & institutions. That is, I felt in him the sort of interest in ideas that goes with a certain lack of good will towards people. I'm skipping his lectures, but gather he's had quite a field day with American education—phrases like "nation-wide play-pen" and the like.

[159] At four o'clock I went over to talk to the church students in Stevenson House.[153] The topic was supposed to be the Christ the preacher should present to his congregation. I suppose it's some good for me to do that kind of thing, but God how it bores me, & how I wish people would stop forcing me to be a religious special pleader. Nine-tenths of my appearances this year have been religious—both as writer & speaker, & I'm tired of it.

Thursday, March 6

[160] At Council yesterday Archie Hare presented the report of the Committee on Extra-Curricular Activities, based on a questionnaire sent out to the students, of whom 392 replied. That in itself seems to me significant of a curious attitude of students—they knew it was official, and as students don't get all that mail it seems to follow that two-thirds of our students are distinctively scatterbrained, lazy, or sulky. The report

showed nothing surprising, except that Bennett had been evidently convincing himself that we do 50% of our teaching. The report indicated that it was more like 20%, which of course it is, and he seemed chagrined. Victoria is certainly being carried by the University of Toronto, and I suppose our (largely meaningless) independence will soon go: if it survives as a genuine decentralization I think we'll be all right. I'd rather see us cling to Toronto than to the Church. In the evening I listened to an indifferent dramatization of *1066* by that idiot Eric Christmas.[154]

[161] The nine o'clock today was on Spenser's imitative harmony and general verbal stunting. The difference between sound-wit and meaning-wit isn't clear to me yet, and I don't know—yes, I do—I mean verbal mimesis would naturally come in the high mimetic period. The twelve o'clock was very enjoyable—on the concrete universal. The kids made a real effort and kept asking me to repeat things. The fundamentalist wasn't there. I think now I have a fair table of archetypes, and with that on one side and the table of thematic elements on the other I ought to crack the central chapter on quest narratives readily enough. Only maybe that way it would follow archetypes & not precede. In the afternoon I harangued the third year again on my views of comedy for two hours, making a somewhat perfunctory start on *Measure for Measure*. I'm beginning to realize some of the difficulties of the part of my thesis that I hold in common with Stoll. Drama isn't *all* convention. That's a sophisticated & educated notion, & runs counter to the views of any unsophisticated member of my audience.[155] (On the ironic level there is a pretence of a direct appeal to a hypothetical audience of boobs, as in advertising & propaganda, and this, like other forms of irony, is the tomb of mimesis and the womb of spectacular *auto*, where the thing communicated is supposed to be believed). All drama contains a pretence of reality which becomes part of the critic's data sooner or later.

Friday, March 7

[162] Hence the variety of likes & dislikes different critics may have for a character present a critical problem that you can solve, not of course by appealing to the "intentions" of Shakespeare and asserting that you know what they are, but by studying the structure of the play as a whole. That's not only where convention becomes important, but where it's seen to be dependent on structure & genre. Well, the variety of opinions

expressed about Isabella, for instance, are pretty bewildering, & one's first instinct is to take refuge in moral relativism. If Victorian critics thought she was so wonderful, maybe they're right. Well, they aren't right, and I refuse to be bullied by such relativism. The situation Isabella is in, when Claudio finds he is more afraid of death to himself than of dishonor to her, would be a tragic Antigone-like situation if Isabella had the weight for a tragic role. Well, she hasn't. There's no trace of real greatness or charity in her: all she thinks of is the insult to herself. It shatters the dream of her virginity that we've seen building up ever since, as a novice in the convent, she was already quite sure the nuns had too much leeway. All through the colloquy with Lucio, even the plea with Angelo, she's half asleep. The Duke (who is heterophonically a Christ-figure) is more obviously a restored father than I think we get anywhere else. So it's clear that Isabella belongs in a comedy, which is a study of "ignoble" characters.

[163] This morning I did some more on Spenser's versification. I still have to work out this notion of a metrical complex: I suppose in English the iambic pentameter is the battlefield of the musical four-thump line and the pictorial long-drawn-out, semi-quantitative line. Also I should try to investigate the phenomenon of parallelism as one of the schemata linking poetry with prose. The rhythm of a character sketch in Earle is closer to the *Essay on Man* than to Addison. Parallelism is to movement what alliteration & assonance are to sound. Things may open up from here, & may not. The graduate group had a paper on Dylan Thomas by Gordon Smith, not too conclusive. I ignored it, very largely, & went on with my thematic elements. The elements of *dianoia*, relating to the poet himself, are coming a bit clearer. *Symbolisme* & the Mallarmé tradition on the ironic level; the romantic & genetic view of the creative imagination in the low mimetic; the loving orator on the high mimetic; the sacramental lover on the romantic & the encyclopedic on the mythical. Or something like that.

Saturday, March 8

[164] In the afternoon Helen felt restless, and came to cruise around the Museum in the afternoon. I picked her up there and we went on to have a few drinks and then dinner at the Lichee Gardens. We both felt like a holiday and it did us a lot of good; also the food was wonderful. As we get more bourgeois and middle-aged in our tastes we gradually find

ourselves having a better time in places like the Lichee Gardens than in places like 22A.[156]

[165] However, today was totally wasted. I don't know why: a certain perversity sweeps over me from time to time. Yesterday I read a book Copp Clark sent me in response to my remark about Lagerkvist's *Barabbas*. This was a novel of his called *The Dwarf*, & which for some reason I read straight through. The dwarf is the Jungian shadow, the accuser inseparably attached to the body (identified with the castle) of a Renaissance prince. The link with Andreyev's play is interesting.

[166] The scheme of the book seems to be simplifying a bit. After the Introduction, I begin with a conspectus or alphabet of themes, based on my five modes. Then I go on to the five (if there are five) narratives of the quest, dealing with the parallel patterns in typical plots of myth, romance and comedy (note that there's no word like romance for the whole narrative of high mimetic from tragic to comic—the nearest word is epic & that's misleading), and, I suppose of Druidism. Third in this series is the meaning chapter, and it concludes in a discussion of the verbal universe, which leads on to archetypes. Then the chapter on genres, which is back again, follows and completes the first half of the book, leading on the second half, which deals with genres in what now seems to me their logical order: drama, lyric, epic, prose fiction, and the final ironic pulverizing of forms that leads to scripture. Then a final chapter as a conclusion, summarizing the techniques of criticism, should now be a possibility if I get the rest of all that stuff stowed away in other chapters.[157] So I come back to my twelve-chapter scheme after all. And of course I'll drop the last chapter if it doesn't come out in one clear piece by itself. But the main themes of the book are beginning to come together and form a unity, and my original notion of a collection of essays is as dead as the great auk. One or two more bits of crystallization like this five modes business and I'm all set. I think, too, that I have a genuine fear of reading that isn't all just laziness: a fear of being driven too far in any one direction before I get the whole picture.

Sunday, March 9

[167] Another wasted day, spent mainly in doing crossword puzzles.

My usual reaction when faced with things I don't want to do: but I'm overdoing it. Enough said. I heard Irving on Critically Speaking, and his voice was good, though he gave a terrific plug to a book by Lewis Mumford, an author I'd always thought of as mostly blatherskite. In the evening we heard a good but confusing performance of Etherege's *Man of Mode*, with Don Harron in it.

[168] My 4k ideas seem to be forming links, which will be useful if I ever start to write that essay on Morris. In *News from Nowhere* there seem to be fewer people, which suggests what the real socialist answer to Malthus is. Savages & animals don't have meals: they fast & feast, & in very primitive conditions there is no such vice as greed. Similarly, we spawn and rut out of panic, frustration, boredom and the sort of ingrown concupiscence that results from a lack of creative outlets. To say nothing of simpler things like the ten-year (at least) interval between erecting the Tower of Babel and penetrating heaven with it. In a more relaxed society sex would be as well under control as hunger, & birth control would be within the organism, not a mechanical brake on an organism assumed to be out of control. There shouldn't be any mystery like Shaw's "leave it to nature" about it. Well, since I got that idea about democracy as a recovery of natural society that forms a secular analogy to Christianity, Rousseau & the whole Rousseauist tradition has [have] become so much clearer. For Morris, seizure of the instruments of production means seizing control of one's own hands, and that's the direct action that destroys the state and the machine at once. The *real* moral of *Past & Present* is that, as you obviously can't argue from a monastery to an empire, the shape of human society is a decentralized community. The *real* moral of *Sartor Resartus* is that the central heroic act on the low mimetic level, an act of work that destroys the twin dragons of dandyism and drudgery at once, is an act of manufacture in Morris's sense: George Fox's suit of leather.[158] This is a very important aspect of low mimetic dianoia: the conception I mean of work as creative act. It's the ethical reference of the whole romantic movement. From that point of view, the ironic vision is an essential complement, as it illustrates the distinction between free human nature & human nature in bondage to institutions. I suppose that's partly why the Communists have gone back to bourgeois realism for their own norms of art. And as the conception of "human nature set free" clarifies, the heroic modes are added.

Monday, March 10

[169] The nine o'clock was on Browne, but didn't get much said. The twelve o'clock, on Morris, got a little more said. I'm certainly glad to have my kids asking questions, but I'm still depressed by the wariness and cynicism of their questions. My guess is that the whole educational process that, as I've said so often, fails to distinguish interest, which is a conditioned reflex or response to a stimulus, from concentration which is the habit of learning, has left them utterly bored and exhausted, like the man on his wedding night who had eight performances and a rehearsal (same as performance, only nobody comes). Next time I have to work out the progress of the words art & nature through the course from Burke's repudiation of natural society to Morris' repudiation of artifice, thence to Huxley's statement of the antithesis.

[170] In the afternoon John Findlay [Finlay] came in with Pat Grandy and Walt Stewart to talk about the Acta kids' party. The girl won't be much use, and John wants beer, which annoys and irritates me, as it's an adolescent reaction to Methodist hypocrisy which I approve of but don't particularly want to get stuck with. I'll wait and see: I don't even know if it's legal—but of course that's why they want it at our place and not at Wymilwood. But there are thirty people coming, and *they* certainly can't guarantee that nobody is going to run home squealing to mamma that Professor Frye tried to rape her with a beer bottle. Well, at four I went over to waste time at a Department meeting, which ended very quickly, as we cut out the main item of business. This was a report to Innes [Innis] about what we think the place of the humanities in education ought to be. Knowing what that Department's like on the most specific & concrete questions, I wouldn't even imagine what they would do to an assignment like that. But fortunately Woodhouse said U.C. had already turned in a brief, a committee of the Graduate School (I hadn't heard of that: it sounds like a pretty arbitrary procedure on Woodhouse's part) had turned in another, that he knew Trinity had turned in a third (as College, I believe); at that point Shook said St. Mike's had finished the first sentence or so of theirs, Robins said that in that case we'd go into the matter at Victoria, and so, unless we wanted a sixth brief—well. Ken Maclean [MacLean], in that bemused way he gets, hung on to the notion for a while, and Mcdougall [McDougall] even spoke & voted for it, but

the upshot was that we got out of there by five-thirty, quite lost and wondering what to do and where to go.

Tuesday, March 11

[171] Well, what I decided to do was go & have some Martinis. Silly of me, but after I'd had two who should come in but Don Harron. I can't imagine why, unless somehow he knew that I was there. He's playing in *Arms & the Man* next week, and Gloria is up at Gravenhurst nursing young Martha, who's nine months old now. Donald is the same as ever: a good deal of probably brilliant conversation I didn't hear much of. I was very tired, and the Martinis stewed me. The waiter recognized him & joined the discussion. Then I had a brief dinner at Murray's & went to the Forum meeting. We decided to hold a special strategic meeting, and at it I'm going to make a speech about how we've manoeuvered ourselves from a CCF rag into an even tighter corner, an intellectual-bloc-within-the-CCF rag. In other words, the Morrises don't like Alan [Allan] Sangster's feud with the CBC, but seem unconscious of the fact that their own feud with the CCF has gone quite far enough. Otherwise the meeting went well enough: Al Shea & Andrew [Hebb] were there, [A.F.B.] Clark not. Two beers completed my rout.

[172] This morning I discovered I'd caught a mean cold, as I richly deserved. So I didn't do the one thing that would have given some point to the day: go over and hear Havelock give the special lecture on Semantics in Greek Philosophy he'd been brought up here to give by the Department of Classics. It means that I see nothing of Eric during his visit her [here]: I heard of two parties, but naturally wasn't asked to either. The rest of the day was routine. The nine o'clock was awful: it was a cold dull morning and about two-thirds of the class was there. I have never had a class before who cut so many lectures so cheerfully. I don't know whether it's the fuss I made over latecomers or not; it's not, I'm pretty sure, the quality of my lectures, which are very good in 4k. I finished Morris and began on Huxley, and the tall musical girl seemed struck by my differentiation between the doctrines of evolution in biology and of progress in history. The twelve o'clock, on Judaistic analogies of Christian symbols, wasn't too bad: but my pacing of that course has been bad all year, and as they're a dull class they haven't helped. I sound

as though I were just gloomy from the cold, which of course is true, but it's also true that my long holiday with returned students and a year off is over, and I'm back to kindergarten teaching again.

Wednesday, March 12

[173] Speaking of kindergartens reminds me of a current silly story about the teacher of a progressive school who found a little puddle outside the door. She then proposed that she & the whole class should cover their eyes while the offender, thus unidentified, slipped out to wipe it up. So they did, and the patter of little feet was duly heard going out the door and in again. When the teacher next opened the door she found *two* little puddles there, with a note reading "The Black Hand strikes again."

[174] The cold continues, though the weather was better. I didn't think I could get down to my ten o'clock, but I did, and gargled my way through Browne, who doesn't much thrill me as a subject to lecture on. The sunshine encouraged me to stay down for a semi-official staff "colloquium," as it was called; "cackloquium," as I called it in my date pad. Joe's [Joe Fisher's] idea. I honestly don't know what the hell gets into Joe some times. All that high-priced help kept down till late in the afternoon spending over an hour to talk about—what do you suppose? The "seminar method" of teaching as opposed to lectures! Of course I've always known that Joe was the kind of man who would stop you on the street to tell you that he'd just discovered a wonderful little magazine called the Reader's Digest that gives you the cream of current periodical reading. But really! Well, we slugged through it, everybody speaking in turn. We demonstrated the fact that every lecture was as much a seminar as the number of students, the ignorance and immaturity of students, the curriculum, the examination, and the physical shape of the room permitted. Only towards the end did the fact that students hate seminars because they can't take notes except when the professor speaks even emerge, much less any appreciation of the fact that students have a right to the lecture, & the lecturer similarly has a right to talk. Jessie [Macpherson] said that. Irving mentioned the great expense of the "preceptorial" system introduced by Woodrow Wilson into Princeton, & Archie [Hare] neatly punctured what point there would have been to that by saying that when *he* was in Princeton he heard preceptorials over a partition,

and there was the lecturer yacking away the whole time just as he does in a classroom. The only thing I got out of it was a dim perception of the value of a first-year course designed especially to break the receptive habits inherited from high school and encourage the habit of participation—in short, a course in remedial education.

Thursday, March 13

[175] The cold was no better and I've been sleeping very badly, with some diarrhoea in the mornings. Thank God Ned [Pratt] thinks he'll be back soon—in fact next week, beginning with his Liberal Arts talk on Tuesday. So this will be my last two-hour stretch Thursday afternoons. I couldn't take any more of it—it's buggered my graduate group on Fridays as well. I got through a certain amount of Spenser at nine, and if I skip all the minor episodes like the Fradubio business I should finish in good time. The twelve o'clock continued to be very good: the pacing and accommodation there is just right, and I have very good kids. A smaller group possessed of their Bibles is certainly the answer in that course, whatever year it's given to.

[176] Well, in the afternoon I managed to get through some remarkably bad lectures on *Measure for Measure*. Actually they weren't so bad except that there was a bit too much of my theory of comedy & too little about the play. I'm too tired to organize a new lecture in this much of a hurry. I worked out my point about Isabella's being a comic character because she hasn't the weight for a tragic character, and applied it to Claudio's fear of death and Angelo's moral hybris. I also suggested that it could be applied to the Duke. Then I discussed Isabella's father-complex, somewhat to their amusement, and thinking of the way the play is paired with *All's Well*, where it's a sulky Adonis of a boy with a bad mother-fixation that everybody including his mother is out to break. Then I explained my second-world point and said the problem-plays were experiments in bringing the second world into the disguise of a central character, and exploding it when the character is undisguised and regrouping the characters in a tighter social unit—"so they look better," as that very thoughtful lad Bob Davenport remarked. I noted the symmetry of the four couples (which seems to run through a great many of the comedies), and the fact that all the men—Claudio, Angelo, the Duke, Lucio, even Bernardine—are threatened with death, though absolutely nobody gets

hurt. The Sir Gawain theme of mock death may be pretty deeply embed-ded in comedy even apart from the tricky-slave business in which the Duke himself, as a disguised vice, is involved. It's a part of the business of evading the absurd law, a law that often involves the death penalty. The agon in Aristophanes has of course a similar function.

Friday, March 14

[177] I'm getting through the second book of Spenser, and at this rate I'll soon be through. I think Ned's [Ned Pratt's] probably right that they're over-lectured to anyway. We're certainly teaching children again, though: of course I want them to ask questions, but it's a problem to know how to answer a question which means simply a lack of comprehension. It brings into the focus of a practical problem my own point that the teacher doesn't answer a question so much as try to raise the question-er's mental level to where he can outgrow the question. When I say the Church of England tried to be moderate, they say "isn't that smug?" and when I say the dungeon of Orgoglio means Kierkegaard's "shut-upness," they say "can't you ever be alone?" and when I say Huxley stressed evol-ution in moral questions they say "isn't it unrealistic to talk that way now that we're civilized?" I'm certainly not complaining because they ask these questions: I'm just wondering why they come in this particular form. I think they'd prefer me to be less impartial in my exposition than I am: if I overstated a case and made a writer obviously guilty of a glaring fallacy, they'd find that exposition easier to remember.

[178] The graduate group had Francis Chapman's paper on *Heart of Darkness*. A very poor and disappointing paper, because all he did was summarize the story and then say the symbolism was "confusing": I suppose he means he's confused about graduate work generally, but it was a bit shocking all the same. Our kids are so immature, and their intellectual and cultural adolescence so artificially delayed, that when they're graduated they keep hanging around the graduate school be-cause they don't know how to graduate mentally. And as their social conscience is being outraged and they haven't any vocation for the profession, they get pretty neurotic.

[179] After lunch I went home. John [Finlay] & Walter [Stewart]—and Patricia [Grandy]—arrived with the beer and skittles in the afternoon,

we had an early dinner, and by 7:30 Patricia was back again, with Joyce Bingleman, to help Helen get ready. It was a simply beautiful party, and Helen enjoyed it as much as I did. I'd been stewing about the beer, but they really were completely mature about it. The younger ones, especially the girls, had cokes, and no group of people could have behaved more naturally or pleasantly. There were thirty-one there altogether, but they got into our front room all right for the meeting before they spread out into the dining room. Only one couple spooned; the others were just pleasant guests to have around.

Saturday, March 15

[180] John [Finlay] had gone to some pains to arrange an exhibition of copy, layout, stages of prints, and so on, all neatly lettered, out on the floor of the living room. Then he gave them a speech about why he'd asked them all there (I hadn't realized until he reminded me of it that the original idea for a "Friends of Acta" party had been mine) and I gave a speech complimenting him and his staff. Then we broke out the beer and soft drinks, and finally trooped into the dining room, where they'd laid in a hell of a stock of cheese and ham and pickles and rye bread and stuff. Never again will I try to feed them doughnuts and apples. We talked about everything: the suppression of the Varsity (I think the S.A.C. [Students' Administrative Council] made fools of themselves over that),[159] college gossip, movies & so on. They started going at midnight, but the party wasn't over until half-past one.

[181] Today John [Finlay] came back to pick up the virgins and dead soldiers, and I rode with him down to the Acta office, where I helped carry it in, and back again. How these youngsters ate! For the rest, I did very little during the day. In the evening the English staff came in to discuss the President's letter about the humanities. I'd suggested that they meet at our place over a bottle as the most painless way of doing it. That was a very pleasant party too, but with less vigor. Ned [Pratt] of course was out; Ruth [Jenking] phoned up an hour before to say that the nervous exhaustion was too much for her; Kay [Coburn] and I had colds: Joe [Fisher] & John [Robins] are both invalids who ought to be in bed by nine every night, and Joe couldn't eat any of our food. That left Chris [Love] & Ken [MacLean] in relatively normal health, and anyway they all had drinks & I think all enjoyed themselves. And we went through

the letter like a buzz-saw: I've never seen John Robins in better form as a chairman. We covered the eight points in a little over an hour: I was secretary. We said the humanities dealt with the culture of the past (thus including history & all philosophy) and recommended (this was largely due to me) a first year General Education course along Harvard lines. With great reluctance and hesitation I've finally come to the point of believing that most of our honour courses are not the planned areas of concentrated study I used to think they were, but special technical trainings assimilated to the professional schools and not to the idea of a university. And as the pass course is no damn use, we have to try this General Education scheme, if we can prevent it from becoming an education in generalities.

Sunday, March 16

[182] Not surprisingly I went to bed for the afternoon, not to sleep, but to do crossword puzzles, the only form of activity I seem to be capable of. In the middle of it I dictated to Helen the brief from the Department to the Graduate School: in other words the notes from last night. In the evening I went out to Woodsworth House and slugged through another god-damned job. That was a speech on the relation of the artist to society based on a discussion of *The God that Failed.* I'd picked that because I'd done it for the radio and was damned if I was going to do any special work for this. It was a pretty poor and empty job, although the discussion was fair. But if people get me to do jobs I don't want to do that's a logical result. I think they expected me to bring students over, but there was only one first-year lad there. Something to check off the list. I hope with the muscle job they did I can check it off for good.

[183] Now the opening chapter, after the introduction, is to be called "Levels of Imitation." It starts by distinguishing the rhythm and pattern of the poem (actually it starts with a recognition of the ambiguity of the word "poem") as "narrative" and "meaning" respectively. Then I distinguish from narrative the imitation of actions, and call it "plot," the Aristotelian *mythos.* I establish the point that imitation means the incorporation of content, and is not an external relation of words to things. (It would be interesting if the Aristotelian conception of mimesis *involved,* as a necessary part of itself, the archetypal approach to criticism. For imitation in his sense refers to the archetypal and not the sigmatic level

of symbolism). Of course on the sigmatic level one could call the mimesis a representation of events in life, and an abstraction of the gross events of the narrative. *Mythos* is the soul of art because it's the living organic part of it which is also capable of being looked at as an entelechy. This latter brings us to the imitation of meaning, which I call "thought," the Aristotelian *dianoia*, the kind of thing the "history of ideas" people study—for that too can be looked at externally as a representation of ideas. On the archetypal level it's a union of form and idea—a point I may keep in reserve. Each aspect is tied to two ethical poles: the *mythos*, to the hero and his society; *dianoia*, to the poet and *his* society. The two societies join: but there are five levels of action indicated by the hero, and five levels of thought indicated by the poet, each with its social pole.

Monday, March 17

[184] A busy day, of a kind I don't mind once in a while. The nine o'clock did, and nearly did for, Religio Medici. I don't know why I suddenly felt dead on the subject of Browne: I sure as hell hope I can get rid of 2i next year. Then Anne Carnwath came in—the girls say she's still neurotic—the current slang for such a situation is "doesn't cope"—but she sure as hell looks normal enough to me, and very charming too. Neither do I know why I make hell so tedious a symbol of security. A job that permits one to spend an hour in the line of duty talking to an attractive young girl with a quick mind is a pleasant job. The twelve o'clock was on Huxley, and a most uncomfortable hour it was. A raw, bleak day; the university heating plant no damn use at best—Bill James says the new one will start functioning in the fall; Monday is bad anyway because they go easy on Sundays, & in Room 36, where for some reason they didn't bother putting the partitions up to the ceiling in the first place and which is too big anyhow for the rods, and you've got a dead ringer for the return of the Ice Age. I wonder if that sentence is grammatical. My kids begged me to find another room, but there just isn't one available.

[185] In the afternoon I went over to the Forum office and read through a large amount of crap. There are still a great many stories (including Pacey & Ken Maclean [MacLean]) but not many poems. It took me a couple of hours, including the time I spent whacking out a stupid editorial on education,[160] in which I forgot everything I was going to say.

Especially the point about the survival of political shibboleths, according to which there's a vague overhang of the notion that supporters of Deweyism are politically progressive & supporters of the humanities stuffy and reactionary. John Nicol was doubtful about it and so was I, but I finally shoved it in. Then I went over to Hart House, where I picked Helen up, to hear the first of Crane's Alexander lectures.[161] He says he's going to assume a kind of critical pluralism or relativism: that the disagreements among critics are due to the use of different and incommensurable frames of reference, & that many of the agreements are actually only verbal similarities. Some people, he says, understand by distinguishing & others by unifying. Well, I understand by unifying, and ultimately I certainly won't accept any *ultimate* pluralism, though I can quite see that the kind of differentiating analysis he's proposing to do would have to be done first, and should be.

Tuesday, March 18

[186] Helen hated the lecture, but she was in a black mood, in between cold and curse. I took her out for a couple of drinks and then we went down to Angelo's for dinner, but the party wasn't too big a success, and ended in a tantrum when she got home. She'd been working very hard all day, hanging clothes in the basement, and Crane's cold-boiled cabbage prose didn't give her much of a spiritual uplift.

[187] Today I did a brilliant nine o'clock, one of the best lectures I've ever given this year, but the twelve o'clock, the last R.K. lecture, was largely a frost. I think my general sense of failure in that course is partly my fault—bad pacing and proportioning of material to start with, and then a profound reluctance to handle my central conception of Jesus as effective mythically rather than historically. And it's partly theirs: they're a sleepy and bored class, without anything of the feeling that there used to be in that course—it's just one more course to them, and a twelve o'clock one that keeps them from lunch. One of my social science people came to talk to somebody, and ducked out as soon as I began, which put me off to start with. There was no clap at the end either, which I always miss if I don't get it. I'm quite seriously thinking of chucking the whole course next year, because it's not worth the extra effort for me if it's nothing extra for them. The rest of the day was relatively uneventful. I finished the appraisal of Cotter's thesis and the damned survey of poetry

for the UTQ,[162] and went over to hear Crane's second lecture, which was on Aristotle. A very careful, conscientious analytical exposition: he left out a good deal, such as the discussion of the unities—in fact he left out everything that interests me about the *Poetics*. I phoned Helen and told her I'd be staying down to hear Ned [Pratt] reading his poetry at Wymilwood, but as soon as she heard my voice (I'm still fighting a cold, and of course I felt dismal enough anyway) she told me to come home and go to bed, which I did.

[188] That conception of the democratic revolution as the recovery of natural society is certainly bringing a lot of things into focus for me: all through Crane's lecture I was trying to fit it to the idea of mimesis. In Morris (I really *must* do an essay on him) there's the final tie-up of the art-nature theme. At least, Blake says that the state of nature for man is a state of art: Morris says the same. One works it out on an evolutionary and the other on a revolutionary basis. Crane says that in Aristotle mimesis is an internal relation of form to matter, which suggests that "nature" in human contexts is the starting-point of a dialectic.

Wednesday, March 19

[189] Today I took a holiday, after a fashion. I got up very early, got down and read until my ten o'clock, got through a (to me) commonplace but I suppose entertaining enough lecture on Burton, and then cruised down to Eaton's for lunch. Then I went down to Heintzmans & bought three Macdowell [MacDowell] sonatas, the first, third & fourth (they're called the Tragic, Norse & Keltic), and the Liszt B minor sonata. I got back at a quarter to two feeling I'd had a terrific carouse. It's difficult to explain why, but when I get to feeling down in the mouth I buy piano music, and to me it's exactly what buying a red hat would be to a woman. The quality of the music isn't so very important—if it's good enough to fill a missing space in my library that's all I want. I read through the Norse sonata in the evening & realized it was just a crop of corn, but I knew it would be anyway. (Actually, I'm quite fond of that kind of corn). But there's so much in that eager, starved life of mine that began when I was about nine and lasted until it began to break when I went to Chicago at fourteen that still needs satisfying. A fixation on the word "sonata" and a curious interest in any piano composition that has that name is something I still can't quite understand. But because of a

dithyrambic (and I now realize very silly) article on Scriabine in the Etude of (I think) May, 1925,[163] I shall sooner or later have to acquire all ten of his piano sonatas. The fact that he had really nothing on the ball was a great disappointment to me, but doesn't affect my resolution. I will never play these great floundering sonatas, nor ever much want to. But I have always thought of music, and to lesser extent of literature, as a rich and glowing paradise of variegated genius, and it is with the greatest unwillingness that I have recognized the presence of stupidity, dullness and ineptitude in it.

[190] Well, Crane's third lecture was a little easier to follow: more names and historical connections. But his relativism and pluralism are breaking down into an Aristotle (and Crane) *contra mundum* attitude. *Everybody's* in the other camp—the camp where poetry is treated as a form of discourse. Now I've lost Aristotle: I don't understand how he's distinguishable from this. Anyway, the discourse people include the Latin rhetoricians, the medieval people, the critics of the Renaissance who thought they were Aristotelians but weren't, the romantics, and the romantic tradition extending to the new critics & the myth critics. The last group includes Edmund Wilson, Lionel Trilling, Francis Ferguson [Fergusson], Wilson Knight, and me.

Thursday, March 20

[191] The nine o'clock started Book Three of Spenser and got *me* started on the kind of complex it represents. It's the same as that of Shakespearean comedy, more or less: the disguised active heroine who pursues her man through a forest. The twelve o'clock—the last first year lecture—gave a little more detail on the ark and dove business in the Bible. Creation: spirit (breath; bird (dove); life force; beneficent dragon or body of life) vs. tehom (dead water; chaos). Flood: ark (total body of life; dove; boat floating on sea) vs. flood (all living things united in death). Paradise: garden (terrible angel, with mother links) vs. serpent. History: Israel (Aaron's breastplate) vs. Leviathan (Egypt-Pharaoh-Red Sea-Nile-leviathan as Egypt and Babylon-Nebuchadnezzar ones, also the Prince of Tyre with *his* breastplate). Prophecy & Psalms: God as kingly dragon killer riding on the cherub or on a throne with beasts & eyes vs. leviathan or power of sea—also Job in a wisdom context. Gospels: Jesus as sea-calmer and fisher of men (also, in connection with the Grail & the fisher

king, a provider of endless food for thousands out of bread & fish: Jesus himself is the fish) vs. death & hell as a leviathan body. Revelation: God on his throne vs. the dragon & the whore (the dragon as nature or the provider of food, the rain-dragon of China, is a mother principle, the body out of which we came like Jonah). I don't [know] why I scribble all this out, except in the hope that the process itself will start my mind working.

[192] Crane's lecture was about the errors & excesses of the pseudo-Aristotelian people, Wimsatt & the new critics, and of the Platonists or archetypal people. He played it for laughs, & the graduate people obediently tittered. Finally he distinguished me as the most articulate of the group, & the most aware of the difficulties in the position. Well, I suppose I'm that all right, but I think I see in him the sort of pseudo-Aristotelianism I thought I saw in Elder Olson at the Institute.[164] That is, the view that you're "misunderstanding" Aristotle unless you relate what he said about poetics to his whole system of thought and then swallow that. If biology is a science, anything Aristotle said about the parts & generation of animals must be judged by the authority of biology and anything of permanent value in it should be kidnapped by biology. If literary criticism is a systematic study of literature, Aristotle's Poetics should be kidnapped by criticism, which has in the main decided that literature is a form of discourse.

Friday, March 21

[193] More about Book Three and the Trojan myth. I wonder why my 4k lectures build up such terrific organization, also my Milton lectures, but the Spenser ones don't at all? Mainly, I suppose, it's just because I'm starting new stuff when I'm tired and bored. It's partly too that I've set up to be an authority on Spenser when I know nothing about him. Well, the graduate group had a paper by the Jap, whose name incidentally is not Akiro, as I've been calling him, but Nishio—Akiro is his first name. A surprisingly good paper, on dragon symbols. So I talked about dragons for over an hour, and then laid into Crane. Well, I made remarks about the fallacy of misplaced concreteness which says in effect "the damn botanists can have their leguminous dicotyledons, but as for me and Joe Doakes, we'll string along with good old beans." At the same time it's only fair to say that Crane was right in singling me out as the only

archetypal critic who isn't just playing around but thinks of archetypes as organizing conceptions of a systematic science.

[194] His final lecture was rather curious. After a criticism of criticism that left one feeling that no critic would meet his approval who wasn't God Almighty, he outlined his own theory. I was touched, because he threw away the invulnerability he'd been assuming and became just one more damn critic. He said that in all writing there's a structural principle involved that is the informing cause of the writing—you become more and more aware that you're hanging on to a formative principle that acts as though it had an independent life (note the reappearance here of the theme of the quasi-organism one gets in Spengler—it's the Aristotelian equivalent of the difficulty about the Platonic form). Hence the primary activity of the critic is to recover the informing cause (I suppose one could call it theme) of the work of art he's dealing with. This, he said rather recklessly, is a question of empirical fact, thereby assimilating criticism into other ascertainable disciplines like bibliography. However, he also talked about alternative hypotheses and a balance of probabilities. This, he said, was one thing the rhetoricians and archetypalists alike had left out. He then reverted to his pluralism, but said the different schools should keep on schooling. Norman Endicott thanked him afterwards, and quoted Oscar Wilde as saying he didn't know whether the critics of *Hamlet* were really mad or just pretended to be.

Saturday, March 22

[195] In the evening the Macleans [MacLeans] had a supper party for the Cranes, and a very good party it was. (Very good of Ken too, as Crane wrote one of his typically slaughterous reviews of Ken's book).[165] The Grants, the Loves, the Ropers, and Ronald Williams (I suppose because of the Chicago connection)[166] were there (I suppose Mrs. Williams is pregnant again). Martinis to begin with, and whisky afterward, so what with a very late dinner I got sick again afterward. My own damn fault. I was well into my fifth drink before I realized that I'd had practically no lunch. The party did a men-women split, unusual for the Macleans [MacLeans], and we gossiped about jobs and they about curtains. We were, as I faintly remember, beginning to get slightly maudlin about Eliot and Auden just at the end. Douglas Grant of course talked very well, and remained sober enough to drive us home. I suppose a car, to

say nothing of children and sitters and things, *does* make one very temperate. Crane is a very charming man, but remains a most elusive one.

[196] This morning I was very badly hung over, having had another vomiting spell, but I staggered down to 44 Hoskin to be second in command at Graham Cotter's oral. My appraisal was, I think, pretty good. It agreed closely with Priestley's, at any rate. But Cotter surprised us by coming through very well on his oral: he surprised and impressed Woodhouse, which I trust will help him get a job. As Barker said to me afterwards, the thesis doesn't jell, and in fact I think it will be a long time before anything Cotter writes does jell. He's confused by over-ambitiousness, and Barker feels that Chicago in general & Crane in particular probably confused him most of all.

[197] Then I went home and to bed for the afternoon. The Harrons came in for dinner, bless their hearts. Don told me all about Fry's play *A Sleep of Prisoners* and about his tour with it through New York, Hershey, Pa., I think Youngstown, and other stations of the actor's cross. The agent plans to do another tour with it in the fall and so won't let Donald put it on here, to his very considerable disappointment. He's going to be in a production of Sartre's *Crime Passionel*, as they call it—I think it's his *Mains Sales*.[167] Evidently the Fry play is a series of Biblical archetypes involved with a group of four soldiers—I must read it. He's reading me, anyway, according to Donald, as he wants to do a play on Blake.

Sunday, March 23

[198] We then went out to hear *Arms and the Man*. The New Play Society buggered itself up by giving too many bad Canadian plays, so their output is restricted to their revue, *Spring Thaw*, and one or two others.[168] We sat with Gloria [Harron] and watched Donald [Harron] do his stuff as Sergius. I thought the play was very well received, mainly because it's utterly foolproof comedy and they emphasized the comic points very heavily. I had the feeling too, which Donald confirmed later, that the players were being taken over by the audience: he talked about "bomb laughs," and they seemed to fall into the slightly coarsened rhythm of farce in their response to it.

[199] Otherwise, I hardly knew what to say. The acting was really pretty

bad, and I thought Donald was really outstandingly bad. I lied like a gentleman, but I don't really know what to make of Donald as an actor. The others all muffed a great many of their points, but still they held together after a fashion: I think their main trouble was the miserably small stage they have at the Museum, which prevented them from timing their business very subtly. The best acting was Robert Christie as Bluntschli in the first act. Pegi Brown was Raina, and she's an excellent broad-comedy trouper. Donald did Sergius in a nervous, excitable, bawling way—all the pose of gloom and self-mockery simply had to be read in if you knew the play. Maybe he's just too intelligent to be a good actor: that is, there's too solid a core of his own personality.[169]

[200] Afterwards we went to their studio on Yonge & Bloor, over Ely's, where Dora Mavor Moore was giving a party. It was quite an old home week. I hadn't realized how many of our best actors—Robert Christie, Donald Harron, Vernon Chapman, Pegi Brown—were Vic graduates. I talked to Mrs. Earle Grey, who's in some danger of trying to get me to do Shakespeare lectures again—not that I did them before. Earle Grey directed the play, and they made a presentation to him afterwards. Everybody treated me with great respect—actors are leery of critics. But it's a shame that they can only rent the Museum theatre for the one week: they make their money on the second week, and only had full houses Friday & Saturday, so they'll only just break even.

[201] Today (Sunday) was buggered in the usual fashion. I hate myself.

Monday, March 24

[202] Got up early and did a rather perfunctory and unprepared lecture on Izaak Walton. I always dislike the bits and pieces of litter to be cleared away in that course, particularly when it's major literature that has to be treated as litter. *Force majeure* constrains me to add "instead of letters." The twelve o'clock was wonderful: one of the best lectures I've given all year. On Butler, and fitted together his social and biological views very neatly and concisely. For some reason it always makes them giggle to be told that there's no such thing as nature. Dick Burgener came in to talk to me in the morning: evidently he's one of the people concerned with editing Reid MacCallum's stuff.[170] He says Reid left four and a half volumes of impersonal or academic diary material, much of it

unpublishable, but much of it very good. The series is called "Nulla Dies," which I suggested meant "no dice." It confirms my impression that Reid would never have made a writer of books, but was primarily a writer of aphorisms or *pensées*. Our literary or book production is so conventionalized these days that a man has to die and leave a diary behind before what he has to say can be published at all, if he thinks in an unconventional form.

[203] In the afternoon I read most of Bert Hamilton's thesis, which is much better written than I expected: he says Tillyard has been giving him intensive training in writing. He's still a graceless unlicked cub, and proves it by the fanatical insistence with which he beats the bejeezus out of his thesis in the sense of main argument. He practically never mentions a poem by Spenser except the first book of the *Faerie Queene*, and his point that the critical principles of Sidney's *Apology* throw a good deal of light on Spenser's practice—sound enough in itself—is ground down practically to the vanishing point. He wants to add another chapter, but didn't condescend to say what on. Oh, well, another job done. Or on the way to being done. Helen came down and we had a drink or two and then back to the Lichee Gardens. But it was an anticlimax—the service was demoralized and the atmosphere wasn't there. I suppose it's the dullness of the preceding Sunday that hangs us over on Mondays. Helen was worried by the news from Roy [Kemp] that Mary [Kemp] has rheumatic fever—worried because of the chance that she'll drop the divorce proceedings and he'll be stuck with her.

Tuesday, March 25

[204] The nine o'clock, the last one for that course, continued outstanding. I manage to make Butler's ideas pretty interesting to the kids, and for a nine o'clock the response was pretty good. But I'm getting crotchical, and have to make a deliberate effort to recover my good temper. It's the stampeding of the old aggressive ego: I've been thinking a good deal lately about the primacy of the aggressive instinct. I suppose I have a lot dammed back, what with my childhood: physical and social disadvantages combined with a terrific will to power in my own sphere. Well, the hell with that. The twelve o'clock dealt with the term test I'd set my kids. For some absurd reason I'd got panicky about it, and told them if they finished in twenty minutes I'd be pained but not surprised. What I'd

done was give them Vaughan's *Regeneration* poem "A ward, and still in bonds,"[171] and told them to figure out the Biblical symbols. Naturally they all scribbled frantically right up to the last minute. I spent most of the afternoon reading them and felt a little more encouraged about that course. That is, while about six people failed it, there were some remarkably good and perceptive analyses of the poem—by no means all from my English people, two of whom, Evelyn Linton and Nancy Curran, were among the failures.

[205] At lunch I learned of two new Emmanuel appointments. The man to be brought in to replace Dow is Johnson of Hartford, whom I met last term—he was included in the V.C.U. [Victoria College Union] chapel series to be looked over. He's a Scotchman (I suppose his name is Johnston)[172] who'll stay here only just long enough to get his bid from Scotland and scram. Oh, well, I suppose it'll do us good to have people around who can go somewhere else. The one to replace [John] Line is—Charlie Leslie. So *that's* what he was hinting about so darkly last year. Well, it gets him out from under Irving; it provides Emmanuel with some administrative competence (Line couldn't have made a terrific registrar and after all Matheson is still Dean), and otherwise it seems a damned silly appointment. Technically he's the senior theologian of the United Church of Canada now, and he's actually not a theologian at all. George McMullen explained to me that they were actually trying to work Bill Fennell into the job, and that there's a lot of prejudice against Fennell in the Church (I suppose because he's been tarred with the "Barthian" brush) so they have to bring him along under cover of what is technically a Leslie appointment.

Wednesday, March 26

[206] Another thing I heard was that the celebrated undertaking firm of [George W.] Brown and Macdougall [McDougall], of the Department of Modern History, are planning to bury Walter Stewart—hasn't gone to groups or done enough term work. Looks as though he'll lose his year. I'd be sorry to see that happen: it would be quite a loss to Acta, and I think a basically unhealthy shock for him. Young people dramatize themselves in certain roles, but haven't the experience not to get stuck with them.

[207] In the afternoon the Armstrong lecture was given by Strachan, a

Presbyterian parson from Cambridge. On religion and life in Thomas Hardy.[173] He's in his eighties, and wandered and yammered, as old men will, and towards the end he was just preaching a sermon. I suppose Crane has something: as long as you have your virility the informing cause can erect itself in your work. However, it really wasn't so bad except that it costs $150, and Irving figured out afterward that a very pointless anecdote cost us (or rather the foundation) $30. His main point of course was that Hardy and the Presbyterians have the same view of life at bottom. I suppose a Protestant intellectual would have the same kind of interest in Hardy that a Catholic would have in, say, Baudelaire.

[208] Today I didn't do much except give a half-assed lecture on Herbert. I don't know why those kids put up with me. Victoria Reports is out again, with that dismal shit I wrote about Pearson's lunch in it under my name.[174] Archie Hare said he assumed it was Bill James writing it, until he turned over the page to find me under it, or at the bottom of it, like Oscar Wilde in a hotel.[175] It snowed frantically all day, and I sat around wishing the chair in my office was more comfortable, wishing I didn't have to read that goddamned Edgar book again,[176] wishing I didn't have to go to the Senior Dinner, wishing I could get started at my book and the hell with all this bloody niggling, wishing the college weren't getting into such a rah-rah Joe College state, and so on. Regarding this last, Ken Maclean [MacLean] made the very interesting suggestion that Canada was having a post-war Jazz age of its own. It missed, very largely, the 1920 one, but now that we're getting the post-war children, a lot of prosperity, and a tendency to make the Americans do the responsible jobs, along with a certain backlog of "progressive" education, we seem to be starting where the Americans have left off.

Thursday, March 27

[209] The Senior Dinner last night was the first I'd been to since we abolished it. I thought that Bennett was just vetoing the Council, but apparently not: Staples said it worked out to everybody paying for his or her own dinner. It was in the King Edward Hotel, a far better place than the Arcadian Court—smaller and with better food. (The reason we didn't have it in a hotel before was [Walter] Brown's fear that somebody might sneak off and have a beer afterward.) I think on the whole it's a good idea to have students run the dinner: they had a higher percentage of attend-

ance and there was less of a rush for the exit gates as soon as the speeches began. Also their chairman didn't talk so much. On the other hand everything students do at Victoria these days has a dreadful hey-fellas corniness about it, and Moore & Bennett, who spoke, played right along with it. Partly because no institution retains any sort of hold over 80% of our students. I enjoyed myself because I sat beside Barbara Smith, who is a thoroughly nice girl, but Helen got stuck with Evelyn Linton and Beverley Pearson, and had a miserable time, even to the point of recommending that I leave Victoria. Anne Carnwath had taken a room in the hotel and was giving a party afterward, to which Jessie Mac [Macpherson] was going, but she didn't ask us until the Tretheweys, who had arranged to drive us home, had collected our coat checks (the long wait for that was the worst thing about the party) and it would have been intolerably rude then to change our minds.

[210] Today I gave my last lecture to the Milton class, on the Mutability Cantoes. Peggy Haig, the girl who got married last year and wanted me to do it, was there—her husband's at Yale doing some graduate course— I think in drama. He used to be—perhaps still is—in social work and was the one who wrote me all the letters when I gave my lecture there.[177] She says Betty (Kay) Fowler hooked her Boyd man after all—I'd thought that had fallen through. My twelve o'clock was the test for first year. I note that that nice boy who read Kafka[178] is named Fowler—he must be Betty's kid brother, as he's much the same physical type. Reading the tests convinced me that I'm right about sticking to the fourth year for that course: I got them interested, and up to a point instructed, but it's too mature a conception for them. (It is for fourth year too, but that's as far as the car goes[.])

Friday, March 28

[211] Well, in the afternoon I got a lucky break. Betty Endicott phoned and told Helen about a concert at Eaton Auditorium—one of those Women's Musical Society affairs. So Helen phoned me and I met her there. A small string ensemble called the Virtuosi di Roma, a group of Italians whose names I didn't altogether believe. One of the two cellists was called Massimo Amphitheatrof and the pianist—the only woman in the group—was Ornella Santoliquido.[179] They played eight Baroque concerti, four by Vivaldi and one by Rossini at the age of twelve. As

everyone was a first-class musician in his own right, they took turns doing the solos. The effect of an ensemble of genuine virtuosi was utterly different from the ordinary processed orchestra with a megalomaniac conductor shaking a stick at a mass of unruly children. Every one brought a sense of new possibilities—that lovely bel canto tone that Italians seem to get into everything was there all right, but there was no blurring of the fine crisp outlines. The performances were pretty scholarly too: one was done on the viola d'amore, which I'd never seen before.

[212] Today I went down with Hilliard [Trethewey], but of course didn't have a nine o'clock. The graduate group produced a paper by young Woodbury on Joyce's *The Dead*. I don't know why I say young Woodbury—he's married and is older than some of the others. I tried to develop the cluster of ironic hero-motives represented by the Shem of Finnegans Wake, and promised to tie everything together next week. In the afternoon, I finished up two god-damned jobs that had been staring at me for weeks—at least it seemed like weeks, but isn't. I read Bert Hamilton's thesis and got a note off to him saying I wasn't too keen about it. And I finished with the Edgar MS and sent Lorne Pierce a letter recommending further cuts. That'll rejoice his heart and infuriate Dona, but I don't give a damn. I've utterly and completely lost what interest I ever had in that project, and am concerned now only to put it where I won't have to hear of it again.

Saturday, March 29

[213] Last evening we went out to Hart House to the Faculty evening. We heard Robert Finch and a lad named Douglas Bodle or Bogle[180] play some of the Mozart four-hand stuff. To be specific, they played the F major sonata and the G major variations for an encore. The audience wasn't too receptive, I thought: the seats in the Debates Room are magnificently uncomfortable and for some reason they waited nearly half an hour, with everybody there, before starting the program. Well, Robert & his partner played superbly. Then Ned [Pratt] gave readings from his "Last Spike" poem. He tells me the connective tissue is in prose this time, and that he'd wanted it in prose for both *Behind the Log* & *Breboeuf* [*Brébeuf*]. I'm afraid the poem is not very good, and that it turns on a number of very labored conceits. If the Gospels didn't specifically warn against worrying over the future I sure would worry about how to

review it next year.[181] But he put on a good show, & nobody who didn't know him well, and recently, would think he was under a nervous strain. Anyway he got what Donald [Harron] calls "bomb laughs" all through. Then we went in for coffee and talked to various people, including the Priestleys and Helen Ignatieff.

[214] [Nicholas] Ignatieff died that night of a heart attack, probably before we'd left the building. He was at the party, but left during it, and was found by his wife where he'd collapsed fixing a flat tire. Chris Love was intercepted by a porter just as he was leaving and asked if he knew anything about an inhalator sent up from downtown—the Star had been phoning about it. He said he didn't know, and why didn't they ask the Warden. 1950 will stand out in my mind as the year none of my friends died. 1949 was Reid [MacCallum] & 1951 Jerry [Riddell],[182] both, with the Warden, at this time of year. The series has completely destroyed my belief in the grip of the life force. That is, I used to feel a Victorian confidence that nature took a very strong hold of people, and that a young man in the full flush of health couldn't just drop dead. Well, he can, and what impresses me now is the tenuousness of the relation between intelligence and organic life. Ignatieff was the right man in a very difficult job—the absurd paradox of an all-male recreational centre in the middle of a coeducational campus is finally beginning to catch up with Hart House, I think, and the apathy of students for the kind of thing they could get without sexual stimulation was worrying him a good deal—but I notice that I never feel sorry for people who die, only for their survivors, beginning with myself.

Sunday, March 30

[215] Yesterday Helen came down to the office in the morning to help me tie up the Hamilton and Edgar stuff, but we finished too late to get it over to the post office. We went to lunch and then on to a special Forum meeting supposed to be concerned with strategic planning of articles. Actually it developed into a discussion of our circulation in which Lew [Lou] Morris took every suggestion as a personal reflection on his efficiency. It was, to put it mildly, a difficult meeting to chair—I told Peter Morgan afterwards that for the day of judgement I was putting a lot of stock in the "Blessed are the peacemakers" clause. He drove us home. I shouldn't be surprised if Lew will soon drive Allan Sangster off the

board—the kind of thing the Morrises have done all along to the Forum is exactly what makes them shudder with horror when the CCF does it. Bugger the god-damned Forum—it bores me to write about it.

[216] This morning was the Baccalaureate sermon—Seeley of Trinity, and very good. I played the piano, but as I was still something of a wreck from yesterday I made a lot of fluffs—however, I got compliments afterwards. Not very good attendance either from students or staff. For some reason they decided to pull back the chairs on the platform during the singing of the hymn, and Seeley went on his provostorial arse—not too obtrusively, but he must have wondered about his sister college. The general performance was unmemorable but dignified—anyway, John Finlay, whom I went home with, was deeply impressed by Seeley. His father, after giving up religion, is now dipping a cautious toe back in, via Unitarianism, and John wanted to know why most clergymen didn't try to translate Christian ideas out of clichés. I said it was because nine-tenths of the church's energy was preoccupied with just keeping the mechanism going.

[217] Another blasted bore was waiting for me at home—Helen had asked her mother and father to dinner and we had three dead-weight problems in geriatrics to lift. Well, Helen's mother is all right, but her father was hopeless, and a double load. Then we went in to tea at the Haddows, given for a visitor we didn't meet, as she was stuck behind a sofa. That beautiful Swede Mrs. Forstner was there, and she asked me whether I thought Trinity or University College was the best place to send her daughter. Ho hum. She didn't even react when I told her I was from Victoria.

Monday, March 31

[218] The 2i course hangs on like the Old Man of the Sea: I did the metaphysical poets, or tried to do them, to an utterly apathetic class. Crashaw, Vaughan, Traherne, all going by in a cloud of dust. I got a letter from the Hudson Review asking if I'd review *Inquiring Spirit*,[183] the usual letter from David Hoeniger demanding the usual recommendation by return mail, and Erdman's book. The last item is 750 pages. I'm beginning to feel like the fly in that Katherine Mansfield story.[184] I went in to lunch as early as I could. The warden's funeral was this afternoon[185]

at the exact time the Trinitarian Society was supposed to be being addressed by one N. Frye in the Debates Room on the subject of Christianity and Culture. They transferred the meeting to Rosedale Presbyterian
Church, as it never occurred to them that I ought to be at the funeral too.
I didn't protest—I knew the Great Hall would be crowded anyway and I
wanted to get this assignment done, not just postponed. However, the
meeting was badly messed up: they put a member on guard at Hart
House but the police wouldn't allow cars near the place. So the meeting
finally came to rest in Rosedale, a charming little church and a far better
place for it, and if the group had been congenial I'd have enjoyed myself
immensely. They weren't. It was Art Young who got me into it, and then
he couldn't go because he had a funeral, so I was picked up by a man
named [Stuart] Coles from Oshawa, who then picked up two more
members on the way. I'd forgotten how awful parsons could be when
they're by themselves. Coles said it was too bad Young wouldn't be
there, as he was the mediator between me and them (he knew what I
knew, in other words, and they're so ingrown an outfit they have to read
papers at each other and of course didn't know me) and a parson in the
back seat promptly said: "We awll have another mediator." Nuts. Bob
Miller, a former student of mine, did what introducing was done. They
turned out to be a largely Presbyterian and Barthian outfit, and read in
their minutes a letter of resignation from Bill Fennell, so evidently it
wasn't too congenial to him. Diltz was there: he's the only layman. Well,
I was pleased to be able to summarize what I had to say in twenty-five
minutes instead of twice that. I split it into two parts, political & cultural,
and based each on an application of the term analogy. The first half was
the straight *Bias* article line about democracy as the natural analogy or
secular analogy to the idea of Christian society,[186] which latter of course
cannot take a definite form by itself.

Tuesday, April 1

[219] They let that go without comment, but the second half, a piece
of my chapter three and dealing with art as the hypothetical analogy of
faith, got them going, as by that time I realized it would do, on a line
of Barthian chatter about the analogy of being and how awful that
doctrine was. Well, I rolled through like a tank, because I've read the first
two pages of Barth's *Dogmatics* too, and all they had in reserve was
straight Philistine prudery. Diltz stood up for me, and so did the host,

the parson of the church, and we parted on good terms, but I didn't feel like joining the society. The reason I give it all this space is partly that I have a recurrent Yeatsian nostalgia for an ideal symposium group, and this group raised the nostalgia without of course satisfying it. One of the men of God—quite a decent bird actually—drove me to the Park Plaza, where I met Helen and sank a couple of Martinis.

[220] Today I did precisely what I'd been promising myself I'd do for weeks: I didn't go to the office, as I had no lectures, but went to the Reference Library and started writing my book. I felt it was necessary to make a gesture of that kind to break in my stage fright and get things moving inside. I think I put in a fair day: I didn't write as much as I expected, but I expected not to, if I make myself clear. I had lunch at Eaton's and went home after four—my notion that I can't write after four may have been artificially introduced, but it seems to work. I stopped at the new Murray's at Bay and College for tea and found they had a squallbox—a very unobtrusive one, but still a squallbox. Beginning of the end. It was a gloomy day and I should have been in high spirits, but for some reason wasn't. The reason was perhaps that I was aware there wouldn't be another day like that for some time, so I couldn't abandon my nagging worries about when I'd get those bloody essays done and the like. The opening chapter though is pretty straightforward—almost too much so, as I think the best thing to do is scribble out a brief outline, type it, and then work up the typed copy. After I get it and the meaning chapters done I think I'll go to work, not perhaps directly on archetypes, but on a draft of the epic chapter (9, I think) with the object of trying to separate what should go into it from the archetypes. If that succeeds the whole book will fold up like a pup tent, as I told Erdman his would. It didn't, obviously. Oh, well, it's still the kind of thing I should be doing instead of explaining culture to people who want to know only one thing about it and that is how to get rid of it.

Wednesday, April 2

[221] More 2i, and there'll be another one, as I had to stop in the middle of Herrick. They wanted it next Monday, to my chagrin, so I have one more nine o'clock. From then until the council meeting I marked their essays. The council was mostly Joe Fisher again, who seems anxious to become the successor of Sissons in the art of prolonging meetings unnec-

essarily. This time he went into a committee of the whole after business
was over to discuss housing for younger members of staff. More serious,
he wants another cackiloquium, this time on general education, and of
course who has to lead the discussion but Norrie Frye. So I have to get
through a couple of American blatherbooks about education for a free
society, including the Harvard report, by next Tuesday, and then I have
to spend a fucking evening on it. Oh well, Moff Woodside told me a
story that I thought was funny. A man whose wife wanted children
consulted a doctor, who asked him about sexual intercourse, particularly
the position assumed. The man said dog style, and the doctor advised
him to return to the more conventional pattern. The man said "What,
and miss the television?"

[222] It is true that my feeling that the honour course was perfect has
altered slightly in the past year. I still don't want much tinkering done
with it, but it's possible to maintain that departmental autonomy (in his
final year the honour-course student is practically adopted by one department) does tend to make for vocational training rather than liberal
education. That's no doubt most true of the natural sciences, but household economics produces dietitians, classics schoolteachers, & only English seems to turn out housewives. So perhaps we might consider first-year
courses like the General Education ones at Harvard, trying to give a view
of literature as a whole, with some sense of the relevance of history and
philosophy to it. (I think we should draw the line at St. John's total
breakdown of all barriers).[187] A Humanities course roughly parallel to
the present Soc & Phil. course, making English, Moderns & perhaps
Classics three-year courses, is a possibility I'm doubtful about. But if we
kept the Honour courses as they are, but introduce the principle of unity
of course taking precedence over departmental considerations, so that,
say, whatever course a student was in & whatever options he took, he'd
be doing the Renaissance in second year, or options in the ancient world
that fitted the Renaissance, I think we'd have something pretty exciting,
not just for the first-class student who makes his own connections anyway, but for the ordinary, docile, interested student.

Thursday, April 3

[223] Today I took another day off, in a manner of speaking. I stayed
home all day, and finished marking the 2i essays. I think I marked
twenty-three—there were thirty-eight altogether, and I'd done a fair

number yesterday. I was all finished by four o'clock, though my eyes were slightly crossed, and of course I couldn't read or write for the rest of the day. The topic was comparing the *Utopia* with another book in the tradition. I assign that subject every year, because I think they're interested in it and they do quite well at it. I'm interested to notice too that it's a General Education type of topic. Also for some reason it excites me. I seem to get in a vaguely creative state of mind just reading essays about it. I feel that I know when a *situation* of ideas is a fruitful one: this Utopia pattern has already given me part of my *Living Church* essay,[188] but there's more to be got out of it. Also I periodically recur to my idea of writing a Utopia myself, making the ideal state a state of watchers in Bardo, occupying the same time & space that we do.

[224] This last is connected with a scheme that's been in my head for at least ten years, and to which an extraordinary number of hunches have been attaching themselves. If it is really true that I'm released from the obligation to do any more specific critical studies, except incidentally or episodically, and that two more books might actually include about all I have to say about literature, I might turn my energies to something different. That has always been, since I got over my adolescence, a gigantic anatomy based on the theme of initiation or hierarchic degrees of knowledge. Several themes have been included in it, and they feature the Utopia I speak of and some comprehensive treatment of the Bardo world. Ever since I read Dante, I have been fascinated by the possibilities of the ascent or anabasis form (less by the Inferno, because so many others, like Orwell and Sartre & Koestler, have done that better than I can do). I think vaguely of seven or eight metamorphoses on various levels of the spiritual world that a dead man's soul goes through, including a Utopia, a vision of Bardo, an apocalypse, and finally a withdrawal into the Lankavatara "mind itself." The "novel" interest would consist in the fact that his whole earthly life would have to be reassembled in the process. I should start collecting notes for it, anyway.

Friday, April 4

[225] Today I held the grand finale of the graduate group, which I think was a success all right, though not as big a one as I had thought I might pull off. I didn't learn a great deal from it either: that first chapter (which was what it was mostly) is hampered by its schematism. However, I split the four levels of meaning into five, and put the "between" levels in—

music & painting, events & ideas, examples & precepts, ritual and oracle. The fact that on the tropological level poetry *contains* ritual explains why there are ritual elements in poems without any necessary historical traditions—or even historical facts: it's not necessary to assume that the ritual patterns involved in a given poem ever existed or not in any society—if they did, the question is a separate one. I know this, but haven't realized it. Then I filled in the levels of criticism: textual and ambiguous rhetoric on level one, historical background on two, structural (Crane's Aristotelianism) on three, & archetypal on four. Re anagogy, I simply said that we read poetry & criticism & anagogy is what we have as a result. I'm not satisfied with this. They naturally asked me what poetry was between on the anagogic level, and I said in the Middle Ages it would be the Word between the Power (archetype of events) and the Spirit (archetype of ideas, though that doesn't work too well either. If Christ is on the *right* hand of the Father, it may be the other way round. It depends whether we're looking at their faces or, like Moses, at their arses). Later it might be between becoming and being, which may be a point about the Mutability Cantoes.[189]

[226] In the evening I went to Woodhouse's final party for Crane. McLuhan, Priestley, Harold Wilson, [Norman J.] Endicott, Grant, Knox. Crane takes to liquor very well. The discussion was fitful: Woodhouse, like myself, loves the symposium, but I find that the tendency to break up in smaller units is very strong. I talked rather uncertainly to Harold Wilson, who promised as usual to phone us, & talked about *Troilus & Cressida*. He thought I'd written on it at length. I said Machiavelli's Prince, if he had a courtier to advise him, wouldn't draw Castiglione's *Courtier*: he'd get something more like Ulysses, full of melancholy Luciferian knowledge of good & evil, of time & the chain of being. Well, Crane said he thought there wasn't much political conversation in Canada. They discussed a recent article by Al Capp in *Life* announcing that he wasn't going to be America's only good social satirist any more, because he (or his syndicate: I couldn't make out which) thought that satire was getting un-American.[190]

Saturday, April 5

[227] They debated whether it was ironical or not, & it was suggested that the recent marriage to Daisy Mae meant he was going in exclusively for domestic humour. But Marshall [McLuhan] pooh-poohed the idea:

he said Capp was just getting started, beginning with the projected birth of a son on July 4 called Yankee Doodle Yokum. I sat between Woodhouse & Crane & listened to a good deal of gossip.

[228] Today I did very little except go over to help Helen shop. It's been consistently cold, raw, bleak weather for several days, with no break in sight, and sunshine is a matter of a few glints a day. Getting 22 students fed and watered is quite a little chore, but what with our bundle buggy we got all the grub lugged back before noon. Helen got a big ham and her Spanish rice materials, and spent a good part of the afternoon getting ready.

[229] It was a delightful evening. The same thing happened exactly that happens in lectures. I'd asked Anne Ward for this evening, and she sparked all the others. Only one man came, out of the three that had been asked, and he was no use conversationally, though a nice lad—James Davies, going into theology. I didn't realize Anne Ward was an actress— I *must* go to Hart House plays more—she was Medea when they did that. And then, somewhat surprisingly, Dorothy Meen developed an astonishing personality. She's had dramatic training too, and has been through England in a car. She told a long story, very well, of being admitted to the grounds of Balmoral Castle because she was wearing a plaid skirt, and seeing Margaret Rose and little Prince Charles & others all having tea. She's older than the others—class of 47, I think, back to get a second on her 4k because she needs it for her O.C.E. specialist—and shared the lead with Anne Ward. Then Barbara Smith, who's also from England, Janet Waite, a friend of Anne's, and Carol Mackinnon [MacKinnon] chimed in, and the conversation got very friendly and relaxed. They're nice kids, and, as usual, I wish I'd had them up earlier and oftener. My belief in the fundamental good will of students is pretty important to me, and I need to talk to them frequently to get that belief reinforced. They asked me to play—Dorothy Meen's idea—and for some reason I played quite well— the Spanish things. Not much was said—the usual discussion of plays and movies one always gets into with students—but it was a completely successful party and we both loved it. So did they, I think. They kept coming back to the subject of exams like mice to cheese.[191]

Sunday, April 6

[230] Today I did very little except sit around and wait for tonight's

party.[192] Helen wasn't feeling too well, and I felt a bit out of sorts myself, in spite of the general success of last night. The party, when it came, was an anticlimax. It sounds brutal to say I got the culls, & would be perhaps fairer to say that there wasn't a leader. After all, last night we had two actresses. There were too many there, for one thing: kids who will make efforts when they're relatively alone will freeze up like clams when there's more of a crowd. Also—I expected this, of course—they hadn't even conceived the possibility of talking to each other, so it was an informal seminar group with me conducting the discussion.

[231] However, they did their best to avoid talking about exams. I played for them—not as well as last night, but I played. I played a bit more, in fact, as Catharine Turnbull asked me if I thought this "modern" music would survive. I said I thought Hindemith would, and she hadn't heard of Hindemith. And she was the girl I saw in Lady Macmillan's [MacMillan's] entourage the night of a Mendelssohn choir concert, a solid Toronto bourgeois product—B.S.S. and an address on Walmer Road.[193] The fact that I'm back teaching children again, as Barker [Fairley] said, still takes a bit of getting used to. Anyway, I played some of the *Ludus Tonalis*[194] for them. They, & the kids last night, explained why they'd dissolved in giggles during a Samuel Butler lecture, which had puzzled me, as what I'd said wasn't as funny as all that. It was in a Monday 12 o'clock that I was expounding on how Butler's views of society developed out of his biological theories, & explaining how for him conventional judgements from strong, handsome, socially secure people drop with so terrific a weight, like Towneley's "Oh my dear fellar," in *The Way of All Flesh*.[195] The kids were scribbling busily and looking at their watches to see how soon they could eat. I paused, & in the silence young Janet Waite's stomach gave a mighty rumble, which I didn't hear. The next sentence was, "That is the voice of nature in society." They stayed even later than the other lot, & we both felt worn out with the effort of trying to lift the party. I had an impression that they didn't even know each other so very well. I got a better impression of Evelyn Linton, who I think now is a very decent girl,[196] but Pat Smith didn't take the lead I hoped she would take, and the two boys were hopeless—Innis [Innes] Allan, the only male left in English. I don't understand why men avoid that course.

Monday, April 7

[232] Dug myself out and went down to my nine o'clock. Do you know that that infernal course isn't even finished yet? I gave them back their essays with strict orders to come and discuss them with me. One did—a lad named Francis, and young Langford did too, only he'd skipped the lecture and came in to get his essay. Oh well, it gave me more time to mark the third year essays, which I finished. The lecture on Herrick made the point that a so-called Epicurean or *carpe diem* philosophy about seizing the passing moment has a lot to do with writing a very brief poem. Something there for the lyric chapter. Otherwise, of course, it was the usual nonsense. Then Anne Carnwath came in and we chatted for a while—she's very excited about the prospect of learning Greek next year. She's interested in the relation of men and women, naturally, and we discussed it: like many of her elders, she thinks it's possible to arrive at some conception of what men and women are like as men & women, as distinct from the type of behavior suggested to them by the society they're in. I don't. I suppose that in any society the fact that women bear children will condition some of their behavior, but beyond that I doubt that it's possible to risk a single generalization about what men or women are like that doesn't amount merely to an observation of a certain kind of society.

[233] After a dull day marking essays it was dreary enough to have to go out to a Forum meeting. But I did. It was better than the previous one. [A.F.B.] Clark was there, and I think Al Shea will shape up as one of our most useful people. He's very handsome, and I think Edith [Fowke] likes to show off a little when he's present, which is useful, as it makes her fertile in suggestions. There's an article by Brewin attacking Underhill and several letters, pro and con.[197] The flow of stuff seems to keep coming, and this time more strategic suggestions were made. Kay [Morris] still goes on yammering about the ruthlessness of the CCF, and it bores and bothers me, as it seems completely out of perspective.

[234] I was reading a Haydn sonata the other day that had a "minuet al rovescio"—an eight-bar period leading to the dominant, then you play the eight bars backward, reading the music right to left, and you have the second period leading back to the tonic. It struck me that this "rovescio"

stunt has actually succeeded in defining the germinal or radical idea of the whole binary form, which, in pure forms like the Scarlatti sonata, is simply variegated mirror-writing.

Tuesday, April 8

[235] Didn't do much today, but the evening was the occasion for our special colloquium. Joe [Fisher] was very excited about it and had prepared a paper, which had a good deal of wit and made out a highly theoretical case for general education, though, as Hilliard [Trethewey] said afterwards, he never quite got down to earth. His was a much better piece of rhetoric than mine, but I think on the whole mine was better received—I got a lot of compliments on it afterward and most of the discussion was based on it. I said the things I've already said about the honour course, but Bennett ruled them out of order—he didn't think it was possible to upset departmental autonomy there. However, I did say that the General Course was the place to experiment. The trouble was that in the course of reading up my assignment I'd got profoundly suspicious of General Education courses. The St. John's one struck me as most effective as a graduate's crammer course—the exact opposite of what it's supposed to be, assuming that it works. Even the Harvard one began to look pretty dubious under close examination, & most of the others were obviously a lot of shit. Some of the more honest universities simply quoted the high school curricula and said, well, here we are. To my surprise Ken Maclean [MacLean] came out strongly for me and so did Irving—the two with most American experience. I came out for lowering our entrance requirements to take in younger students, and then said the problem was not one of curricula at all, but of the passive & receptive attitude of students coming from high school, who can't make the transition to an active, participating, voluntary form of education. That brought Moff Woodside into the discussion, who pointed out that if we brought a General Education course into first year as an option against language or science, they'd all take it not because they cared anything about it but because they wanted to duck out of language or science, and if it were in the other group they'd be utterly apathetic unless it were taught by a spellbinder. In other words, tinkering with the present machinery won't help. We kicked a few other ideas around for a while, and some of the older ones like Alvin Surerus compared earlier curricula. But the prospect of having, say, a first-year course on epic,

reading everything except *Paradise Lost* in translation, didn't seem to thrill anybody: I suggested that the individual departments might start by liberalizing their own courses and that the colleges might make a start in their R.K. departments, as I've done.

Wednesday, April 9

[236] Well, two unexpected things happened today. For one thing, I learned that I was included in Jean Elder's invitation to go to New York for Easter. She seemed to assume it, or Helen had misunderstood her. So I shan't get the long writing spell in over the weekend that I thought I would, but a dramatic break is probably better for me anyway. The other thing is that Duke has renewed the offer that I turned down last year at this time, as flatly as I could without taking a tone that nobody with any manners would take.[198] A man named Benjamin Boyce wrote me to ask me if I'd be at all interested in going down to Duke to give a lecture & be looked over. They think of me as directing graduate studies in the 19th century field—I don't know why they think I'd be any use there. The thought of making a permanent change is appalling in itself, but a change that's really no promotion strikes me as silly for a man who loves quiet and routine.

[237] I finally gave my last damn lecture to Second Year, and they gave me a most appreciative clap, bless their hearts. I told them about various things like the Cowley Pindaric on the emblem.[199] For some reason Irving poked his nose through the door at five minutes to eleven, just as I was trying to conclude an impressive peroration with the aid of King's *Exequy*. Then I went down to Amen House[200] to see Johnston, who had Dan Davin in tow. I thought Dan would be still a fighting red-eyed Irish drunken novelist,[201] but nothing of the sort: he's evidently quite a big shot in O.U.P. [Oxford University Press] now, lives in Oxford, has severed his connections with New Zealand, has married Winnie and has several children, and obviously leads a most respectable existence. Whether he's still a practising Catholic or not I don't know: Helen Garrett had reported no, but with Winnie around I imagine he's still making the rounds. He said he thought Oxford had treated Kay [Coburn] pretty badly over the Coleridge notebook business—Kay blames Chambers' jealousy for that. She's seeing him tonight, and I left him after a beer with Johnston (who's not too impressive a man at close quarters) about

to have lunch with Barker Fairley. I went home and went to bed early for the first time in five nights. The kids' little thank-you notes are coming in now, and it's a great pleasure to see them. It really was a good idea to have them in, and I think even a late date in the year helped.

Thursday, April 10

[238] First I went to the Forum office and decided on the correspondence about Underhill's article about Woodsworth House. I put in Brewin's article[202] & cut the others. Kay [Morris] wanted me to cut a sentence out of it that she said was "misrepresentation," but I said nothing doing. I got out of there and went on to Robins' office and discussed the Duke offer with him, picking up a wad of dough ($250 altogether) from the bank on the way.[203] I also ran into Alice Eedy, with her dabs of powder and her rat's-nest hair-do, who told me she was working on a novel. I hope that girl has something—anyone who takes writing as seriously as she does deserves to have. I was also glad to see that her lunatic lover hasn't exterminated her yet. Well, Robins hadn't much to say, nor had Bennett, whom I went to see afterwards. Except that my salary is going up, as per schedule. He advised against my accepting the Duke invitation to put pressure on the Board—I think in good faith. Then I met Dan Davin, whom I'd asked to lunch, and we went and had a few beers at the Park Plaza, which is where he's staying, and then on to lunch. Ken Maclean [MacLean] was there, bless him—it always helps so much to have Ken around when one has a guest. Dan advises my trying Bonamy Dobrée with another letter. I said goodbye and, rather too full of beer, typed out a letter to Boyce saying sorry nothing doing. What I actually said was "it would be a poor return for your hospitality and friendliness not to say as frankly as I can that my feelings have not changed." Useful formula to remember. I hope the first-class offers will start coming in about this time next year, if I can get a book out by then.

[239] Jean's [Jean Elder's] car came along at about 3:30 and we left for New York, with that wonderful sense of release and exhilaration that beginning a long trip with a car always gives me. We struck out along the Queen Elizabeth highway, through the Burlington cut-off, and on to Niagara Falls. We crossed the border there, without incident, and drove around the park in the quickly fading light. It was bitterly cold and bleak, or seemed so to us in our light coats, and we didn't contemplate

the cataract very long. We had dinner at a wonderful place called the Mayflower, where they served us a terrific dinner centring on Southern fried chicken. It took us a good two hours to eat it, which put us pleasantly behind schedule—there was no great hurry and it gave us an appropriate feeling of luxury. Cost us about four bucks apiece.

Friday, April 11

[240] Then we headed east, or rather south, towards Buffalo, and across the great bridges over the Niagara river. There was a big sign saying the highway would be closed in the event of an enemy attack—we assumed they didn't mean us, and after we passed Batavia we began to think about quitting. Places seemed crowded, but we got a good enough one in a tiny place called Wallace. The woman gave us the whole upstairs, and it was relatively cheap ($2.50 for each room) and clean. Next morning we had breakfast in a slightly larger place named Bath, and at Painted Post we swung over into Pennsylvania and drove through beautiful rolling country for the rest of the morning. We passed a sign on a movie theatre reading "Closed for Holy Week. Attend your Church." There were historical signs up, but seemed mostly interested in a march by a Revolutionary general named Sullivan, who spread himself all over the map. Lunch in a burg named Tuckhannock, and we passed through Scranton, a depressed looking town. Up to that point I'd been sitting in the middle, and the ache in my back really got me down, so I changed with Helen. It suddenly occurred to me why Helen had made me sit in the middle: she'd heard that that was the safer place to be in an accident—had in fact found it so when we had ours—and was trying to save my life. Well, we went through the Delaware Water Gap, which was pretty but hardly what a sign boasted it to be, the eighth wonder of the world. Then we went into New Jersey, which was dreadful, as New Jersey always is. I can't put my figure[204] on the impression of squalid meanness that a highway in flat country surrounded by service stations, hot dog stands, second-hand car lots (one a bright mauve), telephone poles and billboards always manages to give. The elements of it are the elements of what with all its faults is a wonderful civilization—what makes it so unspeakably dreary? I suppose it's just its presence: in retrospect it would take on quaintness, as 19th c. dreariness begins to do now. We were tired when we hit New York, and Jean's one weak spot as a driver—traffic lights—began to become more obvious. However, we got

in all right, with the absurd consequence one so often gets in New York: Helen and I got a single room at the Barbizon Plaza with an extra cot shoved into it, and Jean got a double at the Commodore. It was clear that the Commodore could have taken all of us quite comfortably: the B.P. is nearer the Easter Parade and was frantically crowded all weekend.

Saturday, April 12

[241] We had dinner at Jean's hotel and I went along with the two girls to the theatre: they had tickets to Shaw's *Caesar & Cleopatra* but I couldn't get one, as it was the last performance. I waited until the man said it was a waste of time to wait longer, then went home and had a couple of Scotches & went to bed early.

[242] This morning I was up in fair time and went off by myself while Helen went with Jean to shop. I walked along 57th Street and dropped into several galleries. One had a collection of 15th–16th cs. Temptations of St. Anthony, which gave me an idea of the possibilities and range of that subject as calling up a phantasmagoric world, a sort of counterpart to the apocalypse—a satiric apocalypse, really. The rest were mainly standard modern French—I note that the vogue for primitives continues, and I don't wonder—I'm a pushover for people like Bombois myself. I saw a lovely Utrillo somewhere, and some good Matisse at Rosenberg's. I also dropped into Carl Fischer's for some music and asked for Weber, but could only get Vol. II, the D minor & E Minor sonatas—they're the most interesting, but I want the whole four. I drifted over to 5th Avenue and into Brentano's, where I got the New Directions translation of Mallarmé, a book I could have bought just as well at Britnell's. Then to Schrafft's for an early lunch and then to theatres to pick up tickets. A half-hearted effort to find another music store was unsuccessful, and I eventually landed in the Museum of Modern Art, where there was a fine variegated show. Posters in the basement, including some interesting Kollwitzes, drawings by Picasso and—to me infinitely more interesting, because I'd seen a lot of the Picasso before—Minotaur stuff— —Odilon Redon. Several walls full of that wonderful haunting stuff with its weird echoing captions. The impression I got in the morning was repeated— one wall of St. Anthony scenes opposite another of Revelation ones. I got there before there was too big a crowd to react to them. The third floor had contemporary Americans, including the Mark Rothko that Douglas

McAgy [MacAgy] knows. For me, it was a kind of facile formula-paint-ing—a development of exhibition painting in which a man gets to be known as a type—that's the fellow who paints like marble, or does two color splashes broken by a black horizontal line. However, I'm probably wrong. The last one did "Lumia" paintings—twenty minutes of cloudy shifting shapes in a lighted box in a darkened room.

Sunday, April 13

[243] That drew a big crowd, which amused me—it was the analogy to the movie that interested them, & the analogy to the kaleidoscope that struck me. Well, I eventually found my way to the Commodore and met the girls, then on to see Antony & Cleopatra. I'd got a ticket for $8.40, and was very close. Olivier & Vivian Leigh. A revolving stage, with busted columns representing the Forum on one side & a gateway looking vaguely like Karnak on the other. It was all right. They acted it. Octavius—Robert Helpmann—I quite liked, but found the show as a whole pretty infertile in suggestiveness. Overdramatized, I thought: the *intimacy* of the great verse seemed lost. But I was interested enough. The monument was, Helen said, the same Sphinx they'd had for the opening of the Shaw,[205] which was nice. We walked home in a pouring rain and Helen got into another tantrum—natural enough for a girl with a new hat.

[244] This morning, on Jean's suggestion, we headed for Harlem to go to a Negro Baptist Church called the Abyssinian. The pastor, who is—or was—also a Congressman, is called Clayton Powell, and his wife is the pianist Hazel Scott. We got there in time to line up for the second service, beginning at twelve. It was jammed to the roof (the first one we were told was more so) and we were evidently the only white people present, though nobody was self-conscious about it. The great majority of the congregation were in our own 30–50 age group, and just like any other middle-class Nonconformist congregation, but some of the grand-mammies and aunties who had been born further south wanted to swing it, and kept punctuating the preacher's cadences with "Amen," "that's the pint," "praise de Lawd," and the like. One old girl jumped up, waved her arms, and hugged the woman next her, but it was clear that most disapproved of such goings on, and the congealing of something rural-evangelical (it's just that: there's nothing specifically Negro about it) into Walmer Rd. or Yorkminster amused me. I wasn't very keen on the

sermon, which struck me as neither simple nor sincere, but was impressed by his efforts to get people a church home in New York—he was clear that it didn't have to be a Baptist one. They were selling tickets for a fashion show in which the models were to be "our own Hazel Scott" and a Texas girl who'd made good in Paris. The notion of a minister's wife (usually a sartorial scapegoat) being a model seems to me an excellent one. We'd gone partly for the colorful costumes, but the cold weather had subdued them.

Monday, April 14

[245] I had never seen an evangelical service before in which the preacher gets taken over by his audience: it's an interesting dramatic form. We filed out & were greeted by a man who called himself "Professor" Howse, a teacher & graduate of Tuskegee. Jean told him she'd been teaching the life of Carver to her class, and he said "You must be a very brilliant woman." Kenneth Leslie belongs to that church, or did.[206] We ate at the Y.W.C.A. cafeteria and then went out to the Cloisters.[207] I couldn't understand being with two women who had no interest in the Easter Parade, but we let the people with stuffed chickens in their hats have it their own way. Jean looked at the cloisters: we sat and listened to the lovely medieval records. A long bus trip back tired both girls out: Helen and I wandered around Fifth Avenue looking at the debris of the parade, had a drink and then went down to the Commodore for a meal which had to be rather hurried. Then we went on to the Plymouth Theatre to hear Charles Laughton, Charles Boyer, Agnes Moorhead and Sir Cedric Hardwick read "Don Juan in Hell," the third act of Man and Superman. That impressed me far more than the Shakespeare thing did—as an exhibition of the mechanics of good acting, of the sort of thing you have to be able to do to be a good actor, it was unique in my experience. I note too that pure symposium, like the masque, brings the personalities of the actors very close to the audience. And I suppose the concentration of symposium needs a Bardo setting—Shaw's hell is entered after death and at the end there's a prophecy of rebirth. There were a few people in the audience who shouldn't have been there, & two of them were unfortunately right in front of us, but on the whole it was an excellent audience. (I note that, writing this some days after the event, I've confused two evenings: it was after this show that we walked home in a gradually increasing downpour).

[246] Today was the day I'd been waiting for. I started out half-heartedly to look for a music store, and found one, on 56th Street, just beside Carnegie Hall. Exactly the place I'd been looking for, with stacks of second-hand music to look over instead of having to ask for something specific. I got the first three volumes of the Ricardi edition of Scarlatti—there are five available altogether, I understand—a volume containing the ten Scriabine sonatas, a book I didn't even know existed, and which fell into my hands like the wish-fulfilment of a dream, some Fux and Glyn's edition of Weelkes.

Tuesday, April 15

[247] Every one of these was something I'd been panting to get—as I've said before, these things are symbols to me: I don't pretend there's anything rational about the feeling. They even had a copy of the Fitzwilliam Virginal Book there—it's still $33.75, and I shrank from buying—perhaps silly when I had a car to transport it in. More important, I now have a spiritual home in New York, an anchor to hold me there.

[248] Well, I went on to get a haircut and a lunch, and walked home, in something of a daze. Helen came soon afterwards and Jean eventually turned up, though she'd been considerably delayed. We left New York in overcast, misty weather, and went directly north. We intended to go up the Hudson, but got on to an inland highway called the Taconic State Parkway. It was a superb divided highway, with no towns on it, and we made good time on it. It ran out at a place called Red Hook, where we had dinner, and we set out from there across the Hudson to the village of Catskill, where we bedded down in a huge house run by people who'd just got back from Florida. Pleasant life. Cost $6.50 this time. The man was a horse breeder, I think. Jean seemed tired, which is unusual for her.

[249] This morning we started out again across a highway that wound through the valleys of the Catskills, though there was one point where we could have seen five states, according to the sign, if there hadn't been a heavy mist. The country is full of tourist resorts for foreign-born people, and have curious things, like swimming pools beside the road. Around noon we hit Cooperstown, the home of the baseball. I started to write Mecca, because that's what Jean said it was.[208] We approached the

baseball museum and peeked through the window, but the admission was 80 cents and none of us could have distinguished Babe Ruth's balls from his bat at seven paces, so we thought the hell with it. We got some maple syrup for Dad—it's always a problem to know what kind of souvenir to bring him—and, after an indifferent lunch, made for the other museums up the road. The Farmer's Museum, a miniature antique village of the 1820 period (Cooper is James Fenimore) wasn't open and obviously isn't finished, but what we saw looked interesting—a grocery store, a blacksmith shop—that we did get into, because the blacksmith was there—a law office & apothecary's shop, and the like. Cooperstown hasn't added itself up yet as a tourist centre, but no doubt will.

Wednesday, April 16

[250] We went through a trashy junkshop and then drove up to a big house left by the local Clarence Webster, a man named Clark.[209] That was a museum too, and the admission was still 80¢. Helen pushed us in, but there wasn't much to it—mementos & MSS of Cooper, odd bits of Shaker furniture, and the like. The only thing of interest was a large exhibition of American folk art in the basement—primitive paintings, carved weathervanes, and the like. That I was glad to see. But it was a relief to get on our way. The rest of the trip, along Highway 20, wasn't of great interest. We put off dinner until we got to Niagara Falls, which was fairly late, and then crossed the border. No difficulty at customs, though the woman asked me what the "book" (Mallarmé) was that I had on my list. She didn't ask to see it, but naturally I resented the question. I spotted her as a French Canadian who'd got her job by a pull with the Federal government, and I suppose female Micks have a special interest in naughty books, what with me looking intellectual and just putting down one. The rest of the trip we spent talking about Roy & Mary [Kemp]—we hadn't seen Roy because he hasn't a New York telephone any more—and it was clear that Toronto affairs were increasingly taking hold of us. We got home at midnight exactly.

[251] Dad hadn't heard us come in, but he hadn't done badly: his Lucy [Lucy Massey] is in town now, and Helen's mother and Jean Haddow had both fed him. I went down to the office. There was no great crush of mail, but still there's a lot of stuff on my desk. I compiled a Renaissance paper and took it over to U.C. expecting a busy beehive of activity there,

but nothing doing. So I went home. I note that the more senior and responsible one is in university work, the more of one's energy is absorbed in keeping the machine going. In the evening I went out to Wymilwood, where Anne Bolgan had collected my allegory people for an informal meeting. I was a bit miffed to find that Hugh MacCallum & Francis Chapman, who both knew about it, hadn't bothered to come. Neither had the Jap, so a lot of people aren't going to know that the exam is to be on May 12. I spent the time answering questions, mainly repetitions of previous questions. Even Mary Waugh went over to Chez Paris [Paree] for a drink—it was largely because of her that I hadn't served drinks at that disastrous evening at my house. Some of them thought the course was continuing, & I suppose I am cutting it short a bit cavalierly, but what the hell. I'm tired talking, and want to write.

Thursday, April 17

[252] Went down first to the Forum and read the page proofs. Allan Sangster's column contained an outrageous plug for one of his own features that (under pressure from Edith [Fowke]) I cut. I expect however that Allan is getting bored with the Forum, and, like Grube before him, is working up to making an issue of his own temperament. The rest of the day I spent mainly in reading Erdman's book, which is 750 pages long. Yet it's full of good stuff, and it'll be difficult to know where to cut it. The main things—the influence of Barlow on *America*, of Gillray on *Europe*, of the Steadman [Stedman] drawings on VDA [*Visions of the Daughters of Albion*], are clearly spotlighted, and the development from Blake's (presumed but probable) early Wilkite sympathies[210] through the two revolutions to a gradual withdrawal from political questions in the major prophecies is clearly traced. His (Erdman's) political prejudices rather spoil the end of the book—I don't mean his contemporary political views; I mean a general prejudice in favor of Blake's having a political interest. He greatly underestimates Blake's quite genuine disillusionment with Deism, plays down the "I am sorry to see my countrymen trouble themselves with politics" passage,[211] and regards his later attitude as dictated partly by personal cowardice and partly by what he calls a "fetishistic" view of art. Within limits—and they are limits that commend themselves to a good many Americans—his evidence & argument is very strong, and no doubt somebody will say that he's made a fool of people like me. In fact the exactness of his research makes me feel

very grateful that, unlike Schorer & Bronowski, I didn't commit myself to more guesses about the historical allegory. As I told him, I assumed that somebody like him would come along sooner or later, and so I went straight ahead on the central dialectic issue. He treats me with great respect, no doubt because he's obliged to me, but his lack of sympathy with anything like a religious, much less an apocalyptic, attitude is not going to clarify Blake criticism to the extent that I feel so good a book should. I don't know what recommendations to make about cutting, except in general that the end of the book is fatiguing, and there are certainly some prolixities. But he suggests cutting footnotes, and he's the sort of writer who is at his best in footnotes. It's really a terrific job, and he certainly shouldn't have any trouble with his career once it's out.

Friday, April 18

[253] In the morning I managed to waste some time collecting the committee for Sanborn's exam. Roper, McLuhan, [Norman J.] Endicott & myself, in Endicott's office. McLuhan suggested a single overall question, which I had to fight. It's bad enough having to struggle with Woodhouse over exam questions, trying to get something that's less Woodhouse party line, trying to make him see that what he's not interested in isn't necessarily always peripheral to the subject, and now here's Marshall, a worse party-liner even than Woodhouse. His question followed exactly the general outline of (a) his course (b) Hugh Kenner's book on Pound, and even though Sanborn had taken the course I thought it was bad for discipline to accept the single-question formula. Marshall didn't give in too gracefully, identifying me with Toronto prissiness as he did so.

[254] In the afternoon I ate maple sugar & finished Erdman's book, which will probably have sugar-crumbs all through it as a result. In the evening we went out to dinner at Ella Martin's. She had in a charming young couple named Dunning. He's a returned man,[212] and now an undergraduate in anthropology; she's a gorgeous blonde, originally from New Zealand, and a teacher. They spend their summers teaching Indian children up on the Ontario-Manitoba border, and say that the quality of H.B.C. [Hudson's Bay Company] traders is going down very rapidly. Instead of fur traders and empire builders, they get storekeepers and mangy social misfits who compensate for their own deficiencies by

ascribing them to the Indians. The Indians as a result are hard to get the confidence of. They hand out school supplies to the children and the children snitch them and hide them in trees, and keep on doing that until it's clear to them that they don't need to. They made me feel very nostalgic for the days when I had returned men for students.

[255] I think my anatomy project should have seven stages, along the lines of my general seven pillars idea. First will be satiric, based on some central scheme of a shift of perspective; the second will be the Utopia, and the third Bardo. That'll take up most of my current ideas. Fourth is the assault on the gods, the clarifying of religious ideas; fifth is the dissolution of nature, where all the ideas I get when I read popular science ought to go. Sixth is apocalypse and seventh the Lankavatara "mind itself" or total void. For the present, collecting ideas for this is an end in itself.

Saturday, April 19

[256] Review of Buckley's *God and Man at Yale* I may or may not put into the *Forum*:[213] Mr. Buckley was graduated from Yale in 1951 and was editor of the college paper in his final year. He was an extreme rightist politically, and as he got more brickbats than his predecessor, who was a leftist, he concluded that he represented the opinion of a minority of students and staff at Yale, and of a majority of alumni. He examines the teaching at Yale, directing his main attention to Christianity and economics. He finds that Christianity is ineffectively taught and that a doctrinaire secularism is much more fashionable; he finds that a majority of teachers of economics are suspicious of laissez faire, recommend Keynesian texts, and express sympathy with British socialism. Those who pay for a university, he says, ought to buy the product they are paying for, and if a majority of the alumni and board of governors favor Christianity and capitalism, the present witch-hunt against Communists ought to be extended to socialists and secularists. This book has been very highly praised & widely and favorably reviewed—another melancholy illustration of the murderous dither American public opinion is now in. The subtitle of his book is "The Superstition of Academic Freedom."

[257] Several things are missing from Mr. Buckley's argument. One is

that as soon as you define a *general* area within which a scholar's teaching must operate, you are forced to define that area more & more exactly until it becomes clear that the teacher must say, not what the alumni want him to say, but what they can be prodded into thinking they want him to say by astute propagandists like Mr. Buckley. Another is that most of a student's radicalism in religion & politics merely expresses his own social detachment: he has not yet taken root in society. People with families & bigger incomes develop more interest in established religion and capitalism, because their relation to society has changed. Like many propagandists, Mr. Buckley considerably overestimates the power of indoctrination. It's highly significant, too, that he says nothing about the duty of a student to spot his instructor's bias and discount it. He thinks of the student simply as taught, and thereby shows that he has no real interest in forming public opinion, but only in stampeding it.

Sunday, April 20

[258] My reason for spending all that space on so foolish a book is that it's an example of the fact that Christianity has been alien to American culture since the Revolution, in the sense that the roots of American secularism are in the Constitution. This bird, like all of his stripe, deals not in lies, but in half-truths. It *is* true that the universities are full of fanatical sectarian bigots—I mean secularist bigots—who have projected their childhood resentments on established religion, and who, under the pretext of "waking up the student," "shaking him out of his complacency," and the like, do their best to convert him to the same kind of dogmatism. Christians have little defence against this demonic zeal for souls, because they are committed to charity, and cannot smear & caricature their opponents in the way that their opponents smear and caricature them. The real objection to such people is not that they do not say they believe what some people want them to believe, but simply that they are badly educated and intellectually dishonest. And their effectiveness is in their immaturity, because students are immature.

[259] I spent the day reading my music. The two Weber sonatas are considerably beyond my expectations—well, the E minor is. It's a completely delightful piece of romantic music, melodious and eloquent, with a fine tarantella in the last movement. I think I'll get it up and then do what that man in Seattle did: see who can guess the authorship. And Scarlatti I think must be just about the wittiest man that ever lived. I'm

not sure about this Ricardi edition—I suppose suppressing the word sonata and arranging all the pieces into "suites" by key is just the editor's notion of accurate musical scholarship.[214] In the evening we went out to a party the Cronins were giving for the French consul here, a man named [Paul] Martin who's going back to France. Pat [Cronin] was there, & stayed up for nearly the whole party: his vitality is amazing, though of course it's a little tedious to be with him for very long, as I was. Larry Shook was there, and I tried to tell him about what I'd done the previous Sunday, but he wasn't much interested, and Helen reported the same result from the Cronins.[215] I'm afraid that Catholics show their broad-mindedness only in assuming that Protestants will have some interest in Catholicism, but it doesn't seem to reverse.

Monday, April 21

[260] In the morning Norma Arnett (Coles) came in to collect her thesis, one of the little jobs I'd had to do last week after I came back. I don't know what to make of that girl—she expected that the copy I was reading would be the final one, and she has no notion of grammar, punctuation or spelling: I had corrections on every page, which was why it took me so long. The thesis itself is [a] very dogmatic one—the kind we expect from Catholics but isn't normally done by Protestants. I criticized it for talking about Traherne as though he got his Platonism straight from Plato instead of from 17th c. highbrow gossip. I certainly hope the Coles family can get socially adjusted: they certainly aren't now.

[261] The afternoon was my stint to supervise the R.K. exams, so I sat in the chapel from 2 till 4:30. It wasn't even my exam—that was in the morning—so I didn't even have the gloomy satisfaction of watching their reactions. Kids seem very defenceless and rather appealing when they're scribbling exams, but, as Bill Fennell said at lunch, invigilating is about as close to hell as I ever want to get. That is, the feeling of time crawling on is paramount. Nothing happens—well, one boy did want to go to the can, so I let him go. I'm supposed to go with him, and I'm not supposed to leave the room—I don't know how one works that out. With the girls, I guess you just pass out lots of blotting paper & hope for the best.

[262] I'd suggested to Helen that she might pick me up for a drink afterwards, and I found that she'd collected Betty Endicott & Kay Coburn

on the way, so we had quite a party. And Kay had the best news. She'd been applying to the Bollingen Foundation for assistance on the Coleridge notebooks. They've got lots of money—Mellon money—but I always thought they were a completely wacky and irresponsible outfit, what with the Ezra Pound schlemozzle[216] and those god-damned books they publish.[217] And when Kay was talking about them the night of the colloquium, she was still hopeful, but it sounded to me like a brush-off. Well, she's heard from them, and they want to know where & when she'll have the first five thousand dollars. So I let her pay for a round. They say of course they'd like to publish the notebooks, but don't in any way make that a stipulation. So Kay's going to England this summer after all, and all her expenses are taken care of from here out. She's also been asked to do something for an MLA supplementary volume on the romantics.[218]

Tuesday, April 22

[263] Today I made a terrific effort and actually read all my R.K. exams, both first year and fourth year. I can't claim that I read them all with fanatical conscientiousness, but I got a good enough impression of each one to feel that I'd given it a fair mark. The first year ones I did first— they were quite short, as nobody wrote more than a book, and their writing hadn't yet been ruined by the intensive training in bullshooting we give them here. I didn't plough anybody, not even that poor Fowler boy who messed up the test. He only wrote on two of my three questions, but was trying to write well, so I let him through. The fourth year papers made me feel just a little bit better about that course. I managed to get across a terrific amount of information, and they reproduced it with a docility that seemed to me at least consistent with interest. I still feel that it's just one more course to them and that they haven't the maturity to feel that there's any special revelation, or even integration, about it. If so, then it's hardly worth the extra effort it involves me in. The hostility I felt in the classroom all year I still recognized—some of it from that un-housebroken young bastard Yalden, and some more located in the social sciences, probably Carpenter influence.[219] But I'll try it again to see if it was just an unlucky combination of bad pacing on my part and of an accidentally dull year. After all, 48 was largely a post-war year. I wonder too if my repetition isn't beginning to exacerbate their little adolescent egos—who does this guy Frye think he is anyway? and the like. One of

my students was a Bahai convert, and preached Bahai at me for several pages.

[264] In the evening we went out to the Ballet. It was pouring rain, but we got the Haddows to take us down—the taxis didn't answer. Neither of us was in much of a mood for ballet. The first, some Tschaikowsky nonsense, was dull, the second, L'Apres midi d'un Faune, was stodgy, the third was one of their own, and at the end they did the Nutcracker Suite again. The evening socially was a fair success—we talked to the Owens in one intermission, and to Mary Jackman and Kay Coburn in the other. At the end we met Grace Workman and her husband John Scott, & they drove us home. He's attached to the university and hospital here, and lectures on (I think he said) Electro-Encephalography, which he translated as brain waves.

Wednesday, April 23

[265] The third ballet last night was a history of ballet: from Louis XIV's time, or possibly Louis XIII, to the present. The music was bits & pieces from Lully to Duke Ellington, and Donald [David] Adams, one of the main dancers in the group, thought it up. The costumes were fine & some of the satiric touches were good—a takeoff of Isadora Duncan, for instance, but they clowned it far too much, in Trudi Schoop fashion, and labored their points far too much. (It was presented as the projection of a history read by a dull pupil). It was interesting though as a native product, and one that didn't rest exclusively on overdone symbolism.

[266] I slept in and was late getting down this morning, which made me nervous, in the mood I get when I pick something up & put it down & pick something else up & put it down on top of what I just put down before, and then wonder where the hell I mislaid it. So naturally I didn't get much done. The vast mass of crap handed in for the E.J. Pratt poetry award dissolves away fairly soon when one gets down to it—there's so much that can just be tossed aside: three or four things seem to have something, though what they have is mostly Eliot.

[267] Maggie Newton came for dinner in the evening, bless her heart. She's changed her job over now, and my mind went woolgathering when she explained what it was, so I don't know, but it's well paid—

I did hear that. I think it's in the fall that she's planning to get married and move out of her flat. Her husband will be making far less than she for quite some time—always, most likely—Maggie's not the type to marry a man of strength & experience equal to her own. She says children's aid at present, with so many foreigners, is concerned almost entirely with desertions and not at all with cruelty—I suggested that that was the result of a nomadic floating society of easy mobility—it's when you feel trapped in a permanent relation with a kid that you're likely to turn sadistic. She seemed to think that had something. At present her roommate Connie Harrison is being persecuted by a lunatic who's been stuck in the funny jug twenty-one times, but always gets out again through some incompetent psychiatrist she's talked over or through her husband signing her out, and comes & screams at them or tears up clothes or pours a pot of coffee over the broadloom.

Thursday, April 24

[268] Today I got out & went down to Simcoe Hall to collect papers. All the pass papers were being given out. Ken Maclean [MacLean] was supposed to run the meeting, but seemed quite nervous, & asked me to take charge of distributing the first year papers, which I did, apparently with great efficiency: he told me afterwards I was "wonderful." There were more 1b than was expected, so we transferred Sister St. Francis from third year, where we thought there were fewer, & then discovered that Priestley, who was distributing third year, was over a hundred out in his addition, so Kay Coburn was transferred to third year from second year. That sort of thing. Woodhouse brought along the graduate Renaissance papers: they'd all flunked his section of it, as he'd set spotting & quite hard spotting, I think—and they panicked. So I took my papers home & read them & they all got firsts for me. All except Parr, that is, who isn't at all ready to come up yet, but who, being a terrifically glib talker, did some unfortunate guessing. His paper on Bacon guessed the titles of a lot of essays Bacon hadn't written, for instance, and when asked for an example of Elizabethan verse satire he produced *The Faerie Queene.*

[269] I don't know why I'm getting like this. I read first year papers until I could feel my brain beginning to soften, and then went in to tea. When they start telling you that Hamlet is a very knoble character it's time to

knock off. At tea we got into a discussion of existentialism, prompted by the fact that Jessie [Macpherson] had just seen the Sartre play that Don Harron is in—they call it *Crime Passionel* here, although I think its original title was *Mains Sales*.²²⁰ I seemed to be the only one present who had much notion of existentialism, & of course I know very little, but we kept quite an animated discussion going—Ned [Pratt], Joe [Fisher], Archie [Hare], Jessie, Bert Arnold & I. Helen came into the middle of it, & afterwards we drifted over to the Park Plaza, after inspecting a seven-branched candelabra, Norwegian workmanship, in that new shop at the end of Petticoat Lane. It's only $12.60 and I expect she'll buy it. The cocktail lounge was full of an enormous party of fat women whose coordination got pretty poor after a bit, but we had our two drinks & went out to have dinner. We settled on a new place on Bloor east of Yonge where the new subway station is to be—quite good & unpretentious, except that it calls itself 5th Avenue through a foolish habit of our newspapers of applying that term to Bloor St.

Friday, April 25

[270] We then saw that the theatre next door, which I think is called the Towne, was running something we tried to see in New York & missed: "The Emperor's Nightingale." It turned out to be a Czech film with puppets, telling the Andersen fairy tale. I quite liked it, and the color was good, but it was very slow-moving and sentimental and heavily moralizing, in a romantic way (nature vs. artifice) that didn't seem very convincing. And I *don't* see any point in close-ups of puppets, which were a painfully frequent feature. The supporting programme was quite good— a National Film Board short on the Canadian Ballet festival of 1949, which I hadn't seen, an account of an island near Puerto Rico where psychologists study six hundred monkeys, and, most interesting of all, a documentary on life in a small Chinese hamlet in the far south among the rice paddies.

[271] Today I got down early again, or relatively early, and we did term marks in Robins' office. I dislike that job, but by God we got it all done by lunch time, which is a record, I think. That's the one occasion when I get really impatient with Ned [Pratt] & John [Robins] & feel it's about time they stopped filibustering. Ned looks at his A's & B's & tries to remember whether he likes the student or not, & whether he'll give him 80 or

50, talking of course all the time. I have no business being irritable—I don't quite know why I am. Ruth's [Ruth Jenking's] father died Sunday & was buried (I think) Wednesday.

[272] I asked Ted Nicholls [Nichols] to lunch—he's Hart House chaplain & was proposing to complicate my life with a weekend at Caledon[221] with S.C.M. faculty & a discussion about the university in the modern world, but that, thank heaven, looks as though it'll fall through. They'd originally planned to have the Warden do it. Ted tells me that Ignatieff had already decided to resign the Hart House job anyway. He didn't make it very clear why, except that the Warden had a very strong sense of finishing chapters in his life, and didn't perhaps realize that he was at the end of the book. I say perhaps because Ted said he often dropped into his office to talk about death, particularly about whether it just happened to you or whether it came from inside. I'd never talked seriously to Ted Nicholls [Nichols] before, and got a very favorable impression of it [him]—like Charlie Leslie in many ways, but I think less melancholy in temperament. He says his instincts are for rural life, & while he doesn't question the will of God, he thinks it landed him in a funny spot.

Saturday, April 26

[273] Went down in the morning to Parr's oral, followed by Schranzer's— I mean Schanzer's. Parr won't make it, though he got through all right on his special period. Woodhouse and I gave him 43 and Ken MacLean 25. He came up long before he was ready. Schanzer, however, did very well, and will probably get a first. He was very collected and composed, had his own point of view on every question, and stuck stubbornly to it. I don't think he's as good as Norman [J.] Endicott does, but maybe I'm just sore because he didn't take a course with me. I was the only one not concerned with the exam who stayed for it, but I didn't see how to get out, so I sat there exacerbating my bum and cursing myself for a fool. At intervals I tried to read Butterfield's new book on *History and Human Relations*, which the CBC has sent me to review, and found it disappointing. He seems a master of graceful platitude.[222] I learn that Innes [Innis] is in the hospital with cancer and is not expected to recover.[223]

[274] Very late for lunch, I walked up to Bloor St. and met Barker Fairley,

who's busy writing his paper now. He was out walking because he was in flight from exams—when he has them to do he can't do them and yet can't do anything else. He says he thinks the examination system may work in England but has completely failed here, and was not impressed by my argument that cramming for exams gives a great many of our students the only intellectual excitement they get. Knox came up: he and Woodhouse are doing the summer school and he feels very browned off over the prospect. I went over to Murray's and choked down some concoction or other, then went back to my office and, by God, I finished the blasted first year pass papers, extra ones and all. It gave me a terrific lift to do it, as they were *very* dull, and I shan't have any more (apart from Barker's rereads, which will come God knows when) until 4k arrives on the 12th. One bewildered infant told me that Hamlet was caught between the motor and the pedestal, which he spelled "pedestle." I stared at that for some time before it dawned on me that he'd read somewhere that Hamlet was caught between the mortar and the pestle, and as he'd never seen a mortar or a pestle he'd just transposed it into his own terms. I marked 51 and ploughed I think eight.

Sunday, April 27

[275] When I got home Helen was sore because she'd spent all afternoon digging up the boulevard and had expected me to help her. I was rather glad I hadn't, actually, because this was the day the spring hay fever took to give me hell. However, I mowed the front lawn and changed some screens on the windows and sawed dead branches off trees to put on the boulevard & keep the kids off. Meanwhile Lucy Massey was having tea with Dad waiting for her son to come and collect her, which he did about half-past five. Just as we were about to get supper the Cronins dropped in. They'd had tea at the Ursulines, but they said it was a sloppy wishwashy tea, and could they have some real tea with us and share a cake they brought, a noble erection with red and yellow roses on it. So we had a second tea and they left about eight. They gave us, or at least Helen, some details about Quebec, & will write to the Mother Superior of the Ursuline convent there so Helen can see it & all its seventeenth-century stuff. They claim that Indians couldn't embroider a single moccasin until the Ursulines taught them how, which, if true, would explain why so many Indian beadwork designs look like French rococo & chinoiserie.

1953 Diary

[1–4 March 1953]

This brief diary is in the NFF, 1991, box 28, file 3. It is written on four leaves of light green notebook paper.

Mar. 1. [Sunday]

[1] Got up and read somewhat aimlessly until it was time to go to London.[1] We took a taxi and the man chattered about hockey games. He's been a coach in Ottawa and was homesick for it. The train trip was unbelievably dull. The windows were frosted over so we couldn't even see the bleak wintry landscape. Mary Waugh was on the same train, being interviewed for a teaching job in Woodstock. I gave Helen Henry James' *Other House* to read (I must check Rose Arminger & her red dress & white parasol—no, the other way round),[2] but I had nothing to read myself. I diddled at my archetypes a bit. The city of destruction and the dangerous Acrasia[3] garden need more pairing, and the hero barking orders into the air, being admired by fatuous goons like Carlyle & leaving subordinates to apply them to reality with a comfortable feeling that he's done something brainy and strategic that takes a large view—all that is the analogy of the creative Word or fiat. Both exceedingly obvious, but so many things are.

[2] George [Birtch] met us, a bit subdued—two of his five youngsters had flu. Joan & Ann. The oldest & only boy, Ralph, is in his teens, or near it. The little ones, Susan & Lorraine, are very sweet, and blonde. Mary the same as ever. It was a horrible house, designed by old Fatass Johnson,[4] who obviously should have been forcibly restrained from designing

houses, as well as lecture courses. C.V. Maclean was recruited from the same church, though he didn't live in the—er—manse. If they'd get George down to replace Matheson they'd be getting somewhere.[5] Well, we had to stay in the Hotel London, but we had supper with the Birtches & of course went to the evening service. George is doing a series on hymnody & had reached the Reformation. He gave a little talk about Luther & had them try to sing Ein Feste Burg, Lobe den Herrn, Nun Danket, & others. Very good, and certainly one way to beat the evening service problem. The United Church Carpet Ball League worshipped with us. That's a game for older men, an interesting-looking group of lower-middle class types. Evidently they bowl or something on a carpet—anyway it's not a reading group, to judge from their president, who acted as clerk & struggled with Isaiah.

[4] In the evening the Miseners & the Naylors came in. The Bateses were asked, but didn't show up—however they live fifty miles away. Rudy Eberhard, who runs an ornamental iron works (there are four in London, I discovered from the yellow pages, so London must fancy pokers wreathed in true-love knots. However, they do fire escapes & filing cabinets & such: I suppose it's only the Maritimes who have risen to the sublime *laissez faire* of the wooden fire escape). Rudy's wife, whose name is Helen, was home suckling a baby, and Rudy only stayed half an hour. Carman [Naylor] looks older, but is more interesting, & his wife Peggy did the talking. She belongs to a Great Books club & seems to be keen on it: they have leaders, who aren't allowed to express opinions, but no lecturers. It's a better arrangement than a female lecture group. They have men too. I still like Don [Misener] as much as ever, but I no longer feel that Agnes' [Agnes Misener's] grouch is really sardonic humor. It's just grouch, and she is beginning to look very unattractive—as though she'd just bitten into life and found it a lemon. I can't recall all the conversation. John Bates has moved from his Ohio place (Worcester [Wooster] College) to Greenwich, Conn.

[5] I was driven out of the churches largely by having been dragged off to listen to that old shit sack Glendenning in my youth. That is, I don't think I'd attend church anyway, but I wouldn't have so intense a feeling of wasted time about it. As it is, I associate Church with evenings, & the evening service is going to become more & more obviously an unnecessary evil. This church of George's is very Methodist in design, with the

choir as big as possible & the minister as nearly in the centre as possible. In the morning, with the sun shining, such architecture makes sense: it looks festive and pleasant. In the evening, with all color blotted out of the windows, harsh lights glaring from the ceiling, and a depressed, scanty, & demoralized congregation, it looks like a police court. Evenings should be spent at home.

Mar. 2. [Monday]

[6] Didn't sleep too well, but we were up in good time & had breakfast in the hotel, very gay with blue-green walls and yellow-green chairs. George came around and drove me to the Metropolitan Church. They had a hymn (I played) a prayer & they plunged into what they evidently considered business. I kicked myself for playing, & played a wrong note, but Don Stewart, who was there in an Air Force uniform, pushed me into it. The "business" was a lot of yatter & yack about whether there should be a reporter allowed in. He was there, and people kept jumping up and saying "I move no action be taken." They sounded like a lot of petulant old men (the old ones were the worst) without enough to do. The meeting began at ten, I was supposed to start at 10:30 and finish at 11:30, & I actually got started at 10:50, & then only after George had moved that the "business" be postponed till after the talk. Thank God they had a blackboard—without that it would have been an utter shambles. But with the board I could at least write down the table of apocalyptic symbols. I had a feeling of let-down about it, as it was such a waste of my time and their money to bring me there for a half-hour (they paid my hotel bill & gave me fifteen bucks besides, which covered train expenses for the two of us). I got a few questions and a long, silly, incoherent speech from Pete Colgrove's father. They'd warned me about him. Like his son, he has an amateurish interest in science—Pete's fourth-dimension paper was an earlier one in the series.[6] I couldn't make any sense out of what he said. One of the worst of the filibusterers, however, asked some intelligent questions, & I thought if I'd had a full hour & a half might have converted some of them to Christianity. But I don't know. They have to preach two sermons every Sunday, & somewhere or other they've picked up from the traditions of Protestantism the notion that each sermon has to present, not a facet of doctrine, but an opinion. And nobody can produce two opinions a week without becoming opinion-

ated, and a bore. Even Don Stewart asked me if I were sure I knew what I was talking about. Fred Stokes' father was there, & Miriam Collins.

[7] George saw me off to the train, & seemed eager to have me write out my ideas in a book. I think I shall after I finish the EP [Essay on Poetics]: if I finish *that* the way I want to, I'll write pot boilers out of it the rest of my life. I went back a bit dejected. The windows were frosted still in the coaches, but not in the first-class accommodation, so we went in to lunch. I drafted the outline of a book I might write along the lines George suggested. At Hamilton three women got on, one with an exceptionally loud & persistent voice who laughed exactly like a hen: clook, clook, clook. I suppose one could write a story about an Erewhon where there's a general opinion that *every* form of animal life has a human descendant, so human beings are classified into pig-men, horse-men, cock-men & the like. I listened to her—she was right opposite me and I had no choice— and tried to analyze the elements in the impression of plebianism she gave. I thought the essence of it was the fact that education through adjustment to environment produces the completely uneducable being. She had reached her adjustment, and gave the impression of a Robot. It wasn't lack of intelligence; it was the absorption of intelligence into automatism. There was no receptivity, as there is in a genuinely intelligent woman like Mary Birtch, and hence no charm, for charm, as its etymology shows, is magic, the sense of the indefinite range of reality. Behaviorism is senility. When an organism has reached its adjustment, it stops evolving, & a man who has stopped evolving in this world is still only an ape.

[8] We got home & Helen stirred up a dish full of baked beans & ancient meat. We had to have something because of Dad. I ate it, puked into the toilet bowl, & went to bed. Barker phoned. The Moderns committee set up by Jeanneret came through with a demand for four more (pass) English courses, & as he thinks Woodhouse will jump at the idea he wants me to help him resist. I said I'd certainly resist for next year, though I couldn't promise the total indefinite opposition he suggested. He also suggested our doing a saw-off on 2c & 3c, Victoria to do half, Trinity the other half. That's all right for next year, with Kay away, but I'd like to become self-sufficient. I don't like having to arrange for the marking of essays in 4n, for instance.[7]

Mar. 3. [Tuesday]

[9] Got up with a sore throat & a hoarse voice & struggled down to my nine o'clock, on Morris. I said that the basis of social theorizing was needs, food, shelter, clothing: that under civilization as Morris (and Rousseau) conceived it needs were specialized into class wants. That this movement from need to want was a perversion of the development of the real society from need to creativity. I linked Morris with anarchist & Jeffersonian trends, of course, & I'm gradually working toward something epiphanic about society & the mind, & the myth of where they meet.

[10] At four I went down to see Arnold Walter about Lister Sinclair's course. Funny rabbit warren the Conservatory is: one sees a grey-haired professor (Boris [Ronbaking?] as it happened) coming out of one door & a little girl scurrying upstairs to her music lesson. Music is the most philoprogenitive of the arts, with Bach & his twenty children at the head of it: no other art has anything like the child's teaching piece. Well, Walter was pretty bothered about Lister's having run away without setting an exam or giving me any details about what he's done. I said I'd do the Shakespeare-Milton-Dryden period with music attached, nothing else. (After all, I haven't even Robins' book any more.) I gather that Lister had ranged pretty freely, & probably confused them completely. He showed me the Library, a pretty melancholy looking one and the absurdly small record collection. I went home in a cold rain & found a letter from Blodwen Davies, who wants a grant to go to Holland to prove that her Mennonites are an apostolic church, pre-Protestant & pre-Waldensian even, going back to the fourth century. As her other references are Marius Barbeau, Dick Davis & Chuck Hendry, I'm the one to pronounce on her competence as a church historian. Ah me. Went to bed, finished the *Genealogy of Morals* and started *Ecce Homo*. During the day I went over to Britnells [Britnell's] & bought Keats's letters, the revised Mona Wilson Blake,[8] Herbert Muller's *Uses of the Past*, & a collection of Santayana's four "realm books."[9] Ken Maclean [MacLean] is going to Virginia, I think in April, to lecture on Thurber in a special series.[10]

Mar. 4. [Wednesday]

[11] The mail brought a note from that drivelling dithering idiot Carol Harper. Like a fool, I'd told her I'd be out on the West Coast next

summer, in a panic to keep her from coming down to bugger me up this summer. Now she says she'll move to Vancouver, and, says she, leave your wife at home, husbands & wives are unnatural. What she imagines gives her the right to talk to me that way I don't know. I threw the letter away: if I tried to answer it I'd get stomach ulcers. Victor Whatton & Ted Sawyer were in: the former is in rather a bad way—working too hard. I advised him to try Woodhouse for a readership next year. The ten o'clock did most of Sidney's Apology, to a lazy, sulky, unwilling looking class. I wish I knew whether I'm really dull, or whether students are less interested in ideas than they were. I think an educational system that proceeds by age groups and basic vocabularies has a very harmful influence on them, as it deadens their curiosity in favor of practical adjustment. But still the main responsibility has to be on the students. I must tell them sometime that it's only as fellow-students they interest me: as pupils in front of a teacher, they're senile children.

[12] The twelve o'clock was a very able lecture, on Morris, & finished Morris. I'm not quite clear why *News from Nowhere* has been so wonderfully productive a book for me, but it has been. I talked about active & contemplative ideals in education, about the central governor-principle, the magnetic great man & his disciples in Carlyle, the area of free discussion in Mill, culture in Arnold, the church in Newman, & the natural society in Rousseau. A link appeared between Morris's doctrine of creative spontaneity & Renaissance *sprezzatura*[11] in Castiglione. But the main thing is what's apparently becoming the centre of my conclusion: it's hypothetical or artistic production that resolves the antithesis of the existential & the essential. As I realized while talking about Sidney, the essential is abstract, remote & withdrawn from life, but the hypothetical and imaginative isn't.

[13] I came home earlyish, deliberately skipping the Council meeting, more for discipline than anything else. I felt—I think the word is lazy, a word I dislike. Anyway, I couldn't write & had to relapse into reading instead. I finished *Ecce Homo* and started *Zarathustra* again. The way Nietzsche talks about himself in *Ecce Homo* is wrong in fact, but not in conception: it's the way a Communist would talk about Marx, so it isn't impossible. Given ever so slight a list to port, the history of the future might have gone through Nietzsche instead of through Marx. By the future I mean his future, our present. But still Nietzsche had no sense of

dialectic incarnation: he couldn't organize or produce the form of the Pauline or Leninist epistle, hence his views about his own historical importance are a *post hoc propter hoc* fallacy. That is, he's not a genuinely existential thinker, but a hypothetical one who thinks he ought to be. Speaking of Marxist dialectic incarnations, the morning paper brought out its second-coming headlines to announce that Stalin was dying: I don't suppose even we expected him to live forever, though whenever we believe someone to be demonic something of the immortality of the devil gets attached to him. No one attracts so much fascinated speculation as an enemy: I suppose one of the things Nietzsche was trying to say is that if man could only think of God as an enemy he might get interested in him—the point behind a good deal of the anti-Nietzschean too, such as conviction of sin and Barth's *ganz anders*.[12]

1955 Diary

[1 January – 22 March 1955]

This diary is in a small, red leatherette book (11.2 × 7.3 cm), having space for two days' entries on each page. Frye sometimes used an entire page or more than a single page for a day's entry. The diary is in the NFF, 1993, box 2, file 2.

Jan. 1. [Saturday]

[1] Quiet but pleasant New Year's Eve party featured Gordon Wood, in excellent spirits & evidently quite recovered, Ella Martin, & of course Vera [Frye] & Dad. Jay Macpherson & Daryl Hine dropped in, & so did Harold Whitley. There was no place for young Hine to stay, as it was not very discreet putting him in the spare room of a girls' residence, so he stayed with us. Got up early and got Vera & Dad off on the morning train, leaving them in charge of the Passenger Agent. The rest of the day *very* quiet, with a good deal of sleeping. Hine gave me an unbound copy of Five Poems—some very good stuff in it.[1]

Jan. 2. [Sunday]

[2] Also quiet, cleaning up the Christmas mess, undressing & burning the tree, writing answers to cards, & the like. Wrote cards to Birtches, Buckleys, Velma Holt, George Johnston, Margaret Allen (the sick girl), Dan Seltzer (in Oxford), Jim Hurlock, Frances Croft (53),[2] Chitticks, Nancy Orwen (Bill is starting over again in Syracuse) & the [William] Thompsons [Thomsons] at Harvard. Then we murdered ourselves with an overdose of Martinis and were let in for a largely sleepless night, full of dreams on the surface of dozing.

Jan. 3. [Monday]

[3] Spent the day, perhaps for the first time in my life, preparing my lectures. The promise I made to take over Ken's [Ken MacLean's] 4j course[3] caught up with me and I read a book on Rossetti all day, also Sam Slick,[4] as that too falls due tomorrow. Attended Hilliard Trethewey's committee on building, inspected Room 30, which isn't bad. It's pretty clear that 30 is what the Administration wants & wants us to back, and 18 is the Property Committee's idea. Irving back from Philosophy Conference at Baltimore, and very chipper at having taken part in a discussion.

Jan. 4. [Tuesday]

[4] Started Arnold at 9, with the diagram. Talked more this time about the aesthetic judgement in terms of a sense of proportion & good taste. It may make things simpler. The special Canadian group went surprisingly well, on Pratt, & so did the other one, starting Sam Slick. The graduate group I didn't feel was quite so good: I couldn't seem to get started on Little Gidding. However, I promised them better things for next week. The catch about David Hoeniger and the Nuffield is that Wally Field is applying for one too, and two would be expensive, or so Hal says. Charlie Leslie is now probation officer in Muskoka district.

Jan. 5. [Wednesday]

[5] Dug myself out for a Wednesday 9 o'clock & started on Rossetti. Gossipy & entertaining, but no ideas: I don't have any on Rossetti as yet. I must do an illustrated lecture when I find out how to run that damn machine. Then I ran over to the library & got Wicksteed,[5] ran back in time to meet David Walker of TV. He had a script ready, and I think the programme will go all right.[6] The twelve o'clock on Arnold went fairly well & then two o'clock on the Eliot quartets was the usual sort of struggle. Council went on till six discussing faculty-student relations with two cute kids on the V.C.U. [Victoria College Union], both in my Can Lit class.

Jan. 6. [Thursday]

[6] The first Milton lecture of the year was, if I do say so myself, a

beautifully organized job on Book IX. Just the stock stuff, of course, but it came off well. The twelve o'clock drew a big crowd for some reason: I suppose the rumor that I do the Eliot quartets rather well does spread. Only I didn't do it too well, my best lecture, the one on Burnt Norton, having been done yesterday. In the evening we went to see the Victoria Dramatic Society (it's called a club now) do Obey's "Noah."[7] I thought it came off reasonably well: I had reservations about Herbert Whittaker's direction, but it depended on Noah (John Douglas) who was good.

Jan. 7. [Friday]

[7] The second Milton lecture wasn't as good as the first, but it wasn't too bad. In the afternoon I went down to Lou Morris' new book shop. Tremendous space, but a fire trap. It costs him $33 a day, takings so far $36, which I think is remarkably good for a start. I asked him about Roy Clark, who was our taxi driver last night, & one of the innumerable stray cats that Morrises have picked up and sheltered. He says Clark is a manic depressive, which I can well believe. I bought an Imperial standard typewriter for $180. Helen went to a Museum lecture on Chinese silk, & we went then to dinner at the new chicken place on Bloor St—chicken & finger bowls.[8]

Jan. 8 and 9. [Saturday and Sunday]

[8] Overslept & so didn't go down to do all the desk jobs that were waiting for me. I shopped around for the morning: lunch at Murrays, & then Yvonne Housser dropped in just before Yvonne Williams came to take us to the opening of Will Ogilvie's show at the Picture Loan. I found the stuff—South African scenes—a trifle disappointing—pink & purple confections that in Canada we associate with calendars. Then to Bessie MacAgy's cocktail party, where we met a bunch of bridge players: Mrs. [Currie?], whose son is engaged to Joan Haggert, & Peggy of Peggy's hats on Bloor. Peggy was plump, corseted in a way that stuck her breasts away out, & had once been cute. Husband in succession duties. Today we took things pretty easy, going only to tea at John Nicol's & meeting there a Mrs. [Becker?] who teaches speech at the Conservatory. I quite liked her: a little like mother with her dark sombre voice & rather readily emotional temperament. I think Jim Wood's scheme of getting her to speak to the Liberal Arts Club an excellent one, as they can pay her.

Helen searched the New York Times in vain in search of Douglas MacAgy's new troth plighter.[9] Divorce is a catastrophic business: the sombreness of Protestantism is linked with it, I think.

Jan. 10. [Monday]

[9] Got down latish and dithered around reading stuff on the pre-Raphaelites as an excuse for not working. Not a very good excuse. I did get started on the essay schedule, a week late, wrote a letter or two, got my hair cut, saw Kay Morris on the subway—she seems to be very pleased about the Yonge Street move[10]—got Daniel de Montmollin to show me how to run the slide projector machine, arranged to get some slides, saw David Hoeniger about the Nuffield business, & tried to give myself a feeble illusion of efficiency. Sometimes I bore myself. The typewriter arrived tonight & I typed a bit on it: it's certainly a beautiful one.

Jan. 11. [Tuesday]

[10] Got out in good time for my nine o'clock, which did up Arnold: another lecture should finish him. There was a considerable drop in the voluntary Can. lit.: also the sitters disappeared from the other class, all but Jay. This is the last year I allow indiscriminate auditing: their enthusiasm has to be prepared to last. The Sam Slick lecture went very well, on language. So did the graduate group, reading Dylan Thomas. But all the auditors except three disappeared. Anne Carnwath wants to take graduate work. I went over for slides in the afternoon, & hope all goes well tomorrow. The Macleans [MacLeans] are rented.

Jan. 12. [Wednesday]

[11] Well, operating the slide projector turned out to be easy enough, except that I got in a lot of pictures backsided—I mean wrongside out. The other half of the machine, showing book illustrations, doesn't work too well. The twelve o'clock on Arnold was rather poor, as I'd really finished that. The two o'clock 3c finished the quartets, after a fashion. Karl Kenteroff came in & picked up his essay—his trouble is his family's Belgian & they don't speak English at home. Then a committee meeting on 2c and 3c: we changed the 3c prose around some, adding Gosse & Macneile Dixon, and a new anthology of criticism by Bate.[11]

Jan. 13. [Thursday]

[12] The nine o'clock on Milton staggered through the creation—I hope to finish P.L. [*Paradise Lost*] tomorrow. Then I sat around on my fanny through office hours, doing bugger & all. Having a number of uncongenial jobs to do has really got me with my gears fouled up. The twelve o'clock started Ned [Pratt], who teaches very well. Chris Love says Ned fainted on the street last night, but of course he hasn't been feeding himself properly. Building committee at 2, looking at a plan of Horwood's to put all administration on the west side of the main hall—a net gain of two offices. Then Moderns, putting the g options in English. They shifted the years around to avoid time-table difficulties.

Jan. 14. [Friday]

[13] I finished Paradise Lost all right & drew up a schedule of lectures for the next month. 3j will last two more weeks, & the four nine o'clocks with it. 4j will perhaps stagger on for another week. Hugh MacCallum's oral (M.A.) was held in my office at 2, and lasted until 4. He got through, of course, but is still very inarticulate. Woodhouse lectured him—and me—on reason in Milton. He says his mother's operation for cataracts seems to have been very successful. Dinner was late and I skipped the Senate: I've decided to feel a bit off, evidently: the feeling is real, of course.

Jan. 15. [Saturday]

[14] This was the day I had planned for work on the book. But what I did was quite different. The Forum sent me Joan Evans' new book on Ruskin, so what did I do but sit down and read it through to the end, then write my review of it.[12] The fact that I at least wrote the review saves a bit. I'm doing what I always do when confronted with uncongenial tasks: just withdraw from everything. One trouble is that I've kept the bliss of reading steadily & systematically as a donkey's carrot to get me through this writing, & when I haven't time to write I feel disposed to nibble.

Jan. 16. [Sunday]

[15] Well, in spite of myself I worked like a nigger today. I had to go

down to the television studio at 2:30, got made up, & had a total of three rehearsals before the show finally came off at 6 o'clock. Technically it was amateurish, I felt. I think I'm being objective when I say that my essential part, writing the script, choosing the poems and pictures, & timing it was pretty well done. The reading (an actor named Barry Morse) was excellent too. My own delivery was so-so. Edith Fowke came to see me & we brought her home (in her car) for dinner, & then I went to bed early.

Jan. 17. [Monday]

[16] Post-mortems today: an astonishing number of people saw it. General agreement that the photography, especially of me, which of course I didn't see, was pretty awful. However, Robin Harris said it was the best one all year in that series. Priestley & [Arthur] Barker saw it with him. Petitions committee meeting giving Montreal's B.A. in English Grade 13 standing, & Laval's a qualified first year. At the Department Meeting, which was mostly calendar, Woodhouse fought the Gosse & another measure, but lost both counts. We cleared up pretty well the whole calendar, with relatively little change.

Jan. 18. [Tuesday]

[17] The nine o'clock started Ruskin & got over the double parabola business. Attendance at the special Canadian group continues small, but I worried through Sam Slick. I know it's good to leave decisions to them, but still their morale sinks when they're not led by the nose. Auditors are dropping out of 4j, but the class is good, and I did all right on Wacousta.[13] The graduate group read The Fall of the House of Usher—Pat Carraway: if she stays away only Jay [Macpherson] and [Youmans?] will be left. Damn auditors. Without Jay I wouldn't have much morale left. A student wanted me to take part in a panel discussion with Carpenter. I said no.

Jan. 19. [Wednesday]

[18] The nine o'clock finished the Rossettis, I hope: anyway I "covered" them. Irving came in to urge me to give the panel discussion a miss (I'd mentioned it last night to him) & told me of Carpenter's habit of carica-

turing his colleagues to his class. I don't mind that—the idea just doesn't appeal. The Varsity sharply but very honestly critical of my show— Wendy Michener.[14] More Ruskin at twelve: an ineffectual closing of Pratt at two. The exact formula for Pratt still eludes me. Home early & coaxed Helen into a good humor. Dick Ellmann has asked me for a Joyce paper at MLA[15] & Bald has finally written about the Chicago visit.

Jan. 20. [Thursday]

[19] The nine o'clock made quite a dent in Paradise Regained, & impressed me so much I sat down to write that paper I always think of doing on it every year. However, a sentence or two in it soon derailed me back to the book. For the twelve o'clock I set my second test on Eliot & Shelley & Auden. Then I had the 4m people in to lunch & we put Pratt & Pound & Dylan Thomas on the poetry & threw all the junk off.[16] Now I'm being consulted about whether we ought to get a Schlicker Baroque organ or not for the college. I feel at the moment very much in favor of it.

Jan. 21. [Friday]

[20] Busy but pleasant day. The nine o'clock finished Paradise Regained, after a fashion, nothing new emerging. At two o'clock I went down to the Ph.D. Committee meeting where we discussed one M'Intyre for most of the afternoon. Seems he hasn't got a first in his special field. We co-opted Knox and [Harold S.] Wilson, but all they said was they were doubtful about M'Intyre. So were we, so that didn't help. The graduate school is depressing. I got back for the tail end of the tea for Yvonne Housser. Blodwen Davies said she heard my programme & "got a lot out of it": Mary Jackman objected to the "mystery" part of it. Leila Robins also saw it. Then we adjourned to Jessie Mac's [Macpherson's] for cocktails.

Jan. 22. [Saturday]

[21] At the cocktail party I talked mainly to Charles Comfort. Dalton Wells & his wife liked the show, but wished I'd read the poems myself. Not many people have taken *that* line. Charles' second daughter Anna is getting married in Williamstown, Mass. Helen enjoyed the party immensely, as she talked to a lot of people she hadn't seen for a long time. Then she & I went down to the King Edward Hotel for dinner—she still

feels shy about the downtown hotels here, although she's been to many bigger ones in bigger cities. She found it small, dull & corny, which was a most educational experience for her. Then we got a taxi & got to Sunshine Town,[17] just in time.

Jan. 23 and 24. [Sunday and Monday]

[22] I quite liked Sunshine Town: it was very limited in its objectives, but was pleasant, stuck closely to Leacock, and was, as Helen said, "wholesome." Yesterday my efforts to work on the book were interrupted by Helen's desire to heave furniture around. Not too successful anyway: I started on the rhetoric chapter,[18] but got a lot of it wrong. In the evening we went out to Mary Campbell's & met Bob & Jean Macdonald [McDonald]. He seems older, tired & weak, but Jean as lovely (as I think) as ever. Today there was more heaving & grunting, the upshot of which was that my study was shifted about & the whole of the pine furniture ensemble put together for the first time since we left Bathurst St.[19] It gives me a lot more space to put depressing objects out of sight. In the evening we went to the MacLures for a nightcap. Greta didn't play any too well, as she said, but it's always wonderful to hear that instrument. She did a superb Couperin Passacaille & the Mxnxstrxdxsx thing,[20] if that's right. Today I read Chew's old book on Swinburne[21] & went to a Graduate Department meeting where we discussed—guess what—M'Intyre. Hell of a dull damn meeting. Otherwise nothing much happened today.

Jan. 25. [Tuesday]

[23] Ruskin at nine, & a small Canadian Literature group at ten. Leacock. Jay's [Jay Macpherson's] taken to going to it, which is a wrong decision. None of them had seen Sunshine Town. The twelve o'clock did Wacousta, and was quite a lot better: that course holds up well. And that, of course, was it for today, as the graduate group was moved on. I feel a bit bothered about my lecturing this year—part of the general sense of being harried. I saw Ned [Pratt], and he says Claire [Pratt] is over her third operation and past the crucial infection period. She's to be home in about three weeks, he says. It's too soon to take the beaten look out of his face, but time should improve it if Claire does too.

Jan. 26. [Wednesday]

[24] Swinburne at nine, moderately successful, and an almost total failure on *Unto This Last* at twelve. I just suddenly decided I didn't want to talk about that book, and didn't know or care enough about it. The two o'clock was much better, beginning Browne's Religio Medici. I have an extremely bright class in that 3c, and I wish the group was smaller and the texts less crowded and difficult. I stayed around in the afternoon and went down to the Royal Society dinner. A mathematician whose name I didn't get made a rather dull speech and the discussion afterward was pretty aimless.

Jan. 27 and 28. [Thursday and Friday]

[25] The nine o'clock did half of Samson Agonistes, talking a bit about the nature of tragedy. I was tired & broke my consulting hours to go out for a New Yorker & a cup of coffee. The twelve o'clock did some more Browne, in fact practically finished it. Good class: that yawny girl wasn't there. Helen had phoned a drunk piano tuner who got maudlin but agreed to come today, so I phoned her to see how her virtue was, but he didn't show up & it wasn't attempted. The first library committee under the new or Senate regime was held today & was mildly eventful: it'll be a better set up. We accepted the Coleridge collection[22] & got some new business organized: committees to revise periodicals & the like. In the evening the graduate students came in: Cowie is intelligent & Kleiman interested, but the others, especially the women, are the clammiest bunch of cretins I've ever seen. Tiring dull evening on The Phoenix & the Turtle. Today I finished 3j and wasted half the afternoon on a silly special meeting of the Administrative Committee of Division P. All about the three year residence rule for the Ph.D. Grube made an impassioned speech against it, & told me afterwards that he'd asked to have the special meeting called: I couldn't figure it all out.

Jan. 29. [Saturday]

[26] Today I did a very little at the book, in the intervals of rearranging the living room furniture and going out for shopping with Helen. We had lunch at Murray's, and staggered home with enough food for a

regiment. I've begun reorganizing the genres & rhetoric chapters into a single chapter. Harvey Olnick phoned up about the Baroque, & he mentioned some European firms that might do better than Schlicker. Anyway he's got dope on it that he'll send me. The fourth year came in for dinner, seven of them, Arnold Bailey, Alicia File, Marion Woods, Ishbel Junor, Jean Little, Sally McCrae, Lillian Mitchell, exactly half the English class.

Jan. 30. [Sunday]

[27] Tonight the other seven came: Allen Bentley, Joan Haggert, Nora Wilson, Margaret Kell, Glorya Gillies, Mary Leslie, Allison Roach. Nice kids. Everyone came, & everyone except Alicia stayed the evening. The conversation Sunday was better, largely because the one man present had so much more on the ball. Joan Haggert emerged as one of the best personalities in the group—that's the kind of thing you don't learn from lectures. She's going to Europe next year, with Allison; Margaret and Glorya are getting married; Jean Little is to teach handicapped children in Guelph, Lillian [Mitchell] & I think Sally [McCrae] (another nice kid) are for O.C.E.

Jan. 31. [Monday]

[28] Today I felt a bit hung over—both lots had stayed till midnight—but my throat kicked up at 7:45, so it did me no good not to have a nine o'clock. I got some correspondence attended to that had been bothering—and boring—me, notably [Heming?] Vaughan's packet of protest. The afternoon was another donkey job—I'd called Woodhouse, Priestley, [Arthur] Barker, Shook & Mallon in to do that Moderns job (options for non-English people), so we had tea at Victoria and then adjourned to Room 14 to finish the examination schedule. I have 36, the comprehensive, and 4g to convene, besides a couple of rereads & my own courses.

Feb. 1. [Tuesday]

[29] The nine o'clock started Morris, on the to-hell-with Ruskin principle. I can always lecture on Morris. The Canadian special group got a lecture on Wacousta, as I didn't want to waste it, and the twelve o'clock people got Roughing It in the Bush.[23] Not bad. The graduate group was a

straight lecture—they'd asked for the Grecian urn, & I gave them Endymion. They're awfully dull, but I'm bad too—I think it was a poor idea to take the whole course over and organize it without papers. Out to Mary Lou Kilgour's for dinner, with David Knight: pleasant & relaxing evening.

Feb. 2 and 3. [Wednesday and Thursday]

[30] The nine o'clock practically finished Swinburne, and worked fairly well. Then I went over to the Library School to give the first of two lectures on Canadian poetry. I had stuff, but the organization was only so-so, and they didn't get used to my voice. Better luck next time. The twelve o'clock was Morris again, and quite good. The two o'clock began Sartor Resartus—I ran out of Browne material very quickly—and was all right, I think. Council meeting at four, uneventful, and Bill Staple's lecture at 5 on Ecclesiastes. He linked it not with pessimism but with resigned optimism of the "Whatever is is right" variety. We went home with Hilliard [Trethewey] and to bed early. Today I suddenly decided to play hookey, and stayed home all day, the first Monday-to-Friday day I've stayed home since September. I begged off a dinner at and evening with [David] Stevenson of Western Reserve, and explained that I was trying to avoid the flu. I seem to do this at least once every February, and I think perhaps it pays off. Anyway it helps to keep my mind on the fact that my book is more important than anything else I'm doing. I'd cut my 3c lecture, but I still had a curious guilty feeling. Partly because *Helen* was giving a lecture—a talk on her Princeton venture to the VWA [Victoria Women's Association], along with Kay Coburn.

Feb. 4. [Friday]

[31] Today I went down to the office solely & simply because I hadn't the strength of mind to stay home. I did nothing when I got there, of course. No lectures now, and I further wasted my time by going to the Senate meeting because I thought Art Cragg would be there and I'd more or less tentatively asked him up for dinner the next time he came. He didn't come, but as he didn't send his regrets either I was more or less stuck. However, some interesting things turned up. We're going to open a new Spanish department, & are bringing Art Fox in. I suggested putting him in the French department to simplify the constitutional issues.

Feb. 5. [Saturday]

[32] Well, yesterday the piano tuner came—the proper one, that is—so I dug out some Scarlatti again. We stayed in all day, waiting for Yvonne Williams to come & drive us out to Blodwen's [Blodwen Davies's], but she didn't come. I'm signed up to go to Chicago Feb. 27, so I may take the last 4j hour for a Butler 4k in order to finish both courses by then. It would be wonderful to have no more nine o'clocks. I do a talk to students at tea (shades of Cornell!) Monday. Talk to Bald's seminar Tuesday, & give a public lecture Wednesday. I plumped for Pericles for the seminar. I'm probably a fool: the rest will be stalling from the book, I suppose.

Feb. 6 and 7. [Sunday and Monday]

[33] Peter Fisher came down this weekend, & came up here for midday dinner. He's far more relaxed and cheerful than he was before: time heals all wounds, & certainly seems to be taking care of the Fisher situation. He feels a bit peripheral at RMC [Royal Military College]—the buttons on the uniform, he called it—but still I think he's well adjusted to the situation. After that we found out what the trouble was yesterday— the Blodwen Davies visit was for today. So Yvonne came just as Peter left & drove us out. Christopher Chapman's movie "The Seasons," was the feature.[24] He was there, with Peter Stokes, people called Lovens (sp?)— he's a big shot in Maclean-Hunter, & a brigadier in the war, the [Reesors?], & another girl who's name I didn't get. There were two movies, & I found the second more interesting. Chris has a theory which interests me, that parasites accompany poor soil. Restore the organic balance of the soil, he says, and the parasites go away. This doctrine conflicts with commercial interests that sell poison sprays, & that's big business because it's an important peace-time sideline of armaments concerns. Almost too good to be true—parasites, waste land soil and armaments concerns all linked together. (Nothing much happened today anyway.)

Feb. 8 and 9. [Tuesday and Wednesday]

[34] Morris continued to go well, & the Canadian lit. groups were so-so. Roughing It in the Bush doesn't present what you might call inexhaustible riches. I left early because I'd arranged a lunch at the Students'

Union for Elder Olson. There to get Kay [Coburn] in (Ruth [Jenking] begged off), but I'd said S.C.R. [Senior Common Room] to Woodhouse, tried to send him a message via [Joseph] Fisher, who forgot. Twenty minutes late, & at that they gave us two separate tables: I must make sure they never do that again. So Chris [Love] & Ken Kee & I ate at one table & the others with Olson. I put Ned [Pratt] at the head, but he'd never heard of Ned, or of Kay, who was opposite, & then there was Millar [MacLure] with his murderous UTQ review of Olson coming.[25] However, no teeth sank in. The graduate group was a little better. Comedy: I was of course too busy to wade into The Winter's Tale, so I stalled with my beautiful stalling apparatus. Afterwards I went to dinner at Hart House, again with Olson, & then to hear his paper on Wallace Stevens. He's a pretty dull & humourless bastard, but the paper was a lot better than most of his work. Except of course that Stevens himself has more humor. People can get more damn reputation in the States on less damn mental ability. Not only the States either: there's Empson.

Feb. 10 and 11. [*Thursday and Friday*]

[35] Well, yesterday I sailed into Morris & Meredith at nine, & I think I'll finish easily enough next week. Nothing to do but Clough & stuff. Then I ankled over to the Library school again. This time things went better. There's a preternaturally wise young man who's nailed me both times. Bertha seemed pleased, & suggested an extra lecture next year. A girl from Ottawa showed me the plan of the new National Library: looks superb, with a fine view across the Ottawa. The twelve o'clock on Huxley was fair, but I'll be glad to get to Butler. In the afternoon I killed time until Archie's [Archie Hare's] lecture, which was quite good, on Maurice Barrès, a civilized and tolerant presentation of a man who's obviously a poisonous old bastard. After that we all went to a special dinner given for the staff by the Board of Regents: the idea was for the Board to meet staff. Tables of four: mine had John Line, Grant, & Mrs. Bennett. She & Morley Smith got presented with things for their work on residence committees. Stupid but amiable speeches all round. Party at Jessie's [Jessie Macpherson's] afterwards for Archie. Two Board members there, Eve Powell Plewes & Lois Girvan Wilson. Gradually our own generation becomes senior. Jessie played a long record, "The Investigator," a CBC skit on McCarthy. McCarthy's own voice, done by Drainie, was superb: the rest a bit tedious.

Feb. 12 and 13. [Saturday and Sunday]

[36] Let's see: what happened the last day or so? My 3c lectures were on Sartor Resartus, & not bad. Theall was in, asking me whether he should take a job in Ohio he hasn't got yet. St. Mike's doesn't pay him enough to keep a family on, and whenever he says so the Council votes him a "gift" of $100. I don't know why he consulted me, but I'm glad he did. Irving says Sparshott is to come on the Vic Ethics staff. I quite like that idea. Smith has announced another raise at Toronto, & the Board said they'd play along. No doubt the same way they did last time: publicly, they equalled Toronto salaries; privately, they explained it would take several years to get to the "floor." Carpenter's Explorations 4 is out, in a most handsome Kandinskyish cover. It has my archetypes thing[26] and Millar's [Millar MacLure's] Dylan Thomas article,[27] but is otherwise as silly as ever. Except that article by Ong saying the Hebrews talked in terms of the ear & the Greeks the eye, & our conceptual language has got steadily more spiritual ever since, let the cat out of the bag as far as Marshall's [Marshall McLuhan's] main thesis is concerned. I mean, now I know what he thinks he's talking about. Back to oral tradition, the ear, and the Word of God. People have told me Anthony Frisch was back in Austria: he phoned from Brampton today. Ah me.

Feb. 14. [Monday]

[37] Quiet day, partly because it snowed the whole goddam day. I had no lectures, but I did have a Ph.D. Coe [Committee] meeting at 3, a Dept. Mtg. at 4, stayed down for dinner, & then gave a lecture at the School of Social Work at 7:30. Underhill in the chair. I did all right, but the audience was badly cut down by the weather. I talked on "The Liberal Spirit" and gave them a lot of my [P4?] line. Chuck Hendry seemed on the whole pleased. Nancy sent me a Valentine & her picture—she's going to be a lovely young woman.[28] Carpenter, whom I met, says the cover of Ex 4 [*Explorations*, no. 4] *is* Kandinsky—swiped. I hope he doesn't get in trouble. Marshall has issued "Counter Blast":[29] his love affair with the twenties is getting indecent. Ph.D.'s include Pat Carr on Pope & Ross Woodman on Shelley.

Feb. 15. [Tuesday]

[38] The nine o'clock finished Huxley, so there's only Butler to do. The

Canadian groups were not bad—Grove, and an idea or two emerged. Thoreau's "the only true America" line[30] fits him pretty well. Then I dashed down to look at myself doing Blake on a TV retake. Millar [MacLure] came along, & Carpenter & McLuhan were supposed to, but didn't. I wasn't as awful as I expected, but I sure don't want any goddamn script next time. I still think I had a pretty good idea for the program & he (David Walker) said his reports were favorable & he'd enjoyed doing it more than his other programs. The graduate group had all my auditors back: things have come to a Pretty Pass when I depend on auditors for morale, but I do with that lot.

Feb. 16 and 17. [Wednesday and Thursday]

[39] The nine o'clock did Fitzgerald & Clough, & I found they went surprisingly well, especially Fitzgerald. I said his poem was the bourgeois conscience on holiday. He's a very interesting man, & so is Clough. The twelve o'clock started Butler, the Life & Habit stuff. Not bad, but for some reason I don't get it to go so well. Then I met disaster in the two o'clock—Sartor—where I was faced with so dense an audience that I was goaded into saying that these hero ideas nearly conquered the world ten years ago, so naturally some dim bulb of a boy wanted to know why this book was considered good. I can't handle that sort of situation. Tea at Alta Lind's [Alta Lind Cook's] for Jessie [Macpherson]: Leila Robins, Coxeters, Irvings, Marshall [McLuhan] and others. Jessie's lecture had an excellent crowd: the first good one. It was a fair lecture, on the "public" level, given with apparent ease, though naturally she was very easy. We then went to Kay's for a drink & I met various friends. Helen James, Greta Kraus, the Andersons & Laure [Rièse] were there. Laure's anthology of French Canadian poetry is out:[31] she said she had a hell of a time getting the Quebec poets to let her print the poems she wanted. They seem worse than our English lot: then they get religious.

Feb. 18. [Friday]

[40] Today I got down at ten to start the American literature course— Frost. Not good: I hadn't prepared anything, and anyway I'd heard about it only late last night. Nice class, though. Of course, it was ten o'clock. I had Norman Endicott in to lunch, but we didn't get anything done on 3b, except a general plan. Then I went home early and did some

more typing. Yesterday I struggled into some Butler with 3c and had [Robert] McDougall over to SCR [Senior Common Room] for lunch and the 4g paper. He'd set most of it before he arrived. Norman was unusually frank about ASPW's [Woodhouse's] favoritism: I didn't know Ken's book was turned down by the UT press.[32]

Feb. 19. [Saturday]

[41] Stayed in all day but we went to the Grant's in the evening— Douglas Grant, that is. New house up on Manor Road. They've done a great deal of papering & painting & rebuilding of decor, & it looks fine. Douglas is still a good deal inclined to the typical English grouches & clichés about Americans, but being put in charge of the Quarterly has certainly given him a new interest, and I think he'll do extremely well in raising circulation and general morale. There's no reason at all why the UTQ shouldn't go over well, and Douglas will certainly do a hell of a lot better job on it than I'd do.

Feb. 20. [Sunday]

[42] Holed up all day & wrote & typed. The third chapter is shaping up fairly well, and all the stuff I used to think was a separate chapter on rhetoric is folding up like a pup tent inside the genres. What I do is start with the old introduction to the theory of genres, then work out what I call "initiatives" for epos, prose, drama and lyric in turn, showing in each one what the melos and opsis links are. Then I go on to a specific-form section, & wind up with a peroration on ratio & oratio. That's mainly the praxis & theoria aspects (extensions) of melos & opsis in prose, leading to a new idea of a conceptual rhetoric.[33]

Feb. 21. [Monday]

[43] The usual rather aimless Monday: Gord Roper for lunch on the comprehensive, but again nothing much done on it. Two letters: one for someone named Donald Davie in Dublin, getting a book out (Routledge Kegan Paul) & wants to make extensive use of LML ["Levels of Meaning in Literature"].[34] Gives you a feeling that you do do something for somebody, sometimes. The other was a note from Woodhouse in New

York, adding as a kind of afterthought that my name had been stuck on the MLA executive ballot. Fortunately I haven't a hope of getting in, not that it's a hope: I have a mild curiosity to see how the wheels go round, but I daresay they go round & round.

Feb. 22. [Tuesday]

[44] The nine o'clock struggled through some Butler, but the class was sleepy, and I couldn't seem to get going. The quality of my lectures is that of a public performance; it depends entirely on the quality of response I get, and with me a dull lecture always (well, *nearly* always), means a dull class, not a dull professor. I don't know why I say this to a diary: I ought to say it to them. The Can. lit. groups were, as usual, indifferent & very good, respectively. Again it's brightness in the class: they catch things. The graduate group (Pat Carr missing, but all the others there) went fairly well on The Winter's Tale: I gave them more chance to talk & they took it.

Feb. 23 and 24. [Wednesday and Thursday]

[45] In the evening the Macdonalds [McDonalds]—well, Bob—came around and took us to hear Robin Harris's paper. It was on the contrast between English essay questions & our own Grade 13, where everything's prescribed for you by the form of the question. He proposed shoving matriculation back to Grade 12. Discussion was blocked by MacDougall, who's president of ATE [Association of Teachers of English] and had a plan of research to sell us. Baloney, I think. Today I took the nine o'clock (the last one until September, I trust) for the 4k Butler. Butler doesn't go nearly as well as usual this year. The special Can. lit. group will quit after one more session, and the 12 o'clock remains my pride and joy. I'm also doing Butler for 3c, and that doesn't help matters. In any case I've broken the back of my last eleven-hour week. Today I got Butler finished in 3c, & yesterday I wound up fourth year. I played it down because the lecture was bad. This afternoon Mrs. Kirkwood came over with the 4k exam & I went over to Douglas Grant's for the 3c. Douglas took us in to tea & Mrs. K[irkwood] & Theall & George Falle talked very pleasantly for quite a while, mostly about the ATE meeting. [Arthur] Barker phoned about the 3j on Monday, but the hell with that. Now for the comprehensive.

Feb. 25. [Friday]

[46] Nothing much happened in the morning: the 1i lecture was on Eliot, and not so good—all my best lecturing subjects are turning sour on me. Helen went to see her doctor about a very painful foot. She's got flat feet. In the afternoon was a tea for Jack Nicholls.[35] Small but pleasant occasion: Helen's mother & father turned up & even they had a good time. Munro Beattie was there & took us and Jay Macpherson out to a restaurant called the Candlelight on Bloor West: one of those places for Europeans recently opened & for celebrated Negroes like Eartha Kitt & Louis Armstrong.[36]

Feb. 26. [Saturday]

[47] Stayed in all day, except for doing the shopping: Helen's foot was better but still bothering her. Earl Wasserman of Johns Hopkins, whom I think I met, wrote to ask me to read a paper in his group, which is 1750–1800. He wants me to do a key paper revising all our ideas about that period.[37] That's two. I've heard from [Noelan?], & *he's* in the goddam business and wants to *sell* me an organ. Ah me. More letters of recommendation for Fred Sternfeld & (earlier) David Erdman. Staying in Canada & looking inscrutable has its disadvantages. I left the comprehensive on Gordon Wood's doorstep, and packed up without writing any of the letters I should have written.

Feb. 27. [Sunday]

[48] Caught the train all right & spent the world's dullest day on it. It was raining in Toronto, snowing in London, overcast in Detroit, & foggy in Chicago. I had a long wait in Detroit, & walked along mean streets. Planes were, as I heard, grounded, so it's as well I went by train. I read the Comedy of Errors. Sirluck met me, ensconced me in the Quadrangle Club,[38] which is fine, & then I went back to his place on Blackstone for a drink. Two drinks, very strong ones. Rumor Earle & Esther Birney have split—undoubtedly a canard. Leslie [Lesley Sirluck] more beautiful than ever, if possible, and less sharp-tongued. I'm to be left a good deal by myself, I trust.

Feb. 28. [Monday]

[49] Cecil Bald called around at 7:30 and took me over to meet some of

the English staff. Williamson, Wilt, as unbuttoned as ever, Sledd, some-
one named Tave who's read my history article,[39] a girl named Hamm, a
southerner, & others. Lunch at Quadrangle with Blair—uneventful.
Then wandered about, up to 55th & down to 63rd, came back to
Wieboldt[40] for my first job: "ratio & oratio" to graduate students at tea.
About a dozen, and *no* staff, for Bald, who took me there, promptly left.
As some of them hung around until half-past five I think they were
interested enough. Then to dinner at Bald's, where I met the
Williamsons, a very pleasant couple called Silbersteins [Silversteins],
who drove me home, a woman harpsichordist, Elder Olson and (I
think) his second wife.

Mar. 1. [Tuesday]

[50] Nothing much happened in the morning except a bit of lecture
preparing: went to lunch with Sirluck & Bald, & then went to the seminar on Pericles. My stuff was fair, but in my judgement about an even
grade B. There were some searching questions: my impression is of
earnest & habitually analytic minds. The last part of the lecture, on
romantic narrative, was pretty scrambled. Then a cocktail party at
Blair's for the English department. I went out with the Olsons, Sirlucks
& Silversteins to dinner at the Q.C. [Quadrangle Club], then to
Silversteins['] afterwards. He's quite the liveliest mind I've met in this
English Department.

Mar. 2. [Wednesday]

[51] Quiet morning; a beautiful day. Wandered about, went up to the
Fountain of Time at the West end of the Midway, which I still quite
like,[41] dropped in to the Harper Library & wrote out the notes for my
lecture, went to the Q.C. for lunch, where I talked to a man in Chinese
who said the Communists have spent a lot of money vilifying Chiang
Kai Shek, drifted over to Bald's office at 3:30, went in to tea, & gave my
lecture to about 80 or 90 people in a small theatre (Social Science 122). I
tried my system of notes on filing cards (about 16 for a 50 minute lecture)
and it seemed to work fairly well. I yelled too loud, I think, & too
monotonously. Vera [Frye], Dad & Esta [Aldrich] were all at the lecture:
then we went to [Cate's?] for cocktails, meeting Betty & Larry, & then out
to dinner nearby.

Mar. 3. [Thursday]

[52] Relaxed in the morning, and went over to Charlie Bell's for lunch. Extremely pleasant, Danny[42] a sensible looking girl, and about what I expected in fact. Two little girls, Carol [Carola] & Sandra. I got the impression that Danny would prefer boys. Charles tells me Rodney [Baine] is now head of English at Mississippi State Teachers College, Cleveland, Miss. Charles is still very isolated from the department—no one knows him, & college & division are evidently sharply separated.[43] Charles seems a natural lone wolf. Then I went to Evergreen Park in a hail storm and had dinner with Vera & Dad, the Ricketts, & the Holts (they seem to be reconciled) coming over in the evening. Driven home by Ricketts.

Mar. 4. [Friday]

[53] Elder Olson came to take me to lunch at the Q.C. [Quadrangle Club]. Not so much—he hasn't read my stuff nor I his—& it was largely a matter of feeling that we were both relatively honest & respectable. Then I got downtown, dropped briefly into the Art Institute, but couldn't find stores—I can't make much sense of Chicago. The evening I went over to Lesley Sirluck's for a drink & met a couple called Cushing & Margaret Smith. Then we went to the "Revels," the skit the faculty puts on at their own expense. The theme was slum clearance, an electronic bulldozer, the operator (who was Kimpton) going berserk & destroying the university, which then moved out to Utopia, Texas. Some good songs. Dancing I didn't stay for.

Mar. 5. [Saturday]

[54] Waited for Vera to collect me, & we drove out to Evergreen Park, where she gave me a chicken-pie dinner. Then she started early to drive me out to Evanston, a long dreary ride through Chicago's back streets. Dick & Mary [Ellmann] look wonderful; they have two kids, a boy & a girl (Stephen & Esther) besides their irrepressible Pierre. People called (I think) the [Hayforths?] were for dinner, & miscellaneous people, mostly English of course, for the evening. Somebody brought along that record "The Investigator," & I emerged as a central figure of interest because I came from the country that produced it.[44] Drank too much & too fast.

Vera called for me & I drove home along the waterfront, a very pleasant ride.

Mar. 6. [Sunday]

[55] Hung over & with no breakfast served at the Q.C. [Quadrangle Club], but got a taxi to the station & stood around getting a headache. However, the train was on time & I filled up on coffee. The train—I mean my car—was full of senior officers discussing approaching exercises & manoeuvres at Detroit. The usual dull wait in Detroit, very cold day. My mental processes were badly deranged by hangover, loss of sleep & routine, so I could hardly do anything but buy a crossword puzzle book & work cryptograms. The train was on time up to Galt, so sat in a cow pasture & meditated until it was time to be late again. Got home at midnight. Helen had had a busy but apparently sociable & pleasant week.

Mar. 7. [Monday]

[56] Got out to get my mail, but there wasn't so much. The [Raising?] Committee has certainly been busy, as Woodhouse is on it. My 3b had "style & thought" changed to "thought & style" in his handwriting. I blew my top over the Department of Education's refusing to prescribe *The Red Badge of Courage* through "objections," & wrote an angry letter. Lecture by Boase on the pre-Raphaelites, beautifully organized. Talked to Mary Campbell who quite approved of my letter. Helen said the Armstrong lecture was good[45] & the Senior Dinner excellent—at least [A.B.B.] Moore was,[46] but now Moore's been laid out again with a cold. Jean Elder is looking for a new house & thinking of changing her job to Forest Hill.

Mar. 8. [Tuesday]

[57] Dug myself out for my special group at ten but nobody came but Allen Bentley, Jay [Macpherson], & May Leslie. However, they got a better lecture on Ethel Wilson's *Equations of Love*, for once, than the twelve o'clock people did. Margaret Prang keeps coming regularly. [Robert] MacDougall came over to set a supplemental Can. lit. paper. Not much chance of its ever being written. The graduate group went

fairly well, on spectacular & mimetic drama & a certain amount of my *Pericles* stuff. I left it early & went down with Helen to a cocktail party for Boase of Magdalen at Oxford Press. Martin Baldwin surprisingly friendly. Then to Angelo's for a spaghetti supper, & to Chinatown to buy soup service plates. Drank too much & slept very badly as usual.

Mar. 9. [Wednesday]

[58] Got up badly hung over and staggered down at ten to meet Boase, whom I'd asked over to see Victoria. He's an astonishingly lively person, picked out our staircase as our most interesting feature, looked over our Goetzs (actually I never knew the damn crucifixion in the chapel was a Goetz), was evidently less interested in the Students' Union, & went over to the Museum. I had an eleven on the Waste Land & a 3c at two on Huxley, both fair. Seminar with Boase again, mainly on Turner, partly on [John] Martin, Fuseli, Blake & Denby. Sherry in Norman's [Norman Endicott's] office afterwards. Then dinner at Hart House for rehearsal of tomorrow's jack with Carl Williams & a man named Schrader.

Mar. 10, 11, 12, 13. [Thursday–Sunday]

[59] The only lecture today was the twelve o'clock on Huxley and Franklin. I'm getting more reconciled to that 3c lot. At lunch I gave Archie [Hare] half a dozen words for his puzzle—I mention this because my sense of harassed pressure is all in my eye. At four o'clock I went over to 48 U.C. [University College] for F.W. Bateson's seminar in Wordsworth. He's a funny gnomelike little man looking a little like the late B.K. Sandwell, but with a very bad delivery. I got very little of the talk, went with Helen to dinner & got up to the Unitarian Church on the nose. The "panel discussion" seemed to go very well, though my own distinction between the informative & the educational, interest & concentration, stimulus & habit, certainly applies to things like panel discussions. (It was supposed to be on democracy & mass media.) Jay Macpherson was there, and we took her home with us afterwards. Today I got through some Eliot—a bright class that first year—& went to lunch in the Students' Union, given by Kay, for Bateson. Kay did the honors very well, but Bateson seems bored by everything, just as Boase was interested in everything. Another seminar, on Blake, put me behind a large eight ball, as obviously nobody would speak until I did, & what I

had to do was tell him he'd completely missed Blake by inventing a "private symbolism" for him. I'm sure we're wrong to bring staff in. Then I went to dinner with him at Hart House, and on to a meeting of the Graduate Club at which he talked about "the novel's original sin." The novel's original sin is that novels bore Bateson. Ho hum. Paton is here as a guest of philosophy & was introduced to Bateson: the point is that both are at Corpus, but P. is a fellow and B. isn't. Sounds like a bit of a masochist, an Oxonian Leavis. Anne Bolgan drove me home & talked about her prospects. Today I went down to help Douglas Duncan & Helen hang the new Victoria show, a loan exhibition from Charles Band.[47] Douglas has disc trouble, so I heaved the pictures around, & then we had a very late lunch. Douglas was unusually outspoken about the local art situation. Evidently the directors of the Art Gallery say there's no money to buy pictures when they happen to want those pictures themselves. He misses J.S. Maclean, the only collector he's been advising who had a taste of his own. We got home for dinner but the rest of the day was a bit shot, and today too I didn't seem to get very much done. It's a harassing busy time: it isn't really all in my eye. I'm getting a bit hysterical over the number of visitors, & I think we should cut down, out of protest if for nothing else.

Mar. 14. [Monday]

[60] This was the day I thought was going to be a "free" day. A pile of graduate fellowship applications arrived from Shook and I'd just got through them when I had to go over to lunch to meet a Rockefeller commissioner who was inquiring about F.R. Scott's Kingston affair.[48] I didn't realize it still had to be sold. So I said it was an experiment that ought to be tried, & he seemed satisfied. In the evening [Lester] Pearson came to speak to the Alumni. I got asked because Helen had set up the picture exhibition & because I could play the College song. Big crowd & I talked to a lot of people, but very dull & Pearson said bugger-all. Adlai Stevenson woulda said something.

Mar. 15 and 16. [Tuesday and Wednesday]

[61] A good day, on the whole, because I felt I was on the bit all day, full of ideas & expressing them properly, & I can be very happy when I'm doing that with no feeling of wasted time. The twelve o'clock was on

Morley Callaghan's book, about which I put up a pretty good line, about tragedy being a rare form that needed either heroism or innocence & that Peggy's [Peggy] Sanderson's innocence made her story tragic.[49] The graduate group was pretty good too: my stuff on comedy hasn't run out yet. Then at two o'clock Allan Anderson & an assistant came along & set up a tape recorder and shoved it into my puss & said talk & relax. Well, of course I only talked, but I didn't talk so badly. My opinion of the younger generation. I said their attitude, if one could define an attitude in it, made sense enough to me. I said they had no faith in any external society better than their own, and were trying for detachment rather than conversion or revolt. Anderson seemed considerably impressed, but as Helen says he always has been by me. Today I talked about Eliot to first year and about Wordsworth to third year. I wanted to hear Paton, but through indolence I didn't get across the park.

Mar. 17. [Thursday]

[62] Today there was only the twelve o'clock on Shelley, and I got through *that* all right. In the evening we went over to the Knoxes for dinner, and the Sirlucks were there, in advance of my bread & butter letter to them. Ernest talks very well, if still loudly, and I wish I could be as fluent on financial matters: saying government bonds were good because they finance deficit operations that don't create a market—I'm easily impressed by that sort of thing. In the afternoon Surerus & Cousland & Peggy Ray & I discussed library policy at great length.

Mar. 18. [Friday]

[63] This morning I went down to talk about Lampman, who came off all right, and then I decided that if I were ever going to get to see the Dutch show at the Art Gallery this was the time. So I met Helen there & we looked over it. Helen was nearly driven crazy by her old association with the place & by being constantly harried & closed about by lecturers, including Isabelle. I didn't like the feel of the place much either. So we came home quickly and had supper, & then I went on to Ryerson House to talk to some very bright boys about Finnegans Wake. That kind of thing is university teaching at its best, & it happens far too seldom.

Mar. 19 and 20. [Saturday and Sunday]

[64] Today I holed up & really tried to get some writing done. So not much "happened." Helen was busy painting the attic floor, & I addressed myself to the third essay, which promptly began to fold up like a pup tent. That is, there's of course a lot of work to do on it yet, but I'm laying out a pretty solid draft. The first part, on initiatives, is about in rough shape, what I call the "smooth yellow" stage; then there follows my drama article, my fiction article,[50] the stuff on prose rhetoric, and a conclusion taken mainly from my Myth as Information article,[51] which stands up surprisingly well. I got also the yellow part of two in white (except for the conclusion) and a fair smooth yellow draft of Four, down to the mythoi. At present I've decided to put the section on specific forms of lyric and the zodiac in a couple of appendixes. That, of course, only simplifies my problem on the postponing-the-visit-to-the-dentist principle, but still I get a terrific lift out of seeing all the parts come together, so that as far as I can see there's no really unknown territory left. What I shall do now is make a frontal assault on the mythoi, & that will bring the whole structure into focus. I'm really beginning to feel that I might soon be rid of it.

Mar. 21. [Monday and Tuesday]

[65] Went down earlyish & finished reading Two Solitudes, a last-minute piece of plugging I'm rather ashamed of. Lunch with a self-appointed committee on the organ: Carscallen, Francis, Bert Arnold, Jessie & I.[52] Uneventful: naturally, I'm stuck with the report. In the afternoon I went over to hear Harbage's first Alexander lecture.[53] He promises to be one of our most popular people: nothing in it except a certain amount of elementary common sense, but beautiful timing in jokes and a genial way with various Aunt Sallies. Stayed out for drinks and dinner.

Mar. 22. [Wednesday]

[66] Last lecture in Canadian literature at twelve, on Two Solitudes. Not my best work: I seem to be deliberately throwing away my last lectures this year. Harbage was on again in the afternoon, still simple-minded, but still carrying most of his audience. I noticed Eric Gill saying he

agreed. He came out for a fluid plain stage with minimal action inner &
upper—as he says, Granville Barker knew it all thirty years ago.[54] Went
out for dinner with Mary Campbell at the Candlelight (not too good:
shan't go back) & then on to the A.T.E. meeting, where Laurette Riese & I
were doing the speeches. Laure [Rièse] gave a very competent survey of
French Canadian poetry.

Appendix 1
Directory of People Mentioned in the Diaries

NOTE: Page numbers for directory entrants, as well as their life dates, where available, have been included in the index to the present volume. The absence of a death date for a given entrant does not necessarily mean that the individual was still living at the time of publication of the volume, but only that the date of death could not be ascertained.

Abrams, M.H. (Mike). Member of the English department at Cornell University.

Adam, Adolphe. French composer of operas, ballet, and choral and church music.

Adams, David. First principal male dancer of the National Ballet of Canada.

Adams, (Douglas) Ernest. Canadian baritone.

Adaskin, Murray. Orchestral and chamber musician; became head of music at USk in 1952; conductor of Saskatoon Symphony Orchestra, 1957–60.

Adeney, Marcus. Well-known cellist; member of faculty of music, U of T; played for the TSO from 1928 to 1948 and taught for thirty-five years at the RCMT.

Alabaster, William. English divine and poet.

Alderson, Gordon. Teacher at the Eastern High School of Commerce, Toronto.

Aldrich, Esta. Friend and housemate of Vera Frye.

Alexander, Henry. Head of the English department at Queen's University; became the first president of the Canadian Linguistic Association in 1954; elected as a fellow of the Royal Society of Canada in 1948.

Alford, (Edward) John Gregory. Professor of fine arts, U of T, in the 1930s and 1940s; later taught at the Rhode Island School of Design.

Allan, Innes M. VC, 5T2.

Allen, Don Cameron. Professor of English at Johns Hopkins University; specialist in Renaissance literature.

Allen, Margaret. VC, 5T1; member of NF's 1951 graduate course in allegory; later, Margaret J. Ritchie.

Anderson, Allan. Produced freelance public affairs documentaries for CBC
  Radio.
Anderson, Fulton Henry (Andy). Head of the philosophy department at U of T
  and a member of the department of ethics at UC.
Anderson, William. VC, 5T2.
Andrew, Richard William. VC, 5T2; member of the VC Union Executive.
Anfiteatroff, Massimo. Cellist with the Italian ensemble Virtuosi di Roma.
Arne, Thomas Augustine. English composer of operas, other stage works, and
  songs.
Arnett, Norma. VC, 4T9.
Arnold, Joan. Daughter of Robert and Magda Arnold.
Arnold, Magda. Wife of Robert K. (Bert) Arnold; wrote a series of books on
  emotion, personality, and motivation.
Arnold, Richard C.A. (Ricky). VC, 5T4.
Arnold, Robert Karl (Bert). Member of the German department at VC; husband
  of Magda Arnold.
Arnott, Barbara. Hope Arnott's twin sister.
Arnott, Hope. VC, 5T1; later, Hope Arnott Lee.
Arnup, John D. (Johnny). VC, 3T2; the Fryes' lawyer; later, member of the
  senate, U of T, 1945–50, and member of the board of regents, VU, 1960–70.
Arthos, John. Professor of English at University of Michigan.
Arthur, Paul. Toronto graphic artist and typographic designer; editor of the
  short-lived literary magazine *Here & Now.*
Auld, Frederick Clyde. Attorney; joined the staff of the department of law,
  U of T, in 1929, and later became professor of Roman law.
Avison, Margaret. VC, 4T0; friend of NF: they often met over lunch to discuss
  her poetry in the 1940s and 1950s; M.A., U of T, 1964; became a well-known
  Canadian poet.
Ayres, Harold. Artist friend of HKF's family.

Babbitt, Thomas Parlee. Mayor of Moncton, N.B., 1950–52; later, provincial
  minister of municipal affairs; killed in a plane crash at age 41 in 1957.
Bailey, Arnold T. VC, 5T5.
Baine, Alice. Wife of Rodney Baine.
Baine, Rodney Montgomery. Rhodes scholar at Merton College, 1936–39; B.A.,
  Southwestern at Memphis; B.A. in English, Oxford, 1938; B.Litt., 1939; taught
  at Mississippi State Teachers College, MIT, and the universities of Missouri,
  Richmond, and Georgia.
Baker, Eleanor. Public school teacher in Toronto.
Bald, Robert Cecil. Professor of English, University of Chicago; authority on
  Donne; lectured at U of T in 1950.
Balding, C.D. Mining-engineer consultant; employer of Beth Jenking.

Baldwin, Martin. Director of the AGT.

Band, Charles S. Member of the council of the AGT and chair of the educational committee of the gallery.

Banting, Sir Frederick G. U of T medical researcher who in 1921, along with his assistant Charles H. Best, isolated insulin; received the Nobel Prize for chemistry in 1923.

Barbeau, Charles Marius. Ethnologist; founder of professional folklore studies in Canada.

Barker, Arthur. Member of the English faculty at TC; moved to the University of Illinois as a research professor in 1961; later returned to Canada to teach at UWO.

Barker, Belva. VC, 4T9; enrolled at VC after serving in the Royal Canadian Air Force and finished her course in three years.

Barlow, Joel. American poet and politician; Blake was indebted to his *Vision of Columbus: A Poem in Nine Books* (1787).

Barth, Karl. Swiss Protestant theologian.

Bartlett, Arthur R. Teacher at the RCMT.

Bates, John. VC, 3T3, EC, 3T6; brother of Bob Bates.

Bates, Maxwell. Canadian artist, architect, and author; was part of the Calgary Group of artists formed in 1947 by J.W.G. Macdonald and others.

Bates, Robert Philip (Bob). VC, 3T3, EC, 3T6; brother of John Bates.

Bates, Ronald Gordon Nudell. One of NF's students; completed a dissertation on Joyce under NF's supervision (Ph.D., U of T, 1960), went on to teach at UWO, and later wrote a monograph on NF in the Canadian Writers series.

Bateson, F.W. University lecturer, fellow, and tutor in English, Oxford University, 1946–60; founding editor of *Essays in Criticism*.

Baxter, John S. Graduate student in English, U of T, 1949–51; taught at UC, 1952–54; Ph.D., U of T, 1963; taught at Queen's University.

Bayefsky, Aba. Canadian watercolourist, oil painter, muralist, and teacher whose work concentrated on the human figure.

Baynton, Barbara. Australian short story writer.

Beattie, Alexander Munro. VC, 3T3; taught for his entire career at Carleton University in Ottawa.

Beattie, George. One of NF's pub companions in the 1940s; worked in public relations; helped to publicize FS through various news services.

Beckjord, Eric S. B.A., Harvard College, 1951; became a nuclear physicist.

Beharriell, (Stanley) Ross. VC, 4T4; he and his wife Patricia met NF when Beharriell was completing his M.A. requirements at Toronto in 1948; Ph.D., Wisconsin, 1954; taught at Wabash College and Niagara University; returned to Canada in 1958 to teach at the Royal Military College, Kingston.

Bell, Andrew James. UC, class of 1878; long-time professor of Latin at VC and of comparative philology at U of T.

Bell, Charles Greenleaf. Rhodes Scholar from Mississippi; Exeter College, 1936–39; B.A., University of Virginia; B.A. in English, Oxford, 1938; B.Litt., Oxford, 1939; traveled with NF through Italy in 1937; assistant professor of humanities, University of Chicago, 1949–56.

Bell, Graydon. VC, 5T1.

Bell, Leslie Richard. Choir conductor and arranger; founded the Leslie Bell Singers, a women's choir, in 1939.

Bennett, Ethel. Wife of Harold Bennett.

Bennett, Harold. Professor of Latin, VC; appointed dean of VC in 1944; acting president and dean, 1949–51; principal of VC from 1951 until NF assumed that post in 1959.

Bentley, Allen B. VC, 5T5.

Bentley, John Albert. Professor of English, USk, 1925–60; music critic for the *Saskatoon Star-Phoenix*.

Beny, Roloff. An abstract expressionist Canadian painter; later took up photography and moved to Rome.

Bernanos, Georges. Catholic novelist and polemicist.

Bernhardt, Karl. VC, 2T6; member of the U of T psychology department and on the staff of the Institute of Child Study at U of T; author of *Basic Principles of Pre-School Education* (1942), published by the Institute for Child Study at the U of T.

Berton, Pierre. Well-known Canadian journalist, historian, and media personality; wrote for *Maclean's* magazine, 1947–58.

Best, Sandy. Eldest son of Charles Best, co-discoverer of insulin; as a student, a member of the Hart House art committee.

Bevan, Allan. Ph.D., U of T, 1953; wrote his dissertation on *Dryden as a Dramatic Artist* under the direction of W.B. Douglas Grant; taught at Dalhousie University until his death in 1983.

Beynon, Josephine (Jodine). VC, 4T4; studied *The Golden Bough* with NF in a noncredit course, enrolled in NF's first graduate course in Blake (1946–47), and then became a secondary-school teacher of literature; later, Josephine Boos.

Bice, Clare. Canadian graphic artist and illustrator.

Bickersteth, John Burgon. Warden of Hart House, U of T, 1921–47.

Biggs, E(dward) Power. English-born concert organist and editor of organ music.

Bigio. See Franciabigio.

Birchard, May. Six-term Toronto alderman (1946, 1957–60, 1964); worked on behalf of the aged and needy; an inveterate writer of letters to newspapers; executive of the Rosedale Liberal Association; retired from politics following her defeat in the 1964 alderman election.

Birney, Earle. Canadian poet known for his experimental verse; teacher, novelist, playwright, and editor; taught at UC, 1936–46, and then at UBC until his retirement in 1963.

Birney, Esther. Wife of Earle Birney.

Birtch, George. VC, 3T3; EC, 3T6; a UCC minister who held pastorates in London, Ont., and elsewhere.

Birtch, Mary. George Birtch's wife.

Bissell, Claude T. Member of the English department at UC, 1941–56; president of U of T, 1958–71.

Blackmur, Richard P. American poet and critic; taught at Princeton, 1948–65.

Blair, Walter. Member of the English department, University of Chicago.

Blanshard, Brand. American rationalist philosopher.

Blatz, William E. Professor of psychology and director of the Institute of Child Study, U of T.

Bledsoe, Tom. NF's editor for the Holt, Rinehart and Winston edition of Milton's *"Paradise Lost" and Selected Poetry and Prose* (1951).

Blewett, Constance (Connie). VC, 3T6; assistant to the registrar at VC.

Blissett, William. Member of the English department, UC, 1948–50; Ph.D., U of T, 1950; taught at USk and at Huron College, UWO, and returned to UC in 1965.

Bloch, Ernest. Swiss-born American composer.

Bloore, Ronald L. Canadian painter and organizer of progressive exhibitions; in 1949 he was studying at U of T, where he was a member of the Hart House art committee.

Blunden, Edmund. NF's tutor at Oxford, 1936–37, 1938–39; poet and critic.

Boase, Thomas Sherrer Ross. British art historian.

Bochner, Lloyd. Actor for radio and the New Play Society; his wife, Ruth (née Roher), was a pianist.

Bodle, (George Talbot) Douglas. Organist, harpsichordist, pianist; began teaching keyboard at the RCMT in 1957; joined the Faculty of Music, U of T, in 1969.

Boeschenstein, Hermann. Professor of German at UC.

Boissonneau, Arthur N. B.S. in forestry, U of T, 4T3.

Bolgan, Anne C. Reader in English, VC, 1951–52; one of NF's Ph.D. students; did a dissertation on T.S. Eliot, supervised by NF (Ph.D., U of T, 1960); taught at the University of Alaska (1959–64) and then at UWO.

Bomberger, Madeline. VC, 4T9.

Bombois, Camille. French primitive painter.

Bond, Marie. VC, 4T8; OCE, 1949; she and her husband, Kenneth S. Gardner, VC, 4T8, taught in the Ont. secondary school system until their retirement.

Bondy, Fr. Louis J. Superior of the Basilians and professor of French at SMC; was instrumental in getting Marshall McLuhan to join the English faculty at SMC.

Bonnycastle, Murray. Canadian painter and watercolourist; studied at OCA, 1928–31; also a poet, who published his work in the *Canadian Forum*, among other places.

Böszörmenyi-Nagy, Béla. Hungarian-born pianist; taught at the TCM (after 1947, the RCMT).

Boulton, Mary. HKF's aunt on her father's side; sister of Charlotte Boulton Cronin.

Bower, Frances. VC, 4T2.

Bowles, Richard P. (Dick). VC, 5T0.

Bowman, Archibald Allan. Professor of moral philosophy, University of Glasgow; in 1934, delivered the Vanuxem lectures at Princeton, where he taught from 1912 to 1926.

Bowman, Walter P(arker). Member of the English department at Western Reserve University; taught at Flora Stone Mather College (the women's college at Western Reserve) and in the graduate school, 1947–50.

Boyce, Benjamin. Ph.D., Harvard, 1933; specialist in seventeenth- and eighteenth-century literature; head of the department at Duke University.

Boyce, William. English composer and organist.

Boyd, Josephine. VC, 5T3.

Boyd, Sophie. Member of the staff of the School of Social Work, U of T.

Bradley, F.H. Welsh idealist philosopher; became a fellow at Merton College in 1924.

Brady, Alexander. Professor of political science, U of T; associate editor of the *University of Toronto Quarterly*.

Brailey, F.W.L. Member of the Commission on Culture of the UCC and UCC minister.

Brandt, Art. VC, 3T2.

Brandtner, Fritz. Modernist Canadian painter; credited with having introduced German expressionism to Canada.

Branscombe, John. Born in Moncton, N.B.; B.Th., Acadia University, 1949; attended Southern Baptist Seminary, Louisville, Ky.; ordained Baptist minister who served pastorates in N.S., Ont., and N.B.

Brant, Joseph. Mohawk war chief, Loyalist, and statesman.

Bredvold, Louis I(gnatius). Professor of English, University of Michigan.

Breen, Mel. Student at UC; contemporary of Don Harron; had been a prominent amateur actor even before he reached college; eventually became a journalist, but died quite suddenly in his mid-thirties.

Breithaupt, Edna. Artist; formed the Toronto Art Students' League after Arthur Lismer resigned from OCA.

Breithaupt, Louis Orville. Lieutenant governor of Ont., 1952–57; appointed chancellor of VU in 1959.

Brett, George S. Professor of philosophy, chair of the philosophy department at

UC, and dean of the Graduate School at U of T; conceived the course in philosophy, English, and history at U of T, modeling it on the Oxford Modern Greats.

Brett, Gerard. Became director of the ROM in 1948; husband of Beatrice (Betty) Brett.

Brett, Katherine Beatrice (Betty). Director of the textile department at the ROM; wife of Gerard Brett.

Brewing, Willard. Minister of St. George's United Church in Toronto; served as moderator of the UCC, 1948–50; began his ecclesiastical career in Philadelphia with the Reformed Episcopal Church; joined the UCC in 1929 and accepted a pastoral charge in Vancouver.

Brieger, Barbara. Wife of Peter Brieger.

Brieger, Peter. Lecturer in fine arts, U of T.

Bright, James Robert Alexander. VC, 3To.

Britnell, George E. Ph.D., U of T, 1938; head of the department of economics and political science at USk.

Brittain, Miller G. New Brunswick painter known for his bleak Depression pictures, his treatment of Biblical themes, and, after World War II, his surrealistic techniques.

Britten, Benjamin. English composer, pianist, and conductor.

Broad, C.D. English philosopher.

Brooker, Bertram. Painter, writer, illustrator, music critic, advertising executive; was an active member of Toronto's cultural and intellectual life; his exhibition at the Arts and Letters Club in February 1927 was the first show of abstract art in Canada; had no formal art training.

Brooks, Cleanth. Professor of English at Louisiana State and Yale Universities; became one of the influential New Critics.

Brooks, Gordon. VC, 4T7; graduate student in English at U of T, 1949–50.

Brooks, Van Wyck. American biographer and cultural critic.

Broun, Heywood. American newspaper columnist and critic.

Brown, Alan. VC, 4T8.

Brown, Audrey Alexandra. Canadian poet; author of a half-dozen volumes of verse; first woman writer to receive the Lorne Pierce medal for literary achievement.

Brown, E(dward) K. Member of the English department at University of Manitoba, 1935–37, UC, 1929–35, 1937–41, Cornell, 1941–44, and University of Chicago, 1944–51.

Brown, Elizabeth Eedy. Classmate of NF and HKF; married NF on 27 July 1988.

Brown, George W. Professor of history at U of T and editor of the University of Toronto Press.

Brown, James E. Lawyer from Brantford, Ont.; elected to Parliament in 1953; married Elizabeth Eedy, who later became NF's second wife.

Brown, Kathleen (Kay). VC, 5To; member of the writers' group at VC; became a
   journalist and editor.
Brown, Maud. Walter T. Brown's wife.
Brown, Pegi. VC, 4T8.
Brown, Walter T. Professor of philosophy, VC, 1912–28, and Yale, 1928–32;
   principal of VC, 1932–41; president of VC, 1941–49.
Brown, William J. Vice-principal of Northern Vocational School.
Bruchovsky, Olga. VC, 5T3.
Brunner, Emil. Swiss Protestant theologian.
Buchan, John, 1st Baron Tweedsmuir. Prolific writer of fiction and history;
   Governor General of Canada, 1935–40.
Bucke, Richard Maurice. Canadian psychiatrist; his popular *Cosmic Conscious-
   ness* (1901) speculated about an imminent psychic revolution.
Buckley, Jerome H. (Jerry). VC, 3T9; member of the English department at the
   University of Wisconsin, 1942–54; later, professor of English at Harvard.
Burgener, Richard J.C. (Dick). Ph.D. in philosophy, U of T; friend of Ted Saw-
   yer; founding chair of the department of philosophy, University of Waterloo,
   where he taught from 1961 to 1965, when he took a disability leave.
Burke, Kenneth. American literary critic, best known for his theory of literary
   forms and his studies of rhetoric, history, and philosophy.
Burwash, Nathanael. President and chancellor, VU, 1887–1913.
Burwell, Willard Beverley (Bev). VC, 3T9; M.A., University of London, 1952;
   S.T.B., TC, 6To; served in the diocese of Toronto, becoming rector of St.
   Alban's in 1963; one-time secretary of Hart House, U of T.
Bush, Douglas. Teaching fellow at U of T, 1920–21; M.A., U of T, 1921; Ph.D.,
   Harvard; professor of English at Harvard, beginning in 1936.
Bush, Geoffrey. Son of Douglas Bush; gave up an academic career to become a
   newspaper film critic; also wrote plays for small theatre groups.
Butler, Joseph. English bishop and theologian; his best-known work is *Analogy
   of Religion* (1736).

Caesar, Cameron Hull (Cam). VC, 3T3; did postgraduate work at the University
   of London in 1935–36, when HKF was studying at the Courtauld Institute;
   worked for Standard Oil as a chemist.
Calendino, M. Graduate student in English at U of T, 1949–50.
Callaghan, Morley. Novelist, short story writer, and playwright; began his
   career as a newspaper reporter and was admitted to the Ont. Bar in 1928, but
   from 1929 on he devoted himself to his writing.
Cameron, Ethel. Friend of HKF's mother, Gertrude Kemp; they often
   vacationed together at Gordon Bay, where the Kemps had a cottage.
Cameron, Jean Elizabeth. VC, 3T3.
Cameron, Mary Louise Clarke. VC, 4T1; sister of Dorothy Clarke Hay.

Cameron, M.G. Peter. Husband of Mary Louise Clarke Cameron; a physician at
the Christie Street Hospital, Toronto, following World War II, and later
resident physician at St. Michael's Hospital, Toronto.

Campbell, Mary A. Taught secondary English at Parkdale Collegiate Institute,
Toronto, where she was department head; later chaired the English section of
the joint U of T-Toronto Board of Education committee on which NF served.

Capling, Mabel M. Alto with the Toronto Mendelssohn Choir.

Card, Catharine. VC, 5T1; a member of the writers' group at VC and close
friend of Jean Inglis; associate editor of *Acta Victoriana*, 1949–50.

Carnwath, Anne F. VC, 5T3; a member of the writers' group at VC.

Carpenter, Edmund. Member of the anthropology department, U of T; with
Marshall McLuhan, a colleague and lifelong friend, edited Canada's first
postmodern literary magazine, *Explorations* (1953–59).

Carr, Patricia (Pat). Ph.D. student, U of T; received her degree in 1961, having
written a dissertation on Pope under the supervision of Kenneth MacLean.

Cassidy, Eugene. Born in Japan of missionary parents; attended UBC; returned
to Japan in 1930, where he taught and became interested in photography;
returned to Canada in 1938 and eventually became a successful contract
photographer in New York City.

Cassidy, Harry M. Social reformer and head of the School of Social Work.

Casson, A.J. Canadian painter and watercolourist; began his career as an
apprentice at the commercial art firm of Franklin Carmichael, who took him
sketching and introduced him to the other members of the Group of Seven.

Catto, Charles R. VC, 5T1.

Cavell, H. Elmer. Public school inspector for the Toronto Board of Education.

Chalmers, Randolph Carleton. Professor of systematic theology at St. Andrew's
College, Saskatoon, Sask.; later taught systematic theology and philosophy of
religion at Pine Hill Divinity Hall, Halifax, N.S.; secretary of the Commission
on Culture, UCC.

Chambers, Sir E.K. English scholar and critic; knighted in 1925.

Chapman, Christopher. Canadian film director; achieved success with his first
short film, *The Seasons*.

Chapman, Francis S. VC, 5To. Graduate student in English, U of T, 1950–52.

Child, Philip Albert Gillette. Chancellor's professor of English at TC, 1923–26,
1941–64.

Chisholm, Brock. Canadian psychiatrist and medical administrator; helped
draft the constitution for and became the first director-general of the World
Health Organization.

Chittick, Victor Lovitt Oscar. Along with his wife Edna, became friends with
the Fryes during the summer of 1951 when NF taught at the University of
Washington; taught English at Reed College for twenty-seven years and was
visiting professor at the University of Washington, 1948–49.

Christie, Robert. Author; wrote for the *Calgary Albertan*; script writer in Hollywood.

Christmas, Eric. Canadian thespian and film maker; spent ten years of his early
career at the Stratford Shakespeare Festival, Stratford, Ont.; became a successful filmographer and actor in the U.S.

Ciardi, John. American poet, critic, and translator.

Clark, Alexander Frederick Bruce. Professor of French, U.B.C., 1918–49; became
a member of the editorial board of the *Canadian Forum* in August 1952.

Clark, John Abbott. Member of the English department, Michigan State University, 1928–65.

Clark, June. VC, 4T9.

Clark, Paraskeva. Russian artist who came to Toronto in 1931; worked for René
Cera at Eaton's College Street in Toronto.

Clark, Philip T. Treasurer of Ont., husband of Paraskeva Clark, and part of the
circle that included leading artists, writers, and musicians of the time in Toronto.

Clark, Samuel Delbert. Canadian sociologist; professor of political economy at
U of T.

Clarke, Irene. One of the founders of Clarke, Irwin and Company, a book
publishing house; wife of William Henry Clarke; graduate of VC.

Clarke, William Henry (Bill). President of Clarke, Irwin and Company, a book
publishing house he and his wife Irene founded in 1930; graduate of VC;
manager of the Canadian Oxford University Press, 1936–49.

Clawson, William Hall. Member of the department of English at UC, 1907–50.

Coburn, Caroll Langford. Kathleen Coburn's brother.

Coburn, Frank Emerson. Kathleen Coburn's brother.

Coburn, John Wesley (Wes). Kathleen Coburn's brother.

Coburn, Kathleen (Kay). NF's colleague in the English department at VC;
became a distinguished Coleridge scholar.

Code, Muriel. VC, 3T3.

Code, Winifred Horwood. VC, 3T4.

Cody, Canon Henry John. Canadian clergyman and educator; president of
U of T, 1932–44; chancellor, 1944–47.

Cohen, Jacob Lawrence. Influential Canadian labour lawyer.

Coldwell, Major James William. Member of Parliament from Sask. and one of
the founders of the CCF, later NDP.

Cole, Desmond W. Graduate student in English, U of T, 1949–50.

Coleman, Elliott. American poet; taught at Johns Hopkins University.

Coles, Donald. VC, 4T9; one of the editors of *Acta Victoriana* in 1948–49; M.A. in
English, U of T, 1952, studied at Cambridge, and returned to Canada after a
decade abroad; began teaching at York University in 1965.

Coles, Stuart. Minister of Knox Presbyterian Church in Oshawa, Ont.

Colet, John. English scholar and theologian.

Colgrove, Rogers G. (Pete). VC, 3T3.

Collin, W(illiam) E(dwin). Professor of romance languages at UWO, 1925–60;
taught French Canadian literature.

Collins, Miriam. VC, 3T8; EC, 4T1.

Colonna, Vittoria. Italian poet, friend of Michelangelo, and intimate associate of
the reforming party at the papal court.

Coltham, Harriett. VC, 5T0; attended OCE and taught high school English;
later, Harriett Armson.

Colville, Alex. Canadian realistic painter; studied and taught at Mount Allison
University.

Comfort, Charles. Portrait, landscape, and mural painter; director of the department of mural painting at OCA; taught at U of T, 1938–60, after which he
became director of the NGC in Ottawa.

Comfort, Louise. Charles Comfort's wife.

Conklin, Nora. Sister of Bill Conklin, a classmate of NF at VC; studied at
Julliard School of Music; later Nora Conklin Skitch.

Constant, Danuta Landau. VC, 4T7.

Cook, Alta Lind. VC 1T3; member of the French department at VC.

Cook, Donald. VC, 2T8; president of VC alumni.

Copley, John Singleton. American portrait and historical painter.

Corbett, Edward Annand. Educator; first director of the Canadian Association
of Adult Education, 1936–51; founder of the Banff School of Fine Arts, initia-
tor of the *Citizens' Forum* radio program.

Corbett, Paul Martin. Professor of chemical ceramic engineering, U of T.

Cosgrove, Stanley M. Canadian painter who taught art in Montreal; was known
as an excellent draftsman and colourist.

Cotter, Graham. Graduate student in English at U of T; member of the English
department at UC, 1952–57, after which he left for the clergy.

Coulter, John. Canadian biographer and playwright, best known for his dramatic trilogy *Riel*.

Cousland, Kenneth. Professor of church history, EC; appointed principal of EC
in 1956.

Coutts, Eleanor. B.A., U of T, 4T7; M.A., University of Wisconsin, 1948; Ph.D.,
University of Wisconsin, 1956; reader in English, VC, 1952–53.

Cowan, Tillie. Instructor in children's art at the AGT.

Cowie, Vic. Member of NF's graduate course in Blake, 1952–53, and in literary
symbolism, 1954–55; did his M.A. thesis on W.H. Auden under NF's supervision; taught at the University of Manitoba.

Coxeter, Harold S.M. Professor of mathematics, U of T.

Cragg, Arthur Richard. VC, 3T3 and EC, 3T7; friend of NF from the time of
their student days at VC; brother of Laurence Cragg; performed the Fryes'
marriage ceremony in 1937.

Cragg, Florence (née Clare). VC, 3T3; wife of Arthur Cragg; friend of NF and
HKF from the time of their student days at VC.

Cragg, Laurence H. (Laurie). VC, 3T4; M.A., U of T, 1935; Ph.D., U of T, 1937; brother of Arthur Cragg.

Craig, Peggy (Peg). Vera Frye's roommate in Chicago; NF first met her during his 1933 visit to Chicago.

Crane, R.S. Member of the English department, University of Chicago, and a central figure among the Chicago neo-Aristotelians; Alexander lecturer at U of T for 1951–52; the following year, visiting professor in the School of Graduate Studies for one term.

Crang, James Carscellan. B. Arch., School of Architecture, U of T, 5T0.

Creighton, Alan. Corresponding editor and, later, business manager of the *Canadian Forum*; authored two books of poetry.

Creighton, Donald G. Member of the history department at U of T, 1927–70; known for the literary style he brought to the writing of Canadian history.

Creighton, Luella Sanders Bruce. Wife of Donald Creighton.

Croft, Frances. VC, 5T3.

Cronin, Catherine A. HKF's cousin on her father's side, the daughter of Patrick and Charlotte Boulton Cronin.

Cronin, Helen B. HKF's cousin on her father's side; daughter of Patrick and Charlotte Cronin.

Cronin, Margaret. HKF's cousin on her father's side; daughter of Patrick and Charlotte Cronin.

Cronin, Patrick (Pat). HKF's great uncle on her father's side; husband of Charlotte Boulton Cronin; father of nine children, including, Catherine, Helen, Margaret, and Martha.

Cronin, Sister St. Martha, I.B.V.M. HKF's cousin on her father's side; daughter of Patrick and Charlotte Cronin.

Cronyn, Hume. Canadian-born actor, screenwriter, theatre director; husband of Jessica Tandy.

Cumberland, Dorothy (née Darling). VC, 3T3; wife of Jack Cumberland.

Cumberland, John D.W. (Jack). VC, 3T2; lawyer for the Goodyear Tire and Rubber Co.; married Dorothy Darling.

Cumberlege, Geoffrey Fenwick Jocelyn. Publisher to the University of Oxford and, beginning in 1945, chair of Oxford University Press.

Cummings, Harold. Canadian businessman who worked in New York for Cadbury-Fry, the chocolate manufacturer.

Curran, Nancy. VC, 5T2.

Currelly, Charles Trick. Professor of the history of industrial art, U of T, during NF and HKF's student days; later, professor of archaeology and director of the ROM; NF edited Currelly's autobiography, *I Brought the Ages Home* (1956).

Dale, E(rnest) A(bell). Member of the Classics department at UC.

Daly, Reginald Alworth. VC, class of 1892; geologist known for his work in plate techtonics.

Daly, Thomas Cullen (Tom). Filmmaker and film producer; began working for the National Film Board in 1940.

Daniells, Roy. Poet, professor, and critic who had a long-time friendship and correspondence with NF; spent most of his teaching career at UBC; taught at VC, 1934–36.

Darte, Marion. Friend of Ray and Eleanor Godfrey from high school days; married Jack Johnson, a corporate lawyer and collector of miniature prints; their home on Bedford Park Rd. was the scene of many parties attended by the Godfreys, Fryes, McLuhans, and other Toronto literati.

Davenport, Robert (Bob). VC, 5T3.

Davey, Keith. VC, 4T9; later worked in radio and Liberal Party politics; devised a strategy for defeating the conservatives in the early 1960s; was made a senator in 1965 by Prime Minister Lester Pearson; continued to be active in Liberal Party politics through the mid-1980s.

Davies, Blodwen. Author of travel books combining local history, description, and legend; born in Que., but spent most of her adult life near Toronto; friend of the artist Yvonne McKague; contributed numerous book reviews to the *Canadian Forum*.

Davies, Gordon. Toronto artist; worked for Simpson's Photo Engravers.

Davies, James W. VC, 5T2.

Davies, Raymond Arthur. Toronto author and journalist; had a special interest in the Canadian north.

Davies, Trevor H. Minister emeritus at Timothy Eaton Memorial Church, Toronto; chair, library board, VU.

Davin, Daniel M. (Dan). New Zealander who came to Oxford as a Rhodes scholar in 1936; NF first made his acquaintance at Oxford in 1938; earned a First in Greats at Balliol College; became an editor at Oxford University Press, where he eventually served as secretary and academic publisher.

Davin, Winifred Kathleen. Wife of Daniel Davin.

Davis, Herbert J. Member of the English department at UC; when NF was at EC, he enrolled in Davis's graduate seminar in Blake; left U of T in 1938 to teach at Cornell; a distinguished Swift scholar; later became reader in bibliography at and then president of Smith College.

Davison, J.A. Visiting professor of Classics, VC, 1949–50.

Dawson, Robert MacGregor. Professor of political economy, U of T.

Day, Jessie. VC, 3T7; her sister Eleanor had been a classmate of NF and HKF; she and her husband Douglas were godparents of Hilary Whitley.

Deacon, William Arthur. Writer, critic, essayist, and syndicated reviewer for the Toronto *Globe and Mail*, 1938–60; literary editor of *Saturday Night*, 1922–28.

Dean, Helen. Employee of the Toronto Public Library.

de Beaumont, Victor. Member of the French department at VC, 1907–52.

Deichman, Kjeld and Erica. Ceramists from N.B.

Delworth, William Thomas (Tom). VC, 5T1; editor of *Acta Victoriana*, 1950–51; later became Canadian ambassador to Germany and then principal of TC.

de Montmollin, Daniel. Member of the French department at VC; later transferred to the Classics department at VC.

Dempsey, Lotta. Journalist and television host; wrote for the Toronto *Globe and Mail*; in 1952 became the editor of *Chatelaine*.

Denomy, Fr. Alexander Joseph. Professor of French and of the history of comparative literature at SMC.

DeTolnay, Charles. Art historian whose chief specialty was Renaissance painting; lectured at U of T in 1949.

DeWitt, N(orman)W(entworth). Emeritus member of the department of Classics at VC.

de Wulf, Maurice. Belgian philosopher; best known for his studies in the history of medieval philosophy.

Dickinson, William James Condy. VC, 5T0.

Dillon, Margaret (Marg). VC, 4T3; at the time of NF's 1949 Diary, was working on an M.A. in sociology at U of T and serving as a don in the VC women's residences.

Diltz, Bert Case. Faculty member at OCE who was effectively responsible for training secondary teachers of English in Ont. from 1931 to 1958; dean of OCE, U of T, 1958–63.

Dilworth, Ira. Taught English at UBC until 1938, when he became manager of radio station CBR in Vancouver; later, supervisor of CBC International Service in Montreal and then national director of CBC programming in Toronto; one of the executors of the Emily Carr Trust.

Dobrée, Bonamy. British literary critic.

Domm, Gordon. Minister at Bathurst United Church, Toronto, 1937–58; active in the temperance movement and in social outreach programs.

Dougherty, Charles T. Ph.D., U of T, 1953; wrote a dissertation on Ruskin under the direction of A.S.P. Woodhouse.

Douglas, John Ryerson Moore. VC, 5T7.

Dow, John. Professor of New Testament literature and exegesis, EC; retired 1952.

Dow, Sterling. Professor of history and Greek, Harvard University; later president of the Archaeological Institute of America.

Drainie, John Robert Roy. Versatile radio actor who began performing in the late 1930s and quickly emerged as the leading actor in the CBC *Stage* series; performed hundreds of roles in classical and Canadian drama.

Drever, Dorothy. VC, 3T3.

Drew, George Alexander. Lawyer and politician; was elected head of the Ont. Conservative party in 1938 and was premier of Ont., 1943–48; leader of the Federal Conservative Party, 1948–56.

Drugan, Bridget. VC, 5T0.

Dryer, Douglas Poole. A member of the philosophy department, U of T.

Dunbar, Helen Flanders. Physician, theologian, and author; founding editor of the journal *Psychosomatic Medicine*; known for her integration of religion and psychiatry and for her book on Dante.

Duncan, Douglas M. Toronto art dealer who in 1936 helped to found the Picture Loan Society and was responsible for the first exhibitions of Carl Schaefer, Will Ogilvie, and others; consultant on art at VC.

Dunn, Charles William (Charlie). Member of the English faculty (medievalist with specialty in Celtic studies) at UC, 1946–56; later taught at NYU and Harvard.

Dunning, R.W. U of T, 5T2.

Duplessis, Maurice Le Nobelet. Prime minister and attorney-general of Que., 1936–39 and 1944–59.

Duthie, George Ian. Professor of English at McGill University, specializing in textual editing of Shakespeare.

Dyer-Bennett, Richard. Major figure in the folk music revival of the 1950s and 1960s.

Dyke, J.T.W. (Tom). VC, 5T1.

Easterbrook, W(illiam) Thomas (Tom). Associate professor of political economy, U of T.

Eberhard, Rudy. VC, 3T4.

Eberhart, Richard. American poet; founded the Poet's Theater in Cambridge, Mass., in 1951.

Eddis, Joan. UC, 5T1; women's editor of the *Varsity*, 1949–50; became a public relations officer, columnist for the *Globe and Mail*, CBC host, and teacher of journalism at Carleton University.

Edgar, Dona. Wife of Pelham Edgar.

Edgar, Pelham. Member of the English department at VC, 1909–38; one of NF's teachers.

Edison, George. Ph.D., U of T, 1941; professor of ethics at TC.

Edmonds, Robert B. (Bob). VC, 5To

Eedy, Alice. VC, 3T9; sister of Elizabeth Eedy Brown (later Frye); became a social worker in the hospitals of B.C.; NF encouraged her early efforts to write when she was a student, and she published a number of short stories, two novels, and a poetic memoir about Toronto; later, Alice Boissonneau.

Elder, Jean. VC, 3T3. Classmate and long-time friend of NF and HKF.

Elder, Ruth. Sister of Jean Elder.

Elliott, William Yandel. Professor of government at Harvard; a member of the Southern Fugitives poets; Rhodes scholar; organized the poetry conference at Harvard, summer 1950.

Ellmann, Mary. Professor of English, Wellesley University; wife of Richard Ellmann.

Ellmann, Richard. Well-known Joyce and Yeats scholar; taught at Harvard, Northwestern, and Oxford; husband of Mary Ellmann.

Emmanuel, Pierre. Contemplative French poet in the tradition of Claudel.

Endicott, Betty. Wife of Norman Endicott.

Endicott, James G(areth) (Jim). VC, 2T3; M.A., U of T, 1924; D.D., EC, 1924; UCC missionary in China; called himself "a Christian Marxist"; after the 1949 World Peace Conference in Paris, helped found the Canadian Peace Congress; older brother of Norman J. Endicott.

Endicott, Norman A. VC, 5T0; eldest son of James G. Endicott; as a student, head of the Labour Progressive Party at U of T; later practised law.

Endicott, Norman Jamieson. Member of the English department at UC; younger brother of James G. Endicott.

Endicott, Shirley. VC, 5T2; daughter of James G. Endicott; taught sociology at U of T, was a pioneer in the movement to end violence against woman, and became a creative writer; later, Shirley Endicott Small.

Erdman, David V(orse). Blake scholar at the University of Minnesota; later taught at the State University of New York, Stony Brook.

Erichsen-Brown, Frank. Artist and attorney; senior partner in Erichsen-Brown and Hopkins; married Isabel Russell.

Evans, Joseph Cooper. Registrar, U of T.

Ewing, Barbara. VC, 4T7; worked in intelligence for the communications branch of the National Research Council.

Fackenheim, Emil Ludvig. Lecturer in philosophy, U of T.

Fadiman, Clifton. American writer and critic.

Fahrni, Mildred. Secretary of the Fellowship of Reconciliation, a pacifist organization.

Fairley, Barker. Member of the German department at U of T, 1915–57, well-known Goethe scholar, and a painter; husband of Margaret Fairley; founder, and for a time editor, of the *Canadian Forum*.

Fairley, Joan. Daughter of Margaret and Barker Fairley.

Fairley, Margaret. One of the founders of the Labour Progressive Party and editor of *New Frontiers*; devoted her life to the Communist cause.

Falle, George Gray. Member of the English department, TC, 1957–81.

Fauré, Gabriel. French composer.

Feilding, Charles Rudolph. Professor of moral and pastoral theology, TC, 1940–70, and dean of divinity at TC, 1946–61; member of the editorial board of the *Canadian Forum*.

Fennell, William Oscar (Bill). VC, 3T9; EC, 4T2; taught systematic theology at EC; member of the Commission on Culture of the UCC.

Fenwick, Kathleen. Curator of prints and drawings at the NGC in Ottawa.

Ferguson, Max. CBC radio personality for fifty years; host of *The Max Ferguson Show*; known in the 1950s and 1960s as "Ol' Rawhide."

Fernald, Helen Elizabeth. Assistant professor of East Asiatic studies, U of T; curator of East Asiatic department, ROM.

Fewster, Stanley. Advertising manager of the TTC.

Field, George Wallis (Wally). Appointed to a permanent position in the German department at VC in 1948.

File, Alicia M. VC, 5T5; later, Alicia Gallow.

File, Edgar (Ed). VC, 5T4; M.Div., EC, 5T6.

Fillmore, Herbert Stanley. VC, 5T0; editor of the *Varsity*, 1949–50.

Finch, Robert D.C. Scholar, artist, musician, and modernist poet; taught French at UC, 1928–68.

Finlay, John Baird. VC, 5T1; editor of *Acta Victoriana*, 1950–51; became a member of Parliament for Oxford, Ont.

Fisher, Douglas Mason. VC, 4T9; CCF-NDP politician; later became a syndicated columnist for the Toronto *Telegraph* and Toronto *Sun* and a television host.

Fisher, Gloria. VC, 4T9; one of NF's students; married Don Harron following her graduation in 1949.

Fisher, Joseph (Joe). Member of the English faculty at VC, 1936–52.

Fisher, Peter. One of NF's students; NF directed his dissertation on Blake, later published as *The Valley of Vision*; Ph.D., U of T, 1949; began his teaching career at the Royal Military College in the fall of 1949; drowned in a sailing accident in 1958.

FitzGerald, R.D. One of the important Australian poets to emerge in the 1920s.

Flahiff, Frederick T. Member of the English department at TC and later SMC.

Flenley, Ralph. Member of the history department at U of T.

Ford, Ella Priscilla. Wife of Harry Edgerton Ford.

Ford, Harry E. Member of the French department at VC; retired in 1940.

Foreman, Phyllis. VC, 3T3; married Hugh Moorhouse.

Fowke, Edith. Folklorist, teacher, and writer; member of the editorial staff of the *Canadian Forum* when NF was editor; became a prolific writer on folklore, especially folk songs; presented a CBC program on folk songs, 1950–63.

Fowler, Catherine E. (Betty/Kay). VC, 4T8.

Fox, Arthur M. (Art). Member of the French department, VC.

Franciabigio (Francesco de Christofano). Italian painter.

Fraser, Blair. Toronto journalist; became a CBC Radio commentator in 1944.

Fraser, Elizabeth. Canadian book designer who lived in London and who was a friend of Norah McCullough; she befriended NF when he was at Oxford.

Fricker, Herbert Austin. Conductor of the Toronto Mendelssohn Choir, 1917–42.

Frost, Leslie Miscampbell. Premier of Ont., 1949–61.

Fry, Christopher. British dramatist.

Frye, (Eratus) Howard. NF's brother; thirteen years older than NF; killed in the Amiens drive by a German bomb on 18 August 1918—one of the relatively few air casualties of World War I.

Frye, Helen Kemp. VC, 3T3; married NF on 24 August 1937.

Frye, Herman Edward. NF's father, a hardware salesman.

Frye, Richard Nelson. Ph.D., Harvard, 1946; became a distinguished Near Eastern scholar and Aga Khan professor of Iranian at Harvard.

Frye, Vera. NF's sister, twelve and one-half years his senior; born in Lowell, Mass., on 25 December 1900; B.A., Mount Allison University; did graduate work in both English and psychology at the University of Chicago; taught school in Chicago most of her life; died in Los Angeles, California, on Good Friday, 1966.

Fulford, Edna. Rented the attic of the Fryes' Clifton Rd. home in the 1940s.

Fulford, Kenneth R. VC, 5To.

Fulford, Nancy. Child of Edna Fulford; NF's goddaughter.

Fulton, Edmund Davie. Canadian lawyer, politician, and judge; first elected to the House in 1945; ran for the Progressive Conservative Party leadership in 1956.

Fulton, Janet Angel. VC, 5To; her mother was a friend of NF's sister Vera; later, Janet Fulton Hibberd.

Furphy, Joseph. Australian writer, best known for his picaresque novel *Such Is Life* (1903).

Fux, Johann Joseph. Austrian composer of operas and church music.

Fyles, Harold. Member of the English department at McGill University.

Gannett, Lewis Stiles. Literary critic for the *New York Herald Tribune* and novelist.

Gardener, Donald H. (Don). Public educator; taught at the Canadian Institute of International Affairs.

Garratt, Elthea Annie Howard (Dolly). NF's maternal aunt, married to Rev. Rufus Garratt.

Garrett, Helen. Wife of Jack Garrett.

Garrett, John C. (Jack). Canadian Rhodes Scholar who taught in the English department at TC, 1945–49, and later at the University of Canterbury in New Zealand; member of the editorial board of the *Canadian Forum*.

Garrod, Dolores. One of Carl Klink's students at UWO; in honour English; member of the Hesperian Club (literary society).

Garrod, Heathcote William. Fellow, Merton College, Oxford University.

Gayfer, Margaret. VC, 4T8.

Gelber, Marvin. Canadian politician and diplomat; member of Parliament for South York; long-time supporter of the AGO.

George, Henry. American economist; his basic platform for curing poverty was to levy a "single tax" on the value of land and to abolish all other taxes.

Germain, Edythe O'Brien. VC, 4T9.

Gibbs, Wolcott. Drama critic for the *New Yorker* and author of *Season in the Sun and Other Pleasures* (1946), a collection of his pieces from that magazine.

Gibson, Mary. VC, 4To; sister of Stephen Gibson; student of NF; taught at OCA for thirteen years; became a lifelong student of Bhakti Yoga.

Gibson, Stephen Hamilton. VC, 4To; was an admirer of Marshall McLuhan; husband of Georgiana Green, VC, 3T3, and later of Audrey Renwicke.

Gieseking, Walter W. German pianist of international reputation, particularly in French music; made his debut in 1915 and toured widely.

Gillies, Glorya M. VC, 5T5; later, Glorya Eades.

Gillray, James. English caricaturist whose prints influenced William Blake.

Gillson, Henry S. President of the University of Manitoba, 1948–54; a mathematical physicist.

Gilmour, Clyde. Well-known film critic and broadcaster; with his *CBC Movie Critic* in 1947, he became the first regular North American film reviewer on radio; his program *Gilmour's Albums* ran on CBC for four decades.

Gilson, Étienne. Professor of philosophy, SMC; leading French Thomist philosopher, attached to Pontifical Institute, SMC, during the war years.

Ginsberg, Morris. British sociologist and moral philosopher; taught at the London School of Economics.

Glaz, Herta. Austrian contralto; made her debut with the Metropolitan Opera in New York in 1942; sang widely in the U.S. in the following years and soloed for the Toronto Mendelssohn Choir.

Godfrey, Eleanor. Editor of the *Canadian Forum*; later edited an adult education magazine, *Food for Thought*, and did volunteer work with a child care program; also wrote short stories and radio scripts; married Bill Graham in March 1940.

Godfrey, (Ethel) Ray. Sister of Eleanor Godfrey; a social worker in the 1940s; later taught at the School of Social Work, U of T.

Goggio, Emilio. Head of the department of Italian, Spanish, and Portuguese, U of T.

Goldring, Cecil Charles. Superintendent of schools in Toronto.

Goldschmidt, Nicholas. Musical conductor who helped to establish opera in Canada and who was well-known for his organizing of musical festivals.

Gordon, Lois. Social worker at the Children's Aid Society, Toronto.

Goudge, Helen. Wife of Thomas A. Goudge.

Goudge, Stephen. VC, 6T4; son of Helen and Thomas A. Goudge.

Goudge, Thomas A. (Tommy). Professor of philosophy at U of T, 1938–76; taught at Waterloo and Queen's before coming to Toronto in 1938; best known for his study of C.S. Pierce.

Gould, Earnest (Ernie). VC, 3T3; younger brother of Sid Gould.

Gould, Margaret. VC, 4T4; poet; married David Parsons.

Gould, Sydney (Sid). VC, 2T9; returned to VC to teach Classics in 1935; later taught at Purdue University.

Graf, Uta. German soprano who came to the U.S. in 1948; sang for the San Francisco Opera Company in 1949.

Graff, William. Student of NF in the early 1940s; wounded in World War II in Italy; became a librarian in Peterborough, Ont.

Graham, Bill. Husband of Eleanor Godfrey; worked in advertising with McLaren's; after retirement, published two social histories of Ont.

Graham, John. Member of the English department at UWO; received his Ph.D. from Toronto in 1952, writing a dissertation on Virginia Woolf under the supervision of NF.

Grandy, Patricia K. VC, 5T2; married Walter Stewart's brother, Sandy.

Grant, Abigail. Daughter of Joan and Douglas Grant.

Grant, George Munro. Principal of Queen's University.

Grant, Joan. Wife of Douglas Grant.

Grant, John Douglas. Ph.D., U of T, 1947; wrote a dissertation on Samuel Butler under the direction of A.S.P. Woodhouse; taught at UBC.; died suddenly in 1952.

Grant, Peter. VC, 5T1.

Grant, (William) Douglas (Beattie). Member of the English department at UC, 1948–61; editor of the *University of Toronto Quarterly*, 1956–60.

Green, Harry H. VC, 5T0; editor-in-chief of *Acta Victoriana*, 1949–50; studied political science at VC and later became a Presbyterian minister.

Green, T.H. English idealist philosopher.

Grey, Earle. Canadian film and television actor; since 1986, the Earle Grey Award has been bestowed annually to recognize special achievement in television.

Grier, Sir Wyly. Canadian portrait painter; came to Canada from Australia in 1876, studied in Europe, and returned to Canada in 1891; was knighted in 1935 for his contributions to Canadian arts and letters.

Griffin, Frederick. Feature writer and war correspondent for the *Toronto Daily Star* and the *Star Weekly*, 1919–46.

Grimshaw, Joyce C. Contributor to the *Canadian Forum*; worked for five years in the economics and research branch of the Department of Labour, Ottawa.

Group of Seven. Important Canadian art movement that drew its inspiration from northern Ont. landscapes; the seven members were Frank Carmichael, Lawren Harris, A.Y. Jackson, Frank Johnston, Arthur Lismer, J.E.H. MacDonald, and F.H. Varley.

Grove, Frederick Philip. Canadian poet, novelist, teacher, and translator.

Grube, G(eorge) M(aximillian) A(nthony). Professor of Classics, U of T; had been book review editor and managing editor of the *Canadian Forum* before NF was associated with the magazine.

Grube, John D. Son of G.M.A. Grube.

Gummow, J.J. Graduate student in English, U of T, 1951–52.

Gustafson, Ralph Barker. Canadian poet and professor; taught at Bishop's University, 1963–79.

Guthrie, James Rattray. Assistant professor of Christian education, EC.

Hackenbroch, Yvonne Alix. Curator of the Lee Fareham Collection at U of T from 1945 to 1949, when she became curator of the Irwin Untermeyer Collection at the Metropolitan Museum of Art in New York.

Haddow, Bill. Neighbour of the Fryes, living next door at 125 Clifton Rd., one house south of the Fryes; taught forestry at U of T and later worked with the Ont. government as a forest pathologist; husband of Jean Haddow.

Haddow, Don (Donny). Son of Jean and Bill Haddow.

Haddow, George. Brother of Bill Haddow; member of the English department at McMaster University, where he later became department head.

Haddow, Jean. Neighbour of the Fryes; an accomplished vocalist, having sung with the Boston Symphony, New York Philharmonic, and numerous other groups; also a pianist, she often helped NF with his Bach; wife of Bill Haddow.

Hagan, Fred. Head of the art department at Pickering College.

Haggert, Joan. VC, 5T5; later, Joan Ellis.

Haig, Margaret (Peggy). VC, 4T8.

Hall, John Alexander. Canadian painter who supported his fine art career through commercial art and illustration; taught in York township schools, 1938–42; began as a lecturer in fine art, U of T, in 1945, and as a lecturer in architecture in 1946.

Hallam, Bishop William Thomas. Professor at Wycliffe College; principal at Emmanuel College, Saskatoon, Sask.; dean of divinity at Huron College, London, Ont.; father of Isabel Whitley, the Fryes' neighbour.

Hallman, Eugene Sanborn. Friend of the Fryes; a broadcast executive for CBC.

Hallman, Margaret (née Torrance). VC, 3T3; wife of Eugene Hallman.

Hamilton, Albert C. (Bert). M.A. in English, U of T, 1948; Ph.D, Cambridge, 1953; began his teaching career at the University of Washington, but returned to Canada in 1968 to teach Renaissance literature at Queen's University; became an authority on Renaissance literature; author of *Northrop Frye: Anatomy of His Criticism*.

Hamm, Catherine. Secretary of the English department at the University of Chicago.

Harbage, Alfred Bennett. American Shakespearean scholar; appointed to the English department at Harvard University in 1952; authority on Shakespeare's theatre.

Hare, F. Archibald (Archie). Member of the French department at VC.

Harper, Carol Ely. Poet and novelist; at the time of NF's 1952 Diary, was managing editor of *Experiment: An International Review of New Poetry*; published a number of poems and short stories in the *Canadian Forum*.

Harris, Howie. Younger son of Lawren Harris; his wife was Peggy.

Harris, Lawren. Influential Canadian painter, prime mover of the Group of Seven, and founding member of the Arts and Letters Club.

Harris, Robert. Canadian artist.

Harris, Robin Sutton. Member of department of English, UC, 1952–64; principal, Innis College, 1964–71.

Harrison, Constance (Connie). Social worker with the Children's Aid Society.

Harrison, G(eorge) B(agshaw). Head of the English department at Queen's University, 1943–49; following that, taught at University of Michigan; Shakespeare scholar.

Harron, Don. VC, 4T8; one of NF's students; later became a Canadian radio and television personality; married Gloria Fisher after graduating from VC.

Harron, Gloria. See Fisher, Gloria.

Havelock, Eric. Member of the Classics department at VC, 1929–47; one of the board of editors of the *Canadian Forum*; taught at Harvard, 1947–63, and then at Yale.

Haworth, Peter. Canadian watercolourist and stained glass designer; director of the Central Technical School in Toronto, 1929–55.

Hay, Dorothy Clarke. Wife of Harvey Hay of Bruce Beach, Ont.; sister of Mary Louise Clarke Cameron; later Dorothy (Dottie) Clarke Wilson.

Haydon, Benjamin Robert. English historical painter and diarist.

Hebb, Andrew. B.A., Dalhousie University, 1928; edited the *Rural Co-operator* magazine; was an occasional contributor to and a board member of the *Canadian Forum*; husband of Ruth Dingman Hebb.

Hebb, Ruth Dingman. VC, 3T3; during the time of the diaries she and her husband Andrew lived on Moore Ave., adjacent to Clifton Rd., near the Fryes.

Helpmann, Sir Robert. Australian dancer, actor, and choreographer.

Hendry, Charles Eric (Chuck). Chair, graduate department of social work, School of Social Work.

Hepburn, Mitchell. Liberal Premier of Ont., 1934–42.

Hersenhoren, Samuel. Musical conductor and director; founder of the New World Orchestra; violinist with the Parlow String Quartet, 1942–51.

Heywood, Percy Kilbourn. President of Evangeline Shops in Toronto and one of the organizers of the Toronto Better Business Bureau; president of the alumni association, VC.

Hicklin, Ralph Craig. Member of NF's Spenser seminar, 1947–48; taught briefly at UNB; became drama and ballet critic for the *Globe and Mail* before an early death.

Hicks, Rivers Keith. Dean of arts, U of T, and professor of French and registrar, UC.

Hicks, Wesley. Columnist for the Toronto *Telegram* and Canadian correspondent for *Time* magazine.

Hiller, Arthur Garfin. Producer for CBC Radio.

Hine, Daryl. Canadian poet who spent most of his life in the U.S.

Hitchcock, Henry-Russell. Distinguished architectural historian; came to Smith College from Wesleyan College in 1947 as director of the Smith College Museum of Art and professor of architectural history.

Hoeniger, F(rederick) J(ulius) David. Former student of NF; appointed to the English faculty at VC when NF became chair in 1953; founder of the Centre for Reformation and Renaissance Studies, VC.

Hogg, Frank. Astronomer; director of the Dunlap Observatory in Richmond Hill; husband of the well-known astronomer Helen Battles Sawyer Hogg.

Holt, Helen. VC, 5To; attended OCE, 1950–51, where she received her certificate and then taught French in the Ont. secondary school system (Erin and London); later, Helen Holt Heath.

Home, Ruth. Lecturer and guide at the ROM.

Honeyford, Bruce Wilson. Graduate student in English at U of T; received his Ph.D. in 1952, writing a dissertation, directed by Robert S. Knox, on Jacobean tragedy.

Honig, Edwin. Instructor in English, Harvard University, 1949–52; later, professor of English at Brown University.

Hooke, Samuel Henry. Professor of Oriental languages and literature at VU; widely published Biblical scholar and Ancient Near Eastern historian.

Hopper, Frances. VC, 5To.

Hopwood, Victor G. Ph.D., U of T, 1950; taught English at UBC.

Hornett, Bert M. VC student; died of pneumonia in 1952, his second year in college.

Hornyansky, Michael. Son of artist Nicholas and musician Joyce Hornyansky; later won a Rhodes Scholarship and became chair of the English department at Brock University.

Horwood, Eric. VC, 2T2; architect retained by VC for various remodelling projects.

Horwood, Marjorie. VC, 3To; married Howe Martyn.

Horwood, Winifred (Wyn). Marjorie Horwood's sister; married Richard B. Code, Muriel Code's brother.

Housser, Yvonne. See McKague, Yvonne.

Howard, Connie. Wife of William A. Howard; she and her husband spent time during the early years of their marriage at the summer cottage of HKF's parents at Lake Joseph.

Howard, John Albert S. NF's maternal uncle.

Howard, Olive. Wife of NF's first cousin, Wilbert Howard; her father-in-law, Daniel Hersey Howard, was the brother of NF's mother.

Howard, William A. (Bill). Interior designer with the Thornton-Smith Co., and, after World War II, head of design in Eaton's fine furniture department; member of the Arts and Letters Club.

Howarth, Dorothy. Reporter for the Toronto *Telegram*.

Howson, Richard V. VC, 5T1.

Hubener, Jean Isabel. Special lecturer in English at VC; received a Guggenheim in 1950, the same year NF received his, to study at Harvard.

Hubler, Edward Lorenzo. Professor of English, Princeton University.

Huggett, Lillie M. VC, 4T9.

Hughes, Merritt Yerkes. Ph.D., Harvard, 1921; Milton scholar; professor of English, University of Wisconsin, where he was chair, 1952–55.

Humphrey, Jack W. Figurative and abstract Canadian painter, many of whose watercolours were of New Brunswick subjects; his self-portrait, *Draped Head*, is in Hart House, U of T.

Hutchins, Robert Maynard. President of the University of Chicago.

Hutchinson, Sybil. Editor at McClelland and Stewart and literary agent.

Hyatt, Glen C. B.A. in honour English, UWO, 1950; member of the Hesperian Club (literary society); after college, returned to Victoria, B.C., where he ran his father's printing firm.

Hyrchenuk, Stephen. Mary Kemp's brother.

Ignatieff, George. Canadian diplomat; became provost of TC, 1972–79, and chancellor of U of T, 1980–86.

Ignatieff, Helen. Wife of Nicholas Ignatieff.

Ignatieff, Nicholas. Warden of Hart House, U of T.

Infeld, Leopold. Refugee from Poland who taught mathematics at U of T; along with J.L. Synge, helped lay the groundwork for work in theoretical physics in Canada.

Inglis, Jean. VC, 5T0; a member of the writers' group at VC; her story *And the Green Hills Laugh* was published posthumously in the *Canadian Forum* when NF was editor.

Innis, Harold A. Dean of the graduate school, U of T; political economist and pioneer in communication studies.

Innis, Mrs. Harold A. Member of the Commission on Culture of the UCC.

Ironside, Diana Joan. VC, 4T9; she enrolled in a number of NF's courses.

Irving, Allan. Son of John A. Irving.

Irving, John Allan. M.A. Princeton, 1928; professor of ethics and social philosophy at VC; taught at Princeton and UBC before coming to VC in 1945.

Jackman, Mary Coyne Rowell. VC, 2T5; a friend of Douglas Duncan, Will Ogilvie, Charles Comfort, and other artists; opened the first day-care centre in Ont.; became a Virginia Woolf scholar; in 1950, at age 46, returned to U of

T to study art; subsequently accumulated a substantial collection of modern art.

Jackson, A.Y. Canadian landscape painter and member of the Group of Seven.

Jacobi, Lou. Well-known stage, television, and film actor.

Jaffary, Stuart King. Professor in the School of Social Work, U of T.

Jaffe, Adrian. Member of the English department, Michigan State University, 1947–67.

James, Helen. Began working at CBC Radio in 1945 as an assistant producer; in 1953 became assistant supervisor of talks and public affairs, where she assumed the direction of women's programming; resigned from CBC in 1965 to enter social work.

James, Percy N. VC, 4T8; became a novelist, poet, and short story writer, most of his books having been published in Newfoundland.

James, William C. (Bill). VC, 1T6; chair of the board of regents of VC, 1942–51; later became bursar and secretary of the board.

Jarrell, Randall. American poet.

Jarvis, Lucy. Canadian painter, art teacher, filmmaker, and television producer; in 1942 she and Pegi Nicol MacLeod opened the Observatory Art Centre in Fredericton, N.B.

Jeanneret, F.C.A. Principal of UC and member of the department of French.

Jeffries, Alison. VC, 5T0; excelled in athletics and graduated with first-class honours in the four-year General Course, having taken two of NF's courses; later, Alison Hall.

Jenking, Beth. VC, 3T5.

Jenking, Ruth I. Member of the English department at VC, 1945–70.

Joblin, Kingsley (King). VC, 3T2; EC, 3T6; NF's colleague at VC in the department of religious knowledge.

Johnston, Alfred John. Professor of homiletics at EC.

Johnston, George. Studied at U of T; taught English at Mount Allison University, 1947–50, and at Carleton University, 1950–79; poet and translator; he and NF became lifelong friends.

Johnston, George. Professor of New Testament literature and exegesis at EC; replaced John Dow, who retired in 1952.

Jolliffe, Edward Bigelow. Attorney and politician; leader of CCF in Ont., 1942; leader of the official opposition in the legislature, 1943–45, 1948–56.

Joseph, M.K. (Mike). NF's New Zealand friend from their Oxford days in the 1930s; became an English professor and novelist.

Junor, Ishbel. VC, 5T5; later, Ishbel Sikorski.

Kain, Richard Morgan. Professor of English, University of Louisville; Joyce scholar; taught in the Harvard summer school in 1950.

Kee, Kenneth Orville. VC, 4T9; became a member of the English department at

VC in 1953; received his Ph.D. from U of T in 1955, having done a dissertation on *Sir Gawain*, directed by John Robins, C.W. Dunn, and L.K. Shook.

Keeping, Hugh. Friend of HKF's family; had been a classmate of HKF's younger brother Harold during the 1930s.

Keeping, Margaret. Wife of Hugh Keeping.

Kell, Margaret E. VC, 5T5; later, Margaret Virany.

Kemp, Gertrude. HKF's mother.

Kemp, Harold. HKF's younger brother; killed in action in World War II.

Kemp, Hugh. Writer for the CBC national drama series, established in 1947; later worked for NBC in New York.

Kemp, Marion. HKF's younger sister; went to South Africa in 1936 to marry Ernie Harrison, the first of her three husbands; died in Rhodesia on 2 February 1977.

Kemp, Mary. Roy Kemp's wife.

Kemp, Peter. NF and HKF's nephew, the son of Roy and Mary Kemp.

Kemp, Roy. HKF's younger brother; became a photographer, working most of his professional life in New York City.

Kemp, Stanley Heber Franklin. HKF's father; U of T, oT6; had to give up his intention to enter the ministry because he was quite deaf, becoming instead a commercial artist in a photoengraving business, Grip Ltd., where early in his career he worked with Arthur Lismer and Tom Thomson; the chief designer for the Crown Cork and Seal Co. for twenty-five years.

Kenmare, Dallas. British poet and critic.

Kenner, (William) Hugh. B.A., UC, 4T5; M.A., U of T, 1946; wrote thesis under Marshall McLuhan; Ph.D., Yale, 1950; became a well-known writer on modernism; taught at the University of California, Santa Barbara, and Johns Hopkins.

Ketchum, J(ohn) D(avidson). Professor of psychology, U of T.

Kettle, Horace Garnard (Rik). Founding member of the Picture Loan Society, Canada's first art rental.

Key, Sidney James. Curator, AGT; instructor in art and archaeology, U of T.

Keynes, Sir Geoffrey. Well-known Blake scholar; when NF was a student at Oxford, he had visited Keynes and sent him an early version of his manuscript on Blake.

Kidd, James Robbins (Roby). Teacher and adult educator; director of the Canadian Association for Adult Education, 1951–82; first chair of adult education at the Ont. Institute of Adult Education.

Kieran, John Francis. One of the panelists on the *Information Please* radio program.

Kilgour, Mary Louise. VC, 4T9; married David J. Knight.

Kimpton, Lawrence A. Chancellor of the University of Chicago.

King, Anthony S. (Tony). Son of Marjorie and Harold King.

King, Harold S. Toronto artist; studied at McMaster University and in Europe; began teaching at the Northern Vocational School in 1933.

King, Marjorie. Wife of Harold King.

King, Ralph E. VC, 4T8; EC, 5T1; graduate student in English, U of T, 1950–51.

King, William Lyon Mackenzie. Liberal prime minister of Canada, 1921–30, 1935–48.

Kirkconnell, Watson. Professor of English and head of the department at Mc-Master University, 1940–48; became president of Acadia University in 1948.

Kirkwood, Mossie May. Member of the English department at TC and principal of St. Hilda's College, U of T, 1936–59; wife of W.A. Kirkwood.

Kirkwood, W.A. Professor emeritus of Latin, TC; formerly dean, faculty of arts, TC; husband of Mossie May Kirkwood.

Kleiman, Edward (Ed). B.A., University of Manitoba; M.A. in English, U of T; member of NF's graduate course in literary symbolism, 1954–55; did an M.A. thesis on *King Lear* under NF's supervision; taught at the University of Manitoba; short story writer.

Klein, A.M. Canadian poet and leading figure in Jewish-Canadian culture; studied at McGill University, where he became a close friend of A.J.M. Smith and F.R. Scott.

Klinck, Carl Frederick. Member of the English department at UWO.

Knight, David J. VC, 4T8; Ph.D. in English, Yale University; began teaching at VC in 1952; married Mary Louise Kilgour.

Knight, John (Jack). Brother of David Knight; at the time of NF's diaries, a musician; later worked for Columbia Artists Management and the National Film Board.

Knight, Norm. VC, 3T4.

Knowles, Robert. Son of Robert Edward Knowles; journalist who wrote for the *Toronto Daily Star*, *Saturday Night*, and other publications; was killed in a motorcycle accident while serving in the armed forces in England.

Knowles, Robert Edward. Left the ministry to become a journalist, writing chiefly for the *Toronto Daily Star*.

Knox, Kenneth W. VC, 4T9; New Church Theological School, 1949–52; became a minister of the New Church, serving churches in California, and devoted his life to the writings of Emmanuel Swedenborg.

Knox, Robert S. Member of the English department, UC, 1920–57.

Kolessa, Lubka. Canadian piano teacher.

Kraus, Greta. Harpsichordist; played often with flutist Robert Morris Aitken.

Kreisel, Henry. Member of the English faculty at the University of Alberta, where he began teaching in 1947 after he had received his M.A. from U of T; Ph.D., University of London, 1954; also a novelist, short story writer, and playwright.

Kubik, Gail. American violinist, conductor, and composer.

Lacey, Alexander. Member of the French department at VC.

Laidlaw, George Norman. Member of the French department at VC.

Lambert, Jessica and Richard. Children of Richard Stanton Lambert.

Lambert, Richard Stanton. Supervisor of educational broadcasts for CBC.

Lamport, Allan A. Toronto politician; served as alderman for many terms and then as mayor, 1952–54.

Lane, Mary Liz. VC, 5T0; acted in the productions of the Vic Dramatic Society and wrote reviews for the *Varsity*; taught high school English for thirty-three years, mainly in Scarborough, Ont.; later, Mary Culley.

Lane, Wilmot B. Ryerson professor of ethics at EC and a member of the department of ethics at VC.

Langford, Norman. VC, 3T5; EC, 4T4; ordained in the UCC; in 1949, left the UCC for the Westminster Press of the Presbyterian Church in Philadelphia.

Latimer, Douglas L. VC, 5T1.

Latimer, Elspeth. VC, 4T6.

Lautenslager, Earl. VC, 3T1; EC, 3T5; at the time of NF's 1949 Diary, a minister at Howard Park United Church in west Toronto; in 1963, appointed principal of EC.

Laverty, Alexander Marshall (Marsh). VC, 3T4; EC, 3T7; minister of the UCC; chaplain, First Canadian Army, 1942–45; became university chaplain of Queen's University, Kingston, Ont., in 1947.

Lawrence, Elwood Parsons. Member of the English department, Michigan State University.

Lawson, Clinton David. VC, 5T1; M.Div., EC, 5T4; later became librarian.

Lawson, James S. (Jim). Assistant librarian at VU and library tutor in EC.

Layhew, Howard. NF's first cousin, the son of his maternal aunt, Harriet (Hatty) Howard Layhew.

Layhew, Hugh. NF's first cousin, the son of his maternal aunt, Harriet (Hatty) Howard Layhew.

Leacock, Stephen. Canadian humourist, essayist, teacher, political economist, and historian.

LeBourdais, Donat Marc. Canadian freelance writer; for six years, director of the division of education for the National Committee for Mental Hygiene; frequent contributor to the *Canadian Forum*.

LeBourdais, Mrs. D.M. Daughter of Frank and Isabel Erichsen-Brown.

Leddy, J. Francis. Dean of the College of Arts and Sciences, USk; first president, University of Windsor.

Lederman, Robert S. (Bob). Minister of the Evangelical United Brethren Church (currently Calvary United Church) in Listowel, Ont., 1948–51.

Lees, Gene. Student at OCA in 1950; left college to become a newspaper reporter; became a widely published jazz critic and historian.

Lemke, Clarence D. EC, 5T3; held pastorates in the UCC and was involved in its educational work, 1954–75.

Leo, Ulrich. Special lecturer in Italian, Spanish, and Portuguese, U of T.

LePan, Arthur. Father of Douglas LePan; supervisor of buildings and grounds, U of T.

LePan, Dorothy. Mother of Douglas LePan.

LePan, Douglas Valentine. UC, 3T5; later taught at Harvard, served in the department of external affairs, and was principal of UC; published four books of poetry, a novel, and a memoir.

Leslie, Charles Whitney (Charlie). VC, 3T0; member of the department of ethics, VC, and professor of systematic theology, EC.

Leslie, Kenneth. Canadian poet and journalist; spent some time in New York as a magazine editor; winner of the Governor General's prize for poetry in 1938.

Leslie, Mary C. VC, 5T5; later, Mary Anderson.

Le Sueur, William Dawson. Popular Canadian thinker; author of *Count Frontenac* (1907), *William Lyon Mackenzie* (1907), and other works.

Levin, Harry (Tuchman). Chair of comparative literature, Harvard University.

Lewis, David. Socialist politician, labour lawyer, and professor; a key theorist for the CCF in the late 1930s; later played an important role in designing the New Democratic Party; national secretary for the CFF, 1937–50.

Lewis, Ivor Evan Gerwyn. Canadian graphic artist; member of the Canadian Society for Graphic Art.

Line, John. Professor of philosophy and history of religion at EC.

Line, William (Bill). Professor of psychology, U of T.

Linton, Evelyn. VC, 5T2.

Lipset, Seymour Martin. Well-known sociologist and member of the editorial board of the *Canadian Forum*.

Lismer, Arthur. Painter, art teacher, and member of the Group of Seven; from 1927 to 1938 was educational supervisor at the AGT, where HKF worked, beginning in 1936; a friend of HKF's father.

Little, Jean. VC, 5T5.

Little, William J. Bursar at VC.

Livesay, Dorothy. Canadian poet, journalist, fiction writer, and critic.

Livingston, Judith (Judy). VC, 5T1; later taught English, worked as a travel adviser, and directed comic plays for children.

Lockhart, Wilfred Cornett. VC, 2T9, and EC, 3T3; later became president of the University of Winnipeg.

Long, Marcus. Member of the philosophy department, U of T.

Love, Christopher C. (Chris). Member of the English department at VC, 1948–77.

Love, Viola (Vo). Wife of Christopher C. Love.

Lowell, Robert. American poet.

Lower, Arthur Reginald Marsden. Canadian historian; taught at Wesley College in Winnipeg, 1929–47, and at Queen's University, 1947–59; following the views of Harold Innis, wrote on the role of the forest in the development of Canada.

Lowery, Mary. Journalist; wrote for the *Toronto Daily Star* and *Star Weekly*, *Saturday Night*, and *Maclean's*; married Eustace Ross.

Luce, Henry Robinson. American magazine publisher and editor of *Life*, *Time*, and *Fortune*.

Luz, Virginia Erskine. Artist; taught illustration at the Central Technical School in Toronto, 1940–74.

Lynch, Lawrence E. (Larry). Professor of philosophy at SMC.

Lytle, Andrew (Andy). Writer for the *Toronto Daily Star*.

MacAgy, Douglas G. Friend of the Fryes; in the 1930s, worked at the Barnes Collection in Pennsylvania and the Cleveland and San Francisco Museums of Art, eventually ending up in New York; at the time of NF's 1952 Diary, was executive secretary of the New York museums committee for UNESCO; in 1953, became consultant to the director of the Museum of Modern Art.

MacAgy, Elisabeth B. (Bessie). Douglas MacAgy's mother.

MacAgy, Jermayne S. (Jerry). First wife of Douglas MacAgy.

McAree, John V. Dean of Canadian newspaper columnists; wrote for the Toronto *Globe and Mail* and its predecessor, the *Mail and Empire*.

MacCallum, Alice. Wife of Reid MacCallum.

MacCallum, H. Reid. Member of the philosophy department at U of T; NF's undergraduate aesthetics teacher; a graduate of Queen's University and a Rhodes Scholar at Oxford; the Fryes bought their home on Clifton Rd. from McCallum in 1946.

MacCallum, Hugh R. Graduate student in English at U of T, 1952; later did a dissertation on Milton under the direction of A.S.P. Woodhouse and then taught at UC; son of Reid and Alice MacCallum.

McCann, J.J. Liberal member of Parliament for Renfrew South; became minister of national revenue for Canada in 1945.

McCarthy, Doris Jean. Artist; taught at the Central Technical School in Toronto, 1932–72.

McCarthy, Mary. American novelist, essayist, and critic.

McCosh, Mary. VC, 5To; majored in French and Spanish and taught secondary school French for a number of years in Wingham, Ont.

McCrae, Sally E.A. VC, 5T5.

McCullagh, George. Founded the Toronto *Globe and Mail* in 1936 by uniting two dailies, the *Globe* and the *Mail and Empire*; bought the Toronto *Evening Telegram* in 1949.

McCulley, Joseph (Joe). Tutor, VC, 1926–27; headmaster Pickering College, 1927–47; became warden of Hart House, U of T, 1952.

McCullough, Norah. Close friend of HKF, with whom she worked for a number of years at the AGT; along with Arthur Lismer, was especially instrumental in developing art education programs.

McCullough, William Stewart. Professor of Oriental languages at UC.

McCurdy, Jarvis. Member of the department of ethics at UC.

Macdonald, Allistair. B.A., Acadia, 1942; M.A., McGill, 1947; Ph.D. in English, U of T, 1973; taught at Acadia from 1965 until his retirement in 1988.

Macdonald, E.A. (Alex). General secretary of the Students' Administrative Council, U of T.

McDonald, Evelyn. Teacher at the Bloor Collegiate Institute.

McDonald, Jean. VC, 3T7; taught English at North Toronto Collegiate Institute; husband of Robert P. McDonald; later taught at Oakwood Collegiate Institute and Thornlea Secondary School.

Macdonald, J.E.H. Canadian artist; a founder of the Group of Seven.

Macdonald, J.W.G. (Jock). Canadian artist and educator; taught at OCA, 1947–60.

MacDonald, John Ford. Member of the department of English at UC, 1925–48; chair of the Commission on Culture of the UCC, 1948–50.

MacDonald, John Sandfield. Premier of Ont., 1867–72.

MacDonald, Ramsay. Scottish politician and the first British Labour prime minister.

McDonald, Robert P. (Bob). VC, 3T7; taught English at North Toronto Collegiate Institute and, like his wife Jean, was active in the Association of Teachers of English; later taught at Oakwood Collegiate Institute and Thornlea Secondary School.

Macdonald, Rose. Reporter for the Toronto *Telegram*.

Macdonald, Ross Hazelton. VC, 3T6; was studying for his Ph.D. in Russian history during NF's Guggenheim year (1950–51); returned to U of T to teach history and, later, religious studies.

McDougall, D(onald) J(ames). Professor of history, U of T.

MacDougall, Robert L. Ph.D. in English, U of T, 1950; his dissertation, *A Study of Canadian Periodical Literature of the 19th Century*, was directed by Claude T. Bissell; taught at UC, 1950–57.

MacDowell, Edward Alexander. American composer and pianist.

MacEachren, Clara F. Member of the board of regents of VU, representing the general council of the UCC.

MacFarlane, Joseph Arthur. Dean of the faculty of medicine, U of T.

McFarlane, Mary E. Ph.D. student at U of T, where she had come from United College in Winnipeg; did not complete her dissertation on Christopher Smart; married A.C. Hamilton and became a writer and editor.

McGee, W.H. Reader in the English department at VC; later taught at Univ. of
  Alaska.

McGibbon, Don. Husband of Pauline McGibbon.

McGibbon, Pauline (née Mills). VC, 3T3; later became the lieutenant governor
  of Ont., 1974–80, the first woman to hold that position in Canada.

MacGillivray, Elinor. Wife of J.R. MacGillivray.

MacGillivray, James Robertson. A member of the English department at UC,
  1930–71.

McKague, Yvonne. Canadian painter who closely followed the prototypes of
  the Group of Seven during her early years; taught at OCA from the early
  1920s until 1949; in 1935, married Frederick Broughton Housser.

McKee, David. Ph.D. student in English at U of T; left academic life, took up
  newspaper work, became an ordained Anglican priest, and then returned to
  the Toronto *Globe & Mail*.

Mackenzie, Laura Mabel. Ph.D. in English, U of T, 1955; her dissertation on *The
  Scottish Ballad in the Eighteenth Century* was supervised by F.E.L. Priestley;
  taught at UBC.

MacKenzie, Norman Archibald MacRae (Larry). Toronto lawyer; taught international law, U of T, in the 1930s; became president of UBC.

McKeon, Richard. Professor of philosophy at the University of Chicago and
  central figure among the neo-Aristotelians there.

MacKinder, Sir Halford John. English geographer and politician.

McKinnon, Alastair. VC, 4T7; M.A., U of T, 1948; taught at McGill University.

MacKinnon, Carol F. VC, 5T2; became a high school teacher; with her classmates in language and literature, formed a book club, which in the late 1980s
  was continuing to meet monthly for book discussions; later, Carol
  McDermott.

MacKinnon, Malcolm Hugh Murdoch (Murdo). Member of the English department at UWO, 1946–64; Ph.D., U of T, 1948; wrote a dissertation on Milton
  under A.S.P. Woodhouse; dean of arts at the University of Guelph, 1964–78;
  principal, University of Guelph.

Mackintosh, William Archibald. Economic historian and civil servant; principal
  of Queen's University, 1951–61.

McLachlan, Matthew. Assistant to the warden at Hart House.

McLaughlin, Isabel. Early modernist Canadian painter; studied with Arthur
  Lismer and Yvonne McKague (Housser); was influenced by the Group of
  Seven.

McLean, C.V. Member of the religious knowledge department at VC.

Maclean, Hugh N. Ph.D. in English, U of T, 1950; wrote a dissertation on Fulke
  Greville, directed by H.S. Wilson; taught at the Royal Military College, 1950–
  56, and subsequently taught at the University of Cincinnati and SUNY,
  Albany.

MacLean, Kenneth (Ken). Member of the English department at VC, 1938–75.

MacLean, Rita. VC, 5To.

MacLean, Sara. Wife of Kenneth MacLean; mother of Kenny and Sally.

McLellan, Ruth Elizabeth. VC, 5To; M.A., 1967; M.Phil., 1968.

MacLennan, David Alexander. Minister at Timothy Eaton Memorial Church, Toronto, 1936–49; became professor of preaching and pastoral care at Yale Divinity School in 1949.

McLuhan, Corinne Lewis. Wife of Marshall McLuhan.

McLuhan, Marshall. Member of the English department at SMC, 1946–79; well-known communications theorist.

MacLure, Millar. Ph.D. in English, U of T, 1949; his dissertation, *The St. Paul's Cross Sermons*, was supervised by H.S. Wilson; taught at United College in Winnipeg, 1949–53, and then returned to U of T as a member of the English department at VC.

MacMillan, Sir Ernest. Internationally known conductor of symphonic and choral music; conducted the TSO, 1931–56.

McMullen, George. Taught public speaking at EC and at Wycliffe and Knox Colleges.

McNabb, Barbara. VC, 4T4; one of NF's students; worked at Ryerson Press, 1946–47, after which she became an editor of a business magazine devoted to pottery, chinaware, and glass.

McNaught, Carlton. Advertising writer; author.

McNaught, Kenneth William Kirkpatrick (Ken). Ph.D. in history, U of T, 1950; professor of history, University of Manitoba; son of Carlton McNaught.

McNicol, John. Principal, Toronto Bible College, 1940–46.

Macphail, Agnes G. Politician and reformer; first woman in the Canadian House of Commons, elected to Parliament in 1921.

Macphail, Sir Andrew. Canadian physician, man of letters, professor of medicine, and soldier; taught history of medicine at McGill, 1907–37.

Macpherson, C(rawford). Professor of political economy, U of T.

Macpherson, Jay. Canadian poet and critic; NF's student and, later, colleague at VC.

Macpherson, Jessie Hill Knox. Dean of women at VC.

Macpherson, John. Member of the departments of Oriental languages and religious knowledge at VC.

MacRae, C. Fred. Ph.D. in English, U of T, 1953; wrote a dissertation, directed by Claude Bissell, on *The Victorian Age and Canadian Poetry*.

McRae, John R.Y. Ph.D., U of T, 1953; member of the English department at UWO, 1949–54; later taught at SUNY, Buffalo, and at William Patterson College.

McRae, Robert F. (Bob). Assistant professor of philosophy, U of T.

Mactaggart, Hugh Carmichael. VC, 3T3; became a UCC minister.

Madden, Fr. John. Member of the English department at SMC, 1948–69; later, St. Thomas Univ., Houston.

Magoun, Francis Peabody, Jr. Professor of Anglo-Saxon at Harvard.

Maidment, Lilly Catherine. HKF's maternal aunt; two years older than HKF's mother, both having been born on 3 February.

Mallett, Jane Keenleyside. Well-known Canadian actress whose career began at Hart House Theatre when she was a student.

Mallinson, Jean. Graduate student in English at U of T; became a writer and a teacher of English as a second language in Vancouver.

Mallon, Fr. Hugh Vincent. Member of the English department, SMC.

Mandel, Eli. Canadian poet and teacher; Ph.D., U of T, 1957; taught at University of Alberta and York University.

Manifold, John S. Australian poet.

Manning, Ed. Neighbour of the Fryes; he and his wife lived at 104 Heath St. East, two blocks west of the Fryes' Clifton Rd. home.

Manning, Ruth. VC, 5To; later, Ruth Alexander.

Manson, Alexander MacLeod (Alec). VC, 4T3, EC, 4T6.

Markowitz, Jacob. Toronto physician; professor of research in experimental surgery, U of T; contributor to the *Canadian Forum* and supporter of *Canadian Poetry Magazine*.

Marks, Dorothy. Interior decorator at Eaton's department store; wife of Oscar Rogers.

Marshall, Lois. Canadian soprano whose first major performance was in 1947 as soloist in Bach's St. Matthew Passion with the Toronto Mendelssohn Choir and the TSO.

Martin, Chester B. Professor of history and head of the department, U of T.

Martin, Ella. Don in the women's residences at VC from the 1930s to the 1950s.

Martin, John. English Romantic painter and mezzotint engraver.

Martin, Paul Joseph James. Politician; diplomat; French consul in Toronto, 1949–52.

Martin, Thomas H.W. Public school inspector for the Board of Education, Toronto.

Martyn, Howe. VC, 3To; after a sojourn in England working for Lever Brothers, became a professor of international studies in Washington, D.C.; married Marjorie Horewood.

Massey, Lionel. Canadian museum director.

Massey, Lucy. Friend of NF's father.

Mathers, William D.M. (Bill). Student at VC in 1950.

Matheson, Alexander Dawson. Dean and later principal of Emmanuel College, 1945–56.

Matthiesen, F.O. Professor of English at Harvard University; gave the Alexander Lectures on Henry James, 1944–45.

Maugham, W. Somerset. British novelist and short story writer.

Mauriac, François. French Catholic novelist.

Maynard, Fredelle Bruser. Canadian journalist; articulated the experience of Canadian Jewry and wrote on the creative education of children; winner of the Governor General's award; wife of artist and professor Max Maynard.

Mazzoleni, Ettore. Conductor and music educator; came to Toronto in 1929 and taught music and English at Upper Canada College; became conductor of the TCM Symphony Orchestra in 1934; married Winifred Macmillan on 27 June 1933.

Mehlberg, Henry. Came from Poland to Toronto in 1949, where he was appointed as a special lecturer in philosophy; left U of T in 1956 for the University of Chicago, where he taught for fourteen years.

Meisel, Jan (John). VC, 4T8; editor of *Acta Victoriana* during his fourth year; he and his sister had escaped from Czechoslovakia during World War II and gradually made their way to Canada; was a member of the editorial board of the *Canadian Forum* during his M.A. year (1949); the following year, joined the department of political science at Queen's University.

Mendelssohn, Eleanora. Film and stage actress.

Merezhkovsky, Dmitry Sergeyevich. Russian poet, novelist, and critic; wrote a historical trilogy, *Christ and Anti-Christ* (1896–1905).

Michael, John Hugh. Professor of New Testament at EC.

Michener, Wendy Roland. TC, 5T6; arts editor and later co-editor of the *Varsity*; became a widely published cultural critic, writing for the *Toronto Daily Star*, *Maclean's*, *Saturday Night*, and the *Globe and Mail*; daughter of Roland Michener, Governor General of Canada, 1967–74.

Milford, Theodore Richard. Canon and prebendary of Lincoln Cathedral; chancellor, beginning in 1947.

Millar, Graham. VC classmate of NF and HKF; married Mildred Oldfield, also a classmate, in June 1935.

Miller, Robert W. (Bob). VC, 4T1.

Milne, W.S. Member of the staff of Northern Vocational School; contributor to the *Canadian Forum*.

Misener, Agnes. Wife of Don Misener.

Misener, Benton. VC, 4T8; entered college after serving in the Navy, did a year of graduate work, attended teachers' college, and served for thirty-two years as principal of elementary schools in Etobicoke, Ont.

Misener, Don. VC, 3T3.

Mitchell, Lillian. VC, 5T5; later, Lillian Watson.

Moffit, Margaret. VC, 4T7.

Montague, William Pepperell. American new realist philosopher.

Moore, Arthur Bruce Barbour. Principal of St. Andrews College, Saskatoon, Sask., 1946–50; president of VU, 1950–70.

Moore, Dora Mavor. Well-known Canadian actress and teacher; organized the New Play Society, which performed from 1946 to 1956 and which presented an annual satiric revue, *Spring Thaw*.

Moore, James Mavor. Actor, playwright, and producer; helped launch the New Play Society, and in 1950 became the chief producer for CBC television; the son of Dora Mavor Moore.

Moore, Marianne. American poet.

Moorhouse, Hugh. VC, 3T3, EC, 3T6; lived next door to NF during their EC days, 1933–36; returned to EC for an M.A. in philosophy and theology in 1950, during which time he was a residence house supervisor at VC; married Phyllis Foreman. ·

Morawetz, Oskar. Czech musician who came to Canada in 1940 and studied at the U of T; one of Canada's most frequently performed composers.

Morgan, Dorothy Coulter. VC, 3T4; daughter of Al Coulter, mayor of Weston; wife of Harry Coulter, a teacher.

Morgan, John. VC, 4T9.

Morgan, John Stewart. Associate professor of social work at the School of Social Work, U of T; M.A., Oxford.

Moritsugu, Frank. Editor of the *Varsity*, 1950–51; had a career in journalism and public relations; later, worked on behalf of the Japanese-Canadians who had been interned in the 1940s.

Morris, Kay. Staff member of the *Canadian Forum*; along with her husband, Louis A. Morris, managed the business affairs of the magazine and helped to keep it afloat.

Morris, Louis A. (Lew, Lou). With wife Kay, long-time business manager of the *Canadian Forum*.

Morris, William James (Bill). VC, 5T4; attended EC, but left theology school to do a Ph.D. in anthropology; worked for the department of Indian affairs in Ottawa; later entered business.

Morrison, George. Director of the Community Life Training Institute, Barrie, Ont.

Morrison, Mary Louise. Soprano who began her career as an opera singer on CBC and with the Canadian Opera Company, of which she was a founding member.

Morrison, R.P. (Bobby). U of T graduate student from Winnipeg.

Morse, Barry. Actor, producer, and director; in 1951 moved from England to Canada, where he began work in live theatre and on CBC Radio.

Morton, William (Bill). Canadian tenor; from 1938 to 1951, sang the Evangelist in the annual performances of the *St. Matthew Passion* by the Toronto Mendelssohn Choir; a regular performer on CBC Light Opera and CBC Opera.

Mosdell, Doris. VC, 4To; one of NF's students in 1939; member of the editorial board of the *Canadian Forum*, for which she wrote a regular column of movie reviews; during the time of NF's diaries she also had a weekly spot on CJBC radio; wife of Allan Sangster.

Moss, Sylvia. VC, 5To; worked for CBC for twenty-five years, where she was in charge of school broadcasts.

Mott, Hawley S. Judge of the family court in Toronto.

Muckle, Fr. J.T. Professor of Latin and Latin palaeography and of medieval Latin literature at SMC.

Mure, Geoffrey R(eginald) G(ilchrist). Appointed warden of Merton College, Oxford, in 1947.

Murray, (William Ewart) Gladstone. First general manager of CBC Radio.

Murton, Walter. VC, 5To.

Mustard, Thornton. Key figure in the curriculum branch of the Ont. Department of Education.

Naylor, Carman A. VC, 3T3.

Needler, Winifred. Curator of the Near Eastern department of the ROM.

Nelles, Samuel Sobieski. Principal, VU, 1851–54; president, 1854–87.

Nelson, Winifred. VC, 4T7.

Nestroy, Johann. Austrian comic dramatist.

Newlin, Claude M(ilton). Member of the English department, Michigan State University, 1929–60.

Newton, Margaret (Maggie). Social worker who rented the Fryes' attic and a second floor living room at 127 Clifton Rd. in the late 1940s; had previously worked for the United Nations relief organization, seeking homes for European war orphans; later joined the faculty of the School of Social Work, U of T.

Newton, Robert. President of the University of Alberta, 1941–50.

Nichols, E.M. (Ted). Chaplain of Hart House.

Nichols, Jack. Painter.

Nicholson, Ben. British painter; after 1933 he produced only abstract work, including a series of white, low-relief carvings.

Nicholson, J(ohn)W(illiam) A(ngus). Methodist minister and CCF member from the Maritimes; was interested in the Social Gospel movement after the Depression and associated with other younger leaders of the movement in the Fellowship for a Christian Social Order.

Nicol, John. VC, 4T8; employed by the Department of Transport, Coral Harbour, Southhampton Island, Northwest Territories; in 1949, published a series of articles in the *Canadian Forum* on the subarctic region; became a member of the editorial board of the *Forum* in 1950.

Nicolson, Marjorie Hope. Widely published scholar on sixteenth- and seventeenth-century English literature; interested especially in the relation between literature and science; gave the Alexander lectures at U of T in 1946–47.

Niebuhr, Reinhold. American theologian; professor of Christian ethics, Union Theological Seminary, New York, N.Y., 1928–60.

Nims, Sister (Margaret) Frances. Lecturer in English at SMC.

Nishio, Akiro. Member of NF's graduate seminar on allegory, 1951–52.

Nitchie, Elizabeth. Professor of English at Goucher College; specialist in British Romanticism, particularly Mary Shelley.

Norman, Madeleine (Sister Marion). Member of the English department at SMC (Loretto), U of T, 1944–46 and 1954–70.

Northrop, F.S.C. Sterling professor of both philosophy and law at Yale University, where he taught for thirty-nine years; devoted his life to resolving international ideological conflicts.

Noseworthy, Joseph William (Joe). Popular high school teacher who defeated Arthur Meighen, national leader of the Conservative party, in the 1942 federal by-election, the first CCF victory in Ont.

Noyes, Lilian. Niece of NF's father, Herman Edward.

Nye, Russell B(laine). Member of the English department, Michigan State University.

Ochino, Bernardino. Italian Protestant reformer.

O'Donnell, Fr. James Reginald. Professor of Latin palaeography and medieval Latin at SMC.

Olnick, Harvey. Founder of serious musicological teaching in Canada; taught at U of T, 1954–83.

Olson, Elder James. Member of the English department, University of Chicago; one of the neo-Aristotelians.

Oppenheimer, Ernst M. VC, 4T9; did graduate study in German at Columbia and Harvard; in 1957 became the first full-time appointee at Carleton College (later, University) in Ottawa, where he remained until his retirement.

Ostade, Adriaen van. Dutch painter and printmaker.

Oughton, Jack. Close friend of HKF; in the 1930s, lived around the corner from the Kemps at 882 Carlaw St.; assistant in biology at U of T, 1934–35; became an associate in zoology at the ROM; later taught at the Ont. Agricultural College and worked for twenty years for the World Health Organization of the United Nations.

Oughton, Phillis. Wife of Jack Oughton; studied biology at U of T.

Ouimet, Roger. Attorney and judge; became a justice of the superior court of Que. in 1955.

Outerbridge, Ian Worrall. VC, 5T1; president of the student body during his final year.

Overstreet, H.A. Popular American author; his *The Mature Mind* was a Book-of-the-Month Club selection in 1949.

Owen, Derwyn Randulph Grier. B.A., TC; associate professor of ethics, head of the religious knowledge program, and lecturer in divinity, TC; became provost of TC in 1957.

Owen, Ivon. Associate editor and contributor to the *Canadian Forum*; later became head of Oxford University Press in Canada.

Pacey, Desmond (Des). Teacher, editor, short story writer, and literary critic; studied at U of T and Cambridge; taught at Brandon College in Manitoba, 1940–44, and UNB, 1944–75, where he also served as vice-president; early champion of Canadian literature.

Page, Madelaine. Graduate student in English at U of T, 1949–51.

Panton, L(awrence) A(rthur) C(olley). Canadian landscape painter; was principal of OCA, 1951–54; became president of the Arts and Letters Club in 1953.

Parkes, A.E. Associate secretary of the Students' Administrative Council, U of T.

Parlow, Kathleen. Violinist who taught at the TCM; founded the Parlow String Quartet, the best-known Canadian quartet of its day (1943–58).

Parr, Roger P(hillip). Graduate student at U of T in 1951–52; received his Ph.D. in 1956, having written a dissertation, directed by L.K. Shook, on Chaucer; began teaching at Marquette University, Wisc., in 1953.

Parsons, David Stewart. VC, 4T8; M.A. in English, U of T, 1951; wrote a dissertation on G.B. Shaw under the supervision of Claude Bissell; married Margaret Gould; taught English at USk, 1958–91.

Patchell, Robert W. UC, 4T8; audited NF's courses; friend of James Reaney and Richard Stingle; later worked for CBC Radio and became a producer for CBC television.

Paton, Herbert James. Professor of moral philosophy at Oxford and fellow of Corpus Christi College.

Peacock, Kenneth (Ken) Howard. Composer, pianist, and musicologist; at the time of NF's 1949 Diary, was teaching music in Ottawa.

Peacock, Ronald. Member of the German department at Manchester University.

Pearce, Donald. Member of the English department at the University of Michigan; later taught at the University of California, Santa Barbara.

Pearson, Beverley. VC, 5T2.

Pearson, Lester Bowles (Mike). VC, 1T9; well-known Canadian diplomat, public servant, and politician; chancellor of VU, 1952–59; prime minister of Canada, 1963–68.

Peers, Frank Wayne. Supervisor of public affairs talks for CBC Radio, 1948–60; later, professor of political science, U of T.

Pegis, Anton C. Professor of the history of philosophy at the Pontifical Institute of Mediaeval Studies and the U of T; Ph.D., U of T, 1931; taught at Marquette and Fordham Universities, and returned to U of T in 1946.

Pentland, Barbara. Well-known composer; one of the first Canadian composers to use avant-garde techniques; taught at the TCM, 1943–49, and at UBC, 1949–63.

Pepper, George. Canadian painter; studied with J.E.H. MacDonald and was strongly influenced by the Group of Seven; taught at OCA.

Pergolesi, Giovanni Battista. Italian composer, violinist, and church organist.

Perry, Ralph Barton. American philosopher; proponent of new realism.

Peterson, Doris E. Joined the English department at United College (Manitoba) in 1945, and was head of the department from 1947 to 1949, when she was succeeded by Millar MacLure.

Peterson, Leonard (Len). Canadian playwright and novelist, best known for his many CBC radio dramas.

Petrella, Enrico. Italian operatic composer.

Phelps, Arthur L. (Art). VC, 1T3; member of the English department at McGill University, 1947–53, and CBC broadcaster; the voice of CBC Radio's *Neighbourly News* for fifteen years.

Pierce, Lorne. Editor, writer, publisher; editor-in-chief of Ryerson Press, 1922–60, where he championed Canadian authors.

Piper, John. English abstract painter, decorative designer, and art critic for the *Listener* and the *Nation*.

Pitkin, Walter B. American new realist philosopher.

Pitt, David G. Ph.D. in English, U of T, 1960; wrote a dissertation on *Language and the Poetic Theory of English Romanticism*, directed by F.E.L. Priestley; taught for his entire career at Memorial University of Newfoundland; biographer of E.J. Pratt.

Playfair, William Henry. One of the principal architects of the Greek revival in Scotland.

Plewes, Eve Powell. VC, 2T8; member of the board of regents, VU.

Pope, Isabel. Tutor in Romance languages, Radcliffe College.

Pope, John Collins. Medievalist; specialist on *Beowulf*.

Porter, Dana Harris. Tory attorney-general of Ont. and later Ont.'s chief justice.

Potts, Abbie. Author, educator; wrote books on Shakespeare, Wordsworth, and Spenser; member of the advisory committee of the English Institute, 1953–56; taught at Vassar and Rockford Colleges.

Prang, Margaret. Member of the history department, UBC.

Pratt, E(dwin) J(ohn) (Ned). Well-known Canadian poet and member of the English department at VC, 1920–53.

Pratt, (Mildred) Claire. Daughter of E.J. Pratt; VC, 4T4; artist, writer, editor, and poet.

Pratt, Viola (Vi). Wife of E.J. Pratt; graduate of VC and OCE; editor, UCC Publishing House; short story writer; social activist.

Preston, Melvin Alexander. Member of the physics department at U of T, 1949–53; later, taught at McMaster University.

Preston, Richard Arthur (Dick). One of the original members of the history department at the Royal Military College when it reopened after World War II; wrote a two-volume history of the Royal Military College; later became head of the Canadian studies program at Duke University.

Price, Hereward Thimbleby. Professor of English, University of Michigan.

Priestley, F.E.L. Member of the English department at UC, 1944–70; had taught previously at the University of Alberta, 1931–36, and UBC, 1940–44.

Priestley, J.B. British novelist, playwright, and broadcaster.

Puccetti, Roland Peter. M.A., U of T, 1950; D. de l'Univ., Paris, 1952; taught at the American University in Beirut, the University of Singapore, and Dalhousie University.

Purcell, Henry. English composer.

Quiggin, Margaret J. (Peggy). VC, 5T1.

Quintana, Ricardo Beckwith. Member of the English department at the University of Wisconsin and a scholar of eighteenth-century literature, especially Jonathan Swift.

Ransom, John Crowe. American poet and critic; leading theorist of the Southern literary renaissance; founder and editor of the *Kenyon Review*; taught at Kenyon College, 1937–58.

Rapee, Erno. Silent film composer; conductor of the Grand Orchestra at the Capitol Theater in New York City, the largest theatre orchestra in the 1920s.

Rathburn, Eldon. Staff composer for the National Film Board, 1944–76; wrote scores for more than one hundred films.

Ray, Margaret (Peggy). Associate librarian at VC, 1935–52; appointed librarian in 1952.

Ready, Jack. Member of the English department at UWO; specialist in Anglo-Saxon; later went to the University of Michigan to work on the Old English lexicon.

Reaney, James Crerar. Poet, playwright, and teacher; attended UC as an undergraduate, taught at the University of Manitoba, returned to Toronto to complete a Ph.D. under NF's supervision, and taught for many years at UWO; married Colleen Thibaudeau in 1951.

Reid, Thomas. Scottish philosopher.

Reinhardt, Max. Austrian theatre manager.

Renwicke, Audrey. VC, 5T0; married Stephen Gibson.

Reymes-King, John. Ph.D., U of T, 1950; wrote a dissertation on Morley's madrigals; first professor of music at the University of Alberta.

Ribera, Jusepe de. Spanish artist.

Rice, Philip Blair. Managing editor and later associate editor of the *Kenyon Review* when John Crowe Ransom was editor; taught philosophy at Kenyon College.

Rice, Warner G(renelle). Professor of English, University of Michigan.

Riddell, Robert Gerald (Jerry). Senior tutor when NF was a student at VC; later became the permanent Canadian delegate to the United Nations; died suddenly in 1951 while representing Canada at the UN.

Ridley, Maurice Roy. Professor of English, Harvard University.

Rièse, Laure (Laurette). VC, 3T3; member of the French department at VC.

Rinehart, Keith. Ph.D. student at the University of Wisconsin in 1950; completed his dissertation on Victorian autobiography in 1951; later became chair of the English department at Central Washington College, Ellensburg, Wash.

Roach, Allison. VC, 5T5.

Roberts, Sir Charles G.D. Canadian poet and writer of animal stories.

Robertson, Duncan Crosby. Ph.D. student in English at U of T in 1950; completed his degree in 1965, writing a dissertation on modern criticism under NF's supervision; taught at Queen's University.

Robertson, (Hartley) Grant. Member of the Classics department at VC.

Robins, John D. One of NF's teachers at VC and later a colleague in the English department; began his career at VC in the German department, but in 1925 moved to English where he taught until his retirement in 1952; head of the department, 1938–52.

Robins, Leila. Wife of John D. Robins.

Robinson, F.N. Professor of English at Harvard University; Chaucer specialist.

Robinson, Judith. Journalist who wrote first for the Toronto *Globe and Mail*, 1937–40, and then, as a daily columnist from Ottawa, for the Toronto *Telegram*.

Robson, Albert Henry. Vice-president of the council of the AGT; authored several books on Canadian painters and painting; art director at Grip, Ltd., which employed HKF's father; was a supporter of the Group of Seven painters before they enjoyed public favour.

Robson, D.O. Member of the Classics department at VC.

Roethke, Theodore. American poet.

Rogers, Diane (Di). VC, 5T0.

Rogers, Oscar. Teacher at the Davisville Ave. School in Toronto; husband of Dorothy Marks.

Rogers, Robert Wentworth. Ph.D., Harvard, 1942; became professor of English, head of the department, and dean of the College of Liberal Arts and Sciences at the University of Illinois, Champaign-Urbana.

Romans, Gordon. VC classmate of NF and HKF.

Romans, Lois (née Hampson). VC, 3T3; wife of Gordon Romans.

Rooke, Barbara E. VC, 4T5; lecturer in English at VC; professor of English at Trent University.

Roper, Gordon. Member of the English department at TC, 1946–69, and later at Trent University.

Rose, Albert (Al). Member of the faculty at the School of Social Work, U of T; contributor to the *Canadian Forum*.

Roseborough, Margaret. *See* Stobie, Margaret.

Rosenmeyer, Thomas G(ustav). Member of the Classics department, University of Iowa; later, professor of Classics at University of California, Berkeley.

Roskolenko, Harry. Journalist and author; born in Canada but spent most of his life in New York.

Ross, Glenn. VC, 5T1; later named permanent president of the class; became an accountant and worked both in private practice and for the government.

Ross, Harold. Editor of the *New Yorker*, 1925–51.

Ross, Malcolm (Mac). M.A., U of T, 1934; Ph.D., Cornell, 1941; taught at the University of Manitoba, 1945–50, Queen's University, 1950–62, TC, 1962–68, and Dalhousie University, 1968–82.

Ross, Mary Lowery. *See* Lowery, Mary.

Rossi, Mario Manlio. Visiting professor of philosophy at U of T, 1950–51.

Rowe, John Gordon. After his undergraduate and seminary training in the U.S., became chaplain of Hart House, 1950–54; first editor of *Bias*, a magazine of the Student Christian Movement; began his teaching career at UWO in 1955; later, Dean of Arts, Huron College, UWO.

Rowland, Nancy. VC, 4T6; Ph.D., 1965; member of the English department, SMC; married Bill Orwen.

Russell, Lillian. American singer and actress, known for her beauty, charm, and talent in light opera.

Russell, Stanley. Minister of Deer Park United Church in Toronto.

Rutherford, John T. VC, 5T3; active in the film society and in drama as a student, and was president of the student CCF group; had a career with CBC television.

Sagar, Barbara E. VC, 5T1; in the first class to graduate in the anthropology course.

Sagar, W.L. Associate professor of civil engineering, School of Practical Science, U of T.

Saint Francis, Sister M. *See* Nims, Sister (Margaret) Francis.

Saltmarche, Kenneth Charles. Curator of the Willistead Art Gallery, Windsor, Ont.

Saminsky, Lazare. Russian-born composer and conductor known for his music for Jewish worship.

Sanborn, C. Earle. Taught elementary school for nine years before graduating from VC in 1948; instructor in English at UC in the early 1950s; Ph.D. in English, U of T, 1959; wrote a dissertation on Yeats under the supervision of Marshall McLuhan; taught at UWO until his retirement.

Sanderson, Charles Rupert. Chief librarian of the Toronto public libraries.

Sandwell, B.K. Author, teacher, and editor of *Saturday Night*, 1932–51.

Sangster, Allan. Member of the editorial board of the *Canadian Forum*; wrote a regular column of radio reviews; formerly music critic for the Toronto *Globe and Mail*; husband of Doris Mosdell.

Sansom, William. British short story writer, novelist, and travel writer.

Santoliquido, Ornella Pulite. Pianist with the Italian emsemble Virtuosi di Roma.

Saunders, Sir Charles Edward. Cerealist who in 1907 developed Marquis wheat, a faster-maturing variety of wheat, which led to greater production in the prairies.

Savan, David. Member of the philosophy department at U of T, 1943–81; came to Toronto from the College of William and Mary in 1943.

Sawyer, A(rthur) Edward (Ted). Graduate student at U of T; Ph.D. in English, U of T, 1960; wrote a dissertation on Joseph Conrad; a committed Anglo-Catholic interested in church affairs.

Schanzer, Ernest. Member of the English department, UC; Shakespearean scholar.

Schawlow, Rosemarie. VC, 4T1; was in NF's classes the first year he taught at VC, 1937–38; studied English at Harvard for a semester; later, Rosemarie Wolfe.

Schikaneder, Emanuel. Librettist for Mozart's *The Magic Flute*.

Scholem, Gershom. Professor of Jewish mysticism at Hebrew Union University, 1933–63.

Schoop, Trudi. Swiss dancer and comedienne; organized her Comic Ballet in 1931; toured Canada in 1947.

Sclater, J(ohn) R(obert) P(aterson). Minister at Old St. Andrews United Church, located at Carlton and Jarvis Streets in Toronto.

Sclater, William. Canadian author and journalist; his book *Haida*, about a World War II destroyer, won the Governor General's Award for nonfiction in 1947.

Scott, Elizabeth. Wife of James Richardson Scott, political organizer and secretary of the National Liberal Federation.

Scott, Frank R. Canadian poet and social philosopher; taught at McGill, 1927–64; founder of the League for Social Reconstruction.

Scott, James Richardson (Jim). Lecturer in English at UC; subsequently went into journalism, then taught at UWO, and later became a political organizer.

Scott, John Wilson. Lecturer (later professor) in physiology and clinical teacher in medicine and surgery, U of T; husband of Grace Workman.

Sedgewick, Garnett Gladwin. Head of the English department at UBC; a medievalist; social activist; gave the Alexander Lectures at U of T, 1935.

Seeley, R(eginald) S(idney) K(ingsley). Provost of TC; lecturer in religious knowledge and in divinity at TC.

Seltzer, Dan. B.A., Princeton, 1954; Ph.D., Harvard, 1959; professor of English at Harvard and then at Princeton, where he also directed the university's theatre program; became acquainted with NF in 1954 when the latter was Class of 1932 visiting lecturer at Princeton.

Service, James D. (Jim). VC, 5T0; business manager of *Acta Victoriana*, 1948–50.

Shabaeff, Grace Dempster. VC, 4T1.

Shannon, Edgar F., Jr. Ph.D., Oxford, 1949; instructor in the English department at Harvard University, 1950–56; later, professor of English, and then president, University of Virginia.

Shapley, Harlow. American astronomer; director of the Harvard University Observatory, 1921–52.

Shea, Albert A. (Al). Political economist; contributor to the *Canadian Forum*; in 1950 he had just returned from New York where he had served as consultant to UNESCO on mass communications.

Sherburn, George Wiley. Professor of eighteenth-century literature at Harvard University.

Shields, Thomas Todhunter. Self-educated Baptist clergyman and minister at the Jarvis St. Baptist Church in Toronto for forty-five years; fiercely antiCatholic, he founded his own denomination and seminary after he was expelled from the Baptist convention of Ont. and Que. for intolerance.

Shook, Fr. Lawrence Kennedy. Member of the English department at SMC; superior of the Basilian order.

Short, Robert (Bob). Brother-in-law of Margaret Gayfer; a school teacher.

Shovel, Sir Cloudesby. English admiral.

Shubik, Martin. B.A., U of T, 4T7, M.A., U of T, 1949; Ph.D., Princeton, 1953; became a professor of mathematical economics at Yale; as a student, contributed reviews and satirical poems to the *Canadian Forum*, the latter under the pseudonym of Thersites.

Siddall, Ruth Ellen. Graduate student in English, U of T, 1947–49.

Silcox, Claris Edwin. UCC minister.

Silverstein, Theodore. Member of the English department, University of Chicago.

Simmons, R.B. Keeper of the prints at the Hart House gallery, U of T, 1949–50.

Sinclair, Gordon. Broadcaster and writer for the *Toronto Daily Star*; his opinionated "news and comments" were heard on CFRB in Toronto in the 1940s and 1950s.

Sinclair, Lister. Playwright and producer for CBC.

Sirluck, Ernest. M.A., U of T, 1941, Ph.D., U of T, 1948; member of the English faculty at UC, 1946–47; at the time of NF's 1949 Diary, was teaching English at the University of Chicago; returned to teach at UC and became dean of graduate studies at U of T in 1961; president of the University of Manitoba, 1971–76.

Sirluck, Lesley. Wife of Ernest Sirluck; occasional reviewer for the *Canadian Forum*; sister of Kenneth McNaught.

Sisco, Gordon. Official of the UCC; appointed secretary of the General Council of the UCC in 1936.

Sissons, Charles Bruce. Member of the Classics faculty at VC; author of *A History of Victoria University* (1952).

Sitwell, Edith. Well-known English poet; sister of Osbert and Sacheverell Sitwell; reviewed NF's *FS* in the *Spectator*.

Sitwell, Osbert. British satirical poet; novelist and autobiographer; brother of Edith and Sacheverell Sitwell.

Skitch, Russell. Canadian opera singer.

Skoggard, Jean Ross. VC, 3T9; artist who lived in China for a while and developed a Chinese style of painting.

Sledd, James H(inton). Member of the English department, University of Chicago.

Smallbridge, J.E. Graduate student in English, U of T, in 1952.

Smiberts, John. Scottish portrait painter; first artist of note to produce paintings in America.

Smith, A.E. Methodist minister whose support of the labour struggles in Manitoba caused his dismissal from the church; was elected to the Manitoba legislature and became one of the founding members of the Canadian Labour Party.

Smith, A.J.M. (Art). Canadian poet and critic; produced a number of important anthologies of Canadian poetry and prose; left Canada in 1936 to teach at Michigan State University, where he remained until his retirement in 1972.

Smith, Barbara Jean. VC, 5T2.

Smith, Datus C., Jr. Editor, Princeton University Press, 1941–53; director, 1943–53.

Smith, Gordon Elmer. B.A., U of T, 5T1; M.A. in philosophy, 1952; member of NF's graduate seminar on allegory, 1951–52.

Smith, Kathlyn. VC, 5T0; on the editorial staff of the *Varsity* and *Acta Victoriana*.

Smith, Patricia J. VC, 5T2.

Smith, Sidney E. President of U of T, 1945–57.

Smith, W(illiam) Lyndon. Professor of church history at TC.

Sorokin, Pitirim A. First professor of sociology at Harvard, where he taught from 1930 to 1955; pioneer of sociological research.

Spaulding, Edward G. American new realist philosopher.

Speers, John Edward. VC, 4T5; one of NF's students; went to the University of Manitoba for an M.A., returning to Toronto to study for the Anglican ministry at TC.

Spencer, Alexander Charles. Engineer; chancellor of VU, 1944–52.

Spencer, Theodore. American poet and critic.

Spender, Sir Stephen Harold. English poet, critic, and man of letters; held many academic posts in England and the U.S.

Spring, David. Lecturer in the history department at U of T, 1946–48; accepted an appointment at Johns Hopkins University in 1949.

Spry, Graham. Journalist, diplomat, and political activist; was a staunch advocate of public broadcasting in Canada and the co-founder of the Canadian Radio League; director of Saskatchewan House, London.

Stapleford, Ernest William. President of Regina College for twenty-three years; in 1937, became assistant to the president at VU, and in 1948, assistant minister at Metropolitan United Church, Toronto.

Staples, William Ewart (Bill). Professor of Oriental languages, VC.

Stedman, John Gabriel. British writer whose *Narrative* Blake helped to illustrate and which in turn influenced several of his poems.

Stedmond, John Mitchell. Member of the English department at USk; later moved to Queen's University, where he taught until his retirement.

Stern, Max. Proprietor of the Dominion Gallery in Montreal, which introduced the sculpture of Henry Moore to Canada; his gallery was the first to give contracts to artists.

Sternfeld, Frederick William. British musicologist; Ph.D., Yale, 1943; taught at Wesleyan and Dartmouth before becoming a lecturer, and eventually a reader in the history of music, at Oxford.

Stevenson, David L(loyd). Member of the English department at Western Reserve University, 1947–64; later taught at Hunter College in New York, N.Y.

Stevenson, Ellen. Graduate student in English, U of T, 1949–50.

Stewart, Douglas Bruce. Student in fine arts at U of T and member of the Hart House art committee, 1947–49; secretary, 1949; B.S. in library science, U of T, 5T8; spent career as librarian in Ont. and N.S.

Stewart, Dugald. Scottish philosopher.

Stewart, Isobel Routly. VC, 3T9; helped to organize the student writers' group and was on the staff of *Acta Victoriana*.

Stewart, Walter D. Attended VC, 1949–53; managing editor of *Acta Victoriana*, 1952; became a well-known newspaper editor and writer.

Stiling, Frank. B.A., McMaster, 1926; Ph.D., University of Michigan, 1949; joined the English department at UWO in 1949; subsequently became dean of the faculty of arts and sciences.

Stingle, Richard M. VC, 4T8; reader in the English department at VC, 1948–49; M.A., U of T, 1950; taught at United College in Winnipeg and later at UWO.

Stobie, Bill. Member of the English department, University of Manitoba; husband of Margaret Roseborough Stobie.

Stobie, Margaret (Peggy). Margaret (née Roseborough) was a member of the graduate seminar on Blake given by Herbert J. Davis that NF enrolled in during his first year at EC; Ph.D., U of T, 1937; member of the English department at the University of Manitoba, 1946–50, 1959–72.

Stokes, Frederick C. VC, 4T3.

Stoll, E.E. Shakespearean scholar who argued that Shakespeare's plays represent the actualities of history; taught at the University of Minnesota.

Strachan, R(obert) H(arvey). Minister from Cambridge, Eng.; delivered the Armstrong Lecture at VC in 1952.

Stykolt, Stefan. VC, 4T6; he and his sister Janina had escaped from Poland during World War II; after studying at Harvard and Cambridge, accepted a position in the department of economics and political science at U of T; in 1954, succeeded NF as editor of the *Canadian Forum*; died at age thirty-eight after a painful illness.

Summer, John and Eileen. Friends of Muriel Code.

Summersgill, W.J. Graduate student in English at U of T, 1949–50.

Surerus, J(ohn) Alvin. Member of the German department at VC.

Sutherland, James R. Professor of modern English literature, University College, London; had been an instructor in English at USk, 1921–23.

Sutherland, John. Poet and editor; founded the First Statement Press, which issued a number of important chapbooks; edited the *Northern Review*, 1945–56.

Sword, John Howe. Secretary, School of Graduate Studies, U of T; later, provost of U of T.

Tait, Marcus D.C. Member of the department of Classics, UC.

Tandy, Jessica. American actress; co-starred in many films with her husband Hume Cronyn.

Tatham, George Sidford. Member of the geography department at U of T.

Tave, Stuart M(alcolm). Member of the English department, University of Chicago.

Tawney, Richard Henry. English economic historian.

Taylor, Griffith. Professor of geography and head of the department at U of T.

Theall, Donald F. Ph.D., U of T, 1954; wrote a dissertation on modern poetry, directed by Marshall McLuhan; taught at SMC, 1954–65; professor, later president, Trent University.

Thibaudeau, Colleen. Canadian poet; UC, 4T8; M.A., 1949; worked in publishing in 1949–50; married James Reaney in 1951.

Thomas, Isabel Martin. M.A., U of T, 1924; one of the original faculty members

and head of the English department at York Memorial Collegiate Institute,
  which opened in 1929; active in the League for Social Reconstruction.

Thompson, Callum. Member of the Commission on Culture of the UCC; a UCC
  minister.

Thompson, Eleanor F. VC, 4T9; M.A., Ph.D.; became senior tutor at Woodsworth College, U of T; later Eleanor Morgan.

Thompson, Francis. English poet of the Aesthetic movement of the 1890s.

Thompson, Gloria. VC, 5T0; member of the writers' group at VC; enrolled in all
  of the courses NF taught in her years at VC; later became a teacher, tutor,
  student of medieval history (M.A., 1988), writer, and editor.

Thompson, Margot I. Toronto editor.

Thomson, Beth. VC, 4T9.

Thomson, D(ouglas) F(erguson) S(cott). Lecturer, later professor, in Latin, UC.

Thomson, Edgar B. (Ted). VC, 4T4, with a degree in commerce; brother of
  Eleanor M. Thomson.

Thomson, Eleanor M. VC, 4T9; later, Eleanor David (not to be confused with
  Eleanor F. Thompson).

Thomson, J.S. Dean of the faculty of divinity, McGill University, 1946–56;
  elected for a two-year term as moderator of the general council of the UCC in
  1956; delivered the Armstrong Lecture at VC in 1950.

Thomson, Murray. U of T, 4T7; worked in adult education in Sask. Canadian
  peace activist; peace education secretary of the Canadian Friends Service
  Committee, 1962–69.

Thomson, William. Taught Arabic at Harvard beginning in 1924; James Richard
  Jewett Professor from 1939.

Thorburn, John. Visiting professor of philosophy, U of T, 1950–51, after the
  death of Reid MacCallum.

Thornhill, Reginald (Reg). Friend, along with his wife Mary, of HKF's father
  and mother, S.H.F. and Gertrude Kemp; at his instigation, S.H.F. Kemp
  joined the Commercial Artists Guild.

Thorpe, Clarence DeWitt. Member of the English department, University of
  Michigan.

Thurber, James. American writer and cartoonist; began writing for Harold
  Ross's *New Yorker* in 1927.

Thurston, David Erwin. SMC, 5T0.

Tillich, Paul. German-born American theologian and philosopher; taught
  theology at Union Theological Seminary, New York, Harvard Divinity
  School, and the Divinity School at the University of Chicago.

Tindall, William York. Professor of English, Columbia University.

Tinker, Chauncey Brewster. Professor of English at Yale University; medievalist; *Beowulf* bibliographer; critic of eighteenth- and nineteenth-century literature.

Toll, LeRoy. VC, 3T5; Toronto portrait photographer, with a studio at 119 Williamson Rd.

Tracy, Clarence Rupert. Member of the English department at UNB and later at USk and Acadia.

Trethewey, Della Mae (Del). Wife of Hilliard Trethewey.

Trethewey, (William) Hilliard. Member of the French department at VC, 1936–67; chair, 1952–67.

Trilling, Lionel. American literary critic; taught at Columbia University.

Trimble, H. Harrison. Teacher and principal in the Moncton, N.B., school system; appointed superintendent and secretary of the Moncton school board in 1925, a position he held for almost four decades.

Tubman, Barbara. VC, 4T9.

Tupper, K(enneth) F(ranklin). Dean of the faculty of applied science and engineering, U of T.

Turnbull, Catharine J. VC, 5T2.

Tuve, Rosemond. Professor of English, University of Pennsylvania.

Tyrell, Joseph Burr. VC, 8T9; eminent geologist, explorer, and historian.

Underhill, Frank. Member of the history department at U of T, 1927–55; a political journalist who helped found the *Canadian Forum* and the League for Social Reconstruction.

Upshall, Joyce. VC, 5T2.

Urquhart, Donald A. (Don). VC, 5T2; one of the literary editors of *Acta Victoriana*, 1949–50; became an elementary school teacher and later principal in the Toronto school system.

Urwick, E.J. Author of a number of books in social philosophy; NF's colleague in philosophy, John A. Irving, edited Urwick's *The Values of Life* (1948).

Valdes, Juan de. Spanish humanist and religious reformer.

Valentin, Gottfried. German painter.

Valleau, Douglas John. VC, 4T9; became a secondary school teacher.

van Barentzen, Aline. American-born French pianist; began her musical education in Boston and at age nine entered the National Conservatory of Music in Paris.

Van Doren, Mark. American poet, novelist, and critic.

Vaughan, Harold W. (Hal). VC, 3T1, and EC, 3T6; minister of Zion United Church in Brantford, Ont.

Vickers, George Stephen. Member of the faculty of art and architecture, U of T.

Vickery, John B. (Jack). VC, 4T7; M.A., Colgate; Ph.D., University of Wisconsin; married Olga Westland.

Viereck, Peter. American poet.

Vinci, Ernesto. Teacher, baritone, physician; joined the faculty of music at U of T, 1945; one of Canada's leading voice teachers.

Vlastos, Gregory. Professor of Classics at Queens University; moved to Cornell University in 1950.

Voaden, Herman Arthur. Playwright, director, editor, and educator; after World War II, began a second career as a national arts lobbyist; first president of the Canadian Arts Council, 1945–48; director of the Canadian Conference of the Arts.

Volkoff, Boris. Well-known dancer and choreographer; after coming to Canada from Moscow, established a dance school.

Waite, Janet Katherine. VC, 5T2; later, Janet Burnie.

Wallace, Edward Wilson. President and chancellor of VU, 1930–41.

Wallace, Malcolm. Professor of English at UC, 1905–44.

Wallace, Robert Charles. President of the University of Alberta, 1928–36; principal of Queen's University, 1936–50.

Wallerstein, Ruth. Member of the English department at the University of Wisconsin; seventeenth-century scholar.

Walter, Arnold M. Canadian musicologist and educator; became an influential leader on the music faculty at U of T, helping to develop an extensive research library; established an opera school at the TCM in 1949.

Walter, Onalee. VC, 4T9; received her M.A. in psychology in 1950 and became a school psychologist.

Wanless, Dawn. VC, 4T9; had worked for three years and spent five years in the Navy before entering VC in the fall of 1945.

Ward, Anne. VC, 5T2; later, Anne Maxwell.

Warren, Alba H(oughton). Member of the English department at Princeton; friend of NF from their student days at Merton College; a Rhodes Scholar from Texas.

Watson, Homer. Canadian landscape painter and one of the founders of the Canadian Art Club; president of the Royal Canadian Academy, 1918–21.

Watson, John. Canada's foremost early philosopher and the only Canadian ever invited to give the Gifford Lectures in Edinburgh; his books on Kant were classics in the field.

Watson, Stanley A. Key figure in the curriculum branch of the Ont. Department of Education.

Watson, Sydney Hollinger. Toronto designer, artist, and muralist; became principal of OCA in 1955.

Watson, Wilfred. Innovative poet and playwright; taught English at the University of Alberta.

Waugh. Mary. VC, 5T1; M.A., U of T, 1952.

Weaver, Robert. Editor, broadcaster, and founder of the *Tamarack Review*;

originated the CBC *Critically Speaking* series, and was responsible for the CBC's *Tuesday Night* and *Anthology* programs.

Webber, Gordon M. Canadian artist; chief assistant of Arthur Lismer at the AGT, beginning work there in 1930; taught classes at the Children's Art Centre of the AGT, 1935–39.

Webster, Joan. VC, 5T0.

Webster, John Clarence. Canadian physician, historian, nationalist; taught obstetrics and gynaecology at the University of Chicago's Rush Medical Center; returned to Canada in 1919 to begin a new career as a historian and collector of artefacts.

Wechsler, Dora. Canadian ceramic sculptor.

Wedgwood, Sir John Hamilton. Son of Sir Ralph Wedgwood and brother of Veronica Wedgwood.

Wedgwood, Sir Ralph Lewis. Railway administrator; father of Veronica and Sir John Wedgwood and great-grandson of Josiah Wedgwood, the potter.

Wedgwood, Veronica. Daughter of Sir Ralph Wedgwood; became a distinguished historian, influenced by her father's friendship with W.G.M. Trevelyan; NF met her and her father shortly after he arrived at Merton College in 1936.

Weelkes, Thomas. English madrigal composer.

Wees, Frances. Prolific author of mystery novels.

Weinert, Donald L. VC, 4T9.

Wells, Dalton Courtright. Justice of the Supreme Court of Ont.; married Kathleen P. Irwin.

Westaway, James Whitlock. Insurance executive; bass singer with the Toronto Mendelssohn Choir; later, president of the TSO.

Westland, Olga. UC, 4T7. M.A. Wellesley; Ph.D., University of Wisconsin; married John B. Vickery; changed her name from Wasylchuk to Westland when she was at Wellesley.

Wetmore, F(rank) E(llsworth) W(aring). Member of the department of chemistry, U of T.

Wevers, J(ohn) W(illiam). Professor of Oriental languages, UC.

Whatton, W. Victor. M.A., U of T, 1950.

White, Helen C. Professor of English at the University of Wisconsin; scholar of sixteenth- and seventeenth-century literature.

White, Lois G. VC, 5T2; member of the VC Union Executive.

White, Mary E. Professor of Classics, TC.

Whitley, Harold. Neighbour of the Fryes; school principal in Toronto and school inspector for the Toronto Board of Education; husband of Isabel.

Whitley, Hilary. Daughter of Harold and Isabel Whitley.

Whitley, Isabel. Neighbour of the Fryes; teacher at Leaside High School; wife of Harold; daughter of Bishop William Thomas Hallam.

Whittaker, Herbert. Director of amateur and professional theatre; drama critic for the *Globe and Mail*, 1949–75.

Whyte, Peter and Catharine. Students at the Museum of Fine Arts in Boston in the late 1920s; they married in 1930 and moved to Banff, which was Peter's home, where they devoted their lives to painting the landscape and the native people of the area.

Wilbur, Richard. American poet.

Wilkes, John. English politician; despite his outrageous personal behaviour, became a symbol of free speech.

Wilkinson, K. Jerome. Member of the English department at the University of Michigan.

Will, (Joseph) Stanley. Professor of French at UC.

Willan, Healey. Composer, organist, choir director, and educator; a dominant force in Canadian music for more than fifty years; taught at the TCM, 1913–37, and at U of T, 1937–50.

Williams, Ronald J. Assistant professor of Oriental languages at UC.

Williams, Yvonne. Stained glass artist; NF had known her since the mid-1930s, when she had lectured on the windows of Chartres Cathedral at the AGT.

Williamson, George. Professor of English, University of Chicago; specialized in seventeenth-century literature.

Wilson, Earl W. Graduated from OCA in 1946.

Wilson, Edmund. Well-known literary and cultural critic who assimilated Marxist and Freudian ideas; became literary editor of the *New Republic* in 1926.

Wilson, George Earl. Dean of the faculty of arts and sciences at Dalhousie University.

Wilson, Harold Sowerby. Member of the English faculty at UC, 1946–59.

Wilson, Lois Girvan. VC, 3To; member of the board of regents, VU.

Wilson, Nora R. VC, 5T5.

Wilt, Napier. Member of the English department, University of Chicago.

Wimsatt, William K., Jr. Professor of English at Yale University; one of the influential New Critics.

Winspear, Mary. Friend of NF from his student days; they had both been in Herbert Davis's Blake seminar during NF's first year at EC.

Winwood, Estelle. Well-known character actress; starred in *Quality Street* (1937) and numerous subsequent films.

Wolf, Hugo. Austrian composer, chiefly of songs.

Wolfe, Rosemarie. *See* Schawlow, Rosemarie.

Wolfe, Roy. Husband of Rosemarie Schawlow Wolfe.

Wood, Gordon. VC, 4T3; returned to VC in 1946 after serving in the army, enrolled in NF's Blake and Spenser courses, received his M.A. in 1947, and began his teaching career at Carleton University in 1951.

Wood, John Sinclair. Professor of French at VC.

Woodbury, J.C. (Jack). Member of NF's graduate seminar on allegory, 1951–52; attended U of T, 1951–54.

Woodhouse, A.S.P. Member of the English department at UC, 1929–64; chair of the department during the time of NF's 1949 Diary.

Woodman, Ross Grieg. One of NF's students in the 1949 Blake seminar; NF, along with F.E.L. Priestley, later supervised Woodman's Ph.D. dissertation on *The Apocalyptic Vision in the Work of Percy Bysshe Shelley*; taught at UWO.

Woods, Marion L. VC, 5T5; later, Marion Kirkwood.

Woodside, Moffat St. Andrew (Moff). Professor of ancient history, VC; registrar at VC, 1944–52; dean of arts, U of T, 1952–57; appointed principal of UC, 1959.

Woodsworth, J.S. Founding leader of the Co-operative Commonwealth Federation (CCF).

Woolsey, Theodore Dwight. President of Yale University, 1846–71.

Workman, Grace. VC, 3T6; M.A., 3T9; Ph.D., 4T3; don in the women's residences at VC, 1939–41; later, Grace Workman Scott.

Wright, Cecil Augustus. Dean of the School of Law, U of T.

Yalden, Maxwell Freeman. VC, 5T2; later minister of External Affairs and ambassador to various countries, including Belgium.

Yeats-Brown, Francis. British author; assistant editor of the *Spectator*, 1926–28.

Young, Art. VC, 3T9; EC, 4T3; UCC minister.

Young, Harold. Secretary of the board of colleges and universities of the UCC.

Appendix 2
Radio Talks and Published Writings
of Helen Kemp Frye

NOTE: This list includes the articles Helen Kemp Frye wrote for the *Star Weekly* and the *Montreal Standard*. No search has yet been undertaken to locate her other newspaper articles.

"The Heretic" [short story]. *Acta Victoriana*, 55, no. 4 (1932): 16–19.

"A New Outlook on Crime." *Acta Victoriana*, 56, no. 4 (April 1932): 24–7.

"The Library, Old and New." *Acta Victoriana*, 57, no. 3 (1933): 18–22.

"The University and the Fine Arts." *Acta Victoriana*, 57, no. 5 (April 1933): 5–10.

"Loan Collections from the Art Gallery of Toronto." *The School*, 25 (October 1936): 105–9.

"Children in the Gallery." CBC Radio talk, broadcast on 30 March (read by Judge Frank Denton).

"The Permanent Collection." CBC Radio talk, broadcast on 25 May 1937.

"Children at the Art Gallery of Toronto." *The School*, 26 (September 1937): 10–13.

"The Christmas Story in Art." CBC Radio talk, broadcast on 14 December 1937.

"Yvonne Williams." *Canadian Forum*, 18 (June 1938): 30.

"Yvonne McKague Housser." *Canadian Forum*, 18 (September 1938): 176.

"Henri Masson." *Canadian Forum*, 18 (November 1938): 241.

"Fritz Brandtner." *Canadian Forum*, 18 (December 1938): 272.

"Art for Everyman." *Curtain Call*, 10 (January 1939): 13–14. Originally broadcast on CBC Radio, 1 November 1938.

Review of *Portinari: His Life and Art*, intro. by Rockwell Kent. *Canadian Forum*, 21 (April 1941): 25.

"Economy and the Arts." *Canadian Forum*, 21 (July 1941): 116–17.

"Societies and Society." *Canadian Forum*, 21 (August 1941): 150–1.

"Art in the Nineteenth Century" [review of *The Story of Modern Art*, by Sheldon Cheney]. *Canadian Forum*, 21 (January 1942): 316.

"Portrait of the Artist in a Young Magazine." *Canadian Forum*, 22 (May 1942): 53–5.

"Manhandling the Arts." *Canadian Forum*, 22 (June 1942): 82–5.

"Help Yourself to Field Flowers." *The Standard* (Montreal), 15 August 1942, 13.

"American Folk Arts." *Canadian Forum*, 22 (December 1942): 276–7.

Review of *The St. Lawrence* by Henry Beston. *Canadian Forum*, 22 (December 1942): 286–7.

"Artists' Post-war Plan." *Canadian Forum*, 24 (August 1944): 113.

"UNESCO Program." *Canadian Forum*, 26 (February 1947): 252–3.

"Design in Industry." *Canadian Forum*, 27 (April 1947): 12–13.

"Two Art Conferences." *Canadian Forum*, 27 (May 1947): 37–8.

"Canadian Handicrafts Abroad." *Star Weekly*, 12 February 1949, 8.

Review of *Francisco de Goya*, by José Lopez-Rey. *Canadian Forum*, 31 (December 1951): 213–14.

Review of *A.J. Casson*, by Paul Duval. *Canadian Forum*, 32 (June 1952): 72.

Review of *Duveen*, by S.N. Behrman. *Canadian Forum*, 32 (September 1952): 140–1.

Review of *A History of Victoria University*, by C.B. Sissons, and *A History of the University of Trinity College, 1852–1952*, ed. T.A. Reed. *Canadian Forum*, 33 (May 1953): 45.

Review of *University College, 1853–1953*, ed. Claude T. Bissell. *Canadian Forum*, 33 (March 1954): 283.

Review of *Emily Carr as I Knew Her*, by Carol Pearson. *Canadian Forum*, 35 (April 1955): 24.

Review of *The Noble Savage: A Life of Paul Gauguin*, by Lawrence and Elizabeth Hanson. *Canadian Forum*, 35 (May 1955): 43.

"Our Art Gallery." *Victoria Reports*, 5, no. 1 (1955): 27.

"Alumni Hall Exhibition of Pictures by Isabel McLaughlin." *Victoria Reports*, 5, no. 2 (1955): 22–3.

"Exhibitions in Alumni Hall." *Victoria Reports*, [6, no. 1] (1956): 32.

"Picture Exhibitions in Alumni Hall." *Victoria Reports*, 8, no. 1 (1958): 28–9.

"Picture Exhibitions." *Victoria Reports*, 8, no. 2 (1958): 11.

"Class of '33—25th Reunion." *Victoria Reports*, 8, no. 2 (1958): 25–7.

Notes

Introduction

1 *Further Extracts from the Note-Books of Samuel Butler*, ed. A.T. Bartholomew (London: Jonathan Cape, 1934), 156.

2 *The Diary of Samuel Pepys* contains a million and a quarter words. NF's notebooks approach that size, even exceed it if the various holograph drafts in the notebooks are included in the total.

3 Some 5,000 letters are in NF's general correspondence files. The files of his correspondence with publishers, letters relating to speaking engagements, various media projects, and University of Toronto business contain several thousand more letters. NF's letters of recommendation number more than 650. After 1968, when NF's secretary Jane Widdicombe began making carbon copies of his correspondence, the record is fairly complete, but many of the letters NF wrote before 1968 have not been preserved, or at least their whereabouts is unknown.

4 50.385. We should allow for the possibility that NF may be referring to a form of writing that Michael Dolzani and I have labelled a notebook. In the early 1940s the distinction for NF between a notebook and a diary was not always clearly delineated: in NB 4, for example, he refers to material that is not a chronological, dated narrative as a diary (par. 24).

5 "Curious experience, throwing out all the various excreta I'd been saving since before my Oxford days. Notebooks full of dead wood. I don't know why I have such a passion for collecting notebooks when I don't think I've ever filled one completely up. Even the original Blake one has a couple of blank pages at the end" (50.423). NF's "original Blake" notebook has not survived. Whether or not it was included in the notebooks that NF disposed of here is uncertain. After he had completed *AC*, NF wrote, "I've begun notes on this [his novel] many times, but threw away my best notebook, written in Seattle, in a London (Ont.) hotel" (NB 20, par. 1).

6 "Several efforts" seems to imply more than two, but it is possible that NF is referring to his 1942 and 1943 efforts only.

7 See Michael Dolzani, ed., *The "Third Book" Notebooks of Northrop Frye, 1964–1972: The Critical Comedy* (Toronto: University of Toronto Press, forthcoming).

8 *A Book of One's Own: People and Their Diaries* [2nd ed.] (St. Paul, Minn.: Hungry Mind Press, 1995).

9 For Ayre's use of NF's 1949 Diary, see *Northrop Frye: A Biography* (Toronto: Random House, 1989), 212–17.

10 42.84, 140; 49.1.

11 We do "keep" records, in the sense of recording regularly. But we don't "keep" novels, plays, poems, autobiographies, essays, and the like.

12 *A Book of One's Own*, xi.

13 49.2, 4, 9, 10, 3 and 7.

14 See Dolzani, "The Ruins of Time: Frye and the City, 1977," *Northrop Frye Newsletter*, 8 (Summer 1999): 1–7, and "On Earth as It Is in Heaven: The Problem of Wish-Fulfilment in Frye's Visionary Criticism" [unpublished typescript but forthcoming in a collection of essays edited by Jean O'Grady and Wang Ning].

15 See *The Bulletin of Victoria College in the University of Toronto, 1949–1950*, 21. Other Religious Knowledge courses included the Semitic world, the history of Christianity, the Old Testament, philosophy of religion, and world religions. The Religious Knowledge offerings for students in the three-year Pass Course were a series of courses similar in content to those in the Honour Course option, but including Hebrew and Greek; these courses met for three hours each week.

16 See *NFC*, 142.

17 NF's own version of the "seven ages of life" is recorded in NB 20, written in the late 1950s: "In this world life has, as Shakespeare says, seven ages, of approximately a decade in length. The first years, up to ten, are the age of gluttony. Of the acquisitive appetite in its simplest & most directly demanding form. The teens are the age of wrath, of the resentments of parent-rebellion and violent aggressiveness. The next decade is the age of lechery, when the coming of sexual experience brings with it idealisms, ambitions, & similar emotions. These focus into more practical & limited objectives as the 30–40 age of envy begins & one struggles for a career. The forty-year mark is the menopause era for women or something similar for me, & brings the seed of avarice or anxious inventories of resources. Then full maturity, or the age of pride, sets in & lasts until the end of life when it modulates into the age of sloth" (par. 3).

18 42.31, 110; 49.21, 26, 41, 57, 78, 91, 189 (three dreams), 221, 284 (two dreams), 319, 336, 374; 50.148; and 52.17.

19 For NF's holograph notes on his reading of *Psychology of the Unconscious*, see the first three pages of NB 42 (NFF, 1993, box 3, file 10).

20 See 49.11, 161, 140, 201, and 294.

21 49.235. The paper never got written, probably because by the time of *AC* NF wanted to distance himself from Jung's notion of the archetype. NF's notes on Jung's *Psychology of the Unconscious* (see n. 19, above) call attention to a number of parallels between Blake and Jung: they may be notes toward the paper NF planned to write. A few years later he did review Jung's *Two Essays in Analytical Psychology* and *Psychology and Alchemy* in the *Hudson Review*, 6 (Winter 1954): 611–19; rpt. as "Forming Fours" in *NFCL*, 117–29.

22 50.124 and 58.

23 49.91, 333, and 361.

24 According to Jung most people have one of the four functions (thinking, feeling, sensation, intuition) as their "habitus" or preferred function, with a second, auxiliary function. Thus, those who have a scientific or empirical bent engage in thinking about sensations; those who are theorists (this is NF), thinking about intuitions; those who are artists, feeling about intuition; and those who are sensualists, feeling about sensations.

25 Elizabeth Fraser, twelve years NF's senior, was a Canadian book designer who lived in London and Oxford when NF was at Merton College. If Fraser's letters to NF during this time are to be believed, they had an affair.

26 A sampler of such labels: "that cute Mallinson girl" (49.254), "and a cute little (or big rather) fourth year girl with a snub nose & breasts bursting out of her dress" (49.307); "a juicy cutie from Hungary" (50.7), "Colleen Thibaudeau . . . is really a very cute little girl" (49.299); Becker has "a cute American wife (50.372)"; "we had an excellent dinner served by a cute little German girl" (50.475); "that very cute Margaret Allen girl" (52.147); even Sister Marion of SMC is said to be a "cute nun" (49.156). For "pretty," "attractive," and "beautiful," see 49.256, 275; 50.30, 196, 221, 420, 484; 52.137, 184.

27 See, e.g., 50.255: "More sitting—Helen obviously didn't want me to go to the office, though there was a lot of work to do there. More Plautus, and the general drift of the exposition is beginning to shape up. After all, I can always leave my letters another day, and it's certainly luxurious to work on a book."

28 Unpublished typescript in NFF, 1991, box 50, file 1.

29 51.10. By January 1952 he had changed the title to *Essay on Poetics* (52.1).

30 Michael Dolzani, "The Book of the Dead: A Skeleton Key to Northrop Frye's Notebooks," in *Rereading Frye: The Published and Unpublished Work*, ed. David Boyd and Imre Salusinszky (Toronto: University of Toronto Press, 1999), 19–30. See also Dolzani's introduction to *The "Third Book" Notebooks of Northrop Frye, 1964–1972: The Critical Comedy*, and Robert D. Denham,

introduction to *Northrop Frye's Late Notebooks, 1982–1990: Architecture of the Spiritual World* (Toronto: University of Toronto press, 2000), xl–xlv.

31 The chart draws from the following diary entries: 49.119, 353; 50.60, 107, 128, 157, 181, 228, 234, 246, 306, 310, 316, 427, 452

32 Held at McMaster University in May 2000, this was the twelfth symposium on NF's work. The others were "Northrop Frye and Contemporary Criticism," at the annual meeting of the English Institute, September 1965; "Portrait of Northrop Frye," at the University of Rome "La Sapienza," May 1987; "Northrop Frye and the Contexts of Criticism" and *"Anatomy of Criticism* in Retrospect," at the meeting of the Modern Language Association, San Francisco, December 1987; "Northrop Frye and Eighteenth-Century Studies," at the meeting of the American Society for Eighteenth-Century Studies," University of Minnesota, April 1990; "Northrop Frye and Contemporary Literary Theory," at the meeting of the Canadian Comparative Literature Association, Queen's University, May 1991; "Northrop Frye Festival," in Moncton, N.B., November 1991; "The Legacy of Northrop Frye in the East and West," at Sookmyung Women's University, Seoul, Korea, May 1992; "The Legacy of Northrop Frye: An International Conference," at the University of Toronto, October 1992; "Northrop Frye Research Seminar," at the University of Newcastle, New South Wales, Australia, July 1994; "Northrop Frye and China," at Peking University, Beijing, July 1994; "International Symposium on Northrop Frye Studies," at Inner Mongolia University, Hoh-Hot, China, July 1999.

33 See, e.g., 49.66, 49.262, 49.280, 49.363, 50.126, 50.259, 50.277.

34 Published in *The Living Church*, ed. Harold Vaughan (Toronto: United Church Publishing House, 1949), 152–72; rpt. *NFR*, 253–67.

35 Michel de Montaigne, "On the Inconstancy of Our Actions," in *The Complete Essays*, trans. and ed. M.A. Screech (Harmondsworth, England: Penguin, 1991), 377 (bk. 2, essay 1).

1942 Diary

1 Port Credit, about twenty kilometres west of Toronto, was, at the time, an affluent unincorporated area in Peel.

2 Beth Jenking's boss was C.D. Balding, a mining-engineer consultant. His home, Mississauga House, was eventually sold to Roy Thomson, the newspaper tycoon.

3 When NF returned from his study at Oxford in 1939, he and HKF rented a walk-up apartment at 1574 Bathurst St. (just south of St. Clair Ave.). They lived there for six years. See Ayre, 160.

4 *Bruyères, La Terrasse des audiences au claire de lune, Ondine,* and *Feux d'artifice* are four of Claude Debussy's *Douze Préludes*, second book (1912); *Des Pas sur la neige*, one of his *Douze Préludes*, first book (1910).

5 Herman Melville, *Moby Dick*, ed. Harrison Hayford and Hershel Parker (New York: Norton, 1967), 169 (chap. 42); "The Narrative of Arthur Gordon Pym," in *The Works of Edgar Allan Poe*, ed. Edmund Clarence Stedman and George Edward Woodberry (Chicago: Stone and Kimball, 1895), 5:244–50 (chap. 25). From 1935 to 1939 Ben Nicholson did a series of relief paintings in various shades of white.

6 Jean Philippe Rameau, *Traité de l'harmonie* (1722). In his *Autobiography* Mill speaks of being "seriously tormented by the thought of the exhaustibility of musical combinations" (chap. 5).

7 See "Ronsard contre Rabelais" in Jules Michelet, *Oeuvres Complètes*, ed. Paul Viallaneix (Paris: Flammarion, 1980), 7:118. Here Michelet sets up the opposition between Ronsard and Rabelais as cultural models, and he maintains that the elites chose Ronsard. The "hesitation" to which NF refers appears to be his own invention. Michelet simply presents Ronsard as the poet of the aristocracy, a writer who was touted as the great poet of the age by another aristocratic poet who hated Rabelais, Joachim du Bellay.

8 Wanda Landowska's essays on Couperin and Rameau are found in her *Musique ancienne* (1909). An accessible trans. is in *Landowska on Music*, ed. and trans. Denise Restout (New York: Stein and Day, 1981), 259–73.

9 This is apparently the Jenkings' father, although it could be C.D. Balding, Beth Jenking's boss.

10 Arthur Symons, *The Symbolist Movement in Literature* (London: Heinemann, 1899), 15–18.

11 See Gérard de Nerval, *Aurélia*, in *Oeuvres*, ed. Albert Béguin and Jean Richter (Paris: Gallimard, 1960), 1:357–412. The quotations in this par. come from pp. 363, 374, 385, and 399 in the Gallimard edition. Which edition NF was using is uncertain. The parenthetical phrase in the penultimate quotation is NF's addition.

12 NF repeats the point in *FS*, 213.

13 The quotations in this par. come from *Oeuvres*: 1:366, 370, 371, 375, 376, 377–8, 377, 377, and 379.

14 The quotations in this par. come from *Oeuvres*: 1:381, 412, 413.

15 The quotations in this par. come from *Oeuvres*: 1:410, 411, and 412. The material in parentheses is NF's addition.

16 Yeats says that "the student of *A Vision* will understand [Blake's *Mental Traveller*] at once" (*A Vision*, rev. ed. [N.p.: Macmillan, 1956], 189). He sees the man and woman of Blake's poem as representing, respectively, the symbolically masculine Will and Creative Mind and the symbolically feminine Mask and Body of Fate (262). "Mathematic form" is a phrase from Blake's *On Virgil* (Erdman, 270).

17 "Such a writer as Gérard de Nerval, who had presumably not read Blake, is much closer to him than Yeats, who edited him. In the study of Blake it is the analogue that is important, not the source" (*FS*, 12).

18 See Helen Frye, "Help Yourself to Field Flowers," *The Standard* (Montreal), 15 August 1942, 13.

19 A town located about twenty-five kilometres north of Toronto.

20 A beer parlour, where students and faculty often gathered to talk comfortably with each other, at 1163 Bay St., just south of Bloor.

21 "Pahits" is apparently a nonsense word, as is "cheroots" in this context.

22 Major James William Coldwell and J.J. McCann (rather than McMann, as NF has it) were members of the 1942 Radio Committee, established to examine the annual reports of the CBC. The committee was critical of Murray's handling of his expense accounts and asked him to step down as general manager of CBC Radio. See "Review Expenses Paid to Gladstone Murray," *Toronto Daily Star*, 10 July 1942, 3, and "Demands the 'Truth' on CBC Finances," ibid., 13 July 1942, 2.

23 See par. 15, above.

24 The allusion is to a remark by Mammon to Dol Common in Ben Jonson's The *Alchemist* (1610): "Had your father / Slept all the happy remnant of his life / After the act, lien but there still, and panted, / He'd done enough to make himself, his issue, / And his posterity noble" (4.1.60–4).

25 NF is apparently referring to the *Canadian Review of Music and Art*, which began publication in 1942 and for which Adeney had served as book editor in the late 1940s.

26 *Think*, a magazine of the International Business Corporation, began publication in 1935.

27 *The Closed Book (An Epic of the Soul's Quest)* (Toronto: Macmillan, 1943), a narrative poem by Wilmot B. Lane, professor of ethics at VC and EC.

28 This is almost certainly Eleanor Godfrey, editor of the *Canadian Forum*, as her sister Ray, a social worker, is mentioned later in the entry.

29 NF's proposed activities conclude with a fictional bird and an equally fictional Latin name: Accinus and Pacuvius were two second-century B.C. Roman tragic poets.

30 The novel by Wilkie Collins (1868).

31 NF was a lifelong reader of detective stories. His library, now housed in the special collections of the Victoria University Library, contains a great deal of such fiction, including three detective stories by Dorothy Sayers, two by Carr, four by Allingham; these titles, however, were all added to the collection after NF was writing the present diary.

32 IODE = Imperial Order Daughters of the Empire, a patriotic and philanthropic women's organization.

33 The reference is to Raymond Chandler's private detective, Philip Marlowe.

34 See Edgar Allan Poe's "The Murders in the Rue Morgue."

35 Mitchell Hepburn, premier of Ontario from 1934 to 1942, had supported Tory leader Arthur Meighen in the 1942 by-election. Meighen was defeated by J.W. Noseworthy, a popular high school teacher and CCF candi-

date, in the North York by-election. The constituency had been Conservative, and because of the wartime political truce the Liberals did not nominate a candidate to oppose Meighen, the newly chosen Tory leader. Many Liberals wanted a contest and crossed over to elect Noseworthy. On 10 February 1942 the American press reported Hepburn's remark that the Japanese navy was superior to the American navy, which was "in hiding"—a remark that caused the Canadian government some embarrassment and resulted in Mackenzie King's sending a note of apology to Franklin Roosevelt.

36 A 1933 film directed by Walter Forde and based upon Arnold Ridley's *Ghost Train: A Play in Three Acts* (1931).

37 The titles come, respectively, from *Hamlet*, 1.3.78; Christopher Marlowe, *The Passionate Shepherd to His Love*, l. 1; *King Lear*, 5.3.325; James Shirley, *The Contention of Ajax and Ulysses*, sec. 3, l. 23; Julia Ward Howe, *The Battle Hymn of the Republic*, l. 2; Song of Songs, 2:15; *The Tempest*, 5.1.182; Milton, *Paradise Lost*, bk. 1, l. 105; Christopher Marlowe, *Edward II*, 1.1.59; Milton, *Lycidas*, l. 163.

38 A popular radio quiz show that began airing on more than one hundred NBC stations in 1945.

39 The reference is to Lytton Strachey (1880–1932) and Philip Guedalla (1899–1944), English writers known respectively for their biographies and popular histories.

40 Hugh I'Anson Fausset, *Tennyson: A Modern Portrait* (London: Selwyn and Blount, 1923).

41 This paper was published as "The Nature of Satire" in the *University of Toronto Quarterly*, 14 (October 1944): 75–89. NF's essay draws on a number of the ideas and examples in the eight-section outline here.

42 *The Drag-Iron*, in *The Collected Poems of E.J. Pratt*, ed. Northrop Frye, 2nd ed. (Toronto: Macmillan, 1958), 57.

43 On the invectives Calvin used to vilify those who did not believe in Scripture, see Vilfredo Pareto, *A Treatise on General Sociology* (New York: Harcourt, Brace, 1935), 1:380–1.

44 The most caustic of Thomas Nashe's attacks on Gabriel Harvey was his *Have with You to Saffron Walden, or Gabriel Harvey's Hunt Is Up* (1596).

45 This seems to be a reference to Burton's long catalogue of human transgressions that result from the failure to practice Christian charity. See *Anatomy of Melancholy* (New York: Tudor, 1955), 638.

46 *Colasterion: A Reply to a Nameless Answer against the Doctrine and Discipline of Divorce* (1645), one of Milton's four pamphlets on divorce.

47 On Socrates' argument with Thrasymachus regarding the nature of justice, see the *Republic*, bk. 1, 326b–54b.

48 *Boswell's Life of Johnson*, 2nd ed., ed. L.F. Powell and G.B. Hill (Oxford: Clarendon Press, 1964), 2:54.

49 NF is perhaps referring to the speech of the chorus at the end of act 4 of

Auden and Isherwood's *The Dog beneath the Skin* (1935), though numerous other passages would qualify as negativism.

50 Harry Levin, *James Joyce: A Critical Introduction* (Norfolk, Conn.: New Directions, 1941); David Daiches, *Virginia Woolf* (Norfolk, Conn.: New Directions, 1942).

51 G. Wilson Knight, *Chariot of Wrath: The Message of John Milton to Democracy at War* (London: Faber and Faber, 1942).

52 Georges Simenon, *Affairs of Destiny* (London: G. Routledge, 1942). The book contains *New Haven, Dieppe*, and *A Woman of the Grey House.*

53 "We live meanly, like ants . . . and our best virtue has for its occasion a superfluous and evitable wretchedness" (Henry David Thoreau, *Walden*, ed. Bill McKibben [Boston: Beacon Press, 1997], 86).

54 Each of Sibelius's *Five Pieces* (op. 75) is named after a tree.

55 Audrey Alexandra Brown (b. 1904), an author and poet from B.C.

56 That is, to the home of HKF's parents, S.H.F. and Gertrude Kemp.

57 "But the liberal deviseth liberal things; and by liberal things shall he stand." NF used "By Liberal Things" as the title of his installation address as principal of Victoria College.

58 Jack and Regillus are characters in the novel NF was working on, *Locust-Eaters*, the first part of a larger fictional project entitled *Quiet Consummation*, after *Cymbeline*, 4.2.280. See the flyleaf of Notebook 5 and NF's undated letter to Roy Daniells in the Roy Daniells Fonds, University of British Columbia archives, box 42, file 5. "Craggish" refers to Art Cragg, NF's college friend and classmate, and a UCC minister. NF never completed the novel, but see NBs 1 and 2 for the chaps. that survived (NFF, 1991, box 22). Some of the material in the latter notebook exists in a revised fifteen-page typescript, in the NFF, 1991, box 37, file 2. For an account of NF's fiction-writing efforts, see Jonathan Hart, "The Quest for the Creative Word: Writing in Northrop Frye's Notebooks," in *Rereading Frye*, 55–71.

59 A 1942 film based on a play by James Thurber and Elliott Nugent (who directed the film) and starring Henry Fonda and Olivia de Havilland.

60 The movie playing on a double bill with *The Male Animal* was *Poison Pen.* NF saw the movies at the Alhambra Theatre at Bloor and Bathurst Streets.

61 Centre Island, one of the Toronto Islands in Lake Ontario, about one mile south of downtown Toronto.

62 Ernest Sirluck was married to Lesley Caroline McNaught on 10 August 1942.

63 The Diet Kitchen was a restaurant and tea room located at 72 Bloor St. West.

64 Lytle, a sports reporter for the *Toronto Star*, was referring to the penalty box in hockey.

65 Howard Wilcox Haggard, *Devils, Drugs and Doctors: The Story of the Science of Healing from Medicine-Man to Doctor* (New York: Simon and Schuster, 1946). A copy is in the NFL. The numbers in square brackets refer to the pages in Haggard from which NF is drawing his notes for this entry.

66 *The Natural and Moral History of the Indies* (1602; Eng. trans. 1604), ed. Clements R. Markham (New York: Burt Franklin, 1970), 1:136. NF is quoting from a different trans.

67 Robert Burton, *Anatomy of Melancholy*, 79.

68 A reference apparently to Kenneth Sisam, ed., *Fourteenth Century Verse and Prose* (Oxford: Clarendon Press, 1921–22), an annotated copy of which is in the NFL.

69 Charles II.

70 The works referred to in this entry: S.L. Wolff, *The Greek Romances in Elizabethan Prose Fiction* (New York: Columbia University Press, 1912); William Guild Howard, "Ut Pictura Poesis," *PMLA*, 24, no. 1 (1909): 40–123; Elizabeth Manwaring, *Italian Landscape Painting in Eighteenth-Century England* (New York: Oxford University Press, 1925); Sir Uvedale Price, *A Dialogue on the Distinct Characters of the Picturesque and the Beautiful* (Hereford, England: D. Walker, 1801); Richard Graves, *Columella, or the Distres't Anchoret: A Colloquial Tale* (London: J. Dodsley, 1779).

71 "Notes and Comments," in "The Talk of the Town," *New Yorker*, 15 (9 September 1939): 9–10.

72 *The Shadow Man*, in Wallace, *The Guv'nor and Other Stories* (London: Collins, 1932).

73 A 1942 film with screenplay by Ring Lardner, Jr., directed by George Stevens and starring, in addition to Hepburn, Spencer Tracy.

74 A 1941 20th Century Fox film directed by Archie Mayo, starring Don Ameche, Joan Bennett, and Roddy McDowall.

75 The reference is to the last section of the final chap. of Logan Pearsall Smith's *The English Language* (New York: Holt, 1912), 233–51.

76 John Evelyn, *Diary*, begun in 1631 but not published until 1818.

77 Feinsod's was a delicatessen at 693 Yonge St. Camp Borden was the military base where Harold Kemp trained before being sent to Europe as a flying officer for the 100th squadron of the Royal Canadian Air Force. He was killed in action a year and a half later—on 24 February 1944—at the age of twenty-one.

78 The edition NF is reading is *Love & Freindship* [sic]: *and Other Early Works, Now First Printed from the Original ms.* (Toronto: F.D. Goodchild, n.d.).

79 A Toronto bookstore at 765 Yonge Street just north of Bloor.

80 The film, playing at the Eglinton Theatre, was *Through Different Eyes*, starring Frank Craven, Mary Howard, June Walker, Donald Woods, and Vivian Blake.

81 "And I must be a country wife still too, I find, for I can't, like a city one, be rid of my musty husband and do what I list" (William Wycherley, *The Country Wife* [1675], 5.4.389–90).

82 The film, on a double bill with *Through Different Eyes*, was *Rings on Her Fingers*, starring Henry Fonda and Gene Tierney.

83 *The Vicar of Bray* is a ballad about a priest who changes his religious affiliation

according to whether the King of England happens to be Protestant or Catholic; the tenure of Simon Aleyn, the vicar of Bray from 1540 to 1588, involved several changes of faith from Protestant to Catholic and back again.

84 The Braybrooke Pepys was first published in 1825 by Richard Neville, Lord Braybrooke. An annotated copy of the Everyman edition (London: Dent, 1927) is in the NFL.

85 The reference is to a quotation by Sebastian Evans about an earlier editor of *Geoffrey of Monmouth*, J.A. Giles, who had revised and corrected Aaron Thompson's 1718 trans. of *Geoffrey*. Giles had written about his edition that "the translation of Thompson has been followed, revised and corrected wherever the phraseology appeared to be unsuited to the more accurate ears of the present day." Evans quotes these words and then remarks, "As I have been under no obligation to either edition, it is perhaps better not to speak further about them" (*Geoffrey of Monmouth* [London: Dent, 1912], 248).

86 That is, Walter Bradford Cannon (1871–1945), the American physiologist. Carl Georg Lange (1834–1900), the Danish psychologist, advanced a theory of emotion that was developed independently by William James.

87 NF's braces. Riddell, who had been a senior tutor at VC during NF's student days, had joined the Canadian Department of External Affairs.

88 The attack on Dieppe took place on 19 August 1942. Of the 6,100 troops involved roughly 5,000 were Canadians. In the ill-fated mission the Canadian forces suffered the heaviest toll of any Canadian battalion in a single day throughout the entire war.

89 Oscar Levant, *Smattering of Ignorance* (Garden City, N.Y.: Garden City Pub. Co., 1940), 134–5.

90 The reference is apparently to Eleanor Godfrey; her husband Bill Graham worked for a while in advertising.

91 "Reflections at a Movie," which picks up some phrases from this diary entry, appeared in *Canadian Forum*, 22 (October 1942): 212–13; rpt. in *RW*, 287–91. There is space enough on the last line of this entry for NF later to have added the note about "Reflections at a Movie," which is apparently what he did.

92 *Caroline of England: An Augustan Portrait* (London: Collins, 1939).

93 Howard K. Smith, *Last Train from Berlin* (New York: Knopf, 1942).

94 Smith, who later became a well-known CBS commentator, was a Rhodes Scholar at Merton College during the time NF studied there. NF is apparently remembering this incident from their student days.

95 A 1935 Paramount film adapted from Dashiell Hammet's novel of that title and directed by Frank Tuttle.

96 The "downtown" location of Diana Sweets coffee shop and restaurant was at 187 Yonge St.

97 James Holly Hanford, *A Milton Handbook* (New York: F.S. Crofts, 1926). This edition of Hanford's book is in the NFL.

98 *Maria Chapdelaine* (1916) is a novel of *habitant* life by Louis Hémon.

99 A reference to "Reflections at a Movie" (n. 91, above).

100 The reference is to the Athenian statesman Aristides the Just (ca. 530–ca. 468 B.C.). An illiterate citizen voted to banish Aristides from Athens on the sole grounds that he was tired of hearing everyone refer to him as "the Just." See Plutarch, *Lives*, chap. 7.

101 A 1940 Parmount film written and directed by Preston Sturges and starring Brian Donlevy, Muriel Angelus, and William Demarest.

102 Davies was actually from Montreal; he had been practising journalism in Toronto.

103 Apparently a reference to the controversial depiction of the Jews by Alfonso de Espina (15th century), the chief originator of the Spanish Inquisition. Alan Mendelson notes that NF is ridiculing Krating for expressing a common prejudice at the time—that the Sephardic Jews are acceptable, because they are good candidates for assimilation and conversion, but the more recent immigrant Jews from Eastern Europe are not, because they are ignorant of "our ways." The prejudice was common also in England at the time. Mendelson points out that George Grant also refers to "the coal in the bathtub" example in one of his own journal entries at about the same time (28 October 1942). See *Collected Works of George Grant*, ed. Peter C. Emberley and Arthur Davis (Toronto: University of Toronto Press, 2000), 1:21 (Alan Mendelson to Robert D. Denham, 24 December 2000).

104 An RKO film, with screenplay by Orson Welles, based on a novel by Booth Tarkington and starring Joseph Cotten and Anne Baxter.

105 This is probably the essay on Byrd in NB 17 (NFF, 1991, box 24).

106 Leo Rosten, *Hollywood: The Movie Makers, The Movie Colony* (1941). Under the pseudonym of Leonard Q. Ross, Rosten wrote *The Education of H*Y*M*A*N K*A*P*L*A*N*.

107 In Vedantic philosophy, two of the three qualities of *prakriti* (nature or primal matter): *rajas* refers to activity, striving, or the force that can overcome indolence; *tamas*, to the dull, passive forces of nature manifest in darkness and ignorance.

108 The article, "Music in the Movies," was published in *Canadian Forum*, 22 (December 1942): 275–6; rpt. in *RW*, 24–8. NF used practically all of the notes in the present entry in writing his article.

109 See par. 88, above.

110 *A Smattering of Ignorance*, 142–3.

111 Eric Havelock's volumes on Socrates were never published. His *Preface to Plato* (Cambridge: Harvard University Press, 1963) was based on lectures he gave in the 1950s.

112 Probably a reference to HKF's parents and her younger brother Harold.

113 A course in Restoration and eighteenth-century literature.

114 Marion and Helen Darte had become close friends with Eleanor and Ray
    Godfrey when all four were students (Ray began at U of T in 1930; Eleanor,
    in 1929). The Godfrey sisters had roomed with Marion Darte at St. Joseph's
    High School. Ray Godfrey remembers the man from Winnipeg as a friend
    of her brother-in-law who had lost his leg in a horse-riding accident; he
    was passing through Toronto and stayed with Eleanor and Bill Graham
    (telephone conversation with Ray Godfrey, 8 March 1999).

115 A restaurant at 772 Yonge St. This was one of the three Murray's restau-
    rants the Fryes frequented.

116 Leonard Wooley, *Ur Excavations* (Oxford: Oxford University Press, 1939).

117 *Men at War: The Best War Stories of All Time*, ed. Ernest Hemingway (New
    York: Crown, 1942), xxvii.

118 Franklin P. Adams, ed., *Innocent Merriment: An Anthology of Light Verse*
    (Garden City, N.Y.: Garden City Pub. Co., 1942). W.H. Auden, ed., *The
    Oxford Book of Light Verse* (Oxford: Clarendon Press, 1939).

119 Christopher Isherwood, "Take It or Leave It," *New Yorker*, 18 (24 October
    1942): 17–19.

120 "Reflections at a Movie"; see par. 99, above.

121 "Why, seeing things are not hidden from the Almighty, do they that know
    him not see his days?"

122 "The Anatomy in Prose Fiction," *Manitoba Arts Review*, 3 (Spring 1942):
    35–47.

123 J.S. Lawson and Edith Grace Coombs had been married on 7 May 1942.

1949 Diary

1 One of the undated diaries NF might be referring to is the material at the
  beginning of NB4, a notebook that also contains the 1942 Diary. He refers
  to that initial material as a "diary" (NB4, par. 24). See the headnote to the
  1942 Diary.

2 This paper became the original version of "The Function of Criticism at
  the Present Time," which was published in the *University of Toronto Quarterly*, 19 (October 1949): 1–16; it was subsequently developed into the
  Polemical Introduction of *AC*. NF presented the paper at the humanities
  colloquium on 28 February 1949.

3 Ayer's Cliff is on Lake Massiwippi, south of Sherbrooke, P.Q.; Burges is a
  small town on the southern coast of Newfoundland.

4 *"The Literary Instinct*: A man will show this by writing at all odd times as
  people show the artistic instinct by sketching in season and out of season"
  (*Further Extracts from the Note-Books of Samuel Butler*, 156). NF may also
  have in mind Butler's remarks on the habit of writing in *Life and Habit*
  (London: Jonathan Cape, 1910), 6–8.

5 If Chauvin, a graduate student at U of T, wrote a review of *Refus Global*, the

1948 manifesto by the Canadian painter Paul-Émile Borduas that pro-
claimed total freedom of expression, it was not published in the *Canadian
Forum*. He did, however, publish an article on the French Canadian poet
Émile Nelligan in the *Canadian Forum*, 28 (March 1948): 277. NF had become
managing editor of the *Canadian Forum* in 1948.

6 NF perhaps has in mind asking Allan Sangster about having someone review
the English trans. of Thomas Mann's *Dr. Faustus*, which was published in
1948 (New York: Knopf), a year after it had appeared in German. Gordon J.
Wood reviewed the book in the *Canadian Forum*, 29 (April 1949): 16, 18.

7 Probably a reference to George and Jean Johnston. During the 1940s George
Johnston would occasionally send his short stories to NF for comment.

8 The Maynards are apparently Fredelle and Max Maynard. "Baby Nancy,"
NF's godchild, is the daughter of a woman named Edna who rented the attic
of the Fryes' Clifton Road home in the early 1940s. In 50.445, NF indicates
that Nancy is five years old; Edna later married a man named Fulford. See
Ayre, 197.

9 Tickets that Harron had sent to the Fryes for to a play he was to act in on
22 January, Morley Callaghan's *To Tell the Truth* (Don Harron to Robert D.
Denham, 28 February 1994). See par. 114, below.

10 NF's father, Herman Edward Frye, was a hardware salesman; he was
seventy-eight years old when NF was writing the present diary.

11 See n. 2, above.

12 L, or Liberal, represented the first phase of NF's writing plans after he
finished *FS*. These plans, as he outlines them in his notebooks, tended to
change over the years. In a series of autobiographical notes he gave a brief
outline of his plans in the late 1940s, saying that the books he intended to
write

> took shape at first as a Pentateuch or series of five. Blake was the Genesis;
> a study of drama, esp. Shakespearean comedy, was the Exodus; Leviticus
> was to be philosophical (a dream of a "Summa" of modern thought had
> got into my skull very early). Numbers was to be a study of Romanticism
> & its after-effect, & Deuteronomy was to deal with general aesthetic
> problems. Suddenly, & simultaneously with the final & complete conver-
> sion to criticism, my old adolescent dream of eight masterpieces rose up
> again and hit me finally and irresistibly. Blake became Liberal, the study
> of drama Tragicomedy, the philosophical book, now a study of prose
> fiction, became Anticlimax, Numbers became Rencontre, Deuteronomy
> Mirage, & three others took nebulous shape. For several years I dithered,
> doodled, dawdled, dreamed & dallied. It was silly to let an adolescent
> pipe-dream haunt me like that: on the other hand, it did correspond to
> some major divisions in my actual thinking. So I kept on with it. When I
> finished the Blake, it became zero instead of one, & its place was taken by

a study of epic. In my notes the initial letters of the eight books were cut down to hieratic forms: L for Liberal; ⅂ for Tragicomedy; ∧ for Anticlimax; ⋏ for Rencontre; V for Mirage; ⊢ for Paradox; ⊥ for Ignoramus; T for Twilight. The last three seldom appear. (NB 1991, box 50, file 1)

For a commentary on NF's ogdoad project, see Michael Dolzani, "The Book of the Dead: A Skeleton Key to Northrop Frye's Notebooks," in *Rereading Frye*, 19–38, and Robert D. Denham, introduction to *Northrop Frye's Late Notebooks, 1982–1990: Architecture of the Spiritual World*, xli–xlv.

13 Selfhood is Blake's term for innate human selfishness that is opposed to the imagination; if selfhood is not annihilated it becomes, for Blake, a Satanic "spectre."

14 Brother Ass was the name St. Francis of Assisi frequently used to refer to his body.

15 NF grew up in Moncton, N.B.

16 NF's colloquium paper. See n. 2, above.

17 Marie Bond, who was enrolled at OCE, had visited campus to tell NF about her wild and humorous experiences in practice teaching (Marie Bond Gardner to Robert D. Denham, 9 March 1994).

18 A 1947 film directed by Herbert Kline; made with amateur actors in Palestine and partially financed by the Jewish National Fund.

19 A 1948 Polish film by Wanda Jakubowska.

20 See n. 14, above.

21 This lecture was for English 4k, "Nineteenth-Century Thought." The reading list included Newman, Burke, James Mill, John Stuart Mill, Carlyle, Ruskin, Huxley, Arnold, Morris, and Butler. The course met for two hours a week.

22 NF is thirty-six at the time.

23 That is, the lecture for the RK course, taught by the department of religious knowledge at VC, assisted by the staff of EC. In 1949–50, NF taught the first- and fourth-year RK courses, both of which were on the English Bible.

24 The new course in "Nineteenth-Century Literature."

25 NF has been asked to speak to a women's group in Peterborough, Ont., on 21 January.

26 E.J. Pratt had gone to New York for a reading at the Poetry Society; he had left on 28 December and returned on New Year's Day. See David G. Pitt, *E.J. Pratt: The Truant Years, 1882–1927* (Toronto: University of Toronto Press, 1984), 398–9.

27 In 1936 Thornton Mustard of the Toronto Normal School and Stanley Watson of the Keele Street Public School had been tapped to prepare a proposal for curriculum reform. Their *Programme of Studies*, issued in 1937, was in many respects based on the progressive education movement in the

U.S. See Robert M. Stamp, *The Schools of Ontario, 1876–1976* (Toronto: University of Toronto Press, 1982), 164–71.

28 *CBC Wednesday Night* was a regular series of cultural radio programs; it had been launched on 3 December 1947, and it lasted for almost thirty years, though it was shifted first to Sunday and then, in 1965, to Tuesday. For the program of 5 January Arnold Walter prepared the music for the production of *Twelfth Night*, which was adapted for radio by Lister Sinclair and which aired at 8:00 P.M. For the final hour of *Wednesday Night* Aline van Barentzen played Beethoven's Sonata in F Minor (op. 57) and two works from Debussy's second book of Twelve Preludes, *Ondine* and *Feux d'Artifice*. The French government had sponsored a North American tour for van Barentzen, which she was just beginning.

29 A reference, apparently, to the fall of the natural order and Satan's pact with Chaos in *Paradise Lost*.

30 The reference is to the graduate seminar in Blake. Ross Woodman's paper was the first of a series of student papers presented throughout the second term. NF had lectured on Blake during the first term. Woodman had come to Toronto to do a dissertation on Milton under A.S.P. Woodhouse. After registering for NF's seminar, he decided to shift from Milton to Blake; but when *FS* came out, he concluded there was little left to say, so he turned to another apocalyptic poet, Shelley, for his dissertation, directed by both Woodhouse and NF. Woodman's paper for the Blake seminar was mainly about the echoes of *Paradise Lost* in Blake's *Milton* (Ross Woodman to Robert D. Denham, 18 February 1994).

31 "On the Question of Whether or Not Penelope Is Being Whitewashed," chap. 5 of Butler's *The Authoress of the Odyssey* (1897).

32 Probably a reference to Arthur Barker, but NF could be referring to Barker Fairley.

33 Margaret Avison had reviewed Roy Daniells's *Deeper into the Forest* and Robert Finch's *The Strength of the Hills* in the *Canadian Forum*, 28 (March 1949): 287.

34 NF's parents had planned to name their second son, born in 1902, Northrop: he was stillborn or else lived only a short while. See Ayre, 21.

35 From a 1936–37 choral work by John Ireland.

36 NF apparently has in mind this passage from Sir Thomas Browne: "To this (as calling my self a scholar), I am obliged by the duty of my condition: I make not therefore my head a grave, but a treasure, of knowledge; I intend no Monopoly, but a community, in learning; I study not for my own sake only, but for theirs that study not for themselves. I envy no man that knows more than my self, but pity them that know less. I instruct no man as an exercise of my knowledge, or with an intent rather to nourish and keep it alive in mine own head then [*sic*] beget and propagate it in his" (*Religio*

Medici, Letters to a Friend, &c. and Christian Morals, ed. W.A. Greenhill [London: Macmillan, 1926], 97 [pt. 2, sec. 3]).

37 NF is apparently planning for someone to do an article for the *Canadian Forum* on T.D. Lysenko's politically motivated and now completely discredited theories of plant genetics, which held sway in the Soviet Union for more than three decades; the article never appeared in the *Canadian Forum*. See also par. 17, above, where NF suggests he would like Jack Oughton to write the article.

38 Elizabeth Fraser, twelve years NF's senior, was a Canadian book designer who lived in London and Oxford when NF was at Merton College. In some ways their relationship was an attraction of kindred spirits. If Fraser's letters to NF during this time are to be believed, the relationship was more than that.

39 The allusion is to Keats's *Ode to a Nightingale,* l. 52.

40 This is doubtless Eleanor Godfrey.

41 See par. 46, above.

42 See n. 36, above.

43 Short, who was a teacher, was actually not connected with the School of Social Work. He was at the lecture, no doubt, because of Margaret Gayfer's interest in NF, and he had read *FS* (Margaret Gayfer to Robert D. Denham, 25 May 1994).

44 Harold King had helped HKF speed up the process of painting decorative trays, an activity she had begun in 1941 to earn spare money. See Ayre, 174–5. HKF's brother Harold had been killed in World War II. See 42.n. 77.

45 The allusion is to Evelyn Waugh's macabre novel about California funeral practices, *The Loved One* (1948).

46 Hatfield Hall School, located in Cobourg, Ont., was an Anglican elementary and secondary school for girls.

47 "Annals of Crime: The Wily Wilby, I and II," *New Yorker,* 24 (1 January and 8 January 1949): 23–33, 34–45. The article is about a Canadian citizen, Ralph Marshall Wilby, who was caught for embezzlement in both Canada and the U.S.

48 The Beanery Boys were members of a Toronto teenage gang that had received a great deal of public criticism, much of it unwarranted. Rev. Gordon Domm of Bathurst United Church had opened his church halls to the boys in an effort to reform them. For the article NF refers to, see "Pierre Berton and C.G. Gifford, "The Beanery Gang," *Maclean's,* 15 December 1948, 12, 50–3.

49 English 2i, "English Prose and Poetry, 1500–1660."

50 See n. 44, above, and 42.n. 77.

51 Wellek reviewed *FS* in *Modern Language Notes,* 64 (January 1949): 62–3. He judged the book to be "one of the major achievements of modern Blake scholarship," but he faulted NF for ignoring evaluation and for not

analysing poetry as poetry; he concluded that something was wrong with NF's mythopoeic conception of poetry because, even if Blake's work were symbolically coherent, it could not be defended as poetry.

52 The reference is to Mark Schorer's *William Blake: The Politics of Vision*, which was published the year before *FS* appeared. The two books were sometimes reviewed together, and Wellek does compare *FS* with Schorer's book.

53 Judy Livingston was eighteen at the time, one of about twenty students in the English language and literature course at VC; she remembers especially the "*Paradise Lost* lectures by the 'Great God Frye,' as he was known even then" (Judy Livingston Bowler to Robert D. Denham, 18 February 1994).

54 Apparently, Margaret Avison.

55 Apparently, Eleanor Godfrey.

56 "The Argument of Comedy," in *English Institute Essays: 1948*, ed. D.A. Robertson, Jr. (New York: Columbia University Press, 1949), 58–73.

57 The staff of the *Canadian Forum* met in a carriage house at 16 Huntley Street, which was also the home of Kay and Louis Morris; that remained the *Forum* address until 1954.

58 "The Four Forms of Prose Fiction," *Hudson Review*, 2 (Winter 1950): 582–95.

59 Donald L. Weinert was twenty-six at the time, a fourth-year student in political science and economics. He was enrolled in NF's RK class, a first-year arts elective in the Pass Course. Weinert remembers the interview with NF, who "was most gracious in his treatment of my request for a letter of recommendation." After graduating, Weinert wrote and edited radio news scripts, but left that in 1952 for a career in pipelining in Canada and the U.S. He recalls that NF "was a brilliant lecturer with a vast command of his subject, and the course made a deep impression on me that lasted all my life. There was a concept in the course that much of the Old Testament was tribal history and anecdote of Israel and is common to most societies in history. But he never allowed you to forget that it was one people's concept of the Divine and that the truths in it were universal and significant. I had grown up in a small Ontario town, Baptist. To hear the Bible treated as literature and, horrors, as something allegorical and not literal was a concept that I had never encountered" (Donald L. Weinert to Robert D. Denham, 15 February 1994).

60 J.W.A. Nicholson had written an article entitled "Maritime Labor Irritation" for the *Canadian Forum*, 21 (August 1941): 143–5.

61 Rowland and Orwen did, in fact, get married.

62 According to Beynon the letter to her was doubtless in response to her writing to thank him for what he had taught her: he was "the one who made my university education a spiritual one, setting the mode for the rest of my life" (Josephine ["Jodine"] Beynon Boos to Robert D. Denham, 20 August 1994).

63 That is, Arthur Barker's Milton students from TC. See par. 62, above.

64 "There is a Moment in each Day that Satan cannot find" (William Blake, *Milton*, pl. 35, l. 42 [Erdman, 136]).

65 H.P. Blavatsky, *Isis Unveiled* (New York: J.W. Bouton, 1877), 1:179–80.

66 "Bardo" is ordinarily used to denote the intermediate stage between death and rebirth, but in *The Tibetan Book of the Dead* "bardos" also means the series of constantly changing realities between birth and death.

67 "The Pursuit of Form," *Canadian Art* (Christmas 1948): 54–7.

68 The syntax here goes awry. NF seems to have intended to write: "It occurs to me that the Cartesian view . . . "

69 See n. 12, above.

70 Jnana-yoga, the way or path of abstract knowledge, is one of the four primary yogas in Hinduism.

71 O.J. Silverthorne was chair of the Motion Picture Censorship and Theatre Inspection Branch of the Ontario attorney general's office; this meant that he was, in effect, the chief censor of movies and plays in Ontario. The "Bawling Boys" would have included groups such as the IODE (Imperial Order Daughters of the Empire). Any questions regarding censorship at the time would have had to do with sex in the movies, not with politics. Mosdell apparently never wrote the article, at least not for the *Canadian Forum*.

72 Likely a reference to Gerard and Betty Brett.

73 The educational program at St. John's College, Annapolis, Md., was based on the philosophy that the best route to a liberal education was for students to engage in a four-year, nonelective program of reading, discussing, and writing about the great books of Western civilization. In some ways the program was quite similar to the one developed by Mortimer Adler and others under Robert Hutchins's leadership at the University of Chicago.

74 See n. 27, above.

75 Arnold J. Toynbee, *A Study of History* (London: Oxford University Press, 1939), 4:222.

76 Tantramar Marshes, near Sackville, N.B.

77 The humanist utopia that Rabelais constructs in bk. 1 of *Gargantua and Pantagruel*.

78 Harry Roskolenko had published a poem, *New Year View*, in the *Canadian Forum*, 28 (January 1949): 235.

79 John Henry Cardinal Newman, *Apologia Pro Vita Sua*, ed. David J. DeLaura (New York: Norton, 1968), 98. The phrase—"the world judges with assurance"—is from Augustine's *Contra epistolam Parmeniani*, 3.4.24: Newman had picked it up from a citation by Cardinal Wiseman.

80 NF had written, "in the two amazing portraits of John Robins and Salem Bland, in which two very human and warm-blooded people are stylized into contemplative yogis, we again feel that the subject has been transmuted rather than evoked" ("The Pursuit of Form," 54 [n. 67, above].)

81 See n. 2, above.

82 Shubik did contribute to the *Canadian Forum*, publishing satiric political verse under the pseudonym of Thersites, as well as book reviews.

83 "That St John the Evangelist was bed-fellow to Christ and leaned always in his bosom; and that he used him as the sinners of Sodoma" (Richard Baines, "A Note Concerning the Opinion of One Christopher Marly, Concerning His Damnable Judgment of Religion and the Scorn of God's Word," Christopher Marlowe, *Complete Poems and Plays* [London: Dent, 1976], 513). The so-called "Baines's Note" is a series of opinions on religion, said to have been Marlowe's but apparently penned by Baines in an effort to bring Marlowe before the Court of the Star Chamber.

84 For an account of the issues of Federation NF refers to here, including the Clergy Reserves agreement, see C.B. Sissons, *A History of Victoria University* (Toronto: University of Toronto Press, 1952), especially chap. 8. S.S. Nelles was appointed president of VU in 1854; Nathanael Burwash became president and chancellor of VC in 1887; Macdonald was the first premier of Ontario.

85 "Creation without toil," says Yeats, "is the chief temptation of the artist" (*Autobiographies* [London: Macmillan, 1955], 202).

86 Milton uses these images in chap. 5 of *The Reason of Church Government Used against Prelaty*.

87 For the Blake seminar David Pitt read a paper on Blakean antecedents in certain eighteenth-century poets: Thomson, Collins, Young, Warton, Smart, and Cowper (David G. Pitt to Robert D. Denham, 3 March 1994).

88 A student named Reta Horner was enrolled in the English language and literature course at VC; she graduated in 1949. But NF seems to have mistaken Reta, whom he calls "Rita," for another student. At least Reta Horner has no memory of asking NF about taking an M.A., and, as her mother had died while she was in high school, NF's statement about taking a "holiday from mamma" obviously refers to someone else (Reta Horner Parna to Robert D. Denham, 19 February 1994).

89 Darrell Figgis, *The Paintings of William Blake* (London: Ernest Benn, 1925), a collection of Blake's most famous paintings.

90 NF is jesting with the name of the group, which was "Fudger," an informal association that met several times annually for discussion, often in response to a paper presented by a faculty or community member. The group had been initiated in 1924 by VU president and chancellor R.P. Bowles, with the financial assistance of the Toronto benefactor H.H. Fudger, one of the owners of the Robert Simpson Company. NF was a dues-paying member of the group and, in fact, presented a paper to the membership on 21 April 1949 (see par. 335, below).

91 That is, living on war-service gratuities provided by the Department of Veterans' Affairs.

92 Isobel Routly Stewart and *Acta Victoriana* editor Rowell Bowles organized a

Writers' Group in 1938 as a way of creating student interest in writing (it was essentially a poetry group) and of promoting submissions to the magazine; it was a student-initiated group, although John Robins and E.J. Pratt occasionally attended the meetings. Stewart took courses at Columbia from William York Tindall and Lionel Trilling; her short story class was from Caroline Gordon; and at Union Theological Seminary two of her teachers were Reinhold Niebuhr and Paul Tillich (phone conversation with Isobel Routly Stewart, 17 February 1993).

93 After Norma Arnett graduated from VC in 1949, she began writing NF, averaging a letter a day for almost ten years. In a letter to William Fennell, dated 14 May 1980, NF refers to Arnett's letters, as well as the writing she submitted to him, as "psychotic blither" (NFF, 1990, box 3, file 1). NF finally had to ask that the letters be stopped. She continued to write at intervals, but NF instructed his secretary to return them unopened. As the letters had no return address, they were simply discarded (conversation with Jane Widdicombe, 8 March 2000). The *Varsity* was the student newspaper at U of T.

94 Harron played the leading role in Callaghan's play—that of a teetotalling bartender in a New York gin mill; he befriends the mistress of a gangster who then falls in love with him. Harron was a member of the New Play Society, which mostly staged classics by Shakespeare, Shaw, Sheridan, Goldsmith, Synge, and O'Casey. In 1949, however, the Society performed the world premiere of *To Tell the Truth*. Harron reports that "he hated doing the role, and made fun of it in front of Morley Callaghan, but it had some success in front of our New Play audiences." The production later transferred to the Royal Alexandra Theatre in Toronto, where it had a one-week run. NF's reference to the play as "a Saroyanesque fantasy" is fairly accurate, as the play is something of a rehash of William Saroyan's *Time of Your Life* (Don Harron to Robert D. Denham, 28 February 1994). For an account of the production, see Martha Harron, *Don Harron: A Parent Contradiction* (Toronto: Collins, 1988), 107.

95 John Milton, *Areopagitica* (Hughes, 720).

96 Fibber McGee and Molly of the popular radio show lived at 79 Wistful Vista.

97 Arthur S. Turberville, *Johnson's England: An Account of the Life & Manners of His Age* (Oxford: Clarendon Press, 1933).

98 In 1901 two wealthy Edwardian ladies, while exploring the grounds of the palace of Versailles, claimed to have wandered into the time of Marie Antoinette and to have seen the queen and members of her court. The story was first told by C.A.E. Moberly and E.F. Jourdain in *An Adventure* (London: Macmillan, 1911). A study of the case, including all previously published accounts, is in *The Ghosts of Trianon: The Complete "An Adventure,"* ed. Michael H. Coleman (Wellingborough, England: Aquarius Press, 1988).

99   Throughout his notebooks NF uses several symbols to represent the eighth
      book (Twilight), ordinarily ⊤ or Γ."
100 "But the idea of beauty and of human nature perfect on all sides, which is
      the dominant idea of poetry, is a true and invaluable idea" (Matthew
      Arnold, *Culture and Anarchy, with Friendship's Garland and Some Literary
      Essays*, ed. R.H. Super [Ann Arbor: University of Michigan Press, 1965],
      99).
101 This would seem to be Rosemarie Schawlow, one of NF's graduate stu-
      dents, but she has no recollection of the Wordsworth bibliography (tel-
      ephone conversation with Rosemarie Schawlow, 15 February 1994).
102 Eleanor Thompson Morgan recalls that June Clark had been in the Royal
      Canadian Air Force, had completed all of her high school in six months
      after the war, and intended to be a UCC minister. From a rough working-
      class background, "she was small and intense, boyish, and completely
      outside the experience of our small-town, genteelly brought-up, repressed
      selves. . . . She was also refreshingly vigorous, funny, and direct. She was
      something of a protégé of the Dean of Women; to the extent that when
      some of her shenanigans in the Graduate house we lived in, in 1951, were
      duly complained of by the House Head, the message was that we were to
      put up with them" (Eleanor Thompson Morgan to Robert D. Denham,
      26 August 1994). Clark left the university after 1951.
103 The *Athenia* sank in 1939, having been torpedoed by the Germans.
104 Thorstein Veblen, *The Theory of the Leisure Class: An Economic Study of
      Institutions* (New York: Modern Library, 1934).
105 The line, slightly misquoted, is from Henry Vaughan's *Peace*.
106 Douglas was the bestselling author of such books as *Magnificent Obsession*
      (1929).
107 Above "obscurities" NF wrote "allusions."
108 This book, like a number of the books NF planned to write, never came to
      fruition.
109 The Fryes had been invited to a social evening with classmates and friends
      at the home of Jack and Dorothy Cumberland in Mimico, then a Toronto
      suburb. Jack Cumberland, a lawyer for the Goodyear Tire and Rubber
      Company west of Mimico, and his wife Dorothy (née Darling), had re-
      cently moved to Queen's Avenue in Mimico. Eugene and Margaret (née
      Torrance) Hallman lived in the Kingsway area just north of Mimico. John
      and Eileen Summer were friends of Muriel Code: they had moved to the
      area from British Columbia and had also bought a home on Queen's
      Avenue (Muriel Code to Robert D. Denham, 11 March 1994). The class-
      mates of NF and HKF at this gathering were Dorothy Cumberland, Muriel
      Code, and Margaret Hallman. Jack Cumberland had graduated from VC a
      year earlier.

110 Muriel Code's brother, Richard B. Code, married Winifred (Wyn) Horwood, who was the sister of Howe Martyn's wife, Marjorie Horwood. Howe Martyn and Marjorie Horwood were 1930 graduates of VC.

111 *Six Novels of the Supernatural*, ed. Edward Wagenknecht (New York: Viking, 1944).

112 The novel by Mrs. Oliphant was *A Beleaguered City*, and the other two in the collection were Frances H. Burnett's *The White People* and Mary Johnston's *Sweet Rocket*.

113 HKF was still in the hospital.

114 Friedrich Nietzsche, *Thus Spoke Zarathustra*, trans. Walter Kaufmann (New York: Modern Library, 1995), 264.

115 Norman Mailer's best-selling war novel (New York: Holt, 1948).

116 Charles Williams, *Arthurian Torso: Containing the Posthumous Fragment of the Figure of Arthur* (London: Oxford University Press, 1948).

117 MacLean's VC public lecture was on John Locke (Kenneth MacLean to Robert D. Denham, 11 May 1994).

118 The ATE [Association of Teachers of English] was a secondary school organization, devoted to improving the quality of teaching of English in grades 12 and 13.

119 MacLean's lecture was never published.

120 For an account of Pratt's ten-day Newfoundland visit, see David G. Pitt, *E.J. Pratt: The Master Years, 1927–1964* (St. John's, Newfoundland: Jesperson Press, 1987), 399–403.

121 Alexander Pope, *Essay on Man*, sec. 1, l. 200.

122 C.C. Goldring, appointed director of education by the Toronto Board of Education in 1933, had been influenced by the progressive education movement in the U.S. and was interested in aligning the public school curriculum with current social realities. See Robert M. Stamp, *The Schools of Ontario, 1876–1976*, 165–6.

123 This is almost certainly Robert P. (Bob) McDonald, who, along with his wife Jean, taught English at North Toronto Collegiate Institute.

124 HKF's mother, Gertrude Maidment Kemp, was exactly two years younger than her sister, Lilly.

125 See n. 2, above.

126 See n. 21, above.

127 Denis Saurat, *Milton: Man and Thinker* (London: J. Cape, 1924), first published in French under the title *La pensée de Milton*.

128 Oppenheimer was applying for graduate studies in German at Illinois; he ended up doing his graduate work at Columbia and Harvard.

129 The editors or editorial board of *Acta Victoriana*, the student magazine at VC.

130 The committee that was to set the exam for English 2i, "English Prose and Poetry, 1500–1660."

131 For bardo, see n. 66, above. *Paravritti* is a term that NF takes from Mahayana Buddhism, meaning the complete conversion of the mind. In 50.278 he defines it as "epistemological apocalypse." In his notebooks, NF sometimes uses the word to mean a break or reversal of movement. In *MD* he refers to it as a "turning around" (13).

132 One of the two hours of NF's class conflicted with a history class that Belva Barker needed to complete her third-year course. When she approached NF with the problem, he volunteered to repeat the one 9:00 lecture she would miss each week. Barker would go to his office at 10:00, listen to the lecture, and take notes; because she rarely asked questions, these sessions did not ordinarily take the full hour (Belva Barker Walker to Robert D. Denham, 15 March 1994).

133 An Ontario town about 120 kilometres west of Toronto.

134 Morley Callaghan, *To Tell the Truth*. See par. 114, above.

135 NF is referring to the statement he wrote for *Acta Victoriana* on 7 February.

136 This experience is also recounted in Ayre, 200.

137 A brief, unsigned entry in many editions of the *Encyclopaedia Britannica*. The passage NF refers to: "The chief exposition of this doctrine is that of Dr. Watts (*Works*, v, 274, etc.); it has received little support" (1952 ed., 18:434).

138 "Culture and the Cabinet," *Canadian Forum*, 28 (March 1949): 265–6. NF laments the failure of the Canadian government, which lacks a genuine interest in culture, to establish a national theatre, a national library, and a policy on education. NF actually wrote the editorial on 15 February (see par. 190, below).

139 "Cardinal Mindszenty," *Canadian Forum*, 28 (March 1949): 267. NF condemns the Mindszenty trial for the illegal procedures used by the police in kidnapping Mindszenty and the government's use of the case as a propaganda stunt.

140 A popular Parisian theatre presenting gruesome plays, similar to the Punch and Judy puppet-show dramas.

141 That is, the English language and literature graduates in the class of 1948.

142 Robert Patchell had begun work on his M.A. in 1948–49, but ran out of money about mid-year and became a fire underwriter and eventually a CBC producer. There were twenty graduates in English language and literature in the class of 1948 at VC: five became university teachers and eight secondary school teachers. Here NF is referring to the members of that class who had returned to U of T to do graduate work. He had a somewhat different opinion of these students as undergraduates. In a CBC radio program on James Reaney, broadcast in September 1976, he re-

marked that "when Jamie was an undergrad he went to University College. It was just as well he did, because that class at Victoria was the most brilliant class I ever taught, and with Jamie in it, it might have been a bit overpowering" (Margaret Gayfer to Robert D. Denham, 17 April 1994).

143 *The Petition for an Absolute Retreat* (1713) is a poem by Anne Kingsmill Finch, Countess of Winchilsea.

144 The *Star Weekly* was a popular Saturday supplement to newspapers throughout Ont. HKF's article was "Canadian Handicrafts Abroad," *Star Weekly*, 12 February 1949, 8.

145 See n. 2, above.

146 See n. 139, above.

147 *The Madonna of Alsace*, a sculpture by Émile Antoine Bourdelle (1861–1929), in the Phillips Memorial Gallery in Washington, D.C.

148 Friedrich Heinrich de la Motte Fouqué (1777–1843), German romantic writer of novels, romances, plays, *Märchen*, and epics, the best known of which is *Undine* (1811), one of the early *Märchen*. "Young Chapman" is apparently Francis Chapman, mentioned in par. 188, above.

149 "Culture and the Cabinet" (n. 138, above).

150 Edith Birkhead, *The Tale of Terror: A Study of the Gothic Romance* (New York: Dutton, 1920).

151 The reference here is to the museum lecture mentioned in par. 192.

152 "Sterne," in *The Essays of Virginia Woolf, 1904–1912*, ed. Andrew McNeillie (San Diego: Harcourt Brace Jovanovich, 1986), 1:280–8. The essay first appeared in *TLS*, 12 August 1909.

153 The reference is to the short stories of Ludwig Bemelman (1898–1962).

154 At the meeting of the general council of the UCC in Montreal in 1946 the Board of Evangelism and Social Service was instructed to appoint a Commission on Culture which was to write a report on modern culture from the perspective of the church. NF attended several meetings of the commission, spearheaded by Randolph C. Chalmers, through the summer of 1950, and he made several presentations to the commission, one on modern literature. The report was presented to the general council in 1950 and was published as *The Church and the Secular World* (Toronto: Board of Evangelism and Social Service, 1950). NF wrote two brief sections of the report, "Tenets of Modern Culture" (pp. 13–14), and "Literature" (pp. 42–4); the former he revised and expanded into "Trends in Modern Culture" for the volume of essays that emerged from the commission, *The Heritage of Western Culture: Essays on the Origin and Development of Modern Culture*, ed. Randolph C. Chalmers (Toronto: Ryerson Press, 1952), 102–17.

155 See n. 66, above. For a number of years NF entertained the notion of writing a bardo novel. See, e.g., NB 2 (NFF, 1991, box 22). See also 42.n. 58.

156 Norma Arnett, "Ars Poetica—A Controversy," *Acta Victoriana*, 73, no. 4 (1949): 40–2.

157 The *Citizens' Forum* was a popular weekly radio program, broadcast over CBC, that made use of listening groups. The program was initiated in 1941 and lasted until the mid-1960s. The Canadian Association for Adult Education issued study outlines covering the subjects of the programs. The topic for 18 February was "Is World Government Possible for the Near Future?"

158 See par. 140.

159 The reference is to the treatment of space, time, and immortality in the work of John William Dunne (1875–1949). See, e.g., Dunne's *An Experiment with Time* (London: Faber and Faber, 1937), *Nothing Dies* (London: Faber and Faber, 1946), *The Serial Universe* (London: Faber and Faber, 1942), and *The New Immortality* (New York: Harper, 1937).

160 "Pure religion and undefiled before God and the Father is this, To visit the fatherless and widows in their affliction, and to keep himself unspotted from the world."

161 The first bardo, as opposed to the second (Chönyid) and the third (Sidpa). See *The Tibetan Book of the Dead*, ed. W.Y. Evans-Wentz (London: Oxford University Press, 1960), 89–101.

162 See n. 64, above.

163 A regulation issued by the government under general provisions of an Act of Parliament but not specifically submitted to Parliament.

164 Bulwer-Lytton's short story (1862), in which he introduces occult powers.

165 Richard Brinsley Sheridan's farce, first performed in 1779. For the New Play Society, see n. 242, below.

166 NF's colloquium paper. See n. 2, above.

167 Kilgour was literary editor of *Acta Victoriana*. Arnett had written a letter to the editor of *Acta* in response to a criticism of three of her poems that had appeared in the magazine: *At Parting* (72 [October 1948]: 9), *Alder Song* (72 [December 1948]: 25), and *To Youth: 1949* (72 [February 1949]: 34–5). The critique by Winifred Ruth Julian, VC, 5To, and her brother, along with Arnett's reply, are in *Acta Victoriana*, 72 (March 1949): 39–42 (Mary Louise Knight [neé Kilgour] to Robert D. Denham, 25 February 1994).

168 Green was a third-year student in political science who had been tapped by Fisher as his successor for the editorship of *Acta Victoriana*; Green was willing to waive a student government post for the editorship (Douglas Fisher to Robert D. Denham, 29 March 1994).

169 The reference is to Louis Morris (NF sometimes refers to him as Lew, rather than the customary Lou). Morris had the habit of taking a strong stand on the editorial policy of the *Canadian Forum* even though his position was business manager; he was especially anxious that the leftist political slant of the *Forum* not be confused with Communist theory. Morris, e.g., argued strongly that the *Forum* should reject a manuscript on theatre submitted by Nathan Cohen because Cohen was rumoured to have been a Communist; Morris prevailed in this case, but several members of

the editorial board resigned in protest (Doris Mosdell Sangster to Robert D. Denham, 30 March 1994).

170 The reference here is uncertain. See par. 276, below, where NF refers to having bungled the Shubik matter. Perhaps the issue had to do with a conflict between Martin Shubik and Allan Sangster, a board member and media reviewer for the *Canadian Forum*, over the political satire that Shubik was contributing to the *Forum*. See n. 82, above.

171 NF was commissioned to do an edition of Milton, eventually published as *"Paradise Lost" and Selected Poetry and Prose* (New York: Holt, Rinehart and Winston, 1951).

172 Simon the Clerk in Charles Williams's *All Hallows' Eve*.

173 The pre-Buddhist religion of Tibet.

174 The orthodox view is that *para* means something more like transcendent; *Parabrahman*, e.g., means the transcendent form of Vishnu.

175 The reference is apparently to Alfred Korzybski's *Science and Sanity* (1933). Korzybski was the founder of the General Semantics movement.

176 The leader of the Peasants' Revolt of 1381 and the subject of William Morris's romance *The Dream of John Ball* (1888).

177 These are members of the women's group to whom NF spoke on chivalric romance and courtly love on 7 and 14 February.

178 At the opening of the seventh seal, when four of the seven angels sound their trumpets, plagues and other forms of destruction of the "third part" result. See Revelation 8:7–12.

179 NF's colloquium paper. See n. 2, above.

180 The book was Martin Ellehauge's *The Position of Bernard Shaw in European Drama and Philosophy* (Copenhagen: Levin and Munksgaard, 1931). The book helped Parsons determine the eventual title of his dissertation, *The Development of Bernard Shaw's Theory of the Superman* (1951), directed by Claude Bissell (David Parsons to Robert D. Denham, 5 March 1994).

181 A monthly magazine published in Toronto between 1927 and 1957.

182 Harron, who had graduated from VC in 1948, was not a-member of NF's class, but he went to an occasional lecture with his fiancée Gloria Fisher, who, because of NF, had changed her course from modern languages to English (Don Harron to Robert D. Denham, 28 February 1994).

183 Pratt sometimes prefaced the reading of his *A Feline Silhouette* with a similar story. See David G. Pitt, *E.J. Pratt: The Master Years*, 99.

184 The Rinehart editions; NF had contracted with Rinehart to prepare an edition of Milton. See n. 171, above.

185 NF eventually did complete his essay on Morris—thirty-three years later: "The Meeting of Past and Future in William Morris," *Studies in Romanticism*, 21 (Fall 1982): 303–18; rpt. in *MM*, 322–39.

186 The reference is to people in the attic apartment, which the Fryes were renting to Margaret Newton.

187 The quadrangle at the southwest corner of Merton College; the origin of the word "Mob" remains unknown.

188 See n. 157, above. The topic for the Citizens' Forum program for 25 February was "What Are the Current Parliamentary Issues?"

189 See n. 161 above.

190 See n. 64, above.

191 See T.S. Eliot, introduction to *All Hallows' Eve* (New York: Pellegrini and Cudahy, 1948), xiv.

192 NF's comment was apparently not used by the reporter; it did not, in any case, appear in the *Telegram* during the following two weeks. George McCullagh, owner of the Toronto *Globe and Mail,* had bought the Toronto *Evening Telegram* earlier in the year with the goal of competing with the *Toronto Star.* On the state of affairs created by the McCullagh purchase, see the editorial in the *Canadian Forum,* 29 (May 1949): 25–6.

193 NF's colloquium paper. See n. 2, above.

194 Ibid.

195 The Maison Doré was at 38 Asquith Ave.

196 The race of people in bk. 3 of *Gulliver's Travels* who are endowed with immortality but who turn out to be the most miserable of humankind because of advanced senility.

197 The code, again, refers to NF's writing plans. See n. 12, above.

198 C.G. Jung, *Psychology of the Unconscious,* trans. Beatrice M. Hinkle (New York: Moffat, Yard, 1916). Nearly forty years later Jung radically revised the work, which was published in English as *Symbols of Transformation.* An annotated copy of *Psychology of the Unconscious* (New York: Dodd, Mead, 1963) is in the NFL.

199 The code refers to NF's writing plans. See n. 12, above. NF is suggesting that it is easier to relate Jung to *AC* than to *FS.*

200 Those written for "English Prose and Poetry, 1500–1660."

201 The review was by Kathleen Raine of Mona Wilson's *The Life of William Blake* in the *New Statesman and Nation,* 37 (5 February 1949): 136. NF's letter of protest was not published.

202 *Tat Tvam Asi,* in Sanscrit, meaning that the Absolute is in essence one with oneself. The expression was one of NF's shorthand ways of referring to the final metaphorical vision beyond the literary experience—what he also called "ecstatic identification."

203 CBC Stage was the general title of a weekly drama series of CBC Radio; it began in 1944 as "Stage 44."

204 These were the essays on More's *Utopia* written by the students in English 2i, which NF finished marking on 4 March.

205 See par. 208, above.

206 Kafka's *A Report to an Academy* is narrated by an ape.

207 See, e.g., Michelangelo's *Sketch of the Sorrowing Virgin* and *Study of Ma-*

donna in the Louvre and *Our Lady of the Annunciation* and *Madonna and Child* in the British Museum.

208 In bk. 2 of *The Faerie Queene* Maleger is the captain of the shadowy forces who attack the bulwarks of the House of Alma, the stronghold of Temperance. Guyon is the stern knight of Temperance.

209 The Nuffield Trust offered travelling fellowships for study in the U.K.

210 Rosie was Eleanor Godfrey and Bill Graham's dog.

211 This was the student evening service NF had agreed to hold at Earl Lautenslager's Howard Park United Church (see par. 232, above). The flock is a reference to his own students: Gayfer, Patchell, and Stingle, 1948 graduates of VC, were in the graduate program in English at U of T in 1949; Reaney was a graduate of UC. Eleanor Thomson, 4T9, her brother Ted (4T5), and Dawn Wanless (4T9, a returned serviceman) and his wife were members of the Howard Park Church. Barbara Ewing was in the Pass Arts course. In the entry for 13 March 1949 of his college diary James Reaney made the following note: "Heard Dr Frye preach a very good sermon on Wisdom at Howard Park United. God's Candle" (James Reaney to Robert D. Denham, 2 March 1994, and Dawn Wanless to Robert D. Denham, 12 March 1994).

212 See n. 254, below.

213 The Hart House Art Committee was a combination (what NF means by "joint") of U of T staff members and artists, on the one hand, and student volunteers, on the other; the students were put up for election by the various undergraduate colleges at U of T; the committee's function was to choose and organize the series of exhibitions for the year and to advise on purchases for the permanent collection at Hart House. The Hart House records identify committee members by initials only: P.R. Day, J.D. Boggs, D.E. Thurston (second-year student at SMC), P. Christenson, C.S. Noxon, and D.B. Stewart (third-year student at TC). (Douglas B. Stewart to Robert D. Denham, 19 July 1999). Donald Creighton and G.M.A. Grube were the faculty members on the committee.

214 NF is referring to a program of exchange lectureships that had been established among U of T and universities in the U.S., including Cornell, Wayne State, Western Reserve, Michigan, and Chicago.

215 The effects on those who "tarry long at the wine," according to Proverbs 23:32.

216 "Music in Poetry," *University of Toronto Quarterly*, 11 (January 1942): 167–79.

217 "The wild tulip, at the end of its tube, blows out its great red bell / Like a thin clear bubble of blood, for the children to pick and sell" (Robert Browning, *Up at a Villa—Down in the City*, ll. 24–5).

218 Which poem by Robert Finch NF has in mind is uncertain, but a likely

candidate would be the quick sketch entitled *Still Life* in *The Strength of the Hills* (Toronto: McClelland, 1948), 61. Margaret Avison had reviewed this volume, which contains a half-dozen poems on painting, in the *Canadian Forum* (see par. 41, above).

219 That is, at an annual celebration at Jesus College.

220 The manuscript David Erdman sent NF eventually became *Blake: Prophet against Empire* (Princeton: Princeton University Press, 1954).

221 The Heliconian Club, located at 35 Hazelton Ave., was an association of professional women in the arts and literature; membership in the club, which was founded in 1908, was by invitation to those who had "achieved distinction in their particular field."

222 See par. 200, above.

223 This is apparently Arthur N. Boissonneau, who was earlier (par. 170, above) in the company of Clarence Lemke.

224 NF's point is that these Greek words can be translated in a variety of ways; the usual translations would be, respectively, church, repentance, daily bread, elder, and bishop.

225 Max Stirner, *Der Einzige und Sein Eigentum*, originally published in 1945 and trans. as *The Ego and Its Own* (New York: Dover, 1973).

226 In Hinduism, the real immortal self of human beings.

227 HKF's parents lived at 205 Fulton Ave., the home where HKF grew up.

228 "The Two Camps," *Canadian Forum*, 29 (April 1949): 3. NF comments on the impasse in the confrontation of communism and democracy, maintaining that the violations of civil liberties in the U.S. and Canada do nothing but aid the communist position.

229 Osbert Sitwell, *The Man Who Lost Himself* (London: Duckworth, 1929). James Reaney remembers NF's discussing Sitwell and James's *The Jolly Corner* at the King Cole Room of the Park Plaza Hotel in April of 1949 (James Reaney to Robert D. Denham, 2 March 1994). This was probably the occasion on 9 April that is mentioned in par. 319, below.

230 "That was the prick of the spindle to me that gave me the keys to dreamland" (James Joyce, *Finnegans Wake* [New York: Viking, 1958], 615).

231 Clark's letter criticized NF's view of Jesus as a mythic rather than a historical figure. See Ayre, 215. One student, Mary Louise Knight (née Kilgour), reports that she remembers very clearly how NF ended the lecture: "The bell rang, over a scene of almost unimaginable tension. It was a loud bell, in an old and reverberating Methodist classroom. NF said, with great courtesy, 'I regret that time has given me the last word'" (Mary Louise Knight to Robert D. Denham, 25 February 1994). June Clark, or Clarkie as she was called by her peers, had been spurred to issue her manifesto by something in a previous class NF had said that she considered heretical. Eleanor Morgan (née Thompson) also recalls the episode: "I don't remem-

ber Frye's answer, but I do remember thinking he handled it very well, quietly, giving no real quarter, but not putting [June Clark] down either, or being in any way thrown by this unusual outburst. After the class . . . Clarkie was pretty upset and angry. She claimed that Frye had not answered her legitimate intellectual arguments and had sloughed it off as a joke, so that she had no respect for him. We were all relieved and pleased with his response, though she may have had a point. The whole course was his real answer" (Eleanor Morgan to Robert D. Denham, 26 August 1994).

232 The Oxford Movement, which began at Oxford in 1833, was an Anglican High Church reform movement led by John Keble, John Henry Cardinal Newman, and Charles Froude. The movement, which lasted for a dozen years, was prompted by a perceived decline in religious life, an anxiety about political changes, and a fear of liberal thought.

233 The references are to Butler's *The Authoress of the Odyssey* (1897) and to the 1865 pamphlet he published at his own expense, *The Resurrection of Jesus Christ as given by the Four Evangelists critically examined*; a large part of the latter work was incorporated into *The Fair Haven* (1873).

234 St. Hilda's College was the women's residence of Trinity College.

235 Charles Williams, *The Greater Trumps* (London: V. Gollancz, 1932).

236 "Color-bar of BBC English," *Canadian Forum*, 29 (April 1949): 9–10. McLuhan's editorial commentary is about the prejudices associated with the "educated" British accent.

237 NF's manuscript on Robert Smith Surtees' *Handley Cross* is in NB 41 (NFF, 1991, box 26).

238 NF is referring to either "The Eternal Tramp," *Here and Now*, 1, no. 1 (December 1947): 8–11, or "The Great Charlie," *Canadian Forum*, 21 (August 1941): 148–50.

239 A year-long course on "The Development of the English Drama to 1642," taught principally by E.J. Pratt. NF gave a half-dozen or so lectures on Jacobean drama toward the end of the course.

240 See 42.n. 79.

241 *The Philosophical Lectures of Samuel Taylor Coleridge*, ed. Kathleen Coburn (London: Pilot Press, 1949); *The Grandmothers* (Toronto: Oxford University Press, 1949).

242 The New Play Society was a nonprofit, professional theatre group founded by Dora Mavor Moore in 1946; forty-seven of the seventy-two plays it presented over ten seasons were original; *Spring Thaw* was the annual satiric revue that the New Play Society presented for twenty-five years, beginning in 1948.

243 John Knight, the brother of David Knight, had just returned from his successful debut at Town Hall in New York City; the Toronto recital on

9 April was his first subsequent performance (David Knight to Robert D. Denham, 29 March 1994).

244 See par. 296, above.

245 In Mahayana Buddhism, the one who enters into nirvana as the intended goal of unassisted effort; in Sanskrit, literally, "the solitary awakened one."

246 There is no entry for 29 March.

247 The source of the joke is that Mossie May Kirkwood, the principal of St. Hilda's College, was fond of the word "intercourse" for social relations. She once asked A.Y. Jackson, e.g., how many years it had been since he had had intercourse with the girls at St. Hilda's.

248 The talk NF gave at the Senior Dinner. "Dana Porter . . . gave the usual clichéd blather about leaving the ivory tower of university and going out into the real world. Unfortunately, he then left and so did not hear Frye's rejoinder in the next speech. Frye told us: 'You are now leaving the real world and entering Bay Street where every businessman is tied to his desk by an umbilical cord of telephone wire'" (Richard M. Stingle to Robert D. Denham, 7 March 1994).

249 G.G. Sedgewick had given the 1934–35 Alexander Lectures at U of T, which were published as *Of Irony, Especially in Drama* (Toronto: University of Toronto Press, 1934). For Stoll on *Othello*, see Elmer Edgar Stoll, *Othello: A Historical and Comparative Study*, University of Minnesota Studies in Language and Literature, no. 2 (Minneapolis: Bulletin of the University of Minnesota, 1915). In *Of Irony* Sedgewick does criticize Stoll's views on *Othello* (see pp. 89–93), though not in the way NF reports what Sedgewick had said in the Alexander Lectures.

250 John Webster, *The Duchess of Malfi*, 4.2.146.

251 See n. 239, above.

252 That is, use in the lecture at the School of Social Work.

253 Rosemarie Schawlow's brother, Arthur Leonard Schawlow, a physicist, had gone to Washington, D.C., to deliver a scientific paper; in 1981 he was awarded the Nobel Prize in physics.

254 This row had been occasioned by the publication, the year before, of Peter Grant's poem *Abstract Conception I* in *Acta Victoriana*, 73, (December 1948): 17–20. The poem was a parody of the virgin birth, which had won a literary contest judged by Marshall McLuhan. The editor of *Acta*, Douglas Fisher, had been summoned by the principal of VC and raked over the coals for publishing an "obscene" poem. According to Fisher, NF said that McLuhan had "picked by far the best entry, a poem of worth, not just a good try by a student. 'Leave the principal to me,' he said, and despite rumors galore we heard no more from on high" (Douglas Fisher, "The Symbol of an Era," *Toronto Sun*, 7 January 1981, 11). See also Ayre, 214. Fisher was quoted in the student newspaper as saying that Grant's poem

"motivated a great deal of student criticism on moral and religious grounds" ("No Contributions Cause of Gripes Says Acta Editor," *Varsity*, 14 January 1949, 3). Grant followed this news story with a letter to the editor, maintaining that his poem contained "no allegories, no hidden meanings" ("Misconception," *Varsity*, 18 January 1949, 6).

255 See n. 171, above.

256 The reference is to NF's lecture for the School of Social Work.

257 Albert Rose and Alison Hopwood, "Regent Park: Milestone or Millstone," *Canadian Forum*, 29 (May 1949): 34–6.

258 See pars. 44 and 54, above.

259 As we learn in the previous entry, NF did not give his lecture at the School of Social Work, which was located in the old McMaster University Building at 273 Bloor St. West.

260 Ross Woodman recalls that NF read the poem aloud in a somewhat monotonous and mechanical tone for two hours (Ross Woodman to Robert D. Denham, 18 February 1994).

261 Entuthon Benython is the forest of lost direction outside of Golgonooza. See *Jerusalem*, pl. 14, l. 34 (Erdman, 158).

262 Harron did an adaptation of Webster's play for CBC Radio, though he doesn't recall asking NF to collaborate. "Knowing [NF's] ultra-generous nature," says Harron, "he probably gave me loads of sage advice and then backed away from sharing in the proceeds" (Don Harron to Robert D. Denham, 28 February 1994).

263 Both McFarlane and McKee had come to Toronto from Winnipeg, where they had known each other in college.

264 See par. 74, above.

265 A competition in which students voluntarily wrote essays on a prescribed topic given out by the presiding professor.

266 The King Cole Room at the Park Plaza Hotel at Bloor St. and Avenue Rd. Less attractive than it sounds, the men's section of the King Cole Room was a narrow bleak corridor in the basement of the hotel; the "ladies' section" was a bit less dismal.

267 That is, as opposed to Joe Fisher and Ken MacLean, members of the English department at VC. Peter Fisher and Hugh N. Maclean were both graduate students in English at U of T.

268 David Pitt was offered the position at Michigan State University, but, deciding to return to his native province, he became instead the first appointee to the faculty of Memorial University of Newfoundland (David G. Pitt to Robert D. Denham, 3 March 1994).

269 Peacock's *Bridal Suite* was composed in 1947 and was first performed in Toronto during that year.

270 Maurice Ravel, *Pavane pour une Infante défunte* (1899); Claude Debussy, *La*

cathédrale engloutie (from *Préludes*, bk. 1) (1910); Vincent Youmans, *Tea for Two* (from the musical comedy *No, No, Nanette*) (1924).

271 Grace Shabaeff, who had been in one of NF's 1937 classes, had returned to Toronto to arrange an exhibition of her husband's ceramic wall plaques at Eaton's College Art Gallery. She was married in 1946, her husband having come to the U.S. by way of Shanghai in 1929 and ending up in Montreal, where he eked out a precarious living by selling his paintings privately (Grace Demster Shabaeff to Robert D. Denham, 12 March 1994).

272 Madeline Bomberger Lavender remembers the effect of NF's course this way: "Part of what our church did was to have evangelistic services, usually at Easter time. As a child of 12 or 13, these were very disturbing to me. . . . Some of what I heard . . . meant, among other things, that I had to abandon intellectual, logical considerations. When I attended Frye's R.K. course . . . I found things that he said reconciled both faith and reason. And I resonated to many parts of the Bible he spoke about and quoted. I believe that the comment I made at the end of the exam made brief reference to my previous church experience and what his course had meant to me as a result" (Madeline Bomberger Lavender to Robert D. Denham, 17 March 1994).

273 Diana Ironside recalls this visit to NF during her fourth year, remembering that he was "gracious and helpful" in advising her to pursue graduate work. She left Canada after graduating from VC in 1949, returned in 1968, and taught at the Ontario Institute for Studies in Education until her retirement in 1991. She remembers the RK course as an "exciting challenge" (Diana Ironside to Robert D. Denham, 9 February 1994).

274 English 3j was the Honour Course NF taught on Spenser and Milton.

275 Frances Wickes, *The Inner World of Man: With Psychological Drawings and Paintings* (New York: Holt, 1948).

276 A translation of *Tai i chin hua tsung chih*, for which Jung wrote a fifty-six-page commentary; published as *Secret of the Golden Flower: A Chinese Book of Life* (New York: Harcourt, Brace, 1931). Jung's commentary touches on topics and works that would make their way into NF's later notebooks; among them are *wu-wei* (action through nonaction), Kundalini Yoga, the *I Ching*, *The Tibetan Book of the Dead*, the Eros–Logos opposition, Lévy-Bruhl's *participation mystique*, Meister Eckhart, and Jacob Boehme.

277 Jolande S. Jacobi, *The Psychology of C.G. Jung* (London: Routledge and Kegan Paul, 1942).

278 See par. 317, above.

279 Harold King had died on 6 January. See par. 44, above.

280 That is, to NF's in-laws' home at 205 Fulton Ave.

281 HKF's younger brother and younger sister. Roy and his wife Mary lived in New York, where he was a photographer. Marion lived in Rhodesia. Her

second husband, Daniel P. Erasmus, had deserted her only three days before NF's diary entry, and Erasmus was found dead on 8 May 1949, apparently having died two weeks earlier.

282 Mrs. Agnes Hickman and her husband Walter were members of the Stone parish, one of three charges NF served when he was a student minister in southwestern Sask. during the summer of 1934. For NF's account of the Hickmans, see *Correspondence* 1:267, 275, 302, 307, 308, and 316.

283 See Owen's editorial, ". . . And Then There Were Ten," *Canadian Forum*, 29 (April 1949): 1–2.

284 See par. 324, above.

285 See par. 332, above.

286 On the Fudger group, see n. 90, above.

287 NF was doubtless reading the translation by W.Y. Evans-Wentz (Oxford: Oxford University Press, 1949), an annotated copy of which, acquired later, is in the NFL. NF may have been pointed to *The Tibetan Book of the Dead* by the reference to it in Jung's commentary on *The Secret of the Golden Flower*, 111.

288 The lectures on Spenser and Joyce that NF is to give at the University of Michigan at Ann Arbor.

289 John Arthos, *The Language of Natural Description in Eighteenth-Century Poetry* (Ann Arbor: University of Michigan Press, 1949).

290 Donald Pearce had completed his Ph.D. dissertation on Yeats the year before: *The Significance of Ireland in the Work of W.B. Yeats* (University of Michigan).

291 See n. 289, above.

292 Roger P. Hinks, *Myth and Allegory in Ancient Art* (London: Warburg Institute, 1939).

293 Clarence D. Thorpe, *The Mind of John Keats* (New York: Oxford University Press, 1926).

294 A.J.M. Smith's *The Book of Canadian Prose* (Toronto: W.J. Gage) was not published until 1965.

295 Nathaniel West, *Miss Lonelyhearts* (New York: James Laughlin, 1933).

296 *Monsieur Vincent*, directed by Maurice Cloche and starring Pierre Fresnay; the film won an Oscar for the best foreign film in 1947.

297 A collection of essays in memory of Richard Davidson, principal of Emmanuel College. NF contributed an article, "The Church: Its Relation to Society" (introduction, n. 34).

298 As it turned out, the three students NF recommended *were* "blind leads": James Reaney accepted the position.

299 This is the manuscript for Len Peterson's *Chipmunk*, published later in the year by McClelland and Stewart; NF critiques it in the next entry, par. 348.

300 The lecture that NF gave on 6 April.

301 Harold Vaughan, *The Living Church* (see introduction, n. 34).

302 Reid MacCallum and Robert Finch had been close friends.

303 Pratt was invited to lecture on Canadian poetry at the University of Michigan, Ann Arbor, on 29 June 1949. See David G. Pitt, *E.J. Pratt: The Master Years*, 403–4.

304 Op. 121a, Variations, G, on Wenzel Müller's *Ich bin der Schneider Kakadu*.

305 Because of failing health, Walter T. Brown resigned as president of VC in June 1949 (he had suffered a cerebral hemorrhage in December 1948). Before the appointment of A.B.B. Moore as president of VU in 1950, Harold Bennett served as acting president and dean; in 1951 his title was changed to principal of VC.

306 William James, *The Varieties of Religious Experience* (New York: New American Library, 1958), 76–111 (Lectures 4 and 5).

307 William Herbert Carruth, *Each in His Own Tongue*, ll. 15–16.

308 See par. 351.

309 See 42.n. 58.

310 The women's residence of VC, located in the former home of Edward Rogers Wood at 84 Queen's Park Crescent directly west of EC; the building was named after Wood's two children, William (Wy) and Mildred, and was presented as a gift to the university by Mrs. Wood and Lady Flavelle in 1926; today the building is called Falconer Hall and is part of the Faculty of Law at U of T.

311 The movie of Margery Sharp's *Nutmeg Tree* (London: Collins, 1937) was *Julie Misbehaves*, a 1948 MGM production starring Greer Garson, Walter Pidgeon, Peter Lawford, Cesar Romero, and Elizabeth Taylor.

312 Colgrove, whose course was math and physics, with a speciality in astrophysics, had become interested in the fourth dimension during his senior year at VC and had developed a lecture on the subject during his early years as a math teacher at Forest Hill Collegiate. On the occasion NF mentions here, Colgrove was trying out the lecture, which was later televised for META, on a group of admired friends (Pete Colgrove to Robert D. Denham, 22 February 1994).

313 See n. 8, above.

314 Hilary Hallam Whitley, the daughter of Isabel Hallam Whitley and Harold Whitley. Isabel's father was Bishop Hallam, who was a friend of Archdeacon Marsh from their Wycliffe College days. The "girl named Day" was Jessie Adams (née Day). Her husband Douglas, a long-time friend of the Whitleys, was the godfather of baby Hilary, and HKF was the godmother. Katherine Beatrice (Betty) Brett was a friend of Isabel Whitley from their school days (Jessie Day Adams to Robert D. Denham, 9 March 1994, and 29 July 1994).

315 The *Isa*, also called the *Isavasya Upanishad*, derives its name from the opening word of the text, Isavasya or Isa; it belongs to the Vajasaneyi

school of the Yajur Veda; the Vajasaneyi Samhita consists of forty chaps. of which this Upanishad is the last.

316 See Ivon Owen's unsigned editorial, "Coming Soon," *Canadian Forum*, 29 (June 1949): 49–50.

317 Hebb, editor of the *Rural Co-operator*, an independent, nonpartisan, semi-monthly newspaper published by the Ontario Federation of Agriculture, was a member of the board of the *Canadian Forum* but did not permit his name to be included on the masthead: he felt that the *Forum* was losing its political independence under the strong CCF influence of George Grube; under NF's editorship the *Forum* recovered a great deal of its former independence (Ruth D. Hebb to Robert D. Denham, 3 March 1994).

318 The examinations for English 2b, a Pass Course in "Poetry."

319 "On Book Reviewing," *Here and Now*, 2 (June 1949): 19–20.

320 NF's practice on the Blake exam was to ask students to write as much as they could on as many of the quotations as they could. Some students would write for six or seven hours.

321 The Ontario Hospital at Whitby, established in 1913, was the first hospital named as such (as opposed to "asylum") in Ontario for the care and treatment of the mentally ill.

322 In the preface to his *Blake Studies* Sir Geoffrey Keynes wrote: "Books on William Blake have become fashionable in recent years and their value has usually borne a definite relation to the amount of study expended by the author on his subject. The climax has been seen recently in the magnificent interpretive study of Blake written by Northrop Frye in Canada and published by Princeton University" (*Blake Studies: Notes on His Life and Work* [London: R. Hart-Davis, 1949], xi).

323 H.M. Margoliouth, review of *Fearful Symmetry*, in *Review of English Studies*, 24 (October 1948): 334–5. As for the "joke" NF mentions, Margoliouth says, "The Stone of Scone is not used 'to crown the kings of England'" (335), as opposed to what NF had said in *FS*, 224.

324 The editing of the Rinehart Milton. See n. 171, above.

325 On this occasion, according to Wood, they discussed the references to Zen Buddhism in *Fearful Symmetry* (Gordon Wood to Robert D. Denham, 10 March 1994).

326 Marshall McLuhan had long had a dream of starting a magazine to advance his ideas about the communication media; while this dream was never realized, he did become associate editor of the magazine *Explorations* (1953–59), founded by his colleague Edmund Carpenter.

327 Manufacturers of farm machinery and other equipment; the Massey Manufacturing Co. merged with A. Harris, Son & Co. in 1891.

328 NF has almost certainly written "3e," but there was no English course with that designation. He perhaps meant to write "3c," a course in nineteenth-

century poetry that served as an option for the religious knowledge requirement for students in the Honour Courses.

329 The Pontifical Institute of Mediaeval Studies in Toronto was established in
1929 and received its papal charter ten years later. Run by the Basilian
Fathers, it was substantially influenced by the thought of Étienne Gilson

330 This is a reference to Millar MacLure's defence of his Ph.D. dissertation,
The Paul's Cross Sermons, 1534–1641: An Introductory Survey, which had
been directed by H.S. Wilson. MacLure left Toronto to become head of the
English department at United College, Winnipeg, where he stayed until
1953, when he joined the faculty at VC.

331 G.B. Harrison, who had directed MacLure's M.A. thesis at Queen's, was
the external examiner for MacLure's Ph.D. orals.

332 MacCallum had died at the monastery of the Cowley Fathers, Bracebridge,
Ont.

333 See n. 220, above.

334 Bernard Blackstone, *English Blake* (Cambridge: Cambridge University
Press, 1949). NF's review of the book appeared in *Modern Language Notes*,
64 (January 1951): 55–7.

335 NF's introduction for the Milton ed. was twenty-six pages in the published
version.

336 Apparently a review of Pitirim A. Sorokin's *Reconstruction of Humanity*
(1948), a research project carried out by Sorokin and other scholars at
Harvard, focusing on what society must do to avoid a new catastrophe.

337 Cotter had written a two-part commentary, "Toward Responsible Government in Jamaica," for the *Canadian Forum*, November and December 1948.

338 Dix's book was published in London by Dacre Press in 1945.

1950 Diary

1 The Colloquium was a UC event, which met irregularly in the Croft Chapter House. The paper NF presented on 28 February 1949, "First Steps in
Literary Criticism," became the original version of "The Function of Criticism at the Present Time" (see 49.n. 2). NF delivered his "Social Work" talk
on 6 April 1949. He gave his Senior Dinner speech at VC on 30 March 1949,
and his speech at St. Hilda's College on 2 April. On 13 March 1949 NF held
the student evening service at Earl Lautenslager's Howard Park United
Church in Toronto.

2 L or Liberal, represented the first phase of NF's writing plans after he
finished *FS*. See 49.n. 12. Often during this and the other surviving diaries
NF speaks of L as a book on the epic, particularly *The Faerie Queene*, though
many of his references to L involve material that was to become a part of
AC. The dictation NF refers to here was a running commentary on *The*

Faerie Queene that survives as a ninety-three page holograph manuscript in the NFF, 1991, box 37, file 1. The notes for bk. 1 and the first canto of bk. 2 are in NF's hand; HKF took dictation for bk. 3 and the first ten cantos of bk. 4, at which point the manuscript ends.

3 A paper NF presented to the Philosophical Club at U of T; it developed into "Levels of Meaning in Literature," *Kenyon Review*, 12 (Spring 1950): 246–62.

4 "The Church: Its Relation to Society"; see introduction, n. 34.

5 For the shorthand notation for NF's eight-part writing project, see 49.n. 12. As NF later speaks of Paradox as the foundation for a study of archetypes and a conspectus for the verbal universe (par. 310, below), he conceives of Paradox at this stage as *AC*, or at least a large part of it.

6 "The Four Forms of Prose Fiction" (49.n. 58); "The Argument of Comedy" (49.n. 56); and "The Function of Criticism at the Present Time" (49.n. 2).

7 Roy Daniells taught at UBC, and Desmond Pacey at UNB. They were both heads of departments and thus able to make appointments.

8 NF and HKF had travelled to Cambridge, Mass., by way of Moncton during early September of 1949.

9 NF's older sister Vera, who taught school in Evergreen Park in Chicago, and their father were regular visitors to Toronto during the Christmas holidays.

10 The three books that NF anticipated writing after *FS*, which he referred to as Tragicomedy, Anticlimax, and Rencontre.

11 "The Four Forms of Prose Fiction" (49.n. 58).

12 Dr. Ella Priscilla Ford, wife of Professor Edgerton Ford, died on 2 January 1950.

13 Birchard had served one term as an alderman in 1946 and was elected for five subsequent terms, beginning in 1957. She campaigned on behalf of Toronto's needy, the elderly population, and day nurseries.

14 The reference is to a plebiscite on whether to legalize Sunday sports, an issue that was on the ballot with the Toronto municipal elections. Those in favour of permitting sports events on Sunday won by a small margin. For NF's unsigned editorial on the subject see, "Man and the Sabbath," *Canadian Forum*, 29 (February 1950): 241, 245.

15 Allan Lamport had been elected controller of the Toronto Board of Control in 1949 and served as a member of that board through 1950; he was not contesting an election at the time, though he had previously served as an alderman and would so later serve.

16 Malcolm Ross had resigned his position in the English department at the University of Manitoba in 1950. Clarence Tracy, an associate professor at UNB, did go to USk as a full professor. NF apparently means that he had recommended Christopher Love for Tracy's vacant position, but Love, who had been appointed lecturer in English at VC in 1948, remained at VC, where he became an assistant professor and senior tutor in the men's residences.

17 NF is referring, not to Discourse 9, the final discourse in *The Idea of a University*, but to Discourse 8, where Newman holds up Julian the Apostate as an example of intellectual religion. See secs. 8–10 of Discourse 8.

18 NF is to give a talk on modern culture in Huntsville, Ont., on 4 January.

19 Gershom Scholem, *Major Trends in Jewish Mysticism* (New York: Schoken, 1941).

20 John B. Vickery, who had been an undergraduate at VC, was working on his Ph.D. at the University of Wisconsin.

21 Jerome Buckley, VC, 3T9, who had begun teaching English at the University of Wisconsin in 1942. Both Jack Vickery and Richard Stingle were in Buckley's Romanticism seminar during the fall of 1949, their first semester at Wisconsin.

22 The Spenser professor was not a man, but Helen C. White. Wisconsin's Renaissance faculty included (in addition to White) Merritt Y. Hughes, Madeleine Doran, and Ruth Wallerstein. Vickery and Stingle were able to get White, who was engaged in quasi-political activities in Washington at the time, to agree to their reading Spenser independently (John B. Vickery to Robert D. Denham, 28 September 1998).

23 The rooftop restaurant at the Park Plaza Hotel at Bloor St. and Avenue Rd.

24 See 49.n. 154.

25 The general offices of the United Church were at 299 Queen St. West in Toronto.

26 This "paper" is the introduction (NF calls it a "preface" in par. 57, below) to Milton's *Paradise Lost and Selected Poetry and Prose*, the book he was editing for Holt, Rinehart and Winston; it was published in 1951.

27 Yvonne Williams's home and studio was located at 3 Caribou Ave., near the intersection of Dupont and Dundas St. West.

28 Joan Evans was a prolific art historian; NF could be thinking about any one of a number of her books on medieval art.

29 Robins was joking about the answer of the student, who had conflated Frances (Fanny) Burney and Earle Birney, the author of *Turvey: A Military Picaresque* (Toronto: McClelland and Stewart, 1949).

30 NF's father, Herman, had been a widower for ten years. Lucy Massey was one of two widows from Moncton who had been pursuing him for some time, and as Ayre says, "had a way of turning up wherever he was" (234); her son Lloyd lived in Toronto at the time. She corresponded occasionally with the Fryes in later years, even after NF's father's death in 1959.

31 A 1949 comedy directed by John Paddy Carstairs and based on a play by William Douglas Home.

32 MacKinnon never did write the book. On the Nuffield, see 49.n. 209.

33 See par. 12, above.

34 That is, the obligation to shovel the snow from his sidewalk.

35 Kenmare had written on 10 November 1949 from Barnt Green, Worcester-shire, about his enthusiasm for *FS*. His letter is in the NFF, 1991, box 6, file 4.

36 Peter Kemp, NF's nephew.

37 C.G. Jung, *Symbols of Transformation* (Princeton, N.J.: Princeton University Press, 1991), 266–7. See also Jung's *Psychology of the Unconscious*; NF had read the original edition of this book, published in 1916.

38 The student officers for the class of 1951; NF was the faculty sponsor for the group. Toll, a Toronto photographer, took group photos for *Acta Victoriana*.

39 See introduction, n. 34.

40 The Function of Criticism at the Present Time" (49.n. 2), "The Four Forms of Prose Fiction" (49.n. 58) and "The Argument of Comedy" (49.n. 56).

41 The editor was Philip Blair Rice.

42 The members of the Tuesday afternoon writing group were Sylvia Moss, Kay Brown, Jean Inglis, Catherine Card, Kathlyn Smith, Mary Lane, Rita MacLean, and Gloria Thompson. Ruth Elizabeth McLellan joined the group later in the year. If NF doesn't remember quite how the group got born, neither do the members of the group from this era. But see 49.n. 92. Accord-ing to Mary Lane, the sessions were "quite informal, not exactly intimate. I cannot recall Professor Frye ever addressing any of us directly by our first name, nor did he analyse in depth, though he made suggestions. While we criticized each other's work, he was intent, missing nothing. We watched too for any little sign of his approval. He was pretty good at keeping a poker face! We trotted back to the barracks, content that he had listened and commented. . . . I think the purpose of our sessions with Dr. Frye must have been to drum up new material for *Acta Victoriana*. Or he may have wanted to foster 'the creative individual'—who knows? At any rate, these meetings were a pleasant break from the course essays we had to write, and he, to mark" (Mary Lane Culley to Robert D. Denham, 7 June 1994).

43 NF is referring to the first of the Armstrong Lectures (see n. 47, below), presented in the VC chapel by J.S. Thomson on "The Mysticism of Francis Thompson," 10–11 January 1950.

44 *English Institute Essays, 1948*, which contained NF's "The Argument of Comedy" (49.n. 56).

45 The reference is to Joseph Butler's *Analogy of Religion* (1736), an argument against the contemporary Deists that natural and revealed religion were not incompatible.

46 The reference is to NF's unsigned editorial "Merry Christmas," *Canadian Forum*, 29 (December 1949): 193–4; NF briefly surveys the history of Christ-mas and laments the panic and compulsion of its present commercialism. J.V. McAree quoted the first par. of the editorial in his own editorial, "Christmas Old and New," *Globe and Mail*, 24 December 1949, 6.

47 An annual VC lecture series on education and religion, established by an

endowment from George H. Armstrong in 1938. The first Armstrong lecture was given in 1939 by A.J.B. Wace, professor of Classical anthropology at Cambridge.

48 Porter, Ontario's minister of education, had protested the schools' using novels as models of prose. See 49.225 and 255. The meeting was apparently devoted to this issue. Late in 1949 Porter had caused quite a stir when he recommended abolishing the Ontario high school examinations and regrouping grades 1–13 into four larger divisions. NF may be referring to an English department meeting late in 1949 at which this issue was discussed. On the Porter recommendations, see "Hiroshima, Ontario," *Saturday Night,* 20 December 1949, 20.

49 In the context of other members of the faculty, this is an apparent reference to Harold Innis and his wife. NF refers to Harold Innis as "Innes" in the 1950 and 1952 Diaries.

50 For the staff photograph, see *Acta Victoriana,* 74 (January 1950): 4.

51 See 49.n. 154.

52 Francis Bacon's theory of the four "idols" or false appearances is developed in his *Novum Organum* (1622).

53 John Irving's presentation to the Commission on Culture appeared in a condensed form in chap. 5 of the commission's report, "The Sciences and Philosophy in Modern Culture," in *The Church and the Secular World,* 11–13. Irving expanded his views into an essay with the same title, which was published in the book that emerged from the work of the commission, *The Heritage of Western Culture,* 88–101 (49.n. 154).

54 See n. 3, above.

55 "The Function of Criticism at the Present Time" (49.n. 2).

56 A public library at 40 St. Clair Ave. East.

57 William Henry Hudson, *The Purple Land that England Lost* (1885), a series of short stories set in South America.

58 After graduating from UC in 1948, David Parsons taught for several years at Meisterschaft College, which was located at 84 Woodlawn Ave. in Toronto.

59 Doubtless a reference to the John S. Morgans.

60 Kathleen Coburn, *The Grandmothers* (49.n. 241).

61 That is, the department of Oriental (Near Eastern) languages at VC.

62 A.F.B. Clark, *Boileau and the French Classical Critics in England (1660–1830)* (Paris: E. Champion, 1925). NF's saying that Clark "was there" apparently means he was present at the colloquium.

63 "The Four Forms of Prose Fiction" (49.n. 58). The passage in the essay NF refers to: "Romance is older than the novel, a fact that has developed the historical illusion that it is something to be outgrown, a juvenile and undeveloped form. The social affinities of the romance, with its grave idealizing of heroism and purity, are with the aristocracy, and it revived in the period we

call Romantic as part of the Romantic tendency to archaic feudalism and a cult of the hero, or idealized libido. In England the romances of Scott and, in less degree, the Brontës, are part of a mysterious Northumbrian renaissance, a Romantic reaction against the new industrialism in the Midlands, which also produced the poetry of Wordsworth and Burns and the philosophy of Carlyle. It is not surprising, therefore, that an important theme in the more bourgeois novel should be the parody of the romance and its ideals" (585). In *AC* the ideas about aristocratic and proletarian romance were incorporated, not into the section on prose fiction in the Fourth Essay, but into the introduction to "The Mythos of Summer: Romance" in the Third Essay.

64 "Man and the Sabbath," 241, 245 (n. 14, above).

65 George Johnston had tried to persuade the committee to buy a religious painting by Brittain (George Johnston to Robert D. Denham, 15 May 1999).

66 See n. 3, above.

67 "Turning New Leaves," *Canadian Forum*, 29 (December 1949): 209–11. This begins as a review of Samuel Putnam's trans. of *Don Quixote* but turns into a short essay on the novel. The passage that bothered Endicott: "But great art comes from the harnessing of a conscious intention to the creative powers beneath consciousness, and we do not get closer to the author's meaning by getting closer to the book's meaning" (*NFCL*, 160).

68 Desmond Pacey, head of the English department at UNB, had been in Toronto looking for a replacement for Clarence Tracy, an eighteenth-century scholar, at UNB. Wood had already taught at UNB on two occasions, the spring semester of 1946 and in 1947–48, after his M.A. year at U of T. NF had been prodding John Robins to keep Wood, who had a one-year appointment at VC. In 1951 Wood went to Carleton University (Gordon Wood to Robert D. Denham, 10 March 1994).

69 Johnston completed all of the Ph.D. requirements except the writing of his dissertation: "Mme. Blavatsky was too much for me & to tell the truth so was Blake's *Jerusalem*" (George Johnston to Robert D. Denham, 15 May 1994).

70 Archibald Allan Bowman, *A Sacramental Universe: Being a Study in the Metaphysics of Experience* (Princeton: Princeton University Press, 1939).

71 John A. Irving, "Dr. Bowman's Lectures," *Princeton Alumni Weekly*, 6 April 1934, 599–600.

72 See n. 14 above.

73 See 42.n. 77.

74 The anonymous reviewer of William Saroyan's *The Assyrian and Other Stories* quotes Saroyan as saying that children are "the only aristocracy of the human race" (*The New Yorker*, 25 [1 January 1950]: 86).

75 The Chez Paree was located at 220 Bloor St. W.

76 See par. 50, above.

77 The student NF had in mind was Richard V. Howson.

78 Lucille Hoffman was not a member of the 1951 VC executive and she never dined at the Fryes' home (Lucille Hoffman McBeth to Robert D. Denham, 17 May 1994). NF has confused her with Lucille Hammond, VC, 5T1, who was a member of the executive.

79 A 1949 comedy, directed by Leslie Arliss and starring Kieron Moore and Christina Norden.

80 The pieces the Fryes heard at the TSO concert were Oscar Morawetz's *Overture "Carnival,"* Benjamin Britten's *Soirées Musicales,* Haydn's *Piano Concerto in D Major,* Eldon Rathburn's *Images of Childhood,* Tchaikovsky's *Italian Caprice,* and, after intermission, Sibelius's *Symphony No. 2 in D Major.* The special concert, conducted by Sir Ernest MacMillan, was dedicated to the United Nations International Children's Emergency Fund. The fourteen-year-old pianist was Elizabeth Auld.

81 A conference on religion sponsored by the Edward Hazen Foundation.

82 Johnston read his paper to the Graduate English Club.

83 For NF's notes on *The Phoenix and the Turtle,* see NBs 12 and 14, in the NFF, 1991, box 24.

84 John Sutherland, "Old Dog Trait—An Extended Analysis," *Contemporary Verse,* 29 (Fall 1949): 17–23. The "old Forum article" was NF's "Canada and Its Poetry," *Canadian Forum,* 23 (December 1943): 207–10; rpt. in *BG,* 131–45.

85 On the *Citizen's Forum,* see 49.n. 157.

86 Fraser, a journalist, was at the time the overseas editor of *Maclean's*; Ouimet, an attorney, later became justice of the Superior Court of Quebec; Sinclair was a broadcaster and newspaper writer whose opinionated "news and comments" were heard on CFRB in Toronto in the 1940s and 1950s; Macphail, a politician and reformer, was the first woman in the Canadian House of Commons, elected to Parliament in 1921.

87 On the *Citizens' Forum,* see 49.n. 157. Forty-eight years later a group of twenty-seven panelists for *Maclean's* magazine selected NF as the second most important person in Canadian history and the first among the category of thinkers and writers. See the cover story of *Maclean's,* 1 July 1998.

88 See par. 46, above.

89 See par. 2, above.

90 The allusion is to John Henry Cardinal Newman's *Lead, Kindly Light* (1833), which was set to music as a hymn by John B. Dykes.

91 Sten Bodvar Liljegren, *Studies in Milton* (Lund: Gleerups, 1918).

92 See n. 3, above.

93 Harry Allen Overstreet, *The Mature Mind* (New York: Norton, 1949).

94 Evan Harrington is the protagonist of George Mededith's novel of that name (1860).

95 Wood did not in fact accept Desmond Pacey's offer from UNB, where he

had taught in the Veterans' College in 1946 and again in 1947–48 following his M.A. exam. See n. 68, above.

96 The paper NF ended up presenting was "Blake's Treatment of the Archetype," which was published in *English Institute Essays, 1950*, ed. Alan S. Downer (New York: Columbia University Press, 1951), 170–96.

97 NF's uncertainty about the name "Drury" seems to be justified.

98 A 1934 novel by Christina Stead.

99 Grant's poem *Abstract Conceptions I* had appeared in *Acta Victoriana*. See 49.266 and n. 254.

100 NF had suggested that the group have lunch "off the campus" so that Kathleen Coburn could be included in the party. Women were excluded from the Senior Common Room until 1968.

101 Godfrey Goodman (1586–1655) was the bishop of Gloucester, a position to which he was appointed in 1625, the process of his appointment not unlike that of Donne's election as the Dean of St. Paul's; William Hakewell (1574–1655), a friend of Donne, was a member of the Inns of Court. For the ways they figure in Donne's life, see R.C. Bald's posthumous *John Donne: A Life* (New York: Oxford University Press, 1970), 114, 193–4, 286–7, 376–8 (Goodman), 44–5, 82, 498 (Hakewell).

102 Richard F. Jones, "Science and Criticism in the Neo-classical Age," *Journal of the History of Ideas*, 1 (1940): 381–412; and Charles Monroe Coffin, *John Donne and the New Philosophy* (Morningside Heights, N.Y.: Columbia University Press, 1937).

103 "The Ideal of Democracy," *Varsity*, 7 February 1950, 3.

104 The Grange, a restored Georgian mansion, was the original home of the Art Gallery of Toronto.

105 "The Church: Its Relation to Society" (introduction, n. 34).

106 "Levels of Meaning in Literature" (n. 3, above).

107 R.B. Simmons was keeper of the prints at Hart House from September 1949 until February 1950. He and his committee of three managed the print room, rematted drawings, lent books from the Hart House art library, and changed drawings in the print cabinet. According to Judi Schwartz, the present curator of the Hart House gallery, Simmons seems to have assumed the position by default. In any event, the secretary of the art committee thanks Simmons in the annual report for accepting the job on short notice (Judi Schwartz to Robert D. Denham, 29 September 1998). The warden of Hart House was Nicholas Ignatieff.

108 See Professor Douglas P. Dryer's editorial on communism in the *Varsity*, 7 February 1950, 3.

109 After World War II Johnston decided to spend his veteran's allowance on graduate studies at Toronto. NF directed his M.A. thesis on Blake's poetry, which was granted after one year. He then did another year of graduate

study, taught for two years at Mt. Allison University, and returned to Toronto for further graduate work (George Johnston to Robert D. Denham, 15 May 1994).

110 More than a half-dozen books with this title are in the catalogues of the Online Computer Library Center and the National Library of Canada, but none is written by a man named Murphy. The book was apparently published privately.

111 1b was a Pass Course in "Poetry and Drama."

112 "George Orwell," *Canadian Forum*, 29 (March 1950): 265–6.

113 In NB 3.145, NF wrote: "Λ [Anticlimax] 1. An article on the four forms of prose fiction (done, offered to Virginia, & completely superseding the Manitoba Anatomy article, though some material in the latter is still good & unused)." "The Four Forms of Prose Fiction," which appeared in the *Hudson Review*, 2 (Winter 1950): 582–95, was apparently first offered to the *Virginia Quarterly Review*. Precisely what NF means by "fiasco" is uncertain, but the suggestion is that the article was rejected. The "Manitoba article" was "The Anatomy in Prose Fiction," *Manitoba Arts Review*, 3 (Spring 1942): 35–47.

114 Victor G. Hopwood, *A Critique of Objective Standards in Poetic Judgment*," Ph.D. diss., U of T, 1950.

115 The *Lankavatara Sutra* is one of the sutras of Mahayana Buddhism; *paratantra-laksana* ("the dependent character") is, in the Yogacara school of Indian Buddhism, one of the three characteristics of entities—a doctrine embodied in the *Samdhinirmocana Sutra*. "Mind-only" or *citta-matra*, the central doctrine of the Yogacara school, means that the world is considered as nothing but mind or consciousness.

116 In 1949, NF had written his "colloquium paper," which was developed into "The Function of Criticism at the Present Time" (49.n. 2). Elizabeth Nitchie of Goucher College was the director of the English Institute session on Blake.

117 NF is referring to his article on "Levels of Meaning in Literature" (n. 3, above).

118 See n. 112, above.

119 A copy of the letter from the Guggenheim committee, along with NF's reply, is in the NFF, 1988, box 39, file 4.

120 M.H. Abrams was to visit Toronto to speak on the annual round-robin exchange of lecturers. See 49.n. 214.

121 The reference is to NF's first-year RK class, which met on Thursday at 12:00, and his fourth-year RK class, which met on Tuesday at 12:00.

122 HKF's mother had been keeping Roy and Mary Kemp's infant son Peter.

123 That is, NF's introduction to the Rinehart Milton (49.n. 171).

124 On the Citizens' Forum, see 49.n. 157.

125 See n. 120, above.

126 Duncan Robertson did eventually do a Ph.D. dissertation under NF's supervision, receiving his degree in 1965. The other student was almost certainly Ross Woodman, whose dissertation on the apocalyptic vision in Shelley was directed by NF: he received his degree in 1957.

127 A small group of indigenous people from an isolated fishing village of the same name on the central west coast of B.C.

128 See 49.n. 213.

129 The remark is occasioned by the printed note in the diary that 22 February is Ash Wednesday in Quebec.

130 *Representative Poetry* was a two-volume anthology used by the combined English departments at U of T. The first edition was published in 1912. The edition NF refers to here was the third; NF had assisted Norman J. Endicott in preparing the notes for the first volume of this edition in May 1935.

131 "Levels of Meaning in Literature" (n. 3, above).

132 See 49.137.

133 That is, NF had to shovel the snow from his sidewalk again.

134 C.D. Broad, *The Mind and Its Place in Nature* (New York: Humanities Press, 1921).

135 The daughter was Lois G. White.

136 James R. Guthrie came from Edinburgh in 1948 to be a guest lecturer at EC and the United Church Training School. In 1949 he was appointed to a permanent position at EC.

137 See 49.n. 154.

138 *The God that Failed: Six Studies in Communism* (New York: Harper, 1949).

139 See n. 134, above.

140 NF is referring to his forthcoming radio review of *The God that Failed*. See par. 144, above.

141 NF had agreed to edit Pelham Edgar's autobiography, *Across My Path*, which was published two years later (Toronto: Ryerson).

142 See 49.n. 185.

143 Gloria Thompson does not recall NF's showing off for the writing group, but that was perhaps because she "did not think of him as an ordinary human being, only as a great mind." She does, however, remember that NF would blush when she would speak up in class, and she and her friends always left his classes "feeling elated" (Gloria Thompson Dent to Robert D. Denham, 23 October 1998).

144 NF was not elected a fellow of the Royal Society of Canada until 1951.

145 Daniells had edited Thomas Traherne's *A Serious and Pathetical Contemplation of the Mercies of God, in Several Most Devout and Sublime Thanksgivings for the Same* (Toronto: University of Toronto Press, 1941).

146 NF apparently meant to write "the fragmentation epic" or "epic fragmentation lyric" for "epic fragmentation epic." The sense, in any case, is that

the epic breaks down into three kinds of lyric: diffuse, brief, and micro-cosmic.

147 The Famous Door was a tavern and cocktail lounge located at 665 Yonge St.

148 See n. 134, above.

149 NF never wrote the paper on poetry for the *Kenyon Review*, though he did write one on the forms of drama, "A Conspectus of Dramatic Genres," *Kenyon Review*, 13 (Autumn 1951): 543–62.

150 That is, without the money from Margaret Newton, who had earlier rented an upstairs room in the Fryes' home.

151 Barbara McNabb was the editor of a business magazine devoted to chinaware and other decorative accessories, and it was in this capacity that she met and interviewed Josiah Wedgwood when he came to Toronto. She was aware that NF had known Veronica Wedgwood. McNabb lived close to St. Clair and Avenue Road, and often ran into the Fryes in that area when they were out for their walks. (Barbara McNabb, phone conversation with Margaret Burgess, 31 March 2000). Veronica Wedgwood had be-friended NF when he was a student at Oxford in 1936–37. See *Correspondence* 2:566, 578, 589, 675, 677.

152 In Hughes, the sonnets numbered respectively 18, 19, 23, 10, 22, 11, 16, and 17.

153 Munro Beattie was recruiting a replacement for William Wilgar, who had retired from Carleton in December because of tuberculosis (George Johnston to Robert D. Denham, 15 May 1994). Johnston accepted the position at Carleton, where he remained until he retired.

154 "When God gave him [Adam] reason, he gave him freedom to choose, for reason is but choosing" (John Milton, *Areopagitica*, in Hughes, 733).

155 Richard Henry Tawney, *Religion and the Rise of Capitalism* (1926); "Darcy" is apparently a reference to M.C. D'arcy, *The Mind and Heart of Love* (1945), a book, according to William Blissett, that was much talked about at the time, by Peter Fisher among others.

156 This is an apparent reference to the paper Woodhouse presented later in the year, "Romanticism and the History of Ideas," at a conference of the International Association of University Professors of English. The paper was given at Oxford and published in London in *English Studies Today*, ed. C.L. Wrenn and G. Bullough (Oxford University Press, 1951), 120–40.

157 Inglis's story, "The Gentle Wind," was published in the *Canadian Forum*, 31 (October 1951): 153–5, 157.

158 NF was the supervisor of William Blissett's dissertation on *The Historical Imagination in the English Renaissance: Studies in Spenser and Milton*, com-pleted in 1950.

159 That is, an egg without a shell; thus, imperfect or unproductive. According to superstition the hen that lays a wind egg was impregnated by the wind.

160 Mad Margaret in Gilbert and Sullivan's *Ruddigore* (1887), which the Fryes
    had seen on 4 February (par. 89, above).

161 M.H. Abrams developed this idea in "The Poem as Heterocosm," in *The
    Mirror and The Lamp: Romantic Theory and the Critical Tradition* (New York:
    Norton, 1958; orig. pub., 1953), 272–85. Abrams quotes the analogy from
    W.R. Inge's *God and the Astronomers* (1933) on p. 262.

162 Woodhouse was chiefly responsible for bringing Abrams back to Toronto
    in 1964 to present the Alexander lectures (M.H. Abrams to Robert D.
    Denham, 20 April 1994).

163 A.S.P. Woodhouse, "Collins and the Creative Imagination," in *Studies in
    English*, ed. Malcolm W. Wallace (Toronto: University of Toronto Press,
    1931), 59–130. Abrams's compliment to Woodhouse is found as well in a
    note in *The Mirror and the Lamp*, 381.

164 Kathleen Coburn was to lecture at Cornell under the round-robin arrange-
    ment described in 49.n. 214.

165 NF has at least entertained the idea of spending his sabbatical year at the
    University of Chicago, where R.S. Crane was at the centre of a group of
    critics who would become known as the Neo-Aristotelians.

166 A.S.P. Woodhouse presented a paper, "The Historical Criticism of Milton,"
    to the Milton section at the annual meeting of the Modern Language
    Association on 28 December 1950; it was followed by Cleanth Brooks's
    paper, "Milton and Critical Re-estimates." Both papers were published in
    PMLA, 66 (December 1951): 1033–54.

167 Abrams develops the point about these two Swiss critics in *The Mirror and
    the Lamp*, 276–8.

168 The reference is to David Erdman's Blake manuscript (49.272).

169 The payment for NF's editing of the Rinehart Milton.

170 See par. 82, above.

171 The Rinehart edition of *Wuthering Heights* was published in 1950.

172 That is, the introduction to NF's edition of the Rinehart Milton.

173 The position at Carleton University. See par. 173, above.

174 John Donne, *A Litany*, l. 142.

175 Douglas Grant's personal World War II narrative was *The Fuel of the Fire*
    (London: Cressett Press, 1950). "For war is energy Enslavd" is from Blake's
    The Four Zoas, Night the Ninth, l. 151 (Erdman, 390, l. 42).

176 U.S. customs had refused Barker Fairley a visa to lecture on Goethe at Bryn
    Mawr because of his leftist sympathies (he had supported a Soviet friend-
    ship organization) and his wife Margaret's association with the Commu-
    nist party. See 49.296. Later in the year NF wrote an editorial criticizing
    U.S. immigration policies: "Nothing to Fear but Fear," *Canadian Forum*, 29
    (November 1949): 169–70; rpt. in *RW*, 395–8.

177 The reference is to the debate over the Neo-Lamarckian theories advanced

by T.D. Lysenko, whose attacks on Mendelian genetics were endorsed by the Communist party. Lysenko's agenda (politics disguised as science) ultimately did great damage to Soviet science.

178 See n. 158, above.

179 Samuel Butler, *Erewhon* (1872), chap. 23.

180 NF gave the Senior Dinner speech on 30 March 1949. He did record that day's events in his diary, although he did not indicate what he had said in his Butler lecture.

181 Dorothy Howarth, "Professor of English Abhors Horses, Tales of $5 'Millionaires,'" *Toronto Telegram*, 25 March 1950, 39. Howarth's feature is largely a biographical account: anecdotes from NF's school days in Moncton, his stint on the Sask. prairies, his Oxford years, and his work on Blake.

182 Most likely William C. (Bill) James, chair of the board of regents of VU.

183 Nicholas Ignatieff.

184 The reference is uncertain. NF's fullest references to the sonata are in NB 5 (see pars. 2, 5, 6, 8–9, 13–16), and in NB 8, par. 131, he refers in passing to the "comedy structure" of the sonata form.

185 "Why the Sun Stood Still: A Preview by Fulton Ousler of Dr. Immanuel Velikovsky's New Book: *Worlds in Collision*," *Readers' Digest*, [29] (March 1950): 155–70. This article appeared only in the Canadian ed. of *Readers' Digest*. *Worlds in Collision* was published by Macmillan later in 1950.

186 See 49.n. 239.

187 Kitely, the jealous husband of Jonson's play, figures in eight scenes (acts 2–4); which of these episodes NF has in mind is uncertain.

188 Eli Mandel did get his Ph.D. in 1957, writing a dissertation on Christopher Smart under the direction of F.E.L. Priestley.

189 Mary McFarlane abandoned her plans to finish a dissertation on Christopher Smart in order to raise a family.

190 Reid MacCallum had died the previous year. William Blissett edited, under the title *Imitation and Design and Other Essays* (Toronto: University of Toronto Press, 1953), the same unfinished book, with reprinted articles, that Irving declined doing.

191 See NF's introduction to John Milton, *Paradise Lost and Selected Poetry and Prose*, v.

192 See n. 141, above.

193 See par. 82, above.

194 Eleanor Godfrey, her husband Bill Graham, and Eleanor's sister, Ray.

195 Stan Fillmore was editor of the *Varsity*; Joan Eddis was women's editor; Eddis had the title "women's editor" changed to "associate editor" for those who followed her (Joan Eddis to Robert D. Denham, 28 May 1999).

196 E.J. Pratt was to retire from teaching at the end of the 1949–50 academic year.

197 See n. 181, above.

198 See par. 194, above.

199 The housecleaning was apparently in connection with the birth of Joan Grant's baby (see par. 205, above). In par. 317, however, the Fryes visit the Grants in their "new flat," so a plan to move seems also to be involved.

200 See 49.285, where NF recounts the episode: June Clark had read an open letter on the last day of class criticizing the course.

201 Renwicke was something of a nonconformist and rebel as a student at VC; Endicott was head of the Labour Progressive Party at U of T. NF apparently considered their attitude toward the course as somewhat hostile or supercilious.

202 Ruth Elizabeth McLellan joined the writing group sometime after its inception.

203 See 49.n. 239.

204 Philaster is the rightful heir to the crown of Sicily in Beaumont and Fletcher's *Philaster* (1609); he is in love with and loved by Arethusa, the daughter of the usurper, the king of Calabria. Arethusa ("the waterer") is the numph who fled to Sicily to escape the advances of the river-god Alpheus; there she was saved by Artemis, who changed her into a fountain.

205 Onalee Walter (later, Lee Gage), one of the presidents of the class of 1949, had given a short valedictory address the year before. She enumerated the various things her class would remember about their years at VC, including some lines from Tennyson's *Flower in the Crannied Wall*, often quoted by philosophy professor Marcus Long (Lee Gage to Robert D. Denham, 29 April 1994). NF, who was honorary professor for the class of 1949, had himself given the Senior Dinner speech when he was a student.

206 That is, Bruce Honeyford's oral exam.

207 See par. 225, above.

208 Matthiessen committed suicide on 31 March 1950. He had been suffering severe depression, especially after the death of his longtime companion, the painter Russell Cheney.

209 Di Rogers was a member of this delegation, appointed along with Alison Jeffries by the other students in the RK course, charged with asking NF whether he believed in the power of prayer. Rogers reports that she has never forgotten NF's reply: "He first made it clear that he did believe in the power of prayer and that one could not only benefit oneself but others as well through prayer. He asked us to picture a wheel with spokes, God on the hub and all people of the world on the circumference. A person on the circumference could, in his view, pray directly to God on the hub for spiritual guidance and strength or request God to direct the same to a specific individual or any person or persons on the circumference of the

wheel in need of His help" (Di Rogers to Robert D. Denham, 26 April 1994).

210 That is, the news that he could not serve as editor of the *Canadian Forum* for the next year because of the Guggenheim fellowship.

211 See n. 181, above.

212 NF's courses in the Renaissance (2i), nineteenth-century (4k), and Spenser and Milton (3j).

213 Tom Delworth did serve as editor of *Acta Victoriana* for 1950–51, and Hope Arnott served as associate editor; she and Delworth shared the duties of literary editor during 1949–50. Delworth "greatly enjoyed working with Kay Coburn," who assumed the role of staff advisor for *Acta* during NF's Guggenheim year (W. Thomas Delworth to Robert D. Denham, 4 March 1997).

214 Harold Bennett was serving as acting president of VU, and the search had begun for a new president.

215 In May, A.B.B. Moore was appointed president of VU, as NF later reports (par. 386, below).

216 Harold Creasser's bookshop was at 5 Rowanwood Ave. It had previously been located at 856 Yonge St.

217 This edition of Austen, *Love and Freindship* [sic] *and Other Early Works, Now First Printed from the Original MS* (Toronto: F.D. Goodchild, n.d.), is in the NFL.

218 A 1949 British comedy, directed by Alexander MacKendrick.

219 For her Ph.D. dissertation at the University of Wisconsin, Coutts was working on a study of the poetry of William Alabaster. Wallerstein and White were colleagues at the University of Wisconsin.

220 See 42.n. 77.

221 See n. 176, above.

222 Hubener proposed to study the German literary and scholarly publications during World War II and immediately following.

223 Vlastos, who had been a professor of philosophy at Queen's University before moving to Cornell, was considered a Canadian recipient of the Guggenheim. He proposed to study the development of moral and political concepts of Greek philosophy.

224 Kenneth M. Setton, head of the Department of History at the University of Manitoba, had received a Guggenheim fellowship in 1949. One of the scientists was Nicholas Polunin, professor of botany at McGill University.

225 Stapleford's nickname was apparently "Billy Goat": his given name was William, and he had a goatee.

226 Joyce Cary's *The Horse's Mouth* (1944) contains more than forty catchwords and quotations from Blake. Cary quotes extensively from *The Mental Traveller* in chaps. 12–17.

227 "It's my own invention": the White Knight's words to Alice when he sees

her admiring his little wooden box (Lewis Carroll, *Through the Looking Glass and What Alice Found There* [1871], chap. 8).

228 Margaret Ray, who had been associate librarian since 1935, was appointed librarian when John Robins retired in 1952.

229 "The Canadian Forum," *Saturday Night*, 65 (11 April 1950): 6.

230 The reference is to NF's agreeing to edit Pelham Edgar's autobiography. See n. 141, above.

231 Lees's book was actually a series of twelve short stories. NF apparently felt that the book had promise, as he recommended Sybil Hutchinson, a literary agent, to Lees; she sold his first short story (Gene Lees to Robert D. Denham, 13 October 1998). See par. 294, below.

232 See 49.n. 154. The chair of the commission was J.F. Macdonald; Randolph C. Chalmers was the secretary.

233 NF has listed six influential Canadian social scientists. The historian Frank Underhill was a telling commentator on public affairs in Canada and the first president of the League for Social Reconstruction. Harold Innis was one of Canada's pre-eminent political economists and a pioneer in communications studies. Donald Creighton was the foremost English Canadian historian of his generation. MacGregor Dawson was an influential teacher and constitutional scholar; his *The Government of Canada* (1947) became a standard textbook. Samuel D. Clark was known for a series of studies interpreting Canadian social development in terms of economic frontiers; the book of his that NF mentions is *Church and Sect in Canada* (Toronto: University of Toronto Press, 1948).

234 Which Bolgan in fact did, completing a dissertation on T.S. Eliot, directed by NF, ten years later.

235 Christopher Love wrote his dissertation, directed by A.S.P. Woodhouse, on *The Scriptural Latin Plays of the Renaissance and Milton's Cambridge ms*; he received his Ph.D. from U of T in 1950.

236 See par. 264, above.

237 "As when some one peculiar quality / Doth so possess a Man, that it doth draw / All his affects, his spirits, and his powers, / In their constructions, all to run one way. / This may be truly said to be a humour" (Ben Jonson, *Every Man out of His Humour*, Prologue, "After the Second Sounding," ll. 105–9).

238 For the "living well" passage, see *The Faerie Queene*, bk. 1, canto 2, st. 43; for Maleger, bk. 2, canto 9; for Tantalus, bk. 2, canto 7.

239 See par. 272, above.

240 Moorhouse, a VC and EC classmate of NF, had returned to Emmanuel for his M.A. in philosophy and theology; he and Phyllis Foreman were married shortly thereafter.

241 "Levels of Meaning in Literature" (n. 3, above).

242 Bach's B Minor Mass, the second event in the Bach Festival, was presented
by the TSO and the Mendelssohn Choir on Wednesday evening, following
E. Power Biggs's performance in the afternoon. For a review of both performances, see Ronald Hambleton, "Music in Toronto," *Globe and Mail*,
20 April 1950, 10.

243 For a review of the concert by the Conservatory Chamber Players, the third
event in the Bach Festival, see Court Stone, "Bach Festival," *Globe and Mail*,
21 April 1950, 8.

244 Beny had changed his given name from Wilfred Roy to Roloff. In the mid-
1950s he turned from printmaking and painting to photography and spent
most of the rest of his life in Rome. Years later he photographed NF for
Italian magazines when the latter made his 1979 trip to Italy.

245 *Time* never did publish a story on the *Canadian Forum* or on NF's
Guggenheim, even though as late as 30 May NF receives word from Roy
Kemp that the story may still appear. Hicks's article may have been passed
over because *Time* at this point was devoting ten to fifteen pages a week to
a special section on the Korean War.

246 The reference is to Lois Marshall's limp; she was crippled by polio as a child.

247 Child's Restaurant was at 9 King St. W. The Arts and Letters Club of
Toronto, founded in 1908 and located at 14 Elm Street in downtown Toronto, was, and still is, a meeting place for professionals in the arts.

248 That is, presiding over the RK exam (see par. 287, above).

249 "The only unfortunate circumstance [of NF's receiving a Guggenheim
fellowship] is that Professor Frye's absence will interrupt and possibly end
the ablest editorship the Canadian Forum has ever had" (W.A. Deacon,
"The Fly Leaf," *Globe and Mail*, 22 April 1950, 11).

250 Frank S. Hogg, "The Capers of a Comet Before Becoming Venus," *Globe
and Mail*, 22 April 1950, 10—a review of Immanuel Velikovsky's *Worlds in
Collision*. Hogg was director of the Dunlop Observatory in Richmond Hill
until his death from a heart attack in 1951.

251 Apparently these are duplicate copies of sample editions of the Rinehart
series that the publisher had sent to NF.

252 William Blake, "Annotations to Swedenborg," Erdman, 605.

253 "What can *Adonis horti* among the Poets meane other than *Moses* his *Eden*,
or terrestriall Paradise? The Hebrew *Eden* being *Voluptas* or *Delitie*, whence
the Greeke ηδονη [edone] (or pleasure) seems necessarily deriued" (Henry
Reynolds, *Mythomystes*, intro. Arthur F. Kinney [Menston, Yorkshire:
Scolar Press, 1972]; a facsimile rpt. of the 1632 ed. [London: Henry Seyle],
76). NF knew *Mythomystes* through *Critical Essays of the Seventeenth Century*, ed. J.E. Spingarn (Oxford: Clarendon Press, 1908), 1:141–78, an annotated copy of which is in the NFL. Spingarn's edition of Reynolds was on
the bibliography of NF's course in literary symbolism.

254 A proposal to produce a collection of prose texts, following the model of the English department's successful *Representative Poetry*, a prescribed text for students in the Pass Course.

255 The astrolabe, currently in a glass case in the office of VU head librarian Robert Brandeis, was given to the university by Mrs. Ann Starr; bearing the date 1595, it was found on the site of a seventeenth-century mission on Christian Island near Penetang, Ont.

256 Karl Barth, "The Word of God in its Threefold Form," in *The Doctrine of the Word of God*, pt. 1 of *Church Dogmatics*, trans. G.T. Thomson (Edinburgh: T. and T. Clark, 1936), 1:98–135.

257 The letter was to encourage Charles R. Feilding to assume the editorship of the *Canadian Forum*.

258 See par. 294, above.

259 A 1949 film based on a novel by Graham Greene, directed by Carol Reed and starring Joseph Cotten, Orson Welles, and Trevor Howard.

260 Mary Kemp, NF's sister-in-law; HKF's mother and father; and Peter Kemp, Mary and Roy Kemp's infant son.

261 Doris Mosdell, "Theatre," *Canadian Forum*, 30 (April 1950): 15.

262 Béla Böszörmenyi-Nagy.

263 Mary Kemp's parents and her brother Stephen.

264 See n. 177, above.

265 For P.J. Proudhon's views on the revolutionary cycle of Christianity, see *De la justice dans la révolution et dans l'Église* (1858), especially vol. 1, chap. 6. For Ivan Karamazov's view of the failures of Christ, see his story of the Grand Inquisitor in Dostoevsky's *The Brothers Karamazov* (1879–80), bk. 4, chap. 5. NF would later draw attention to the Dostoevsky parallel in *RE*, 134.

266 Burke's critique of the metaphysics of the French National Assembly, with its appeal to the rights of man, appears throughout his *Reflections on the Revolution in France* (1791). For his attack on Rousseau's role in the "revolution of consciousness," see his *Letter to a Member of the National Assembly* (1791).

267 NF did write a report on "Literature" for the Commission on Culture; it was published under that title in the section of the commission's report on "Organs of Cultural Expression." See 49.n. 154.

268 For Spring Thaw, see 49.n. 242.

269 An annual satiric and musical revue at VU, the oldest in Canada, formally baptizing the freshmen into the life of the college. It was begun in 1872— when VC was in Cobourg—as a "Bob party" for the benefit of the college janitor, Robert Beare, from whom the show took its name. See NF's comment on the 1931 Bob in *Acta Victoriana*, 56 (October–November 1931): 30.

270 The pair are Don Harron and his wife Gloria (née Fisher). For an account of *Spring Thaw '50*, see Martha Harron, *Don Harron: A Parent Contradiction*, 118–22; on NF's delight over Harron's puns, see p. 121.

271 Pete Colgrove and NF had been classmates at VC, where they had developed something of a rivalry at the piano. During their student days NF was known for his playing of classical music; Colgrove, for jazz.

272 Jacobi, a Toronto native, went on to become a well-known stage and Hollywood actor.

273 Supplementary examinations taken by students who had failed the exams the previous semester.

274 NF did write his essays on Morris and Butler, but not until more than thirty years later: "The Meeting of Past and Future in William Morris" (49.n. 185), and "Some Reflections on Life and Habit," *Northrop Frye Newsletter*, 1 (Spring 1989): 1–9; rpt. in *MM*, 141–54.

275 Bates ended up writing a dissertation on Joyce, receiving his Ph.D. in 1960. NF directed the dissertation.

276 NF is referring to the current issues of the *Canadian Forum*.

277 "Music in Poetry" (49.n. 216).

278 Richard Ellmann, *Yeats: The Man and the Masks* (New York: Macmillan, 1948); *The Permanence of Yeats*, ed. James Hall and Martin Steinmann (New York: Macmillan, 1950). NF reviewed the books on CBC Radio on 28 May. See par. 379, below.

279 The reference is to Joseph Hone's *W.B. Yeats, 1865–1939* (New York: Macmillan, 1943).

280 See *Yeats: The Man and the Masks*, chap. 7 ff.

281 W.B. Yeats, *Autobiographies* (London: Macmillan, 1955), 202.

282 See 49.196.

283 "Yeats and the Language of Symbolism," *University of Toronto Quarterly*, 17 (October 1947): 1–17; rpt. in *FI*, 218–37.

284 The allusions here are to the first and last lines of st. 3 of Yeats's *Sailing to Byzantium*.

285 In the elaborate psychological theory that Yeats set down in *A Vision*, the "mask," representing that which should be, is the opposite of the "will" or ego. For the "true" and "false" masks in each of Yeats's phases of "the great wheel" or personality types, see *A Vision*, rev. ed. (N.p.: Macmillan, 1956), 96–9. For Yeats's views on the "creative minority," see his *Autobiographies* (London: Macmillan, 1927), 361, and his 1925 Senate speech in Seanad Eirann, *Parliamentary Debates*, 5 (11 June 1925): 443.

286 Here NF is drawing on *Yeats: The Man and the Masks*, 264–6.

287 NF is apparently remembering Eliot's reference to the supernatural world in Yeats's poetry as a "lower mythology" (*After Strange Gods: A Primer of Modern Heresy* [New York: Harcourt, Brace, 1934], 50).

288 At the 1948 English Institute NF had presented his paper, "The Argument of Comedy," on the second day of the conference (8 September) at 1:30 P.M. See 49.n. 56.

289 G.I. Duthie presented a paper on "Shakespearian Editorial Problems

Requiring Eclectic-Text Solutions." A selection of the papers of the English Institute was published in *English Institute Essays, 1950*, ed. Alan S. Downer (New York: Columbia University Press, 1951), which contains the complete program.

290 On successive Wednesdays in February of 1951, the VC College Council sponsored four lectures under the series title "The Epic Romance." In addition to the lectures by Robertson and Surerus, John Robins lectured on *Beowulf* and A.J. Denomy on *The Song of Roland*.

291 Hugh Keeping had been a close friend of HKF's brother Harold. The Keepings, who were married in 1948, rented an apartment for a few years before looking for their first home to rent or buy. They eventually bought a home in another Toronto neighbourhood. Later they and their children were frequent guests at HKF's parents' cottage on Lake Joseph in the Muskoka Lakes region north of Toronto, and in 1958 they bought the cottage from the Kemps (Hugh Keeping [son of the Keepings referred to in this entry] to Robert D. Denham, 27 October 1998).

292 John Colet (ca. 1467–1519) lectured at Oxford on Paul's epistles (1496–1504), opposing the interpretations of the scholastic theologians.

293 That is, a walk around the Mt. Pleasant cemetery, which was near their home.

294 The reference is to Madelaine Page. See par. 300, above.

295 Benedict M. Greene, president of International Press, Ltd., which published *Who's Who in Canada*, and Margaret Lawrence, a Toronto writer (not to be confused with the well-known fiction writer Margaret Laurence), were married in 1943 and lived at 6 Crescent Rd. in Toronto.

296 HKF's Cronin relatives were all Roman Catholics.

297 William Sclater, *Haida* (Toronto: Oxford University Press, 1947), a book about the World War II destroyer Haida; the book won the Governor General's Award for non-fiction in 1947.

298 The School of Graduate Studies, located at the corner of Hoskin Ave. and Devonshire Pl.

299 John Reymes-King, *An Aesthetic Analysis of the Madrigals of Thomas Morley*, Ph.D. diss., U of T, 1950. The dissertation ran to 642 pp.

300 "And There Is No Peace," *Canadian Forum*, 30 (June 1950): 52.

301 Much of Winnipeg had to be rebuilt after the disastrous Red River flood in 1950. The relief effort included the rescue of trapped residents by military personnel and their transport to safety by special trains. The same year Rimouski, Quebec, experienced a devastating fire.

302 See 49.n. 154 and par. 318, above.

303 The Pilot Tavern, opened in 1944 and still in operation at time of publication, was in Yorkville at 22 Cumberland St. near Yonge St.

304 A 1946 play by Jean Giraudoux. Royal Alec = Royal Alexandra Theatre in

Toronto, an Edwardian playhouse at 260 King St. W., designed by John Lyle, which opened in 1907.

305 Sir James Frazer, *The Dying God* (vol. 4 of *The Golden Bough*) (London: St. Martin's, 1930), 197. Frazer is actually writing about the people of Calabar, not the Senegambians.

306 Reymes-King did complete his dissertation for the Ph.D. See n. 299, above. The reference to Hunter is uncertain.

307 NF repeats the line in "Literature as Context: Milton's *Lycidas*," in *FI*, 128.

308 David Lewis's two boys were Stephen and Michael; the twin girls, Janet and Nina.

309 The reference is almost certainly to the influential Canadian labour lawyer Jacob Laurence Cohen. As the obituaries for Cohen in both the *Globe and Mail* and the *Toronto Star* give his date of death as 24 May 1950, it is clear that NF is composing his entries here after having made the trip to Brantford on 24 May.

310 The reference is to the Canadian Peace Congress, founded by James Endicott, which was begun after he returned from the World Peace Congress in Paris in April 1949; Endicott called himself a "Christian Marxist." There were parallels between the careers of J.S. Woodsworth, the well-known pacifist and founder of the CCF, and Endicott. Woodsworth had been arrested and charged with sedition in 1919 because of editorials he wrote during the Winnipeg general strike. Both Woodsworth and Endicott had attended VC, both were ordained ministers, both faced strong opposition within the church, and both resigned from the active ministry to champion social and political justice through institutions outside the church. For an account of Endicott's conflict with the United Church of Canada, see Stephen Endicott, *James G. Endicott: Rebel out of China* (Toronto: University of Toronto Press, 1980), chap. 23.

311 Victoria Day.

312 Elizabeth Brown (née Eedy) had been a classmate of NF and HKF at VC. Thirty-eight years later—on 27 July 1988—she and NF were married, the ceremony performed by another classmate, Bob Bates. Elizabeth Eedy Brown's first husband, James Brown, had died in 1974. Brantford is an Ontario town about 85 kilometres southwest of Toronto.

313 Benjamin Ingham founded the Inghamites, or Moravian Methodists, in 1741.

314 See par. 363, above.

315 The subtitle of *Waverley* is "'Tis Sixty Years Since."

316 Kathleen Coburn and Jessie Macpherson owned a summer cottage at Georgian Bay; they had bought a five-and-a-half acre island sixteen miles southwest of Parry Sound and had their cottage built there in 1939.

317 On Love's dissertation, see n. 235, above.

318 See par. 362, above.

319 See par. 335, above.

320 NF's talk on Yeats, ostensibly a review of Richard Ellmann's *Yeats: The Man and the Masks* and *The Permanence of Yeats*, ed. James Hall and Martin Steinman, will be published in *Northrop Frye on Literature and Society: Unpublished Papers*, volume 10 of the Collected Works of Northrop Frye (Toronto: University of Toronto Press, forthcoming). The typescript is in the NFF, 1988, box 48, file 3.

321 Gordon Sinclair, *Foot-Loose in India* (1933), one of four books that Sinclair wrote about his adventures as a wandering reporter for the *Toronto Star*.

322 Sinclair recounts the story of Baby Stella and Hemingway's resignation from the *Toronto Star* in *Will the Real Gordon Sinclair Please Stand Up* (Toronto: McClelland and Stewart, 1966), 130–1. See also Sinclair's account of Baby Stella in *Will Gordon Sinclair Please Sit Down* (Toronto: McClelland and Stewart, 1975), 22, where he gives a somewhat different report from the one NF records here: the story Hemingway was asked to write that "caused the really big blow-up" had to do with a white peacock that was to replace Stella in the zoo after the baby elephant had died.

323 Hemingway's story on the Japanese earthquake appeared in the *Toronto Star*, 25 September 1923. Sinclair has embellished the account: Hemingway wrote only of a "quite beautiful daughter in a Japanese kimono." Sinclair may have told Hemingway that the girl had come from her bath and that her breasts were exposed, but Hemingway includes no such details in his newspaper story. See Ernest Hemingway, *Dateline: Toronto, The Complete Toronto Star Dispatches, 1920–1924*, ed. William White (New York: Scribner's, 1985), 308–13.

324 Stingle recalls that NF took him to the Prince Arthur Room of the Park Plaza Hotel (Richard Stingle to Robert D. Denham, 7 March 1994).

325 Olga Wasylchuk changed her name to Westland, an approximate translation into English from Ukrainian, when she went to Wellesley for her M.A. In August 1950, during the summer vacation in Toronto, she married Jack Vickery, whom she had met as an undergraduate at U of T (John B. Vickery to Robert D. Denham, 28 September 1998).

326 Frederick J. Hoffman, according to Jack Vickery, was responsible for coining the "small fry" label for the Toronto contingent at Wisconsin. Ricardo Quintana was an admirer of NF, reports Vickery, "principally because his [Quintana's] mind was adventuresome, open, and interested at that time in expanding his historical scholarship into new and fresh critical insights and theories of satire and irony in particular" (John B. Vickery to Robert D. Denham, 28 September 1998).

327 Undergraduates could enrol in all graduate courses except graduate seminars and pro-seminars.

328 That is, did not make the mistake of accepting an offer to teach at the University of Wisconsin.

329 The "last 1000" was NF's "Tenets of Modern Culture" for the Commission on Culture. The "another 1000 words" became his report on "Literature" in *The Church and the Secular World*, 45–6. See 49.n. 154, and n. 267, above.

330 NF ended up doing talks on Milton, Swift, Blake, and Shaw in the CBC "Writer as Prophet" series. The talks were given on four consecutive Fridays—16 June, 23 June, 30 June, and 7 July. The radio talks will be published in *Northrop Frye on Literature and Society*, forthcoming. The typescripts—seven double-spaced pages each—are in the NFF, 1988, box 48, file 3.

331 Mosdell was the regular film reviewer for the *Canadian Forum*. *Critically Speaking* was a national radio program on the arts, originated by Clyde Gilmour.

332 Harold Wilson, "Dramatic Emphasis in *All's Well That Ends Well*," *Huntington Library Quarterly*, 13 (1950): 222–40.

333 This is likely Eleanor Godfrey.

334 Little had begun work at VU as an accountant; he then became senior tutor and still later superintendent of buildings and grounds, combining these several functions when he was appointed bursar in 1932; in 1944 he had become secretary to the Board of Regents.

335 St. Michael's, Trinity, and University Colleges.

336 See n. 141, above.

337 NF decided eventually to omit the essay on Macphail, which had originally appeared in the *Queen's Quarterly*, and he added Edgar's essays on Barker Fairley and Charles Cochrane.

338 NF omitted from the published volume Edgar's review of Macnaughton's *Essays and Addresses* (1946).

339 See par. 384, above.

340 NF may mean Thomas Hill Green, Watson's contemporary; or he could be referring to T.M. (Theodore Meyer) Greene, the Kantian religious philosopher.

341 This seems most likely to be D.F.S. Thomson.

342 Frank Roncarelli, whose case had begun in 1946 when police raided his restaurant looking for Jehovah's Witnesses literature. Because Roncarelli had been posting bail for the Jehovah's Witnesses, Prime Minister Duplessis had instructed the head of the liquor commission to cancel Roncarelli's license. Scott, along with A.L. Stein, defended Roncarelli, who was awarded more than $33,000 by the Supreme Court in January 1959. For an account of the case, see Sandra Djwa, *The Politics of Imagination: A Life of F.R. Scott* (Toronto: McClelland and Stewart, 1987), 297–317.

343 That is, the introduction to Pelham Edgar's autobiography (n. 141, above)

344 Roy Wolfe had studied geography at U of T, where Taylor was head of the department.

345 Gargary is the blacksmith, married to Pip's sister, in Dickens's *Great Expectations*. He remarks to Pip that when his wife goes on a rampage, "candour compels fur to admit that she is a Buster" (Charles Dickens, *Great Expectations* [New York: Dodd, Mead, 1949], 58 [chap. 7]).

346 The editing of Pelham Edgar's memoirs, articles, and manuscripts (n. 141, above).

347 The University Settlement, established in 1910 and still in existence at the time of publication, was a community centre development at 23 Grange Rd. that worked with the poor, new immigrants, and delinquent youth.

348 John Irving read his paper on "The Development of Philosophy in Central Canada from 1850 to 1900" at the regional conference of the Humanities Research Council of Canada on 10 June 1950. The paper was published in the *Canadian Historical Review*, 31 (September 1950): 252–87.

349 Janet Fulton was not one of NF's students, but he knew her indirectly: her mother had been a good friend of his sister Vera since their undergraduate days at Mt. Allison University (Janet Fulton Hibberd to Robert D. Denham, 11 May 1994). As Janet Fulton was a student in the Pass Course, NF was obviously hoping she and her parents would come to the reception.

350 Jones worked for the Hobbs Glass Company.

351 Pelham Edgar, "Matthew Arnold as a Writer of Prose," *Dalhousie Review*, October 1921: 248–62; and "Matthew Arnold as a Poet," *Transactions of the Royal Society of Canada*, 3rd series, sec. 2, 1914: 309–20. NF says in his introduction to Edgar's *Across My Path* that he "regretfully excluded" both of the Arnold essays (vii).

352 Lorne Pierce was editor-in-chief of Ryerson Press, which published Edgar's *Across My Path*. "Egypt" was the fourth chap. of pt. 1 of *Across My Path*. Edgar and his first wife Helen had travelled through Egypt with Charles T. Currelly and his wife in 1908.

353 See par. 364, above.

354 In his letter to Sir Watkin Phillips, Jeremy Melford writes "that every person who pretended to nauseate the smell of another's excretions, snuffed up his own with particular complacency" (Tobias Smollett, *Humphry Clinker*, ed. James L. Thorson [New York: Norton, 1983], 16).

355 NF makes the point in the last par. of his talk on Milton. See the typescript in the NFF, 1988, box 48, file 3, or *Northrop Frye on Literature and Society*, forthcoming.

356 NF expanded this point in *AC*, 140.

357 See Pelham Edgar, "Duncan Campbell Scott, *Dalhousie Review*, April 1927, 38–46; and "George Meredith," *Living Age*, 12 October 1907, 95–110.

358 The brief essay on "Literature" that NF wrote for the Culture Commission. See 49.n. 154 and n. 267, above.

359 The Fryes leased their house to H.J. Bright for $135 per month from 15 July 1950 through 14 September 1951. A copy of the lease is in the NFF, 1993, box 5, file 1.

360 In chap. 11 of Carroll's *Alice's Adventures in Wonderland* the guinea-pigs, who had applauded at the Mad Hatter's testimony, were thrust into bags and then sat upon by the officers of the court.

361 "Appropriately" because, as NF shortly notes, Luella Creighton's husband Donald had been a Guggenheim recipient.

362 Creighton actually received his Guggenheim in 1940 for a study of the development of Canadian nationality.

363 Frederick W. Sternfeld, *Goethe and Music* (New York: New York Public Library, 1954). NF and Sternfeld met on several later occasions at the English Institute.

364 Edith Fowke had begun her CBC radio program on folk songs in 1950. *Food for Thought* was a periodical of the Canadian Association for Adult Education.

365 Roy Daniells had attended the meeting of the Humanities Research Council of Canada in Kingston, 10 June 1950.

366 Earle Birney, *Turvey: A Military Picaresque* (Toronto: McClelland and Stewart, 1949).

367 Apparently the J.S. Morgans because of the connection with Margaret Newton and social work.

368 Jonathan Swift, *Irish Tracts, 1720–1723*, and *Sermons*, ed. Herbert Davis and Louis Landa (Oxford: Basil Blackwell, 1963), 74.

369 "Caution or Dither?" *Canadian Forum*, 30 (July 1950): 75.

370 That is, the scheme proposed by Lou Morris, managing editor of the *Canadian Forum*, to rotate editors. See pars. 410 and 416, above.

371 *Neurotica*, a periodical devoted to neuroses in literature, was published from 1948 to 1952, first in St. Louis, then in Stamford, Conn., and finally in New York; it was edited by Jay Landesman (1948–51) and Gershon Legman (1952).

372 The proper spelling: Böszörmenyi-Nagy.

373 Harold King had died the previous year; Harold Kemp, NF's brother-in-law, had been killed in World War II.

374 See n. 348, above.

375 Richard Maurice Bucke, *Cosmic Consciousness: A Study in the Evolution of the Human Mind* (New York: Dutton, 1901). John Irving's footnote indicated that while both William Dawson Le Sueur and Bucke were influential thinkers neither was a philosopher. See Irving's "The Development of Philosophy in Central Canada from 1850 to 1900," 252 (n. 348, above).

376 Irving incorporated this information in a footnote. See "The Development of Philosophy in Central Canada from 1850 to 1900," 252.

377 Ibid., 269.

378 NF did write his archetype paper, "The Archetypes of Literature," which was published in *Kenyon Review*, 13 (Winter 1951): 91–110; rpt. *FI*, 7–20. The paper turned out to be the most anthologized of all NF's essays. The article on the forms of poetry was never written. The editor of the *Kenyon Review* was John Crowe Ransom. The person who actually wrote NF was Philip Rice, the managing editor.

379 James Scott, "Author's Progeny," *Telegram*, 17 June 1950. NF repeats practically everything Scott wrote about daughter S.

380 In 1950 Douglas MacAgy left the California School of Fine Arts, where he had been director, and served for a brief period as vice-president of sales for Orbit films. See David Beasley, *Douglas MacAgy and the Foundations of Modern Art Curatorship* (Simcoe, Ont.: Davus Publishing, 1998), 43.

381 See the Logos diagram in the entry for 20 May, p. 356, above.

382 That is, to HKF's mother and father's home at 205 Fulton Ave.

383 HKF's father S.H.F. Kemp had attended Wycliffe College, the Anglican theological college at U of T, but he had to abandon his plans to enter the ministry because he was quite deaf, becoming instead a commercial artist in a photoengraving business, Grip Ltd., where Albert H. Robson was art director. Grip, Ltd. had employed J.E.H. Macdonald, Tom Thomson, and other Group of Seven artists, as well as Ivor Lewis. S.H.F. Kemp had earned an M.A. from U of T in 1908, writing a thesis on *The Life of Palladio and His Place in the Evolution of Architecture*.

384 See par. 161, above.

385 This is the paper on Blake that NF was preparing for the CBC Radio's "Writer as Prophet" series. For the typescript of what NF eventually read in the studio, see NFF, 1988, box 48, file 3, or *Northrop Frye on Literature and Society*, forthcoming.

386 See 49.n. 8.

387 North Korea had invaded South Korea on 25 June 1950.

388 See n. 385, above.

389 When he was on a visit to the home of classmate Graham Miller during the summer of 1933, NF wrote to Helen Kemp that "the family here has all of Shaw's plays in one volume and I have read six since Wednesday. I read all of Shaw at fifteen and he turned me from a precocious child into an adolescent fool. Therefore he has had far more influence on me than any other writer" (*Correspondence*, 1:98).

390 Shaw's proposal that the representative unit should be a man *and* a woman so that every elected body would have equal numbers of men and women. See the preface to *"In Good King Charles's Golden Days,"* in *Complete Plays with Prefaces* (New York: Dodd, Mead, 1962), 6:7–9.

391 "In good King Charles's golden days, / When loyalty no harm meant" (*The Vicar of Bray*, ll. 1–2).

392 Pelham Edgar's autobiography, *Across My Path*, which NF had edited.

393 That is, the question of NF's becoming editor-in-chief at Ryerson Press, a position Pierce had held since 1922.

394 Margaret Ray, the librarian at VC, had prepared the bibliography for *Across My Path* and, as NF says in the acknowledgments, provided "much other assistance which, to put it briefly, made the book possible" (v).

395 This apparently occurred in the mid-1930s. Spry had taken over the *Canadian Forum* in 1935, and the next year the control of the *Forum* passed to the League for Social Reconstruction.

396 That is, only one more CBC radio talk—on Shaw.

397 The paper NF presented at the English Institute later in the year, "Blake's Treatment of the Archetype" (see n. 96, above).

398 See n. 348 above.

399 "Naturally" is used hundreds of times in the *Summa Theologiae*, and which one NF has in mind is uncertain. Perhaps the most likely candidate is in Q. 90, A. 4, Reply to Obj. 1

400 The offprint was John Irving's "The Evolution of the Social Credit Movement," *Canadian Journal of Economic and Political Science*, 14 (1948): 321–41. Almost a decade passed before his book appeared: *The Social Credit Movement in Alberta* (Toronto: University of Toronto Press, 1959).

401 Whether NF is alluding here to Karl Barth's *ganz Anderes*, usually translated as "Wholly Other," or whether he means *ganz anderes*, "completely different," is not altogether certain, though the latter seems more probable. Reacting in his early work to certain views of God's immanence he saw in the more extreme forms of liberalism, Barth used *ganz Anderes* to refer to the absolute transcendence of God. But because the syntax here calls for an adjectival phrase modifying "nature of the babe," it does seem more likely that NF means "completely different." Since "nature" is feminine in German, one would ordinarily expect *ganz andere*, but NF is apparently not aware of (or concerned with) the adjectival declension. NF later (53.13) refers to "Barth's *ganz anders*," using the adverb phrase "completely differently." In this case, both the context and the syntax suggest that NF should have written *ganz Anderes* or "*das ganz Andere*," the Wholly Other, which Barth also refers to as the "*totaliter aliter*." See his *The Word of God and the Word of Man*, trans. Douglas Horton (New York: Harper, 1957), 74–5, 91, an annotated copy of which is in the NFL.

402 Mary Kemp was pregnant with their second child, Susan.

403 See par. 453, above.

404 See n. 400, above.

405 The book on the Arctic was apparently *Stéfansson: Ambassador of the North* (Montreal: Harvest House, 1962). Which of LeBourdais's books would qualify as a textbook is uncertain, but see his *Canada's Century* (London:

Methuen, 1951) and *Nation of the North: Canada since Confederation* (London: Methuen, 1953).

406 NF's "paper" is his radio talk on Shaw.

407 Six days later General Douglas MacArthur, Commander in Chief of the United Nations forces, announced to the Joint Chiefs of Staff that the Korean conflict was going to be a major operation.

408 This is perhaps the wife of Richard Davidson, the principal of EC, 1932–44.

409 This paper, "Philosophical Trends in Canada," was published as chap. 6 of John A. Irving's *Science and Values: Explorations in Philosophy and the Social Sciences* (Toronto: Ryerson Press, 1952), 56–82. About NF's debt to George Brett, Irving wrote: "Many leading scholars in fields other than philosophy also received their principal intellectual stimulation from Brett, but it must suffice to mention only Northrop Frye, the most dynamic and productive of the younger literary critics" (78). Why NF refers to Irving's article as "the American edition" is not clear. NF later writes (par. 585) that Irving sent him "his new essay for the Americans." This could be a reference to Irving's typescript for "One Hundred Years of Canadian Philosophy," in *Philosophy in Canada: A Symposium* (Toronto: University of Toronto Press, 1952), which incorporates a good deal of material from his "The Development of Philosophy in Central Canada" and does contain a section on George Brett (though it does not mention NF). Perhaps NF thinks that a University of Toronto Press publication will reach an American audience in a way that Irving's journal articles would not. Irving may have decided to delete the reference to NF between the time of this entry and 31 August, when NF received the article from Irving.

410 NF's references are to Shaw's *The Perfect Wagnerite* (1898) and to Wagner's *Parsifal*.

411 Diana Sweets was a coffee shop and restaurant located at 188 Bloor St. West near Avenue Rd.

412 See par. 458, above.

413 The reference is to the process of individuation, which, according to Jung, takes place between the ages of thirty-five and forty. NF is six days from his thirty-eighth birthday.

414 See par. 469, above.

415 The Fryes had bought their Clifton Rd. home from Reid MacCallum.

416 Witch grass is a bush-like weed.

417 *The Fireside Book of Folk Songs*, ed. Margaret B. Boni (New York: Simon and Schuster), 1947. Elizabeth Brown (née Eedy) would become NF's second wife thirty-eight years later. See n. 312, above.

418 On pp. 24–6 of his 1951 Diary, which do not contain diary entries themselves, NF gives a ten-section chronological outline for what he has entitled "A Musical Companion to English Literature." Each section contains a list of songs: there are eighty-four altogether.

419 Hilliard Trethewey's project was to edit the French text of the *Ancrene Riwle* from the manuscript at Trinity College, Cambridge, with variants from the manuscripts in the Bibliothèque Nationale and the British Library (then Museum). He eventually completed the text, which was published in London in 1958 by Oxford University Press for the Early English Text Society.

420 NF has begun writing what became one of his best-known essays, "The Archetypes of Literature" (n. 378, above).

421 Maugham edited several anthologies of short stories, but NF was likely reading from the 1526–page collection entitled *Tellers of Tales: 100 Short Stories from the United States, England, France, Russia and Germany* (New York: Doubleday and Doran), 1941.

422 See n. 222, above.

423 NF's neologism is perhaps a pun; otherwise, he meant to write "button-holer."

424 NF is still referring to his paper "The Archetypes of Literature" (n. 378, above).

425 The outline NF gives here is essentially the one he followed for the pub. version of "The Archetypes of Literature" (n. 378, above). He does refer to Auden's *The Enchaféd Flood* (p. 12). The Blake article is one that NF had agreed to present at the 1950 English Institute, "Blake's Treatment of the Archetype" (n. 96, above).

426 A reference to Victor Hopwood's dissertation (see par. 105, above).

427 NF meant to write "Kenway Street," which was the address of their summer house in Cambridge.

428 Jean Elder and her father.

429 The Botantical Museum, which housed the Garden in Glass, was popularly known as the "Glass Flowers."

430 See 49.206.

431 The sender of the letter had perhaps misheard "wun-tzu" for *Wen-tzu*, a compilation of Taoist thought and practice.

432 A reference to Sir Halford John MacKinder, *Democratic Ideals and Reality* (1919), where he develops his thesis about the Eurasian heartland.

433 Mount Allison University, in Sackville, N.B., a largely undergraduate institution with a solid academic reputation and an excellent physical plant.

434 Hanns-Erich Kaminski, *Céline en chemise brune*, published originally by Nouvelles Éditions Excelsior in 1938.

435 Karl Julius Holzknecht, *The Backgrounds of Shakespeare's Plays* (New York: American Book Co., 1950). (If NF did publish a review of Holzknecht's book, I have been unable to locate it. Ed.)

436 Ruth C. Wallerstein, *Studies in Seventeenth-Century Poetic* (Madison: University of Wisconsin Press, 1950).

437 *The Country of the Blind* (1911).

438 The reference is to the paper on Blake NF is going to write for the English Institute. "Sneezon" is NF's blend for the sneezing season.

439 A New England department store, headquartered in Boston.

440 The native inhabitants of Newfoundland; they were Algonquin-speaking hunter-gatherers.

441 See Friedrich von Schiller, *On Naive and Sentimental Poetry* (1795–96)— speculations about the differences between primitive and later, more sophisticated poetry.

442 See Williamson's *Senecan Amble: A Study in Prose from Bacon to Collier* (London: Faber and Faber; Chicago: University of Chicago Press, 1951). *A Reader's Guide to T.S. Eliot* was published three years later (New York: Noonday Press, 1953). Williamson's Ph.D. dissertation, Stanford University, 1928, was published as *The Donne Tradition* (Cambridge: Harvard University Press, 1930). Ruth Wallerstein's "book" was *Studies in Seventeenth-Century Poetic* (n. 436, above). George Williamson's article was "Strong Lines," *English Studies*, 18 (1936): 152–9.

443 "Special significance attaches to . . . Professor Frye's [essay] on the church's relation to society because of its uncompromising declaration that 'there is no liberty except Christian liberty' and that 'the natural man cannot desire freedom: he can only desire mastery'" ("Concerning Preachers," *Saturday Night*, 1 August 1950, 6–7).

444 That is, in preparation for the anticipated visit of NF's father to his niece in Lowell, Mass.

445 "The Archetypes of Literature" (n. 378, above).

446 The conference (14–17 August 1950) was organized by the director of the summer school, William Yandell Elliott. On Monday, 14 August, John Crowe Ransom spoke on "Poetry and the Academy" and Stephen Spender on "Modern Poetry and Science." Peter Viereck provided a "Commentary" on the topic of the first night's forum, "Poetry and the Modern World." For the proceedings of the conference, see *Harvard Summer School Conference on the Defense of Poetry, August 14–17, 1950* (Cambridge: Harvard University, n.d.). For an account of the Canadians at the conference, see Sandra Djwa, *Politics of the Imagination: A Life of F.R. Scott*, 271–2.

447 For an edited transcript of the discussion, see the *Harvard Summer School Conference on the Defense of Poetry*, 43–63.

448 The 15 August meeting that NF did not attend, devoted to "The Poem and The Public," featured talks by Marianne Moore ("Impact, Moral and Technical; Independence versus Exhibitionism; and Concerning Contagion"), Randall Jarrell ("The Obscurity of the Poet"), and Pierre Emmanuel ("Poetry and Mass Communication").

449 Kenneth Burke provided his commentary on the previous evening's proceedings the next day, 16 August, in the Sanders Theater.

450 This was likely the classics scholar Gerald Else, who taught at the University of Iowa in the 1950s.

451 Lily Ross Taylor, *The Divinity of the Roman Emperor* (Middletown, Conn.: American Philological Society, 1931).

452 A poem by John Crowe Ransom.

453 A British ballad.

454 The letter that Brébeuf writes in pt. 3 of E.J. Pratt's *Brébeuf and His Brethren*. Sandra Djwa reports NF's saying that "Pratt read very badly and nobody could make much of it. I was embarrassed and I wished they'd either left it out or had something a bit better" (*The Politics of Imagination: A Life of F.R. Scott*, 271–2).

455 The other Canadian poet who read was either A.J.M. Smith or F.R. Scott.

456 In Rhode Island.

457 Robert M. Hutchins taught and served as dean of the law school at Yale from 1925 to 1929. He and M.C. Winternitz, dean of the medical school, actually organized the Institute of Human Relations.

458 As it turned out, Kenneth MacLean spent his entire academic career at VC. He had lectured at Duke University during the summer term.

459 *Boswell's London Journal: 1762–63*, ed. Frederick A. Pottle (New York: McGraw-Hill, 1950). Many of the private papers of Boswell that Pottle spent a lifetime editing came from the collections at Malahide Castle and the Fettercairn House.

460 Kenneth MacLean, *Agrarian Age: A Background for Wordsworth* (New Haven: Yale University Press, 1950).

461 This was apparently Marion Florence Lansing, the prolific author of children's books.

462 Baine, a Rhodes scholar, and NF had been friends since their days together at Merton College in the 1930s.

463 Charlie Bell, like Baine, a Rhodes scholar from Mississippi, had been friends with NF and Baine at Merton College in 1937–39; Bell married Mildred Winfree, with whom he had been more or less living during their Oxford years; in 1949, following his divorce from Winfree, he married Diana (Danny) Mason.

464 Baine did publish his dissertation some fifteen years later: *Thomas Holcroft and the Revolutionary Novel* (Athens: University of Georgia Press, 1965).

465 Marion was HKF's younger sister. See 49.n. 281.

466 The author, who was both a physician and a theologian, was in fact the "same person." The books in question were *Emotions and Bodily Changes: A Survey of Literature on Psychosomatic Interrelationships, 1919–1945* (New York: Columbia University Press, 1946); *Symbolism in Medieval Thought and Its Consummation in the "Divine Comedy"* (New Haven: Yale University Press, 1929).

467 "Music in Poetry" (49.n. 216).

468 "The Archetypes of Literature" (n. 378, above).

469 See 49.nn. 56 and 58.

470 It is not clear what paper of Irving's is meant here; it appears to be a different one from those referred to in nn. 348 and 400, above.

471 NF doubtless meant to write "steamer trunk."

472 There are no diary entries for 2–4 September.

473 Barbara Tubman had been married on 29 June 1950 in the Emmanuel College Chapel. She remembers Beth Thomson's having told her about the chance meeting with NF at Harvard: Thomson "was living on Ellice Avenue in Cambridge—the shortest route to the subway was to walk through the Harvard campus." Both Tubman and Thomson had been in English Language and Literature at VC, which meant they had courses with NF for their final three years. They had both gone to Boston in September 1949, Tubman returning to Toronto in May 1950, the month before her wedding. Thomson had hitched a ride back to Boston with Ruth Jenking (Barbara Beardsley [née Tubman] to Robert D. Denham, 6 July 1999). On 5 September 1950, Beth Thomson wrote to Barbara Tubman, "Today was the day of all days—I am elated, bursting—from the effect of one personality who makes me realize the joy, sweetness, significance, of just being alive. . . . Who else but Frye? He is here on a Guggenheim, and every day I walk through the Harvard Yard, or in the square, I think of him, first of him as just 'Frye,' then of his thoughts, and of his vision, which inspired his lectures and in turn had so deep a meaning for 'ses petits idolateurs.' . . . I was just crossing the street, when whom should I see but Mrs. Huebner [Hubener], striding hell-bent along Mass. Ave. I called to her and her face jumped out of its accustomed pattern with surprise. . . . In the middle of a fireworkish exchange of news and reminiscences, 'my heart leapt up when I beheld' a small, shy, white head mincing along in the crowd—and Frye was with us. . . . We three stood, talking of Barker Fairley, Ernst Oppenheimer, Boston, where everyone was living, and what their telephone numbers were—and now FRYE has mine in his little black book. I can now die. Finally Hueby went on her way and Frye and I proceeded towards the Yard. And, Barbara, I felt completely at ease. We talked about kids who had graduated, life, his new book. He said, 'Well, with this Guggenheim thing, I'm doing something with the epic form, allegory and symbolism— you know, on Spenser's *Faerie Queene*.' Miss Jenking had told him that you and I had lived together, and he asked, 'How is Barbara? Did she marry anyone I know?' . . . He's going to New York next week to give a paper on Blake—'It's an awful job—dull! I've finished with Blake,' he said. As we parted he said, 'I'm awfully glad I ran into you, Beth. I'll see you again.' It was very thrilling because that adolescent, teacher-pupil relationship had disappeared, and I didn't feel a bit shy or tongue-tied. It was the most

perfectly natural thing to be standing on the corner of Mass. Avenue, talking with one of the greatest geniuses living today. Am so happy that I have had a few moments of knowing him as a person—it is a feeling of deep admiration and warmth; and I am, as you see, overflowing with the strength and sweetness of his presence. He would hate this, but it's true: he has the prophetic light which gives fuller life to those he touches, and today has held one of the rarest moments of meaningful pleasure I have known. Amen." (Beth Lerbinger [née Thomson], quoting from the letter that Barbara Tubman Beardsley had returned to her, to Robert D. Denham, 15 July 1999).

474 There is no diary entry for 6 September.

475 The Fryes are headed for New York where NF is to present his paper on Blake at the English Institute at Columbia University, 8–11 September. See n. 96, above.

476 Among NF's extant diaries none records his activities for an entire year. NF might have continued to write in this diary had he not, following the English Institute meeting, 8–11 September at Columbia University, broken his right arm in an automobile accident. The Fryes and Philip Wheelwright, the driver of the car, were on their way from New York to Princeton to see a production of Eliot's *Family Reunion* when the accident, which hospitalized NF for a week, occurred. See Ayre, 226.

1951 Diary

1 Eights Week is the main annual rowing event at Oxford, held during the fifth week of Trinity term during May. "Henley" refers to the Henley Regatta, an annual amateur rowing contest, dating back to 1839, at Henley-on-Thames.

2 Douglas Grant, *James Thomson: Poet of "The Seasons"* (London: Cresset Press, 1951); and *The Fuel of the Fire* (London: Cresset Press, 1950), a personal narrative about World War II. See "A Selected List of Autumn Books," *The New Statesman and Nation*, 40 (18 November 1950): 472.

3 See 50.n. 175.

4 Frederick W. Sternfeld taught at Dartmouth College in Hanover, N.H.

5 Frederick W. Sternfeld's first article was "Kubik's McBoing Score," *Film Music Notes*, 10 (November–December 1950): 8–19; his second one, "Musical Score of C-Man," *Musical Quarterly*, 361 (April 1950): 274–6.

6 See 50.n. 429.

7 See 50.n. 149.

8 NF had been asked by Robert Heilman to teach a summer course on the Romantic period at the University of Washington in Seattle.

9 E.K. Chambers, *Samuel Taylor Coleridge: A Biographical Study* (Oxford: Clarendon Press, 1938).

10 "Poetry and Design in William Blake," which was published in the *Journal of Aesthetics and Art Criticism*, 10 (September 1951): 35–42. For the drama article, see 50.n. 149.

11 Two months earlier NF, who was recovering from a broken arm, had dictated to Helen an extensive series of notes on *The Faerie Queene*. These notes are in NB 43, in the NFF, 1991, box 37, file 1.

12 NF published his article on *Paradise Regained* five years later: "The Typology of *Paradise Regained*," *Modern Philology*, 53 (May 1956): 227–38.

13 This is apparently a reference to some comments that NF had written in response to a request by Ernst M. Oppenheimer, who was doing graduate work at Harvard during NF's Guggenheim year. Oppenheimer had told NF of a problem he was having with Rilke's *Sonette an Orpheus*, and NF, "made some very helpful comments," according to Oppenheimer, the next time they met. If NF's comments were, in fact, written, they have not survived, nor has Oppenheimer's seminar paper (Ernest M. Oppenheimer to Robert D. Denham, 9 July 1999).

14 NF's *Kenyon Review* articles: "Levels of Meaning in Literature," "A Conspectus of Dramatic Genres," and "The Archetypes of Literature" (50.nn. 3, 149, and 378). NF's Guggenheim application is in the NFF, 1988, box 39, file 4.

15 "The Church: Its Relation to Society" (introduction, n. 34).

16 NF was responsible for organizing and directing the 1951 English Institute conference on "Sources and Analogues in Criticism," which was held at Yale University, 5–8 September. Josephine Bennett of Hunter College did present a paper at the conference. The other speakers NF was able to secure were Harold Wilson and Marshall McLuhan, both of U of T, and Frederick Sternfeld of Dartmouth College.

17 Under the pseudonym of Simon Paynter, Owen reviewed Aldous Huxley's *Themes and Variations* in the *Canadian Forum*, 30 (January 1951): 238.

18 NF's review was published as "The Young Boswell," *Hudson Review*, 4 (Spring 1951): 143–6.

19 A printed note in the diary itself indicates that 8 January was the day the Battle of New Orleans was fought.

20 "Novels on Several Occasions," *Hudson Review*, 3 (Winter 1950–51): 611–19.

21 That is, Rinehart wants NF to prepare notes for his edition of Milton (49.n. 171).

22 See 49.n. 210.

23 Harris Fletcher, *The Complete Poetical Works of John Milton* (Boston: Houghton Mifflin, 1941), a revision of the Cambridge edition, ed. William Vaughan Moody; and John Milton, *Paradise Lost* (New York: Odyssey Press, 1935), ed. Merritt Y. Hughes.

24 James Holly Hanford, *The Poems of John Milton* (New York: Ronald Press, 1936).

25 A reference apparently to the six-volume edition of *Paradise Lost* (1892) by

A.W. Verity. NF is perhaps punning on the Harvard Classics, which are im-
printed with the university's "Veritas" insignia. Vols. 3 and 4 of the Harvard
Classics contained Milton's prose and poems, respectively, ed. Charles W. Eliot.

26 "One must imagine Sisyphus happy"—the final sentence of Albert Camus's
   The Myth of Sisyphus, trans. Justin O'Brien (New York: Knopf, 1955).

27 NF was to spend the summer teaching at the University of Washington.

28 The Fryes were making arrangements to move from their cramped quarters
   in the Brattle Inn on Story St., where they had been living since 1 September
   1950 (see 50.586). Isabel Pope lived at 37 Kirkland St., just to the northwest
   of the Harvard University campus.

29 The reference is to the notes NF is preparing for the Rinehart Milton.

30 A.S.P. Woodhouse, "Notes on Milton's Views on the Creation: The Initial
   Phases," *Philological Quarterly*, 28 (1949): 211–36.

31 NF is still seeking speakers for the English Institute session he is organizing
   for September. See par. 11, above. Alba Warren's book was published by
   Princeton in 1950.

1952 Diary

1 English 2i, "English Prose and Poetry, 1500–1660."

2 The allusion is to Psalm 16:6.

3 The poetry article is NF's "Letters in Canada: 1951, Poetry," *University of
   Toronto Quarterly*, 21 (April 1952): 252–8; the Edgar book is Pelham Edgar's
   Across My Path (50.n. 141); and the Royal Society paper is "Comic Myth in
   Shakespeare," *Transactions of the Royal Society of Canada*, ser. 3, 46, sec. 2
   (June 1952): 47–58.

4 NF incorporated portions of the Royal Society paper, "Comic Myth in
   Shakespeare," into the Third Essay of *AC*.

5 Benedict M. Greene, who lived at 6 Crescent Rd. in Toronto, was the publisher of *Who's Who in Canada*. See 50.352.

6 The radio talk was a review of Alessandro Manzoni's *The Betrothed* and Pär
   Lagerkvist's *Barabbas*, the typescript for which is in the NFF, 1993, box 3, file
   11. See also *Northrop Frye on Literature and Society*, forthcoming. For the
   Forum, NF reviewed Peter and Iona Opie's edition of the *Oxford Dictionary of
   Nursery Rhymes*, published in the book-review column "Turning New
   Leaves," *Canadian Forum*, 31 (February 1952): 258–60.

7 "Shakespeare and the Here and Now," *PMLA*, 67 (February 1952): 87–94.

8 A.S.P. Woodhouse was elected for a three-year term (1952–55) to the MLA
   executive council.

9 The book manuscript by Albert S. Roe that NF agreed to read was subsequently published as *Blake's Illustrations to the Divine Comedy* (Princeton:
   Princeton University Press, 1953). For Erdman's book, see 49.n. 220.

10 See 49.n. 83

11 Henri Peyre has asked NF to submit a paper on symbolism for *Yale French Studies*; it was published later in the year as "Three Meanings of Symbolism," *Yale French Studies*, 9 (1952): 11–19.

12 A 1951 United Artists film, starring Nora Swinburne, Esmond Knight, Thomas E. Breen, Arthur Shields, and Patricia Walters; adapted by Renoir from a novel by Rumer Godden.

13 The heroine of Virginia Woolf's *To the Lighthouse* (1927), Mrs. Ramsay is a strong and consolidating presence at the Hebrides home where she, her husband, their children, and family friends gather each summer.

14 "The Three Meanings of Symbolism" (n. 11, above).

15 Bill and Jean Haddow and their son Donny were the Fryes' next-door neighbours.

16 "Morals for the Masses," *Canadian Forum*, 31 (January 1952): 217–19.

17 The *Defensor Pacis* (*Defender of the Peace*), written by Marsilius of Padua in 1324, argued that the clergy should have no governmental power.

18 Alessandro Manzoni, *The Betrothed, "I Promessi Sposi": A Tale of XVII Century Milan*, trans. Archibald Colquhoun (London: Dent, 1956), 339 (chap. 25).

19 The first of two horses NF rode on the Sask. mission field during the summer of 1934.

20 Roy Daniells's radio talk. See par. 15, above.

21 University of Toronto Schools, located at 371 Bloor St. West, prepared bright students for U of T.

22 The lecture for English 4k, "Nineteenth-Century Thought."

23 R.S. Crane of the University of Chicago was giving the Alexander lectures at U of T for 1951–52. His lectures were published as *The Languages of Criticism and the Structure of Poetry* (Toronto: University of Toronto Press, 1953).

24 The trans. by Henry Alexander and Llewellyn Jones of Pär Lagerkvist's one-act play *Let Man Live* is in *Scandinavian Plays of the Twentieth Century* (Princeton: Princeton University Press, 1951), 103–21. Henry Alexander taught at Queen's University.

25 NF did debate Edmund Carpenter on 21 February. See par. 132, below.

26 "Three Meanings of Symbolism" (n. 11, above).

27 Charles Lamb, "Mrs. Battle's Opinions on Whist," in *English Romantic Poetry and Prose*, ed. Russell Noyes (New York: Oxford University Press, 1956), 600–1.

28 That is, a candidate for a teaching position in the English department at VC. He did get the job.

29 Beverley Burwell, who had been secretary of Hart House, U of T, 1942–46, had gone to England in 1948, where he was Scarborough research scholar at the Courtauld Institute of Art, University of London. He returned to Canada in 1953 and did take his degree in Sacred Theology at TC in 1960. He then

served as assistant executive secretary of the Diocesan Council of Social Services and associate director of the Anglican Information Centre.

30 NF is participating in a *Citizens' Forum* program on "Why Do Canadians Leave Home?" On the *Citizens' Forum*, see 49.n. 157. The program for 10 January paired three Canadians living in New York with three Torontonians who might well have moved abroad, given the nature of their work, but who stayed in Canada. As the three Canadians in New York were Hugh Kemp, Harold Cummings, and Helen Porter (the teacher), Geary must have been a Canadian, rather than an American. See *CBC Times*, 4, no. 25 (6–12 January 1952): 1.

31 NF's graduate course for the 1951–52 academic year was "The Methods and Techniques of Allegory." The course focused on NF's five levels of allegory (which became the five levels of meaning in the Second Essay of *AC*). Students were required to present to the class an analysis of any work of literature using NF's five-level scheme. NF would sit at the back of the classroom during the presentations, coming forward at the conclusion to give his comments (Margaret J. Ritchie [née Allen] to Robert D. Denham, 28 July 1998).

32 See n. 23, above.

33 See 50.n. 176.

34 Fairley's lectures were published as *Goethe's Faust: Six Essays* (Oxford: Clarendon Press, 1953).

35 NF apparently meant to write, "difficulty of trying to sense the unity."

36 NF did write the article, "The Analogy of Democracy," which appeared in *Bias*, 1 (February 1952): 2–6.

37 The article on J.S. Woodsworth in the March issue of the *Canadian Forum* was written, not by NF, but by Lloyd Harrington.

38 See par. 110, below.

39 *The Heritage of Western Culture: Essays on the Origin and Development of Modern Culture* (49.n. 154).

40 A 1947 psychological mystery drama, the major production of the VC Dramatic Society for the year; directed by Donald Glen.

41 See par. 23, above.

42 See par. 26, above.

43 This is doubtless the Mrs. Wilbur who had been a member of NF's extension class in 1950. See 50.301.

44 NF has been lecturing to a group of women in an extension course.

45 See par. 18, above.

46 "Phalanx of Particulars," review of Hugh Kenner's *The Poetry of Ezra Pound*, in *Hudson Review*, 4 (Winter 1952): 627–31; rpt. in *NFCL*, 197–203.

47 A reference to Rossell Hope Robbins's *The T.S. Eliot Myth* (New York: H. Schuman, 1951).

48 "ation of ation": NF's shorthand for the Canadian Association of Adult
   Education. Roby Kidd had replaced Edward Annand Corbett as director of
   the association in 1951.

49 For Edward J. Pratt's somewhat incoherent letter about the transportation
   strike, see "Coals on the Heads," *Globe and Mail*, 17 January 1952, 6. Ned
   Pratt's middle initial was also J.

50 Gordon V. Thompson Ltd., a music publishing enterprise, was located at
   902 Yonge St.

51 "The Analogy of Democracy" (n. 36, above).

52 Adaskin left Toronto in 1952 to become head of the music department at
   USk.

53 Emily Carr's journals were published in 1966, though not edited by Dilworth,
   Carr's literary executor, who died before her journals were published.

54 William Arthur Deacon, "Church Presents Culture Society's Inner Pattern,"
   Globe and Mail, 19 January 1952, 22. About NF's contribution to *The Heritage
   of Western Culture* (49.n. 154) Deacon wrote: "The brilliant Northrop Frye . . .
   ignores the creative arts in his chapter on Trends in Modern Culture. He
   deals extensively with political thought in a changing world, with aspects of
   democracy and similar topics as related to the unformulated or semi-formu-
   lated religious views of typical living persons." Deacon then quotes a long
   passage from the last page of NF's essay, "Trends in Modern Culture."

55 "The Church: Its Relation to Society," in *The Living Church* (introduction, n.
   34).

56 NF is referring to the *Citizens' Forum* program on Canadians who migrate to
   the U.S. (see par. 23, above). The letter from Helen James is in the NFF, 1991,
   box 3, file 5, along with a one-page typescript of the editorial in the *Ottawa
   Citizen* of 15 January. The editorial noted that the "Toronto group contained
   an educationist who offered some effective counter-arguments" to those
   who maintained there was greater opportunity and a "climate of democracy" in the U.S. On the *Citizens' Forum*, see 49.n. 157.

57 A documentary film on the visit of Princess Elizabeth and the Duke of
   Edinburgh to Canada and the U.S. in the fall of 1951.

58 *Ti-Coq* (*L'il Rooster*) was a 1948 play by the Canadian actor and playwright
   Gratien Gélinas. Daly had seen the stage version: it was not made into a film
   until 1953.

59 "The Analogy of Democracy" (n. 36, above).

60 NF reviewed Child's *The Victorian House and Other Poems*, Bruce's *The
   Mulgrave Road*, Smith's *Footnote to the Lord's Prayer and Other Poems*, and
   Brewster's *East Coast*, along with several other books of Canadian poetry, in
   "Letters in Canada: 1951, Poetry," *University of Toronto Quarterly*, 21 (April
   1952): 252–8.

61 Merritt Y. Hughes, who was the chair of the English I section of the Modern

Language Association for 1952, asked NF to present a paper at the 1952 annual convention in Boston. NF obliged with "Characterization in Shakespearean Comedy," which was published in *Shakespeare Quarterly*, 4 (July 1953): 271–7.

62 NF had met Carol Ely Harper during the summer of 1951 when he had taught a course at the University of Washington in Seattle. NF's comments here appear to refer not simply to Harper's fixation on him but also to the automatic writing of her multiform poem, *The City* (see par. 36, above), which eventually expanded to a seven-volume epic. The poem was never published.

63 The reference is to NF's review of Canadian poetry (par. 50, above).

64 The reference is to the chap. NF had written for the book edited by Randolph C. Chalmers, *The Heritage of Western Culture* (49.n. 154).

65 For the "chilly review" (unsigned), see "Summarize Heritage of Western Culture in Church's Report," *Varsity*, 22 January 1952, 5. The Niblock cartoon is on p. 8. Ursula Niebuhr, professor of religion at Barnard College and wife of Reinhold Niebuhr, had lectured on "A Christian Understanding of Sex" earlier in the day at the Victoria College Chapel. Her talk was part of the week-long University Christian Mission.

66 NF had been elected a Fellow of the Royal Society of Canada in 1951; Henry Alexander of Queen's University, in 1948.

67 See par. 50, above.

68 See n. 11, above.

69 See introduction, n.34.

70 This does seem to be a piece of gossip—at least in most of its details. Endicott had met Mary Austin in January 1925, six months before they were married on 19 June. For the account of their romance and for the difficulty of the separation between Endicott and Nina Yeomans, see Stephen Endicott, *James G. Endicott: Rebel out of China*, 62. Stephen Endicott reports that Marion Hilliard, an old friend of Jim Endicott, had been "particularly offended by his disloyalty and infidelity to Nina and accused him of having 'no sense of honour,'" but she later "recovered her trust in him" (63).

71 U of T president Sidney Smith had released his annual report over the weekend. See "Lectures, High Schools Cause Failures—Smith," *Varsity*, 28 January 1952, 1. Portions of Smith's report are on p. 3 of the *Varsity*.

72 The "lad" from SMC was Stephen Somerville. See his "God Again Proved," *Varsity*, 25 January 1952, 8, and "Religion: A Human Necessity," *Varsity*, 29 January 1952, 8.

73 Anne Bolgan did complete her dissertation on T.S. Eliot, supervised by NF, eight years later.

74 "President's Report (1): Ciceros Wanted," *Varsity*, 29 January 1952, 8.

75 "A Conspectus of Dramatic Genres" (50.n. 149).

76 Hilliard Trethewey was chair of the French department at VC; Joe Fisher had been appointed chair of the English department in July 1952; NF did not become chair until after Joe Fisher's death later in the year, although, as Ayre notes, he did serve as *de facto* chair after Fisher's health deteriorated (238–9).

77 See n. 9, above.

78 Robert Graves, *Wife to Mr. Milton: The Story of Marie Powell* (London: Cassell, 1943).

79 The phases of the hero outlined here became a part of the First Essay of *AC*.

80 The day of the installation of Lester B. Pearson as chancellor of VU.

81 Gilbert and Sullivan's *H.M.S. Pinafore* had been presented by the VC Music Club, under the direction of Godfrey Ridout and Geoffrey Hatton.

82 Carnwath and Upshall, executive members of the VC Liberal Arts Club, had been delegated to ask NF to address members of the club. NF obliged, addressing the club at Wymilwood later in the year (Joyce Upshall Fleming to Robert D. Denham, 25 July 1998).

83 J.B. Tyrrell, who had graduated from VC in 1889, was ninety-four years old.

84 See Lester B. Pearson, "The Chancellor's Inaugural Address," *Victoria Reports*, 2, no. 2 [1952]: 7–14.

85 NF used the engraved invitation for Pearson's installation to jot down a series of notes for *AC*, and he may well have written these notes, which have survived, during the luncheon itself. See the NFF, 1992, box 3, file 7. See also Ayre, 236–8.

86 A reference, apparently, to certain quirks of speech by Walter T. Brown, president of VU, 1941–49, and Alexander Charles Spencer, chancellor of VU, 1944–52.

87 W.A. Mackintosh, the new principal of Queen's University, delivered greetings from the other universities of Canada. His remarks were published in *Victoria Reports*, 2, no. 2 [1952]: 15, 18–19.

88 Lester B. Pearson roomed in Gate House when he was a student at VC. The Gate House undergraduates showered Pearson with confetti, feathers, and the like from their strategic location above the platform in Convocation Hall.

89 A position Jacques Maritain argues in "Poetry and Beauty," chap. 5 of *Creative Intuition in Art and Poetry* (New York: Meridian Books, 1955). The statement "poetry has no object" is on p. 130.

90 Walt Stewart did not in fact return to VC for his final year, but his name did remain on the masthead as editor of *Acta Victoriana* for the 1952–53 academic year.

91 John Rutherford was book review editor for the 1952–53 academic year; Ricky Arnold was literary editor but did not serve as an adviser.

92 Aldous Huxley, *Point Counter Point* (New York: Modern Library, 1928), 143–4 (end of chap. 10).

93 The miracle of the draught of fishes.

94 Geoffrey Bush was the son of Douglas Bush, professor of English at Harvard who had taken his M.A. at U of T. After publishing an early critical book based on his Lowell lectures, Geoffrey Bush told his father that he had no desire to pursue an academic career. This was doubtless a disappointment to his father, and NF seems to have been right in suspecting a developing tension between father and son over the latter's decision. Regarding the offer that had been made to Geoffrey Bush from Toronto, Douglas Bush apparently indicated that his son had turned it down because, living in Canada, he would be exempt from the draft. Douglas Bush may well have been reluctant to tell the people at VC of his son's decision to abandon the academy. (Jerome H. Buckley provided some of the information in this note; letter to Robert D. Denham, 8 October 1998.)

95 See n. 18, above.

96 On Fairley's exclusion from the U.S., see 50.n. 176.

97 Douglas LePan, who was a member of the Department of External Affairs, 1945–59, was serving in Washington as minister-counsellor. The "LePans," his mother and father, were Dorothy and Arthur, a military officer.

98 "The Function of Criticism at the Present Time (49.n. 2).

99 "Levels of Meaning in Literature" (50.n. 3).

100 "The Archetypes of Literature" (50.n. 378).

101 "A Conspectus of Dramatic Genres" (50.n. 149).

102 "Comic Myth in Shakespeare" (n. 4, above).

103 The reference is to Robert Graves's *The White Goddess* (1948). Graves's *In Dedication* is a poem to the nature goddess (or Blake's Vala).

104 James's "The Moral Equivalent of War," an essay based on a speech delivered at Stanford University in 1906, advances the idea of an organized national service.

105 Pratt had fallen a few days after his seventieth birthday. On the injury and its effects, see Pitt, *E.J. Pratt: The Master Years*, 418–19.

106 That is, the 12:00 lecture for the class in "Nineteenth-Century Thought" NF had forgotten about. The class also met on Tuesdays at 9:00.

107 The "sermon books" were small, paper-covered notebooks, some of which have survived. Notebook 30e, on the front cover of which NF wrote "II," is material for the Second Essay of *AC*, and Notebook 30f, with "IV" on the front cover, is material for the Third Essay. Notebook 30d, with "III" on the front cover, is mostly a draft of material for what turned out to be the First Essay. These notebooks are in the NFF, 1991, box 25.

108 A.F.B. Clark became a member of the editorial board of the *Canadian Forum* in August 1952.

109 For Sandwell's review of *The Heritage of Western Culture* (49.n. 154), see "Church Looks at Culture," *Saturday Night*, 23 February 1952, 3, 28.

Sandwell quotes two sentences from NF's "Trends in Modern Culture" (one on American Deism, the other on the need for spiritual power) "with some hope that they may send some readers in search of the pages which lead up to them" (3).

110 "going phut" = fizzling out, failing.

111 As it turned out, Barker Fairley did not give a paper on Keller, or, as it is suggested he might in par. 138, on Heine, at the 1952 meeting of the Royal Society. NF did give his paper on "Comic Myth in Shakespeare" (n. 4, above). His MLA paper was "Characterization in Shakespearean Comedy" (n. 61, above).

112 See 50.n. 151.

113 The ink in NF's pen is flowing too freely.

114 Ben Jonson, *Every Man in His Humour* (1599) and *The Alchemist* (1610).

115 This would have been the branch of Murray's Lunch Limited at 1500 Yonge St.

116 The heroine of Woolf's *To the Lighthouse* (1927).

117 "If you knew time as well as I do," said the Hatter [to Alice], "you wouldn't talk about wasting *it*. It's *him*" (Lewis Carroll, *Alice's Adventures in Wonderland*, chap. 7).

118 In September 1950 NF had broken his right arm in an automobile accident. See 50.n. 476.

119 "Installation Luncheon," *Victoria Reports*, 2 (March 1952): 5–6.

120 "For Whom the Dunce Cap Fits," *Canadian Forum*, 31 (March 1952): 265–6; rpt. in *WE*, 55–6.

121 Woodsworth House, the headquarters of the Woodsworth Memorial Foundation, was on Jarvis St. The purpose of the foundation was to encourage educational activities and to promote the socialist ideals of J.S. Woodsworth.

122 The political conflict to which NF alludes here had to do with whether Woodsworth House would remain primarily an independent centre for education or whether it would become a political advocacy group for the CCF and the trade unions. This was the debate that in fact emerged at the annual meeting of the Woodsworth Foundation on 27 February. Woodsworth House was the headquarters of the CCF, whose membership had been largely responsible for acquiring the property through subscriptions. The issue was the degree of control the CCF would exercise over the work of the foundation. The Morrises, who were managing editors of the *Canadian Forum*, were strongly opposed to the policies of the CCF in this controversy.

123 The painting is Harris's *The Meeting of the School Trustees* (1885), owned by the National Gallery of Canada. A tipped-in colour reproduction appears on the inside back cover of *New Frontiers*, 1, no. 1 (Winter 1952): following p. 48.

124 Pearl Parnes, "Campus Profile: Prof Northrop Frye," *Varsity*, 21 February 1952, 4.

125 Jane Reddick Schofield does not recall NF's talk to the Dramatic Society, but does remember that the Fryes attended a meeting of a book club she and several of her classmates organized following their graduation (Jane Reddick Schofield to Robert D. Denham, 23 September 1998).

126 Stella Harrison, "Letter from London," *Canadian Forum*, 31 (March 1952): 270–1.

127 NF meant to write "had a right to do *that*."

128 In an interview with Philip Marchand, NF recalled that "Carpenter was quite an aggressive, belligerent person. He could be a real son of a bitch. It was all quite impersonal, but he tended to tackle people on their own ground, and of course he would always win. Although I don't think either of us won that debate, particularly" (Philip Marchand, *Marshall McLuhan: The Medium and the Messenger* [Toronto: Random House, 1989], 117).

129 In reviewing Ernst Jünger's *On the Marble Cliffs*, NF had compared Warner's *Aerodrome* to Jünger's novel. See "Turning New Leaves," *Canadian Forum*, 27 (March 1948): 283.

130 "Professors Duel on 'Universality,'" *Varsity*, 22 February 1952, 1.

131 See par. 112, above.

132 NF had done a CBC review of Pär Lagerkvist's *Barabbas* on CBC Radio on 6 January. See par. 15, above. For Britnell's, see 42.n. 79.

133 That is, the people influenced by Arthur O. Lovejoy's studies in the history of ideas. A version of Crane's paper, "Philosophy, Literature, and the History of Ideas," was published in *Modern Philology*, 52 (1954): 77–83, and rpt. in *The Idea of the Humanities and Other Essays Critical and Historical* (Chicago: University of Chicago Press, 1967), 1:173–87.

134 Tamino was played by Robert Price, an opera star originally from Wichita, Kan.

135 Papageno was performed by Andrew MacMillan.

136 It is not clear what NF means by "Moncton man": Adams was born in Winnipeg, grew up in Vancouver, and moved to Toronto in 1948.

137 As Barker Fairley had lectured on Heine on 7 February at U of T, it seems likely that the context of NF's remarks here is the Royal Society session he had assumed responsibility for planning. See par. 113 and n. 111, above.

138 The first-year RK course.

139 NF is recording here his activities on Thursday, 28 February.

140 See 49.n. 157. The question for the Citizens' Forum program that aired on CBC Radio on 28 February was "Does the Federal Surplus Mean Our Taxes Are Too High?"

141 The "cute girl" happened to be a married woman. The previous year Margaret J. Ritchie had married Richard Allen shortly after graduating

from VC; their wedding was on Bastille Day, which was also NF's birthday.

142 NF reviewed Hyde's *Southern Cross* and Iona and Peter Opie's *The Oxford Dictionary of Nursery Rhymes* on CBC radio. The typescripts of these reviews are in the NFF, 1993, box 3, file 11, and the reviews will appear in the forthcoming *Northrop Frye on Literature and Society*. For the "Forum article," see n. 6, above.

143 NF saw the performance of Smetana's opera, presented by the Royal Conservatory Opera Company, at the Royal Alexandra Theatre. *The Bartered Bride* (1866) had, incidentally, been the first production of the Royal Conservatory Opera School in 1947.

144 The Opera Festival had begun in 1950, when it presented three operas.

145 *leno* = go-between, procurer.

146 Bill Andrew and Lois White were two of the twelve members of the Victoria College Union Executive. White has no recollection of ever being involved with a religious service or ever speaking with NF while at VC; she thinks NF may have confused her with another member of the executive (Lois G. Taylor to Robert D. Denham, 4 August 1998). Andrew thinks he may have had a meeting with NF but doesn't recall the service (William Andrew to Robert D. Denham, 22 October 1998). In announcing the Victoria College Union chapel service, however, the *Varsity* reported that "VCU special directoress Lois White and treasurer Bill Andrew will assist Prof. Frye at the 7:30 p.m. service in the Victoria College Chapel" ("Northrop Frye Talks to Vic This Sunday," *Varsity*, 29 February 1952, 1).

147 At this VU Sunday Evening Concert, Kraus also played Couperin and Byrd.

148 Evelyn Linton and Joyce Upshall.

149 NF is referring to his 12:00 class on Monday, 3 March, English 4k, "Nineteenth-Century Thought."

150 NF was editing Pelham Edgar's autobiography. See 50.n. 141.

151 See 49.n. 14.

152 NF almost certainly meant to write Innis.

153 NF means Stephenson House, a VU co-operative residence for undergraduates at 77 Charles St. West; it was one of several properties on Charles St. given to VU by F.C. Stephenson.

154 A dramatization of W.C. Sellar and R.J. Yeatman's tongue-in-cheek history of England, *1066 and All That* (New York: Dutton, 1931).

155 NF is referring to the view of E.E. Stoll that Shakespearean drama reflects the actualities of history and that many critics are confused by dramatic conventions and conventional characters in the plays.

156 The Lichee Gardens, located at 118 Elizabeth St., was a landmark Toronto restaurant for many years; it moved to another location in the early 1980s.

22A refers to the restaurant at the Windsor Arms Hotel, located at 22 St. Thomas St.; the bar there, known as Club Twenty-Two, was a popular hangout for writers. The Windsor Arms was converted into condominiums in the 1990s.

157 The shape of the book as outlined here (modes, levels of meaning, archetypes, and genres) is the general shape that *AC* finally took.

158 The famous pair of leather breeches made by George Fox (1624–91), the itinerant Quaker preacher; in the middle of the seventeenth century the established church feared the man dressed in that famous suit as much as John the Baptist, in his leather girdle, was feared centuries before.

159 The Students' Administrative Council (SAC) at U of T had suspended publication of the *Varsity* because of its view that a humorous issue of the newspaper that had been published on 5 March was in bad taste. For an account of the controversy, see "The 'Varsity' Story," *Varsity*, 18 March 1952, 1–2, 4. This was a special edition of the *Varsity*, published under the authority of the SAC by the Publications Commission.

160 "Have We a National Education?" *Canadian Forum*, 32 (April 1952): 3; rpt. in *WE*, 57–8.

161 See n. 23, above.

162 See n. 3, above.

163 *Étude* published no articles on Scriabin in 1925. NF is doubtless referring to Ellen Von Tidebohl, "Musical Voyage Down the Volga," *Étude*, 44 (December 1926): 905–6.

164 NF had heard Olson give his talk on "The Poetic Method of Aristotle: Its Powers and Limitations" at the annual meeting of the English Institute the previous September.

165 R.S. Crane reviewed Kenneth MacLean's *John Locke and English Literature of the Eighteenth Century* (New Haven: Yale University Press, 1936) in *Philological Quarterly*, 16 (1937): 180–1. Crane found the book to be unscholarly and disorganized.

166 Ronald Williams had received his Ph.D. from the University of Chicago.

167 Sartre's *Les Mains sales* (1952) was filmed as *Crime Passionel*.

168 For the The New Play Society and its annual production of *Spring Thaw*, see 49.n. 242.

169 For a review of the play—a performance from earlier in the week— see Herbert Whittaker, "Show Business," *Globe and Mail*, 18 March 1950, 19.

170 Reid MacCallum's essays, *Imitation and Design and Other Essays* (Toronto: University of Toronto Press, 1953), were actually edited by William Blissett, who notes in his preface that "Mr. Richard Burgener has taken a helpful interest in the whole project from the beginning" (v).

171 The phrase is from the first line of Vaughan's poem.

172 George Johnston replaced John Dow as professor of New Testament literature and exegesis at EC. This is not the George Johnston, poet and Carleton University professor, who was NF's longtime friend.

173 R.H. Strachan delivered the 1951–52 Armstrong Lecture on "Religion and Life in the Writings of Thomas Hardy," 25 March, in the VC chapel.

174 See n. 119, above.

175 A suggestive reference perhaps to Wilde's having spent much time at the Savoy Hotel entertaining his young male friends.

176 See par. 155, above, and 50.n. 141.

177 NF's lecture was "The Argument of Comedy" (49.n. 56), which he gave at the English Institute, hosted by Yale University, on 8 September 1948.

178 See par. 81, above.

179 NF has the name of the cellist slightly misspelled, but Massimo Anfiteatroff and Ornella Pulite Santoliquido were the actual names of two of the musicians in the ensemble, which was conducted by Renato Fasano.

180 The young pianist was Douglas George Talbot Bodle.

181 The two poems had been published, respectively, in 1947 and 1940. NF reviewed Pratt's *Towards the Last Spike* in "Letters in Canada: 1952, Poetry," *University of Toronto Quarterly*, 22 (April 1953): 269–80.

182 On MacCallum's death, see 49.354. Jerry Riddell, who for many years had been senior tutor in the men's residences at VC and a lecturer in the history department at U of T and who later joined the Department of External Affairs, died suddenly while representing Canada at the United Nations.

183 NF did review Kathleen Coburn's *The Inquiring Spirit*, an edition of Coleridge's prose, in *Hudson Review*, 6 (Autumn 1953): 170–7; rpt. in *NFCL*, 170–7.

184 Katherine Mansfield, "The Fly" (1922), a story of victimization in which a fly in a businessman's inkwell unsuccessfully struggles to escape from the man's sadistic mistreatment of the small creature.

185 That is, the funeral of Nicholas Ignatieff.

186 See n. 36, above.

187 The reference is to the great books program at St. John's College, Annapolis, Md.

188 See introduction, n. 34.

189 The material NF refers to here as his "first chapter" is an embryonic version of what turned out to be the Second Essay of *AC*.

190 Al Capp, "'It's Hideously True': Creator of Li'l Abner Tells Why His Hero Is (Sob!) Wed," *Life*, 32 (31 March 1952): 101–8.

191 After graduating from VC several of the twenty-two language and literature students formed a book club to discuss current works of literature; a half-century later the members of the club, including Janet Waite Burnie, Carol MacKinnon McDermott, and Anne Ward Maxwell, were still meeting monthly.

192 The party is for the students in NF's English 4k course, "Nineteenth-Century Thought."

193 Walmer Rd., which is one block west of Spadina Ave., runs north from Bloor St. to Heath St.

194 A piano work by Paul Hindemith, first performed in 1944.

195 "Towneley is a good fellow," said I [the narrator], gravely, "and you should not have cut him." "Towneley," he [Ernest Pontifex] answered, "is not only a good fellow, but he is without exception the very best man I ever saw in my life—except," he paid me the compliment of saying, "yourself" (Samuel Butler, *The Way of All Flesh* [New York: Modern Library, n.d.], 361–5).

196 NF later indicated to Evelyn Linton that if she wanted to take her M.A. degree with him he would respond favourably (Evelyn Linton to Robert D. Denham, 11 August 1998).

197 Frank H. Underhill, "Power Politics in the Ontario C.C.F," *Canadian Forum*, 32 (April 1952): 7–8; F.A. Brewin, "Woodsworth Foundation," *Canadian Forum*, 32 (May 1952): 34–5, 37. For reasons of space none of the letters was published.

198 The letter containing the 1951 offer tendered by Duke University is in the NFF, 1993, box 5, file 4.

199 The reference is uncertain. The word "emblem" does not appear in any of Abraham Cowley's Pindaric odes, and none of the Pindarics is devoted to the general subject. Cowley does speak of "emblemata" in the opening lines of bk. 1 of his *Plantarum*, and the Latin form of the word appears elsewhere in this poem, though, again, Cowley is not addressing the emblem as a subject. It seems most likely that NF is referring to Cowley's *Of Wit*, which is an ode although not exactly a Pindaric.

200 The name of the building for the Toronto offices of Oxford University Press from 1929 to 1963, located at 480 University Ave.

201 NF had met Davin in 1938 when they were students together at Oxford. For NF's account of Davin then, see *Correspondence*, 2:804–5.

202 See par. 233, above.

203 Money for the trip to New York.

204 NF apparently meant to write "finger."

205 That is, for *Caesar and Cleopatra*, which HKF and Jean Elder had seen on 11 April.

206 Leslie was a member of the church when he was a magazine editor in New York.

207 The Cloisters, in Ft. Tryon Park, New York City, is a branch of the Metropolitan Museum of Art containing an outstanding collection of Gothic tapestries, including *The Hunt of the Unicorn*.

208 Before "baseball" in the previous sentence NF wrote and then cancelled "Me."

209 John Clarence Webster was a Canadian physician who, after retiring, began a second career as a historian; he amassed a large library of books on North American history, as well as thousands of artefacts and pictures of that history.

210 The reference is to Blake's sympathies with the fierce criticism of George III by the politician John Wilkes. For Erdman's Blake manuscript, see 49.n. 220.

211 "I am really sorry to see my Countrymen trouble themselves about Politics" (William Blake, *Public Address*, Erdman, 580).

212 That is, a military veteran.

213 NF decided against publishing the review in the *Canadian Forum*.

214 Alessandro Longo (1864–1945) organized Scarlatti's sonatas for the harpsichord into suites, which were published in 11 vols. (Milan, 1906–10).

215 The previous Sunday the Fryes had attended the service at Adam Clayton Powell's Baptist church in Harlem.

216 In 1949 the Bollingen Prize, administered by the Library of Congress, was awarded to Ezra Pound for achievement in American poetry. Pound's receipt of the prize caused a heated controversy because he was at the time under indictment as a traitor for his pro-fascist and anti-Semitic radio broadcasts from Italy. A congressional committee subsequently asked the Library of Congress to dissociate itself from the award, which it did.

217 The Bollingen Series, a publishing enterprise begun by Paul and Mary Mellon in 1943, had already published more than thirty titles by the early 1950s. The series focused on mythological subjects.

218 Kathleen Coburn did not contribute to either the rev. ed. (1956) or the 3rd ed. (1976) of *The English Romantic Poets: A Guide to Research*, ed. Thomas Raysor (New York: Modern Language Association), the 1st ed. of which appeared in 1950.

219 That is, the influence of Edmund Carpenter, a member of the anthropology department at U of T, with whom NF had had the debate on the nature of universal symbols. See pars. 19, 123, 126, 128, and 132–5, above.

220 See n. 167, above.

221 A town fifteen kilometres northwest of Toronto, where U of T has a farm and accommodations for visitors and meetings.

222 The typescript for NF's review of Butterfield's book is in the NFF, 1993, box 3, file 11.

223 Harold Innis died on 8 November 1952.

1953 Diary

1 The Fryes were going to London, Ont., to visit VC and EC classmate George Birtch and his wife Mary. NF had been invited to give a talk at a conference held in the Metropolitan Church in London, where Birtch was the minister.

2 Cf. *AC*, 101: "When a critic meets St. George the Redcross Knight in Spenser, bearing a red cross on a white ground, he has some idea what to do with this figure. When he meets a female in Henry James's *The Other House* called Rose Arminger with a white dress and a red parasol, he is, in the current slang, clueless."

3 Acrasia = the character in Spenser's *Faerie Queene* (bk. 2, canto 12) who symbolizes self-indulgence and whose Bower of Bliss is destroyed.

4 Rev. Alfred H. Johnston, who had been NF's professor of homiletics at EC. See Ayre, 241, and *Correspondence*, 2:423, 439, 463, 491.

5 That is, to replace A.D. Matheson as principal of EC.

6 For Pete Colgrove's fourth-dimension paper, see 49.369 and n. 312.

7 English 2c, "The Novel"; English 3c, "Nineteenth-Century Poetry"; English 4n, "The Modern Novel." English 4n was an Honour Course; English 2c and 3c were for General Course students.

8 *The Life of William Blake*, published in 1927 and reissued with corrections in 1948.

9 George Santayana, *Realms of Being* (1927–40).

10 James Thurber was a neighbour of the MacLeans at their summer home in Cornwall, Conn. See MacLean's *James Thurber* (1953), a twelve-page monograph published in the Peter Rushton Seminar series on contemporary prose and poetry.

11 An "untranslatable word conveying the sense of masterly ease, spontaneity, the tossed-off quality that shows nothing of the long practice that has led up to it" (*MM*, 314).

12 For NF's use of Barth's phrase, see 50.n. 401.

1955 Diary

1 Daryl Hine, *Five Poems* (Toronto, 1954).

2 "53" means that Croft graduated from VC in 1953.

3 A course in Victorian poetry.

4 Sam Slick was a comic character made famous by Thomas C. Haliburton in a series of sketches and books.

5 Joseph Wicksteed, *Blake's Innocence and Experience: A Study of the Songs and Manuscripts* (London: Dent, 1928).

6 NF is to appear on a television program on William Blake. See pars. 15–16, 18, 21, and 38, below.

7 André Obey, *Noah: A Play in Five Scenes* (1935). The VC Dramatic Society's production was directed by Herbert Whittaker, with John Douglas in the title role.

8 The restaurant referred to is the Swiss Chalet, opened at 234 Bloor St. West in 1954 and still going strong as part of a large chain at the time of publication.

9 Douglas MacAgy, the well-known art curator and museum director, had married Elizabeth Tillett in early 1955. HKF and Douglas MacAgy had been friends since the mid-1930s when she worked at the AGT and he was studying art in Toronto and at the Barnes Foundation in Philadelphia. This was the second marriage for MacAgy: he and his first wife Jermayne, also a noted art curator, were divorced on 16 December 1954.

10 The reference is to the new bookshop Kay and Lou Morris have opened. See par. 7, above.

11 Walter Jackson Bate was the editor of *Criticism: The Major Texts* (New York: Harcourt, Brace, 1952).

12 NF's untitled review is in the *Canadian Forum*, 34 (March 1955): 285.

13 John Richardson, *Wacousta; or, The Prophecy* (1832), a historical romance.

14 See Wendy Michener, "Frye Explores Blake," *Varsity*, 19 January 1955, 5. Michener felt that there was a lack of connection between NF's "professorial delivery," the images of Blake's engravings, and Barry Morse's reading of Blake's poems.

15 NF did present a paper on "Quest and Cycle in *Finnegans Wake*" at the 1955 annual meeting of the Modern Language Association in Chicago. Ellmann chaired the session—"English 11: Contemporary Literature." NF's essay was published in the *James Joyce Review*, 1 (February 1957): 39–47, and rpt. in *FI*, 256–64.

16 4m, "Modern Drama and Poetry."

17 *Sunshine Town*, a musical comedy with lyrics and music by Mavor Moore, premiered at the New Play Society on 10 January 1955. The play was based on Stephen Leacock's *Sunshine Sketches of a Little Town* (1922).

18 The Fourth Essay of *AC*.

19 See 42.n. 3.

20 The Fryes and the MacLures had listened to a radio program with harpsichordist Greta Kraus playing Couperin's *Passacaille in B Minor* and *Les fastes de la grande et ancient ménestrandise*. NF substituted an "x" for each of the vowels in his effort to spell *ménestrandise*; for the consonants he forgot only the second "n."

21 Samuel C. Chew, *Swinburne* (Boston: Little, Brown, 1929).

22 Through the efforts of Kathleen Coburn, a substantial collection of papers from the Coleridge family and family editors were presented to the VU Library by the J.S. McLean Foundation in 1954.

23 Susanna Moodie, *Roughing It in the Bush; or, Forest Life in Canada* (1852), an account of Moodie's early life and observations in Canada.

24 A 1954 ciné-poem in which Vivaldi's symphony *The Seasons* is given visual form through the pageantry of the passing year; filmed at Lake Simcoe, Ont., by Christopher Chapman, *The Seasons* was voted film of the year by the Canadian Film Awards.

25 Millar MacLure, "Dylan Thomas Paraphrased," *University of Toronto Quarterly*, 24 (July 1955): 435–7.

26 "The Language of Poetry," *Explorations: Studies in Culture and Communication*, 4 (February 1955): 80–90.

27 Millar MacLure, "Tower of Words," *Explorations: Studies in Communication and Culture*, 4 (February 1955): 40–51.

28 No doubt a reference to Nancy Fulford, NF's god-daughter.

29 McLuhan's privately published pamphlet *Counterblast* (1954; 17 pp.) was a response to the recommendations of the Canadian Royal Commission (Massey Report) on the arts and sciences.

30 "The only true America is that country where you are at liberty to pursue such a mode of life as may enable you to do without these [coffee, tea, and meat], and where the state does not endeavor to compel you to sustain the slavery and war and other superfluous expenses which directly or indirectly result from the use of such things" (Henry David Thoreau, *Walden*, in *Walden and Other Writings*, ed. Brooks Atkinson (New York: Modern Library, 1937), 185.

31 *L'âme de la poésie canadienne française*, ed. Laure Rièse (Toronto: Macmillan, 1955).

32 NF is apparently referring to Ken MacLean's *The Agrarian Age* (50.n. 460).

33 This is material that made its way into the Fourth Essay of *AC*.

34 Davie did devote some attention to NF's views in *Articulate Energy: An Inquiry into the Syntax of English Poetry* (London: Routledge and Kegan Paul, 1955), 130–41, 161–5.

35 This is apparently a reference to the painter Jack Nichols (b. 1921), whose subjects were typically servicemen; he taught at UBC and U of T following World War II.

36 The Candlelight was at 376 Bloor St. West.

37 NF obliged Earl Wasserman's request, writing a paper entitled "Towards Defining an Age of Sensibility" and presenting it on 29 December 1955 to the English 8 section, chaired by Wasserman, at the annual convention of the Modern Language Association in Chicago. The paper was subsequently published in *ELH*, 23 (June 1956): 144–52, and rpt. in *FI*, 130–7.

38 The Quadrangle Club was the faculty club at the University of Chicago.

39 "Towards a Theory of Cultural History," *University of Toronto Quarterly*, 22 (July 1953): 325–41.

40 Wiebolt Hall housed the English department at the University of Chicago.

41 NF had seen the Fountain of Time when he visited the Chicago World's Fair in June of 1933.

42 Danny = Diana Mason Bell, Charles Bell's second wife; they were married 23 July 1949.

43 Bell was teaching at the time in the humanities division at the University of Chicago.

44 See par. 35, above.

45 The Armstrong Lecture, on "The Great Divorce: Intellectual Education vs. the Education of the Emotions," was delivered at VC on 1 March by A. Victor Murray, president of Chestnut College, Cambridge, Eng. NF was in Chicago at the time.

46 President A.B.B. Moore had given the address at the senior dinner, held on 3 March in the Great Hall at Hart House.

47 Helen Frye was chair of the VC Picture Exhibition Committee. The show from the collection of Mr. and Mrs. Charles S. Band, which included oil paintings by Lawren Harris, A.Y. Jackson, Arthur Lismer, Emily Carr, and Paul-Émile Borduas, opened in Alumni Hall on 14 March.

48 F.R. Scott had organized a national poetry conference to be held in Kingston, Ont., 28–31 July 1955. As Scott's proposal for funding had by this time already met the Rockefeller requirements, the purpose of the commissioner's inquiry may have had to do with some of the problems that faced the organizing committee. In November NF had helped to arrange a meeting between Scott and Robert Weaver of CBC to discuss the Kingston conference. See Sandra Djwa, *The Politics of Imagination: A Life of F.R. Scott*, 275–7.

49 Peggy Sanderson is the tragic heroine of Morley Callaghan's *The Loved and the Lost* (1951). A white girl who wants to associate with Montreal's black community, she is cut off from both societies and is eventually murdered by uncomprehending whites.

50 "A Conspectus of Dramatic Genres" (50.n. 149); "The Four Forms of Prose Fiction" (49.n. 58).

51 "Myth as Information," *Hudson Review*, 7 (Summer 1954): 228–35.

52 VU ended up buying, not the Schlicker organ (see par. 19, above), but a two-manual electronic organ from the J.C. Hallman Co. of Waterloo, Ont.

53 Alfred Harbage's Alexander Lectures were published as *Theatre for Shakespeare* (Toronto: University of Toronto Press, 1955).

54 That is, Harbage argued against any kind of strict adherence to the view advocated by most stage manuals: that the action of Shakespeare's plays took place in various enclosures ("inner" and "upper" stages) at the rear of the projecting platform. See chap. 2 of Harbage's Alexander lectures, *Theatre for Shakespeare*, 19–40. The reference to Granville-Barker's view also appears in the published lectures (pp. 32–3).

Index

NOTE: When NF refers in passing to a married couple, their name is indexed at the end of the entry for one of the individuals. Dates of works are for the first edition; for foreign works translated into English, the date is that of the English translation.